Cambridge Tracts in Theoretical Computer Science

Titles in the series

1. G. Chaitin *Algorithmic Information Theory*
2. L.C. Paulson *Logic and Computation*
3. M. Spivey *Understanding Z*
4. G. Revesz *Lambda Calculus, Combinators and Functional Programming*
5. A. Ramsay *Formal Methods in Artificial Intelligence*
6. S. Vickers *Topology via Logic*
7. J-Y. Girard, Y. Lafont & P. Taylor *Proofs and Types*
8. J. Clifford *Formal Semantics & Pragmatics for Natural Language Processing*
9. M. Winslett *Updating Logical Databases*
10. K. McEvoy & J.V. Tucker (eds) *Theoretical Foundations of VLSI Design*
11. T.H. Tse *A Unifying Framework for Stuctured Analysis and Design Models*
12. G. Brewka *Nonmonotonic Reasoning*
14. S.G. Hoggar *Mathematics for Computer Graphics*
15. S. Dasgupta *Design Theory and Computer Science*
17. J.C.M. Baeten (ed) *Applications of Process Algebra*
18. J.C.M. Baeten & W. P. Weijland *Process Algebra*
23. E.-R. Olderog *Nets, Terms and Formulas*
27. W.H. Hesselink *Programs, Recursion and Unbounded Choice*
29. P. Gärdenfors (ed) *Belief Revision*
30. M. Anthony & N. Biggs *Computational Learning Theory*
34. F. Nielson & H.R. Nielson *Two Level Functional Languages*

MATHEMATICS FOR COMPUTER GRAPHICS

Study of regular division of the plane with angels and devils

MATHEMATICS FOR COMPUTER GRAPHICS

S.G. HOGGAR
Department of Mathematics
Glasgow University

CAMBRIDGE
UNIVERSITY PRESS

Published by the Press Syndicate of the University of Cambridge
The Pitt Building, Trumpington Street, Cambridge CB2 1RP
40 West 20th Street, New York, NY 10011–4211, USA
10 Stamford Road, Oakleigh, Melbourne 3166, Australia

First published 1992
Reprinted with corrections 1993, 1994

Printed in Great Britain at the University Press, Cambridge

Library of Congress cataloguing in publication data available

British Library cataloguing in publication data available

ISBN 0 521 37574 6 hardback

Table of contents

To my wife, Elisabeth

Preface

The purpose of this book is to further the applying of mathematics to computer graphics. It is written from the conviction that not only is mathematics beautiful in itself, but that applying mathematics is a beautiful thing to do.

We include sections giving the reader what can serve as a reminder of, or as a compact introduction to vectors, matrices, groups, and complex numbers, to the level required for the main exposition. A high priority is given to visual illustration and examples. There are exercises which the reader can use if desired, at strategic points in the text, gathered together and sometimes extended at the end of each chapter. When an exercise number is marked thus √, there is an answer or hint in *selected answers* just before the index. In the introduction we suggest some easy ways in, where to find purely pictures, light reading, or material requiring diligent commitment, depending on what rewards one seeks at the time.

These days, the mathematics of computer graphics could surely not be compassed in a single book. We do not for example build up from scratch the apparatus of elementary calculus and coordinate geometry. However we do offer a study of transformations and symmetry in the plane, with applications to producing patterns by computer (Chapters 1-6). We classify length-preserving transformations in 3-space, with techniques from vectors, matrices and geometry, and show how to actually *do* a considerable variety of things, culminating in rotation by quaternions and in-betweening solid motions in 3-space (Chapters 7-9). The topology part of the book (Chapters 10-13) contains a variety of applications, interesting and important in their own right, such as Newton's method of solution, extrema of continuous maps, and the Principle of Linear Programming. At the same time it gives the base for properties and constructions of fractal images via iterated function systems and Mandelbrot and Julia sets (Chapters 14-16).

Much of the material of this book began as a graduate course in the Summer of 1988, for PhD students in computer graphics at the Ohio State University. My thanks are due to Rick Parent for encouraging the idea of such a course, to Phil Huneke for enabling me to give it as a visiting faculty member in the mathematics department, and to Charles Csuri for encouraging the idea of the book. I thank Eiichi Bannai for his original invitation to come to Ohio for our joint work (on t-designs). I am indebted to Robin McLeod and Tektronix for an Academic Scholarship award and for an instructive week of computer graphics at Tektronix Beaverton, Oregon.

A further part of the book was developed from a course for Final Year mathematics students at the University of Glasgow. I thank my department for three months leave to begin the book. I thank the Glasgow Mathematical Association, Maclaurin Society, and St. Andrews University mathematics department, for opportunities to air some ideas to an audience.

I am much indebted to John Patterson for checking the draft text with care and detail beyond the call of duty, and for many helpful comments. My thanks too for comments on parts of the text, to Ian Anderson, John Jeacocke, Alistair Kilgour, James Logie, Adam McBride, Finlay Mc Naughtan, Ian Murphy, and Edmund Robertson. In a different vein, I thank Keiran Clenaghan for running Computing Science student projects based on Chapters 1-6, and the many enthusiastic school students who spur my faith in the seventeen plane patterns each Open Day. Also Jim McNally for finance and publicity via our Enterprise in Higher Education department. On the last two counts thanks are due to Scotsys Computers for their kind loans of equipment. Also on the British scene, I thank Rae Earnshaw for organising excellent international conferences that helped acquaint me with the people and ideas in computer graphics.

The text was prepared as camera-ready copy by the author in Microsoft Word on an Apple Macintosh IIci and printed on an Apple Laserwriter. Typesetting of mathematical formula was done mainly with Formulator, and diagrams drawn with Superpaint. Further software used, in addition to Pascal programs written by the author, was: The Game of fractal images (H.-O.Peitgen, H.Jürgens, D.Saupe, M.Parmet), The Desktop fractal design system (M.F. Barnsley), and Explorer (J.Dirksen, β-test copy). In this connection, my thanks to Adrian Bowman, who lent me his IIcx when the latter two programs failed on the IIci, and as a source of images for the colour plates (care of the Glasgow University photographic unit).

Final thanks to Keith van Rijsbergen, head of computing science at Glasgow, who created the series in which this book appears, and to Cambridge University Press for their resolute patience until the book was finished.

Stuart G. Hoggar
Glasgow, January 1992

Introduction

> The person in the being mode will come to the lecture with an idea, a question, in mind. He will not attempt to write down everything he hears, but will afterwards emerge knowing more than the person who did. (Freely quoted from Erich Fromm *To have or to be*.)

It is expected that, rather than work through the whole book, readers will wish to browse or to look up particular topics. To this end we give a fairly extended introduction, list of symbols, and index. Each chapter begins with a table of its contents. The book is in four interconnected parts (the connections are outlined at the end of the Introduction):

I	*The plane*	Chapters 1-6.
II	*3-space*	Chapters 7-9.
III	*Topology*	Chapters 10-13.
IV	*Fractals*	Chapters 14-16.

In each case the easiest chapter is the first cited, but it would be a pity to stop there. Indeed the results of Chapters 1-2 are foundational for all four parts, sometimes leading to very pleasant shortcuts of an argument or calculation. On the other hand Chapter 10, whilst essentially avoiding topology, may be used as a pointer to the rest of the book. One aid to taking in information is first to go through following a substructure and let the rest take care of itself (a surprising amount of the rest gets tacked on). To facilitate this, each description of a part is followed by a quick trip through that part, which the reader may care to follow.

An easy way in. If it is true that one picture is worth a thousand words then an easy but fruitful way into this book is to browse through selected pictures. Here is one suggestion. Start with the plane pattern examples of Chapter 5: Section 5.7 and Exercises 5. For some more, see Examples 4.20 and Exercises 4. An early illustration of a Julia set is Figure 11.14. More illustrations of fractal sets in black and white (not to be despised) are found in (most of) Figures 10.6 to 10.18 (curves), Figures 14.10 to 14.25, Figure 15.9, and Figures 16.18 to 16.26. Finally, move to the colour plates.

Chapters 1-6 (Part I.) The mathematics is geared towards producing patterns automatically by computer, allocating some design decisions to a user. We begin with isometries - those transformations of the plane which preserve distance and hence shape, but which may switch left handed objects into right handed ones (such isometries are called indirect). In this part of the book we work geometrically, without recourse to matrices. In Chapter 1 we show that isometries fall into two classes: the direct ones are rotations or translation, and the indirect ones reflections or glides. In Chapter 2 we derive the rules for combining isometries and introduce groups and the Dihedral group in particular. In a short Chapter 3 we apply the theory so far to classifying all 1-dimensional or 'braid' patterns into seven types (Table 3.1).

From Chapter 4 especially we consider symmetries or 'symmetry operations' on a plane pattern. That is, those isometries which send a pattern onto itself, each part going to another with the same size and shape (see Figure 1.3 and ff.). A plane pattern is one having translation symmetries in two non-parallel directions. Thus examples are wallpaper patterns, floor tilings, carpets, patterned textiles, and the Escher interlocking pattern of the frontispiece. We prove the Crystallographic restriction, that rotational symmetries of a plane pattern must be multiples of a 1/2, 1/3, 1/4, or 1/6 turn (1/5 is not allowed). We show that plane patterns, are made up of parallelogram shaped cells, falling into five types (Figure 4.9). The chapter concludes with examples.

In Chapter 5, guided by the conclusions of Chapter 4, we deduce the existence of seventeen pattern types, each with its own set of interacting symmetry operations. In Section 5.8 we include a flow chart for deciding into which type any given pattern fits, plus a fund of test examples. In Chapter 6 we draw some threads together by proving that the seventeen proposed categories really are distinct according to a rigorous definition of 'equivalent' patterns (Section 6.1), and that every pattern must fall into one of the categories provided it is 'discrete' (there is a *lower* limit on how far any of its symmetries can move the pattern). By this stage we increasingly use the idea that, because the composition of two symmetries is a third, the set of all symmetries of a pattern form a group (the definition is recalled in Section 2.5). In Section 6.3 we consider various kinds of regularity upon which a pattern may be based, via techniques of Coxeter graphs and Wythoff's construction (they apply in higher dimensions to give polyhedra). Finally in Section 6.4 we concentrate the theory towards building an algorithm to construct (e.g. by computer) a pattern of any type from a modest user input, based on a smallest replicating unit called a fundamental region (we also offer software on a disc, see the end of the chapter).

Chapters 1-6: *a quick trip*. Read the introduction to Chapter 1 then note Theorem 1.18 on what isometries of the plane turn out to be. Note from Theorem 2.1 how they can all be expressed in terms of reflections, and the application of this in Example 2.6 to composing rotations about distinct points. Look through Table 2.2 for anything that surprises you. Theorem 2.12 is vital information and this will become apparent later. Do the exercise above Figure 2.19. Omit Chapter 3 for now. Read the first four pages of Chapter 4 then pause for the Crystallographic restriction (Theorem 4.15). Proceed to Figure 4.9, Genesis of the five net types, note Examples 4.20, and try Exercise 6 at the end of the chapter yourself. Get the main message of Chapter 5 by using the scheme of Section 5.8 to identify pattern types in Exercises 5 at the end of the chapter (examples with answers are given in Section 5.7). Finish in Chapter 6 by looking through Section 6.4 on 'Creating plane patterns' and recreate the one in question 13 of Exercises 6 (end of the chapter) by finding one fundamental region.

Chapters 7-9 (Part II.) These chapters build from two to three-dimensional geometry and, by contrast with earlier chapters, are matrix oriented. In Chapter 7, after recapitulating the basics of 3-d vectors and coordinates we explain left handed versus right handed triples of vectors and their use in coordinate systems. The scalar product of vectors is introduced, with its relation to geometry. Now we consider matrices, determinants, and some applications such as: calculating areas and volumes, determining whether a triple is left or right handed, calculating various types of vector products. Finally we show how to determine the matrix of any plane isometry, using a 3 by 3 matrix if translation is involved.

Chapter 8 is about isometries in 3-space (now translation is included in a 4 by 4 matrix). We begin by proving that isometries can necessarily be represented in matrix form, determine the effect of a change of coordinate axes, and characterise isometries by their determinant as always preserving or always reversing right handedness. We determine the matrices for general reflection, rotation, translation, glides, rotary reflections and screw isometries, showing that these exhaust the possibilities for 3-d isometries. We introduce a number of techniques for going back and forth between the geometry and matrix of an isometry. For example determining from a rotation matrix the direction and position of the axis, the angle and its sense. Thus we easily compute the composition of any two of the six types of isometry. Example 8.29 is an application in Molecular graphics. The usefulness of eigenvalues and eigenvectors for some of these calculations appears. Along the way we derive some formulae and methods of practical value which deserve to be better known, such as (8.11), Example 8.40, Theorems 8.42, 8.49 and Corollary 8.52. We conclude with a list of where twenty such 'how to' solutions are found in the chapter (a possible quick way in).

Chapter 9 aims to show some benefits of using quaternions as a technique for calculating with rotations, which comes into its own especially when, in setting up animation of solid objects, we wish to move smoothly between a whole sequence of translated and rotated images (key frames) of the object. We cover first the basics of complex numbers a+b**i**, where a,b are real and **i** is a symbol whose square is -1. Indeed the complex numbers are the smallest set of 'numbers' to include both the real numbers (which they do in the form a+0**i**) and a square root of -1. A remarkable consequence of this inclusion is that not only does every quadratic equation now have a solution, but so does every polynomial equation, of whatever degree. This is the famous 'Fundamental Theorem of Algebra' (proved in Chapter 13 but first used, for eigenvalues, in Chapter 8). However the fact that generalises into 3-d rotations by quaternions is this: a complex number may be viewed as a point in the plane with polar coordinates r,θ. Then, to multiply two numbers, we multiply the values of r, but *add* the angles (see Figure 9.5). We introduce the special arithmetic rules (9.15) for quaternions a+b**i**+c**j**+d**k**, where **j**,**k** are further square roots of -1. On reaching Example 9.36 we are ready to calculate compositions of 3-d rotations by using quaternions. Some nice test cases are provided by composing symmetry operations of Platonic solids (tetrahedron, square, icosahedron..). Finally in Section 9.4 we show how in-betweening over a series of key frames may be done by constructing a Bézier-type curve through corresponding points (unit quaternions) on the three-dimensional sphere in real 4-space.

Chapters 7-9: *a quick trip*. Do Exercise 7.11 at the end of Chapter 7, checking out the background of vectors, matrices and determinants in (7.4), Definitions 7.3 and 7.29, Theorem 7.31 (c),(d), Theorem 7.32, Rules 7.20 and preceding definition. For Chapter 8, pick out three things that look new or interesting from the how to do list on page 177. If inclined, follow an example and do an exercise on each. In Chapter 9, if new to complex numbers, first read pages 180 to 186 and note Figure 9.7. For quaternions and rotations look through Section 9.2.1. Use Theorem 9.30 to do Exercise 25 on page 216, using the method of Example 9.38.

Chapters 10-13 (Part III.) Chapter 10 is a fairly easy intoduction to ideas which reappear throughout the rest of the book, with plenty of diagrams and pictures. We show first how some phenomena of coastlines and land frontiers can now be 'explained' in fractal terms. It proves very instructive to introduce Mandelbrot's initiator-generator construction for curves, from snowflake, to the Sierpinski gasket as curve, to the plane-filling type. Its reformulation in terms of plane transformations (going beyond isometries but using them) points to powerful techniques for fractals, which appear first in Chapter 13.

With Chapter 11 we come for the first time to topology. The basics of metric spaces are covered, where 'metric' signifies that we allow a variety of concepts of distance. This is emphatically not the esoteric for its own sake, for from Chapter 13 on we reap the benefit of laws of distance applying to a concept of distance between visual images. The idea of distance leads to open sets, closed sets, and thence to rigorous and usable definitions of interior and boundary. Then to a definition of continuous function which dispenses with ε's and δ's and makes some otherwise hard-to-prove results much easier.

Chapter 12 plays the role of topology, part 2. We define compact sets and prove their important equivalence in n-space to closed and bounded sets. Some famous results follow on the benefits of compactness. Much flows from: the image of a compact set under a continuous function is compact. For example (i) every linear function from n- to m-space has a bound on the factor $|f(\mathbf{x})|/|\mathbf{x}|$ by which it scales the length of a vector **x** (important for iterated function systems in Chapter 14), and (ii) a real linear function on a compact subset of n-space attains its maximum and minimum on the boundary, from which follows the Principle of Linear Programming, (12.9). The other key idea in this chapter is connectedness, agreeing with an intuitive idea in obvious cases. Similarly to the compact case, the image of a connected set under a continuous function is connected. This has easy applications to a proof of the Intermediate Value Theorem and working with 'sides' of a (hyper)plane. Many results here (as in Chapter 11) are the basis of later study of Mandelbrot, Julia, and other fractal sets.

Chapter 13 introduces the Hausdorff distance between two pictures interpreted as subsets of the plane. We prove that the distance laws of Chapter 11 for a metric space are satisfied. Now we define the 'collage map', sending a plane set E to a new set ψE determined by N plane transformations. We prove the far-reaching Contraction Mapping Theorem, 13.14 which shows via Theorem 13.28 when the successive image pictures $\psi^k E$ approach a unique one (this is followed up in Chapter 14). Hausdorff distance also plays an important role in Chapter 15. A second and interesting application of the Contraction Mapping Theorem is to the iterative solution of polynomial equations, showing why Newton's method is better than most. We also use it to show the existence and uniqueness of a class of differential equations. In the final Section, 13.4, we tie some loose ends such as the approximation of a continuous function by a sequence of step functions (see the 'measures' part of Chapter 15) and a proof of the Fundamental Theorem of Algebra by topology and winding numbers.

Chapters 10-13 : A quick trip. Use (10.7) to calculate the dimension of the Sierpinski gasket in Figure 10.7. Examine Figure 10.14 and read page 232. In Chapter 11 note Definitions 11.1, 11.2 and 11.34 then follow Examples 11.41, using the index as necessary. In Chapter 12, take the meaning of *compact* from Theorem 12.26, note Theorem 12.28, and follow the proof of Application 12.29. Do Exercise 12.8 on page 301 similarly to Example 12.30 (but don't forget the hint). For Chapter 13, start by reading the first two pages. Note the (fact of) applications of Theorem 13.14 to solving equations in Section 13.2.2. Note the existence and uniqueness of fractals (Theorem 13.28) following from the topology Theorem 13.27 (again, use the index as necessary), and its illustration in Figures 13.8. You may like to see how winding numbers are applied in Section 13.4.2. For the idea of distance between two pictures, try Exercise 13.7 on page 327.

Chapters 14-16 (Part IV.) This last part of the book is mostly about fractals. Whilst it contains material of a technical nature (after all, we are dealing with foundations), there is much that is relatively easy to pick up. Chapter 14 covers the iterated function systems (IFS) highlighted and developed especially by Barnsley (1988) and co-workers. We define an IFS, based on N contractive maps w_i of the plane that are affine (linear plus translation), and its attractor $\mathcal{A}$, a subset of the plane to be interpreted and viewed as an 'image', or picture. In a framework from Chapter 13, $\mathcal{A}$ is the limit of a sequence of sets A_n, where A_{n+1} is the collage $w_1(A_n) \cup w_2(A_n) \cup ... \cup w_N(A_n)$. After some classic attractors, such as Barnsley's fern, we study affine maps and how to work with them in the IFS and computer screen context. Now we take the reader through some typical attractors with small N (tree, anvil, 'Moscow by night') and give practice in recognising the transformations that produce such results. We consider the possibility of finding the component transformations of an IFS to produce more general images and show the value of the Contraction Mapping Theorem and its accompanying bound (often translated as the 'Collage Theorem'). We demonstrate the process for a face requiring twelve transformations.

Chapter 15 is about the Random Iteration Algorithm (RIA) of Barnsley and Demko (1985). It produces the attractor of an IFS not by a series of approximations $\psi^k E$ but as a sequence of points which build up to it. Each successive point is obtained by applying a random choice of transformation w_i from those of the IFS (Definition 15.23). We analyse the algorithm's effectiveness using an addressing scheme for attractors which is a generalisation of the binary, ternary or decimal expansions of numbers on the real line. We investigate whether the RIA might work more efficiently with a less 'random' number generator for choosing the w_i. Hutchinson's idea (1981), that measure theory ought to help in working with attractors, comes to fruition very naturally via the RIA (Barnsley and Demko). Not only shades of grey but of colour are 'measured out', even down to the pixel level. By Section 15.4, having covered some of the technicalities, we are well placed to introduce Hausdorff dimension, based as it is on measures. (We take a fractal set as one whose Hausdorff dimension differs from its topological dimension.) We include the result that a self-similar set has Hausdorff dimension equal to its easily calculated similarity dimension.

In Chapter 16 we come to some of the hardest and yet some of the most spectacular things covered in this book, arising from the dynamics of iterated complex functions f(z). Thus we start with a function f: **C** $\to$ **C** (where **C** is the plane regarded as complex numbers), an initial point z_0, and observe the behaviour of the sequence $z_0, z_1, z_2, \ldots$, (called the *orbit* of z_0) where $z_{n+1} = f(z_n)$. Importantly, this process could be the iterative solution of an equation (see later). Very influential on the overall outcome is the orbit's behaviour near a fixed point α of f(z), i.e. one for which $f(\alpha) = \alpha$. If the derivative $f'(\alpha)$ has modulus less than 1 then points z sufficiently near α are drawn towards it ($f^n(z) \to \alpha$ as $n \to \infty$). Such points constitute the *basin of attraction* $A(\alpha)$, whose boundary is the *Julia set* of f. We prove results leading to the computer generation of Julia sets (Constructions 16.44 to 16.46) and to their colour codings which produce some increasingly well-known beautiful effects. As is commonly done, we study especially the effectively representative case $f(z) = f_c(z) = z^2+c$ and introduce its Mandelbrot set M, the set of points c for which J(f) is connected, or alternatively (a theorem) those c for which $f_c{}^n(c)$ does *not* tend to infinity as n does (see Construction 16.51). We explore the anatomy of M, which has further interesting detail at every level of magnification. Indeed M acts as an encyclopaedia of Julia sets in ways which even include 'snapshots'. Nevertheless M is connected, and we sketch the Douady-Hubbard proof of this. Finally we investigate the Julia set and basins of attraction for Newton's iterative method of solution, starting from any complex number, and shed new light on an old problem.

Chapters 14-16 : a quick trip. Read page 330 and see in Figure 14.1 how frame 2 arises from frame 1 in the same way as frame 1 arises from frame 0. Consider Figure 14.10 and Examples 14.19, 14.21, 14.26. Read pages 355-356 then try the exercise below Figure 14.22 **or** use colour plate 7 to help you understand Figure 14.21. In Chapter 15 look at the following figures and their explanations: 15.4, 15.8, 15.9, 15.12. Apply ten steps of the RIA for a Sierpinski gasket by throwing dice. In Chapter 16, start with the Mandelbrot set of Figure 16.18 in conjunction with page 424 (read Theorem 16.50 rather than the lemma). Take a look at Seahorse valley via colour plates 9-19. For Julia sets look quickly through pages 407-409, then pick up on Figure 16.20 and its preceding explanation. See this exemplified in colour plates 20-24, 27, 28. Note the construction *methods* on pages 422 to 423 and 425. Finally, look at Theorem 16.68 (Newton's method) and its illustration on colour plate 30.

Which chapters depend on which

1-6	Each chapter depends on the previous ones.
7	All depends on Chapter 1; only Section 7.4 depends on Chapter 2.
8	Matrices and vector products from Chapter 7, and Chapters 1,2.
9	As for Chapter 8, plus a little calculus towards the end.
10	Vectors and plane isometries from Chapter 1.
11	Elementary vectors (Section 1.2.1).
12	The definitions and results of Chapter 11; Elementary vectors (Section 1.2.1). Linear functions (Definition 8.4 ff.).
13	Isometries and vectors (Chapter 1). Section 13.4 requires complex numbers (Section 9.1). Topology: the results and definitions of Chapters 11, 12.
14	Vectors and plane isometries from Chapters 1, 2. Matrices (Chapter 7). Certain recapitulated results and the idea of convergence, from Chapter 13.
15	As for Chapter 14, plus iterated function systems (Section 14.1). Continuity (Section 11.4).
16	Complex numbers (Section 9.1). Topology: the results and definitions of Chapters 11, 12 and Section 13.4.1. Note: Sections 16.2.5 to 16.3.2 essentially rely only on results of Chapter 16.

Table of crude chapter dependencies.

A Chapter depends on those it can 'reach' by going down the graph.

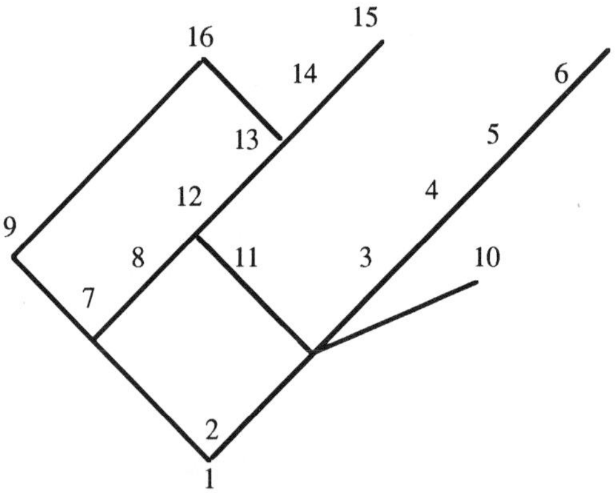

Chapter 1 ISOMETRIES

1.1 Introduction

One practical aim in Part 1 is to equip the reader to build a pattern generating computer engine. The patterns we have in mind come from two main streams. Firstly the *geometrical tradition*, represented for example in the fine Moslem art in the Alhambra at Granada in Spain, but found very widely.

Figure 1.1 Variation on an Islamic theme. For the original, see Critchlow (1976), page 112. The arrows indicate symmetry in two independent directions, and the pattern is considered to continue indefinitely, filling the plane.

Less abundant but still noteworthy are the patterns left by the ancient Romans (Field, 1988). The second type is that for which the Dutch artist M. C. Escher is famous, exemplified in the frontispiece, in which (stylised) motifs of living forms are dovetailed together in remarkable ways. Useful references are Coxeter (1987), MacGillavry (1976), and especially Escher (1989). In Figure 1.2 we imitate a classic Escher-type pattern.

The magic is due partly to the designers' skill and partly to their discovery of certain rules and techniques. We describe the underlying mathematical theory and how it may be applied in practice by someone claiming no particular artistic skills.

The patterns to which we refer are true *plane* patterns, that is, there are translations in two non-parallel directions (opposite directions count as parallel) which move every submotif of the pattern onto a copy of itself elsewhere in the pattern. A *translation* is a movement of everything, in the same direction, by the same amount. Thus in Figure 1.2 piece A can be moved to piece B by the translation represented by arrow **a**, but no translation will transform it to piece C. A reflection would have to be incorporated.

%%

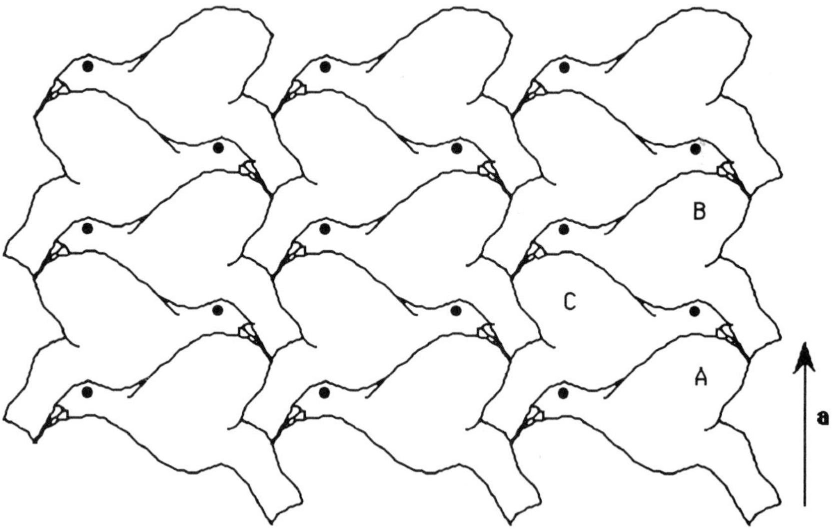

%%

Figure 1.2 Plane pattern of interlocking birds, after M. C. Escher.

EXERCISE The reader may like to verify that, in Figure 1.1, two smallest such translations are represented in their length and direction by the arrows shown, and determine corresponding arrows for Figure 1.2. These should be horizontal and vertical.

But there may be much more to it.

More generally, we lay a basis for understanding *isometries* - those transformations of the plane which preserve distance - and look for the easiest ways to see how they combine or can be decomposed. Examples are translations, rotations, and reflections. Our approach is essentially geometrical. An important tool is the idea of a *symmetry* of a plane figure; that is, an isometry which sends every submotif of the pattern onto another of the same size and shape. (The translations we cited for Figure 1.2 are thus symmetries, but we reiterate the idea here.) For example, the head in Figure 1.3(a) below is symmetrical about the line AB and, corresponding to this fact, the isometry obtained by reflecting the plane in line AB is called a *symmetry* of the head. Of course we call AB a *line of symmetry*. In Figure 1.3(b) the isometry consisting of a one third turn about O is a symmetry, and O is called a 3-fold centre of symmetry. In general, if the 1/n turn about a point A (n maximal) is a symmetry of a pattern we say A is an *n-fold centre of symmetry*, of the pattern.

Figure 1.3(a)

Figure 1.3(b)

The key idea is that the collection of all symmetries, or *symmetry operations,* of a figure, form a *group* G (see Section 2.5). Here this means simply that the composition of any two symmetries is another, which is sometimes expressed by saying that the set of symmetries is closed under composition. Thus, for Figure 1.3(a) the symmetry group G consists of the *identity* I (do nothing) and reflection in line AB. For Figure 1.3(b), G consists of I, a 1/3 turn τ about the central point, and a 2/3 turn which may be written τ^2 since it is the composition of two 1/3 turns τ. In fact, every plane pattern falls into one of 17 classes determined by its symmetry group, as we shall see in Chapter 5. That is, provided one insists, as we do, that the patterns be *discrete*, in the sense that no pattern can be transformed onto itself by arbitrarily small movements. This rules out for example a pattern consisting of copies of an infinite bar ·· ▬▬▬ ··· .

EXERCISE What symmetries of the pattern represented in Figure 1.1 leave the central point unmoved?

Section 6.3 on tilings, or tessellations of the plane is obviously relevant to pattern generation and surface filling. However, I am indebted to Alan Fournier for the comment that it touches another issue: how in future will we wish to divide up a screen into pixels, and what should be their shape? The answer is not obvious, but we introduce some of the options. cf. Ulichney (1987), Chapter 2.

A remarkable survey of tilings and patterns is given in Grünbaum and Shephard (1987), in which also the origins of many familiar and not-so-familiar patterns are recorded. For a study of isometries and symmetry, including the 'non-discrete' case, see Lockwood & Macmillan (1978), and for a connection with manifolds Montesinos (1987).

Now, a plane pattern has a smallest replicating unit known as a *fundamental region* $\mathfrak{F}$ of its symmetry group: the copies of $\mathfrak{F}$ obtained by applying each symmetry operation of the group in turn, form a *tiling* of the plane. That is, they cover the plane without area overlap. In Figure 1.2 we may take any one of A, B, C as fundamental region. Usually several copies of this region form together a *cell,* or smallest replicating unit which can be made to tile the plane using *translations only.* Referring again to Figure 1.2, the combination of A and C is such a cell.

The last section of Part 1 shows how the idea of a fundamental region of the symmetry group, plus a small number of basic generating symmetries, gives on the one hand much insight, and on the other, a compact and effective method of both analysing and automating the production of patterns. This forms the basis of our marketed program 'Polynet' (page 113). This text contains commercial possibilities, not least of which is the production of books of patterns and teach-yourself pattern construction. See for example Oliver (1979), Devaney (1989), Schattschneider and Walker (1982), or inspect sample books of wallpaper, linoleum, carpeting, and so on.

We conclude by noting the application of plane patterns as a test bed for techniques and research in the area of texture mapping. cf. Heckbert (1989), Chapter 3.

1.2 Isometries and their sense

We start by reviewing some basic things needed which the reader may have once known but not used for a long time.

1.2.1 The plane and vectors

Coordinates Points in the plane will be denoted by capital letters A, B, C, ... It is often convenient to specify the position of points by means of a *Cartesian coordinate system.* This consists of (i) a fixed reference point normally labelled O and called the *origin*, (ii) a pair of perpendicular lines through O, called the *x-axis* and *y-axis,* and (iii) a chosen direction along each axis in which movements are measured as positive.

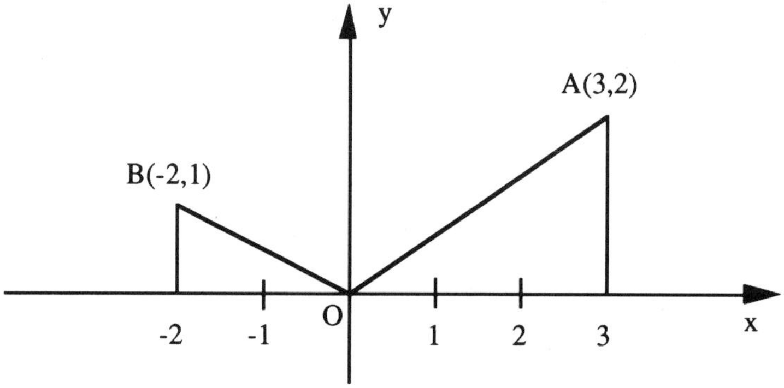

Figure 1.4 Coordinate axes. The x-axis and y-axis are labelled by lower case x, y and often called Ox, Oy. Positive directions are arrowed.

Thus in Figure 1.4 the point A has coordinates (3,2), meaning that A is reached from O by a movement of 3 units in the positive direction along the x-axis then 2 units in the positive y direction. Compare B(-2,1), reached by a movement of 2 units in the negative (opposite to positive) x direction and 1 unit in the y direction. Of course the two component movements could be made in either order.

Lines The straight line joining two points A, B is called the *line segment* AB. As in the case of coordinates, we need the technique of assigning to AB one of the two possible directions, giving us the *directed line segments* <u>AB</u> or <u>BA</u>, according as the direction is towards B or towards A. This is illustrated in Figure 1.5(a) below.

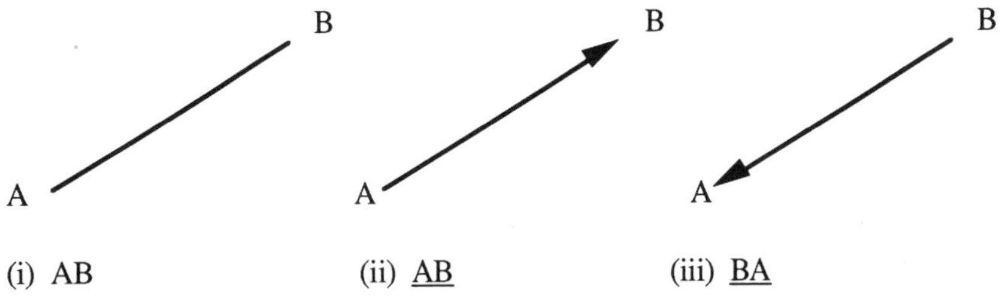

Figure 1.5(a) Directed and undirected line segments.

Length $|AB|$ denotes the length of the line segment AB, which equals of course the distance between A and B. Sometimes it is useful to have a formula for this in terms of the coordinates $A(a_1,a_2)$ and $B(b_1,b_2)$:

$$|AB| \quad = \quad \sqrt{(b_1 - a_1)^2 + (b_2 - a_2)^2}\,. \tag{1.1}$$

EXERCISE Prove formula (1.1) by using the theorem of Pythagoras.

Vectors A vital concept as soon as we come to translation [Section 1.2.2(a)], a *vector* is any combination of a distance, or magnitude, and a direction in space. (For now, the plane.) Thus every directed line segment represents some vector by its direction and length, but the same vector is represented by *any* line segment with this length and direction, as depicted in Figure 1.5(b) below.

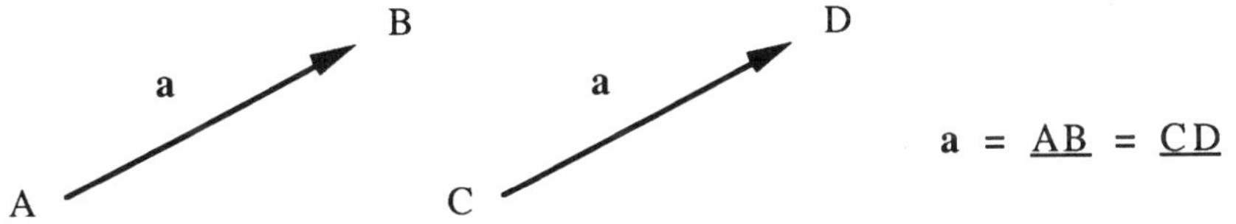

Figure 1.5(b) Directed line segments representing the same vector **a**.

A letter representing a vector will normally be printed in bold lower case thus: **a**, and although the directed line segment <u>AB</u> of Figure 1.5(b), for example, has the additional property of an *initial point* A and *end point* B we will sometimes allow ourselves to write for example $\mathbf{a} = \underline{AB} = \underline{CD} = \mathbf{b}$, to mean that all four have the same magnitude and direction With the length (magnitude) of a vector **x** denoted by $|\mathbf{x}|$, the statement then includes $|\mathbf{a}| = |\underline{AB}| = |\underline{CD}| = |\mathbf{b}|$. Also it is often convenient to drop the letters, in a diagram, leaving an arrow of the correct length and direction thus: ⟶. The *angle between two vectors* means the angle between representative directed line segments <u>AB</u>, <u>AC</u> with the same inital point.

Components and position vectors By contrast with the previous paragraph, we may standardise on the origin as initial point, representing a vector **a** by segment <u>OA</u>. Then we write

$$\mathbf{a} = (a_1,a_2),$$

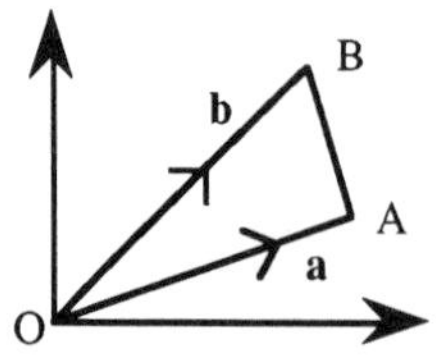

Figure 1.6

where a_1,a_2 play a double role as the *coordinates* of point A, and the *components* of vector **a**. Further, since **a** now defines uniquely the position of the point A, we call **a** the *position vector* of A (with respect to origin O). Similarly a point B has position vector $\mathbf{b} = (b_1,b_2)$, and so on (Figure 1.6). Alternatively we may write $\mathbf{r}_A$ for the position vector of A.

Of course x,y will remain alternative notation for the coordinates, especially if we consider a variable point, or an equation in Cartesian coordinates, such as $x = m$ for the line perpendicular to the x-axis, crossing it at the point (m,0).

Scalar times vector In the context of vectors we often refer to numbers as *scalars*, to emphasise that they are not vectors. We recall that the *magnitude* or *absolute value* of a scalar λ is obtained by dropping its minus sign if there is one. Thus $|\lambda| = -\lambda$ if $\lambda < 0$, otherwise $|\lambda| = \lambda$. If **a** is a vector and λ a scalar then we define $\lambda\mathbf{a}$ as the vector whose magnitude equals the product $|\lambda|\,|\mathbf{a}|$, and whose direction is that of **a** if $\lambda > 0$ and opposite to **a** if $\lambda < 0$. If $\lambda = 0$ then we define the result to be the anomalous vector **0**, with zero magnitude and direction undefined. As in the illustration below, we usually abbreviate (-1)**a** to -**a**, (-2)**a** to -2**a**, and so on. Also (1/c)**a** may be shortened to **a**/c ($c \neq 0$).

EXAMPLES

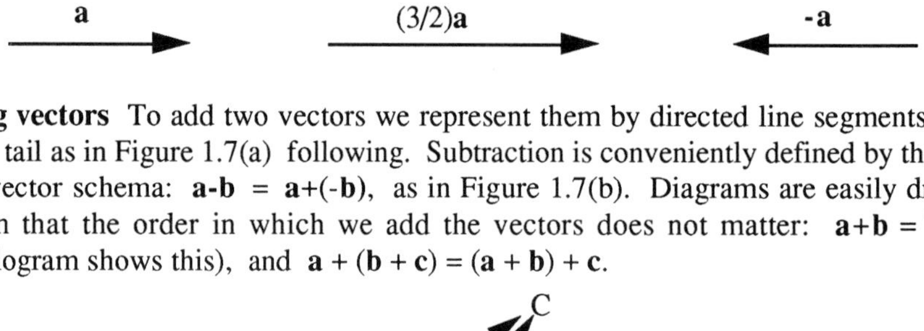

Adding vectors To add two vectors we represent them by directed line segments placed nose to tail as in Figure 1.7(a) following. Subtraction is conveniently defined by the scalar times vector schema: **a-b** = **a+(-b)**, as in Figure 1.7(b). Diagrams are easily drawn to confirm that the order in which we add the vectors does not matter: **a+b** = **b+a** (a parallelogram shows this), and **a** + (**b** + **c**) = (**a** + **b**) + **c**.

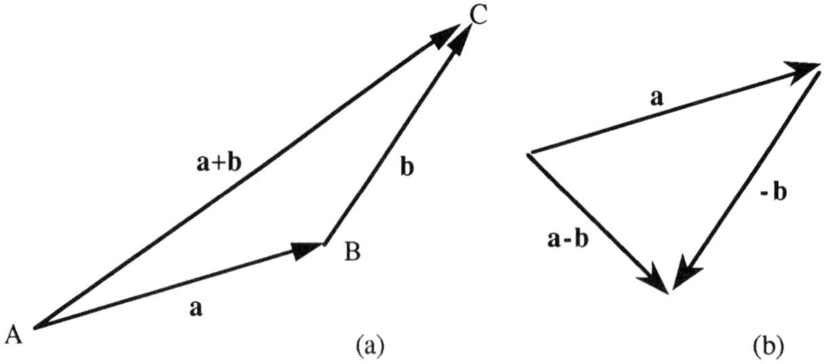

Figure 1.7 Finding (a) the sum and (b) the difference of two vectors by placing them nose to tail.

RULES Let **a**, **b** be the position vectors of A, B. Then

$$\mathbf{a} + \mathbf{b} = (a_1 + b_1, a_2 + b_2) \qquad (1.2A)$$
$$\lambda\mathbf{a} = (\lambda a_1, \lambda a_2) \qquad (1.2B)$$
$$\underline{AB} = \mathbf{b} - \mathbf{a}. \qquad (1.2C)$$

Proof For (1.2A) we refer to Figure 1.7(a), and imagine coordinate axes with point A as origin, taking the x-direction as due East. Then $a_1 + b_1$ = (amount B is East of A) + (amount C is East of B) = amount C is East of A = first component of C. The second components may be handled similarly. (1.2B) is left to the reader. To establish (1.2C), we note that the journey from A to B in Figure 1.6 may be made via the origin: $\underline{AB} = \underline{AO} + \underline{OB} = (-\mathbf{a}) + \mathbf{b}$.

The section formula The point P on AB with AP : PB = m : n (illustrated below) has position vector **p** given by

$$\mathbf{p} = \frac{1}{m+n}(m\mathbf{b} + n\mathbf{a}). \qquad (1.3)$$

Often called the *section formula*, this is extremely useful, and has the virtue of covering cases such as (i), (ii) shown below in which P does not lie between A and B.

(i)

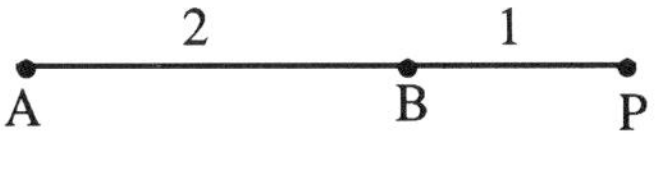

(ii)

This means that $\underline{AP}$ and $\underline{PB}$ are in opposite directions and so m, n have opposite signs. Thus in Case (i) $\underline{AP} = -3\underline{PB}$ and we may write $\underline{AP} : \underline{PB}$ = 3 : -1 (or equally, -3:1), whilst Case (ii) entails $\underline{AP} = -(3/5)\,\underline{PB}$, or $\underline{AP} : \underline{PB}$ = -3 : 5.

This said, (1.3) is easily proved, for $n\underline{AP} = m\underline{PB}$, so by (1.2) $n(\mathbf{p} - \mathbf{a}) = m(\mathbf{b} - \mathbf{p})$, which rearranges as $(m+n)\mathbf{p} = m\mathbf{b} + n\mathbf{a}$.

EXERCISE Draw the diagram for proving (1.2A), marking in the components of **a** and **b**.

APPLICATION 1.1 This is a handy illustration of the use of vectors to prove a well known fact we will need in Chapter 6 : The medians of a triangle ABC all pass through the point G (centre of gravity), whose position vector is

$$\mathbf{g} = \tfrac{1}{3}(\mathbf{a} + \mathbf{b} + \mathbf{c}) .$$

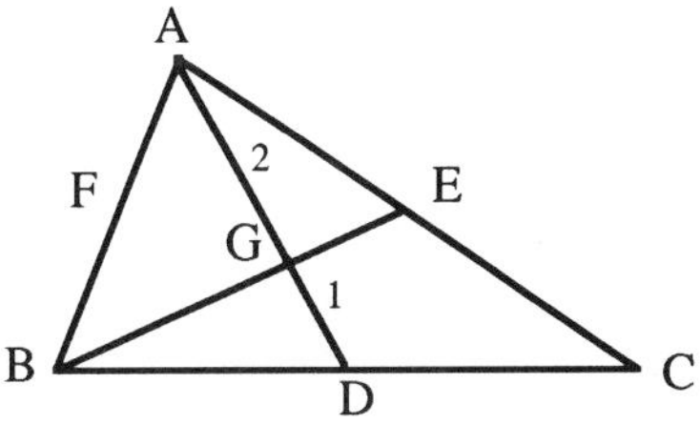

To prove this, label the midpoints of the sides by D,E,F as shown. By (1.3), D has position vector $\mathbf{d} = (1/2)(\mathbf{b} + \mathbf{c})$. So, again by (1.3), the point that divides median AD in the ratio 2 : 1 has position vector $(1/3)(2\mathbf{d} + 1\mathbf{a})$, which equals $(1/3)(\mathbf{a} + \mathbf{b} + \mathbf{c})$ on substituting for **d**. But this expression is symmetrical in **a**, **b**, **c**, and so lies on all three medians, dividing each in the ratio 2 : 1.

NOTE The use of components gives an important way to calculate with vectors, which will come into its own in Chapter 7. Before then, our arguments will be mostly geometrical, with components as a tool in some exercises. However, we give both a geometrical and a coordinate proof of (1.14) a little further on, which the reader may find interesting for comparison purposes at that point.

EXERCISE Use position vectors and (1.3), which applies equally in 3- space (indeed, in any dimension), to prove the following facts about any tetrahedron ABCD. (i) The four lines join-ing a vertex to the centroid of its opposite face are concurrent at a point G which divides each such line in the ratio 3:1, (ii) The three lines joining midpoints of pairs of opposite edges all meet in G.

1.2.2 Isometries

DEFINITION 1.2 A *transformation* g of the plane is a rule which assigns to each point P a unique point P^g, or P', called the *image of P under g*. (Note that P^g does not mean P 'to the power of' g.) We think of g as moving points around in the plane. We also call g a *map* or *mapping* of the plane onto itself, and say g *maps* P to P'. An ***isometry*** of the plane is a transformation g of the plane which preserves distances. That is, for any two points P, Q:

$$|P'Q'| = |PQ|. \tag{1.4}$$

The reader is advised not to think first of the formula (1.4) but to start from the idea of isometries preserving distance. Of course the same definition is applicable to 3-space or even higher dimensions, and we pursue this in Part two (Chapters 7-9). An important first consequence of the definition is as follows:

An isometry g transforms straight lines into straight lines, and preserves the (unsigned) size of angles. (1.5)

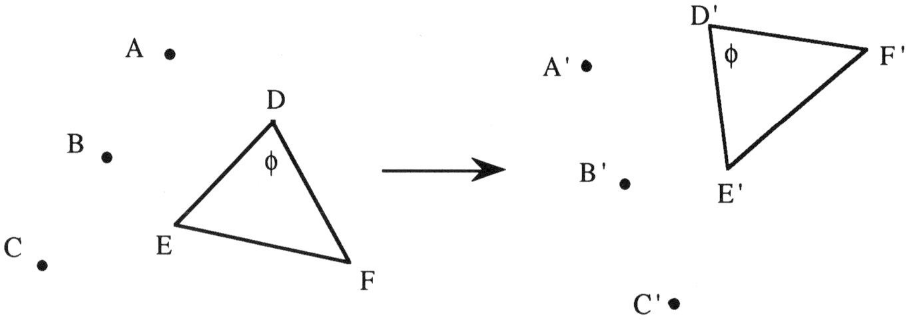

Figure 1.8 Points A, B, C on a straight line, a triangle DEF, and their images under an isometry. The magnitude of angle ϕ is preserved.

Proof of (1.5). We refer to Figure 1.8. It suffices to show that if points A, B, C lie on a straight line, then so do their images A', B', C'. Suppose B lies between A and C. Then elementary geometry tells us that

$$|AC| = |AB| + |BC|,$$

and therefore from condition (1.4) of an isometry, the same holds with A, B, C replaced by A', B', C'. Consequently, A', B', C' also lie on a straight line, and the first assertion of (1.5) is established: straight lines are transformed to straight lines. Now, given this, let us view the angle ϕ between two lines as the vertex angle of some triangle DEF, transformed by g into another triangle, D'E'F' - which must be congruent to DEF because the lengths of the sides are unchanged by g. Thus the vertex angle is unchanged, laying aside considerations of sign. This completes the proof.

NOTATION 1.3 The following are convenient at different times for referring to the image of P under a transformation g:

(i) P' (ii) P^g (iii) g(P).

We shall explain in Section 1.3.1 the significance of our choosing (ii) rather than (iii). In each case the notation allows us to replace P by any figure or subset F in the plane. Thus figure F^g consists of the images of the points of F, or $F^g = \{x^g: x \in F\}$. For example, if F is the lower palm tree in Figure 1.9 , with $g = T_{\mathbf{a}}$ (see just above the figure) then F^g is the upper. The heads of Figure 1.11 provide a further example.

Three types of isometry At this juncture it is appropriate to discuss the three most familiar types of isometry in the plane. The remaining type is introduced in Section 1.3.2.

(a) **Translation** For any vector **a** the translation $T_{\mathbf{a}}$ of the plane is the transformation in which every point is moved in the direction of **a**, through a distance equal to its magnitude $|\mathbf{a}|$.

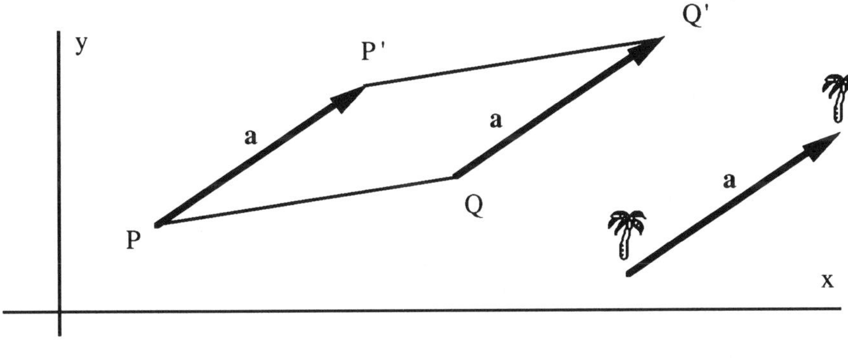

Figure 1.9 The translation $T_{\mathbf{a}}$ is an isometry as $|P'Q'| = |PQ|$ always.

Thus $\underline{PP'} = \mathbf{a}$ (in magnitude and direction). To show that $T_{\mathbf{a}}$ is an isometry, suppose it sends another point Q to Q'. Then $\mathbf{a} = \underline{QQ'}$, so that PP' and QQ' are parallel and equal, making a parallelogram PP'Q'Q. Hence by an elementary theorem in Geometry, $|P'Q'| = |PQ|$, and $T_{\mathbf{a}}$ has indeed preserved distances.

NOTATION 1.4 P' is also called the *translate* of P (by $T_{\mathbf{a}}$). Notice that $T_{\mathbf{a}}$ sends **x** to **x**+**a**, when we identify a point X with its position vector **x**. More geometrically, if $\mathbf{a} = \underline{PQ}$ we may write unambiguously $T_{\mathbf{a}} = T_{PQ}$, the translation which takes P to Q.

(b) **Rotation** As illustrated in Figure 1.10, let the transformation $R_A(\phi)$ be

$$R_A(\phi) \;=\; \text{rotation about the point A through the angle } \phi.$$

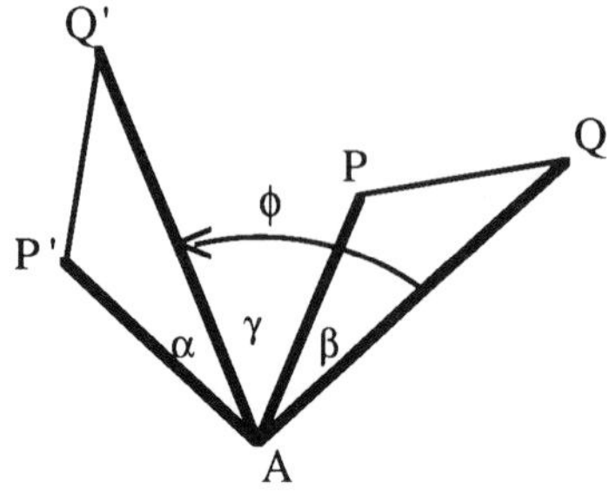

Figure 1.10 Rotation about the point A through positive angle ϕ.

Notice that ϕ is a *signed* angle; it is positive if the rotation is anti-clockwise (counterclockwise), negative in the clockwise case. In Figure 1.10 we see why rotation is an isometry: By definition, $|AP'| = |AP|$, $|AQ'| = |AQ|$ and, signs excluded, $\beta+\gamma = \phi = \alpha+\gamma$, hence $\alpha = \beta$. This establishes congruence of triangles PAQ, P'AQ' (two sides and the included angle), which includes the equality $|P'Q'| = |PQ|$. Thus $R_A(\phi)$ preserves distance and so is an isometry.

REMARKS 1.5

1. We will often use the special notation $R_A(1/n)$ for a 1/n turn about point A and $R_A(m/n)$ for m n'ths of a turn, negative m denoting a clockwise direction. Thus $R_A(2/3)$ is a 2/3 turn about A. Note that $R_A(\phi)$ is distinguished from reflection notation below by the '(ϕ)' part.

2. A rotation through any number of complete turns leaves every point where it began, and so is the *identity isometry* I of Section 1.1 One whole turn is the angle 2π, measured in radians. Thus rotation through $\phi+2\pi$ is the same isometry as rotation through ϕ. We only count the final position of each point, not its route to get there.

3 A 1/2 turn $R_A(\pi)$, or $R_A(1/2)$, reverses the direction of every line segment AB starting at A. In particular the 1/2 turn about the origin sends the point (x,y) to (-x,-y).

4 The effect of a rotation through angle ϕ may be obtained by rotation in the opposite direction, for example through angle $-(2\pi-\phi)$. So $R_A(2/3)$ is equivalent to $R_A(-1/3)$, a clockwise 1/3 turn.

(c) **Reflection** Let $R_{\boldsymbol{m}}$ denote the transformation of the plane obtained by reflecting every point P in the line $\boldsymbol{m}$. That is, as we indicate below in Figure 1.11, PP' is perpendicular to $\boldsymbol{m}$ and P, P' are at equal distances from $\boldsymbol{m}$ but on opposite sides.

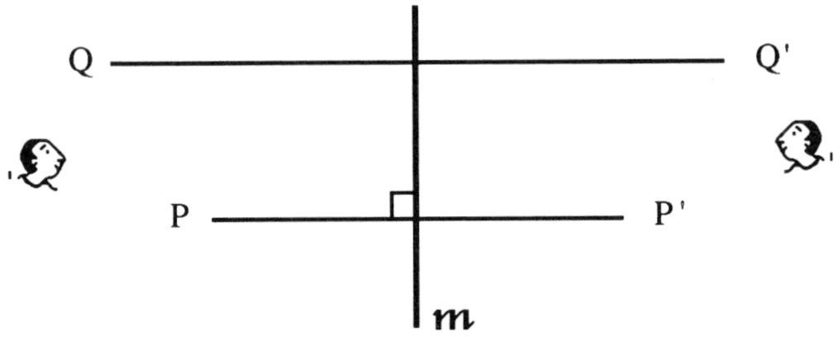

Figure 1.11 Reflection in a line m.

NOTATION 1.6 We may call m the *mirror*, or *mirror line* for the reflection. It is often useful to let R_{AB} denote reflection in a line m which contains points A, B, and let $R_{ax+by=c}$ denote reflection in the line $ax + by = c$.

EXAMPLE 1.7 The following simple formula will be especially useful in Section 6.4.4, and meanwhile for alternative ways to establish many results in the text (cf. the second part of Theorem 1.18) and Exercises. It states that, in coordinates, *reflection in the line* $x = m$ is given by

$$(x, y) \rightarrow (2m - x, y), \tag{1.6}$$

meaning that the isometry $R_{x=m}$ sends the point (x,y) to $(2m-x,y)$.

Proof From the definition of reflection, the y coordinate is unchanged since the mirror is parallel to the y-axis, but x becomes $m + (m-x)$, which equals $2m-x$.

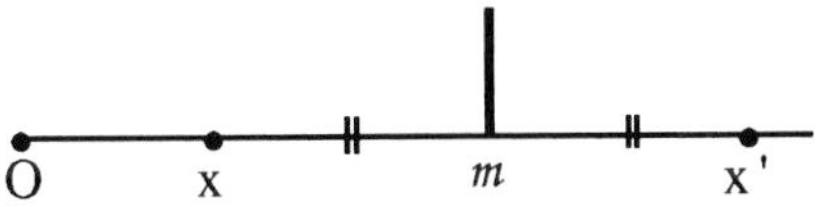

EXAMPLE 1.8 We use coordinates to show that reflection is an isometry. We may choose the coordinate system so that the mirror is the y-axis, giving $m = 0$ in the reflection formula (1.6). Referring to Figure 1.11, suppose the coordinates are $P(p_1,p_2)$, and so on. Then the distance formula (1.1) gives

$$\begin{aligned} |P'Q'|^2 &= (q_1' - p_1')^2 + (q_2' - p_2')^2 \\ &= (-q_1 + p_1)^2 + (q_2 - p_2)^2 \\ &= |PQ|^2, \text{ as required.} \end{aligned}$$

EXERCISE Give a geometrical proof that, in Figure 1.11, we have $|P'Q'| = |PQ|$ and hence that R_m is an isometry, considering also the case where P, Q are on opposite sides of the mirror.

1.2.3 The sense of an isometry

In Figure 1.11 the reflection transforms the right looking face into one that looks to the left (and vice versa). We will see in Theorem 1.10 that an isometry which reverses one face will consistently reverse all. In more directly geometrical terms, it reverses the direction of an arrow round a circle as in Figure 1.12 below, so we proceed as follows.

SENSE Any three non-collinear points A, B, C lie on a unique circle, and the *sense* of an ordered triple ABC means the corresponding direction round the circle, as in Figure1.12. This is also the direction of rotation of BC (about B) towards BA. We give angle ABC (letters in that order) a positive sign if triple ABC is anticlockwise; then CBA is clockwise and angle CBA is negative.

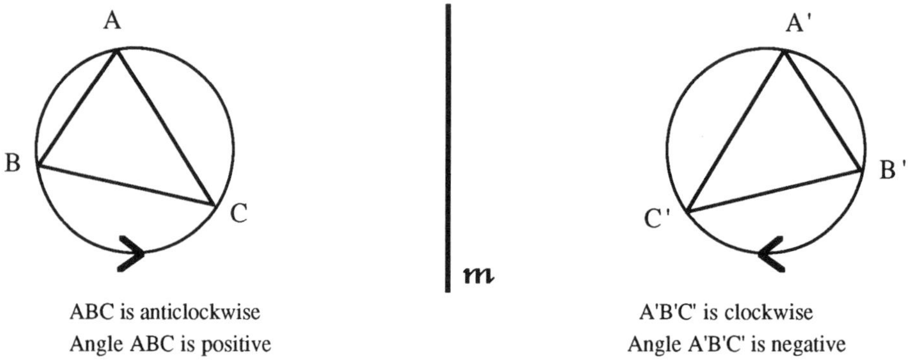

Figure 1.12 Reflection R_m reverses the sense of ordered triple ABC.

Notice that the cyclically related triples ABC, BCA, CAB all specify the same direction round a circle (anticlockwise in Figure 1.12) and that their reverses CBA, ACB, BAC correspond to the opposite direction. Now we are ready for a definition which, happily, accounts for all isometries.

DEFINITION 1.9 An isometry is *direct* if it preserves the sense of any non-collinear triple and *indirect* if it reverses every such sense. We note that the reflection isometry R_m in Figure 1.12 is indirect, since it reverses the sense of ABC (it must be one or the other by Theorem 1.10 below).

THEOREM 1.10 (a) Every isometry is either direct or indirect, (b) An isometry is determined by its effect on any two points and whether it is direct or indirect. Or alternatively by its effect on three non-collinear points.

Proof (a) Let g be an isometry and let A, B, P, Q be points with P and Q on the same side of the line AB, as in Figure 1.13(a) below.

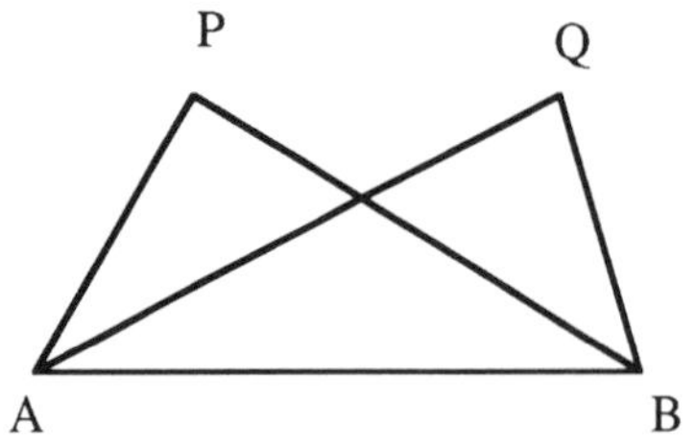

Figure 1.13 (a)

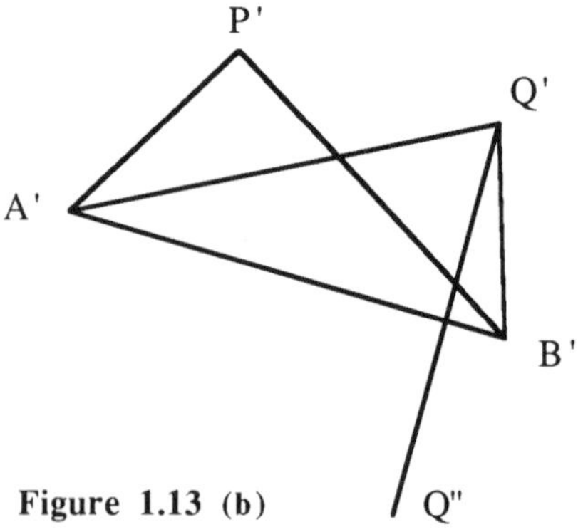

Figure 1.13 (b)

Then the images P' and Q' must be on the same side of A'B' as shown in Figure 1.13(b) above since: given A', B' and P', there are exactly two possible positions Q', Q" for the image of Q, and by elementary geometry $|P'Q''| \neq |PQ|$, which rules out Q". Since, therefore, points on the same side of a line are transformed to points on the same side of its image, we have that for any two points A, B:

if the isometry g preserves (reverses) the sense of one triple containing A, B then it preserves (reverses) the sense of every such triple. (1.7)

where the parentheses mean that the statement holds with 'reverses' in place of 'preserves', and all triples referred to are non-collinear. Let g preserve the sense of PQR. We must deduce that g preserves the sense of an arbitrary triple XYZ, and we shall do this with (1.7) by changing one point at a time.

g preserves the sense of PQR
$\Rightarrow$ g preserves the sense of PQZ (unless P,Q,Z are collinear - cf. Figure 1.14(b))
$\Rightarrow$ g preserves the sense of PYZ (unless P,Y,Z are collinear - cf. Figure 1.14(c))
$\Rightarrow$ g preserves the sense of XYZ (since X,Y,Z are not collinear).

Special cases can be handled by judicious use of (1.7). For example, in Figure 1.14(b) we may proceed in the order PQR $\rightarrow$ XQR $\rightarrow$ XQZ $\rightarrow$ XYZ. This completes the proof of Part(a), reversal cases being handled similarly.

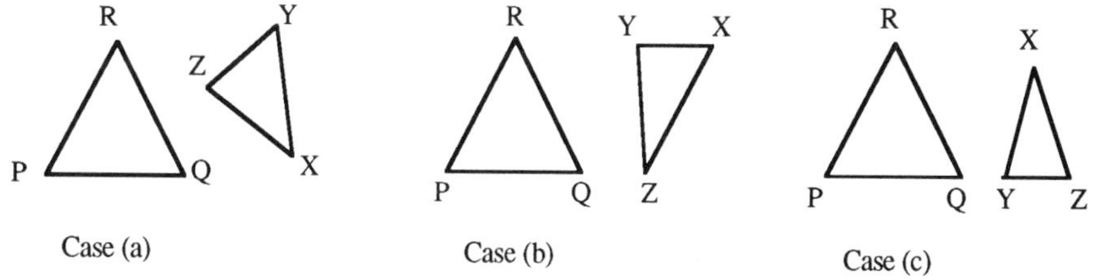

Figure 1.14 Diagram for the proof that if g preserves the sense of triple PQR then it preserves the sense of XYZ. (a) is the general case and (b), (c) are sample special cases.

Proof (b) we refer to Figure 1.13. Suppose the images A', B' of A, B under the isometry g are given. Let Q be any point. If Q happens to lie on AB then Q' lies on A'B', by (1.5), and the equalities $|Q'A'| = |QA|$, $|Q'B'| = |QB|$ determine its exact position. Otherwise these equalities leave two possibilites, represented by Q', Q" in Figure 1.13(b). Since Triples A'B'Q' and A'B'Q" have opposite senses, the image of Q is now determined by whether g is direct or indirect. Alternatively, if we specify the image C' of a third point C, (C not collinear with A, B), then the distances of Q' from the other three images determine its position. This completes the proof of (b).

EXAMPLE 1.11 By considering when the sense of a triple is preserved we have the following categorisation from Theorem 1.10.

Rotation, Translation	DIRECT.
Reflection	INDIRECT.

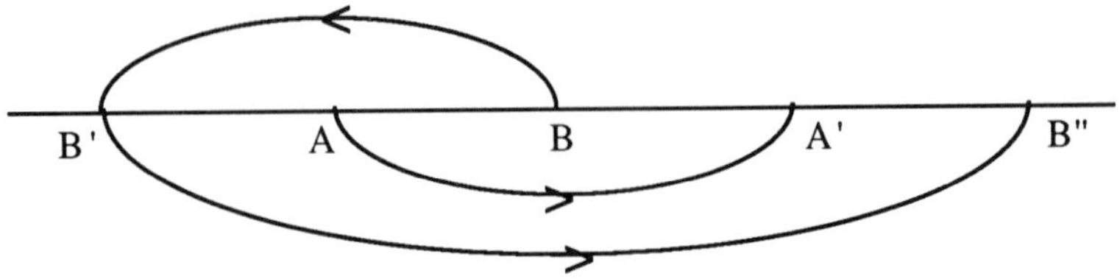

We shall determine the result of performing first a half turn about the point A shown above, then a half turn about B. Since both operations preserve distance and the senses of all triples, the result must be a direct isometry g. But which one? According to Theorem 1.10 we will have it when we find an isometry which is direct and which has the right effect on two points. Now, the result of g is that A moves to A', and B to B" via B'. But A $\rightarrow$ A', B $\rightarrow$ B" is achieved by the direct isometry T_{2AB}, which is therefore (by Theorem 1.10) the one we seek.

EXERCISE Find the result of a half turn about the point A (diagram shortly above), followed by a reflection in a mirror through B at right angles to AB **or** Give the argument in the proof of Theorem 1.10 for special case (c) (cf. the argument for Case (b)).

1.3 The classification of isometries

1.3.1 Composing isometries

We wish to prove Theorem 1.15, a simple and useful result which will assist us in classifying all possible isometries of the plane. First some notation is required. If g, h are two isometries, then their *composition*, or *product*, gh, is the transformation obtained by performing *first* g *then* h. Since g and h both preserve distances, so does their composition, which is therefore also an isometry. In denoting this composition by gh (or g.h), we are deliberately writing the transformations in the order in which they are performed, by contrast with the other standard system defined by (gh)(A) = g(h(A)) where gh means 'perform h then g'. Occasionally, the latter will be convenient. Normally (until Chapter 10) we will use our present definition, which is equivalent to

$$A^{gh} = (A^g)^h . \tag{1.8}$$

In words this says: 'to apply the isometry gh to an arbitrary point A, apply g then h'. In the sense of (1.8), A^g behaves like A to the power of g. It follows that, for a composition of three isometries f, g, h we have the *associative law*

$$f(gh) = (fg)h. \tag{1.9}$$

POWER NOTATION g^m denotes m successive repetitions g.g...g of an isometry g, where $m \geq 1$. Consequently we have the power law (1.10) below for m, n = 0, 1, 2, ... in which we write write $g^0 = I$, the identity (do nothing) isometry.

$$g^m g^n = g^{m+n} = g^n g^m, \qquad (g^m)^n = g^{mn}. \qquad (1.10)$$

EXAMPLES 1.12 The composition of a 1/7 turn, a 2/7 turn, and a 4/7 turn about a given point A is a complete turn. Thus all points are returned to their original positions and the resulting isometry is the identity. We may write $R_A(1/7)\,R_A(2/7)\,R_A(4/7) = I$, without bracketing any pair together. On the other hand, two successive reflections $R_m R_m$ in the same mirror, or n successive 1/n turns about a point A also give the identity, so we may write

$$R_m{}^2 = I = [R_A(1/n)]^n. \qquad (1.11)$$

Composition of translations The rule is

$$T_{\mathbf{a}}\,T_{\mathbf{b}} = T_{\mathbf{a+b}} = T_{\mathbf{b}}\,T_{\mathbf{a}} \qquad (1.12)$$

where the vector sum **a+b** is obtained by placing representatives of **a** and **b** nose to tail in the manner of Figure 1.7 The first equality is a definition and the second is a consequence, conveniently placed here, which the reader is asked to prove below.

EXERCISE Use a parallelogram to show that $T_{\mathbf{a}}\,T_{\mathbf{b}} = T_{\mathbf{b}}\,T_{\mathbf{a}}$, where $T_{\mathbf{a}}$ is translation by the vector **a**. Express $(T_{\mathbf{a}})^n$ as a single translation ***or*** Let g denote a 3/10 turn about some point. Show that $(g^5)^3$ has the effect of a 1/2 turn.

Resolving a translation into components This means re-expressing the corresponding vector as a sum of two others. See below.

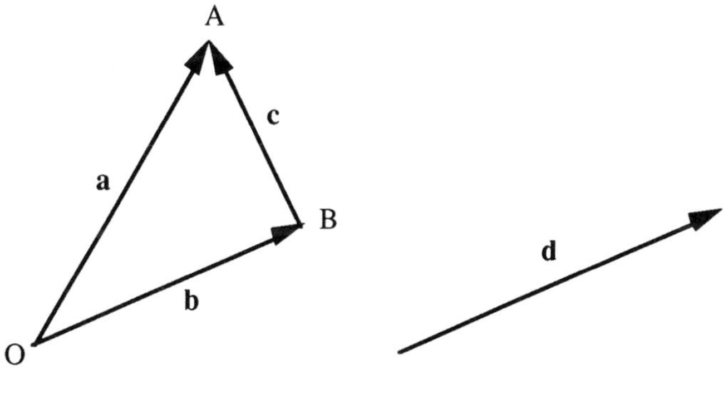

Figure 1.15 Resolving vector **a** along and perpendicular to **d** : **a** = **b+c.**

Referring to Figure 1.15 above, suppose we are given a fixed direction, say that of a vector **d**. Then we may express any vector **a** as the sum of a vector **b** in the direction of **d** plus a vector **c** perpendicular to **d**:

$$\mathbf{a} = \mathbf{b} + \mathbf{c}.$$

This is called *resolving* **a** into components along and perpendicular to **d**. To achieve this, we represent **a** by a directed line segment <u>OA</u>, and then position a point B so that <u>OB</u> has the direction of **d** and BA is perpendicular to **d**. Then the required components are **b** = <u>OB</u> and **c** = <u>BA</u>. Note that we do not require <u>OB</u> = **d**.

At the same time we have *resolved* the translation T_a into *components* along and perpendicular to **d** in the sense that

$$T_a = T_c T_b = T_b T_c. \tag{1.13}$$

REMARKS 1.13 (1) Resolving **a** with respect to the positive x-direction gives the (Cartesian) components of **a.** (2) T_{AB} is the unique translation which sends point A to point B. In particular, we interpret T_{AA} as the identity isometry I (do nothing).

EXERCISE Resolve the vector **a** = (4,0) along and perpendicular to the direction of $\underline{OA}$, where A is the point (1,1).

1.3.2 The classification of isometries

DEFINITION 1.14 We say an isometry g *fixes* a point A if $A^g = A$. This is especially pertinent since a rotation fixes its centre (the point about which rotation is made), and a reflection fixes the points of its mirror, whilst a translation moves everything. For this culminating section of Chapter 1 we first reduce (Theorem 1.15) the classification problem to that of isometries that fix some point (Theorem 1.16), plus the question of what happens when one of these is combined with a translation (cf. (1.14), (1.15)).

THEOREM 1.15 Let A be any point in the plane. Then every isometry g is the composition of an isometry that fixes A, and a translation. Either order may be assumed.

Proof Let the isometry g send A to A'. Then $T = T_{A'A}$ is a translation that sends A' back to A. We have

$$A \xrightarrow{g} A' \xrightarrow{T} A,$$

so the isometry h = g.T fixes A. The argument then runs:

$$\begin{aligned} h &= g\,T_{A'A} \\ \text{therefore} \quad h\,T_{AA'} &= g\,T_{A'A}\,T_{AA'} = g, \end{aligned}$$

the last equality being because the combined effect of translation $T_{A'A}$ followed by $T_{AA'}$ is to do nothing (ie their composition is the identity isometry). In conclusion, we have g = h T_1, where, as required, h fixes A and T_1 is a translation (here $T_{AA'}$). A slight variation of the argument gives g in the form T_2 h, for different h fixing A, and translation T_2.

EXERCISE Adapt the proof above, to obtain the isometry g as a composition g = T h.

THEOREM 1.16 An isometry that fixes a point O is either
(a) *a rotation about O (direct case), or*
(b) *reflection in a line through O (indirect case).*
Proof Let an isometry g fix O and send A to A', B to B'.
Case g direct Here angles AOB, A'OB' are equal in sign as well as magnitude and so, as in Figure 1.16(a) below, angles AOA', BOB' enjoy the same property. Hence g is rotation about O.
Case g indirect. Now angles AOB, A'OB' are equal in magnitude but opposite in sign, as

in Figure 1.16(b), so in the case B = C, for any point C on the bisector m of angle AOA', we see that g fixes C. Since g preserves length and angles (in magnitude) g reflects points B not on m to their mirror image in m.

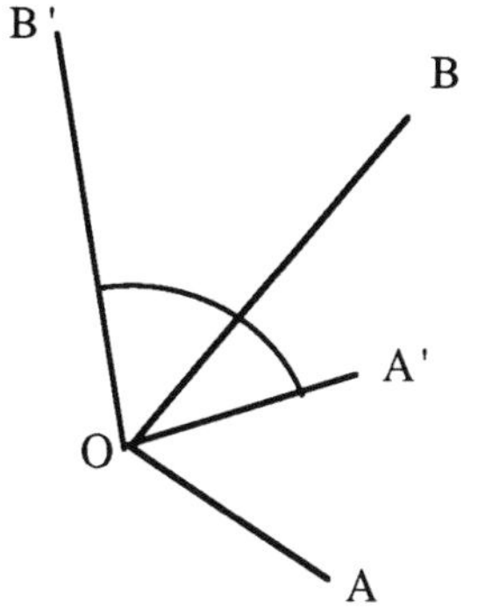

Figure 1.16(a)

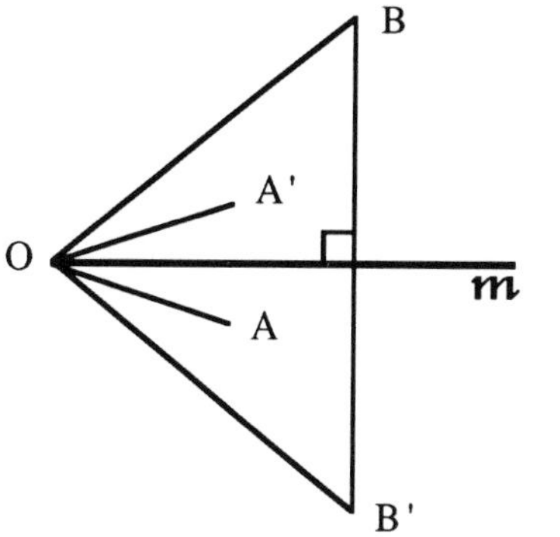

Figure 1.16(b)

Notice that we have incidentally shown that a rotation is direct and a reflection is indirect. Theorem 1.16 classifies isomorphisms that fix one or more points. What about those that fix none? We know from Theorem 1.15 that, given any point A we care to choose, we can represent any such isometry g as a composition h.T, where T is a translation and h is an isometry that fixes A. Thus such isometries are obtainable from the point-fixing ones, rotation and reflection, by composing them with translations. The result includes a fourth type of isometry called a glide, which we shall now introduce.

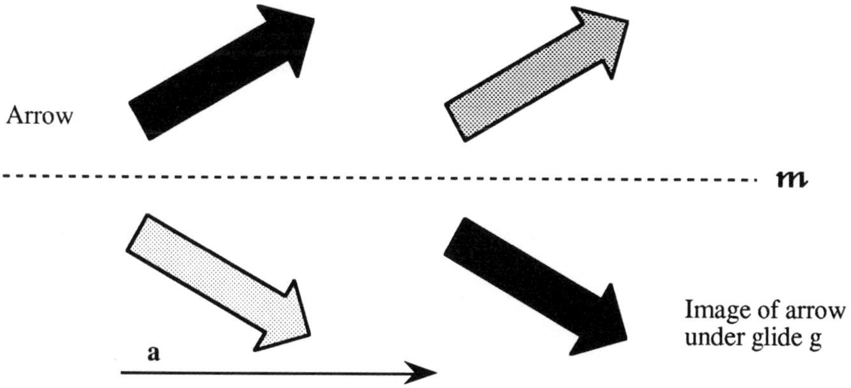

Figure 1.17 Black arrow, and its image under glide reflection g, composed of reflection R_m and translation T_a, in either order. The lightest arrow is an intermediate image, after reflection first. The darker shows translation done first.

Glides A *glide reflection,* or *glide,* with (mirror) line m is the composition of the reflection R_m in m with a translation T_a parallel to m. Obviously it does not matter in what order these two operations are done. The result is the same, as we can see in Figure 1.17 above. *By convention,* the mirror of a glide is drawn as a line of dashes. Notice that the composition of a glide R_mT_a with itself is the translation T_{2a}, as illustrated in Figure 1.18

below, in which the first ladder yields the rest by repeated application of the glide. This illustrates the easy to see, but very useful Remark 1.17.

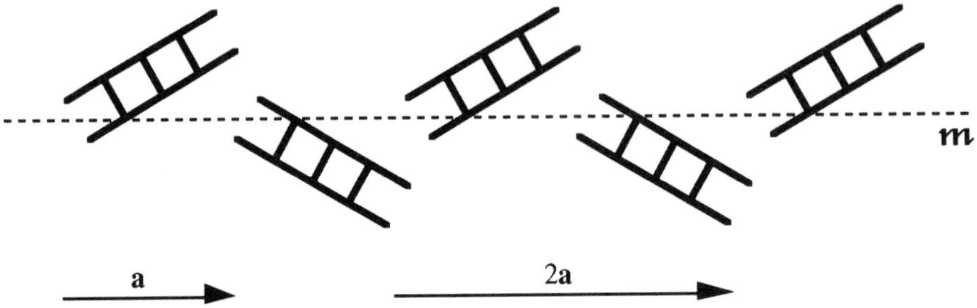

Figure 1.18 Images of ladder under repeated application of glide T_aR_m.

REMARK 1.17 The composition of two indirect isometries is direct. The composition of a direct and an indirect isometry is an indirect isometry.

Proof The composition of two indirect isometries reverses the sense of every ordered triple *twice*, and therefore leaves their sense unchanged. If just one of the isometries is indirect, then the result is one reversal only, and so we obtain an indirect isometry.

THEOREM 1.18 (Classification.) Every isometry is one of the four types:

Direct - translation or rotation.

Indirect - reflection or glide.

Proof Suppose we are given an isometry g. Then by Theorem 1.15 g is the composition of a translation with a point-fixing isometry. By Theorem 1.16, the latter isometry is a rotation or reflection, according as it is direct or indirect. Therefore it suffices to establish the following composition rules, in which the composition may be carried out in either order (though the order will affect precisely *which* rotation or glide results). We give the proofs for only one order, the other being proved similary.

rotation . translation = rotation. (1.14)

reflection . translation = glide. (1.15)

To prove (1.14), suppose that the rotation is τ and the translation is T_a. Referring to Figure 1.19(a) below, a line parallel to **a**, suitably placed relative to the centre of rotation O, contains a point A and its image A' under τ such that the vector $\underline{A'A}$ equals **a**. Then $\tau.T_a$ fixes A and is direct, so by Theorem 1.16 it is a rotation.

To establish (1.15), let the reflection be R_m, followed by translation T_a. Since this translation resolves into components T_v parallel to m and T_w perpendicular to m, we only need show that R_mT_w is reflection in a mirror n parallel to m and at a distance $(1/2)|w|$ from m, as indicated in Figure 1.19(b). But Theorem 1.10 tells us that an isometry is determined by its effect on any two points and whether it is direct or indirect. Now, R_mT_w, like the reflection R_n, is indirect (Remark 1.17), being the composition of an indirect and a direct isometry. Like R_n, it fixes every point A on n, and so by Theorem

1.10 it is indeed the reflection R_n. Finally, we have

$$R_m T_a = R_m(T_w T_v) = (R_m T_w)T_v = R_n T_v,$$

which is a glide, as asserted.

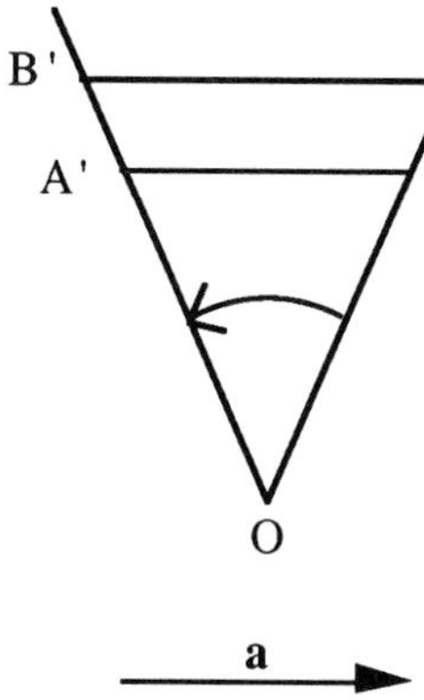

Figure 1.19(a)

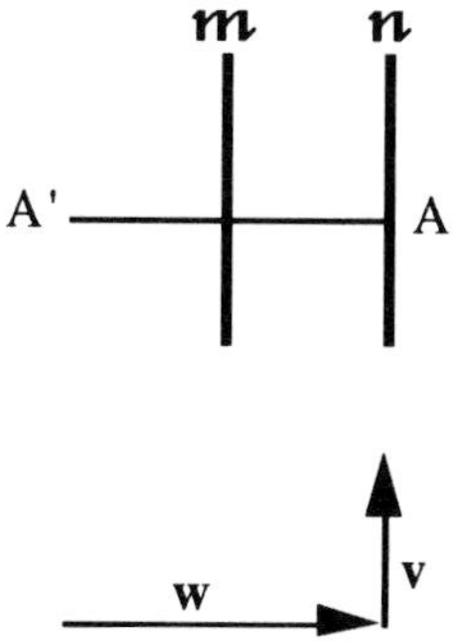

Figure 1.19(b)

Proof of (1.15) using coordinates. We may (and do) choose the coordinate system so that the mirror of the glide is the y-axis x = 0. Let the translation part be $T_{(t,u)}$. Then the reflection followed by translation has the effect $(x,y) \to (-x,y) \to (-x+t, y+u)$. But by the reflection formula (1.6) this is also the result of reflection in the line x = t/2 followed by translation $T_{(0,u)}$, thus it is a glide, since $T_{(0,u)}$ is parallel to the y-axis. If the translation is performed first, the corresponding reflection is in the line x = -t/2, with same translation part as before.

EXERCISES 1

1 Verify that, in Figure 1.1, two smallest translations are represented in their length and direction by the arrows shown, and determine corresponding arrows for Figure 1.2. These should be horizontal and vertical.

2 √ (i) What symmetries of the pattern represented in Figure 1.1 leave the central point unmoved? (ii) Prove formula (1.1) by using the Theorem of Pythagoras. (iii) Draw the diagram for proving (1.2A), marking in the components of **a** and **b**.

3 Use position vectors and (1.3), which applies equally in 3- space (indeed, in any dimension), to prove the following facts about any tetrahedron ABCD. (i) The four lines joining a vertex to the centroid of its opposite face are concurrent at a point G which divides each such line in the ratio 3:1, (ii) The three lines joining midpoints of pairs of opposite edges all meet in G.

4 Give a geometrical proof that, in Figure 1.11, we have |P'Q'| = |PQ| and hence that R_m is an isometry, considering also the case where P, Q are on opposite sides of the mirror.

5 √ Find the result of a half turn about the point A in the diagram of *Example 1.11*, followed by a reflection in a mirror through B at right angles to AB **or** Give the argument in the proof of Theorem 1.10 for the special case in Figure 1.14 (c) (cf. the argument for Case (b)).

6 √ Use a parallelogram to show that $T_{\mathbf{a}} T_{\mathbf{b}} = T_{\mathbf{b}} T_{\mathbf{a}}$, where $T_{\mathbf{a}}$ is translation by the vector **a**. Express $(T_{\mathbf{a}})^n$ as a single translation ***or*** If g denotes a 3/10 turn about some point, what fraction of a turn is $(g^5)^3$?

7 √ Resolve the vector $\mathbf{a} = (4,0)$ along and perpendicular to the direction of $\underline{OB}$, where B is the point (1,1).

8 √ (i) Use coordinates to prove that the composition of reflections in parallel mirrors at distance d apart is translation through a distance 2d perpendicular to the mirrors. (ii) What is the result of reflection in the x-axis followed by reflection in the y-axis?

9 For distinct points A, B determine the composition of a half turn about A followed by the translation T_{AB}, by considering the net effect upon A, B.

10 Mirror lines m, n intersect in a point A at angle ϕ. Determine the composition $R_m R_n R_m$, using Theorem 1.16, and following the motion of a point on one of the mirrors.

11 √ The vertices A, B, C of an equilateral triangle have the positive sense. (i) Prove that $R_C(1/3) R_B(1/3) = R_A(2/3)$, by considering the images of A and C, or otherwise (cf. Theorem 1.10). (ii) Determine the composition $R_A(-1/3) R_B(1/3)$ [Hint: let D be the midpoint of BC].

12 The vertices A,B,C,D of a square are counterclockwise and E, F are the respective midpoints of AD, DC. Show that $R_E(1/2) R_{BD}$ is a glide with translation vector $\underline{EF}$.

13 √ Find a formula for reflection in the line with equation ax+by = 1. [Hint for gradients: recall that $\tan(\theta + \pi/2) = -\cot\theta$. In Section 7.4 we develop a more streamlined method for the occasions when it is expedient to work with isometries in terms of coordinates.]

Chapter 2 HOW ISOMETRIES COMBINE

In Chapter 1 we combined two isometries g, h to produce a third by taking their compositions gh (do g then h) and hg. There is another way to combine two isometries, of great practical use in the context of plane patterns, and which we will introduce in Section 2.3. We begin by highlighting two geometrical ways to find the composition (or product) of isometries. The first was already used in the proof of Theorem 1.18, namely:

Method 1

(A) Determine the sense of the composition from those of its parts (Remark 1.17).
(B) Determine the effect of the composition on two convenient points P, Q.
(C) Find an isometry with the right sense, and effect on P, Q. This must be the one required, by Theorem 1.10.

Notice that (C) is now made easier by our knowledge of the four isometry types (Theorem 1.18). This method can be beautifully simple and effective for otherwise tricky compositions, but the second approach, given by Theorem 2.1 and Corollary 2.2, is perhaps more powerful for getting general results and insights. With Theorems 1.15 and 1.16 it says that every isometry can be decomposed into reflections, *and* it tells us how to combine reflections

Method 2 Decompose the given isometries into reflections, using available freedom of choice, so that certain reflections in the composition cancel each other out. See Examples 2.3 to 2.7. We note for later:

Method 3 Use Cartesian coordinates (See Chapter 7).

NOTATION We take this opportunity to recall some standard abbreviations from the list of symbols on page 451 that will be useful from time to time. Each one is a subset of the next.

N The set of *natural numbers* 1,2,3,...
Z The *integers* ...,-2,-1,0,1,2,...
Q The *rationals*, or rational numbers, $\{m/n\text{: } m,n \text{ are integers and } n \neq 0\}$
R The *reals*, or *real numbers*, corresponding to the points of a line extending indefinitely in both direction (the *real line*). Certain postulates are involved, which we do not need to touch on until Definition 12.6 (cf. Simmons, 1963).

2.1 Reflections are the key

THEOREM 2.1. Composing isometries.

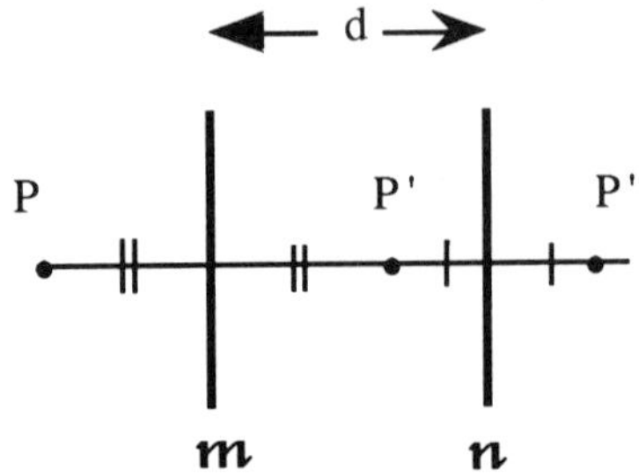

Figure 2.1(a)

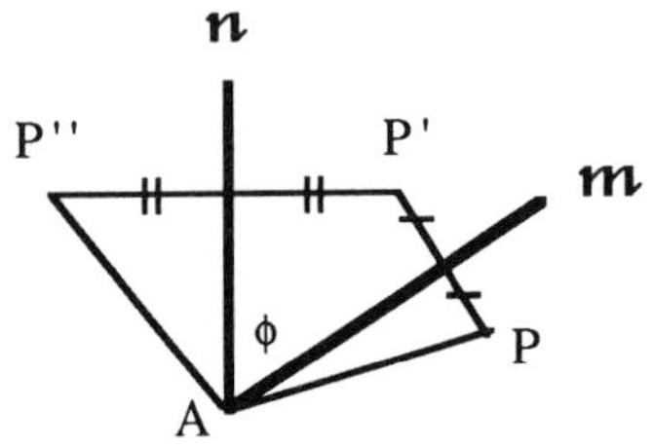

Figure 2.1(b)

(a) If lines **m, n** *are parallel at distance d then the composition of reflections R_mR_n is a translation of magnitude 2d perpendicular to these lines,*
(b) If lines **m, n** *intersect in the point A at angle ϕ then R_mR_n is rotation through angle 2ϕ about A :* $R_mR_n = R_A(2\phi)$.

The proof (omitted) is by elementary geometry in Figure 2.1. Notice in Figure 2.2 that crossing lines offer us two angles to choose from. Signs apart, these angles add up to π, so unless the lines are perpendicular, one angle is acute and is taken as *the* angle between the lines. Also, by mentioning **m** first, we imply a *signed* turn of ϕ from **m** to **n** (if no order is implied then the angle may be taken as unsigned).

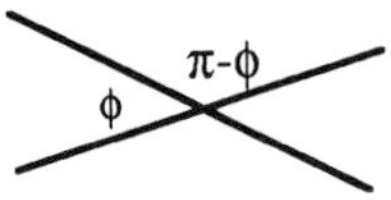

Figure 2.2

COROLLARY 2.2 **Decomposing isometries.**
(i) *A rotation about a point A may be expressed as the product* R_mR_n *of reflections in lines through A at half the rotation angle.*
(ii) *A translation may be expressed as the product* R_mR_n *of reflections in lines perpendicular to the translation direction, at one half the translation distance.*
(iii) *In case (i) the direction, and in (ii) the position of one line may be chosen arbitrarily. The other line is then determined.*

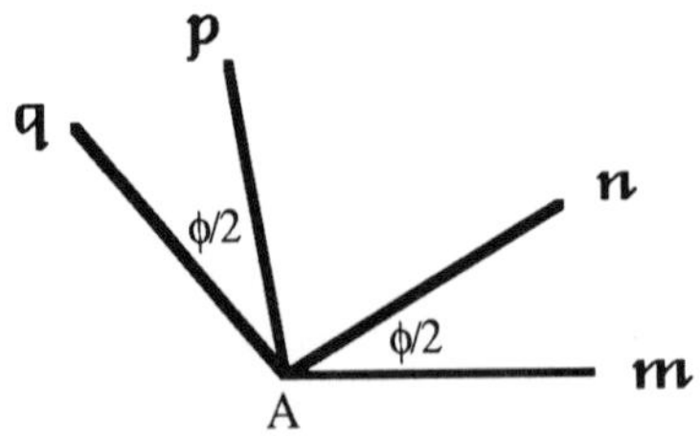

Figure 2.3 Two alternatives : $R_A(\phi) = R_mR_n = R_pR_q$.

REMARK 2.2A For a rotation of 1/n of a turn, ie an angle of $2\pi/n$, the mirrors should be at angle π/n. Examples of using this second method are given in Section 2.2.

2.2 Some useful compositions

At the end of this section we give Table 2.2, showing the result of all types of products of isometries. First, we gain practice with special cases which are foundational to the study of isometries and plane patterns, and whose first use will be in the classification of braid patterns in Chapter 3. The notation of Table 2.1 below will help to visualise what is going on.

TABLE 2.1 Notation for the four isometry types in the plane.

———➤	Translation symmetry. Distance and direction is that of the arrow.
———	Continous line, representing position of mirror.
- - - - - - - - - - -	Broken line, representing mirror line of glide.
- - - - - - - - -➤	Glide, with its translation component indicated.
0 △ □	1/2 turn, 1/3 turn, 1/4 turn, ...
═══	Two coincident mirrors.

First we try a composition problem already solved in the proof of Theorem 1.18 (the four isometry types). For clarity, a small 'x' denotes composition.

EXAMPLE 2.3

Reflection $R_m \times$ Translation T_a perpendicular to mirror
= *reflection in a mirror* ***n*** *parallel to the original one,* (2.1)
at one half translation distance, $|\mathbf{a}|/2$, *from it.*

Thus, by repeatedly composing the latest mirror reflection with the translation $T_{\mathbf{a}}$, we get a whole string of mirror positions :

| | | | | ....

at intervals of half translation distance.

Proof of (2.1) By Corollary 2.2 we can express the translation $T_{\mathbf{a}}$ as the product of reflections in two parallel mirrors, one of which we may choose to be ***m*** itself. If the second mirror is ***n*** then we can compute as follows, with successive diagrams below each other to show relative horizontal positions. The argument is expressed geometrically on the left, and algebraically on the right.

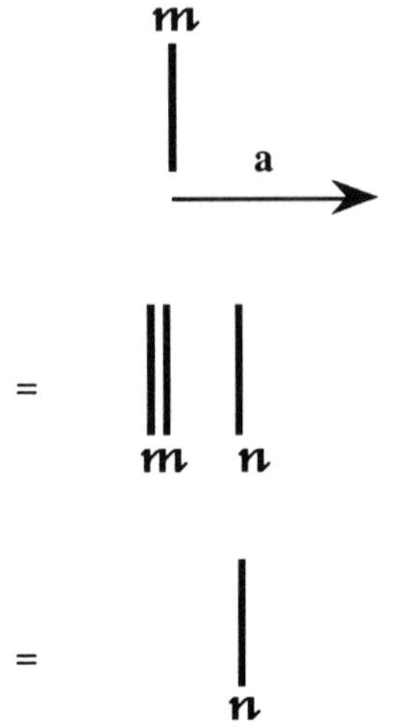

$$R_m T_a$$

$$= R_m (R_m R_n) = (R_m R_m) R_n$$

$$= R_n, \quad \text{since } R_m R_m = I.$$

Figure 2.4 Computing the result of reflection followed by translation. The argument is represented geometrically on the left and algebraically on the right.

EXAMPLE 2.4

Reflection R_m x *Rotation with centre on the mirror* (2.2)
= *Reflection R_n in mirror at one half rotation angle to* $\boldsymbol{m}$.

We include this example before any further illustration, because it is exactly analogous to Example 2.3, with translation regarded as a special case of rotation in the manner of Theorem 2.1(b). It will be used soon to investigate the group of all symmetries of the regular n-gon, in Section 2.4, the Dihedral group. Now, if the rotation is $R_A(\phi)$ then the argument for Example 2.4 can be put simply in terms of geometry (below left) or in terms of algebra (below right), after the pattern of Example 2.3.

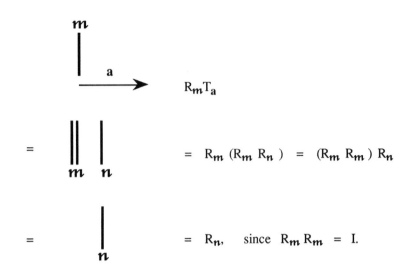

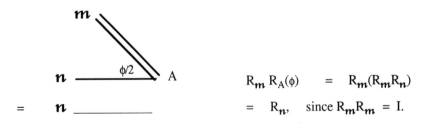

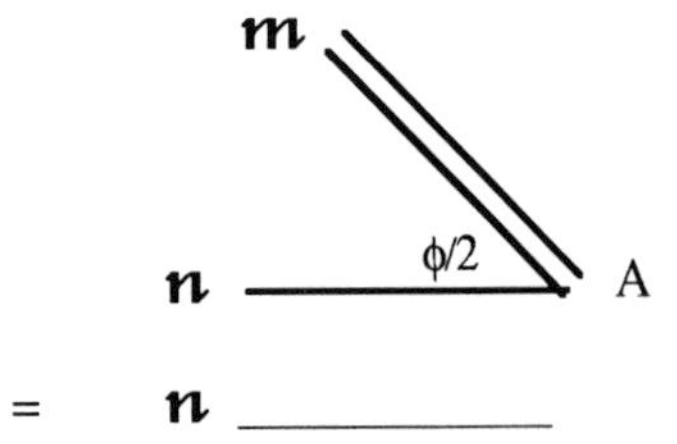

$$R_m R_A(\phi) = R_m(R_m R_n)$$

$$= R_n, \quad \text{since } R_m R_m = I.$$

Figure 2.5 Rotation plus reflection computed (geometry on the left, algebra on the right).

EXAMPLE 2.5 ***Rotation*** x ***Translation*** = ***Rotation*** *(same angle).* This adds to the Composition statement (1.14) the fact that the result of composing translation with a rotation is a rotation through the *same angle*. In Exercise 3 the reader is asked to establish this by the methods of Examples 2.3 to 2.7. The argument will of course be a slight generalisation of what we give below for an important special case.

1/2 turn x *Translation*
= *1/2 turn at half translation distance away from the original.* (2.3)

Proof of (2.3) As before, the left side is both a geometric proof , and an illustration of the result, using results (2.1) and (2.2).

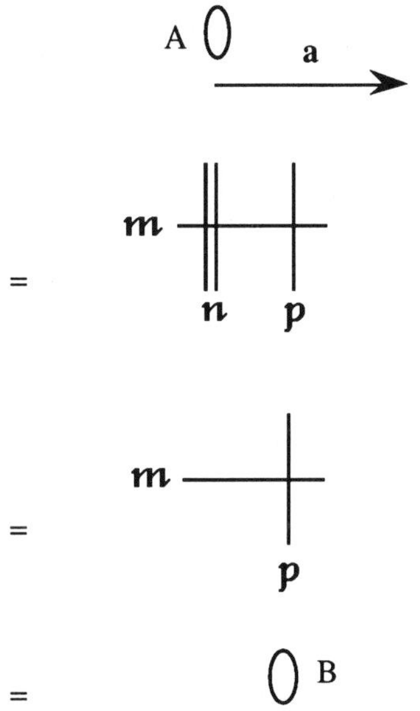

$$R_A(1/2)\ T_{\mathbf{a}}$$

$$= (R_m R_n)(R_n R_p)$$

$$= R_m R_p, \quad \text{since} \quad R_n^2 = I$$

$$= R_B(1/2).$$

Figure 2.6 Calculating 1/2 turn x translation.

Analogously to Example 2.3, by repeatedly following the latest 1/2 turn with the translation we get a line of 1/2 turns at intervals of one half translation distance thus:

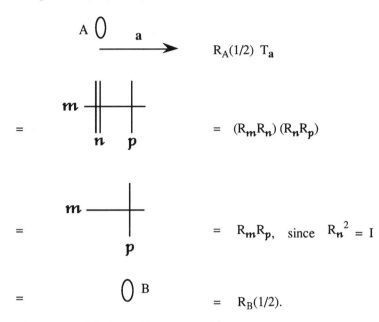

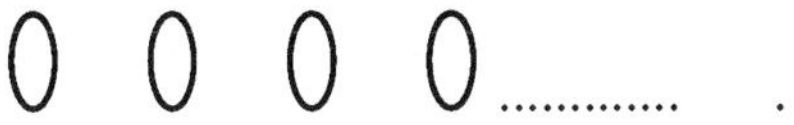

We emphasise that the composition of translation with *any* rotation is a rotation about some point, through the same angle, as the reader is invited to prove below.

EXERCISE Use the methods above, (a) to establish the general case of Example 2.5, (b) to show that the product of two 1/2 turns is a translation through twice the distance between them.

Application *Symmetries of a braid pattern.* We recall from Section 1.1 that a *symmetry* of a figure F is an isometry which sends every subfigure of F into a congruent subfigure (i.e one of the same size and shape). It is important to appreciate that

any composition of symmetries of a figure is also a symmetry of the figure. (2.4)

The reason is simply that such a composition, being the result of performing one symmetry then the other, also satisfies the above criteria for being itself a symmetry. Figure 2.7(a) below is *a braid pattern.* That is, a pattern F with a translation symmetry T_a such that the translation symmetries of F are all the repetitions, ie powers,

$$T_a^n = T_{na}, \tag{2.5}$$

where n is a positive or negative integer. Indeed, F actually consists of the translates $T_{na}(M)$ ($n = 0, \pm1, \pm2, \ldots$) of a basic motif M, for example the woman's head in Figure 2.7(a). There we have also indicated the translation vector **a** (it could equally well be taken as -**a**) [see (3.1)] . By implication, F extends infinitely to the left and right of the representative part we have drawn.

(a)

(b)

(c)

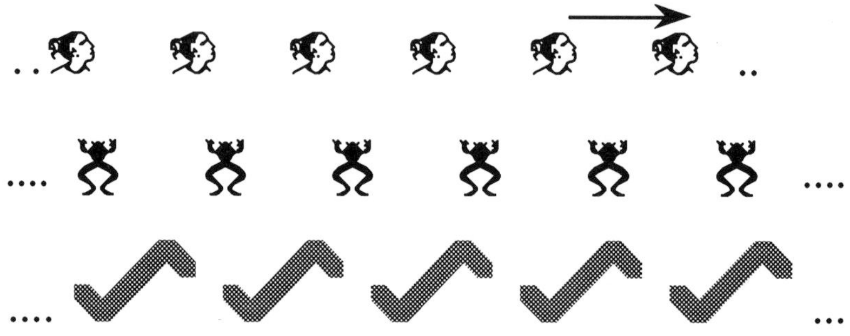

Figure 2.7 Some braid patterns.

The above remarks hold true for Figure 2.7(b), but with basic motif , which has a reflection symmetry R_m. Clearly, whichever copy of the frog we choose as basic motif, R_m is a symmetry of the whole pattern. Since any composition of symmetries is a symmetry, Example 2.3 tells us that there are also reflection symmetries R_n with n midway between every two successive copies of the frog. Here, this conclusion is also easily reached by inspection, but some of its two dimensional relatives are rather less obvious. Theorem 2.12 expresses such symmetries in terms of a small number of 'basic' ones.

In Figure 2.7(c) the basic motif has a 1/2 turn symmetry and so, in accordance with Example 3, there are 1/2 turn symmetries with centres spaced at a half the repetition distance of the basic motif. Thus the symmetries include 1/2 turns halfway between successive copies of the motif. In more complicated examples these 'extra' 1/2 turns are harder to spot visually, especially if we don't know that they must be there (see Figure 2.11 later in the chapter). It was convenient to introduce braid patterns here because they give rise to some nice but not too hard applications of our theory and techniques so far. Their classification is completed in Chapter 3, the shortest chapter of the book.

EXAMPLE 2.6 **Composing rotations: Euler's construction.** Since a rotation is a direct isometry, the product of two rotations is also direct so, of the four types, it must be a translation or rotation (Theorem 1.18). *Euler's construction* is to draw the lines m, n, p as in diagram (a) or (b) below and so determine the new rotation centre and angle, or direction and distance of the translation. Here is the result.

The plane is turned through the sum of the component rotation angles, and we have a translation precisely when this sum is a multiple of the complete turn 2π. (2.6)

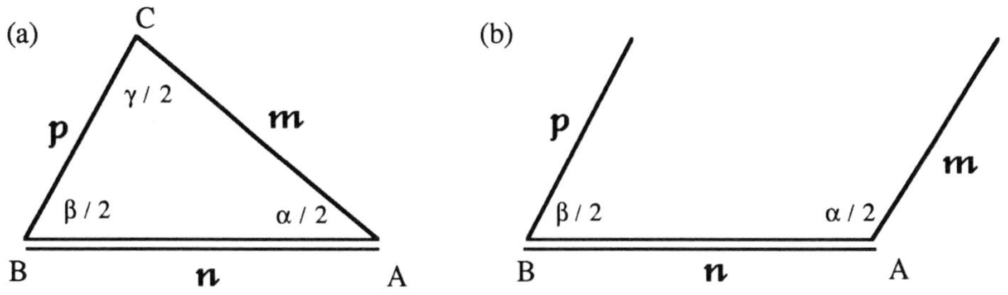

Figure 2.8 Euler's construction for the composition of two rotations.

Proof in Case (a)

$$\begin{aligned} R_A(\alpha)\,R_B(\beta) &= (R_m R_n)(R_n R_p) \\ &= R_m R_p, \quad \text{since} \quad R_n^2 = I \\ &= R_C(-\gamma) \\ &= R_C(\alpha+\beta), \quad \text{since } \alpha+\beta = 2\pi-\gamma. \end{aligned}$$

EXERCISE Use Euler's construction in the triangle of Figure 2.8 made equilateral to show the following, and find such implied 3-fold centres in Figure 1.1:

The existence of 1/3 turn symmetries of a figure, at two vertices of an equilateral triangle, implies the same symmetry at the third vertex. (2.7)

EXAMPLE 2.7 **The product of glides and reflections**

*The product of two glides, or of reflection and glide, is a rotation through twice the angle between their lines - **unless** the lines are parallel, when the result is a translation.* (2.8)

Proof of (2.8) A reflection is a glide with zero translation part, so we need only consider the product of two glides. Suppose first that the mirrors are not parallel, but intersect at angle ϕ. Then since we may switch the translation and reflection parts of a glide, and combine reflection with rotations (Theorem 2.1), the two glides may be combined as

$$(T_a R_m)(T_b R_n) = T_a(R_m R_n)T_b = T_a R_A(2\phi) T_b,$$

But by Example 2.5, rotation combined with translation is a rotation through the same angle, so the result follows. In the parallel case $R_A(2\phi)$ is replaced by a translation (Theorem 2.1), so the result is a translation. Figure 2.9 below shows the specifics when the mirror lines cross at right angles, in the notation of Table 2.1. Case (i) is part of Theorem 2.1.

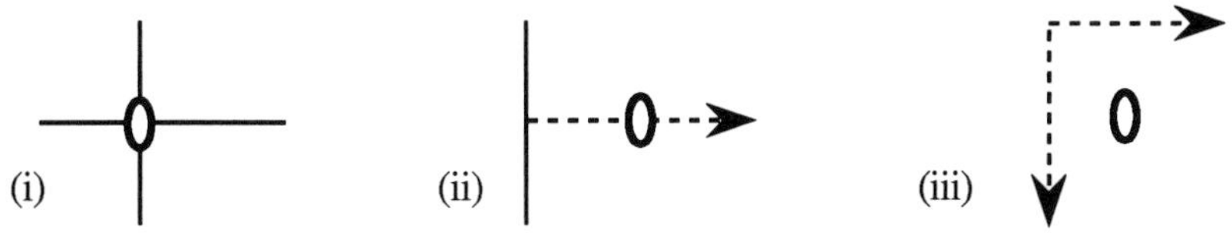

Figure 2.9 The right angle crossing of symmetry and glide lines of a pattern implies the presence of 2-fold centres as shown (cf. Table 2.1). We may think of each glide as pulling the 2-fold centre a 1/2 translation distance from the crossing.

Proof of (iii) We compute the product of glides $h = T_a R_m$, $g = T_b R_p$, as indicated in the diagram below. This can also be established as $R_A(1/2)$ by verifying that hg fixes the point A and sends the intersection of mirrors p and n to the same point as does $R_A(1/2)$. This is sufficient, by Theorem 1.10, since the product of two glides must be direct.

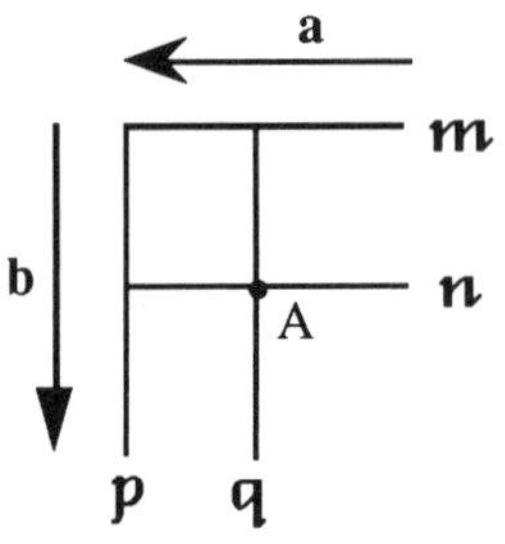

$$\begin{aligned}
& (T_a R_m)(T_b R_p) & \\
= \ & (R_q R_p R_m)(R_m R_n R_p) & \text{(Theorem 2.1)} \\
= \ & R_q R_p\, R_n R_p, & \text{since } R_m^2 = I \\
= \ & R_q R_p\, R_p R_n, & \text{since } p \perp n \\
= \ & R_q R_n, & \text{since } R_p^2 = I \\
= \ & R_A(1/2) & \text{(Theorem 2.1).}
\end{aligned}$$

Figure 2.10 Proof of the assertion in Figure 2.9 (iii). $p \perp n$ means 'p, n perpendicular'.

EXAMPLE 2.8 The symmetries of the plane pattern below include horizontal glides in the positions indicated by dotted lines thus ' .... ' , and vertical glide lines too. The three emphasised points show successive images of one such glide (which?), illustrating that a glide performed twice gives a translation.

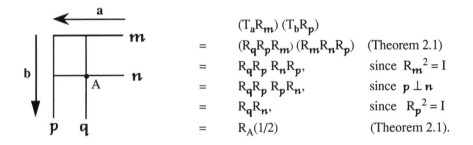

Figure 2.11 A plane pattern with perpendicular glide lines. Finding the vertical ones is part of the next exercise.

EXERCISE (a) Follow the successive images of a white subfigure under repetitions of a glide, noting that a horizontal glide must map horizontal lines to horizontal lines (suitable observations of this kind can greatly facilitate analysis of a pattern). (b) Find the *vertical* glide symmetries of the pattern represented, and verify that each small 'box' bounded by horizontal and vertical glide lines has a 2-fold centre of symmetry at its centre, as predicted in Figure 2.9 (iii).

We conclude this section with Table 2.2, showing all possible compositions of isometry types, derived from Theorem 2.1 (and Corollary 2.2), the composition and decomposition Theorems. Examples 2.3 to 2.7 contain derivations or special cases for the rows indicated. The last row follows also from the fact that the composition of a direct and an indirect isometry must be indirect (Remark 1.17) and therefore a glide (Theorem 1.18), with reflection as the special case of a glide with zero translation part. The table is unaffected by changing orders of composition.

TABLE 2.2 How isometry types combine.

Every line is a consequence of Theorem 2.1. Rows (a) and (b) come from Examples 2.5 to 2.7, whilst Examples 2.3 and 2.4 supply important special cases in row (c). The table is unaffected by changing orders of composition. It justifies the idea of the *point group* in Chapter 6, a key step in the classification of plane patterns into 17 types.

Isometries combined		Type of the product	
(a) DIRECT	DIRECT	ROTATION *	
Rotation ϕ	Translation	Rotation ϕ	(Example 2.5)
Rotation α	Rotation β	Rotation $\alpha+\beta$	(Example 2.6)
(b) INDIRECT	INDIRECT	ROTATION *	
Reflection/glide	Reflection/glide at angle ϕ	Rotation 2ϕ	(Example 2.7)
(c) INDIRECT	DIRECT	GLIDE **	
Reflection/glide	Translation	line parallel to original	
Reflection/glide	Rotation α	line at $\alpha/2$ to original	

* *Translation,* if this angle is a whole number of turns.
** *Pure reflection* (glide with zero translation part) in the following cases:-

EXAMPLE 2.3 : Reflection x translation at right angles to mirror.
EXAMPLE 2.4 : Reflection x rotation with centre on mirror.

EXERCISE Verify line (c) of the above table.

2.3 The image of a line of symmetry

NOTATION 2.9 Let F be some figure in the plane. By definition, a line $\mathbf{m}$ is a *line of symmetry* of F if $R_{\mathbf{m}}$ is a symmetry of F, that is if $R_{\mathbf{m}}$ maps F onto itself; point A is an *n-fold centre* (of symmetry) if $R_A(1/n)$ is a symmetry of F. We normally take n to be largest possible. For example the centre of a regular square is thought of as a 4-fold centre and only in a secondary sense as 2-fold. Sometimes 2,3,..6 -fold centres are called *dyad, triad, tetrad, pentad, hexad* respectively.

A typical consequence of the main result of this section, Theorem 2.12, is that if A is an n-fold centre then so is the image of A under any translation symmetry T_v of F. Thus we get at least a whole line of n-fold centres $\{T_{mv}(A)\colon\ m = 1,2,3, ...\}$ at a translation distance $|\mathbf{a}|$ apart. (A stronger result holds for lines of symmetry perpendicular to the translations, one gets them at $|\mathbf{a}|/2$ apart: see Example 2.3.) All four parts of Theorem 2.12 follow from one basic fact which implies that an isometry sends lines of symmetry to lines of symmetry, proved as Lemma 2.10. For this, we need the idea of an inverse isometry.

Inverse isometries The list of isometry types in Theorem 1.18 shows that every isometry g is a *bijection*. That is, g transforms distinct points to distinct points and every point is the transform of *some* point. Thus every isometry g has a unique *inverse transformation* g^{-1}, sending P^g back to the point P.

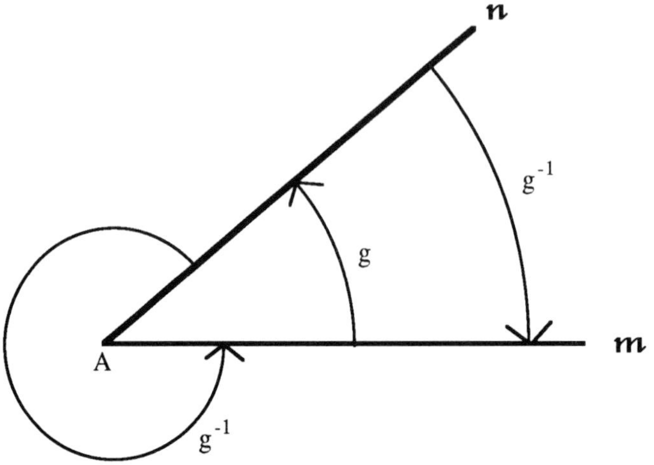

Figure 2.12 A rotation g and its inverse isometry. Here $g = R_A(1/6)$ maps a line $\boldsymbol{m}$ to line $\boldsymbol{n}$, and $g^{-1} = R_A(-1/6) = R_A(5/6)$ maps $\boldsymbol{n}$ back to $\boldsymbol{m}$.

The inverse mapping g^{-1} obviously preserves distances because g does, and so is also an isometry. Also, if g reverses the sense of a triple then g^{-1} undoes the effect, so directness and indirectness are preserved by taking inverses. Further, if g is a symmetry of a figure F then so is g^{-1}. If g fixes a point P then g^{-1} fixes P too because g is bijective. More formally $P = P^{(gg^{-1})} = (P^g)^{g^{-1}} = P^{g^{-1}}$.We observe too that either property, gf = I or fg = I, implies that $f = g^{-1}$. It follows from the associative property (1.8) that

$$(gh)^{-1} = h^{-1}g^{-1} \quad \text{(g, h isometries)}, \tag{2.9}$$

the argument being: $(h^{-1}g^{-1})(gh) = h^{-1}(g^{-1}g)h = h^{-1}I\,h = h^{-1}h = I$. We therefore have the following table of inverse isometries, which may also be deduced directly.

TABLE 2.3 Inverse isometries.

g	R_m	T_a	$R_A(\phi)$	$R_A(1/n)$	R_mT_a	
g^{-1}	R_m	T_{-a}	$R_A(-\phi)$	$R_A(1/n)^{n-1}$	R_mT_{-a}	(2.10)

Proof of (2.10) We will verify the last two columns of the table. Firstly, $R_A(1/n).R_A(1/n)^{n-1} = R_A(1/n)^n = I$ [see (1.11)], hence the inverse of $R_A(1/n)$ is $R_A(1/n)^{n-1}$.

For the glide we have $(R_mT_a)(T_{-a}R_m) = R_m(T_aT_{-a})R_m = R_m\,I\,R_m = R_m\,R_m = I$.

Conjugates Here is a widely used piece of notation which we shall immediately require for Lemma 2.11. It will appear at intervals throughout the whole book. We recall that $\boldsymbol{m}^g$

denotes the image of a line m under an isometry g. A suggestively similar notation R^g is used for the *conjugate of an isometry* R by an isometry g, defined as the composition

$$R^g \equiv g^{-1}Rg. \qquad (2.11)$$

As we recall from (2.4), the composition of two (hence any number of) symmetries of a figure is also a symmetry, so if R, g are symmetries then so is R^g. We now show that if S is a third isometry, then

$$(RS)^g = R^g \cdot S^g. \qquad (2.12)$$

Proof of (2.12) Starting from the right of (2.12), we have

$$\begin{aligned} R^g S^g &= g^{-1}Rg \,.\, g^{-1}Sg\,, && \text{by (2.11)},\\ &= g^{-1}R(g.g^{-1})Sg, && \text{by associativity (1.8)},\\ &= g^{-1}R\, I\, Sg \\ &= g^{-1}(R\,S)g \\ &= (RS)^g\,, && \text{by (2.11)}. \end{aligned}$$

LEMMA 2.10 Let g be an isometry, m a line. If R is reflection in m then R^g is reflection in m^g.

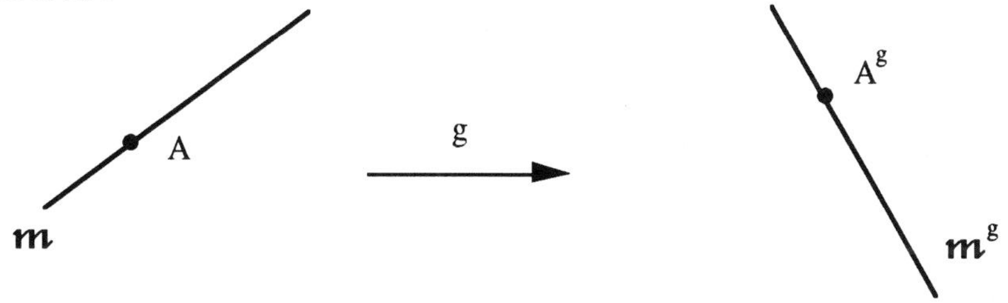

Figure 2.13 The image of a mirror is a mirror.

Proof Clearly $R^g \equiv g^{-1}Rg$ is an indirect isometry, R being indirect, so it suffices to show that R^g has the same effect as reflection in m^g, on any two points (Theorem 1.10). In fact R^g fixes the point A^g for every point A in m, for

$$\begin{aligned} (A^g)^{g^{-1}Rg} &= A^{g\,g^{-1}Rg} && \text{by (1.8)},\\ &= A^{Rg}, && \text{since } g\,g^{-1} = I,\\ &= (A^R)^g && \text{by (1.8)},\\ &= A^g, && \text{since R fixes A (A being in } m). \end{aligned}$$

This proves Lemma 2.10.

DEFINITION 2.11 Let $\mathbf{a} = \underline{AB}$ and g be an isometry. Then $\mathbf{a}^g = \underline{(AB)^g}$.

This means that the new vector $\mathbf{a}^g$ is represented in magnitude and direction by the image under g of any directed line segment which represents $\mathbf{a}$. The significance of this appears in the proof of Theorem 2.12(c) below, where it is shown that, in terms of the expression (2.11) for a conjugate,

$$(T_a)^g = T_b, \text{ where } \mathbf{b} = \mathbf{a}^g. \qquad (2.13)$$

THEOREM 2.12 Any symmetry g of a figure F maps as follows:
(a) lines of symmetry to lines of symmetry,
(b) n-fold centres to n-fold centres,
(c) the direction of one translation symmetry to the direction of another of the same magnitude (Figure 2.15),
(d) glide lines to glide lines with same translation magnitude.
In each case, if R is the old symmetry then the conjugate R^g $(=g^{-1}Rg)$ *is the new.*

Proof Let g be a symmetry of the figure F. To prove (a), suppose that m in Figure 2.14 is a line of symmetry of F. Then $R = R_m$ is a symmetry, hence so is $R^g \equiv g^{-1}Rg$. But by Lemma 2.10 this symmetry is the operation of reflection in the image m^g of m under g, ie m^g is a line of symmetry of F.

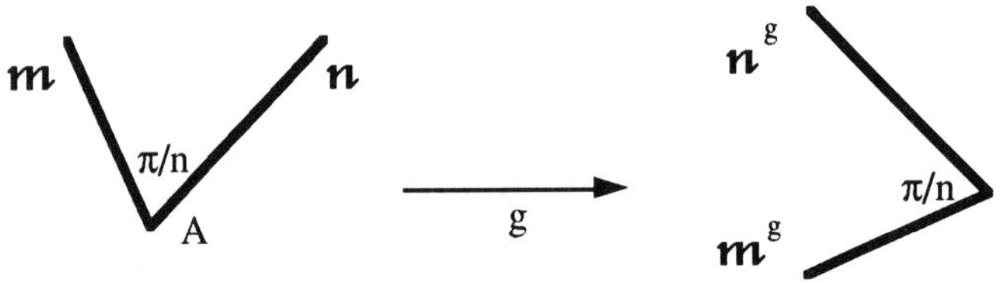

Figure 2.14 An isometry g maps one n-fold centre to another.

(b) Let A be an n-fold centre of symmetry of F. We wish to prove that Ag is an n-fold centre. That is, RAg (1/n) is a symmetry of F. The key observation is that, by Corollary 2.2 we can decompose the symmetry $R_A(1/n)$ as $R_m R_n$, where m, n are lines intersecting in A at angle π/n. This is illustrated in Figure 2.14 above. Since g and $R_A(1/n)$ are symmetries of F, so is the composition

$$
\begin{aligned}
g^{-1} R_A(1/n)\, g &= g^{-1}(R_m R_n)g \\
&= (R_m R_n)^g && \text{by (2.11),} \\
&= (R_m)^g\, (R_n)^g, && \text{by (2.12),} \\
&= R_{m^g}\, R_{n^g}, && \text{by Lemma 2.10,}
\end{aligned}
$$

where the last expression equals $R_{A^g}(1/n)$ or $R_{A^g}(-1/n)$, according as g is direct or not, since the angle between m^g and n^g is the same in magnitude as that between m and n (see(1.5)). In the indirect case of g it still follows that $R_{A^g}(1/n)$ is a symmetry, being the inverse of $R_{A^g}(-1/n)$.

(c) This time we use Corollary 2.2 to write any translation $T_{\mathbf{a}}$ as a product of reflections $R_m R_n$ in parallel mirrors, as in Figure 2.15 below.

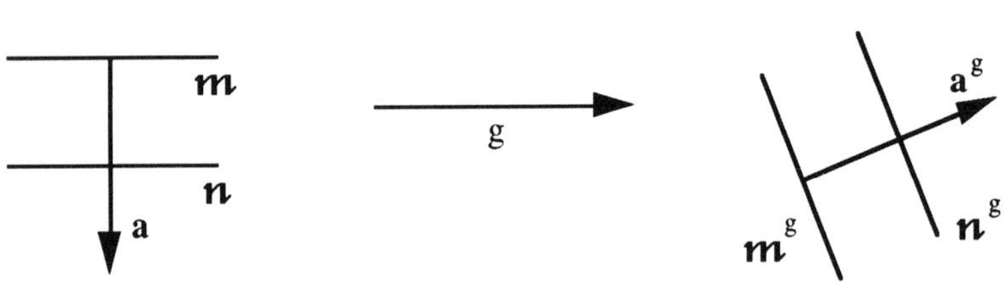

Figure 2.15 An isometry g maps translation vector **a** to $\mathbf{a}^g$.

Then, arguing as in (b), we obtain $g^{-1} T_a g = R_{m^g} R_{n^g}$. Since m and n are parallel and at a distance $|\mathbf{a}|/2$, the same holds for m^g and n^g. Therefore the new isometry is a translation through distance $|\mathbf{a}|$ at right angles to m^g and n^g, as indicated in Figure 2.15 above. The change in direction is found by applying g to a representative directed line segment <u>AB</u> for **a**. With Figure 2.15, this justifies (2.13): $(T_a)^g = T_b$, where $\mathbf{b} = \mathbf{a}^g$.

(d) Let m be a glide line and $R_m T_a$ the corresponding glide symmetry. Since g is an isometry, so is

$$(R_m T_a)^g = (R_m)^g (T_a)^g \quad \text{by (2.12)},$$
$$= (R_m)^g T_b, \quad \text{where } \mathbf{b} = \mathbf{a}^g, \quad \text{by Part(c)}.$$

Here the new translation vector $\mathbf{a}^g$ is parallel to m^g, and of the same magnitude as **a**, so m^g is indeed a glide line, as claimed. The proof is complete.

EXAMPLE 2.13 The first part of Figure 2.16 represents a finite portion of a plane pattern, whose translation symmetries include two of equal length but at right angles. We see also points of 4-fold rotational symmetry, such as the one marked 'A'. By its side we represent the same area but this time we indicate (in the notation of Table 2.1) all the centres of rotational symmetry. They are either 2-fold or 4-fold.

Figure 2.16 A plane pattern and, side by side with it, a representation of where its 1/2 and 1/4 turn symmetries are located. The points A correspond. The notation is found in Table 2.1.

It is useful to know, and a nice application of results so far to show, that

the presence of all the rotational symmetries in Figure 2.16 is implied by the translations, together with a single 1/4 turn at the point A. (2.14)

We consider three stages.

(i) The images of A under translation must be 4-fold centres, by the key Theorem, 2.12, accounting for about a half of those shown, and forming the vertices of a division of the plane into squares.

(ii) By Euler's construction (Example 2.6) 1/4 turns at the vertices of a square imply 1/4 turns at the centre (see Exercise 2 at the Chapter's end), and hence the presence of a second lattice of 4-fold centres.

(iii) There are points which are *not* 4-fold centres but *are* 2-fold centres, and this may be seen as follows. The 1/2 turn about A is a symmetry, since it equals the square of a 1/4 turn, and by (2.3) it combines with a translation to form a 1/2 turn about a further point which is not a 4-fold centre. This accounts for the 2-fold centres.

The remaining symmetries There are many more symmetries of Figure 2.16, both reflections and glides, and the presence of all of them may be predicted once we observe that AB is a line of symmetry. They are shown in Figure 2.17 to the right. Many lines of symmetry are obvious, but finding them all *by inspection of the pattern* is harder in this case. The theory does aid our intuition.

The (thickened) glidelines divide the plane into squares, and the side of a square gives the magnitude of every glide's translation part.

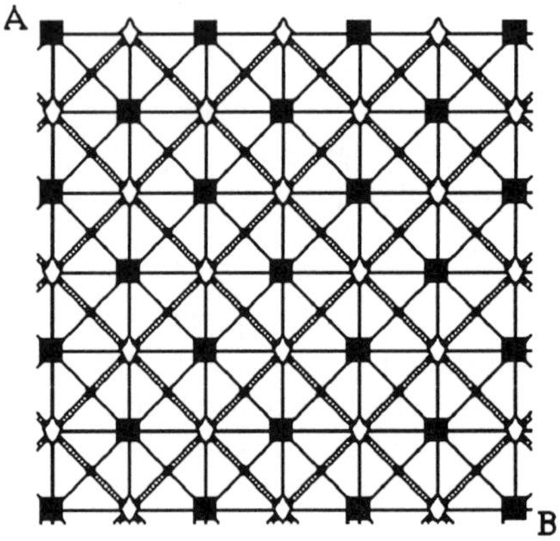

Figure 2.17 All the symmetries of the pattern of Figure 2.16. Here the glidelines are shown thickened for emphasis (cf. Table 2.1).

EXERCISE Satisfy yourself that each symmetry portrayed in Figure 2.17 maps symmetry elements like to like. That is, n-fold centres to n-fold centres, and so on.

EXERCISE Find examples of mirrors, glide lines, and 1/n turn symmetries in the (plane-filling) pattern of Figure 2.18 on the right (made, incidentally, from repetitions of the letter 'M').

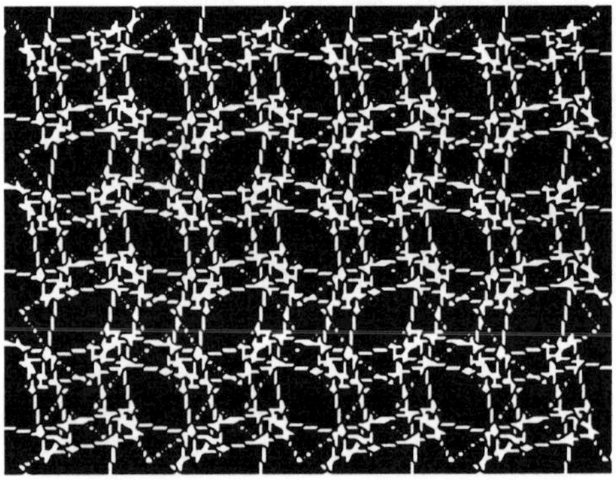

Figure 2.18 (by Mary Small)

EXERCISE Draw a diagram showing all the symmetries of the pattern in Figure 2.19 below, with translation symmetries T_u, T_v in two independent directions. Verify that these translations map lines of symmetry to other lines of symmetry, dyad centres to dyad centres, and glide lines to glide lines.

Figure 2.19 Imitation Escher. The symmetries include reflection, glides, and 1/2 turns.

2.4 The Dihedral group

This section leads to a more general look at groups in the next one. For now, we simply observe that the collection G of all symmetries of a figure F, with the usual law of composition (gh means 'do g then h'), satisfies

(i) The composition of any two symmetries of F is a third.
(ii) If f, g, h are symmetries of F then f(gh) = (fg)h.
(iii) There is a symmetry I (do nothing) of F such that gI = g = Ig for every symmetry g of F.
(iv) For every symmetry g of F there is a unique symmetry g^{-1} (the *inverse* of g) with $g\,g^{-1} = I = g^{-1}g$.

This means that G satisfies the requirements to be a *group* (see Section 2.5) and so is called the *symmetry group*, or *group of symmetries*, of F. Much that is useful flows from this, not least that we can now classify patterns by their symmetry groups. We begin not with plane or even 1-dimensional patterns, but with the regular n-gon, since its symmetry group provides building blocks for classifying more general patterns (as we shall see especially in Section 6.2).

DEFINITION 2.14 The *Dihedral group* D_{2n} $(n \geq 2)$ is the symmetry group of a regular n-gon. The regular 2-gon is thought of as a special case, with 'curved' sides:

.

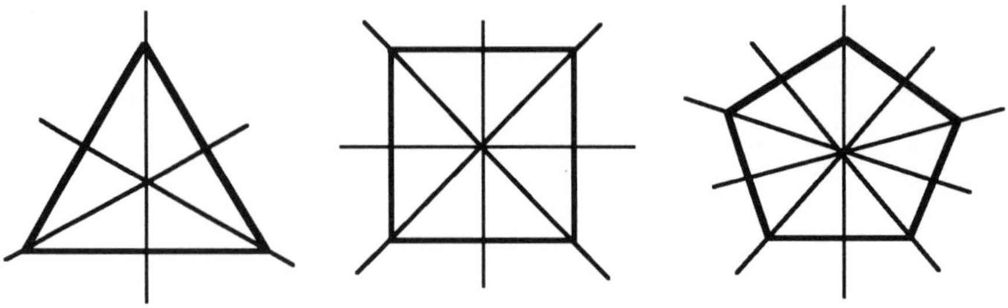

Figure 2.20 Lines of symmetry of some regular n-gons.

EXAMPLE 2.15 It is easy to see from Figure 2.20 above that D_{10}, the symmetry group of a regular pentagon, consists of :

5 reflections - one in each line of symmetry,
5 rotations - the identity I, 1/5 turn, ... , 4/5 turn about the centre,
TOTAL = 10.

There is a slight difference for polygons with an even number of edges, exemplified above by the square, whose lines of symmetry join *either* opposite vertices *or* mid points of opposite edges. However we can see that in all cases

D_{2n} consists of reflections in n equally spaced lines of symmetry through the centre C, and n rotations $I, \tau, \tau^2, \ldots, \tau^{n-1}$, where $\tau = R_C(1/n)$, and $\tau^n = I$. In particular, D_{2n} has exactly 2n elements. (2.15)

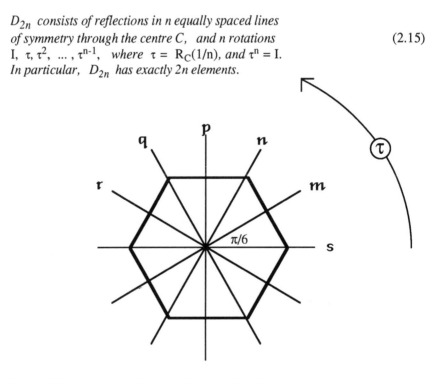

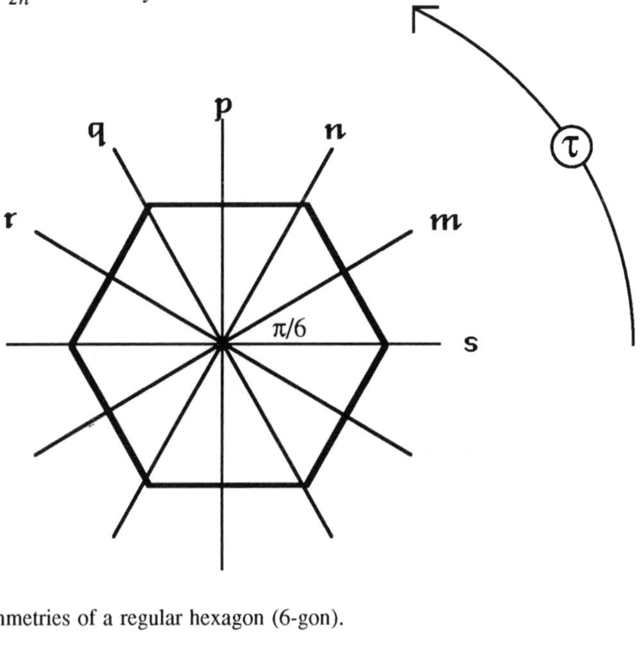

Figure 2.21 Symmetries of a regular hexagon (6-gon).

THE ROTATION SUBGROUP Since the product of two rotations about C is a third, the collection $C_n = I, \tau, \tau^2, \ldots, \tau^{n-1}$ of all rotations, forms itself a group, the *rotation*

subgroup of D_{2n}. It is *cyclic of order n,* meaning that the elements of C_n consist of the powers of a single element, and the size of the group is n. The name C_n is given to groups with this structure in widely varying contexts. See e.g. Birkhoff and MacLane (1963).

EXAMPLE 2.16 Relationships in D_{12}. Let τ be the 1/6 turn about the centre of a regular hexagon, as in Figure 2.21 above, with symmetry lines **s**, ***m***, ***n***, .., ***r***. We give two points of view, each useful for its insights.

VIEW 1 τ maps **s** to ***n***, so $R_n = R_s^{\tau}$ $(= \tau^{-1}R_s\tau)$, by Theorem 2.12. But R_m also maps **s** to ***n***, so

$$R_n = R_s^{R_m},$$
$$= R_m R_s R_m, \quad \text{since } R_m^{-1} = R_m.$$

The two expressions for R_n must be equal, and they are, since $\tau = R_sR_m$ (Theorem 2.1) and $\tau^{-1} = R_mR_s$ (see (2.9)).

VIEW 2 By Example 2.4 in Section 2.2 the composition of a turn about the hexagon centre with reflection in a line of symmetry equals reflection in a line at *half the rotation angle* to the original line. So taking the various powers of τ we obtain, with reference to Figure 2.21 :

$$R_s\tau = R_m,$$
$$R_s\tau^2 = R_n,$$
$$\dots\dots\dots\dots$$
$$R_s\tau^5 = R_r.$$

DEFINITION 2.17 We say a symmetry group G is *generated by* a subset $g_1, g_2, ..., g_s$ if every element g of G is expressible as a product of certain g_i (with or without repetition or powers greater than one). That is, g is a *word* in the g_i. We express this by writing G = Gp{$g_1, g_2, ..., g_s$}. An *odd* (*even*) word will mean one whose length is odd (even). Correspondingly, we say a word has even or odd *parity*. [The definitions are the same for any group.]

THEOREM 2.18 Let R, S be reflections in any two adjacent lines of symmetry of an n-gon, and τ the 1/n turn about the centre. Then
(a) D_{2n} consists of n rotations: $I, \tau, \tau^2, \dots, \tau^{n-1}$ and n reflections, which may be written $R, R\tau, R\tau^2, \dots, R\tau^{n-1}$,
(b) We have $D_{2n} = \langle R, S : R^2 = S^2 = (RS)^n = I \rangle$, the notation $\langle \dots \rangle$ meaning that *D_{2n} is generated by R, S subject only to the given relations and their consequences. Moreover, however they are expressed, a reflection symmetry is an odd word and a rotation is an even word in R, S.*

Proof Part (a) is (2.15) with View 2 applied to general D_{2n}. For (b) we first substitute τ = RS . Then clearly $R^2 = S^2 = I$ and $(RS)^n = \tau^n = I$ (cf. (1.11)), so the given relations do hold. But any relation *independent of these* would imply equalites amongst the 2n distinct elements we have enumerated, a contradiction. Concerning parity, any expression for a rotation (reflection) as a word in R, S must be even (odd) by Remark 1.17, because a rotation isometry is direct and a reflection indirect.

EXERCISES for Section 2.4 The symmetry groups of the figures below are all cyclic or dihedral. Name them. Answers are given after the section following.

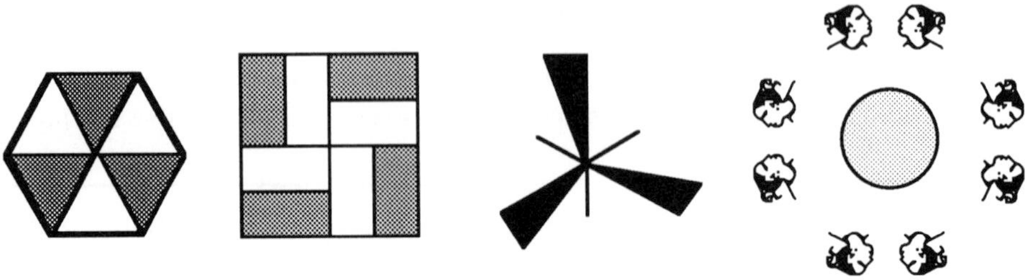

(a) (b) (c) (d)

2.5 Appendix on Groups

DEFINITION 2.19 A set G is a *group* with respect to a composition rule g,h $\rightarrow$ gh if the following axioms hold.

(A) [Associativity] f(gh) = (fg)h for all f,g,h in G.
(B) [Identity] G contains an *identity element*, that is, an element I, such that for every g in G we have Ig = g = gI.
(C) [Inverses] Every element g in G has an *inverse*. That is, a corresponding element g^{-1} exists in G such that $gg^{-1} = I = g^{-1}g$.

THEOREM 2.20 The set of all symmetries of a figure F forms a group under composition.

For a proof, see the beginning of Section 2.4. The following theorem is often useful for finding an identity or inverse.

THEOREM 2.21 Let J be an element of a group G.
(i) *The identity of G is unique, and if* **gJ** = **g** *or* **Jg** = **g** *for some g in G, then J is that identity.*
(ii) *The inverse of an element is unique, and if* **gh** = ***I*** *for some pair g, h in G, then g and h are inverses of each other.*

Proof (i) Let J, K be identities in G. Then J equals JK as K is an identity, which equals K because J is an identity. Thus the identity is unique, and now we have the following chain of implications for any inverse g^{-1} of g: $gJ = J \Rightarrow g^{-1}gJ = g^{-1}g \Rightarrow J = I$. The other proofs are in the same spirit but require more work. They may be found in Birkhoff and MacLane (1963).

DEFINITION 2.22 The *order* of an element g of a group is the least positive integer r such that $g^r = I$; if no such r exists we say g has *infinite order*.

EXAMPLES 2.23 A reflection has order 2, a 1/n turn has order n, but a translation has infinite order. In D_{12}, with t = 1/6 turn, the element t has order 6, and τ^3 has order 2, whilst

$$\begin{aligned} \textit{order of } \tau^4 &= \text{least r such that } \tau^{4r} \text{ is a whole number of turns} \\ &= \text{least r such that } 6 \mid 4r \text{ ('6 is a factor of 4r')} \\ &= 3. \end{aligned}$$

When are groups 'the same'? The symmetry group of a regular n-gon has the same structure wherever the particular n-gon is situated in the plane. This means that we can write any two such groups as $G = Gp\{g_1, ..., g_m\}$, $H = Gp\{h_1, ..., h_m\}$, so that replacing g by h transforms the multiplication table of G into that of H. We then say that the map ϕ from G to H defined by $\phi(g_i) = h_i$ is an *isomorphism* between G and H, and that G and H are *isomorphic*. (A multiplication table for G shows the product $g_r g_s$ at the intersection of a row labelled g_r with a column g_s. It is common to use the word 'multiplication' where, as here, we write a composition in the notation associated with multiplication and call it also a product.) But an isomorphism alone does not satisfy us in the present context of symmetries. For example, if R is a reflection and τ is a 1/2 turn, then the groups $G = \{I, R\}$ and $H = \{I, \tau\}$ are isomorphic, with $\phi(I) = I$, $\phi(R) = \tau$. Their multiplication tables are shown below.

	I	R
I	I	R
R	R	I

	I	τ
I	I	τ
τ	τ	I

Figure 2.22 Multiplication tables of isomorphic but not equivalent symmetry groups $G = \{I, R\}$ and $H = \{I, \tau\}$, where $R^2 = I = \tau^2$.

But we don't want to regard these two as essentially the same. A satisfactory tactic is to impose the additional restriction that ϕ must pair like with like: reflections with reflections, m/n turns with m/n turns, glides with glides, and translations with translations (not necessarily with the same direction or distance). If ϕ satisfies this, we call ϕ an *equivalence*, and say G and H are *equivalent* or 'the same'. In particular, the isometry groups of all regular n-gons, for a fixed n, are not only isomorphic but equivalent, and we call any one (an instance of) the Dihedral group D_{2n}. Equivalence will be the basis of our classification of plane patterns into seventeen types. [See Chapter 5 and Section 6.1 to 6.2 for more details.] *Answers for Section 2.4* : D_6, C_4, C_3, D_8.

EXERCISE In D_{14}, what are the orders of each of $\tau, \tau^2, \ldots, \tau^7$?
EXERCISE Write out the multiplication tables of C_4 and D_4.

EXERCISES 2

---

1 Use Euler's construction to show that some combination of 1/4 turns at the vertices of a square is a 1/4 turn about the centre or show that this result can be obtained from a 1/4 turn at a vertex and a vertex to vertex translation.

2 √ Show that the existence of 1/3 turn symmetries at two vertices of an equilateral triangle implies the existence of 1/3 turn symmetries about the third vertex and that a further symmetry translating one vertex to another implies a 1/3 turn symmetry about the triangle centre.

3 Show that (i) the composition of a rotation through angle ϕ, with a translation, is rotation about some point, through the same angle ϕ [use decomposition into reflections].

4 Verify that the product of a reflection in line m, followed by a glide at right angles to m, is that given in Figure 2.9(ii). [Express the glide as a product of reflections.]

5 √ What kind of isometry can be the result of three reflections? Of four?

6 (a) For the pattern of Figure 2.18, draw a diagram showing all 2- and 4-fold centres of symmetry. (b) Find a glideline, and verify that the corresponding glide g sends n-fold centres to n-fold centres for n = 2, 4. (c) Choose a 1/4 turn symmetry and verify that successive applications of it map the above glide line into successive glidelines.

7 Indicate in a diagram the reflection, glide, and 1/n turn symmetries of Figure 2.19. Choose a symmetry and satisfy yourself that it sends mirrors to mirrors, glidelines to glidelines, and n-fold centres to n-fold centres.

8 √ Let A be a point and g be the isometry $R_A(2/7)$. Express in the form g^n (for smallest positive integer n) the isometries g^2, g^{-1}, g^5.

9 √ Show that, if $(R_m R_n)^2 = I$, for lines m, n, then $(R_n R_m)^2 = I$. Do this first by algebra, using the fact that a reflection has order two, then by geometry, considering turns. How do you know that m and n are not parallel?

10 √ What is the inverse of an isometry of the form $R_m R_n R_p$, where m, n, p are mirror lines?

11 Indicate in suitable diagrams the lines of symmetry of (a) a regular pentagon, (b) a regular octagon. What is the rotation subgroup C_n of the symmetry group in each case?

12 Let R, S be the reflections in successive lines of symmetry round a regular hexagon. Write each element of the Dihedral group as a word in R, S. Determine the order of each element.

13 Construct multiplication tables for the Dihedral groups D_4 and D_6.

14 √ What are the symmetry groups of (a) to (c) below?

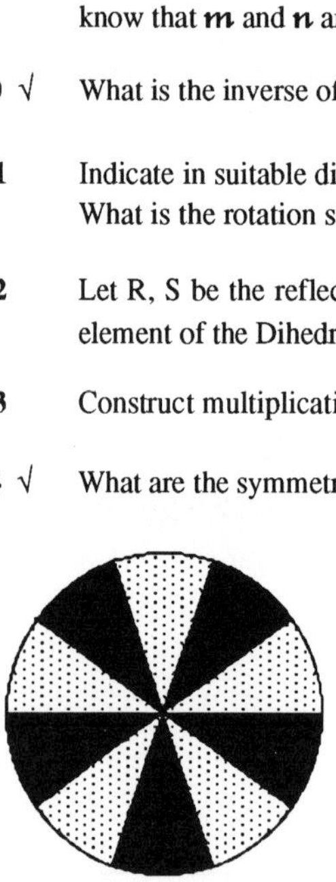

(a)

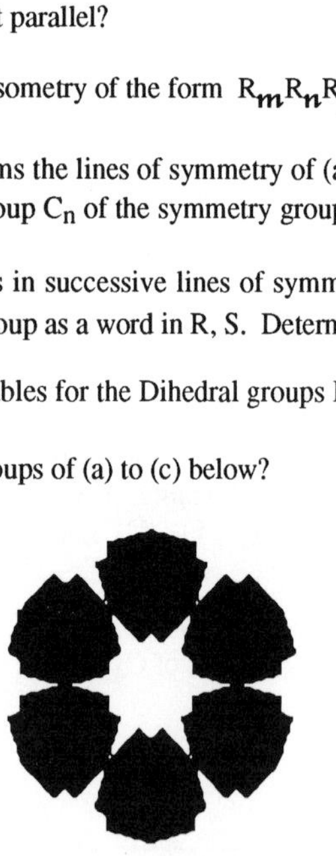

(b)

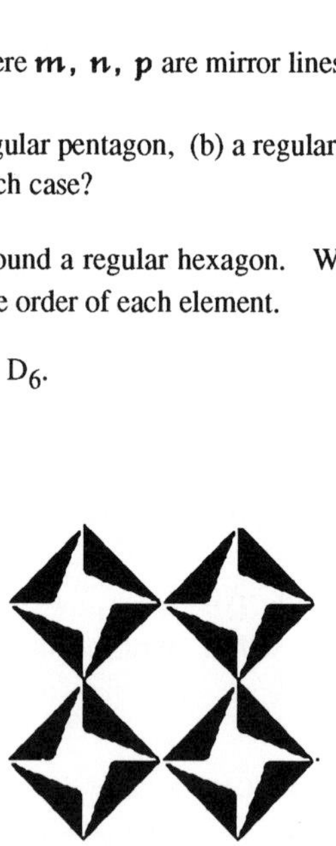

(c)

15 √ Prove that, in any group, the order of an element g equals the order of its inverse, g^{-1}. Verify this for the group D_{14}. Show that the groups C_{14} and D_{14} cannot be isomorphic.

Chapter 3 THE 7 BRAID PATTERNS

In Chapters 1 and 2 we have classified plane isometries, discovered some important principles of how they combine, and made a first application to patterns whose symmetry group is either the dihedral group D_{2n} or its rotation subgroup C_n. Before investigating plane patterns it is a logical and useful step to classify the 1-dimensional, or braid patterns, be aware of their symmetries, and get a little practice in both recognizing and creating them.

DEFINITION 3.1 We say **v** is a *translation vector* of pattern F if $T_\mathbf{v}$ is a translation symmetry. Then a *braid (band, frieze)* pattern is a pattern in the plane, all of whose translation vectors are parallel. In particular, **a** and -**a** are parallel. We will usually call this parallel direction *horizontal*, and the perpendicular direction *vertical*. Other names used are *longitudinal* and *transverse* respectively. A symmetry group of a braid is sometimes called a *line group*.

As noted in Section 1.1, we are investigating patterns which are *discrete*: they do not have translation or other symmetries which move the pattern by arbitrarily small amounts. Thus, amongst the collection of all translation symmetries of the pattern there is a translation $T_\mathbf{a}$ of least but not zero magnitude. Of course it is not unique, for example $T_{-\mathbf{a}}$ has the same magnitude $|\mathbf{a}|$ as $T_\mathbf{a}$. We rephrase an observation from the preliminary discussion of braids preceding Figure 2.7. It may be derived more formally from Theorem 3.3.

*A braid pattern F consists of a finite motif M repeated along a line at regular intervals |**u**|, where **u** is a translation vector of F of least magnitude.* (3.1)

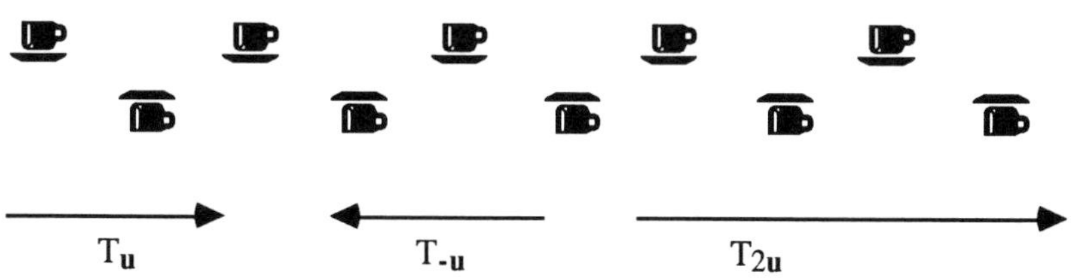

Figure 3.1 Braid pattern with least translations $T_\mathbf{u}$, $T_{-\mathbf{u}}$.

Note on glides If a figure F has translation vectors **a** parallel to lines of symmetry m, then every composition $g = R_m T_\mathbf{a}$ is both a glide and a symmetry of F. However we do not wish to emphasise this. In fact it is customary to restrict mention of 'glide lines' and 'glide symmetries' to the case in which neither R_m nor $T_\mathbf{a}$ alone is a symmetry of F even though their composition *is* a symmetry of this figure. We note that $g^2 = T_{2\mathbf{a}}$, and therefore *twice* the translation part of a glide symmetry *must* be a translation vector of the figure. Hence the following convention.

CONVENTION 3.2 A *glide symmetry* or *glideline* of a figure F will normally refer to a composition $R_m T_{a/2}$, where **a** is a translation vector of F parallel to m, of *minimum possible length.*

THEOREM 3.3 The symmetries of a braid pattern F.
(a) The translation symmetries of F are the iterates T_{nu} of a translation symmetry T_u of least possible magnitude $|u|$, where $n = 0, \pm 1, \pm 2, \ldots$.
(b) The only possible 1/n rotation symmetries of F are the identity (n = 1), and 1/2 turns (n = 2).
(c) Any line of symmetry of F is either horizontal or vertical.
(d) A glide line of F must be horizontal.

Proof (a) Let T_u have least possible magnitude among the translation symmetries of F. Suppose **v** is a translation vector. Then by repeated subtraction or addition of **u** we obtain **v** = n**u**+**w** for some positive or negative integer n, where the vector **w** satisfies $0 \leq |\mathbf{w}| < |\mathbf{u}|$. Hence another translation vector is **v**-n**u** = **w**. Since $|\mathbf{u}|$ is least possible and $0 \leq |\mathbf{w}| < |\mathbf{u}|$, we must have **w** = 0, so **v** has the form n**u** as asserted.
(b) Let **v** be a translation vector. If some 1/n turn is a symmetry then [by Theorem 2.12(c)] so is the translation of magnitude $|\mathbf{v}|$ in the direction of a 1/n turn of **v**. But the only translations of magnitude $|\mathbf{v}|$ are $\pm$**v**, so n equals 1 or 2.
(c) A reflection symmetry in a line which is not parallel or perpendicular to a translation vector **v** conjugates T_v to give a translation not parallel to **v** [by Theorem 2.12(c)]. But this is impossible, since F is a braid pattern.
(d) If g is a non-horizontal glide symmetry then g^2 is a translation not parallel to the translation vectors of F. As in (c) above, this is not possible .

The classification of braids In fact, everything which is not explicitly forbidden by Theorem 3.1 is possible *except* that the presence of certain combinations of symmetries implies other symmetries. The following observations enable us to complete the classification.

A horizontal and a vertical line of symmetry intersect in a 2-fold centre of symmetry. (3.2)

Vertical mirrors are separated by 1/2 the minimum translation distance. (3.3)

The presence of reflection and glide as in (a) below implies 2-fold centres of symmetry A at points 1/4 the minimum translation distance from the mirror, as in Figure 3.2 (b). (3.4)

Figure 3.2 How half turn symmetries of a braid pattern arise from reflections and glides.

EXERCISE Verify assertions (3.2) to (3.4).

NOTATION 3.4 Each braid pattern type is specified by four symbols

r	n	x	y

with the following meaning.

r	Initial symbol denoting a braid as distinct from plane pattern.
n	The highest degree of rotational symmetry in the pattern. That is, n is the largest integer for which the pattern has a 1/n turn symmetry.
x	m if F has a vertical line of symmetry, g if F has a vertical glide line, 1 if F has neither.
y	The same as above, but for horizontal lines. In both cases, the '1' is omitted if it would be the last symbol.

REMARK 3.5 Case x = g is ruled out for braids by Theorem 3.3, but the xy symbols will be used later with similar meanings for plane patterns. Our preparatory work in Theorem 3.3 and (3.1) to (3.4) shows not only that there are seven braid types, but that each has a fixed configuration of symmetries. In Table 3.1 below we give a simple example of each type with the symmetries indicated. The notation is that of Table 2.1 (a continuous line is a mirror and a broken one a glide, and so on). To prevent a glut of symbols, the basic translation symmetry is the same for each example, and is given only in the first one.

Note The symmetry configuration is useful for pattern identification.

CONSTRUCTING BRAID PATTERNS

The idea is to construct a motif M for translation in accordance with (3.1). To achieve the necessary symmetries in M we can start with a sub-motif, say , and append its images under suitable isometries. For example, in the pattern for r2mm in Table 3.1 we reflect in a vertical mirror corresponding to the first 'm', to get , then reflect in a horizontal mirror, obtaining  as translation motif M. Inspection will show how each example in Table 3.1 was created in this way from the same sub-motif. For more refined braids, a subtler choice of sub-motif is required.

Identifying braid patterns We ask

(1) Are there vertical mirrors?
(2) Is there a horizontal mirror or glide line?

Note that there are 1/2 turn symmetries *if and only if* the answer to both (1) and (2) is affirmative.

TABLE 3.1 The seven braid pattern types and their symmetries.

	**r1**
	**r2** 1/2 turns
	**r1m** vertical mirrors
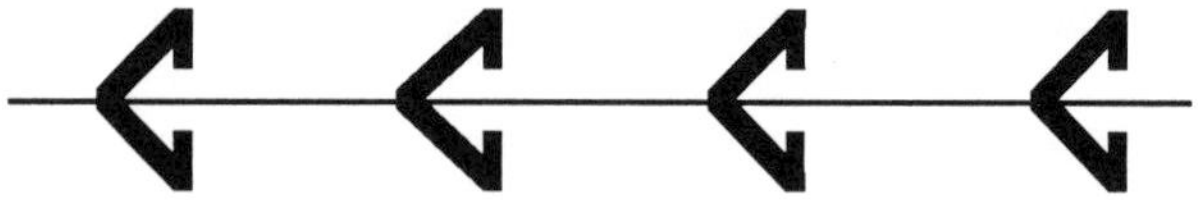	**r11m** horizontal mirror
	**r11g** horizontal glide
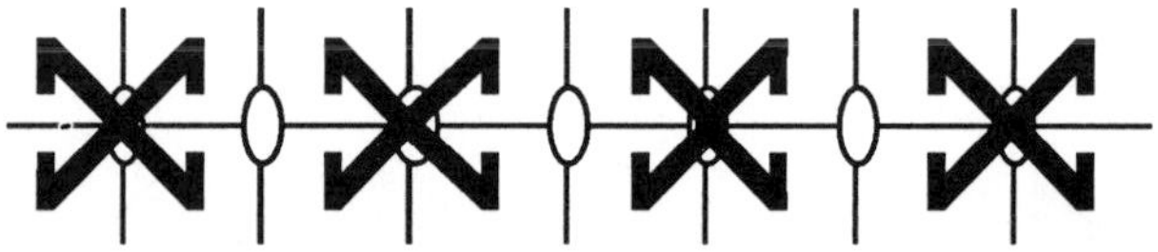	**r2mm** horizontal and vertical mirrors
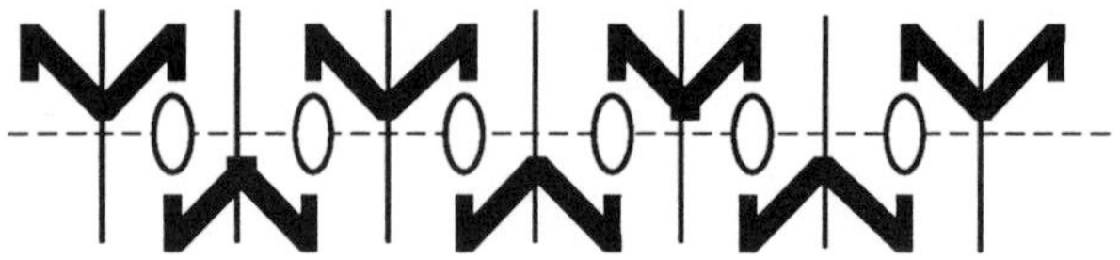	**r2mg** vertical mirror & horizontal glide

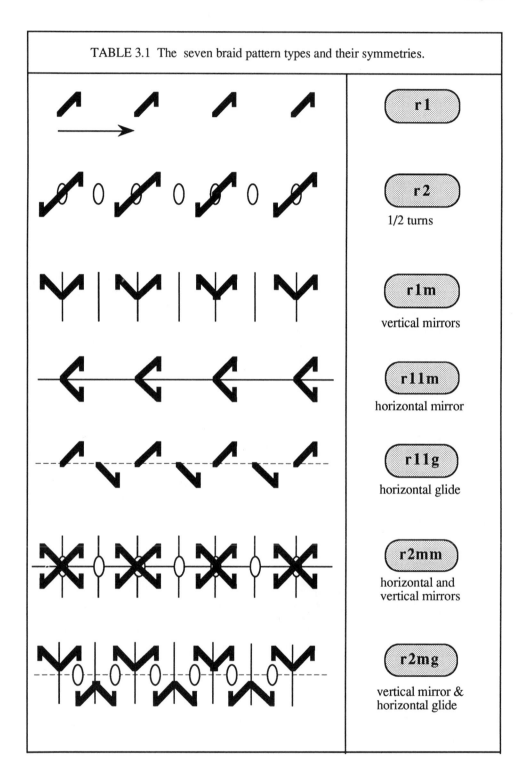

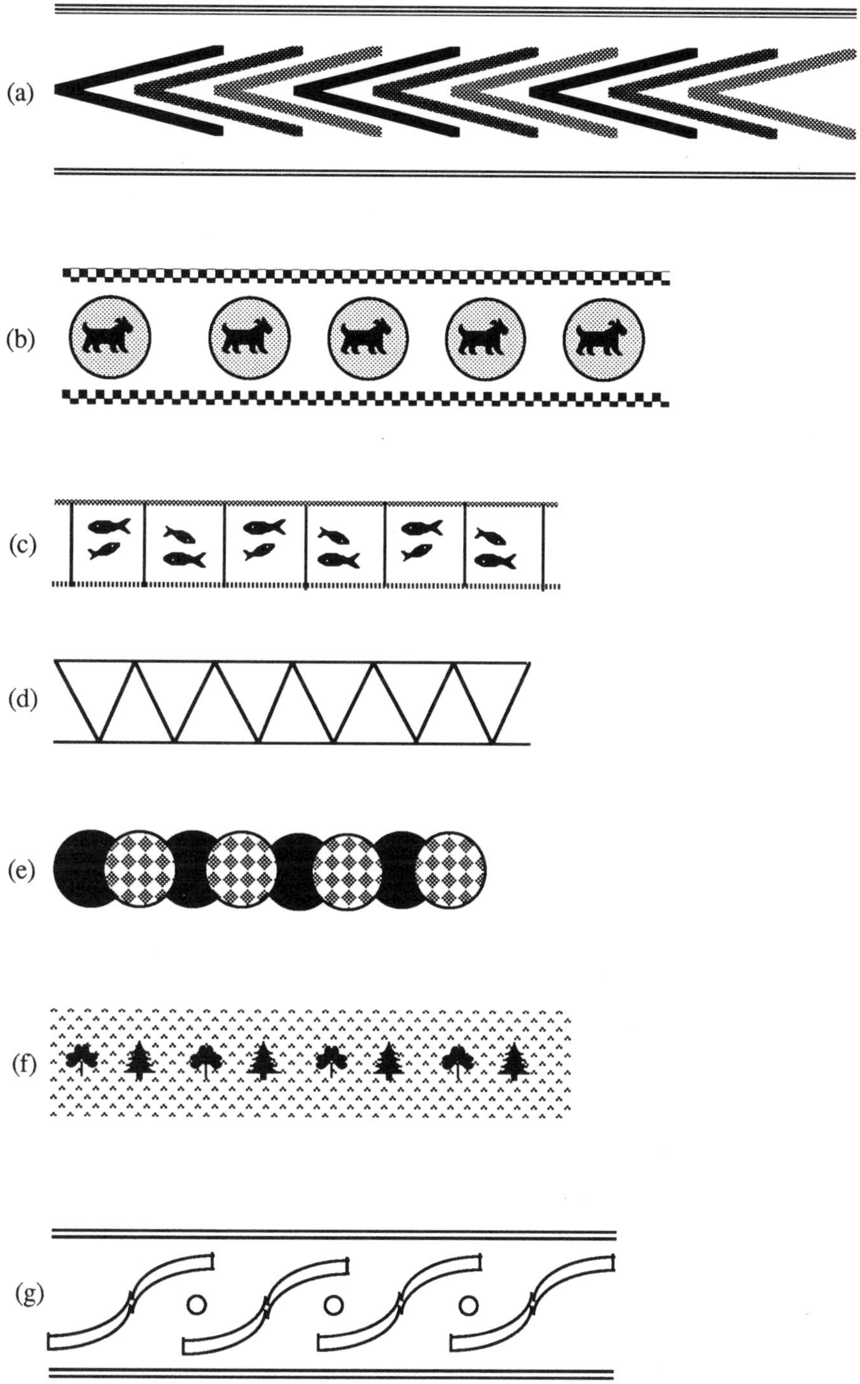

Figure 3.3 Braid patterns (a) to (g) for Exercise 3.2 below.

EXERCISES 3

1 √ Determine the braid types in Figure 2.7, the first row of Figure 2.19, and Figure 3.1.

2 √ Determine the braid types in Figure 3.3 (see above). Suggest a motif and sub-motif in each case.

3 Verify your answers to Exercise 2 by predicting the total pattern of symmetries and checking with Table 3.1.

4 Prove statements (3.2) to (3.4).

5 Construct a flow chart for identifying braid types, building on the two suggested questions.

6 Write a computer program to produce a braid pattern for which the user specifies the type and a submotif. You may wish to extend this to optional printing of the symmetry pattern in the background.

Chapter 4 PLANE PATTERNS & SYMMETRIES

4.1 Translations and nets

REVIEW 4.1 We recapitulate on some basic ideas. An *isometry* of the plane is a transformation of the plane which preserves distances, and is consequently a translation, rotation, reflection or glide (by Theorem 1.18). We may refer to any subset F of the plane as a *pattern*, but in doing so we normally imply that F has symmetry. That is, there is an isometry g which maps F onto itself. In this case g is called a *symmetry* or *symmetry operation* of F. Again, a *motif* M in (of) F is in principle any subset of F, but we generally have in mind a subset that is striking, attractive, and/or significant for our understanding of the structure of F.

Since the symmetry g has the two properties, of preserving distance and sending every point of F to another point of F, it sends M to another motif M' of F, which we may describe as being of the same size and shape as M, or *congruent to* M. By now we have many examples of this situation. An early case is that of the bird motifs of Figure 1.2, mapped onto other birds by translations and reflections. We observed that the composition of two symmetries of F, the result of applying one symmetry then the other, qualifies also as a symmetry, and so the collection of all symmetries of F forms a group G (see Section 2.5). We call G the *symmetry group* of F. Chapter 3 dealt with braid patterns F, in which F has translation vectors but they are all parallel. The term *plane pattern* is reserved for F if there are translation vectors of F (vectors v for which T_v is a symmetry) in two non-parallel directions , and F may be assumed to denote such a pattern from now on.

The discreteness hypothesis As noted from time to time we are restricting attention to patterns F, whose symmetries do not move F continuously, that is by arbitrarily small amounts. Thus there is some least nonzero distance achieved by the translations, and if F has rotation symmetries then they too have a least nonzero magnitude. The same applies to the translation part of any glides, since a glide followed by itself is a translation. By the end of Chapter 6 we will have met at least two patterns corresponding to each possible discrete symmetry group, therefore we note a pattern-independent characterisation of such groups G:

for any point O in the plane, a circle of finite size around O contains only a finite number of G-images of O. (4.1)

By *G-images* of the point O we mean the images O^g for all isometries g belonging to G. By criterion (4.1), a non-discrete example is Figure 4.1(a) below.

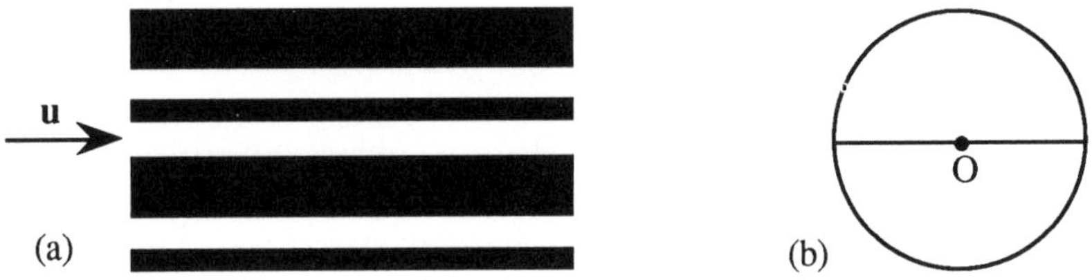

Figure 4.1 (a) Part of a plane pattern, whose translations include $T_{r\mathbf{u}}$ for all r, however small. The G-images of a point O centering a circle of any radius include, for example, a diameter of the circle as shown in (b), hence infinitely many points. This infringes (4.1), so the pattern is not discrete.

By contrast, we easily see that the plane pattern of Figure 4.2 has the property:

The translation vectors of the plane pattern F have a BASIS, that is, a pair **u,v** *such that any translation vector of F can be uniquely expressed as m***u** *+ n***v** *(m,n = 0, ±1, ±2, ...).* (4.2)

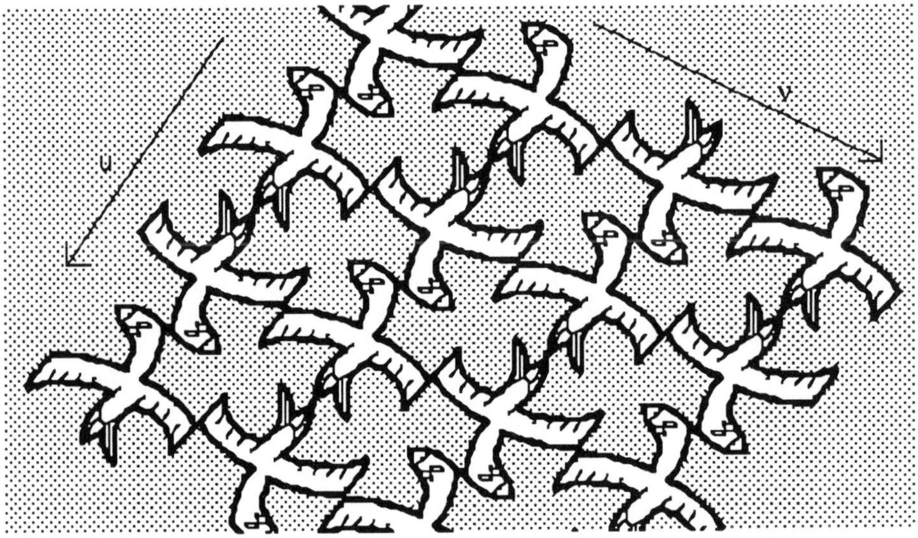

Figure 4.2 Escher-type birds (the pattern extends indefinitely over the plane).

In Theorem 4.6 we give a formal proof that (4.2) holds for all (discrete) plane patterns. Consequently here, as for braid patterns, the whole of F consists of the translations of one part, which we have called the *basic motif* M. A simple choice of M in Figure 4.2 is a square containing exactly four birds (can you suggest a suitable selection?). Later we discuss the options for M.

DEFINITION 4.2 **The translation subgroup.** Let **T** denote the set of all translation symmetries of a plane pattern F, including the identity $I = T_0$. It is easy to verify that **T** is a group [see Section 2.5], from a relation recalled from (1.12):

$$T_v T_w = T_{v+w}. \qquad (4.3)$$

We call **T** the *translation subgroup* of G and say **T** is *2-dimensional* or *plane* , since it contains vectors in two non-parallel directions. By *'the vector v is in T'* we will mean 'the translation T_v is in **T** ', or equivalently '**v** is a translation vector of F'. From the definition of scalar times vector in Section 1.2.1 we have for vectors **v**,**w**:

$$\mathbf{v}, \mathbf{w} \text{ are parallel} \Leftrightarrow \mathbf{v} = \alpha\mathbf{w} \text{ for some nonzero } \alpha. \qquad (4.4)$$

DEFINITION 4.3 A ***net*** N representing the plane translation group **T** is the *orbit,* or set of **T** -images, of some point O in the plane. In symbols:

$$N = \{O^g : g \text{ is in } \mathbf{T}\} = O^{\mathbf{T}}. \qquad (4.5)$$

We may call O the *basepoint* or *initial point* of the net (this point need not be the origin of x,y coordinates). For Figure 4.2 we obtain a 'square' net of which a part is portrayed below (rotated slightly and scaled down for convenience).

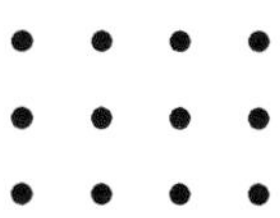

We note that changing the basepoint to any other point of the net gives back the same set of points. Yet the net of translations of a pattern is not unique: choosing a new basepoint A that is not in the net we already have gives an alternative net A^T representing the same set of translations. This freedom facilitates our classifying plane patterns by allowing Convention 4.4 below. We divide them into five classes by net type then investigate what symmetries are allowed by each type.

CONVENTION 4.4 We choose the basepoint of the net to lie on both

(i) a point of highest rotational symmetry of the pattern and,

(ii) a line of symmetry of the pattern,

where condition (i) takes precedence over (ii) if they are incompatible, and refers to an n-fold centre with n as large as possible.

EXERCISE Find suitable net basepoints for Figures 4.2 and 1.1.

4.2 Cells

CONSTRUCTION 4.5 The vertices of a net may be joined up to form congruent parallelograms called **cells.** A cell for a plane translation group **T** or its net N is by definition a parallelogram whose adjacent sides, when directed, represent some basis **u**,**v** for T. If we locate this cell so that one of its vertices is the basepoint of the net we call it a *base cell* or *unit cell,* and its translates occupy the net points as vertices and *tile* or *tesselate* the plane. That is, they fill the plane, with no area overlap. We say N *admits* this unit cell. In Figure 4.3 we show three choices of unit cell admitted by what is called a *hexagonal net* (see Section 4.3.3). These *diamond-shaped* cells are congruent but produce different tesselations (remember all cells in the tiling were to be translates of one cell). Figure 4.4 exhibits a pattern with the hexagonal net, whilst Figure 4.6 shows some non-congruent cells and their tilings for a different net.

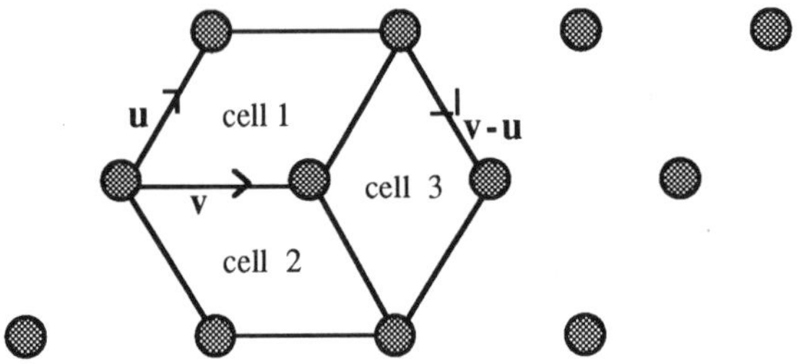

cell	basis
1	**u,v**
2	**v, v-u**
3	**u, v-u**

Figure 4.3 Three rows of a 'hexagonal' net portrayed. The cells of the three bases together form a regular hexagon.

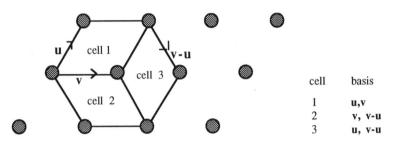

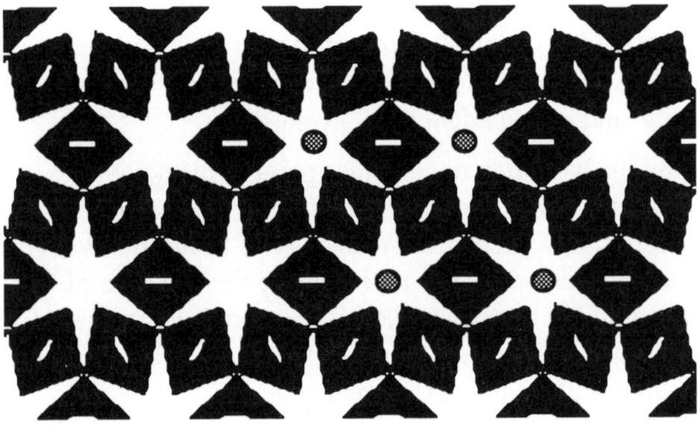

Figure 4.4 Plane pattern with hexagonal net. Convention 4.4 allows the basepoint at the centre of any white star, a six-fold centre of symmetry which also lies on a line of symmetry. We indicate four net points giving cell 2 of Figure 4.3. The points where three dark 'lozenges' meet are points of only three-fold rotational symmetry, not the highest in the figure.

EXERCISE Find net points in Figure 4.4 giving cell 1 and cell 3 of Figure 4.3. Locate a cell which violates Convention 4.4 for basepoints.

Surprisingly, not only does each choice of cell type have the same area, namely the least possible area of a parallelogram made by joining up points of the net, but also..... there are *infinitely many* possible cells of different shape. Our starting point, Theorem 4.6, tells us how to make the most useful choice (for the one exception see Section 4.3.3, Type (iii)).

*THEOREM 4.6 Every plane translation group **T** contains a basis **u,v**. We may take **u,v** to satisfy a **minimum length condition** :*

> ***u*** *is a nonzero vector in T of least possible length, and*
> ***v*** *is a nonzero vector in T, not parallel to **u**, and as short as possible (note : |**u**| ≤ |**v**|).* (4.6)

Proof Since **T** is discrete, **T** does contain vectors **u**,**v** satisfying (4.6). Certainly the set U = {m**u**+n**v** : m,n = 0, ±1, ±2, ...} is a subgroup of **T**, since the composition of two translation symmetries is another. We require to prove that every vector **w** of **T** is in U. To this end we apply the subgroup U to some basepoint O, to obtain a net N. Then U = {$\underline{OR}$: R ∈ N}. Let **w** = $\underline{OP}$. We must prove that (i) the point P is in N, and will do so by obtaining a contradiction in the contrary cases (ii) and (iii) below for the position of P relative to a cell ABCD of the net N.

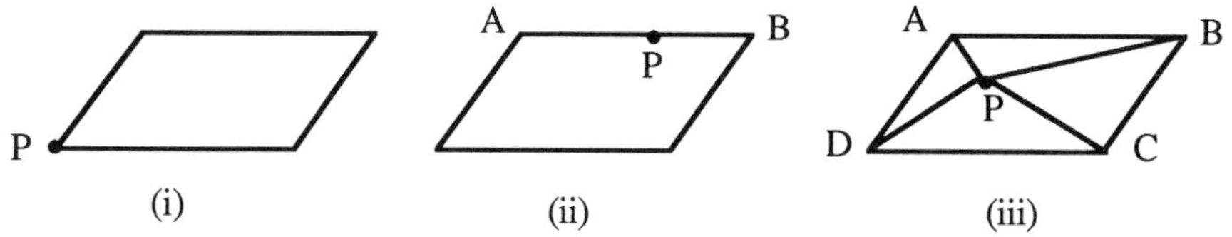

(i) *P is a point of the net N.*

(ii) *P is in the interior of an edge AB of a cell.* Thus $|AP| < |AB|$.
The vector $\underline{AP}$ = $\underline{OP}$ - $\underline{OA}$ is in **T** (since $\underline{OP}$ ∈ **T** and $\underline{OA}$ ∈ U, a subgroup of **T**) and furthermore AB, being a cell edge, has length $|\mathbf{u}|$ or $|\mathbf{v}|$. Therefore $|AP| < |AB|$ contradicts the fact that **u** and **v** satisfy the minimum length condition (4.6) for **T**.

(iii) *P is in the interior of a cell ABCD.*
Since the four (unsigned) angles which P subtends at the cell edges sum to 360°, at least one, say angle APB, is at least 90°. Therefore in triangle APB we have APB as the greatest angle and hence AB as greatest side. Thus $|AP| < |AB|$. Similarly to Case (ii), this contradicts the fact that **u**,**v** satisfy the minimum length condition (4.6) (note that $\underline{AP}$ cannot be parallel to **u** since P is in the interior of the cell).

It remains to prove the uniqueness of an expression for a vector **w** in **T**. Suppose that **w** = m**u** + n**v** = r**u** + s**v** for integers m,n,r,s. Subtracting, we obtain (m-r)**u** = (s-n)**v**. Since **u**,**v** are independent it follows that m-r = 0 = n-s (cf. (4.4)), hence m = r, n = s, and the expression is unique.

NOTATION 4.7 For vectors **a**,**b** we define *area(**a**,**b**)* to be the area of a parallelogram with adjacent sides representing **a**,**b** if these vectors are non-parallel, and otherwise zero. Let **u**,**v** be a basis of the plane translation group **T**. Then area(**u**,**v**) is the area of a *cell* defined by **u**,**v**. Suppose **a**,**b** are related to **u**,**v** by (i) below.

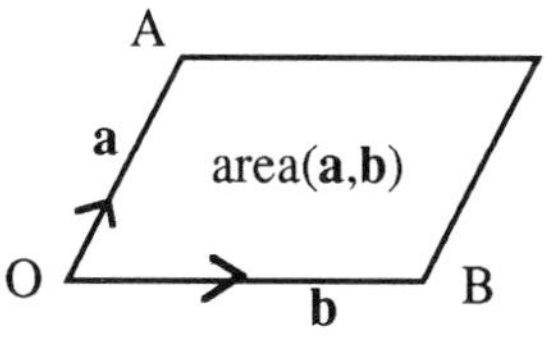

$$\text{(i)}\quad \begin{aligned}\mathbf{a} &= a\mathbf{u} + b\mathbf{v}\\ \mathbf{b} &= c\mathbf{u} + d\mathbf{v}\end{aligned} \qquad \text{(ii)}\quad A = \begin{bmatrix} a & b \\ c & d \end{bmatrix}, \quad \det A = ad - bc. \qquad (4.7)$$

The equations (i) may be specified by their *matrix of coefficients* A, an array of numbers in two rows and two columns called a *2 by 2 matrix*. Thus we may define A by its *column vectors*, writing A = [**x** **y**], where **x** = (a,c), **y** = (b,d). Here A is called an *integral* matrix because its *entries* a,b,c,d happen to be integers. The *determinant* of A, denoted by det(A) or simply det A, is the number ad-bc. The following lemma suggests its importance.

LEMMA 4.8 (Determinant formulae for areas.) We have

(a) area(**a**,**b**) = $|\det M|$, *where* M = [**a b**] *(**a**,**b** arbitrary vectors),*
(b) area(**a**,**b**) = $|\det A|$ area(**u**,**v**), *if **a**,**b** are related to **u**,**v** by (4.7).*

Proof (a) We begin with **a**,**b** non-parallel in the manner of Figure 4.5. Thus the coordinates satisfy $0 < b_1 < a_1$ and $0 < a_2 < b_2$, and we have

area(**a**,**b**)
= 2 (area of OAB)
= 2(area OBC + area ABCD - area OAD)
= $b_1b_2 + (a_1 - b_1)(a_2 + b_2) - a_1a_2$
= $a_1b_2 - a_2b_1$
= $|\det M|$, as required.

If we interchange the positions of A, B the area becomes -(det M), hence the need to take the absolute value (areas are unsigned in this context).

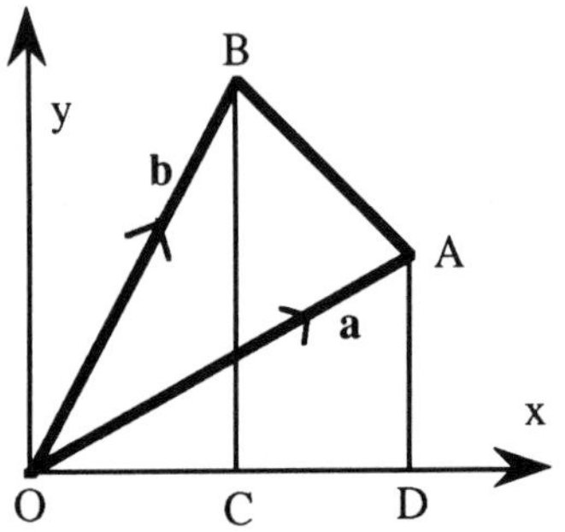

Figure 4.5 Diagram for proof of Lemma 4.8.

Considering variants of Figure 4.5 we find that the determinant formula (a) holds in all cases of **a**,**b** non-parallel. In the case $\mathbf{a} = \alpha\mathbf{b}$ for some scalar α we have $\det M = \alpha b_1b_2 - \alpha b_2b_1 = 0 =$ area(**a**,**b**), so the formula remains true. Cases $\mathbf{a} = \mathbf{0}$ and $\mathbf{b} = \mathbf{0}$ are trivial.

Proof (b) Applying Part(a) to both area(**a**,**b**) and area(**u**,**v**), we obtain

$$\begin{aligned} \text{area}(\mathbf{a},\mathbf{b}) &= |a_1b_2 - a_2b_1| \\ &= |(au_1 + bv_1)(cu_2 + dv_2) - (au_2 + bv_2)(cu_1 + dv_1)|, \quad \text{by (4.7)} \\ &= |(ad - bc)(u_1v_2 - u_2v_1)| \\ &= |\det A| \text{ area}(\mathbf{u},\mathbf{v}), \text{ as required.} \end{aligned}$$

EXERCISE Prove that area(**a**,**b**) = $|\det[\mathbf{a}\ \mathbf{b}]|$ for A,B on opposite sides of the y-axis.

*THEOREM 4.9 Let **u**,**v** be a basis of **T** and **a**,**b** a pair of non-parallel vectors in **T**. Then*

$$\text{area}(\mathbf{a},\mathbf{b}) \geq \text{area}(\mathbf{u},\mathbf{v}),$$

*with equality (i.e. $|\det A| = 1$) if and only if **a**,**b** is also a basis.*

Proof The vital fact that **u**,**v** is a basis allows **a**,**b** to be expressed in terms of **u**,**v** by a relation (4.7)(i), giving area(**a**,**b**) = $|\det A|$ area(**u**,**v**), by Lemma 4.8. We require that $|\det A| \geq 1$, and it is true for reasons so simple they are easily missed. By definition of *basis* in (4.2) the entries in matrix A are integers, so det A itself is an integer from its definition. It cannot be zero because area(**a**,**b**) is nonzero, hence $|\det A| \geq 1$, and the first assertion follows.

For the equality assertion, suppose **a**,**b** as well as **u**,**v** is a basis. Then by the first part, area(**u**,**v**) $\geq$ area(**a**,**b**) $\geq$ area(**u**,**v**), so the areas are equal. For the converse assume that **u**,**v** is a basis and the two areas are equal, implying that $\det A = \pm 1$ by Lemma 4.8. Then equations (4.7)(i) have a unique solution

$$\mathbf{u} = (d\mathbf{a} - b\mathbf{b})/\det A, \qquad \mathbf{v} = (-c\mathbf{a} + a\mathbf{b})/\det A \tag{4.8}$$

for **u**,**v** in terms of **a**,**b**. Furthermore the coefficients of **a**,**b** are integers, since det A equals ±1 and a,b,c,d are integers. Thus any vector **w** in **T** may be expressed in the form **w** = m**a** + n**b** by, for example, expressing **w** in terms of the basis **u**,**v** then applying (4.8). The expression is unique as required, because **w** = m**a** + n**b** = r**a** + s**b** implies (m - r)**a** = (s - n)**b**, and hence m = r, n = s, since **a**,**b** are not parallel (see (4.4)). Thus **a**,**b** is a basis.

REMARKS 4.10 (1) We develop matrices in Chapter 7, so we have here a nice flier or motivation for later. In effect we have proved for the occasion some basic results such as Lemma 4.8. With Chapter 7 behind us it would be natural to invoke 'matrix inverses' in the proof of Theorem 4.9.
(2) We recall for the next Corollary that a cell for a plane translation group **T** is a parallelogram whose adjacent sides, directed, represent basis vectors for **T**.

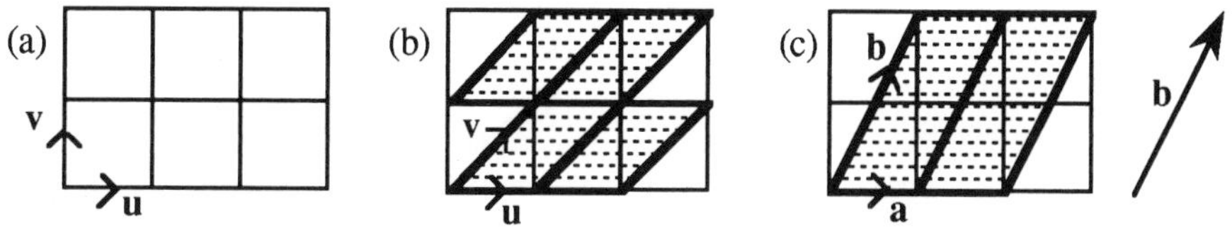

Figure 4.6 Three candidates for cell of a square net (one that admits a square cell). (a) A cell (square) which satisfies the minimum length condition (4.6) and (b), one which does not. By Corollary 4.11(d), every cell satisfying (4.6) is square, for this net. By Corollary 4.11(c), infinitely many parallelograms have the right area for a cell, but by Corollary 4.11(b) the long parallelograms (c) above do not. So **a**,**b** is not a basis of **T**.

COROLLARY 4.11
*(a) A pair **u**,**v** in **T** is a basis if and only if area(**u**,**v**) is least possible for non-parallel vectors in **T**.*
(b) All cells have this least area.
(c) There are infinitely many cell shapes.
(d) All cells satisfying the minimum length condition (4.6) are congruent.

Proof (a) and (b) follow from the observation that by Theorem 4.9, if **x**,**y** is a basis and area(**a**,**b**) is least possible, then area(**a**,**b**) ≥ area(**x**,**y**) ≥ area(**a**,**b**), so the areas are equal. In (c) we start with, say, the basis **u**,**v** given by Theorem 4.6. Then for every 2 by 2 matrix A with integer entries and determinant 1 there is (Theorem 4.9, last part) a new basis **a**,**b** given by (4.7). Also, unless two matrices have identical entries they cannot yield the same pair **a**,**b**, because of the uniqueness of their expression in terms of the basis **u**,**v**.

To produce an infinitude of matrices establishing (c) we shall use two facts from elementary Number Theory (Niven & Zuckerman, 1980, Theorems 1.3 and 1.17): (i) there are infinitely many choices for a pair of distinct prime numbers p,q, and (ii) for any such pair of integers with no common factor there are integers x,y such that px+qy=1.

Then the matrix $A = \begin{bmatrix} p & -q \\ y & x \end{bmatrix}$ has determinant px -(-q)y = 1, and (c) is proved. (Other matrices will do: see Example 4.12.)

For (d), we note that if a cell satisfies (4.6) then the *lengths* of **u**,**v** are determined, though not necessarily their directions. But by Part (b), the cell's area is determined. It equals |**u**| |**v**| sin ϕ, where ϕ is the (unsigned) angle between **u** and **v**, with $0 < \phi < \pi$, and |**u**| sin ϕ is the 'height' of the cell. Thus sin ϕ is determined and hence, although there is an apparent ambiguity in that sinϕ = sin(π-ϕ), the two possible parallelograms are congruent.

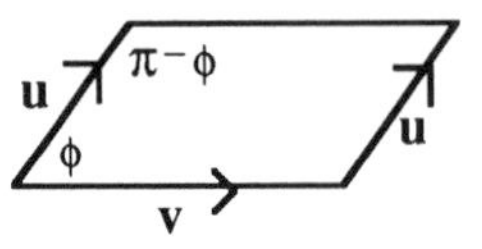

EXAMPLES 4.12 Some integral matrices with determinant ±1.

$$\begin{bmatrix} 2 & 1 \\ 1 & 1 \end{bmatrix} \quad \begin{bmatrix} 1 & -1 \\ 0 & 1 \end{bmatrix} \quad \begin{bmatrix} 2 & 3 \\ 1 & 2 \end{bmatrix} \quad \begin{bmatrix} 3 & 2 \\ 4 & 3 \end{bmatrix} \quad \begin{bmatrix} 2 & 3 \\ 5 & 7 \end{bmatrix}$$

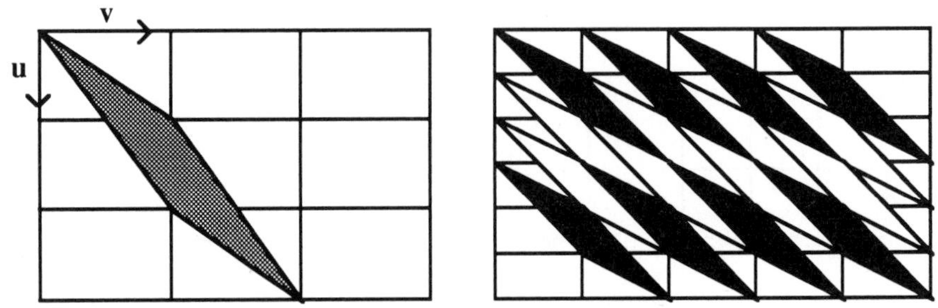

Figure 4.7 New cells from old by the first matrix of Examples 4.12.

The second part of Figure 4.7 is a scaled down version of the first, and indicates how a tiling would proceed. The tiles are in alternate black and white layers.

What the eye sees The cell designs which the eye sees first are usually those with least edge length, our choice of cell in Theorem 4.6. As we take more complicated matrices to make new cells from this original, the new cells become rather thin and elongated. However, if we are looking for a tiling from which to begin a design, we can always use a matrix of determinant say 4, and/or scale the earlier net, to suit our purposes.

EXERCISE Do as in Figure 4.6 with your own matrix.

4.3 The five net types

We are moving towards a classification of plane patterns by symmetries, which will aid both their recognition and creation. This section motivates the first step, of dividing them into five classes by net type.

REVIEW 4.13 Soon (in Chapter 5) we will make extensive use of the notation in Table 2.1, of a continuous line for a mirror, broken line for glide, arrow for translation, and regular n-gon for n-fold centre of symmetry. Where construction lines or cell edges are required in addition, the mirror lines will usually be thickened. We choose a basepoint, at first arbitrarily, and join up the points of the resulting net so as to obtain cells of the **unique size and shape which satisfy the minimum length condition** (4.6) (see Corollary 4.11(d)). Later we will need to reposition the basepoint, for example to satisfy Convention

4.4 and to take advantage of the powerful Net Invariance Theorem 4.14 to come. To recapitulate, we let

F = a given plane pattern
G = the group of all symmetries of F
T = the subgroup comprising all translation symmetries
N = net: all translates of some basepoint by the elements of **T**
M = motif: a part of pattern F whose translates form the whole.

*THEOREM 4.14 (Net invariance.) Let g be a symmetry of a pattern. If g fixes a point of some net for **T** then the net is invariant under g. That is, g maps net points to net points.*

Proof Let g fix the net point A. Then so does g^{-1} (see Notation 2.9ff). In symbols, the double equality $A^g = A = A^{g^{-1}}$ holds. Noting too that any other net point P is the image A^T of a translation symmetry T, we have:

$$P^g = (A^T)^g = A^{Tg} = \left(A^{g^{-1}}\right)^{Tg} = A^{g^{-1}Tg}.$$

But by Theorem 2.12(c), $g^{-1}Tg$ is a translation symmetry of the pattern, and therefore $P^g = A^{g^{-1}Tg}$ is a point of the net, as required.

EXERCISE Verify Theorem 4.14 in Figure 4.4, for a 1/6 turn and a reflection.

4.3.1 Nets allowing a reflection

In spite of Theorem 4.14, we cannot guarantee that cells will be mapped into cells, no matter how carefully we choose the position of the net and the division into cells. What we do find is that the alternative properties a net may have in order to allow a mirror symmetry already suggest the five net types required for a full classification of plane isometries. Naturally enough, since a study of reflections reveals so much about plane isometries.

Suppose the pattern F has at least one mirror line m. It will have others too because of translation symmetries, and perhaps glides and rotations, but we focus attention on the effect of m alone. Since there either is or is not a cell edge parallel to m, we may divide considerations into these two cases. For simplicity we will consider m as horizontal in Case 1, and other convenient directions in Case 2. We will not go into full detail, since we are using these cases simply to highlight the likely relevance of three criteria for a potential cell: are its edges at right angles, are they equal, does one edge have the same length as one diagonal?

CASE 1 *The mirror m is parallel to a cell edge.* We position the net so that m lies *along* a cell edge. Let A be a vertex (net point) as close to m as possible but not actually on it. Then the mirror m reflects A into another vertex A' (Theorem 4.14), and the minimum length condition, it may be verified, allows no *more* than the two possibilites shown below. Note that the three horizontal lines in each diagram are successive lines composed of cell edges.

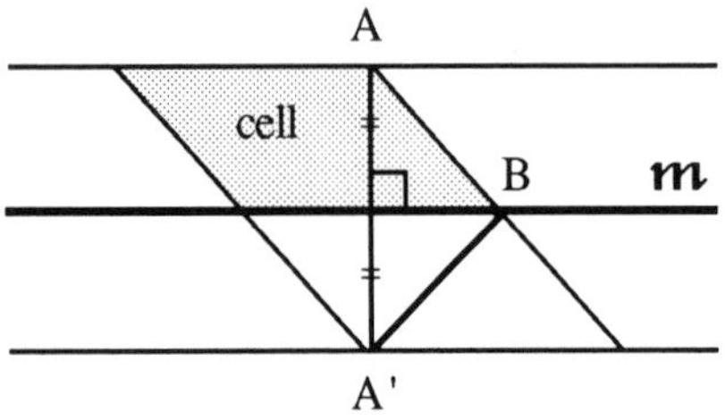

1a. One edge AB equals a diagonal BA' in length

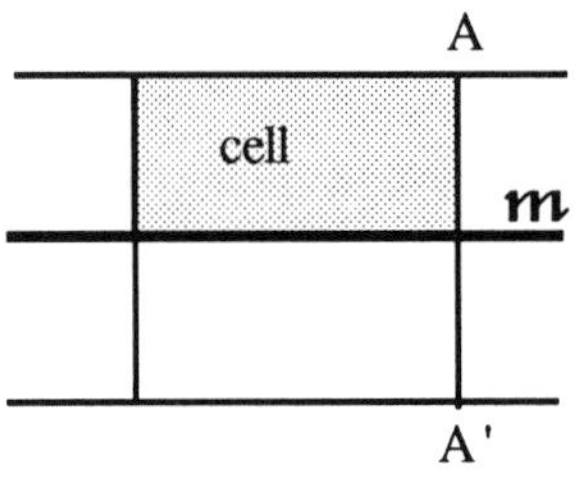

1b. Adjacent cell edges are perpendicular.

CASE 2 The mirror m is parallel to no cell edge. Place the net so that m contains a vertex A. Let AB be an edge. In particular, B is not on m. Then again there are two subcases.

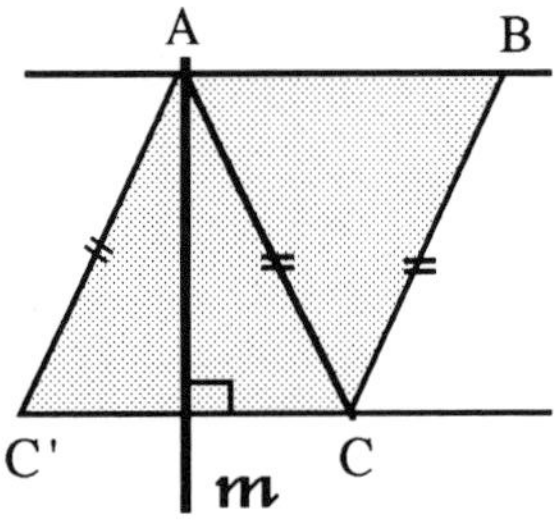

2a. m is at right angles to AB.
One edge equals a diagonal in length.

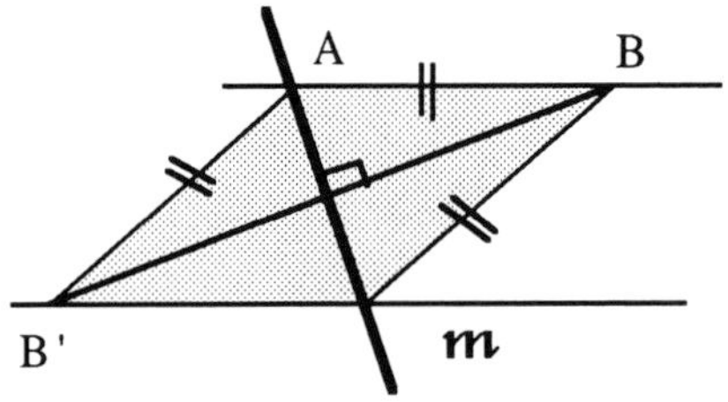

2b. m is not at right angles to AB.
Adjacent cell edges are equal.

4.3.2 Rotations - the Crystallographic restriction

We begin with some consequences of our discreteness hypothesis which don't depend on the presence of translation symmetries of the pattern F. Let F have rotation symmetries about a point A and let α be the smallest positive angle for which $R = R_A(\alpha)$ is a symmetry. We claim that *α is $1/n$ of a turn for some integer n.* Firstly, α must be some fraction of a turn, for if not then $R, R^2, R^3, \ldots$ are all different. Imagine their angles marked on a circle. Since there are infinitely many the marks must come arbitrarily close, contradicting the minimality of α. So now we have $\alpha = 2\pi r/n$ for some integers r,n with no common factor.

Appealing (again) to elementary Number Theory (Niven & Zuckerman, 1980), there is some integer multiple k of r/n which differs from 1/n by an integer. Thus $R^k = R_A(2\pi/p)$ is a symmetry. Since the least rotation is $2\pi r/n$ we must have $r = 1$, and $\alpha = 2\pi/n$ as asserted. Now we are ready to prove the famous Crystallographic restriction for plane patterns, so named for its relation to the early work of crystallographers in classifying crystals by their symmetry groups. See e.g. Phillips (1971).

THEOREM 4.15 ***The Crystallographic restriction.*** *If a plane pattern has an n-fold centre of symmetry, then n = 2,3,4 or 6.*

Proof Let A,B be n-fold centres of symmetry as close together as possible and R,S the corresponding 1/n turns, $R = R_A(1/n)$, $S = R_B(-1/n)$. Our proof refers to the diagrams below. There are two cases to consider: (a) general n, (b) case n = 5.

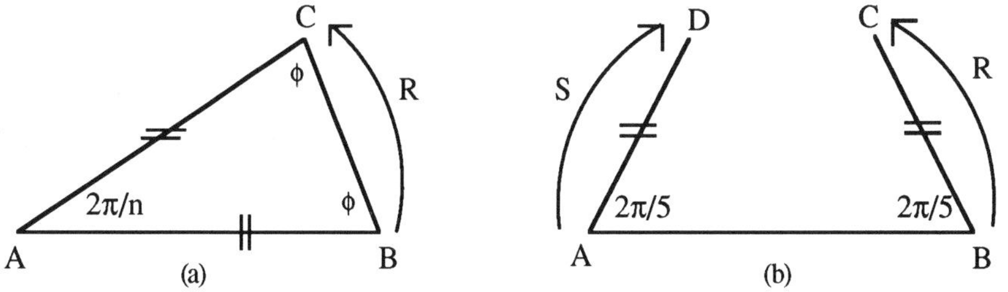

Figure 4.8 Diagram for proof of the Crystallographic restriction

We first establish that $n \le 6$, using Figure 4.8(a). The image $C = B^R$ of B under R is by Theorem 2.12(b) an n-fold centre, so from the hypothesis that $|AB|$ is least possible we have $|AB| \le |BC|$. By elementary Geometry, the same inequality holds for their opposite angles in triangle ABC: $\phi \le 2\pi/n$. Since the angles of triangle ABC must sum to π, we have $2\phi = \pi - 2\pi/n$, whence $\pi/2 - \pi/n \le 2\pi/n$, or $\pi/2 \le 3\pi/n$, and so $n \le 6$. It remains to rule out $n = 5$, using Figure 4.8(b). So let $n = 5$ and consider the points $C = B^R$, $D = A^S$. Then, since $2\pi/5 < \pi/2$ we have the contradiction $|CD| < |AB|$.

4.3.3 The five net types

We are now in a good position to motivate the classification of nets. Consider the following Venn diagram, in which an enclosed subregion represents the set of all cells ABCD with a certain property and the intersection of two such regions represents cells having *both* respective properties. The universal set, represented by an enclosing rectangle, is all possible cells (parallelograms). Section 4.3.1 on reflections suggests highlighting properties $AB = BC$ and $AB \perp BC$. These define the two large regions, and hence *four* possible net types, labelled (i) to (iv) in Figure 4.9 following.

The third property appearing in 4.3.1, that one side of a cell has the same length as one of the diagonals (the diamond shape), is put in as subcase (v) of (iii). According to the Net Invariance Theorem 4.14 this is the only net type to allow the 1/6 and 1/3 turns of the Crystallographic restriction, since such a turn about any net point must send every net point into another. The net is called *hexagonal* because its points form the vertices and centres of a tiling of the plane by hexagons (cf.Figure 6.12). Again, it is not hard to see from Theorem 4.14 that (iv), the *square net*, is the only type to allow 1/4 turn symmetries. The discussion continues after Figure 4.9.

Thus far we have divided nets into five types by their uniquely shaped cells which satisfy the minimum length condition (4.6) (Corollary 4.11(d)): rectangular, square, diamond, rhombus (other than square or diamond), and general parallelogram (none of those preceding). To complete the classification we extend the rhombus class to include all nets which admit a rhombus cell, even if it does not satisfy (4.6). Thus nets such as that of Figure 4.10 are reallocated from the general parallelogram to this type which, because of the Definition and Lemma following, is known as *centred rectangular*. This is how type (iii) in Figure 4.9 is to be interpreted.

DEFINITION 4.16 A net is *centred* if its points are the vertices and centres of a set of rectangles tiling the plane (all being translates of one rectangle).

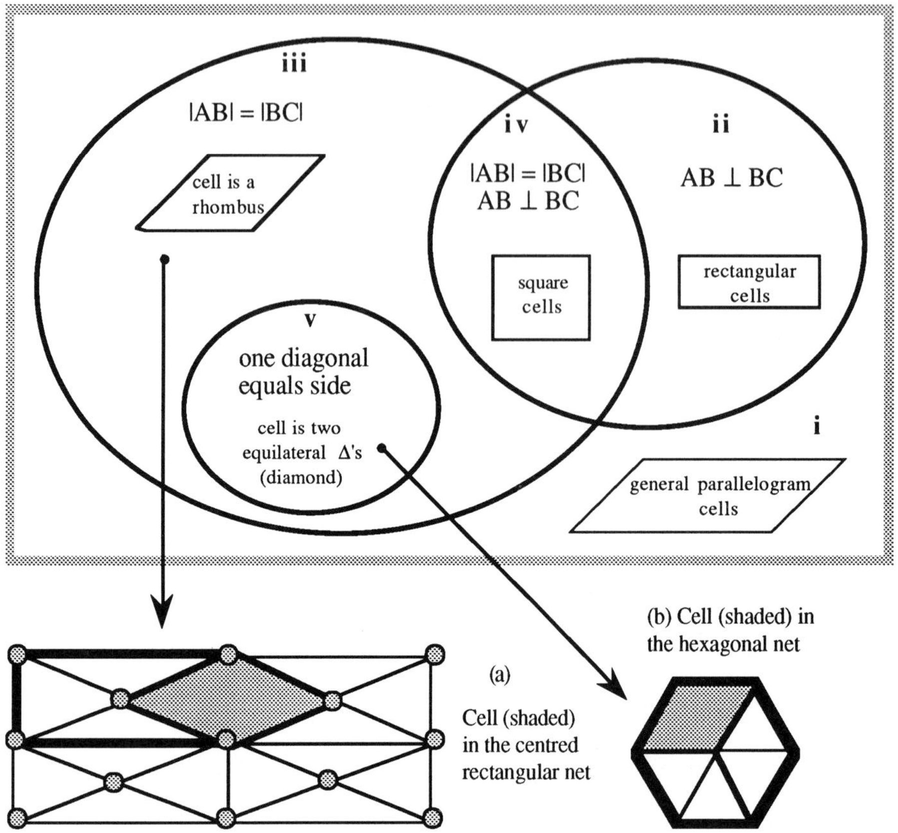

Figure 4.9 Genesis of the five net types

LEMMA 4.17 A net is centred if and only if it admits a rhombus cell.

Proof Figure 4.9(a) shows how a centred net admits a rhombus cell. For the reverse implication we recall that a parallelogram is a rhombus (all four sides equal in length) if and only if its diagonals bisect each other at right angles. In Figure 4.10 the diagonal AC is common edge of two rectangles whose definitions are completed by our specifying that their centres are the vertices D, B of the other diagonal. In this way we recover Figure 4.9(a). (On the other hand, the parallelograms ACDE and FADE are cells of the net which do satisfy the minimum length condition (4.6).)

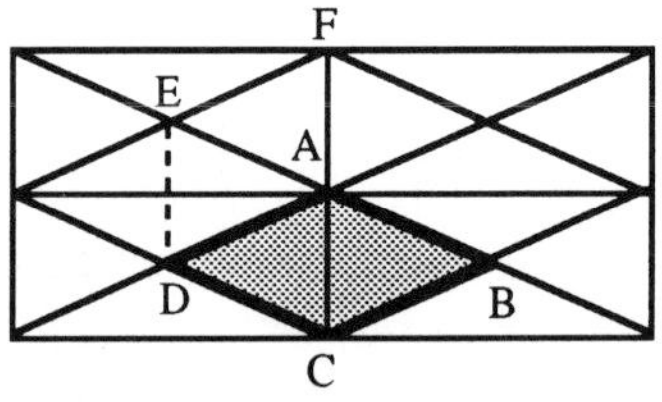

Figure 4.10 Constructing the centred rectangles from a rhombus cell. FADE is an alternative cell which satisfies the minimum length condition (4.6).

REMARK 4.18 In view of Lemma 4.17, the square and hexagonal nets are centred, since the square and diamond are special cases of a rhombus. To avoid confusion we do not emphasise this, but we show in Figure 4.11 the centred rectangles superimposed in dotted outline on these two types.

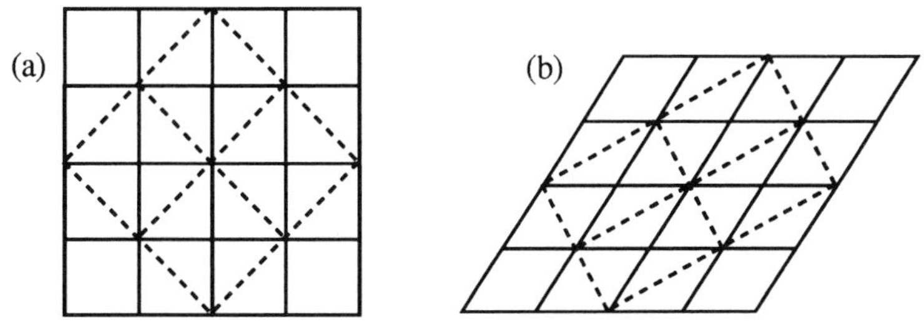

Figure 4.11 How (a) the square net and (b) the hexagonal net with its diamond cells may be exhibited as centred. In the first case the centred rectangle is square.

RESUMÉ 4.19 **The net types** (numbered i to v in Figure 4.9).

(i) *The general parallelogram net* with no special properties, nevertheless has 1/2 turn symmetries about the vertex of each cell, the midpoint of each cell edge, and the cell centre. See Section 5.2.

(ii) *The rectangular net* gives the option of mirrors in either one or two directions, and 1/2 turn symmetries.

(iii) *The centred rectangular net.* Because the diagonals of a rhombus bisect each other at right angles, the points of this net can be grouped as the vertices of *centred rectangles*, as indicated in Figure 4.9(a). This insight not only gives the net its name, but is important in practice, for it is usually easier to see that copies of a motif mark the vertices and centre of a rectangle than to be sure that they are equidistant from their neighbours, especially if the motif has a very irregular shape. Mirror and rotation properties are as for (ii).

Note that a rhombus, though it will have least possible area (Corollary 4.11), may violate the minimum length condition (4.6). (This unavoidable exception causes no harm in the sequel.) It can nevertheless occur as Case 2b in Section 4.3.1.

(iv) *The square net.* This is the first in our list which Theorem 4.14 (net invariance) allows to have 4-fold rotational symmetry. As a result it can support mirrors at 45° as well as 90°. On the other hand, Theorem 4.14 forbids 1/3 or 1/6 turns for this net.

(v) *The hexagonal net.* The cell is a diamond, formed from two equilateral triangles, whose internal angles are of course 60°, or $\pi/3$. Consequently, each point of the net is in six equilateral triangles, tiling a regular hexagon. The hexagons in turn tile the plane. Thus it makes sense to call this net *hexagonal*. Later we see the various possibilities for reflections and glides. Here we note that 1/3 and 1/6 turns are permitted (for the first time), whilst 1/4 turns are not, by Theorem 4.14.

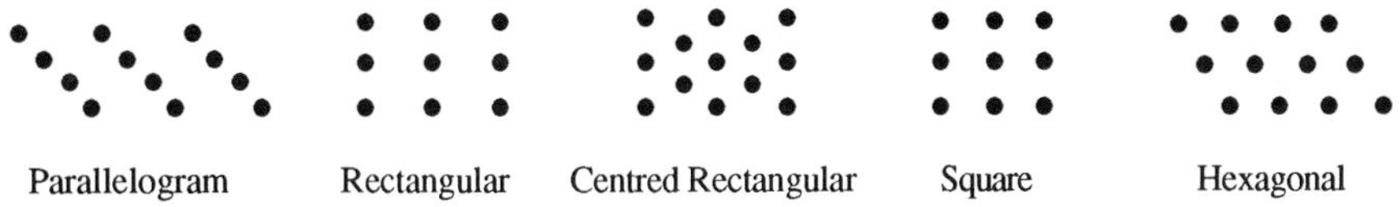

Figure 4.12 Dot patterns representing the five net types.

EXAMPLES 4.20 One pattern of each net type.

Parallelogram net

Rectangular net

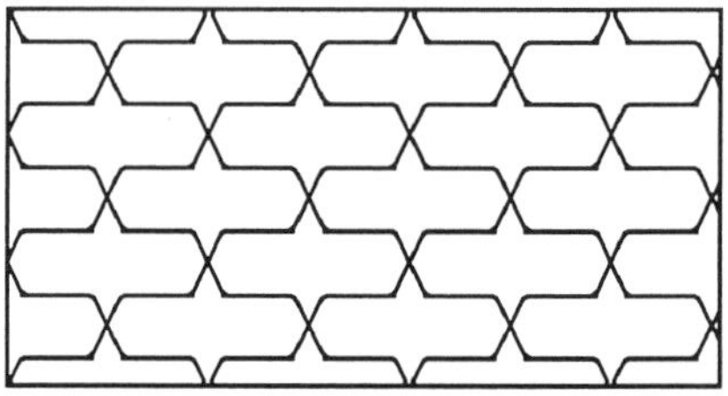

Centred rectangular net

Square net

Hexagonal net

EXERCISES 4

---

1 √ What is the highest rotational symmetry in Figure 4.2, and where?

2 √ Find suitable net basepoints for Figures 4.2 and 1.1.

3 Find net points in Figure 4.4 giving cell 1 and cell 3 of Figure 4.3. Locate a cell which violates Convention 4.4 for basepoints.

4 Write down a matrix A with integer entries and determinant ±1. Starting with a tiling of the plane by rectangles, use matrix A to derive a tiling by parallelograms of the same area, as in Figure 4.4. Repeat for other such matrices A.

5 Prove that the diagonals of a rhombus (parallelogram with all four sides equal) bisect each other at right angles. Draw a tiling of the plane by rhombi and convert it into the corresponding tiling by (centred) rectangles.

6 √ Identify the nets of the plane patterns (a) to (g) represented below.

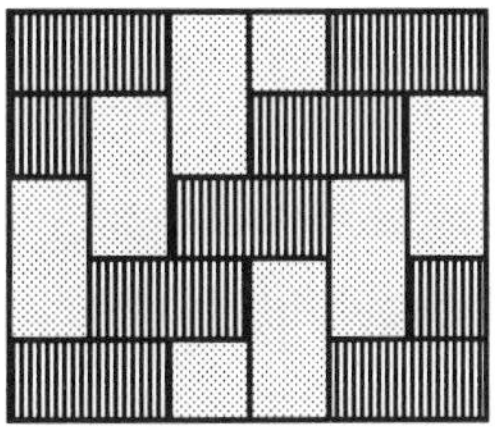

(a)

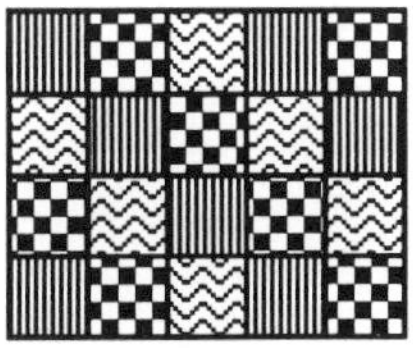

(b)

(c)

(d)

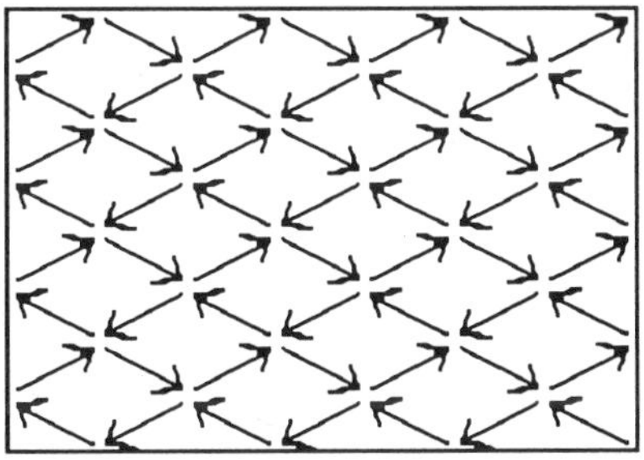

(e)

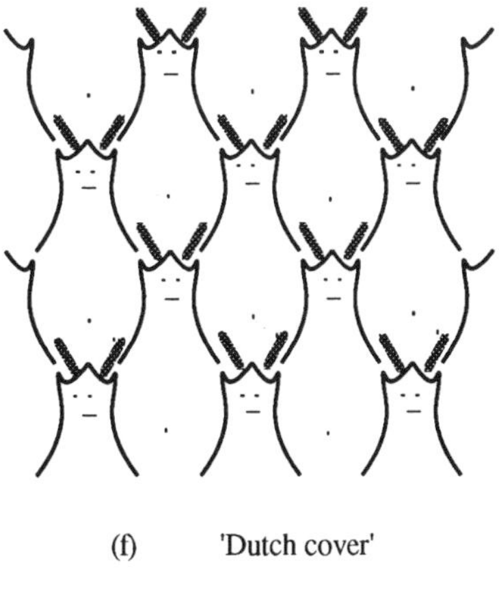

(f) 'Dutch cover'

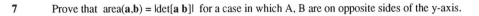

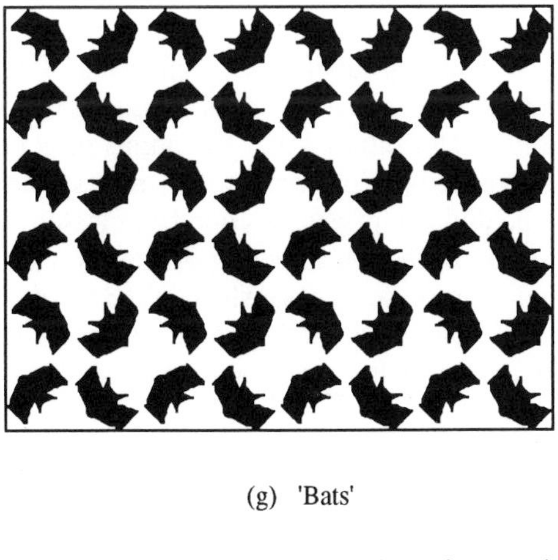

(g) 'Bats'

7 Prove that area(**a**,**b**) = |det[**a b**]| for a case in which A, B are on opposite sides of the y-axis.

8 Verify Theorem 4.14 for the indicated net, in Figure 4.4, using a 1/6 turn, a 1/3 turn, a 1/2, and a reflection.

Chapter 5 THE 17 PLANE PATTERNS

In this chapter we introduce and exemplify the division of plane patterns into seventeen types by symmetry group. This begins with the broad division into net type. The chapter concludes with a scheme for identifying pattern types, plus examples and exercises. It then remains to show that all the types are distinct and that there are no more; this will be done in Chapter 6.

5.1 Preliminaries

Here we recapitulate on some important ideas and results, then introduce the signature system which will label each type of plane pattern according to its symmetry group. For the basics of a plane pattern F and its group of symmetries G, see Review 4.1. We have introduced the subgroup **T** of G, consisting of all translation symmetries of F (Definition 4.2), and the representation of those translations by a net N of points relative to a chosen basepoint O (Definition 4.3). The points of N are the vertices of a tiling of the plane by parallelogram cells (Construction 4.5 - see especially Figure 4.3).

The division of patterns into five classes according to net type (determined by **T**) is motivated by reflection issues in Section 4.3.1. In Section 4.3.3 we described the five types, indicating case by case which of the feasible rotational symmetries for a plane pattern (Section 4.3.2) are permitted by net invariance, Theorem 4.14. The result is a very natural fit, for example the last type, the hexagonal net, allows 3-fold and 6-fold centres but not 4-fold. Indeed, we might have led up to the net types by starting with rotations rather than reflections.

Translations **u**, **v**, represented by adjacent sides of a cell, will denote a basis for the translation symmetries, except in the case of a centred net when it is convenient to use a three vector approach to integrate the rhombus and centred rectangle viewpoints (see Section

Glide symmetries, we recall, are appropriately limited to the kind $R_m T_{w/2}$ whose translation component has one half the length of the shortest translation vector **w** parallel to it, and $R_m T_{w/2} = T_{w/2} R_m$ (see Convention 3.2 and preceding discussion).

New symmetries from old. We remind the reader of two main ways of deducing the presence of further symmetries of a figure from those already identified: (a) Any symmetry maps mirrors to mirrors, glide lines to glide lines, n-fold centres to n-fold centres, and translation directions to translation directions, in accordance with Theorem 2.12. (b) The composition of two symmetries is another, details being given in Table 2.2. This said, the following observations as to what symmetries can exist or coexist for a given pattern, are important ingredients in classifying plane patterns. The first results from (a), because a rotation moves any mirror to the position of another, non-parallel mirror.

The presence of both rotation and reflection symmetries implies at least two mirror directions. Similarly for glides. (5.1)

The presence of non-parallel mirrors, glides, or a combination, implies rotations. [Table 2.2(b).] (5.2)

*The **least** angle between the lines of two mirrors, glides, or a combination, is π/n for $n = 2,3,4$, or 6.* (5.3)

Observation (5.3) holds because the product of reflections in mirrors at angle θ is rotation through angle 2θ, which the Crystallographic restriction Theorem 4.15 lays down to be a multiple of $2\pi/n$, $n = 2,3,4,6$. We will append $n = 1$ as representing the case of no rotational symmetry. A special case of (5.2), the *mirror-glide combination*, was considered in Chapter 3 on braids, for lines at right angles [see (3.4)]. For convenience we reproduce as Figure 5.1 the three situations portrayed in Figure 2.9: the position of one of the 1/2 turns produced by right angle crossing of glide/reflection lines with each other. In summary, the translation component **w** of a crossing glide ensures that the implied 2-fold centre is a translation by (1/2)**w** from the intersection. This happens in two directions for the glide/glide crossing, as seen in Figure 5.1(iii).

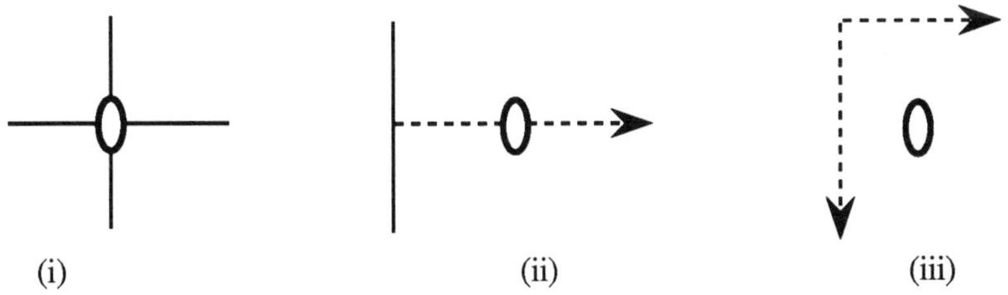

Figure 5. 1. The crossing at right angles of the line of a mirror/glide symmetry with another in either category implies 2-fold centres in the positions shown. This notation was given in Table 2.1.

NOTATION 5.1 Each plane pattern type is specified by four symbols

| z | n | x | y |, a development of the braid Notation 3.4, interpreted as follows.

| z | Initial symbol c if net is centred rectangular, otherwise p for 'primitive'.

| n | The highest degree of rotational symmetry in the pattern. That is, n is the largest integer for which the pattern has an n-fold centre.

| x | m if F has a line of symmetry,
g if, failing the above, F has a glide line,
1 if F has neither.

| y | The same as for x, but for lines in a 'second direction'
In both cases the 1 is omitted if it would be the last symbol.

Interpreting x, y. As with the braid patterns of Chapter 3 it is convenient to consider one mirror direction as horizontal for the purpose of illustration, but we do not wish to consider patterns to be of different type simply because of our choice of which mirror is 'horizontal'. Again, we don't want a pattern to change its type by being rotated through 90 degrees or any other angle. Thus the formulation above allows xy = mg but not xy = gm, because the distinction is not required. In the hexagonal net the distinction for mirror directions is between perpendicular and parallel to the sides of a triangle. This will be explained in its own place, Section 5.6, but see below.

CONVENTION 5.2 We have just noted that it makes sense for certain patterns to be considered as of the same type (or 'equivalent'). Since we are about to draw representative cases of patterns we will anticipate the formal definition of Equivalence in Chapter 6 by agreeing that a pattern remains the same type if we (a) transform the plane by an isometry - reflect, rotate, translate or glide, (b) change scale uniformly - i.e. we simply enlarge or contract, (c) change scale in one direction so as not to change the net type. equivalence: of symmetry groups

Presenting the cases. The order of cases for each net is guided by (5.1) to (5.3). We proceed from low to high rotational symmetry, with increasing number of mirrors or glides. In each case, after the symbol znxy, with its usual shortening highlighted, we give

1. The outline of a representative cell, normally with vertices following the Basepoint Convention, 4.4, at the end of Section 4.1.
2. An Example motif M, whose images under all the translation symmetries in a group of the given type znxy form a pattern of that type. M in turn consists of images of a very simple submotif  placed at the cell vertices, and at other positions and in other ways required by the symmetries in znxy. Notice that M does not include the cell itself.
3. Below the cell, a representation of the rotation centres, mirrors and glide lines which intersect it. cf. Figure 2.17, in which this is continued over nine cells.
4. A small list of symmetries (*generators*) which generate (Definition 2.17) the whole group.
5. Any outstanding explanation of the symmetry configuration.

5.2 The general parallelogram net

Possible 1/n turns: n = 1,2. No mirrors, by 4.3.1.

	p1	p2
EXAMPLE	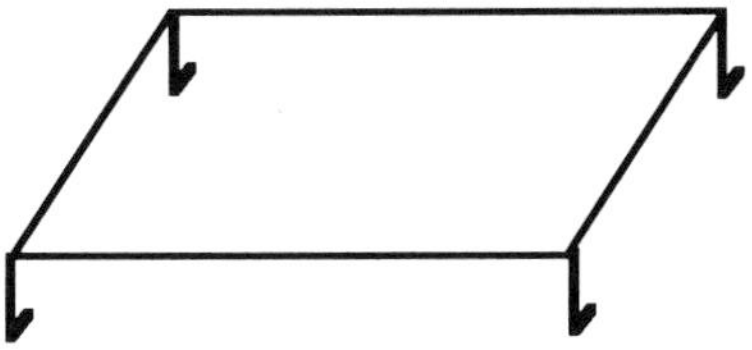	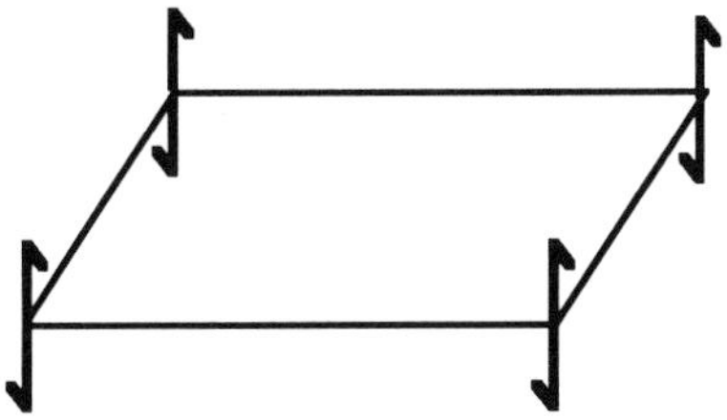
SYMMETRIES	None besides translation	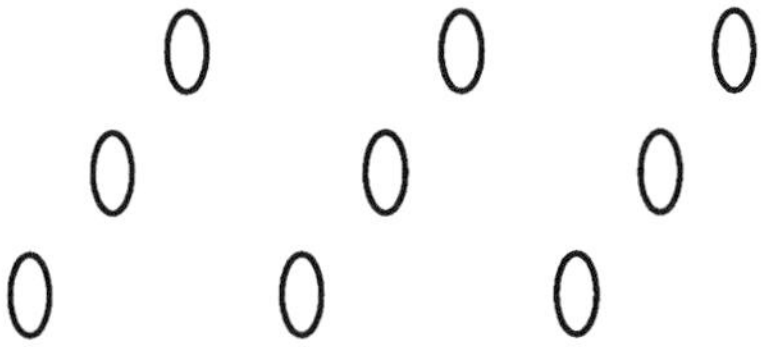
Generators:	Translations **u**,**v**	**u**,**v** plus one 1/2 turn (see (2.3))

5.3 The rectangular net

Possible 1/n turns: n = 1, 2. The case of no m/g is covered under p1, p2.

CASE n = 1 One reflection or glide.

	pm p1m	pg p1g
EXAMPLE	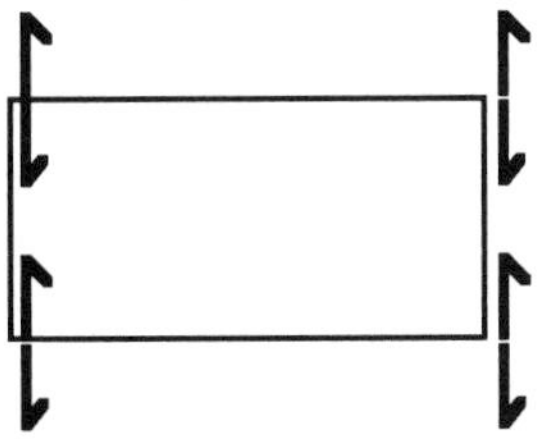	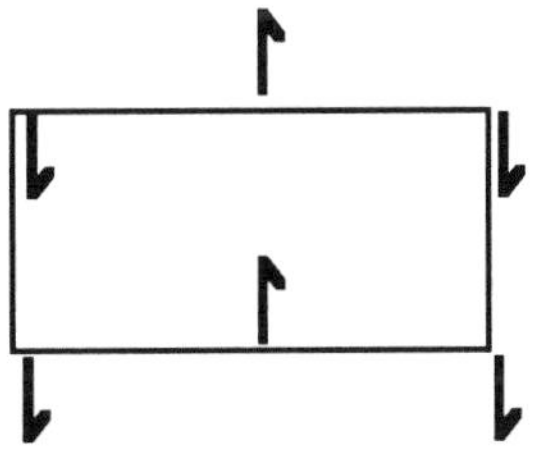
SYMMETRIES		
Generators:	Translations **u**,**v**, one reflection	**u**,**v** plus one glide

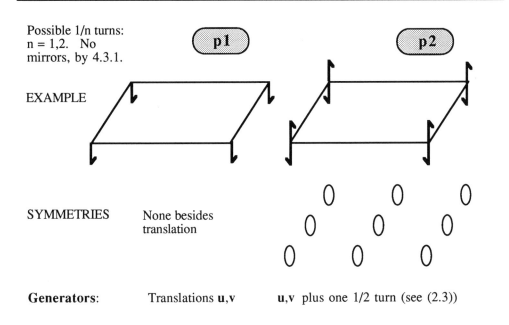

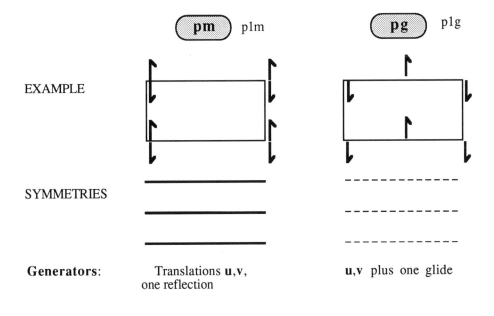

CASE n = 2 Two reflection or glide directions (note: neither need be horizontal).

pmm p2mm	**pmg** p2mg	**pgg** p2gg

EXAMPLE

SYMMETRIES

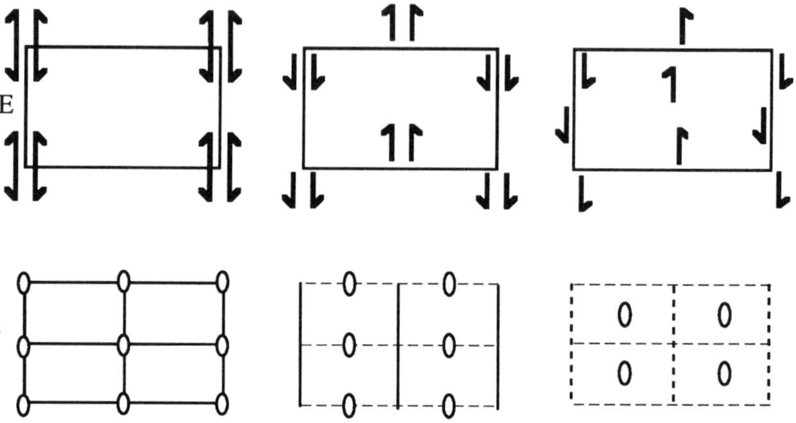

Generators: (See Figures 5.1, 5.2).	Translations **u**,**v** 2 perpendicular reflections	Translations **u**,**v** a reflection a glide	Translations **u**,**v** 2 perpendicular glides

Basepoint position. For convenience in drawing the motif in cases pmg and pgg we have (only) here set the net basepoint at an intersection of mirror lines which is not a centre of symmetry, giving priority to the second rather than the first criterion of Convention 4.4.

EXERCISE Redraw the diagrams for pmg, pgg so as to follow basepoint Convention 4.4. **or** Satisfy yourself that the given generators do result in the configurations of symmetries shown in Cases 1 and 2 for the Rectangular net.

5.4 The centred rectangular net

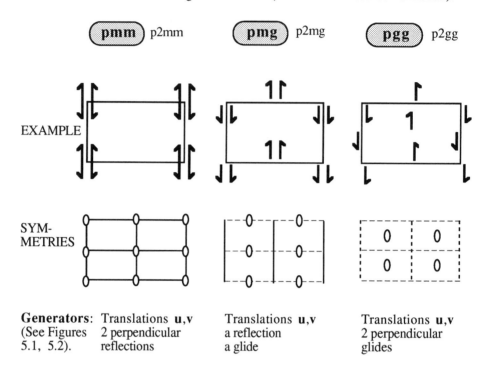

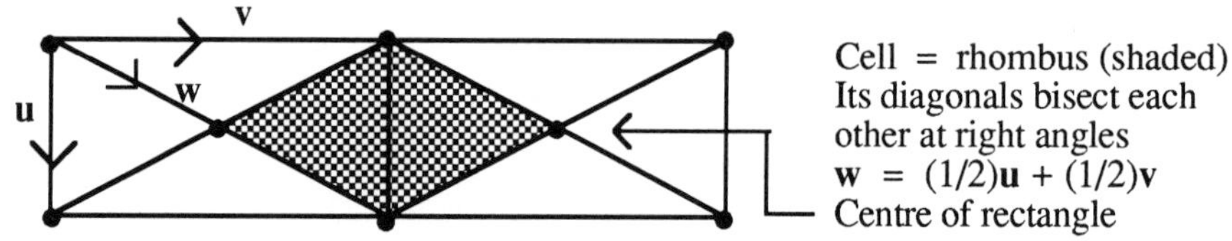

Figure 5.2 Translations, net and cell in the centred case.

'Centred' entails that, in addition to translations along the sides of the rectangle, there is a translation symmetry $T_{-\mathbf{w}}$ from centre to one (and hence to every) corner. In some patterns it is easier to spot a rhombus, in others a centred rectangle. Note that *a rhombus is a parallelogram with diagonals perpendicular.* To get from the rectangle model to a rhombus, start at the centre. Lines to two adjacent vertices form adjacent edges of a rhombus cell, as illustrated in Figure 5.2. For the reverse step, see the proof of Lemma 4.17. Here we get two of the seventeen types.

	CASE n = 1	**CASE n = 2**
	 c1m	 c2mm
EXAMPLE	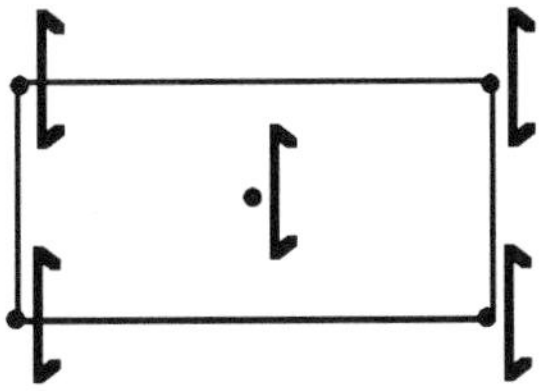	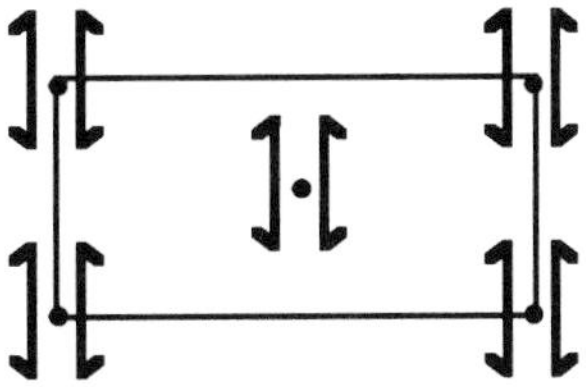
SYMMETRIES	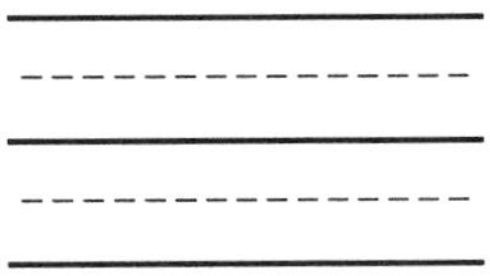	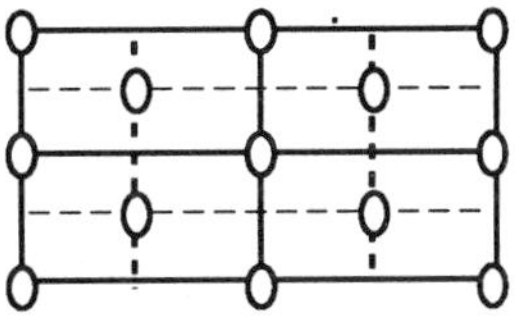
Generators:	Translations **u**,**w** or **v**,**w** one reflection	Translations **u**,**w** or **v**,**w** two perp. reflections

Explanation for symmetries The 1/2 turns in cmm arise from mirror-mirror and mirror-glide crossings, see Figure 5.1. For the glides, suppose we have a horizontal mirror line m, along a cell wall, and translations **u**, **v**, **w** as in Figure 5.2. Then the symmetries of the pattern include the composition $R_m T_w$, which is shown below to be one of the horizontal glides indicated, whose line cuts off 1/4 of a cell. Combining it with a vertical translation **u** gives the other glides of cm. A second mirror direction explains the glides of cmm.

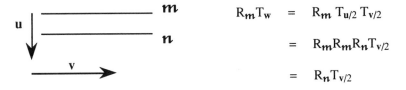

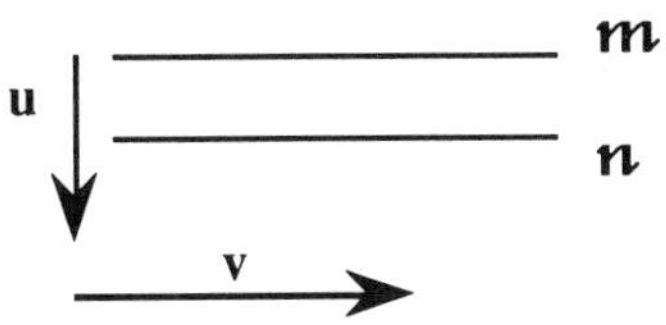

$$R_m T_w = R_m T_{u/2} T_{v/2}$$
$$= R_m R_m R_n T_{v/2}$$
$$= R_n T_{v/2}$$

Figure 5.3 How reflection then diagonal translation produces a glide.

This completes the net types with highest rotational symmetry n = 2.

5.5 The square net

The square net is the only one to allow 1/4 turn symmetries. With only 1/2 turns or none it counts as a special case of the rectangular net, so we consider only the square net with 1/4 turns: n = 4. There are three associated pattern types. The last two are distinguished by having *either* a mirror diagonally across the cell, *or* a glide (not both), and we choose generators accordingly.

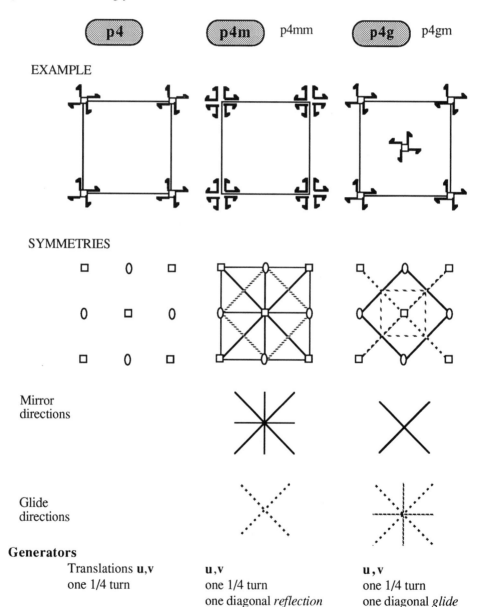

p4	p4m p4mm	p4g p4gm

EXAMPLE

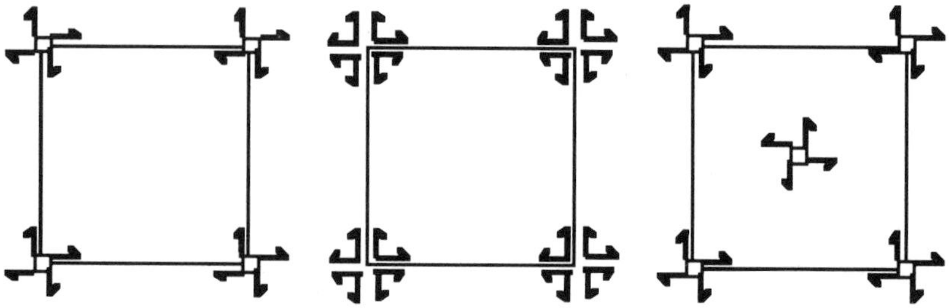

SYMMETRIES

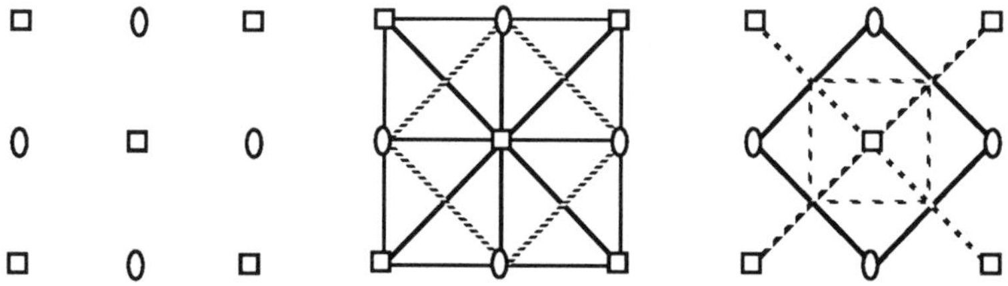

Mirror directions

Glide directions

Generators

p4	p4m	p4g
Translations **u,v**	**u,v**	**u,v**
one 1/4 turn	one 1/4 turn	one 1/4 turn
	one diagonal *reflection*	one diagonal *glide*

Explanation for symmetries

Rotations in all 3 types. The translations **u**,**v** map a 4-fold centre at one vertex of the cell to 4-fold centres at the other vertices (Theorem 2.12). A 1/4 turn at the centre can be obtained as the product of a translation with a 1/4 turn at a vertex [See the solution to Exercise 2.1.] A 1/2 turn at the midpoint of an edge is the product of a translation with a 1/2 turn (= two 1/4 turns) at a vertex (Example 2.5).

Mirrors and glides in p4m. It is an easy exercise to show that translations **u**,**v** plus the known rotations produce the mirrors of p4m from any one mirror, in particular from the diagonal one we take as generator. Assuming these, consider Figure 5.4(a) below. The combination of the 1/2 turn and reflection indicated in boldface is $R_A(1/2)R_n = (R_\ell R_m)R_n = R_\ell(R_m R_n) = R_\ell T_{AB}$, which is a glide since $\underline{AB} = \mathbf{u}/2 + \mathbf{v}/2$. The 1/4 turn symmetry about the cell centre rotates the glideline AB successively into three others, forming the 'box' of glidelines as indicated.

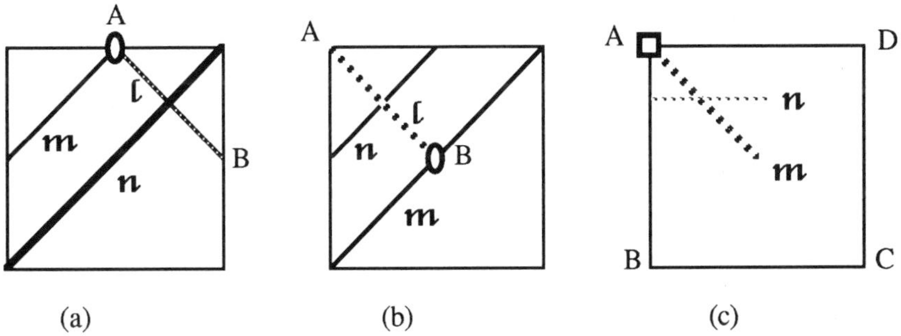

Figure 5.4 (a) Origin of side AB of the box bounded by glidelines in p4m, (b) origin of one side of the box, now formed from mirrors, in case p4g, (c) start of the glide box for p4g.

Mirrors of p4g. We are given one diagonal glide, so rotation about the centre gives the other. In Figure 5.4 (b) above, the combination of glide and 1/2 turn shown boldface equals $(T_{AB} R_\ell)(R_\ell R_m) = T_{AB} R_m = (R_n R_m)R_m = R_n$. Then by rotation we have the 'box' of mirrors shown, included in the symmetries of p4g.

Glides of p4g. In Figure 5.4(c) let g be the diagonal glide in bold (a generator for p4g by assumption), and h the horizontal glide backwards along mirror n, both through the distances indicated. Then $gh = (R_m T_{AC/2})(T_{DA/2} R_n) = R_m T_{DC/2} R_n$. This isometry is direct, being the product of one direct and two indirect isometries, so is determined by its effect on any two points (Theorem 1.10). Since gh fixes A and sends B to D, as does $R_A(1/4)$, we have $gh = R_A(1/4)$, whence $h = g^{-1}R_A(1/4)$. Now since the glide h is the product of two symmetries in the group, h is itself a symmetry, and rotation gives the 'box' of glide lines appertaining to p4g.

5.6 The hexagonal net

Cell = 60° rhombus = 2 equilateral triangles, called a *diamond*.

Rotation symmetries of the net

6-fold at triangle vertices
3-fold at triangle centres
2-fold at mid points of triangle edges

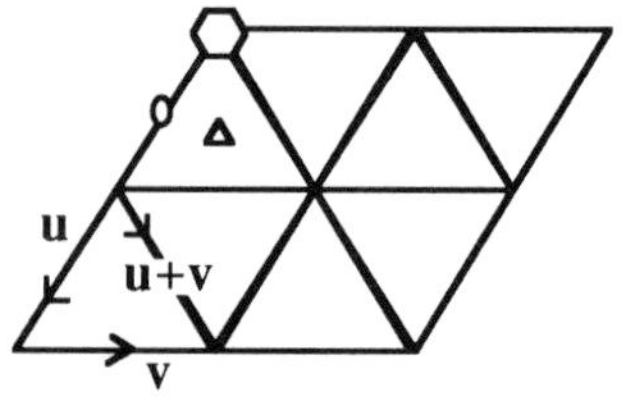

CASE n = 3 Here we suppose that the symmetries include a 1/3 turn (at one triangle vertex), but no 1/6 turn. For the illustrations we take a change of motif.

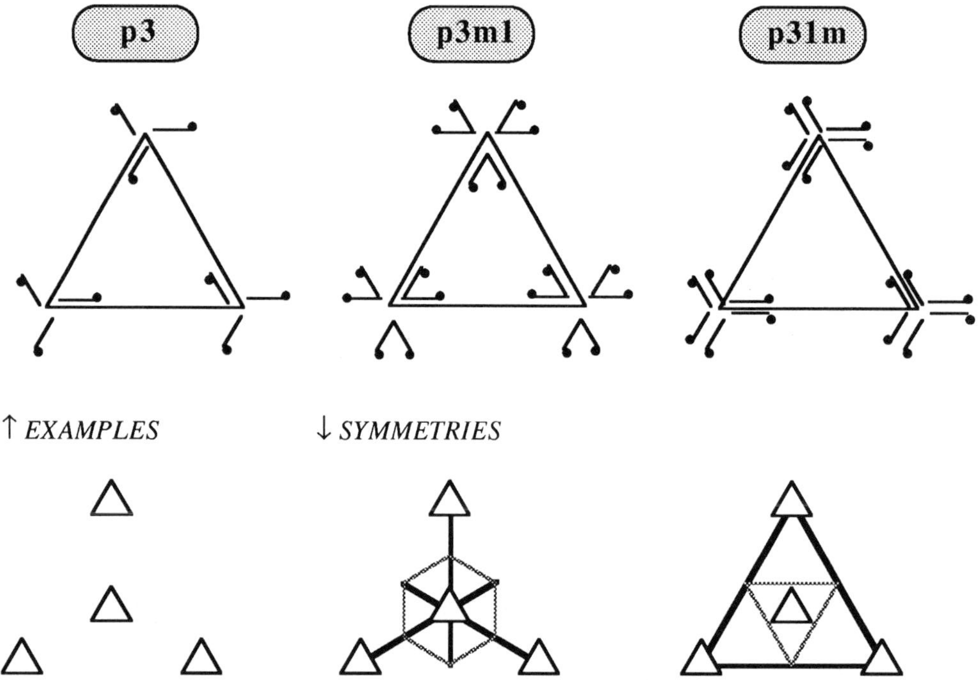

↑ *EXAMPLES* ↓ *SYMMETRIES*

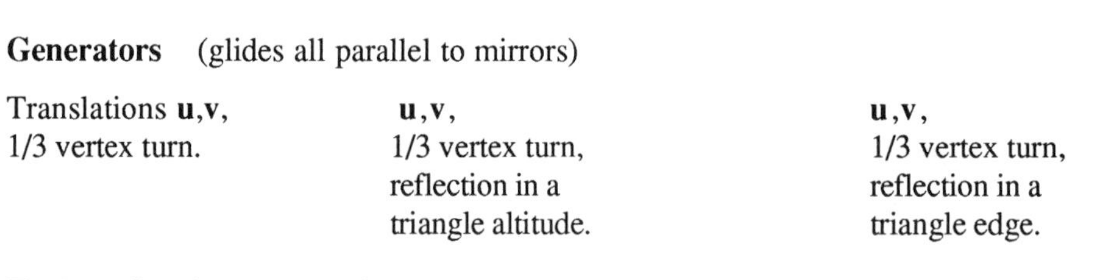

Generators (glides all parallel to mirrors)

p3	p3m1	p31m
Translations **u**,**v**, 1/3 vertex turn.	**u**,**v**, 1/3 vertex turn, reflection in a triangle altitude.	**u**,**v**, 1/3 vertex turn, reflection in a triangle edge.

Explanation for symmetries *Rotations.* By Theorem 2.10 the translation symmetries map the 3-fold centre onto 3-fold centres at every triangle vertex. By Euler's construction, Example 2.6, the 1/3 turns at two adjacent triangle vertices may be combined to produce a

1/3 turn about the triangle centre (see the solution to Exercise 2.2), which now translates to every triangle centre. Introducing no reflections or glides we now have case p3.

The two sets of mirror directions. Combining 1/3 turns with a reflection produces mirrors at angles of 60°, the angle in a triangle of the net. Hence, starting with a mirror perpendicular to the **u**-direction, along the altitude of one triangle, we obtain mirrors along the altitudes of all triangles. This is case p3m1. It is notationally convenient to consider this as a case of one mirror direction only, counting all the altitude directions as one, via 1/3 turns. On the other hand, a mirror in the **u**-direction, along a triangle edge, yields mirrors along the sides of all triangles, via the 1/3 turns, giving case p31m.

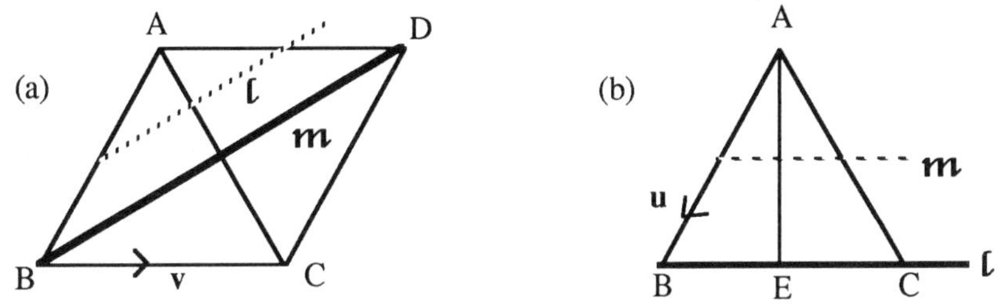

Figure 5.5 Source of the glides in (a) p3m1, (b) p31m. To achieve a more readable picture the dotted glide lines represent position only. A glide *distance* is, as always, one half the shortest translation in a parallel direction.

Glides of p3m1. In Figure 5.5(a) the glide $g = T_{BD/2} R_\ell$ may be followed by R_m to satisfiy $gR_m = T_{BD/2}(R_\ell R_m) = T_{BD/2} T_{AC/2} = T_v$. Hence g equals $T_v R_m$, which is a product of symmetries, hence itself a symmetry. The reader can now see how all other glide lines of p3m1 are generated from this one by reflection and rotation.

Glides of p31m. In Figure 5.5(b), the glide $g = T_{CB/2} R_m$ may be followed by R_ℓ to satisfiy $gR_\ell = T_{CB/2} T_{AE} = T_u$, so that g equals $T_u R_\ell$ and is itself a symmetry. Rotating the glide line by 1/3 turns about the triangle centres gives us the triangle of glides shown.

CASE n = 6

Rotations. On the one hand, a 1/6 turn squared is a 1/3 turn, so we have all the 1/3 turn symmetries of Case n = 3. On the other hand, a 1/6 turn cubed is a 1/2 turn, giving us a 1/2 turn at the midpoint of every triangle edge via translation, in the manner of (2.3). There are thus two cases, according as we do (p6m) or do not (p6) have reflections at all (see below).

Reflections and glides. In case p6m we may compose a 1/6 turn about a triangle vertex with reflection in a mirror along the side of a triangle. The result is reflection in an altitude. Therefore we have the mirror directions of both p3m1 and p31m.

p6

EXAMPLE

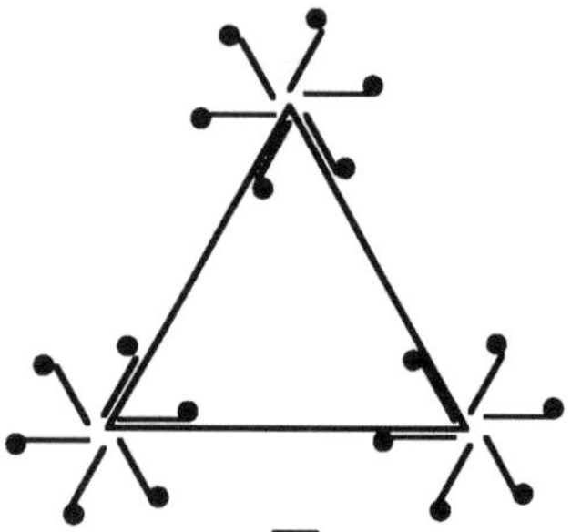

SYMMETRIES

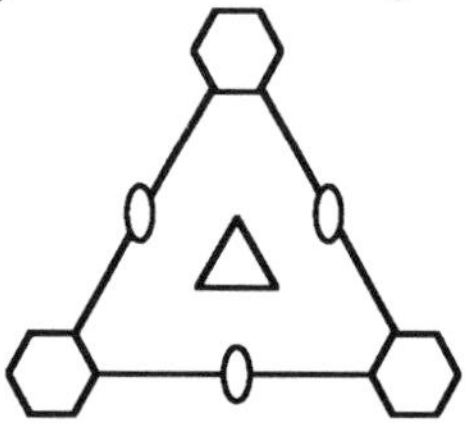

Generators Translations **u**,**v**, a 1/6 vertex turn,

p6m p6mm

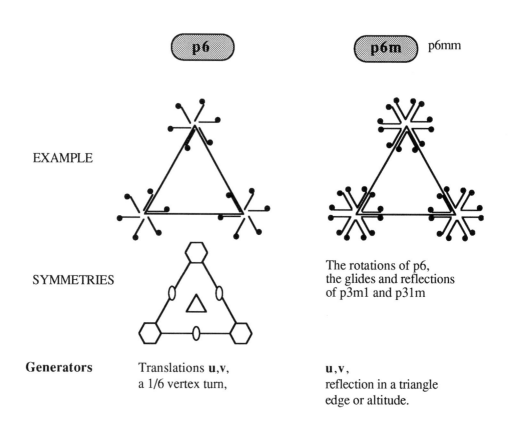

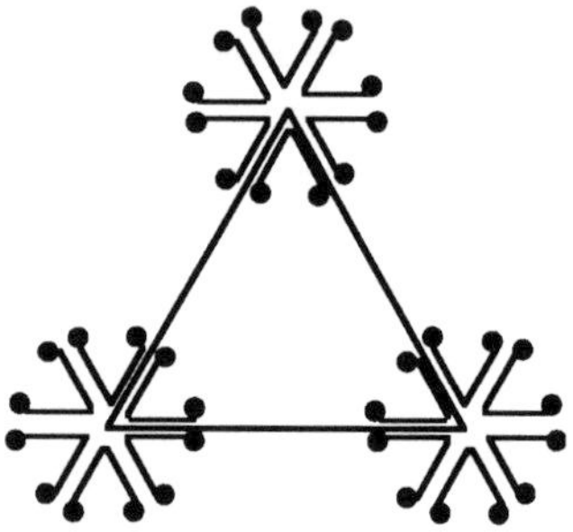

The rotations of p6, the glides and reflections of p3m1 and p31m

u,**v**, reflection in a triangle edge or altitude.

This concludes the seventeen plane patterns and their symmetries, and one choice for the generators of those symmetries. There follows a set of examples, a scheme for identifying the type, and a series of identification exercises for the reader. In the next chapter we see how to generate examples of any type to order.

5.7 Examples of the 17 plane pattern types

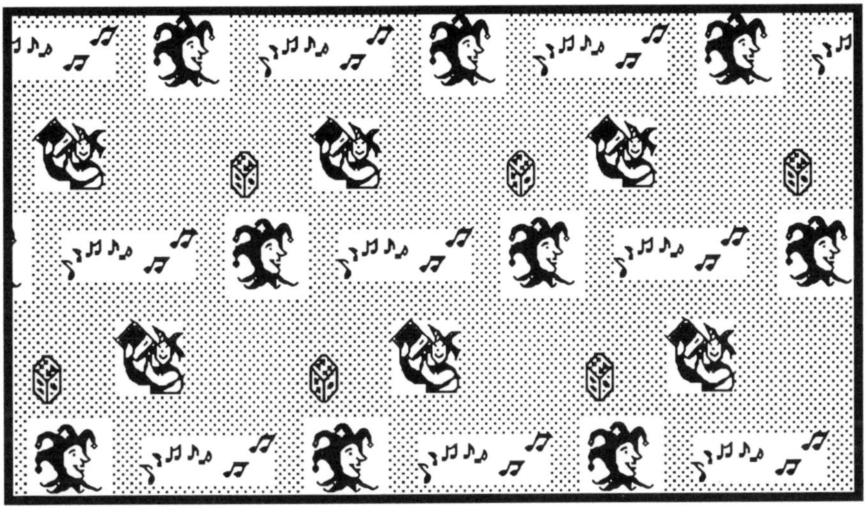

p1: 'The jokers'

p2: 'Roman mosaic'

pg: 'Trees'

pmm

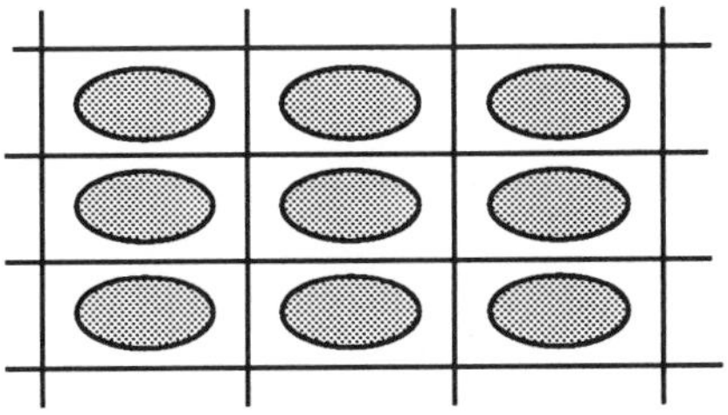

pm

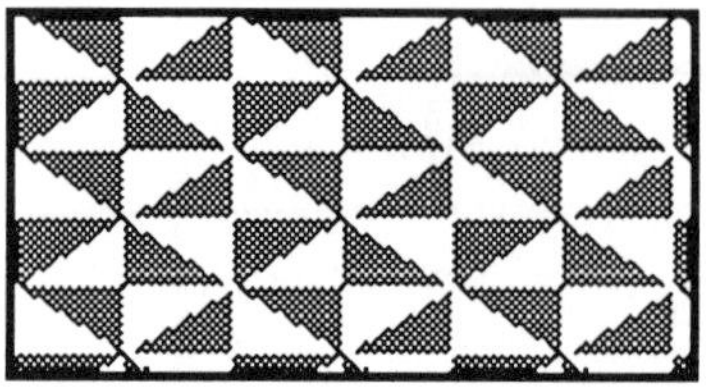

pgg

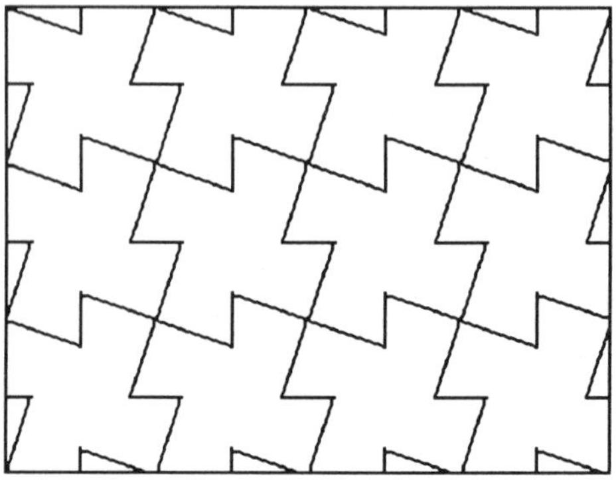

p4: 'Jigsaw 1'

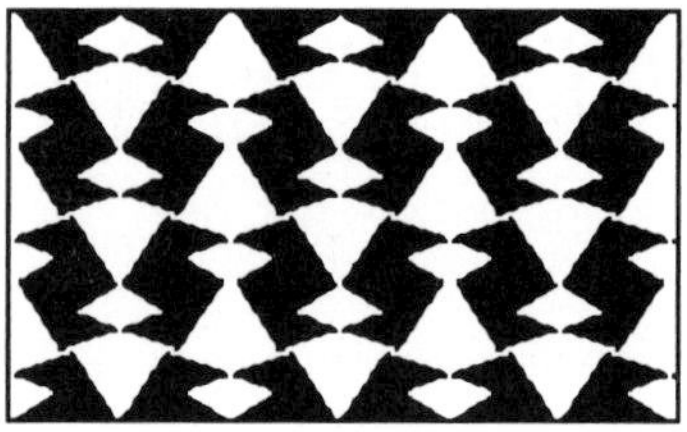

pmg

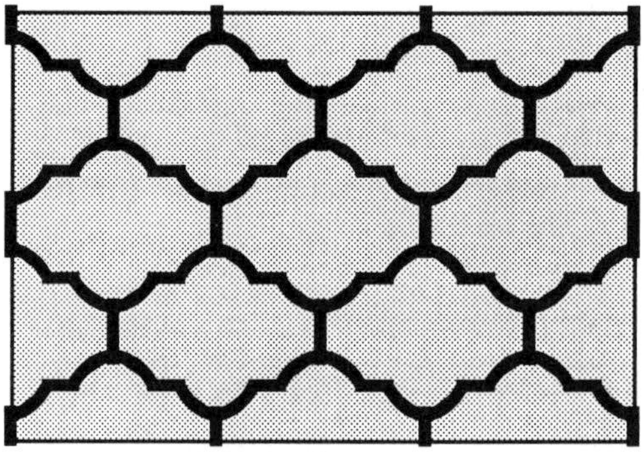

cmm: 'Carpet 1'

cm: 'In clover'

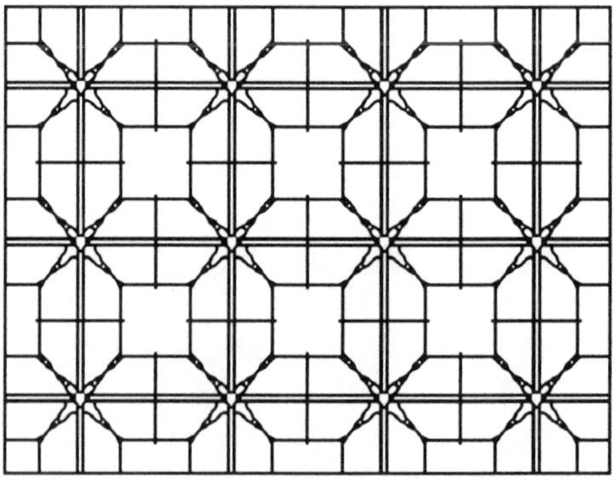

p4m: 'Windows'

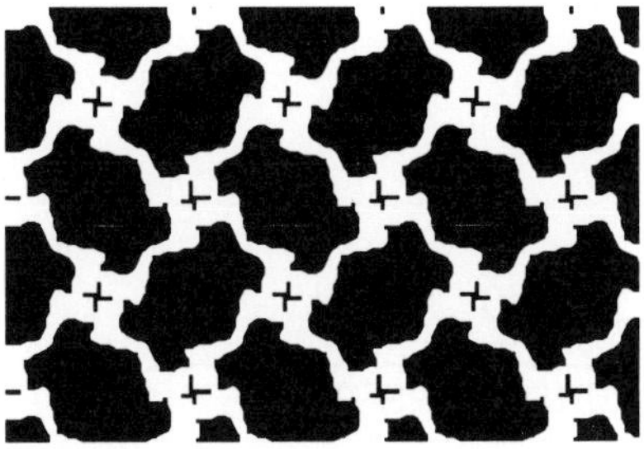

p4g

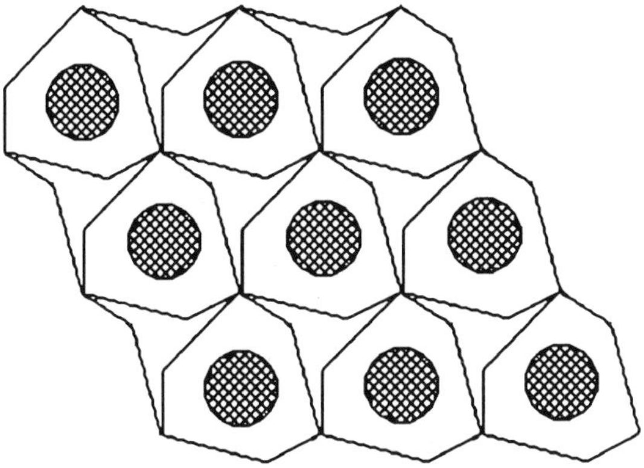

p3

p3m1

p31m

p6

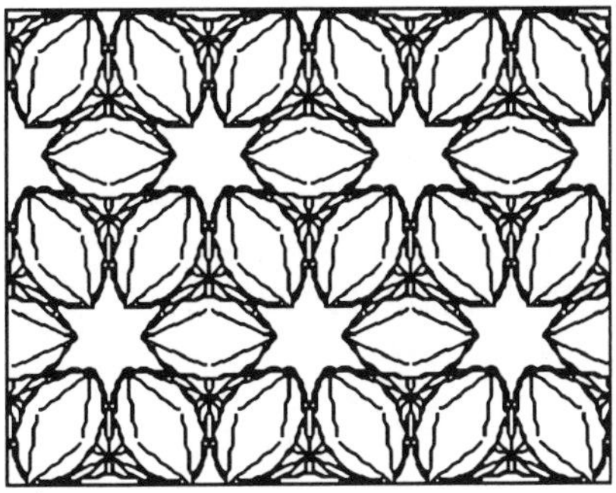

p6m

5.8 Scheme for identifying pattern types

Case A Pattern has 1/2 turns or none.

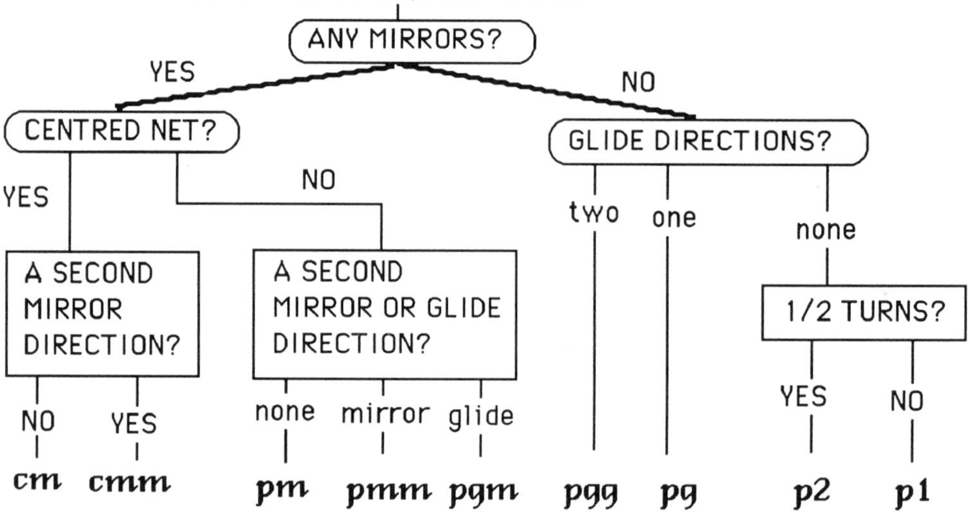

Case B Pattern has 1/n turns: n = 3, 4, or 6.

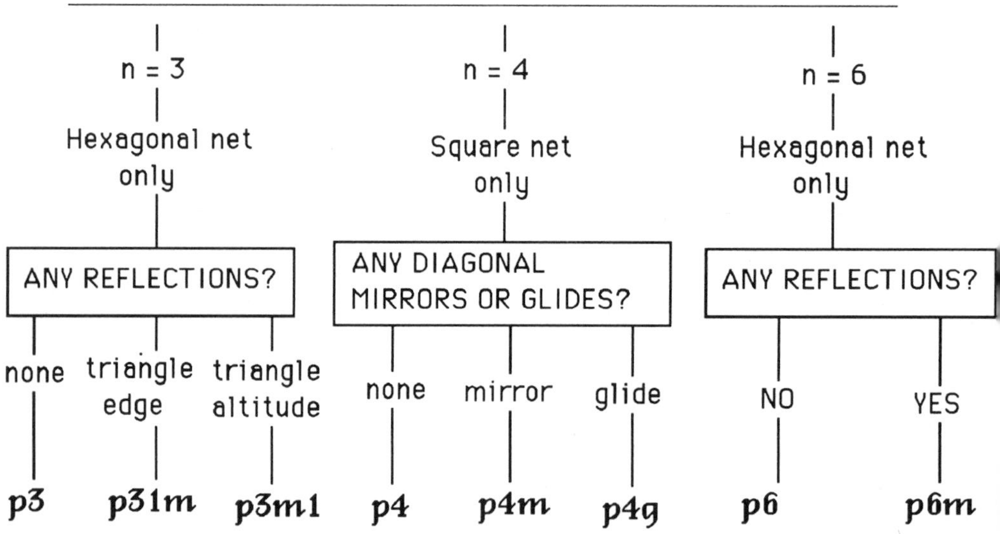

EXERCISE Use the above scheme to check the type of one pattern from each net, in 5.7.

NOTES

(i) *Nets versus rotation.* The first question in our identification algorithm concerns rotations rather than nets, because of possible ambiguity. For example the square is a special case of a rectangle, which is in turn a parallelogram. Indeed, the net of a p1 or p2 pattern can coincidentally be any one of the five net types, though counted as a parallelogram for classification purposes. On the other hand, n = 3 or 6 *requires* the hexagonal net and n = 4 the square, giving an important check as we proceed.

(ii) *1/2 turns* can be hard to spot, and therefore we use them (in the first instance) only to distinguish between p1 and p2. Notice that (i) does not require us to identify 1/2 turns, but simply to decide whether 1/3, 1/4, or 1/6 turn symmetries are present

(iii) *Glides.* As remarked earlier, for glide spotting it may help to think of a fish gliding left-right as it proceeds forwards.

(iv) *Confirming the decision.* Having decided the type of a pattern from the scheme above, we can test this not only by the net but by the presence of any symmetries we choose which are predicted for this type (see Sections 5.2 to 5.6).

EXAMPLE 5.3 (Roman 'Pelta' design.) Following the scheme to find the pattern type, we see that there are 1/4 turn symmetries, and so go to Case B: n = 4. We confirm that the net is square, choosing 4-fold centres as net points (Convention 4.4). But notice that a valid square cell, satisfying the minimum length condition (4.6) has edges not horizontal and vertical, but at 45 degrees to the horizontal. This is seen by focussing on one net point and noting its nearest net points. Sample vertices for a cell are marked in the pattern with a small square: □. Now we can truthfully answer the question relative to this cell: "is there a diagonal mirror, glideline, or neither?" *There is a diagonal glide* (horizontal on this page), so the pattern has type p4g.

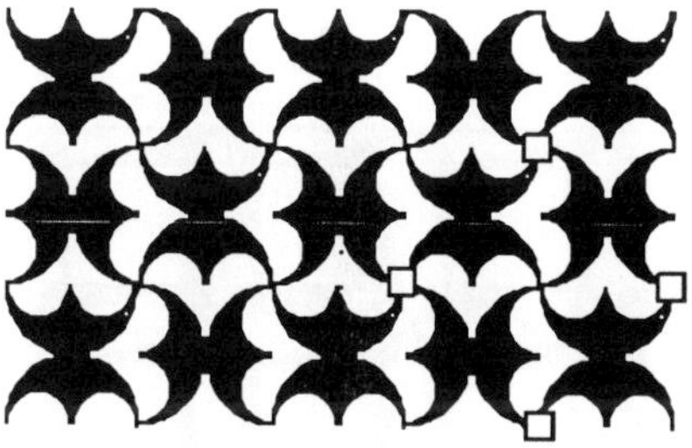

Roman 'Pelta' design

EXERCISE Show that the perpendicular glides below imply the 1/2 turns. Note: Each 2-fold centre is 1/4 translation distance from a glide line.

(a) 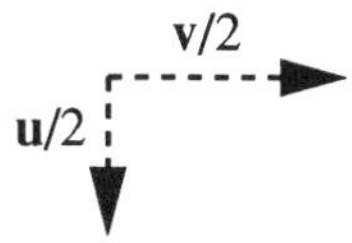

implies (b) 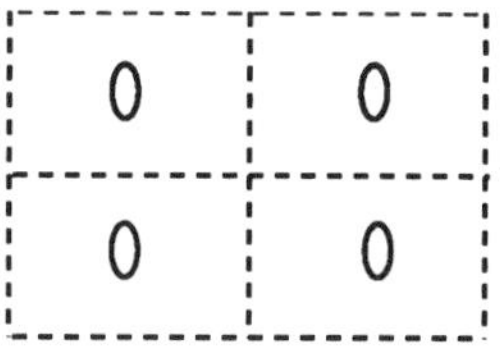

(5.4)

Figure 5.6 Some half turns that must be present in a symmetry group having translations **u**, **v** and glidelines as in (a).

EXERCISES 5

1 √ Identify the type of each of the following patterns.

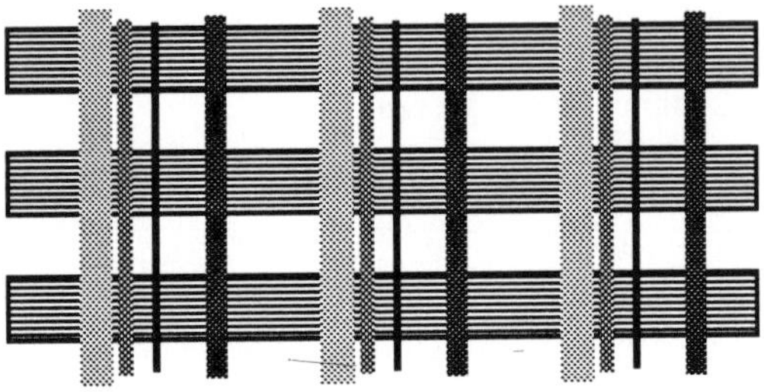

(a) 'Clan fencing'

(b) Roman mosaic, Ostia

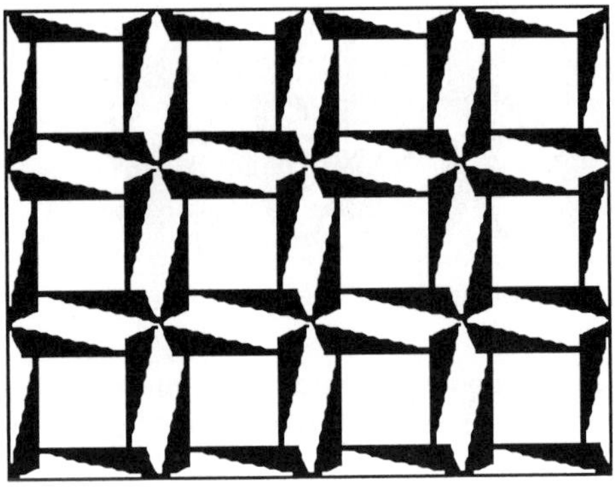

(c) Windmills

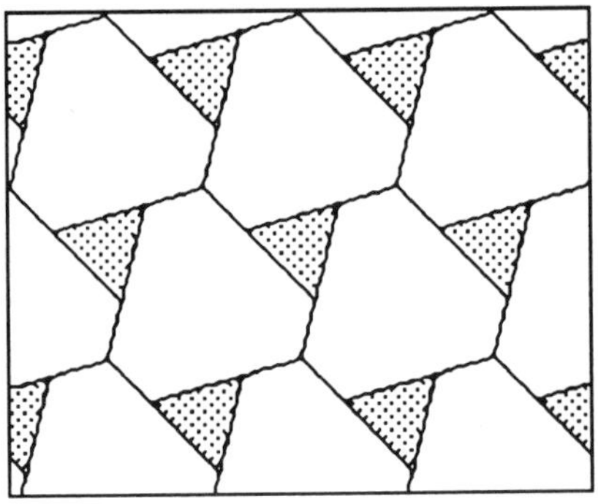

(d) Crazy paving

(e) Persian tiling

(f)

2 √ Identify the type of each pattern below.

(a)

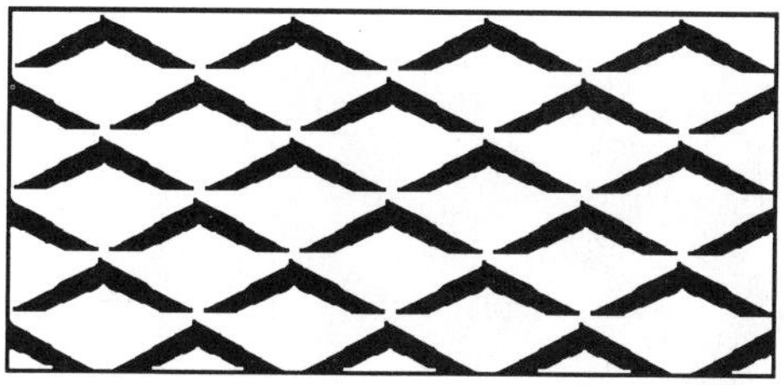

(b)

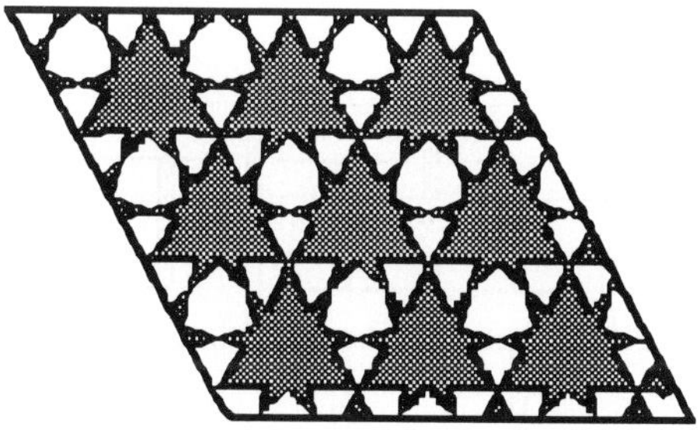

(c)

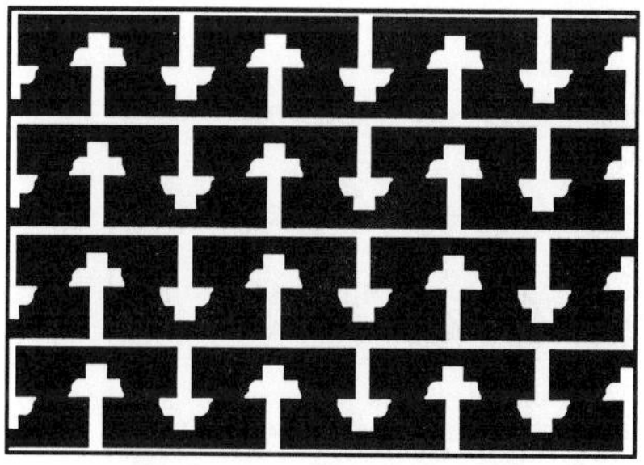

(d)

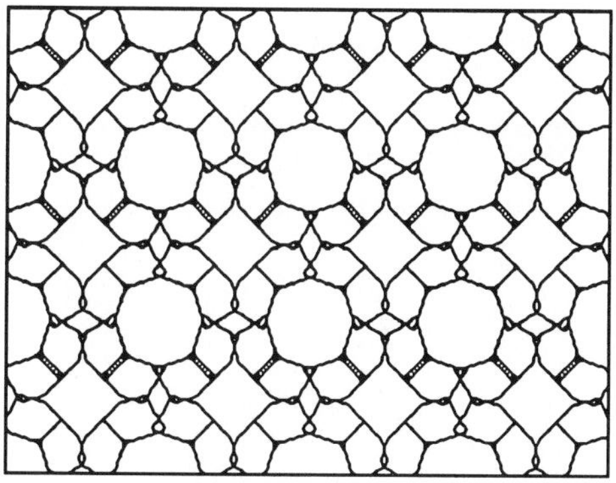

(e)

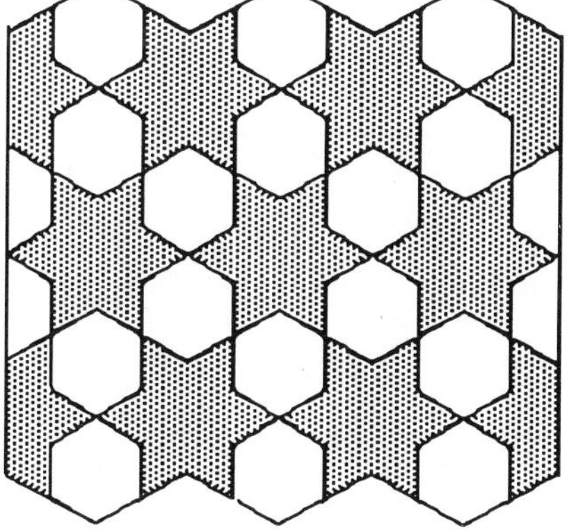

(f) Arabic pattern

3 √ Determine the type of each pattern represented below.

(a) Roman, from Ostia

(b)

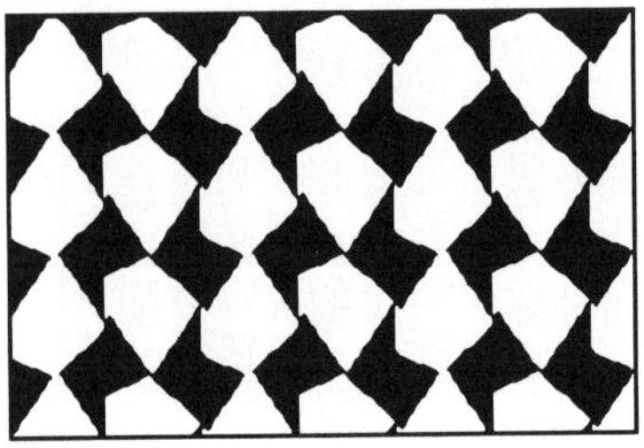

(c) 'Boots'

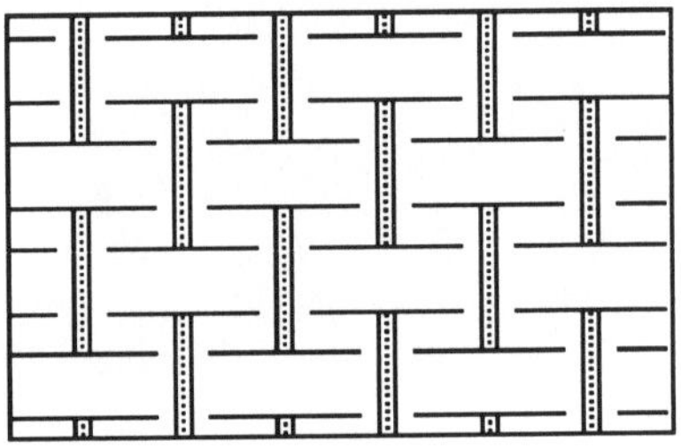

(d) Wicker fence

(e)

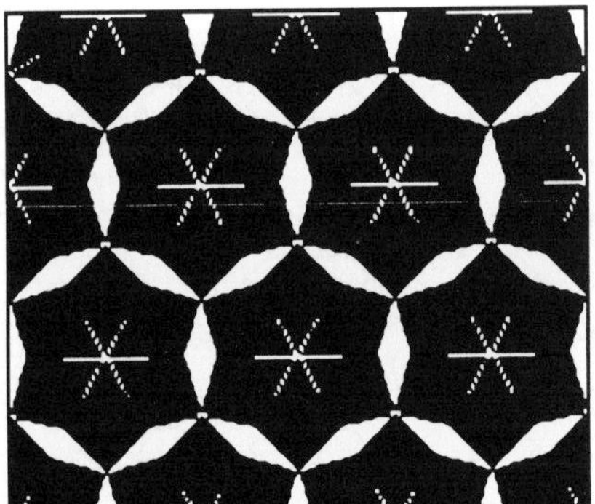

(f)

Chapter 6 MORE PLANE TRUTH

We have indicated how nets fall naturally into five types for the purpose of classifying plane patterns, and found seventeen possible configurations or groups of symmetries. But should they all be considered different, and are there more? After dealing with these questions via sections 6.1 and 6.2, we look at some techniques for producing plane patterns to order. The most important for our purposes will be the use of a fundamental region, developed in 6.4.3, and concluded with the algorithm of Table 6.7, by which most plane pattern examples in this book were produced.

6.1 Equivalent symmetry groups

Here we recapitulate and enlarge upon some material of Section 2.5 on groups in general. For two symmetry groups G, H to be considered 'the same', or equivalent, there must be a pairing between their elements so that their multiplication tables are the same apart from names of elements (cf. Exercises for 2.5, Question 2). So far, this says that G and H are abstractly isomorphic. But we impose the additional requirement that like symmetries must pair with like.

EXAMPLE 6.1 G = $\{I, R_{\boldsymbol{m}}\}$ H = $\{I, R_{\mathbf{p}}\}$, where $\boldsymbol{m}$, $\mathbf{p}$ are different lines. (We permit ourselves to use the same symbol for the identity in either group.) Here G and H are equivalent according to the definitions that follow.

DEFINITION 6.2 Groups G, H are *isomorphic* if there is a *bijection*, or pairing, $\phi: G \to H$ such that

$$\phi(fg) = \phi(f)\phi(g), \quad \text{for all f, g in G,} \tag{6.1}$$

where $\phi(f)$ means the image of element f under map ϕ. Then ϕ is called an *isomorphism* from G to H. Informally, (6.1) is described as saying that ϕ *preserves multiplication*. It follows that for all g in G,

$$\phi(I) = I \qquad (6.2)$$

$$\phi(g^{-1}) = \phi(g)^{-1} \qquad (6.3)$$

$$g \text{ and } \phi(g) \text{ have the same order} \qquad (6.4)$$

where the I's in (6.2) denote in order the identity elements in G and H. If necessary we may distinguish them by subscripts thus: I_G, I_H.

Proof (6.2) We have

$$\phi(I) = \phi(I^2), \quad \text{since } I = I^2,$$
$$= \phi(I)\,\phi(I), \quad \text{by (6.1), } \phi \text{ being an isomorphism.}$$

By Theorem 2.21(i) on uniqueness of identities this is sufficient to prove that $\phi(I) = I$.
Proof (6.3) Here we argue that

$$\phi(g^{-1})\phi(g) = \phi(g^{-1}g), \quad \phi \text{ being an isomorphism,}$$
$$= \phi(I), \quad \text{which equals I by (6.2).}$$

This time we apply Theorem 2.21(ii), and Statement (6.3) follows.
Proof (6.4) We observe, firstly, that $\phi(g^r) = \phi(g.g.....g) = \phi(g)\phi(g)....\phi(g) = \phi(g)^r$. Hence if $\phi(g)^r = I$ we may write $\phi(g^r) = I = \phi(I)$, which implies that $g^r = I$, since ϕ is bijective (part of the definition of isomorphism). Now, this argument reverses: if $g^r = I$ then $\phi(g)^r = I$, so the least power which equals the identity is the same for both g and $\phi(g)$. That is, they have the same order.

EXAMPLE 6.3 The cyclic group C_4 and dihedral group D_4 both have size 4 [see Section 2.4]. Are they isomorphic? Let us first try a sledgehammer approach and use Theorem 2.18 to write out the multiplication tables of these groups (the answer to Exercises for 2.5, Question 2). Let C_4 have a 1/4 turn T as generator, and let D_4 contain a reflection R and 1/2 turn τ. Then with elements listed as first row of their table we have:

TABLE 6.1 The multiplication tables of C_4 and of D_4.

C_4	I	T	T^2	T^3
I	I	T	T^2	T^3
T	T	T^2	T^3	I
T^2	T^2	T^3	I	T
T^3	T^3	I	T	T^2

D_4	I	τ	R	$R\tau$
I	I	τ	R	$R\tau$
τ	τ	I	$R\tau$	R
R	R	$R\tau$	I	τ
$R\tau$	$R\tau$	R	τ	I

We observe that in the C_4 table row 2 is a cyclic shift of row 1, and so on down the rows, whilst the entries for D_4 partition into four quarters. It follows that the elements of D_4, say, cannot be reordered so as to give the same table as C_4 apart from the names. We will not give a more detailed argument because there is a very simple reason based on (6.4) above, why the two groups are not isomorphic. That is, that C_4 has an element of order four, whilst D_4 has not. However, the tables are instructive.

EXAMPLE 6.4 The symmetry group of a cube is isomorphic to the group S_4 of all permutations of four objects. In fact, the symmetries of a cube permute its four main diagonals (see eg Coxeter, 1973).

DEFINITION 6.5 Symmetry groups G, H are *equivalent* if there is an isomorphism $\phi: G \to H$ that sends like to like (then ϕ is called an *equivalence*), that is

$$\text{reflections to reflections, translations to translations, glides to glides, and 1/n turns to 1/n turns.} \qquad (6.5)$$

EXAMPLE 6.6 In the notation of Definition 2.17, let $\mathbf{T}_1 = \mathrm{Gp}\{T_\mathbf{u}, T_\mathbf{v}\}$, $\mathbf{T}_2 = \mathrm{Gp}\{T_\mathbf{w}, T_\mathbf{x}\}$, where vectors **u**,**v** are at right angles and **w**,**x** at 60°. A typical element of $\mathbf{T}_1$ is $T_{m\mathbf{u}+n\mathbf{v}}$ with m,n integers. Then

$$\phi(T_{m\mathbf{u}+n\mathbf{v}}) = T_{m\mathbf{w}+n\mathbf{x}} \qquad (6.6)$$

is an isomorphism satisfying (6.5). Thus $\mathbf{T}_1$ and $\mathbf{T}_2$ are equivalent, as are all plane translation subgroups, by an isomorphism ϕ which pairs the elements of a basis of the one group with a basis (see (4.2)) of the other.

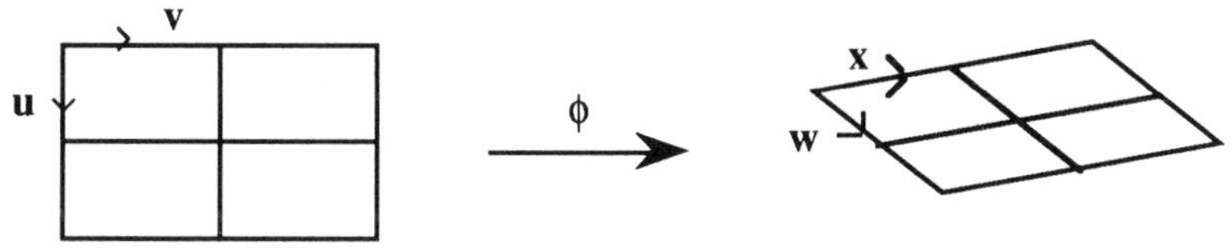

Figure 6.1 Equivalence ϕ between translation groups with bases **u**,**v** and **w**,**x**.

EXAMPLE 6.7 The groups G = {I, R} and H = {I, τ} are isomorphic, where R is a reflection and τ a 1/2 turn, both therefore of order 2. But they are not equivalent, since the only possible isomorphism from G to H maps a reflection to a 1/2 turn, infringing (6.5). In fact the conclusion follows without considering isomorphisms: we may simply note that G has a reflection whilst H does not.

EXAMPLE 6.8 Pattern (a) below is stretched to form pattern (b). This destroys the vertical symmetry, and so the symmetry groups of the two are not equivalent.

Figure 6.2 Two patterns (a), (b) whose symmetry groups are not equivalent.

According to the scheme described in Section 5.8, the first pattern has type cm, whilst the second is designated p1. Of course if we had instead stretched (a) equally in all directions we would still have the 'same' symmetry group for (b).

TABLE 6.2 Tests for equivalence. If any property in the list is possessed by symmetry group G but not H then they are inequivalent, by Definition 6.5.

1. G has an n-fold centre	4. G has both reflections and glides
2. G has reflections	5. G has reflections in at least two directions
3. G has glides	6. G has glides in at least two directions

EXERCISE Why cannot the groups C_6 and D_6 be isormorphic?

REMARK 6.9 (1) An *isometry* g of the plane sends every pattern F to one of the same type. That is, their symmetry groups are equivalent. For by Theorem 2.12, the isometry g maps like to like, satisfying (6.5), and this theorem gives us the equivalence $\phi(R) = g^{-1}Rg$. For example if $\boldsymbol{m}$ is a mirror line of F then $g^{-1}R_{\boldsymbol{m}}g$ is the operation of reflection in the mirror line $\boldsymbol{m}^g$ of F^g. As required, ϕ satisfies the definition of an isomorphism; in detail $\phi(RS) = g^{-1}(RS)g = (g^{-1}Rg)(g^{-1}Sg) = \phi(R)\,\phi(S)$.

(2) *Uniform scaling* of the plane with respect to some origin, namely enlargement or scaling down, fortunately does not change the type of a pattern (if it did the inconvenience would prompt a change of definition of equivalence). If $g(\mathbf{x}) = r\mathbf{x}$ $(r > 0)$ defines such a transformation then the formal equivalence required is given by $\phi(R) = g^{-1}Rg$. Note in particular that g preserves angles, shapes, and the ratios between distances.

(3) Let g be a stretch (or contraction) in one direction, say $g(x,y) = (rx,y)$ $(r > 0)$.
(a) The groups of F and F^g are not equivalent if F has 3,4 or 6-fold centres, since g changes angles.
(b) g does map 2-fold centres to 2-fold centres, for if A,B,C are collinear points with $|AB| = |BC|$ then the same holds for their images.
(c) A stretch parallel to an edge sends a rectangle cell to a rectangle cell.

6.2 Plane patterns classified

We have in Chapter 5 a description of 17 types of plane group, each with a distinct *signature* or *symbol*, of the form znxy. To establish that this list does classify plane patterns up to equivalence, we must prove assertions A, B, C below.

A. Plane groups with different signatures are not equivalent,
B. Plane groups with the same signature *are* equivalent,
C. All plane groups are included in the signature system.

Besides their nets, which concentrate on translation, a further powerful tool we shall use for distinguishing between symmetry groups is their *Point group* $\mathcal{P}$ which, in a complementary way, ignores translation and uses only reflection and rotation.

6.2.1 Patterns with different signatures - the point group

DEFINITION 6.10 Let A be any given point of the plane. Then the *point group* $\mathcal{P}$ of a plane group G consists of the identity and:

(1) all those $R_A(m/n)$ for which there is a m/n turn in G,
(2) for every mirror or glide line of G, the reflection in the parallel mirror through A.

If A needs to be specified, we refer to *'the point group at A'*. That **$\mathcal{P}$ is indeed a group** may be seen as follows (see Section 2.5). From Table 2.2, the product of every two elements of $\mathcal{P}$ is also in $\mathcal{P}$. For example if $\mathcal{P}$ contains $R_A(\alpha)$, $R_A(\beta)$ then G contains $R_P(\alpha)$, $R_Q(\beta)$ for some points P,Q and hence their product $R_S(\alpha+\beta)$, say. Thus, by definition of $\mathcal{P}$, we have $R_A(\alpha+\beta)$ in $\mathcal{P}$. Multiplication in $\mathcal{P}$ is *associative* simply because its elements are transformations, $\mathcal{P}$ contains an *identity* by definition. The *inverse* of an element of $\mathcal{P}$ is in $\mathcal{P}$ because (i) a reflection is its own inverse, and (ii) if $R_A(\phi)$ is in $\mathcal{P}$ then $R_D(\phi)$ is in G for some point D, so is the inverse $R_D(-\phi)$, and hence $R_A(-\phi)$ is in $\mathcal{P}$.

EXAMPLE 6.11 Here is an example, with glidelines thickened and lightened

(a) Plane pattern. (b) Symmetries near a cell. c) The symmetries in the point group $\mathcal{P}$, except the 1/2 turn.

Figure 6.3 From pattern to point group $\mathcal{P} = D_8$.

All the mirrors of $\mathcal{P}$ are shown in Figure 6.3(c) above, understood to intersect at the basepoint A, and we see that they are the lines of symmetry of a square, the regular 4-gon. The rest of $\mathcal{P}$ consists of I, R, R^2, R^3, where R is a 1/4 turn about A. Hence $\mathcal{P}$ is the dihedral group D_8, discussed in Section 2.4. Now we prove a key result for the usefulness of the point group.

THEOREM 6.12 ***The net is invariant under the point group.***
(a) For any plane pattern group G, the net at a given point A is mapped onto itself by the point group $\mathcal{P}$ at A, and consequently,
(b) $\mathcal{P}$ is contained in the point group of the net.

Proof Let B be a net point. Then $B = A^T$ for some translation T. Suppose that g is an element of $\mathcal{P}$. Then we have $B^g = (A^T)^g = A^{Tg} = A^{g^{-1}Tg}$. But $g^{-1}Tg$ is a translation of the net, by Theorem 2.12, so B^g is indeed a point of the net.
The basis for using the point group $\mathcal{P}$ is that if plane groups G, H are equivalent then so are their point groups, and hence:

if the point groups of G and H are not equivalent, then neither are G and H. (6.7)

It is customary to denote the point group by nxy analogously to the plane groups, except that now both 'm' and 'g' are replaced by M. We recall that n corresponds to the smallest 1/n turn in G. In Table 6.3 we list the point group of each net and of each of the seventeen plane pattern types. These may be inferred in each case from the rotation, glide and mirror symmetries given in Sections 5.2 to 5.6 (cf. Figure 6.3). The cyclic and dihedral notation is given also. Note that it does not cover the group 1M, consisting of the identity and a single reflection, $\{I, R_m\}$. The point group of each *net* (itself a plane pattern) is given in parenthesis beneath its name, and must contain the point group of each corresponding plane group, by Theorem 6.12. Dihedral groups D_{2m} and rotation groups C_m are reviewed in

Section 2.4. We are now ready to prove assertion A as the next theorem.

THEOREM 6.13 Plane groups with distinct signatures are inequivalent.

Proof We must prove inequivalence of all pairs chosen from the seventeen types listed in Sections 5.2 to 5.6. The number of such pairs is 17.16/2 = 136. Since patterns with different point groups are inequivalent by (6.7), Table 6.3 shows that all pairs are distinguished by the point group except for the 11 pairs dealt with under four cases, next.

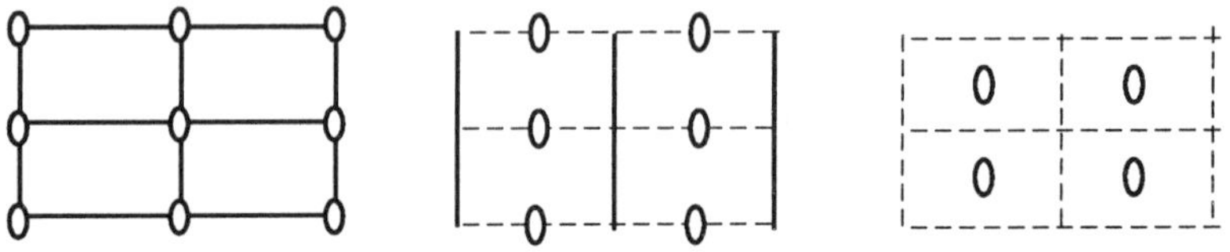

Figure 6.4 Recapitulation of some symmetry configurations.

TABLE 6.3 The plane pattern types by net and point group

NET	Plane group G	Point group of G	
Parallelogram	p1	1	{I}
(2)	p2	2	C_2
Rectangular	pm, pg	1M	
(2MM)	pmm, pmg, pgg	2MM	D_4
Centred rectangular	cm	1M	
(2MM)	cmm	2MM	D_4
Square	p4	4	C_4
(4MM)	p4m, p4g	4MM	D_8
Hexagonal	p3	3	C_3
(6MM)	p3m1, p31m	3M	D_6
	p6	6	C_6
	p6m	6MM	D_{12}

Now we continue the proof of Theorem 6.13.
Case 1M : 3 pairs from pm, pg, cm. These are handled easily by Table 6.2, since pm has one mirror direction but no glides, pg one glide direction but no reflections, whilst cm has both.
Case D_4 : 6 pairs from pmm, pmg, pgg, cmm. None of the first three groups are equivalent by an argument similar to Case 1M (see Figure 6.4). Further, cmm, differs from both pmm and pgg by having both glides and reflections, and from pmg by having two mirror directions (see Section 5.4 for the symmetries in cmm).
Case D_6 : the pair p3m1, p31m. In the first group, reflection may be composed with

translation of minimum length to obtain a reflection, but not in the second.
Case D_8 : the pair p4m, p4g. The first has more mirror directions than the second.

EXERCISE Verify some of the point groups given in Table 6.3.

6.2.2 The classification is complete

Starting from a series of seventeen hypotheses which are easily seen to cover all possible discrete plane pattern groups G, we arrive each time at one of the types listed in Chapter 5. We exhibit equivalence by having the correct net type, and symmetries in the correct positions relative to a basis **u**,**v** for the translation vectors (5.2) of G. The equivalence map ϕ is a natural extension of (6.6) in Example 6.6. Let us temporarily denote a listed group in Chapter 5 by H, with basis **x**,**y**. If a point A has position vector $\mathbf{a} = r\mathbf{u} + s\mathbf{v}$ let A' be the point with position vector $\mathbf{a}' = r\mathbf{x} + s\mathbf{y}$. Then ϕ: G $\to$ H is given by $T_\mathbf{a} \to T_{\mathbf{a}'}$, $R_{AB} \to R_{A'B'}$, $R_A(m/n) \to R_{A'}(m/n)$. We will incidentally confirm that there are no more symmetries than stated in each case of H. Much use will be made of discreteness: as examples, **u** and **v** will always be shortest translation vectors in their respective directions, and we can always choose a mirror and glideline to be as close as possible without coinciding. At the finish we will have established assertions A,B,C at the head of Section 6.2 and so shown that discrete plane patterns may be classified into the 17 types of Chapter 5, distinguished by their labels znxy.

TABLE 6.4 Categories of discrete plane group to be identified with the 17 types of Chapter 5. In each case n is the largest integer for which there is a 1/n turn symmetry. Parentheses denote an inference from what is given. For each row of the table it is shown there are no more possibilites.

mirrors/glidelines	All possible situations that can arise			
None	n = 1, 2, 3, 4, or 6		(p1, p2, p3, p4, p6)	
1 direction only (n = 1)	Mirrors only (pm)	glides only (pg)	mirrors and glides (cm)	
2 directions only (n = 2)	mirrors only (pmm)	glides only (pgg)	mirrors and glides: no m/g parallel (pmg)	mirrors and glides: some m/g parallel (cmm)
Mirrors, n = 4 (square net, no 1/3, 1/6 turns)	some 4-fold (but no 2-fold) centre on a mirror (p4m)		some 2-fold (but no 4-fold) centre on a mirror (p4g)	
Mirrors, n = 3, 6 (hexagonal net, no 1/4 turns)	n = 3 mirror = triangle edge (p31m)	n = 3 mirror = triangle altitude (p3m1)	n = 6 mirror = edge / altitude (p6m)	

CASE 1 Discrete plane groups with no reflections or glides

Case 1.1 (Only translation symmetries.) All such groups are equivalent by Example 6.6, and form type p1.

Case 1.2 $(n = 2.)$ We assume G has a 1/2 turn at the basepoint O, and deduce that G has all the symmetries of p2 and no more. We recall for here and future use

$$R_O(1/2)R_A(1/2) = T_{2OA} \qquad (6.8)$$
$$R_A(1/2) = R_O(1/2)T_{2OA} \qquad (6.9)$$

In fact (6.9) is proved in Figure 2.6 and implies (6.8) (multiply both sides by $R_O(1/2)$). We now have: $2\underline{OA} \in \mathbf{T} \Rightarrow R_A(1/2) \in G$ (by (6.9)) $\Rightarrow 2\underline{OA} \in \mathbf{T}$ (by (6.8)). Thus the 1/2 turns of G are at the same points as for p2, namely those A for which $2\underline{OA}$ is a translation vector, geometrically the cell vertices, midpoints of edges, and centres (see Section 5.2). The position vectors of these points are all $(1/2)(r\mathbf{u}+s\mathbf{v})$, for r,s in **Z**, the set of integers, including zero and the negatives. Thus G is of type p2.

Case 1.3 $(n = 4.)$ We assume G contains $R_O(1/4)$. Then the net is square and there are no 1/3 turns (Resumé 4.19). By the argument of Section 5.5, G contains the rotational symmetries listed for p4, namely 1/4 turns at the cell vertices and centres, and 1/2 turns at the midpoints of the edges. We record the position vectors $r\mathbf{u} + s\mathbf{v}$ or $(r + 1/2)\mathbf{u} + (s + 1/2)\mathbf{v}$ for the 1/4 turns, and $r\mathbf{u} + (s + 1/2)\mathbf{v}$ or $(r + 1/2)\mathbf{u} + s\mathbf{v}$ for the 1/2 turns (r,s in **Z**). There are no more 1/2 turns $R_A(1/2)$ (so no 1/4 turns) because (6.8) implies $2\underline{OA} = r\mathbf{u} + s\mathbf{v}$ (r,s in **Z**); and we have accounted for all such points, since the 4-fold centres also supply 1/2 turns. Thus G is of type p4.

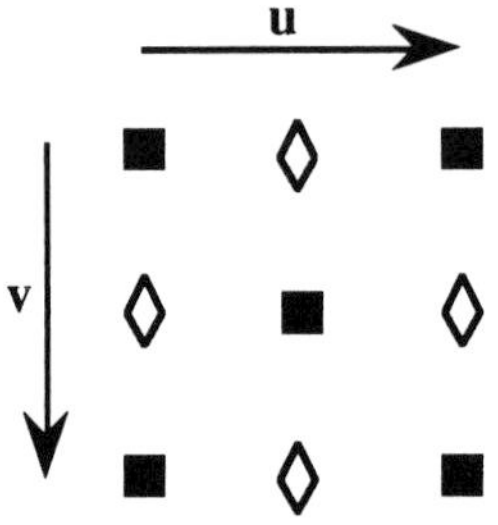

Case 1.4 $(n = 3.)$ We suppose G contains $R_O(1/3)$, and set the basepoint as usual at O. The net is necessarily hexagonal (Resumé 4.19), with basis **u**,**v** along the sides of one of the equilateral triangles making up the unit cell. There are the 3-fold centres at the vertices and centres of every equilateral triangles in the net (see Section 5.6), the position vectors being $(1/3)(r\mathbf{u}+s\mathbf{v})$, for r,s in **Z.** However there are no 1/2 turns, for such would imply a 1/6 turn, say $R_A(1/2)R_O(-1/3) = R_B(1/6)$. It remains to show that there are no more 1/3 turns $R_A(1/3)$, for which we make use of Figure 6.5.

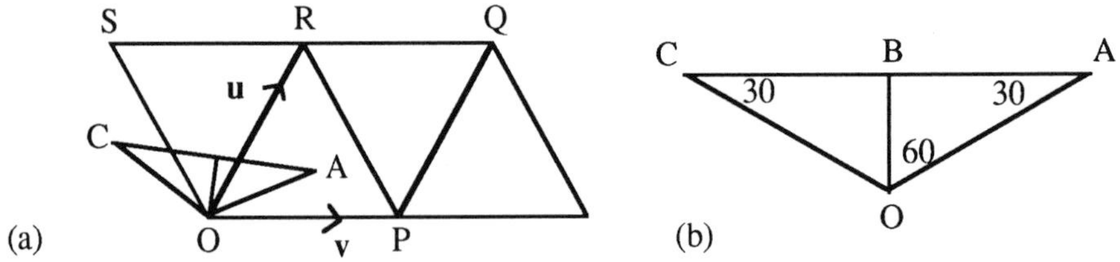

Figure 6.5 There is no 1/3 turn at a point A which is not a triangle vertex or centre.

Suppose $R_A(1/3)$ is a symmetry but A is not a vertex. We need only deduce it must be a triangle centre. We have $R_A(2/3)R_O(1/3) = T_{AC}$, shown enlarged in Figure 6.5(b). By relocating the basepoint if necessary we may assume $|OA| < |OP|$, and then AC is shorter than the long diagonal of a cell OPQR. Since $\underline{AC}$ is a translation vector of G we have $\underline{AC} = \underline{QR}$ for a triangle edge QR. By elementary geometry A is the centre of triangle OPQ. Thus there are no more 1/3 turns and G is of type p3.

Case 1.5 (n = 6.) Our hypothesis is that G contains $R_O(1/6)$ (but still no reflections or glides). As in Case 1.4, this implies that the net is hexagonal and that there are no 1/4 turns. But this time there are 1/2 turns. By taking the square and cube of the 1/6 turn we obtain the rotation symmetries deduced for p6 in Section 5.6: 1/6 turns at the triangle vertices, 1/3 turns at their centres, and 1/2 turns at the midpoints of edges. Our task is to explain why there can be no more symmetries. This was done for 1/3 turns in Case 1.4 . We will rule out new 1/6 turns by ruling out new 1/2 turns (their cubes). Suppose $R_A(1/2)$ is a symmetry. We may suppose $|OA| < |OP|$ as illustrated in Figure 6.5. Then there is a translation symmetry $R_O(1/2)R_A(1/2) = T_{2OA}$, by (6.8). Therefore A is the midpoint of an edge, so is already accounted for. Hence G is of type p6.

CASE 2 Discrete plane groups with reflections/glides all parallel

Case 2.1 (Mirrors only.) Let G have reflection in a mirror m. Since all mirrors of G are parallel there is no rotation symmetry, for it would rotate the mirrors to new directions. We find a basis **u**,**v** of **T** as shortest translation vectors respectively parallel and perpendicular to m. To prove this is so we note that in **T**, every vector parallel to some vector **x** of **T** equals $\alpha\mathbf{x}$ for some constant α, and so the set of all such vectors forms a line group (Definition 3.1). Then Theorem 3.3(a) gives the first assertion below. The second is an elementary observation, illustrated in Figure 6.6(b).

*In **T**, all vectors parallel to a given line n are integer multiples $r\mathbf{u}$, where **u** is a shortest vector parallel to n.* (6.10)

*If **x** is parallel to **u** then subtracting a suitable multiple $t\mathbf{u}$ leaves $\mathbf{w}_1 = \mathbf{x} - t\mathbf{u}$, with $|\mathbf{w}_1| \leq (1/2)|\mathbf{u}|$.* (6.11)

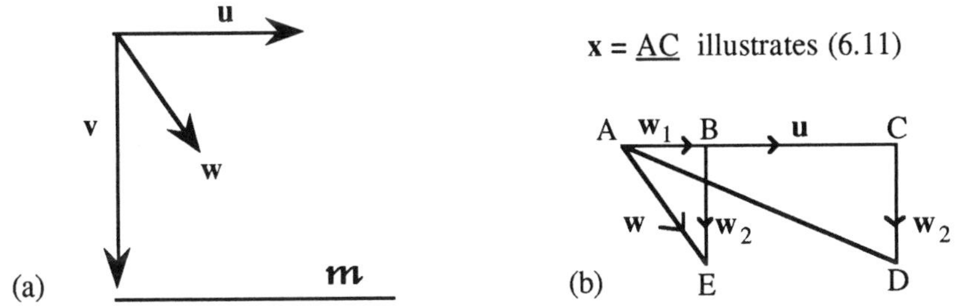

Figure 6.6 (a) Vector **w** is not expressible in the basis **u**,**v**. (b) How the **u** component of **w** can be shortened until $|\mathbf{w}| \leq (1/2)|\mathbf{u}|$.

Suppose **u**,**v** is not a basis and that **w** is a shortest translation vector they do not express (**w** need not be unique). We obtain a contradiction. Resolve **w** parallel to **u** and **v**, say $\mathbf{w} = \mathbf{w}_1 + \mathbf{w}_2$, as in Figure 6.6(b). By (6.11) we may suppose that $|\mathbf{w}_1| \leq (1/2)|\mathbf{u}|$, for otherwise we could subtract multiples of **u** to ensure this, and **w** would still not be expressible in terms of **u**,**v**, but would be shorter. This is illustrated in Figure 6.6(b) by the replacing of <u>AD</u> by <u>AE</u> for **w**. But now $R_m T_w = (R_m T_{w_2})T_{w_1}$, which is a (non-allowed) glide since $R_m T_{w_2}$ is a reflection (see (2.1)), and its translation part $\mathbf{w}_1$ is shorter than **u**. This contradiction shows that, after all, **u**,**v** is a basis of **T**. Finally, combining R_m with multiples $t\mathbf{v}$ (t in **Z**) gives precisely the reflections of pm.

Case 2.2 (Glides only.) As in the previous case there can be no rotations. Let $g = R_m T_x$ be a glide in G with shortest translation part. Let **u**,**v** be shortest translation vectors respectively parallel and perpendicular to the mirror *m*. Then since **x** is as short as possible we have $|\mathbf{x}| \le (1/2)|\mathbf{u}|$ by (6.11). But $g^2 = T_{2x}$, so $|2\mathbf{x}| \ge |\mathbf{u}|$ by minimality of $|\mathbf{u}|$. Hence $|\mathbf{x}| = (1/2)|\mathbf{u}|$ and we may take $g = R_m T_{u/2}$. We have derived a useful ancillary result for other cases:

*If G has glides parallel to translation vector **u**, shortest in its own direction, then G has a glide with translation part **u**/2, and this is least for glides parallel to **u**.* (6.12)

If **u**,**v** is not a basis for the translation symmetries, let **w** be a shortest vector not expressible in terms of them. Decompose **w** parallel to **u** and **v** as in Figure 6.6(b): $\mathbf{w} = \mathbf{w}_1 + \mathbf{w}_2$. As before, we have $|\mathbf{w}_2| \le (1/2)|\mathbf{u}|$ by (6.11). Now, gT_w or gT_{-w} is a glide with translation part (parallel to **u**) strictly shorter than **u**/2. The only way this can be true is for g to be a reflection, but these are not allowed in this case, so we have a contradiction and **u**,**v** do indeed form a basis (in the next case they are allowed, and we infer a centred net). Combining g with translations *r***v**, perpendicular to *m*, we obtain all the glides of pg. The presence of further glides in G would imply translations which are not integral multiples of **v**, contradicting (6.10). Hence G is of type pg.

Case 2.3 (Mirrors and glides.) There are still no rotations because all mirrors and glidelines are in one direction. Let **u** be a shortest vector in that direction. We shall construct a centred rectangular cell for G. As in Case 2.2, we may assume by (6.12) that G contains a glide $g = R_m T_{u/2}$. Let *n* be a mirror of G as close as possible to the mirror line *m* of this glide. Represent **u** by AB with *n* lying along AB. We have $R_n g = R_n R_m T_{u/2} = T_w$, say. Now let <u>AE</u> represent **w** and <u>AD</u>, <u>BC</u> both represent $\mathbf{v} = 2\mathbf{w} - \mathbf{u}$. Then we have the rectangle ABCD with centre E of Figure 6.7.

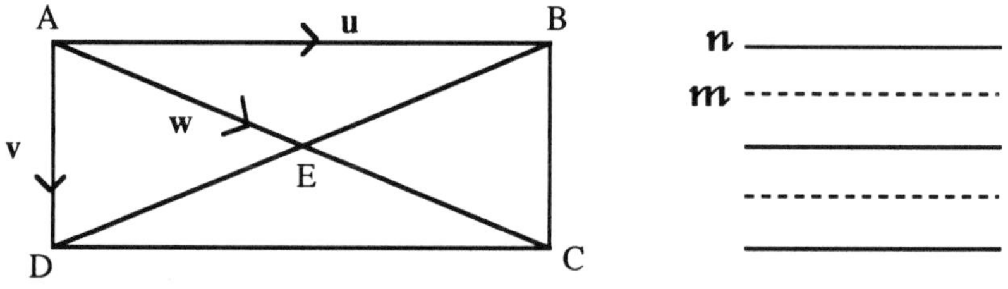

Figure 6.7 The centred rectangular cell, found from parallel mirrors and glides.

Notice that **w** is a shortest translation vector in its own direction, else it would combine with R_n to give a glide too close to *n*. We prove that **u**,**w** (hence also **v**,**w**) is a basis for the translation vectors in the group. Let **x** be such a vector. Then since **u**,**w** are not parallel we have $\mathbf{x} = \lambda\mathbf{u} + \mu\mathbf{w}$ for some constants λ, μ which must be shown to be integers to establish the basis assertion. By (6.11) we may subtract integer multiples of **u**,**w** from **x** so as to leave $|\lambda|, |\mu| < 1$. But then $\mu = 0$, else $R_n T_x$ would be a glide with line closer to *n* than that of g. Thus $\mathbf{x} = \lambda\mathbf{u}$. Now, by the minimality of $|\mathbf{u}|$ we may infer that $\lambda = 0$, which means that the original λ, μ were integers. Thus we have shown that **u**,**w** is a basis. Finally, T_v generates all the reflections and glides of cm by composition with R_n and g. Further glides or reflections cannot be present, for they would generate translations which cannot belong to the group. We have established that G has type cm.

CASE 3 **Discrete groups with reflections/glides in exactly two directions**

Case 3.1 (Mirrors only.) Here n = 2. The two directions must be at right angles, or mirrors would reflect each other into new directions. The shortest translation vectors **u**,**v** in the respective directions form a basis by the argument of Case 2.1. But now we obtain the mirrors and 2-fold centres of pmm, reproduced in Figure 6.4. The existence of further mirrors or 1/2 turn symmetries would contradict the minimality of $|\mathbf{u}|$, $|\mathbf{v}|$. Thus G has type pmm.

Case 3.2 (Glides only.) Again n = 2; the glides are in two perpendicular directions or they would generate more glide directions. The argument of Case 2.2 (glides only, one direction) applies here also to show that shortest vectors **u**,**v** in the respective directions form a basis. By (6.12) there are glides $R_m T_{u/2}$ and $R_n T_{v/2}$ with least translation parts. They generate the symmetry configuration of pgg, shown in Figure 6.4. Further glides or 1/2 turns would contradict the minimality of $|\mathbf{u}|$, $|\mathbf{v}|$. In short, G is of type pgg.

Case 3.3 (Glides and mirrors, no glide and mirror parallel.) As before, n = 2 is implied. The mirrors are all in one direction and the glides in another, perpendicular to the first. The usual arguments show that shortest vectors **u**,**v** in the respective directions form a basis. A glide with shortest translation part has the form $R_n T_{v/2}$, by (6.12). One mirror and this glide, together with translations, generate the symmetry configuration of pmg (see Figure 6.4) and no more. We have G of type pmg.

Case 3.4 (Glides and mirrors: some mirror and glide parallel.) As before, we have n = 2 and two perpendicular directions for mirrors and/or glides. However, things work out a little differently because glides and mirrors are allowed to be parallel.

Let mirror n have glidelines parallel to it and let the glide $g = R_m T_{u/2}$ be as close as possible, where **u** is a shortest translation vector parallel to m (cf. (6.12)). We perform the construction of Case 2.3 (cm) to obtain the centred rectangle ABCD, with **u**,**w** or **v**,**w** equally valid as bases, and **u**,**v**,**w** shortest translation vectors in their respective directions (see Figure 6.7). Now consider the mirror/glides in our second direction. We choose the basepoint as A, lying at the right angle intersection with n of a mirror p along AD.

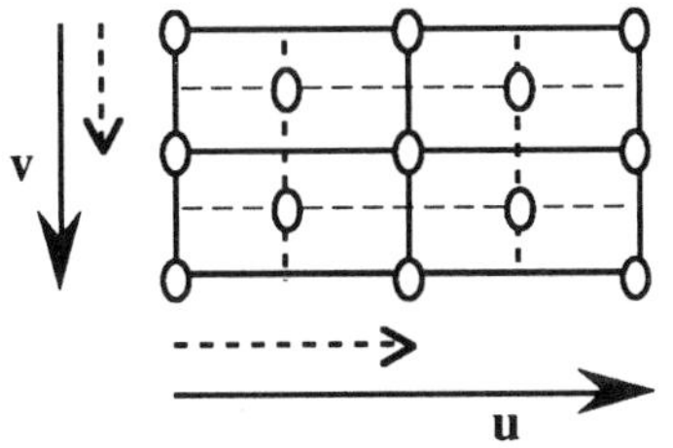

Figure 6.8 The cmm symmetries.

Then $g = R_n T_{u/2}$ is a glide parallel to **u** with least possible translation part. Now R_p and g, together with translations T_{ru} (r in **Z**) generate the remaining mirrors and glides of cmm, combining with those in the first direction to give the 1/2 turns. We have exactly the symmetry configuration of cmm (and no more), as reproduced in Figure 6.8, and so G falls into type cmm.

CASE 4 **Discrete plane groups with mirrors and 1/4 turns**

Case 4.1 (Some mirror contains a 4-fold centre.) We recall from Case 1.3 that as a consequence of 1/4 turns being present, the net is square, no 1/3 or 1/6 turns are possible, and the rotational symmetries are those of p4 and no more as depicted in Figure 6.9. It remains to decide what configurations of mirrors and glides are possible. Now, every mirror must reflect r-fold centres to r-fold centres (Theorem 2.12), and this restricts its position to one of those shown in p4m or p4g. It may or may not pass through a 4-fold centre, and in this present case we suppose that one mirror does so. Whichever mirror we choose for this role, its presence implies (by combination with rotations and translations) that of all mirrors in p4m. Also, combining 1/2 turns and diagonal reflections gives the box of glides in p4m (see Section 5.5). Any further reflections or glides imply the presence of disallowed translations or rotations, and so are ruled out. Hence the present choice of first mirror considered leads to G being of type p4m.

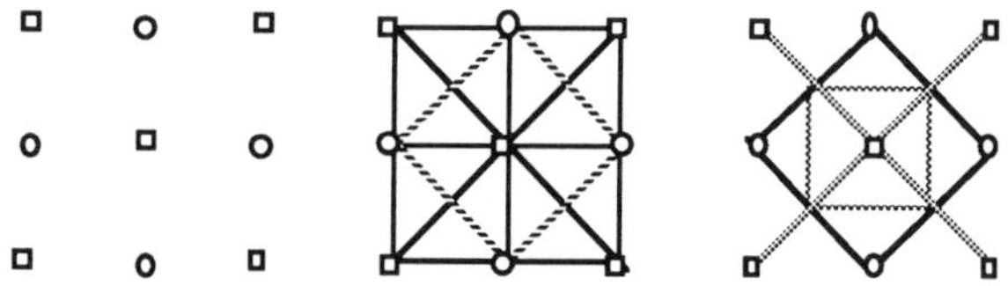

Figure 6.9 Possible symmetry configurations over a cell for a discrete plane pattern with 1/4 turn symmetries. cf. Figure 6.3.

Case 4.2 (No mirror contains a 4-fold centre.) From the discussion of Case 4.1 up to choice of mirror, the remaining choice is to have a mirror containing a 2-fold but not a 4-fold centre. This generates the mirrors and glides of p4g (Section 5.5). Again, the configuration is complete, or contradictions arise, and so G has type p4g.

CASE 5 Discrete plane groups with mirrors and 1/3 turns

Case 5.1 (Mirrors along triangle edges, no 1/6 turn.) In Case 1.4 we dealt with the consequences of allowing a 1/3 turn. The net is hexagonal, meaning that a cell is diamond-shaped, consisting of two equilateral triangles back to back. 1/4 turns are ruled out, but there are 1/3 turns at every vertex and centre, as depicted for p3 in Figure 6.10. What are the options for a mirror? It must reflect 3-fold centres to 3-fold centres (Theorem 2.12), and consequently lies along a triangle edge or altitude. Both cases cannot arise at once, for then we would have a 1/6 turn (this situation is dealt with as Case 5.3). (*) So let us suppose that there is a mirror along some triangle altitude. Invoking translations and rotations we generate the reflections and glides of p3m1, recalled in Figure 6.10 (see also Figure 6.5 for the argument). As usual, a check shows that no more are possible without contradiction. We conclude that G is of type p3m1.

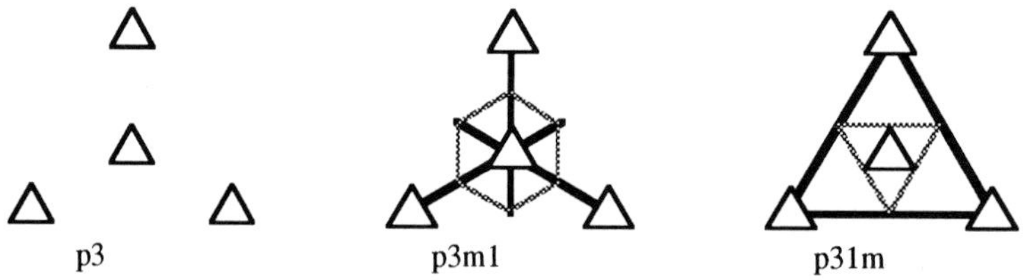

Figure 6.10 Possible symmetry configurations over a half cell for a discrete plane pattern with 1/3 turn symmetries.

Case 5.2 (Mirrors in triangle edges, no 1/6 turn.) Here we follow Case 5.1 up to the choice of mirror direction (*). Then we specify that some mirror lies along a triangle edge. Again referring to Figures 6.10 and 6.5 we obtain precisely the symmetries of p31m, and so G is of this type.

Case 5.3 (Mirrors and 1/6 turns.) The 1/6 turn combines with an altitude reflection to give an edge reflection, and therefore we have the glide/mirror symmetries of both p3m1 and p31m. A 1/6 turn at one vertex is translated to all (Theorem 2.12). Its square is a 1/3 turn, ensuring that the rotational symmetries of p3 are included, and its cube is a 1/2 turn which combines with translations to produce a 1/2 turn at the midpoint of every triangle edge. A little checking shows that further symmetries would violate the hypotheses of this case. Thus G is of type p6m.

This completes a fairly rigorous justification of the standard classification of discrete plane groups of symmetries, and hence of plane patterns. A concise 'pure mathematical' derivation may be found in Schwarzenberger (1980), and a more geometrical approach in Lockwood and Macmillan (1976).

EXERCISE Verify some of the point groups given in Table 6.4.

6.3 Tilings and Coxeter graphs

DEFINITION 6.14 A plane *tiling* or *tessellation* is a countable set of regions $F_1, F_2, \ldots$ called *tiles or faces*, which cover the plane without area overlap. To say the faces are *countable* means that we can index them by integers 1, 2, 3, ... as we have just done. Two tiles may have a common boundary, say a line segment, but this contributes no area. For our purposes we may assume each face is continuously deformable to a closed disk $D = \{(a,b) : a, b \text{ real}, \ a^2 + b^2 \le 1\}$. Thus a tile is not allowed to have 'holes'. A tiling is *polygonal* if every tile is a (not necessarily regular) polygon.

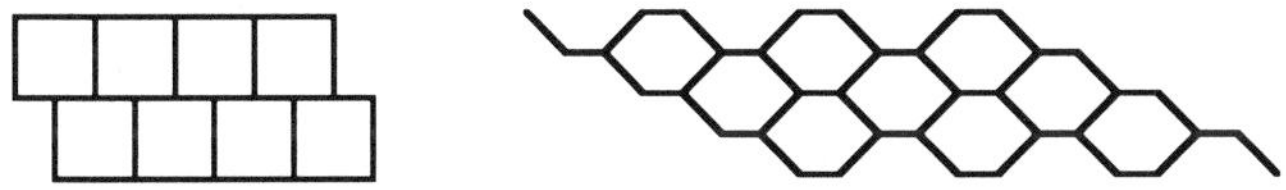

(a) (b)

Figure 6.11 General tilings.

6.3.1 Archimedean tilings

We consider tilings by polygons which fit *edge to edge*, that is, each edge of a polygon is an edge of exactly one other. This rules out (a) of Figure 6.11 above, even though the tiles are polygons. Nevertheless it will prove a very convenient starting point. A simple but important special case is that of the *regular tilings* $\{m, n\}$ by regular m-gons, n at a point. It is easy to prove directly by the approach of (6.13) shortly below that the three well-known ones of Figure 6.12 following are the only possibilities. Note that we exhibit $\{3,6\}$ as the *dual* of $\{6,3\}$, *dual* being defined after Figure 6.12.

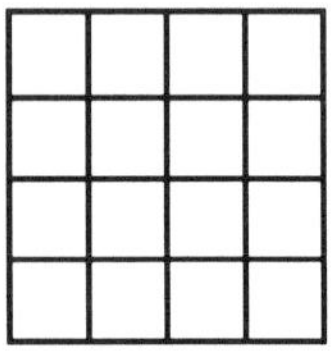

{4,4}

{3,6} light,
{6,3} in bold

Figure 6.12 The regular tilings, with {3,6} as dual of {6,3}.

DEFINITION 6.15 The *dual* of a polygonal tiling is the division into polygonal regions obtained by joining the centre of each polygon to that of every polygon with which it has a common edge. Of course the dual of {4,4} is a translated copy of itself, and taking the dual of {3,6} in Figure 6.12 gives us back {6,3}. We require some notation introduced by Ludwig Schläfli (see Coxeter, 1973).

NOTATION 6.16 (See Figure 6.13.) A vertex around which we have in cyclic order an n_1-gon, an n_2-gon, ... , an n_r-gon, is said to have *type* $(n_1, n_2, \ldots, n_r)$. We abbreviate repeated numbers by an index. Thus (4,6,12), (6,12,4) and (12,6,4) are the same vertex type, as are (4,8,8) and $(4,8^2)$.

DEFINITION 6.17 A tiling by regular polygons is *Archimedean of type* (a,b,...) if each vertex has the same type, (a,b,...). This of course includes the regular tilings, of types (4^4), (6^3), (3^6). We now investigate what other Archimedean tilings exist. Firstly, consider the situation at an individual vertex. We may anticipate that some possibilities for arranging polygons around this point will not extend to a tiling, but we will not miss any that do by starting this way. (Archimedes' name is given to these tilings because he studied polyhedra with faces obeying similar rules to this plane case. See Coxeter, 1973.)

Since the interior angle of a regular n-gon ($n \geq 3$) has angle $\pi - 2\pi/n$ and the angles at a point sum to 2π, we have for a vertex of type $(n_1, n_2, \ldots, n_r)$ that r is at least 3 and: $(\pi-2\pi/n_1) + (\pi-2\pi/n_2) + \ldots + (\pi-2\pi/n_r) = 2\pi$, or

$$(1-2/n_1) + (1-2/n_2) + \ldots + (1-2/n_r) = 2. \tag{6.13}$$

We show that this equation can have, fortunately, only a finite number of solutions, and enumerate them. Since the equation (6.13) is unaffected by the order of the integers n_i we may assume they are arranged in non-decreasing order. Further, $n \geq 3$ implies $1-2/n \geq 1/3$, so there cannot be more than six terms on the left hand side of (6.13), thus

$$3 \leq n_1 \leq n_2 \leq \ldots \leq n_r, \quad \text{and} \quad 3 \leq r \leq 6. \tag{6.14}$$

And now, since $1-2/n$ ($n \geq 3$) is increasing with n, the number of solutions is finite. They are found as follows. For each of r = 3, 4, 5, 6 we test the r-tuples $(n_1, .., n_r)$, in lexicographical order, to see if they satisfy (6.13), until $r(1-2/n_1) \geq 2$. The last condition means of course that the left hand side of (6.13) must now be at least 2. The solutions are given below, lexicographically for each r.

TABLE 6.5 Solution sets for r regular n-gons surrounding a point.

r = 3		r = 4	r = 5	r = 6
3, 7, 42	4, 5, 20	3^2, 4,12	3^4, 6	3^6
3, 8, 24	4, 6, 12	3^2, 6^2	3^3, 4^2	
3, 9,18	4, 8^2	3, 4^2, 6		
3, 10, 15	5^2,10	4^4		
3, 12^2	6^3			

We may pick out the regular tilings as special cases. Four of the solutions as given can be rearranged to produce, up to cyclic permutations and reverse ordering, exactly one further point type each, as shown below in Figure 6.13.

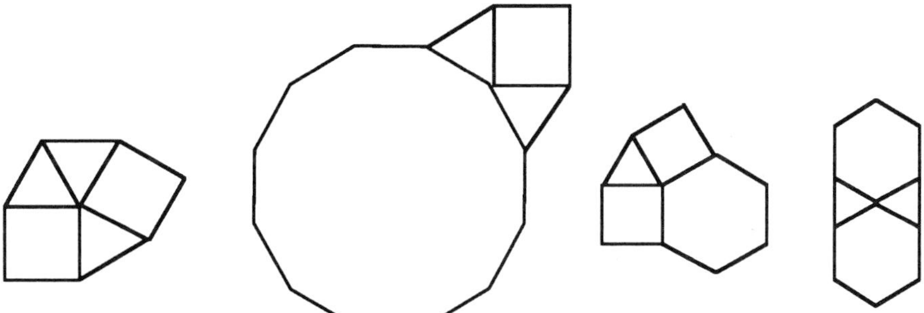

{3, 3, 4, 3, 4} {3, 4, 3, 12} {3, 4, 6, 4} {3, 6, 3, 6}

Figure 6.13 New vertex types by rearrangement of entries in Table 6.5.

We now have twenty one point types that are guaranteed to exist as the surroundings of a single point, but how many extend to a tiling? We will shortly give a list (Table 6.6) but, as noted in Grünbaum & Shephard (1987), a finite diagram does not automatically prove the existence of a tiling. We have to give, in effect, an algorithm for constructing the constructible to an arbitrary number of tiles. We take the opportunity to do so in terms of isometries, applying and reinforcing ideas already built up. There are far-reaching extensions to three and higher dimensions (Coxeter 1973, 1974).

EXERCISE Verify that the solutions of equation (6.13) for r = 3 are as given in Table 6.5.

6.3.2 Coxeter graphs and Wythoff's construction

This construction applies to a configuration of mirrors whose mutual angles are all of the form π/p, $p \geq 2$. It can be used in three dimensions, and more generally in n dimensions, but our concern here will be the 2-dimensional plane. The *Coxeter graph* of a group generated by reflections R, S,... has *nodes* labelled R, S,.. . We join typical nodes R, S by an *edge* marked p if their mirrors are at angle π/p, $p \geq 3$. But we do not join these nodes if p = 2. Corresponding mirror lines are likewise labelled R, S,... as illustrated below.

KEY EXAMPLE 6.18 Mirrors forming a right-angled triangle thus:

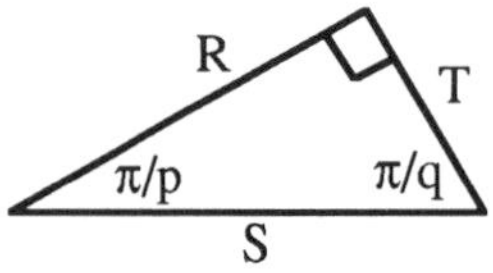

gives Coxeter graph:

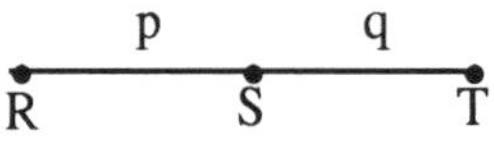

NOTE 6.19 The Coxeter graph here depicted denotes the Dihedral group D_{2p} = Gp{R, S}, the symmetry group of a regular p-gon, generated by reflections R, S in two mirrors at angle π/p. (See Section 2.4 and especially Theorem 2.18.)

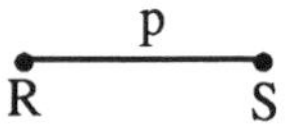

Wythoff's construction The 3-node graph above gives in principle up to seven distinct tilings of the plane for each allowable pair p, q ≥ 3, corresponding to our assigning a special significance to one or more nodes by placing a small circle round each. This works as follows. The vertices of the tiling are the images under the group of one fixed *initial point.* The construction allocates these points to edges, and edges to polygonal faces, based on their belonging to *initial edges*, which belong in turn to *initial faces.* This works consistently because, for example, if A is a vertex of an edge e then A^g is a vertex of edge e^g for any isometry g. We begin with the simplest case.

ONE NODE RINGED

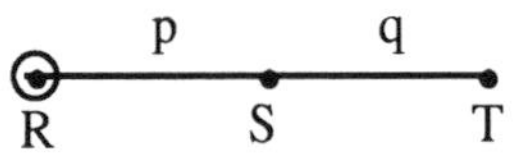

The instructions are:

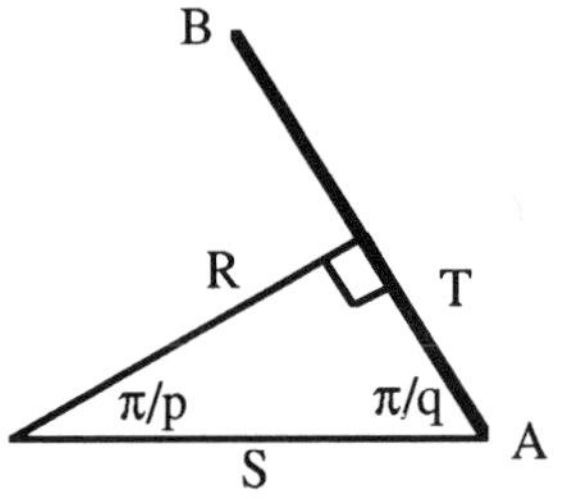

(a) Choose an initial point A on the intersection of all mirrors with unringed nodes, here S and T.

(b) Form an initial edge AB, symbolised as

, where B = A^R.

(c) Form an *initial polygon* (tile) t_0, symbolised as

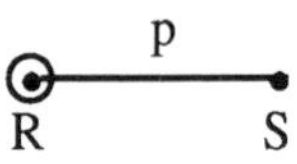

whose edges are the images of AB under Gp{R,S}, namely the rotated copies of AB through successive 1/p turns SR: AB, BC, CD, ... It is shown here as a regular hexagon.

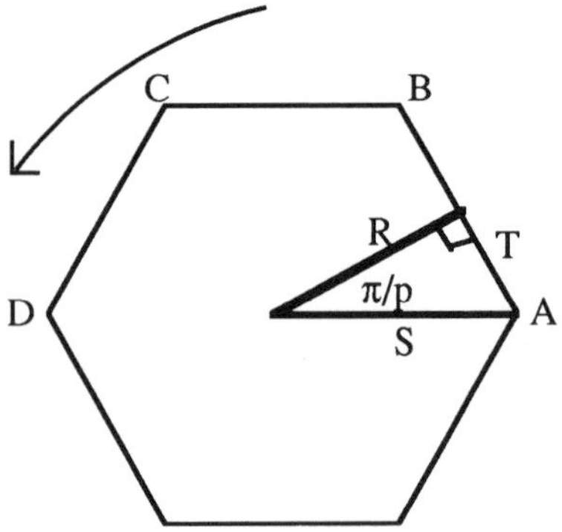

(d) Our tiling is defined to consist of the images of the initial polygonal tile t_0 under Gp{R, S, T}. The **inductive step** as applied to A is given below.

Form the q images of t_0 under successive 1/q turns TS about A

In the diagram, p = 6 and q = 3.

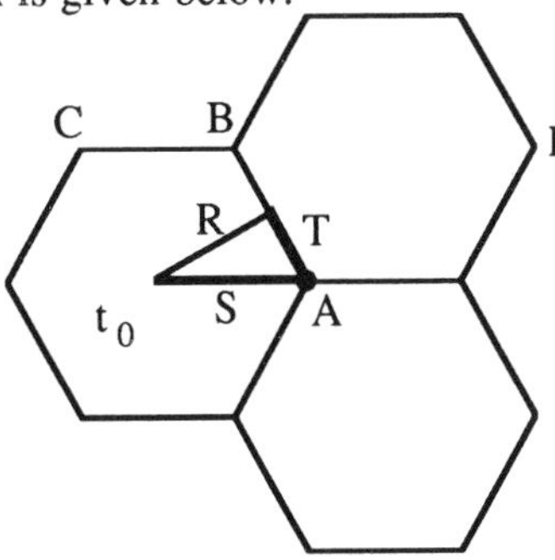

At every stage, a vertex P of the tiling formed so far has 1/q turns in terms of R, S, T and we use them to surround P with q copies of t_0 as was done the first time for A. For example

$R_A(1/q) = TS$, so by Theorem 2.12 we have (see next line)
$R_B(1/q) = TS^{SR}$, since the 1/p turn SR maps A to B, and
$R_C(1/q) = TS^{(SR)^2}$, since $(SR)^2$ maps A to C,
.... and so on.

It remains to observe that all the isometries we have, such as the above, for t_0, go over into any adjacent p-gon via a reflection $T^{(SR)^r}$ in their common edge.

EXERCISE Find a basis for the translation symmetries of {6,3} in terms of R, S, T above.

EXERCISE 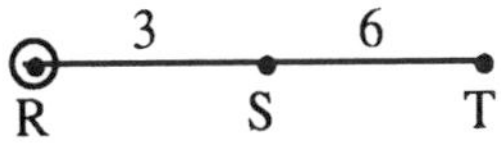

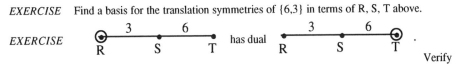

has dual 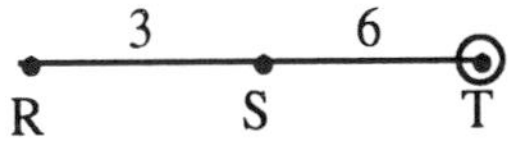

. Verify this by constructing both from the same mirrors R, S, T as shown in Figure 6.12.

It is very useful to understand this basic procedure first before going beyond what we have just constructed, namely a regular tiling {p,q} for each allowable p,q that gives a right-angled triangle: (4,4), (3,6), or (6,3).

INITIAL POLYGONS The general rule is: For each node, if deleting it and the adjacent edges leaves a 2-node subgraph with at least one node ringed, then this subgraph defines an initial polygon (unless the corresponding mirrors are at angle $\pi/2$). More details below.

A NON-REGULAR TILING Now let us obtain something new, still with only one node ringed, by interpreting Wythoff instructions (a) to (d) for this graph.

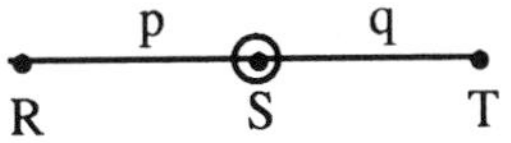

To show the relationship of this to {p,q} and {q,p} we put our right-angled RST triangle as before within a regular p-gon (p = 6 in the diagram below right). The initial point A is on the intersection of mirrors R and T [by Wythoff rule (a) above].

The initial edge ⊙ S = AB

is common to two initial faces: the p-gon

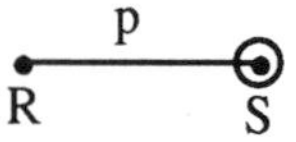

= ABCDEF,

and q-gon

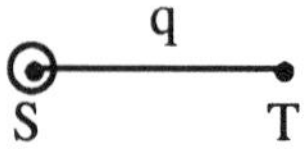

= ABG.

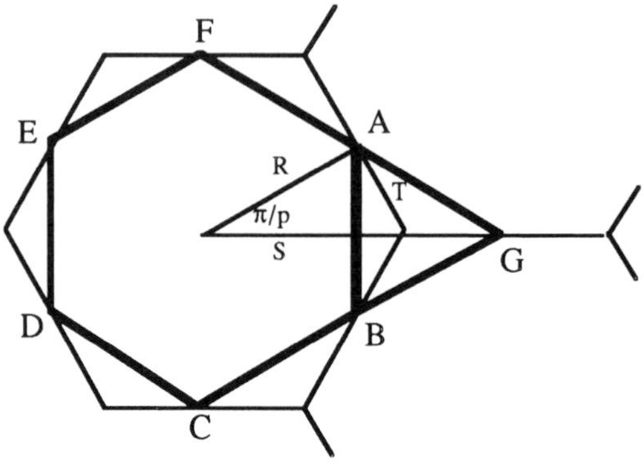

We note that FAG is a straight line because $\pi/p + \pi/q = \pi/2$. Thus, in the tiling, A is surrounded by the initial pair of tiles plus their images under the 1/2 turn RT, as shown here. Furthermore, it is clear from the construction, by a discussion similar to that for the preceding cases, that every point of the tiling is surrounded in the same way. Thus we have an Archimedean tiling of type (p,q,p,q). *The one new case is (3,6,3,6).* In three and higher dimensions we get rather more (see remarks at the end of this chapter).

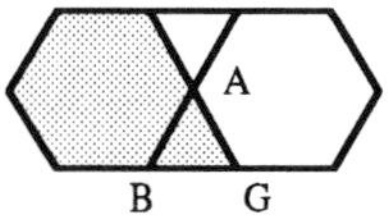

CASES WITH TWO RINGS

CASE 1

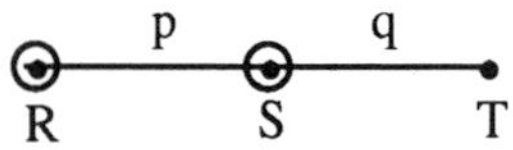

Initial vertices and edges. The only unringed vertex is T. On mirror T we place initial vertex A at the intersection with the angle bisector of mirrors R, S, as in diagram (a) shortly below. This is the unique position which ensures that the initial edges

⊙ R = AB and ⊙ S = AL

have the same length. Further, this is half the side length of the regular p-gon in which we place the RST triangle. See diagram (b) below.

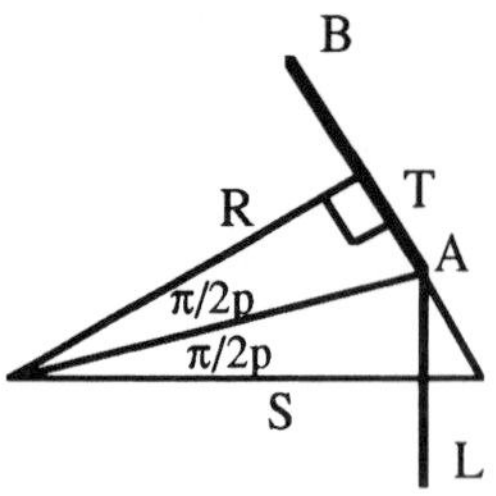

(a)

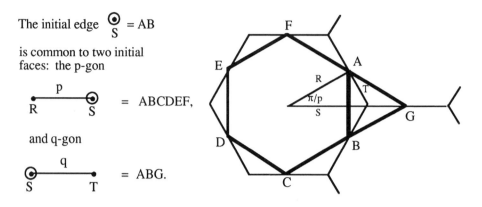

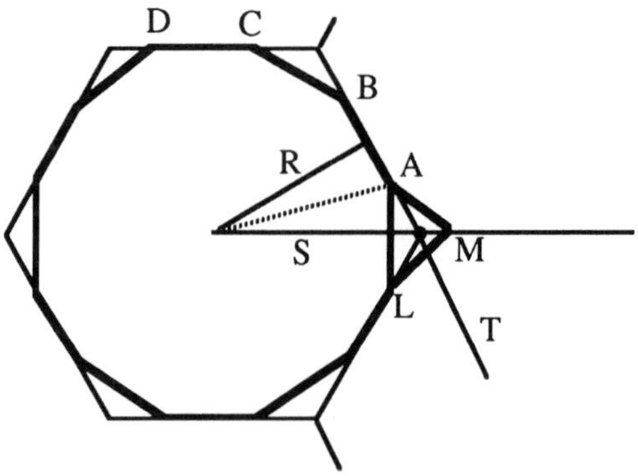

(b)

Initial faces (=tiles, polygons)

(i) 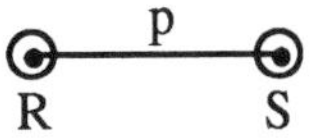

The edges are the images of both AB and AL under 1/p turns SR, giving a regular 2p-gon ABC ... L, inscribed as shown above in diagram (b).

(ii) 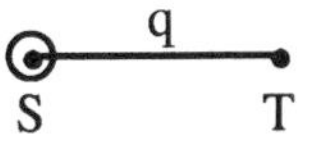

A regular q-gon AL ... M formed from the images of AL under 1/q turns TS.

Conclusion. Polygons (i) and (ii) with their images under the 1/2 turn RT surround vertex A, giving it type (q, 2p, 2p). Hence we have a tiling of this type. Altogether the p,q pairs 4,4 3,6 6,3 yield two new tilings, of types $(3, 12^2)$ and $(4, 8^2)$.

CASE 2

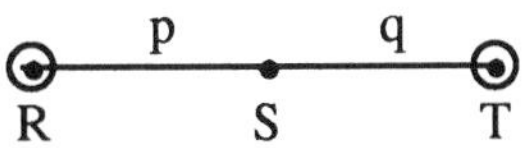

The initial point A is the intersection of mirror S with the bisector of the angle between mirrors R and T, hence the initial edges

= AB, and

= AL

have the same length, as shown in diagram (a) below.

(a)

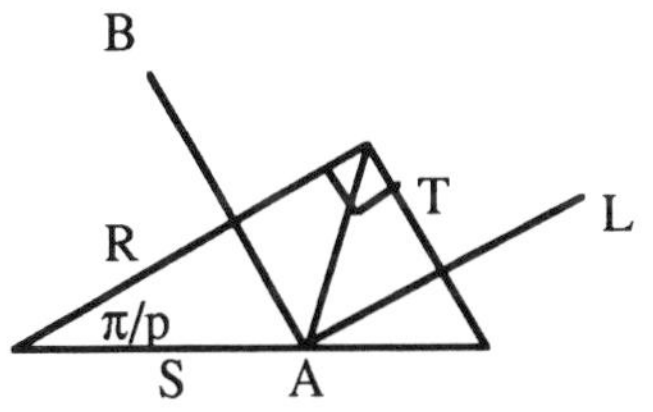

(b)

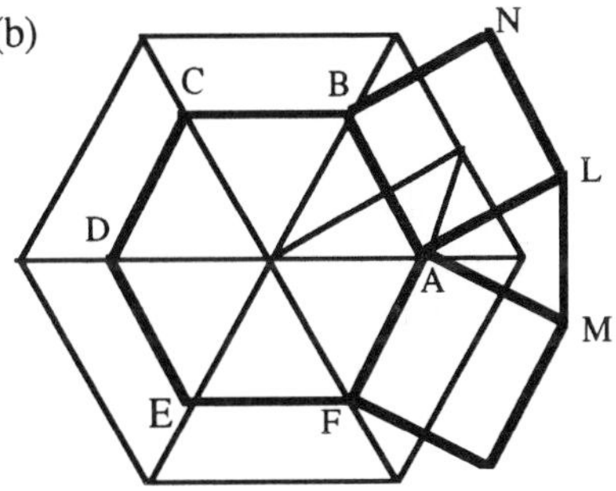

Initial faces (tiles) : (i) 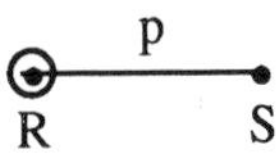

and (ii) 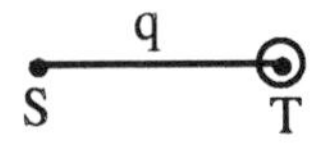

.

(i) is a p-gon ABC ... F whose edges are the images of AB under 1/p turns SR and are parallel to corresponding edges of the background polygon. (ii) is the q-gon AL ... M bounded by q images of AL (q = 3 in diagram (b) above). Now we apply the 1/2 turn RT to (i) and (ii). They, with their copies, each provide one edge of a square ABNL. We see that A has type (p, 4, q, 4). This gives one new tiling, of type (3, 4, 6, 4).

CASES WITH THREE RINGS

CASE 1

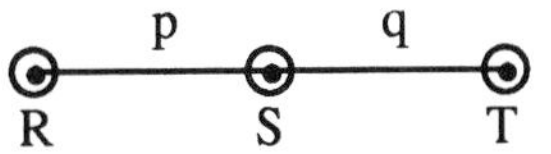

In the previous cases, with just two rings, the potential ambiguity of *initial vertex* A was resolved by using an angle bisector. Now we specify that A lie on two (hence all three) angle bisectors of the RST triangle. Thus A is the centroid of the triangle, and is equidistant from all three sides. The initial edges are:

$$\underset{R}{\odot} = AL, \quad \underset{S}{\odot} = AM, \quad \underset{T}{\odot} = AN,$$

shown in diagram (a) below, have equal lengths. L, M, N are the centroids of the images of the RST triangle under respective reflections R, S, T.

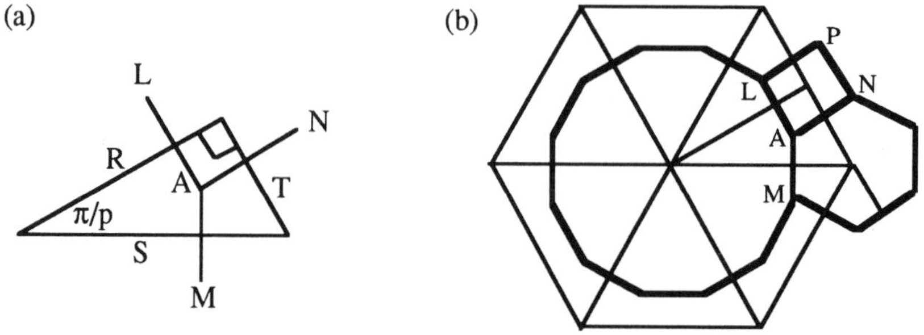

Initial faces : (i) 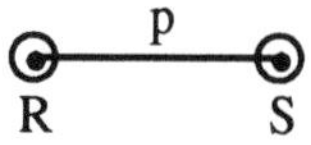

and (ii) 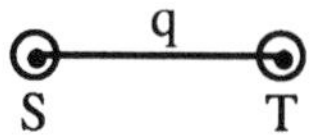

.

Here (i) is a 2p-gon AL .. M inscribed within the background p-gon as in diagram (b) above, whilst (ii) is a 2q-gon AN ... M (q = 3 above). These, together with their images under the 1/2 turn RT, contribute one edge each to bounding a square ANPL, also with A as a vertex. The type is (4, 2q, 2p), giving us (besides some old ones) a new tiling type, (4,6,12). The point types we have not covered are $(3^4,6)$, $(3^3,4^2)$, $(3^2,4,3,4)$. They are not difficult, but we refer to Grünbaum and Shephard (1987) and give now a finite sample of all Archimedean tilings and their types. There appear ten of the twenty one types we identified as possible around a single point. One, $(3^4,6)$, has a right handed, and a left handed form obtained from it by an indirect isometry.

6.4 Creating plane patterns

6.4.1 Using nets and cells

Given a net type and a cell, we can do a little design work focussed on any or all of vertices, edges, or cell interior, whilst keeping the same translation symmetries. A simple example is Figure 6.14 (a). From a viewpoint which may intersect this, we can redraw the left edge with a meaningful cavity provided we put a corresponding bulge on the right edge. Similarly for horizontal edges, as in Figure 6.14(b). See also the excellent discussion in McGregor and Watt (1984), p. 237.

Here are two examples, followed by an exercise for the reader. Creative experimentation can reveal a great diversity of possibilities.

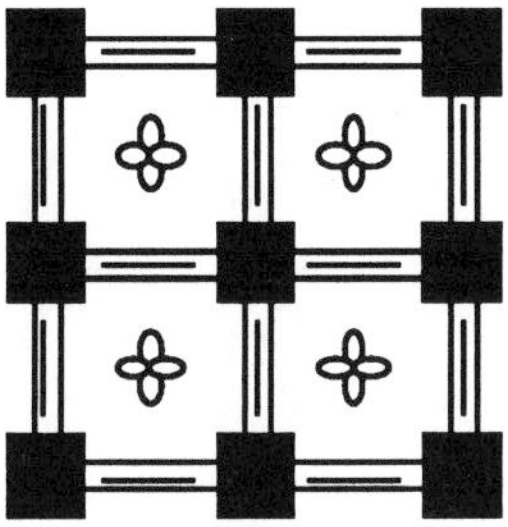

(a) Type p4m

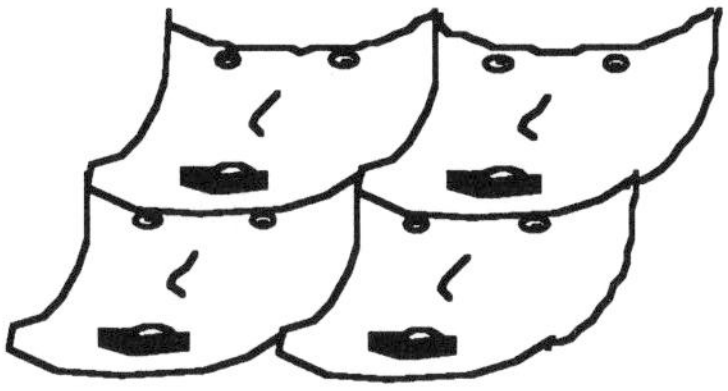

(b) Type p1

Figure 6.14 Patterns formed by modifying aspects of a cell which is (a) a square, (b) general parallelogram type.

EXERCISE Design a pattern by embellishing the hexagonal net.

6.4.2 Patterns from tilings

Every tiling of the plane has a symmetry group. A great variety of tilings are described in Grunbaum & Shephard (1987). In particular, our Archimedean tilings have independent translations in two directions, their symmetry groups are clearly discrete (see Review 4.1 ff.), and therefore they must be some of the seventeen plane groups. The first three tilings in Table 6.6 are already nets, but the last nine give new examples in their own right. However we can modify them in many ways, such as shown below.

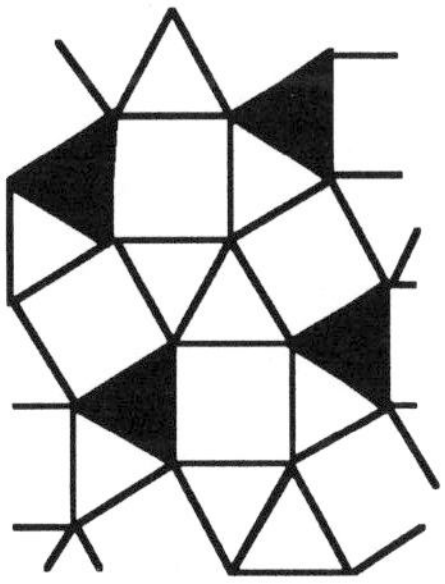

Type p1 from $(3^2,4,3,4)$

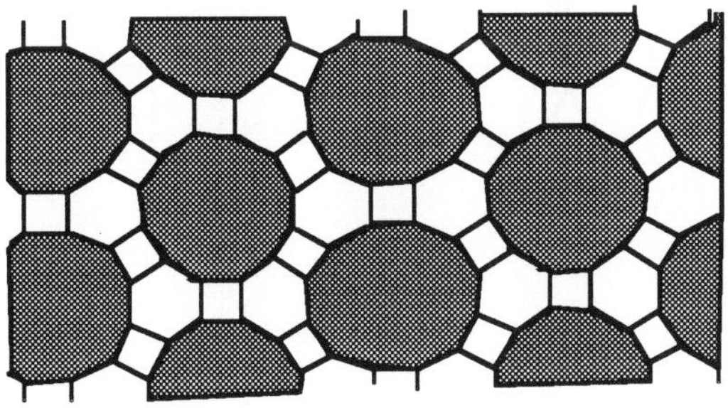

Type p6mm from (4,6,12)

Figure 6.15 Two plane patterns from simple additions to Archimedean tilings.

EXERCISE Design a sweater pattern by embellishing Archimedean tiling $(3^3, 4^2)$.

TABLE 6.6 The Archimedean tilings

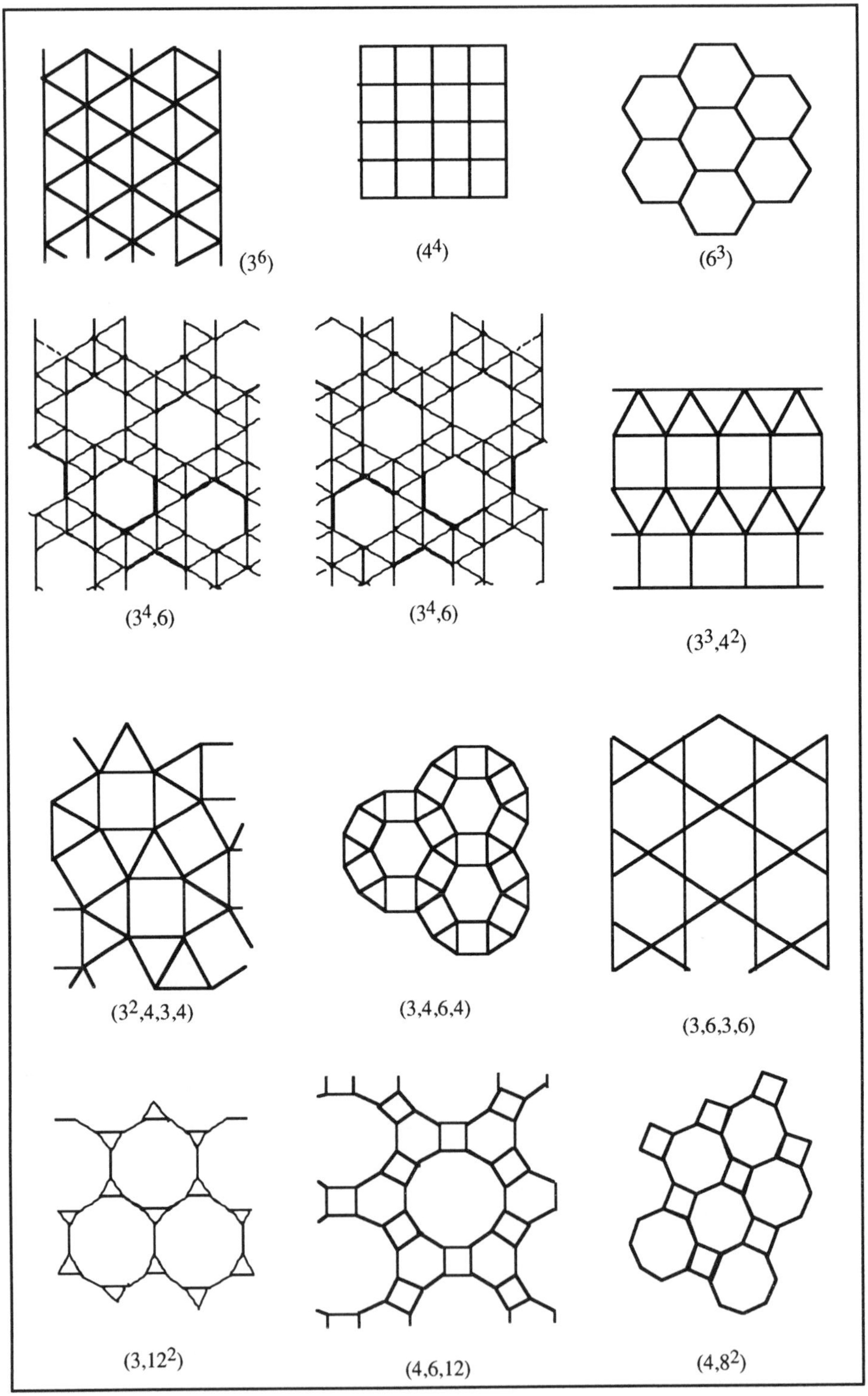

6.4.3 Using the fundamental region

DEFINITION 6.20 A *fundamental region* $\mathcal{F}$ for a discrete group G of isometries of the plane is a closed region satisfying (see Definition 6.14)

the images of $\mathcal{F}$ under G tile the plane. (6.15)

That is, the images cover the plane with no area overlap. It will be useful in the sequel to restate this no-overlap condition as :

no point of $\mathcal{F}$ is mapped to any other by an element of G (except boundary to boundary). (6.16)

What about a single cell as candidate for $\mathcal{F}$? Its images cover the plane, and for group p1 condition (6.16) holds also, so the cell is indeed a fundamental region. But in all other cases (6.16) fails to hold and, in a sense, that is our opportunity.

EXAMPLE 6.21 The plane group pm has a rectangular cell which, with basepoint on one of the parallel mirrors, is bisected by another of these mirrors, as illustrated to the right with vertical mirror m. Because m reflects each half of the cell into the other, condition (6.16) fails. But either the shaded or the unshaded half may be taken as fundamental region. Two step-by-step examples will illustrate how we may use the fundamental region as a tool to obtain patterns of any given type 'to order'.

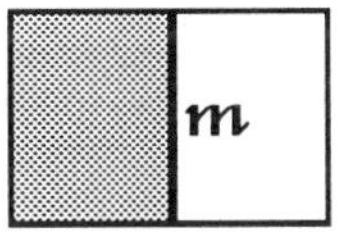

CONSTRUCTION 6.22 ***A pattern generation method:*** *Cut a cell down to a fundamental region, insert a submotif, then rebuild the cell.*

EXAMPLE 6.23 We make a p2 pattern by Construction 6.22; first we need a suitable fundamental region, and we can get it as a subarea of a cell. Three ways to do this are shown in Figure 6.16.

Figure 6.16 The pg cell with its 1/2 turns, and three choices of fundamental region (shaded). Condition (6.16) is satisfied (no overlap) because the central 1/2 turn sends the fundamental region onto an unshaded area. There are no mirrors here.

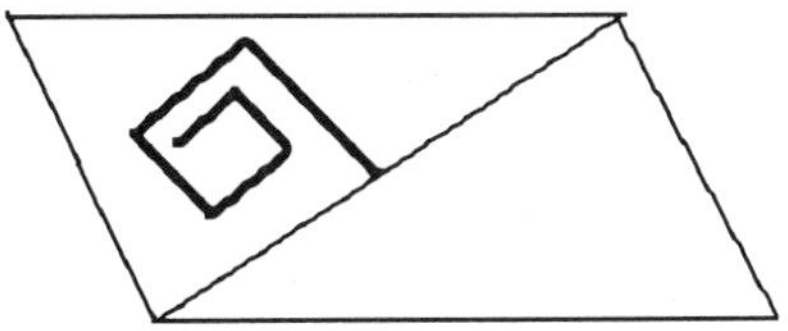

1. Draw an asymmetric motif in the chosen fundamental region.

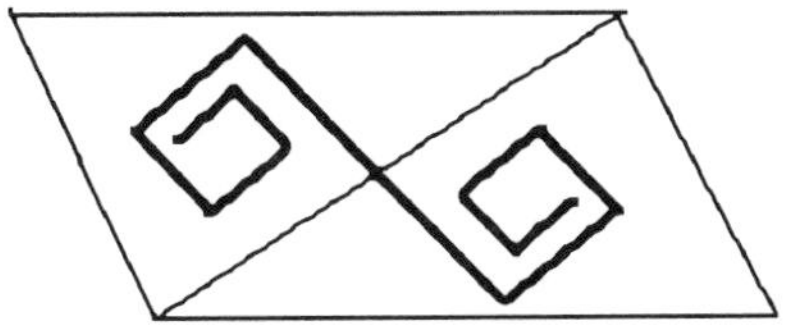

2. Add in its image under the central 1/2 turn.

3. Now put in the p2 translates of this combined motif. The guidelines may or may not be part of the pattern. They are *not* mirrors.

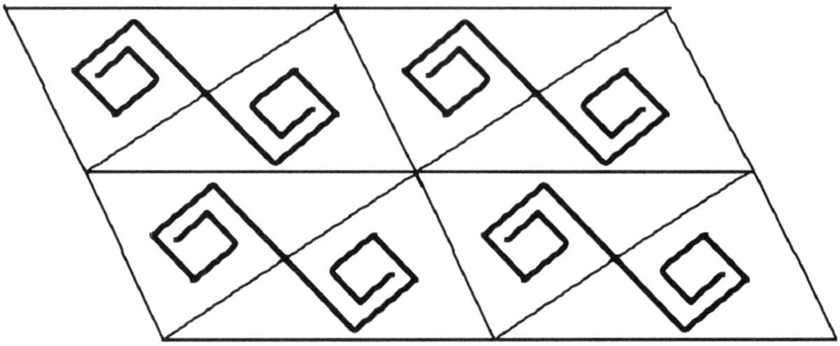

Figure 6.17 Stages in constructing a pattern of type p2 from an initial motif.

EXAMPLE 6.24 We create a pattern of type cmm, again by Construction 6.22. This time finding a fundamental region $\mathcal{F}$ takes several steps, shown in Figure 6.18, in which we start with a cell and repeatedly discard an area because it is the image of another part of the cell under a symmetry in cmm, and so is not required for $\mathcal{F}$, by (6.16). Unlike in the previous example, we may take the cell edges as mirrors. There are glides too, as well as 1/2 turns (Section 5.4).

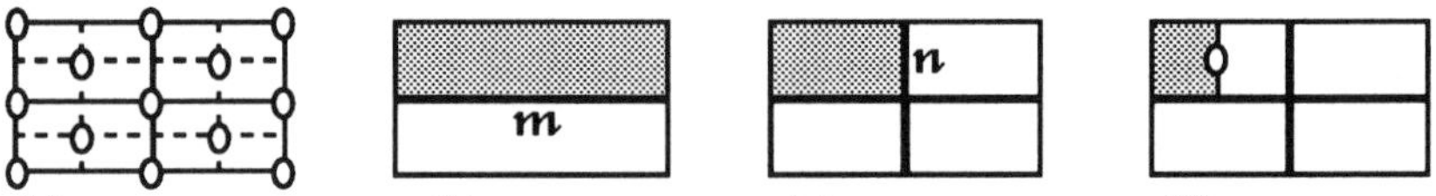

(a) (b) (c) (d)

Figure 6.18 (a) The symmetries of cmm. In cutting down the cell to a fundamental region we discard (b) the lower (white) half of the cell since it is the image of the shaded half under the mirror m, (c) the right half of the cell because of mirror n, (d) another 1/8 'th because of the 1/2 turn shown.

The shaded area (d) of Figure 6.18 is a fundamental region $\mathcal{F}$, since it cannot be further subdivided by symmetries of cmm (Condition (6.16)), and its images fill the cell

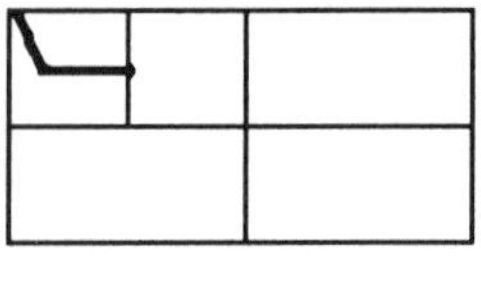

(without overlap) and hence the whole plane after translations are applied (Condition (6.15)). Now we put a simple motif M = 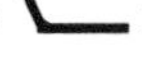 in $\mathcal{F}$ and rebuild the cell, working back the way we came, and including the motif in each image of $\mathcal{F}$.

Rebuilding the cell

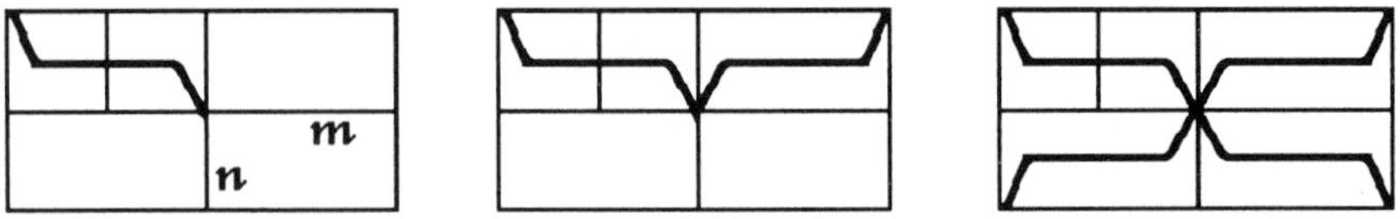

Apply the 1/2 turn reflect in mirror n reflect in mirror m

And finally....

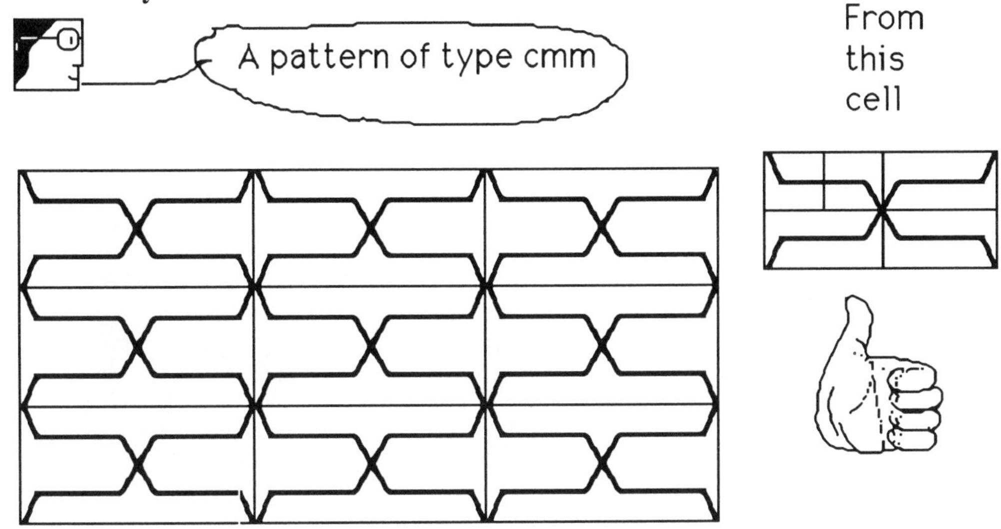

Figure 6.19 Building a cmm type pattern. 1: draw motif in fundamental region, 2: fill the cell, 3: tile the plane.

REMARKS 6.25

(i) As in Examples 6.23 and 6.24 above, it often helps to create a pleasing result if the motif is in contact with the boundary of the fundamental region.

(ii) There are many possible choices of fundamental region, and in choosing a succession of symmetries in G to reduce the cell to a fundamental region, we have in fact found a set of generators for G. A diagram of the configuration of symmetries around a cell, as in Sections 5.2 to 5.6, enables us to assess the choices. For a given effect, some may be more convenient than others.

1	2	3	4
5	6	7	8

Figure 6.20 Eight congruent choices of $\mathcal{F}$ in Example 6.24.

Convenient generators are the horizontal and vertical mirrors crossing the cell, as in Example 6.24, together with a suitable choice of one of the four half turns at a point P interior to the cell. One way this can work is shown below.

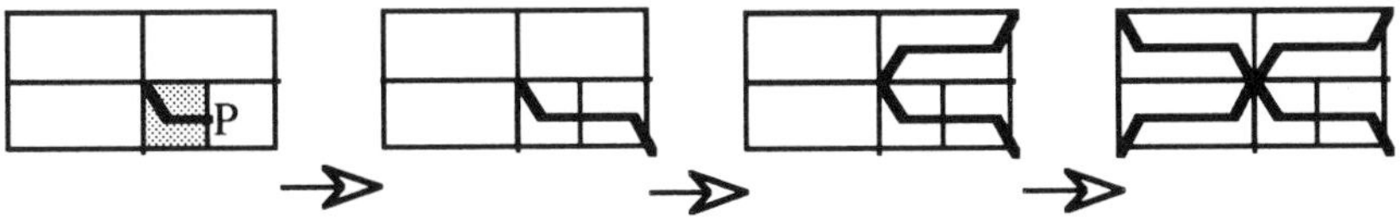

Figure 6.21 Reconstruction of cell contents from fundamental region 7.

(iii) The fundamental region emphatically need not be a parallelogram, or even a polygon. See for example Figure 1.2, an Escher-like picture of type pg in which this region may be taken to be one bird (cf. Escher (1989), p. 30). For a non-polygonal cell, see the p1 pattern in Figure 6.14.

(iv) By trying out various submotifs it is not unusual to hit on an Escher-type dovetailing that we did not design. This occurred, to the good fortune of the present writer, in Figure 6.22, in which the submotif was a roughly 'mouse-drawn' bird, shaded in black.

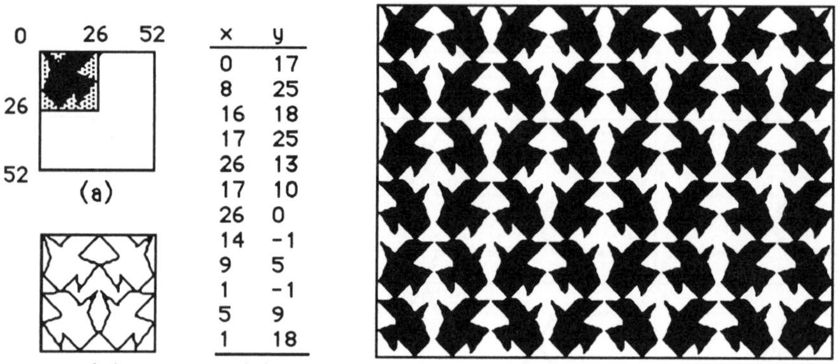

(b)

x	y
0	17
8	25
16	18
17	25
26	13
17	10
26	0
14	-1
9	5
1	-1
5	9
1	18

(c)

(d) Lady-birds

Figure 6.22 Stages in computer generation of a cm pattern with square cell. (a) Bird motif in fundamental region. The scale is in pixels. (b) Copies of unshaded motif filling the cell, corresponding to generators of cm. (c) Local pixel coordinates of 'moused-in' submotif. (d) The cm pattern obtained by tiling the plane with cells. Note the Chinese ladies outlined in white.

(v) To reproduce an existing pattern by the fundamental region method, we may

(a) decide on a cell,
(b) cut it down to a fundamental region $\mathfrak{F}$,
(c) note the portion of the picture contained in $\mathfrak{F}$,
(d) recreate this submotif and apply to it the group of symmetries, building up to a cell then to the plane area it is desired to cover. See Figure 6.23.

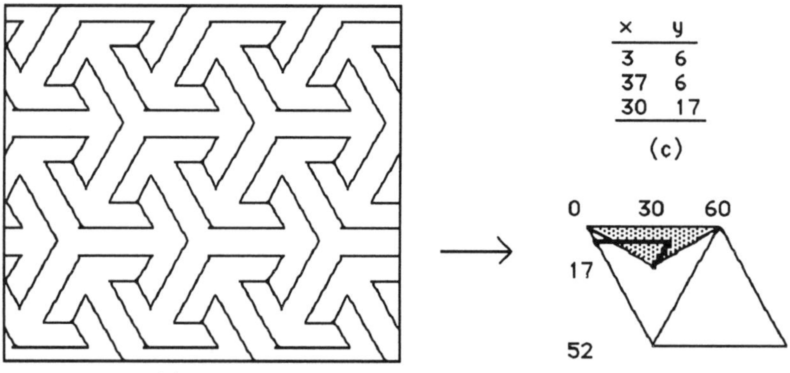

x	y
3	6
37	6
30	17

(c)

(a) (b)

Figure 6.23 Converting a plane pattern to a generating submotif. (a) A common Islamic pattern, (b) a suitable submotif, (c) its calculated coordinates.

EXERCISE Notice that in Figure 6.23 the submotif does not quite lie within the fundamental region. What is gained by this? Redraw diagram (b) to produce the same pattern (a), but this time starting from a submotif lying entirely within the fundamental region. Use your diagram to reconstruct the pattern by hand.

6.4.4 Algorithm for the 17 plane patterns

Nomenclature Coordinates are rectangular, measured in pixels or otherwise, from an origin at O, the top left hand corner of the given cell. G is the centroid of the cell, with coordinates (xg, yg). For the hexagonal net only, G_1 and G_2 are the centroids of the two equilateral triangles shown forming a cell. Their coordinates are (xg_1, yg_1), (xg_2, yg_2). On the other hand, the subscripted g_1 and g_2 are glides, with mirror position and translation component together represented by a dashed directed line segment ----> . Without the arrowhead thus: ------, only the position of the glideline is being specified, but its translation component may be taken to be one half the shortest translation symmetry along its line (see (6.12)).

How to read the table Table 6.7 below describes the algorithm by listing isometries to be applied in succession to a cell, starting with a submotif in the fundamental region, so that tiling the plane with the drawn-in cell will produce a pattern of prescribed type. This was the procedure followed in Examples 6.23 and 6.24. Thus for example "Do: R_m , R_n" in pmm means: In addition to the pixels already illuminated in the cell, turn on all their images under R_m (but don't turn any off). Then repeat this for R_n.

TABLE 6.7 (*Algorithm for the 17 plane patterns.*) Isometry sequence to fill a cell, starting with a submotif in the fundamental region.

p1

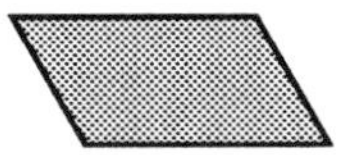

None

p2

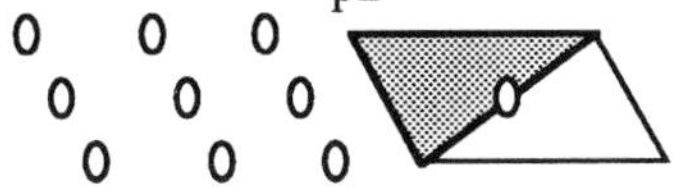

Do: $R_G(1/2)$

pm

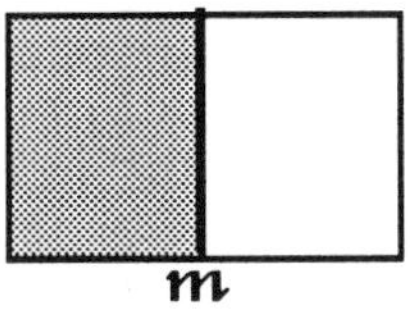

Do: R_m

pg

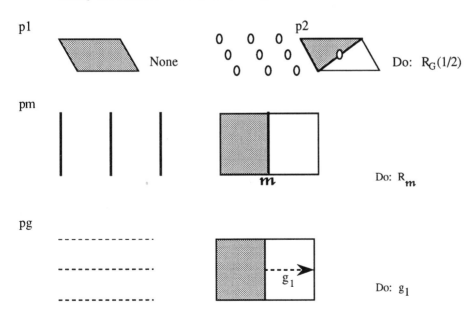

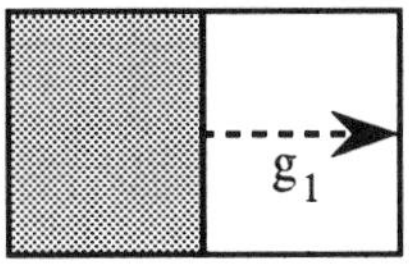

Do: g_1

pmm

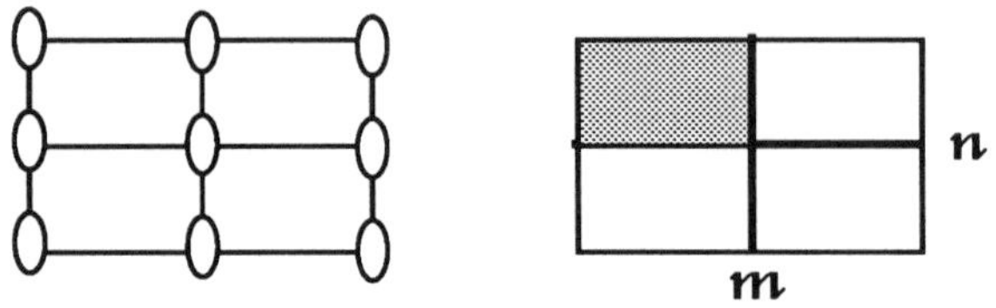

Do: R_m , R_n

pmg

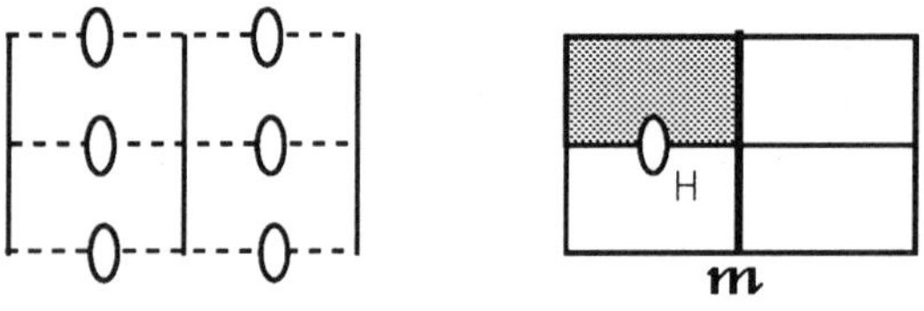

Do: $R_H(1/2)$, R_m

EXERCISE Reposition the pmg cell so that the vertices are 2-fold centres, and obtain a new fundamental region and generator system.

pgg

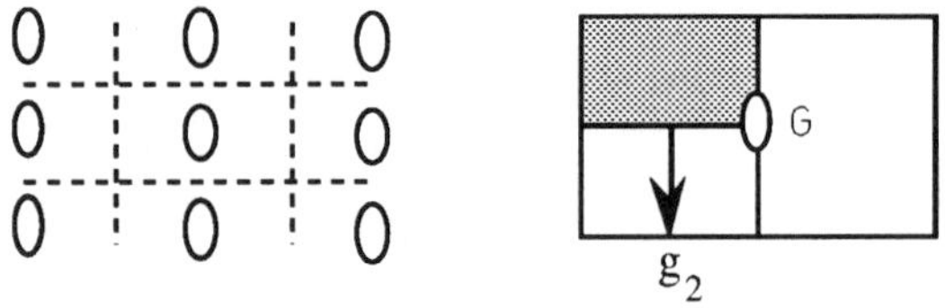

Do: g_2, $R_G(1/2)$

EXERCISE Follow through the steps by which the fundamental region is made to tile the cell in case pgg.

cm

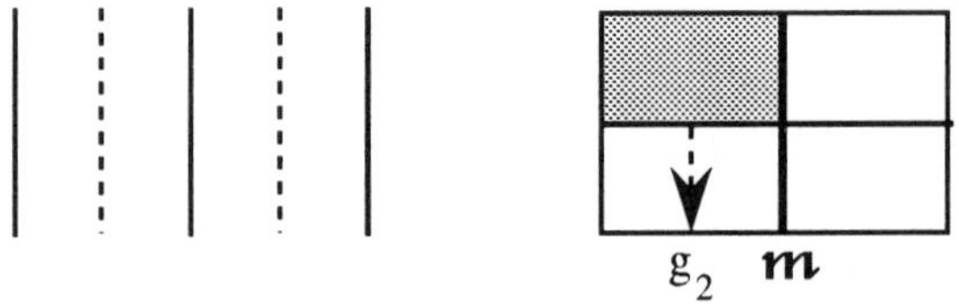

Do: g_2, R_m

cmm

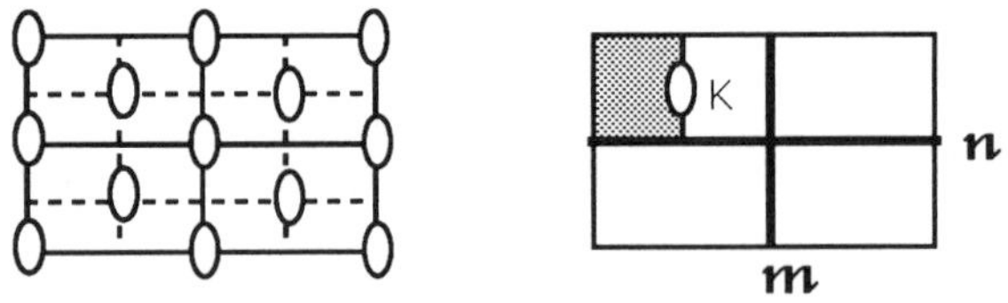

Do: $R_K(1/2)$, R_m, R_n

p4

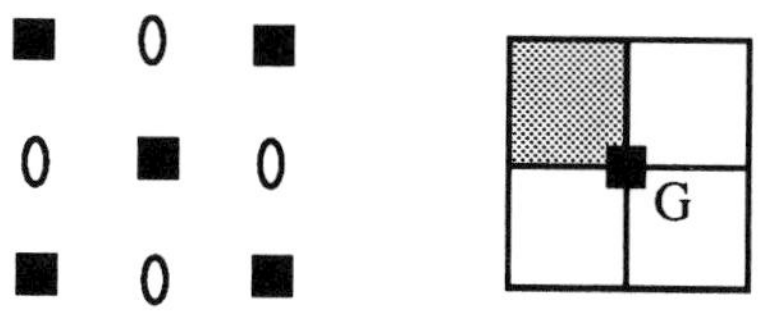

Do: $R_G(1/4)$, $R_G(1/2)$

p4m

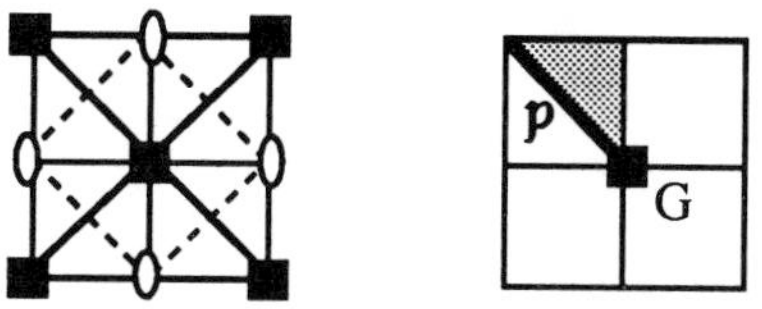

Do: R_p, $R_G(1/4)$, $R_G(1/2)$

p4g

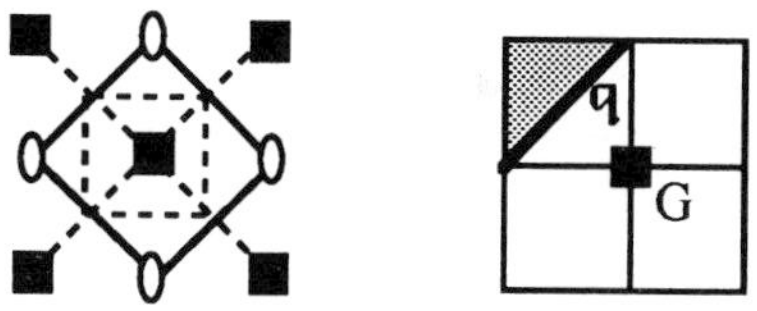

Do: R_q, $R_G(1/4)$, $R_G(1/2)$

EXERCISE Verify that the cell of p4g is rebuilt from the fundamental region as implied. Can you suggest a way to do it using a glide?

p3

Do: $R_{G_1}(1/3)$, $R_{G_1}(1/3)$, $R_{G_2}(1/3)$, $R_{G_2}(1/3)$

p3m1

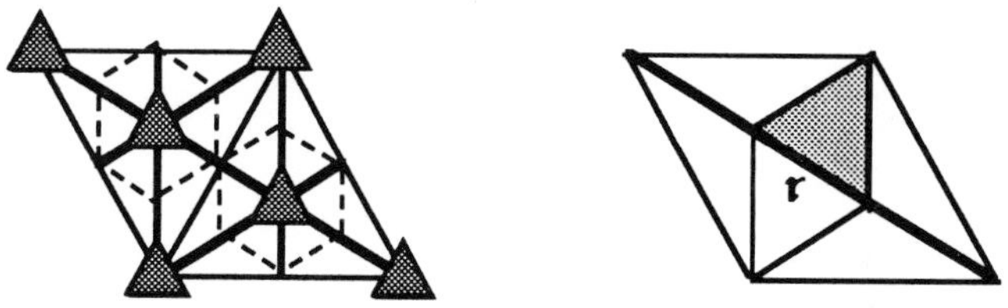

Do: R_r then [*as for* p3] $R_{G_1}(1/3)$, $R_{G_1}(1/3)$, $R_{G_2}(1/3)$, $R_{G_2}(1/3)$

p31m

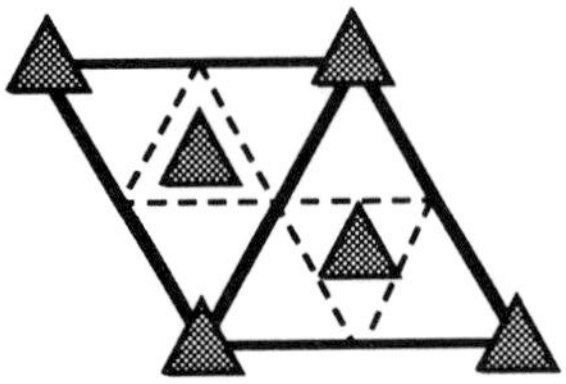

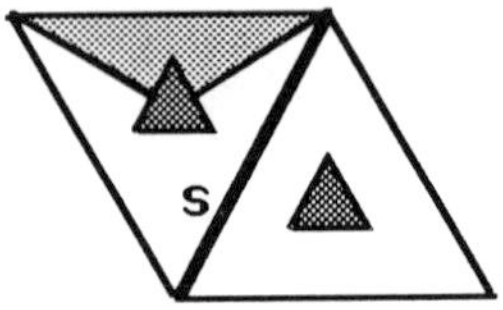

Do: R_S then [*as for p3*] $R_{G_1}(1/3)$, $R_{G_1}(1/3)$, $R_{G_2}(1/3)$, $R_{G_2}(1/3)$

p6

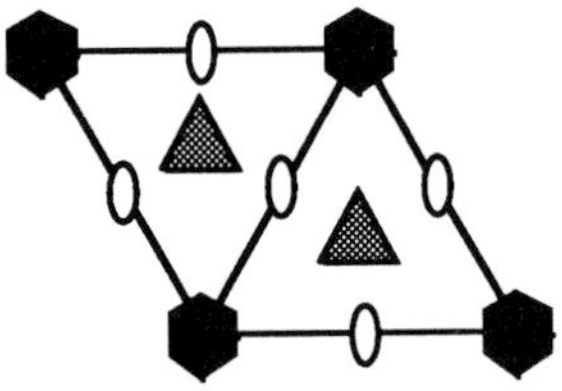

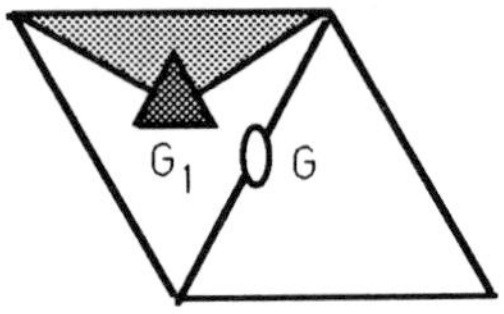

Do: $R_{G_1}(1/3)$, $R_{G_1}(1/3)$, $R_G(1/2)$

p6m

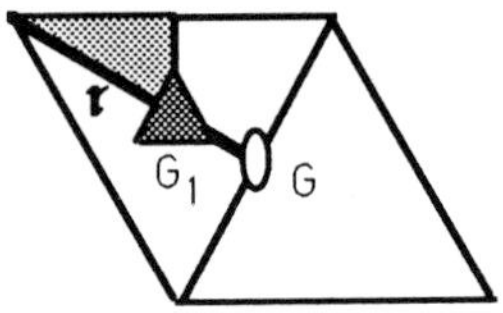

Do: $R_{\mathfrak{t}}$ then [*as for p6*] $R_{G_1}(1/3)$, $R_{G_1}(1/3)$, $R_G(1/2)$

EXERCISE Explain why no 1/6 turn is required as generator in case p6m.

Other approaches Having followed Table 6.7, the reader will be able to find other formulations of fundamental region $\mathfrak{F}$ and associated isometries f, g, h,.... If it is desirable or necessary to fill the cell by straight copies of $\mathfrak{F}$ rather than the procedure above, the way to do this may be inferred by noting that, for example: $(\mathfrak{F} \cup \mathfrak{F}^f)^g = \mathfrak{F}^g \cup \mathfrak{F}^{fg}$, so that we have the following table.

Done so far	Result
f	$\mathfrak{F} \cup \mathfrak{F}^f$
f,g	$\mathfrak{F} \cup \mathfrak{F}^f \cup \mathfrak{F}^g \cup \mathfrak{F}^{fg}$
f,g,h	$\mathfrak{F} \cup \mathfrak{F}^f \cup \mathfrak{F}^g \cup \mathfrak{F}^{fg} \cup \mathfrak{F}^h \cup \mathfrak{F}^{fh} \cup \mathfrak{F}^{gh} \cup \mathfrak{F}^{fgh}$

There may well now be redundancies, enabling us to delete some of the terms above in the unions.

EXERCISE Suppose the above method is applied. Can any terms in the union be dropped in the case of p4g or of p3?

TABLE 6.8 Coordinate form for generators of the 17 plane groups. G(xg, yg) is centre of gravity of a cell. In hexagonal net, yg = xg/√3, G_1 and G_2 have respective coordinates (2/3)(xg,yg) and (4/3)(xg,yg).

Generating isometry	First appearance	Result (x,y) —> (x',y'), x'	y'
R_m	pm	2xg-x	y
R_n	pmm	x	2yg-y
R_p	p4m	y	x
R_q	p4g	xg-y	xg-x
R_r	p3m1	(x+y√3)/2	(x√3-y)/2
R_s	p31m	(4xg-x-y√3)/2	(4yg-x√3+y)/2
$R_G(1/2)$	p2	2xg-x	2yg-y
$R_H(1/2)$	pmg	xg-x	2yg-y
$R_K(1/2)$	cmm	2xg-x	yg-y
$R_G(1/4)$	p4	y	2xg-x
g_1	pg	x+xg	2yg-y
g_2	pgg	xg-x	y+yg
$R_O(1/3)$		-(x+y√3)/2	(x√3-y)/2
$R_{G_1}(1/3)$	p3	4xg/3-(x+y√3)/2	(x√3-y)/2
$R_{G_2}(1/3)$	p3	8xg/3-(x+y√3)/2	(x√3-y)/2

NOTE: Some of the formulae above are conveniently derived by techniques found in section 7.4 : "The matrix of a plane isometry", though they could be done by a judicious combination of Theorem 2.1 and brute force. Many are straightforward, and are set as exercises.

EXERCISE Derive the formulae for R_m and $R_G(1/4)$ (hint: use Corollary 2.2).

REMARKS

1 There is a useful method of tiling the plane or higher dimensions starting from a collections of points. This is the Voronoi triangulation and has been found useful in computer graphics (see for example Dobkin, 1988).

2 In Wythoff's construction for 3-space, mirror lines become firstly the intersection of planes with the surface of a sphere (great circles). We get a fundamental region bounded by such curves and a unifying approach to the polyhedra with some degree of regularity such as the Platonic solids (cube, icosahedron, ..) and many others. The techniques cover tilings of 3-space and beyond (Coxeter 1973, 1974).

3 All this is intimately connected with the construction of 'error-correcting codes' for communications (Conway and Sloane 1988) and one may guess that it will in due course find use in computer graphics. An indication of how this might be so is found in Section 15.2.3.

EXERCISES 6

1 √ Why cannot the groups C_{12} and D_{12} be isomorphic? Give an example of two symmetry groups which are isomorphic but not equivalent (not from amongst the 17 types). See Section 2.4 and Table 6.2.

2 Write out the ten elements of D_{10} in terms of reflections R, S in mirrors at the least possible angle (see Section 2.4).

3 In a pattern of type pgg pick out symmetries which yield the elements of the point group. (cf. Example 6.11. See Section 5.7 and Exercise 1 of Chapter 5.) Do the same for one of type p3m1.

4 √ Prove that there are only three regular tilings of the plane.

5 Write a computer program to produce the solutions of Table 6.5 for Archimedean plane tilings.

6 Find a basis for the translation symmetries of the plane tiling by squares, in terms of three generating reflections R,S,T for the symmetry group.

7 This Coxeter diagram, with p = 3, q = 6, produces an Archimedean plane tiling of type (3,6,3,6) by Wythoff's construction. Apply this construction by hand up to at least six hexagons.

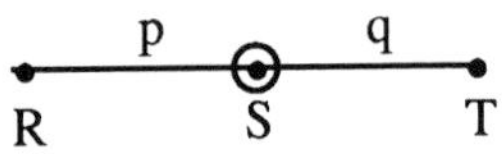

8 Obtain a tiling of type (3,4,6,4) from the Coxeter diagram shown, with p = 3, q = 6.

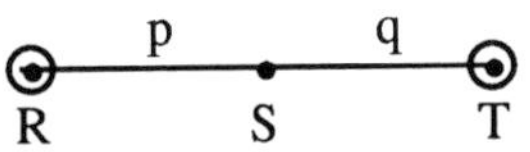

9 Obtain a plane pattern by suitable shading of one of the Archimedean tilings of Table 6.6. Which of the 17 types results? Find the plane pattern type of each example in the table.

10 Starting with the hexagonal net, design plane patterns of type (i) p6m, (ii) p3m1.

11 For each plane pattern in Examples 4.20, find a fundamental region and submotif, then regenerate the pattern. State the type. Record what you do at each stage.

12 Repeat Exercise 11 for patterns (a) to (g) in Exercise 6 of Chapter 4.

13 √ Identify the pattern type on the right. Find fundamental regions of two distinct shapes and their associated submotifs and generators. Illustrate by regenerating (enough of) each pattern by hand.

14 √ Referring to Table 6.7, type pmg, reposition the basepoint at a 2-fold centre. Can you find a fundamental region $\mathfrak{F}$ within the cell. If so, give at least one possible list of symmetries with their images of $\mathfrak{F}$ which tile the cell. Does this work for pgg with basepoint at the intersection of two glidelines?

15 For one pattern type in each net type, use Table 6.7 to design a plane pattern, using the same submotif in the fundamental region for each case.

16 Extend Exercise 15 to all 17 types.

17 Write a computer program implementing the method of Table 6.7 for pattern type cmm, in which the user specifies what lies inside the fundamental region.

18 Extend Exercise 17 to all patterns with rectangular cell.

19 Derive at least four lines of Table 6.8.

20 Project: Implement all procedures of Table 6.7.

Chapter 7 MATRIX AND VECTOR ALGEBRA

7.1 Vectors and handedness

This section is something like an appendix. The reader may wish to scan quickly through or refer back later for various formulae and notations. We reviewed vectors in the plane in Section 1.2.1. Soon we will see how the vector properties of having direction and length are even more useful in 3-space. The results of 1.2.1 still hold, but vectors now have three components rather than two.

7.1.1 Recapitulation - vectors

A *vector* **u** consists of a magnitude |**u**|, also called the *length* of **u**, and a direction, so is representable by any directed line segment <u>AB</u> with the same length and direction. Note that |**u**| = |AB|. Vectors may be *added* 'nose to tail' as indicated in Figure 7.1. Also, if α is a real number, often called in this context a *scalar*, we can form the *product* α**u** : scale the length of **u** by a factor |α|, and reverse direction if α is negative. This is a very convenient system, allowing us to write -α**a** for (-α)**a**, -**a** for (-1)**a**, and **a**/α for (1/α)**a**, and to define subtraction by **a** - **b** = **a** + (-**b**) (cf. Figure 1.7).

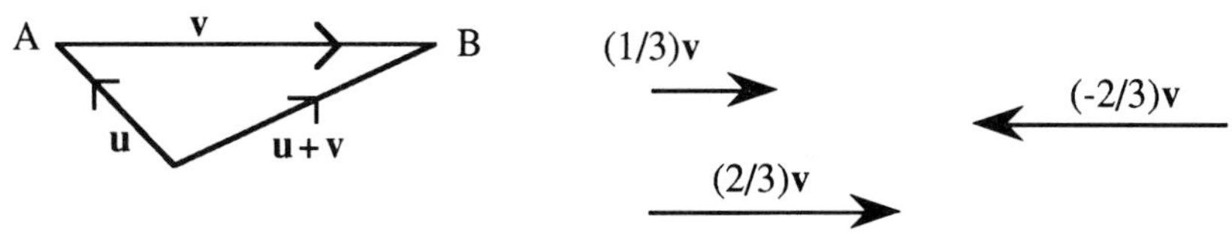

Figure 7.1 Vector addition, and multipllying a vector by a scalar.

We use **0** for the anomalous vector with length 0 and direction undefined, and refer to vector **a** as being nonzero if $\mathbf{a} \neq \mathbf{0}$. Two vectors are (by definition) equal if they have the same magnitude and direction. We follow the custom of writing $\mathbf{a} = \underline{PQ} = \underline{RS}$ to mean that the length and direction of all three are the same, although $\underline{PQ}$ and $\underline{RS}$ have the additional property of a position in space (not necessarily the same position). Now we give a simple definition and remark with far-reaching usefulness in the sequel. Note that in forming $|\mathbf{a}|/|\mathbf{a}|$ we are scaling the length $|\mathbf{a}|$ of **a** by a factor $1/|\mathbf{a}|$, so the new length is 1.

DEFINITION 7.1 A *unit vector* is a vector of length 1.

*If **a** is any nonzero vector then* $\mathbf{a}/|\mathbf{a}|$ *is a unit vector.* (7.1)

7.1.2 Recapitulation - coordinate axes

In ordinary Euclidean 3-space, three mutually orthogonal (= perpendicular) unit vectors **i**, **j**, **k**, starting from a chosen origin O, define coordinate axes as in Figure 7.2. A directional convention we will normally use is that vectors arrowed down and to the left point out of the paper towards the reader.

Figure 7.2 How coordinates (x,y,z) define the position of a point P, starting from the origin. Vector **i** points towards the reader, with **j**,**k** in the plane of the paper.

This means that any point P has unique *coordinates* x, y, z (with respect to **i**, **j**, **k**), defined by

$$\underline{OP} = x\mathbf{i} + y\mathbf{j} + z\mathbf{k}. \tag{7.2}$$

We use (x,y,z) to mean, according to context,

1. The point P,
2. The *position vector* $\underline{OP}$ of P,
3. Any vector with the same magnitude and direction as $\underline{OP}$.

In 2, 3 we call x,y,z the *components* of the vector with respect to **i**,**j**,**k**, which itself is called an *orthonormal set*, meaning that **i,j,k** are *orthogonal* in the sense of being mutually perpendicular, and furthermore have length one. They are also called a *basis* for 3-space because any vector is a unique linear combination (7.2) of them. To add vectors, we add corresponding components. To multiply by a scalar, we multiply each component by that scalar.

NOTATION 7.2 The point A will have position vector **a**, with components (a_1,a_2,a_3). Similarly for other letters, except P(x,y,z). For the distance |OP| we have

$$|OP|^2 = x^2 + y^2 + z^2, \text{ by Pythagoras,}$$

hence
$$|AB| = \sqrt{(a_1 - b_1)^2 + (a_2 - b_2)^2 + (a_3 - b_3)^2}\,. \tag{7.3}$$

DIRECTION COSINES For general OP these are the cosines of the angles α, β, γ between OP and the positive directions on the x, y, and z axes. Thus with $|OP| = r$ we have $x = r\cos\alpha$, $y = r\cos\beta$, $z = r\cos\gamma$.

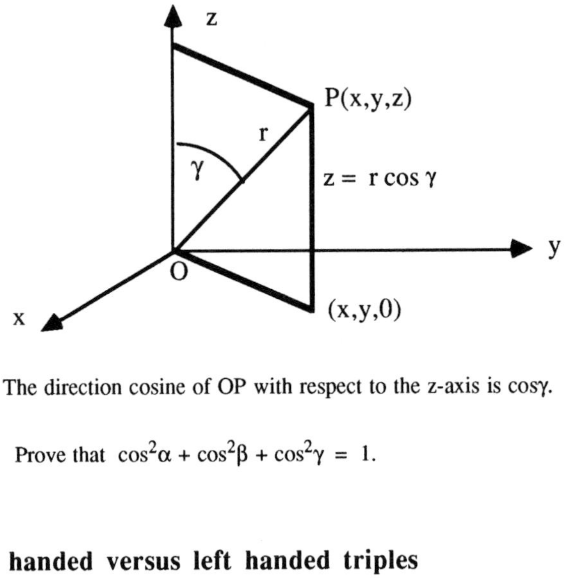

Figure 7.3 The direction cosine of OP with respect to the z-axis is cosγ.

EXERCISE Prove that $\cos^2\alpha + \cos^2\beta + \cos^2\gamma = 1$.

7.1.3 Right handed versus left handed triples

In Section 1.2.3 we used the idea of the sense (clockwise or anticlockwise) of a non-collinear triple of points in the plane. Here we investigate its analogy in 3-space. By convention **i,j,k** is always a *right handed* system or triple, as in the definition below.

DEFINITION 7.3 Vectors **a,b,c** are *coplanar* if the points O,A,B,C are coplanar. An ordered triple **a,b,c** of non-coplanar vectors is *right handed* if:

> *in plane OAB viewed from C, the rotation about O that moves A to B by the shorter route is anticlockwise, (ie the sense of OAB is anticlockwise),*

otherwise **a,b,c** is a left handed triple (NB. **a,b,c** need not be orthogonal in this definition).

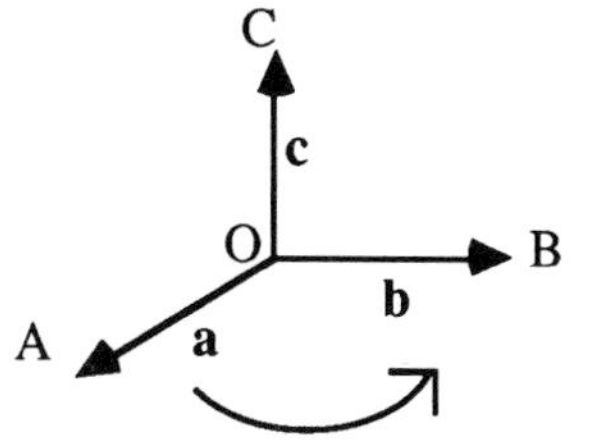

Right handed: **a,b,c** **b,c,a** **c,a,b**
Left handed : **c,b,a** **a,c,b** **b,a,c**

Figure 7.4 Right handed versus left handed triples, with **a** towards the reader.

*We see that if **a,b,c** is right handed then so are the cyclic shifts of this ordering, namely **b,c,a** and **c,a,b**. The other possible orderings, the reverses of the above, are then the left handed ones.*

RIGHT HAND CORKSCREW RULE. The righthandedness condition is equivalent to the statement: **c** points to the same side of plane OAB as the direction of motion of a right handed screw placed at O perpendicular to this plane, and turning OA towards OB.

With a computer screen in mind it is quite usual to take our **b,c** as defining respectively x,y axes, in the plane of the page/screen. Then the z-axis points towards the reader in a right handed system and into the page/screen in the left handed case.

EXERCISE Is the triple **a,b,c** right or left handed, where **a** = (0,0,-1), **b** = (-1,1,0), and **c** = (1,0,2)? What if the order of **a,b** is interchanged? [Answers may be checked from Theorem 7.31.]

7.1.4 The scalar product

A systematic and short way to calculate from vector components both (1) the angles between vectors and (2) whether a triple is right handed, flows from the following definition of *scalar product*, in which a number is associated with a pair of vectors.

DEFINITION 7.4 The *scalar* (or *inner*) *product* of vectors **u** and **v** is

$$\mathbf{u.v} = u_1v_1 + u_2v_2 + u_3v_3. \tag{7.4}$$

Other notations are (**u,v**), <**u,v**>, (**u**|**v**). The angle properties of this product stem from (7.5) to (7.7) following.

$$\mathbf{u.u} = |\mathbf{u}|^2. \tag{7.5}$$

*If ϕ is the angle between nonzero vectors **u**, **v** (that is, the one satisfying $0 \le \phi \le \pi$) then*

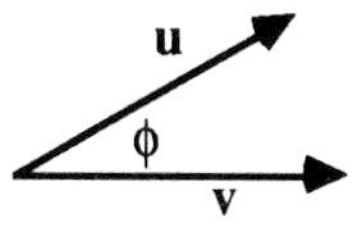

$$\cos\phi = \mathbf{u.v}/|\mathbf{u}||\mathbf{v}|. \tag{7.6A}$$

*The component formula: a vector **u** has components **u.i**, **u.j**, **u.k**, which are the direction cosines if **u** is a unit vector.* (7.6B)

$$2\mathbf{u.v} = |\mathbf{u}|^2 + |\mathbf{v}|^2 - |\mathbf{u}-\mathbf{v}|^2, \tag{7.7}$$

expressing the inner product in terms of distances.

Proof (7.5) is the trivial but useful observation that $\mathbf{u.u} = u_1^2 + u_2^2 + u_3^2$, whilst (7.6) comes from the Cosine Rule in triangle OUV below and (7.7) is a direct calculation, as follows:

$$\begin{aligned} 2|\mathbf{u}||\mathbf{v}|\cos\phi &= |\mathbf{u}|^2 + |\mathbf{v}|^2 - |\mathbf{u}-\mathbf{v}|^2 \quad \text{(Cosine Rule)} \\ &= (u_1^2 + u_2^2 + u_3^2) + (v_1^2 + v_2^2 + v_3^2) \\ &\quad - (u_1-v_1)^2 - (u_2-v_2)^2 - (u_3-v_3)^2 \\ &= 2u_1v_1 + 2u_2v_2 + 2u_3v_3. \end{aligned}$$

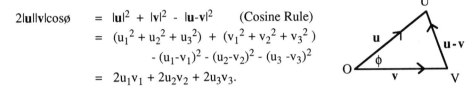

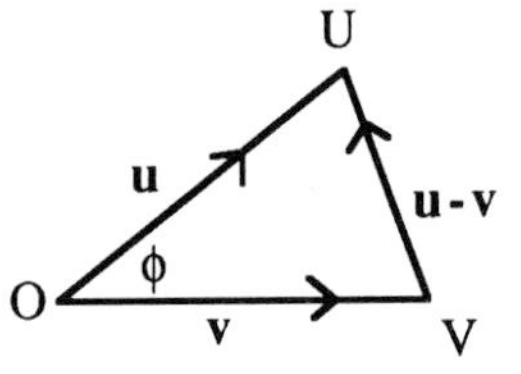

The deduction (7.6B) about components is typified by $u_1 = |\mathbf{u}|\cos\alpha$ (where α is the angle between **u** and the x-axis) $= |\mathbf{i}||\mathbf{u}|\cos\alpha$ (as $|\mathbf{i}| = 1$) $= \mathbf{u.i}$ (by (7.6A)). Thus, if $|\mathbf{u}| = 1$ then $u_1 = \cos\alpha$.

BASIC PROPERTIES Definition 7.4 of scalar product **u.v** was given in coordinates, but by (7.7) it is independent of the choice of **i,j,k**, even if we should choose a left handed system. The basic commutative and distributive laws stated below are calculated from (7.4).

$$\begin{aligned} \mathbf{v.u} &= \mathbf{u.v} \\ \mathbf{u.(v+w)} &= \mathbf{u.v} + \mathbf{u.w} \\ \mathbf{u.}(\alpha\mathbf{v}) &= \alpha(\mathbf{u.v}) = (\alpha\mathbf{u})\mathbf{.v} \end{aligned} \tag{7.8}$$

*THEOREM 7.5 (a) Two nonzero vectors **u,v** .are perpendicular if and only if **u.v** = 0.*
(b) Three vectors $\mathbf{e}_1, \mathbf{e}_2, \mathbf{e}_3$ are mutually orthogonal unit vectors (form an orthonormal set) if and only if

$$\mathbf{e}_i.\mathbf{e}_k = \delta_{ik}, \tag{7.9}$$

where δ_{ik} is the Kronecker delta, defined as 1 if i = k, otherwise 0.

Proof The argument is simple but important. We use the notation of (7.6).
(a): $\mathbf{u.v} = 0 \Leftrightarrow \cos\phi = 0 \Leftrightarrow \phi = \pi/2$ (i.e. **u** and **v** are perpendicular).
(b): (7.9) combines two statements. (i) $\mathbf{e}_i.\mathbf{e}_i = 1$. That is, $|\mathbf{e}_i|^2 = 1$, or equivalently $\mathbf{e}_i$ is a unit vector. (ii) $\mathbf{e}_i.\mathbf{e}_k = 0$ if $i \neq k$. That is, the three vectors are mutually perpendicular.

Notice that $\mathbf{e}_1, \mathbf{e}_2, \mathbf{e}_3$ play the same role as the orthonormal **i,j,k**. This often helps notationally, as in Chapter 8. Further results about vector products must be postponed until we have reviewed matrices in the next section.

EXERCISE Show that the vectors **a** = (1,2,3) and **b** = (6,3,-4) are perpendicular (Theorem 7.5). Find the angle between a diagonal OA of a cube and an adjacent face diagonal by using suitable coordinates for A [Use (7.6).]

7.1.5 A quick trip through n-space

Though 3-space is our concern in this chapter and the next, there are advantages in considering vectors with more than three components, particularly of the type (x,y,z,1) to be introduced in Section 8.5 for isometries of $\mathbf{R}^3$ which include translation. The current Section, 7.1.5, will be more abstract than most, yet also serves as an introduction to general abstract vector spaces, as well as providing a necessary basis for our particular cases. For other applications of greater than three dimensions to computer graphics, see for example Avis and Doskas (1988).

We define $\mathbf{R}^n$ to be the set of all n-tuples $\mathbf{x} = (x_1, x_2, \ldots, x_n)$, where we call $\mathbf{x}$ both a *vector with components* x_i, and a *point with coordinates* x_i, as in the case n = 3. The *unit sphere* in n-space is $S^{n-1} = \{\mathbf{x} \in \mathbf{R}^n : |\mathbf{x}| = 1\}$. Thus S^1 is a circle in the plane and S^2 the usual sphere in 3-space. We perform the same calculations with coordinates as before, for example adding vectors and multiplying by a scalar. The result is that (7.1) to (7.9) extend to $\mathbf{R}^n$ with the proviso that the angle between vectors **u**, **v** is now *defined* by (7.6A): $\cos\phi = \mathbf{u}.\mathbf{v}/|\mathbf{u}||\mathbf{v}|$. Setting n = 3, we obtain the usual model of our three dimensional world. However, proving the component formula (7.6B) is not so simple, and takes us, not unhelpfully into the idea of n as the dimension of $\mathbf{R}^n$.

DEFINITION 7.6 Vectors $\mathbf{u}_1, \mathbf{u}_2, \ldots, \mathbf{u}_k$ in $\mathbf{R}^n$ are called *(linearly) dependent* if some *linear combination* $\lambda_1\mathbf{u}_1 + \lambda_2\mathbf{u}_2 \ldots + \lambda_k\mathbf{u}_k$ equals $\mathbf{0}$ (i.e. the *zero vector* (0,0, ... ,0)), where not all the coefficients λ_i are zero. In this case any vector with nonzero coefficient, say $\lambda_1 \neq 0$, equals a linear combination of the rest, $\mathbf{u}_1 = (-\lambda_2/\lambda_1)\mathbf{u}_2 + \ldots + (-\lambda_k/\lambda_1)\mathbf{u}_k$. The $\mathbf{u}_i$ are called *independent* if they are not dependent.

THEOREM 7.7 Any n+1 vectors in $\mathbf{R}^n$ *are linearly dependent.*

Proof We use the Principle of Mathematical Induction. That is, if the result holds for n=1, and its truth for n = k implies its truth for n = k+1 for k = 1,2,3, ..., then the result holds for all n ≥1. Proceeding with the proof we check the case n=1: if a, b are two numbers then there are coefficients λ, μ, not both zero, such that λa+μb = 0. This is almost trivial, for if a=b=0 we may take λ=μ=1, whilst if a ≠0 say, then λ=1, μ = -a/b will do. So suppose that Theorem 7.7 is true for some positive integer n=k. We are to deduce the truth for n = k+1. We demonstrate the argument with k=2, the general case being no harder. Write the k+1 (= 3) vectors in a column thus:

$$\mathbf{u}_1 = (a_1, a_2, a_3),$$
$$\mathbf{u}_2 = (b_1, b_2, b_3),$$
$$\mathbf{u}_3 = (c_1, c_2, c_3).$$

Since linear dependence is unaffected by reordering the components of each vector in the same way, we may assume a_1 is nonzero (relabel $\mathbf{u}_1, \mathbf{u}_2, \mathbf{u}_3$ too if necessary). Then the new vectors $\mathbf{v}_2 = \mathbf{u}_2 + (-b_1/a_1)\mathbf{u}_1$ and $\mathbf{v}_3 = \mathbf{u}_3 + (-c_1/a_1)\mathbf{u}_1$ have first coordinate zero, so by the assumed truth of Theorem 7.7 for k = 2 there are coefficients λ, μ not both zero such that $\lambda\mathbf{v}_2 + \mu\mathbf{v}_3 = \mathbf{0}$, which simplifies to $\lambda\mathbf{u}_2 + \mu\mathbf{u}_3 + \nu\mathbf{u}_1 = \mathbf{0}$ with the scalar ν given by $\nu = (-\lambda b_1 - \mu c_1)/a_1$, showing that $\mathbf{u}_1, \mathbf{u}_2, \mathbf{u}_3$ are dependent.

THEOREM 7.8 If $\mathbf{u}_1, \mathbf{u}_2, \ldots, \mathbf{u}_n$ *are linearly independent vectors of* $\mathbf{R}^n$ *then they form a basis of* $\mathbf{R}^n$*, that is, any* **a** *in* $\mathbf{R}^n$ *is a unique linear combination of* $\mathbf{u}_1, \mathbf{u}_2, \ldots, \mathbf{u}_n$.

Proof The n+1 vectors $\mathbf{a}, \mathbf{u}_1, \mathbf{u}_2, \dots, \mathbf{u}_n$ are dependent by Theorem 7.7, so we have that $\lambda_0\mathbf{a} + \lambda_1\mathbf{u}_1 + \lambda_2\mathbf{u}_2 + \dots + \lambda_n\mathbf{u}_n = \mathbf{0}$ with not all coefficients zero. In fact λ_0 is nonzero, else the $\mathbf{u}_i$ would be dependent. Thus $\mathbf{a}$ is some combination of the vectors $\mathbf{u}_i$. Furthermore, the combination is unique, because $\mathbf{a} = \Sigma\lambda_i\mathbf{u}_i = \Sigma\,\lambda_i'\mathbf{u}_i$ implies $\Sigma(\lambda_i - \lambda_i')\mathbf{u}_i = \mathbf{0}$ and hence, since the $\mathbf{u}_i$ are independent, each coefficient $\lambda_i - \lambda_i'$ is zero, or $\lambda_i = \lambda_i'$.

DEFINITION 7.9 The *dimension* of a general abstract vector space (see Whitelaw, 1988) is the number of linearly independent vectors required for a basis, which Theorem 7.8 shows to be n for $\mathbf{R}^n$, as we would hope. An *orthonormal basis* is by definition a basis which is an orthonormal set.

THEOREM 7.10 **(The component formula)** *Suppose that the n vectors $\boldsymbol{e}_1, \boldsymbol{e}_2, \dots, \boldsymbol{e}_n$ in $\boldsymbol{R}^n$ are an orthonormal set, that is, $\boldsymbol{e}_i.\boldsymbol{e}_k = \delta_{ik}$ (=1 if i=k, else zero). Then the $\boldsymbol{e}_i$ form an orthonormal basis of $\boldsymbol{R}^n$, and any vector $\boldsymbol{a}$ in $\boldsymbol{R}^n$ has components $a_i = \boldsymbol{a}.\boldsymbol{e}_i$ with respect to this basis. That is, $\boldsymbol{a} = a_1\boldsymbol{e}_1 + \dots + a_n\boldsymbol{e}_n$.*

Proof Firstly, the $\mathbf{e}_i$ are independent. For suppose $\lambda_1\mathbf{e}_1 + \lambda_2\mathbf{e}_2 + \dots + \lambda_k\mathbf{e}_k = \mathbf{0}$. Take the scalar product of each side with $\mathbf{e}_1$, say. Then $\mathbf{e}_1.(\lambda_1\mathbf{e}_1 + \lambda_2\mathbf{e}_2 + .. + \lambda_k\mathbf{e}_k) = \mathbf{e}_1.\mathbf{0}$, which gives $\lambda_1\mathbf{e}_1.\mathbf{e}_1 = 0$ since $\mathbf{e}_1.\mathbf{e}_i = 0$ if $i \neq 1$. Thus λ_1 is zero, and similarly so are the other λ_i. So the e_i cannot be dependent. Hence by Theorem 7.8, $\mathbf{a} = a_1\mathbf{e}_1 + \dots + a_n\mathbf{e}_n$ for unique coefficients a_i. Take the scalar product of each side with $\mathbf{e}_1$, say. We obtain $\mathbf{a}.\mathbf{e}_1 = (a_1\mathbf{e}_1 + \dots + a_n\mathbf{e}_n).\mathbf{e}_1$ which (again since $\mathbf{e}_1.\mathbf{e}_i = 0$ if $i \neq 1$) gives $\mathbf{a}.\mathbf{e}_1 = a_1\mathbf{e}_1.\mathbf{e}_1 = a_1$ as required. Similarly for the other coefficients a_i.

DEFINITION 7.11 The coordinates x_i of the point $\mathbf{x} = (x_1, x_2, \dots, x_n)$ are the components of $\mathbf{x}$ w.r.t. the ***standard basis*** $\mathbf{e}_1, \mathbf{e}_2, \dots, \mathbf{e}_n$, where $\mathbf{e}_i$ has a 1 in the i'th place and zeros everywhere else. That is, $\mathbf{x} = x_1\mathbf{e}_1 + x_2\mathbf{e}_2 + \dots + x_n\mathbf{e}_n$ with $\mathbf{e}_1 = (1,0,\dots,0)$, $\mathbf{e}_2 = (0,1,0,\dots,)$, $\mathbf{e}_n = (0,0,\dots 0,1)$. Note that the $\mathbf{e}_i$ are used to refer to basis vectors generally, so cannot be assumed to be the standard basis unless explicitly defined to be, as in this paragraph. In ordinary 3-space, whatever orthonormal basis **i, j, k** we choose is the standard basis by definition, for in coordinate terms $\mathbf{i} = (1,0,0)$, $\mathbf{j} = (0,1,0)$, $\mathbf{k} = (0,0,1)$.

EXAMPLE One orthonormal basis of $\mathbf{R}^4$ is $\mathbf{e}_1 = (1/2)(1,1,1,1)$, $\mathbf{e}_2 = (1/2)(1,1,-1,-1)$, $\mathbf{e}_3 = (1/2)(1,-1,1,-1)$, $\mathbf{e}_4 = (1/2)(1,-1,-1,1)$. The components of $\mathbf{a} = (1,2,3,4)$ with respect to this basis are $\mathbf{a}.\mathbf{e}_1 = (1/2)(1+2+3+4) = 5$, $\mathbf{a}.\mathbf{e}_2 = (1/2)(1+2-3-4) = -2$, $\mathbf{a}.\mathbf{e}_3 = (1/2)(1-2+3-4) = -1$, $\mathbf{a}.\mathbf{e}_4 = (1/2)(1-2-3+4) = 0$. So in fact $\mathbf{a}$ is a linear combination of just the first three basis vectors.

EXERCISE Express the vector (2,1,0,1) as a linear combination of the basis vectors in the example above. Check your answer.

REMARK 7.12 The following result is used in various forms throughout the book. See e.g. metric spaces in Chapter 11, address space in Chapter 15, and complex numbers in Chapters 9, 16. It states: *for vectors $\boldsymbol{x}, \boldsymbol{y}$ in $\mathbf{R}^n$ we have* (a) $\mathbf{x}.\mathbf{y} \le |\mathbf{x}||\mathbf{y}|$, *and therefore* (b) $|\mathbf{x} + \mathbf{y}| \le |\mathbf{x}| + |\mathbf{y}|$, *and* (c) $|\mathbf{x} - \mathbf{y}| \le |\mathbf{x} - \mathbf{z}| + |\mathbf{z} - \mathbf{y}|$, the last called the *triangle inequality* because it states that (not only in the plane but in n-space) the length of one side of a triangle does not exceed the sum of the lengths of the other two sides.

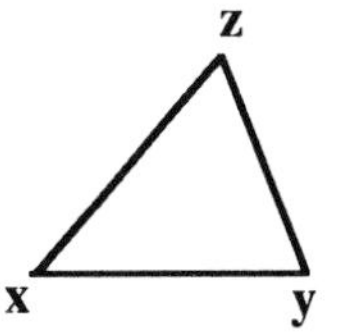

Proof For all values of a real number t we have the inequality $0 \le (t\mathbf{x} + \mathbf{y}).(t\mathbf{x} + \mathbf{y}) = |\mathbf{x}|^2t^2 + 2(\mathbf{x}.\mathbf{y})t + |\mathbf{y}|^2$, by the formula $\mathbf{c}.\mathbf{c} = |\mathbf{c}|^2$ and (7.8). Since this quadratic in t can never be negative, it cannot have two distinct roots

$$-\mathbf{x}.\mathbf{y} \pm \sqrt{(\mathbf{x}.\mathbf{y})^2 - |\mathbf{x}|^2|\mathbf{y}|^2},$$

and so $(\mathbf{x}.\mathbf{y})^2 \le |\mathbf{x}|^2|\mathbf{y}|^2$. Because $|\mathbf{x}|^2 |\mathbf{y}|^2 \ge 0$, we may infer assertion (a). Furthermore, (b) is equivalent to $|\mathbf{x} + \mathbf{y}|^2 \le |\mathbf{x}|^2 + |\mathbf{y}|^2 + 2|\mathbf{x}||\mathbf{y}|$, or, by the formula $|\mathbf{c}|^2 = \mathbf{c}.\mathbf{c}$, to Part (a). Finally, $|\mathbf{x} - \mathbf{y}| = |(\mathbf{x} - \mathbf{z}) + (\mathbf{z} - \mathbf{y})| \le |\mathbf{x} - \mathbf{z}| + |\mathbf{z} - \mathbf{y}|$, by (b).

7.2 Matrices and determinants

7.2.1 Matrices

Let $A = \begin{bmatrix} a_{11} & a_{12} & \cdots & a_{1n} \\ a_{21} & a_{22} & \cdots & a_{2n} \\ \cdots & \cdots & \cdots & \cdots \\ a_{m1} & a_{m2} & \cdots & a_{mn} \end{bmatrix}$, an array of m rows of numbers arranged in n columns.

Then we say A is the *m x n matrix* $[a_{ik}]$, and call a_{ik} the ik'th *entry*, or *element*. Thus the rows of A are indexed by the first subscript, i, and the columns by the second, k. Especially in proving results, it is sometimes useful to write $(A)_{ik}$ for a_{ik}. Equality of matrices, say A = B, means that A and B have the same *type* m x n (i.e., the same number of rows and columns) and that $a_{ik} = b_{ik}$ for each pair i, k.

DEFINITION 7.13 (Two special matrices.) The sequence of all elements of type a_{ii} (the *diagonal elements*) is called the *main diagonal*. The ***identity*** *n x n* ***matrix*** I (written I_n if ambiguity might arise) has diagonal elements 1 and the rest zero. The *zero* m x n matrix has all its entries zero, and is usually denoted by '0', the context making clear that this is the intended meaning. If necessary we write O_{mxn}, or O_n if m = n. Thus for example:

$$O_3 = \begin{bmatrix} 0 & 0 & 0 \\ 0 & 0 & 0 \\ 0 & 0 & 0 \end{bmatrix}, \qquad I_3 = \begin{bmatrix} 1 & 0 & 0 \\ 0 & 1 & 0 \\ 0 & 0 & 1 \end{bmatrix}.$$

ROW VECTORS Any row $[a_{i1} \ldots a_{in}]$ forms a 1 x n matrix or *row vector*, which may be identified with a vector in Euclidean n-space, $\mathbf{a} = (a_{i1}, \ldots, a_{in})$. Similarly for columns.

MATRIX SUMS AND PRODUCTS Matrices may be added, and multiplied by scalars, in the same way as vectors. Multiplication is different. If (and only if) the rows of matrix A have the same length n as the columns of matrix B, then the *product* AB exists, defined by

$$(AB)_{ik} = (\text{row i of A}).(\text{column k of B}) = \sum_{s=1}^{n} a_{is}b_{sk}, \qquad (7.10)$$

the inner product of row i of A and column k of B, regarded as vectors. Thus if A is m x n and B is n x p then AB exists and is m x p. We emphasise that n is the row length of A and column length of B. In forming AB we say B is *premultiplied by* A, or A is *postmultiplied by* B.

EXAMPLES 7.14

(1)
$$[a_1 \;\; a_2 \;\; a_3]\begin{bmatrix} b_1 \\ b_2 \\ b_3 \end{bmatrix} = a_1b_1 + a_2b_2 + a_3b_3 = \mathbf{a}.\mathbf{b},$$

(2)
$$\begin{bmatrix} 1 & 2 & 1 \\ 2 & 3 & 5 \end{bmatrix}\begin{bmatrix} 2 & 1 \\ 0 & 3 \\ 0 & 1 \end{bmatrix} = \begin{bmatrix} 2 & 8 \\ 4 & 16 \end{bmatrix}.$$

2 x 3   3 x 2   2 x 2

EXERCISE Write down the products AB and BA for several pairs of 2 by 2 matrices A, B until you obtain AB different from BA. Can you get this using only the numbers 0 and 1?

DEFINITION 7.15 A *diagonal* matrix D is one which is square and has all its off-diagonal entries zero: $d_{ij} = 0$ whenever $i \neq j$. Thus D may be defined by its diagonal entries, $D = \text{diag}(d_{11}, d_{22}, \ldots, d_{nn})$. The identity matrix D = I is an important special case, as we begin to see soon in (7.13).

EXAMPLE 7.16 The case n = 3.

$$\begin{bmatrix} \lambda_1 & 0 & 0 \\ 0 & \lambda_2 & 0 \\ 0 & 0 & \lambda_3 \end{bmatrix}\begin{bmatrix} 1 & 2 & 5 \\ 6 & 5 & 9 \\ 1 & 0 & 7 \end{bmatrix} = \begin{bmatrix} \lambda_1 & 2\lambda_1 & 5\lambda_1 \\ 6\lambda_2 & 5\lambda_2 & 9\lambda_2 \\ \lambda_3 & 0 & 7\lambda_3 \end{bmatrix}.$$

This leads us to see that, D being an n x n diagonal matrix,

if we premultiply an n x n matrix A by D, i.e. we form DA, this has the effect of multiplying all the elements of row i of A by the i'th entry on the diagonal of D , for $1 \leq i \leq n$. Similarly for AD (postmultiplication by D) and the columns of A. (7.11)

In particular,

$$\text{diag}(a_1, \ldots, a_n)\, \text{diag}(b_1, \ldots b_n) = \text{diag}(a_1b_1, \ldots, a_nb_n), \qquad (7.12)$$

a matrix multiplied by the identity is unchanged,
AI = A and IB = B. (7.13)

EXAMPLE 7.17 The product of n copies of A is written A^n, with A^0 defined to be I. The usual index laws hold: $A^m A^n = A^{m+n}$, $(A^m)^n = A^{mn}$.

EXERCISE Find the product A of the 2 x 2 and the 2 x 3 matrices of Example 2. Does only one way round allow multiplication? Write down a diagonal matrix D so that DA is matrix A with the first row unchanged and the second row multiplied by -2.

TRANSPOSES The *transpose* A^T of a matrix A is obtained by rewriting the successive rows as columns. In symbols, $(A^T)_{ik} = (A)_{ki} = a_{ki}$. Thus for example

$$A = \begin{bmatrix} 1 & 2 & 3 \\ 4 & 5 & 6 \end{bmatrix}, \qquad A^T = \begin{bmatrix} 1 & 4 \\ 2 & 5 \\ 3 & 6 \end{bmatrix}$$

Notice that we now have the option of writing a column vector horizontally as the transpose of a row vector, thus: $[x_1\ x_2\ \dots\ x_n]^T$. We have the following three calculation rules of which the second, $(AB)^T = B^T A^T$, is often called the *reversal rule for matrix transposes.*

$$(A+B)^T = A^T + B^T, \qquad (AB)^T = B^T A^T, \qquad (A^T)^T = A. \tag{7.14}$$

Proof We prove the reversal rule by showing that $(AB)^T$ and $B^T A^T$ have the same ik entry for each pair i,k. We have

$$\begin{aligned} ((AB)^T)_{ik} &= (AB)_{ki} && \text{by definition of transpose,} \\ &= \textstyle\sum_s a_{ks} b_{si} && \text{by definition of AB,} \\ &= \textstyle\sum_s (B^T)_{is} (A^T)_{sk} && \text{by definition of transpose,} \\ &= (B^T A^T)_{ik} && \text{by definition of } B^T A^T. \end{aligned}$$

In the context of transposition, two useful concepts are the following. A square matrix A is *symmetric* if $A^T = A$, and *skew-symmetric* (*anti-symmetric*) if $A^T = -A$. Notice that in the skew case every diagonal element a_{ii} satisfies $a_{ii} = -a_{ii}$, hence the main diagonal consists of zeros.

$$\text{Symmetric: } \begin{bmatrix} 1 & 3 & 7 \\ 3 & -2 & 5 \\ 7 & 5 & 6 \end{bmatrix} \qquad \text{Skew-symmetric: } \begin{bmatrix} 0 & 5 & -6 \\ -5 & 0 & 2 \\ 6 & -2 & 0 \end{bmatrix}$$

In particular, a symmetric matrix is determined by its elements on or above the main diagonal, whilst a skew symmetric matrix requires only those above. As we see above, a 3 x 3 skew-symmetric matrix requires only three elements to specify it.

EXAMPLE 7.18 AA^T is symmetric for any matrix A, whilst for square A, $A+A^T$ is always symmetric and $A-A^T$ is always skew-symmetric.

Proof $(AA^T)^T = (A^T)^T A^T = AA^T$, by (7.14), whereas $(A+A^T)^T = A^T + (A^T)^T = A^T + A$, again by (7.14). The rest is similar.

EXERCISE Prove that if matrix A is square then $A - A^T$ is skew-symmetric.

Finally we observe that: *Every square matrix A can be expressed uniquely as the sum of a symmetric and a skew-symmetric matrix, namely*

$$A = (1/2)(A + A^T) + (1/2)(A - A^T), \qquad (7.15)$$

called respectively the *symmetric* and *skew-symmetric* parts of A.

Proof The equality holds trivially. For uniqueness, suppose that A has two expressions $A_1 + B_1 = A_2 + B_2$ (i). Then taking the transpose of each side yields a second equation $A_1 - B_1 = A_2 - B_2$ (ii). Adding (i) and (ii) we obtain $2A_1 = 2A_2$ and subtracting, $2B_1 = 2B_2$.

EXAMPLE 7.19 The matrix A below splits into symmetric and skew-symmetric parts as shown.

$$A = \begin{bmatrix} 1 & 5 & 7 \\ 3 & 2 & 1 \\ 2 & 6 & 0 \end{bmatrix} = \begin{bmatrix} 1 & 4 & 4.5 \\ 4 & 2 & 3.5 \\ 4.5 & 3.5 & 0 \end{bmatrix} + \begin{bmatrix} 0 & 1 & 2.5 \\ -1 & 0 & -2.5 \\ -2.5 & 2.5 & 0 \end{bmatrix}$$

This technique is useful for determining the axis of a rotation in 3-space from its matrix (Corollary 8.20 of Chapter 8)).

EXERCISE Find the symmetric and skew-symmetric parts of one matrix of Example 7.16.

Finally in this section we note that, fortunately matrix multiplication is associative, that is, if all the implied products exist then

$$(AB)C = A(BC) \qquad (7.16)$$

As a result, we may bracket the product of any number of matrices in any way we wish, or omit the brackets altogether when writing such a product. The proof involves writing out the ik element of (AB)C as a double summation and reversing the order of summation, which gives the ik element of A(BC). See Whitelaw (1983).

7.2.2 Determinants

Determinants are invaluable for computing with vectors and for distinguishing between direct and indirect isometries, in the plane, 3-space and higher dimensions. For an n x n square matrix A, the *determinant*, denoted |A| or det A, may be defined step by step as follows (its absolute value is written |det A|).

n = 1: $|a_{11}| = a_{11}$. n = 2: $\begin{vmatrix} a & b \\ c & d \end{vmatrix} = ad - bc$.

n = 3: $$\begin{vmatrix} a_1 & a_2 & a_3 \\ b_1 & b_2 & b_3 \\ c_1 & c_2 & c_3 \end{vmatrix} = a_1 \begin{vmatrix} b_2 & b_3 \\ c_2 & c_3 \end{vmatrix} - a_2 \begin{vmatrix} b_1 & b_3 \\ c_1 & c_3 \end{vmatrix} + a_3 \begin{vmatrix} b_1 & b_2 \\ c_1 & c_2 \end{vmatrix}.$$

We have already previewed 2 by 2 determinants for proving certain results and making constructions for cells of plane patterns, in Chapter 4 (see Notation 4.7 ff.). Notice that each row element a_i multiplies the determinant obtained by striking out the row and column containing a_i, and that the appended signs alternate as we progress along the row. This generalises to expanding a determinant of any size in terms of determinants of one size less. There follow some rules that can greatly simplify computation. The general method is to convert our determinant to one of equal value, but with many zero entries.

RULES 7.20 (*Evaluating determinants.*)

1. Switching two rows or columns changes the sign of a determinant. Hence a determinant with two identical rows or columns must equal zero.
2. Multiplying each element of a row (or each element of a column) by the same scalar α, multiplies the determinant by α.
3. The value of a determinant is unaffected by the addition of a multiple of one row to another. Similarly for columns.
4. $|AB| = |A|\,|B|$ and $|A^T| = |A|$.
5. $|A| = 0$ if and only if some linear combination $a_1C_1 + a_2C_2 + \ldots + a_nC_n$ of the columns (or of the rows) of A is zero. Of course, not all the coefficients a_i are allowed to be zero. [For case n = 3 see Theorems 7.31(c) and 7.32.]

EXAMPLE 7.21 (1) In evaluating the determinant below we first simplify by subtracting twice row 2 from row 1 (Rule 3).

$$\begin{vmatrix} 5 & 2 & 6 \\ 2 & 1 & 3 \\ 1 & 0 & 1 \end{vmatrix} = \begin{vmatrix} 1 & 0 & 0 \\ 2 & 1 & 3 \\ 1 & 0 & 1 \end{vmatrix} = \begin{vmatrix} 1 & 3 \\ 0 & 1 \end{vmatrix} = 1.$$

(2) The diagonal case: $$\begin{vmatrix} d & 0 & 0 \\ 0 & e & 0 \\ 0 & 0 & f \end{vmatrix} = d\begin{vmatrix} e & 0 \\ 0 & f \end{vmatrix} \text{ (plus two zero terms) } = def.$$

More generally, the determinant of $\mathrm{diag}(d_1, \ldots, d_n)$ equals $d_1d_2\ldots d_n$, the product of the diagonal elements. Indeed, this formula still holds if only the subdiagonal elements (those below the main diagonal) are zero.

Notice that when we evaluate the determinant of a matrix the result is a *polynomial* in the matrix elements, since we use multiplication, addition and subtraction, but not division. We lead up to a result which may give this polynomial in a factorised form, bypassing a potentially tedious calculation. Suppose we divide $x-\alpha$ into a polynomial $f(x)$, obtaining quotient $q(x)$ and remainder R. That is, $f(x) = q(x)(x-\alpha) + R$. Setting $x = \alpha$, we obtain $R = f(\alpha)$ and hence the Lemma now stated.

LEMMA 7.22 *$x-\alpha$ is a factor of a polynomial $f(x)$ if and only if $f(\alpha) = 0$.*

EXAMPLE 7.23 *VanderMonde determinants.*

The 3 x 3 case is $$D = \begin{vmatrix} 1 & 1 & 1 \\ a & b & c \\ a^2 & b^2 & c^2 \end{vmatrix} = \begin{vmatrix} 1 & a & a^2 \\ 1 & b & b^2 \\ 1 & c & c^2 \end{vmatrix}.$$

The following simple argument generalises to the n x n case, in which variables $x_1, \ldots, x_n$

appear up to the power n-1. Firstly, D is a polynomial of total degree three in a, b, c. Now think of D as a polynomial in the variable b: setting b = a makes two columns identical, giving a zero determinant by Rule 1. Hence a-b is a factor of D, by Lemma 7.22. Similarly, so are b-c and c-a, and so $D = \lambda(a-b)(b-c)(c-a)$ for some constant, λ. Since this is an identity, i.e., holds for all values of the variables, let us set a = 0, b = 1, c = 2.

From the second version of D (equal to it by Rule 4), we have $D = \begin{vmatrix} 1 & 1 \\ 2 & 4 \end{vmatrix} = 2$, showing that $\lambda = 1$ and $D = (a-b)(b-c)(c-a)$. We may calculate this directly (in case n = 3) as a check of the argument.

EXERCISE Use some of Rules 1 to 5 to evaluate the determinant of Example 7.21(1) differently. The answer of course should be the same. Give the argument of Example 7.23 corresponding to n = 4.

7.2.3 The inverse of a matrix

Let A be an n x n matrix. If (and only if) det A ≠ there is an *inverse matrix* of A, i.e. an n x n matrix A^{-1} such that

$$A A^{-1} = I = A^{-1} A.$$

It can be shown that an inverse is unique, and that, *for an n x n matrix B*

If either $AB = I$ or $BA = I$ (or both) then B is the inverse of A, (7.17)

and $(AB)^{-1} = B^{-1}A^{-1}$, $(A^T)^{-1} = (A^{-1})^T$, *and* $|A^{-1}| = |A|^{-1}$
if these inverses exist (reversal rule). (7.18)

The formula (7.18) is called the *reversal rule for matrix inverses.* Compare the similar rule for transposes in (7.14).

EXAMPLE 7.24 (Formulae for the inverse.)

$$\text{Let } A = \begin{bmatrix} a & b \\ c & d \end{bmatrix}. \quad \text{Then } A^{-1} = \frac{1}{|A|}\begin{bmatrix} d & -b \\ -c & a \end{bmatrix}, \quad \text{if } |A| \neq 0. \tag{7.19}$$

To verify the formula, denote by B the matrix claimed to be inverse to A, then

$$AB = \begin{bmatrix} a & b \\ c & d \end{bmatrix}\begin{bmatrix} d & -b \\ -c & a \end{bmatrix}.\frac{1}{|A|} = \begin{bmatrix} ad-bc & 0 \\ 0 & ad-bc \end{bmatrix}.\frac{1}{|A|}.$$

This equals the identity matrix I because |A| = ad-bc. Hence B is indeed inverse to A, by (7.17). The formula above is the case n = 2 of *Cramer's rule* for the inverse of an n x n matrix with nonzero determinant: $A^{-1} = |A|^{-1}$ adj A, where the *adjoint* adj A of A has ij element equal to $(-1)^{i+j}$ times the determinant of the (smaller) matrix that results on striking out row i and column j from A. Though convenient to state, this formula involves much arithmetic if n > 2, and we give it only for completeness, since all the inverses we shall require will be geometrically evident. As a simple example the matrix corresponding to a rotation through angle θ has inverse corresponding to $-\theta$ (see Example 7.25 and Sections 7.4, 8.4, and 8.5). For an algorithm based on row operations, involving less calculation than Cramer's rule, see Foley and van Dam (1990), or for full details Whitelaw (1991).

Here we note the following.

A diagonal matrix D = diag(d_1, ... , d_n) is invertible if and only if its diagonal elements are nonzero, and then

$$D^{-1} = \text{diag}(d_1^{-1}, \dots , d_n^{-1}). \tag{7.20}$$

EXERCISE Deduce the reversal rule (7.18) for matrix inverses from (7.17), by rebracketing the product $(AB).(B^{-1}A^{-1})$. [i.e. use the associative property (7.16).]

7.2.4 Orthogonal matrices

These will turn out to be exactly the matrices that describe point fixing isometries in 3-space. An n x n matrix is A called *orthogonal* if $A A^T = I$. This is equivalent to each of

(a) $A^TA = I$,

(b) A has an inverse, and $A^{-1} = A^T$,

(c) The rows (or columns) of A form a set of n *orthonormal vectors*, that is, mutually orthogonal unit vectors.

Proof

$A^TA = I$ ⇔ A^T is the inverse of A, by (7.17),

⇔ $AA^T = I$ by (7.17),

⇔ $(AA^T)_{ik} = \delta_{ik}$ (1 if i=k, otherwise 0)

⇔ (row i of A).(column k of A^T) = δ_{ik}

⇔ (row i of A).(row k of A) = δ_{ik}

⇔ the rows of A form an orthonormal set of vectors.

A slight addition to the argument justifies the assertion about columns of A, and is left as an exercise.

EXAMPLE 7.25 (Prime example.) In Section 7.4.1 we show how the matrix given below describes rotations,

$$A = \begin{bmatrix} \cos\phi & \sin\phi \\ -\sin\phi & \cos\phi \end{bmatrix} \text{ is orthogonal, for any angle } \phi.$$

EXAMPLE 7.26 A classical use of matrices is to write equations in compact form. Thus the system of three equations

$$\begin{aligned} x + 2y - z &= 6 \\ 2x + y + 2z &= 9 \\ 2x - 2y - x &= -3 \end{aligned} \quad \text{becomes} \quad \frac{1}{3}\begin{bmatrix} 1 & 2 & -1 \\ 2 & 1 & 2 \\ 2 & -2 & -1 \end{bmatrix}\begin{bmatrix} x \\ y \\ z \end{bmatrix} = \begin{bmatrix} 2 \\ 3 \\ -1 \end{bmatrix}$$

which we write as AX = H, where $X = [x\ y\ z]^T$. It happens here that A is orthogonal, a frequent occurrence in Chapters 8 and 9, so the inverse of A is immediately known to be A^T. Multiplying both sides of the equation by A^{-1} we have a standard argument: AX = H ⇒ $A^TAX = A^TH$ ⇒ $X = A^TH$, whence x = 2, y = 3, z = 5/3. Notice that AX = H is equivalent to the transposed equation $X^TA^T = H^T$, that is to $[x\ y\ z]\ A^T = [2\ 3\ -1]$. In the introduction to Section 7.4 we see why, apart from typographical reasons, this way round is often preferred.

REMARK 7.27 If A is orthogonal then $|A|^2 = |A||A^T| = |AA^T| = |I| = 1$, hence A has determinant ±1 [which of Rules 7.20 were used here?].

DEFINITION 7.28 The set of all n by n orthogonal matrices, with multiplication as its law of composition, is called the *orthogonal group* O(n) (it *is* a group, see Definition 2.19).

EXERCISES Verify that the matrices of Examples 7.25 and 7.26 are orthogonal by considering their rows (does the determinant of either equal -1?). **or** Use (7.14) to show that the product of two orthogonal matrices is another and hence that the orthogonal group is indeed a group.

7.3 Further products of vectors

Besides the scalar product of two vectors, there are three other ways of forming new vectors or scalars, from vectors, which will be very useful, partly because they provide effective methods of calculation in terms of coordinates.

7.3.1 The standard vector product

DEFINITION 7.29 Let non-parallel nonzero vectors **a**,**b** be at angle ϕ. Thus $0 < \phi < \pi$. The *vector product* **c** = **a** x **b** of the ordered pair **a**,**b** is defined by:

(a) |**a** x **b**| = |**a**| |**b**| sin ϕ. Note that this is the area of the parallelogram with **a**,**b** as adjacent edges, since this area equals base length |**a**| times height |**b**|sinϕ.

(b) **a** x **b** is perpendicular to both **a**, **b** and such that **a**, **b**, **c** = **a** x **b**, is a right handed triple. We define **a** x **b** to be the zero vector if **a**,**b** are parallel or either vector is zero.

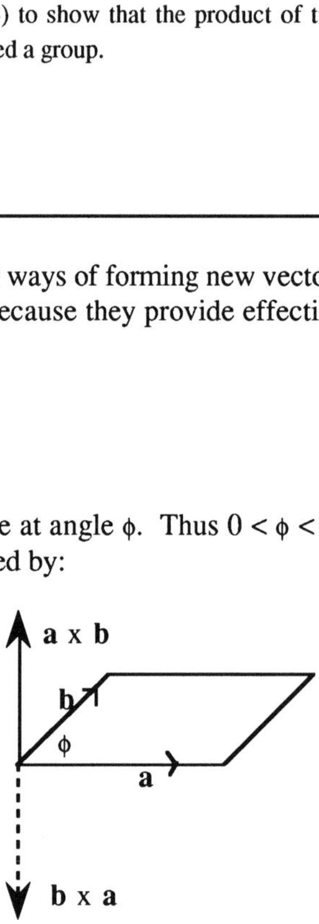

PROPERTIES

$$\mathbf{a} \times \mathbf{a} = \mathbf{0} \qquad (7.21)$$
$$\mathbf{b} \times \mathbf{a} = -\mathbf{a} \times \mathbf{b}, \qquad (7.22)$$
$$\alpha\mathbf{a} \times \mathbf{b} = \mathbf{a} \times \alpha\mathbf{b} = \alpha(\mathbf{a} \times \mathbf{b}), \text{ if } \alpha \text{ is a scalar}, \qquad (7.23)$$
$$\mathbf{a} \times (\mathbf{b} + \mathbf{c}) = (\mathbf{a} \times \mathbf{b}) + (\mathbf{a} \times \mathbf{c}) \qquad (7.24)$$

The hardest to prove is (7.24), and we will shortly do this using the scalar triple product, defined below. Once available, (7.24) gives the connection to an exceedingly important and useful determinant formula (Theorem 7.32) for the vector product, starting with the immediately deducible products from the right handed system **i, j, k** of Section 7.1.3 :

$$\begin{array}{lllll} \mathbf{i} \times \mathbf{j} = \mathbf{k} = -\mathbf{j} \times \mathbf{i} & & \mathbf{i} \times \mathbf{i} = \mathbf{0} \\ \mathbf{j} \times \mathbf{k} = \mathbf{i} = -\mathbf{k} \times \mathbf{j} & & \mathbf{j} \times \mathbf{j} = \mathbf{0} \\ \mathbf{k} \times \mathbf{i} = \mathbf{j} = -\mathbf{i} \times \mathbf{k} & & \mathbf{k} \times \mathbf{k} = \mathbf{0}. \end{array} \qquad (7.25)$$

Notice that the cyclic permutation **i** $\rightarrow$ **j** $\rightarrow$ **k** $\rightarrow$ **i** applied to each line above yields another.

7.3.2 Triple products of vectors

DEFINITION 7.30 The *scalar triple product* of vectors **a**,**b**,**c** is the scalar [**a**,**b**,**c**] = **a**.(**b** x **c**).

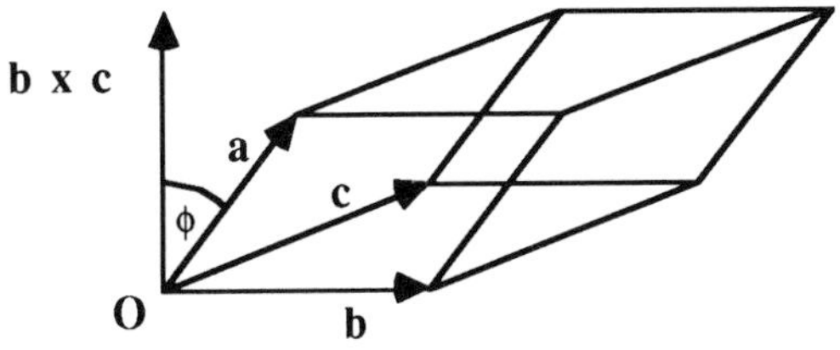

Figure 7.5 A solid bounded by parallelograms whose volume is ±**a**.(**b** x **c**).

*THEOREM 7.31 Let **a**,**b**,**c** be nonzero vectors. Then*
(a) *[**a**,**b**,**c**] equals ± the volume of the figure (parallelepiped) with opposite faces parallel and **a**,**b**,**c** represented by adjacent edges, as shown above,*
(b) *[**a**,**b**,**c**] is constant under cyclic shifts of **a**,**b**,**c** and changes sign under non-cyclic permutations,*
(c) *[**a**,**b**,**c**] = 0 if and only if **a**,**b**,**c** are coplanar; in particular*
*[**a**,**b**,**c**] = 0 if any two of **a**,**b**,**c** are equal or parallel,*
(d) *The triple **a**,**b**,**c** is right handed if [**a**,**b**,**c**] > 0 and left handed if [**a**,**b**,**c**] < 0.*
(e) *Let **a**,**b**,**c** be unit vectors. Then **a**,**b**,**c** is a right handed or left handed* **orthonormal** *set according as [**a**,**b**,**c**] = 1 or -1 (it may be neither).*

Proof We think of the volume as V = (area of base) times (height) = |**b** x **c**| |**a**| |cosϕ| = ± [**a**,**b**,**c**]. If **a**,**b**,**c** is right handed then **b** x **c** points to the same side of the base as does **a** and so $0 \leq \phi < \pi/2$, cosϕ > 0. Consequently we have V = |**a**| |**b** x **c**| cosϕ = [**a**,**b**,**c**]. In the left handed case $-\pi \leq \phi < -\pi/2$, and cosϕ < 0, therefore V = |**a**| |**b** x **c**| (-cosϕ) = -[**a**,**b**,**c**]. This is sufficient to establish (a) to (d).

To prove (e), we observe that with **a**,**b**,**c** as unit vectors, the greatest value of the volume V of the figure diagrammed above, is 1, by elementary geometry, and occurs precisely when **a**,**b**,**c** are mutually perpendicular, thus forming an orthonormal set. By part (a), [**a**,**b**,**c**] = ±V, so **a**,**b**,**c** is an orthonormal set if and only if [**a**,**b**,**c**] = ±1. But by part (d), 1 and -1 here correspond respectively to right and left handedness.

Proof of (7.24) : **a** x (**b** + **c**) = (**a** x **b**) + (**a** x **c**). The key idea is to consider the difference **d** = **a** x (**b** + **c**) - (**a** x **b**) - (**a** x **c**). It suffices to prove that **d**.**d** = 0, for then **d** = 0 by (7.5). We have

d.**d**	=	**d**.{**a** x (**b** + **c**)- (**a** x **b**) - (**a** x **c**)}	
	=	**d**.{**a** x (**b** + **c**)} - **d**.(**a** x **b**) - **d**.(**a** x **c**),	by (7.8)
	=	(**b** + **c**).(**d** x **a**) - **d**.(**a** x **b**) - **d**.(**a** x **c**),	by Theorem 7.31(b)
	=	**b**.(**d** x **a**) + **c**.(**d** x **a**) - **d**.(**a** x **b**) - **d**.(**a** x **c**),	by (7.8)
	=	**d**.(**a** x **b**) + **d**.(**a** x **c**) - **d**.(**a** x **b**) - **d**.(**a** x **c**),	by Theorem 7.31(b)
	=	0, by cancellation.	

THEOREM 7.32 Vector products and scalar triple products are given by the following determinants.

$$\mathbf{a} \times \mathbf{b} = \begin{vmatrix} \mathbf{i} & \mathbf{j} & \mathbf{k} \\ a_1 & a_2 & a_3 \\ b_1 & b_2 & b_3 \end{vmatrix}, \qquad [\mathbf{a},\mathbf{b},\mathbf{c}] = \begin{vmatrix} a_1 & a_2 & a_3 \\ b_1 & b_2 & b_3 \\ c_1 & c_2 & c_3 \end{vmatrix}$$

Proof We have, in the usual component notation,

$$\begin{aligned} \mathbf{a} \times \mathbf{b} &= (a_1\mathbf{i} + a_2\mathbf{j} + a_3\mathbf{k}) \times (b_1\mathbf{i} + b_2\mathbf{j} + b_3\mathbf{k}) \\ &= a_1b_1\, \mathbf{i} \times \mathbf{i} + a_2b_2\, \mathbf{j} \times \mathbf{j} + a_3b_3\, \mathbf{k} \times \mathbf{k} \qquad (= 0 \text{ by } (7.21)) \\ &\quad + a_1b_2\, \mathbf{i} \times \mathbf{j} + a_2b_1\, \mathbf{j} \times \mathbf{i} \\ &\quad + a_2b_3\, \mathbf{j} \times \mathbf{k} + a_3b_2\, \mathbf{k} \times \mathbf{j} \\ &\quad + a_3b_1\, \mathbf{k} \times \mathbf{i} + a_1b_3\, \mathbf{i} \times \mathbf{k} \qquad \text{by } (7.23), (7.24), \\ &= \begin{vmatrix} a_1 & a_2 \\ b_1 & b_2 \end{vmatrix}\mathbf{k} + \begin{vmatrix} a_2 & a_3 \\ b_2 & b_3 \end{vmatrix}\mathbf{i} + \begin{vmatrix} a_3 & a_1 \\ b_3 & b_1 \end{vmatrix}\mathbf{j} \end{aligned}$$

by (7.25), which equals the given determinant. The formula for $[\mathbf{a},\mathbf{b},\mathbf{c}]$ follows from the determinant for $\mathbf{b} \times \mathbf{c}$ and Definition 7.4 of scalar product.

REMARK 7.33 (1) For a left handed coordinate system we must switch the last two rows in each determinant formula of Theorem 7.32 above.
(2) Theorem 7.32 has a nice spinoff in two dimensions. In Chapter 4 we used a determinant fomula for area and proved it 'barehandedly' in a special case (Lemma 4.8). Now we can deduce it from Theorem 7.32 along with an application in the plane to the sense of a rotation and to collinearity. This is Corollary 7.34A.

EXERCISE Determine whether the following ordered triple of vectors forms a right handed triple, a left handed triple, or is coplanar: (1,1,1), (1,-1,1), (0,1,0).

COROLLARY 7.34A Let $A(a_1,a_2,0)$, $B(b_1,b_2,0)$ be points in the xy-plane, distinct from the origin. Then $\mathbf{a} \times \mathbf{b} = (0,0,D)$, *where*

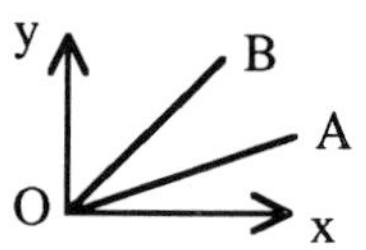

$$D = \begin{vmatrix} a_1 & a_2 \\ b_1 & b_2 \end{vmatrix}.$$

If $D = 0$ then the points O, A, B are collinear or $A = B$. If $D \neq 0$ then rotation of OA about O towards OB is anticlockwise if $D > 0$, and clockwise if $D < 0$. In any case, the triangle with adjacent sides OA, OB has area half the absolute value $|D|$.

Proof We view **a**, **b** as vectors in 3-space with third coordinate zero and the determinant formula of Theorem 7.32 gives $\mathbf{a} \times \mathbf{b} = (0, 0, D)$. Thus if $D > 0$ then $\mathbf{a} \times \mathbf{b}$ is in the positive z-direction so **a**, **b**, **k** is a right handed triple, whereas $D < 0$ makes it left handed. This translates to the Corollary's assertion about the position of OA relative to OB. Let $D = 0$, i.e. $a_1b_2 = a_2b_1$. Since neither A nor B is the origin, the supposition that one of the four coordinates, say b_1, is zero entails $a_1 = 0$ and the other two being nonzero. Hence $(a_1,a_2) = (a_2/b_2)(b_1,b_2)$ and O, A, B are collinear (or A = B). This leaves the case of all four coordinates nonzero, when we may legitimately infer that $(a_1/b_1) = (a_2/b_2)$, so again O, A, B are collinear (or A = B). Finally, By Definition 7.29 for vector product, the triangle has area $(1/2)|\mathbf{a} \times \mathbf{b}| = (1/2)|(0, 0, D)| = (1/2)\,|D|$.

COROLLARY 7.34B The area of a triangle in the xy-plane with vertices A,B,C is

$$1/2 \text{ the absolute value of } \begin{vmatrix} 1 & 1 & 1 \\ a_1 & b_1 & c_1 \\ a_2 & b_2 & c_2 \end{vmatrix}.$$

Proof From Definition 7.29, twice the area is

$$\begin{aligned} |\underline{AB} \times \underline{AC}| &= |(\mathbf{b} - \mathbf{a}) \times (\mathbf{c} - \mathbf{a})| && \text{by (1.2C),} \\ &= |\mathbf{b} \times \mathbf{c} - \mathbf{b} \times \mathbf{a} - \mathbf{a} \times \mathbf{c} + \mathbf{a} \times \mathbf{a}| && \text{by (7.24),} \\ &= |\mathbf{b} \times \mathbf{c} - \mathbf{b} \times \mathbf{a} - \mathbf{a} \times \mathbf{c}| && \text{by (7.21), (7.22),} \\ &= |(0, 0, D_1 - D_2 + D_3)| && \text{by Corollary 7.34A,} \\ &= |D_1 - D_2 + D_3|, \end{aligned}$$

where D_1, D_2, D_3 are the respective z-coordinates of $\mathbf{b} \times \mathbf{c}$, $\mathbf{b} \times \mathbf{a}$, $\mathbf{a} \times \mathbf{c}$, giving the three 2 x 2 determinants in the expansion of the displayed 3 x 3 determinant.

REMARK (Complexity of calculations.) If we calculate twice the area of a triangle by the determinant of Corollary 7.34B, without considering how labour may be saved, we use 6 multiplications and 5 additions (we here include subtraction under 'addition'). Taking out common factors gives $a_1(b_2-c_2) + b_1(c_2-a_2) + c_1(a_2-b_2)$, with just 3 multiplications and 5 additions. However we may reduce the multiplications to 2 by the expression $(a_1-c_1)(b_2-c_2) + (b_1-c_1)(c_2-a_2)$. It is really quite unexpected that the area of a plane quadrilateral ABCD can be computed with no more operations than the triangle requires, by the felicitous formula $(c_1-a_1)(d_2-b_2) + (b_1-d_1)(c_2-a_2)$. These observations are part of a wider study by Shamos (1978). Such are important for computer graphical calculations involving many thousands of facets of a subdivided surface. See e.g. Foley et al (1990).

THEOREM 7.35 Evaluating vector and scalar triple products.

$$\begin{aligned} \mathbf{a} \times (\mathbf{b} \times \mathbf{c}) &= (\mathbf{a}.\mathbf{c})\,\mathbf{b} - (\mathbf{a}.\mathbf{b})\,\mathbf{c}, \\ [\alpha\mathbf{a}+\beta\mathbf{b}, \mathbf{c}, \mathbf{d}] &= \alpha[\mathbf{a},\mathbf{c},\mathbf{d}] + \beta[\mathbf{b},\mathbf{c},\mathbf{d}], \\ [\mathbf{d}, \alpha\mathbf{a}+\beta\mathbf{b}, \mathbf{c}] &= \alpha[\mathbf{d},\mathbf{a},\mathbf{c}] + \beta[\mathbf{d},\mathbf{b},\mathbf{c}], \\ [\mathbf{c}, \mathbf{d}, \alpha\mathbf{a}+\beta\mathbf{b}] &= \alpha[\mathbf{c},\mathbf{d},\mathbf{a}] + \beta[\mathbf{c},\mathbf{d},\mathbf{b}]. \end{aligned}$$

Proof The most straightforward way to prove the first formula is by components, but notice first that since $\mathbf{b} \times \mathbf{c}$ is perpendicular to the plane of $\mathbf{b},\mathbf{c}$ (if started at the origin, say), its product with $\mathbf{a}$ lies in that plane, and so equals $\lambda\mathbf{b} + \mu\mathbf{c}$ for some scalars λ,μ. For the first coordinates in the formula we have

$$
\begin{aligned}
[\mathbf{a} \times (\mathbf{b} \times \mathbf{c})]_1 &= a_2(\mathbf{b} \times \mathbf{c})_3 - a_3(\mathbf{b} \times \mathbf{c})_2 && \text{by Theorem 7.32,}\\
&= a_2(b_1c_2 - b_2c_1) - a_3(b_3c_1 - b_1c_3) && \text{by Theorem 7.32,}\\
&= (a_2c_2 + a_3c_3)b_1 - (a_2b_2 + a_3b_3)c_1 &&\\
&= (a_1c_1 + a_2c_2 + a_3c_3)b_1 - (a_1b_1 + a_2b_2 + a_3b_3)c_1 &&\\
&= (\mathbf{a}.\mathbf{c})b_1 - (\mathbf{a}.\mathbf{b})c_1 && \text{by (7.4).}
\end{aligned}
$$

The corresponding results for the other coordinates are obtained by cyclically permuting the subscripts $1 \to 2 \to 3 \to 1$. The second formula follows from (7.8) and the definition $[\mathbf{u},\mathbf{v},\mathbf{w}] = \mathbf{u}.(\mathbf{v} \times \mathbf{w})$. The rest follows from the fact that $[\mathbf{u},\mathbf{v},\mathbf{w}]$ is unchanged under cyclic shifts of **u**,**v**,**w** (Theorem 7.31).

EXAMPLE 7.36 $[\mathbf{a},\mathbf{b},\mathbf{a}+\mathbf{c}] = [\mathbf{a},\mathbf{b},\mathbf{a}] + [\mathbf{a},\mathbf{b},\mathbf{c}]$ (by Theorem 7.35) $= [\mathbf{a},\mathbf{b},\mathbf{c}]$, since $[\mathbf{a},\mathbf{b},\mathbf{a}]$ has two entries equal and so is zero by Theorem 7.31(c). See also Exercise 13 at the end of the chapter.

EXERCISE Express $[\mathbf{a}+2\mathbf{b}-3\mathbf{c},\mathbf{a}-\mathbf{c},\mathbf{b}]$ as a multiple of $[\mathbf{a},\mathbf{b},\mathbf{c}]$ or prove more generally that

$$[x_1\mathbf{a}+x_2\mathbf{b}+x_3\mathbf{c},\ y_1\mathbf{a}+y_2\mathbf{b}+y_3\mathbf{c},\ z_1\mathbf{a}+z_2\mathbf{b}+z_3\mathbf{c}] = \begin{vmatrix} x_1 & x_2 & x_3 \\ y_1 & y_2 & y_3 \\ z_1 & z_2 & z_3 \end{vmatrix} [\mathbf{a},\mathbf{b},\mathbf{c}].$$

7.3.3 Vectors and coordinate geometry

We include this short section to give at least a sample of how a judicious use of vectors can simplify calculations and proofs in 3-dimensional coordinate geometry (cf. Application 1.1 in the plane). We will concentrate on lines and planes, starting with their equations.

*EXAMPLE 7.37 The line m through the point A, parallel to the vector **u** has a parametric equation*

$$\mathbf{r} = \mathbf{a} + t\mathbf{u}, \quad \text{i.e.} \quad \left\{\begin{array}{lcl} x &=& a_1 + tu_1 \\ y &=& a_2 + tu_2 \\ z &=& a_3 + tu_3 \end{array}\right\}$$

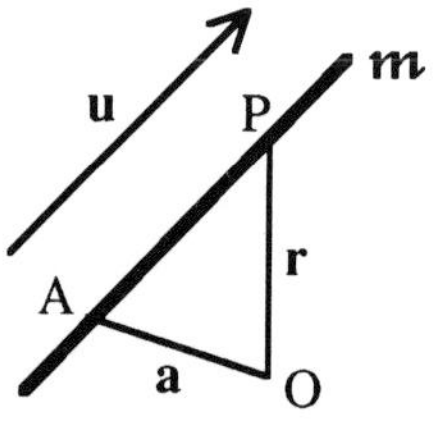

That is to say, all points of this form, with $t \in \mathbf{R}$, are on the line, and every point of the line may be so expressed. We call **u** a *direction vector* for m.

Proof Let the point P have position vector **r**. Then: P is on m $\Leftrightarrow$ $\underline{AP}$ is parallel to **u** $\Leftrightarrow$ $\underline{AP} = t\mathbf{u}$ (some $t \in \mathbf{R}$) $\Leftrightarrow$ $\mathbf{r} - \mathbf{a} = t\mathbf{u}$ i.e. $\mathbf{r} = \mathbf{a} + t\mathbf{u}$ ($t \in \mathbf{R}$). Alternatively we could invoke the Section formula (1.3).

EXAMPLE 7.38 Determine where the line through points A(1,2,1) and B(2,8,4) cuts the sphere $x^2 + y^2 + z^2 = 2$.

Solution A direction vector for the line, $\boldsymbol{m}$ say, is $\underline{AB} = (1,6,3)$. The point on $\boldsymbol{m}$ with parameter t is then $\mathbf{r} = \mathbf{a} + t\underline{AB}$, or in coordinates (1+t, 2+6t, 1+3t), which is on the sphere when t satisfies $(1+t)^2 + (2+6t)^2 + (1+3t)^2 = 2$. The solutions are approximately t = -0.16 and t = -0.53, giving intersection points P(0.84, 1.04, 0.52) and Q(0.47, -1.18, -0.59).

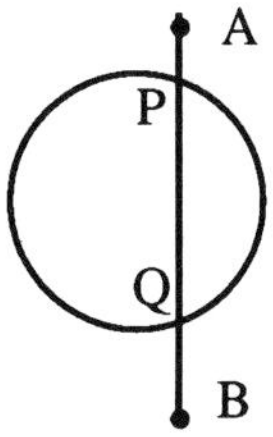

EXAMPLE 7.39 Any vector perpendicular to plane π is called a normal vector to π. The plane π through a point A, having a normal vector $\mathbf{n} = (l,m,n)$ *has equation*

$$lx + my + nz = la_1 + ma_2 + na_3.$$

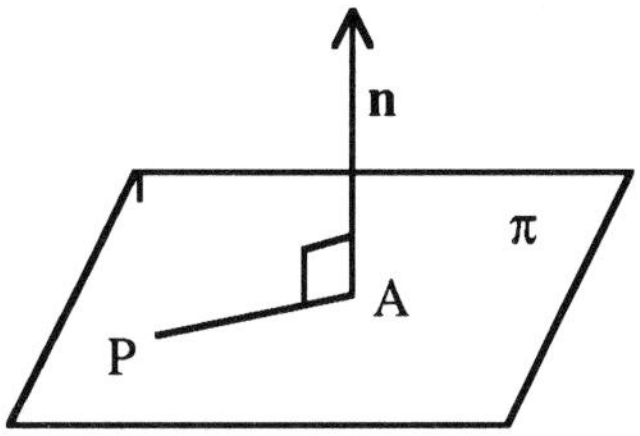

Proof Let the point P have position vector **r**. Then P is on π ⇔ $\underline{AP}$ is perpendicular to **n** ⇔ $(\mathbf{r}-\mathbf{a}).\mathbf{n} = 0$ (by Theorem 7.5) ⇔ $\mathbf{r}.\mathbf{n} = \mathbf{a}.\mathbf{n}$.

One reason why the vector product is so useful is that it gives us a simple way to compute the coordinates of a *vector at right angles to two given vectors*. Here are some applications of this.

EXAMPLE 7.40 Find (i) the equation of the plane π through points A(1,0,1), B(2,-1,3), C(2,3,-2), (ii) the foot of the perpendicular from Q(1,1,-2) to π.

Solution (i) One vector normal to π is $\underline{AB} \times \underline{AC}$ = (1,-1,2) x (1,3,-3) = (-3,5,4) (Theorem 7.32). Since A is on π, the latter has equation -3x+5y+4z = -3(1)+5(0)+4(1) = 1.
(ii) The required point R is on the line through Q(1,1,-2) parallel to the normal (-3,5,4). A typical point on this line is (1-3t,1+5t,-2+4t). At R, on the plane, t satisfies -3(1-3t) + 5(1+5t) +4(-2+4t) = 1, giving t = 7/50. Hence R is (29/50, 17/10, -36/25).

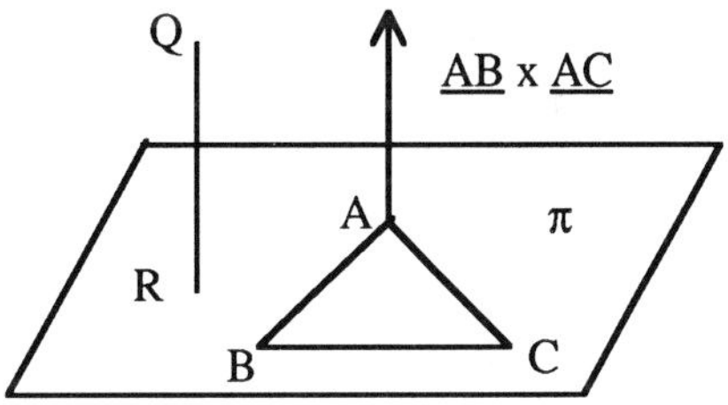

EXAMPLE 7.41 Determine the line of intersection of planes x+2y-5z = 6, 2x–y+4z = -3.

Solution. Since the intersection line $\boldsymbol{m}$ is in both planes a direction vector is perpendicular to both normals and may be taken as (1,2,-5) x (2,-1,4) = (3,-14,-5). We need any point on $\boldsymbol{m}$, so try for one satisfying z = 0, and hence x+2y = 6, 2x-y = -3, giving the point A(0,3,0) and parametric equation for $\boldsymbol{m}$: x=3t, y = 3-14t, z = -5t, or in so-called *symmetric form*:

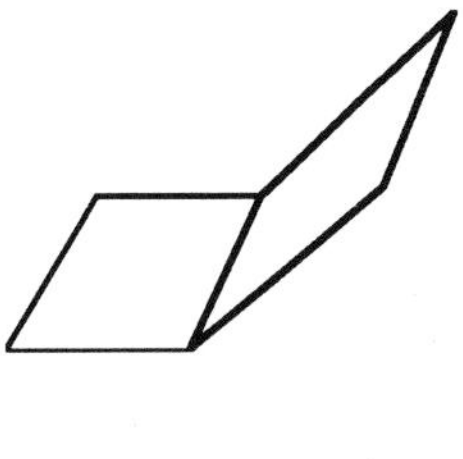

$$\frac{x-0}{3} = \frac{y-3}{-14} = \frac{z-0}{-5} \ (=t).$$

EXERCISE Use the ideas of Examples 7.37 to 7.41 to find an equation for the plane through points A(1,2,3), B(-1,0,1) and at right angles to the plane x-y+2z = 5. [4x-y-3z = -7.]

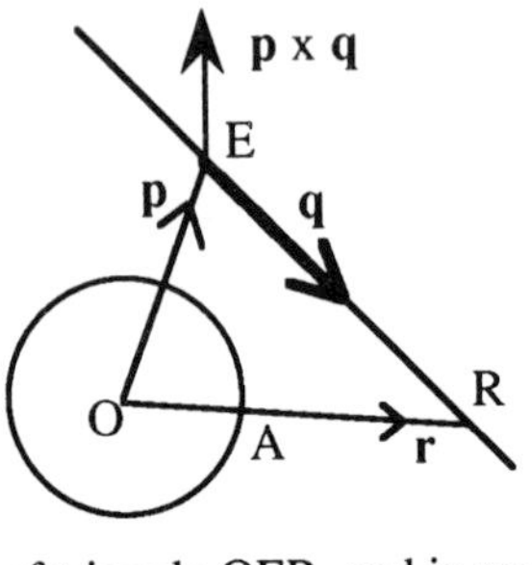

A 'REAL LIFE' APPLICATION This cropped up in work on 'inverse displacement mapping' (see Patterson, Hoggar and Logie, 1991). We have a sample ray (line) for which the parametric equation of Example 7.37 is **r** = **p** + t**q**, as illustrated. The radius vector OR from the origin to the ray meets a unit sphere, centre O, at the point with angular coordinates u, v (think of latitude and longitude). Finding an equation v = f(u) for the ray is rather hard work until we observe that, since **p** x **q** is perpendicular to OE and ER it is perpendicular to the plane of triangle OER, and in particular to OR. Hence (**p** x **q**).**r** = 0, leading after some simplification to the ray equation $v = (2/\pi)\tan^{-1}(k.\cos(\pi u + a))$, where k,a are given by the coordinates of constant vectors **p**,**q**. cf. for example Blinn(1978).

7.4 The matrix of a plane isometry

We find that every transformation of coordinates by a plane isometry can be expressed as [x' y' 1] = [x y 1]A, where A is a 3 x 3 matrix. If a second transformation is applied with matrix B, the result is [x y 1]AB. Thus matrices appear in the order of performance of the corresponding isometries.

7.4.1 Rotations and reflections fixing the origin

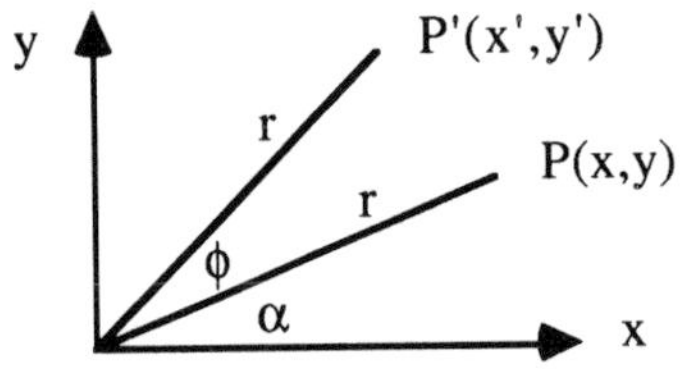

THEOREM 7.42 Rotation through angle f about the origin in the xy-plane is given by (x,y) → (x',y'), where in matrix notation

$$[x'\ y'] = [x\ y]\begin{bmatrix} \cos\phi & \sin\phi \\ -\sin\phi & \cos\phi \end{bmatrix}. \qquad (7.26)$$

The matrices arising in this way form the special orthogonal group SO(2) of 2 by 2 matrices satisfying $MM^T = I$, $|M| = 1$.

Proof In polar coordinates, with |OP| = r = |OQ| in the diagram above, we have x = rcosα, y = rsinα, and so

$$x' = r\cos(\alpha+\phi) = r\cos\alpha\cos\phi - r\sin\alpha\sin\phi = x\cos\phi - y\sin\phi,$$
$$y' = r\sin(\alpha+\phi) = r\cos\alpha\sin\phi + r\sin\alpha\cos\phi = x\sin\phi + y\cos\phi,$$

which together form matrix equation (7.26). For the last part we note first that the matrix of rotation in (7.26) is indeed in SO(2), so it remains to show that every 2 by 2 matrix

$$M = \begin{bmatrix} a & b \\ c & d \end{bmatrix}, \quad \text{with } MM^T = I, \quad |M| = 1 \tag{7.27}$$

arises from a rotation. Now (7.27) implies that $M^T = M^{-1}$, $|M| = 1$, or by the matrix inverse formula (7.19) for the 2 x 2 case,

$$\begin{bmatrix} a & c \\ b & d \end{bmatrix} = \begin{bmatrix} d & -b \\ -c & a \end{bmatrix}, \quad \text{hence } c = -b,\ d = a, \text{ and } \quad M = \begin{bmatrix} a & b \\ -b & a \end{bmatrix}.$$

Thus, from $|M| = 1$, we have $a^2 + b^2 = 1$ and so may write $a = \cos\phi$, $b = \sin\phi$ for some angle ϕ, giving M the rotation form (7.26).

REMARKS 7.43 (1) If M is the matrix for rotation through ϕ then M^{-1} is that for $-\phi$. (2) An orthogonal matrix has determinant ± 1.

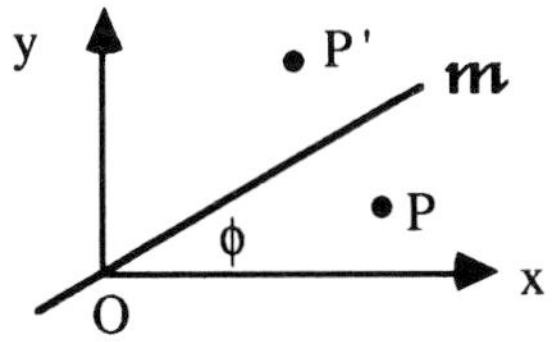

THEOREM 7.44 Reflection in a mirror m *through the origin in the plane, at angle* ϕ *to the x-axis, is given by* $[x\ y] \to [x'\ y']$, *where*

$$[x'\ y'] = [x\ y]\begin{bmatrix} \cos 2\phi & \sin 2\phi \\ \sin 2\phi & -\cos 2\phi \end{bmatrix}. \tag{7.28}$$

Such matrices are those in the orthogonal group O(2) which have determinant -1.

Proof We use the previous Theorem to calculate this matrix as a composition. As in Part 1, let R_m be the reflection in any mirror m. Then

$$R_m = R_{Ox} R_{Ox} R_m \qquad (R_{Ox} \text{ is reflection in the x-axis})$$
$$= R_{Ox} R_O(2\phi), \qquad \text{by Theorem 2.1,}$$

where the last isometry is rotation about the origin through angle 2ϕ. Since these maps are written in their order of application, R_m has matrix

$$\begin{bmatrix} 1 & 0 \\ 0 & -1 \end{bmatrix}\begin{bmatrix} \cos 2\phi & \sin 2\phi \\ -\sin 2\phi & \cos 2\phi \end{bmatrix} = \begin{bmatrix} \cos 2\phi & \sin 2\phi \\ \sin 2\phi & -\cos 2\phi \end{bmatrix}$$

as stated. Now, this matrix is orthogonal, of determinant -1, and the Theorem asserts that every 2 by 2 matrix $M = \begin{bmatrix} a & b \\ c & d \end{bmatrix}$, with $MM^T = I$, of determinant -1, has the form (7.28) for some angle, written as 2ϕ. This follows in the same way as the last part of

Theorem 7.42. Alternatively, with D = diag(1,-1) and so $D^2 = I$, the matrix N = DM satisfies $NN^T = I$, $|N| = |D||M| = 1$ so, by Theorem 7.42,

$$N = \begin{bmatrix} \cos\alpha & \sin\alpha \\ -\sin\alpha & \cos\alpha \end{bmatrix}, \quad \text{for some angle } \alpha .$$

Now $D^2 = I$ gives M = DN, which has stated form (7.28) on our replacing α by 2ϕ.

EXERCISE Compute the product AB, where A is the matrix of rotation about O through 90 degrees and B gives reflection in the line $y = x\sqrt{3}$. Does your answer agree with geometrical predictions?

7.4.2 General plane isometries and 3 x 3 matrices

We note from Theorem 1.15 and 1.16 that every plane isometry is the composition of a translation with a rotation or reflection that fixes the origin. Their matrices are given in (7.31) to (7.33), but first some explanations. A convenient way to incorporate translations into the matrix scheme is to use extended vectors [x,y,1]. Then for *translation* by a vector (a,b) we have

$$[x\ y\ 1] \to [x+a\ \ y+b\ \ 1] = [x\ y\ 1]\begin{bmatrix} 1 & 0 & 0 \\ 0 & 1 & 0 \\ a & b & 1 \end{bmatrix} \qquad (7.29)$$

and in this notation the 3 x 3 matrices for rotation ϕ about the origin, and reflection in a line through the origin at ϕ to the x-axis, are respectively

$$\begin{bmatrix} \cos\phi & \sin\phi & 0 \\ -\sin\phi & \cos\phi & 0 \\ 0 & 0 & 1 \end{bmatrix} \quad \text{and} \quad \begin{bmatrix} \cos 2\phi & \sin 2\phi & 0 \\ \sin 2\phi & -\cos 2\phi & 0 \\ 0 & 0 & 1 \end{bmatrix} \qquad (7.30)$$

REMARK 7.45 Each matrix of (7.29), (7.30) has determinant +1 or -1 according as it represents a direct or an indirect transformation. It follows that an isometry of the plane is direct if its determinant is +1 and indirect if it is -1. (Notice that this statement is independent of our choice of Cartesian coordinate system.) For example, the product of a translation and a reflection is indirect (cf. Remark 1.17) and the product matrix has determinant (1) x (-1) = -1.

EXAMPLE 7.46 Find the matrix for reflection in the line n shown in the diagram

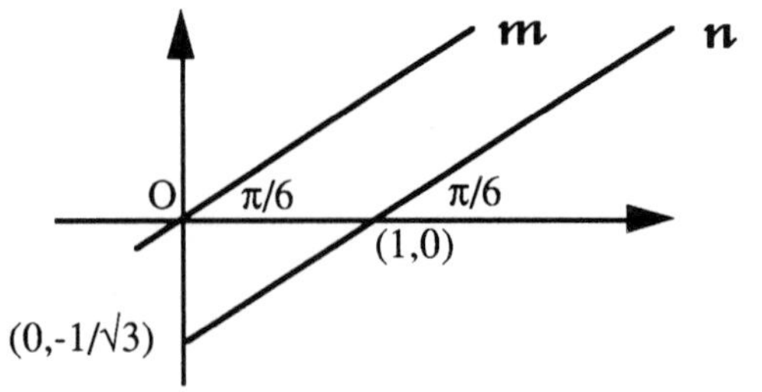

Solution Let T be translation by the vector (1,0). Then T maps line $\boldsymbol{m}$ to line $\boldsymbol{n}$ and so, by the important result Theorem 2.12, we have $R_n = T^{-1}R_mT$. Now cos π/3 = 1/2, sin π/3 = √3/2, so the matrix of R_n is the product

$$\begin{bmatrix} 1 & 0 & 0 \\ 0 & 1 & 0 \\ -1 & 0 & 1 \end{bmatrix} \frac{1}{2}\begin{bmatrix} 1 & \sqrt{3} & 0 \\ \sqrt{3} & -1 & 0 \\ 0 & 0 & 1 \end{bmatrix}\begin{bmatrix} 1 & 0 & 0 \\ 0 & 1 & 0 \\ 1 & 0 & 1 \end{bmatrix} = \frac{1}{2}\begin{bmatrix} 1 & \sqrt{3} & 0 \\ \sqrt{3} & -1 & 0 \\ 1 & -\sqrt{3} & 2 \end{bmatrix}$$

Some checks (i) Having got the answer we have an infallible check that it is correct. Since by Theorem 1.1 an isometry of the plane is determined by whether it is direct or indirect, and its effect on any two points, we have only to check that the matrix has determinant -1 and that it fixes the points (1,0) and (0, -1/√3) where the mirror $\boldsymbol{n}$ cuts the coordinate axes. Note that, for the verification we must convert these coordinates to their matrix forms, namely [1 0 1] and [0 -1/√3 1].
(ii) For the translation part, any one that maps line $\boldsymbol{m}$ to line $\boldsymbol{n}$ will do. In particular we could choose translation (1, -√3)/4 perpendicular to these lines. The calculation is different but the result is the same. The reader may wish to convince him/her self of this

EXERCISE Compute the matrix for an anticlockwise rotation of 3π/4 about (1,1).

NOTATION 7.47 M_g = matrix for plane isometry g (here of 3 by 3 type).

Example 7.46 illustrates the first of three ways to assemble the matrix of a general isometry g as a composition, with translation T, and h fixing the origin.

(i)	$M_g = M_T^{-1} M_h M_T$	(Theorem 2.12)
(ii)	$M_g = M_h M_T$	(Theorem 1.15)
(iii)	$M_g = M_T M_h$	(Theorem 1.15)

Often in practice the most convenient is (ii). We may compute T by the rearrangement $M_T = M_h^{-1} M_g$. Let M_g send the origin to point **a**, then $T = T_{\mathbf{a}}$, since M_h fixes the origin. For (iii) we may use $M_T = M_g M_h^{-1}$: let M_g send O to **a** and M_h^{-1} send **a** to **b**. Then $T = T_{\mathbf{b}}$. Then (ii) looks like the favourite, but how does it work for Example 7.46 ? We require the image of O under reflection in $\boldsymbol{n}$. We can calculate this by trigonometry, but it is actually easier to use the translation by (1,0) and apply method (i) as was done. (ii) comes into its own when we can easily read off the image of O under the given isometry, as in the next example.

EXAMPLE 7.48 (cf. Table 6.8.) Find the matrix for rotating a 1/3 turn about the centroid G_1 of an equilateral triangle with vertices O, A(2,0), and B with positive y-coordinate. The symmetry of the triangle shows that g sends O to A, so the required matrix may be obtained as a product, with c = cos 2π/3, s = sin 2π/3,

$$\begin{bmatrix} c & s & 0 \\ -s & c & 0 \\ 0 & 0 & 1 \end{bmatrix}\begin{bmatrix} 1 & 0 & 0 \\ 0 & 1 & 0 \\ 2 & 0 & 1 \end{bmatrix} = \begin{bmatrix} c & s & 0 \\ -s & c & 0 \\ 2 & 0 & 1 \end{bmatrix}.$$

Notice that we could have written the answer straight by inspection for, multiplying a matrix

M_g (g fixing the origin) on the right by the matrix of translation vector (a,b) simply sets $m_{31} = a$, $m_{32} = b$, and makes no other changes. Indeed,

$$\begin{bmatrix} x & y & 0 \\ z & t & 0 \\ 0 & 0 & 1 \end{bmatrix} \begin{bmatrix} 1 & 0 & 0 \\ 0 & 1 & 0 \\ a & b & 1 \end{bmatrix} = \begin{bmatrix} x & y & 0 \\ z & t & 0 \\ a & b & 1 \end{bmatrix}.$$

Hence if a plane isometry with 3 x 3 matrix M is expressed as an isometry that fixes the origin, followed by a translation, then the translation components may be read off from the third row of M as (m_{31}, m_{32}) (7.31)

For instance, in Example 7.46 , this translation is now easily seen in retrospect to have been $(1, -\sqrt{3})/2$. But the other way round it is different:

$$\begin{bmatrix} 1 & 0 & 0 \\ 0 & 1 & 0 \\ a & b & 1 \end{bmatrix} \begin{bmatrix} x & y & 0 \\ z & t & 0 \\ 0 & 0 & 1 \end{bmatrix} = \begin{bmatrix} x & y & 0 \\ z & t & 0 \\ ax+bz & ay+bt & 1 \end{bmatrix}.$$

In summary (7.31) means that, even starting with the matrix of Case (i) or (iii), *we can read off the translation required* if, we wish to re-express the isometry as in case (ii) with the translation done last.

EXERCISE Translation by (1,2) is followed by rotation through $\pi/6$ about the origin. For the rotation to be done first, what translation must follow to achieve the same effect? (The rotation is the same. cf. Table 2.1.]

Matrices for plane isometries

$$\begin{bmatrix} \cos\phi & \sin\phi & 0 \\ -\sin\phi & \cos\phi & 0 \\ a - a\cos\phi + b\sin\phi & b - a\sin\phi - b\cos\phi & 1 \end{bmatrix} \quad \text{Rotation through angle } \phi \text{ about point } (a,b) \qquad (7.32)$$

$$\begin{bmatrix} \cos 2\phi & \sin 2\phi & 0 \\ \sin 2\phi & -\cos 2\phi & 0 \\ a - a\cos 2\phi & -a\sin 2\phi & 1 \end{bmatrix} \quad \text{Reflection in the line through } (a,0) \text{ at angle } \phi \text{ to the x-axis} \qquad (7.33)$$

$$\begin{bmatrix} \cos 2\phi & \sin 2\phi & 0 \\ \sin 2\phi & -\cos 2\phi & 0 \\ a - a\cos 2\phi + d\cos\phi & -a\sin 2\phi + d\sin\phi & 1 \end{bmatrix} \quad \text{Glide through distance d along a line through } (a,0) \text{ at } \phi \text{ to the x-axis} \qquad (7.34)$$

Reflection in a horizontal mirror y = b is not included above; it sends (x,y) to (x,2b-y).

EXERCISE Find the matrix for the glide from (2,0) to (4,2). Check by the effect on two points, and the sign of the determinant.

Rotations in 3-space What we can readily say at this stage is that, in three dimensions, rotation through ϕ about the z-axis does not change the z-coordinate, and so is given by

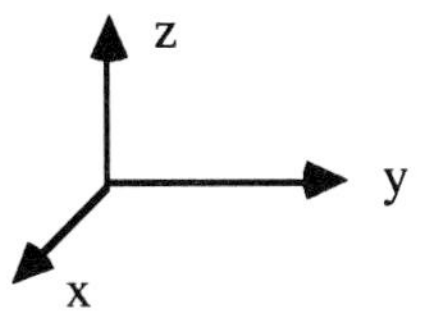

$$[x' \ y' \ z'] \quad = \quad [x \ y \ z]\begin{bmatrix} \cos\phi & \sin\phi & 0 \\ -\sin\phi & \cos\phi & 0 \\ 0 & 0 & 1 \end{bmatrix}. \qquad (7.35)$$

The case of rotation about an arbitrary axis in three dimensions will be taken up in the next chapter, where we classify isometries in 3-space, and again in Chapter 9, where we show how the use of quaternions can be an enabling and simplifying technique.

How to find/determine

The angle between vectors	(7.6)
Multiply by a diagonal matrix	(7.11)
Evaluate a determinant	Rules 7.20
Detect left handed vs right handed system	Theorems 7.31, 7.32
Detect clockwise vs anti clockwise rotation	Corollary 7.34
Evaluate **a** x **b**, [**a**,**b**,**c**], and **a** x (**b** x **c**)	Theorem 7.32, Corollary 7.34
Translation part of isometry from its matrix	(7.31)
Matrix of general plane isometry	(7.32) to (7.34)

EXERCISES 7

---

1 (i) Find the distance between the points (1,4) and (-3,7). (ii) Give an example of a left handed orthonormal triple of vectors.

2 √ By drawing a sketch, decide whether the triple of vectors (1,1,0), (1,-1,0), (0,0,-1) is left or right handed. According to their inner products, should any two of them be at right angles?

3 √ Find the angle between a main diagonal and an adjacent edge of a cube by using suitable coordinates for the endpoints of the diagonal [see (7.4) to (7.6)].

4 Find every possible product of two of the three matrices in Example 7.14(2) (see Section 7.2.1).

5 √ Prove that, when the implied products exist, (i) $(AB)^T = B^TA^T$, (ii) $A^TB + B^TA$ is symmetric, (iii) $A^TB - B^TA$ is skew-symmetric.

6 √ What is the inverse of the matrix diag{2, -1, 3}? A square matrix A satisfies $A^4 = I$. What can we say about (i) the determinant of A, (ii) the inverse of A? Can you find such an example?

7 Solve the simultaneous equations 2x+3y = 1, x-5y = 7 by first inverting a 2 x 2 matrix (c.f. Example 7.20). Show that if the matrix A has an inverse, then so does its transpose, and $(A^T)^{-1} = (A^{-1})^T$. [Use (7.14), (7.18).]

8 Prove that (i) for a 2 x 2 matrix, if the rows are an orthonormal set then so are the columns, (ii) for a 3 by 3 matrix, the determinant of A^T equals the determinant of A. (cf. Rule 4 of 7.20.]

9 √ Prove that the set of all orthogonal n by n matrices forms a group [see Section 2.5].

10 √ After checking that the vectors (1/2)(1,1,1,1), (1/2)(1,1,-1,-1), and (1/2)(1,-1,1,-1) form an orthonormal set, find a fourth vector which, with them, forms the rows of an orthogonal matrix. Is the determinant +1 or -1?

11 √ For each of the following triples of vectors, determine whether it is left handed, right handed, or coplanar. Check the first two by a rough sketch.

(a) (1,1,-3), (2,1,6), (3,-1,4), (b) (1,1,1), (-1,0,0), (0,1,0),

(c) (1,2,3), (4,5,6), (5,4,3), (d) (1,1,0), (0,1,1), (1,0,1).

12 √ For the points A(2,-5), B(-3,-40), determine by evaluating a determinant, whether rotation of OA towards OB (O fixed) is clockwise or anticlockwise. Now check by a sketch.

13 √ Prove the last three formulae of Theorem 7.35. Cyclic symmetry will help (Theorem 7.31(b)). Prove that [**a**+**b**, **b**+**c**, **c**+**a**] = 2[**a**,**b**,**c**], using cyclic symmetry and Theorem 7.35.

NOTE There follow examples on the coordinate form of a plane isometry. Recall that we can be sure we have the right isometry (given that it *is* an isometry) by verifying its effect on two points, and that it is direct or indirect as required. For the last, see Exercise 15.

14 √ Find the coordinate change (x,y) to (x',y') caused by reflections in each of the following lines in the plane. Do this first by a matrix then rederive the answer by a geometrical argument if possible. Note formula (1.6).

(i) *m* : x = a,

(ii) **p** : y = x,

(iii) **q** : x + y = c, (Geometry: first consider y = -x)

(iv) **r** : the line through O at π/6 to the x-axis,

(v) **s** : the side AB of an equilateral triangle OAB with O the origin, A at (a,0), B with positive y coordinate.

[Diagrams in Table 6.7, answers in Table 6.8.]

15 Verify that the matrix for a plane isometry has determinant +1 in the direct, and -1 in the indirect case by writing out matrices for all types.

16 √ Find the transformation (x,y) to (x',y') of a 1/2 turn about a point G(a,b) using two mirror reflections (no matrices). Does this check with the directly calculated matrix (7.32)? [Answer is in the p2 row of Table 6.8.]

17 √ Write down the matrix for a 1/4 turn about the point (a,a). Now express this as a rotation about the origin followed by a translation. [cf. The p4 row of Table 6.8, where the turn is clockwise because the y-axis points downwards.]

18 Express a 1/3 turn about the point (1,1) as a 1/3 turn about (2,2) followed by a translation.

19 √ Show that the composition of a clockwise 1/3 turn about the origin followed by a 1/2 turn about (2,0) is a 1/6 turn, and determine the centre of rotation.

20 Show that reflection in the mirror $y = x\tan \phi$ followed by translation (2a,2b) is a glide along $y = (x-a)\tan \phi + b$, the original line translated. What is the translation component of the glide?

21 (i) Determine, without using a matrix, the coordinate change corresponding to a glide of length d along the line $y = b$. (ii) Use a formula to find the matrix for a glide from A(1,0) to B(3,1). (iii) What is the result if this is followed by translation by the vector (0,1)? [The solution to Exercise 20 may be useful.]

Chapter 8 ISOMETRIES IN 3-SPACE

The object of this chapter is to classify, and find out how to calculate with, isometries in 3-space. We begin by proving the plausible but not quite obvious fact that a fixed point isometry, one that fixes at least one point, is always linear if that point be taken as the origin of coordinates. We may take linear as 'representable by a matrix'. Composing such isometries with translations gives all possible isometries, which can therefore be represented by 4 by 4 matrices analogously to the situation in two dimensions with 3 x 3 matrices. Furthermore, we use scalar triple products of vectors to show that an isometry consistently preserves or reverses right-handedness.

In Section 8.4 we classify fixed point isometries in three dimensions, assisted by a small section on matrix eigenvalues. This entails the interesting feature that the product of rotations about two axes through a point A is a rotation about a third axis through A (Corollary 8.43). An isometry is now rotation, reflection in a plane, or one called a *rotary reflection* [Section 8.4.4], in which the axis is at right angles to the reflection plane.

Finally, in Section 8.5, we allow composition with translation. This produces two new types of isometry. The first is a *glide in 3-space*, that is the composition of reflection in a plane with translation in a direction parallel to the plane. The second is called a *screw*, in which rotation is combined with translation along its axis. Thus there is a total of six isometry types in three dimensions. We stop short of more general transformations, e.g. the projective type, for reasons of space. See for example Foley et al (1990).

We note but do not stress that, given the basic properties of general $\mathbf{R}^n$ established in Section 7.1.5, the definitions and results of Sections 8.1 and 8.2 carry over to $\mathbf{R}^n$ with the same proofs, except where orientation is concerned. This requires more work to set up in $\mathbf{R}^n$ and we shall not need it. The interested reader may consult Husemoller (1966). We return briefly to the study of general $\mathbf{R}^n$ for eigenvalues, in Section 8.4.5, since we will need them for the 4 x 4 isometry matrices, as well as the two 3 x 3 kinds.

NOTATION 8.1 Let transformations R, T of 3-space be represented by matrices M, N. Then the image of a vector $\mathbf{x}$ under RT (do R then T) is $\mathbf{x}$MN. Composition apart, it is often convenient to write T($\mathbf{x}$) or just T$\mathbf{x}$ for the image of $\mathbf{x}$ under transformation T, as we do generally in this Chapter. Finally a reminder. In coordinatising 3-space we choose an origin, and an orthonormal triple $\mathbf{i}, \mathbf{j}, \mathbf{k}$ to define the axes. In these coordinates, $\mathbf{i} = (1,0,0)$, $\mathbf{j} = (0,1,0)$, $\mathbf{k} = (0,0,1)$.

8.1 Which isometries are linear?

Here is our first step in classifying isometries. Let us suppose that the origin O is fixed once for all.

8.1.1 The matrix of a linear map, and isometries

DEFINITION 8.2 A transformation T of 3-space is an *isometry* if T preserves distances:

$$|T\mathbf{x} - T\mathbf{y}| = |\mathbf{x} - \mathbf{y}| \quad \textit{for all } \mathbf{x},\mathbf{y} \textit{ in } \mathbf{R}^3, \tag{8.1}$$

and hence T preserves angles (up to sign), areas, and volumes Especially important for us is: *If T fixes the origin , TO = O, then*

$$T\mathbf{x} \cdot T\mathbf{y} = \mathbf{x} \cdot \mathbf{y} \quad \textit{for all } \mathbf{x},\mathbf{y} \textit{ in } \mathbf{R}^3, \tag{8.2}$$

and hence

$$\textit{if } \mathbf{e}_1, \mathbf{e}_2, \mathbf{e}_3 \textit{ is an orthonormal basis of 3-space then so is } T\mathbf{e}_1, T\mathbf{e}_2, T\mathbf{e}_3 . \tag{8.3}$$

Proof (8.2) follows from (8.1) because an inner product is completely expressible in terms of distances, by (7.7). The argument begins with $|T\mathbf{x}| = |T\mathbf{x} - T\mathbf{O}| = |\mathbf{x} - \mathbf{O}| = |\mathbf{x}|$, and then

$$\begin{aligned} 2\, T\mathbf{x} \cdot T\mathbf{y} &= |T\mathbf{x}|^2 + |T\mathbf{y}|^2 - |T\mathbf{x} - T\mathbf{y}|^2 && \text{by (7.7)},\\ &= |\mathbf{x}|^2 + |\mathbf{y}|^2 - |\mathbf{x} - \mathbf{y}|^2 && \text{by (8.1)},\\ &= 2\, \mathbf{x} \cdot \mathbf{y} && \text{by (7.7)}. \end{aligned}$$

For (8.3) we now have $T\mathbf{e}_i \cdot T\mathbf{e}_j = \mathbf{e}_i \cdot \mathbf{e}_j = \delta_{ij}$, by (8.2) .

In this Chapter we will often need the coordinate formula (7.6B) which is therefore requoted here for convenience.

The i'th coordinate of a vector **u** *in an orthonormal basis* $\mathbf{e}_1, \mathbf{e}_2, \mathbf{e}_3$ *is* $\mathbf{u}.\mathbf{e}_i$. (8.4)

The following theorem was stated in Chapter 1 for the plane, but the proof given there is clearly valid for general $\mathbf{R}^n$. It is simple and useful, and we shall need to keep it in mind.

THEOREM 8.3 If A is any point of 3-space then any isometry T is composed of a translation, and an isometry that fixes A.

Now we concentrate on the isometries that fix the origin O, and prove the important facts that they are linear, that their matrices form the orthogonal group, and that the determinant distinguishes between direct and indirect isometries.

DEFINITION 8.4 A transformation T of n-space is *linear* if, for all vectors **x**, and real numbers α,

$$T(\mathbf{x} + \mathbf{y}) = T(\mathbf{x}) + T(\mathbf{y}), \qquad T(\alpha\mathbf{x}) = \alpha T(\mathbf{x}). \tag{8.5}$$

This certainly holds if T is given by a matrix, $T(\mathbf{x}) = \mathbf{x}M$, for $T(\mathbf{x} + \mathbf{y}) = (\mathbf{x}+\mathbf{y})M = \mathbf{x}M + \mathbf{y}M = T(\mathbf{x}) + T(\mathbf{y})$, and $T(\alpha\mathbf{x}) = (\alpha\mathbf{x})M = \alpha(\mathbf{x}M) = \alpha T(\mathbf{x})$. The converse is proved in Theorem 8.5. Note though that a linear map must fix the origin, since $T(\mathbf{O}) = T(0\mathbf{x}) = 0T(\mathbf{x}) = \mathbf{O}$, for any x. The definition of *linear* applies to any map (function) from n-space to m-space, though we do not yet require this degree of generality.

We know that origin-fixing isometries of the plane are linear because we have classified them and produced matrices for each case. Let us note here, however, that linear maps go way beyond isometries, for example in dilation and shear (see Figures 8.1, 8.2). This will be fully explored in Chapter 14.

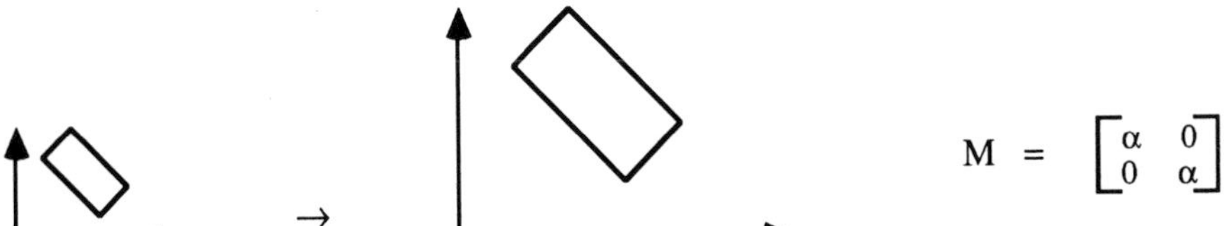

Figure 8.1 Dilation $\mathbf{x} \to \alpha\mathbf{x}$, $\alpha > 0$.

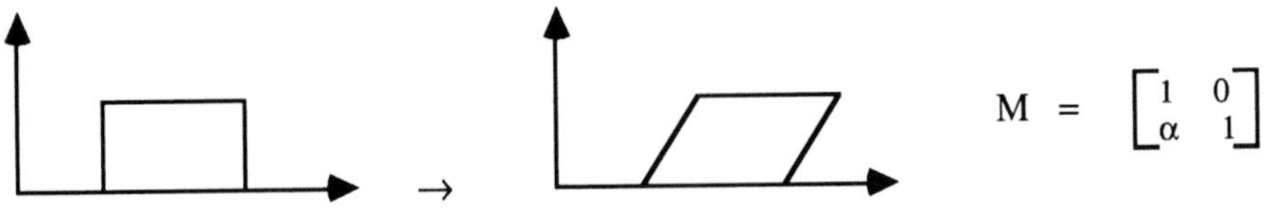

Figure 8.2 Shear $(x,y) \to (x+\alpha y, y)$, $\alpha > 0$.

In fact, it is very useful to define certain transformations to be of the same type if one can be obtained from the other by composition with an isometry. We note here though that, as is fitting, a linear transformation T maps lines to lines, for the line L joining points **a**, **b** consists of the points **x** = **a** + t(**b**-**a**) for all real numbers t, and T**x** = T**a** + t(T**b** - T**a**). Hence T maps L to the line joining points T**a** and T**b**.

THEOREM 8.5 *If T is a linear transformation of 3-space, then it is given by a matrix M as follows.*

$$T(\mathbf{x}) = \mathbf{x}M, \quad M = [m_{ij}], \quad m_{ij} = T(\mathbf{e}_i).\mathbf{e}_j \tag{8.6}$$

where the coordinates of **x** *are taken with respect to an orthonormal basis* $\mathbf{e}_1, \mathbf{e}_2, \mathbf{e}_3$. *In particular, the* ***i'th row*** *of M consists of the coordinates* m_{i1}, m_{i2}, m_{i3} *of* $T(\mathbf{e}_i)$.

Proof Let T be linear. $T(\mathbf{e}_i)$ is a vector and so is expressible in coordinates with respect to $\mathbf{e}_1, \mathbf{e}_2, \mathbf{e}_3$. Let these coordinates be in order m_{i1}, m_{i2}, m_{i3}. Then by the coordinate formula (8.4),

$$m_{ij} = T(\mathbf{e}_i).\mathbf{e}_j \quad \text{for } 1 \le i,j \le 3. \tag{8.6A}$$

With the usual notation $\mathbf{x} = (x_1,x_2,x_3)$ we have

$$\begin{aligned} T(\mathbf{x}) &= T(x_1\mathbf{e}_1 + x_2\mathbf{e}_2 + x_3\mathbf{e}_3) \\ &= x_1T(\mathbf{e}_1) + x_2T(\mathbf{e}_2) + x_3T(\mathbf{e}_3) && \text{by linearity, (8.5)} \\ &= x_1(m_{11}\mathbf{e}_1 + m_{12}\mathbf{e}_2 + m_{13}\mathbf{e}_3) \\ &\quad + x_2(m_{21}\mathbf{e}_1 + m_{22}\mathbf{e}_2 + m_{23}\mathbf{e}_3) \\ &\quad + x_3(m_{31}\mathbf{e}_1 + m_{32}\mathbf{e}_2 + m_{33}\mathbf{e}_3), && \text{by (*).} \end{aligned}$$

The first coordinate of the right hand side, namely the coefficient of $\mathbf{e}_1$, equals $(x_1,x_2,x_3).(m_{11}, m_{21}, m_{31})$, the inner product of **x** with the first column of M. Similarly for the other coordinates, and the proof is complete.

NOTE 8.6 The proof above holds if any three non-coplanar vectors are taken as basis, except that we no longer have the explicit formula $m_{ij} = T(\mathbf{e}_i).\mathbf{e}_j$. This is not emphasised here since we will have virtually no occasion to use a non-orthonormal basis. Essentially the same argument shows that any linear map (function) from n-space to m-space is similarly representable by a matrix.

EXAMPLE 8.7 Find the matrices of the linear transformations of $\mathbf{R}^3$ given by (a) T(x,y,z) = (2x+y, x+z, x+y-3z), (b) T(**i**) = **j**+**k**, T(**j**) = **i**-**j**+**k**, T(**k**) = 2**i**-**j**.

Solution (a) The matrix M of the transformation is defined by T(x,y,z) = [x y z]M, so the coefficients of x, y, z in successive coordinates form the columns of M, which is the first matrix on the right.

$$\begin{bmatrix} 2 & 1 & 1 \\ 1 & 0 & 1 \\ 0 & 1 & -3 \end{bmatrix}, \quad \begin{bmatrix} 0 & 1 & 1 \\ 1 & -1 & 1 \\ 2 & -1 & 0 \end{bmatrix}$$

(b) Theorem 8.5 applies with basis **i**, **j**, **k**. For instance T(**i**) = **j**+**k**, so the first row of M consists of the components (0,1,1). Thus M is the second matrix above.

EXERCISE Find the matrix M when basis **i**,**j**,**k** is transformed to **j**, (**i**+**k**)/√2, (**i**-**k**)/√2. Verify that M is orthogonal and state its determinant.

8.1.2 The proof of linearity

THEOREM 8.8 (Isometries and the orthogonal group.) An isometry T of 3-space which fixes the origin is linear. With respect to any orthonormal basis $\mathbf{e}_1, \mathbf{e}_2, \mathbf{e}_3$ *the matrix of T is orthogonal.*

Proof Let $\mathbf{e}_1, \mathbf{e}_2, \mathbf{e}_3$ be an orthonormal basis. Then by (8.3) so is $\mathbf{f}_1, \mathbf{f}_2, \mathbf{f}_3$, where $\mathbf{f}_i = T\mathbf{e}_i$. Now we express a vector $\mathbf{x}$ in one system and $T\mathbf{x}$ in the other; let us write $\mathbf{x} = x_1\mathbf{e}_1 + x_2\mathbf{e}_2 + x_3\mathbf{e}_3$ and $T\mathbf{x} = y_1\mathbf{f}_1 + y_2\mathbf{f}_2 + y_3\mathbf{f}_3$. Then we have

$$\begin{aligned} y_i &= T\mathbf{x} \,.\, \mathbf{f}_i, && \text{by the coordinate formula (8.4),} \\ &= T\mathbf{x} \,.\, T\mathbf{e}_i && \text{by definition of } \mathbf{f}_i, \\ &= \mathbf{x} \,.\, \mathbf{e}_i && \text{since T is an isometry fixing } \mathbf{O}\text{, by (8.2),} \\ &= x_i, && \text{by (8.4).} \end{aligned}$$

Note that $y_i = x_i$ is obvious if T is linear. We are using other facts. Now express $\mathbf{f}_i$ in $\mathbf{e}_j$ coordinates: $\mathbf{f}_i = \Sigma_j\, m_{ij}\mathbf{e}_j$ (j = 1 to 3), where $m_{ij} = \mathbf{f}_i \,.\, \mathbf{e}_j$ by (8.4). Then

$$\begin{aligned} T\mathbf{x} &= \Sigma_i\, x_i\mathbf{f}_i, && \text{since } x_i = y_i \\ &= \Sigma_i\, x_i\, (\Sigma_j\, m_{ij}\mathbf{e}_j), && \text{by definition of } m_{ij} \\ &= \Sigma_j\, (\Sigma_i\, x_i m_{ij})\mathbf{e}_j, && \text{on reversing the order of summation.} \end{aligned}$$

Thus the j'th component of $T\mathbf{x}$ above, namely the coefficient of $\mathbf{e}_j$, equals the inner product $(x_1,x_2,x_3).(m_{11}, m_{21}, m_{31})$ of $\mathbf{x}$ with the j'th column of matrix $M = [m_{ij}]$. We have shown that T is linear by obtaining it in matrix form, $T(\mathbf{x}) = \mathbf{x}M$. To prove that the matrix M is orthogonal, it suffices to prove that (row i of M) . (row j of M) = δ_{ij} (see Section 7.2.4). But the left hand side is

$$\begin{aligned} \Sigma_k\, m_{ik}m_{jk} &= \Sigma_k\, (\mathbf{f}_i.\mathbf{e}_k)(\mathbf{f}_j.\mathbf{e}_k) && \text{by definition of } m_{ij} \\ &= \mathbf{f}_i.\mathbf{f}_j && \text{calculated in coordinates with respect to } \mathbf{e}_1, \mathbf{e}_2, \mathbf{e}_3 \;\; [(8.4)] \\ &= \delta_{ij}, \text{ as required.} \end{aligned}$$

REMARKS 8.9 (i) It is easy to see that every orthogonal matrix N produces an isometry by $\mathbf{x} \to \mathbf{x}N$, *in fact* $|\mathbf{x}N|^2 = (\mathbf{x}N)(\mathbf{x}N)^T = \mathbf{x}(NN^T)\mathbf{x}^T = \mathbf{x}\,I\,\mathbf{x}^T = |\mathbf{x}|^2$. *The converse is the hard part, and we have just included it in Theorem 8.8. Thus, using any fixed coordinate system,*

> *the orthogonal group O(3) may be identified with the group of all isometries that fix the origin.*

(ii) We have the expression $m_{ij} = T(\mathbf{e}_i).\mathbf{e}_j$ for the elements of the matrix M of T, assuming only that T is linear, not necessarily an isometry, but that the $\mathbf{e}_i$ are orthonormal. If in addition T is an isometry then the $T\mathbf{e}_i$ are also orthonormal [(8.3)], in particular they are unit vectors, and as a result m_{ij} is the cosine of the angle between $T\mathbf{e}_i$ and $\mathbf{e}_j$. In this situation we call M *the matrix of cosines*. Indeed, Theorem 8.8 shows that every orthogonal matrix can be so represented.

8.2 Change of axes

Still keeping the origin fixed, we may wish to change from one set of coordinate axes to another. Aided by Section 8.1 we identify the effect of this on coordinates, the matrix of an isometry, and its determinant.

8.2.1 The matrix of a change of axes

There is a unique isometry mapping one given set of axes to another .

To see this, suppose that **i**,**j**,**k** is an orthonormal basis for coordinates, that **i'**,**j'**,**k'** is the "new" basis, and that we want an isometry T with T**i** = **i'**, T**j** = **j'**, T**k** = **k'**. Since T fixes the origin and so is linear, its effect on a general point is determined by its effect on a basis, namely T(x**i** + y**j** + z**k**) = x**i'** + y**j'** + z**k'**.

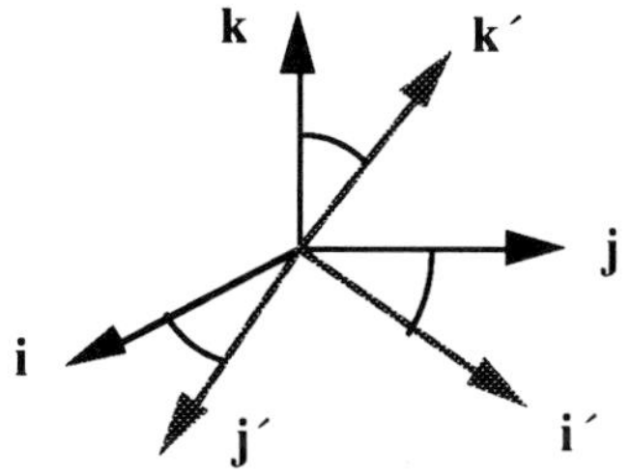

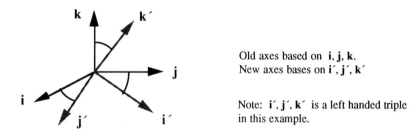

Old axes based on **i**, **j**, **k**.
New axes bases on **i´**, **j´**, **k´**

Note: **i´**, **j´**, **k´** is a left handed triple in this example.

Figure 8.3 Some angles for the direction cosine matrix.

By Remark 8.9 (ii), the matrix of T in terms of basis **i**,**j**,**k** is the *matrix of cosines*, where row i is the i'th new basis vector in terms of the old basis,

$$A = \begin{bmatrix} \mathbf{i}'.\mathbf{i} & \mathbf{i}'.\mathbf{j} & \mathbf{i}'.\mathbf{k} \\ \mathbf{j}'.\mathbf{i} & \mathbf{j}'.\mathbf{j} & \mathbf{j}'.\mathbf{k} \\ \mathbf{k}'.\mathbf{i} & \mathbf{k}'.\mathbf{j} & \mathbf{k}'.\mathbf{k} \end{bmatrix} \qquad (8.7)$$

Notice that the rows are indexed by **i'**, **j'**, **k'** and the columns by **i**, **j**, **k**. This gives a viewpoint which may be easier for calculation, as in the example following.

EXAMPLE 8.10 Find the matrix of any isometry which will map the axes **i**,**j**,**k** so as to send **i** into **u** = (1, 1, 1)/√3.

Solution For this, we complete **u** to a set of three mutually orthogonal unit vectors **u**,**v**,**w**. First we satisfy the orthogonality condition then we divide each vector by its own length. One possibility is **v** = (1, -1, 0)/√2, **w** = (1, 1, -2)/√6. The matrix is now particularly simple to write down, the rows being the coordinates of **u**, **v**, **w** with respect to **i**,**j**,**k**, as indicated by the bordering. We observe that 1/√3 = cos 54.7°, 1/√2 = cos 45°, 1/√6 = cos 65.9°.

$$\begin{array}{c} \\ \mathbf{u} \\ \mathbf{v} \\ \mathbf{w} \end{array} \begin{array}{c} \begin{array}{ccc} \mathbf{i} & \mathbf{j} & \mathbf{k} \end{array} \\ \begin{bmatrix} 1/\sqrt{3} & 1/\sqrt{3} & 1/\sqrt{3} \\ 1/\sqrt{2} & 1/\sqrt{2} & 0 \\ 1/\sqrt{6} & 1/\sqrt{6} & -2/\sqrt{6} \end{bmatrix} \end{array}$$

Second viewpoint : an entry is the scalar product of corresponding vectors on the borders. Thus the **w**, **j** entry is **w**.**j** .

REMARK 8.11 (From single vector to a basis.) The Example above suggests a simple scheme for extending unit vector **u** = (a,b,c) with a,b,c ≠ 0, to an orthonormal basis, by appending (-b,a,0), (a,b,c-1/c) then dividing each vector by its length. We return to this problem in Example 8.29 and ff.

EXERCISE Verify that the scheme of Remark 8.11 does produce an orthonormal basis. Find a matrix for mapping **i**,**j**,**k** into a new basis, where **i** → (3,0,4)/5, and check that the matrix is orthogonal.

8.2.2 The effect on coordinates, of a change of axes

If the basis changes by **e** → **e**A *then coordinates change by* **x** → **x**A^T.

In terms of the **old** basis, here to be called again $\mathbf{e}_1, \mathbf{e}_2, \mathbf{e}_3$, the coordinates of a vector **x** become **x**A. In terms of the new basis $\mathbf{f}_1, \mathbf{f}_2, \mathbf{f}_3$ with $\mathbf{f}_i = T(\mathbf{e}_i)$ and $a_{ij} = \mathbf{f}_i.\mathbf{e}_j$ the i'th coordinate of **x** becomes

$$\begin{aligned} \mathbf{x}.\mathbf{f}_i &= (x_1\mathbf{e}_1 + x_2\mathbf{e}_2 + x_3\mathbf{e}_3).\mathbf{f}_i && \text{by (8.4),} \\ &= x_1\mathbf{e}_1.\mathbf{f}_i + x_2\mathbf{e}_2.\mathbf{f}_i + x_3\mathbf{e}_3.\mathbf{f}_i && \text{by (7.8),} \\ &= x_1a_{i1} + x_2a_{i2} + x_3a_{i3} && \text{by definition of A,} \end{aligned}$$

which equals the inner product of **x** with row i of A, that is with column i of A^T. Thus the new coordinates of **x** are **x**A^T. This may seem too much of a coincidence. The explanation is that moving the axes one way may be regarded as moving points the opposite way. Thus coordinates should change by A^{-1}. But $A^{-1} = A^T$.

EXAMPLE 8.12 What are the new coordinates of point (1,6,4) if the basis ***i,j,k*** *is cycled round to* ***j,k,i****?* The coordinates must be shifted round one place, but which way? Using the matrix here gives a check if required. We must remember to transpose it before converting the coordinates!

$$\begin{array}{c} \\ \mathbf{j} \\ \mathbf{k} \\ \mathbf{i} \end{array} \begin{array}{c} \begin{array}{ccc} \mathbf{i} & \mathbf{j} & \mathbf{k} \end{array} \\ \begin{bmatrix} 0 & 1 & 0 \\ 0 & 0 & 1 \\ 1 & 0 & 0 \end{bmatrix} \end{array} \qquad \begin{bmatrix} 1 & 6 & 4 \end{bmatrix} \begin{bmatrix} 0 & 0 & 1 \\ 1 & 0 & 0 \\ 0 & 1 & 0 \end{bmatrix} = \begin{bmatrix} 6 & 4 & 1 \end{bmatrix}$$

A A^T Result

EXERCISE Verify that the rows of matrix A^T with A as above, are the coordinates of the old basis in terms of the new. Is this true for any change of orthonormal basis?

8.2.3 The effect on the isometry matrix

Under a basis change $\mathbf{e} \to \mathbf{e}A$, *an isometry matrix* M *becomes* AMA^T.

Proof In the usual notation, suppose the old basis $\mathbf{e}_1, \mathbf{e}_2, \mathbf{e}_3$ is changed to the new basis $\mathbf{f}_1, \mathbf{f}_2, \mathbf{f}_3$. Thus (a) $\mathbf{f}_i = \mathbf{e}_i A$, and (b) $a_{ij} = \mathbf{f}_i.\mathbf{e}_j$. We have an isometry T with old matrix M. For the new matrix we calculate the n'th component of $T\mathbf{f}_i$ in terms of the new basis, where i,j,k,n below run from 1 to 3.

$T\mathbf{f}_i$	=	$T(\Sigma_k a_{ik}\mathbf{e}_k)$	by (a),
	=	$\Sigma_k a_{ik} T\mathbf{e}_k$	since T is linear,
	=	$\Sigma_{k,j} a_{ik}m_{kj}\mathbf{e}_j$	as M is the matrix of T.

The n'th component in the new basis is

$(T\mathbf{f}_i).\mathbf{f}_n$	=	$\Sigma_{k,j} a_{ik}m_{kj}\mathbf{e}_j.\mathbf{f}_n$	by the coordinate formula (8.4),
	=	$\Sigma_{k,j} a_{ik}m_{kj}a_{nj}$	by (b),
	=	$(AMA^T)_{in}$,	(the small T denotes transpose)

by definition of matrix multiplication. Since therefore the new components of $T\mathbf{f}_i$ form in order the i'th row of matrix AMA^T, this is the new matrix of T.

EXAMPLE 8.13 What becomes of the matrix of half turn about the z-axis after the basis **i**, **j**, **k** *is changed to* $(\mathbf{j}+\mathbf{k})/\sqrt{2}$, $(\mathbf{k}+\mathbf{i})/\sqrt{2}$, $(\mathbf{i}+\mathbf{j})/\sqrt{2}$? For the matrix M of the 1/2 turn isometry we don't need to recall the sine and cosine of $\pi/2$, since geometry shows us immediately the images of **i**, **j**, **k**, enabling us to write M straight down as in Section 8.2.2. The new matrix AMA^T is, A being symmetric,

$$\frac{1}{\sqrt{2}}\begin{bmatrix} 0 & 1 & 1 \\ 1 & 0 & 1 \\ 1 & 1 & 0 \end{bmatrix}\begin{bmatrix} 0 & 1 & 0 \\ -1 & 0 & 0 \\ 0 & 0 & 1 \end{bmatrix}\frac{1}{\sqrt{2}}\begin{bmatrix} 0 & 1 & 1 \\ 1 & 0 & 1 \\ 1 & 1 & 0 \end{bmatrix} = \frac{1}{2}\begin{bmatrix} 1 & 0 & -1 \\ 2 & 1 & 1 \\ 1 & -1 & 0 \end{bmatrix}.$$

EXERCISE Calculate (7.35) the 3 by 3 matrix for a rotation of $\pi/6$ about the z-axis. Determine by the main result of this section the new matrix N when the axes are changed by $\mathbf{i} \to \mathbf{j} \to \mathbf{k} \to \mathbf{i}$. Verify your answer by geometrical considerations.

8.2.4 The effect on the determinant of M

There is no change. The determinant of the matrix of T, after changing basis by matrix A is, by 8.2.3, $|AMA^T| = |A|\,|M|\,|A^T| = |AA^T|\,|M| = |M|$.

NOTATION 8.14 By Theorem 8.8, if an isometry fixes the origin then it is linear, and the converse is given by Theorem 8.5: linear isometries fix the origin.We will therefore often use the term *'linear isometry'* as the shorter description. Also we shall refer to *'the determinant of T'* since the determinant of the matrix of T is the same for any basis.

8.3 Isometries and orientation

8.3.1 Orientation and the scalar triple product

The possible *orientations* of an ordered triple of vectors **a**,**b**,**c** are right handed and left handed (this defines the term). An isometry preserves angles but may reverse orientation, as in the example below.

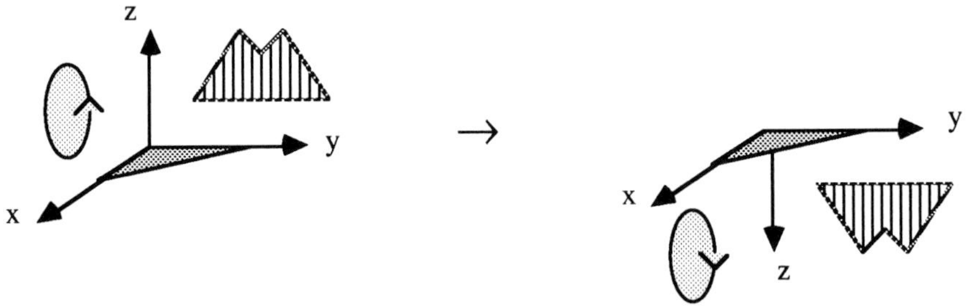

Figure 8.4 Reflection in the xy-plane.

Notice the arrow reversal around the circle above. In fact, reflections play a crucial role in classifying isometries of 3-space, and we will see that, as in the plane case, all isometries can be decomposed into products of reflections.

SIGN CONVENTION 8.15 Henceforth, when speaking of the matrix of an isometry, unless otherwise stated *we will assume a right handed coordinate system.* But note that, for example, reversing the direction of the z-axis does not change the sign of the determinant of a transformation matrix. We covered this point in Section 8.2.4: the change of bases is given by $\mathbf{e}_1, \mathbf{e}_2, \mathbf{e}_3 \to \mathbf{e}_1, \mathbf{e}_2, -\mathbf{e}_3$.

DEFINITION 8.16 An isometry of 3-space is *direct* if it preserves all orientations and *indirect* if it reverses them (we see shortly that there is no other possibility).

REMARK 8.17 It follows logically from the definition that, as in the plane case, the product of two isometries R, S is

DIRECT if R, S are both direct or both indirect,
INDIRECT if one of R, S is direct and the other indirect.

Hence *an isometry is direct if and only if its inverse is direct.* We will soon see how the above definition for 3-space harmonises with the corresponding one for the plane, but meanwhile, for this definition to be useful, it must be impossible for an isometry to preserve some orientations and reverse others. Since translations clearly preserve orientation, we only need check the linear (= origin-fixing) ones, and the following result does this and more for us.

EXERCISE State why an isometry is direct if and only if its inverse is direct.

*THEOREM 8.18 For a linear transformation T of 3-space, with matrix M, we have for any vector triple **a**,**b**,**c** :*

$$[T\mathbf{a}, T\mathbf{b}, T\mathbf{c}] = |M|\,[\mathbf{a},\mathbf{b},\mathbf{c}]. \tag{8.8}$$

Hence a linear isometry either has determinant +1 and preserves all orientations, or has determinant -1 and reverses all orientations.

Proof In the usual notation let $\mathbf{a} = (a_1, a_2, a_3)$ with respect to a right handed orthonormal basis $\mathbf{e}_1, \mathbf{e}_2, \mathbf{e}_3$. Then if $T\mathbf{e}_i = \mathbf{f}_i$ we have, since T is linear, $T\mathbf{a} = a_1\mathbf{f}_1 + a_2\mathbf{f}_2 + a_3\mathbf{f}_3$. Similarly for **b** and **c**. Now, since $[\mathbf{u},\mathbf{v},\mathbf{w}] = 0$ if any two of **u**,**v**,**w** are parallel, we have for example $[a_1\mathbf{f}_1, b_1\mathbf{f}_1, T\mathbf{c}] = 0$, accounting for three out of a possible 3 x 3 x 3 = 27 terms in the expansion by linearity (Theorem 7.35) of [T**a**,T**b**,T**c**]. A cyclic shift $1 \to 2 \to 3 \to 1$ of subscripts reveals another 3 + 3 = 6 zero terms. Hence

$[T\mathbf{a}, T\mathbf{b}, T\mathbf{c}] = [a_1\mathbf{f}_1,\ b_2\mathbf{f}_2 + b_3\mathbf{f}_3,\ c_2\mathbf{f}_2 + c_3\mathbf{f}_3]$ plus two terms obtained by cyclic shifts of the subscripts,

$= a_1\mathbf{f}_1 \cdot (b_2c_3 - b_3c_2)\,\mathbf{f}_2 \times \mathbf{f}_3$ plus two terms, since $\mathbf{f}_3 \times \mathbf{f}_2 = -\mathbf{f}_2 \times \mathbf{f}_3$,

$= a_1\begin{bmatrix} b_2 & b_3 \\ c_2 & c_3 \end{bmatrix}[\mathbf{f}_1, \mathbf{f}_2, \mathbf{f}_3]$ plus two terms,

$= [\mathbf{a}, \mathbf{b}, \mathbf{c}]\,[\mathbf{f}_1, \mathbf{f}_2, \mathbf{f}_3].$

Since by Theorem 8.5 the rows of M are the components of $\mathbf{f}_1, \mathbf{f}_2, \mathbf{f}_3$ in that order, with respect to the right handed orthonormal basis $\mathbf{e}_1, \mathbf{e}_2, \mathbf{e}_3$ it follows from the determinant formula (Theorem 7.32) for the triple scalar product that $[\mathbf{f}_1, \mathbf{f}_2, \mathbf{f}_3] = |M|$. This completes the proof of the formula for [T**a**, T**b**, T**c**]. For the second part we note that a linear isometry has determinant ±1 and that **u**,**v**,**w** is right handed if $[\mathbf{u},\mathbf{v},\mathbf{w}] > 0$ and left handed if $[\mathbf{u},\mathbf{v},\mathbf{w}] < 0$ (Theorem 7.31(d)).

REMARK 8.19 The formula of Theorem 8.18, with Theorem 7.31(a), shows that, up to sign, the determinant of a linear transformation T is a constant factor by which T scales all volumes.

EXAMPLE 8.20 Is the linear transformation defined by $\mathbf{i} \to \mathbf{j}+\mathbf{k}$, $\mathbf{j} \to \mathbf{k}+\mathbf{i}$, $\mathbf{k} \to \mathbf{i}+\mathbf{j}$ *an isometry, and does it preserve orientation? Verify the formula of Theorem 8.18 for the vector triple* $\mathbf{a} = (1,1,1)$, $\mathbf{b} = (1,-2,0)$, $\mathbf{c} = (0,2,1)$.

Solution T has a matrix M whose rows are the coordinates of the images of the orthonormal basis **i**,**j**,**k** under T , by Theorem 8.5. (These images constitute an orthonormal basis if T is an isometry, by (8.3).) Thus M is the matrix on the right. T is not an isometry since M is not an orthogonal matrix. For instance (row 1).(row 2) ≠ 0 (see Section 7.2.4, Assertion (c)). But $|M| = -1(0-1) + 1(1-0) = 2$, so T does preserve orientation by the formula of Theorem 8.18. To verify the formula in this case we compute

$$\begin{bmatrix} 0 & 1 & 1 \\ 1 & 0 & 1 \\ 1 & 1 & 0 \end{bmatrix}$$

$$[\mathbf{a},\mathbf{b},\mathbf{c}] = [\mathbf{b},\mathbf{c},\mathbf{a}] = \begin{vmatrix} 1 & -2 & 0 \\ 0 & 2 & 1 \\ 1 & 1 & 1 \end{vmatrix} = -1, \quad \text{and}$$

$$[T\mathbf{a},T\mathbf{b},T\mathbf{c}] = [\mathbf{a}M,\mathbf{b}M,\mathbf{c}M] = \begin{vmatrix} 2 & 2 & 2 \\ -2 & 1 & -1 \\ 3 & 1 & 2 \end{vmatrix} = -2.$$

Thus $[T\mathbf{a},T\mathbf{b},T\mathbf{c}] = |M|\,[\mathbf{a},\mathbf{b},\mathbf{c}]$, as was to be verified.

EXERCISE Repeat the example above for T defined by $\mathbf{i} \to \mathbf{i}+\mathbf{j}-\mathbf{k}$, $\mathbf{j} \to 2\mathbf{i}+\mathbf{j}$, $\mathbf{k} \to \mathbf{i}-\mathbf{k}$ and $\mathbf{a} = (1,2,3)$, $\mathbf{b} = (3,4,1)$, $\mathbf{c} = (2,-7,6)$.

8.3.2 Consistency with the plane definition

If an isometry T of 3-space fixes the z-axis then T maps the xy-plane to itself (why?). In its action on the *plane* T fixes the origin and preserves distances, so has 3 by 3 matrix of the form

$$\begin{bmatrix} a & b & 0 \\ c & d & 0 \\ 0 & 0 & 1 \end{bmatrix}, \quad \text{with} \quad \begin{bmatrix} a & b \\ c & d \end{bmatrix} \quad \text{in} \quad O(2).$$

We wish to show that our two definitions of directness agree in the plane (they are found in Section 1.2.3 and above Remark 8.17). Let OAB in the plane have anticlockwise sense. Then OA, OB, OZ is a right handed triple in 3-space. Suppose T maps this triple to OC, OD, OZ.

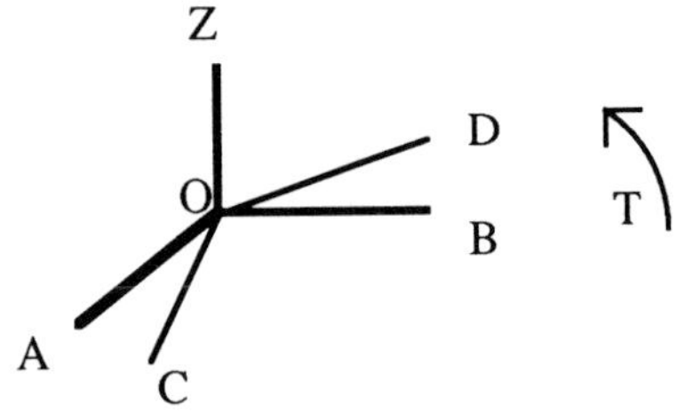

Then: T is direct in 3-space ⇔ OC, OD, OZ is right handed ⇔ OCD is anticlockwise ⇔ T is direct as an isometry of the plane.

8.3.3 4 x 4 Matrices and translation in 3 dimensions

We used extended vectors [x y 1] to include translations in the 2-d matrix formulation, and we use extended vectors [x y z 1] to do the same for 3-space. The 4 x 4 matrix N, for a linear isometry with matrix $M = [m_{ij}]$ FOLLOWED BY translation by vector (a_1, a_2, a_3) is the product given shortly below. It comes out less simply in the reverse order, hence we emphasise putting the translation second. Just as for the plane in Section 7.4.2, if the translation *was* done first we can read off as (a_1,a_2,a_3) the translation which should be done last, *in order to achieve the same effect.*

$$\begin{bmatrix} m_{11} & m_{12} & m_{13} & 0 \\ m_{21} & m_{22} & m_{23} & 0 \\ m_{31} & m_{32} & m_{33} & 0 \\ 0 & 0 & 0 & 1 \end{bmatrix} \begin{bmatrix} 1 & 0 & 0 & 0 \\ 0 & 1 & 0 & 0 \\ 0 & 0 & 1 & 0 \\ a_1 & a_2 & a_3 & 1 \end{bmatrix} = \begin{bmatrix} m_{11} & m_{12} & m_{13} & 0 \\ m_{21} & m_{22} & m_{23} & 0 \\ m_{31} & m_{32} & m_{33} & 0 \\ a_1 & a_2 & a_3 & 1 \end{bmatrix}$$

The nice thing is that the product matrix N has the same determinant as M, so that not only does N represent an arbitrary isometry of 3-space, but this isometry is direct if $|N| = 1$ and indirect if $|N| = -1$, in agreement with Remark 8.17. The three dimensional development continues in the succeeding sections.

COROLLARY 8.21 A general isometry of 3-space is direct or indirect according as the determinant of its 4 by 4 matrix is 1 or -1.

EXERCISE A 90 degree turn about the z-axis is preceded by a translation of (1,-2,4). What translation should instead follow the turn, to achieve the same effect? Verify that the determinant is the same in both cases. How does it square with the isometry products involved?

8.4 Classifying fixed point isometries

In this section we find that, unlike the situation in two dimensions, 3-dimensional reflections and rotations may combine into a new type of isometry named rotary reflection. We derive the important result that the product of rotations about two axes through the origin is rotation about a third, and we show how to compute explicitly the axis, the angle and, importantly, its sign.

8.4.1 Basic theorems and examples

THEOREM 8.22 An isometry g in 3-space is determined by its effect on any three non-collinear points and whether g is direct or indirect. Alternatively, by the effect on four noncoplanar points.

Proof Let g map three non-collinear points A, B, C to A', B', C'.

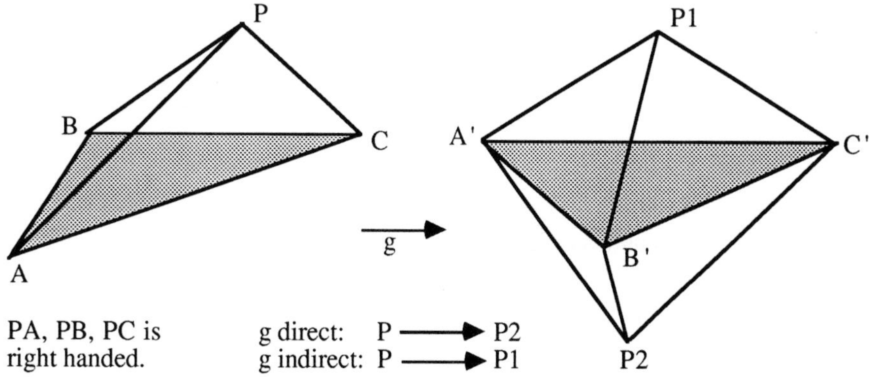

Figure 8.5 An isometry g is determined by its effect on four non-coplanar points.

Elementary geometry shows that, if the distances of a point P from A, B, C are specified then there are just two possible positions for P. Further, we see that the triple PA, PB, PC is right handed for one position of P and left handed for the other. This gives the conclusion of the theorem, illustrated by Figure 8.5 above.

8.4.2 Reflection in a plane

FORMAL DEFINITION We refer to the diagram below. Let B be the projection of a point P onto a plane Π. Thus, if P is not on Π then BP is a normal to Π at B, as shown. Then the *reflection of* P *in* Π is P', where

$$\underline{PP'} = 2\underline{PB}. \tag{8.9}$$

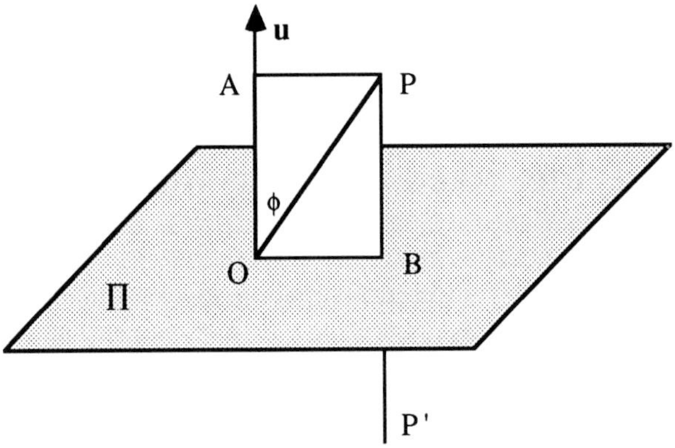

Figure 8.6 Reflection in a plane Π sends P to P', where $\underline{PB} = \underline{BP'}$.

NOTATION 8.23 (Reflections.) Some natural extensions of the notation for reflection in a line will be useful. We recall that a *normal* vector **u** to a plane is one perpendicular to it. If in addition **u** is a unit vector (one of length 1), **u** is called a *unit normal.*

R_Π the operation of reflection in the plane Π,
R_{ABC} reflection in the plane containing non-collinear points A,B,C,
$R_\mathbf{u}$ reflection in the plane through O with a normal vector **u.**

We note that the slightly similar notations for rotation have an argument, which distinguishes them from reflection. Now we present a simple formula for calculation. Reflection $R_\mathbf{u}$ is given by

$$R_\mathbf{u} : \quad \mathbf{x} \to \mathbf{x} - 2(\mathbf{x}.\mathbf{u}/|\mathbf{u}|^2)\,\mathbf{u} \tag{8.10}$$

Proof We refer to Figure 8.6. Let $\mathbf{x} = \underline{OP}$ and let the normal, **u**, start at the origin O, assuming first that **u** is a unit vector. Then we have

$$\begin{aligned}\underline{BP} &= \underline{OA}, && \text{where A is the projection of P onto } \mathbf{u},\\ &= (|OP| \cos\phi)\,\mathbf{u} &&\\ &= (\mathbf{x}.\mathbf{u})\,\mathbf{u}, && \text{by (8.4)},\end{aligned}$$

so by (8.9), $R_\mathbf{u}$ sends **x** to $\mathbf{x} - 2(\mathbf{x}.\mathbf{u})\,\mathbf{u}$. Now we replace **u** by $\mathbf{u}/|\mathbf{u}|$ to obtain a unit normal from the original **u**, and so recover the given formula (8.10).

EXAMPLE 8.24 With **u** = (1, -1, 0), $R_\mathbf{u}$ switches the first two components of a vector, for by (8.10), $R_\mathbf{u}$ sends (x_1,x_2,x_3) to $(x_1,x_2,x_3) - 2(x_1-x_2)(1, -1, 0)/2 = (x_2, x_1, x_3)$.

EXAMPLE 8.25 Find the orbit (= all the images) of point (2,2,2) under the group generated by $R_\mathbf{u}, R_\mathbf{v}, R_\mathbf{w}$, where **u** = (1, 0, 0), **v** = (1, -1, 0), **w** = (0, 1,-1).

Solution $R_\mathbf{u}$: $(x_1,x_2,x_3) \to (x_1,x_2,x_3) - 2x_1(1, 0, 0) = (-x_1,x_2,x_3)$, thus $R_\mathbf{u}$ changes the sign of the first coordinate x_1. Now obviously, in the light of Example 8.24, $R_\mathbf{w}$ switches the last two coordinates, so $R_\mathbf{v}$ and $R_\mathbf{w}$ between them generate all permutations of the coordinates, and so our including $R_\mathbf{u}$ adds the sign changes of all three coordinates. Applying all these transformations to (2, 2, 2) yields the eight vertices (±2, ±2, ±2) of a cube of side 4. The planes $\Pi_\mathbf{u}, \Pi_\mathbf{v}, \Pi_\mathbf{w}$ through the origin with respective normals **u,v,w** are depicted below in Figure 8.7. Reflection in each plane is a symmetry of the cube, and maps every plane of symmetry into another.

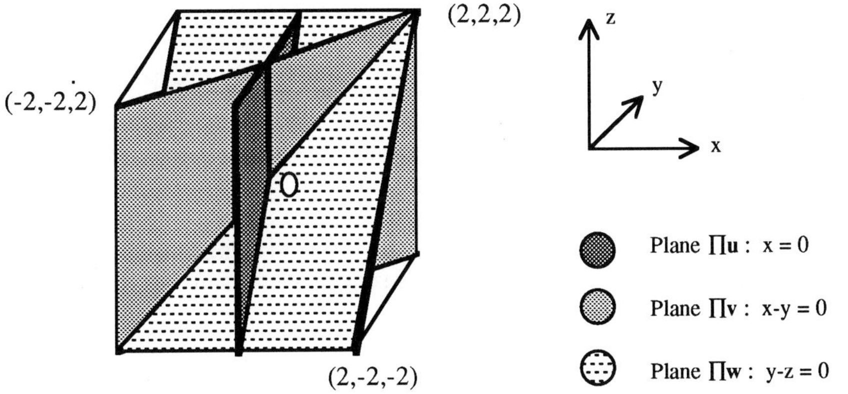

Figure 8.7 Reflection planes generating the symmetries of a cube centred at O.

EXERCISE Determine the effect on coordinates, of reflection in the plane with equation x+y = 0. [The normal is (1,1,0).] Put this in matrix form.

The matrix of a reflection Note that whatever the matrix M of a reflection is, it must satisfy $M^2 = I$ since a reflection applied twice gives the identity transformation. From formula (8.10), reflection in the plane through the origin with <u>unit</u> normal **u** is given by $\mathbf{x} \to \mathbf{x}M$, where

$$M = \begin{bmatrix} 1-2u_1^2 & -2u_1u_2 & -2u_1u_3 \\ -2u_2u_1 & 1-2u_2^2 & -2u_2u_3 \\ -2u_3u_1 & -2u_3u_2 & 1-2u_3^2 \end{bmatrix} = I - 2\mathbf{u}^T\mathbf{u}. \qquad (8.11)$$

Finding the axis A normal vector of the reflection plane for (8.11) is any row of M-I which is not all zero. cf. Example 8.40.

EXERCISE Use (8.11) to find the matrix for reflection in the plane 2x - 5y + z = 0.

THEOREM 8.26 Let planes Π, Π' be at angle ϕ. Then the composition $R_\Pi . R_{\Pi'}$ of reflection in Π followed by reflection in Π' equals rotation through angle 2ϕ about the line of intersection of Π and Π', unless the planes are parallel, when we obtain translation through twice the distance between them.

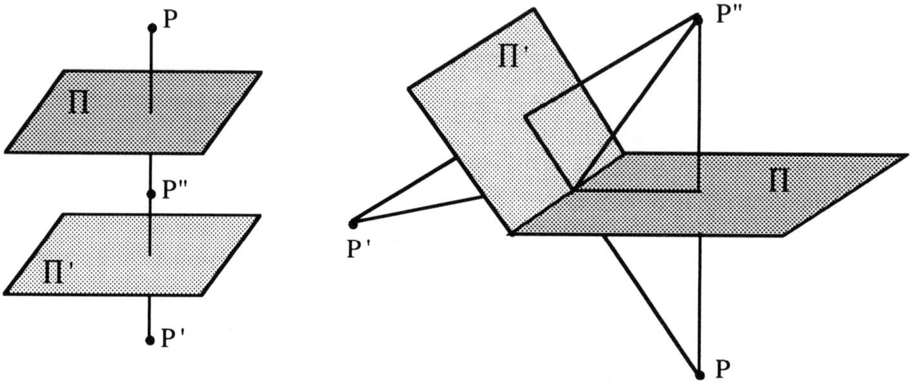

Figure 8.8 Reflection in two successive planes gives rotation about their line of intersection, or translation if they are parallel.

Proof This is essentially the same as in the plane, using the diagram above, in which P → P" → P'. Alternatively, an algebraic proof may be given using formula (8.10) or its matrix form (8.11), for a reflection.

8.4.3 Rotation

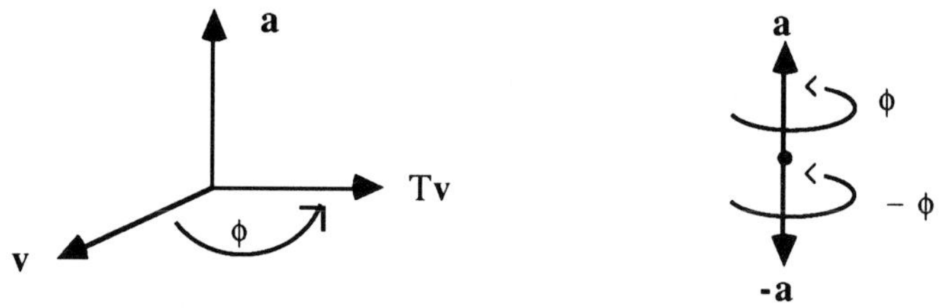

Figure 8.9 Rotation ϕ about axis **a** equals rotation -ϕ about axis -**a**.

NOTATION 8.27

$R_A(\phi)$ = rotation ϕ about a point A in the plane (as before),
$R_{\mathbf{a}}(\phi)$ = rotation ϕ about *axis vector* **a** in 3-space.

Calling **a** an *axis vector* means that

(i) the vector **a** starts at some given point,
(ii) the rotation is about an axis lying along **a**,
(iii) ϕ is defined to be positive if the triple **v**, T**v**, **a** or equivalently **a**, **v**, T**v**, is *right handed*, where **v** is any vector with the same starting point as **a**, and T denotes the rotation transformation. Thus ϕ *has the sign of* [**v**, T**v**, **a**]. In calculations it may be convenient to choose **v** at right angles to **a**. For examples,

see Section 8.4.6.

REMARK 8.28 $R_{\mathbf{a}}(\phi) = R_{-\mathbf{a}}(-\phi)$, as illustrated above. We emphasise that ϕ is a signed angle, and that reversing the direction of the axis reverses the sign of ϕ. We record the 3 by 3 matrices for rotation through angle ϕ about respective axes **i**, **j**, **k** (a right handed system). For rotation about an arbitrary axis, see Theorem 8.49.

$$\begin{bmatrix} 1 & 0 & 0 \\ 0 & \cos\phi & \sin\phi \\ 0 & -\sin\phi & \cos\phi \end{bmatrix}, \quad \begin{bmatrix} \cos\phi & 0 & -\sin\phi \\ 0 & 1 & 0 \\ \sin\phi & 0 & \cos\phi \end{bmatrix}, \quad \begin{bmatrix} \cos\phi & \sin\phi & 0 \\ -\sin\phi & \cos\phi & 0 \\ 0 & 0 & 1 \end{bmatrix} \tag{8.12}$$

EXAMPLE 8.29 (An application in Molecular Graphics.) Thomson, Higgins and Edge (1988) construct a surface depicting electrostatic potential using coloured polygons. Such a polygon, centred at the origin and lying in the xy plane, must be recentred at the point (p,q,r) and realigned to be perpendicular to the unit vector (a,b,c) instead of to (0,0,1). We write $v = \sqrt{(b^2 + c^2)}$, taking **i,j,k** as basis for x,y,z coordinates. Noting that $a^2 + v^2 = 1$, we may use the three stage process indicated by Figures 8.10 (a) to (c) below.

$$M_y = \begin{bmatrix} v & 0 & -a & 0 \\ 0 & 1 & 0 & 0 \\ a & 0 & v & 0 \\ 0 & 0 & 0 & 1 \end{bmatrix}$$

$\cos\phi = v, \quad \sin\phi = a$

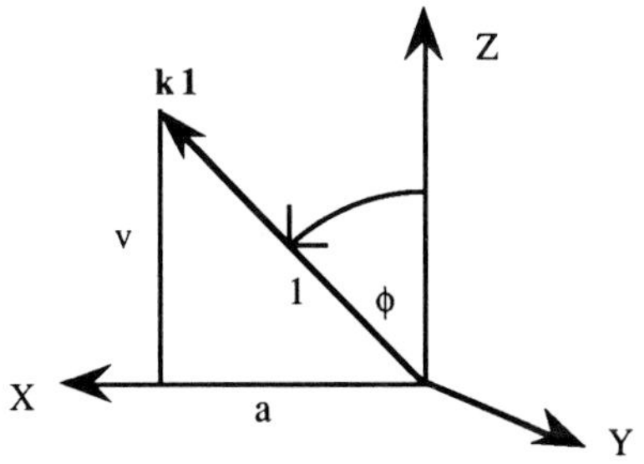

Figure 8.10(a) First stage. The 4 x 4 matrix M_y rotates **k** about the y-axis, into a unit vector **k1** with x-component a.

$$M_x = \begin{bmatrix} 1 & 0 & 0 & 0 \\ 0 & c/v & -b/v & 0 \\ 0 & b/v & c/v & 0 \\ 0 & 0 & 0 & 1 \end{bmatrix}$$

$\cos\theta = c/v, \quad \sin\theta = -b/v$

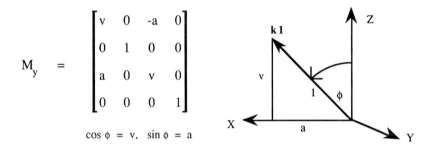

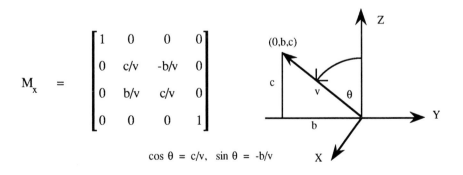

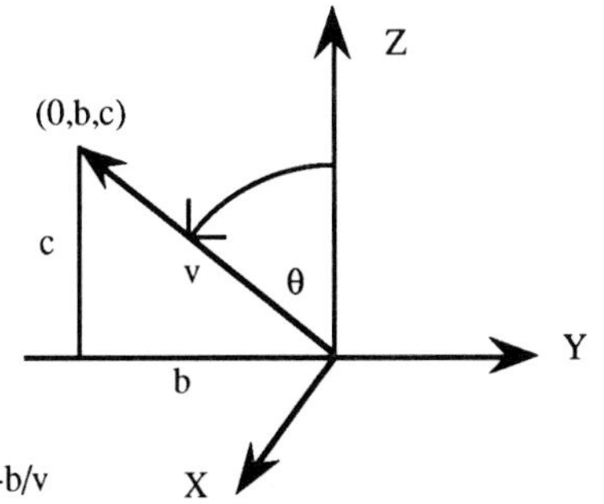

Figure 8.10(b) Stage 2. Matrix M_x rotates **k1** about the x-axis to a vector with y,z-components b,c, so the vector is (a,b,c). The rotation is shown in the yz-plane.

$$M = \begin{bmatrix} v & -ab/v & -ac/v & 0 \\ 0 & c/v & -b/v & 0 \\ a & b & c & 0 \\ p & q & r & 1 \end{bmatrix}$$

Figure 8.10(c) Stage 3. We apply the 4 x 4 translation matrix N for (p,q,r). The complete transformation is therefore $[x\ y\ z\ 1] \to [x\ y\ z\ 1]\ M_yM_x\ N$, with combined matrix $M = M_yM_x\ N$, as shown above.

REMARK 8.30 (Degrees of freedom.) What we gain from the method above is geometrical insight: the result *can* be obtained by successive rotations about the y and x axes (cf. Euler angles in Section 9.4.1). It is easily checked that M is orthogonal with determinant 1, and that M sends the origin to (p,q,r) and **k** to (a,b,c) as required. Theorem 8.22 tells us that infinitely many other matrices would do the job, since we have the freedom to specify the effect also on any vector not parallel to **k**. That is, on any point not collinear with the origin and the point (0,0,1). Of course, this choice must be consistent with the transformation being an isometry, which we wish it to be.

The quickest way to obtain an orthogonal matrix that will send **k** to the unit vector **w** = (a,b,c) is to extend the singleton set {**w**} to an orthonormal triple **u**,**v**,**w** (Remark 8.11) thus:

k → **w** = (a,b,c),
j → any unit vector **v** perpendicular to (a,b,c),
i → either of the two unit vectors ±**u** perpendicular to **v**,**w**.

Notice that the last line amounts to choosing whether the transformation will be direct or indirect. It is direct precisely when the corresponding vector triples have the same orientation (cf. Theorem 8.18). Changing **u** to -**u** interchanges directness and indirectness.

EXERCISE Find matrices of both a direct and an indirect isometry mapping (0,0,1) to (1,2,-2).

8.4.4 Rotary reflections

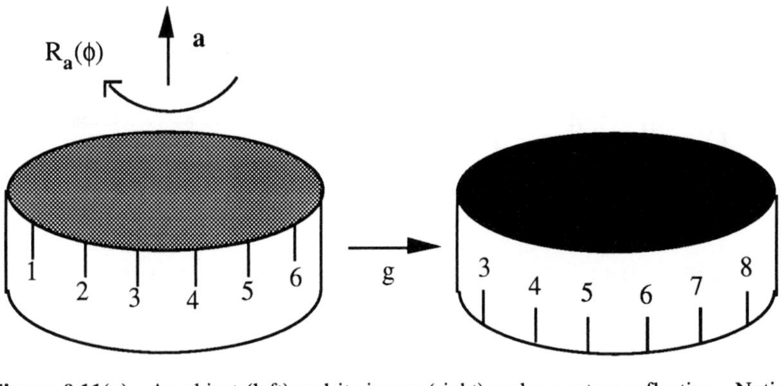

Figure 8.11(a) An object (left) and its image (right) under a rotary reflection. Notice that ϕ is negative, since the rotation is clockwise with **a** as axis.

To preview our next result towards classification of 3-d isometries, it turns out that a linear isometry is a rotation, reflection, or an especially simple combination in which the rotation axis is normal to the mirror. We give a formal definition and an example.

DEFINITION 8.31 A *rotary reflection* is an isometry $g = R_{\mathbf{a}}(\phi).R_{\Pi}$ of 3-space in which $\mathbf{a} \perp \Pi$ ($\mathbf{a}$ is perpendicular to the plane Π). We note that g also equals $R_{\Pi}.R_{\mathbf{a}}(\phi)$, as a consequence of $\mathbf{a} \perp \Pi$.

INVERSION $\mathbf{v} \to -\mathbf{v}$. The special case of a 1/2 turn + reflection (see Figure 8.11(b)).

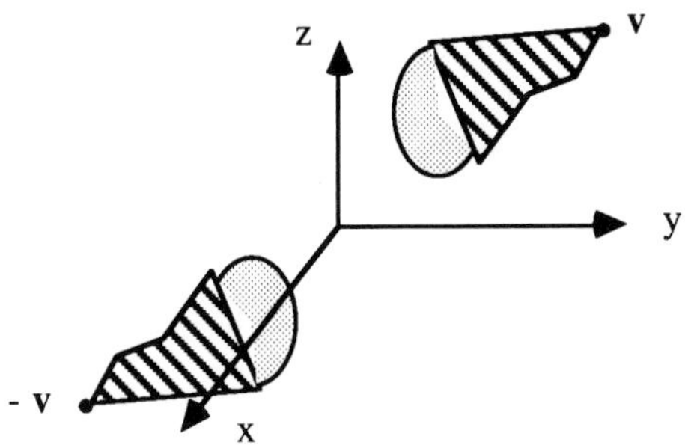

Figure 8.11(b) An object and its image under inversion (special case of rotary reflection). This isometry has order two. Applying it a second time, to the image, we recover the original.

The inversion map is reflection through the origin O, reversing the direction of every line through O. It occurs when the rotation in a rotary reflection is a 1/2 turn, sending $\mathbf{v}$ = (x,y,z) to (-x,-y,z), which is then mapped by the reflection to (-x,-y,-z) = $-\mathbf{v}$. Note: although strictly a special case, inversion is not usually thought of as rotary reflection, because of its obvious symmetry properties in all directions relative to the origin. Indeed it may be decomposed as $R_{OXY}\, R_{OYZ}\, R_{OZX}$, reflection in the three coordinate planes in succession.

EXERCISE Write down the matrix for inversion. Verify by matrices that it is the product of a half turn and a reflection, or the product of three reflections.

REMARK 8.32 Since, clearly, any reflection is an indirect isometry, the same holds for the product of any odd number of reflections, whilst an even product is direct. In particular, a rotation is the product of two reflections so is direct (see Theorem 8.25) and has determinant 1 (Corollary 8.21), but a rotary reflection is the product of three reflections so is indirect, with determinant -1.

8.4.5 Eigenvalues and isometries

To classify linear isometries we need a little of the theory of eigenvalues, reproduced here. For a revision of complex numbers, see Section 9.1, but here is a quick 'fix'. The set **C** of complex numbers is an extension of the real numbers for which *every* quadratic equation has a solution because of the presence of the symbol **i** (not to be confused with a basis vector, though there are connections) which acts as a square root of -1. We may express the complex numbers as $\mathbf{C} = \{x+y\mathbf{i}: x, y \in \mathbf{R}\}$, with multiplication requiring the extra definition $\mathbf{i}^2 = -1$.

Thus for example $(1-2\mathbf{i})(3+\mathbf{i}) = 3-2\mathbf{i}^2-5\mathbf{i} = 5-5\mathbf{i} = 5(1-\mathbf{i})$. And $z^2+2z+5 = 0 \Leftrightarrow (z+1)^2 = -4 = 4\mathbf{i}^2 \Leftrightarrow z = -1\pm2\mathbf{i}$. The complex number $z = x+y\mathbf{i}$ is said to have *real part* x, *imaginary part* y, *conjugate* $x-y\mathbf{i}$, and *modulus* $|z|$, where $|z|^2 = x^2+y^2 = (x+y\mathbf{i})(x-y\mathbf{i})$, the squared length of the vector (x,y) in the plane. The number of unit modulus $\cos\phi + \mathbf{i}\sin\phi$ is denoted by $e^{\mathbf{i}\phi}$, because it behaves like this power for any angle ϕ (see Section 9.1.2).

Complex numbers are invaluable in Science, Mathematics and Engineering (see e.g. Churchill, 1960). Right now we need the fact that every polynomial with complex (which includes real) coefficients is the product of linear factors. This is one version of the *Fundamental theorem of Algebra*, (13.20). We note too that a polynomial equation of degree n cannot have more than n distinct solutions, for each solution α implies a factor $x-\alpha$ of the polynomial, by the argument of Lemma 7.22 applied (unchanged) to complex numbers.

DEFINITION 8.33 The real or complex number λ is an *eigenvalue* of the n x n matrix M, with *eigenvector* $\mathbf{x} = (x_1, \ldots, x_n)$ if

$$\mathbf{x}M = \lambda\mathbf{x} \quad \text{and } \mathbf{x} \neq 0. \tag{8.13}$$

Notice that

(i) $\mathbf{x} \neq 0$ means not *all* entries of $\mathbf{x}$ are zero,

(ii) if $\mathbf{x}$ satisfies (8.13) then so does $\beta\mathbf{x}$ for every complex number β,

(iii) if M and λ are real and (8.13) is satisfied by some complex $\mathbf{x}$ then by taking either the real parts or the imaginary parts of $\mathbf{x}$, which cannot *all* be zero, we obtain a *real* nonzero solution for $\mathbf{x}$.

EXAMPLES 8.34 (a) *Rotation.* For M the matrix of rotation about axis vector $\mathbf{a}$ we have $\mathbf{a}M = 1\mathbf{a}$. Thus M has an eigenvalue 1 with eigenvector $\mathbf{a}$.

(b) *Reflection.* If M is the matrix of reflection in a mirror through O with normal vector $\mathbf{n}$, then $\mathbf{n}M = -\mathbf{n}$. That is, -1 is an eigenvalue, with $\mathbf{n}$ as an eigenvector. From observation (ii), any multiple of $\mathbf{n}$ is also an eigenvector corresponding to 1, as we know it should be. We can say a little more (note that here M is the top left hand 3 x 3 matrix if we are using a 4 x 4 version) :

(8.14)

(A) The axis vectors of a rotation with matrix M are the eigenvectors of M with eigenvalue 1,

(B) The normal vectors to the plane, for a reflection with matrix M, are the eigenvectors of M with eigenvalue -1,

(C) The eigenvalues of a reflection matrix M are ±1.

Proof of (C) $\mathbf{x}M = \lambda\mathbf{x} \Rightarrow \mathbf{x}M^2 = \lambda\mathbf{x}M \Rightarrow \mathbf{x} = \lambda^2\mathbf{x}$ (since $M^2 = 1$) $\Rightarrow \lambda^2 = 1$, as we assume $\mathbf{x} \neq 0$. Notice that the equation $\lambda^2 = 1$ cannot have more than two solutions, even if we admit complex numbers (again, by Lemma 7.22). Next we will see how one may compute eigenvalues in general.

CALCULATING EIGENVALUES We derive an equation whose roots are precisely the eigenvalues of a given n x *n matrix M*. Let λ be any real or complex number, then

$$
\begin{aligned}
&\mathbf{x}M = \lambda\mathbf{x}, \quad \text{for some } \mathbf{x} \neq 0 \\
\Leftrightarrow\quad & \mathbf{x}(M - \lambda I) = \mathbf{0}, \text{ for some } \mathbf{x} \neq \mathbf{0} && (8.15)\\
\Leftrightarrow\quad & \text{some linear combination } \textstyle\sum_i x_i C_i \text{ of the rows} \\
& \text{of } M - \lambda I \text{ is zero (not all } x_i \text{ zero)} \\
\Leftrightarrow\quad & |M - \lambda I| = 0 \quad \text{(by Rule 7.20(5)).} && (8.16)
\end{aligned}
$$

Thus for each solution $\lambda = \alpha$ of the *eigenvalue equation* (8.16) we have a nonzero vector **x** satisfying (8.13). Now we observe that $M - \lambda I$ equals

$$
\begin{bmatrix}
m_{11} - \lambda & m_{12} & \cdots & m_{1n} \\
m_{21} & m_{22} - \lambda & \cdots & m_{2n} \\
\cdots & \cdots & \cdots & \cdots \\
m_{n1} & m_{n2} & \cdots & m_{nn} - \lambda
\end{bmatrix}
$$

and, setting $\lambda = 0$ to obtain the constant term as $|M|$, we argue (below) that, up to a multiple $(-1)^n$ the eigenvalue equation has the form

$$\lambda^n - (\textstyle\sum_i m_{ii})\lambda^{n-1} + .. - ... + (-1)^n |M| = 0. \qquad (8.17)$$

For the coefficient of λ^{n-1} we look back at the inductive definition of a determinant in Section 7.2.2. We have that (a) one term in the expansion of $|M - \lambda I|$ is the product of the diagonal elements of $M - \lambda I$, $D(\lambda) = (m_{11} - \lambda)(m_{22} - \lambda) \ldots (m_{nn} - \lambda)$, (b) every other term contains at most n-2 of the diagonal elements, *because* in forming the subdeterminant which multiplies an element m_{1k} of the first row ($k \geq 2$) we omit row 1 and column k, and hence both $(m_{11} - \lambda)$ and $(m_{kk} - \lambda)$. We conclude therefore that (c), the coefficient of λ^{n-1} in the determinant $|M - \lambda I|$ equals the coefficient of λ^{n-1} in $D(\lambda)$, namely $(m_{11} + m_{22} + .. + m_{nn})$.

Now, by the Fundamental Theorem of Algebra (see the head of Section 8.4.5), the left hand side of the eigenvalue equation (8.17) is the product of n linear factors $\lambda-\alpha_i$, possibly with repetitions, in which some α_i may be complex. We view the equation as having n roots, counted according to their multiplicities. But first some simple examples on 2 x 2 matrices.

EXAMPLE 8.35 Calculate the eigenvalues of the following matrices, and find eigenvectors for the third matrix.

$$
\text{(i)} \begin{bmatrix} 2 & 3 \\ 3 & 4 \end{bmatrix} \quad
\text{(ii)} \begin{bmatrix} 1 & 0 \\ 0 & 2 \end{bmatrix} \quad
\text{(iii)} \begin{bmatrix} 0 & -1 \\ 1 & 0 \end{bmatrix} \quad
\text{(iv)} \begin{bmatrix} 1 & 1 \\ 1 & 1 \end{bmatrix}
$$

Solution In the 2 x 2 case we can read off the eigenvalue equation directly from (8.17).
(i) $\lambda^2 - (2+4)\lambda + (8-9) = 0$, $\lambda^2 - 6\lambda - 1 = 0$; solution $\lambda = 3 \pm \sqrt{(10)}$.
(ii) $\lambda^2 - 3\lambda + 2 = 0$ and $\lambda = 1,2$.
(iii) $\lambda^2 + 1 = 0$, with classic solution $\lambda = \pm\mathbf{i}$.
(iv) $\lambda^2 - 2\lambda = 0$, $\lambda = 0, 2$.

For an eigenvector $\mathbf{x} = [x\ y]$ of (iii) corresponding to eigenvalue $\lambda = \mathbf{i}$ we have the standard equation of (8.15): $\mathbf{x}(M - \lambda I) = \mathbf{0}$. Written out, this is

$$\begin{bmatrix} x & y \end{bmatrix}\begin{bmatrix} -\mathbf{i} & -1 \\ 1 & -\mathbf{i} \end{bmatrix} = \mathbf{0}, \quad \text{or} \quad \begin{cases} -\mathbf{i}x + y = 0 \\ -x - \mathbf{i}y = 0 \end{cases}$$

Now the matrix $(M - \lambda I)$ has determinant 0 so by Rule 7.20(5), each column of the matrix, hence each equation, must be a multiple of the other. And indeed, on inspection we find that the first equation is i times the second, using $\mathbf{i}^2 = -1$. Thus the only condition x, y must satisfy is $x = -\mathbf{i}y$ and we may take $\mathbf{x} = [-\mathbf{i}\ 1]$. Starting again with eigenvalue $\lambda = -\mathbf{i}$ we find a corresponding eigenvector $[\mathbf{i}\ 1]$.

EXERCISE Derive the second eigenvector in part (iii) above.

DEFINITION 8.36 The *trace* of an n x n matrix M is the sum of its diagonal elements, $\text{Tr}\, M = m_{11} + m_{22} + \ldots + m_{nn}$. By Lemma 8.37(ii) below, the trace and determinant of the matrix of an isometry T do not depend on the choice of basis, but only on T itself. Hence they are described as *invariants* of T and referred to as *the trace and determinant of T*. The trace will be useful for, amongst other things, identifying the angle of rotation of T when rotation is present (see Theorem 8.42).

LEMMA 8.37 Let M be an n x n matrix. Then

(i) *Tr M equals the sum of the eigenvalues of M, and |M| equals their product.*

(ii) *The eigenvalue equation of M is unchanged if we replace M by AMA^{-1}, where A is an invertible n x n matrix. In particular, if M is the matrix of an isometry T, then the new matrix under a change of orthonormal basis has the same trace and determinant as M.*

Proof (i) Let the eigenvalues be $\lambda_1, \ldots, \lambda_n$, of which some may be equal. Then the left hand side of the eigenvalue equation (8.17) is identical to $(\lambda - \lambda_1)(\lambda - \lambda_2) \ldots (\lambda - \lambda_n)$. The coefficient of λ^{n-1} is $-\Sigma\lambda_i$, which must therefore equal the coefficient $-\Sigma m_{ii}$ of λ^{n-1} in (8.17). This gives the first assertion of (i). For the second we observe that the two equal constant terms are $(-1)^n \lambda_1\lambda_2 \ldots \lambda_n$ and $(-1)^n|M|$.

(ii) We recall Rule 7.20(4), that $|BC| = |B||C|$ for the determinant of the product of two matrices B, C. Thus, since $|A|\,|A^{-1}| = |AA^{-1}| = 1$, we have $|M-\lambda I| = |A|\,|M-\lambda I|\,|A^{-1}| = |A(M-\lambda I)A^{-1}| = |AMA^{-1} - A\lambda IA^{-1}| = |AMA^{-1} - \lambda I|$. Thus replacing M by AMA^{-1} leaves the eigenvalue equation (8.17) and hence the trace and determinant unchanged. This proves (ii), since the change of basis by a matrix A changes M to AMA^T (Section 8.2.3), and A is an orthogonal matrix (Theorem 8.8), for which $A^T = A^{-1}$ (Section 7.2.4 (b)).

THEOREM 8.38

(i) *The eigenvalues of an orthogonal matrix M have modulus 1.*

(ii) *A linear isometry T of 3-space fixing the origin satisfies $T\mathbf{v} = \pm\mathbf{v}$ for some nonzero real vector $\mathbf{v}$.*

Proof (i) We denote the complex conjugate of a number or matrix by an overbar. Equating the transposed complex conjugate of both sides of (8.13), we obtain $M^T\overline{\mathbf{x}}^T = \overline{\lambda}\,\overline{\mathbf{x}}^T$, which we combine with the original (8.13) to get $\mathbf{x}M\,M^T\overline{\mathbf{x}}^T = \lambda\mathbf{x}\,\overline{\lambda}\,\overline{\mathbf{x}}^T$. This simplifies to $\mathbf{x}\overline{\mathbf{x}}^T = |\lambda|^2 \mathbf{x}\cdot\overline{\mathbf{x}}^T$, and hence to $|\lambda|^2 = 1$, for the reasons that $MM^T = I$, and $\mathbf{x}\overline{\mathbf{x}}^T = \Sigma_i x_i\overline{x}_i = \Sigma_i |x_i|^2$, which is nonzero since $\mathbf{x} \neq 0$.

(ii) Let M be the matrix of T. Since M is 3 x 3 the eigenvalue equation (8.17) is cubic and so has at least one real root α. On the other hand, we know that M is orthogonal and therefore by part (i), $|\alpha| = 1$, implying $\alpha = \pm 1$. Then $\mathbf{x}M = \lambda\mathbf{x}$ becomes $\mathbf{x}M = \pm\mathbf{x}$. Finally, by remark (iii) under (8.13), we may choose $\mathbf{x}$ to be real and so take $\mathbf{v} = \mathbf{x}$.

EXAMPLE 8.39 Find eigenvalues and eigenvectors for the rotation matrix M shown.

$$M = \begin{bmatrix} \cos\phi & \sin\phi & 0 \\ -\sin\phi & \cos\phi & 0 \\ 0 & 0 & 1 \end{bmatrix}$$

We already know 1 is an eigenvalue with eigenvector [0 0 1]. Write $c = \cos\phi$, $s = \sin\phi$, so that $c^2 + s^2 = 1$. Then the eigenvalue equation is $|M - \lambda I| = 0$ (8.16), with

$$M - \lambda I = \begin{bmatrix} c-\lambda & s & 0 \\ -s & c-\lambda & 0 \\ 0 & 0 & 1-\lambda \end{bmatrix}$$

Thus $(\lambda - 1)(\lambda^2 - 2c\lambda + 1) = 0$, with $\lambda = 1$ a solution as predicted. For the others, $\lambda = \cos\phi \pm \mathbf{i}\sin\phi = e^{\pm i\phi}$. These two complex conjugate numbers have modulus $c^2 + s^2 = 1$ in agreement with Theorem 8.38.

Eigenvectors. With $\lambda = e^{i\phi}$ we have $c - \lambda = -\mathbf{i}s$, and further to this the eigenvalue equation $[x,y,z](M - \lambda I) = 0$ gives, on dividing out by $-s$, the three equations: $\mathbf{i}x - y = 0$, $x + \mathbf{i}y = 0$, $(1 - c - \mathbf{i}s)z = 0$. Thus we have only two independent equations, in agreement with $|M - \lambda I| = 0$ (see Rule 7.20(5)). An eigenvector is $(1,\mathbf{i},0)$. Corresponding to $\lambda = e^{-i\phi}$ we may take $(1,-\mathbf{i},0)$.

EXAMPLE 8.40 The matrices M in (i) and (ii) below are for rotation and reflection that fix the origin. Find the axis and plane via eigenvectors (*Remark 8.41).

$$\text{(i)} \quad \frac{1}{9}\begin{bmatrix} -7 & 4 & 4 \\ 4 & -1 & 8 \\ 4 & 8 & -1 \end{bmatrix}, \qquad \text{(ii)} \quad \frac{1}{7}\begin{bmatrix} -2 & 3 & -6 \\ 3 & 6 & 2 \\ -6 & 2 & 3 \end{bmatrix}$$

Solution (i) An axis vector is any eigenvector with eigenvalue 1, by (8.15). The eigenvector equation is $\mathbf{x}(M - \lambda I) = 0$, here $\mathbf{x}(M - I) = 0$. With $\mathbf{x}$ written [x y z] as usual, the first two equations are $-16x + 4y + 4z = 0$, $4x - 10y + 8z = 0$, with solution $z = y = 2x$. An axis vector is (1,2,2).

(ii) Here a normal to the plane is any eigenvector with eigenvalue -1, by (8.14)(B). The eigenvector equation is $\mathbf{x}(M + I) = 0$. It is convenient to take the last two equations: $3x + 13y + 2z = 0$, $-6x + 2y + 10z = 0$, with solution $z = -2y$, $x = -3y$. A normal to the plane is (-3,1,-2), hence its equation $3x - y + 2z = 0$.

REMARK 8.41* For non-eigenvalue methods to obtain the axes, see following (8.11) for reflection, and Corollary 8.52 for rotation. In the next section we see how to identify easily the rotation angle, including its sign. We *could* do it now by changing coordinates so that the axis is along **k and using (8.12), but this will be left as an exercise at the Chapter's end.

EXERCISE Verify that the matrix for reflection in plane x + 2z = 0 has determinant -1 and that all its eigenvalues have modulus 1.

8.4.6 Classification and identification

We have shown that a linear isometry T satisfies Tv = ±v for some nonzero vector **v**, and noted that we may replace **v** by any multiple of itself. Thus we may choose a coordinate system **i**,**j**,**k** with **k** = v, T**k** = ±**k**.

Since T preserves angles it maps the xy-plane onto itself and, by Theorem 1.16, it must do so either by a rotation of some angle ϕ about the origin O, or by reflection in a line m through O with polar angle say ϕ. We consider these two cases in turn.

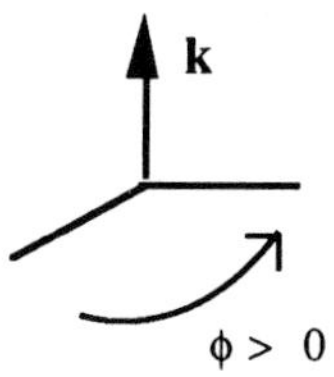

CASE 1 T rotates the xy-plane.

(a) *Suppose* T**k** = **k**. Then by (7.35) T has matrix M as given on the right, Hence |M| = 1 and T is the rotation $R_k(\phi)$.

$$M = \begin{bmatrix} \cos\phi & \sin\phi & 0 \\ -\sin\phi & \cos\phi & 0 \\ 0 & 0 & 1 \end{bmatrix}$$

b) *Suppose* T**k** = -**k**. Then the matrix of T equals that of part (a) times the matrix that sends [x y z] to [x y -z], namely diag(1,1,-1). So we have matrix M as shown, |M| = -1, and T is the product of a reflection z → -z in the x-y plane and the rotation $R_k(\phi)$. Thus T is by definition a rotary reflection.

$$M = \begin{bmatrix} \cos\phi & \sin\phi & 0 \\ -\sin\phi & \cos\phi & 0 \\ 0 & 0 & -1 \end{bmatrix}$$

CASE 2 T acts on the xy-plane as a reflection R_m.

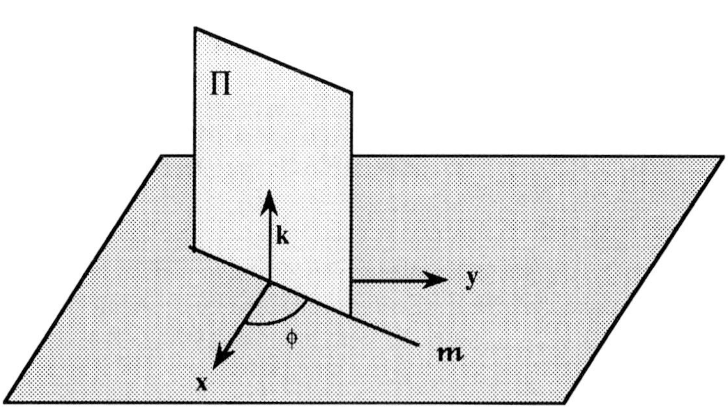

Figure 8.12 Diagram for Case 2.

(a) *Suppose* T**k** = **k**. Then the matrix of T is

$$M = \begin{bmatrix} \cos 2\phi & \sin 2\phi & 0 \\ \sin 2\phi & -\cos 2\phi & 0 \\ 0 & 0 & 1 \end{bmatrix}$$

Here $|M| = -1$ and T is reflection in the plane Π which contains $\boldsymbol{m}$ and **k**.

(b) *Suppose* **Tk** = -**k**. Then M is as above, but with bottom diagonal entry -1 instead of 1. We have for the first time in this situation, the diagonal entry -1 along with $|M| = +1$. Referring to Figure 8.12 again, we see that T is the product of reflection $z \to -z$ in the xy-plane with reflection in the plane Π. Since these planes are at right angles the result is a 1/2 turn about their intersection, the line $\boldsymbol{m}$.

We now have our classification. Note that a rotation angle ϕ, $-\pi \le \phi \le \pi$, is determined only up to sign by its cosine alone. We must in addition know the sign, and this is achieved by means of a suitable scalar triple product as specified in Section 8.4.3. In practice this usually means evaluating a determinant.

THEOREM 8.42 Let T be a linear isometry of 3-space, then there are the following possibilites.
(i) $|T| = 1$. Unless T is the identity it is a rotation, with axis vector **a** *given by* $T\boldsymbol{a} = \boldsymbol{a}$ *(eigenvalue 1). The rotation angle ϕ has the sign of $[\boldsymbol{a},\boldsymbol{v},T\boldsymbol{v}]$ for any non-axial vector* **v**, *and is then determined by $2\cos\phi+1 = Tr\,T$.*
(ii) $|T| = -1$. T is a rotary reflection. If $T\boldsymbol{x} = -\boldsymbol{x}$ for all vectors **x** *(matrix -I) then T is inversion. Otherwise T has an axis vector* **a** *given by $T\boldsymbol{a} = -\boldsymbol{a}$ (eigenvalue -1). The rotation angle ϕ has the sign of $[\boldsymbol{a},\boldsymbol{v},T\boldsymbol{v}]$ for any non-axial vector* **v**, *and is then determined by the equality $2\cos\phi - 1 = Tr\,T$.*

COROLLARY 8.43 The composition of rotations about two axes through a point A, is rotation about a third axis through A.

Proof Take A as origin for right handed coordinates. Let the rotations be T_1, T_2. Then $|T_1| = |T_2| = 1$ and so $|T_1T_2| = |T_1|\,|T_2| = 1$. By the classification Theorem, 8.42, we know that T_1T_2 must be a rotation.

EXAMPLE 8.44 Find the composition of a 1/2 turn about the x axis followed by a 1/4 turn about the y axis.

Solution The matrix for rotation about OY needs care. One way to be sure is to write down the matrix for a 1/4 turn about OX and advance the rows and columns cyclically one place, thus $x \to y \to z \to x$. We go from

$$\begin{bmatrix} 1 & 0 & 0 \\ 0 & 0 & 1 \\ 0 & -1 & 0 \end{bmatrix} \text{ to } \begin{bmatrix} 0 & 0 & -1 \\ 0 & 1 & 0 \\ 1 & 0 & 0 \end{bmatrix}, \quad \text{therefore} \quad \begin{bmatrix} 1 & 0 & 0 \\ 0 & -1 & 0 \\ 0 & 0 & -1 \end{bmatrix}\begin{bmatrix} 0 & 0 & -1 \\ 0 & 1 & 0 \\ 1 & 0 & 0 \end{bmatrix} = \begin{bmatrix} 0 & 0 & -1 \\ 0 & -1 & 0 \\ -1 & 0 & 0 \end{bmatrix}$$

is the required composition. By the Corollary 8.43 this has to be a rotation. As a check, the determinant is 1. It is now routine to determine the axis vector $\mathbf{x} = (x,y,z)$ from $\mathbf{x}(M - I) = 0$. Two independent equations are $-x - z = 0$, $-2y = 0$, so one axis vector is (1,0,-1). We now have a formula for the angle of rotation ϕ: $2\cos\phi + 1 = Tr\,M = -1$, giving in this case $\cos\phi = -1$ and $\phi = \pm\pi$. Thus the result, independently of the sign of ϕ, is a 1/2 turn about (1,0,-1).

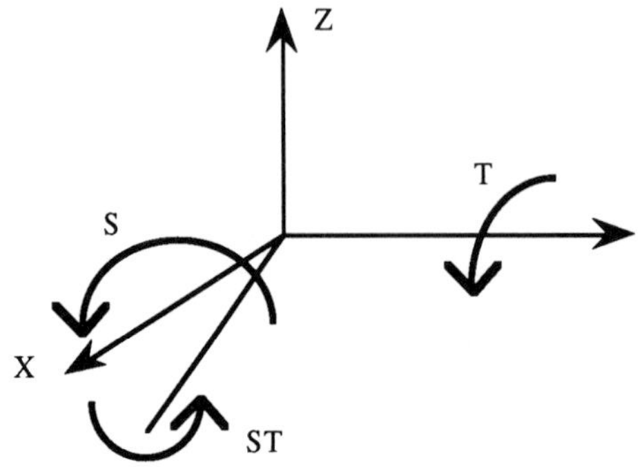

Figure 8.13 Diagram for Example 8.44. Rotations S: 1/2 turn about OX, T: 1/4 turn about OY, and their composition.

EXAMPLE 8.45 Find the result of reflection in the plane x + 2y - z = 0, followed by a rotation of $\pi/3$ about the z-axis.

Solution By the classification Theorem, 8.42, the result T has determinant -1 and so is a rotary reflection, albeit with a different angle, axis and plane. That is, the theory predicts that T can be expressed as rotation about the normal to some plane, followed by reflection in that plane. To begin, the matrix (8.11) for reflection in the original plane, with normal **u** = (1,2,-1) and d = $|\mathbf{u}|^2 = 6$, is $(1/6)(6I - 2\mathbf{u}^T\mathbf{u})$, so the matrix M of the given composition is

$$\frac{1}{3}\begin{bmatrix} 2 & -2 & 1 \\ -2 & -1 & 2 \\ 1 & 2 & 2 \end{bmatrix}\begin{bmatrix} 1/2 & \sqrt{3}/2 & 0 \\ -\sqrt{3}/2 & 1/2 & 0 \\ 0 & 0 & 1 \end{bmatrix} = \frac{1}{6}\begin{bmatrix} 2+2\sqrt{3} & -2+2\sqrt{3} & 2 \\ -2+\sqrt{3} & -1-2\sqrt{3} & 4 \\ 1-2\sqrt{3} & 2+\sqrt{3} & 4 \end{bmatrix}$$

For the *axis* we have T**x** = -**x**, or **x**(M + I) = 0 or, to eliminate fractions, **x**(6M + 6I) = 0. We have the equations $x + 2y + 5z = 0$, $(2\sqrt{3}-2)x + (5-2\sqrt{3})y + (2+\sqrt{3})z = 0$, from the lasst two columns of M. Solving, we avoid fractions by $z = -3+2\sqrt{3}$, and obtain for the axis **a** = $(7-4\sqrt{3}, 4-3\sqrt{3}, -3+2\sqrt{3})$.

For the *angle of rotation* ϕ we have $2\cos\phi - 1 = \text{Tr}\, M = 5/6$, hence $\cos\phi = 11/12$. The sign of ϕ is that of [**a**,**v**,**v**M] = [**v**,**v**M,**a**] where we may take **v** conveniently as (3,0,0). Then ϕ has the sign of the determinant

$$\begin{vmatrix} 3 & 0 & 0 \\ 1+\sqrt{3} & -1+\sqrt{3} & 1 \\ 7-4\sqrt{3} & 4-3\sqrt{3} & -3+2\sqrt{3} \end{vmatrix},$$

which has the positive value $15-6\sqrt{3}$. We conclude that ϕ is $\cos^{-1}(11/12)$, or approximately 23.6 degrees.

EXERCISE Find the product of a 1/4 turn about the x-axis with reflection in plane x + 3z = 0.

REMARK 8.46 (i) A rotary reflection, unlike the case of pure reflection or rotation, does seem to require that the axis be found as an eigenvector. There is no short cut

(ii) By choosing a right handed coordinate system at a point A, we may identify the group of rotations about A with the *special orthogonal group*

$$SO(3) = \{M: \text{ M is in } O(3) \text{ and } |M| = 1\}.$$

The other elements of O(3) are rotary reflections (including reflections as a special case).

(iii) The Classification Theorem, 8.42, with the fact that an isometry in 3-space is determined by its effect on any three non-collinear points and whether it is direct or indirect (Theorem 8.22), yields Table 8.1 below, distinguishing the four types listed. In Section 8.5 we consider also isometries which fix no point.

TABLE 8.1 How to distinguish isometries that fix a point A.

Isometry T	$\|T\|$	Fixed set	Other indicators
rotation	1	the axis	
reflection	-1	the mirror	
inversion	-1	the point A	reverses all lines through A
rotary reflection*	-1	the point A	reverses a unique line through A

* Other than inversions or pure reflections

8.4.7 More calculation techniques

To start this section we prove Theorem 8.47, enabling us to determine matrices and hence compositions for arbitrary rotations and reflections. To exemplify the main idea, suppose we wish to rotate an object about an arbitrary axis. Then to do so we may move the object to the origin, perform the rotation about an axis through the origin, then move the rotated object back to its original position.

THEOREM 8.47 Let the isometry g of 3-space, map vector $\boldsymbol{u} = \underline{AB}$ *to* $\boldsymbol{v} = \underline{CD}$, *and plane* Π *to* Σ. *Then*

(a) (Reflection in plane Σ*)* $\quad R_\Sigma = g^{-1} R_\Pi g$, ie $(R_\Pi)^g$,

(b) (Rotation thro' ϕ *about* $\boldsymbol{u}$*)* $\quad R_{\mathbf{v}}(\phi) = g^{-1} R_{\mathbf{u}}(\phi) g$, ie $R_{\mathbf{u}}(\phi)^g$,

(c) (Translation $\boldsymbol{x} \to \boldsymbol{x} + \boldsymbol{u}$*)* $\quad T_{\mathbf{v}} = g^{-1} T_{\mathbf{u}} g$ ie $(T_{\mathbf{u}})^g$.

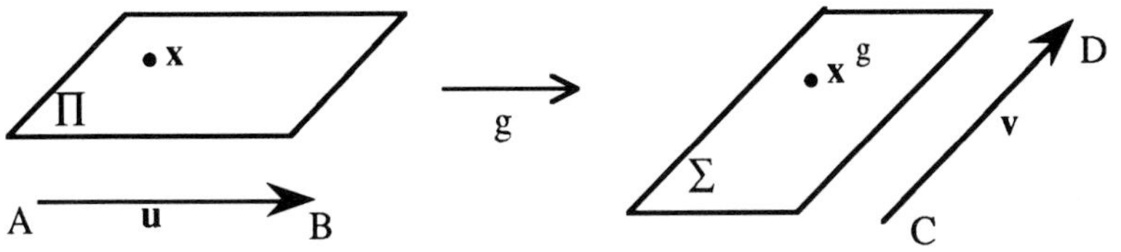

Figure 8.14 Illustration of Theorem 8.47 on how to calculate one reflection, rotation or translation from another.

Proof Firstly, $(R_\Pi)^g$ is indirect because R_Π is, by Remark 8.17. By Table 8.1 above, it suffices to show that the fixed set of $(R_\Pi)^g$ is $\Sigma = \Pi^g$. This exercise is left to the reader, and is identical to the corresponding proof for mirror lines in the plane, found in Theorem 2.12. Now (b), (c) hold because rotations and translations are products of reflections and $(RS)^g = R^g.S^g$ for isometries R, S. Again, the argument is found in Theorem 2.12.

EXAMPLE 8.48 Find the matrix for a half turn about axis vector $\mathbf{a} = (1,-1,1)$. Explain the absence of square roots in the answer.

Solution First we obtain an isometry matrix M which maps **a** onto the x-axis by completing unit vector $\mathbf{a}/|\mathbf{a}| = (1/\surd 3)(1,-1,1)$ to an orthonormal basis in the manner of Remark 8.11. If N is the matrix for a half turn about the x-axis then the required matrix is, by Theorem 8.47 (b), $M^{-1}N\,M = M^TN\,M$, namely

$$\begin{bmatrix} 1/\surd 3 & 1/\surd 2 & 1/\surd 6 \\ -1/\surd 3 & 1/\surd 2 & -1/\surd 6 \\ 1/\surd 3 & 0 & -2/\surd 6 \end{bmatrix} \begin{bmatrix} 1 & 0 & 0 \\ 0 & -1 & 0 \\ 0 & 0 & -1 \end{bmatrix} \begin{bmatrix} 1/\surd 3 & -1/\surd 3 & 1/\surd 3 \\ 1/\surd 2 & 1/\surd 2 & 0 \\ 1/\surd 6 & -1/\surd 6 & -2/\surd 6 \end{bmatrix} = \frac{1}{3}\begin{bmatrix} -1 & -2 & 2 \\ -2 & -1 & -2 \\ 2 & -2 & -1 \end{bmatrix}$$

Why the roots disappear. The first row of M is the axis vector $\mathbf{a} = (a_1,a_2,a_3)$, so we may write *columns* i and j of M as respectively $[a_i,b_i,c_i]^T$, $[a_j,b_j,c_j]^T$. Then the i,j entry in $M^T N\,M$ is

$$\begin{aligned} [a_i,b_i,c_i]\ \mathrm{diag}(1,-1,-1)\ [a_j,b_j,c_j]^T &= [a_i,b_i,c_i]\ [a_j,-b_j,-c_j]^T \\ &= a_ia_j - b_ib_j - c_ic_j \\ &= 2a_ia_j - \delta_{ij} \end{aligned}$$

since $a_ia_j + b_ib_j + c_ic_j = \delta_{ij}$ by orthogonality of matrix M. In matrix terms this says $M^TN\,M = 2\mathbf{a}^T\mathbf{a} - I$, and the argument above applies to any axis vector, hence the remark below. The simplicity is not due to the present **a** having elements ±1 but to the rotation being a half turn.

REMARK The matrix for a half turn about axis vector **a**, with $|\mathbf{a}|^2 = e$ (note the square) , is

$$M = e^{-1}(2\mathbf{a}^T\mathbf{a} - eI). \tag{8.18}$$

EXERCISE Calculate the matrix of Example 8.48 using (8.18).

Now we use Theorem 8.47 to go for a universal formula for rotations, finding some surprising matrix relations along the way. Below is the resulting formula (cf. the equivalent result in quaternions for angle 2ϕ, Theorem 9.10).

*THEOREM 8.49 The matrix for rotation through angle ϕ, about unit axis vector **a** with components (a_1, a_2, a_3), is*

$$M_\mathbf{a} = (\cos\phi)I + (1-\cos\phi)\mathbf{a}^T\mathbf{a} + (\sin\phi)\begin{bmatrix} 0 & a_3 & -a_2 \\ -a_3 & 0 & a_1 \\ a_2 & -a_1 & 0 \end{bmatrix}.$$

Proof By Theorem 8.47 we have $M_\mathbf{a}(\phi) = M^T A\,M$, where A is the matrix of rotation ϕ about the x-axis and M is an orthogonal matrix sending unit vector **i** to axis vector **a**. Thus the first row of M is **a** and the three rows are an orthonormal basis **a**,**b**,**c** of 3-space. It must be possible to eliminate **b** and **c** from $M^T A M$, whichever of the infinite number of choices are taken for them. We do this by simple observations which enable us to avoid various pitfalls of complication. For definiteness, though it is not essential, we suppose that **a**,**b**,**c** (in that order of course) are a right handed triple, which is equivalent to M being a rotation. Then

$$\mathbf{b} \times \mathbf{c} = \mathbf{a}, \tag{8.19}$$

by definition of the vector product. Now, what does the process of forming $M^T A M$ do to A? Suppose E_{ij} is the 3 by 3 matrix with zero entries except for a 1 in the i,j position and that, as a temporary notation the rows of M are R_1, R_2, R_3. Then

$$M^T E_{ij} M = R_i^T R_j \qquad (1 \le i,j \le 3). \tag{8.20}$$

To see this, consider E_{12}. We have for $M^T E_{12} M$ the expression

$$[R_1^T \ R_2^T \ R_3^T] \begin{bmatrix} 0 & 1 & 0 \\ 0 & 0 & 0 \\ 0 & 0 & 0 \end{bmatrix} \begin{bmatrix} R_1 \\ R_2 \\ R_3 \end{bmatrix} = \begin{bmatrix} m_{11} & m_{21} & m_{31} \\ m_{12} & m_{22} & m_{32} \\ m_{13} & m_{23} & m_{33} \end{bmatrix} \begin{bmatrix} R_2 \\ 0 \\ 0 \end{bmatrix} = \begin{bmatrix} m_{11}R_2 \\ m_{12}R_2 \\ m_{13}R_2 \end{bmatrix}$$

which equals $R_1^T R_2$. Now let A be the first matrix shown below, where we write s = sinϕ and c = cosϕ. $M^T A M$ involves the second, with p,q,r to be found.

$$A = \begin{bmatrix} 1 & 0 & 0 \\ 0 & c & s \\ 0 & -s & c \end{bmatrix}, \qquad (\mathbf{b}^T \mathbf{c} - \mathbf{c}^T \mathbf{b})^T = \begin{bmatrix} 0 & r & q \\ -r & 0 & p \\ -q & -p & 0 \end{bmatrix}.$$

Reverting back to **a**,**b**,**c** as rows of M, we have

$$\begin{aligned} M^T A M &= M^T [\, cI + (1-c)E_{11} + s(E_{23} - E_{32})]\, M \\ &= cM^T I M + (1-c)M^T E_{11} M + sM^T(E_{23} - E_{32})M \\ &= cI + (1-c)\mathbf{a}^T\mathbf{a} + s(\mathbf{b}^T\mathbf{c} - \mathbf{c}^T\mathbf{b}), \quad \text{by}(8.20). \end{aligned}$$

Now, the last term (matrix) is skew symmetric, as is shown by the equalities $(\mathbf{b}^T \mathbf{c} - \mathbf{c}^T \mathbf{b})^T = \mathbf{c}^T \mathbf{b} - \mathbf{b}^T \mathbf{c} = -(\mathbf{b}^T \mathbf{c} - \mathbf{c}^T \mathbf{b})$, and so has the form given above. It remains only to express p, q, r in terms of the coordinates of **a**. But the first row of this matrix is the vector

$$b_1(c_1, c_2, c_3) - c_1(b_1, b_2, b_3) = (0,\ b_1c_2 - b_2c_1,\ b_1c_3 - b_3c_1),$$

which equals $(0, a_3, -a_2)$ by (8.19), as asserted. Similarly the 2,3 entry is a_1, and we are done. For another approach, see Faux and Pratt (1987).

EXAMPLE 8.50 Find the matrix for a 1/4 turn about axis vector (1,2, -2).

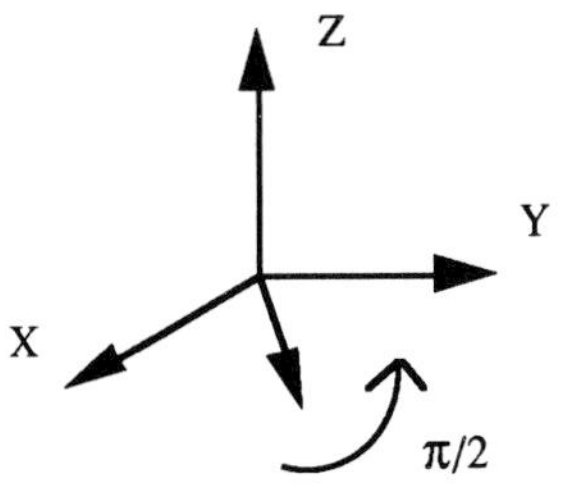

Solution We use Theorem 8.49. The formula simplifes with cosϕ = 0, sinϕ = 1. Notice that we require a *unit* axis vector, **a** = (1/3)(1,2,-2). The first matrix below is $\mathbf{a}^T\mathbf{a}$ and the result is

$$\frac{1}{9}\begin{bmatrix} 1 & 2 & -2 \\ 2 & 4 & -4 \\ -2 & -4 & 4 \end{bmatrix} + \frac{1}{3}\begin{bmatrix} 0 & -2 & -2 \\ 2 & 0 & 1 \\ 2 & -1 & 0 \end{bmatrix} = \frac{1}{9}\begin{bmatrix} 1 & -4 & -8 \\ 8 & 4 & -1 \\ 4 & -7 & 4 \end{bmatrix}.$$

EXERCISE Find the matrix for a 3/4 turn about axis vector (-1,2,2).

EXAMPLE 8.51 Find the matrix for reflection in the plane Π: $x + 3y + 2z = 5$.

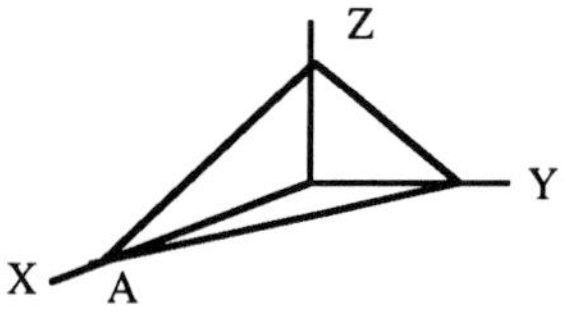

Solution A unit normal vector is $\mathbf{u} = (1,3,2)/\sqrt{14}$. We first require a translation mapping Π to the parallel plane through the origin. Notice that this need *not* be along a normal vector; we need only map some point of Π to the origin. Now Π meets the x-axis at A(5,0,0), so translation by (-5,0,0) is all we require. The composition map prescribed by Theorem 8.47(a) and (8.11) is then

$$\begin{bmatrix} 1 & 0 & 0 & 0 \\ 0 & 1 & 0 & 0 \\ 0 & 0 & 1 & 0 \\ -5 & 0 & 0 & 1 \end{bmatrix} \frac{1}{7}\begin{bmatrix} 6 & -3 & -2 & 0 \\ -3 & -2 & -6 & 0 \\ -2 & -6 & 3 & 0 \\ 0 & 0 & 0 & 7 \end{bmatrix} \begin{bmatrix} 1 & 0 & 0 & 0 \\ 0 & 1 & 0 & 0 \\ 0 & 0 & 1 & 0 \\ 5 & 0 & 0 & 1 \end{bmatrix} = \frac{1}{7}\begin{bmatrix} 6 & -3 & -2 & 0 \\ -3 & -2 & -6 & 0 \\ -2 & -6 & 3 & 0 \\ 5 & 15 & 10 & 7 \end{bmatrix}.$$

EXERCISE Find the 4 x 4 matrix for reflection in the plane $x + 2y + z = 3$.

COROLLARY 8.52 **(Rotation axis from matrix)** *The matrix of a rotation ϕ about unit axis vector **a** has skew-symmetric part (see (7.15))*

$$S = (\sin\phi)\begin{bmatrix} 0 & a_3 & -a_2 \\ -a_3 & 0 & a_1 \\ a_2 & -a_1 & 0 \end{bmatrix},$$

and hence S yields an axis vector provided $\sin\phi \neq 0$. If $\sin\phi = 0$ then, (unless M is the identity matrix), $\phi = \pi$ and an axis vector is any nonzero row (or column) of $M + I$.

Proof Theorem 8.49 gives the rotation matrix M as a sum of the skew-symmetric matrix S and a symmetric matrix. Since by (7.15) the decomposition is unique, S is indeed the skew-symmetric part of M. If $\sin\phi = 0$ (and $M \neq I$) then $\phi = \pi$, $\cos\phi = -1$, resulting in $M = 2\mathbf{a}^T\mathbf{a} - I$. Hence the last assertion of the Theorem.

EXAMPLE 8.53 Determine the axis and angle for the rotation matrix

$$M = \frac{1}{57}\begin{bmatrix} 28 & -23 & -44 \\ -16 & -52 & 17 \\ -47 & 4 & -32 \end{bmatrix}.$$

Solution Note that the determinant of M must be 1, contrary to appearances, but we are not asked to verify this. The skew symmetric part, we recall from (7.15), is the matrix S with $s_{ij} = (m_{ij}-m_{ji})/2$, namely

$$S = \frac{1}{114}\begin{bmatrix} 0 & -7 & 3 \\ 7 & 0 & 13 \\ -3 & -13 & 0 \end{bmatrix}.$$

From Corollary 8.52, if the rotation has axis vector **a** and angle ϕ, then **a** $\sin\phi$ is the vector (13,-3,-7)/114. Taking ϕ to be positive, as we may, an axis vector is (13,-3,-7), with $\sin\phi = \sqrt{227}/114$. Since this still leaves ambiguity (between the angle ϕ and its supplement $\pi-\phi$) we need the trace formula $2\cos\phi + 1 = \text{Tr } M = (28-52-32)/57$, giving $\phi = \cos^{-1}(-113/114)$ or about 172 degrees. [Note. This example comes from the product of reflections in planes $x+2y+z = 0$, $2x-3y+5z = 0$.]

EXERCISE Use Corollary 8.52 to check the axis in the answer to Example 8.40(i).

EXAMPLE 8.54 Find the matrix to rotate vector **i** onto an arbitrary unit vector **u** = (a,b,c), around an axis perpendicular to both. Ensure that the angle of rotation ϕ is positive.

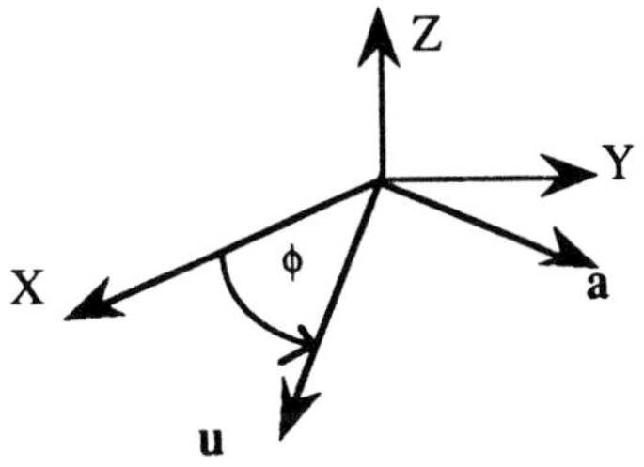

Solution Since **i**, **u** are unit vectors we have $\cos\phi$ = **i.u** = a, and, assuming ϕ to be positive, $\sin\phi = \sqrt{(b^2+c^2)} = \sqrt{(1-a^2)}$. The axis that will make ϕ positive is **a** = (**i** x **u**) / |**i** x **u**|, which equals vector $(0,-c,b)/\sin\phi$. Theorem 8.49 gives, with d = 1+a,

$$aI + \frac{1-a}{1-a^2}\begin{bmatrix} 0 & 0 & 0 \\ 0 & c^2 & -bc \\ 0 & -bc & b^2 \end{bmatrix} + \frac{\sin\phi}{\sin\phi}\begin{bmatrix} 0 & b & c \\ -b & 0 & 0 \\ -c & 0 & 0 \end{bmatrix} = \begin{bmatrix} a & b & c \\ -b & 1-b^2/d & -bc/d \\ -c & -bc/d & 1-c^2/d \end{bmatrix}.$$

THEOREM 8.55 (Mapping one vector pair onto another.) Let ***u,x*** *and* ***a,y*** *be pairs of unit vectors at the same angle* ϕ *:* ***u.x*** *=* ***a.y*** *=* $\cos\phi$*, with* $\sin\phi \neq 0$*. Then a rotation matrix M sending* ***u,x*** *to* ***a,y*** *is given by*

$$M = [\mathbf{u}^T \ \mathbf{v}^T \ \mathbf{w}^T]\begin{bmatrix} \mathbf{a} \\ \mathbf{b} \\ \mathbf{c} \end{bmatrix},$$

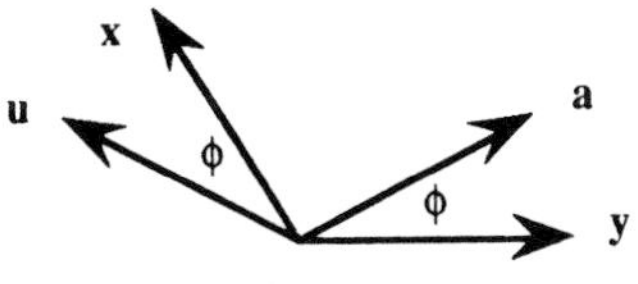

where **v** = (**x** x **u**)/d, **w** = (**x** - **u** $\cos\phi$)/d,
b = (**y** x **a**)/d, **c** = (**y** - **a** $\cos\phi$)/d,

and d = |***x*** x ***u***| = |***y*** x ***a***| = $|\sin\phi|$. *Moreover M is instead a rotary reflection if we replace* ***x*** x ***u*** *by its negative.*

Proof We recall that an orthogonal matrix can be viewed as a square matrix whose rows (or equivalently whose columns) are orthonormal - mutually orthogonal unit vectors. Also, if **a**,**b** are two rows then the third is $\pm$**a** x **b**. Suppose we extend **a**,**u** to orthonormal sets **a**,**b**,**c** and **u**,**v** **w**. We use these vectors to form the columns of orthogonal matrices A, U. That is, $A^T = [\mathbf{a}^T\ \mathbf{b}^T\ \mathbf{c}^T]$, and $U^T = [\mathbf{u}^T\ \mathbf{v}^T\ \mathbf{w}^T]$. Hence **i**U = **u**, **i**A = **a**, and so $\mathbf{i} = \mathbf{u}U^{-1}$, $\mathbf{a} = \mathbf{i}A = \mathbf{u}(U^{-1}A)$. Since $U^{-1} = U^T$, we then have **u**M = **a**, where $M = U^TA$ has the form specified in the Theorem.

The proof is by no means finished, since we have to choose **v**,**w** and **b**,**c** within the orthonormal constraint so that **x**M = **y**. But this is equivalent to $\mathbf{x}U^T = \mathbf{y}A^T$, and so to the simultaneous holding of (i) $\mathbf{xu}^T = \mathbf{ya}^T$, (ii) $\mathbf{xv}^T = \mathbf{yb}^T$, (iii) $\mathbf{xw}^T = \mathbf{yc}^T$. Now, we are already given (i) as hypothesis. To ensure (ii), we define **v**, **b** as in the present theorem. Then $\mathbf{xv}^T = \mathbf{x.v} = 0 = \mathbf{b.y} = \mathbf{yb}^T$, since **x** is perpendicular to **x** x **u** and **b** to **y** x **a**. The equal inner products being *zero* is a particular simplifying choice. Now **c**,**w** are determined up to sign by orthogonality of U, A. Taking the right handed choices of the present theorem and using the formula **p** x (**q** x **r**) = (**p.r**)**q** - (**p.q**)**r** of Theorem 7.35 with **u.u** = 1 = **a.a**, we see

$$\mathbf{w} = \mathbf{u} \times \mathbf{v} = \mathbf{u} \times (\mathbf{x} \times \mathbf{u})/d = (\mathbf{x} - \mathbf{u}\cos\phi)/d, \qquad \cos\phi = \mathbf{u.x},$$
$$\mathbf{c} = \mathbf{a} \times \mathbf{b} = \mathbf{a} \times (\mathbf{y} \times \mathbf{a})/d = (\mathbf{y} - \mathbf{a}\cos\phi)/d, \qquad \cos\phi = \mathbf{a.y}.$$

It remains to check that (iii) holds. We have

$$\begin{aligned} d\mathbf{x.w} - d\mathbf{y.c} &= \mathbf{x.}(\mathbf{x} - \mathbf{u}\cos\phi) - \mathbf{y.}(\mathbf{y} - \mathbf{a}\cos\phi) \\ &= \mathbf{x.x} - (\mathbf{x.u})\cos\phi - \mathbf{y.y} + (\mathbf{y.a})\cos\phi \\ &= 0, \qquad \text{since } \mathbf{x.x} = \mathbf{y.y} = 1, \text{ and } \mathbf{x.u} = \mathbf{y.a} = \cos\phi. \end{aligned}$$

EXAMPLE 8.56 Find a rotation matrix to send **u**,**x** to **y**,**a** where **u** = **i**, **x** = (√3,1,0)/2, **a** = (-1,0,√3)/2, **y** = **k**.

Solution We calculate as follows using the notation of Theorem 8.55 above. Firstl of all, **x** x **u** = (0,0,-1/2), so d = 1/2, **v** = (0,0,-1). With cosϕ = **u.x** = √3/2 we obtain the equalities **w** = 2(**x** - **u** cosϕ) = (0,1,0), **b** = 2(**y** x **a**) = (0,-1,0), **c** = 2(**y** - **a** cosϕ) = (√3/2,0,1). Therefore the required matrix is

$$M = \begin{bmatrix} 1 & 0 & 0 \\ 0 & 0 & 1 \\ 0 & -1 & 0 \end{bmatrix} \begin{bmatrix} -1/2 & 0 & \sqrt{3}/2 \\ 0 & -1 & 0 \\ \sqrt{3}/2 & 0 & 1/2 \end{bmatrix} = \begin{bmatrix} -1/2 & 0 & \sqrt{3}/2 \\ \sqrt{3}/2 & 0 & 1/2 \\ 0 & 1 & 0 \end{bmatrix}.$$

EXERCISE Find a matrix to rotate vector (1,1,0) to (0,1,1) whilst fixing (1,1,1) (Theorem 8.55).

REMARK 8.57 The methods above can be extended to achieve other criteria for M. First of all we can obviously rotate any one vector into any other, around an axis perpendicular to both or otherwise. What leeway do we have for matrices M sending one pair to another inclined at the same angle? We are specifying the action of an isometry on three points: the origin, **a**, and **x**. Therefore there are two possibilities, one direct, the other indirect, and similarly for the matrix in a fixed coordinate system, in spite of our apparent choices in the matrix factors of M.

8.5 3-d isometries in general

Any isometry T can be expressed as a product

$$T = R\,T_{\mathbf{w}}, \qquad (8.21)$$

where R is an isometry fixing some point A and **w** is a translation vector (R is linear if A is the origin). Thus we must discover what happens when an isometry of each type listed below is followed by a translation $T_{\mathbf{w}}$.

a. *REFLECTION* R_{Π}
b. *ROTATION* $R_{\mathbf{a}}(\phi)$
c. *ROTARY REFLECTION* $R_{\mathbf{a}}(\phi)\, R_{\Pi}$, **a** normal to Π.

We obtain two new isometry types which, like rotary reflection, are each the product of two isometries $R_1\, R_2$ which *commute*, that is

$$R_1R_2 = R_2R_1, \tag{8.22}$$

in consequence of their defining planes, lines, etc. being parallel or perpendicular to each other (see Sections 8.5.1 and 8.5.2).

8.5.1 Reflection plus translation equals glide

The name is not new in this context. We have already considered this construction in two dimensions, and essentially the same argument goes through.

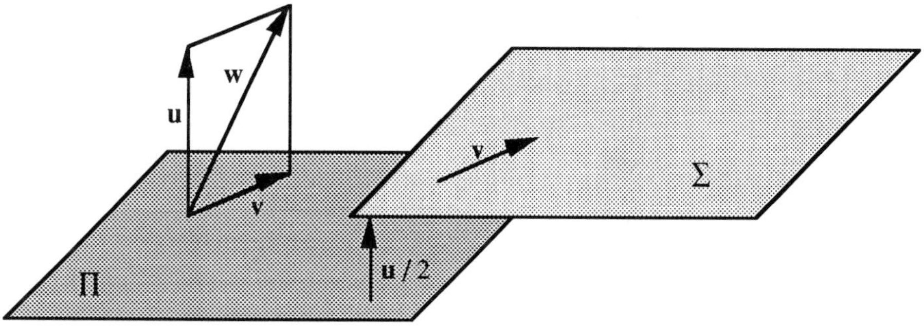

Figure 8.15 Computing $R_{\Pi}T_{\mathbf{w}}$ by expressing $T_{\mathbf{w}}$ as a translation parallel to Π plus one perpendicular to Π.

For $R_{\Pi}T_{\mathbf{w}}$ we split **w** into vectors **u** normal to Π and **v** parallel to Π. Thus $\mathbf{w} = \mathbf{u}+\mathbf{v}$, as in Figure 8.15 above. Then

$$T = R_{\Pi}T_{\mathbf{u}}T_{\mathbf{v}} = R_{\Sigma}\, T_{\mathbf{v}}, \qquad \text{by Theorem 8.26,}$$

where Σ is a plane parallel to Π at distance $|\mathbf{u}|/2$ from Π in the direction of **u**. Thus T is a glide according to the definition below.

DEFINITION 8.58 A *glide in 3-space* is a composition $R_{\Pi}T_{\mathbf{v}}$ where the vector **v** is parallel to the plane Π. We emphasise that the two isometries commute: $R_{\Pi}T_{\mathbf{v}} = T_{\mathbf{v}}R_{\Pi}$. For the connection with plane glides we note that restriction to a plane Σ', perpendicular to Σ but parallel to **v**, gives us a plane glide in Σ' along its intersection with Σ.

REMARK 8.59 Let the plane Π have normal **n** and contain the point with position vector **a**. Write $\mathbf{r} = (x,y,z)$. Then an equation for Π is $\mathbf{r}.\mathbf{n} = \mathbf{a}.\mathbf{n}$ (see Example 7.39 & Figure 8.16).

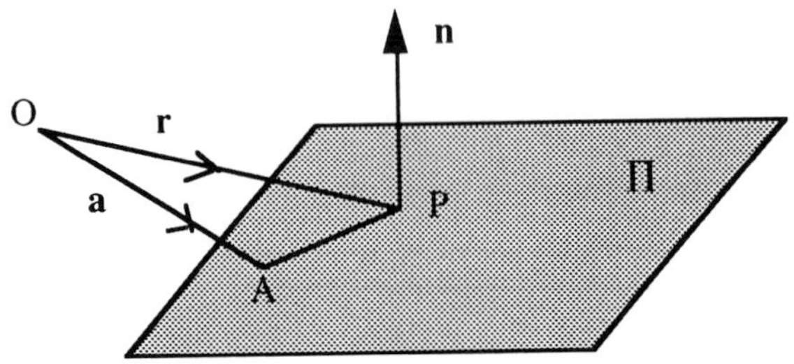

Figure 8.16 Finding an equation for a plane through A with normal vector **n**

EXAMPLE 8.60 Reflection in the plane Π: x + y + z = 8 is followed by translation by (1,2,5). Find the equation of the plane and its matrix, for the resulting glide.

Solution Following the above remark, we may take **a** = (8,0,0), **n** = (1,1,1) in Figure 8.16. The component of **w** = (1,2,5) along the normal is **u** = $(\mathbf{w}.\mathbf{n}/|\mathbf{n}|^2)\mathbf{n}$ = (8/3)(1,1,1). Therefore a point on the glide plane is **a** + (1/2)**u** = (4/3)(7,1,1) (cf. Figure 8.15), and the new equation is **r**.**n** = (4/3)(7,1,1).(1,1,1), or x+y+z = 12.

For the matrix, we need not calculate the component of **w** parallel to the plane (either of them). Let Γ be the plane through the origin which is parallel to Π. Since Π meets the x-axis at (8,0,0), the glide is $R_\Pi T_w = T_{(-8,0,0)} R_\Gamma T_{(8,0,0)} T_{(1,2,5)}$ (cf. Example 8.51). Formula (8.11) enables us to write down the matrix for R_Γ. Remembering that the translation matrices do not change the 3 x 3 part of the reflection matrix, we obtain:

$$\begin{bmatrix} 1 & 0 & 0 & 0 \\ 0 & 1 & 0 & 0 \\ 0 & 0 & 1 & 0 \\ -8 & 0 & 0 & 1 \end{bmatrix} \frac{1}{3}\begin{bmatrix} 1 & -2 & -2 & 0 \\ -2 & 1 & -2 & 0 \\ -2 & -2 & 1 & 0 \\ 0 & 0 & 0 & 3 \end{bmatrix} \begin{bmatrix} 1 & 0 & 0 & 0 \\ 0 & 1 & 0 & 0 \\ 0 & 0 & 1 & 0 \\ 9 & 2 & 5 & 1 \end{bmatrix} = \frac{1}{3}\begin{bmatrix} 1 & -2 & -2 & 0 \\ -2 & 1 & -2 & 0 \\ -2 & -2 & 1 & 0 \\ 19 & 43 & 31 & 3 \end{bmatrix}.$$

EXERCISE Find the glide plane for reflection in x + y + 2 = 0 is followed by translation of 3**k**.

8.5.2 Rotation plus translation equals screw

Here we get something with no real counterpart in the plane. Let the rotation be $R_\mathbf{k}(\phi)$, where **k** is based at a point A. Similarly to the previous case, we resolve the translation vector **w** into **u** parallel to **k** and **v** perpendicular to **k**, as indicated in Figure 8.17. Then we have $R_\mathbf{k}T_\mathbf{w} = [R_\mathbf{k}(\phi)T_\mathbf{v}]T_\mathbf{u} = R_\mathbf{u}(\phi)T_\mathbf{u}$, by Example 2.5, with axis vector **u** based at some point B in the plane Π through A with normal **k** (or **u**). This is a SCREW, as defined below.

DEFINITION 8.61 A *screw* in 3-space is a product $R_\mathbf{k}(\phi)T_\mathbf{u}$, where the translation vector **u** is parallel to the axis vector **k**. Note: The two component isometries commute: $R_\mathbf{k}(\phi)T_\mathbf{u} = T_\mathbf{u}R_\mathbf{k}(\phi)$. The successive images of an object F are shown in Figure 8.17.

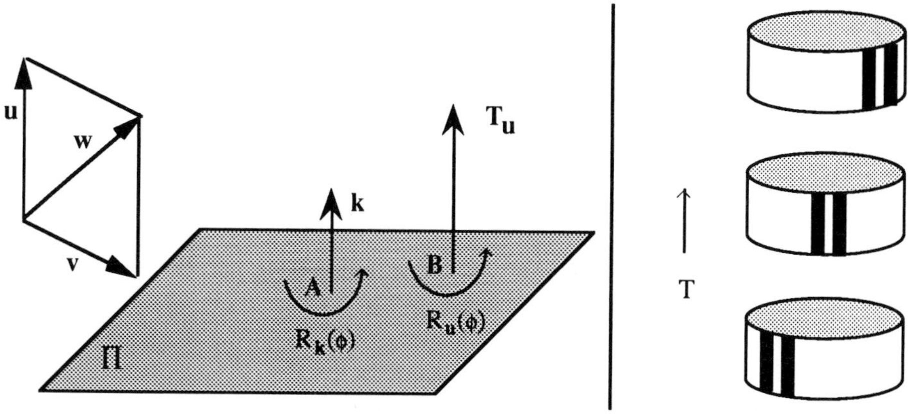

Figure 8.17 (a) Let the axis of a rotation be normal to plane Π. The translation to follow the rotation is resolved parallel and perpendicular to Π, showing that this composition is a screw: rotation about a new parallel axis plus translation along that axis. (b) Successive images of an object under a repeated screw isometry.

EXAMPLE 8.62 A rotation of ϕ about the z-axis is followed by translation (p,q,r). Determine the resulting screw isometry.

Solution With $c = \cos\phi$, $s = \sin\phi$, the resulting isometry matrix may be written as the following product:

$$\begin{bmatrix} c & s & 0 & 0 \\ -s & c & 0 & 0 \\ 0 & 0 & 1 & 0 \\ p & q & 0 & 1 \end{bmatrix} \begin{bmatrix} 1 & 0 & 0 & 0 \\ 0 & 1 & 0 & 0 \\ 0 & 0 & 1 & 0 \\ 0 & 0 & r & 1 \end{bmatrix}$$

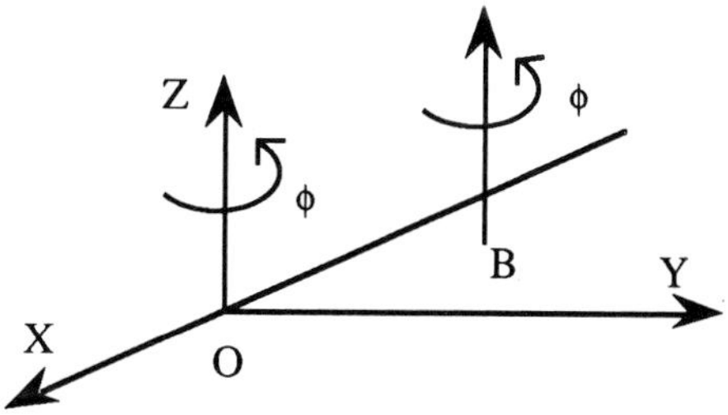

Figure 8.18 Rotation x translation = screw

These two matrices commute. The first incorporates the translation component perpendicular to the original axis, whilst the second gives the component parallel to that axis which will form the translation part of the screw. We know from Example 2.5 that the first matrix gives rotation ϕ about an axis parallel to **k** and we may determine it by finding the vectors [x y z 1] fixed by this matrix. They are the solutions of: $(c-1)x - sy + p = 0$, $sx + (c-1)y + q = 0$, $0z = 0$, namely $x = (p - q\cot(\phi/2))/2$, $y = q + p\cot(\phi/2)$, z arbitrary. Thus the new axis is in the direction expected, passing through the point (x,y) found above. The diagram above sketches the result for $\phi = \pi/3$, $(p,q) = (2,3)$, with B as $(2-3\sqrt{3}, 3+2\sqrt{3})/2$.

REMARK 8.63 The 4 x 4 matrix of a screw has the form $\begin{bmatrix} M & 0 \\ \mathbf{u} & 1 \end{bmatrix}$.
The screw axis is parallel to the axis of rotation matrix M. If **u** is replaced by its component perpendicular to the axis then the eigenvectors of eigenvalue 1 are the points of the screw axis. This is how we found the axis in Example 8.62 above, the component being (p,q,0),

EXERCISE A 1/3 turn about axis (1,1,1) is followed by translation by 3**k**. Find the axis of the resulting screw.

8.5.3 Rotary reflection plus translation

Consider the rotary reflection $R_k(\phi)\ R_\Pi$ with **k** based at a point A in the mirror plane Π, followed by translation T_w.

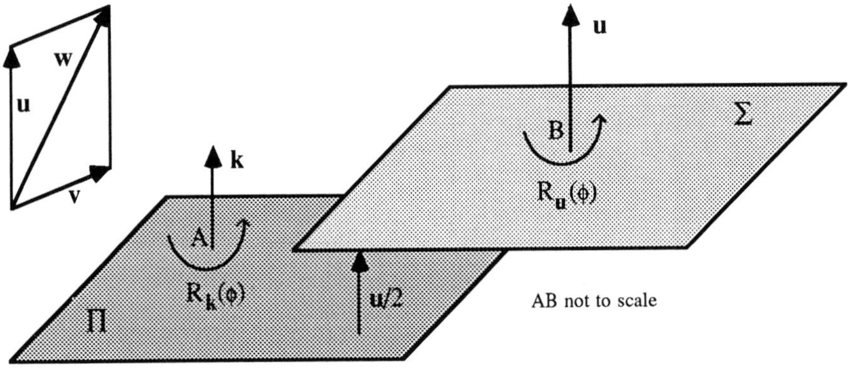

Figure 8.19 Translation is to be added to a rotary reflection whose plane is Π. Resolving this translation parallel and perpendicular to Π shows that the result is a parallel rotary reflection.

We resolve the translation vector **w** into **u** parallel to **k** plus **v** perpendicular to **k**. Then since T_u ,T_v commute and R_π,T_v commute,

$$R_k(\phi).R_\Pi \cdot T_w \;=\; R_k(\phi)\ R_\Pi T_u\ T_v \;=\; R_k(\phi)T_v \cdot R_\Pi T_u \;=\; R_u(\phi).\ R_\Sigma,$$

where **u** is based at some point B in a plane Σ parallel to Π and distance $|\mathbf{u}|/2$ from it in the direction of **u**. Thus the result is another rotary reflection, with new plane and axis parallel to the old ones, and angle the same.

8.5.4 The final classification

We have now shown that every isometry of 3-space may be expressed as one out of the following two lists.

DIRECT	INDIRECT
Rotation	Reflection
Translation	Glide
Screw	Rotary reflection / inversion

EXERCISE Find the product of a glide and a rotary reflection.

Identification As an example, T may be given as the product of several known isometries. Table 8.1 show us how geometrically to identify an isometry amongst those that fix a point. If T is not known to fix a point but $O^T = A$ then the product $T.T_{\underline{AO}}$ fixes the origin O and we are back to the table. More generally we have Theorem 8.22: if we know whether T is direct or indirect and can determine its effect on three points, then any isometry we propose with the same effect may be identified with T. On the other hand, given a 4 x 4 matrix known to be that of an isometry, the bottom row gives the translation part and we can handle the rest as in Section 8.4, linear isometries.

RECAPITULATION 8.64 Adding a translation moves a mirror, glideplane, glideline, or rotation axis parallel to itself. It does not affect a rotation angle. It may turn a reflection into a glide, rotation into screw, or vice versa.

How to find/determine:

Components of a vector with respect to a basis	(8.4)
Matrix of a linear transformation	(8.6)
Matrix of a change of orthogonal axes	(8.7)
New coordinates after change of axes	Section 8.2.2
New transformation matrix after change of axes	Section 8.2.3
Whether isometry is direct or indirect	(8.9)
Matrix of a 3-d reflection	(8.11)
Plane of reflection from its matrix	(8.11)ff
Matrix sending **k** to **a** by rotation about x,y-axes	Example 8.29
General orthogonal matrix sending **k** to **a**	Remark 8.30
Eigenvalues and vectors	Section 8.4.5
Rotation axes and mirror normals as eigenvectors	(8.14)
Products of rotations (O fixed) by eigenvectors and trace	Theorem 8.42
Product of rotation and reflection (O fixed) as above	Theorem 8.42
Geometrically distinguish isometries fixing point A	(Table 8.1)
Arbitrary 3-d rotations & reflections in form $T^{-1}gT$	Theorem 8.42
Matrix of a general rotation (O fixed)	Theorem 8.49
Axis from rotation matrix (O fixed)	Corollary 8.52
Matrix to rotate **i** to **a** around axis perpendicular to both	Example 8.47
Orthogonal Matrix to send **a**,**b** to **x**,**y** (unit vectors, **a**.**b** = **x**.**y**)	Theorem 8.55

EXERCISES 8

1 √ Find the matrix of the linear transformation T in the cases (a) T(x,y,z) = (3x-y,2x+z,x-y+z), (b) T maps **i**, **j**, **k** to (**i**+**k**), (**j**+**k**), (**i**-**j**), (c) T(**i**+**j**) = √2**k**, T(**i**-**j**) = √2**i**, T(**k**) = **j**. Are any of these transformations isometries? (Note. |M| = ± 1 is not sufficient to prove that a matrix M is orthogonal.]

2 Check that the following are orthonormal triples, then find the matrix M that sends the first triple to the second (check that $M = N^T$ and MN = I). (a) (1/3)(1,2,2), (1/3)(2,-2,1), (1/3)(2,1,-2), (b) **j**, (1/√2)(**i**+**k**), (1/√2)(**i**-**k**).

3 Find the matrix of any isometry that maps **i**, **j**, **k** so as to send **k** into **w** = (1/√6) (1,2,-1).

4 What are the new coordinates of the triangle vertices (0,0,0), (1,0,1), (1,1,0) after the coordinate axes are changed to lie along the orthonormal triple (b) in Question 2? Determine the new matrices of the isometry T given by rotation of a quarter turn about the z-axis. Now check this by calculating the image of the triangle under T, in both coordinate systems.

5 √ Three linear transformations T are defined below. Determine in each case whether T preserves orientation, reverses it, or maps all of 3-space onto a plane (if so, what plane) (a) T(**i**) = **j**, T(**j**) = **i**, T(**k**) = **k**, (b) T(x,y,z) = (x-y, 2x+y+3z, y+z), (c) T(**i**+**j**) = **k**, T(**j**+**k**) = **i**, T(**k**+**i**) = **j**.

6 A translation of (1,2,5) is followed by a 3/4 turn about the z-axis. Use 4 x 4 matrices to determine what translation would instead follow the 3/4 turn, to achieve the same overall transformation. Check your result on the square with vertices (0,0,0), (1,0,0), (1,1,0), (0,1,0).

7 Write down the matrices M for reflection in the yz-plane and N for reflection in the plane x=z. Verify that MN rotates the plane by 1/4 turn about the y-axis, by computing the images of three non-collinear points, and checking that |MN| = 1.

8 √ Calculate the orbit of the point (2,0,0) under the group of symmetries generated by the reflections $R_{\mathbf{u}}$, $R_{\mathbf{v}}$, $R_{\mathbf{w}}$ in planes through the origin with normal vectors **u** = (1,0,0), **v** = (1,1,0), **w** = (0,1,1). The result should be the vertices of a certain polyhedron. Can you name it?

9 Find a composition of a rotation about the x-axis followed by rotation about the y-axis which will map a triangle in the xy-plane to one with normal unit vector (a,b,c). Apply this in case (a,b,c) = (1,1,1) with triangle O(0,0,0), P(0,1,0), Q(1,0,0).

10 (a) Use suitable coordinates to show that, in a rotary reflection, the rotation and reflection commute. (b) Choose three mutually perpendicular planes through the origin. Use matrices to show that the composition of reflections in each plane in turn is inversion.

11 Write down the matrix M for a rotary reflection with angle 45° about the z-axis. What does this matrix become if the axes of x, y, z are transformed (by an isometry) to lie along the vectors **k**, **i**+**j**, **i**-**j**.?

12 Verify that one of the matrices of Question 11 has an eigenvalue -1, with eigenvector (0,0,1).

13 Calculate eigenvalues and vectors for the following matrices, using the trace and determinant to write down the eigenvalue equation.

$$\text{(i)}\ \begin{bmatrix} 3 & 0 \\ 0 & 5 \end{bmatrix} \quad \text{(ii)}\ \begin{bmatrix} 2 & 1 \\ 0 & 3 \end{bmatrix} \quad \text{(iii)}\ \begin{bmatrix} 0 & 1 \\ 1 & 0 \end{bmatrix} \quad \text{(iv)}\ \begin{bmatrix} 2 & -1 \\ 3 & 2 \end{bmatrix}$$

Show that the eigenvalues of a matrix, whose entries below the main diagonal are all zeros, consist of the diagonal elements. What are suitable eigenvectors?

14 √ Of the following two matrices, one describes a rotation and the other a reflection in 3-space. By the easiest way you know, determine which is which and find the respective axis **a** or normal **n**.

$$\frac{1}{7}\begin{bmatrix} 3 & -6 & 2 \\ -6 & -2 & 3 \\ 2 & 3 & 6 \end{bmatrix}, \qquad \frac{1}{9}\begin{bmatrix} -1 & 4 & 8 \\ 4 & -7 & 4 \\ 8 & 4 & -1 \end{bmatrix}$$

15 Find the angle of rotation in Question 14 by first changing coordinates so that the new z-axis lies along **a** (for a quicker way, see Theorem 8.42 or Corollary 8.52).

16 √ Find the compositions: (a) A 1/3 turn about the z-axis followed by a 1/3 turn about the y-axis, (b) A 1/4 turn about OA, where A is (1,1,1), followed by a 1/2 turn about the y-axis (Theorem 8.19 may help).

17 Find the following compositions of isometries fixing the origin. (a) A rotary reflection with axis vector (1,2,2) then a reflection in the xy-plane (see Theorem 8.49). (b) Rotation of 90° about the z-axis followed by reflection in the plane x=z.

18 Find a 3 x 3 matrix to rotate the vector **k** onto (1/3)(1,-2,2) around an axis perpendicular to both (use Theorem 8.49).

19 Find (a) a rotation matrix, (b) the matrix of a rotary reflection, mapping the vectors (1, $\sqrt{2}$, 1), (0, 1, 0) to (1, 0, 0), ($\sqrt{2}$, -1, 1).

20 Reflection in the plane x + 2y - z = 6 is followed by translation by (1,1,0). Find the 4 x 4 matrix for the resulting glide, its plane, and its translation part.

21 A 2/3 turn about axis vector (1,1,-1) is followed by translation 2**i**. Find the axis of the resulting screw and its 4 x 4 matrix.

22 Determine the 4 x 4 matrix of the composition of the answers to Questions 20 and 21. Describe this transformation.

Chapter 9 QUATERNIONS AND ROTATIONS

The Irish mathematician Sir William Rowan Hamilton struggled for fifteen years to extend the 2-component complex numbers to triples, finally discovered it was impossible with the properties he sought (e.g. the product of two nonzero numbers cannot be zero, our (9.23)), but hit on the 4-component quaternions in 1843 (Hamilton, 1844). He inscribed the basic rules on a bridge in Dublin, Ireland. For a time quaternions were very fashionable, then they went out of favour. In this century interest revived with further applications in (Quantum) Physics, apart from a modest place in for example Algebraic topology, group theory and combinatorics (see e.g. Husemoller (1966), Hoggar (1982)). The application of quaternions to rotations has been known for a long time (Cayley, 1845). Already used to calculate with spacecraft rotations (see e.g. Hughes, 1986), quaternions were highlighted to computer animators by Shoemake (1985). Here we develop the properties upon which that application depends, beginning with a quick trip through the most relevant material on complex numbers, the forerunners of quaternions.

9.1 Complex numbers

In many times and places, negative, let alone complex numbers have seemed problematical, unreal. Yet they can be used to solve problems about real numbers, such as differential equations. They find application in electronics, fluid dynamics, electromagnetic theory and elastic deformation, to name only some areas (Churchill, 1960).

But their most immediate application is in the solution of polynomial equations, as evidenced below.

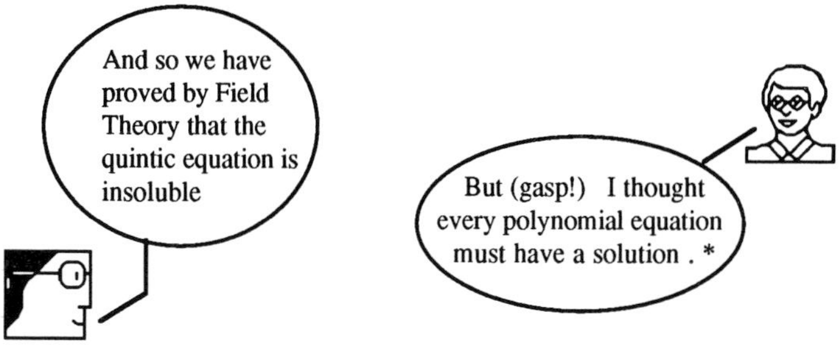

* **Ed.** True if complex numbers are allowed. The classic case is $x^2 + 1 = 0$.

Figure 9.1 Complex numbers yield some surprises. Polynomial equations of degree four or less have a formula for their solution (Remarks 9.16), but since square roots are involved, not every potential solution exists as a real number. If complex numbers are allowed, then although equations of degree five and greater have no general formulae for their solutions, every polynomial equation has a solution.

9.1.1 Basic arithmetic

Just as the real numbers correspond to the points of the x-axis, so does each point (a,b) of the plane represent a *complex number* $z = a+\mathbf{i}b$, treated as an algebraic expression in one unknown, **i**, subject to $\mathbf{i}^2 = -1$ (the significance of this relation is our topic here).

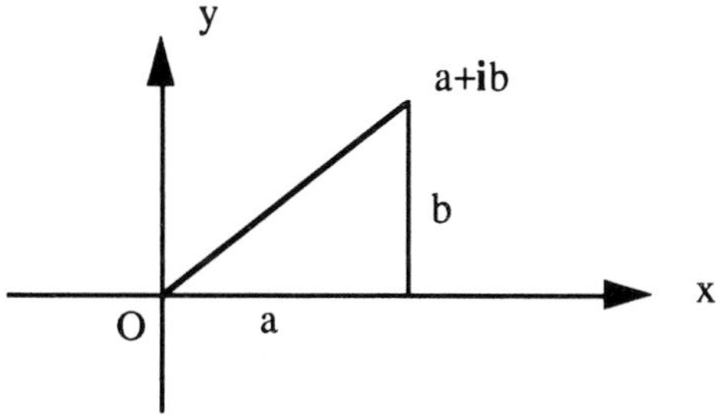

Figure 9.2 The Argand diagram, representing a+**i**b as point (a,b).

The representation of complex numbers by points in the plane is called an *Argand diagram*. Then the x-axis represents numbers x+0**i**, which we may regard as ordinary real numbers x, whilst the y-axis represents type 0+y**i**, also written simply y**i** and called *purely imaginary* numbers. We often omit the word 'represents' and say a complex number 'is' its corresponding point. In particular, **i** is the point (0,1). Incidentally, we will not distinguish between **i**y and y**i**. For purposes of addition, subtraction, and multiplication by a real number, a+**i**b acts like a vector with components a,b. Thus, if c+**i**d is another complex number and α a scalar (real number), then

$$\begin{aligned}(a+\mathbf{i}b) + (c+\mathbf{i}d) &= (a+c) + \mathbf{i}(b+d),\\ \alpha(a+\mathbf{i}b) &= \alpha a + \mathbf{i}(\alpha b)\end{aligned} \tag{9.1}$$

EXAMPLE 9.1 $(1+2\mathbf{i}) + (3-5\mathbf{i}) = 4-3\mathbf{i}$, $5(1+2\mathbf{i}) = 5+10\mathbf{i}$.

Once we get the multiplication rule right, some invaluable results follow. In fact the rules (9.1) are extended to the 'usual' rules of arithmetic via the vital extra definition

$$\mathbf{i}^2 = -1. \tag{9.2}$$

Thus multiplication of two arbitrary complex numbers is given by

$$\begin{aligned}(a+\mathbf{i}b)(c+\mathbf{i}d) &= a(c+\mathbf{i}d) + \mathbf{i}b(c+\mathbf{i}d) \\ &= ac + ad\mathbf{i} + bc\mathbf{i} + bd\mathbf{i}^2 \\ &= (ac-bd) + \mathbf{i}(ad+bc)\end{aligned} \tag{9.3}$$

EXAMPLE 9.2 $(1+2\mathbf{i})(3-5\mathbf{i}) = 3 + 6\mathbf{i} - 5\mathbf{i} - 10\mathbf{i}^2 = 13+\mathbf{i}$.

EXERCISE Calculate $(1-i)(2+i)(-1+3i)$ two ways: (a) by multiplying the first two numbers firstly, (b) by starting with the last two. Your answers should be the same, by the associative law given below.

ASSOCIATIVITY $(z_1.z_2)z_3 = z_1(z_2.z_3)$ for any three complex numbers z_1, z_2, z_3. We cannot assume this in advance, but happily (9.2) and (9.3) do keep the multiplication associative, since each triple product of complex numbers above is a sum of eight products (ab)c or a(bc), in conformity with the bracketing, where each of a,b,c is a real number or a real multiple of **i**. For example $2(3 \times 5i) = 2 \times 15i = 30\mathbf{i}$, and $(2 \times 3)5\mathbf{i} = 6 \times 5\mathbf{i} = 30\mathbf{i}$. The Commutativity property $z_1z_2 = z_2z_1$ is easily checked by straight multiplication. In any case, both properties are clearer from the striking geometrical significance of multiplication, (9.6), shortly below.

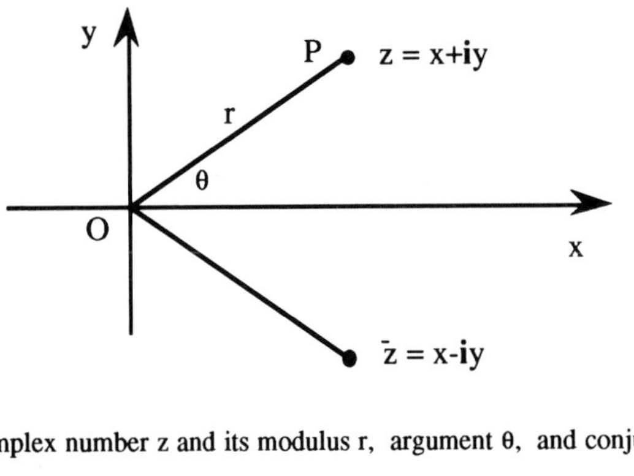

Figure 9.3 Complex number z and its modulus r, argument θ, and conjugate $\bar{z}$.

NOTATION 9.3 **C** is the set of all complex numbers. $z = x+\mathbf{i}y$ will denote an arbitrary complex number, with obvious shortenings: $x+0\mathbf{i} = x$, $0+\mathbf{i}y = \mathbf{i}y$, $1\mathbf{i} = \mathbf{i}$, $(-1)\mathbf{i} = -\mathbf{i}$. Referring to Figure 9.3, we write

Re z	$= x$,	the *real part* of z,
Im z	$= y$,	the *imaginary part* of z,
$\bar{z}$	$= x-\mathbf{i}y$,	the *conjugate* of z, also written z*
$r = \lvert z \rvert$	$= \sqrt{(x^2 + y^2)}$,	the *modulus* of z,
θ	= signed angle XOP,	the *argument* of z, or *arg(z)* *(undefined if z = 0)*.

EXAMPLE 9.4 $z = \sqrt{3} + \mathbf{i}$ has real part $\sqrt{3}$, imaginary part 1, conjugate $\sqrt{3} - \mathbf{i}$, modulus $\sqrt{[(\sqrt{3})^2 + 1^2]} = 2$. To be sure of getting the correct sign for the argument θ we first *plot the point* $(\sqrt{3},1)$, as shown in Figure 9.4 below. Then it is clear that $\theta = \sin^{-1}(1/2) = \pi/6$ (the angle between $-\pi/2$ and $\pi/2$ whose sine is 1/2).

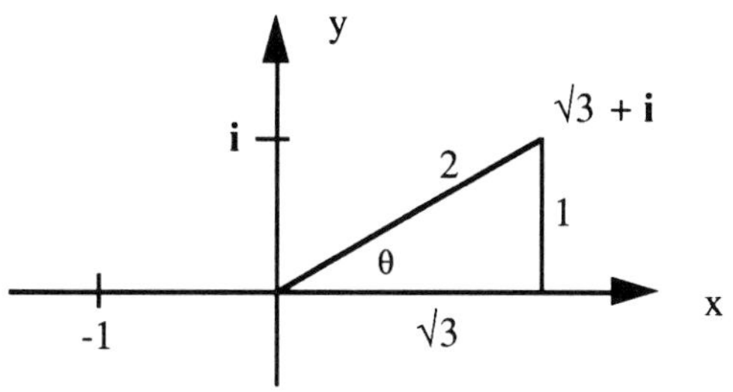

Figure 9.4 Diagram for reliably determining the argument of $\sqrt{3}+\mathbf{i}$.

MODULUS A key property is that $z = 0$ if and only if $|z| = 0$, the significance being that z has two parts, whereas $|z|$ is a single number. Notice too that $|z_1 - z_2|$ is the usual Euclidean distance (1.1) between points in the plane. The next exercise applies this.

EXERCISE Find the modulus and argument of $-1+\mathbf{i}$. **or** Write down in xy coordinates the equation of the plane curve given by $\{Z: |z| = |z - 4|\}$, and hence identify its shape. What theorem in geometry predicts this shape? Harder: do the same for $|z - 2| + |z + 2| = 6$.

INVERSES Now it is convenient to observe that $(x+\mathbf{i}y)(x-\mathbf{i}y) = x^2 - \mathbf{i}^2y^2 = x^2 + y^2$, and that consequently, if the complex number $z = x+\mathbf{i}y$ is nonzero, it has an inverse $z^{-1} = (x-\mathbf{i}y)/(x^2 + y^2)$, which may be written more briefly as $\bar{z}/|z|^2$. This confirms that we can divide by any nonzero complex number β, with $\alpha/\beta = \alpha.\beta^{-1}$.

CONJUGATES Notice that $\bar{z}$ gives the reflection of the point z in the x-axis, providing geometrical content to the useful assertions of (9.4) below, of which the first two lines follow directly from the definition of conjugate:

$$z+\bar{z} = 2x, \quad z-\bar{z} = 2\mathbf{i}y, \quad z\bar{z} = |z|^2, \tag{9.4A}$$

$$z+\bar{z} \text{ is real}, \qquad z = \bar{z} \Leftrightarrow z \text{ is real}, \tag{9.4B}$$

$$\overline{z_1 + z_2} = \bar{z}_1 + \bar{z}_2, \quad \overline{z_1 z_2} = \bar{z}_1 \bar{z}_2, \quad \overline{z_1/ z_2} = \bar{z}_1/ \bar{z}_2. \tag{9.4C}$$

Proof of (9.4C) We obtain the first two equalities by replacing b by -b and d by -d, both in the first line of (9.1), and in (9.3). For the third, which assumes z_2 is nonzero, we have $z_1 = (z_1/z_2)z_2$ and therefore $\bar{z}_1 = \overline{(z_1/z_2)}\,\bar{z}_2$. Finally, we divide both sides by $\bar{z}_2$.

EXAMPLE 9.5 The last part of (9.4A), which we have just checked under 'inverses', implies that if we multiply a number by its conjugate the result is real. This gives a standard way to divide one complex number by another, thus

$$\frac{3+2\mathbf{i}}{3+4\mathbf{i}} = \frac{(3+2\mathbf{i})(3-4\mathbf{i})}{(3+4\mathbf{i})(3-4\mathbf{i})} = \frac{9-12\mathbf{i}+6\mathbf{i}-8\mathbf{i}^2}{3^2 + 4^2} = (1/25)(17-6\mathbf{i}).$$

EXERCISE Divide 4+5i by 5-4i. Is the answer a surprising coincidence? [cf. Theorem 9.7.]

EXAMPLE 9.6 Here is a use of the properties of conjugates (9.4), finishing with a result about real polynomials (those whose coefficients are all real numbers). Given $\alpha = -1+2i$ as a root of the equation $f(z) = z^4 + 3z^3 + 8z^2 + 7z + 5 = 0$, find the others, and factorise the polynomial.

Solution The idea is that, since f(z) has real coefficients, $\overline{\alpha}$ is also a root, for, setting $z = \alpha$ and taking conjugates of both sides of the equation by means of (9.4), we have

$$\overline{\alpha^4} + \overline{3\alpha^3} + \overline{8\alpha^2} + \overline{7\alpha} + \overline{5} = \overline{0}, \quad \text{or} \quad \overline{\alpha}^4 + 3\overline{\alpha}^3 + 8\overline{\alpha}^2 + 7\overline{\alpha} + 5 = 0,$$

since the conjugate of a real number is itself. Now since α and $\overline{\alpha}$ are *both* roots, f(z) is divisible by $(z-\alpha)(z-\overline{\alpha}) = z^2 - (\alpha + \overline{\alpha})z + \alpha\overline{\alpha} = z^2 - 2\mathrm{Re}(\alpha) + |\alpha|^2 = z^2 + 2z + 5$, a real quadratic factor arising from a complex root. Dividing this into f(z) we obtain the factorisation $f(z) = (z^2 + 2z + 5)(z^2 + z + 1)$, a fact about real polynomials. The other two roots of f(z) are those of $z^2 + z + 1$, namely $z = (-1 \pm \sqrt{1-4})/2 = (-1 \pm \mathbf{i}\sqrt{3})/2$.

Notes (1) $(z-\alpha)(z-\overline{\alpha})$ is always a real quadratic polynomial, as we saw above, (2) The reader may reasonably wonder how often we know one complex root of a high degree polynomial. The answer is: sometimes in important cases, of which $z^n - 1$ is an example soon to be considered in Section 9.1.3.

9.1.2 The polar form

We observe that r,θ in Figure 9.3 are the polar coordinates of z as a point in the plane. In fact,

$$\begin{aligned} z &= x + \mathbf{i}y, \\ &= r\cos\theta + \mathbf{i}(r\sin\theta), \\ &= r(\cos\theta + \mathbf{i}\sin\theta), \quad \text{the } \textit{polar form} \text{ of } z. \qquad (9.5) \end{aligned}$$

This points up the first remarkable consequence of $\mathbf{i}^2 = -1$ (cf. Figure 9.5), of which (9.6) and Theorem 9.7 are equivalent statements immediately below.

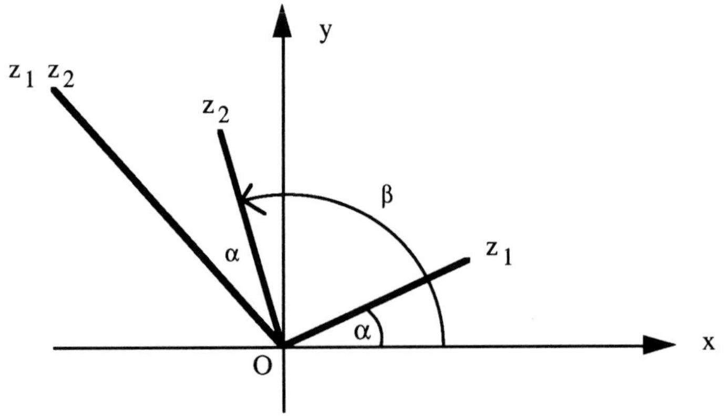

Figure 9.5 The product of two complex numbers z_1, z_2 is formed by adding their arguments and multiplying their moduli. Here z_1z_2 has argument $\alpha+\beta$.

To multiply two complex numbers, we multiply the moduli and add the arguments (9.6)

THEOREM 9.7 We have for any two complex numbers $z_1, z_2 \neq 0$

$$\begin{aligned} \arg(z_1z_2) &= \arg(z_1) + \arg(z_2), && (\text{if } z_1z_2 \neq 0), \\ |z_1z_2| &= |z_1|\,|z_2|, \end{aligned}$$

and consequently

$$\begin{aligned} \arg(z_1/z_2) &= \arg(z_1) - \arg(z_2), && (\text{if } z_1z_2 \neq 0), \\ |z_1/z_2| &= |z_1|\,/\,|z_2| && (\text{if } z_2 \neq 0). \end{aligned}$$

Proof This is well worth doing, as it is both simple and fundamental. We prove the first two assertions of the Theorem using polar forms (9.5).

$$\begin{aligned} &r(\cos\alpha + \mathbf{i}\sin\alpha) \times s(\cos\beta + \mathbf{i}\sin\beta) \quad (r, s > 0) \\ &= rs(\cos\alpha + \mathbf{i}\sin\alpha)(\cos\beta + \mathbf{i}\sin\beta) \\ &= rs\{\cos\alpha\cos\beta - \sin\alpha\sin\beta + \mathbf{i}(\sin\alpha\cos\beta + \cos\alpha\sin\beta)\} \\ &= rs\{\cos(\alpha+\beta) + \mathbf{i}\sin(\alpha+\beta)\}, \text{ by angle formulae.} \end{aligned}$$

On the other hand, if either modulus $r = |z_1|$ or $s = |z_2|$ is zero we have $|z_1z_2| = |z_1|\,|z_2|$ since both sides are zero. Now let z_1, z_2 be nonzero. Then we deduce the last two lines of the Theorem from the first two, similarly to the discussion of conjugates (the case $z_1 = 0$ on the fourth line being trivial), for we have $z_1 = (z_1/z_2)\,z_2$ and, taking arguments, $\arg(z_1) = \arg(z_1/z_2) + \arg(z_2)$; taking moduli, $|z_1| = |(z_1/z_2)|\,|z_2|$. These are easily rearranged to give the required results, and the proof is complete.

A profound and practical consequence of this is that the complex number $\cos\theta+\mathbf{i}\sin\theta$ behaves like a number raised to a power, motivating definition (9.7) below (for further explanation see Remark 9.16).

DEFINITION $e^{i\theta} = \cos\theta + \mathbf{i}\sin\theta.$ (9.7)

CONSEQUENCE $e^{i\alpha}e^{i\beta} = e^{i(\alpha+\beta)}.$ (9.8)

CONSEQUENCE The inverse of $e^{i\theta}$ is its conjugate $e^{-i\theta}$. (9.9)

One should not fail to note that $e^{i\theta}$ has modulus $\sqrt{(\cos^2\theta + \sin^2\theta)} = 1$ and that the polar form of a general complex number with modulus r and argument θ may be written $re^{i\theta}$. The only exception is $z = 0$, for which $r = 0$ and θ is undefined. It is convenient to regard θ as defined only up to adding or subtracting multiples of a complete turn 2π, since this leaves the complex number unchanged (see e.g. Figure 9.3). For example, instead of $e^{3\pi i/2}$ we may write $e^{-i\pi/2}$. In this sense, we should strictly refer to 'one value of arg(z)' in Theorem 9.7. On the other hand, as the reader may wish to check from the definitions

$$e^{i\pi} = -1, \qquad e^{i\pi/2} = \mathbf{i}. \qquad (9.10)$$

Hence multiplying by $e^{i\pi}$ or equivalently adding π to the argument (angle) simply changes the sign of a complex number, whereas multiplying by **i** turns z through a right angle. These facts correspond to the real formulae $\sin(\theta+\pi) = -\sin\theta$, $\cos(\theta+\pi) = -\cos\theta$, and $\sin(\theta+\pi/2) = \cos\theta$, $\cos(\theta+\pi/2) = -\sin\theta$.

More generally the transformation $T(z) = ze^{i\theta}$ rotates the plane through an angle θ, where we regard the transformation itself as being unaffected by the addition of complete turns to θ. Notice that, with $c = \cos\theta$, $s = \sin\theta$, we can recover the rotation matrix by $[x\ \ y] \to x+\mathbf{i}y$ $\to (x+\mathbf{i}y)(c+\mathbf{i}s) \to cx-sy + \mathbf{i}(sx+cy) \to [cx-sy\ \ sx+cy] = [x\ \ y]\begin{bmatrix} c & s \\ -s & c \end{bmatrix}$. Much more importantly, we will see in Section 9.3.2 how to express rotation of q about a general unit vector **a** through the origin in 3-space in terms of a quaternion polar form $e^{\mathbf{a}\theta}$, where, as a quaternion with three components, $\mathbf{a}^2 = -1$.

EXAMPLE 9.8 Find (i) the modulus of the product $(3-4\mathbf{i})(5\mathbf{i}+12)$ and of the quotient $(3-4\mathbf{i})/(5\mathbf{i}+12)$, (ii) the conjugate of $e^{i\pi/7}(-2+17\mathbf{i})$, (iii) $(-1+\mathbf{i}\sqrt{3})^{20}$.

Solution (i) This brings out the fact that we need not multiply out the two numbers in order to find the modulus of their product. By the highlighted statement (9.6), or Theorem 9.7, $|(3-4\mathbf{i})(5\mathbf{i}+12)| = |3-4\mathbf{i}|\,|5\mathbf{i}+12| = 5.13 = 65$, and $|(3-4\mathbf{i})/(5\mathbf{i}+12)| = |3-4\mathbf{i}|/|5\mathbf{i}+12| = 5/13$.
(ii) By (9.4) we may proceed similarly to above and simply take the conjugate of each factor. The answer is $e^{-i\pi/7}(-2-17\mathbf{i})$.
(iii) We wish to avoid a horrendous time with the Binomial theorem. The key is to first plot $-1+\mathbf{i}\sqrt{3}$ in the Argand diagram to determine its modulus and argument r, θ as is done in Figure 9.6 below.

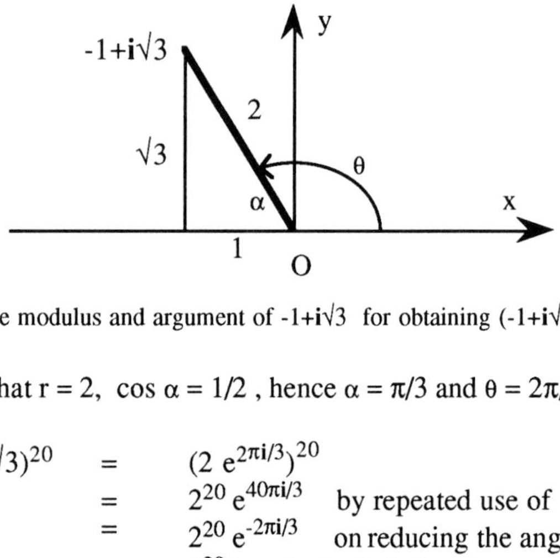

Figure 9.6 The modulus and argument of $-1+\mathbf{i}\sqrt{3}$ for obtaining $(-1+\mathbf{i}\sqrt{3})^{20}$.

The diagram shows that r = 2, $\cos\alpha = 1/2$, hence $\alpha = \pi/3$ and $\theta = 2\pi/3$.
We have

$$\begin{aligned}
(-1+\mathbf{i}\sqrt{3})^{20} &= (2\,e^{2\pi i/3})^{20} \\
&= 2^{20}\,e^{40\pi i/3} && \text{by repeated use of (9.6),} \\
&= 2^{20}\,e^{-2\pi i/3} && \text{on reducing the angle by } 7 \times 2\pi, \\
&= 2^{20}(\cos 2\pi/3 - \mathbf{i}\sin 2\pi/3) \\
&= 2^{19}(-1-\mathbf{i}\sqrt{3}).
\end{aligned}$$

EXERCISE Calculate $(1+\mathbf{i})^5$ (a) by the polar form, (b) by the Binomial theorem.

9.1.3 Further consequences of a square root of -1

NO DIVISORS OF ZERO From the modulus rule $|z_1z_2| = |z_1|\,|z_2|$ of (9.6), it is clear and was already assumed without comment, that the product of two nonzero complex numbers cannot be zero. This would be false with $\mathbf{i}^2 = +1$, for then $(1+\mathbf{i})(1-\mathbf{i})$ would be zero, and we would call $1+\mathbf{i}$, $1-\mathbf{i}$ *divisors of zero.* In fact we take $\mathbf{i}^2 = -1$ and they are *not* divisors of zeros.

THEOREM 9.9 **(De Moivre's Theorem.)** If n is any integer $0, \pm 1, \pm 2, \ldots$, then

$$(e^{i\theta})^n = e^{in\theta}, \text{ or } \quad (\cos\theta + \mathbf{i}\sin\theta)^n = \cos n\theta + \mathbf{i}\sin n\theta. \qquad (9.11)$$

Proof The result is trivially true for n = 0 since any nonzero number to the power zero is defined to be 1. Let n be a positive integer. Then, as in Example 9.8(iii) above, (9.11) holds by repeated application of the multiplication rule (9.6): $e^{i\alpha}.e^{i\beta} = e^{i(\alpha+\beta)}$. Suppose n is a negative integer, then $m = -n$ is positive and we may apply the first part to m:

$(e^{i\theta})^n$	=	$(e^{i\theta})^{-m}$	
	=	$1/(e^{i\theta})^m$	by definition of a negative power,
	=	$1/e^{im\theta}$	by (9.11) for a positive integer,
	=	$e^{-im\theta}$	by definition of a negative power,
	=	$e^{in\theta}$	since m = -n.

EXAMPLE 9.10 Use complex numbers to express $\cos^4\theta$ as a linear combination $A\cos 4\theta + B\cos 3\theta + C\cos 2\theta + D\cos\theta + E$.

Solution Write $z = e^{i\theta}$. Then we have, by De Moivre's Theorem, $z^n = e^{in\theta}$, $z^{-n} = e^{-in\theta}$, and $z^n + z^{-n} = 2\cos n\theta$, whence

$$\begin{aligned}
(2\cos\theta)^4 &= (z + z^{-1})^4 \\
&= z^4 + 4z^2 + 6 + 4z^{-2} + z^{-4} \\
&= (z^4 + z^{-4}) + 4(z^2 + z^{-2}) + 6 \\
&= 2\cos 4\theta + 8\cos 2\theta + 6, \text{ hence} \\
\cos^4\theta &= (1/8)\cos 4\theta + (1/2)\cos 2\theta + 3/8.
\end{aligned}$$

THEOREM 9.11 (From introduction to Section 8.4.5.) Let $f(z)$ be a real or complex polynomial of degree n and α a constant. Then

(i) The remainder on dividing $f(z)$ by $z-\alpha$ is $f(\alpha)$.

(ii) $z-\alpha$ is a factor of $f(z)$ if and only if $f(\alpha) = 0$ (α is a root of $f(z)$).

(iii) $f(z)$ can have at most n distinct roots.

ROOTS OF UNITY The following fact is illustrated in Figure 9.7. It depends on Theorem 9.11, is important in itself, and shows incidentally that De Moivre's Theorem cannot hold for fractional powers: Let n be a positive integer. Then *there are exactly n n'th roots of unity, that is, solutions of the equation* $z^n = 1$, *and they lie equally spaced round the unit circle centred at the origin.*

Proof The reason is simple. If we set $w = e^{2\pi i/n}$ then the n successive powers $w, w^2, w^3, \ldots, w^n$ are distinct, being spaced round the unit circle at angle intervals of $2\pi/n$; but furthermore $w^n = e^{2\pi i} = 1$ and so every power $(w^r)^n$ equals 1. Thus every w^r is an n'th root of unity. (Of course $w^r = e^{2\pi ri/n}$.) This accounts for n distinct roots of unity and, since z^n-1 has degree n, there can be no more, by Theorem 9.11.

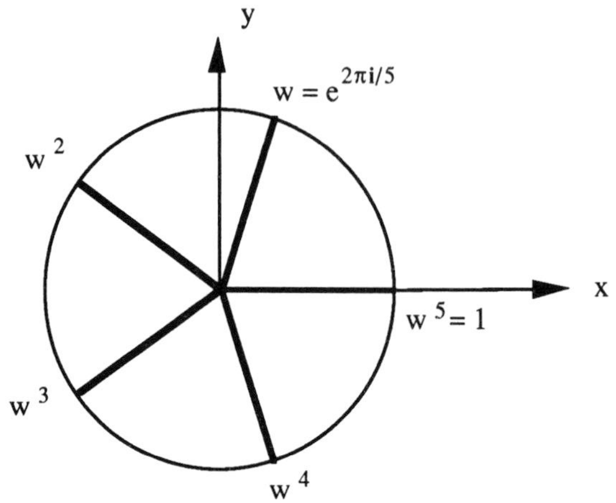

Figure 9.7 Argand diagram showing the fifth roots of unity. For given n, the n'th roots are equally spaced around a circle of radius 1 at the origin (the unit circle).

Some applications of roots of unity We give two examples, besides factorising $z^n - 1$.

(1) *Plane rotations.* We have already observed that the plane transformation $T(z) = zw$ rotates the plane by the argument (angle) of w. Thus if w is the fifth root of unity $e^{2\pi i/5}$ then T is rotation by a 1/5 turn and the set of all fifth roots of unity $\{1, w, w^2, w^3, w^4\}$ is a group under composition by multiplication, which is isomorphic to the group of rotation symmetries $\{I, T, T^2, T^3, T^4\}$ of the regular pentagon (cf. Section 2.4).

(2) *The connection with fractal Julia sets.* See Example 16.22 and (on Newtons' method in the complex plane) Theorem 16.68.

ROOTS IN CONJUGATE PAIRS We know already from Example 9.6 that the roots of $z^n = 1$, or $z^n - 1 = 0$, must occur in conjugate pairs $\alpha, \overline{\alpha}$ (coincident if α is real), since this equation has real coefficients. This pairing is seen in Figure 9.7 where for example the reflection of root w in the x-axis is its conjugate and fellow root w^4. Thus, provided we know which powers are the conjugates of which, actual calculation may be required for no more than half of the roots. And we do have this information; for example (n = 5) $\overline{w} = e^{-2\pi i/5} = w^{-1} = w^{5-1}$ (since $w^5 = 1$) $= w^4$, as we saw. The result is stated as (9.12). Notice that an n'th root of unity must have modulus 1 (why?).

If w has modulus 1 then $\overline{w} = w^{-1}$ *and if w is also an n'th root of unity then the conjugate of* w^r $(r \in N)$ *is* w^{n-r}. (9.12)

EXAMPLE 9.12 The three cube roots of unity are 1 itself and :
$w = e^{2\pi i/3} = \cos 2\pi/3 + \mathbf{i} \sin 2\pi/3 = (1/2)(-1 + \mathbf{i}\sqrt{3})$, and
$\overline{w} = e^{-2\pi i/3} = (1/2)(-1 - \mathbf{i}\sqrt{3})$ (no calculation).

EXERCISE (i) Multiply out w^3 to check that w above is a cube root of 1 (the Binomial Theorem will save some work). (ii) Infer a list of six distinct 6'th roots of 1. (ii) Write down *without calculation* four distinct 4'th roots of 1.

EXAMPLE 9.13 (The argument here applies in any 'field' of numbers.) Prove that if w is an n'th root of unity other than 1 then $1 + w + w^2 + \ldots + w^{n-1} = 0$ $(n \geq 2)$.

Solution $0 = w^n - 1 = (w - 1)(1 + w + w^2 + \ldots + w^{n-1})$. Since w-1 is nonzero, the factor it multiplies is zero, by the 'no divisors of zero' property of complex numbers.

THEOREM 9.14 (A real consequence.) x^n-1 is always a product of real linear factors x±1 and real quadratic factors x^2+ax+1.

Proof From its list of roots, $z^n - 1$ is a product of real linear and/or quadratic factors of the form $(z-w)(z-\overline{w}) = z^2 - 2z\,\mathrm{Re}(w) + 1$. This is illustrated in the table below.

TABLE 9.1 Some factorisations based on complex roots of unity.

n	n'th roots of unity	factorisation of $z^n - 1$
2	1, -1	$(z-1)(z+1)$
3	1, w, $\overline{w}$	$(z-1)(z^2 + z + 1)$
4	±1, ±i	$(z-1)(z+1)(z^2 + 1)$
5	$1, \zeta, \zeta^2, \overline{\zeta}, \overline{\zeta}^2$	$(z-1)(z^2 + \tau z + 1)(z^2 + \sigma z + 1)$
6	±1, ±w, ±$\overline{w}$	$(z-1)(z+1)(z^2 - z + 1)(z^2 + z + 1)$

Here, $w = e^{2\pi i/3}$, $\zeta = e^{2\pi i/5}$ whilst σ, τ are the roots of $x^2-x-1 = 0$, namely $\tau = (1+\sqrt{5})/2$, the 'Golden ratio', and $\sigma = (1-\sqrt{5})/2$. Hence $\sigma\tau = -1$, $\sigma+t = 1$, $\sigma^2+\tau^2 = 3$. Note that although $2\sin(\pi/5)$ equals $\sqrt{(3-\tau)}$ and cannot be expressed conveniently in terms of σ, τ, we do have $\tau = 2\cos(\pi/5)$, and this suffices for applications.

THE FUNDAMENTAL THEOREM OF ALGEBRA This goes beyond roots of unity, and underlines the importance of complex numbers:

every complex polynomial equation f(z) = 0 *has a root, and hence every polynomial of degree n is the product of n linear factors.* (9.13)

For a proof by topology see Section 13.4.2. The second assertion follows from the first because for each root α we can divide out by a factor z-α. Gauss gave his fourth proof of The Theorem at the age of seventy, an age pretty advanced for his times. Thus every real polynomial has a complex root even if it does not have a real one. As illustrated by roots of unity, if we restrict ourselves to real polynomials, then as we saw in Example 9.6 the roots occur in conjugate complex pairs, and hence the polynomial is the product of real linear and/or quadratic factors. And we have deduced this from facts about complex numbers. For applications of the factorisation of z^n-1 see Schroeder (1986).

EXERCISE Derive the factorisation of x^6-1 by using sixth roots of unity.

By a result of elementary geometry, the sum of lengths of two sides of a triangle equals at least the length of the third side. Since the sides of a triangle may represent vectors and hence complex numbers we have the first inequality stated below.

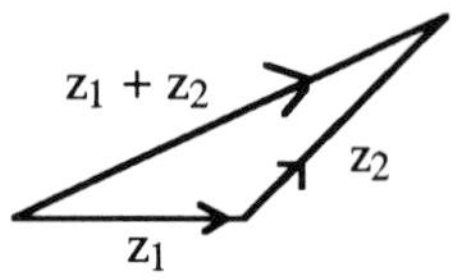

THEOREM 9.15 (The triangle inequality for complex numbers.) For complex numbers z_1 and z_2 we have

$$\text{(a)} \quad |z_1 + z_2| \le |z_1| + |z_2|, \qquad \text{(b)} \quad \big||z_1| - |z_2|\big| \le |z_1 + z_2|.$$

Proof (a) A direct proof can be given using the definition and properties of the modulus but we will be content with having deduced it from elementary geometry. In fact it is a special case of a result for n-space (Remark 7.12). We can now infer (b) by the argument $|z_1| = |(z_1 + z_2) - z_2| \le |z_1 + z_2| + |-z_2|$, for then $|z_1| - |z_2|$ and similarly $|z_2| - |z_1|$ do not exceed $|z_1 + z_2|$, and part (b) follows.

REMARKS 9.16 (1) *(Choosing the e in $e^{i\theta}$.)* The fact that $\cos\theta + \mathbf{i}\sin\theta$ behaves like a number raised to a power suggests we call it $d^{i\theta}$ for some real number d, but how should we choose d? Defining the derivative $[f(\theta) + \mathbf{i}g(\theta)]' = f'(\theta) + \mathbf{i}g'(\theta)$ for f, g real, we obtain $(\cos\theta + \mathbf{i}\sin\theta)' = -\sin\theta + \mathbf{i}\cos\theta = \mathbf{i}(\cos\theta + \mathbf{i}\sin\theta)$. But for real functions, if $d^{c\theta}$ has derivative $cd^{c\theta}$ then d is uniquely e, the base of 'natural logarithms ln(x)'. This may be deduced from the formula $(d^{c\theta})' = cd^{c\theta}$ (see a basic calculus text such as Swokowski, 1979). The result is that writing $\cos\theta + \mathbf{i}\sin\theta$ as $e^{i\theta}$ leads to a nice extension of differential calculus to complex numbers and to new techniques for solving real differential equations.

Some readers may find the series expansion $e^x = 1 + x + x^2/2! + x^3/3! + \dots$ with $x = \mathbf{i}\theta$ more illuminating for (given that this is valid), by separating out the real and imaginary parts we obtain $e^{i\theta} = (1 - \theta^2/2! + \theta^4/4! + \dots) + \mathbf{i}(\theta - \theta^3/3! + \theta^5/5! + \dots)$, and these series are the expansions for $\cos\theta$ and $\sin\theta$.

(2) *(Solving equations.)* We mentioned at the start of this chapter that polynomial equations of degree less than five have a formula for their solution. Of course the quadratic equation $ax^2 + bx + c = 0$ has solutions $x = (-b \pm \sqrt{(b^2 - 4ac)})/2a$, which reduces in the case $x^2 + 2hx + c = 0$ to $x = -h \pm \sqrt{(h^2 - c)}$. The formulae for degrees 3,4 are somewhat more complicated and seem not often to be used, perhaps because Newton's iterative method is so simple to carry out (Example 13.22). However it is interesting to see these formulae and know that they exist, and it seems likely that they will be useful from time to time for equation-solving in computer graphics.

Degree 3. Dividing through by the coefficient of x^3 and setting $z = x + a_2/3$ (a_2 being the new coefficient of x^2) we reduce the cubic to the form (a) below, whose solutions are the cube roots in (b). The six values coincide in pairs.

$$\text{(a)} \quad z^3 + pz + q = 0, \qquad \text{(b)} \quad z = [-q/2 \pm \sqrt{q^2/4 + p^3/27}\,]^{1/3}.$$

Degree 4. As before, we eliminate the coefficient of the second highest power, after dividing through by the leading coefficient, setting now $z = x + a_3/4$. We obtain the form (c) below, whose solutions are those of the two quadratics shown in (d), where u is any solution of the cubic equation in (e) (complex cube roots are obtained by using polar forms, see Section 9.1.2).

(c) $z^4 + pz^2 + qz + r = 0$, (d) $z^2 + u/2 \pm (Az-B) = 0$,

(e) $A = \sqrt{u-p}$, $B = q/2A$, and $(u^2 - 4r)(u - p) - q^2 = 0$.

For more on the practicalities of solving polynomial equations of degree three and higher, see Schwarze et al (1990), and Pross et al (1988). We take the theory of complex numbers further for the purpose of Mandelbrot, Julia sets, and others, in Chapter 16.

EXERCISE Solve the cubic equation $z^3 + 3z + 2 = 0$. It may be helpful to express your answer in terms of $a = (1 + \sqrt{3})^{1/3}$ and $b = (-1 + \sqrt{2})^{1/3}$, noting that $ab = 1$. **or** By first squaring both sides, prove the triangle inequality for complex numbers, using especially the properties $|z|^2 = z\bar{z}$ and $Re(z) \le |z|$.

9.2 The Quaternions

In this section we set up the foundations of quaternions as a preparation to their application to rotations in three dimensions.

9.2.1 Basics of quaternions

A quaternion **a** may be viewed as the extension of a complex number $a_0 + a_1\mathbf{i}$ to an entity with four components:

$$\mathbf{a} = a_0 + a_1\mathbf{i} + a_2\mathbf{j} + a_3\mathbf{k}, \qquad (9.14)$$

where the real numbers a_1, a_2, a_3 are written formally as coefficients of the symbols **i**, **j**, **k**. Quaternions are added, subtracted, multiplied by real numbers and by each other as algebraic expressions, subject to the following laws of multiplication

$$\begin{array}{lllll} \mathbf{ij} = \mathbf{k} = -\mathbf{ji}, & \mathbf{i}^2 = -1, \\ \mathbf{jk} = \mathbf{i} = -\mathbf{kj}, & \mathbf{j}^2 = -1, \\ \mathbf{ki} = \mathbf{j} = -\mathbf{ik}, & \mathbf{k}^2 = -1. \end{array} \qquad (9.15)$$

Note that the cyclic rotation $\mathbf{i} \to \mathbf{j} \to \mathbf{k} \to \mathbf{i}$ transforms each row of (9.15) into another. We say accordingly that these laws are *invariant* under rotation of **i**, **j**, **k** (cf. (7.25)). They can be written more compactly as $\mathbf{i}^2 = \mathbf{j}^2 = \mathbf{k}^2 = \mathbf{ijk} = -1$, once we have established that quaternion multiplication is associative: $(\mathbf{ab})\mathbf{c} = \mathbf{a}(\mathbf{bc})$, in Section 9.2.2.

EXAMPLES 9.17 (1) $2 \times 3\mathbf{j} = 6\mathbf{j} = 3\mathbf{j} \times 2$; multiplication by a real number may be done in either order.

(2) $\mathbf{i}(2\mathbf{j}-1) = 2\mathbf{ij} - \mathbf{i} = 2\mathbf{k}-\mathbf{i}$, but $(2\mathbf{j}-1)\mathbf{i} = 2\mathbf{ji} - \mathbf{i} = -2\mathbf{k} - \mathbf{i}$, a different answer. Thus quaternions do not commute, as is already clear from (9.15). But notice the steps in the multiplications.

(3)
$$\begin{aligned} (\mathbf{i}+2\mathbf{j})^2 &= (\mathbf{i}+2\mathbf{j})(\mathbf{i}+2\mathbf{j}) \\ &= \mathbf{i}(\mathbf{i}+2\mathbf{j}) + 2\mathbf{j}(\mathbf{i}+2\mathbf{j}) \\ &= \mathbf{i}^2 + 2\mathbf{ij} + 2\mathbf{ji} + 4\mathbf{j}^2 \\ &= -5, \quad \text{since } \mathbf{i}^2 = \mathbf{j}^2 = -1 \text{ and } \mathbf{ij} = -\mathbf{ji}. \end{aligned}$$

(4) $(2\mathbf{i}+3)(1+\mathbf{j}+\mathbf{k}) = 2\mathbf{i}(1+\mathbf{j}+\mathbf{k}) + 3(1+\mathbf{j}+\mathbf{k})$
$= 2\mathbf{i}+2\mathbf{k}-2\mathbf{j} + 3+3\mathbf{j}+3\mathbf{k}$
$= 3+2\mathbf{i}+\mathbf{j}+5\mathbf{k}$.

EXERCISE Show that $\mathbf{a}(\mathbf{bc}) = (\mathbf{ab})\mathbf{c}$ in case $\mathbf{a} = \mathbf{i}$, $\mathbf{b} = 3\mathbf{j}-\mathbf{k}$, $\mathbf{c} = 2-5\mathbf{j}+6\mathbf{k}$.

NOTATION 9.18 $\mathbb{H}$ is the set of all quaternions and, based on (9.14): we say $\mathbf{a}$ has *scalar* or *real* part $S\mathbf{a} = a_0$, *vector* or *pure* part $V\mathbf{a}$ (or $\acute{\mathbf{a}}$) $= a_1\mathbf{i} + a_2\mathbf{j} + a_3\mathbf{k}$, and *conjugate* $\bar{\mathbf{a}} = S\mathbf{a}-V\mathbf{a} = a_0 - \acute{\mathbf{a}} = a_0 - a_1\mathbf{i} - a_2\mathbf{j} - a_3\mathbf{k}$. We call the quaternion $\mathbf{a}$ *pure* or a *vector* if it has zero scalar part, i.e. if $a_0 = 0$.

EXAMPLES 9.19 (1) The quaternion $\mathbf{a} = 3 + 2\mathbf{i} - 3\mathbf{j} + \mathbf{k}$ has real part $S\mathbf{a} = 3$, pure part $\acute{\mathbf{a}} = 2\mathbf{i}-3\mathbf{j}+\mathbf{k}$, and conjugate $\bar{\mathbf{a}} = 3-2\mathbf{i}+3\mathbf{j}-\mathbf{k}$.

(2)
$$\begin{aligned}(a_1\mathbf{i} + a_2\mathbf{j} + a_3\mathbf{k})^2 &= a_1\mathbf{i}^2 + a_2\mathbf{j}^2 + a_3\mathbf{k}^2 \\ &\quad + a_1a_2\mathbf{ij} + a_2a_1\mathbf{ji} \\ &\quad + a_2a_3\mathbf{jk} + a_3a_2\mathbf{kj} \\ &\quad + a_3a_1\mathbf{ki} + a_1a_3\mathbf{ik} \\ &= -(a_1^2 + a_2^2 + a_3^2), \quad \text{by e.g. } \mathbf{ij} = -\mathbf{ji}.\end{aligned}$$

(3)
$$\begin{aligned}\mathbf{a}\bar{\mathbf{a}} &= (a_0 + \acute{\mathbf{a}})(a_0 - \acute{\mathbf{a}}) = a_0^2 - a_0\acute{\mathbf{a}} + \acute{\mathbf{a}}a_0 - \acute{\mathbf{a}}\acute{\mathbf{a}} \\ &= a_0^2 - \acute{\mathbf{a}}\acute{\mathbf{a}} \\ &= a_0^2 + a_1^2 + a_2^2 + a_3^2, \quad \text{by (2) above,} \\ &= \bar{\mathbf{a}}\mathbf{a}.\end{aligned}$$

NORM AND CONJUGATES Example (3) above shows that we can usefully define the *norm* or *modulus* $|\mathbf{a}|$ of a quaternion $\mathbf{a}$ by analogy with the complex numbers since it has the crucial property of being positive unless $\mathbf{a}$ is zero. Thus we define $|\mathbf{a}| \geq 0$ by

$$|\mathbf{a}|^2 = \mathbf{a}\bar{\mathbf{a}} = \bar{\mathbf{a}}\mathbf{a} = a_0^2 + a_1^2 + a_2^2 + a_3^2, \quad \textit{then} \tag{9.16}$$

$$|\mathbf{a}| \geq 0 \textit{ for all quaternions } \mathbf{a}, \textit{ and } |\mathbf{a}| = 0 \Leftrightarrow \mathbf{a} = 0, \tag{9.17A}$$

$$\textit{If } \lambda \textit{ is a positive number then } |\lambda\mathbf{a}| = \lambda|\mathbf{a}|. \tag{9.17B}$$

We call $\mathbf{a}$ a *unit quaternion* (cf. unit vectors) if $|\mathbf{a}| = 1$. In due course we will derive the famous and deeper property $|\mathbf{ab}| = |\mathbf{a}||\mathbf{b}|$, for it has important consequences (see Theorem 9.30). The immediately verifiable properties of conjugates are:

$$\overline{\mathbf{a} + \mathbf{b}} = \bar{\mathbf{a}} + \bar{\mathbf{b}}, \quad \overline{\lambda\mathbf{a}} = \bar{\lambda}\bar{\mathbf{a}} \quad (\lambda \in \mathbf{C}) \tag{9.18}$$

$$\mathbf{a} + \bar{\mathbf{a}} = 2S\mathbf{a}, \quad \mathbf{a} - \bar{\mathbf{a}} = 2V\mathbf{a} \tag{9.19}$$

$$\mathbf{a} \text{ is real} \Leftrightarrow \mathbf{a} = \bar{\mathbf{a}} \quad \mathbf{a} \text{ is pure} \Leftrightarrow \mathbf{a} = -\bar{\mathbf{a}} \tag{9.20}$$

The expected property of conjugates, $\overline{\mathbf{ab}} = \bar{\mathbf{a}}\,\bar{\mathbf{b}}$, is more problematical. Indeed it fails to hold. However the situation is saved by the fact that $\overline{\mathbf{ab}} = \bar{\mathbf{b}}\,\bar{\mathbf{a}}$ (Theorem 9.24).

PURE QUATERNIONS AS VECTORS Without even a change of notation the pure quaternion $a_1\mathbf{i} + a_2\mathbf{j} + a_3\mathbf{k}$ represents a vector (a_1, a_2, a_3) in 3-space, the basis being $\mathbf{i} = (1, 0, 0)$, $\mathbf{j} = (0, 1, 0)$, $\mathbf{k} = (0, 0, 1)$. The modulus is the same from both viewpoints, $|\mathbf{a}| =$

$\sqrt{(a_1^2 + a_2^2 + a_3^2)}$, and the calculation in Example 9.19(2) gives the following result, which we state as a theorem because of its centrality.

THEOREM 9.20 The square of a pure quaternion **u** *is real. Specifically,* $\mathbf{u}^2 = -|\mathbf{u}|^2$. *In particular, every unit pure quaternion is a square root of -1.*

This is something quite new after complex numbers, where the equation $z^2 = -1$ can have only two solutions, $\pm\mathbf{i}$. We are saying that if we extend the permitted range of solutions to quaternions then every one of the infinitely many points on the unit sphere in 3-space, $S^2 = \{\mathbf{x} \in \mathbf{R}^3: |\mathbf{x}| = 1\}$, yields such a square root. But does this help? The answer is *yes*, because these solutions enable us to represent a rotation about any axis in $\mathbf{R}^3$ by a quaternion. The mechanism is the *polar form*, introduced in Section 9.2.3 after some groundwork in 9.2.2, where we relate the three ways now available to combine two vectors: **ab**, **a.b**, **a** x **b**.

EXAMPLE 9.21 Could there be square roots of -1 which are *not* pure? We'll clear this up right now. Let $\mathbf{a}^2 = -1$ ($\mathbf{a} \in \mathbf{H}$). Then in the usual notation $(a_0 + \mathbf{á})^2 = a_0^2 + 2a_0\mathbf{á} + \mathbf{áá}$ $= a_0^2 - (a_1^2 + a_2^2 + a_3^2) + 2a_0\mathbf{á}$, by Theorem 9.4. Equating this to -1 gives two equations (i) $a_0^2 - (a_1^2 + a_2^2 + a_3^2) = -1$, (ii) $2a_0\mathbf{á} = 0$. From the second, either $a_0 = 0$ or $\mathbf{á} = 0$. But $\mathbf{á} = 0$ is impossible by (i) since it would involve $a_0^2 = -1$, and the square of a real number cannot be negative. Therefore $a_0 = 0$ and **a** is pure.

EXERCISE Calculate $(1-\mathbf{i}+2\mathbf{j}+5\mathbf{k})^2$ with the help of Theorem 9.20 on pure quaternions.

9.2.2 Theorems on quaternion multiplication

We can't go much further without showing that one thing the quaternions do share with complex numbers is associativity.

THEOREM 9.22 Let **a**, **b**, **c** *be quaternions. Then*

(i) $\mathbf{a}(\mathbf{b}+\mathbf{c}) = \mathbf{ab}+\mathbf{ac}$, $(\mathbf{b}+\mathbf{c})\mathbf{a} = \mathbf{ba}+\mathbf{ca}$ *(bilinearity)*

(ii) $(\mathbf{ab})\mathbf{c} = \mathbf{a}(\mathbf{bc})$ *(associativity)*

Proof (i) Note that the multiplication law for **i**,**j**,**k** extends to quaternions generally by bilinearity. That is, (i) holds by definition when **a**,**b**,**c** are individual terms of a quaternion, such as $a_1\mathbf{i}$. We sketch the verification that (i) holds as expected when **a**,**b**,**c** are general quaternions. The two parts of (i) are similar. Expanding **a(b+c)** we obtain

$$(a_0 + a_1\mathbf{i} + a_2\mathbf{j} + a_3\mathbf{k})\{(b_0+c_0) + (b_1+c_1)\mathbf{i} + (b_2+c_2)\mathbf{j} + (b_3+c_3)\mathbf{k}\}$$

$= a_0(b_0+c_0) + a_0(b_1+c_1)\mathbf{i} + a_0(b_2+c_2)\mathbf{j} + a_0(b_3+c_3)\mathbf{k}$
+ three sets of terms in which a_0 is replaced respectively by $a_1\mathbf{i}$, $a_2\mathbf{j}$, $a_3\mathbf{k}$

$= a_0(b_v + b_1\mathbf{i} + b_2\mathbf{j} + b_3\mathbf{k}) + a_0(c_0 + c_1\mathbf{i} + c_2\mathbf{j} + c_3\mathbf{k})$
+ (as above) $=$ **ab** + **ac**.

Proof (ii) Expanding **(ab)c** with the four terms in each quaternion we obtain 4 x 4 x 4 =

64 terms (pq)r, which we must show equals p(qr). When at least one of p, q, r is real there is nothing to prove, so we are left with proving that (pq)r = p(qr) when p,q,r run through the values **i,j,k**, a total of 3 x 3 x 3 = 27 cases. However the set of rules (9.15) for multiplying these factors is invariant under rotation of **i,j,k** so we need verify only the nine cases shown for readability as a matrix equality below, indexed by the first two factors (the rows correspond to the first factor and the columns to the second).

$$\begin{bmatrix} (\mathbf{ii})\mathbf{i} & (\mathbf{ij})\mathbf{i} & (\mathbf{ik})\mathbf{i} \\ (\mathbf{ji})\mathbf{i} & (\mathbf{jj})\mathbf{i} & (\mathbf{jk})\mathbf{i} \\ (\mathbf{ki})\mathbf{i} & (\mathbf{kj})\mathbf{i} & (\mathbf{kk})\mathbf{i} \end{bmatrix} = \begin{bmatrix} -\mathbf{i} & \mathbf{j} & \mathbf{k} \\ -\mathbf{j} & -\mathbf{i} & -1 \\ -\mathbf{k} & 1 & -\mathbf{i} \end{bmatrix}$$

The same matrix of answers is obtained if each product is bracketed the other way. For example, instead of **(ji)i** we calculate **j(ii)** = **j**(-1) = -**j**, obtaining the same answer. With these verifications the proof is complete.

EXERCISE Explain via rules (9.15) why the second matrix of Proof (ii) above is skew symmetric apart from the main diagonal.

INVERSES AND CANCELLATION If **ab** = 1 we say that **a** is a *left inverse* of **b** and that **b** is a *right inverse* of **a**. If **ab** = **ba** = 1 we call **b** a *2-sided inverse* of **a**, or simply an *inverse* of **a**. Fortunately the formula $\bar{\mathbf{a}} / |\mathbf{a}|^2$ for the inverse of a complex number works for the quaternions also, and for the same reason: $\mathbf{a}\bar{\mathbf{a}} = \bar{\mathbf{a}}\mathbf{a} = |\mathbf{a}|^2$, so that $\mathbf{a}(\bar{\mathbf{a}} / |\mathbf{a}|^2) = 1 = (\bar{\mathbf{a}} / |\mathbf{a}|^2)\mathbf{a}$.

Every nonzero quaternion **a** *has a unique inverse* $\mathbf{a}^{-1} = \bar{\mathbf{a}} / |\mathbf{a}|^2$ (9.21)
and if $\lambda \neq 0$ *is real then* $(\lambda\mathbf{a})^{-1} = \lambda^{-1}\mathbf{a}^{-1}$.

Uniqueness of the inverse is a consequence of associativity, for if **b,c** are both inverses of **a** then **b** = **b(ac)** = **(ba)c** = 1**c** = **c**. An intriguing question remains. Could there be a left or a right inverse which is not a full 2-sided inverse? The simple answer is *no* (cf. the similar situation for square matrices). In fact every left or right inverse equals $\bar{\mathbf{a}} / |\mathbf{a}|^2$(denoted $\mathbf{a}^{-1}$). For example if **b** is a left inverse, i.e. 1 = **ba**, then, multiplying on the right by $\mathbf{a}^{-1}$, we have $\mathbf{a}^{-1} = (\mathbf{ba})\mathbf{a}^{-1} = \mathbf{b}(\mathbf{aa}^{-1}) = \mathbf{b}(1) = \mathbf{b}$. Similarly for 1 = **ab**. More generally, multiplying by $\mathbf{a}^{-1}$ gives us:

The cancellation laws for quaternions. Let $\boldsymbol{a} \neq \boldsymbol{0}$ $(\boldsymbol{a,b,c} \in \boldsymbol{H})$.
If **ab** = **ac** *or* **ba** = **ca** *then* **b** = **c**. (9.22)

The quaternions have no divisors of zero. That is, if **ab** = ***0***
then **a** = ***0*** *or* **b** = ***0***. (9.23)

EXERCISE Write down the inverses of **k** and of 2 - **i** + **k**, and check that they work. Verify in this case the formula $(\mathbf{ab})^{-1} = \mathbf{b}^{-1}\mathbf{a}^{-1}$.

THREE WAYS TO MULTIPLY TWO VECTORS We can now combine a pair of vectors **x** and **y** as follows, and the next theorem gives an important relation between these products.

(1) $\mathbf{x.y} = x_1y_1 + x_2y_2 + x_3y_3$, the *scalar product*,

(2) $\mathbf{x} \times \mathbf{y}$ = $\begin{vmatrix} \mathbf{i} & \mathbf{j} & \mathbf{k} \\ x_1 & x_2 & x_3 \\ y_1 & y_2 & y_3 \end{vmatrix}$,   the *vector product*,

(3) $\mathbf{x}\,\mathbf{y}$ the *quaternion product*.

THEOREM 9.23 Let $\mathbf{x}, \mathbf{y}$ be pure quaternions. Then $\mathbf{xy}$ has scalar part $-\mathbf{x.y}$ and vector part $\mathbf{x} \times \mathbf{y}$, in fact

$$\mathbf{xy} \;=\; -\mathbf{x.y} + \mathbf{x} \times \mathbf{y} \;=\; \overline{\mathbf{yx}} \quad (S\mathbf{x} = S\mathbf{y} = 0) \tag{9.24}$$

Proof   Since $\mathbf{ji} = -\mathbf{ij}, \;\; \mathbf{kj} = -\mathbf{jk}, \;\; \mathbf{ik} = -\mathbf{ki}$ (9.15), we have for $\mathbf{xy}$,

$$(x_1\mathbf{i} + x_2\mathbf{j} + x_3\mathbf{k})(y_1\mathbf{i} + y_2\mathbf{j} + y_3\mathbf{k})$$
$$= \quad x_1 y_1 \mathbf{i}^2 + x_2 y_2 \mathbf{j}^2 + x_3 y_3 \mathbf{k}^2$$
$$+ \quad (x_1 y_2 - x_2 y_1)\mathbf{ij} \;+\; (x_2 y_3 - x_3 y_2)\mathbf{jk} \;+\; (x_3 y_1 - x_1 y_3)\mathbf{ki}.$$

Notice that the simultaneous cyclic interchange 1,2,3 and $\mathbf{i},\mathbf{j},\mathbf{k}$ moves us cyclically round the last three expressions. The last expression may be written $\;-(x_1 y_3 - x_3 y_1)\mathbf{j}\;$ and, applying the multiplication rules (9.15) for $\mathbf{i},\mathbf{j},\mathbf{k}$, we obtain the result $-\mathbf{x.y} + \mathbf{x} \times \mathbf{y}$. For the second equality in (9.24) we interchange $\mathbf{x}$ and $\mathbf{y}$ to get $\mathbf{yx} = -\mathbf{y.x} + \mathbf{y} \times \mathbf{x}$, whose conjugate equals $\mathbf{xy}$ since $\mathbf{y} \times \mathbf{x} = -\mathbf{x} \times \mathbf{y}$. Now for two theorems which contain probably the deepest results of this section.

THEOREM 9.24 Quaternion multiplication satisfies $\;\overline{\mathbf{ab}} \;=\; \overline{\mathbf{b}}\,\overline{\mathbf{a}}$

Proof With $\acute{\mathbf{a}}$ denoting the pure part of quaternion $\mathbf{a}$, we have

$$\mathbf{ab} \quad = \quad (a_0 + \acute{\mathbf{a}})\,(b_0 + \mathbf{b}')$$
$$= \quad a_0 b_0 + a_0\mathbf{b}' + b_0\acute{\mathbf{a}} + \acute{\mathbf{a}}\mathbf{b}'.$$

Hence $\qquad \overline{\mathbf{ab}} \quad = \quad a_0 b_0 - a_0\mathbf{b}' - b_0\acute{\mathbf{a}} + \mathbf{b}'\,\acute{\mathbf{a}},$ by (9.24),

$$= \quad (b_0 - \mathbf{b}')\,(a_0 - \acute{\mathbf{a}}), \qquad \text{by inspection,}$$
$$= \quad \overline{\mathbf{b}}\,\overline{\mathbf{a}}.$$

THEOREM 9.25 The norm of a quaternion product is the product of the norms:

$$|\mathbf{ab}| = |\mathbf{a}||\mathbf{b}|. \tag{9.25}$$

Proof $\qquad |\mathbf{ab}|^2 \;\; = \quad (\mathbf{ab})\,(\overline{\mathbf{ab}}) \qquad$ by definition of norm,

$$= \quad (\mathbf{ab})\,(\overline{\mathbf{b}}\,\overline{\mathbf{a}}) \qquad \text{by Theorem 9.24,}$$
$$= \quad \mathbf{a}(\mathbf{b}\overline{\mathbf{b}})\overline{\mathbf{a}} \qquad \text{as } \mathbf{H} \text{ is associative, Theorem 9.22,}$$
$$= \quad \mathbf{a}\,|\mathbf{b}|^2\overline{\mathbf{a}} \qquad \text{by definition of norm,}$$
$$= \quad \mathbf{a}\overline{\mathbf{a}}\,|\mathbf{b}|^2 \qquad \text{as } |\mathbf{b}|^2 \text{ is real,}$$
$$= \quad |\mathbf{a}|^2\,|\mathbf{b}|^2 \qquad \text{by definition of norm,}$$
$$= \quad (|\mathbf{a}|\,|\mathbf{b}|)^2.$$

Hence the result, since norms are non-negative.

EXAMPLE 9.26 The set of all unit quaternions may be viewed as the set of all unit vectors in 4-space, forming the 3-sphere S^3 (the '3' refers to the number of independent coordinates). This set satisfies the axioms for a group, albeit an infinite one. Firstly it is closed under multiplication for if **a**, **b** are unit quaternions then $|\mathbf{ab}| = |\mathbf{a}||\mathbf{b}| = 1 \times 1 = 1$, by Theorem 9.25. Multiplication is associative by Theorem 9.22. The real number 1 acts as identity, and every unit quaternion, being nonzero (by (9.17A)) has an inverse, by (9.21), namely $\bar{\mathbf{a}}$. Of special interest are finite subgroups related to symmetry groups of polyhedra (see Table 9.4 above Figure 9.13, and Coxeter, 1974). A subgroup with eight elements is the *quaternion group* $Q = \{\pm 1, \pm\mathbf{i}, \pm\mathbf{j}, \pm\mathbf{k}\}$.

EXERCISE Prove that $|\mathbf{axa}^{-1}| = |\mathbf{x}|$ $(\mathbf{a} \neq \mathbf{0})$.

EXERCISE Calculate $(\mathbf{i}+3\mathbf{j}+\mathbf{k})(2\mathbf{i}-\mathbf{j}+5\mathbf{k})$ using (9.24). Check the answer satisfies $|\mathbf{xy}| = |\mathbf{x}||\mathbf{y}|$.

9.2.3 The polar form of a quaternion

*COPIES OF **C** WITHIN **H*** The quaternions of form $a_0 + a_1\mathbf{j}$ form a copy of the complex numbers with **j** in place of **i**. Indeed, if we write suggestively $\mathbf{I} = a_1\mathbf{i} + a_2\mathbf{j} + a_3\mathbf{k}$, of unit norm, then by Theorem 9.20 $\mathbf{I}^2 = -1$, and so

the quaternions $\lambda + \mu\mathbf{I}$ (λ,μ *real) form a copy of the complex numbers.* (9.26)

In particular the set of such numbers is commutative, though we must stick to the same **I**. In fact every polynomial in **I** with real coefficients reduces to the form $\lambda + \mu\mathbf{I}$ because of $\mathbf{I}^2 = -1$. This contrasts with the noncommutativity of the quaternions in general, which we observed as early as Example 9.17.

POLAR FORM Suppose $\mathbf{b} = b_0 + \mathbf{b}'$ is a quaternion of modulus 1. Then $-1 \le b_0 \le 1$ and from Figure 9.8 $b_0 = \cos\theta$ for a unique angle θ with $0 \le \theta \le \pi$ $(\theta = \cos^{-1}(b_0))$, and hence $|\mathbf{b}'|^2 = 1 - b_0^2 = \sin^2\theta$. But from $\sin\theta \ge 0$ for $0 \le \theta \le \pi$, we may infer that $|\mathbf{b}'| = \sin\theta$. We call θ the *argument* of **b**. Now unless **b** is real we have $\sin\theta \neq 0$, so we may write $\mathbf{I} = (1/\sin\theta)\mathbf{b}'$, giving $\mathbf{b} = \cos\theta + \mathbf{I}\sin\theta$. Hence:

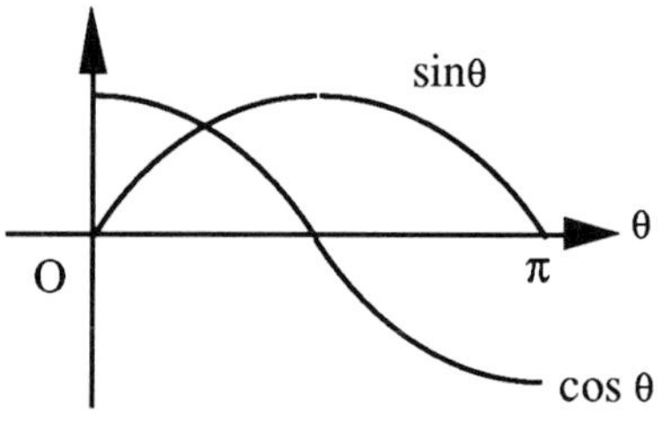

Figure 9.8 sin θ and cos θ for $0 \le \theta \le \pi$.

A non-real unit quaternion has a unique expression in the form $\cos\theta + \mathbf{I}\sin\theta$, $0 \le \theta \le \pi$, where $\mathbf{I}^2 = -1$. (9.27)

Notice that, analogously to the case of complex numbers, the conjugate $\cos\theta - \mathbf{I}\sin\theta$ equals $\cos(-\theta) + \mathbf{I}\sin(-\theta)$. Also, in the special case **b** real, we have the same expression as (9.27) but **I** is arbitrary because its coefficient $\sin\theta$ is zero. Then $b = 1$, $\theta = 0$ or $b = -1$, $\theta = \pi$. Indeed (9.27) to (9.32) go through as they did in case $\mathbf{I} = \mathbf{i}$.

DEFINITION $e^{\mathbf{I}\theta} = \cos\theta + \mathbf{I}\sin\theta$ $(\mathbf{I}^2 = -1)$. (9.28)

CONSEQUENCE $e^{\mathbf{I}\alpha}e^{\mathbf{I}\beta} = e^{\mathbf{I}(\alpha+\beta)} = e^{\mathbf{I}\beta}e^{\mathbf{I}\alpha}$. (9.29)

CONSEQUENCE The inverse of $e^{\mathbf{I}\theta}$ is its conjugate $e^{-\mathbf{I}\theta}$. (9.30)

For a general quaternion **a** of norm $r > 0$ we have $\mathbf{a} = r\mathbf{b}$, with $\mathbf{b} = (1/r)\mathbf{a}$ of unit norm, hence the unique polar form

$$\mathbf{a} = re^{\mathbf{I}\theta} = r(\cos\theta + \mathbf{I}\sin\theta). \tag{9.31}$$

Given that there is a unique θ between 0 and π we allow θ to be changed by multiples of 2π as we do with the complex number polar form, itself a special case of the quaternionic, since this leaves cosθ, sinθ and hence the quaternion unchanged. Notice that all pure quaternions have $\theta = \cos^{-1}(0) = \pi/2$, when we insist that $0 \le \theta \le \pi$. We emphasise that, for a fixed quaternion square root **I** of -1, expressions of the form $e^{\mathbf{I}\alpha}, e^{\mathbf{I}\beta}, e^{\mathbf{I}\gamma}$ may be multiplied in any order, using (9.29). In particular we have *De Moivre's Theorem for quaternions*: if $\mathbf{I}^2 = -1$ and $n = 0, \pm1, \pm2, \ldots,$ then

$$(\cos\theta + \mathbf{I}\sin\theta)^n = \cos n\theta + \mathbf{I}\sin n\theta \tag{9.32}$$

EXAMPLES 9.27 (Some polar forms.) As indicated in Table 9.2 below, we determine **I** by dividing the pure part by its norm, then find the angle, using an Argand diagram if necessary. We emphasise that all pure quaternions can be expressed with $\theta = \pi/2$.

(1) $\mathbf{i} = e^{\mathbf{i}\pi/2}$, $\mathbf{j} = e^{\mathbf{j}\pi/2}$, $\mathbf{k} = e^{\mathbf{k}\pi/2}$. This gives a simple illustration of the need to keep **I** fixed if we are to ensure commutativity, for $e^{\mathbf{i}\pi/2}e^{\mathbf{j}\pi/2} = \mathbf{ij} = \mathbf{k}$, whereas the other order gives $-\mathbf{k}$. Observe that $-\mathbf{k} = e^{\mathbf{I}\pi/2}$ with $\mathbf{I} = -\mathbf{k}$, but still $\theta = \pi/2$.

(2) The polar form of **i+j**. Another pure case, so it has $\theta = \pi/2$. We may highlight I by writing $\mathbf{i}+\mathbf{j} = \sqrt{2}.\frac{\mathbf{i}+\mathbf{j}}{\sqrt{2}} = \sqrt{2}e^{\mathbf{I}\pi/2} = \sqrt{2}e^{(\mathbf{i}+\mathbf{j})\pi/2\sqrt{2}}$.

TABLE 9.2 To find the polar form of a quaternion **a**:

(1) Write **a** as $\mathbf{a} = a_0 + |\mathbf{a}'|(\mathbf{a}'/|\mathbf{a}'|)$,

(2) Plot $(a_0, |\mathbf{a}'|)$ in the Argand diagram to find r,θ.

or

Calculate $r = |\mathbf{a}|$ from the components and identify a_0/r with a known cosine (cf. Example 9.28(2)).

Note: it may be notationally or otherwise convenient to find r,θ for the conjugate then correct the sign.

(3) The polar form of $1 + \mathbf{k}\sqrt{3}$. Not pure, so we may plot $(1,\sqrt{3})$ on an Argand diagram (i.e. in the xy-plane) and obtain $r = 2$, $\theta = \pi/3$. Thus $1 + \mathbf{k}\sqrt{3} = 2e^{\mathbf{k}\pi/3}$. By De Moivre's Theorem $(1/2)(1 + \mathbf{k}\sqrt{3})$ is a cube root of -1 (its cube has angle π).

(4) The polar form of $\sqrt{2} + \mathbf{j} - \mathbf{k} = \sqrt{2} + \sqrt{2}\,\frac{\mathbf{j}-\mathbf{k}}{\sqrt{2}}$. The technique of plotting $(\sqrt{2}, \sqrt{2})$ clarifies that $r = 2$, $\theta = \pi/4$, so $\sqrt{2} + \mathbf{j} - \mathbf{k} = 2e^{(\mathbf{j}-\mathbf{k})\pi/4\sqrt{2}}$. Now De Moivre's Theorem predicts that $(\sqrt{2} + \mathbf{j} - \mathbf{k})^8 = 256$, which is not exactly obvious on inspection.

(5) The polar form of $1+\mathbf{i}+\sqrt{3}\mathbf{j}+2\mathbf{k}$. The pure part has squared norm $1+3+4 = 8$, so $\mathbf{I} = (\mathbf{i}+\sqrt{3}\mathbf{j}+2\mathbf{k})/2\sqrt{2}$, and by the Argand diagram $r = 3$, $\theta = \cos^{-1}(1/3)$, a first example in which θ is not a rational multiple of π. Later we will use this as an example for rotation in 3-space.

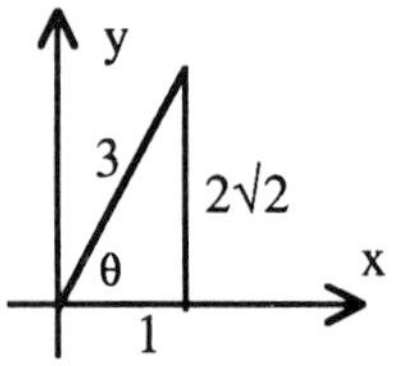

EXAMPLES 9.28 (When quaternions give simpler numbers.) (1) In using quaternions we can sometimes avoid the $\sqrt{}$ signs required in the complex case. A prime example is the cube root of 1, $w = (1/2)(-1+\mathbf{i}\sqrt{3})$. By De Moivre's Theorem, any square root of -3 can replace $\mathbf{i}\sqrt{3}$, and a convenient choice in quaternions is $\mathbf{i}+\mathbf{j}+\mathbf{k}$, giving $w = (1/2)(-1+\mathbf{i}+\mathbf{j}+\mathbf{k})$, an especially simple form which we probably would not guess, starting from the basic multiplication laws (9.15).

(2) We have $\cos \pi/5 + \mathbf{i} \sin \pi/5 = (1 + \sqrt{5})/4 + \mathbf{i}\sqrt{(5 - \sqrt{5})/8}$ as complex tenth root of unity, but having one square root within another. Using quaternions we can take $\cos \pi/5 + \mathbf{I} \sin \pi/5 = (1 + \sqrt{5})/4 + \mathbf{i}/2 - \mathbf{j}(1 - \sqrt{5})/4$, involving only single level square roots. More compactly written this is $(1/2)(\tau + \mathbf{i} - \sigma\mathbf{j})$, where (see Table 9.1 in Section 9.1.3) σ,τ are the solutions of $x^2 - x - 1 = 0$. Then $\mathbf{I} = (\mathbf{i} - \sigma\mathbf{j}) / \sqrt{(1 + \sigma^2)}$.

EXERCISE Find the polar forms of (i) $\sqrt{3}+\mathbf{i}-\mathbf{j}+\mathbf{k}$ and (ii) $-\sigma + \mathbf{j} - \tau\mathbf{k}$ [Harder - see (2) above and use the properties of σ,τ given in Table 9.1]. Deduce a fourth root of -1 from question (i).

9.3 Quaternions and rotation

In this section we bring out three ways in which quaternion multiplication provides isometries, the third being the important representation of rotations in 3-space.

9.3.1 Left and right multiplication

This provides a nice application of results on matrices from Chapters 7 and 8. We identify a quaternion $\mathbf{x} = x_0 + x_1\mathbf{i} + x_2\mathbf{j} + x_3\mathbf{k}$ with the point/vector (x_0, x_1, x_2, x_3) in 4-space $\mathbf{R}^4$ and the standard basis $\mathbf{e}_0, \mathbf{e}_1, \mathbf{e}_2, \mathbf{e}_3$ with respective quaternions $1, \mathbf{i}, \mathbf{j}, \mathbf{k}$, where $\mathbf{e}_0 = (1,0,0,0)$ and so on. Given a quaternion $\mathbf{a}$, the corresponding *left multiplication* transformation $L_\mathbf{a}$ of $\mathbf{R}^4$ sends $\mathbf{x}$ to $\mathbf{ax}$, the *right multiplication* $R_\mathbf{a}$ sends $\mathbf{x}$ to $\mathbf{xa}$. They are linear, for example $L_\mathbf{a}(\mathbf{x}+\alpha\mathbf{y}) = \mathbf{a}(\mathbf{x}+\alpha\mathbf{y}) = \mathbf{ax}+\alpha\mathbf{ay} = L_\mathbf{a}(\mathbf{x}) + \alpha L_\mathbf{a}(\mathbf{y})$ $(\alpha \in \mathbf{R})$, and hence are representable by matrices, where $\mathbf{x} \to \mathbf{x}M_L$ and $\mathbf{x} \to \mathbf{x}M_R$ respectively. The matrix elements may be obtained by a bare-handed approach or by applying the 4-dimensional version of Theorem 8.5 (which systematises the calculation). Thus the rows of M_L correspond to $1, \mathbf{i}, \mathbf{j}, \mathbf{k}$, and the $\mathbf{i}$ row for instance consists of the components of $L_\mathbf{a}(\mathbf{i}) = \mathbf{ai}$. Thus we calculate from (9.15)

$$\mathbf{a}1 = a_0 + a_1\mathbf{i} + a_2\mathbf{j} + a_3\mathbf{k}, \quad \mathbf{ai} = a_0\mathbf{i} - a_1 - a_2\mathbf{k} + a_3\mathbf{j},$$
$$\mathbf{aj} = a_0\mathbf{j} + a_1\mathbf{k} - a_2 - a_3\mathbf{i}, \quad \mathbf{ak} = a_0\mathbf{k} - a_1\mathbf{j} + a_2\mathbf{i} - a_3,$$

and this gives M_L below. For M_R we calculate $1\mathbf{a}, \mathbf{ia}, \mathbf{ja}, \mathbf{ka}$.

$$M_L(\mathbf{a}) = \begin{bmatrix} a_0 & a_1 & a_2 & a_3 \\ -a_1 & a_0 & a_3 & -a_2 \\ -a_2 & -a_3 & a_0 & a_1 \\ -a_3 & a_2 & -a_1 & a_0 \end{bmatrix}, \quad M_R(\mathbf{a}) = \begin{bmatrix} a_0 & a_1 & a_2 & a_3 \\ -a_1 & a_0 & -a_3 & a_2 \\ -a_2 & a_3 & a_0 & -a_1 \\ -a_3 & -a_2 & a_1 & a_0 \end{bmatrix}$$

Considering $M = M_L$, we find that the components a_i are so distributed and signed that the rows of the matrix are mutually orthogonal, and each has length $|\mathbf{a}|$. Equivalently, $MM^T = |\mathbf{a}|^2 I$, where I is the identity matrix. Modifying the argument of Remark 8.9 we have $|\mathbf{x}M|^2 = (\mathbf{x}M)(\mathbf{x}M)^T = \mathbf{x}MM^T\mathbf{x}^T = \mathbf{x}|\mathbf{a}|^2 I\mathbf{x}^T = |\mathbf{a}|^2|\mathbf{x}|^2$. Thus $L_\mathbf{a}$ scales all vectors by a factor $|\mathbf{a}|$, in agreement with $|\mathbf{ax}| = |\mathbf{a}||\mathbf{x}|$ of Theorem 9.25. Now let **a** be a unit quaternion, so that $\mathbf{L_a}$ is an isometry and M is orthogonal. What else can we say about M, apart from $M^{-1} = M^T$? Without going into details we define the isometry in $\mathbf{R}^4$ to be direct if $|M|$ is 1 and indirect if it is -1. Is $|M|$ always the same, independently of **a**?

Calculating $|M|$ directly looks rather formidable, but because the determinant is the product of the eigenvalues, it can be done simply, on the observation that M is skew-symmetric apart from the diagonal terms a_0. That is, $M = a_0 I + S$, where $S^T = -S$. It follows from the eigenvalue equation $|M - \lambda I| = 0$ that the eigenvalues of M are those of S increased by a_0. Now $MM^T = I$ gives $S^2 = (a_0^2-1)I$. This implies that each eigenvalue λ of S satisfies $\lambda^2 = (a_0^2 - 1)$, for $\mathbf{x}S = \lambda\mathbf{x} \Rightarrow \mathbf{x}S^2 = \lambda\mathbf{x}S = \lambda^2\mathbf{x}$. Thus S has eigenvalues $\pm i\sqrt{(1 - a_0^2)}$ and those of M are $a_0 \pm i\sqrt{(1 - a_0^2)}$ (assuming $a_0^2 < 1$). Since their sum equals the trace $4a_0$ of M, the + and - signs occur twice each, and $|M| = (a_0^2 - i^2(1-a_0^2))^2 = 1$. In case $a_0^2 = 1$, we have $M = a_0 I$, $|M| = 1$. (Notice that a_0^2 cannot exceed 1. Why?) A similar analysis holds for $M = M_R$.

EXERCISE Verify that M_R is the matrix given, by determining it in the manner described.

Now, why should M have the essentially skew-symmetric form we observed? According to the component formula of Theorem 8.5 we have discovered that, for $\mathbf{a} \in \mathbf{H}$, and $\mathbf{e}_0,\mathbf{e}_1,\mathbf{e}_2,\mathbf{e}_3$ standing for $1,\mathbf{i},\mathbf{j},\mathbf{k}$ respectively,

$$(\mathbf{ae}_s).\mathbf{e}_t = \begin{cases} -(\mathbf{ae}_t).\mathbf{e}_s, & \text{if } s \neq t \\ a_0, & \text{if } s = t \end{cases} \tag{9.33}$$

This is interesting because for $s \neq t$ it is a unified result, not distinguishing between 1 and any of **i**, **j**, **k**. It must be a consequence of such a result about multiplication of the basis elements; and here is that result, in particular parts (iii) and (iv).

THEOREM 9.29 Let $\mathbf{e}_0, \mathbf{e}_1, \mathbf{e}_2, \mathbf{e}_3$ *denote* $1,\mathbf{i},\mathbf{j},\mathbf{k}$ *respectively. Then for r,s,t taking values 0,1,2,3 we have*

(i) $\mathbf{e}_r^{-1} = \pm\mathbf{e}_r$, (ii) $\mathbf{e}_r\mathbf{e}_s = \pm\mathbf{e}_t$, for some t,
(iii) $\mathbf{e}_s\mathbf{e}_t^{-1} = -\mathbf{e}_t\mathbf{e}_s^{-1}$ $(s \neq t)$, (iv) $(\mathbf{e}_r\mathbf{e}_s).\mathbf{e}_t = -(\mathbf{e}_r\mathbf{e}_t).\mathbf{e}_s$ $(s \neq t)$.

Proof Everything comes from the multiplication table (9.15), with $1\mathbf{e}_r = \mathbf{e}_r$ assumed. Parts (i) and (ii) may be read straight off that table. For example $\mathbf{j}(-\mathbf{j}) = 1$ so $\mathbf{j}^{-1} = -\mathbf{j}$ (inverses are unique by (9.21)), whereas $1^{-1} = 1$. For (iii), suppose firstly that $\mathbf{e}_s = 1$. Then $\mathbf{e}_t = \mathbf{i}, \mathbf{j}$, or **k** so the assertion is $\mathbf{e}_t^{-1} = -\mathbf{e}_t$, which is true by (9.15). Similarly for case $\mathbf{e}_t = 1$. If $s, t \geq 1$ $(s \neq t)$ the result is $\mathbf{ji} = -\mathbf{ij}$ or a cyclic shift of it, hence true by (9.15). Part *(iv)*: From the fact that, as vectors the $\mathbf{e}_i$ satisfy $\mathbf{e}_r.\mathbf{e}_s = \delta_{rs}$ (1 if r = s, else 0) we have the following simple table which establishes (iv).

	Condition	$(\mathbf{e}_r\mathbf{e}_s).\mathbf{e}_t$	$(\mathbf{e}_r\mathbf{e}_t).\mathbf{e}_s$
$\mathbf{e}_r\mathbf{e}_s = \mathbf{e}_t$	i.e. $\mathbf{e}_r = \mathbf{e}_t\mathbf{e}_s^{-1} = -\mathbf{e}_s\mathbf{e}_t^{-1}$	1	-1
$\mathbf{e}_r\mathbf{e}_s = -\mathbf{e}_t$	i.e. $\mathbf{e}_r = -\mathbf{e}_t\mathbf{e}_s^{-1} = \mathbf{e}_s\mathbf{e}_t^{-1}$	-1	1
	$\mathbf{e}_r\mathbf{e}_s \neq \pm\mathbf{e}_t$	0	0

9.3.2 Quaternions and rotation in 3-space

We come now to an important application of quaternions: as an alternative to rotation matrices. The case seems most clear cut in their use for smoothing animation (Section 9.4). Here we explore how quaternions work out in representing rotations in 3-space. The first step is to spot the non-obvious fact that if **x** is a pure quaternion, alias a point in 3-space, then so is $\mathbf{axa}^{-1}$ for *every* quaternion **a**, pure or otherwise. This is not the case for left or right multiplication, so we do not quite have a correspondence with the similar looking isometry combination of Theorem 2.12. For example left multiplication by **i** sends the point **i** = (0,1,0,0) to (-1,0,0,0).

*THEOREM 9.30 (Rotation about unit axis vector **I** through angle 2θ.)*
(a) *If* **x** *is a pure quaternion then so is* $\mathbf{axa}^{-1}$ *for every quaternion* ***a***.
(b) *The transformation of 3-space* T: $\mathbf{R}^3 \to \mathbf{R}^3$ *given by*

$$T(\mathbf{x}) = \mathbf{axa}^{-1}, \quad \textit{with } \mathbf{a} = re^{\mathbf{I}\theta}, \quad (r > 0,\ \mathbf{I}^2 = -1),$$

is rotation through angle 2θ about axis vector I based at the origin.
(c) *With* $\mathbf{a} = t + u\mathbf{i} + v\mathbf{j} + w\mathbf{k}$, $|\mathbf{a}| = 1$, *the matrix for* $T(\mathbf{x}) = \mathbf{x}M$ *is*

$$M(\mathbf{a}) = \begin{bmatrix} 1-2v^2-2w^2 & 2tw+2uv & 2uw-2tv \\ 2vu-2tw & 1-2w^2-2u^2 & 2tu+2vw \\ 2tv+2wu & 2wv-2tu & 1-2u^2-2v^2 \end{bmatrix}.$$

(d) $M(\mathbf{a}^{-1}) = M(\mathbf{a})^{-1} = M(\mathbf{a})^T, \qquad M(\mathbf{a})M(\mathbf{b}) = M(\mathbf{ba}) \quad (\mathbf{a},\mathbf{b} \text{ in } \mathbf{H}).$

REMARKS 9.31 (1) In the matrix (c) we follow the notation of Shoemake (1985), though it may be convenient to replace the diagonal elements by their equivalents $\cos 2\theta + 2u^2$, $\cos 2\theta + 2v^2$, $\cos 2\theta + 2w^2$. The matrix is given in a rather different form in Theorem 8.49. To make the transition from one to the other, we replace 2θ here by φ. However, we shall derive the present formula in terms of quaternions, for completeness. Either formula may be preferable, depending on the precise purpose.

(2) Transposing (d) we have $M(\mathbf{b})^T M(\mathbf{a})^T = M(\mathbf{ba})^T$. These transposes are the matrices required if we work with the matrix formulation $T(\mathbf{x}) = M^T\mathbf{x}^T$, as is often done. We emphasise again that if we know the matrices for one formulation then we know them for the

emphasise again that if we know the matrices for one formulation then we know them for the other: simply transpose.

Notice that if quaternion multiplication were commutative the map T would be the identity.

EXERCISE Demonstrate the equivalence of the two versions of the rotation matrix, in Theorems 8.49 and 9.30.

Proof of Theorem 9.30 Note first that (a) can be proved by multiplying the appropriate matrices $M_L(\mathbf{a})M_R(\mathbf{a})^T$ from the previous section to obtain the first row and column all zeros except for leading entry 1, which shows that this matrix maps a vector of form (0,a,b,c) into another vector with zero first coordinate, i.e. pure quaternions to pure quaternions. We shall carry out a coordinate free proof, obtaining a most useful formula which exhibits the rotation produced. Without loss of generality we may assume that **a** is a unit quaternion, since $(\lambda\mathbf{a})\mathbf{x}(\lambda\mathbf{a})^{-1} = \mathbf{axa}^{-1}$ for a nonzero real number λ, by (9.21). It will be very helpful to have the following three results before us for pure quaternions (hence vectors) **u**, **v**, **w**.

(i) $\mathbf{uv} = -\mathbf{u.v} + \mathbf{u} \times \mathbf{v}$, (9.24)
(ii) $\mathbf{u} \times (\mathbf{v} \times \mathbf{w}) = (\mathbf{w} \times \mathbf{v}) \times \mathbf{u} = (\mathbf{u.w})\mathbf{v} - (\mathbf{u.v})\mathbf{w}$ (Theorem 7.35)
(iii) The product $[\mathbf{u,v,w}] = \mathbf{u}.(\mathbf{v} \times \mathbf{w})$ is unchanged if **u**,**v**,**w** shift cyclically, and is zero if any two are equal (Theorem 7.31).

Suppose the polar form is $\mathbf{a} = c + \mathbf{I}s$, where $c = \cos\theta$, $s = \sin\theta$ for some angle θ, and $\mathbf{I}^2 = -1$. In anticipation of (b) let us write $T(\mathbf{y})$ for $\mathbf{aya}^{-1}$. Then

$$\begin{aligned} T(\mathbf{y}) &= (c + \mathbf{I}s)\,\mathbf{y}\,(c - \mathbf{I}s) && \text{by (9.30) for } \mathbf{a}^{-1}, \\ &= c^2\mathbf{y} + sc(\mathbf{Iy} - \mathbf{yI}) - s^2\,\mathbf{I\,y\,I}, \\ &= c^2\mathbf{y} + 2sc(\mathbf{I} \times \mathbf{y}) - s^2\,\mathbf{I\,y\,I}, && \text{by (i) for } \mathbf{Iy},\ \mathbf{yI}. \end{aligned}$$

$$\begin{aligned} \mathbf{I\,y\,I} &= (\mathbf{Iy})\mathbf{I} \\ &= -(\mathbf{I.y})\mathbf{I} + (\mathbf{I} \times \mathbf{y})\,\mathbf{I} && \text{by (i) for } \mathbf{Iy}, \\ &= -(\mathbf{I.y})\mathbf{I} - (\mathbf{I} \times \mathbf{y}).\mathbf{I} + (\mathbf{I} \times \mathbf{y}) \times \mathbf{I}, && \text{by (i) for } (\mathbf{I} \times \mathbf{y})\mathbf{I} \\ &= -(\mathbf{I.y})\mathbf{I} + (\mathbf{I.I})\,\mathbf{y} - (\mathbf{I.y})\,\mathbf{I}, && \text{by (ii),} \end{aligned}$$

since $(\mathbf{I} \times \mathbf{y}).\mathbf{I} = 0$ by (iii). Finally, $\mathbf{I.I} = |\mathbf{I}|^2 = 1$ simplifies the expression to

$$\mathbf{I\,y\,I} = \mathbf{y} - 2\,(\mathbf{I.y})\mathbf{I}, \tag{9.34}$$

Now we substitute (9.34) in the expression so far for $T(\mathbf{y})$, noting that $c^2 - s^2 = \cos 2\theta$ and $2sc = \sin 2\theta$, to obtain a formula that will be useful again,

$$T(\mathbf{y}) = \mathbf{y}\cos 2\theta + (\mathbf{I} \times \mathbf{y})\sin 2\theta + (1 - \cos 2\theta)\,(\mathbf{I.y})\,\mathbf{I} \tag{9.35}$$

where **y**, **I** are pure and $\mathbf{I}^2 = -1$. Since $\mathbf{I} \times \mathbf{y}$ is also pure, so is $T(\mathbf{y})$, as we wished to show.

(b) There are various ways to show that T is rotation through 2θ about axis vector **I**. We make maximum use of the classification of isometries. *T is an isometry* because the definition (8.1) is satisfied as follows

$$
\begin{aligned}
|T(\mathbf{x}) - T(\mathbf{y})| &= |\mathbf{axa}^{-1} - \mathbf{aya}^{-1}| && (\mathbf{x}, \mathbf{y} \text{ pure}) \\
&= |\mathbf{a}(\mathbf{x}-\mathbf{y})\mathbf{a}^{-1}| \\
&= |\mathbf{a}|\,|\mathbf{x}-\mathbf{y}|\,|\mathbf{a}^{-1}| && \text{by Theorem 9.25,} \\
&= |\mathbf{x}-\mathbf{y}| && \text{as } |\mathbf{a}^{-1}| = 1/|\mathbf{a}|.
\end{aligned}
$$

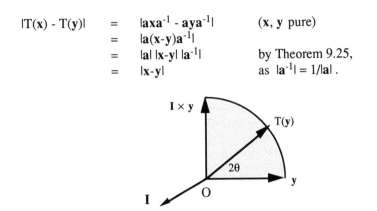

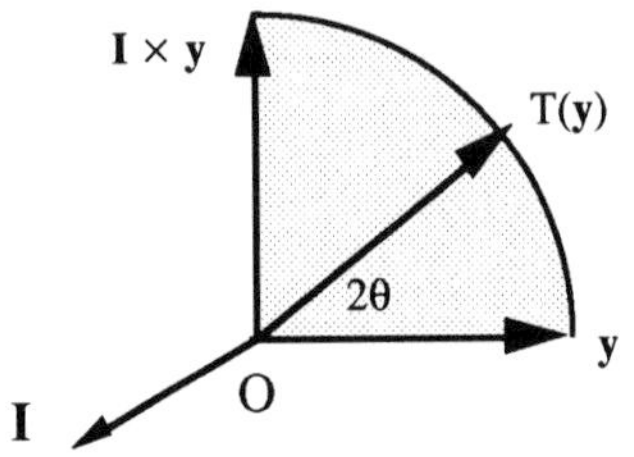

Figure 9.9 Effect of the transformation $T(\mathbf{y}) = \mathbf{aya}^{-1}$, with $\mathbf{a} = e^{\mathbf{I}\phi}$, $\mathbf{I}^2 = -1$.

Let **y** be a vector perpendicular to I, so that $\mathbf{I.y} = 0$, and from (9.35) we have as illustrated in Figure 9.9

$$T(\mathbf{y}) = \mathbf{y}\cos 2\theta + (\mathrm{I} \times \mathbf{y})\sin 2\theta. \qquad (9.36)$$

This shows that T has the same effect as rotation 2θ about axis **I**, on the plane Π through O normal to **I**. By the Classification Theorem 8.42, T is either the rotation claimed or a rotary reflection in Π. But $T(\mathrm{I}) = \mathbf{a\,I\,a}^{-1} = e^{\mathbf{I}\theta}\,\mathrm{I}\,e^{-\mathbf{I}\theta} = e^{\mathbf{I}\theta}\,e^{-\mathbf{I}\theta}\,\mathbf{I} = \mathbf{I}$, so T must be the rotation. Thus the key result is established. (Alternatively, T acts as the rotation on four non-collinear points: the point with position vector **I** and any three non-collinear points in Π. Hence result (b) by the earlier Theorem 8.22.)

(c) We are computing the 3 x 3 submatrix $M = [m_{rs}]$ of $N = M_L(\mathbf{a})M_R(\mathbf{a})^T$ corresponding to the last three rows and columns, numbered 1,2 ,3, from

$$m_{rs} = (\text{row r of } M_L(\mathbf{a})) \,.\, (\text{row s of } M_R(\mathbf{a})) \qquad (*).$$

What is more obvious from $m_{rs} = (\mathbf{ae}_r\mathbf{a}^{-1}) \,.\, \mathbf{e}_s = f(a_0, a_1, a_2, a_3)$, say, is that $m_{r+1,s+1} = f(a_0, a_2, a_3, a_1)$, where $1\to2\to3\to1$ (0 fixed), and that therefore we may obtain the second and third rows of M from the first (this being found from (*)). For example $m_{12} = 2a_1a_2 + 2a_0a_3$ implies that $m_{23} = 2a_2a_3 + 2a_0a_1$. Representing the diagonal we have $m_{11} = a_1^2 + a_0^2 - a_3^2 - a_2^2 = t^2 + u^2 - v^2 - w^2$, which equals $1 - 2v^2 - 2w^2$ (the stated expression) because of $1 = |\mathbf{a}|^2 = t^2 + u^2 + v^2 + w^2$. [The fact that N is orthogonal and sends vectors (0,a,b,c) to (0,d,e,f) implies that its first row and column have the form (1,0,0,0), though we do not need this.]

(d) The matrix result $M(\mathbf{ab}) = M(\mathbf{b})M(\mathbf{a})$ holds, since $(\mathbf{ab})\mathbf{x}(\mathbf{ab})^{-1} = \mathbf{a}(\mathbf{bxb}^{-1})\mathbf{a}^{-1}$ implies that $M(\mathbf{b})$ is applied first. The first statement of (d) now follows from the equalities $M(\mathbf{a}^{-1})M(\mathbf{a}) = M(\mathbf{aa}^{-1}) = M(1) = I$ (the identity matrix), because a 1-sided inverse is 2-sided by (7.17).

EXERCISE Prove that $\mathbf{y}, T(\mathbf{y}), \mathbf{I}$ is a right-handed triple in part (b) above, if $0 < 2\theta < \pi$.

EXERCISE Complete the calculation of $M(\mathbf{a})$ from $M_L(\mathbf{a})M_R(\mathbf{a})^T$.

REMARKS 9.32 The reader may wish to postpone these comments, logically placed here, until after seeing the examples that follow. (1) Sometimes in the literature one finds $T(\mathbf{x}) = \mathbf{a}^{-1}\mathbf{x}\mathbf{a}$, $\mathbf{a} = e^{\mathbf{I}\theta}$. Since $\mathbf{a}^{-1} = e^{-\mathbf{I}\theta}$ the result is rotation, still about axis $\mathbf{I}$, but through -2θ rather than 2θ. There may be applications for which this sign reversal perhaps does not matter, but for computer graphics it seems risky to let in a gratuitous minus sign. Therefore we stick to $T(\mathbf{x}) = \mathbf{a}\mathbf{x}\mathbf{a}^{-1}$.

(2) We emphasise that in contrast with (i), replacing $\mathbf{a}$ by $r\mathbf{a}$ for any $r \neq 0$ leaves T unchanged, since $(r\mathbf{a})\mathbf{x}(r\mathbf{a})^{-1} = r\mathbf{a}\mathbf{x}r^{-1}\mathbf{a}^{-1} = \mathbf{a}\mathbf{x}\mathbf{a}^{-1}$. This is especially useful if obtaining $\mathbf{a}$ of unit modulus requires division by a square root.

(3) Again, replacing $\theta, \mathbf{I}$ by $-\theta, -\mathbf{I}$ leaves the rotation unchanged, since $e^{(-\theta)(-\mathbf{I})} = e^{\mathbf{I}\theta}$. This is illustrated in Section 8.4.3. On the other hand, replacing $\mathbf{a}$ by its conjugate or $\mathbf{I}$ by its negative reverses the turn.

(4) The unit quaternion $\mathbf{a}$ gives a 1/n'th turn if and only if $\mathbf{a}$ has order 2n (is a 2n'th root of unity and nothing less). Reason: rotation $2\pi/n$ requires argument π/n.

To encourage our faith that quaternions accomplish rotations, we start with several examples in which the answer is easy to check.

EXAMPLE 9.33 Calculate the effect on the x-axis, of rotation by $\pi/2$ about the z-axis, using quaternions directly. We use $T(\mathbf{x}) = \mathbf{a}\mathbf{x}\mathbf{a}^{-1}$. In the usual notation $2\theta = \pi/2$, $\mathbf{I} = \mathbf{k}$, and $\mathbf{a} = \cos \pi/4 + \mathbf{k} \sin \pi/4 = (1 + \mathbf{k})/\sqrt{2}$. Since $|\mathbf{a}| = 1$ we have $\mathbf{a}^{-1} = \bar{\mathbf{a}} = (1 - \mathbf{k})/\sqrt{2}$, and so

$$T(\mathbf{i}) = \tfrac{1}{2}(1+\mathbf{k})\,\mathbf{i}\,(1-\mathbf{k}) = \tfrac{1}{2}(\mathbf{i}+\mathbf{k})\,(\mathbf{i}+\mathbf{j}) = \tfrac{1}{2}(\mathbf{i}-\mathbf{ik}+\mathbf{j}-\mathbf{jk}) = \mathbf{j}.$$

Therefore T maps the x-axis into the y-axis, vindicating Remark (1) above. See Figure 9.10 on the right. Also $T(\mathbf{k}) = \mathbf{k}$ (no calculation required - why?) and $T(\mathbf{j}) = -\mathbf{i}$, which confirms by the classification of isometries that we have the correct rotation, since it is correct on four noncoplanar points

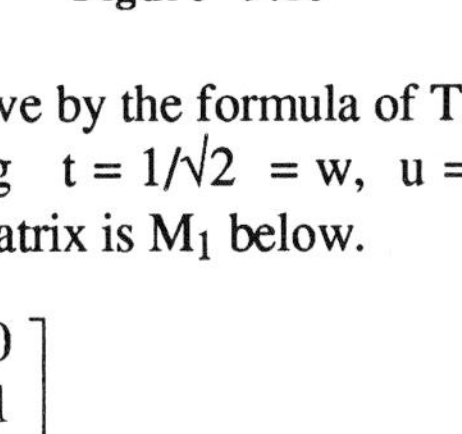

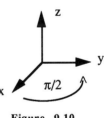

Figure 9.10

EXAMPLE 9.34 We calculate the matrix for the Example above by the formula of Theorem 9.30(c), with $\mathbf{a} = (1 + \mathbf{k})/\sqrt{2} = t + u\mathbf{i} + v\mathbf{j} + w\mathbf{k}$, giving $t = 1/\sqrt{2} = w$, $u = v = 0$. Hence, in agreement with the rotation formula of (7.26), the matrix is M_1 below.

$$M_1 = \begin{bmatrix} 0 & 1 & 0 \\ -1 & 0 & 0 \\ 0 & 0 & 1 \end{bmatrix}, \qquad M_2 = \begin{bmatrix} 0 & 1 & 0 \\ 0 & 0 & 1 \\ 1 & 0 & 0 \end{bmatrix}$$

EXAMPLE 9.35 We use quaternions to find the matrix for rotation about axis vector (1,1,1) through a 1/3 turn. For this we have $2\theta = 2\pi/3$, $\theta = \pi/3$, $\mathbf{I} = (\mathbf{i}+\mathbf{j}+\mathbf{k})/\sqrt{3}$, which gives simply $\mathbf{a} = (1+\mathbf{i}+\mathbf{j}+\mathbf{k})/2$, $t = u = v = w = 1/2$. By Theorem 9.30(c), the matrix is M_2 above. This sends x-axis $\rightarrow$ y-axis $\rightarrow$ z-axis cyclically, as we knew it ought. Indeed, given this, we could write down the matrix straightaway by Theorem 8.5. Notice that $\mathbf{a}$ is a cube root of 1.

TABLE 9.3 A compendium of quaternions **a** for rotation $T(\mathbf{x}) = \mathbf{axa}^{-1}$
For axis **I** replace **k** by **I** except in case (*)

Rotation	θ	axis	quaternion **a**	$\lvert a \rvert$
1/2 turn	$\pi/2$	z-axis	$\mathbf{k}$	1
1/3 turn	$\pi/3$	z-axis	$1 + \sqrt{3}\mathbf{k}$	2
1/4 turn	$\pi/4$	z-axis	$1 + \mathbf{k}$	$\sqrt{2}$
1/5 turn	$\pi/5$	$\tau\mathbf{j} + \mathbf{k}$ (*)	$\tau + \mathbf{j} - \sigma\mathbf{k}$	2
1/6 turn	$\pi/6$	z-axis	$\sqrt{3} + \mathbf{k}$	2

(*) Refers to a 1/5 turn about OA with $A(0,1,-\sigma)$ a vertex of an icosahedron - the regular solid bounded by twenty equilateral triangular faces, five at each of the 12 vertices. Here (see Table 9.1) $\tau = (1+\sqrt{5})/2 = 2\cos\pi/5$ and $\sigma = (1-\sqrt{5})/2$ are the roots of $x^2-x-1 = 0$. Hence $\sigma+\tau = 1$, $\sigma\tau = -1$, $\sigma^2+\tau^2 = 3$, $\sigma^2 = 2-\tau$ and $\tau^2 = 2-\sigma$. The points $(0, \pm\tau, \pm 1)$ and their cyclic shifts serve as vertices. $\sin\pi/5$ cannot be expressed conveniently in the way $\cos\pi/5$ can.

9.3.3 Composition of rotations, by quaternions

EXAMPLE 9.36 We find the composition of a 60° rotation about the y-axis followed by a 60° rotation about the x-axis, without using matrices. Reversing order as prescribed, the appropriate product of quaternions is

$$\frac{\sqrt{3}+\mathbf{i}}{2}\cdot\frac{\sqrt{3}+\mathbf{j}}{2} = \frac{3}{4} + \frac{1}{4}(\mathbf{i}\sqrt{3} + \mathbf{j}\sqrt{3} + \mathbf{k}) = \cos\theta + \mathbf{I}\sin\theta,$$

hence the result is a rotation of $2\cos^{-1}(3/4) = 83^{\circ}$, about an axis vector $(\sqrt{3}, \sqrt{3}, 1)$.

EXAMPLE 9.37 We shall combine rotation symmetries,

$$R_{OE}(1/2)R_{OA}(1/3),$$

of the regular tetrahedron, shown in Figure 9.11. This solid is bounded by four equilateral triangles, three at each of the 4 vertices. Inspection shows that the rotation symmetries are as listed below, with origin O at the centre:

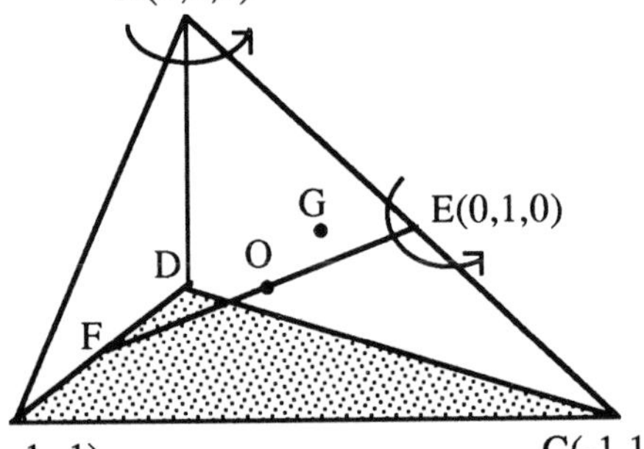

Figure 9.11 The regular tetrahedron. Its vertices are $(\pm 1, \pm 1, \pm 1)$ with none or two minus signs.

(1)	a 1/2 turn about each line EF joining the midpoints of opposite edges	3
(2)	a 1/3 and a 2/3 turn about OA for each vertex A	8
(3)	The identity rotation (do nothing)	<u>1</u>
		12

The product of any two of these symmetries must be a third. We require the result of a 1/2 turn about OE followed by a 1/3 turn about OA. Using Table 9.3 as an aid, we find that suitable rotation quaternions are for $R_{OE}(1/2)$: $\mathbf{a} = \mathbf{j}$, for $R_{OA}(1/3)$: $\mathbf{b} = 1 + (\sqrt{3})\underline{OA}/|\underline{OA}| = 1+\mathbf{i}+\mathbf{j}+\mathbf{k}$. By Theorem 9.30(d), a rotation quaternion for $R_{OE}(1/2)R_{OA}(1/3)$ is $\mathbf{ba} =$

$(1+\mathbf{i}+\mathbf{j}+\mathbf{k})\mathbf{j} = -1-\mathbf{i}+\mathbf{j}+\mathbf{k} = -1 - \sqrt{3}(\underline{OB}/|\underline{OB}|)$. From Table 9.3 (note that **a** and -**a** give the same rotation), the result is a 1/3 turn about OB. Equivalently a 2/3 turn about OG, where G is the centroid of triangle ADC.

EXERCISE Find $R_{OE}(1/2)R_{OB}(1/3)$ in the tetrahedron of Example 9.37. Check your answer by its effect on three suitable points besides the origin, or by using matrices.

EXAMPLE 9.38 The cube of Figure 9.12 contains a symmetrically placed copy of the tetrahedron ABCD of Example 9.37, whose symmetries are thus also symmetries of the cube. We find the product of the cube rotation symmetries indicated:

$$R_{OZ}(1/4)\, R_{OH}(-1/3).$$

An appropriate quaternion product is, by Table 9.3, $(1-\sqrt{3}(\underline{OH}\,/\,|\underline{OH}|) \times (1+\mathbf{k}) = (1-\mathbf{i}-\mathbf{j}+\mathbf{k})(1+\mathbf{k}) = 2(-\mathbf{i}+\mathbf{k})$, giving a 1/2 turn about OL.

For reflections, cf. Example 8.25.

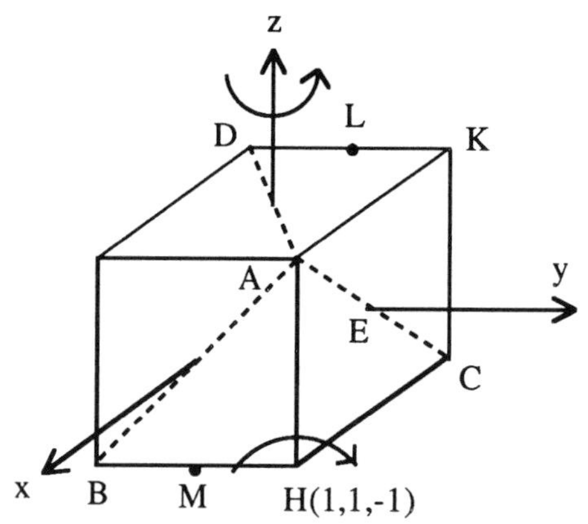

Figure 9.12 The cube, centred at the origin, with vertices (±1, ±1, ±1), and inscribed tetrahedron ABCD from Figure 9.11.

EXERCISE Compute $R_{OY}(3/4)R_{OK}(1/3)$, above. Is this a symmetry of the tetrahedron?

A fund of rotation examples

By rotation *about a point* A of a polyhedron (solid bounded by plane faces) we will mean rotation about axis OA, where as always O is the origin. The *rotation group* of a figure is the group of all its rotational symmetries. For the *cube* of Example 9.38, symbolised by {4,3} because its faces are squares, three at a vertex, the rotation group consists of the identity and all powers of: a 1/2 turn about the midpoint of each edge, a 1/3 turn about each vertex, a 1/4 turn about each *face centre* (centre of face). Total 24. The face centres of a cube form the vertices of its 'dual', the *octahedron* {3,4} with four regular triangular faces at each vertex. Its symmetries are therefore those of a cube, but with face and vertex switched in the description.

The *icosahedron* {3,5} is a solid bounded by twenty regular triangular faces, five at each of the twelve vertices. Rotation symmetries come from: a 1/2 turn about the mid point of each edge, a 1/3 turn about each face centre, and a 1/5 turn about each vertex. A total of sixty in the group. As before we may take the face centres as vertices of a 'dual', this time the *dodecahedron* {5,3}, with regular pentagonal faces, three at a vertex. The five solids enumerated are called the *Platonic solids*, and exhaust the possibilities for a regular polyhedron {p,q} that is *convex*, meaning that any line segment joining two points in the solid is also within the solid.

Table 9.4 gives the unit quaternions for each of the three distinct rotation groups, and a geometrical description of them in terms of *permutations* of certain subfigures. A permutation of a list of objects, say denoted by 1,2, ..., n, is a reordering of them, and is called *even* or *odd* according as it requires an even or odd number of *transpositions* (i.e.

Then for example 1,2,3 may be cyclically shifted to 3,1,2 by transposing 2,3 then 1,3, so is even. The group of all permutations of n objects is called the *symmetric group* S_n, and its subgroup of all even permutations is the *alternating group* A_n.

For further information, see Coxeter (1973) who shows that such a polyhedral group, the rotation group of a polyhedron, has order twice the number of edges in the polyhedron's boundary. The reader may know the Euler polyhedron formula V-E+F = 2 (cf. Table 9.4), holding for a wide variety of surfaces bounded by polygonal faces. For its application to Solid modelling in computer graphics, see Baumgart (1974) and Mäntylä (1988). A useful introduction is found in Foley et al (1990).

TABLE 9.4 Rotation groups of the Platonic solids, and associated quaternions
V, E, F denote the number of vertices, edges, and faces

Solid	Rotation group	V	E	F	Corresponding group of unit quaternions
Tetrahedron	*Tetrahedral group.* The group A_4 of all even permutations of the vertices.	4	6	4	1, **i**, **j**, **k**, 1±**i**±**j**±**k**, and their negatives.
Cube Octahedron	*Octahedral group.* The group S_4 of all permutations of the main diagonals of the cube.	8 6	12 12	6 8	The above, & (1±**i**)/√2, (1±**j**)/√2, (1±**k**)/√2, (**i**±**j**)/√2, (**j**±**k**)/√2, (**k**±**i**)/√2, & negatives.
Icosahedron, Dodecahedron	*Icosahedral group.* The group A_5 of all even permuations of five regular tetrahedra on the dodecahedron's 5 x 4 vertices.	12 20	30 30	20 12	The tetrahedral ones, & (±t±u**i**±v**j**±w**k**)/2, with tuvw an even permutation of -1 0 σ τ.

EXERCISE What group of rotations comes from quaternion group Q = {±1, ±**i**, ±**j**,±**k**}?

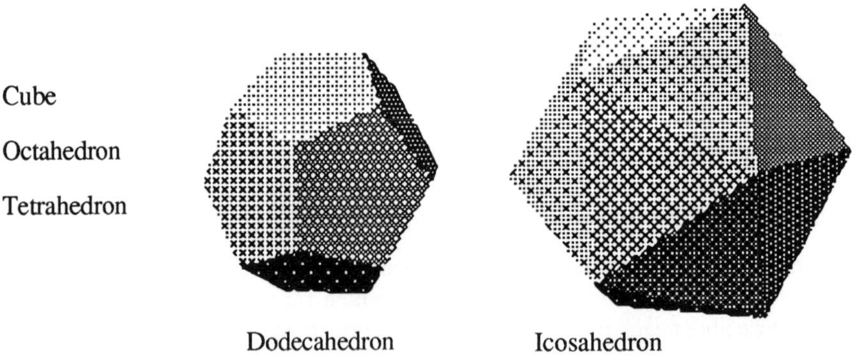

Figure 9.13 The five Platonic solids

A connection with groups We give now a small amount of information concerning a wider context. For further reading on quaternions, see Coxeter (1974) and references therein. Just as the unit pure quaternions can be regarded as the points of the unit 2-sphere S^2, in 3-space, so can the unit quaternions be viewed as forming the 3-dimensional sphere in 4-space:

$$S^3 = \{(a_0, a_1, a_2, a_3): \text{ each } a_i \text{ is real, } \Sigma a_i^2 = 1\},$$

in which the pure quaternion subset S^2 is the "equatorial" subsphere defined by $a_0 = 0$. (In Section 9.4 we consider how to take a smooth path through a sequence of points on S^3 to achieve animation 'in-betweening'). But there is more. Since the product of two unit quaternions is a third, multiplication of quaternions gives S^3 the structure of an infinite group , with identity from the real number 1 (Example 9.26). We have a map

$$F: S^3 \to SO(3),$$

which sends $\pm\mathbf{a}$ to the same matrix $M(\mathbf{a})^T$. And F is a *group homomorphism,* meaning that $F(\mathbf{ab}) = F(\mathbf{a})F(\mathbf{b})$. This is simply $M(\mathbf{ab})^T = M(\mathbf{a})^T M(\mathbf{b})^T$. It is described as *2:1 and onto* because every matrix in SO(3) is the image of exactly two members of S^3. We have just introduced the Platonic solids, whose rotation groups G are finite subgroups of SO(3). The corresponding sets of unit quaternions in Table 9.4 are finite subgroups of S^3, namely the inverse images $F^{-1}(G)$; collectively they are called the *binary* polyhedral groups $2A_4$, $2S_4$, $2A_5$, of orders 24, 48, 120.

Coordinates on the n-sphere We build up from the circle S^1 to S^2 to S^3, and similarly beyond, so that S^n is coordinatised by n angles. For the equatorial circle S^1 in S^2 we have a typical point $\mathbf{u} = (\cos\phi, \sin\phi)$, $0 \le \phi \le 2\pi$. Now take basis vectors $\mathbf{e}_1, \mathbf{e}_2, \mathbf{e}_3, \ldots$ each viewed as belonging to a higher dimensional space as required. Then we extend S^1 to S^2, adding a further coordinate on basis vector $\mathbf{e}_3$, obtaining the points of the ordinary sphere S^2 as $\mathbf{v} = \mathbf{u}\sin\theta + \mathbf{e}_3\cos\theta$, $(0 \le \theta \le \pi)$. In coordinates,

$$\mathbf{v} = (\cos\phi \sin\theta, \sin\phi \sin\theta, \cos\theta).$$

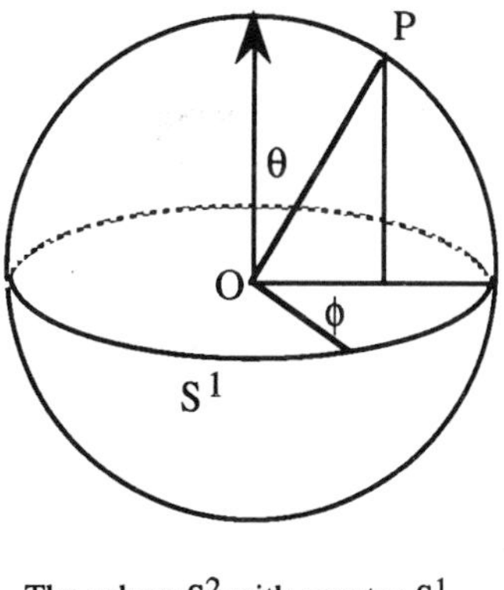

The sphere S^2 with equator S^1.

To coordinatise S^3 we simply apply the same idea again with new basis vector $\mathbf{e}_4$ and angle say ψ, where $0 \le \psi \le \pi$ (we might have chosen $\theta_1, \theta_2, \theta_3$). Then S^3 has points

$$\mathbf{w} = \mathbf{v}\sin\psi + \mathbf{e}_4\cos\psi = (\cos\phi \sin\theta \sin\psi, \sin\phi \sin\theta \sin\psi, \cos\theta \sin\psi, \cos\psi).$$

9.4 Quaternion in-betweening

Background references for this Section are given at the end of the Chapter.

9.4.1 Why in-betweening and why quaternions?

A prime case in which interpolation or 'in-betweening' is required, is that of computer animation. The aspect we address here is that of animation in 3-space with no change in the actual shape of a moving object. A series of *key frames* are established for giving the position and orientation of an object at certain time intervals, and we wish to generate a suitable sequence of intermediate states so that the object will appear to the eye to move smoothly between and past key frames. A key frame may be specified by a 4 by 4 matrix as in Section 8.3.3 describing the position and orientation of an object in 3-space, relative to a chosen origin and three mutually perpendicular coordinate axes. Since we are dealing here with strictly rigid motion, only direct isometries are allowed, which, according to the classification of Section 8.5.4 are

Translation,
Rotation, or
Screw,

where a screw consists of rotation combined with translation parallel to the axis.

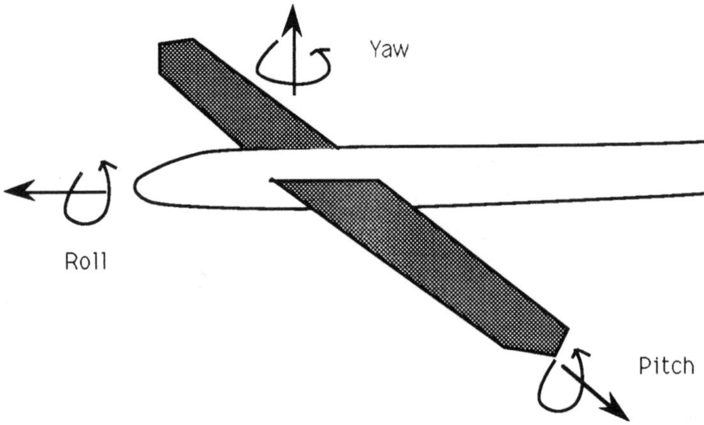

Figure 9.14 Yaw, pitch and roll for an aircraft.

But why quaternions? We cannot interpolate directly beween transformation matrices because their entries are partially dependent, for example a 3 x 3 rotation matrix is subject to six quadratic relations. The traditional set of independent coordinates describing rotation in three dimensions has been Euler angles, introduced successfully by Euler (1758) to solve differential equations, and still useful in this regard (see e.g. Miller (1972)). Euler angles are an extension of the idea of latitude and longitude on the ordinary 2-sphere. They specify rotation as the composition of three independent rotations about given axes through an origin, in a given order. A typical system used in aircraft dynamics (Figure 9.14) is to specify in order:

1. Yaw, or heading, around a vertical axis,
2. Pitch, around a horizontal axis through the wings,
3. Roll, around an axis along the fuselage.

This is not the only system in use. The reader may care to list 12 = 3 x 2 x 2 viable alternate systems with mutually perpendicular axis in the object. See Hughes (1986). On the other hand a quaternion represents orientation as a single rotation, enabling a much simpler approach to interpolation in particular. This is probably the most important gain in using quaternions. The complications of Euler angles for animation are further discussed in Shoemake (1985).

REMARK Robotics is another area where in-betweening is required. See for example the tutorial of Heise and Macdonald (1989).

9.4.2 Interpolating between two orientations

Clearly there is no problem in applying linear interpolation to the translation parts of successive placings of an object in space. Here we address the question of a suitable way to interpolate between two orientations as unit quaternions, that is, as points on the unit sphere S^3 in 4-space.

As we will soon show, any two distinct points **a**, **b** on S^3 lie on a unique circle in this sphere, called the *great circle* through **a**, **b**, divided by these points into two *great arcs* (if one is the shorter we call it *the* great arc between **a**, **b**). Since the points of this circle may be parametrised by angle in the usual way, it is natural to use *spherical linear interpolation* between **a** and **b** as indicated in Figure 9.15: if the angle between vectors **a**, **b** is θ then the interpolated point **q**(t) for time t, where $0 \le t \le 1$, is given by the vector at angle $t\theta$ to **a**.

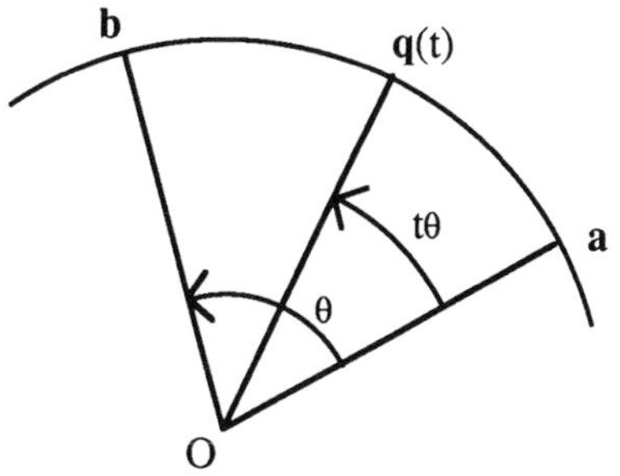

Figure 9.15 Spherical interpolation along a great arc **a b**.

A formula is simple to obtain once we appreciate that **a**, **b** are on an honest circle of radius 1 in an ordinary 2-dimensional plane Π, which happens to be sitting in 4-space. This works as follows. The 4-vectors **a**, **b** define a unique plane Π through the origin consisting by definition of all linear combinations of **a**, **b**,

$$\Pi = \{\lambda \mathbf{a} + \mu \mathbf{b} : \lambda, \mu \text{ are arbitrary real numbers}\}.$$

Angles in Π are defined by innerproducts of its vectors calculated from their coordinates as 4-vectors. But how do we know this is like the usual x-y plane?

APPROACH 1 By similar arguments to the 3-dimensional case, Theorem 8.55, there exists a 4 by 4 orthogonal matrix M sending unit vectors **a**,**b** to unit vectors **a'**,**b'** with last two coordinates zero and with **a'**.**b'** = **a**.**b**. Also M sends $\lambda\mathbf{a} + \mu\mathbf{b}$ to $\lambda\mathbf{a}' + \mu\mathbf{b}'$. Thus geometry in Π is the same as that in

$$\Pi' = \lambda(a_1', a_2', 0\ 0) + \mu(b_1', b_2', 0\ 0): \quad \lambda, \mu \text{ real},$$

and hence the same as a standard plane Σ based on 2 coordinates with, say (a'_1, a'_2) defining one axis and a perpendicular vector (c'_1, c'_2) the other, as in Figure 9.16.

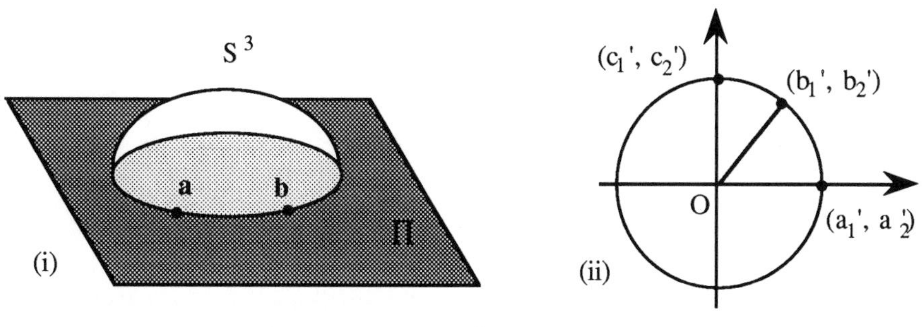

Figure 9.16 (i) Plane Π intersects sphere S^3 in a great circle, (ii) the plane Σ.

APPROACH 2 Π itself contains a unit vector **c** perpendicular to **a**, so that **a**,**c** define axes for x,y coordinates in Π. To obtain **c** we subtract from **b** its component along **a** and make the result into a unit vector. Thus $\mathbf{c} = \mathbf{v} / |\mathbf{v}|$, where $\mathbf{v} = \mathbf{b} - (\mathbf{b.a})\mathbf{a}$. As a check, $\mathbf{v.a} = \mathbf{b.a} - (\mathbf{b.a})\mathbf{a.a} = 0$, since $\mathbf{a.a} = 1$. Using $\mathbf{a.a} = 1 = \mathbf{c.c}$ and $\mathbf{a.c} = 0$ we calculate the inner product in Π (inherited from $\mathbf{R}^4$) as $(x_1\mathbf{a} + x_2\mathbf{c}).(y_1\mathbf{a} + y_2\mathbf{c}) = x_1y_1 + x_2y_2$. Thus Π is a standard plane.

The great circle C through **a**, **b** is by definition the intersection of Π and the sphere S^3, namely the points of Π constituting its unit circle about the origin. We have now justified Figure 9.15, and laid the foundation for later arguments here and in Section 9.4.4. The formula quoted in Shoemake (1985) and Heise and Macdonald (1989) may now be derived simply by an argument in the plane where, if **a**, **b**, **c** are unit vectors at given angles α, β as shown in Figure 9.17 then **c** is a linear combination $\lambda\mathbf{a}+\mu\mathbf{b}$, determined by α, β alone, and this relation continues to hold if the plane consists of 4-vectors as does Π above.

*LEMMA 9.39 For coplanar unit vectors **a**, **b**, **c**, forming nonzero angles α, β as shown in Figure 9.17, we have* $\mathbf{c}\sin(\alpha+\beta) = \mathbf{a}\sin\beta + \mathbf{b}\sin\alpha$.

Proof We find the linear relationship $\mathbf{c} = \lambda\mathbf{a} + \mu\mathbf{b}$ by viewing **a**, **b**, **c** as complex numbers (as we may, by Approach 2), when $\mathbf{a} = \mathbf{c}e^{-i\alpha}$, $\mathbf{b} = \mathbf{c}e^{i\beta}$, and so $\mathbf{c} = \lambda\mathbf{c}e^{-i\alpha} + \mu\mathbf{c}e^{i\beta}$ or, dividing through by **c** as a complex number :

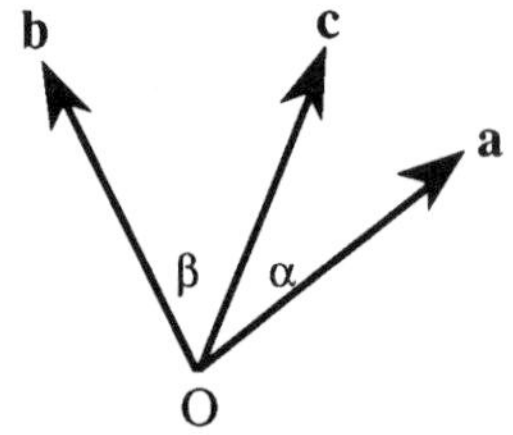

Figure 9.17 Coplanar unit vectors ($\alpha, \beta \neq 0$).

$$1 = \lambda(\cos\alpha - \mathbf{i}\sin\alpha) + \mu(\cos\beta + \mathbf{i}\sin\beta).$$

Equating real and imaginary parts (NB: the real part of the left hand side must equal the real part of the right hand side and similarly for the imaginary parts), we obtain two equations for the unknowns λ, μ:

$$\lambda\cos\alpha + \mu\cos\beta = 1, \qquad -\lambda\sin\alpha + \mu\sin\beta = 0.$$

To complete the proof it remains to solve these easy equations and to apply the relation $\sin(\alpha+\beta) = \sin\alpha\cos\beta + \cos\alpha\sin\beta$.

*COROLLARY 9.40 The quaternion obtained by spherical linear interpolation from **a** to **b** on the unit sphere S^3 in 4-space, with parameter t $(0 \le t \le 1)$, where $\mathbf{a.b} = \cos\theta$, is given by*

$$\mathbf{q}(t) = \frac{\sin(1-t)\theta}{\sin\theta}\mathbf{a} + \frac{\sin t\theta}{\sin\theta}\mathbf{b} \qquad (\sin\theta \neq 0) \qquad (9.37)$$

Proof We apply Lemma 9.39 with $\alpha = \theta t$, $\beta = \theta - \theta t$. (Figure 9.15 is repeated on the right).

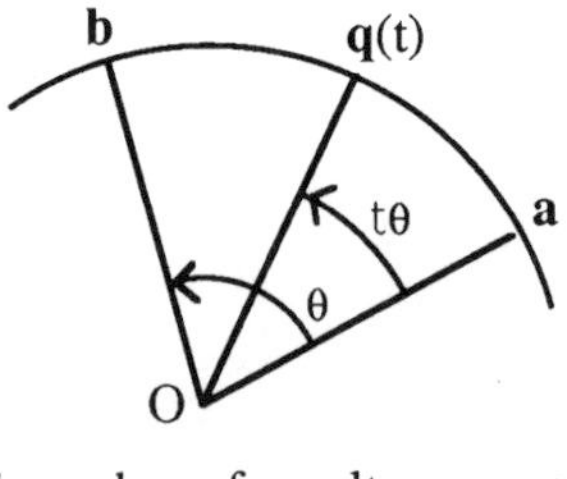

REMARK 9.41 Concerning the case $\sin\theta = 0$, note that $\sin\theta = 0 \Leftrightarrow \cos\theta = \pm 1 \Leftrightarrow \mathbf{b} = \pm\mathbf{a} \Leftrightarrow$ unit quaternions **a**, **b** give the same rotation (see Remark 9.32(2)).

DIFFERENTIATING VECTORS We formulate the small number of results we need in terms of plane vectors, the extension to higher dimensions being straightforward. Suppose the position vector $\mathbf{r}(t) = (x(t), y(t))$ of a point P varies with a parameter t, possibly time. With the usual convention of a dot to denote differentiation with respect to t, we define the derivative of $\mathbf{r}$ as $\dot{\mathbf{r}} = (\dot{x},\dot{y})$ (we say $\mathbf{r}$ is *differentiable* when $\dot{x}$ and $\dot{y}$ exist). Then $\dot{\mathbf{r}}$ is a tangent to the curve traced out by P since it represents the direction in which $\mathbf{r}$ is changing as t varies. Further, the length $|\dot{\mathbf{r}}|$ represents the rate at which $\mathbf{r}$ is changing - how fast P moves along the curve for a given rate of change of t. The following Lemma will suffice.

LEMMA 9.42 If vectors $\mathbf{u}$, $\mathbf{v}$, *and scalar a(t) are differentiable then*
(a) $(d/dt)\, \mathbf{u}.\mathbf{v} = \mathbf{u}.\dot{\mathbf{v}} + \dot{\mathbf{u}}.\mathbf{v}$ (b) $(d/dt)\, a\mathbf{v} = a\dot{\mathbf{v}} + \dot{a}\mathbf{v}$

Proof (a) $(d/dt)\, \mathbf{u}.\mathbf{v} = (d/dt)(u_1v_1 + u_2v_2) = u_1\dot{v}_1 + \dot{u}_1v_1 + u_2\dot{v}_2 + \dot{u}_2v_2 = \mathbf{u}.\dot{\mathbf{v}} + \dot{\mathbf{u}}.\mathbf{v}$ (on regrouping the terms). The second part is slighter shorter.

The classic example is the unit circle with $1 = \mathbf{r}.\mathbf{r}$, hence $2\mathbf{r}.\dot{\mathbf{r}} = 0$ and the tangent is at right angles to the radius, as confirmed by $\mathbf{r}.\dot{\mathbf{r}} = (\cos t, \sin t).(-\sin t, \cos t) = 0$. Now, from (9.37), with $\mathbf{a},\mathbf{b}$ constant, so that $\dot{\mathbf{a}} = \dot{\mathbf{b}} = 0$, we have the derivative of $\mathbf{q}(t)$ as

$$\dot{\mathbf{q}}(t) = \frac{\theta\cos t\theta}{\sin\theta}\mathbf{b} - \frac{\theta\cos(1-t)\theta}{\sin\theta}\mathbf{a} \qquad (\sin\theta \neq 0) \tag{9.38}$$

EXAMPLE 9.43 Show that $|\dot{\mathbf{q}}(t)|^2 = \theta^2$ (which is what we would expect).

Solution We have $|\dot{\mathbf{q}}(t)|^2 = \dot{\mathbf{q}}(t).\,\dot{\mathbf{q}}(t) =$

$$= \left(\frac{\theta\cos t\theta}{\sin\theta}\right)^2 \mathbf{b}.\mathbf{b} - 2\left(\frac{\theta\cos t\theta}{\sin\theta}\right)\left(\frac{\theta\cos(1-t)\theta}{\sin\theta}\right)\mathbf{a}.\mathbf{b} + \left(\frac{\theta\cos(1-t)\theta}{\sin\theta}\right)^2 \mathbf{a}.\mathbf{a}\,.$$

Setting $\mathbf{a}.\mathbf{a} = \mathbf{b}.\mathbf{b} = 1$, $\mathbf{a}.\mathbf{b} = \cos\theta$, expanding $\cos(\theta - t\theta)$, and collecting terms, we obtain $\theta^2[\cos^2 t\theta - \cos^2\theta\cos^2 t\theta + \sin^2\theta\sin^2 t\theta]/\sin^2\theta$. The bracketed expression simplifies to $\sin^2\theta$, and we are done.

EXERCISE Verify that $|\mathbf{q}(t)| = 1$ by direct calculation as in Example 9.43.

9.4.3 Bézier curves

Paul Bézier produced his famous curves in response to a need in the design of car bodies. References for these curves and subsequent developments are given at the end of the chapter. We focus on *cubic* Bézier curves, that is those based on four *knots*, or *control points*, since these are what we require here. The case of n control points is easy to deduce from this.

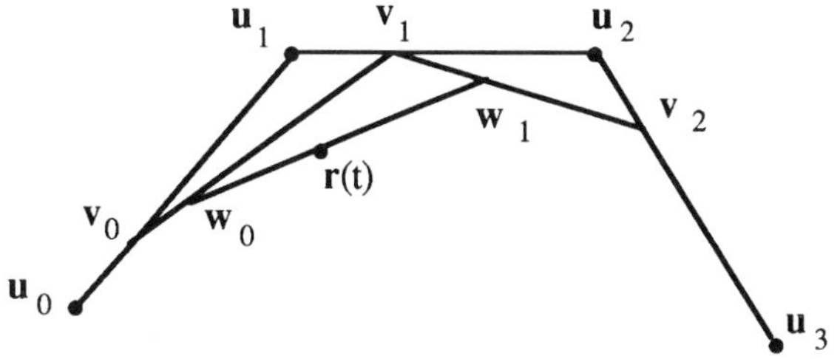

Figure 9.18 Geometrical construction of Bezier curve with four knots.

(a) *Geometrical definition. (Casteljou's construction.)* We refer to Figure 9.18. Let four points $\mathbf{u}_0$, $\mathbf{u}_1$, $\mathbf{u}_2$, $\mathbf{u}_3$ be given in 3-space. Then the corresponding Bezier curve consists of points $\mathbf{r}(t)$, $0 \le t \le 1$, found as follows.

> Let $\mathbf{v}_i$ be the point on line segment $\mathbf{u}_i\mathbf{u}_{i+1}$ dividing it in the ratio t:1 (i = 0,1,2).
> Let $\mathbf{w}_i$ be the point on line segment $\mathbf{v}_i\mathbf{v}_{i+1}$ dividing it in the ratio t:1 (i = 0,1).

Then $\mathbf{r}(t)$ is the point on $\mathbf{w}_i\mathbf{w}_{i+1}$ dividing it in the ratio t :1.

(b) *Algebraic definition.* We shall derive this from (a). We have in order, writing s = 1-t,

$$\mathbf{v}_i = s\mathbf{u}_i + t\mathbf{u}_{i+1} \quad (i = 0,1,2),$$
$$\mathbf{w}_0 = s\mathbf{v}_0 + t\mathbf{v}_1, \quad \mathbf{w}_1 = s\mathbf{v}_1 + t\mathbf{v}_2,$$
$$\mathbf{r}(t) = s\mathbf{w}_0 + t\mathbf{w}_1.$$

Working back, we get a Pascal's triangle effect, giving the binomial coefficients 1,3,3,1 in

$$\mathbf{r}(t) = s^3\mathbf{u}_0 + 3s^2t\mathbf{u}_1 + 3st^2\mathbf{u}_2 + t^3\mathbf{u}_3. \quad (s = 1-t).$$

(c) *Tangents.* An easy differentiation gives $\dot{\mathbf{r}}(0) = 3(\mathbf{u}_1 - \mathbf{u}_0)$, $\dot{\mathbf{r}}(1) = \mathbf{u}_3 - \mathbf{u}_2$, so the Bézier curve is tangent at its end points to respective line segments $\mathbf{u}_0\,\mathbf{u}_1$, $\mathbf{u}_2$ and $\mathbf{u}_3$, as illustrated in Figure 9.19 below.

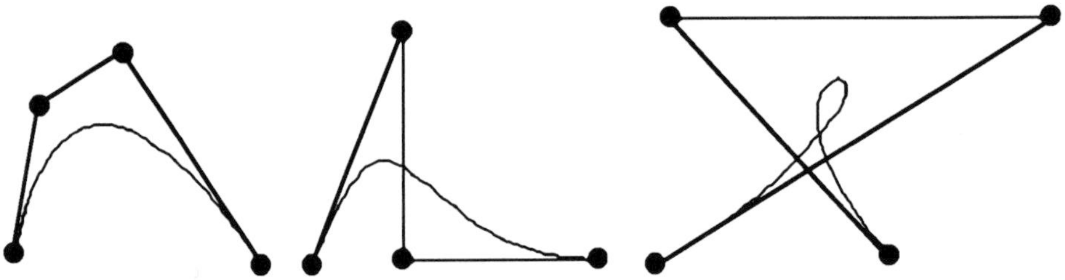

Figure 9.19 Some 4-knot Bezier curves.

In fact the Bzier curve can be shown to lie within the tetrahedron $\mathbf{u}_0\,\mathbf{u}_1\,\mathbf{u}_2\,\mathbf{u}_3$, or within the corresponding polygon if the four knots are coplanar. The third example indicates the circumstances in which the curve may cross itself. We note two special planar cases:

2 knots. This is just a straight line segment: $\mathbf{u}_0$ ________ $\mathbf{u}_1$

3 knots. We obtain a parabola :

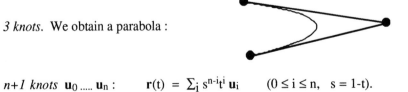

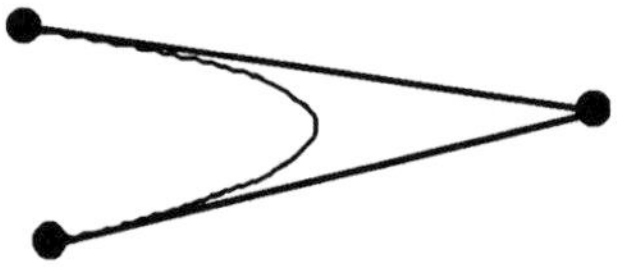

n+1 knots $\mathbf{u}_0 \ldots\ldots \mathbf{u}_n$: $\mathbf{r}(t) = \sum_i s^{n-i}t^i\,\mathbf{u}_i$ $(0 \le i \le n,\ s = 1-t)$.

EXERCISE Prove that a Bezier curve with just 3 knots is a parabola.

9.4.4 In-betweening a sequence of quaternion rotations

Shoemake (1985) proposes interpolation across unit quaternions $\mathbf{q}_1, \mathbf{q}_2, ..., \mathbf{q}_n, \mathbf{q}_{n+1}, ..$ based on Bézier's (1972) splicing together of short Bézier curves from each $\mathbf{q}_n$ to $\mathbf{q}_{n+1}$, with two further control points between, and so that the tangents agree at the curve joins $\mathbf{q}_i$. Thus first order continuity holds, as illustrated in Figure 9.20 below.

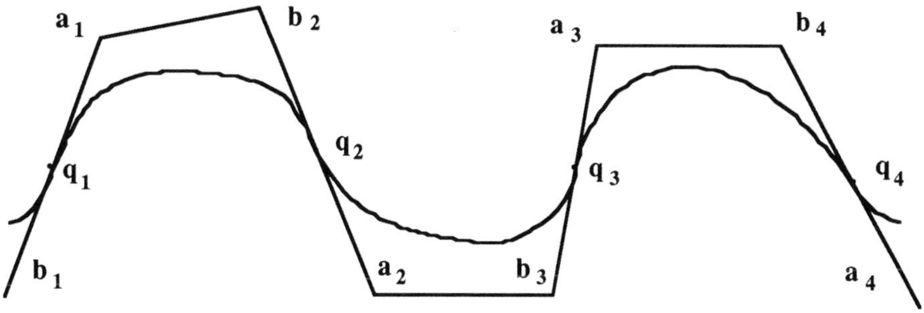

Figure 9.20 Splicing 4-knot Bezier curves so as to keep first order continuity.

The task is to

(a) define additional control points $\mathbf{a}_n$, $\mathbf{b}_n$ on the 3-sphere S^3,
(b) define corresponding 4-knot Bezier curves on S^3, replacing linear interpolation by the spherical formula (9.37),
(c) check the agreement of tangents at the joints $\mathbf{q}_n$.

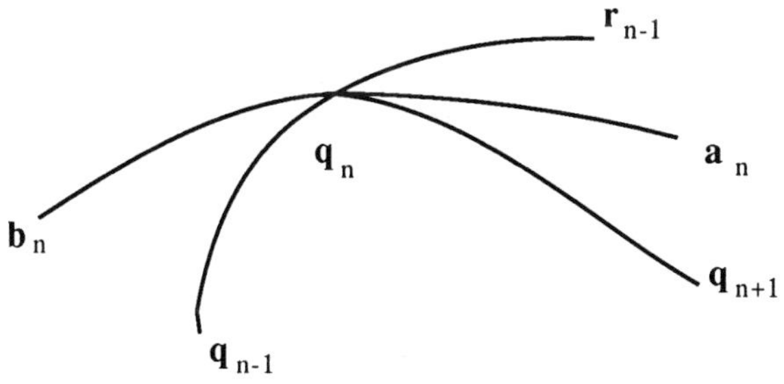

Figure 9.21 Constructing the extra control points.

Choosing $\mathbf{a}_n$, $\mathbf{b}_n$. We refer to Figure 9.21 above, in which all curve segments are great arcs on the sphere S^3, in 4-space. We perform a kind of averaging effect between the incoming arc $\mathbf{q}_{n-1}$, $\mathbf{q}_n$ and outgoing arc $\mathbf{q}_n$, $\mathbf{q}_{n+1}$. We extend arc $\mathbf{q}_{n-1}$, $\mathbf{q}_n$ an equal distance (along the same great circle) to $\mathbf{r}_{n-1}$ say, and call this operation *double*: We write $\mathbf{r}_{n-1}$ = double($\mathbf{q}_{n-1}$, $\mathbf{q}_n$). Let $\mathbf{a}_n$ = bisect($\mathbf{r}_{n-1}$, $\mathbf{q}_{n+1}$), meaning the point which bisects the great arc $\mathbf{r}_{n-1}\,\mathbf{q}_{n+1}$. Finally,

$$\begin{aligned} \mathbf{a}_n &= \text{bisect}(\text{double}(\mathbf{q}_{n-1}, \mathbf{q}_n), \mathbf{q}_{n+1}), \\ \mathbf{b}_n &= \text{double}(\mathbf{a}_n, \mathbf{q}_n). \end{aligned}$$

We may obtain formulae for *bisect*, and *double* as small geometrical exercises *in the plane*. Alternatively, Lemma 9.39 applies in Figure 9.22 (i) below with $\alpha = \beta = \theta$, giving $\mathbf{r}\sin 2\theta$

$= \mathbf{q}\sin\theta + \mathbf{s}\sin\theta$. The stated result follows upon observing that $\sin 2\theta = 2\sin\theta\cos\theta$ and $\cos\theta = \mathbf{q}.\mathbf{r}$. Notice also that, by (8.19), double($\mathbf{q}$,$\mathbf{r}$) is minus the reflection of $\mathbf{q}$ in a line OP through the origin at right angles to $\mathbf{r}$.

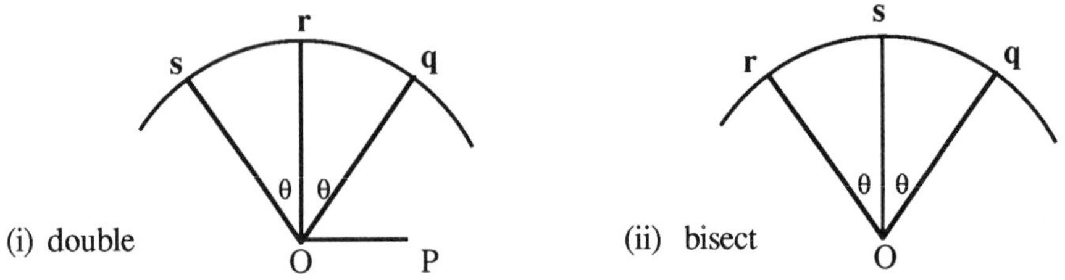

Figure 9.22 (i) $\mathbf{s}$ = double($\mathbf{q}$,$\mathbf{r}$) = $2(\mathbf{q}.\mathbf{r})\mathbf{r} - \mathbf{q}$,
(ii) $\mathbf{s}$ = bisect($\mathbf{q}$,$\mathbf{r}$) = $(\mathbf{q}+\mathbf{r})/|\mathbf{q}+\mathbf{r}|$.

EXERCISE Deduce the formula (ii) above for bisect, from Lemma 9.39.

Agreement of tangents If our interpolation were linear, we would certainly have the magnitude and direction of tangents agreeing as we end one short Bezier curve and enter the next. We now investigate the spherical case via formula (9.37), repeating for convenience Figure 9.18, for a 4-knot Bézier curve.

We need only to determine $\dot{\mathbf{q}}(t)$ at $t = 0$, so we shall leave as an exercise the step by step derivation of $\mathbf{q}(t)$ in terms of $\mathbf{u}_0$, $\mathbf{u}_1$, $\mathbf{u}_2$, $\mathbf{u}_3$ and t. The way is indicated by what follows. Firstly, the spherical linear interpolation formula (9.37) gives, on replacing $\mathbf{r}$ by $\mathbf{q}$ above

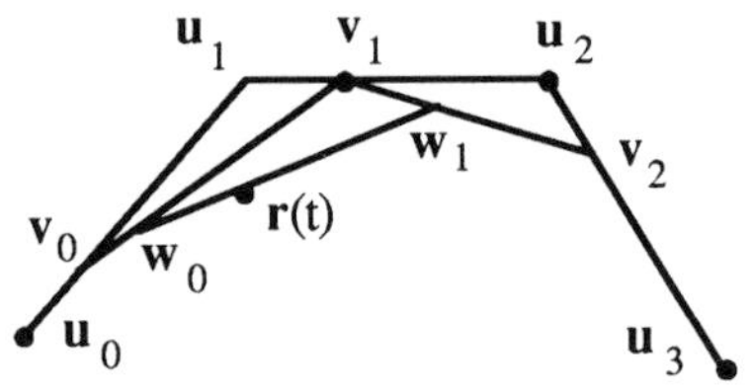

$$\mathbf{q}(t) = g(\theta,t)\mathbf{w}_0 + f(\theta,t)\mathbf{w}_1, \quad \text{where } \cos\theta = \mathbf{w}_0.\mathbf{w}_1, \tag{9.39}$$

and $$f(\theta,t) = \sin\theta t/\sin\theta, \qquad g(\theta,t) = f(\theta,1-t).$$

We note: $\mathbf{w}_0(0) = \mathbf{u}_0$, $\mathbf{w}_1(0) = \mathbf{u}_1$, $\theta(0) = \text{arc}\cos(\mathbf{u}_0.\mathbf{u}_1)$, $= \theta_0$ say,

and $$f(\theta,0) = 0, \quad \frac{\partial f}{\partial t}(\theta,0) = \theta/\sin\theta, \quad \frac{\partial f}{\partial\theta}(\theta,0) = 0,$$

$$g(\theta,0) = 1, \quad \frac{\partial g}{\partial t}(\theta,0) = -\theta\cot\theta, \quad \frac{\partial g}{\partial\theta}(\theta,0) = 0.$$

Now we differentiate (9.39) by the chain rule:

$$\dot{\mathbf{q}}(t) = \left(\frac{\partial g}{\partial\theta}\frac{\partial\theta}{\partial t} + \frac{\partial g}{\partial t}\right)\mathbf{w}_0 + g(\theta,t)\dot{\mathbf{w}}_0 + \left(\frac{\partial f}{\partial\theta}\frac{\partial\theta}{\partial t} + \frac{\partial f}{\partial t}\right)\mathbf{w}_1 + f(\theta,t)\dot{\mathbf{w}}_1.$$

Substituting the values at $t = 0$, we obtain

$$\dot{\mathbf{q}}(0) = -(\theta_0\cot\theta_0)\mathbf{u}_0 + (\theta_0/\sin\theta_0)\mathbf{u}_1 + \dot{\mathbf{w}}_0(0).$$

Similarly

$$\dot{\mathbf{w}}_0(0) = -(\theta_0\cot\theta_0)\mathbf{u}_0 + (\theta_0/\sin\theta_0)\mathbf{u}_1 + \dot{\mathbf{v}}_0(0),$$

$$\dot{\mathbf{v}}_0(0) = -(\theta_0\cot\theta_0)\mathbf{u}_0 + (\theta_0/\sin\theta_0)\mathbf{u}_1 + \dot{\mathbf{u}}_0(0).$$

But of course $\mathbf{u}$ is a fixed point, so $\dot{\mathbf{u}}_0(0) = 0$, and

$$\dot{\mathbf{q}}(0) = 3[-(\theta_0 \cot \theta_0)\mathbf{u}_0 + (\theta_0/\sin \theta_0)\mathbf{u}_1] = 3\dot{\mathbf{v}}_0(0).$$

Now $\dot{\mathbf{q}}(0)$ is a linear combination of $\mathbf{u}_0$ and $\mathbf{u}_1$, and so lies in the plane through the origin and $\mathbf{u}_0, \mathbf{u}_1$. On the other hand $\dot{\mathbf{q}}(0)$ is perpendicular to $\mathbf{q}(0)$ by the standard argument : $\mathbf{q}(t).\mathbf{q}(t) = 1 \Rightarrow 2\mathbf{q}(t).\dot{\mathbf{q}}(t) = 0$. Thus $\dot{\mathbf{q}}(0)$ is tangent to the great arc $\mathbf{u}_0\mathbf{u}_1$ pointing from $\mathbf{u}_0$ to $\mathbf{u}_1$. For the magnitude we have, since $\mathbf{u}_0.\mathbf{u}_0 = 1 = \mathbf{u}_1.\mathbf{u}_1$ and $\mathbf{u}_0.\mathbf{u}_1 = \cos\theta_0$,

$$(1/9)\,\dot{\mathbf{q}}(0).\dot{\mathbf{q}}(0) = \theta_0^2 \cot^2\theta_0 + \theta_0^2/\sin^2\theta_0 - 2\theta_0^2 \cos^2\theta_0/\sin^2\theta_0 = \theta_0^2.$$

Thus the magnitude of the tangent equals three times the length of the arc $\mathbf{u}_0\,\mathbf{u}_1$. This is the analogous result to the 4-knot Bezier case (an extension of the argument to N+1 knots simply replaces 3 by N+1 in both linear and spherical cases). $\dot{\mathbf{q}}(1)$ is similar. Shoemake suggests that, since the factor 3 implies spinning 3 times faster than spherical interpolation (Example 9.43), we should move $\mathbf{a}_n$, $\mathbf{b}_n$ to one third of their original distance from $\mathbf{q}_n$.

REFERENCES ON SPLINES Bartels, Beatty & Barsky (1987), Barsky (1988), Bézier (1972), Burger & Gillies (1989), Faux & Pratt (1979), Foley et al (1990), Rogers & Adams (1990).

EXERCISES 9

---

1 Show that the complex numbers a,b,c satisfy (ab)c = a(bc), where a = 1+**i**, b = 2+**i**, c = 3+**i**.

2 Calculate (5+12**i**)(3+4**i**) and (5+12**i**)/(3+4**i**). Now check that each answer has the correct modulus by |ab| = |a||b|.

3 Prove that multiplication of complex numbers is associative by multiplying out (a+b**i**)(c+d**i**)(e+f**i**) in two ways.

4 √ Find an expression for the conjugate of $(1 + \cos\theta - \mathbf{i}\sin\theta)/(3-\mathbf{i})$ without dividing. Find the real and imaginary parts of (7+13**i**)/(13-7**i**) without dividing.

5 √ Find the four solutions of $z^2+2\bar{z} = 0$, where $z = x+\mathbf{i}y$ ($x,y \in \mathbf{R}$) [$z = 0, -2, 1\pm\mathbf{i}\sqrt{3}$].

6 √ Solve (z+**i**)/(z-**i**) = 2+**i**. [1+2**i**.]

7 √ Find the polar forms of (i) $-\sqrt{3}+\mathbf{i}$, (ii) 1+**i**, (iii) 1-**i**, (iv) $9 + 3\sqrt{3}\mathbf{i}$. Calculate $(-\sqrt{3}+\mathbf{i})^4$ both by De Moivre's Theorem, 9.9, and the Binomial Theorem.

8 Use complex numbers to write as a sum of multiple sines and cosines sin nθ, cos nθ, (i) $\cos^6\theta$, (ii) $\sin^4\theta$, (iii) $\sin^3\theta\cos^4\theta$.

9 (i) List the sixth complex roots of unity and mark them on an Argand diagram. Hence factorise x^6-1 as far as possible into real factors. (ii) Do the same for the fifth roots of unity and x^5-1, writing the factors in terms of the roots of $x^2-x-1 = 0$, namely $\sigma = (1-\sqrt{5})/2$ and $\tau = (1+\sqrt{5})/2 = 2\cos(\pi/5)$.

10 (i) Factorise z^4+1 by solving $z^4 = -1$, (ii) factorise $z^4+\mathbf{i}$.

11 (i) Calculate $(\mathbf{i}+\mathbf{j}+2)^2$. Is the modulus correct? (ii) Calculate $(2\mathbf{i}+\mathbf{j})(1+\mathbf{i})(2-\mathbf{k})$ bracketed both ways.

12 (i) Find which quaternions commute with $\mathbf{k}$, (ii) Use associativity to prove that the multiplication rules (9.15) for $\mathbf{i},\mathbf{j},\mathbf{k}$ are equivalent to $\mathbf{i}^2=\mathbf{j}^2=\mathbf{k}^2 = \mathbf{ijk} = -1$.

13 (i) Find a quaternion square root of -35 with integer coefficients, (ii) find a quaternion $\mathbf{a}$ with integer coefficients whose norm squared is 7. Write down $\mathbf{a}^2$ without any intermediate working.

14 Show that (i) every square root of -2 is pure, (ii) the only quaternion square roots of 1 are ± 1. Find the square roots of $2(\mathbf{i}+\mathbf{j})$. $[\pm(2^{1/4} + 2^{-1/4}(\mathbf{i}+\mathbf{j})]$.

15 Denoting $\mathbf{i},\mathbf{j},\mathbf{k}$ by $\mathbf{e}_1,\mathbf{e}_2,\mathbf{e}_3$, verify the associative law for quaternions by proving equality of the matrices $[(\mathbf{e}_r\mathbf{e}_s)\mathbf{e}_t]$ and $[\mathbf{e}_r(\mathbf{e}_s\mathbf{e}_t)]$ (see the proof of Theorem 9.22(ii)).

16 Deduce the cancellation laws (9.22) from $|\mathbf{ab}| = |\mathbf{a}||\mathbf{b}|$.

17 Calculate the scalar and vector part of $(-\mathbf{i}+\mathbf{j}-\mathbf{k})(\mathbf{j}+\mathbf{k})$ from $\mathbf{xy} = -\mathbf{x}.\mathbf{y} + \mathbf{x} \times \mathbf{y}$ $(S\mathbf{x} = S\mathbf{y} = 0)$. Use this formula to calculate $(2-\mathbf{i}+\mathbf{j}+\mathbf{k})(1-2\mathbf{i}+\mathbf{j}-3\mathbf{k})$. (Check that the norm is correct.]

18 Find the polar forms of the quaternions (i) $\mathbf{j}+\mathbf{k}$, (ii) $1-\mathbf{k}\sqrt{3}$, (iii) $2+\mathbf{i}-\mathbf{j}+\mathbf{k}$. Use De Moivre's Theorem to deduce the cube of each of these quaternions.

19 Use polar forms to show that the quaternions $(1/2)(-1\pm\mathbf{i}\pm\mathbf{j}\pm\mathbf{k})$ are all cube roots of 1. Hence find eight cube roots of -1. Find a fourth root of $\mathbf{i}$ with pure part a real multiple of $\mathbf{i}+\mathbf{j}+\mathbf{k}$.

20 Find the polar form of $t+\sigma\mathbf{i}+\mathbf{j}$ and hence a fifth and a tenth root of unity.

21 Derive the matrix M_R describing right multiplication by a quaternion $\mathbf{a}$ (see 9.3.1). Verify that M_R is orthogonal, $M_R M_R^T = I$, provided $\mathbf{a}$ has norm 1. If $\mathbf{a} = (1/5)(\sqrt{5} + 2\mathbf{j}+4\mathbf{k})$, what is the determinant?

22 (i) Derive the matrix for rotation $T(\mathbf{x}) = \mathbf{axa}^{-1}$ when $\mathbf{a}$ is a unit quaternion, using the matrices M_L and M_R for left and right multiplication by $\mathbf{a}$, (ii) show that this matrix agrees with that derived earlier in Theorem 8.49.

23 Find the quaternion to give rotation $3\pi/2$ about the y-axis and check its effect on all three axes. *Now* determine the matrix (from the formula of Theorem 9.30) and see that it has the same effect.

24 Use quaternions to find the following compositions of rotations in the tetrahedron of Figure 9.11. (i) a 2/3 turn about OB then a 1/2 turn about OF, (ii) a 1/2 turn about OE then a 1/2 turn about OK, where K is the midpoint of BC. In each case, verify your answer if you wish, by the effect on two convenient points not collinear with the origin.

25 √ Use quaternions to find the following compositions of rotations in the cube of Figure 9.12. (i) a 3/4 turn about OX then a 1/3 turn about OC, (ii) a 1/2 turn about OM then a 1/4 turn about OY. In each case, verify your answer if you wish, by the effect on two convenient points not collinear with the origin.

26 Compute independently the rotation quaternions given in Table 9.3. Identify the 2/5 turn about the vertex $(1,0,\tau)$ of an icosahedron (see Tables 9.1, 9.3) with a pair of quaternions listed in Table 9.4.

Chapter 10 FRACTALS AND NATURE

In this first chapter of Part 3, we indicate how fractals arise in nature, explore the aspect of self-similarity and its implications for dimension, and use Mandelbrot's Initiator-generator construction from line segments for a variety of fractal sets, such as the Koch curve. Many of these objects have in recent times changed status from mathematical monster to object of beauty. On our journey we encounter the hitherto infamous but now enlightening plane-filling curves, contradicting old ideas of dimension.

We make a crucial step from geometrical construction of fractal curves to a transformation-oriented description of that process. From this basis, our two examples in Section 10.3.2 point to the remarkable result of Hutchinson (1981) that the final result of such a construction depends not on the starting set, but only on the process. The result is proved in Chapter thirteen after its topological basis (and much else) is established in Chapters eleven and twelve. In Chapter 14 we take up the consequent method for compactly modelling nature by fractals, initiated by the work of Hutchinson and developed by Barnsley (1988) and others. For other approaches see for example Mandelbrot (1983), Peitgen and Saupe (1988), and Lindenmayer-Prusinkiewicz (1990).

But what *is* a fractal? We begin this chapter with a tentative description, and by its end have a working definition (assuming for the present some technical information from Section 15.4).

10.1 Coastlines and dimension

Traditionally and Topologically, a line has dimension 1, so why should coastlines be different? The answer to this question provides a useful introduction to the connection between fractals and nature. We start with a rough idea of a *fractal* as a set whose dimension in the usual sense (1 for a line, 2 for an area, 3 for a volume) misses significant information about the set's intricacy, information which might be retained through a different concept of dimension. Just such a concept is now becoming well established in the

Sciences, and many applications are detailed by Kaye (1989) in a volume of over 400 pages.

Those sets which have come to be regarded as 'fractals' show further detail at every level of magnification, revealing some astonishing effects, such as the reappearing of the whole Mandelbrot set at ever deeper levels within itself (see Colour Plates). The latter example arises in iterating maps of the complex plane (see Chapter 16). The reappearance of a set within itself is even more thoroughgoing in fractal sets which are self similar, and these are the main theme of this chapter. See for example the Koch curve of Figure 10.3, the dragon of Figure 10.11, and Sierpinski gasket of Figure 10.16.

Back to coastlines. The fact is, that the measured length of a coastline or land frontier (henceforth referred to collectively as *'borders'*) depends on the size of your ruler units. This is aptly illustrated by the different lengths of their common frontier given by Belgium and The Netherlands, respectively 449 and 380 Km. The reason is that, as the measurement unit, which we shall call ε, becomes smaller, we pick out greater detail. For a coastline this might be bays and inlets, then subinlets and the shape of jutting cliffs... Figure 10.1 shows the effect of measuring a zigzag line with dividers set at various widths. The reader may like to try out this exercise on other shapes, and indeed on a coastline as presented in an atlas.

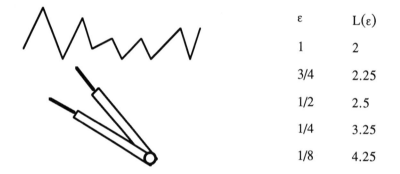

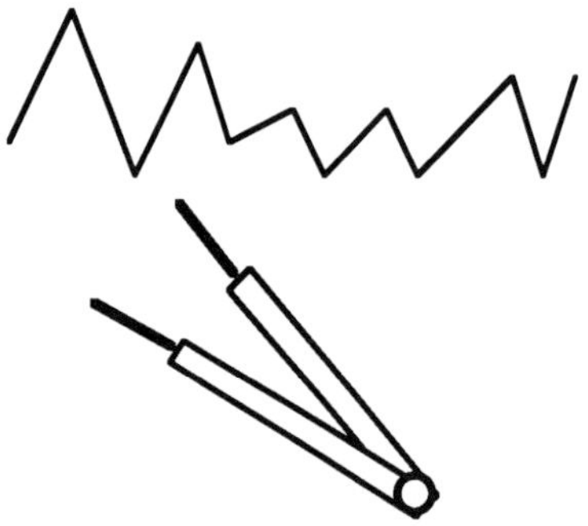

ε	L(ε)
1	2
3/4	2.25
1/2	2.5
1/4	3.25
1/8	4.25

Figure 10.1 Measuring L(ε) for dividers set at width ε. Actual length is about 4.85 inches, or 12.3 centimetres.

We see that, as ε becomes smaller, the measured distance L(ε) approaches the sum of the lengths of the component line segments. How does L(ε) vary with ε for borders the world over? Is there a common theme or structure? The answer is found in the graphs of Figure 10.2 below by L. F. Richardson (1961), who in his day could give no theoretical interpretation for these experimental results. The point to observe is that, within certain limits;

$$\textit{The graph of } \log_{10}(L) \textit{ against } \log_{10}(\varepsilon) \textit{ is a straight line} \tag{10.1}$$

The slope of this line characterises in some way the border it refers to. We will see that the straight line property is explicable on the hypothesis that over a fair range of scales the details of a border look much the same, though they are different details, of a different size. This is formalised in Section 10.3 as the property of *self-similarity,* which in turn leads to a concept of *dimension* D, calculated from the graph slope, and not necessarily a whole number. First, we must reformulate Richardson's result. The straight line graph implies a linear relation.

$$\log_{10} L = a + b \log_{10} \varepsilon \qquad (b < 0), \tag{10.2}$$

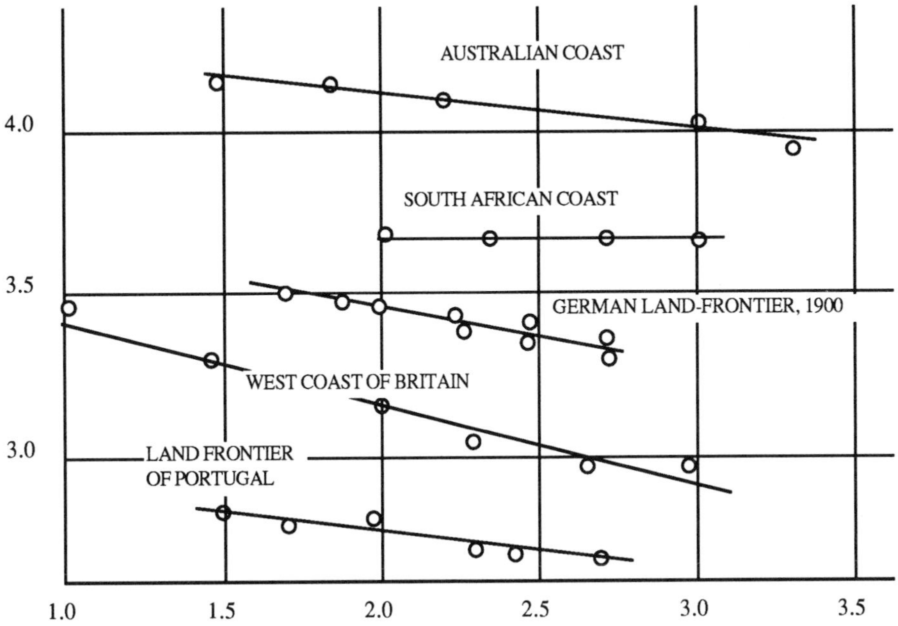

Figure 10.2 Richardson's data on coastline and frontier lengths: $\mathrm{Log}_{10}(\text{Length})$ against $\mathrm{Log}_{10}(\varepsilon)$. Distances are in Kilometers.

in which the slope b is negative. Taking the 10th power of each side, we obtain $L = A\varepsilon^b$ $(A = 10^a)$, or

$$L = A\varepsilon^{1-D}, \quad \text{where} \quad D = 1-b \tag{10.3}$$

But since L equals ε times the number $N(\varepsilon)$ of steps of size ε used to measure L, we have $A\varepsilon^{1-D} = \varepsilon\, N(\varepsilon)$ and so

$$N(\varepsilon) \sim 1/\varepsilon^D, \tag{10.4}$$

where ~ denotes "proportional to".

10.2 Snowflakes, self-similarity, and dimension

10.2.1 Mandelbrot's construction

We begin with a classic example - the snowflake curve $\mathcal{K}$ of Helga von Koch (1904), using Mandelbrot's (1983) *initiator - generator* construction. The construction starts with a rectilinear figure (one made of straight line segments) called the initiator, here simply one line segment. We proceed through a series of stages 1,2,3, ... , at each stage replacing every line segment by a suitably scaled down copy of the generator, itself rectilinear. In the present case the generator C consists of four line segments, each having one third the length of the segment which C will replace. Consequently the total length of the curve is multiplied by a factor 4/3 at each new stage and the length increases without limit.

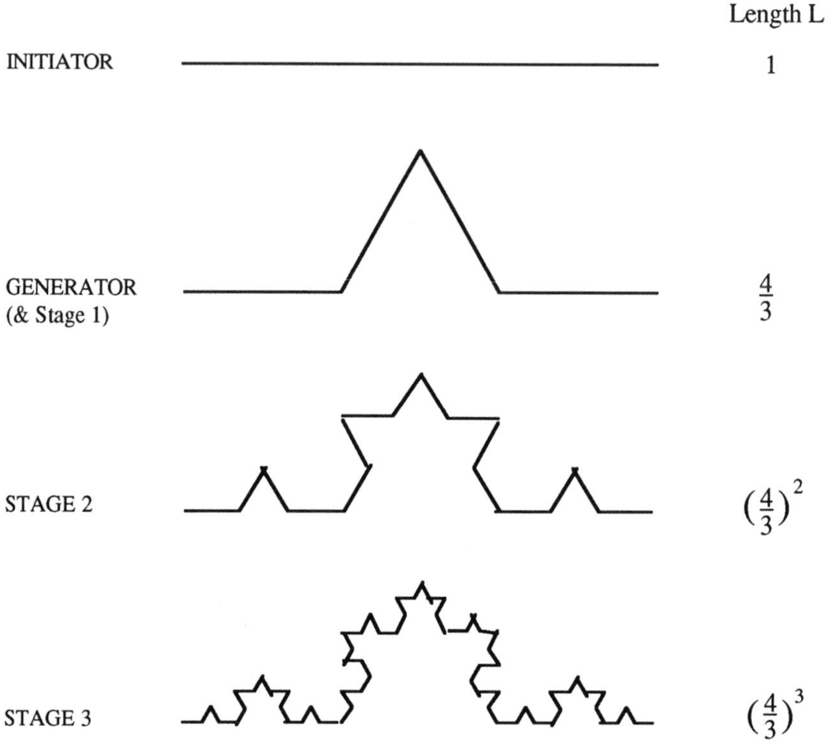

Figure 10.3 Three stages of the Koch curve by Mandelbrot's construction.

However we will show in Chapter 13 that such a process does define a definite 'limit curve', to which we may get as close as desired by taking sufficiently many stages. Figure 10.4 shows three (approximate) Koch curves in a triangle, forming the Koch 'snowflake' .

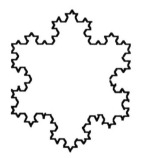

Figure 10.4 An approximation of the Koch snowflake by its third stage.

Two observations are immediate from the construction of the von Koch snowflake curve in Figure 10.3:

(1) Neither the successive approximations nor the limiting curve can cross themselves,

(2) the curve is self-similar, that is, it has the same shape at every level of magnification (shortly to be made more precise).

Of course (2) is not literally true for a snowflake in the real world, nor on the computer or TV screen. It can only hold between certain limits of magnification. For example, if we blow up a coastal detail sufficiently the land-sea boundary becomes ill-defined. On the other hand we can be so far away that the coastline fades into insignificance. We conclude this section with an easy variant of the Koch curve which nevertheless turns out to be quite different in appearance (Figure 10.5). It assumes its essential shape after surprisingly few stages, and the reader is invited to see how this comes about by constructing stages 2,3, 4.

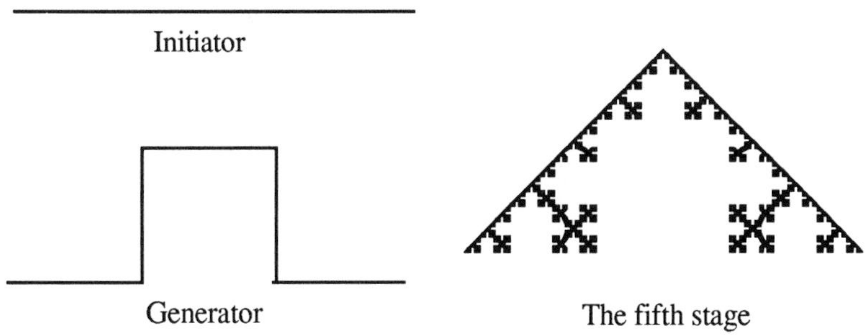

Figure 10.5 'The hat'. Mandelbrot's construction - a generator different from von Koch .

10.2.2 Similarity dimension

Many fractals look the same at every level of magnification, and we will abstract a definition of dimension for this (the self-similar) case from properties of a line segment, square, and cube. The definition allocates respective dimensions 1,2,3 to these latter objects as we would wish. Further details may be found in Mandelbrot (1983), or Voss (1988). Consider Table 10.1 .The generalisation is then: A *D-dimensional self-similar object* is one which can be divided into N smaller copies of itself, each scaled down by a factor

$$r = \frac{1}{N^{1/D}}. \tag{10.5}$$

Notice that each of the N smaller objects, being a scaled down version of the original, may similarly be divided into N smaller copies of itself, and so on ad infinitum. Thus a self-similar object looks the same at every level of magnification. It is understood that, though N may be chosen variously, the relation (10.5) always holds with a corresponding r and the same D. It follows that $r^D = 1/N$, or

$$N = \frac{1}{r^D}, \tag{10.6}$$

which gives the analogy with (10.4) of Richardson's results, r playing the role of ε. Thus in so far as the Richardson graphs are straight lines we may view the corresponding borders as being self-similar. On the other hand, we can calculate the dimension D from the measurable quantities N, r for a self-similar set. Taking logs to any base in (10.6) gives $\log N = D \log(1/r)$, hence

$$D = \frac{\log N}{\log(1/r)}, \tag{10.7}$$

TABLE 10.1 Scaling properties in dimensions 1, 2 and 3.

Dimension	Figure	Result on dividing figure into N equal parts
1	 Line segment	Each part is the original , scaled in the ratio 1/N
2	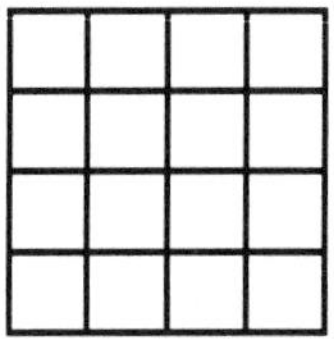 Square	Each part is the original, scaled in the ratio $\frac{1}{N^{1/2}}$
3	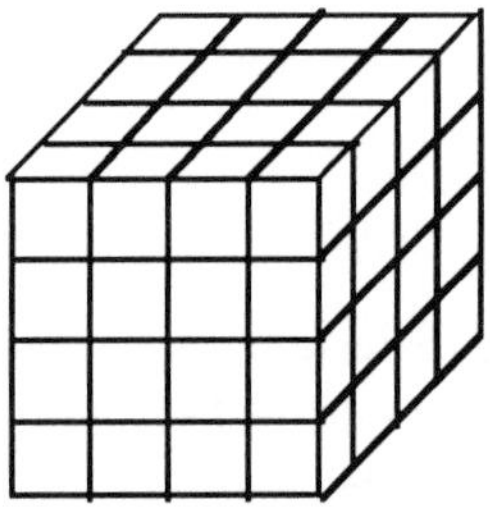 Cube	Each part is the original, scaled in the ratio $\frac{1}{N^{1/3}}$

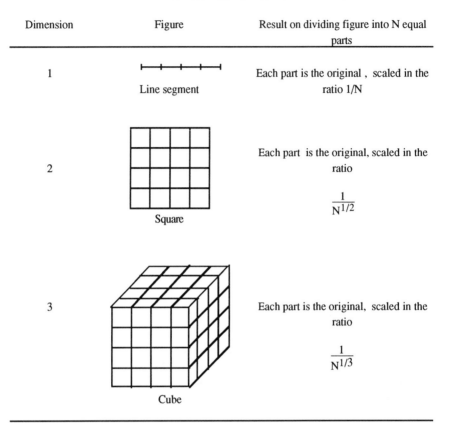

whereas the dimension for a border is obtained from the (negative) slope b of its graph by the relation $D = 1-b$ of (10.3).

EXAMPLE 10.1 The Koch curve is self-similar, as a consequence of the replacement process continuing indefinitely. We have $N = 4$, $r = 1/3$ and so $D = (\text{Log } 4)/(\text{Log } 3) = 1.26...$ This is more than the topological dimension of a line, but less than that of an area.

EXAMPLE 10.2 (Borders yet again.) On the hypothesis that borders are self-similar we have $D = 1-b$, where b is the slope of the graph of Log L against Log ε, and ε the unit of measure. Thus, as observed by Mandelbrot(1983), the Belgian-Dutch frontier has dimension $1 - (-.25) = 1.25$ and the measurement discrepancy of 449 Km on the Belgian side as opposed to 380 on the Dutch is explicable in terms of 'rulers' . Suppose the respective lengths L_1, L_2 are obtained using measurement units of ε_1, ε_2. Then $L = A\varepsilon^b$ from (10.3), with $b = -0.25$, gives $L_1/L_2 = (\varepsilon_1/\varepsilon_2)^{-1/4}$, whence $\varepsilon_2/\varepsilon_1 = 1.95$. The Belgian ruler is twice as long as the Dutch!

EXAMPLE 10.3 For the Koch island, shown in Figure 10.6, each side of the square initiator becomes a self-similar curve with $N = 8$, $r = 1/4$, therefore $D = \log 8/\log 4 = \log_2 8/\log_2 4 = 3/2$ exactly. (Note the convenient rule that the ratio of two logarithms is unchanged if we keep both logarithms to the same base - prove it!)

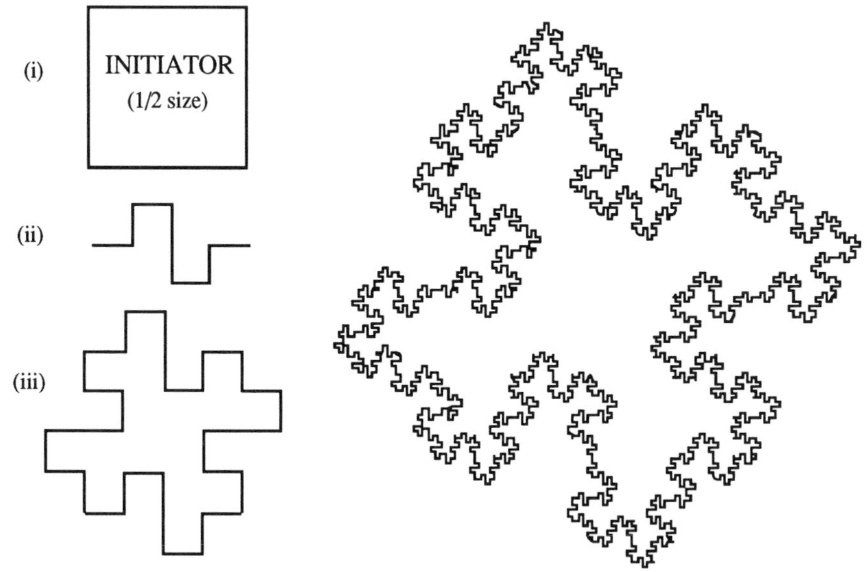

Figure 10.6 The Koch Island (eighth stage) and (i) initiator, (ii) generator, (iii) first stage, all three half size. Its dimension is calculated in Example 10.3.

EXAMPLE 10.4 The Sierpinski curve, whose generator is one half of a regular hexagon, is portrayed in Figure 10.7. It introduces a right-left alternation which was not present in our previous examples of Mandelbrot's construction (replacement was always on the left side). Consider the issue of replacement on the left versus the right, the distinction being defined by direction along the first segment (the initiator), which we may think of as the

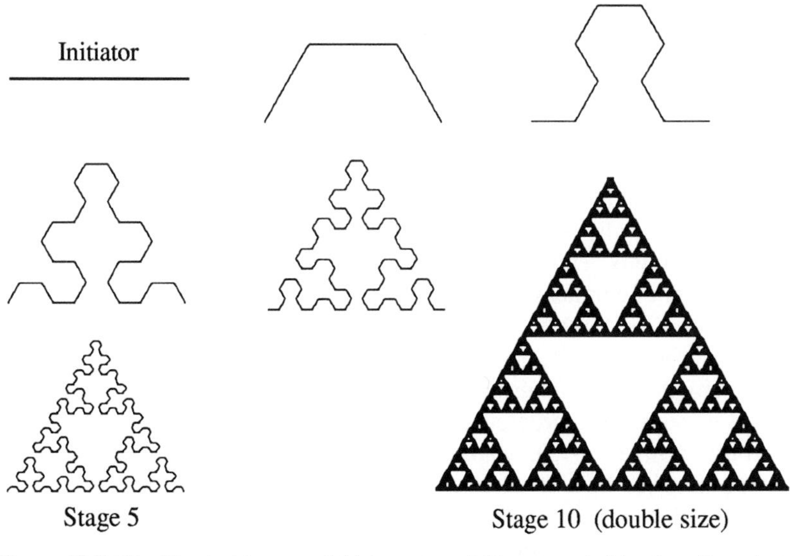

Figure 10.7 The Sierpinski curve. Initiator, stage 1 (the generator) to stage 5, and stage 10. In a stage, the generator replaces successive segments on alternate sides, the global arrangement being by stages: L, RLR, LRLR..., ...

interval [0,1], from 0 to 1 on the x-axis. In the Sierpinski construction, replacement at a given stage is alternatively on the left and the right, but where do we start each time? The answer here is that the first replacement is left for stage 1, right for stage 2, and so on. Symbolically by stages: L, RLR, LRLRLR..., ... The reader is recommended to verify this in Figure 10.7, and then to reconstruct the first few stages without reference to the figure. After a few stages it is evident that the chosen left-right alternation has not held back the tendency of the Mandelbrot construction to give a self-similar result. We have N = 3, r = 1/2, and hence dimension D = log3/log2 = 1.58.., a decent amount greater than 1, as we would expect on seeing stage 10. This remarkable curve exemplifies many aspects of theory and we shall meet it repeatedly in different guises and from different viewpoints. Indeed it first recurs in Section 10.3.2. Because of its appearance the 'curve' is also called the Sierpinski *gasket* (cf. Mandelbrot, 1983).

EXERCISE Calculate the similarity dimension of 'the hat' in Figure 10.5.

10.2.3 Statistical self-similarity

Introducing an element of chance into a construction is liable to give something more, and interesting. Sometimes it gives a very great deal, as in the case of Brownian motion used brilliantly by Mandelbrot and Voss to model landscapes and mountainous terrain. Real coastlines are not exactly self-similar, and we may get a little closer to the reality by introducing an element of randomness into Mandelbrot's construction, for example replacing a line segment by one of two possible generators according to a computerised (or not) toss of the coin. For more information see Mandelbrot (1983), McGregor & Watt (1984), and Voss (1988). Putting the angled part of the generator randomly to left or right in constructing the Koch curve gives a result such as Figure 10.8.

Figure 10.8 Koch construction with generator placed randomly to right or left.

10.2.4 Topological dimension and curves with area

Our discussion of topological dimension in advance of the chapters on topology, though surely in place, is naturally brief. We require a rough idea of *continuous curve* (no jumps), and *area*. Earlier in this century it was assumed that one could define the dimension of a space as the number of continuous parameters required for describing it. An attractive idea, it was much undermined by Peano's invention of a space-filling curve, namely a continuous function from the interval [0,1] in the real line, onto a filled in square (see Kennedy (1973), and Example 10.5). Thus topological dimension was fraught with problems even before fractal dimension entered contention. The situation was saved by Brouwer (see Heyting and Freudenthal, 1975), whose definition of dimension we shall shortly introduce for a set X of points in which the distance d(x,y) between each pair of points x,y is defined. For the axioms a distance is to satisfy, see Definition 11.1. Topological dimension is by definition an integer 0,1,2,.. . This is the key property for the present context, and further details could be left if desired for a second reading (they are more technical than the rest of the chapter). For an extended study see Edgar (1990).

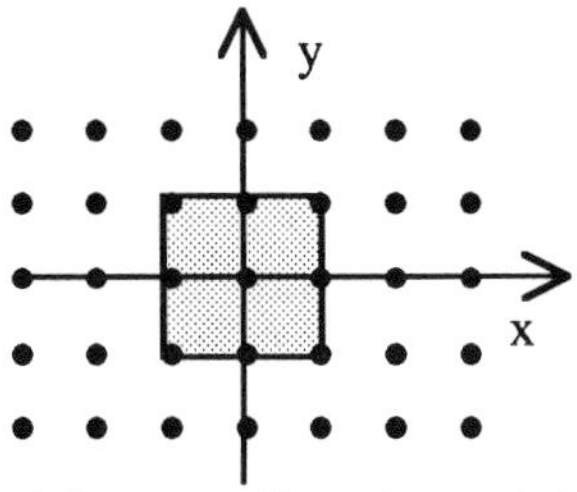

1) We define B_x, the *ball of radius* r *around* x, to be the set of points at distance less than r from x. If X is 3-space then B_x is a ball in the usual spherical sense. In the plane B_x is a disc, and on the line an interval

$$(x-r,\ x+r) = \{y:\ x-r < y < x+r\}.$$

But not all balls are round. For example if X is the space $Z^2 = \{(m,n) \in R^2 :\ m, n \text{ are integers}\}$ then $B_O(2)$ is certainly not a disc; above right, we have represented it as a square, though of course the square is not actually filled with points of Z^2.

(2) The *boundary* ∂A of a subset A of X consists of those points x which are neither 'right in' nor 'right outside' A in this sense: every B_x, however small, contains both points of A and points not in A. Thus $\partial[0,1] = \{0,1\}$. The boundary of a disc in the plane is its circular rim.

(3) A space X has *dimension 0* if every point x of X is *isolated*, that is, some sufficiently small B_x contains no other point of X. Examples are $\{0,1\}$, and Z^2 cited earlier. The space X has dimension n+1 ($n \geq 0$) if each point x of X satisfies: for every $r > 0$, however small, some B_x of radius r has boundary of dimension n.

The real line has dimension 1 for, every point x of it lies in intervals (x-r,x+r) which are arbitrarily short, and whose boundary consists of the 0-dimensional set {x-r,x+r}. Proceeding upward dimension by dimension we see $\mathbf{R}^n$ has dimension n. In any case this definition fixes the outcome as an integer $n \geq 0$ and tells us in turn which spaces have dimension 1, then which have dimension 2, then 3 and so on (not every space need have a well-defined dimension - can you suggest a simple one that does not?). It can be deduced from the definition of dimension that a subspace cannot have greater dimension than the space in which it lies.

EXAMPLE 10.5 Since Peano's original, many curves have been discovered which fill an area of the plane. One such curve which, like Peano's can be obtained by Mandelbrot's construction, is due to Polya, and it fills a triangle. We show in Figure 10.9 the first four stages and the tenth, with endpoints denoted by A, B.

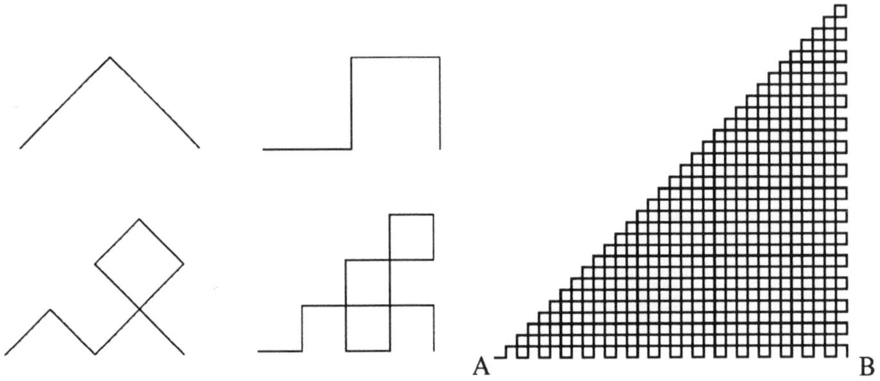

Figure 10.9 First four stages and tenth stage (double size) of Polya's space-filling curve. The end points are A, B. First stage is the generator, which replaces straight segments in successive stages according to the left (L) right (R) formula L, RL, LRLR, RL... .

This construction is one of many in which a line segment is recursively replaced by just two linked segments, always straight lines. This replacement by the generator is on alternate sides, following the same system as the Sierpinski curve of Example 4. Thus by stages: L, RL, LRLR, ... One difference is that the n'th stage in this curve has 2^n segments, compared with 3^n in the Sierpinski case. The reader should find it instructive to check the stages exhibited here.

What about the dimension? This works out very satisfactorily from the similarity dimension formula (10.7), with N = 2 pieces, scaled down from the original in ratio $r = 1/\sqrt{2}$. Thus $D = \log 2/\log(\sqrt{2}) = 2$, as appropriate for a genuine piece of area. The finished product is easily verified to be self-similar, being divided into two $1/\sqrt{2}$ scaled copies of itself by a line bisecting the right angle at B.

EXAMPLE 10.6 The dragon curve is constructed very similarly to Polya's, has dimension 2, and genuinely fills an area, but yet it *looks* dramatically different, suggesting (with a little imagination) a dragon. The only constructional difference is that in each stage alternation starts on the same side. Referring to Figure 10.10, we may represent the process by R, RL, RLRL, ...

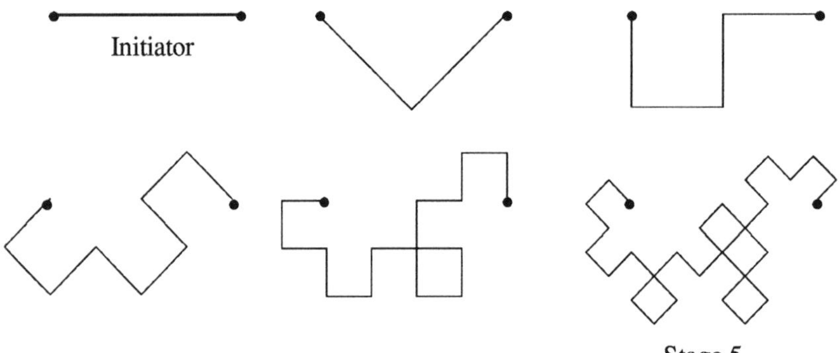

Figure 10.10(a) Dragon curve: generator and first five stages. The first and last point of each stage is emphasised thus •. The alternation is R, RL, RLRL... , ...

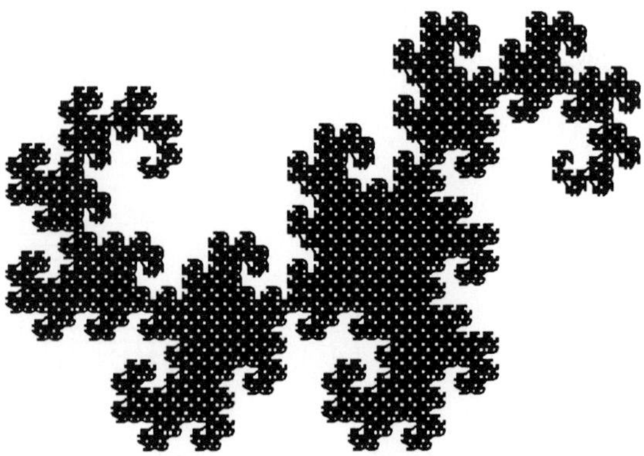

Figure 10.10(b) Complete dragon curve, represented by the fifteenth stage.

EXAMPLE 10.7 (A further construction from the dragon curve.) If a one half turn is applied to a second copy of the dragon then the two copies fit together to form the *twindragon* (see Mandelbrot, 1983), as in Figure 10.11(a).

Figure 10.11(a) The twindragon, formed from the original dragon and a 180° rotated copy. The two halves are shaded differently.

One thing of much interest in the light of Part 1 (Chapters 1 to 6) is that the twin dragon may be tiled by half-sized copies of itself, in the manner indicated in Figure 10.11(b). Thus four tiles make one original. (There is a connection with complex numbers; see Davis and Knuth (1970).)

Figure 10.11(b) The twindragon tiled by scaled down, 90° rotated copies of itself.

EXERCISE Which type of plane pattern is the twindragon tiling of above? [See Section 5.8.]

10.3 Similitudes & generalised similarity

Here we extend the concept of self-similarity by allowing the scaling factor to vary. Now a new viewpoint is most helpful, considering transformations of the plane.

10.3.1 The transformation approach

Imagine we are building a self-similar object such as the Koch curve, stage by stage, as depicted in Figure 10.3. When we take the generator curve C, scale it down, and place that piece in position, we are applying to C a transformation ψ called a *similitude*, a composition of an isometry and a dilation (see below). For information on isometries, see especially Chapters 1 and 2.

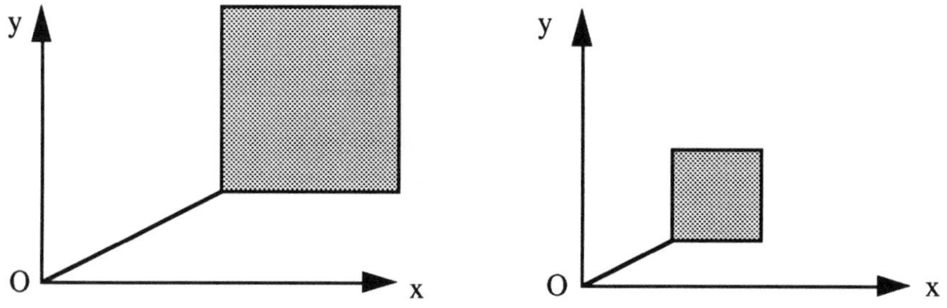

Figure 10.12 Shaded square before and after a dilation with ratio 1/2. Note the halving both of size, and of distance from the dilation centre O.

DEFINITION 10.8 A *dilation* or *uniform scaling* of the plane (with centre the origin) is a transformation of the form ϕ: $\mathbf{x} \to r\mathbf{x}$, where r is a positive number, the *similarity ratio* of ϕ. We think of $\mathbf{x}$ as a vector (x_1,x_2) and then $r\mathbf{x} = (rx_1,rx_2)$. The first thing to observe is that all points are moved radially out from the origin if $r > 1$, and towards the origin if $r < 1$. Thus the precise effect of the dilation depends upon where we choose to locate the origin O.

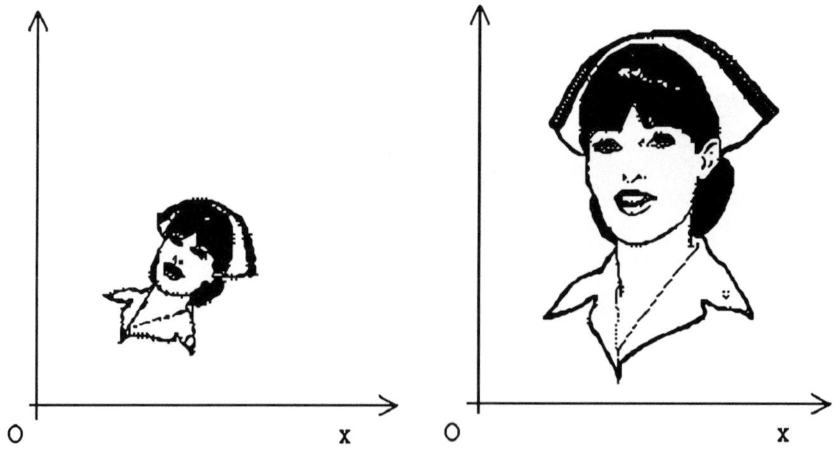

Figure 10.13 Figure in the plane before and after a similitude consisting of a rotation, translation, and dilation.

But secondly, the distance between any two points is scaled in the ratio r, since $|r\mathbf{x} - r\mathbf{y}| = r|\mathbf{x} - \mathbf{y}|$. Thus objects are both scaled in the ratio r, and pulled to r times their original distance from O (similarly for 3-space). If the origin is repositioned so that the centre is at the point with position vector **a**, the map has the expression $\phi(\mathbf{x}) = r\mathbf{x} + (1-r)\mathbf{a}$, by the section formula (1.3). As we indicated, a similitude allows the dilation effect to be composed with translation, rotation, and reflection (or glide). Now let us return to the Koch curve. It is helpful to have right in front of us Figure 10.14, the initiator I and first two stages. The annotations are explained in the ensuing observations.

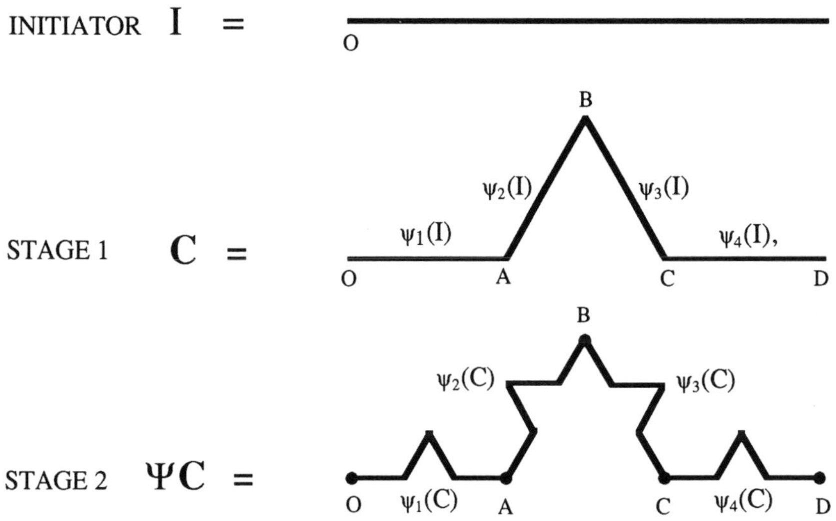

Figure 10.14 Building the Koch snowflake curve by applying similitudes to each stage to obtain the next. Segment OA in stage 1 is replaced by $\psi_1(C)$, whilst AB is replaced by $\psi_2(C)$, and so on. The similarity ratio is 1/3.

Observation 10.9 The generator C is made up of four scaled and rotated and/or translated copies of initiator I, so is expressible as a union $C = \psi_1(I) \cup \psi_2(I) \cup \psi_3(I) \cup \psi_4(I)$ of four sets, the similitudes ψ_i being given by $\psi_1(C)$

$$\psi_1(\mathbf{x}) = \mathbf{x}/3, \qquad \psi_2 = T_{OA}.R_O(\pi/3).\psi$$
$$\psi_3 = T_{OC}.R_O(2\pi/3).\psi_1, \qquad \psi_4 = T_{OC}.\psi_1,$$

where we write mappings in their reverse order of performance. We remind the reader that $R_O(\theta)$ denotes rotation through angle θ about O, and T_{AB} is the translation $\mathbf{x} \to \mathbf{x} + \underline{AB}$ for any vector $\underline{AB}$. (cf. Notation 1.4. We do not require the subscript AB to be underlined.) It is instructive to note that by Theorem 1.10 there is a unique similitude involving no reflection which maps I to any given segment of C and therefore, however arrived at, the ψ_i we have written down is that similitude.

Observation 10.10 The same set of similitudes, now applied to Stage 1, yield the Stage 2 curve, which is therefore the union $\psi_1(C) \cup \psi_2(C) \cup \psi_3(C) \cup \psi_4(C)$. In fact each stage may be obtained from the previous one in this way.

Observation 10.11 The self-similarity of the Koch curve $\mathcal{K}$, as a union of four scaled down versions of itself, may be expressed thus: $\mathcal{K} = \psi_1(\mathcal{K}) \cup \psi_2(\mathcal{K}) \cup \psi_3(\mathcal{K}) \cup \psi_4(\mathcal{K})$.

It follows that the Koch curve, and indeed the others we have formed by Mandelbrot's construction, are special cases for the following definition.

DEFINITION 10.12 Let $\psi_1, .., \psi_N$ be similitudes in the plane, with ratios $r_1, ..., r_N$. For a plane set E the set ΨE is defined by

$$\Psi E = (\psi_1 E) \cup (\psi_2 E) \cup ... \cup (\psi_N). \tag{10.8}$$

Then we say E is *self-similar with respect to* the similitudes ψ_i, or *invariant under* Ψ, if

$$\Psi E = E, \tag{10.9}$$

and provided the sets $\psi_i E$ do not have area overlap (no intersection contains a disc $B_{\mathbf{a}}(r) = \{\mathbf{x}: |\mathbf{x} - \mathbf{a}| < r\}$, for any point **a** and radius r). Thus in the special case where all the ratios r_i are equal, say $r_i = r$, E is self-similar in the ordinary sense (10.5). That is, E is the union of N non-(area)overlapping sets, each congruent to a copy of E scaled down in the ratio r. Having introduced the similitude approach we will look at two further important examples of self similarity in this schema. Note that in any case this curve-forming process is equivalent to starting with an initiator and repeatedly applying a function Ψ of the form (10.8). As a function, Ψ acts on the collection of all subsets of the plane, sending each subset E to a new subset ΨE. We pick up this theme again in Chapter 13. Later we shall emphasise the name *collage map* for Ψ, to recall the fact that it forms a union or 'collage' of sets, (10.8).

EXERCISE Write down suitable similitudes ψ for the Sierpinski curve [cf. (10.11)].

10.3.2 Two classics - Cantor and Sierpinski

Before varying the ratios we shall study the effect of repetitions of Ψ, firstly in a famous 1-dimensional case, the set $\mathcal{C}$ described by Cantor in 1883. In this context, let I denote as before the *closed unit interval*, I = [0,1]. *Closed* implies that the endpoints 0,1 are included, as distinct from an *open* interval (a,b) = $\{x: a < x < b\}$, with endpoints excluded. It is instructive to see why the following three constructions for $\mathcal{C}$ give the same result.

CONSTRUCTION 10.13 This is the classical definition, in which we start with the unit interval I, *delete the open middle third* (1/3, 2/3), then perform this deletion recursively on every line segment remaining. The first few stages are shown in Figure 10.15.

CONSTRUCTION 10.14 $\mathcal{C}$ consists of all points in I which can be written as ternary decimals $0.d_1d_2d_3 ... = \Sigma d_i 3^{-i}$ (i = 1,2,3, ...), with d_i taking the values 0 and 2 but not 1. This includes, for example, 20/27 = 2/3 + 2/27 = 0.202000... .

CONSTRUCTION 10.15 Mandelbrot's construction, with initiator and generator shown in the first two lines of Figure 10.15 below. In transformation terms it is convenient to use subscripts 0, 2 and to define $\psi E = (\psi_0 E) \cup (\psi_2 E)$, where $\psi_0(\mathbf{x}) = \mathbf{x}/3$, $\psi_2(\mathbf{x}) = \mathbf{x}/3 + 2/3$ and, begining with E = I, apply ψ repeatedly. The labelled stages indicate how this works. Note that $\psi_0\psi_2 I$ has ψ_2 performed first.

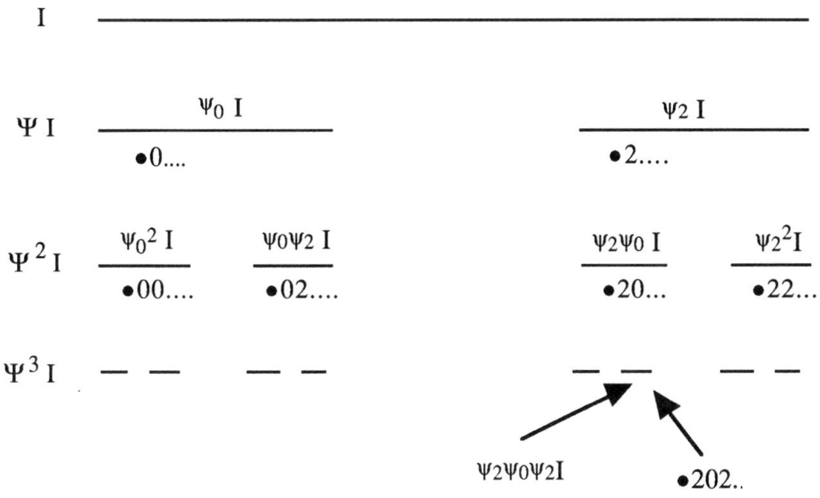

Figure 10.15 Successive approximations to the Cantor set. Note the correspondence between $\psi_0\psi_2$ (ψ_2 done first) and the points with ternary expansion .02...., and so on.

The equivalence of Constructions 10.13 (removing middle thirds) and 10.15 (applying Ψ) may be seen in Figure 10.15. A segment labelled •abc... for example consists of all points whose ternary expansion begins this way, and lies in the image set $\psi_a\psi_b\psi_c(I)$. We may demonstrate the equivalence of Construction 10.14, the ternary decimal, with Construction 10.15 by noting that

$$\begin{aligned}\psi_0(\bullet abc...) &= \bullet 0abc..., \quad \text{whilst}\\ \psi_2(\bullet abc...) &= \bullet 2abc.. \,.\end{aligned}$$

Further, these equalites give

$$C = (\psi_0 C) \cup (\psi_2 C),$$

which equals ΨC by definition, and so C satisfies the condition (10.9) for self-similarity with respect to the transformations ψ_0, ψ_2. For a formal proof of this last assertion we have, taking the ternary decimal form of C, $x \in C \Leftrightarrow x = 0.abc...$(where a,b,c, .. = 0 or 2) $\Leftrightarrow$ $x = 0.0bc...$ or $x = 0.2bc...$ (b,c, .. = 0 or 2) $\Leftrightarrow$ x lies in the union $(\psi_0 C) \cup (\psi_2 C)$.

The Cantor set is self-similar.

EXERCISE Fill in the ψ and ternary labels for the third stage of Figure 10.15.

Because ψ_0, ψ_2 have the same ratio, 1/3, Formula (10.7) gives a value of similarity dimension for the Cantor set, namely log2/log3 = 0.63.. This is less than one, reflecting the idea that the set is akin to a fine dust. Indeed the name *Cantor dust* was coined by Mandelbrot for other sets with a similar sparing spread. This section previews a more detailed development and application in Chapter 15 (address space and the Random Iteration Algorithm). In the next section we define similarity dimension more generally, but a comment called for right now is this: we observed that in some sense the successive $\Psi^k I$ get ever closer to C. It seems reasonable to write

$$\Psi^k I \rightarrow C \quad \text{as } k \rightarrow \infty, \quad or \quad \lim \Psi^k I = C. \tag{10.10}$$

This notation will be given a precise meaning, and the exploration of its significance and truth for fractals begun, in Chapter 13.

Comparison with Sierpinski Here we point back to what has been and forward to what is to come. Looking at the result of the Sierpinski construction, it appears that we could obtain this analogously to the Cantor deletion of middle thirds (Construction 10.13). Namely that we start with a filled-in equilateral triangle E_0 and first remove what we may call the 'middle fourth', the triangle whose vertices are the midpoints of the edges of E_0. This gives E_1 as shown in Figure 10.16. For the second stage E_2 we remove the middle fourth from each triangle of E_1 And so on.

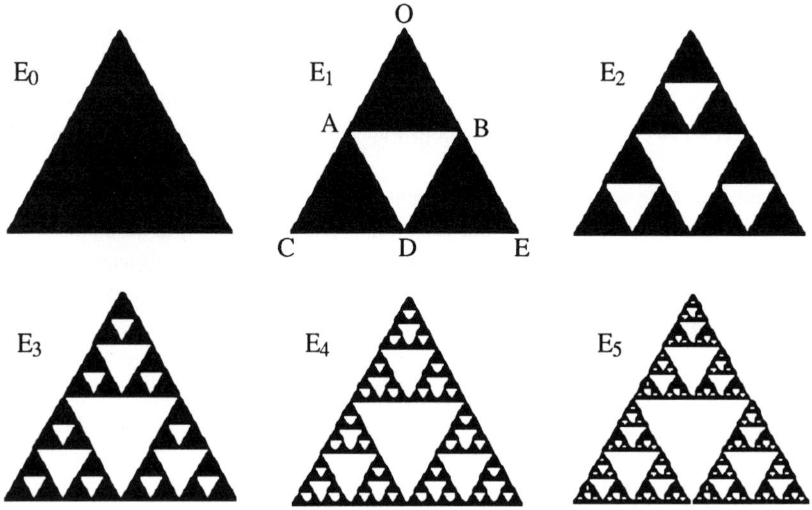

Figure 10.16 Recursively removing the middle fourth triangle to obtain the Sierpinski 'curve' or gasket.

Can we express this as a building up process in terms of similitudes, as we did in Cantor set Construction 10.15? Most certainly. Here are three similitudes which we *could* have used for the original Sierpinski construction (with I as the triangle's base) and which yield E_1, E_2, starting from the filled in triangle E_0. For this we'll *take the origin as the top vertex* and let A, B be midpoints of its adjacent sides, with C, D, E as indicated. Then

$$\begin{aligned} \psi_1(\mathbf{x}) &= \mathbf{x}/2, & \psi_1(E_0) &= \text{triangle OAB}, \\ \psi_2 &= R_A(-1/3)\,.\,\psi_1, & \psi_2(E_0) &= \text{triangle ACD}, \\ \psi_3 &= R_B(+1/3)\,.\,\psi_1, & \psi_3(E_0) &= \text{triangle BDE}. \end{aligned} \tag{10.11}$$

Notice that three natural ψ_i's which give the stages of Figure 10.16 are the dilations ψ_P towards vertex P with ratio 1/2, for P = O,C,E. However these do not suit our present purpose for, starting with initiator I = [0,1], they do not give the Sierpinski curve *stages* shown in Figure 10.7 (try it). Yet this serves only to highlight what we shall prove in Chapter 13, that we must eventually obtain the same figure, albeit by a different route, since the result depends only on the transformations used. The significance of this fact will become more apparent, especially from Chapter 14 on, when we exploit it more fully in the imitation of nature by fractals derived from iterated function systems.

GENERAL SIERPINSKI There is a Sierpinski gasket for every shape of triangle, obtained by deleting the middle fourth triangle as before. The case of a right angled triangle is shown in Figure 13.1

EXERCISE Verify that the similitudes just used for Figure 10.16 do give the successive stages of the Sierpinski curve (Figure 10.7).

10.3.3 Generalised similarity dimension

Now we extend the definition of similarity dimension to allow varying ratios. Self-similarity in this generalised sense was described in Definition 10.12. We recall that ordinary similarity dimension D is defined in terms of the similarity ratio r, and number of copies N of the scaled object making up itself, by $Nr^D = 1$, which we may rewrite suggestively as $r^D + r^D + \dots + r^D = 1$. It is thus reasonable to define *generalised similarity dimension* for a self-similar set with similarity ratios $r_1, r_2, \dots, r_N$, by

$$r_1^D + r_2^D + \dots + r_N^D = 1. \tag{10.12}$$

EXAMPLE 10.16 The twindragon skin of Figure 10.17 is so named because of its relation to the twindragon of Figure 10.12. Here the three segments of the generator connote similitudes with ratios $r_1 = 1/2\sqrt{2}$, $r_2 = 1/\sqrt{2}$, $r_3 = 1/2\sqrt{2}$. Therefore by (10.12) its dimension D satisfies

$$\left(\frac{1}{2\sqrt{2}}\right)^D + \left(\frac{1}{\sqrt{2}}\right)^D + \left(\frac{1}{2\sqrt{2}}\right)^D = 1,$$

hence $(\sqrt{2})^{-D} = x$, where $2x^3 + x - 1 = 0$. The left hand side has derivative $6x^2 + 1$, which is always positive, confirming that the equation has a unique root, approximately D =1.524 (see Example 13.22 for a reminder of Newton's method for solving a polynomial equation).

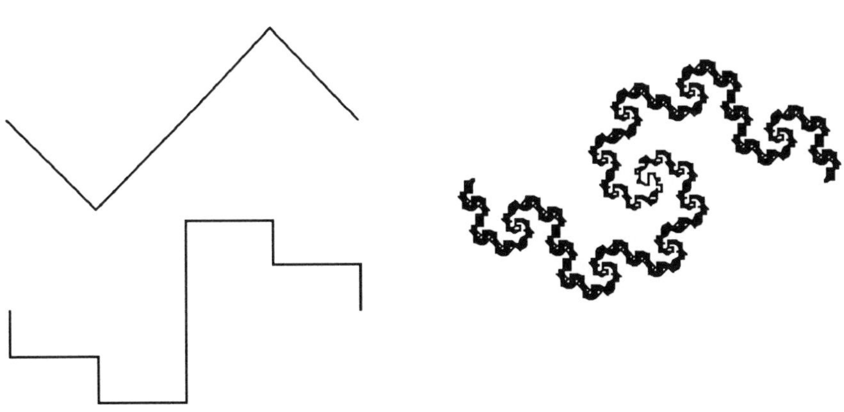

Figure 10.17 The twindragon skin. Initiator, two stages, and final result.

EXERCISE Find expressions for the similitudes ψ_i in the twindragon case.

EXAMPLE 10.17 A neat self-similar set suggested by Falconer (1990) is represented in Figure 10.18.

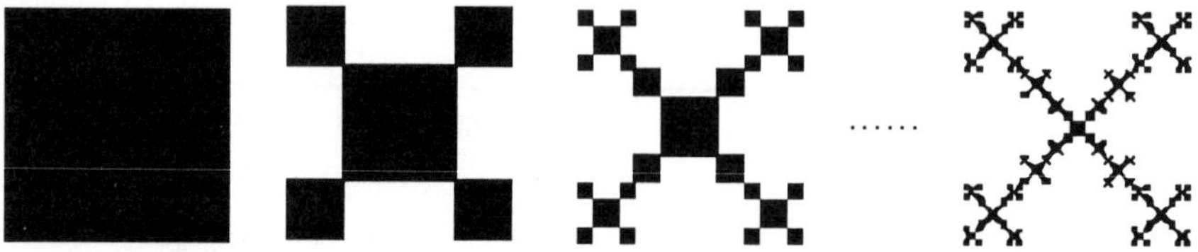

Figure 10.18 A self-similar object with four ratios 1/4 and one ratio 1/2. We show the solid square initiator, first two stages, and final result.

EXERCISE Determine the generalised similarity dimension of the self-similar set above.

We end this chapter as we began, with the question 'what is a fractal?'. Mandelbrot both coined the word, from the Latin *fractus*, meaning *broken*, and gave a working definition which includes most sets that seem to deserve the name, and which we are now in a position to at least understand for the examples given so far. We need to note that, as we discover in Section 15.4 generalised self-similarity dimension is a special case of Hausdorff dimension, which requires a rather technical definition, but applies to all the sets, self-similar or not, which we shall wish to consider. We conclude with the requisite definition.

DEFINITION 10.18 A *fractal*, or *fractal set*, is one whose Hausdorff dimension differs from (Mandelbrot 'is greater than') its topological dimension. For more, see Section 15.4.

In particular the Koch and Sierpinski curves are fractals, whilst the plane-filling curves, monsters that they may be, are not, since they have similarity dimension 2. For further discussion on the meaning of 'fractal' see Edgar (1990), Falconer (1990), and of course its inventor Mandelbrot (1983).

PROJECT Use 'turtle graphics' to produce the curves of this chapter. Commercial programs are available, but it is instructive, and easily done, to implement the individual turtle operations in Pascal code. See for example Becker and Dörfler (1990).

EXERCISES 10

---

1 √ The realms of Greatfract and Littlefract disagree as to the length of their common border, the first measuring it as 185 koch units and the second as 160. How might this discrepancy be explained in terms of their ruler lengths (Research gives a Richardson graph of slope –0.30)?

2 Choose on a suitably scaled map, a coastline or border and, using dividers, obtain a plot of log(ε) against ε, where ε is as usual the 'ruler length' set by the dividers. Approximating the plot by a straight line, estimate the dimension of the chosen boundary.

3 This 'C-curve' results from a single segment initiator, and generator as indicated. Calculate the similarity dimension.

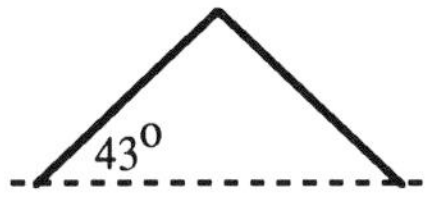

4 Determine the first four stages and the similarity dimension of the 'hat' curve in Figure 10.5.

5 (i) Construct for yourself the first four stages of the Sierpinski curve (Figure 10.7). (ii) Estimate how the final result would look if segments were always replaced on the left.

6 (i) Sketch the first five stages of the 'C-curve' with initiator the hypotenuse, and generator the rest of an isosceles right angled triangle, replacement being always to the left (cf. Figure 10.9). (ii) Repeat, but with replacement scheme L, RR, LLLL, ... What do you expect the final outcome to look like? What is its dimension? (Mandelbrot calls this curve the *Cesaro triangle sweep*, after its inventor.)

7 (i) Draw the first four stages of the Dragon curve (Figure 10.10) with replacement scheme changed to L, LR, LRLR, ... How do these stages relate geometrically to the originals? (ii) Which of the seventeen plane pattern types is obtained in the tiling of the twindragon (Figure 10.11)?

8 (i) Write down suitable similitudes for constructing the stages of the Sierpinski curve shown in Figure 10.7. (ii) Find similitudes for constructing the Sierpinski curve ('gasket') from a solid triangle. Ensure that they also give the curve stages of Figure 10.7. [One answer is given in (10.11).]

9 (i) Continue the construction and labelling of the Cantor set (Figure 10.15). Can you put in similar labelling for stages 1 and 2 of the Sierpinski construction from a solid triangle (Figure 10.16)?

10 √ (i) Find expressions for similitudes suitable for constructing the Twindragon skin curve (Figure 10.17). (ii) Determine the generalised similarity dimension of the set in Figure 10.18.

Chapter 11 BASIC TOPOLOGY

This is Topology with a specific application in mind. We wish not only to explain, but to show *why* certain remarkable techniques work. In particular some equation-solving methods (Sections 13.2.2 and 16.4), the similarity techniques of the previous chapter, the imitation of nature by iterated function systems (Chapter 14), and the Mandelbrot and Julia sets (Chapter 16).

11.1 Metric spaces

The most important 'spaces' for us are the familiar Euclidean spaces, the real line **R**, plane $\mathbf{R}^2$, 3-space $\mathbf{R}^3$, and more generally, as reviewed in Section 7.1.5, n-dimensional Euclidean space $\mathbf{R}^n = \{(x_1, x_2, \ldots, x_n)$: each x_i is in $\mathbf{R}\}$ with the *Pythagorean distance*

$$d(\mathbf{x},\mathbf{y}) \;=\; |\mathbf{x}-\mathbf{y}| \;=\; \sqrt{(x_1 - y_1)^2 + \ldots + (x_n - y_n)^2}\,. \qquad (11.1)$$

where $\mathbf{x} = (x_1, x_2, \ldots, x_n)$ denotes a typical point, defined by its coordinates x_i. Topology has been described as 'Rubber sheet geometry', where objects are considered the same if one can be stretched into the shape of the other. For example a doughnut is a sphere with one handle, a pretzel is a sphere with two handles. This may be seen with a little imagination in Figure 11.1 below, and is handled more rigorously in Section 11.6.

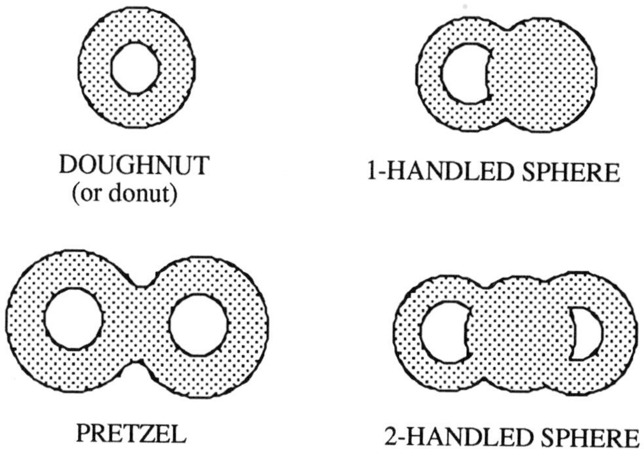

Figure 11.1 The top two objects are topologically the same, as are the bottom two.

Notice that these are all objects in Euclidean 3-space. What the doughnut and the sphere with one handle have in common is that close points in the one correspond to close points in the other, under a bijective mapping between them called a homeomorphism (cf. Definition 11.46), which carries out the necessary stretching. Angles, and straightness need not be preserved, yet stretching does not include breaking, and consequently holes in one object correspond to holes in the other. A fuller description begins with Definition 11.1.

EXERCISE In what sense do the pretzel and 2-handled sphere in Figure 11.1 have 3 holes?

11.1.1 From distance to open sets

Closeness in a general topological space X is defined via open sets. In a full generality which we shall not usually require, X is a set with a rule for deciding which subsets fall in a special class called *open*, in such a way that suitable axioms hold. Namely that the empty set ø, and X, are open sets, as is any arbitrary union or finite intersection of open sets. We specialise as is normally done in the fractals context, to metric spaces, in which openness is derived from the distance between points and the axioms become Property 11.4. We shall shortly define metric spaces and show that they include Euclidean n-space, but we shall see later how some important fractal results come from non-obvious spaces and their distances (see Chapter 13ff).

DEFINITION 11.1 A *metric space* is a pair (X,d), where X is a nonempty set and d is a real function on pairs of points, called *distance*, or a *metric*, satisfying for all x,y,z in X:

(a) $d(x,y) > 0$ if $x \neq y$, and $d(x,y) = 0$ if $x = y$.

(b) *Symmetry* : $d(x,y) = d(y,x)$.

(c) *The triangle inequality* $d(x,z) \leq d(x,y) + d(y,z)$.

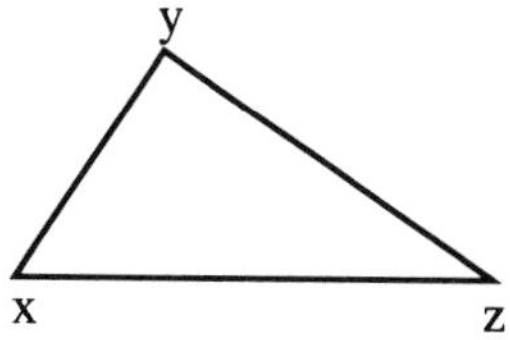

CONVENTION We often say 'X is a metric space', d being understood, or that X is a metric space with respect to distance d. We may also refer to conditions (a) to (c) as

AXIOMS 1 to 3 for a metric space. From now on, all spaces will be metric unless otherwise stated. It is easy to verify that a Euclidean space with the usual distance function (11.1) is a metric space. The triangle inequality (already proved as Remark 7.12) is named after its plane version, in which the length of one side of a triangle does not exceed the sum of the lengths of the other two sides. To define open sets in a metric space X we require the following notation, where the *radius* r is positive.

The *sphere*	$S_a(r)$	$= \{x \in X: d(a,x) = r\}$,
The *open ball*	$B_a(r)$	$= \{x \in X: d(a,x) < r\}$,
The *closed ball*	$B_a[r]$	$= \{x \in X: d(a,x) \le r\}$.

The contrast between $d < r$ and $d \le r$ is typical of the difference between open and closed, as will shortly appear. This motivates the use of round versus square brackets by analogy with the open interval (a,b) and closed interval [a,b]. cf. Examples 11.3 below. We note that an *interval* is a ball in the real line, whilst *disc* (*circle*) refers to a ball (sphere) in the plane.

DEFINITION 11.2 We refer to Figure 11.2. Let X be a metric space. Then a subset A of X is ***open*** if every point a of A is in some open ball $B_a(r)$ contained within A. In particular the empty set ø and the whole of X are open sets. For example we can safely say that every point in ø is in the required open ball, since there *are* no points in ø. Note that, given the point a, the phrase 'some $B_a(r)$' means '$B_a(r)$ for some radius r'. If we need to specify which of several metrics d, d_1, .. is being used, we will describe as *d-open*, *d_1-open*, and so on.

EXERCISE Explain how X satisfies the definition of openness.

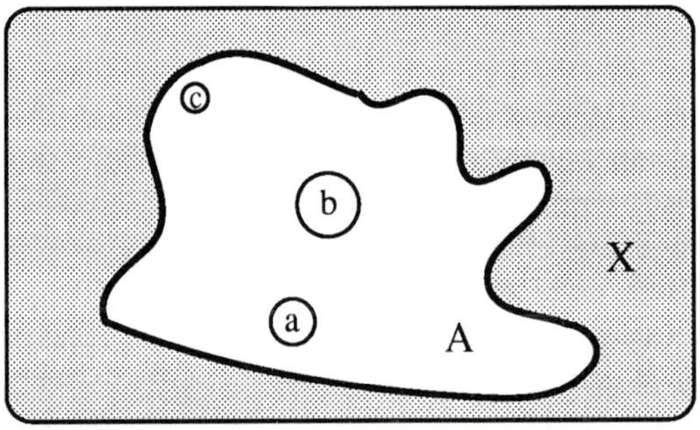

Figure 11.2 Points a,b,c surrounded by open balls in a subset A of X (X is represented by the whole rectangle, A is the unshaded part).

EXAMPLES 11.3 (Some open sets.) (1) An *'open interval'* $A = (\alpha,\beta) = \{x: \alpha < x < \beta\}$, on the real line.

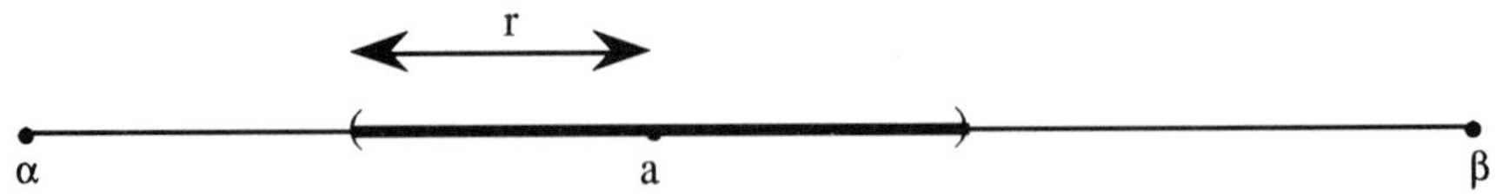

To prove that A is open, as implied by its name, let a be any point of A, both illustrated above. Then a is distinct from α and β, so if $r = (1/2)\min(a-\alpha, \beta-a)$ then the open ball $B_a(r)$ lies inside A. Thus Definition 11.2 is satisfied and A is open. Notice that the factor 1/2 is not necessary. It is added to obtain a more convincing illustration above. Note also the use of round brackets to indicate the limits of the open ball, compared with square brackets for the closed ball (cf. Examples 11.11). Under this heading we may include the infinite intervals, with *a* replaced by the symbol $-\infty$ and/or *b* replaced by ∞. Thus $(-\infty,b)$ represents $\{x: x < b\}$, and so on. The proof of openness in this case is a convenient exercise for the reader.

(2) An *'open Ball'* $B_a(r)$.

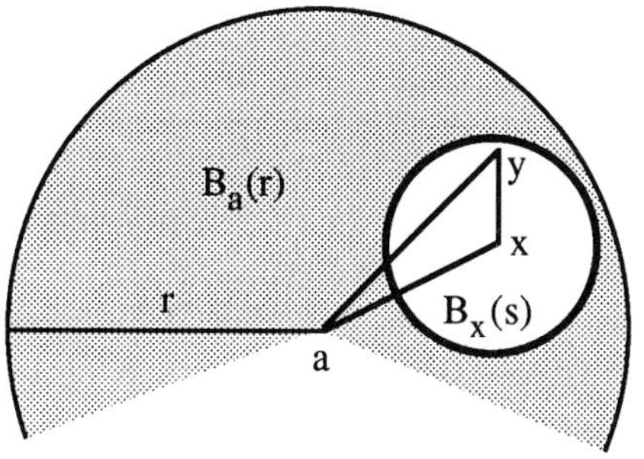

We stress that the open intervals just considered in (1) are the special case of an open ball in which the metric space X is the real line. The diagram here is modelled on the plane but since we are assuming only a general metric space a proof must be based on the distance properties in Definition 11.1. However, with the diagram to aid our intuition this takes very little more work than the plane case (cf. the Exercise below). With labelling as in the diagram, let x be in $B_a(r)$. We define the required open ball $B = B_x(s)$ round x by its radius $s = r - d(x,a)$. Then for any point y in B,

$$\begin{aligned} d(y,a) &\le d(y,x) + d(x,a), && \text{by Definition 11.1(c),} \\ &\le s + d(x,a), && \text{as y is in B,} \\ &= r, && \text{by definition of s.} \end{aligned}$$

Thus B lies within $B_a(r)$, and the proof is complete.

(3) The *half-plane* H_1: $x_1 < \alpha$, with plane coordinates (x_1,x_2). In fact, any strict linear inequality $a_1x_1 + \ldots + a_nx_n < 0$ in general n-space defines an open set, as the reader is invited to prove in Exercise 36 at the end of the chapter. In the present case, any point $x = (x_1,x_2)$ is in an open ball $B_x(r)$ lying within H_1, where $r = (a-x_1)/2$ [$r = a-x_1$ would do].

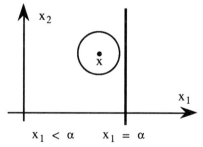

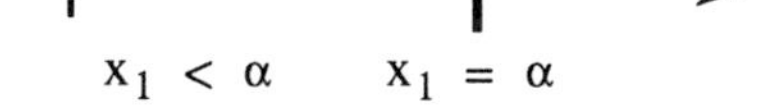

EXERCISE Write down a set that is open and one that is not. What about $A = \{a\}$?

11.1.2 Union, intersection, and basis

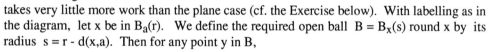

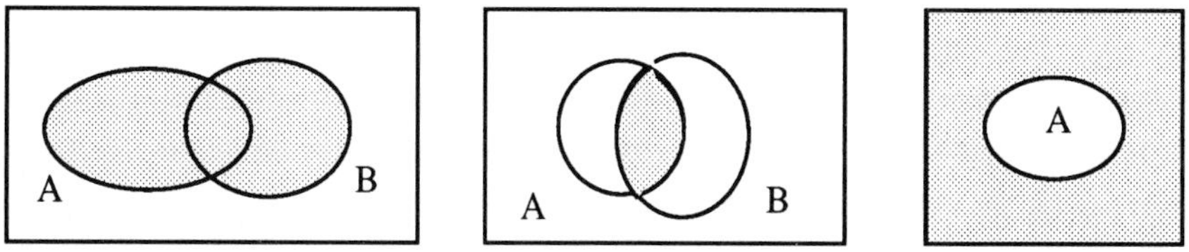

$A \cup B$ shaded $A \cap B$ shaded A^c shaded

Figure 11.3 Basic set operations: intersection, union, and complement.

PROPERTY 11.4
(a) Any union of open sets is open,
(b) The intersection of a finite number of open sets is open.

Proof (a) Any point x in a union of open sets is contained in at least one of them, say A. Since A is open, we have $x \in B_x(r)$, lying within A for some r. Since the ball is in A, it is in the set union, so Definition 11.2 is satisfied.
(b) This is different because we cannot guarantee to produce an open ball lying in the intersection of arbitrarily many sets of decreasing 'size' (cf. the counterexample below). Suppose x is in $A \cap B$, the intersection of two open sets in X. Then for some radii r_1, r_2 we have both $x \in B_x(r_1) \subseteq A$ and $x \in B_x(r_2) \subseteq B$.

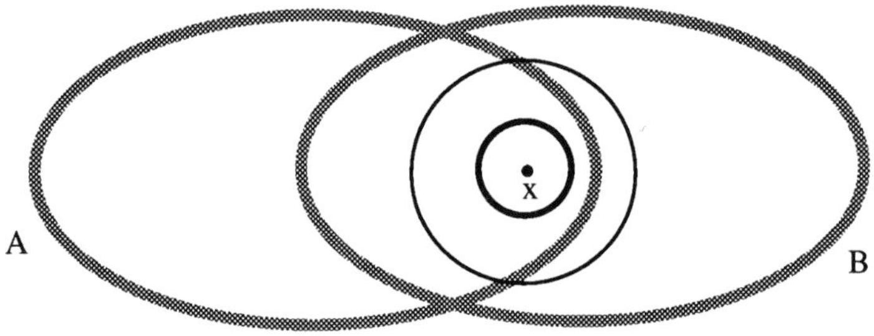

One of these balls lies inside the other, and hence within both A and B as portrayed above, since they have a common centre x. Taking $r = \min(r_1, r_2)$ gives $x \in B_x(r) \subseteq A$. Thus $A \cap B$ is open, and the argument may be repeated any finite number of times. For example if C is another open subset of X then so is $(A \cap B) \cap C = A \cap B \cap C$.

COUNTEREXAMPLE We give an example to show that the intersection of an *infinite* number of open sets need not be open.

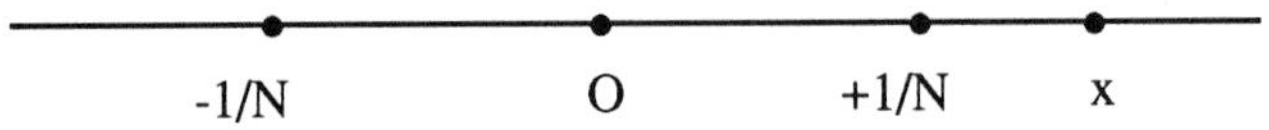

With the real line as metric space X, let A_n be the open interval $(-1/n, 1/n)$ for $n = 1,2,3, \ldots$. Consider the infinite intersection $A = A_1 \cap A_2 \cap \ldots$. We claim that $A = \{0\}$, a single point (and so is not an open set, for no open ball centred at 0 lies within A). Certainly 0 is in A, since it is in every A_i. But no other point $x > 0$ (or similarly $x < 0$) is in A, for we can choose $n = N$ so large that $1/N < x$, and then x is not in A_N and consequently not in the intersection set A *within* A_N.

We may build up significant open sets from intersections and unions of others. Now is the time to revise operations on sets. Figure 11.3 (page 239) recalls the basic operations and Table 11.1 below gives the main definitions and rules, of which (b) to (d) extend to unions and intersections of arbitrarily many sets.

EXAMPLE 11.5 (1) (using Property 11.4.)
The 'interior' of a square, $S = \{(x,y): 0 < x < 1, 0 < y < 1\}$ in the plane, is open.

Proof The interior of the given square is the intersection of four sets, defined respectively by $x > 0$, $x < 1$, $y > 0$, $y < 1$. This is a finite intersection of open sets (of the kind considered in Example 11.3(3)), hence is itself open by Property 11.4.

TABLE 11.1 Rules for operations on subsets A, B of a set X.

DEFINITIONS $x \in A$ means 'x is a member of A', $A \subseteq B$ means 'A is a subset of B'.

$A \cup B = \{x \in X: x \in A$ *or* $x \in B$ (or both)$\}$, the *union* of A and B,

$A \cap B = \{x \in X: x \in A$ *and* $x \in B$ (or both)$\}$, the *intersection* of A and B,

$A \backslash B = \{x \in A: x \notin B\}$, the *complement* of B in A, also written A-B,

$A^c = X \backslash A = \{x \in X: x \notin A\}$, the *complement* of A.

A, B are called *disjoint* or *non-overlapping* if $A \cap B = \emptyset$, the empty set.
A is a *proper* subset of B if it is neither empty, nor the whole of B.
A is a *superset* of B if $A \supseteq B$.

BASIC RULES

(a)	$A \cup B = B \cup A$	$A \cap B = B \cap A$	(Symmetry laws)
(b)	$(A \cup B) \cup C = A \cup (B \cup C)$	$(A \cap B) \cap C = A \cap (B \cap C)$	(Associative laws)
(c)	$A \cap (B \cup C) = (A \cap B) \cup (A \cap C)$	$A \cup (B \cap C) = (A \cup B) \cap (A \cup C)$	(Distributive laws)

(d) *De Morgan's laws* $(A \cup B)^c = A^c \cap B^c$
$(A \cap B)^c = A^c \cup B^c$

(e) *SOME OBVIOUS LAWS*

$A \cup \emptyset = A$	$A \cap X = A$	$(A^c)^c = A$
$A \cap \emptyset = \emptyset$	$A \cup X = X$	$A \cup A = A = A \cap A$

(2) Here is a general technique for proving rules such as those of Table 11.1, applied to the important law $(A \cup B)^c = A^c \cap B^c$. We divide the whole space or *Universal set* X, whose subsets are being considered, into disjoint subsets (1) to (4) as indicated in the diagram. Then $(A \cup B)^c = (1)$, whilst

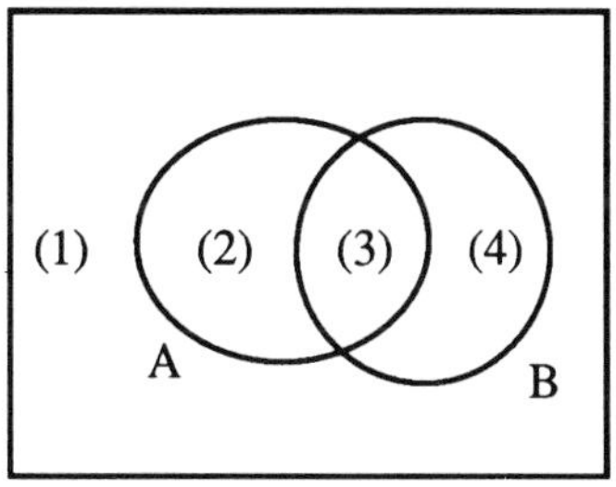

$$\begin{aligned} A^c \cap B^c &= [(2) \cup (3)]^c \cap [(3) \cup (4)]^c \\ &= [(1) \cup (4)] \cap [(1) \cup (2)] \quad (*) \\ &= (1), \text{ as required.} \quad (**) \end{aligned}$$

It is easy to see by inspection that the crucial steps (*) and (**) are valid because sets (1) to (4) are mutually disjoint.

EXERCISE Prove De Morgan's first law in Table 11.1, by the method above.

Basis for the topology The *topology*of a space X means precisely the collection of all its open subsets. It follows from Definition 11.2, not only that every union of open balls is an open set, but that *every* open set A in X may be so expressed, namely

$$A = \bigcup B_x(r) \qquad (x \in A, \; A \supseteq B_x(r)\,), \tag{11.2}$$

the union of all open balls satisfying the condition in parenthesis. The argument runs as follows. Logically, if we denote the union by B, then B ⊇ A since every point x of A is in the open ball $B_x(r)$ it centres. But also A ⊇ B, for each ball in the union lies completely within A, by definition, hence so does their union, B. At first sight this seems outrageous. How could we, for example, have the square shaped open set of Application 11.5? (Consider Figure 11.4 below.)

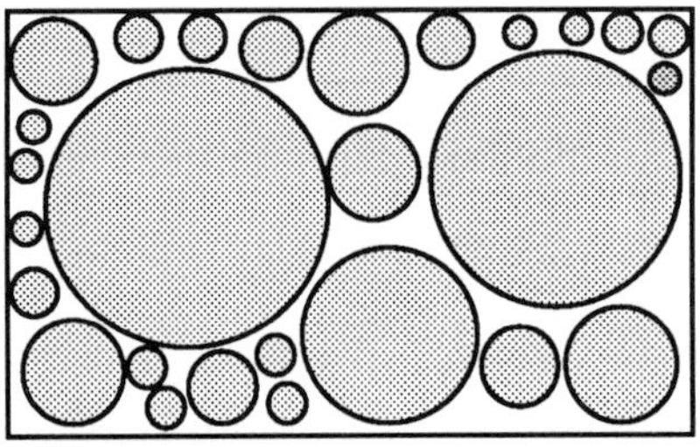

An open set on the line
is a union of open intervals

Figure 11.4 Every open set, even a rectangular one, is a union of open balls though we can only portray a finite number of constituent balls.

The answer is that we have infinity on our side. In general A is the union of infinitely many open balls, down to arbitrarily small sizes. On the real line the proposition is more apparent: every open set is a union of open intervals. These considerations suggest the definition below.

DEFINITION 11.6 A family {U} of subsets is a *basis for the topology* of a space X if the open sets of X are precisely the unions of members of {U}. Thus the set of open balls $B_x(r)$ $(x \in X,\; r > 0)$ is a basis for the topology of the metric space X (see (11.2). This description of the topology of X is called the *open ball topology* . In the case of the plane there is an interesting alternative which we explore in the next section, 11.2. Frequently we can simplify an argument by working with a basis rather with than the larger collection of open sets in general. But there is more. We can sometimes make good use of an even smaller collection of sets called a *sub-basis* : a family of sets whose finite intersections form a basis. (For instance in Section 12.1.4 on 'compact sets'.) An easy example is given immediately above Remark 11.8.

EXERCISE Is there another basis for the topology of the plane, using squares? (cf.Section 11.2).

11.2 Subspaces and product spaces

Subspaces (Inherited distance and open sets.) Any subset A of a metric space X can be viewed as a metric space in its own right, inheriting the distance function of X. Thus an open ball *in A* of radius r, centred at a is $\{x \in A : d(x,a) < r\}$, which may be expressed as $B_x(r) \cap A$, the intersection with A of an open ball in X. Hence the open sets of A are of the form

$$\{U \cap A : \text{ U is an open set in X}\}. \tag{11.3}$$

For a basis, U simply runs through a basis of the topology of X. Thus open sets in the interval [0,1] are unions of open and half-open intervals such as [0,a), (b,c), (d,1], as shown in bold below left. For example, (1/2, 2) is open in **R** and therefore its intersection (1/2, 2) $\cap$ [0,1] = (1/2, 1] is open in [0,1]. Shaded in below right are some open disks of a rectangular subset of the plane. They are bounded by straight segments and circular pieces.

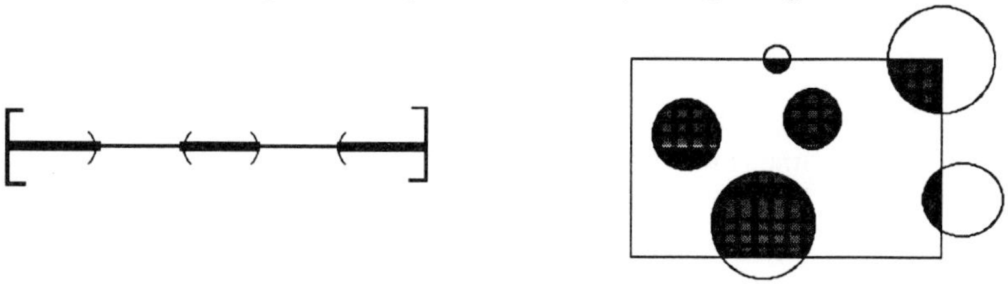

Figure 11.5 The topology of a subspace. Some open sets (darkened) in (i) the interval [0,1] on the line, (ii) a rectangle in the plane.

EXERCISE Deduce from (11.3) a basis for the topology of a plane circle [certain arcs].

EXAMPLE 11.7 (*Discrete spaces.*) (1) The set **N** of positive integers is a subset of **R** and inherits a metric d(m,n) = |m-n|. This makes **N** a useful example of a so-called *discrete space*, one in which every point is an open set, since we may write any point as {m} = $B_m(1/2) \cap$ **N**, the intersection of **N** with an open ball in **R**.

(2) Any finite set of points in a metric space forms a discrete space (prove it).

(3) The rational numbers **Q** $\subseteq$ **R** (cf. Example 11.17(3)) do not form a discrete subspace because every rational number has other rationals arbitrarily close (an easy exercise) and so if x $\in$ **Q** and r > 0 then {x} = $B_x(r) \cap$ **Q** cannot occur. Thus topology distinguishes between the 'spreadoutness' of **N** and **Q**.

Product spaces The plane is an important example of a *product space* X = Y x Z whose points form the *Cartesian product* Y x Z = { (y,z) : y $\in$ Y, z $\in$ Z}, and whose open sets are by definition all unions of products of form

$$\{A \times B: \text{ A is open in Y, B is open in Z}\}. \tag{11.4}$$

That is, the sets (11.4) form a basis for the topology of Y x Z. Again we get an apparent contradiction, which later yields valuable results and insights. Since the plane is, as a set, the Cartesian product **R** x **R**, an open set should be a union of 'open boxes' (a,b) x (c,d). Let us say such unions form the *open box topology* in the plane.

As Figure 11.6 suggests, each point x of an open ball B centres an open box within B, and similarly with ball and box interchanged. Therefore any union of open boxes is a union of open balls and vice versa. Thus the two topologies, *open box* and *open ball*, coincide, and we have for the future a useful second way of viewing the topology of the plane. The family of all open boxes is a second basis. Here is the example promised in Definition 11.7: since an open box is the intersection of four 1/2 planes in the xy-plane, such as x < a, x > b, y < c, y > d, the set of all such 1/2 planes forms a sub-basis for the topology of the plane.

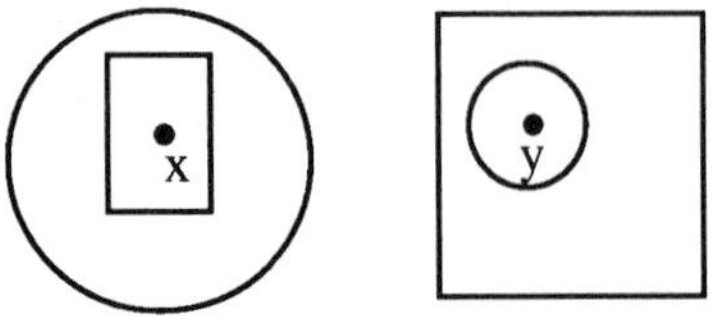

Figure 11.6 In the plane, each point **x** of an open disc centres an open box within that disc, and each point **y** of an open box centres an open disc within the box. Hence the open box and open ball (=disc) topologies of the plane coincide.

REMARK 11.8 We have carefully kept to the one usual metric on the line, plane, and 3-space. However, sometimes another is useful. To round off the discussion above we note a distance which we will call the *box metric* (sometimes called the *Manhattan metric*),

$$d_1((x_1,x_2), (y_1,y_2)) = \max(|x_1-y_1|, |x_2-y_2|),$$

in which a d_1-open ball is simply an open rectangle in the usual sense. The reader is invited to verify that this is so. Thus this distance gives the open box topology of (11.4) above. Most commonly we will meet the product of just two spaces, but the definition extends naturally to the product $X_1 \times X_2 \times \ldots \times X_n = \{(x_1,x_2, \ldots ,x_n): x_i \in X_i, 1 \le i \le n\}$ of any finite number of spaces, with a convenient basis for the topology consisting of all products $\{A_1 \times A_2 \times \ldots \times A_n : A_i$ open in $X_i, 1 \le i \le n\}$. If, as usual, the X_i are metric spaces, this is the (n-dimensional box) topology given by

$$d(x,y) = \max d(x_i,y_i) \ (1 \le i \le n), \tag{11.5}$$

where x and y have the usual coordinates x_i, y_i. Note that the spaces X_i need not be Euclidean. Sometimes the product of infinitely many spaces is required, and this is conveniently dealt with at a later stage, in Section 12.1.4 (after Theorem 12.24).

EXAMPLES 11.9 (*Some product spaces.*) (1) $\mathbf{R}^n = \mathbf{R} \times \mathbf{R} \times .. \times \mathbf{R}$, with n factors. The argument of form 'every ball contains a box and every box contains a ball' which we gave for Case n = 2 applies here too: we may define the topology of $\mathbf{R}^n$ either by open balls or by the open n-dimensional boxes of (11.5). However we will normally use the more familiar Euclidean metric (11.1) which of course gives the open ball topology.

(2) The complex plane **C**. This is simply the plane $\mathbf{R}^2$ with the extra interpretation of a point (x,y) as a complex number x+**i**y. Distances remain the same, as noted in Chapter 9 under 'Modulus', so topologically **C** and $\mathbf{R}^2$ are identical.

(3) $S^1 \times \mathbf{R}$ may be thought of as an infinitely long cyclinder, with neither beginning nor end, and $S^1 \times S^1$, a subspace of $\mathbf{R}^2 \times \mathbf{R}^2$, is the torus or 'doughnut' (or 'donut'). The last assertion requires proof since we regarded the torus as lying in 3-space, and this is given in Section 11.5 on homeomorphisms. See especially Examples 11.48 and 11.56.

EXERCISE Show that the metric (11.5) in the plane satisfies the Triangle inequality of Definition 11.1. **or** Show that the open box topology is the same if we keep to square boxes.

EXERCISE Show that the subspace and product topologies have Property 11.4: 'the collection of open sets is closed under unions and finite intersections'.

11.3 Sequences, limits and closed sets

11.3.1 Closed sets

DEFINITION 11.10 A subset A of X is ***closed*** if its complement is open. In particular, the empty set ø and the whole of X are closed (as well as open). It will follow too (from Test 11.19) that points arbitrarily close to a closed set A must already be members of A, an important feature in what is to come.

EXAMPLES 11.11 (*Some closed sets.*) (1) A 'closed interval' $[a,b] = \{x: a \le x \le b\}$ on the real line.

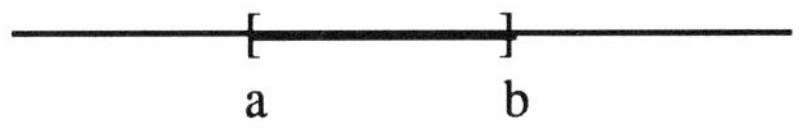

Proof The complementary set is the union of two open sets $(-\infty, a) \cup (b,\infty)$, where for example $(-\infty,a)$ denotes the set $\{x: x < a\}$. This finite union is open by Property 11.4, so [a,b] is closed as asserted.
(2) A closed ball is closed, as is a sphere.
(3) Any finite set is closed.
(4) Any line $y = mx+c$ in the plane is a closed set.
(5) A plane set $E: x_1 \le a$ is closed, for its complement $E^c : x_1 > a$ is open. The same applies to a subset of n-space defined by $a_1x_1 + ... + a_nx_n \le 0$. As a rule non-strict inequalities define a closed set, whilst strict inequalites define an open set.

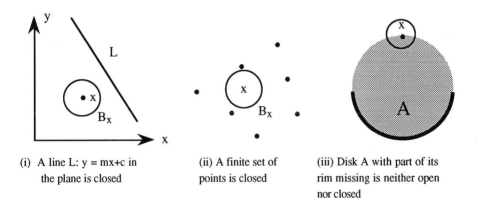

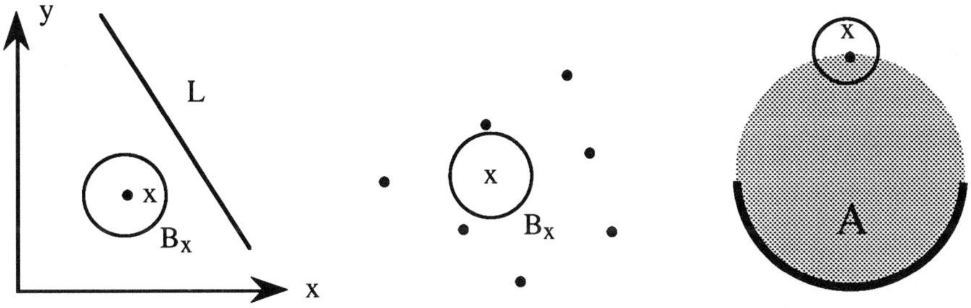

(i) A line L: y = mx+c in the plane is closed

(ii) A finite set of points is closed

(iii) Disk A with part of its rim missing is neither open nor closed

Figure 11.7 Two closed sets and one which is neither open nor closed.

In cases (i) and (ii) of Figure 11.7 any point x in the complement centres a ball lying in that complement. Hence the complement is open and the set itself is closed. The set A in (iii) is not open because a point on the remaining part of the boundary (bold) is not at the centre of a ball in A, no matter how small the radius. On the other hand a point x on the missing boundary has points of A arbitrarily close, so cannot centre a ball lying entirely in the complement of A. This motivates a formal definition of boundary, further on.

EXERCISE In the plane, why is a line segment with endpoints excluded not open ? Is it closed?

Here is a property of closed sets that allows us to build new ones from old. It is deduced from Property 11.4 of open sets, by taking complements.

PROPERTY 11.12

(a) *Any intersection of closed sets is closed,*
(b) *The union of a finite number of closed sets is closed.*

Proof We will be content with a sample of how this goes. Let A, B be closed sets. Then $A \cup B$ is closed because its complement is, by De Morgan's laws (Table 11.1), the same set as $A^c \cap B^c$, the intersection of two open sets.

APPLICATIONS 11.13 (*Some closed sets.*) (1) The first octant in $\mathbf{R}^3$, defined to be $\{(x,y,z): 0 \le x,y,z \}$, is closed, being the intersection of the three closed sets defined respectively by $0 \le x$, $0 \le y$, $0 \le z$.

(2) The plate with a hole,

$$A = \{(x,y) \in \mathbf{R}^2 : x \ge -2,\ y \le 2,\ x^2 + y^2 \ge 1\},$$

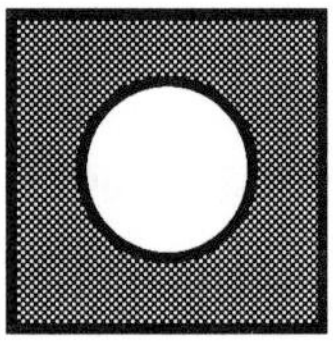

is closed. Of course, if the defining inequalities were made strict we would have an open set, by Property 11.4.

EXERCISE Prove that the intersection of two closed sets is closed.

11.3.2 Sequences and limits

DEFINITION 11.14 Now we establish the important connection with **sequences**. As usual, A will denote a subset of a metric space X. Let $\{x_n\}$ be a sequence $x_1, x_2, \ldots$ of points in A. Formally $x_n = f(n)$, where $f: \mathbf{N} \to A$ is some function, and the same point may appear more than once. Thus one valid sequence in $\mathbf{R}$ is $\{1/2, 1/3, 1/2, 1/3 \ldots \}$. Let x be a point of X which is not necessarily in A. The statement $x_n \to x$ (as $n \to \infty$) means $d(x_n,x) \to 0$: we can get x_n arbitrarily close to x by taking n sufficiently large. Formally again, for any $\varepsilon > 0$, no matter how small, there is an integer N such that $d(x_n,x) < \varepsilon$ whenever $n > N$. Then we say the sequence $\{x_n\}$ *converges to* x, or *has limit* x.

Let's get one thing out of the way. *No sequence can have two limits,* say a,b. Informally, the reason is that the sequence cannot get arbitrarily close to two different numbers simultaneously. More explicitly, if $a \ne b$ with $d(a,b) = \delta > 0$ then we may take N so large that for $n > N$, $d(x_n,a)$ and $d(x_n,b)$ are less than $\delta/2$. This gives a contradiction, namely $d(a,b) \le d(a,x_n) + d(x_n,b) < \delta$. In summary, *if a sequence has a limit, that limit is unique.*

EXAMPLES 11.15 (*Some limits.*) (1) Let $X = \mathbf{R}$, the real numbers, and define a sequence by $x_n = 3 - 1/n$. Then $x_n \to 3$ as $n \to \infty$, as illustrated below.

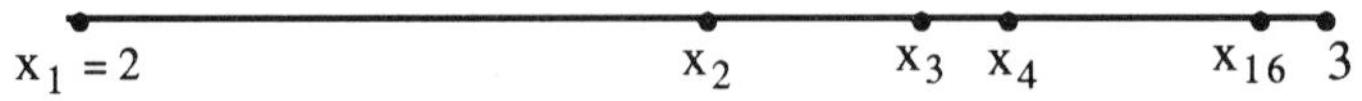

(2) One more example on the line. Let $x_n = n \sin(1/n)$. Then as n increases, $\sin(1/n)$ decreases. Which factor wins out? The answer is a power-sharing $x_n \to 1$, as may be seen

by expanding the sine as a power series (see a basic Calculus textbook such as Swokowski (1979)).

(3) *(Subsequences.)* For later use in Chapter 12 we note that if a sequence $\{x_n\}$ in a metric space has limit L then so does every subsequence $\{x_{n_i}\} = \{x_{n_1}, x_{n_2}, x_{n_3} \ldots\}$. The reason is that if $d(x_n,L) < \varepsilon$ for $n > N$ then $d(x_{n_i}, L) < \varepsilon$ for $n_i > N$. For example the subsequence $\{1/3n\} = \{1/3, 1/6, 1/9, \ldots\}$ of $\{1/n\}$ has the same limit, 0.

(4) *(The umbrella proof that I is uncountable.)* The n'th *partial sum* of a sequence $\{a_i\}$ of real numbers is $S_n = a_1 + a_2 + \ldots + a_n$. If $S_n \to L$ as $n \to \infty$ we say the infinite series $a_1 + a_2 + \ldots$ *has sum L*. In particular there is a formula for the sum of a *geometric series*: $1 + r + r^2 + \ldots = 1/(1-r)$ provided $|r| < 1$. For example

$$1 + 1/3 + 1/9 + 1/27 + \ldots = 1/(1 - 1/3) = 3/2.$$

Further details are given in Table 11.2 (page 270). We can use this to give what is sometimes called the umbrella proof that the set I = [0,1] is *uncountable* - ie cannot be indexed by the positive integers. For suppose that I can be so indexed, its points thus forming a sequence $\{x_n\}$. For each $n \in \mathbf{N}$ we cover x_n on the real line by an interval of width $1/3^n$ (its 'umbrella'). Then the widths of all the umbrellas together have a sum equal to $1/3 + 1/3^2 + 1/3^3 + \ldots = 3/2 - 1 = 1/2$, by our formula above. But this is impossible because the whole of I is covered and it has width 1. So I is uncountable. To tie up the nomenclature, a set whose elements can be indexed by the positive integers is called *countably infinite*. Together with finite sets, such form the *countable* sets. It is a useful short exercise to show that the set Z of positive integers, their negatives, and zero, is countable.

(5) This example is important for later work on the Mandelbrot and Julia sets. We construct a sequence of points x_n moving along a spiral in the plane, as follows. Let R be any positive number, and let x_n have polar coordinates $r = R^n$, $\theta = n\pi/3$. Thus x_n has Cartesian coordinates $x = R^n \cos(n\pi/3)$, $y = R^n \sin(n\pi/3)$. Consider Figure 11.8.

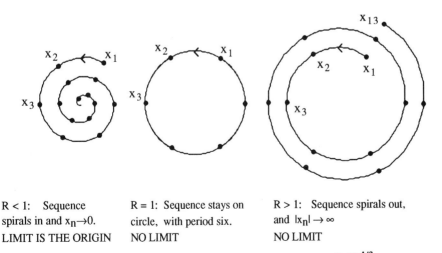

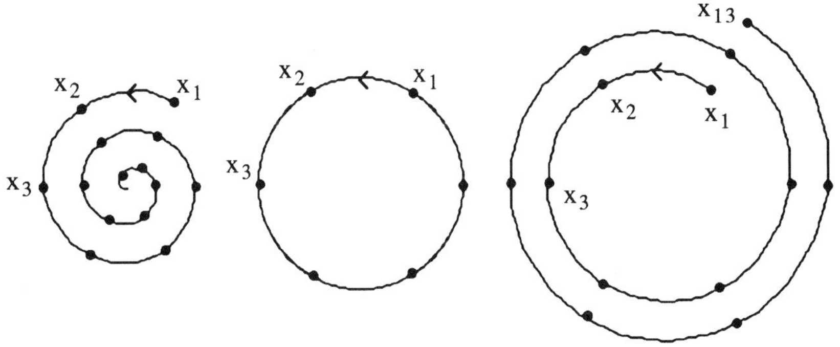

R < 1: Sequence spirals in and $x_n \to 0$. LIMIT IS THE ORIGIN

R = 1: Sequence stays on circle, with period six. NO LIMIT

R > 1: Sequence spirals out, and $|x_n| \to \infty$ NO LIMIT

Figure 11.8 Cases of the sequence $\{x_n\}$, with $x_n = R^n e^{n\pi i/3}$.

In fact successive x_n lie on radial lines spaced at angle $\pi/3$, or 60°, and the sequence moves through the plane in three clearly distinguishable ways according to the value of R, as illustrated in Figure 11.8 above. Note that, as a complex number, x_n is the n'th power of

$Re^{i\pi/3}$, equal by De Moivre's Theorem (9.11) to $R^n e^{n\pi i/3}$.

DEFINITION 11.16 The point x in X is a ***limit point of the subset A*** if x is the limit of a sequence of points in A\{x}. Thus x has points of A arbitrarily close to it. For this reason, such a point x is often called a *cluster point* or *accumulation point.* The reader may be puzzled on seeing A\{x} , with x carefully excluded. The reason is that a point x actually in A, but around which points of A do not cluster, is deservedly called an *isolated point.* Thus for example if A = [0,2] ∪ {3}, looking like ——— . then there is an obvious gap separating 3 from the rest of A, and 3 does not qualify as a limit point but as an isolated point of A. No sequence in the line segment [0,2] can get to within less than one unit of 3.

By definition, every point of A is either isolated or a limit point, but not all limit points need be in A (see the first example below). This said, we drop the isolated points in defining, as we do, the *derived set* A' of A to consist of *all* limit points of A. We give some simple but seminal examples and then prove the connection with closed sets.

EXAMPLES 11.17 (*Limit points on the real line.*) (1) Let A be the open interval (0,1). Every point in A is a limit point, since we can get arbitrarily close to it through points of A. But in addition, still travelling only in A, we can get as close as we wish to the excluded points x = 0,1 which therefore qualify as limit points too. For example with $x_n = 1/(n+1)$ in (0,1) we have $x_n \to 0$. Thus (0,1)' = [0,1].

(2) With A as the closed interval [0,1] there are no limit points (of A) outside A, so [0,1]' = [0,1] and A contains its limit points. This is a property of all closed sets, as we show in Test 11.19 below.

(3) (*Approximating real numbers by rationals .*) A rational number has the form p/q, where p,q are integers, possibly negative, and q is nonzero. Thus we may take q to be positive. The range of numbers that a given computer can represent is a subset of the rationals. Thus an important related fact is:

every real number α can be approximated to arbitrary precision by a rational number (11.6)

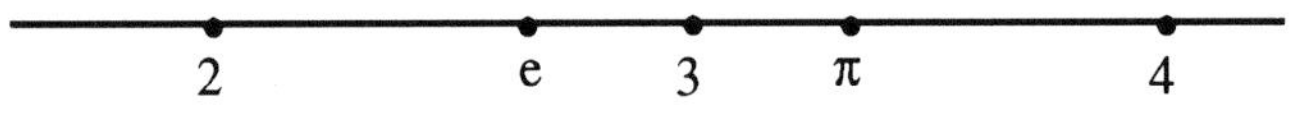

The truth of (11.6) is easily seen, and suggested by the positions of e, the base of natural logarithms (cf. Remark 9.16), and π, as depicted above on the real line. To get a rational number within 1/n of a given number α, divide up the real line so that between successive integer points there are n equally spaced markers. α falls in some subinterval and is then within 1/n of either endpoint, itself a rational number.

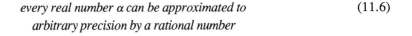

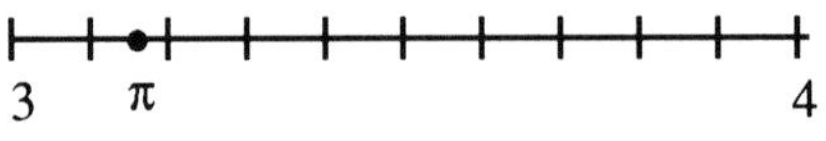

This is really an existence argument, since we don't have a copy of π on the real line to pin down. A practical method is to use continued fractions, see Niven & Zuckerman (1980). Here are some rational numbers within 10^{-n} of e, π for various values of n, obtained this way.

n	1	2	3	6	7
π	$\frac{22}{7}$	$\frac{22}{7}$	$\frac{355}{113}$	$\frac{355}{113}$	$\frac{104348}{33215}$
e	$\frac{11}{4}$	$\frac{19}{7}$	$\frac{106}{39}$	$\frac{2721}{1001}$	$\frac{25946}{9545}$

Where is this leading? The approximation claim of (11.6) may be rephrased as: every open interval centred at α contains a rational number. Then a standard argument gives us a sequence of rationals with α as limit. In fact, for each n the open ball $B_\alpha(1/n)$ contains a rational x_n distinct from α. Since $d(x_n,\alpha) < 1/n$, we have $x_n \to \alpha$.

Conclusions (i) Every real number is the limit of a sequence of rationals. Indeed, **R** is the derived set of the rationals. (ii) The last argument above gives a most useful test, 11.18 below, for limit points, because it may be reversed: the sequence $x_n \to \alpha$ provides every $B_\alpha(r)$ with an element x_n distinct from α (try writing down the (short) proof of Test 11.18).

EXERCISE What are the limit points of the subset $\{(n+2)/(n+1)\}$, n = 1,2,... of **R**?

TEST 11.18 The following are equivalent for a subset A and point x of a metric space X.
(a) x *is a limit point of* A,
(b) *every open ball* $B_x(r)$ *contains points of A besides* x.

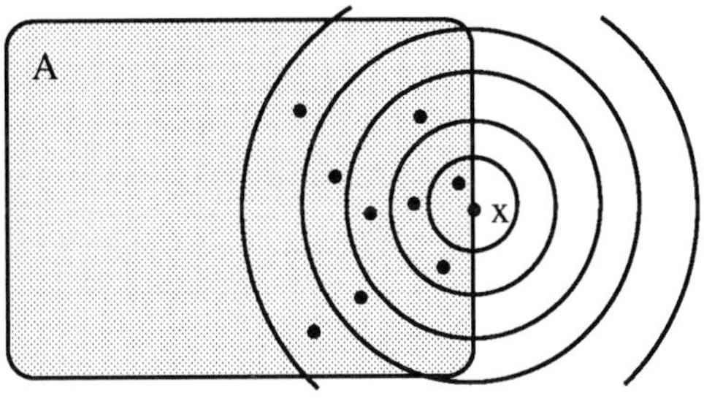

Figure 11.9 x is a limit point of the rectangle A, by Test 11.18, since every open ball centred at x, no matter how small, contains points of A other than x. Note: x need not be a point of A.

11.3.3 Interior, closure, and boundary

TEST 11.19 (A crucial reason for considering closed sets.) A subset A of a space X is closed if and only if A contains all its limit points.

Proof A is closed ⇔ A^c is open, by definition of 'closed'
⇔ for every x in A^c, some $B_x(r)$ is in A^c
⇔ for every x in A^c, some $B_x(r)$ does not intersect A
⇔ for every x in A^c, x is not a limit point of A, (cf. Test 11.18)
⇔ every limit point of A lies in A,

DEFINITION 11.20 The following sets related to a subset A of a metric space are foundational to the dynamics of a discrete system (see Chapter 16).

The *closure*, $\overline{A} = A \cup A'$. The set A together with all its limit points.
The *interior* $A^o = \{x \in A : x \text{ is the centre of an open ball in } A\}$.
The *boundary* $\partial A = \overline{A} \setminus A^o$, The points in or arbitrarily close to A that are not in its interior.

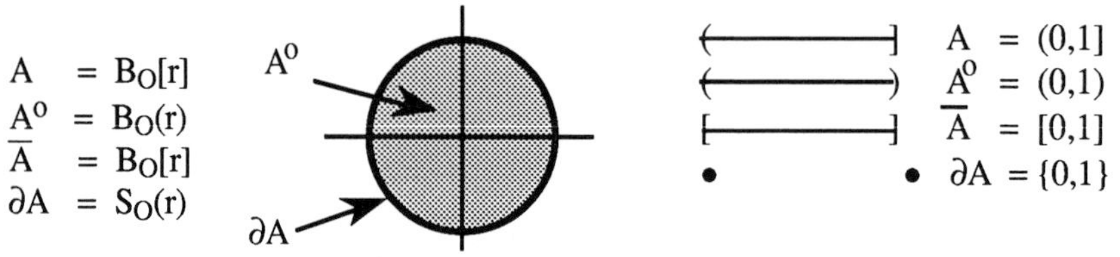

Figure 11.10 In the usual topology on the line and plane, the definitions of 'interior' and 'boundary' correspond well to our intuitive notions.

EXERCISE Find the closure, interior and boundary of $A = (0,1) \cup (1,3]$. Do the same for the closed region between two concentric circles.

Notice from Figure 11.10 that boundary points of A may or may not belong to A. But they do belong to $\overline{A}$ by Definition 11.20, which implies also that, as we shall see, A is sandwiched between its interior (an open set) and its closure (a closed set). We have the following.

$$A^o \subseteq A \subseteq \overline{A} \tag{11.7}$$

$$\overline{A} = A^o \cup \partial A \quad (A^o, \partial A \text{ disjoint}) \tag{11.8}$$

and

$$A \text{ is open} \Leftrightarrow A = A^o \tag{11.9}$$

$$A \text{ is closed} \Leftrightarrow A = \overline{A}. \tag{11.10}$$

Proof (11.7) and (11.8) are true by Definition 11.20. The rest nearly so. To prove (11.9), let A be open. Then any $\alpha \in A$ is in some $B_\alpha(r)$ within A, so $\alpha \in A^o$. Hence $A \subseteq A^o$. But we already know that $A^o \subseteq A$ (11.7), therefore $A = A^o$. Conversely, suppose $A = A^o$. Then any $\alpha \in A$ is in A^o, so is contained in some $B_\alpha(r)$. Hence A is open. For (11.10) we have A is closed $\Leftrightarrow A' \subseteq A$ (Test 11.19) $\Leftrightarrow A = \overline{A}$ (since $\overline{A} = A \cup A'$)

TEST 11.21 A point x is in the boundary of subset A if and only if every open ball centred at x contains

(a) *points of* A [since $x \in \overline{A}$]
(b) *points in the complement of* A [since $x \notin A^o$].

EXERCISE Use Test 11.21 to show that isolated points of A are not in its boundary (are they necessarily in the interior of A? - see (11.8)).

DEFINITION 11.22 A subset A of a space X is *dense* in X if $\overline{A} = X$. This has the effect that A approximates X to any desired degree of accuracy in the following sense: every point of X not already in A has points of A arbitrarily close to it. This important idea is used in producing fractal images (see pages 375,378,414,422). Some immediate examples are:

The rational numbers are dense in **R**, (11.6),
$B_a(r)$ is dense in $B_a[r]$,
The sphere $S_a(r)$ is *not* dense in $B_a[r]$.

EXERCISE Which is dense in which, of : (0,2), (0,2], [1,2), (0,2)\{1}?

11.4 Continuous functions

A continuous function has the benefit that it preserves limits, compactness, and connectedness. The meaning and truth of this will become clearer by Section 11.5 onwards. A major goal in this section is to prove results which enable us to establish continuity for a wide class of functions (= maps, or mappings) easily and conveniently.

11.4.1 The first step - continuity for real functions

DEFINITIONS 11.23 In previous chapters we have used transformations of 2, 3, and 4-space, and isomorphisms between groups. All these are particular cases of a function

$$f: X \to Y, \quad \text{or} \quad X \xrightarrow{f} Y$$

from a set X to a set Y, meaning that f is a rule which associates with every element x of X a unique element y = f(x) of Y, the *image of x under f.* We call X the *domain* and Y the *range* or *codomain* of f, distinguishing Y from the *image* f(X) = $\{f(x): x \in X\}$. The *graph* of f consists of pairs $\{(x,y) \in X \times Y: y = f(x)\}$.

EXAMPLE 11.24 The formula $f(x) = x^2$ defines a function f: $\mathbf{R} \to \mathbf{R}$. Notice that the image is not the whole of **R**, for it excludes negative numbers. The graph is a subset of the product space **R** x **R** which is of course the plane $\mathbf{R}^2$.

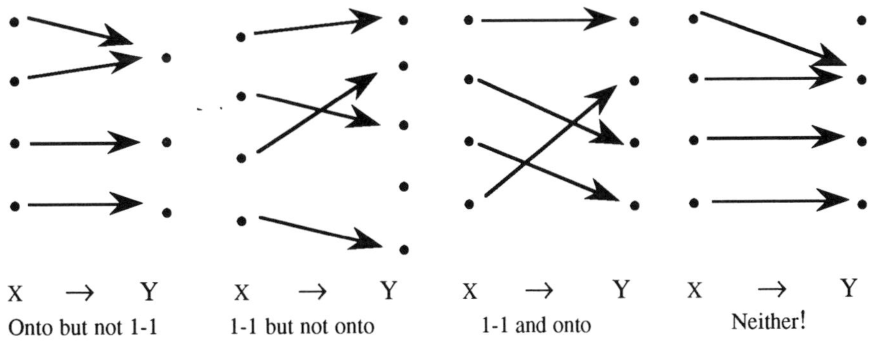

Figure 11.11 Some possibilities for f: X → Y. In which category is (a) f: **R** → **R**, with $f(x) = x^3 - 2$, (b) the above Example 11.24?

DEFINITIONS 11.25 The function f: X → Y is *surjective* or *onto* if f(X) = Y (unlike the example above) and *injective* or 1-1 if it sends distinct elements of X to distinct elements of Y. If f is both 1-1 and onto, it is called *bijective*, or a *pairing*. The *inverse image* of a subset B of Y is $f^{-1}(B) = \{x \in X: f(x) \in B\}$. Thus f is surjective if every point y of Y *has* an inverse image and bijective if also every $f^{-1}(y)$ is a single point. A bijective function f has an inverse function, often written f^{-1}, which sends each point y in Y back to its inverse image, already denoted $f^{-1}(y)$. Isometries are a special instance of such functions (page 30).

DEFINITION 11.26 $X \xrightarrow{f} Y \xrightarrow{g} Z$ denotes the *composition* g.f (or just gf) of functions f and g, with f performed first. Thus $(gf)(x) = g(f(x))$. [This is different from the geometrical superscript notation with x^g for $g(x)$, and $x^{gf} = (x^g)^f$, implying that g is performed first.] We abbreviate to f^n the n-fold composition f.f...f of $f: X \to X$ with itself. The functions f, f^2, f^3, .. are called the *iterates* of f. Even if f(x) is a number, we write $f^n(x)$ to mean a composition rather than the product of n copies of f(x), which may be written as $f(x)^n$ or $(f(x))^n$. The *identity function* 1_X or just 1, sends every element of X to itself. If f has inverse f^{-1} then $f^{-1}f = 1_X$ and $ff^{-1} = 1_Y$. A useful exercise follows.

EXERCISE Show that gf = 1 implies that f is 1-1 and g is onto.

EXAMPLE 11.27 With $f: \mathbf{R} \to \mathbf{R}$, $f(x) = x^2 - 4$, find a formula for f^2. We have $(f.f)(x) = f(x^2 - 4) = (x^2 - 4)^2 - 4$. Such calculations and much more are required for considering Julia sets. Fortunately we do not need to do all this by hand.

NOTATION 11.28 (1) It is frequently useful to specify a function by a formula, such as $f(x) = 1/(x-3)$. This one has a well-defined value for all real numbers except x=3, so whilst it does define $f: [0,1] \to \mathbf{R}$ for example, the *maximal domain* is $\mathbf{R}\backslash\{3\}$.

(2) The example above 'blows up' at x = 3. This phenomenon is usefully incorporated in a definition: given a function $f: X \to \mathbf{R}$ we say $f(x) \to \infty$ as $x \to a$ if $|f(x)|$ can be made arbitrarily large by taking x sufficiently close to a. In particular the symbol ∞ does not represent a real number, though we sometimes append it to **R** or **C** to form a new space, e.g. in studying certain transformations - see Chapter 16. Apart from this, '$y \to \infty$' means 'y becomes arbitrarily large' and positive, with negative counterpart $y \to -\infty$.

Continuity We start with the most basic "hands on" idea of continuity, for the well-known case $f: \mathbf{R} \to \mathbf{R}$, and show how this leads through easy stages to a useful and practical definition for our purposes in terms of open sets. Apart from this last, we define continuity first at a point. Then *f is continuous* if it satisfies such a definition for each point of its domain.

DEFINITION 11.29 A function $f: \mathbf{R} \to \mathbf{R}$ is *continuous at x=a* if, for every $\varepsilon > 0$, there is a number $\delta > 0$ such that $|f(x) - f(a)| < \varepsilon$ whenever $|x-a| < \delta$. The same applies with *subsets* of **R** as domain and codomain. Discontinuity at x = a typically appears as a break in the graph, as depicted below.

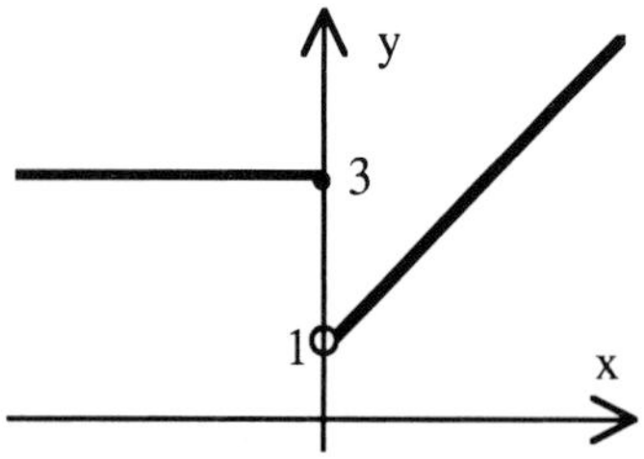

$$f(x) = \begin{cases} 3, & if\ x \le 0 \\ x+1, & if\ x > 0 \end{cases}$$

Note. The ring at (0,1) implies that this point is not in the graph. Instead, the point (0,3) is included.

Figure 11.12 Graph of a function f(x) with discontinuity at x = 0.

To see how Definition 11.29 picks up a break in the graph we rephrase it as 'f(a) is the limit of f(x) as x tends to a'. In symbols,

$$f \text{ is continuous at the point } a \Leftrightarrow \lim_{x \to a} f(x) \text{ exists and equals } f(a). \qquad (11.11)$$

Indeed, we can get f(x) as close to f(a) as we like by taking x close enough to a (with sequences $\{x_n\}$ we get this closeness by taking n large enough). More generally, we say $\lim_{x \to a} f(x) = L$ if f satisfies Definition 11.29 with f(a) replaced by L. The example in Figure 11.12 satisfies, in a natural extension of the notation,

$$\lim_{x \to 0-} f(x) = \lim_{\substack{x \to 0 \\ x < 0}} f(x) \quad \text{(by definition)} \quad = 3$$

while

$$\lim_{x \to 0+} f(x) = \lim_{\substack{x \to 0 \\ x > 0}} f(x) \quad \text{(by definition)} \quad = 1 .$$

Thus f(x) has no unique limit as $x \to 0$ through arbitrary values, and so fails the definition of continuity at x = 0. Such trouble does not arise with f defined by $f(x) = x^2 + 5$, whose limit as $x \to 3$ for example is obviously $3^2 + 5 = 14 = f(3)$, so f is continuous at x = 3. It will soon be clear why such functions are continuous everywhere.

EXERCISE Is f: $\mathbf{R} \to \mathbf{R}$ continuous if $f(x) = 1-2x$, for $x \le 3$ and x^2-4x-1 for $x > 3$?

THEOREM 11.30 Let f,g: $\mathbf{R} \to \mathbf{R}$ be continuous and let $\lambda \in \mathbf{R}$. Then each of the following defines a continuous function h: $\mathbf{R} \to \mathbf{R}$ (denoted by $h = f+\lambda, \lambda f, f+g, fg, f/g$ respectively).

(a) $h(x) = f(x) + \lambda$, *(b) $h(x) = \lambda f(x)$,* *(c) $h(x) = f(x) + g(x)$,*
(d) $h(x) = f(x)g(x)$, *(e) $h(x) = f(x)/g(x)$ (on subsets with $g(x) \neq 0$).*

Let $f(x) \to A$ and $g(x) \to B$, as $x \to a$. Then $f(x)g(x) \to AB$, $f(x)/g(x) \to A/B$ ($B \neq 0$).

Proof (a) is a special case of (c) (an easy exercise), and (b) of (d). For *Case (d)* Let a be an arbitrary point of **R**. As a standard beginning, let $\varepsilon > 0$. Since f, g are continuous we may choose $\delta > 0$ so that $|f(x) - f(a)|$ and $|g(x) - g(a)|$ are both less than ε whenever $|x - a| < \delta$. We note first that this implies limitations on f(x):

$$|f(x)| = |(f(x) - f(a)) + f(a)| \le |(f(x) - f(a)| + |f(a)|,$$

by the triangle inequality. So we can choose δ small enough to ensure that $|f(x)| \le M$ provided $|x - a| < \delta$, for some fixed bound M. We then argue as follows.

$$\begin{aligned} h(x) - h(a) &= f(x)g(x) - f(a)g(a), && \text{by definition of } h(x), \\ &= f(x)[g(x) - g(a)] + g(a)[f(x) - f(a)], && \text{so} \\ |h(x) - h(a)| &\le |f(x)|\,|g(x) - g(a)| + |g(a)|\,|f(x) - f(a)|, && \text{(Triangle inequality)} \\ &\le M\varepsilon + |g(a)|\varepsilon \\ &\le k\varepsilon\ , && \text{with } k = M + |g(a)|. \end{aligned}$$

This suffices, because ε is arbitrarily small.
Case (e) Since $f(x)/g(x) = f(x)\,[1/g(x)]$, we need by Case (d) only to prove that $1/g(x)$ is continuous at points for which $g(x)$ is nonzero. Details are omitted, being similar to those above. For the last part, on limits, we simply replace $f(a)$ by A and $f(b)$ by B in the proofs of (d) and (e).

EXAMPLE 11.31 We use Theorem 11.30 to prove that $f(x) = x^2+2x+3$ is (strictly, *defines*) a continuous function. To do so we construct $f(x)$ by a series of applications of 11.30. The stages are $x \to x+2 \to x(x+2) \to x(x+2)+3$, and they use in succession Cases (a), (d), (a). Obviously any polynomials $p(x)$, $q(x)$ or rational functions $p(x)/q(x)$ can be constructed in this way, hence the following corollary, after which we shall need no more to verify continuity of polynomials or rational functions. However the following exercise is instructive.

EXERCISE Prove that the identity function $f(x) = x$, and any constant function $f(x) = c$, are continuous; prove that if $g: \mathbf{R} \to \mathbf{R}$ is continuous and never zero then so is $1/g(x)$ **or** Prove that the rational function $(x^3 - 5x^2+3x+1)/(x^4+1)$ is continuous. Do it step by step, using Theorem 11.30.

COROLLARY 11.32 All polynomial functions are continuous. A rational function is continuous at all points for which its denominator does not vanish.

11.4.2 Continuity - the wider context

Having established some basics for the familiar real functions of a real variable, $f: \mathbf{R} \to \mathbf{R}$, it is time to take the step of replacing the Euclidean distance $|\mathbf{x}-\mathbf{y}|$ between points $\mathbf{x}$, $\mathbf{y}$ by a general distance function or metric $d(x,y)$. (Now the results of Theorem 11.30 apply by the same arguments to $f,g: X \to \mathbf{R}$, for any metric space X.) Rephrasing the definition in terms of open balls, we have 11.33(a). Then an equivalent condition in terms of sequences and limits is noted, 11.33(b). Finally, and equivalently to the previous ones, we come to the concise test Definition 11.34 for continuity in terms of *open sets*, with distance not even mentioned. This leads to some very streamlined proofs now and later. See for example Corollary 11.35 and Lemma 11.37, following shortly.

DEFINITION 11.33 A function $f: X \to Y$ between metric spaces is *continuous at the point* $a \in X$ if (a) or equivalently (b) below holds. Equivalence is established after the definitions. Property (b) is often known as *sequential continuity*, and is frequently a useful test for, or inference from, Property (a).

(a) For any $\varepsilon > 0$ there is $\delta > 0$ such that
$d(f(x), f(a)) < \varepsilon$ whenever $d(x,a) < \delta$.
That is, $f(B_a(\delta)) \subseteq B_{f(a)}(\varepsilon)$.

(b) For any sequence $\{x_n\}$ in X,
$x_n \to a$ implies $f(x_n) \to f(a)$.
That is, $f(\lim x_n) = \lim f(x_n)$ (if the first limit exists).

DEFINITION 11.34 A function $f: X \to Y$ between metric spaces is *continuous* if the inverse image of every open set is open. That is, if U is an open subset of Y then $f^{-1}(U)$ is an open subset of X.

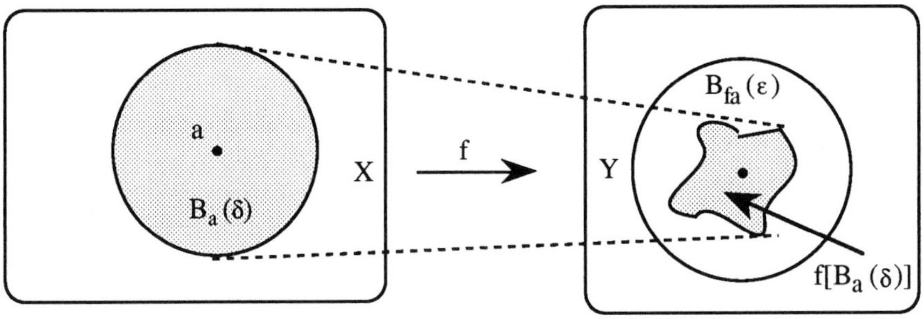

Figure 11.13(a) Function f: X → Y is continuous at a: for every $B_{fa}(\varepsilon)$, f maps some $B_a(\delta)$ into it.

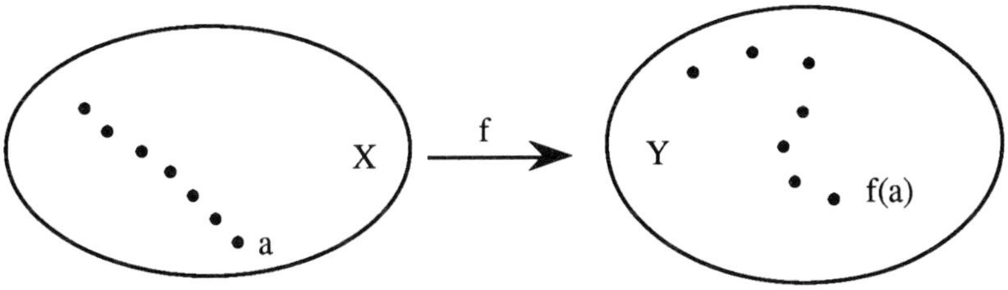

Figure 11.13(b) Function f: X → Y is (sequentially) continuous at a: every sequence with limit a is mapped by f into a sequence with limit f(a).

Proof that the definitions are equivalent. We leave the reader to see that the two statements in 11.33(a) are simply reformulations of each other, and similarly for part (b). We first prove (a) and (b) to be equivalent.

(a) ⇒ (b). Assume (a) and let $x_n \to a$ in X. We must deduce that $f(x_n) \to f(a)$. Suppose we are given a number $\varepsilon > 0$. Then (using (a)) for some $\delta > 0$ we have $|f(x) - f(a)| < \varepsilon$ if $|x-a| < \delta$. Now, since $x_n \to a$, there is an integer $N > 0$ such that $|x_n - a| < \delta$ if $n > N$. Thus $n > N$ implies $|f(x_n) - f(a)| < \varepsilon$, as required to establish that $f(x_n) \to f(a)$.

(b) ⇒ (a). We prove the logically equivalent statement : if (a) is false then (b) is false. Thus, suppose that there exists $\varepsilon > 0$ such that for every $\delta > 0$, no matter how small, $f(B_a(\delta))$ does not lie within $B_{fa}(\varepsilon)$. By taking $\delta = 1/n$ for n = 1,2,3, ... we obtain, for each n, a point x_n in $B_a(1/n)$ whose image $f(x_n)$ does not lie in $B_{fa}(\varepsilon)$. Letting $n \to \infty$ we have $1/n \to 0$, so the radius of $B_a(1/n)$ shrinks towards zero and $x_n \to a$. But $f(x_n)$ does not tend to f(a) because it never enters the fixed open ball $B_{fa}(\varepsilon)$; so (b) is false.

If f satisfies Definition 11.34, then f satisfies Definition 11.33 for each a ∈ X. The argument is illustrated in Figure 11.13(a) above. Assume Definition 11.34 is satisfied by f. That is, U open in Y implies $f^{-1}(U)$ open in X. We will deduce that Definition 11.33 is satisfied in its (a) version for any point a of X. Let $\varepsilon > 0$. We have that $U = B_{fa}(\varepsilon)$ is open, therefore so is $f^{-1}(U)$. Since this set contains a, being the inverse image of a set that contains f(a), it follows by definition of openness that a centres an open ball $B_a(\delta)$ lying within the aforesaid $f^{-1}(U)$. Hence $f(B_a(\delta)) \subseteq B_{fa}(\varepsilon)$, as required. The proof of the converse, *Definition 11.33 (for all a ∈ X) ⇒ Definition 11.34,* is very similar to the proof above, and so is left as an exercise.

EXERCISE Prove that Definition 11.33 (for all $a \in X$) implies Definition 11.34.

COROLLARY 11.35 Composition of functions (diagram below) satisfies $(gf)^{-1} = f^{-1}g^{-1}$ *and hence the composition of continuous functions is continuous.*

$$X \xrightarrow{f} Y \xrightarrow{g} Z$$

Proof This is our first illustration of applying the open set definition for continuity. Notice that unless g has an inverse the expression g^{-1} is only defined as a 'map of sets'. In any case the inverse image $g^{-1}(U)$ is defined for every set U, and similarly for f. With this proviso, we write

$$\begin{aligned}(gf)^{-1}(U) &= \{x \in X: (gf)(x) \in U\} = \{x \in X: g(fx) \in U\} \\ &= \{x \in X: f(x) \in g^{-1}(U)\} = \{x \in X: x \in f^{-1}(g^{-1}U)\} \\ &= f^{-1}(g^{-1}U).\end{aligned}$$

The reader is advised to convince him/herself of this actually very simple argument. For the continuity of composition we suppose U is open. The continuity of g ensures by Definition 11.34 that $g^{-1}(U)$ is open, then that of f ensures $f^{-1}(g^{-1}(U))$ is open. But by the first part, this latter set equals the inverse image $(gf)^{-1}(U)$, which is therefore open. Hence gf is continuous. Obviously we need some information on how f^{-1} behaves on various expressions. The lemma below gives useful rules, as does Theorem 11.37 following it in the next section.

LEMMA 11.36 A function $f: X \to Y$ satisfies for subsets A, B of Y,

(a) $f^{-1}(A^c) = (f^{-1}A)^c$,
(b) $f^{-1}(A \cap B) = f^{-1}(A) \cap f^{-1}(B)$,
(c) $f^{-1}(A \cup B) = f^{-1}(A) \cup f^{-1}(B)$.

Consequently a map $f: X \to Y$ of spaces is continuous iff $f^{-1}(U)$ is open for every open set U in a basis (or even sub-basis) for the topology of Y.

Proof Once one gets the idea, proofs of such results are easy. We shall give a detailed argument for part (b) as representative. The reader may wish to try her/his hand at the others.

$$\begin{aligned}f^{-1}(A \cap B) &= \{x: f(x) \in A \cap B\} \\ &= \{x: f(x) \in A \text{ and } f(x) \in B\} \\ &= \{x: f(x) \in A\} \cap \{x: f(x) \in B\} \\ &= f^{-1}(A) \cap f^{-1}(B).\end{aligned}$$

EXERCISE Use Lemma 11.36 to show that a function is continuous if and only if its inverse image of every closed set is a closed set.

11.4.3 Continuity and product spaces

Under this heading we handle a variety of types of function involving $\mathbf{R}^n$. For simplicity Theorem 11.37 is stated first for the case $n = 2$, then the generalisation is asserted.

THEOREM 11.37 (Continuity of a function into a product space.)

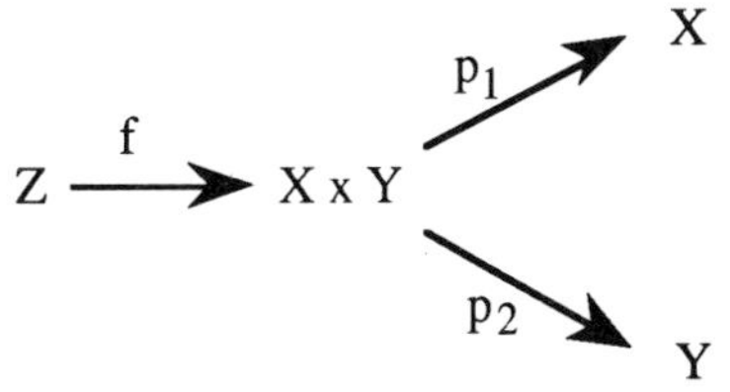

(a) *The* ***projection maps*** *onto each factor of a Cartesian product, given by* $p_1(x,y) = x$, $p_2(x,y) = y$, *are continuous.*
(b) *A function* $f\colon Z \to X \times Y$ *is continuous if and only if both compositions* $p_1.f$ *and* $p_2.f$ *are continuous.*
(c) *The above results hold more generally, for the product of n spaces with projection maps* $p_1, \ldots, p_n$.

Proof (a) Let U be open in X. Then

$$\begin{aligned} p_1^{-1}(U) &= \{(x,y) \in X \times Y : p_1(x,y) \in U\} \\ &= \{(x,y) \in X \times Y : x \in U\} \\ &= U \times Y, \end{aligned} \qquad (11.12)$$

which is open in X x Y since both U and Y are open (see (11.4)). Hence p_1 and similarly p_2, is continuous.

(b) If f is continuous then so are $p_1.f$ and $p_2.f$, by Corollary 11.35. To prove the converse, suppose that $p_1.f$ and $p_2.f$ are continuous. For the continuity of f it suffices to deduce the inverse image $f^{-1}(A \times B)$ is open for A open in X and B open in Y (Lemma 11.36). We have

$$\begin{aligned} f^{-1}(A \times B) &= \{z \in Z : f(z) \in A \times B\} \\ &= \{z \in Z : (p_1.f)(z) \in A \text{ and } (p_2.f)(z) \in B\} \\ &= (p_1.f)^{-1}(A) \cap (p_2.f)^{-1}(B), \end{aligned} \qquad (11.13)$$

which is the intersection of two sets which are open because $p_1.f$ and $p_2.f$ are continuous, and therefore itself open. This completes the proof of (b). The generalisation of (a) and (b) to n-fold products of spaces (see Remark 11.8) takes very little more. The typical difference is that (11.13) becomes

$$f^{-1}(A_1 \times \ldots \times A_n) = (p_1.f)^{-1}(A_1) \cap \ldots \cap (p_n.f)^{-1}(A_n). \qquad (11.13A)$$

EXERCISE Show that if A and B are closed then so is A x B.

COROLLARY 11.38 Let X be a metric space.
(a) *If functions* $f,g\colon X \to \mathbf{R}$ *are continuous then so are their sum, product, and quotient (this, where the denominator is nonzero).*
(b) *The function* $f = (f_1, f_2, \ldots, f_m)\colon X \to \mathbf{R}^m$, *defined in terms of its component functions* $f_i\colon X \to \mathbf{R}$ *by* $f(x) = (f_1(x), f_2(x), \ldots, f_m(x))$, *is continuous if and only if the functions* f_i *are all continuous.*

Proof Part (a) is the argument of Theorem 11.30 with the domain replaced by X. For (b), consider the composition diagram below.

$$X \xrightarrow{f} R^m \xrightarrow{p_i} R$$

$$x \rightarrow (f_1(x), \ldots ,f_m(x)) \rightarrow f_i(x)$$

Since $p_i(x) = f_i(x)$, the result is immediate from Theorem 11.37(c).

EXAMPLE 11.39 Prove continuity for the linear map f: $\mathbf{R}^3 \rightarrow \mathbf{R}^2$, given by

$$\begin{bmatrix} x \\ y \\ z \end{bmatrix} \rightarrow \begin{bmatrix} 2 & 3 & 1 \\ 4 & -1 & 6 \end{bmatrix}\begin{bmatrix} x \\ y \\ z \end{bmatrix} = \begin{bmatrix} 2x + 3y + z \\ 4x - y + 6z \end{bmatrix}.$$

Solution We use this example to illustrate how the next Corollary follows. That result will take care of such details in the future. In the notation of Corollary 11.38(b) we may write $f = (f_1,f_2)$, where $f_1(x,y,z) = 2x+3y+z$, $f_2(x,y,z) = 4x-y+6z$. But these are continuous by Corollary 11.38(a), being formed by sums and products of the continuous projection maps $(x,y,z) \rightarrow x$, $(x,y,z) \rightarrow y$, $(x,y,z) \rightarrow z$, and constant maps $(x,y,z) \rightarrow c$ $(c = -1, 2,3,4,6)$.

COROLLARY 11.40 Let $f = (f_1, f_2, \ldots , f_m)$: $\mathbf{R}^n \rightarrow \mathbf{R}^m$. If the f_i are rational functions of the coordinates in $\mathbf{R}^n$ then f is continuous at the points for which all f_i have nonzero denominators. In particular every linear map g: $\mathbf{R}^n \rightarrow \mathbf{R}^m$ is continuous.

EXAMPLES 11.41 (Some continuous functions)
(1) g: $\mathbf{R}^3 \rightarrow \mathbf{R}^m$, given by $g_i(x,y,z) = x^iyz + (y+z)^3$, for i = 1, 2, ... , m.

(2) f: $\mathbf{C} \rightarrow \mathbf{C}$ with $f(z) = z^2 + c$, where $c = -0.12 + 0.74\mathbf{i}$. Here f is a nonlinear map of the complex plane whose iterates $f^n(z)$ define the Julia set J_c of Figure 11.14 below as a boundary (further described in Chapter 16),

$$J_c = \partial\{z \in \mathbf{C}: |f^{(n)}(z)| \rightarrow \infty \text{ as } n \rightarrow \infty\}. \tag{11.14}$$

We have $f(x+\mathbf{i}y) = (x+\mathbf{i}y)^2 + c = x^2 - y^2 - 0.12 + \mathbf{i}(2xy + 0.74)$ so in coordinates of the real plane $\mathbf{R}^2$, $f(x,y) = (x^2 - y^2 - 0.12, 2xy + 0.74)$, which is continuous by Corollary 11.40.
(3) A *polyhedron* S in 3-space R^3 is the solid bounded by a finite collection of planes $f_i(x,y,z) = a_ix + b_iy + c_iz = d_i$ $(i = 1,2, \ldots,m)$. Examples are the Platonic solids - tetrahedron, cube, octahedron, dodecahedron, and icosahedron (Coxeter, 1973). See Figure 9.13 of Chapter 9. For suitable choice of signs of the coefficients it may be described as the set of points satisfying the inequalites $f_i(x,y,z) \leq d_i$. To put it another way S, may be written as $f_1^{-1}(-\infty, c_1] \cap \ldots \cap f_m^{-1}(-\infty, c_m]$. This is a finite intersection of closed sets and therefore itself closed - an easy application of results so far. [Which ones?]

(4) The General Linear Group GL(n,**R**) is the set of all n by n real invertible matrices. The reader may like to check from the axioms (Section 2.5) that this is indeed a group. At this stage we can easily, as an example, say something about its topology. Since invertible square matrices are those with nonzero determinant, we may view GL(n,**R**) as the inverse image of the open set $\mathbf{R}\backslash\{0\}$ under the determinant map Δ: $\mathbf{R}^{n^2} \rightarrow \mathbf{R}$. We simply represent an n x n matrix as a point in $\mathbf{R}^{n^2}$ by taking the elements row by row as successive coordinates. Since Δ is a polynomial function it is continuous, and so $GL(n,\mathbf{R}) = \Delta^{-1}(\mathbf{R}\backslash\{0\})$ is an open set.

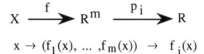

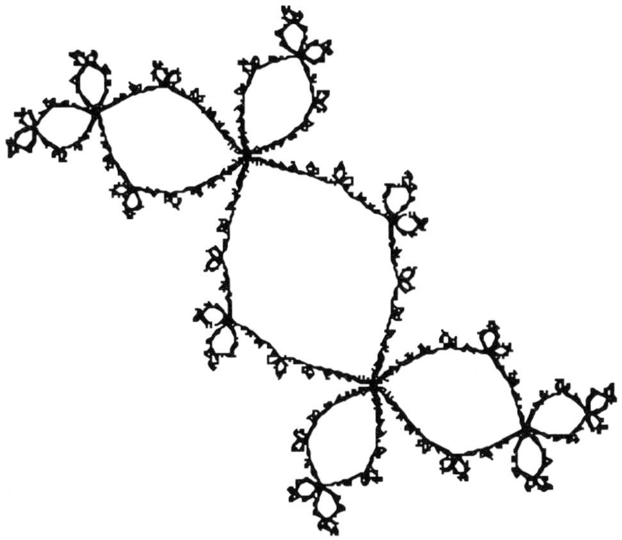

Figure 11.14 Julia set associated with the transformation of the complex plane given by

$f(z) = z^2 + c$, where

$c = -0.12+0.74\mathbf{i}$.

(5) Show that a sequence $\{x_k\}$ in $\mathbf{R}^n$ has a limit a if and only if the coordinates, which we write as $(x_1{}^k, x_2{}^k, \ldots, x_n{}^k)$, satisfy $x_i{}^k \to a_i$ as $k \to \infty$ for each subscript i, $1 \le i \le n$.

Solution We may as well take the sequence more generally in a product of n spaces, $Y = Y_1 \times Y_2 \times \ldots \times Y_n$. With distance (11.5), $d(x,y) = \max d(x_i,y_i)$ $(1 \le i \le n)$, it suffices to note that for every $\varepsilon > 0$,

$$\begin{aligned} d(x_k,a) < \varepsilon &\Leftrightarrow \max d(x_i{}^k,a_i)\ (1 \le i \le n) < \varepsilon, \\ &\Leftrightarrow d(x_i{}^k,a_i) < \varepsilon, \text{ for } 1 \le i \le n. \end{aligned}$$

Thus $x_k \to a$ if and only if $x_i{}^k \to a_i$ for $1 \le i \le n$. Now we take $Y_i = \mathbf{R}$ $(1 \le i \le n)$.

EXERCISE Try any one of the following.

(1) Describe the interior of the cube with vertices $(\pm1,\pm1,\pm1)$ by inequalities of type $ax+by+cz < d$.

(2) What can you say about the topology of the sets of n by n matrices (a) with determinant 1, (b) with determinant ±1?

(3) Use Corollary 11.40 to show that the complex rational function $(3z-5)/(z + \mathbf{i})$ is a continuous map from a subset of the complex plane to itself (think of $\mathbf{C}$ as $\mathbf{R}^2$).

(4) Prove the result of Examples 11.41(5) using basic open sets.

11.4.4 The distance function revisited

The distance function (Definition 11.1) on a metric space X gives a distance $d(x,y) \ge 0$ between every pair of points x, y in X. In other words, d is a function

$$d: X \times X \to \mathbf{R}. \tag{11.15}$$

We say $f: X \times Y \to Z$ is *continuous in the first variable,* if the function $X \to Z$, $x \to f(x,b)$, is continuous for every fixed b in Y. Of course continuity in the second variable requires that $Y \to Z$, $y \to f(a,y)$ be continuous for every fixed a in X, and analogously for the product of any number of spaces. Continuity in each variable for the distance function assists in proving results about fractals in Chapter 13. The property is conveniently established through the idea of injection functions as in the diagram below, with $i_1(x) = (x,b)$, $i_2(y) = (a,y)$ for some $a \in X$, $b \in Y$.

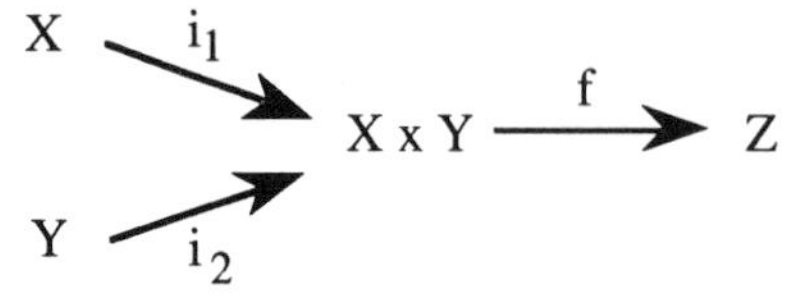

(11.16)

Thus, for example, continuity of f in the first variable means that the composition $f \circ i_1$ is continuous. But i_1 and i_2 are clearly continuous (an exercise given below) for each fixed $a \in X$, $b \in Y$, so if f is continuous then it is continuous in each variable separately [f and i_1 continuous $\Rightarrow$ $f \circ i_1$ continuous, by Corollary 11.35].

EXERCISE Choosing a convenient version of continuity from Definition 11.33, show that an injection map into a Cartesian product space is continuous.

THEOREM 11.42 The distance function $d: X \times X \to \mathbf{R}$ on a metric space X is continuous. Hence d is continuous in each variable separately.

Proof We recall that distance in **R** may be written $d(a,b) = |\mathbf{a}-\mathbf{b}|$. Using this notation will remind us when the space **R** is being referred to. Let us write d = f when thinking of d as a function on X x X. Let $f(a,b) = e$ and $\varepsilon > 0$. Then we must find $\delta > 0$ such that if

$$d((x,y), (a,b)) < \delta. \qquad (*)$$

then $|f(x,y) - e| < \varepsilon$. Suppose that (*) holds with $\delta = \varepsilon/2$. For distance in X x X we may use the Box metric (11.5): $d((x,y), (a,b)) = \max(d(x,a), d(y,b))$. Then (*) gives both inequalities $d(x,a), d(y,b) < \varepsilon/2$. The triangle inequality now shows that

$$\begin{aligned} d(x,y) &\le d(x,a) + d(a,b) + d(b,y) \\ &< \varepsilon/2 + e + \varepsilon/2, \end{aligned}$$

and

$$\begin{aligned} e = d(a,b) &\le d(a,x) + d(x,y) + d(y,b) \\ &< \varepsilon/2 + d(x,y) + \varepsilon/2. \end{aligned}$$

Combining these two, $e - \varepsilon < d(x,y) < e + \varepsilon$; that is, $|f(x,y) - e| < \varepsilon$ as required.

*THEOREM 11.43 (Bounded functions are continuous.) If a function $f: X \to Y$ between metric spaces is **bounded**, that is, for some constant, M,*

$$d(f(x), f(y)) \le M\, d(x,y), \quad \text{for all } x, y \text{ in } X, \qquad (11.17)$$

then f is continuous.

Proof Suppose f is bounded as described. Let $\varepsilon > 0$. Then for $\delta = \varepsilon/M$ and $d(x,y) < \delta$ we have $d(f(x), f(y)) \le Md(x,y) \le M.\varepsilon/M = \varepsilon$. Hence f is continuous by Definition 11.33(a).

NOTE 11.44 Given that f is bounded, there always exists a least possible value of M, which we will call in the general context ρ, the *minimum bound ratio.* (It is also known as the *norm, |f|, of f.*) A proof is given after Definition 12.6, a simple way to determine ρ in the linear case appears in Application 12.29, and a general formula is given at (14.4).

APPLICATION 11.45 The following types of function from n-space to itself are continuous, where λ and μ are constants

(a) *Isometries* : $d(f(x), f(y)) = d(x,y)$.
(b) *Coordinate scaling* : $f(x,y) = (\lambda x, \mu y)$ *in* $\mathbf{R}^2$.
(c) *Dilation* : $f(x) = \lambda x$.
(d) *Similitude* : *The composition of an isometry and a dilation.*
(e) *Contraction maps* : *Bounded functions with* $0 < \rho < 1$.

The continuity of contraction maps plays an essential role in iterative function systems (Chapter 14). The class of similitudes that are contractive is an important subclass.

EXERCISE Give an example of a function f: **R** →**R** which is not bounded. Is it continuous? Does this contradict Theorem 11.43?

11.5 Homeomorphisms

DEFINITION 11.46 Let f: X → Y be a continuous function having a continuous inverse. Then we say f is a *homeomorphism* and X is *homeomorphic to* Y. Alternatively f is a topological equivalence and X is topologically equivalent to Y. The importance of this is not only that f is bijective (1-1 and onto), pairing the elements of X with those of Y, but that f pairs open sets also. That is,

$$U \text{ is open in } X \Leftrightarrow f(U) \text{ is open in } Y. \tag{11.18}$$

For f^{-1} is continuous, so f(U) open in Y implies $f^{-1}(f(U)) = U$ is open in X, and the rest of (11.18) is a similar exercise, with f and f^{-1} interchanged. Immediate from the definition is that f^{-1} is also a homeomorphism, as is the composition of two homeomorphisms.

EXERCISE Prove that, if f: X → Y is a homeomorphism, then U open in X implies f(U) open in Y.

We list some implications of (11.18) which are of special relevance. Let f(U) = V. Then any statement about U that can be phrased in terms of open sets implies the same for V, and vice versa. Having defined open sets via open balls, we may replace 'open ball centred at x' by 'open set containing x' in the definition of interior, closure, boundary, limit. This is because (i) an open ball is a special case of an open set, (ii) if a point x lies in an open subset of A, then x centres an open ball inside A. For example $x \in A^o \Leftrightarrow x \in B \subseteq A$ for some open ball B centred at A (by definition) $\Leftrightarrow x \in V \subseteq A$ for some open set V (by (i) and (ii)). Thus (11.8) gives the following correspondences under a homeomorphism, where A → B means f(A) = B,

$$Uo \to Vo,\ \overline{U} \to \overline{V},\ \partial U \to \partial V\ , \quad (11.19A)$$
$$x_n \to a \quad \Leftrightarrow \quad f(x_n) \to f(a)\ , \quad (11.19B)$$
$$U \text{ is closed} \Leftrightarrow V \text{ is closed}, \quad (11.19C)$$
$$a \text{ is isolated} \Leftrightarrow f(a) \text{ is isolated}, \quad (11.19D)$$

and, to be explained in Chapter 12,

$$U \text{ is compact} \Leftrightarrow V \text{ is compact}, \quad (11.19E)$$
$$U \text{ is connected} \Leftrightarrow V \text{ is connected} \quad (11.19F)$$
$$U \text{ bounds a hole in } X \Leftrightarrow V \text{ bounds a hole in } Y. \quad (11.19G)$$

These can be expressed by saying that f *preserves* interiors, closures, boundaries, limits, and so on. More generally, f preserves any property which can be described in terms of open sets. Such a property is said to be *topological*, and holds for X if and only if it holds for Y. So what kind of bending and stretching or other changes can occur under a homeomorphism? First of all, any changes effected by the list (a) to (e) in Application 11.45, since each, having a continuous inverse, is a homeomorphism. To that list we may add any further types obtainable by an invertible linear transformation. For example, a shear in the plane given by $(x,y) \to (x+\alpha y, y)$, moving points horizontally by an amount proportional to their y-coordinate. More details are given in Chapter 14.

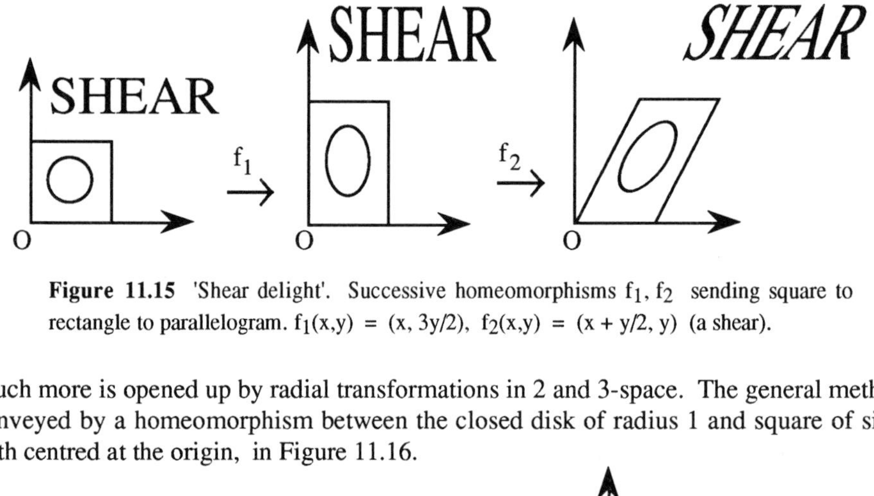

Figure 11.15 'Shear delight'. Successive homeomorphisms f_1, f_2 sending square to rectangle to parallelogram. $f_1(x,y) = (x, 3y/2)$, $f_2(x,y) = (x + y/2, y)$ (a shear).

Much more is opened up by radial transformations in 2 and 3-space. The general method is conveyed by a homeomorphism between the closed disk of radius 1 and square of side 4, both centred at the origin, in Figure 11.16.

In polar coordinates,

$$(r,\theta) \to (R,\theta), \quad \text{where}$$
$$R = 2r \sec\theta \quad (0 \le \theta \le \pi/4).$$

For example, f(P) = Q in the diagram. The rest is dictated by symmetry. Because f is a homeomorphism, the interior of the circle is mapped onto the interior of the square, and the boundary to the boundary, by (11.19A).

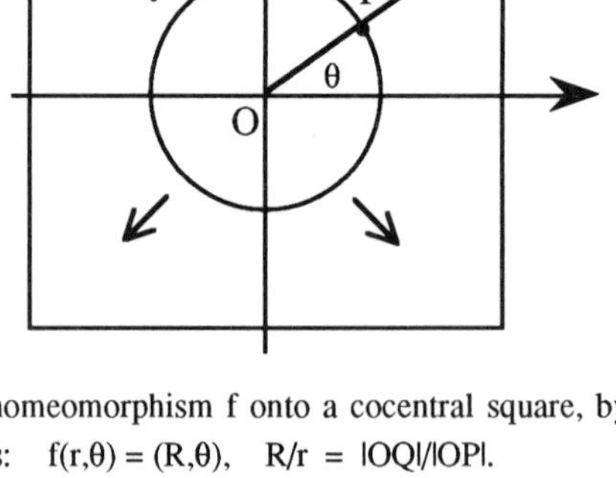

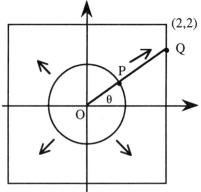

Figure 11.16 Unit circle mapped by a homeomorphism f onto a cocentral square, by proportional stretching along radius vectors: $f(r,\theta) = (R,\theta)$, $R/r = |OQ|/|OP|$.

By the radial method we see that every regular polygon is homeomorphic to a circle and hence to every other regular polygon. With a little more work we can adapt the radial method to irregular and star-shaped polygons such as that of Figure 11.17(a). Right now we'll settle for the following statement.

THEOREM 11.47
(a) *In* $\mathbf{R}$*, all closed intervals are homeomorphic,*
(b) *In the plane,* $\mathbf{R}^2$*, all (filled in) squares, rectangles, parallelograms, regular polygons, and circles are homeomorphic,*
(c) *In 3-space,* $\mathbf{R}^3$*, all closed balls or solid polyhedra are homeomorphic.*

Of course there are many other obvious equivalences, and many that are far from obvious. A standard inference of Part (c) above, using (11.19A), is that the bounding surface of every Platonic solid is homeomorphic to a sphere (the boundary of a ball); the Platonic solids being the cube, octahedron, tetrahedron, dodecahedron and icosahedron (see Coxeter (1973), and Figure 9.13).

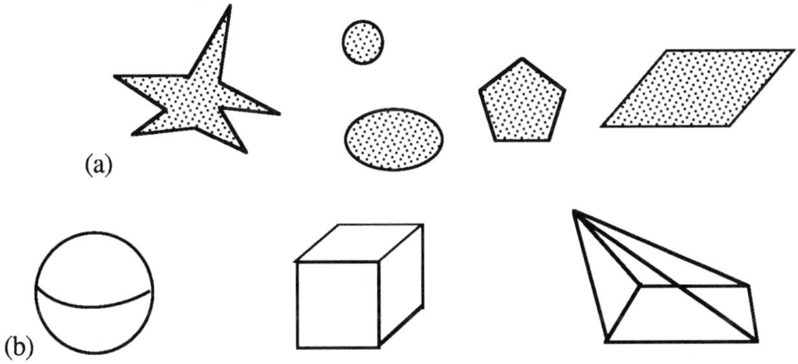

Figure 11.17 (a) Some homeomorphic subspaces in the plane, (b) some homeomorphic subspaces of 3-space.

EXAMPLE 11.48 ($S^1 \times S^1$ *is homeomorphic to the torus in 3-space.*) What exactly is a torus? We use this name for a variety of objects in different sizes, positions in 3-space, and of varying shapes. All are topologically equivalent. We shall take as a standard torus the surface swept out by a circle (the cross-section) of centre A and some radius r, as A itself describes a circle in the xy-plane, centred at the origin, of some radius R > r. The result is roughly represented in Figure 11.18(a).

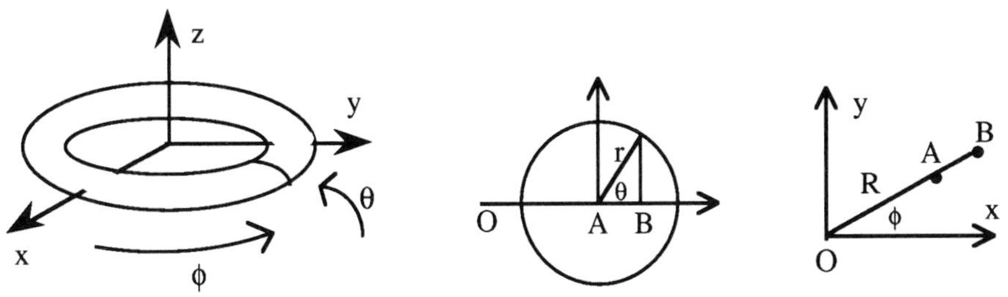

(a) The torus in $\mathbf{R}^3$. (b) Cross-section of torus. (c) Looking down the z-axis.

Figure 11.18 A standard torus.

The centre A of the cross-section lies in the xy-plane, with coordinates (R $\cos\phi$, R $\sin\phi$), and ϕ varying from 0 to 2π. Referring to Figure 11.18(b), let a point P on the cross-section circle project vertically (parallel to the z-axis) onto B in the xy-plane. Then for some angle θ between 0 and 2π the height of P above the plane is $z = r \sin\theta$ and its distance from the z-axis is $|OB| = R + r\cos\theta$ (see Figure 11.18(c)). Thus the torus may be coordinatised as

$$T = \{(R + r\cos\theta)\cos\phi,\ (R + r\cos\theta)\sin\phi,\ r\sin\theta):\ 0 \le \phi,\theta < 2\pi\}.$$

Topologically speaking, every other torus is the image of this under some homeomorphism, and in this sense we can view the torus as, for example, a sphere with one handle (see Figure 11.1). On the other hand, to keep the more familiar torus shape, we may restrict the homeomorphisms to isometries, whilst allowing the radii to vary subject to $R > r > 0$. Finally it is almost trivial now to give a homeomorphism between the subset $S^1 \times S^1$ of 4-space and T. Simply adopt θ, ϕ as coordinates of the respective copies of S^1 and map (θ, ϕ) to the coordinatised point of T exhibited above. Strictly speaking, to prove this is a homeomorphism we should verify that the sine and cosine functions are continuous. For the sine this means that $\sin(\alpha+\varepsilon) \to \sin\alpha$ as $\varepsilon \to 0$, for any angle α. We will be content with the following. Assuming that as $\varepsilon \to 0$ we have $\cos\varepsilon \to 1$ and $\sin\alpha \to 0$, a trigonometric identity gives $\sin(\alpha+\varepsilon) = \sin\alpha\cos\varepsilon + \cos\alpha\sin\varepsilon \to \sin\varepsilon$ as $\varepsilon \to 0$. The cosine is similar.

EXERCISE Construct a homeomorphism between two pyramids on the same base.

EXAMPLE 11.49 (Bracketing product spaces.) If X, Y, Z are metric spaces, or indeed general topological spaces, then $X \times (Y \times Z)$ is homeomorphic to $X \times Y \times Z$, indeed we may bracket the factors in a product of n spaces in any way we choose and still retain a topologically equivalent space.

Proof We have an obvious bijective map $f: X \times (Y \times Z) \to X \times Y \times Z$ with $f(x, (y,z)) = (x,y,z)$. Standard basic open sets for the respective products are $A \times (B \times C)$ and $A \times B \times C$, (cf. (11.4)), where A, B, C are open sets of X, Y, Z in that order. But f pairs such sets, and so is a homeomorphism (by Lemma 11.36). In this way we may prove the corresponding results for variously bracketed products of any finite number of spaces.

One way to show that two spaces are ***not*** **homeomorphic** is to find some topological property possessed by one but not by the other. For example, a closed disc is not homeomorphic to an open one, since the latter has empty boundary (as a subspace of the plane). Other methods arise incidentally in succeeding chapters. [For the methods of Algebraic topology, outside the scope of this text, see e.g. Maunder, 1970.]

11.6 Quotient spaces

Quotient spaces are an important way to obtain new spaces in terms of old simpler ones by glueing. Informally, we glue together points of two spaces, or a set of points of the same space, by designating certain sets of points as 'equivalent', and adjusting the topology accordingly (Definition 11.53). To make this precise we need first of all equivalence relations.

DEFINITION 11.50 (Equivalence relations.) A *relation* R on a set X is defined as a subset

$R \subseteq X \times X$. If $(x,y) \in R$ we say *x is related to y*, or xRy, or simply $x \sim y$. Then R is an *equivalence relation* if it is

Reflexive	:	$x \sim x$ for each x in X,
Symmetric	:	$x \sim y$ implies $y \sim x$, for all x,y in X,
Transitive	:	$x \sim y$ and $y \sim x$ together imply $x \sim z$, for all x,y,z in X.

In this case we say x,y are *R-equivalent* if xRy.

EXERCISE Let $f: X \to Y$ be any function. Show that $R = \{(x,y) : f(x) = f(y)\}$ is an equivalence relation on X.

Equivalence relations crop up in all kinds of places, but before illustrating this and applying them in our context, we note a basic and useful fact: *an equivalence relation R partitions X into nonempty disjoint subsets*. This works as follows. Let $x \in X$. Then we define the *equivalence class containing x*, denoted by $\bar{x}$ or [x], to be

$$[x] \quad = \quad \{y \in X : x \sim y\}, \tag{11.20}$$

the set of all elements related to x. Since every element of X is in *some* equivalence class, the following Theorem establishes the partition

THEOREM 11.51 Equivalence classes [x] and [y] are identical if $x \sim y$, *otherwise they are disjoint.*

Proof We use the symmetry of R without further comment. Let $x \sim y$. If $z \in [x]$ then $x \sim z$ by (11.20), so we have $z \sim x$ and $x \sim y$, giving $z \sim y$ by transitivity. Thus $z \in [y]$. Hence $[x] \subseteq [y]$, and similarly $[y] \subseteq [x]$, proving that $[x] = [y]$. It remains to show that if the intersection $[x] \cap [y]$ is nonempty then $[x] = [y]$. Let $z \in [x] \cap [y]$. Then $x \sim y$, $y \sim z$ so by transitivity $x \sim y$. Hence by the first part, $[x] = [y]$.

Thus X is the disjoint union of the equivalence classes; we can recover R from a knowledge of these subsets (the equivalence classes) by: $xRy \Leftrightarrow x,y$ are in the same subset.

EXAMPLE 11.52 (1) (*The integers mod p*.) Take $X = \mathbf{Z}$, the set of all integers 0, ±1, ±2, ... Let p be a prime number, i.e. $p > 1$ and p is divisible only by itself and 1. We define the relation on **Z** of *equivalence mod p* by: $m\,R\,n \Leftrightarrow p|(m-n)$, usually expressed as $m \equiv n \pmod p$ or "m is congruent to n modulo p". If $p = 7$ then $[3] = \{3,10,17, ...\}$. We define addition and multiplication by $[m]+[n] = [m+n]$, $[m][n] = [mn]$. Then e.g. $[3][5] = [15] = [1]$, which acts as the identity in the set Z_7 of equivalence classes. This structure Z_p is a powerful tool in Number theory, with applications in Cryptology. See e.g. Schroeder (1986). For a compact introduction see Whitelaw (1988).

(2) In (1) we replace integers by $Z_p[x]$, the set of polynomials with coefficients in Z_p, and p by an irreducible such polynomial, i.e. one which cannot be factorised. This leads to the theory of finite fields, an area increasingly important in the design of communications systems. For applications in multi-user theory, see McEliece (1987).

DEFINITION 11.53 Given an equivalence relation R on a space X we define the *quotient space* X/R to be the set of equivalence classes of R with topology obtained from the *quotient map*

$$p: X \to X/R, \quad p(x) = [x] \qquad (11.21)$$

by defining $U \subseteq X/R$ to be open if and only if $p^{-1}(U)$ is open in X. Thus the open sets are the mimimal family of open sets required for p to be continuous. Notice that this is the first time we have defined the topology of a space without reference to a distance function. This is quite all right for topological properties, including those listed as (11.19) (boundaries, limit points ...), since the family of open sets has Property 11.4: a finite intersection or arbitrary union of open sets is open.

EXERCISE Prove that the union or intersection of two open sets in X/R is open, according to definition (11.21).

CONSTRUCTION 11.54

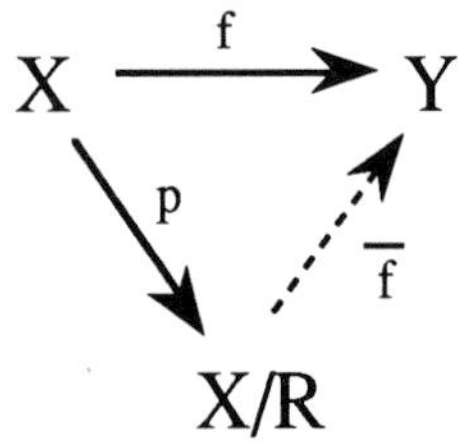

A continuous map f: $X \to Y$ sending R-equivalent points to the same point of Y defines (*'induces'*) a continuous map

$$\bar{f}: X/R \to Y,$$
by $\bar{f}([x]) = f(x)$.

The induced map $\bar{f}$ is well-defined because f, by hypothesis, sends any two points in the same equivalence class to the same point of Y. It is continuous because:

U open in Y	$\Rightarrow$	$f^{-1}(U)$ open in X,	by definition
	$\Rightarrow$	$p^{-1}(\bar{f}^{-1}(U))$ open in X,	as $f = \bar{f} \circ p$
	$\Rightarrow$	$\bar{f}^{-1}(U)$ open in X/R,	Definition 11.53.

We say X/R has the *quotient topology*. However the word *identification* is often used in place of quotient throughout, on the view that we are creating a new space by making identifications between pairs of sets of points of an original space. Indeed this is a standard way to describe the classification (Maunder, 1970) of compact surfaces. (We shall shortly define 'compact' in Chapter 12.) Now we give some examples of quotient spaces.

EXAMPLE 11.55 (The cylinder)

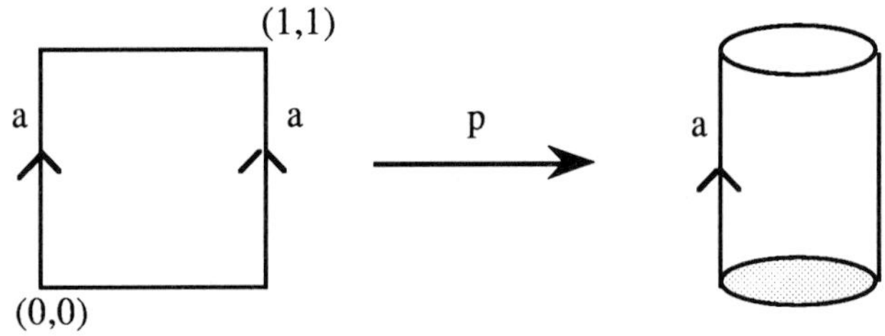

The square represents the subspace $X = \{(x,y) \in \mathbf{R}^2: 0 \le x,y \le 1\}$. The parallel arrows conventionally indicate that we are to identify pairs of points at the same height. That is, $(0,y) \sim (1,y)$, $0 \le y \le 1$. In keeping with this, and essential for more complicated identifications, is the labelling of 'glued' edges by the same letter, a. Commonsense tells us, correctly, that the result is homeomorphic to a cylinder, as indicated. We may represent the cylinder as

$$Y = \{(\cos\phi, \sin\phi, z):\ 0 \le \phi \le 2\pi,\ \ 0 \le z \le 1\}.$$

Following Construction 11.54, define $f: X \to Y$ by $F(x,y) = (\cos 2\pi x, \sin 2\pi x, z)$. Then $f(0,y) = f(1,y)$ as required, so f induces $\bar{f}: X/R \to Y$. This is a continuous bijection. For proving it to be a homeomorphism, we can either use a bare-handed approach, considering the cylinder as a subspace of $\mathbf{R}^3$, and proving f maps open sets to open sets (so that its inverse is continuous) or await Theorem 12.15 .

EXAMPLE 11.56 (*The Möbius band*)

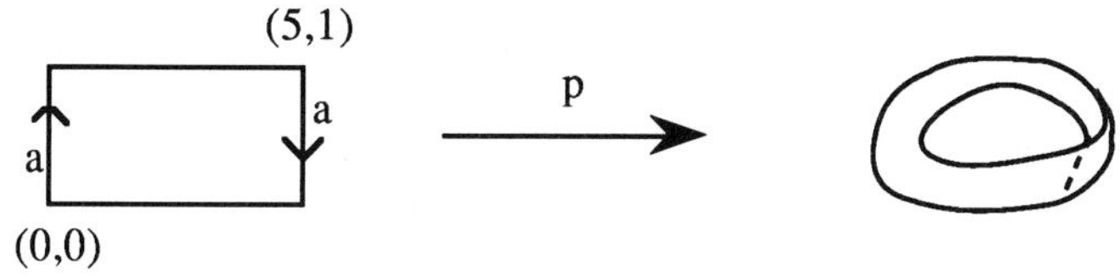

Starting with the indicated rectangle, the arrows now tell us to give one edge a half turn before glueing. More precisely, $(0,y) \sim (5,1-y)$, $0 \le y \le 1$. The result is called a Möbius band and has the strange property that a fly can walk for 5 units and finish on the opposite side of the band, without crossing an edge. Also, cutting a complete circle along the spine, corresponding to the line $y = 1/2$, gives a surprising party trick.

EXAMPLE 11.57 (The torus.)

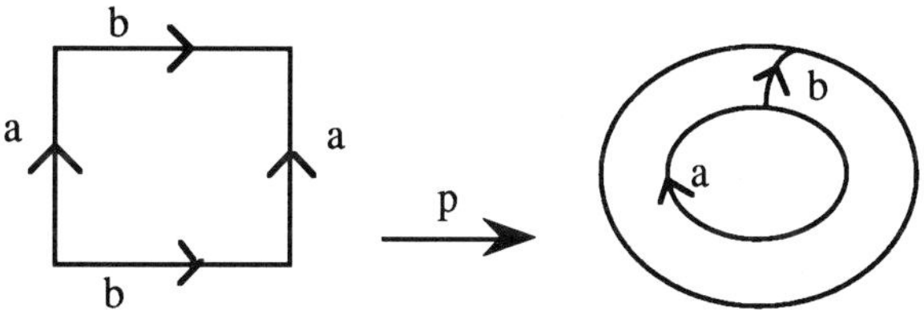

Here we glue the edges marked 'a' together to form a cylinder, then glue the now circular ends together, forming a torus, or doughnut shape.

EXAMPLE 11.58 (The Klein bottle)

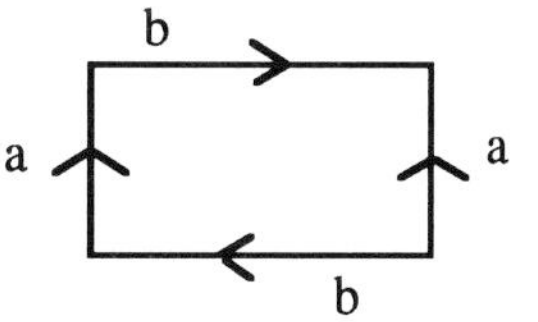

After identifying the a's to get a cylinder we cannot glue the b's the opposite way round as prescribed, in 3-space, without creating self-intersections, but the result is called a Klein bottle. It exists honestly in $\mathbf{R}^4$.

EXAMPLE 11.59 (Making a sphere from a disc.) This and its n-dimensional analogues are useful and well-known to topologists. We take a closed disc D and identify its whole rim S to one point: $x \sim y \Leftrightarrow x,y \in S$. In such a situation we often write D/S rather than D/R. By using an intermediate homeomorphism we see that the result is topologically a 2-sphere, the boundary of a ball in 3-space (see Example 12.17(3) for further details). Imagine we fix the rim and blow the interior as a bubble, obtaining the middle object of Figure 11.19, actually a 2-sphere with an open disc removed. Gradually contract the rim to a point. Whilst the rim has a finite radius the result is still topologicaly a closed disk; only the final finite contraction to a point is the quotient map, giving us a 2-sphere with say the north pole marking the spot where the rim became a point. Proving that the result is a 2-sphere is a nice, short application of compactness, following Theorem 12.15 in the next Chapter.

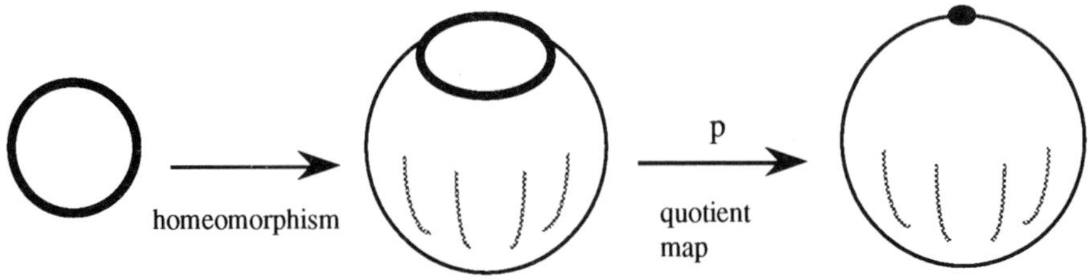

Figure 11.19. Identifying the rim of a disc to a point gives topologically a sphere.

REFERENCES ON METRIC SPACES

1. Real analysis (from limits and compactness to integration). See Murphy (1984).
2. General metric spaces. See Giles (1987), Simmons (1963), or Sutherland (1975).

EXERCISES 11

---

1 In what sense do the pretzel and 2-handled sphere in Figure 11.1 have three holes?

2 Explain how the empty set $\emptyset$ and the whole space X satisfy the definition of openness.

3 √ Write down a set that is open and one that is not. What about $A = \{a\}$?

4 √ Why is an 'open line segment' in the plane not open in the plane? Is it closed?

5 Prove De Morgan's laws by the method of Example 11.5(2).

6 √ Is there another basis for the topology of the plane, besides open discs, rectangles, or squares?

7 Deduce from (11.3) that a basis for the topology of a plane circle is the set of open arcs.

8 Show that (11.5) does define a metric (see Definition 11.1).

9 √ What are the limit points in **R**, of the set of rational numbers?

10 √ What are the limit points of the subset $\{(n+2)/(n+1)\}$, $n = 1,2,\ldots$ of **R**?

11 √ Find the closure, interior and boundary of $A = (0,1) \cup (1,3]$. Do the same for the closed region between two concentric circles.

12 Use Test 11.21 to show that isolated points of subset A of a space are not in its boundary (are they necessarily in its interior? - see (11.8)).

13 Which space is dense in which, in the following list: $(0,2)$, $(0,2]$, $[1,2)$, $(0,2)\backslash\{1\}$?

14 √ Which category of Figure 11.11 applies to $f: \mathbf{R} \to \mathbf{R}$, $f(x) = x^3 - 2$?

15 Show that $gf = 1$ implies that f is 1-1 and g is onto (NB: f is performed before g).

16 Is $f: \mathbf{R} \to \mathbf{R}$ continuous if $f(x) = 1-2x$, for $x \leq 3$ and x^2-4x-1 for $x > 3$? What if $f(x) = |x|$?

17 Prove that the identity function $f(x) = x$, and any constant function $f(x) = c$, are continuous. Prove that if $g: \mathbf{R} \to \mathbf{R}$ is continuous and never zero then $1/g(x)$ is continuous on **R**.

18 Show the rational function $(x^3-5x^2+3x+1)/(x^4+1)$ is continuous (repeatedly apply Theorem 11.30).

19 Prove that a function between topological spaces that satisfies Definition 11.33 for every point also satisfies Definition 11.34.

20 Use Lemma 11.36 to show that a function is continuous if and only if its inverse image of every closed set is a closed set.

21 √ Show that if A and B are closed subsets of a space X then A x B is closed in X x X.

22 √ What can you say about the topology of the sets of n by n matrices (a) with determinant 1, (b) with determinant $\pm$ 1 (open, closed, ...?).

23 Express the complex rational function $f(z) = (3z-5)/(z + i)$ as a continuous map from a subset of the real plane to the real plane.

24 Choosing a convenient definition of continuity, show that that an injection map into a Cartesian product space is continuous.

25 √ Give an example of a function which is not bounded. Is it continuous? (cf. Theorem 11.43.)

26 Prove that, if $f: X \rightarrow Y$ is a homeomorphism, then U open in X implies f(U) open in Y.

27 Describe a homeomorphism between two pyramids on the same base

28 Let $f: X \rightarrow Y$ be any function. Show that $R = \{(x,y) : f(x) = f(y)\}$ is an equivalence relation on X.

29 Prove that the union or intersection of two open sets in a quotient space X/R is open, according to Definition (11.18).

30 For a function $f: X \rightarrow Y$ with $A, B \subseteq Y$, prove the results (a) $f^{-1}(A \cup B) = f^{-1}(A) \cup f^{-1}(B)$, (b) $f^{-1}(A \backslash B) = f^{-1}(A) \backslash f^{-1}(B)$, and hence $f^{-1}(A^c) = (f^{-1}(A))^c$.

31 p_1 and p_2 are projection maps of a product X x Y with A, B subsets of X, Y respectively. Show that $p_1^{-1}(A) = A \times Y$, $p_2^{-1}(B) = X \times B$. By considering their intersection, suggest a sub-basis for the topology of X x Y. Hence describe in three ways the topology of a product $X_1 \times X_2 \times \ldots \times X_n$.

32 **(Further exercises)** For an arbitrary function $f: X \rightarrow Y$, prove the equalities (i) $f(A \cup B) = f(A) \cup f(B)$, and (ii) $f(A \cap B) \subseteq f(A) \cap f(B)$, giving an example in which inequality occurs.

33 Let $f: X \rightarrow Y$ and $g: Y \rightarrow Z$ be functions. Show that if f, g are injective then so is g.f, and similarly for surjections.

34 (i) Let $f, g: X \rightarrow Y$ be continuous maps between metric spaces. Show that if f(x) = f(y) for every x in a nonempty subset A of X then f(x) = g(x) for every point in $\overline{A}$. (ii) Show that the boundary of a set in a metric space is closed

35 (i) Prove that the inequality $a_1x_1 + \ldots + a_nx_n < 0$ in R^n defines an open set, (ii) Describe separately the boundary and interior of a cube, by a series of inequalities.

36 Prove that the map of Example 11.54 is a homeomorphism by the bare-handed approach suggested.

37 √ Let A, B be subsets of a metric space X. Prove that (i) $\overline{A \cup B} = \overline{A} \cup \overline{B}$, (ii) A is dense in X $\Leftrightarrow$ A intersects every nonempty open subset of X, (iii) $\partial(A \cup B) \subseteq \partial A \cup \partial B$.

TABLE 11.2 Real sequences and series

Let $\{x_n\}, \{y_n\}, \{z_n\}$ be sequences of real numbers, with limits $x_n \to a$, $y_n \to b$, $z_n \to c$, and $\lambda \in$ **R.** Usually n runs through the natural numbers $\mathbf{N} = \{1,2,3, ...\}$.

(1) $x_n + \lambda \to a + \lambda$ (2) $\lambda x_n \to \lambda a$ (3) $(x_n + y_n) \to a + b$
(4) $x_n y_n \to ab$ (5) $x_n/y_n \to a/b$ (if all y_n, and b, are nonzero)

(6) If $x_n \leq y_n$ $(n \in \mathbf{N})$ then $a \leq b$ (Similarly with $\geq$ for $\leq$)
(7) If $x_n \leq M$ $(n \in \mathbf{N})$ then $a \leq M$ (Similarly with $\geq$ for $\leq$)
(8) If $x_n + y_n \leq z_n$ $(n \in \mathbf{N})$ then $a + b \leq c$ (Similarly with $\geq$ for $\leq$)
(9) If $\{S_n\}$ satisfies $S_1 \leq S_2 \leq ... \leq M$, then $\{S_n\}$ has a limit $S \leq M$.

SERIES Suppose the *partial sums* $S_1 = a_1$, $S_2 = a_1 + a_2$, $S_3 = a_1 + a_2 + a_3$, ... satisfy $S_n \to S$. Then we say the *infinite sum*

$$\sum_{n=1}^{\infty} a_n = a_1 + a_2 + a_3 + \ ...$$

converges, to the sum S. Special case: the *Geometric series* of n terms, $S_n = 1+r+r^2+... + r^{n-1}$, with $(1-r)S_n = 1-r^n$. Further, if $|r| < 1$ then $r^n \to 0$ as $n \to \infty$. Hence the important formulae below, where we define $|x| = x$ if $x \geq 0$, $|x| = -x$ if $x < 0$.

(10) $1+r+r^2+... + r^{n-1} = (1-r^n)/(1-r)$ $(r \neq 1)$
(11) $1+r+r^2+... = 1/(1-r)$ $(|r| < 1)$

USEFUL SUMS
(12) $1 + 2 + 3 + ... + n = n(n+1)/2$
(13) $1^2 + 2^2 + 3^2 + ... + n^2 = n(n+1)(2n+1)/6$
(14) $1^3 + 2^3 + 3^3 + ... + n^3 = [n(n+1)/2]^2$

INEQUALITES
(15) $|x| - |y| \leq |x + y| \leq |x| + |y|$ (The triangle inequality)
(16) $|a_1 + a_2 + a_3 + ... + a_n| \leq |a_1| + |a_2| + |a_3| + ... + |a_n|$
(17) Let $0 \leq a_n \leq b_n$ $(n \in \mathbf{N})$. If Σb_n converges then so does Σa_n.
(18) If Σa_n converges and $\lambda \in \mathbf{R}$, then $\Sigma \lambda a_n$ converges to $\lambda \Sigma a_n$.
(19) If the second series below converges then so does the first, and

$$\left| \sum_{n=1}^{\infty} a_n \right| \leq \sum_{n=1}^{\infty} |a_n|$$

THE COMPLEX CASE (20) All the above applies to complex numbers also, with $|x+\mathbf{i}y| = \sqrt{(x^2+y^2)}$, except where a statement has meaning only for real numbers, namely (6) to (9) and (17).

TABLE 11.3 Closure, interior, and boundary

DEFINITIONS Let A,B be subsets of a metric space S. Then we say A is *open* if each $x \in A$ centres an open ball $B_x(r) = \{y \in S: d(x,y) < r\}$ in A. The subset B is *closed* if its complement B^c is open. The *topology* of S is its collection of open subsets, which includes S itself and the empty set $\emptyset$. A family $\mathfrak{B}$ of subsets is a *basis for the topology* if the open sets consist of the unions of members of $\mathfrak{B}$. One basis is $\mathfrak{B} = \{B_x(r): x \in S, r > 0\}$, with $A = \bigcup B_x(r)$ $(x \in A, B_x(r) \subseteq A, r > 0)$ whenever A is open.

RULES

(1) Any union of open sets is open, any intersection of closed sets is closed

(2) A finite intersection of open sets is open, a finite union of closed sets is closed

DEFINITIONS $x \in S$ is a *limit point (accumulation point)* of A if every $B_x(r)$ contains a point of A besides x. The *derived set A'* consists of all limit points of A. Then x is an *isolated point of A* if it is *in* A but is not a limit point of A.

$\overline{A} = A \cup A'$, the *closure* of A, also written Cl(A)

$A^o = \{x \in A: B_x(r) \subseteq A \text{ for some } r > 0\}$, the *interior* of A, also written Int(A)

$\partial A = \overline{A} \setminus A^o$, the *boundary*, or *frontier*, of A, also written Fr(A)

RULES

(3) $\overline{(\overline{A})} = \overline{A}$ (4) $A^o \subseteq A \subseteq \overline{A}$ (5) $(A^o)^o = A^o$

(6) $\overline{A}$ is the smallest closed set containing A. That is, if B is closed and contains A then $\overline{A} \subseteq B$

(7) A^o is the largest open set contained in A. That is, if B is open and is contained in A then $B \subseteq A^o$

(8) A is closed $\Leftrightarrow$ $A = \overline{A}$ (9) A is open $\Leftrightarrow$ $A = A^o$

(10) If $A \subseteq B$ then $\overline{A} \subseteq \overline{B}$ (11) If $A \subseteq B$ then $A^o \subseteq B^o$

(12) $\overline{A \cup B} = \overline{A} \cup \overline{B}$ (13) $(A \cup B)^o \supseteq A^o \cup B^o$

(14) $\overline{A \cap B} \subseteq \overline{A} \cap \overline{B}$ (15) $(A \cap B)^o = A^o \cap B^o$

(16) $(\overline{A})^c = (A^c)^o$ (17) $(A^o)^c = \overline{A^c}$

(18) $\partial A = \{x \in S: \text{every } B_x(r) \text{ intersects both A and } A^c\}$

(19) $\partial A = \overline{A} \cap \overline{A^c} = \partial (A^c)$ (20) A' and ∂A are closed sets

(21) $\overline{A} = A \cup \partial A$ (22) $A^o = A \setminus \partial A$

(23) $\partial(A \cup B) \subseteq \partial A \cup \partial B$

TABLE 11.4 Some properties of functions

DEFINITIONS We recall that a function $f: X \to Y$ is called *onto* (or *surjective*) if every $y \in Y$ is the *image* $f(x)$ of some $x \in X$. The function is *1-1* (or *injective*) if it maps distinct points of x to distinct points of Y. That is, $f(a) = f(b) \Rightarrow a = b$. If f is both 1-1 and onto then it is called *bijective*, or *a pairing*. The *image of the subset A of X under f* is $f(A) = \{f(x): x \in X\}$, and the *inverse image of a subset B of Y* is $f^{-1}(B) = \{x \in X: f(x) \in B\}$. The *identity map* $1_X: X \to X$ sends every point to itself. Usually we omit the subscript, unless there is doubt as to what is intended.

We may define a function $f: X \to Y$ between topological spaces to be *continuous* if $f^{-1}(B)$ is open in X whenever B is open in Y. Or equivalently, if $f^{-1}(E)$ is closed in X whenever E is closed in Y. Alternatively B runs through the sets in a basis (or just sub-basis) for the topology of Y.

PROPERTIES of functions

(1) $f: X \to Y$ is 1-1 if and only if there is a function $g: Y \to X$ with $gf = 1$

(2) $f: X \to Y$ is onto if and only if there is a function $g: Y \to X$ with $fg = 1$

(3) If $A \subseteq B$ then $f(A) \subseteq f(B)$

(4) $f(A \cup B) = f(A) \cup f(B)$, more generally $f(\bigcup_i A_i) = \bigcup_i f(A_i)$

(5) $f(A \cap B) \subseteq f(A) \cap f(B)$ (with equality for all $A,B \subseteq X \Leftrightarrow$ f is 1-1)

(6) $(f(A))^c \subseteq f(A^c)$ for all $A \subseteq X \Leftrightarrow$ f is onto. (Equality $\Leftrightarrow$ f is bijective)

(7) If $A \subseteq B$ then $f^{-1}(A) \subseteq f^{-1}(B)$

(8) $f^{-1}(A \cup B) = f^{-1}(A) \cup f^{-1}(B)$, more generally $f^{-1}(\bigcup_i A_i) = \bigcup_i f^{-1}(A_i)$

(9) $f^{-1}(A \cap B) = f^{-1}(A) \cap f^{-1}(B)$, more generally $f^{-1}(\bigcap_i A_i) = \bigcap_i f^{-1}(A_i)$

(10) $f^{-1}(A^c) = (f^{-1}(A))^c$

PROPERTIES of continuous functions

(11) $f(\overline{A}) \subseteq \overline{f(A)}$

(12) *(The union of two functions is continuous.)* Let $X = A \cup B$, with A, B both open (or both closed) in X. Let $g: A \to Y$, and $h: B \to Y$ be continuous, and agree on $A \cap B$. Then $f = g \cup h$ is continuous, where $f(x) = g(x)$ if $x \in A$, and $f(x) = h(x)$ if $x \in B$.

Chapter 12 COMPACT SETS, CONNECTED SETS, HOLES AND HOMEOMORPHISMS

12.1 Compactness

12.1.1 The meaning of compact

We noted in Chapter 1 that closed sets have advantages for sequences; but even more pleasant properties are required, and can be realised, for the theory we shall present and apply. Consider for example the subset of the plane, $S = \{(x,y): 1 \leq x \leq 3\}$. Though closed, it consists of an infinite strip and, correspondingly, we can have sequences with no limit point, as shown in Figure 12.1 (NB 'sequence' will refer to the infinite type of Definition 11.14, unless otherwise stated.)

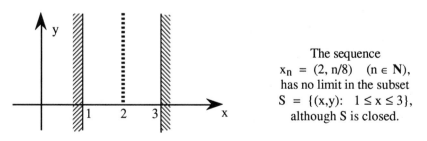

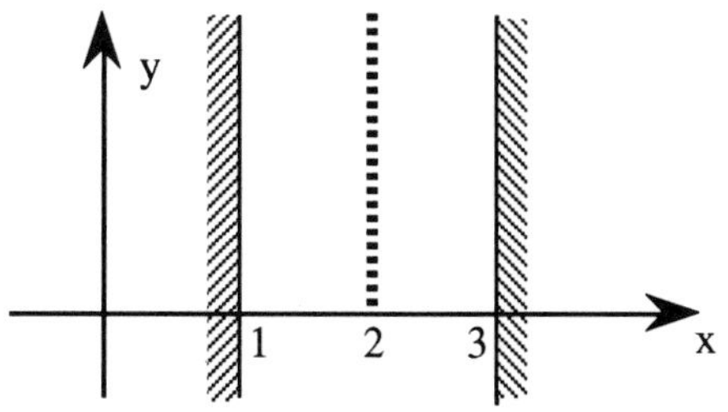

The sequence
$x_n = (2, n/8) \quad (n \in \mathbf{N})$,
has no limit in the subset
$S = \{(x,y): 1 \leq x \leq 3\}$,
although S is closed.

Figure 12.1 Closed sets are not enough.

We eliminate this possibility and obtain many good consequences by specifying that a set be *compact*, as defined shortly. Meanwhile we preview a conclusion:

For a subset of $\boldsymbol{R}^n$, compact means bounded and closed (12.1)

DEFINITION 12.1 A nonempty subset A of a metric space X is *bounded* if A lies within some open ball $B_u(M)$. In fact we may choose any other point v as the centre of the ball and adjust the radius accordingly. For example, let X be n-space, v the origin, and x any point. Then, as indicated in Figure 12.2,

$$\begin{aligned} d(x,O) &\le d(x,u) + d(u,O), && \text{by the triangle inequality,} \\ &\le M + d(u,O), && \text{which is constant,} \\ &\le R, \text{ say.} \end{aligned}$$

Thus A lies within $B_O(R)$. It follows that $A \subseteq \mathbf{R}^n$ is bounded if and only if A lies within a ball centred at the origin, of radius R say, so $|x| < R$ for all x in A.

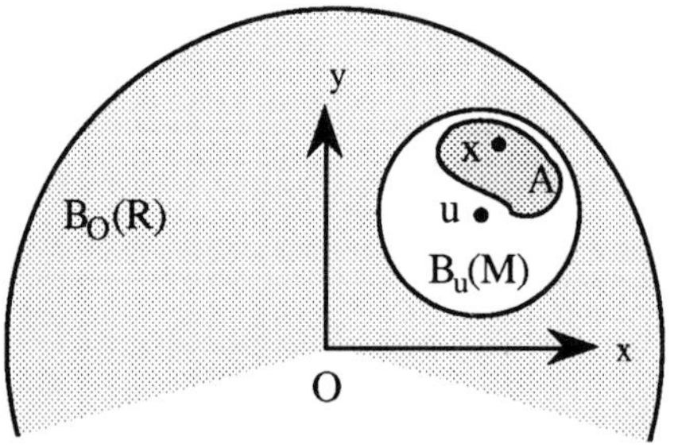

The set A is bounded,

(a) because $A \subseteq B_u(M)$,
(b) because $A \subseteq B_O(R)$.

Figure 12.2 A bounded set in $\mathbf{R}^n$.

Thus the strip in Figure 12.1 is unbounded. We will show that compactness of A ensures that every sequence in A converges, or has a subsequence that does so. Another important result for us is that a continuous real function f: $X \to \mathbf{R}$ on a compact space X attains both a maximum and a minimum. This has interesting applications, for example in linear programming (see Application 12.27).

Closed and bounded was the historical definition of compactness, in the context of Euclidean spaces $\mathbf{R}^n$. However it emerged that in proving results, and in going beyond Euclidean spaces, a certain consequence (called the *Heine-Borel Property)* was the key property and, as remarked by Kelley (1964), like all good theorems its conclusion became the definition. To state it we need the notion of an open cover.

DEFINITION 12.2. Let B be a set. Then a family of sets $\mathcal{A}$ is a *cover* of B if B is a subset of the union $\cup\{A: A \in \mathcal{A}\}$. The family is an *open* cover if each $A \in \mathcal{A}$ is an open set. A *subcover* of $\mathcal{A}$ is a subfamily which is also a cover. Finally, a space X is **compact** if

every open cover of X has a finite subcover. (12.2)

A *subset* A of X is *compact* if A is compact as a subspace (see (11.3)). That is, if every cover of A by open sets of X has a finite subcover.

EXAMPLE 12.3 (1) Any space consisting of a finite number of points is compact (why?).

(2) Recall our infinite plane strip S, reproduced in Figure 12.3. One open cover consists of a single set as shown. This is indeed finite, but Definition 12.2 of compactness requires *every* open cover to have a finite subcover, and one which clearly does not is the *ball cover* (of radius ε)

$$\mathcal{A}_\varepsilon = \{B_x(\varepsilon): x \in S\}. \tag{12.3}$$

The failure is simply because the balls are bounded and S is not. Before going further, we need to review the special case of subsets of the real line.

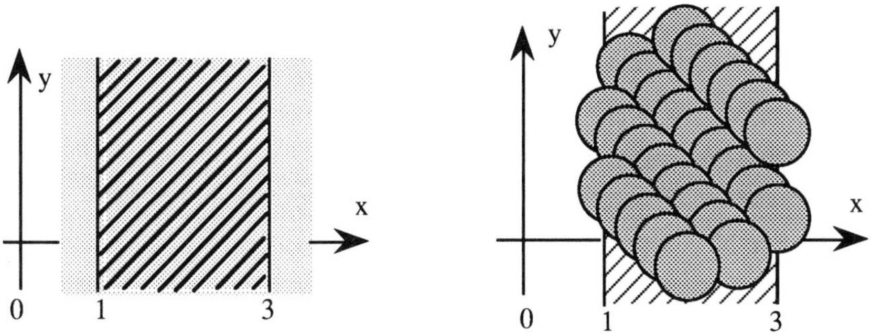

One cover of $S = \{(x,y): 1 \le x \le 3\}$ is $\mathcal{A} = \{A\}$, a family of size 1, where $A = \{(x,y): 1/2 < x < 7/2\}$.

$\mathcal{A}_\varepsilon = \{B_x(\varepsilon): x \in S\}$, is an infinite cover of $S = \{(x,y): 1 \le x \le 3\}$ (by open balls), which contains no finite subcover of S.

Figure 12.3 Two open covers of $S = \{(x,y): 1 \le x \le 3\}$.

EXERCISE Why must a space X be compact if it has only a finite number of points?

EXERCISE Is the discrete space **N** (Example 11.7) compact?

12.1.2 Bounded sets on the real line

We need an extension of the idea of maximum and minimum to the case where the would-be extreme value is not actually in the set.

DEFINITION 12.4 Let A be a subset of **R** and m, M $\in$ **R**. We call M an *upper bound* of A and say A is *bounded above* by M if

$x \le M$ for all x in A

If no $y < M$ is also an upper bound, we call M the *least upper bound* or *supremum* of A, written l.u.b.(A) or sup(A), On the other hand, if $m \le x$ for all x in A, then m is called a *lower bound* of A, and A is said to be *bounded below* by m. If no number greater than m is a lower bound, we call m the *greatest lower bound* or *infimum* of A, written g.l.b.(A) or inf(A). Parentheses may be omitted.

EXAMPLES 12.5 (1) $A = \{1,2,3,4, \dots\} \subseteq$ **R** has no upper bound. However 0, 1 are two of infinitely many lower bounds, of which 1 is the greatest.
(2) $A = [0,3)$, a half open interval in **R**. The number 3, but no lower number, is an upper bound. Hence sup A = 3, though 3 itself is not in A.

DEFINITION 12.6 Let $A \subseteq$ **R.** If inf(A) is contained in A it is called the *minimum*, or *least member* of A. Thus A has least member 1 in Example 12.5 (1) above. Similarly, if sup(A) is contained in A it is the *maximum*, or *greatest member*, of A. In Example 12.5 (2), A has a supremum, but no maximum. Notice that, according to Definition 12.1 of boundedness, A is bounded if and only if it has a supremum and infimum; for a basic postulate of the real line is that if the subset A is bounded below, it has an infimum, and if bounded above, a supremum. Their uniqueness is immediate. For example if M and N are suprema of A then $N \le M$ and $M \le N$, hence $M = N$.

This confirms the existence of the minimum bound ratio ρ of Note 11.44 for a bounded function $f: X \to Y$ between spaces. If $d(fx,fy) \le Md(x,y)$ for all distinct pairs x,y in X, then the set $\{d(fx, fy)/d(x,y)\} \subseteq \mathbf{R}$ has M as an upper bound, and so has a unique least upper bound $\rho \le M$.

EXERCISE Find the supremum of the set $A = \{(x-2)/(x-1): x \ge 3\}$.

EXERCISE Explain why the supremum M of a set A in **R** has points of A arbitrarily close to M (given $\varepsilon > 0$, A must have points $x > M-\varepsilon$ because ...).

LEMMA 12.7 Let A be a subset of **R**. *Then,*

(a) if A is open and contains the point x then, for some $\varepsilon > 0$, A contains a closed interval $[x-\varepsilon, x+\varepsilon]$,

(b) if A is closed and bounded then A has a maximum and minimum.

Proof (a) Since A is open, x is in some open ball $(x-\delta, x+\delta)$ within A. But this in turn contains $[x - \delta/2, x + \delta/2]$, as shown below.

For part (b) we note that A is bounded, so sup A and inf A exist. The definition of sup A shows that it has points of A arbitrarily close, and so is a limit point of A, hence contained in A by Test 11.19 (A being closed). Thus A has a maximum. Similarly A has a minimum.

DEFINITION 12.8 We extend the notions of Definition 12.6 to a real function $f: X \to \mathbf{R}$ on a metric space X, via the image f(X). Thus f is called a *bounded function* if and only if f(X) is bounded. Further, we say that f *attains a maximum* if sup f(X) = f(x) for some x in X, and *attains a minimum* if inf f(X) = f(y) for some y in X.

EXAMPLES 12.9

(1) $f: (0,\infty) \to \mathbf{R}$, $f(x) = 1/x^2$.

f is unbounded; inf f = 0.

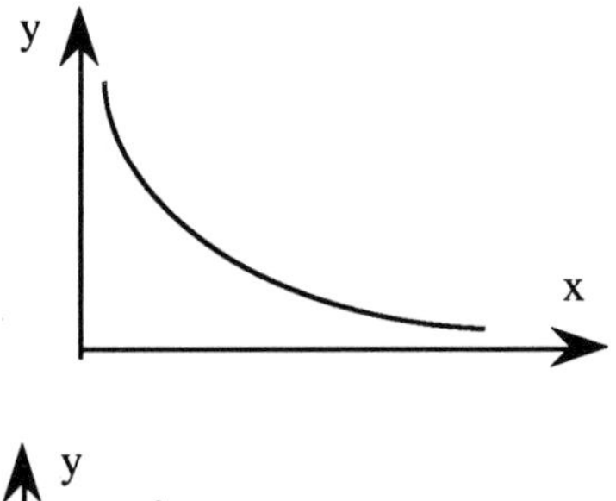

(2) $f: [3,4] \to R$,

$$f(x) = \frac{x-2}{x-1} = 1 - \frac{1}{x-1}$$

f attains a maximum $f(4) = 2/3$ and a minimum $f(3) = 1/2$.

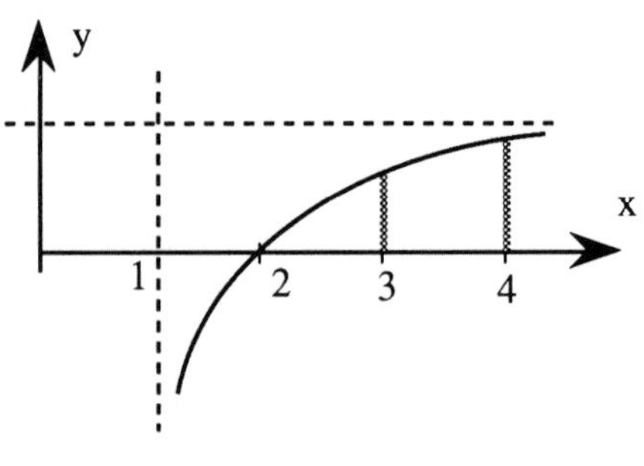

Now for the first, but important step towards classifying the compact subsets of $\mathbf{R}^n$.

THEOREM 12.10 A closed interval on the real line is compact.

Proof Let $\mathcal{A}$ be an open cover of [a,b], $a < b$, and define

$$M = \sup\{x \in [a,b]: \text{a } \textit{finite} \text{ subfamily of } \mathcal{A} \text{ covers } [a,x]\}.$$

Notice that the set is nonempty; it contains the point a because this single point must be in at least one of the open sets A of $\mathcal{A}$, so [a,a] is in a finite subfamily of size one. Further, by Lemma 12.7(a) the point a is in some interval $[a, a+\varepsilon]$ within A, so $a < M$. If $M \geq b$ we are done, so assume $M < b$ (we obtain a contradiction). Then $a < b < M$ as in diagram (a) following.

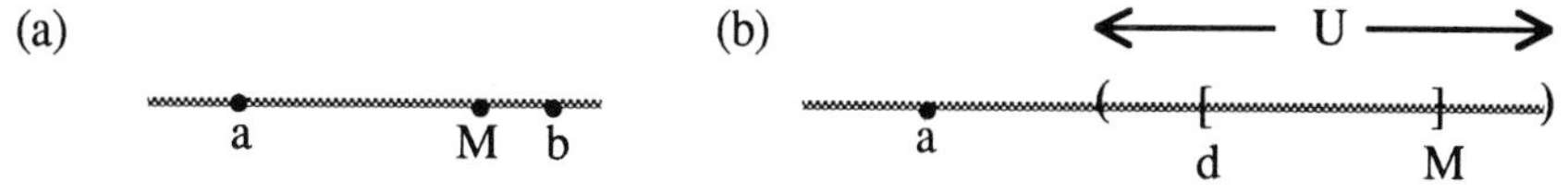

Since $\mathcal{A}$ covers all of [a,b] we may choose U in $\mathcal{A}$ so that $M \in U$, as depicted in diagram (b). By Lemma 12.7(a) again, we may choose $d \in (a,M)$ so that $[d,M] \subseteq U$. By definition of M, some finite subfamily of $\mathcal{A}$ covers [a,d]. But this, with U, covers [a,M]. And since $M < b$, the finite subfamily covers a closed interval to the right of M, say [a, a+e] with $e > 0$. But this contradicts the maximality of M. Hence the proof is complete.

12.1.3 Compactness - the basics

We start by showing how compact sets improve on closed sets, for sequences. It is important to bear in mind that a limit point of a subset need not lie within that set. Whether it does is here a major issue.

THEOREM 12.11 In a compact space, every infinite subset has a limit point.

Proof Let X be a compact space and A any subset with no limit point. The result will follow if we show that A is finite. Let $x \in X$. Since x is not a limit point of A, it lies in some open set O_x (say a ball) containing at most one point of A (x itself, if $x \in A$, otherwise no point). The family $\{O_x\}_{x \in X}$ covers X, therefore by compactness so does some finite subfamily $O_{x_1}, \ldots, O_{x_n}$. But this allows at most n points in A.

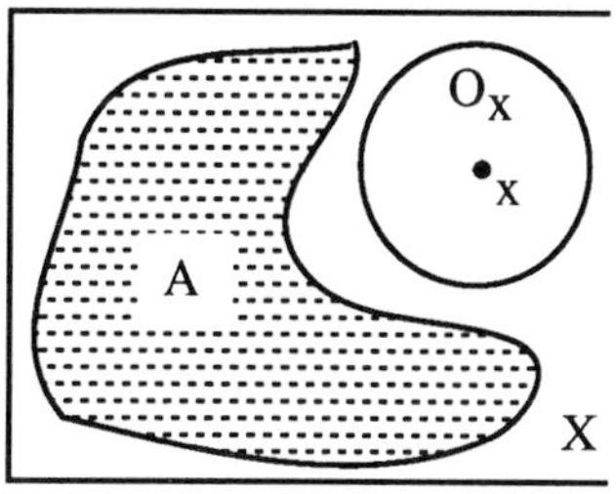

COROLLARY 12.12 In a compact space, every sequence has a convergent subsequence.

Proof If the sequence $\{x_n\}$ contains only a finite number of distinct points, then some point x appears infinitely often, forming the required subsequence. So suppose otherwise. Then by Theorem 12.11 it has a limit point $x \in X$. Therefore for any $m \in \mathbf{N}$, the ball $B_x(1/m)$ contains a point x_{n_m} of the sequence. This gives the required subsequence $\{x_{n_m}\}$, $m = 1,2,3,\ldots$ converging to x.

DEFINITION 12.13 (*Sequential compactness.*) The property just inferred for compact spaces, that every sequence contains a convergent subsequence, is called *sequential compactness*. Thus Corollary 12.12 states that 'compact implies sequentially compact'. One place this will be useful is in proving the 'uniqueness' of fractals in Chapter 13. Before that, we need it for obtaining new compact spaces from old. Although we are not yet ready to characterise compact sets in $\mathbf{R}^n$, the next result takes us half way in the general case (this is the easy half).

THEOREM 12.14 A compact subset of a metric space is bounded and closed.

Proof Let B be a compact subset of the metric space X. We first show that B is *closed*, by proving that B contains all its limit points (Test 11.19). So let $x \in X$ be a limit point of B, with $x_n \to x$ for some sequence $\{x_n\}$ in B. Now B, being a compact subset of X, is itself a compact space (Definition 12.2), to which Corollary 12.12 applies. Thus $\{x_n\}$ has a subsequence converging to a point y in B. But in a convergent sequence, every subsequence converges to the limit of that sequence (see Example 11.15(3)), and so we must have $x = y$. Thus $x \in B$ and B is closed. Furthermore B is *bounded*. For by compactness any ball cover $\mathcal{A}_\varepsilon = \{B_x(\varepsilon): x \in B\}$ has a finite subcovering. And since each ball is bounded, so is B.

The next two results provide excellent building bricks for compact sets.

THEOREM 12.15 (i) Any closed subset of a compact space is compact, (ii) finite unions and intersections of compact spaces are compact.

Proof (i) Let $\mathcal{A}$ be an open covering of the closed subset A of X. Since A is closed, its complement X-A is open, so $\mathcal{A} \cup \{X\text{-}A\}$ is an open covering of X. Since X is compact, this covering contains a finite subcovering of X. Omitting X-A we obtain the required finite subcovering of A. Part (ii) is left as an exercise.

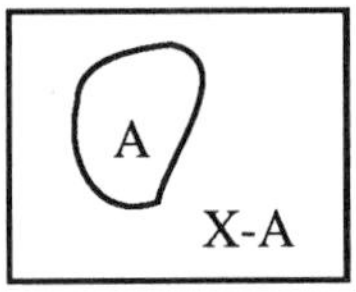

EXERCISE Prove that if A, B are compact subsets of X, then so are $A \cup B$ and $A \cap B$.

THEOREM 12.16 "The continuous image of a compact set is compact". Let $f: X \to Y$ be continuous and onto, X being compact. Then

(a) *Y is compact,*

(b) *if f is also 1-1 then f is a homeomorphism.*

Proof (a) Let $\mathcal{A}$ be any open covering of Y. We must show that there is a finite subcovering. Notice that, since every point of X is mapped to some point of Y, we have $X = f^{-1}(Y)$. On the other hand if $Y = A \cup B$ we have by the properties of the inverse function that $X = f^{-1}(A \cup B) = f^{-1}(A) \cup f^{-1}(B)$ (Lemma 11.36(c)). It follows that the family $\{f^{-1}(A) : A \in \mathcal{A}\}$ is an open covering of X, and so contains, by compactness of X, a finite subcovering $f^{-1}(A_1), \ldots, f^{-1}(A_n)$ of X. But f is onto, so $A_1, \ldots, A_n$ cover Y, and the proof of part (a) is complete.

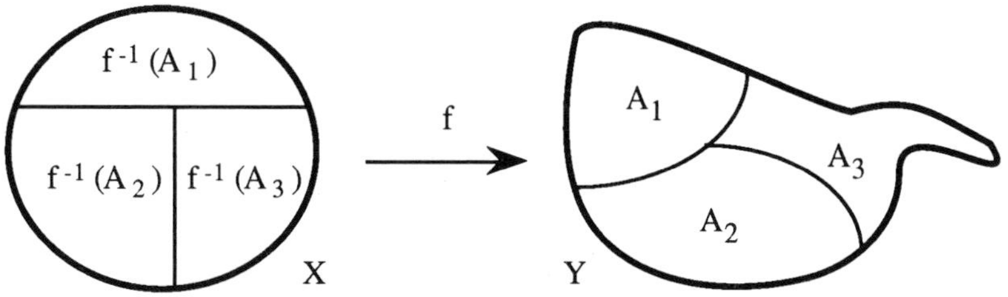

(b) Let f be 1-1 as well as onto. Then f has an inverse function f^{-1}, which we must show to be continuous. Now, a handy test for f^{-1} to be continuous is that its inverse image of a closed set A is closed (see the exercise after Lemma 11.36). That is that $(f^{-1})^{-1}(A)$, which equals f(A), is closed. But A is compact by Theorem 12.15(i), so f(A) is compact by Part(a) of the present theorem and therefore closed by Theorem 12.14. Thus f, having a continuous inverse, is by definition a homeomorphism.

EXERCISE Show that if $f: X \to Y$ is onto and $X = f^{-1}(A) \cup f^{-1}(B)$ then $A \cup B = Y$.

EXAMPLES 12.17 (1) The circle S^1 is compact, since it is the image of the continuous function $f: [0,1] \to \mathbf{C}$ given by $f(x) = e^{2\pi ix}$, and [0,1] is compact by Theorem 12.10. Invoking Theorem 12.15 we see that other compact subsets of the plane are the 'magnifying glass' and finite polygons below. This is so whether they are filled in or not.

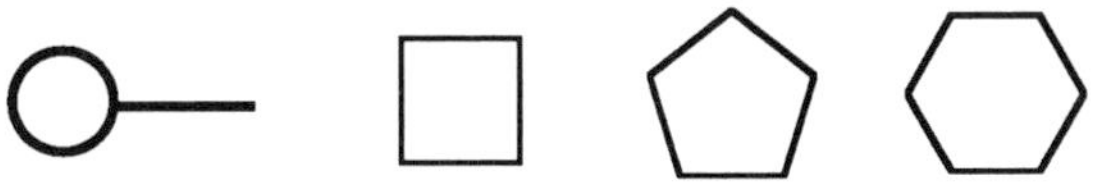

(2) **The Cantor set is compact** by Theorem 12.15, for it is the closed subset of the compact space [0,1] obtained by removing 'open thirds' (Section10.3.2), and any union of open sets is open (Property 11.4). Now here (though not strictly required) is an amazing fact: *every compact metric space is a continuous image of the Cantor set.* A proof is outside the purpose of this book, but may be found in Willard (1970). For more on the Cantor set see Example 12.25 (an infinite product).

(3) *(An application of Theorem 12.16(b).)* This is such a nice application that we include it at this stage although it requires the assumption that a closed disk D in the plane is compact, justified very soon in the next section (Theorem 12.26). It is the homeomorphism promised in Example 11.59 between a disc with its boundary squeezed to a point, and the sphere in 3-space (see the diagram of that example and compare Figure 12.24). The thrust of this example is that the map we produce is easily deduced to be a homeomorphism, by use of Theorem 12.16.

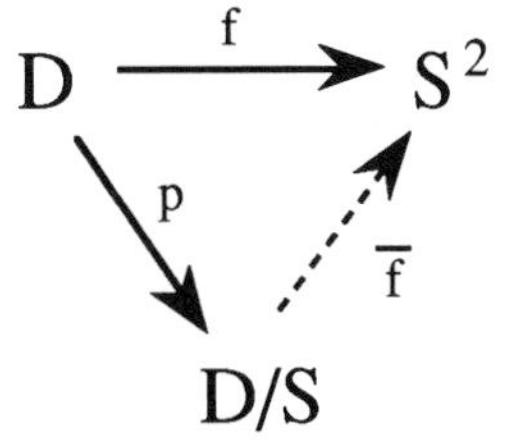

Here is an explicit homeomorphism $\bar{f}: D/S \to S^2$ between the unit disc with boundary squeezed to a point and the sphere. Following Construction 11.54 we define $\bar{f}$ via a continuous map $f: D \to S^2$ which sends the whole boundary to a single point, the North pole, in terms of polar coordinates (r,θ) in D and spherical polars (λ, ϕ) on S^2. This is depicted below in Figure 12.4. The map f sends $P(r,\theta)$ to $P'(\lambda,\phi)$, where $\lambda = \pi(1-r)$, $\phi = \theta$.

Thus f sends origin O to South pole S, radial lines to great circles from the South to North pole, and every point on the boundary r = 1 to the North pole. Note also the images of points Q, R, and the x-axis. Now for the proof that $\bar{f}$ is a homeomorphism. Applying Theorem 12.16(a): D is compact and p is continuous, therefore the image D/S is compact. Applying 12.16(b): D/S is compact, $\bar{f}$ is continuous, 1-1, and onto, therefore $\bar{f}$ is a homeomorphism.

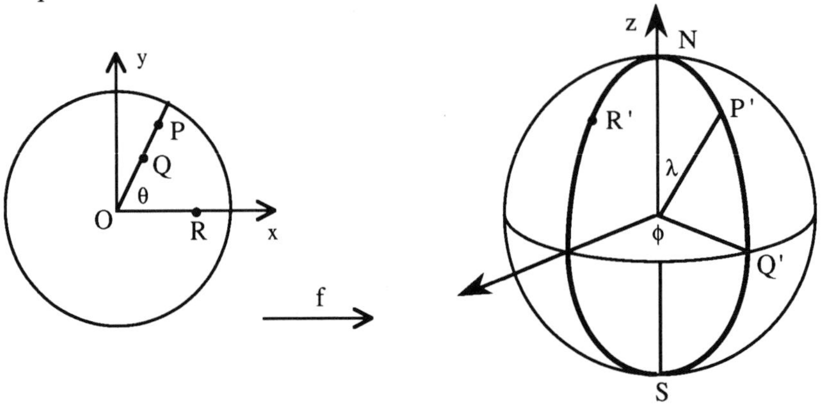

Figure 12.4 A homeomorphism stretching a disc over a 2-sphere.

EXERCISE The projective plane is a quotient space P = D/R (Definition 11.53), where D is the unit disc and xRy ⇔ x = ± y. Thus antipodal points are identified. Why must P be compact?

12.1.4 The product of compact sets is compact

Right now our major goal is to distinguish *compact* subsets of $\mathbf{R}^n$ as those which are bounded and closed, which we shall achieve in Section 12.5. We already know from Theorem 12.14 that compact subsets of any metric space must be bounded and closed. It remains to prove the much harder result, that in the case of $\mathbf{R}^n$ this condition suffices for compactness. The proof depends on establishing the far reaching result of Tychonoff, that products of compact spaces are compact. As an application, we will show that a linear map f is necessarily bounded, and demonstrate how to compute its minimum bound ratio ρ (or norm |f|). First we introduce a new criterion for compactness.

Our major task in proving that products of compact spaces are compact is to characterise compact spaces as being *sequentially compact* (every sequence has a convergent subsequence). We have done the easier part: compact implies sequentially compact (Corollary 12.12). The converse requires a stronger link between sequences and coverings, and in the process of setting this up we introduce some notions and results which will also be useful in the next chapter and beyond.

DEFINITIONS 12.18 (For a metric space X.) (1) We may define the *diameter* of any bounded subset A of X as

$$\text{diam}(A) = \sup d(x,y) \quad (x,y \in A),$$

the least upper bound of distances between pairs of points in A. Thus the diameter of a ball $B_a(r)$ in $\mathbf{R}^n$ is its diameter in the usual sense, 2r, whilst a square of side 1 in the plane has diameter √2.

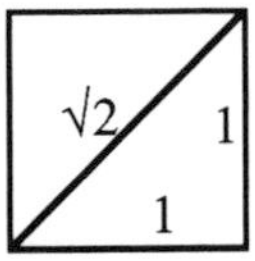

(2) Let $\{U_i\}$ be an open covering of X. Then every point of X is in some U_i. Can we extend this from points to subsets being in U_i? We might expect so if the subsets are small enough in diameter. Accordingly, if for some $\delta > 0$, every subset of diameter less than δ is in some U_i, we call δ a *Lebesgue number* for the covering (thus unbounded subsets are not considered here). It is named after the mathematician who proved the following important result.

THEOREM 12.19 (Lebesgue's covering lemma.) If X is a sequentially compact metric space then every open cover of X has a Lebesgue number.

Proof Let X be a sequentially compact metric space and $\{U_i\}$ be an arbitrary open covering of X. If every subset already lies in some U_i then any positive δ will suffice, so suppose there are some that do not, and call them *large* subsets. Only the bounded large subsets are under consideration. Let the greatest lower bound of their diameters be D. If $D > 0$ we may take $\delta = D$, for then all sets of diameter less than δ are not large. Hence we assume $D = 0$ and obtain a contradiction. Now $D = 0$ entails large sets with arbitrarily small diameters; however these diameters are positive because each such set has at least two points (why ?). So for each $n \in \mathbf{N}$ there is a large set A_n with

$$0 < \mathrm{diam}(A_n) < 1/n.$$

Choose a point x_n in each A_n. Now we invoke the hypothesis that X is sequentially compact to infer that $\{x_n\}$ has a subsequence $\{x_{n_i}\}$ converging to some point x in X. But x, being a single point, lies in some member U_p of the covering, and since U_p is open x lies within a ball $B_x(r)$ in U_p. This is depicted in Figure 12.5(a). Since $x_{n_i} \to x$ as $i \to \infty$ there is an integer $N > 0$ for which $d(x_N,x) < r/2$ and $N > 2/r$. Therefore $\mathrm{diam}(A_N) < 1/N < r/2$, and if $y \in A_N$ then $d(y,x) \le d(y,x_N) + d(x_N,x) < r/2 + r/2 = r$, hence

$$A_N \subseteq B_x(r) \subseteq U_p,$$

as illustrated. This contradicts the hypothesis that A_N is large, so after all $D > 0$ and we have a Lebesgue number $\delta = D$.

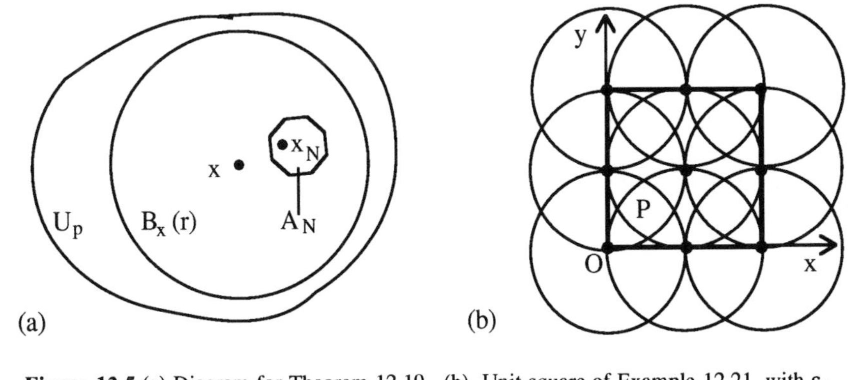

Figure 12.5 (a) Diagram for Theorem 12.19, (b) Unit square of Example 12.21, with ε-net (the circle centres) shown as bold points.

DEFINITION 12.20 Let X be a metric space and let $\varepsilon > 0$. An *ε-ball* is any ball of radius ε in X. (1) We define an *ε-net* (for X) to be a finite subset A for which the ε-balls centred at points of A cover X. Thus A approximates X in the sense that every point of X has a point of A within distance ε. We stress that A must be finite.

(2) X is called *totally bounded* if it has an ε-net for each $\varepsilon > 0$. (If a single subset works for every $\varepsilon > 0$ simultaneously, it is dense in X, by Definition 11.22.)

EXAMPLE 12.21 (1) If X is a square of side 1 in the plane and $\varepsilon = 1/2$, then the set A of circle centres shown bold in Figure 12.5(b) forms an ε-net, since every point P of the square is within distance 1/2 of some point of A. In fact the square is totally bounded, for we can get an ε-net by choosing n so that $1/n < \varepsilon$ and taking $A = \{(p/n, q/n)\colon 0 \le p,q \le n\}$. This net has $(n+1)^2$ points.

(2) It is no coincidence that the space X of (1) was bounded, since totally bounded is a far stronger condition. For, an ε-net being finite, there is a greatest distance $d(a,b) = \text{diam}(A)$ between points of A, so for x,y in X we have

$$d(x,y) \le d(x,a) + d(a,b) + d(b,y) \le \text{diam}(a) + 2\varepsilon.$$

On the other hand if X is bounded the whole space lies within one ball of r of radius say ε, so we have the equivalences

Bounded	:	has an ε-net for some value of ε,
Totally bounded	:	has an ε-net for every value of ε.

EXERCISE How small an ε applies for the set A in figure 12.5(b)?

THEOREM 12.22 If a metric space X is sequentially compact then it is totally bounded.

Proof Let X be a sequentially compact metric space and let $\varepsilon > 0$. Choose a point a_1 in X. If $X \subseteq B_{a_1}(\varepsilon)$ then $\{a_1\}$ is already an ε-net. If not, there is a point a_2 outside this ball. Now, if $X \subseteq B_{a_1}(\varepsilon) \cup B_{a_2}(\varepsilon)$ then $\{a_1, a_2\}$ is an ε-net. Continuing this way we must obtain a finite union of ε-balls which covers X, and hence an ε-net $\{a_1, a_2, \dots, a_n\}$. For otherwise $\{a_n\}$ is a sequence (i.e. is infinite) in which $d(a_r, a_s) \ge \varepsilon$ for all pairs r,s, and so no convergent subsequence is possible, contradicting the sequential compactness of X.

THEOREM 12.23 A metric space is compact if and only if it is sequentially compact.

Proof As we observed, it remains to prove that sequentially compact implies compact. So let $\{U_i\}$ be an open cover of a sequentially compact space X. We must show how to extract a finite subcover. By Theorem 12.19 the cover has a Lebesgue number δ. By Theorem 12.22, X is totally bounded and so has an ε-net $A = \{a_1, \dots, a_k\}$ with $\varepsilon = \delta/4$. Hence for each of $i = 1, 2, \dots, k$ we have

$$\text{diam}(B_{a_i}(\varepsilon)) \le 2\varepsilon < \delta,$$

and so for each such i there is, by definition of the Lebesgue number, a member U_{n_i} of the covering with $B_{a_i}(\varepsilon) \subseteq U_{n_i}$. But $\{B_{a_i}(\varepsilon)\colon 1 \le i \le n\}$ covers X, and hence so does the family $\{U_{n_i}\colon 1 \le i \le n\}$, which is the required finite subcovering of $\{U_i\}$.

THEOREM 12.24 (The little Tychonoff Theorem.) The product of a finite number of compact spaces is compact.

Proof Let X, Y be compact metric spaces. It suffices to prove that X x Y is compact, for the argument may then be repeated: if Z is also compact then so is (X x Y) x Z, and so on. By Theorem 12.23 we may take compact spaces to be precisely those which are sequentially compact (every sequence has a convergent subsequence). We also make crucial use of Example 11.15(3):

$$\text{if a sequence has limit L then so does every subsequence.} \qquad (12.4)$$

Let $\{(x_n, y_n)\}$ be a sequence in X x Y. The proof will be complete when we obtain a convergent subsequence. In the following argument i takes the values 1,2,3, ... We observe firstly that $\{x_n\}$ is a sequence in the compact space X and so has a convergent subsequence $\{x_{n_i}\}$ with limit, say L. Now consider the sequence $\{y_{n_i}\}$ in Y, with the same subscripts. By compactness of Y this sequence has its own convergent subsequence $\{y_{m_i}\}$ with limit, say M. But $\{x_{m_i}\}$ is a subsequence of $\{x_{n_i}\}$ and hence by (12.4) converges to the same limit L. Therefore the sequence $\{(x_n, y_n)\}$ has a subsequence $\{(x_{m_i}, y_{m_i})\}$ converging to (L,M), and the proof is complete.

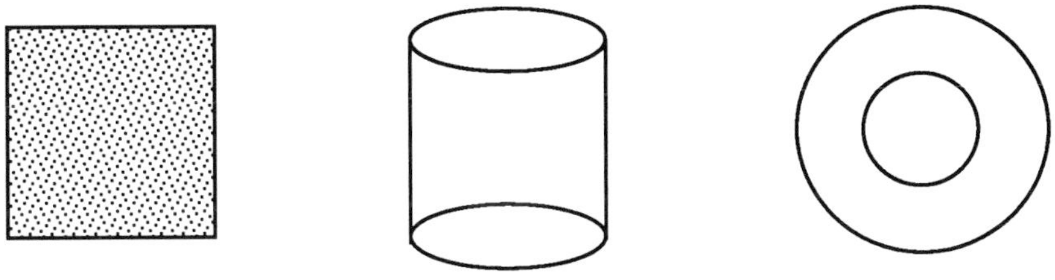

Closed square [0,1] x [0,1] — Cylinder S^1 x [0,1] — Torus ('donut') S^1 x S^1

Figure 12.6 Some compact sets based on Cartesian products.

Arbitrary product spaces We really need only the compactness of a finite product, as in Theorem 12.24, which we are calling the little Tychonoff Theorem. However it is interesting and will sometimes be useful to know that even an infinite product of compact spaces X_i,

$$X = \prod X_i \quad (i \in \mathbf{N}) = X_1 \times X_2 \times \ldots \qquad (12.5)$$

is compact. Here an element or point of X is a sequence, which we may write in the form $x = (x_1, x_2, x_3, \ldots) = (x_i)$, with x_i in X_i. We define projection maps p_n: X $\to X_n$ by $p_n(x) = x_n$. The topology of the product is conveniently defined by a sub-basis (Definition 11.6), namely the family $\{p_n^{-1}(A_n)\}$, where n = 1, 2, ... and A_n runs through all open sets in X_n (or just through a basis of the open sets of X_n). Notice that the sub-basis only allows *finite* intersections, and that we recover the earlier definition when we restrict to a finite number of spaces. For example, if A, B, C are open subsets of spaces X, Y, Z with projections p_1, p_2, p_3 then we have

$$\begin{aligned} p_1^{-1}(A) \cap p_2^{-1}(B) \cap p_2^{-1}(C) &= (A \times Y \times Z) \cap (X \times B \times Z) \cap (X \times Y \times C) \\ &= A \times B \times C. \end{aligned}$$

The proof of Theorem 12.24 may be extended to cover infinite products (12.5). We remark that the full Tychonoff Theorem allows the product of spaces indexed by any set Λ provided with an ordering, a rule for deciding for any pair which comes before the other. Thus Λ could be the unit interval I with points ordered by their position on the real line. (For a proof that the points of I cannot be indexed by the integers, see Example 11.15(4).) Finally, the factors of the product need not be restricted to metric spaces, they may be arbitrary topological spaces. For a proof in this generality see Kelley (1964) or Willard (1970).

EXAMPLE 12.25 (*The Cantor set as an infinite product.*) We can get interesting insights into the topology of an infinite product by seeing how it comes about that the product $X = \{0, 2\} \times \{0, 2\} \times \ldots$ is homeomorphic to the Cantor set $\mathcal{C}$. Each factor $\{0, 2\}$ with its topology as a subspace of **R**, is discrete (each point an open set), and compact because of its finiteness (Example 12.3(1)). Thus our sub-basic open sets in this case are, for each $k \in$ **N**,

$$p_k^{-1}(0) = \{(x_i) : x_k = 0\} \quad \text{and} \quad p_k^{-1}(2) = \{(x_i) : x_k = 2\},$$

and so every open set is a union of sets such as

$$V(*,0,*,*,2,*,*, \ldots\ldots) = \{(xi) : x_2 = 0, x_5 = 2\},$$

in which a finite number of entries is specified and the rest, denoted by asterisks, vary freely. However we don't need all these sets for a basis because some V's are unions of others. For example $V(0,*,2,*,*, \ldots) = V(0,0,2,*,*, \ldots) \cup V(0,2,2,*,*, \ldots)$, since each entry is either 0 or 2. Thus a basis is given by the so-called *cylindrical subsets*

$$V(a_1, a_2, \ldots, a_r) = \{(x_i) : x_1 = a_1, x_2 = a_2, \ldots, x_r = a_r\}, \tag{12.6}$$

where each a_k is 0 or 2 and $r = 1, 2, 3, \ldots$. Notice that the specified entries are consecutive (can you think of a reason for the word 'cylinder'?). Now, there is an obvious bijective map $f: \mathcal{C} \to X$, given by $f(0.x_1x_2x_3 \ldots) = (x_1, x_2, x_3, \ldots)$, where we are using the ternary representation of Construction 10.14 for $\mathcal{C}$, with x_i equal to 0 or 2. We shall prove that f is a homeomorphism by showing that it pairs our basis for the topology of X with a basis for $\mathcal{C}$.

The Cantor set $\mathcal{C}$ has the subspace topology as a subset of **R.** That is, the open subsets of $\mathcal{C}$ are unions of intersections $U \cap \mathcal{C}$ where U is open in **R** and may be taken as an interval. Below we represent the position of such a set U over the second stage of Construction 10.15 for $\mathcal{C}$ (the reader may wish to refer back for the notation).

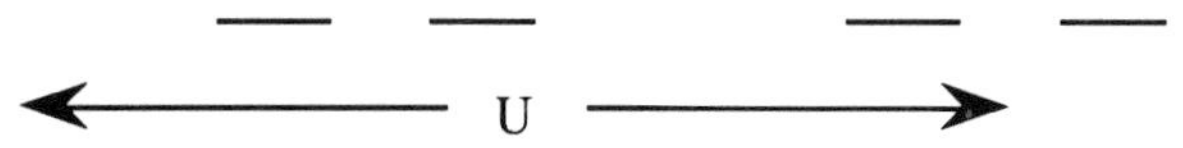

We see that $U \cap \mathcal{C}$ is itself the union of $\psi_0\psi_0(I) \cap \mathcal{C}$, $\psi_0\psi_2(I) \cap \mathcal{C}$, and $\psi_2\psi_0(I) \cap \mathcal{C}$. We conclude that every open set of C is a union of sets of the form

$$\begin{aligned} U(a_1, a_2, \ldots, a_r) &= \psi_{a_1}\psi_{a_2} \ldots \psi_{a_r}(I) \cap \mathcal{C} \qquad \text{(definition)} \\ &= \{0.x_1x_2x_3 \ldots : x_1 = a_1, x_2 = a_2, \ldots, x_r = a_r\}. \end{aligned}$$

But these sets correspond to the cylinder sets of X under the map f, so we have f as a homeomorphism. This proves that the infinite product X of compact spaces {0,2} is compact, as predicted by the Tychonoff Theorem. For more on the Cantor set, see Example 12.57. Now it is time to bring out some important applications of our results on compact sets, especially the characterisation theorem following. Even more will appear in succeeding chapters.

12.1.5 Compact sets and n-space

We need a generalisation of the closed interval $I_r = [-r,r]$, namely the *n-box* in $\mathbf{R}^n$,

$$I_r^n = I_r \times I_r \times \dots I_r \quad \text{(n factors)} \quad = \{(x_1,x_2,\dots,x_n) \in \mathbf{R}^n : -r \le x_i \le r\}.$$

Notice that the closed ball

$$B_O[r] = \{(x_1,x_2,\dots,x_n) \in \mathbf{R}^n : x_1^2 + \dots + x_n^2 \le r^2\}$$

has coordinates satisfying $-r \le x_i \le r$, and hence satisfies $B_O[r] \subseteq I_r^n$, as depicted here in the familiar case n = 2 of the plane.

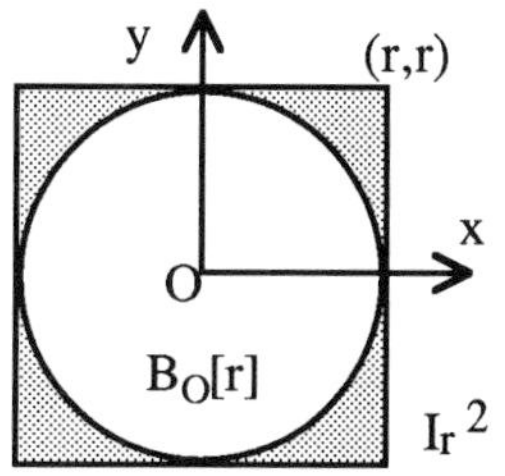

THEOREM 12.26 (Compact sets in n-space.) A subset of $\mathbf{R}^n$ *is compact if and only if it is bounded and closed.*

Proof Let $A \subseteq \mathbf{R}^n$. If A is compact then it is bounded and closed, by Theorem 12.14. To prove the converse, let A be bounded and closed. Then since A is bounded it lies within some closed ball $B_O[r]$, by Definition 12.1. This is where we use the Tychonoff Theorem, 12.24, which implies that, since $I_r = [-r,r]$ is compact by Theorem 12.10, so is the product I_r^n. Now, since $B_O[r] \subseteq I_r^n$, this closed ball is also compact, by Theorem 12.15. Hence, again by Theorem 12.15, so is its closed subset A.

EXAMPLES 12.27 Some compact spaces in $\mathbf{R}^n$ are: the closed ball or sphere, any solid polyhedron or its boundary. In particular a closed disc in the plane is compact, so we have now justified the assumption of Example 12.17(3).

EXERCISE Give two reasons why the torus must be compact. Now another!

The following result is one good reason why compactness is valuable. It has many consequences through the rest of this book.

THEOREM 12.28 A continuous real function on a compact space attains a maximum and minimum.

Proof Let $f: X \to \mathbf{R}$ be continuous and X compact. Then the image f(X) is a compact subset of $\mathbf{R}$, by Theorem 12.16, hence bounded and closed by Theorem 12.26. So it has a maximum and minimum value by Lemma 12.7(b). This completes the proof.

APPLICATION 12.29 A linear map $f: \mathbf{R}^n \to \mathbf{R}^m$ is bounded. The minimum bound ratio ρ exists (cf. Note 11.44) and

$$\rho = \max_{|\mathbf{x}|=1} |f(\mathbf{x})| . \qquad (12.7)$$

Proof Recall that we write $|\mathbf{x}-\mathbf{y}|$ for $d(\mathbf{x},\mathbf{y})$ to denote the Euclidean distance in $\mathbf{R}^n$, $\mathbf{R}^m$. Noting that $\mathbf{x} = \mathbf{y}$ if and only if $|\mathbf{x}-\mathbf{y}| = 0$, we have for $r \ge 0$,

$$|f(\mathbf{x}) - f(\mathbf{y})| \le r|\mathbf{x}-\mathbf{y}|, \qquad \text{for all } \mathbf{x} \ne \mathbf{y} \text{ in } \mathbf{R}^n$$

$$\Leftrightarrow \quad |f(\mathbf{x}) - f(\mathbf{y})| / |\mathbf{x}-\mathbf{y}| \le r, \qquad \text{for all } \mathbf{x} \ne \mathbf{y} \text{ in } \mathbf{R}^n$$

$$\Leftrightarrow \quad |f(\mathbf{x}-\mathbf{y})| / |\mathbf{x}-\mathbf{y}| \le r \qquad \text{(f is linear)} \qquad \text{for all } \mathbf{x} \ne \mathbf{y} \text{ in } \mathbf{R}^n$$

$$\Leftrightarrow \quad \left| f\left(\frac{\mathbf{x}-\mathbf{y}}{|\mathbf{x}-\mathbf{y}|}\right) \right| \le r \qquad \text{(f is linear)} \qquad \text{for all } \mathbf{x} \ne \mathbf{y} \text{ in } \mathbf{R}^n$$

$$\Leftrightarrow \quad |f(\mathbf{w})| \le r \qquad \text{for all } \mathbf{w} \in \mathbf{R}^n \text{ with } |\mathbf{w}| = 1,$$

since $(\mathbf{x}-\mathbf{y})/|\mathbf{x}-\mathbf{y}|$ is an arbitrary vector of length 1. This is a condition on the continuous function $g: S_O[1] \to \mathbf{R}$, $\mathbf{w} \to |f(\mathbf{w})|$. We seek, if it exists, the least r such that $|f(\mathbf{w})| \le r$ for all $\mathbf{w}$ on the sphere $S_O[1]$; but this is precisely the maximum which Theorem 12.28 guarantees will be attained by g, since $S_O[1]$ is compact. Hence the result.

EXAMPLE 12.30 Find the minimum bound ratio ρ, for the linear map f: $\mathbf{R}^2 \to \mathbf{R}^2$ given by

$$f\begin{bmatrix} x \\ y \end{bmatrix} = \begin{bmatrix} 1 & 2 \\ 3 & 4 \end{bmatrix}\begin{bmatrix} x \\ y \end{bmatrix}$$

Solution We have $|f(x,y)|^2 = (x+2y)^2 + (3x+4y)^2 = M$, say. Now ρ is the maximum of M for x,y on the unit circle. That is, for $x = \cos\theta$, $y = \sin\theta$, $0 \le \theta \le 2\pi$. Then $M = (\cos\theta + 2\sin\theta)^2 + (3\cos\theta + 4\sin\theta)^2 = 15 - 5\cos 2\theta + 14\sin 2\theta = 15 + A\cos(2\theta + \lambda)$, where $A = \sqrt{(5^2+14^2)}$, $\tan\lambda = -5/4$. Hence $\rho = \sqrt{(15+A)} = 5.46$ (2 dec. places). For a general formula see (14.4).

Note To find ρ in case f: $\mathbf{R}^n \to \mathbf{R}^m$ we need suitable angle coordinates for the (n-1)-sphere, and these are given in Section 9.3.3.

EXERCISE Find the minimum bound ratio for the transformation of the plane given by (x,y) → (2x-3y+1,5x+y+3). [Hint. First express the map as a composition involving an isometry.]

APPLICATION 12.31 (Linear programming) Let f: A → **R** be a differentiable function on a compact subset A of $\mathbf{R}^n$. Suppose f attains a maximum or minimum on an interior point a ∈ A. The methods of differential calculus show that all the first partial derivatives $\partial f/\partial x_i$ must vanish at the point a. Now assume that f is linear, i.e. that it may be expressed in the form $f(x_1, \dots, x_n) = a_1x_1 + \dots + a_nx_n$, excluding the trivial case $a_1 = \dots = a_n = 0$ when f is constant. Then the first derivatives vanish nowhere, leaving only points on the boundary $\partial A = A \backslash A^o$ on which f can attain the maximum and minimum predicted by Theorem 12.28. Hence we may state:

a real linear function on a compact subset of $\mathbf{R}^n$ attains its maximum and minimum on the boundary. (12.8)

Now suppose further that the compact set A is a *polytope*. That is it is bounded by *hyperplanes*, where a hyperplane is a surface defined by a linear equation of the form $a_1x_1 + \dots + a_nx_n = 0$. In 3-space the object is called a *polyhedron* and is bounded by planes. It is convenient to give the following argument for a polyhedron, for it obviously extends to the general case.

Suppose f: A → **R** attains its maximum at a point a on the boundary. Thus a is in some polygonal face F. But f is continuous as a function on F, hence the maximum occurs on *its* boundary ∂F. Therefore a is in an edge E of F. Repeating the argument we see that a is a vertex of the polyhedron. We may conclude:

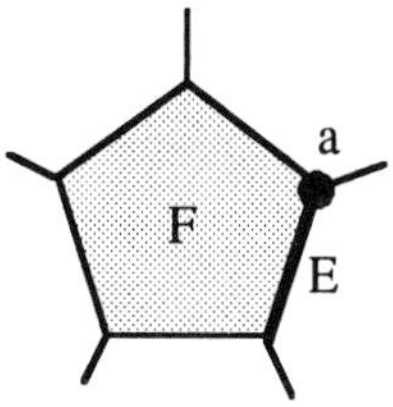

a real linear function on a finite region bounded by hyperplanes in $\boldsymbol{R}^n$ *attains its maximum or minimum at a vertex of the boundary.* (12.9)

This conclusion is the Principle of *Linear Programming*. A simple example follows.

EXAMPLE 12.32 Find the minimum and maximum of f(x,y) = 12x+3y on the plane triangle bounded by lines 3y-5x = 2, x-3y = 2, x+y = 2.

Solution Solving the equations in pairs we find the vertices as P(1/2,3/2), Q(-1,-1), R(2,0). Thus f(P) = 10.5, f(Q) = -15, f(R) = 24. Hence the maximum is 24 and minimum is -15.

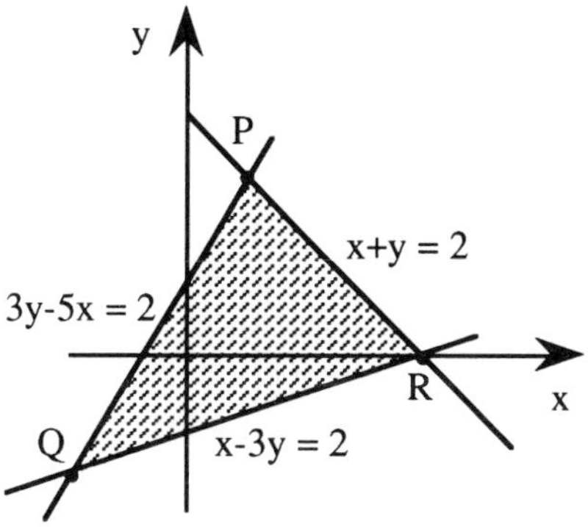

EXERCISE Find the greatest value of x + y + z on the tetrahedron with vertices (0,0,0), (1,2,1), (2,-3,7), (-1,2,3).

12.2 Connectedness

The fact that a continuous function maps connected sets to connected sets is of great assistance in determining the effect of certain homeomorphisms which transform one problem into an equivalent but easier problem. In our case this refers especially to investigation into the dynamics of iterated maps, Chapter 16. In its own right it is an important part of a description of the topology of any set which is of interest to us. Three kinds of connectedness we might consider are, informally,

(1) Connected: if you pick up one piece, the rest comes too.
(2) Path-connected: any two points can be joined by a curve.
(3) Simply connected: there are no holes.

We'll see that path-connected implies connected but not vice versa - both concepts are needed. A considerable achievement was the proof by Douady and Hubbard (1982) that the Mandelbrot set is connected.

12.2.1 Connected spaces

DEFINITION 12.33 A space X is *disconnected (by U, V)* if X = U ∪ V with U, V open, nonempty, and disjoint. Notice that U is the complement of V, so is also closed, and similarly for V. Now X is defined as *connected* if it is not disconnected. And a subset is said to be connected if it is connected as a subspace.

(a) The space X consisting of an interval with one point removed is *not* connected.

(b) The plane with x-axis removed is not connected.

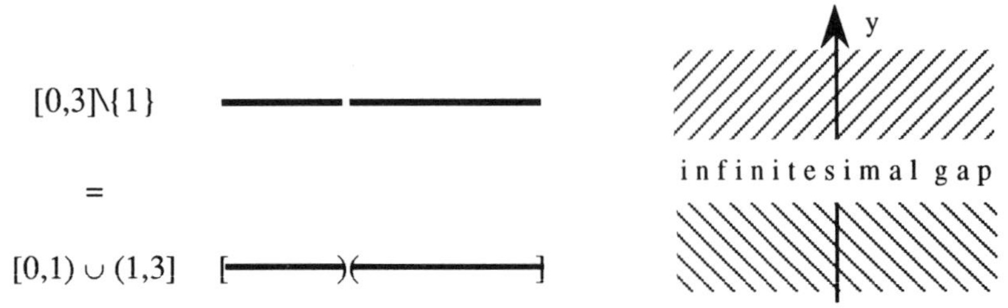

X 'falls apart' into (disjoint) open subsets of itself, [0,1) and (1,3].

X = $H^+ \cup H^-$, the union of the upper and of the lower half-plane.

Figure 12.7 Two spaces X that are not connected.

To take Example (a) above, A = [0,1)∪(1,3] does not at first look like a union of open sets, but of course U = [0,1) and V = (1,3] are open subsets of A as a space in its own right (subspace of **R**) and they are certainly nonempty and disjoint. Thus A is disconnected by U, V. Disconnectedness for a subset A of a space X is sometimes usefully rephrased as: A is *contained in* a union U ∪ V with U, V open, nonempty, and disjoint (this time we say U, V *disconnect* A). Here is an extreme, yet standard, case.

EXAMPLE 12.34 In a space X with the *discrete topology*, such as **N** = {1,2,3, ...} (Example 11.7) every point is an open set, hence so is every subset, and the only connected subsets are the points (an exercise). In such a case we call X *totally disconnected.* Interestingly our old friend the Cantor set is totally disconnected without being discrete (cf. Example 12.57).

Now we prove from the definition that closed intervals on the real line are, as we would hope, connected. The proof follows Gemignani (1967). Notice that, since the definition is given in terms of open sets, if X is connected then so is any homeomorphic set Y. Thus the following theorem shows that *any* closed interval is connected.

THEOREM 12.35 The closed interval [0,1] is connected.

Proof Suppose U, V disconnect [0,1]. Let u ∈ U, v ∈ V and relabel U, V if necessary, so that u < v. Note that, although U, V are represented by intervals in the diagram below, they are assumed only to be open in [0,1], thus in general each is a union of intervals which are open or of type [0,a) or (b,1]. We use Lemma 12.7: each point M in the interior of such a set is contained in an open interval and hence centres a smaller closed interval within that set, as depicted below.

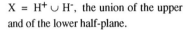

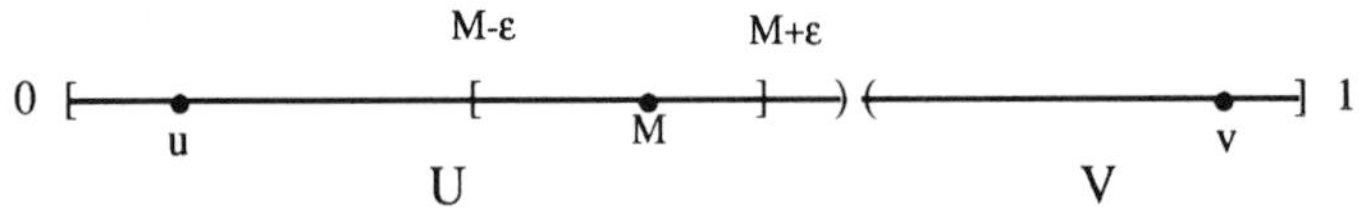

The nonempty set S = {x: x < u or [u,x] ⊆ U } has 1 as an upper bound, so S has a supremum (least upper bound) M with u < M ≤ 1. Since [0,1] = U ∪ V, either M ∈ U or M ∈ V. We show that a contradiction exists in either case, and therefore [0,1] is connected. (1) Suppose $M \in U$. Then, for some $\varepsilon > 0$, we have the inclusion $[M-\varepsilon, M+\varepsilon] \subseteq U$ (Lemma 12.7), and we may take ε sufficiently small that $u < M-\varepsilon$ (as $u < M$). Since also $[u, M-\varepsilon] \subseteq U$ (M being the least upper bound), this gives $[u, M+\varepsilon] \subseteq U$. Hence $M+\varepsilon$ is in S. This contradicts the assumption that M is an upper bound of S. (2) Suppose M is in V. Then since V is open we have the inclusion $[M-\mu, M+\mu] \subseteq V$ for some $\mu > 0$, hence $M-\mu$ is not in U, and so is an upper bound of S. But now this contradicts the assumption that M is the least upper bound of S. We have ruled out possibilites (1), (2) and so [0,1] is connected.

Note Since connectedness is defined negatively, that is, a space is connected if it is not disconnected, proofs of connectedness tend to be by contradiction. We assume a space is disconnected and obtain a contradiction, as we did above. Now we will establish that some familiar spaces are connected. First, we prove a basic Lemma.

LEMMA 12.36 In a space disconnected by U and V, let A be any connected subset. Then A lies within U or V.

Proof Suppose to the contrary that, although a space X is disconnected by U, V, the connected subset A does not lie entirely within U or within V. Then the sets $A \cap U$, $A \cap V$ are (i) nonempty, (ii) disjoint because U, V are so, (iii) open in A because they are the intersections of open sets with A, Hence the fact that $A = (A \cap U) \cup (A \cap V)$ means that these two sets disconnect A. With this contradiction the proof is complete.

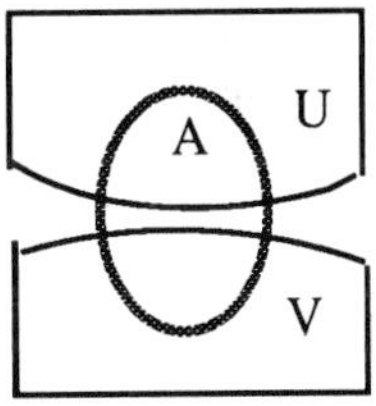

Impossible!

THEOREM 12.37 If the space X is any union of connected subspaces with a common point, then X itself is connected.

Proof Suppose X is the union of connected subspaces A_λ where λ runs through some index set Λ, and x is a common point of all these spaces. But suppose for a contradiction that X is disconnected by U, V. Then for each λ, either $A_\lambda \subseteq U$ or $A_\lambda \subseteq V$, by Lemma 12.36 above. If *some* $A_\lambda \subseteq U$ then an element (certainly x) from each A_λ must be in U, and hence every A_λ is in U. Therefore X, being their union, is in U. But this is impossible because U,V disconnect X. Similarly $A_\lambda \subseteq V$ gives a contradiction, and the proof is complete.

EXAMPLES 12.38 (Applications of Theorem 12.37.) (1) **R** is connected, being the infinite union of connected sets [-n,n] with the origin as common point (n = 1,2,3, ...). This may seem surprising since [-n,n] is a closed interval, but any real number x is in [-n,n] for sufficiently large n, so the result is true. Essentially we have been here before. It is an example of infinity as an ally rather than an opponent.

(2) Real n-space $\mathbf{R}^n$ is connected, being the union of all rays through the origin (see diagram), each homeomorphic to **R** and hence connected.

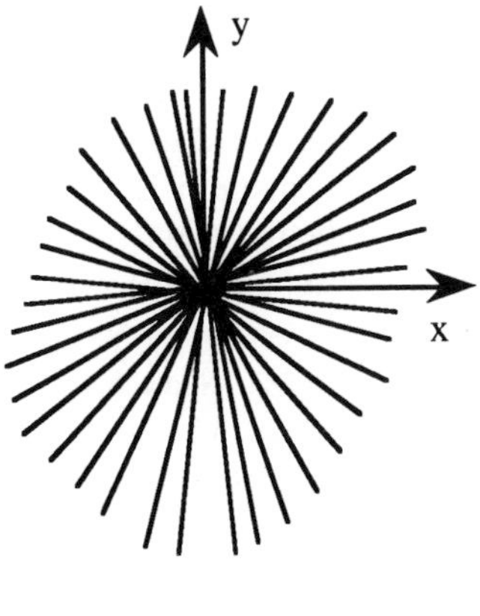

EXERCISE Show that open or closed balls in $\mathbf{R}^n$ are connected.

*THEOREM 12.39 (An easy application of results so far.) The only connected subsets of **R** are **R** itself and all intervals, finite or infinite, closed, half-open, or open.*

12.2.2 Continuous images, and components

One application of results in this section is to give a foundation for distinguishing between the inside and outside of a sphere, or between one side and the other of a hyperplane in Euclidean spaces. The following theorem has many consequences.

THEOREM 12.40 The continuous image of a connected set is connected.

Proof Suppose f: $X \to Y$ is continuous and onto. Let Y be disconnected by U, V. The result will follow if we can deduce that X is disconnected by $f^{-1}(U)$, $f^{-1}(V)$. Firstly, $X = f^{-1}(Y) = f^{-1}(U \cup V) = f^{-1}(U) \cup f^{-1}(V)$; secondly, $f^{-1}(U) \cap f^{-1}(V) = f^{-1}(U \cap V) = f^{-1}(\emptyset) = \emptyset$ (cf. Lemma 11.36). Thirdly, $f^{-1}(U)$ and $f^{-1}(V)$ are open by continuity of f, and finally they are nonempty because f is onto and U, V are nonempty. Thus X is disconnected as claimed, and this proves the result.

EXAMPLES 12.41 (Applications of Theorem 12.40.) (1) The sphere $S_O[1]$ in $\mathbf{R}^n$ is connected, as we show by means of a continuous onto map g from $\mathbf{R}^n \backslash \{O\}$ to $S_O[1]$, given by $g(\mathbf{x}) = \mathbf{x}/|\mathbf{x}|^2$ (= $\mathbf{y}$, where $y_i = x_i/(x_1^2 + x_2^2 + .. + x_n^2)$). This is easily seen to be onto, and is continuous by Corollary 11.38. Assuming that $\mathbf{R}^n \backslash \{O\}$ is connected, as the reader is invited to prove below, we have that the continuous image $S_O[1]$ is connected by Theorem 12.40.

(2) We see may the torus is connected as follows. We can produce a torus T by starting with a square S and identifying opposite edges (Example 11.57). This means that T is the image of S under a continuous map p: $S \to T$ (the quotient map of Definition 11.53). Since the square is connected (eg by Theorem 12.37), so is its continuous image T, by Theorem 12.40.

(3) **The Intermediate Value Theorem.** *Let f: $X \to \mathbf{R}$ be continuous, with X connected and f(a), f(b) of opposite sign. Then there is a real number c such that f(c) = 0. If X is an interval [a,b] then a < c < b.*

Proof We shall give the proof in case X = [a,b], as the rest is a natural extension. By Theorem 12.40 the continuous image f([a,b]) is connected because [a,b] is connected, and so is an interval by Theorem 12.39. This image contains f(a), f(b), and hence the interval [f(a), f(b)], or [f(b), f(a)], which in turn contains zero. Thus f(c) = 0 for some c in (a,b).

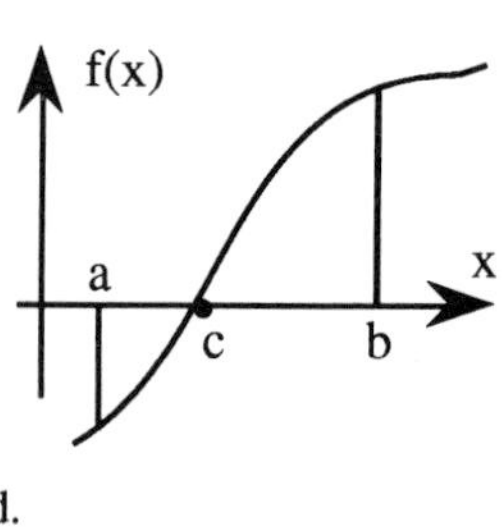

EXERCISE Show that $\mathbf{R}^n$ with the origin deleted is still connected.

EXERCISE Use the Intermediate Value Theorem to show that every real polynomial of odd degree must have a real root. Find such a root to within 1 unit , for $x^5 + 32x^4 + 1$.

(4) *(Showing that two spaces X, Y are not homeomorphic.)* Suppose we can remove a

point x from X so as to leave $X\backslash\{x\}$ disconnected. By Theorem 12.40, if there is a homeomorphism $f: X \to Y$ then $Y\backslash\{f(x)\}$ must be disconnected too (why?). So if there is no point whose removal from Y leaves a disconnected space, then there can be no such homeomorphism f. Some pairs shown up as non-homeomorphic by this test are (a) $X = R$, $Y = \mathbf{R}^n$ $(n > 1)$, (b) $X = [0,1]$, $Y = S^1$.

DEFINITION 12.42 A *(connected) component* of a space X is a maximal connected subset. That is, a connected subset which is *properly* contained in no other connected subset.

THEOREM 12.43 (a) Each point of a space X lies in a unique component. (b) A continuous map $f: X \to Y$ sends any component of X into (not necessarily onto) a unique component of Y.

Proof (a) Let $\{A_\lambda\}$ be the family of all connected subsets that contain $x \in X$. Then the union of all A_λ is by Theorem 12.37 a connected subset. It contains x and is maximal from its definition. (b) The image of a component is connected by Theorem 12.40 and so lies within a component by Lemma 12.36.

How many components? 6 components

Figure 12.8 Subsets of the plane with several components. cf. Figure 12.7.

EXERCISE By considering how they may be disconnected, show that S^2, in fact S^n (for $n > 1$) is not homeomorphic to S^1.

EXAMPLE 12.44 In the totally disconnected space $\mathbf{N} = \{1,2,3, ...\}$ of Example 12.34, each point is itself a component, for even a 2-element subset $\{a,b\}$ is disconnected by open sets $\{a\}$, $\{b\}$. Therefore, since $\mathbf{R}$ is connected, Theorem 12.43(b) dictates that any continuous map $f: \mathbf{R} \to \mathbf{N}$ must be a constant map. Now we give a short formal proof with the present tools of a fundamental fact about Euclidean space.

THEOREM 12.45 (See diagrams (a) and (b) following.)
(a) *The plane with x-axis removed has two components, the upper and lower half-planes* $H^+ = \{(x,y: y > 0\}$, $H^- = \{(x,y): y < 0\}$.
(b) *The plane with unit circle removed has two components, the inside* $\{(r,\theta): r < 1\}$, *and outside* $\{(r,\theta): r > 1\}$, *the latter characterised as unbounded.*

Proof (a) We show that H^+ is a component (a maximal connected subset). The statement for H^- follows similarly, though see also the next exercise. Firstly, H^+ is connected, since any point z is on the line segment zz_0 from a fixed point $z_0 = (0,1)$ (cf. Example 12.38(2)).

(a)

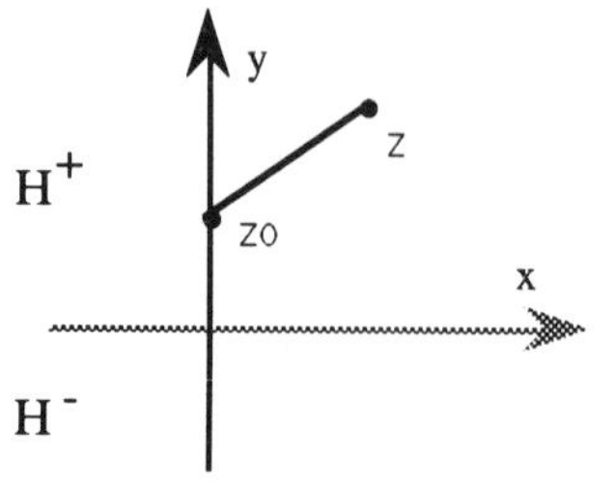

(b)

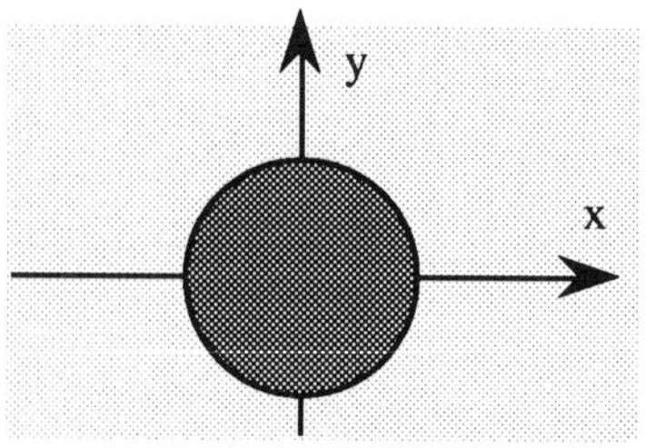

Now, H^+ is a component, by the following argument. A set $V \subseteq \mathbf{R}^2 \setminus \{x\text{-axis}\}$ which properly contains H^+ must include points with negative y-coordinate. Therefore the projection map $p: \mathbf{R}^2 \to \mathbf{R}$ given by $p(x,y) = y$ maps V to a set containing positive and negative values but not zero. This is impossible if V is connected, by the Intermediate Value Theorem (Example 12.41), hence H^+ is a component. For (b) we apply the same argument, with the continuous map $(x,y) \to \sqrt{(x^2 + y^2)}$.

EXERCISE Show that H^+ is connected by defining a homeomorphism onto it from the whole plane [use the exponential function on the second coordinate].

EXERCISE Are the points (1,2,1) and (4,0,1) on the same side of the plane π: $2x-y+z = 5$ (i.e. in the same component of $\mathbf{R}^3 \setminus \pi$)?

REMARK 12.46 In Case (a) above the two components are what we think of as two 'sides' of the removed line. More generally, if removing a subset S from a space X leaves exactly two components, we may call these the *sides* of S.

Of course every line L in the plane has two sides, as we can show formally by a homeomorphism which maps L onto the x-axis (or equally the y-axis) and applying Theorem 12.45(a). Similarly for removal of any subset homeomorphic to a line, such as the curve $y = x^2$. In the same way, the unit circle could be any circle, ellipse, or more general non-crossing closed curve homeomorphic to a circle. The analogous arguments hold for general $\mathbf{R}^n$ and planes, hyperplanes, spheres etc. Notice that if the removed set has equation $f(x) = 0$ $(x \in \mathbf{R}^n)$ then the two sides are defined respectively by $f(x) < 0$ and $f(x) > 0$, simply because $f: \mathbf{R}^n \to \mathbf{R}$ is continuous.

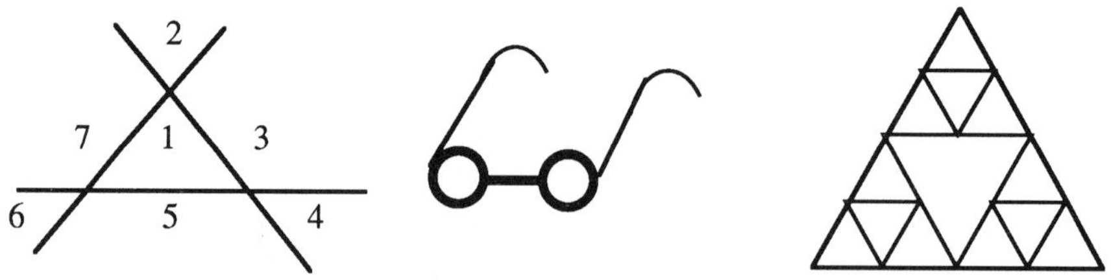

In general three lines divide the plane into seven regions.

This object divides the plane into three regions, one unbounded.

Stage 2 of the Sierpinski gasket. How many regions?

Figure 12.9 Some plane sets whose removal leaves several components.

EXAMPLE 12.47 Verify that the line L: $x/2 + y/3 = 1$ divides $\mathbf{R}^2 \setminus L$ into connected components L^+ : $x/2 + y/3 > 1$, and L^- : $x/2 + y/3 < 1$, by mapping these regions homeomorphically onto the left and right half-planes.

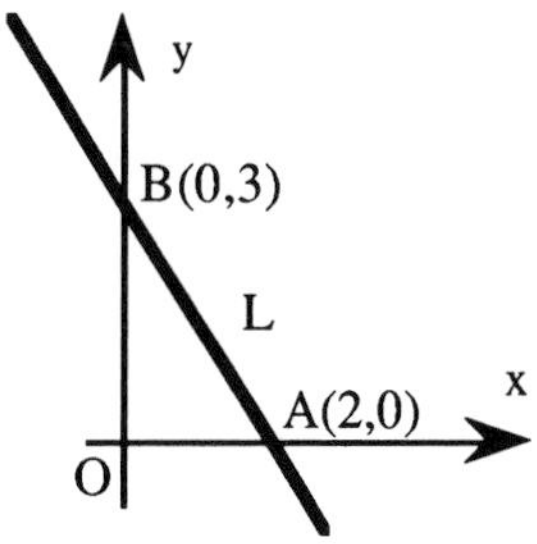

Solution According to theory, *any* homeomorphism of the plane onto itself which sends L to the y-axis *will* map the regions as required (cf. Theorems 12.43, 12.45). The reader may notice, in the light of Chapters 1-2, several obvious isometries that will do. For instance we could rotate L about B until L coincides with the y-axis. But we are not bound to use an isometry. Indeed we might wish to avoid the square roots introduced here by sines and cosines, by going for the more general (*affine*) transformation

$$f\begin{bmatrix}x\\y\end{bmatrix} = \begin{bmatrix}a & b\\c & d\end{bmatrix}\begin{bmatrix}x\\y\end{bmatrix} + \begin{bmatrix}e\\f\end{bmatrix}.$$

It suffices to have f(B) = B, whence $3b+e = 0$, $3d+f = 3$, and f(A) = 0, giving $2a-3b = 0$, $2c-3d = 0$. This leaves us free to choose, say, $b = d = 1$, then $f(x,y) = (1.5x+y-3,y)$, which is a shear as we would expect geometrically [cf. Figure 11.16]. Calling this image (X,Y), we obtain $x = (2/3)(X-Y+3)$, $y = Y$, whence $x/2 + y/3 < 1$ (resp. > 1) $\Leftrightarrow X < 0$ (resp. > 0). Thus the specified regions are mapped to the left and right half-planes as specified.

EXERCISE (i) Which one of the seven regions in Example 12.47 may be defined by $x < 0$, $y > 0$, $g > 0$, where $g(x,y) = x/2 + y/3$? Label the other six similarly. (ii) Find another homeomorphism for Example 12.47.

12.2.3 Further criteria for connectedness

We recall the result from (11.9), (11.10) that for a subset S of a space X

$$S \text{ is closed} \Leftrightarrow S = \overline{S}; \qquad S \text{ is open} \Leftrightarrow S = S^o. \qquad (12.10)$$

THEOREM 12.48 The following are each equivalent to a space X being connected.
(a) *X is not the union of two disjoint nonempty closed subsets.*
(b) *The only subsets of X which are both open and closed are X and* $\emptyset$.
(c) *If A is any subset of X other than X or* $\emptyset$ *then* $\partial A \neq \emptyset$.

Proof Rather than a circle of proofs by contradiction, we prove an equivalent 'circle of falsity', in which (a)~ denotes the contradiction of (a), etc.
(a)~ ⇒ X disconnected. Assume (a) is false: $X = A \cup B$, with A, B disjoint, nonempty and closed. Then $B = A^c$, and $A = B^c$ are open sets which disconnect X.
(b)~ ⇒ (a)~. Suppose (b) is false. Let A be open and closed in X, but distinct from X and $\emptyset$. Then the complement X-A is closed and nonempty, so $X = (X-A) \cup A$ contradicts (a).
(c)~ ⇒ (b)~. Assume that (b) is false and A is distinct from X and $\emptyset$, with $\partial A = \emptyset$. Then since $\overline{A} = A^o \cup \partial A$, (11.8), we have $\overline{A} = A^o$. But $A^o \subseteq A \subseteq \overline{A}$, hence $A^o = A = \overline{A}$. Thus A is both open and closed in X, (12.10), and (b) is false.
X disconnected ⇒ (c)~. Suppose U, V disconnect X. Then $U = V^c$ and $V = U^c$ are also closed, so $U^o = U = \overline{U}$. Therefore $\partial U = \overline{U} - U^o = \emptyset$, and (c) is false.

The basic definition of disconnectedness involves sets which must be open. The next definition enables us to trade that restriction for another that can be easier to apply.

DEFINITION 12.49 Nonempty subsets S, T of a space X are *mutually separated* if $S \cap \overline{T} = \emptyset = \overline{S} \cap T$. They *separate a subset* A if also $A = S \cup T$. Thus S, T need not be open in X but must satisfy a stronger condition than disjointness : not even a limit point of one may be in the other. We emphasise that $\overline{S}$ refers to closure in the 'big' space X; the *closure of* $\overline{S}$ *in A* is $\overline{S} \cap A$ (exercise).

THEOREM 12.50 Subsets S, T of a space X disconnect the subset A if and only if they separate A.

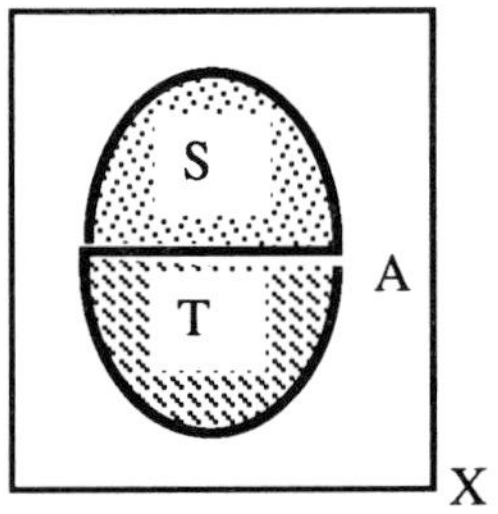

Proof Suppose S, T disconnect A. Then $A = S \cup T$, with S,T nonempty, open, disjoint. We have: $S \cap \overline{T} \subseteq A \cap \overline{T}$ (since $S \subseteq A$) = closure of T in A = T (as T is closed in A). But $S \cap \overline{T}$ is also in S, hence in $S \cap T$, which is empty by hypothesis. Similarly $\overline{S} \cap T = \emptyset$. Thus S, T are mutually separated as required.

Conversely, suppose that $A = S \cup T$ with S, T mutually separated. Then we have that: closure of S in $A = A \cap \overline{S} =$ $(S \cup T) \cap \overline{S} = (S \cap \overline{S}) \cup (T \cap \overline{S})$ (Table 11.1) = S, since $S \subseteq \overline{S}$ and $T \cap \overline{S} = \emptyset$. Therefore S is closed in A, (12.10), and $T = A - S$ is open. Similarly S is open, so S, T disconnect A.

THEOREM 12.51 Let A be a connected subset of X, with

$$A \subseteq Y \subseteq \overline{A}. \tag{12.11}$$

Then Y is connected. In particular, $\overline{A}$ *itself is connected.*

Proof Suppose A is connected and $A \subseteq Y \subseteq \overline{A}$. We shall assume Y is disconnected and obtain a contradiction Here it is convenient to use the mutually separated concept, thus $Y = S \cup T$, where S, T are mutually separated, by Theorem 12.50. Since A is connected, $A \subseteq S$ or $A \subseteq T$ by Lemma 12.36. If $A \subseteq S$ then we have in succession $T \subseteq Y \subseteq \overline{A} \subseteq \overline{S}$, contradicting $T \cap \overline{S} = \emptyset$, with a similar contradiction in case $A \subseteq T$. Thus, after all, Y is connected.

COROLLARY 12.52 The components of a space are closed subsets.

Proof Let A be a component of a space X. By Theorem 12.51 $\overline{A}$ is also connected. But $A \subseteq \overline{A}$ and A is a maximal connected subspace. Hence $A = \overline{A}$ and so is closed by (12.10).

DEFINITION 12.53 Another technique for proving spaces or subsets to be connected is to use the slightly stronger property of being *path-connected.* A *path* in X from a to b (*an a-b path*) is the image of a continuous function $f: [0,1] \to X$ with $f(0) = a$, $f(1) = b$. Since [0,1] is compact and connected, so is every path. The space X is called *path-connected* if there is an a-b path for every pair a, b in X. A subset A of X is path connected if it is so as a subspace.

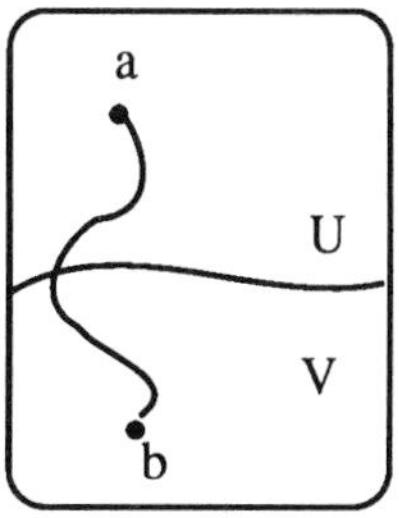

THEOREM 12.54 Path-connected implies connected.

Proof Let X be path-connected, but separated by sets U, V. Then there are distinct points $a \in U$, $b \in V$ and a continuous function $f: [0,1] \to X$ with $f(0) = a$, $f(1) = b$. Therefore the sets $S = U \cap f([0,1])$, $T = V \cap [0,1]$ separate $f([0,1])$, implying the contradiction that $[0,1]$ is disconnected.

EXAMPLES 12.55 (Path connected spaces.)

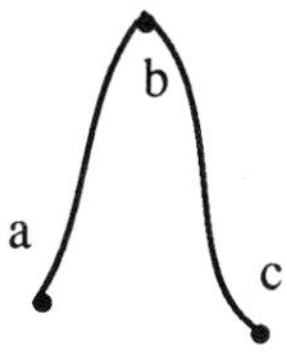

(1) *Show that the 2-sphere is path-connected.* Of course, if there is an a-b path f(t) and a b-c path g(t) then there is an a-c path h(t), and the standard way to combine them is to define

$$h(t) = \begin{cases} f(2t) & 0 \le t \le 1/2 \\ g(2t-1) & 1/2 \le t \le 1 \end{cases} \qquad (12.12)$$

Thus we need only exhibit a path from the North pole to any given point with spherical polar coordinates (θ,ϕ), and this is easily done using a great circle, say $f(t) = (t\theta,\phi)$.

(2) *Show that the orthogonal group* $O(3) = \{$ 3 by 3 real matrices A: $AA^T = I\}$ *is not connected, but that its subgroup* $SO(3) = \{A \in O(3): |A| = 1\}$ *is connected.*

(i) As discussed in Examples 11.41(4) the entries of an n by n real matrix may be taken as coordinates in $\mathbf{R}^{n^2}$, with O(n) defined by the equality $AA^T = I$. Consider the continuous map $O(n) \to \mathbf{R}$, $A \to |A|$. The image is the disconnected set $\{1,-1\}$, so by Theorem 12.40, O(n) is not connected.

(ii) We may show that SO(3) is connected by showing it to be path-connected. We earlier defined a continuous onto map $S^3 \to SO(3)$, $\mathbf{a} \to M(\mathbf{a})$, in which the 3-sphere is identified with the set (group) of all unit quaternions **a** and M(**a**) is the matrix giving the same rotation, including same axis, as the map $\mathbf{x} \to \mathbf{q}^{-1}\mathbf{x}\mathbf{q}$ induced by quaternion multiplication (see Section 9.3.3: Further comments), so it suffices to show that S^3 is path-connected (cf. the two exercises below). But any unit quaternion has the form $e^{\mathbf{I}\theta} = \cos\theta + \mathbf{I}\sin\theta$, where 2θ is the rotation and the axis is given by unit vector (a,b,c), corresponding to $\mathbf{I} = a\mathbf{i} + b\mathbf{j} + c\mathbf{k}$. Thus a path to this point from the North pole (1,0,0,0) is given by $f(t) = e^{\mathbf{I}t\theta}$.

(3) *The topologist's sine curve.*

$$y = \begin{cases} 0 & x \le 0 \\ \sin(1/x) & x > 0 \end{cases}$$

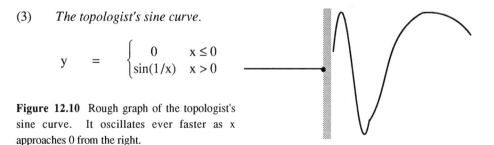

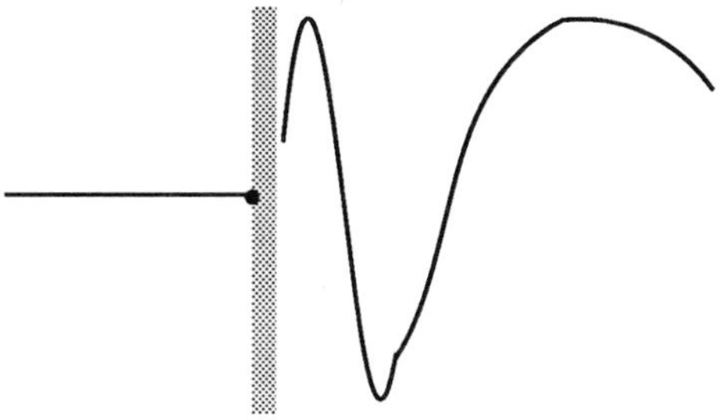

Figure 12.10 Rough graph of the topologist's sine curve. It oscillates ever faster as x approaches 0 from the right.

This is a standard example to show that connected does not imply path-connected, although the converse is true by Theorem 12.54. The curve in Figure 12.10 is a subset $V = S \cup T$ of the plane consisting of line $S = \{(x,0): x \leq 0\}$ and sine part $T = \{(x, \sin 1/x): x > 0\}$ which oscillates always between y = -1 and 1, but ever faster as x becomes smaller.

(i) *V is connected.* Clearly S and T individually are connected. For instance T is a continuous image of $(0,\infty)$. However it is not obvious that $S \cup T$ is connected, for S and T have no common point. But the origin (0,0) comes to our rescue - it is in the closure of T since every $B_O(r)$ intersects T. Thus $T \cup \{(0,0)\}$ lies between the connected set T and its closure, and so is connected by Theorem 12.51. And now V, as the union of two connected sets with the origin as common point, is connected by Theorem 12.37.

(ii) *V is not path-connected.* It may seem intuitively that V actually is path-connected, but the infinite vibration near x = 0 is its undoing in this respect, as we shall see. We assume that V is path-connected and obtain a contradiction. Let $f: I \to V$ be a path from the origin to a point on the curved part T, say (1, sin(1)). Then the set f(I) is compact by Theorem 12.16, but contains the sequence $\{(x_n, \sin(1/x_n))\}$, where $1/x_n = \pi(2n+1)/2$. Now $\sin(1/x_n) = 1$, and $x_n \to 0$ as $n \to \infty$, therefore the sequence has limit (0,1) in $\mathbf{R}^2$. But this point is not in V and hence not in f(I), contrary to the compactness of f(I) (cf. Theorem 12.14 and Test 11.19). This contradiction proves that V is not path-connected.

EXERCISE Prove that the Platonic solids (Figure 9.13) are path-connected.

EXERCISE Is the projective plane path-connected (see Exercise after Example 12.17)?

Now we prove a result for connected spaces that corresponds to the Tychonoff Theorem for compact spaces: a product of connected spaces is connected. In this case the proof can be conveniently given for a finite or infinite product of general topological spaces, with the translation of 'an open ball centred at x' into 'a basic open set B_x containing x'.

THEOREM 12.56 A product space $X = \prod X_i\ (i \in \Lambda)$ *is connected if and only if each factor space is connected, where the index set* Λ *is* **N** *or a finite set.*

Proof We assume that we are dealing with nonempty factors. Suppose the product space X is connected. Then each factor X_i is the image of the continuous projection p_i, so is connected (Theorem 12.40). Conversely, the hard part, assume that each X_i is connected. Let $a = (a_i)$ be any point of X and let E denote its connected component in X. We shall prove X is connected by proving that X equals the connected (Theorem 12.51) subset $\overline{E} \subseteq X$. For any x in X we have

$$x \in \overline{E} \iff x \in E \text{ or } x \text{ is a limit point of } E \qquad \text{(Definition 11.20)}$$
$$\iff \text{each } B_x \text{ intersects } E \text{ (in } x \text{ and/or another point)} \qquad \text{(Test 11.19).}$$

It thus suffices to prove that an arbitrary basic open set U of X meets E. We may label the factors of X so that $U = p_1^{-1}(U_1) \cap \ldots \cap p_n^{-1}(U_n)$, for some n. We recall that $p_\alpha(a) = a_\alpha$ where p_α is projection onto the factor with subscript α, and define a point b of X which will be seen to lie in both E and U by choosing any points $b_i \in U_i$, $i = 1,2,\ldots,n$, as illustrated above, and defining $b_a = a_\alpha$ otherwise. We further define $E_1, \ldots, E_n$ by

$$E_1 = \{x \in X: x_1 \text{ is arbitrary}, \quad x_\alpha = a_\alpha \text{ otherwise}\},$$
$$E_2 = \{x \in X: x_1 = b_1,\ x_2 \text{ is arbitrary}, \quad x_\alpha = a_\alpha \text{ otherwise}\},$$
$$\ldots\ldots\ldots\ldots$$
$$E_n = \{x \in X: x_i = b_i \text{ for } 1 \leq i \leq n-1, \quad x_\alpha = a_\alpha \text{ otherwise}\}.$$

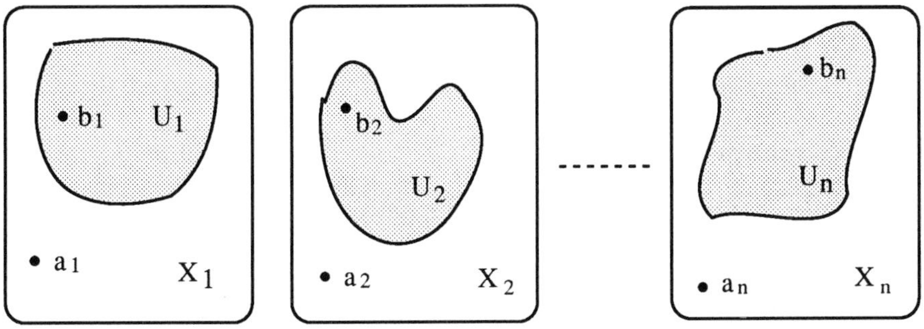

Then E_k is homeomorphic to X_k , which is connected by hypothesis. We verify that the intersection $E_k \cap E_{k+1}$ is nonempty for k = 1, 2, ..., n-1. For example $E_1 \cap E_2$ contains the point y defined by $y_1 = b_1$, $y_\alpha = a_\alpha$ ($\alpha \neq 1$). Hence the set $F = E_1 \cup ... \cup E_n$ is connected, by Theorem 12.37. Now $a \in F$ (in fact $a \in E_1$), F is connected, and E is by definition the maximal connected subset of X containing a. Therefore $F \subseteq E$ and we have in succession $b \in E_n \subseteq F \subseteq E$. Thus $b \in E$. But $b \in U$ by definition of b, and so we have shown as required that U intersects E, completing the proof that X is connected.

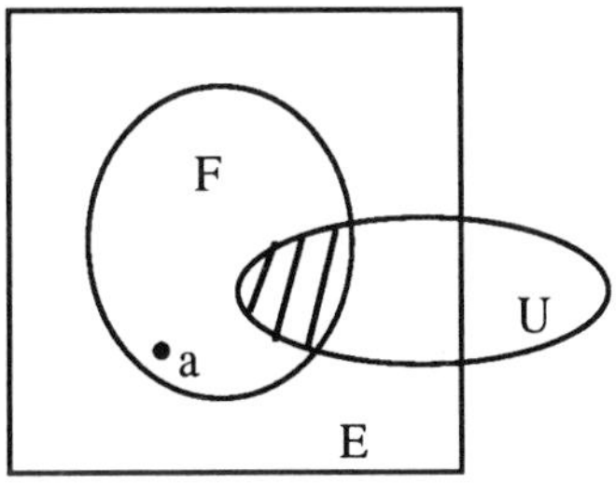

The overall scheme

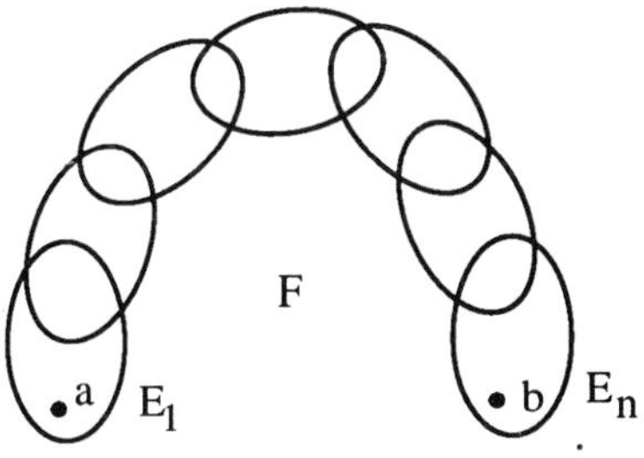

Blow-up of F

EXERCISE Give two reasons why the torus is connected. What is the maximum number of connected components that can be left when we remove two circles from the torus?

EXAMPLE 12.57 (The Cantor set C.) We showed in Example 12.25 that C is homeomorphic to the product of infinitely many copies of the totally disconnected set {0,2}, so according to Theorem 12.56 C is certainly not connected. It can be shown moreover that, with index set **N** or a finite set,

a product of totally disconnected sets is totally disconnected, (12.13)

which includes C. However we will first give an explicit proof that C is totally disconnected. We may think of C as the ternary decimals 0.abc..., with digits taking the values 0 or 2 but not 1, as described in Section 10.3.2. Let α, β be distinct points of C. We will show the first digit position in which they differ by writing $\alpha = 0.d_1...d_n0...$, and $\beta = 0.d_1...d_n2...$, though the argument still holds if there are no initial d_i's . Now α, β lie in distinct intervals [a,b], [c,d] as shown below, where a dot above the digit 2 means that it is repeated indefinitely.

Hence any subset V of C which contains α, β is separated by the sets $\{x \in V: x \le b\}$ and $\{x \in V: c \le x\}$, and so is disconnected (Theorem 12.50). Since, therefore, no point can be contained in a larger connected set, it follows that C is totally disconnected (exercise: C is not discrete).

The reader may wish to compare the 'bare handed' approach above to the proof of the general result (12.13) which turns out to be surprisingly easy. Let A be a connected subset of the product $X = \prod X_i$ $(i \in \Lambda)$. With each factor X_i totally disconnected, the connected set $p_i(A)$ must be a single point a_i, and so $A = \{(x_i): x_i = a_i\ (i \in \Lambda)\} = (a_i)$, itself a single point. Since therefore the only connected subsets of X are single points, X is totally disconnected.

REMARK 12.58 There is a remarkable theorem that one further restriction added to compact and totally disconnected, characterises the Cantor set completely (Willard, 1970, page 217). This in turn enables us to characterise any disconnected *Julia set* as being homeomorphic to the Cantor set C, a surprising result, considered further in Chapter 16. The extra property is that of having no isolated points. Let $x = 0.x_1x_2..$ be a point of C. Then x is not isolated for, given $\varepsilon > 0$, we obtain a second point y within distance ε of x by changing the N'th digit of x from 0 to 2 or vice versa, where N is so large that the difference $d(x,y) = 2/3^N$ is less than ε.

DEFINITION 12.59 Let the space X be path-connected. A pair of points a, b of X are said to be *simply connected in X* if, given any two a-b paths f_0, f_1 in X we can continuously deform f_0 to f_1 through a 1-parameter family of paths $\{f_t : 0 \le t \le 1\}$. More precisely, there is a continuous map $F: I \times I \to X$ with $F(x,t) = f_t(x)$. We then call X itself *simply connected* if any two such paths can be deformed into each other.

Here is an example in which deformation is possible in the plane between two O-B paths $f_0(x) = (x,0)$ and $f_1(x) = (x, x(1-x))$. One simple way to do this is given by

$$f_t(x) = (x, tx(1-x)).$$

What can prevent the deformation is a 'hole' as portrayed in Figure 12.11(a) below.

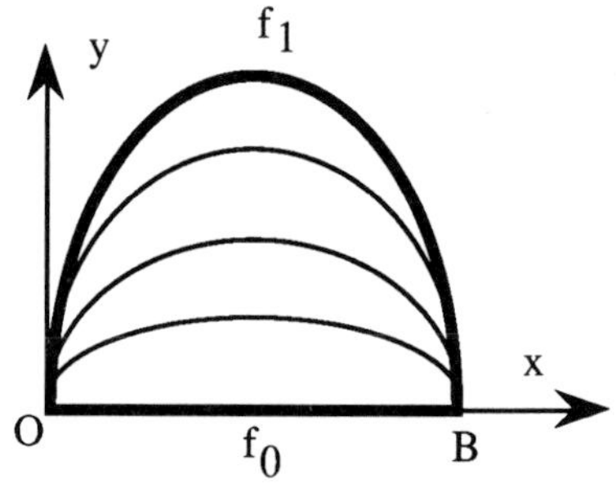

REMARK 12.60 The connection with holes is even clearer when we convert the issue to a question about *loops*, which is done as follows. Call $f^{-1}(t) = f(1-t)$ the *inverse path.* If f is an A-B path and g is a B-A path then composition of paths (12.12) gives a loop (i.e. an A-A path) $f.g^{-1}$ through A, depicted in Figure 12.11(b). Writing $f \sim h$ to mean that path f is deformable into h, we may show that $f \sim g$ if and only if $f.g^{-1}$ is deformable to the constant path at A (an exercise). We may conclude that *X is simply connected if and only if every loop in X may be shrunk to a* point.

EXAMPLES 12.61 $\mathbf{R}^n$ is simply connected for all n, as is every interval in **R**. So is S^n provided $n \ge 2$, the circle being an obvious exception. The torus (=doughnut, or donut), we have seen, is compact, connected, even path-connected, but it is *not* simply connected, for the loop indicated in Figure 12.11(c) cannot be shrunk to a point.

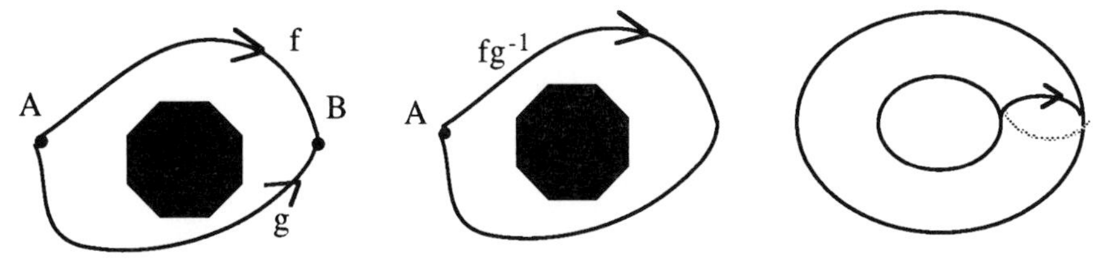

(a) Paths f, g

(b) Path $f.g^{-1}$ is a loop at A. It cannot shrink to A because of the (black) hole.

(c) Unshrinkable loop on a torus (traced out as one angle coordinate varies).

Figure 12.11 The connection between paths and holes.

EXERCISE Show the surface $z = x^2+y^2$ is connected, path-connected, and simply connected.

NOTE 12.62 (*The fundamental group*) If F(x,t) deforms path f into g then g may be deformed into f by F(x,1-t). In the example of Figure 12.11(b), this equals (x,(1-t)x(1-x)). Continuing the notation of Remark 12.60, let $x_0 \in X$ be given. Then ~ is an equivalence relation on the set of loops at x_0. Then composition of paths gives composition of path classes by [f][g] = [f.g]. With a little more work one can show that the set of classes of loops through a given point x_0 satisfy the axioms of Section 2.5 for a group, called the *fundamental group* $\pi(X,x_0)$. Further, a homeomorphism f: X → Y induces an isomorphism $\pi(X,x_0) \to \pi(Y,f(x_0))$ with the result that if the two groups are not isomorphic then X, Y cannot be homeomorphic Here we have probably the most basic element of the machinery of Algebraic Topology. For more information see Hocking and Young (1961) or Maunder (1970).

A final irresistible comment. We may regard a loop in X as a continuous map f: $S^1 \to X$. The idea extends to maps $S^n \to X$, and we have a measure of the n-dimensional holes in X, for n = 1, 2, ... There are many other algebraic structures, even ways to prove algebraic facts by Topology in cases where no direct algebraic proof is known (see Porteous, 1969).

REMARK 12.63 We may extend the list, begun in (11.19A) to (11.19G), of properties preserved under a homeomorphism f: X → Y.

X is compact ⇔ Y is compact
X is connected ⇔ Y is connected
X is path-connected ⇔ Y is path-connected
X is simply connected ⇔ Y is simply connected.

EXERCISE Prove the last two statements of Remark 12.63.

It can be shown that an open simply connected subset of the plane is homeomorphic to an open unit disc. This is the famous Riemann Mapping Theorem (See Ahlfors, 1966), which shows that the final result of this chapter is more general than it looks. It assists us to establish two important properties of Mandelbrot and Julia sets in Chapter 16 (Theorems 16.53 and 16.56).

*THEOREM 12.64 Let $D_1 \supseteq D_2 \supseteq$ ... be subsets of the plane, each homeomorphic to a closed unit disk. Let $D = \cap D_n$ ($n \in$ **N**). Then D and its boundary are connected.*

Proof Notice that by hypothesis there are infinitely many sets D_n, for they correspond to the infinite set of integers 1, 2, .. . Also, D_n may become a fixed set when n reaches some integer k: $D_k = D_{k+1} = D_{k+2} = ..$. But this need not be the case. To show that D is connected, we suppose it to be disconnected by open sets U, V and obtain a contradiction. Thus we assume that D is contained in $U \cup V$ with $D \cap U$ and $D \cap V$ nonempty and disjoint. Now, although each D_n is connected, it contains D and so $D_n \cap U$ and $D_n \cap V$ are nonempty and disjoint. Therefore D_n is not contained in $U \cup V$. So there is a point x_n lying in $D_n \setminus U \cup V$, for each n in **N**.

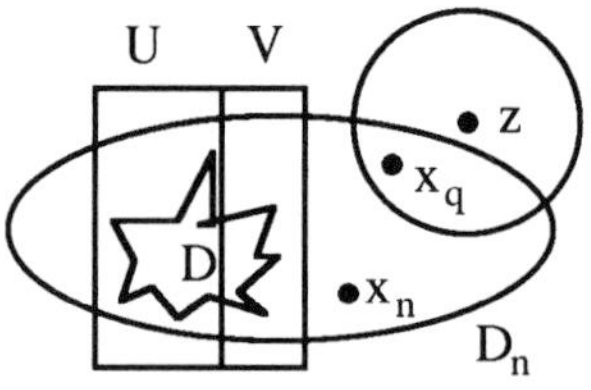

As an infinite subset of the compact space D_1, $\{x_n\}$ has a limit point z in D_1, by Theorem 12.11. Choose $n \in$ **N**. We claim that for every $r > 0$, the ball $B_z(r)$ intersects D_n in a point other than z. For since z is a limit point of $\{x_i\}$ there is a sufficiently high value $q \geq n$ for which $x_q \in B_z(r)$, and so $x_q \in D_q \subseteq D_n$. Hence the point z is in the closure of D_n (Test 11.18), which is D_n itself (by (11.10)) since it is closed.

We have shown that $z \in D_n$ for every $n \in$ **N**, and so $z \in D$ by definition of D. This is the required contradiction: $\{x_n\}$ lies within the closed set $(U \cup V)^c$, which therefore contains its limit point z (Test 11.19), and so z cannot lie within the subset D of $U \cup V$.
Therefore D is connected after all. The proof that ∂D is connected is somewhat similar, and is omitted.

REMARK 12.65 We have shown that the Cantor set is (for later use):

1	Compact	:	Example 12.17(2),
2	An infinite product	:	Example 12.25,
3	Totally disconnected	:	Example 12.57,
4	Perfect	:	Example 12.58.

EXERCISES 12

---

1 √ Find the supremum of the set $A = \{(x-2)/(x-1): x \geq 3\}$

2 Explain why the supremum of a set A has points of A arbitrarily close.

3 √ Prove that if A, B are compact subsets of X, then so are $A \cup B$ and $A \cap B$. Is the discrete space **N** (Example 11.7) compact?

4 Show that if $f: X \to Y$ is onto and $X = f^{-1}(A) \cup f^{-1}(B)$ then $A \cup B = Y$.

5 Show that the closure of subset S in subspace A is $\overline{S} \cap A$ (all within a metric space X).

6 √ Prove for a function $f: X \to Y$, that $f(A \cap B) \subseteq f(A) \cap f(B)$ and find the relation between $f(A \cup B)$ and $f(A) \cup f(B)$.

7 √ The projective plane is a quotient space P = D/R (Definition 11.53), where D is the unit disc and $xRy \Leftrightarrow x = \pm y$ (thus antipodal points are identified). Why must P be compact?

8 √ Find the minimum bound ratio for the transformation of the plane sending the point (x,y) to the point (2x-3y+1,5x+y+3). [Hint: first express the map as a composition involving an isometry.]

9 √ Find the greatest value of $x^2 + y^2 + z^2$ on the tetrahedron with vertices (0,0,0), (1,2,1), (2,-3,7), (-1,2,3). This may involve checking that the derivatives are not zero in the interior.

10 √ Show that open or closed balls in $\mathbf{R}^n$ are connected.

11 √ Show that $\mathbf{R}^n$ with the origin deleted is still connected.

12 Use the Intermediate Value Theorem to show that every real polynomial of odd degree must have a real root. Find such a root to within 1 unit, for $x^5 + 32x^4 + 1$.

13 √ By considering how they may be disconnected, show that S^2 is not homeomorphic to the circle S^1 or to a torus.

14 √ Show that H^+ is connected by expressing it as the image of a connected set under a homeomorphism. Use another map to deduce that H^- is connected.

15 (i) Which of the seven regions in Example 12.47 is defined by $x < 0$, $y > 0$, $g > 0$, where $g(x,y) = x/2 + y/3$? Label the other six similarly. (ii) Find another homeomorphism for the above example.

16 √ (i) Prove that the Platonic solids are path-connected. Can you generalise this? (ii) Is the projective plane path-connected?

17 √ Give two reasons why the torus is connected. What is the maximum number of connected components that can be left when we remove two circles from the torus?

18 Show that the surface $z = x^2+y^2$ is connected, path-connected, and simply connected.

19 Let $f: X \to Y$ be a homeomorphism. Prove from the definitions that X is path-connected if and only if Y is, and similarly for simply connectedness.

Chapter 13 The existence and uniqueness of fractals

13.1 The Hausdorff distance

A general reference for this section is Hutchinson (1981). Recalling some notation from Section 10.3.1, let $\psi_1, .., \psi_N$ be similitudes in the plane (or more generally, n-space), with ratios $r_1, ..., r_N$ $(0 < r_i < 1)$. That is, each ψ_i is the composition in either order of a dilation $\mathbf{x} \to r_i\mathbf{x}$ and an isometry (translation, rotation, reflection, glide - see Section 1.3.2). For every subset E of the plane, these similitudes define a new subset ΨE by

$$\Psi E = (\psi_1 E) \cup (\psi_2 E) \cup ... \cup (\psi_N E). \tag{13.1}$$

Thus ΨE may be understood as a map from the collection $P(\mathbf{R}^2)$ of all subsets of $\mathbf{R}^2$, to itself. To emphasise, and to remind ourselves of, Ψ's construction as a union or 'collage' (3.1) we shall call Ψ the *collage map* determined by the ψ_i ('union map' is not quite so evocative). By repeated application ('iteration') of Ψ we transform E through a sequence of subsets

$$E_0 \ (= E),\ E_1,\ E_2, ... \qquad (E_{n+1} = \Psi E_n), \tag{13.2}$$

as illustrated earlier in Figure 10.14 for the Koch snowflake curve, Figure 10.15 for the Cantor set, and Figure 10.16 for the Sierpinski gasket. In these and in many other cases of interest E_n approaches a 'limit set', giving an important method of constructing fractal images which we shall exploit especially in Chapter 14. The existence of this limit under reasonable conditions is what is meant by the first part of the present chapter's heading, whilst uniqueness refers to the seeming paradox that, by a truly remarkable theorem of Hutchinson (1981) the limit set is independent of the choice of starting set E, but is completely determined by the choice of Ψ, that is, of the maps ψ_i.

In the successive images E_n the structure of E becomes less and less visible, whilst structure inherited from the ψ_i comes to the fore, as we illustrate in Figure 13.1 by the Sierpinski gasket obtained from two different starting sets (see also Figures 10.7 and 13.8(b)). The iterated function systems of Chapter 14 show that it is well worth while allowing the maps ψ_i to be more general than similitudes. A convenient restriction for which the desired results still hold is that each map is *contractive* (is a *contraction mapping*) That is, for all **x**, **y** in $\mathbf{R}^n$,

$$d(\psi_i(\mathbf{x}),\psi_i(\mathbf{y})) \leq r_i\, d(\mathbf{x},\mathbf{y}), \qquad (13.3)$$

where $0 \le r_i < 1$. This is a special case of boundedness, (11.17), so for each ψ_i there is a *least* such constant r_i (it is the minimum bound ratio of Note 11.44). We will assume this least value to have been selected unless noted to the contrary. In the context of contraction maps, it will be called the *contraction ratio* (or just *ratio*) of ψ_i. For a practical method of calculation, Application 12.29 shows that if ψ_i is *linear* then it is bounded, with

$$r_i = \max_{|\mathbf{x}|=1} |\psi_i(\mathbf{x})|.$$

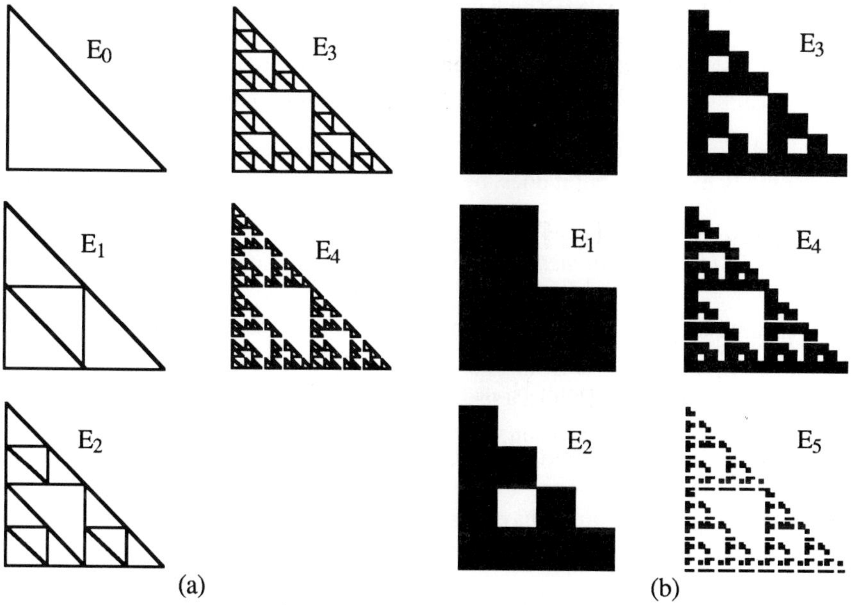

Figure 13.1 A right angled Sierpinski gasket from two different starting sets E: (a) the sides of a right angled triangle, (b) a solid square. If the horizontal side has length 2, with the origin at its left endpoint, the contraction maps for cases (a), (b) are $\psi_1(\mathbf{x}) = (1/2)\mathbf{x}$, $\psi_2(\mathbf{x}) = (1/2)\mathbf{x} + (1,0)$, $\psi_3(\mathbf{x}) = (1/2)\mathbf{x} + (0,1)$. After a few more iterations, (b) looks like (a)

When are two sets close? In order to be precise about E_n (= $\Psi^n(E)$) approaching a limit set as n increases we need a definition of when two sets are close to each other. In other words we need the idea of a distance d(A,B) between two sets. One candidate is d(A,B) = inf{d(a,b): a ∈ A, b ∈ B}, the greatest lower bound of all the d(a,b). This has its uses (Kelley, 1964) but from our point of view it suffers from the defect that two sets can be at zero distance without actually coinciding. This occurs if distinct A, B overlap, as for example in the case A = [0,2], B = [1,3]. Fortunately there is another candidate, the *Hausdorff distance*, or *Hausdorff metric*, for which d(A,B) = 0 entails A = B. Another crucial benefit is that now the triangle inequality holds: d(A,C) ≤ d(A,B) + d(B,C). Is there a catch? The only restriction needed to ensure that the distance axioms hold (Definition 11.1) is that we keep to compact nonempty subsets of our metric space X. Hence we define

$$\mathcal{H}(X) = \{\text{All nonempty compact subsets of } X\}. \tag{13.4}$$

This is called the 'space of fractals' by Barnsley (1988). Now let $E \in \mathcal{H}(X)$. Then since bounded implies continuous (Theorem 11.43) each $\psi_i(E)$ is the continuous image of a compact set so is itself compact (Theorem 12.16). Consequently ΨE is a finite union of compact sets, so it too is compact (Theorem 12.15). Thus we have a function

$$\Psi : \mathcal{H}(X) \rightarrow \mathcal{H}(X). \tag{13.5}$$

DEFINITION 13.1 Our first task is to define Hausdorff distance, conveniently done in two stages, and to show that, equipped with this, $\mathcal{H}(X)$ becomes a metric space and Ψ a contractive map.The *distance* between a point a and compact subset B in the metric space X is given by

$$d(a,B) = \min_{b \in B} d(a,b), \tag{13.6}$$

where d(a,b) denotes distance in X. The validity of this definition depends on the cited minimum actually existing, but it does, by compactness, as we now show.

LEMMA 13.2 The point to set distance (13.6) exists and $d(x,B) = 0$ if and only if $x \in B$.

Proof We showed that the distance function is continuous in each variable (Theorem 11.42). Thus $B \rightarrow R$, defined by $x \rightarrow d(a,x)$, is a continuous function on a compact set, so has a minimum, attained at some point b_0 in B (Theorem 12.28). That is, $\min d(a,b)$ $(b \in B)$ does exist.

For the 'if and only if' part, let $d(x,B) = 0$. Then by the first part we may write $d(x,b_0) = 0$ for some $b_0 \in B$, hence $x = b_0$ by definition of distance function. Thus $x \in B$. Conversely, let $x \in B$. Then we have a series of inequalites sandwiched between zeros either end: $0 \leq d(x,B) = \min d(x,b)$ $(b \in B) \leq d(x,x) = 0$, and hence $d(x,B) = 0$.

EXAMPLE 13.3 For the distance from a point a to plane B in $\mathbf{R}^3$ we have $d(a,B) = d(a,b_0)$, where b_0 is the foot of the perpendicular from a to the plane. Let B be the plane $2x+3y-z = 4$, and let a have coordinates (-1,7,1). A normal vector to B is (2,3,-1), so an arbitrary point on the line through a and b_0 is $(-1,7,1) + t(2,3,-1)$, where t is a parameter. This is b_0 itself if $2(-1+2t) + 3(7+3t) - (1-t) = 4$, ie if $t = -1$. Hence b_0 is (-3,4,2) and $d(a,B) = \sqrt{(2^2 + 3^2 + 1^2)} = \sqrt{14}$.

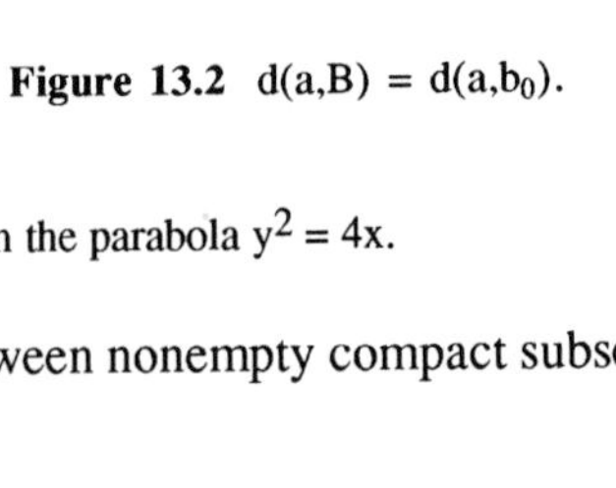

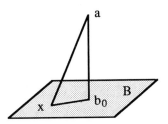

Figure 13.2 $d(a,B) = d(a,b_0)$.

EXERCISE Calculate the distance of the point (2,27) from the parabola $y^2 = 4x$.

DEFINITION 13.4 The *Hausdorff distance* d(A,B) between nonempty compact subsets of a metric space X is given by (cf. Lemma 13.5)

$$d(A,B) = \max(d_A(B), d_B(A)), \text{ where} \tag{13.7}$$

$$d_A(B) = \max_{a \in A} d(a,B)$$

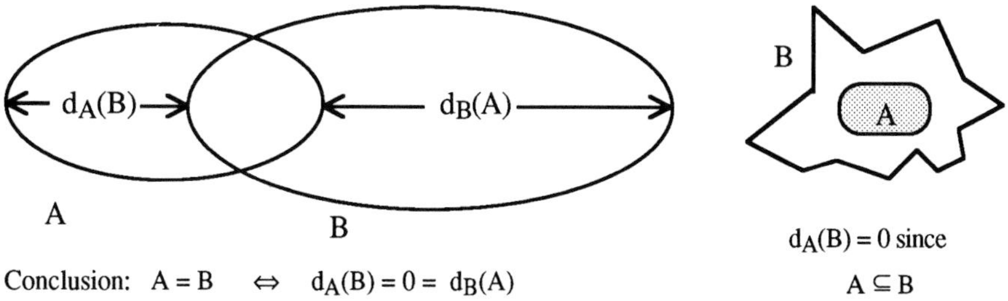

Figure 13.3 The difference between $d_A(B)$ and $d_B(A)$.

LEMMA 13.5 For A, B compact nonempty subsets of a metric space X,
(a) $d_A(B)$ *exists, and equals* $d(a_0,b_0)$, *for some* a_0 *in A, and* b_0 *in B,*
(b) $d_A(B) = 0 \Leftrightarrow A \subseteq B$,
(c) $d(A,B) = d(a_0,b_0)$, *for some* a_0 *in A,* b_0 *in B.*

Proof (a) The details of this can be hard to pin down, and so we shall give them. Once we show that the map f: $A \to \mathbf{R}$, given by $a \to d(a,B)$, is continuous, the existence of $d_A(B)$ as its maximum value is guaranteed by compactness of A (Theorem 12.28); thus $d_A(B) = d(a_0,B)$ for some a_0 in A, which in turn equals $d(a_0,b_0)$ for some b_0 in B. To establish the continuity of f, it suffices to show that for all x,y in A: $|d(x,B) - d(y,B)| \le d(x,y)$. But for any $b \in B$ we have by the triangle inequality, $d(x,b) \le d(x,y) + d(y,b)$ and therefore $d(x,b) - d(y,b) \le d(x,y)$. Similarly with d(x,b) and d(y,b) interchanged. These two facts together give $|d(x,b) - d(y,b)| \le d(x,y)$. Since this holds for every b in B, there follows $|d(x,B) - d(y,B)| \le d(x,y)$, which we noted was sufficient to show that f is continuous. Thus the proof of (a) is complete.

(b) Let $d_A(B) = 0$ and let $a \in A$. Then $d(a,B) \le d_A(B)$ (by definition) therefore $d(a,B) = 0$. Hence $a \in B$ by Lemma 13.2. Thus $A \subseteq B$. Conversely, if we assume that $A \subseteq B$ then $d_A(B) = 0$ is clear (why?). (c) is immediate from part(a).

EXERCISE Deduce Lemma 13.5(c) from 13.5(a).

THEOREM 13.6. The Hausdorff distance is a metric on the set $\mathcal{H}(X)$ *of nonempty compact subsets of a metric space X.*

Proof The assertions we have to prove are (a), (b), (c) of Definition 11.1 for a metric space. Let A, B, C be arbitrary members of $\mathcal{H}(X)$. That is, nonempty compact subsets of X. For (a) we have trivially $d(A,A) = 0$, and the logical equivalences $d(A,B) = 0 \Leftrightarrow [d_A(B) = 0 = d_B(A)] \Leftrightarrow (A \subseteq B \text{ and } B \subseteq A) \Leftrightarrow A = B$. Assertion (b), that $d(A,B) = d(B,A)$, is immediate from the symmetry of their definition. The proof of (c), the triangle inequality, is more substantial. Let a,b,c be points of A, B, C respectively. Then for all a,b,c

$d(c,A)$	$\le d(c,a)$,	by Definition 13.1,
	$\le d(c,b) + d(b,a)$,	by the triangle inequality in X.

So for all b, c,

$d(c,A)$	$\le d(c,b) + d(b,A)$	[Put $a = a_0$ above: $d(b,A) = d(b,a_0,)$],
	$\le d(c,b) + d_B(A)$	by Definition 13.4.

So for all c,

$d(c,A)$	$\le d(c,B) + d(A,B)$	[Put $b = b_0$ above: $d(c,B) = d(c,b_0)$],

$$\leq\ d_C(B) + d(A,B) \qquad \text{by Definition 13.4,}$$
$$\leq\ d(A,B) + d(B,C) \qquad \text{by Definition 13.4.}$$
Hence $d_C(A) \leq d(A,B) + d(B,C)$ [Put $c = c_0$ above: $d_C(A) = d(c_0, A)$].

Similarly $d_A(C)$ is less than or equal to the above sum, and therefore so is $\max(d_A(C), d_C(A))$, which equals $d(A,C)$. Thus we have the required triangle inequality.

EXAMPLES 13.7 (1) On the real line, let $A = [0,2]$, $B = [1,5]$.

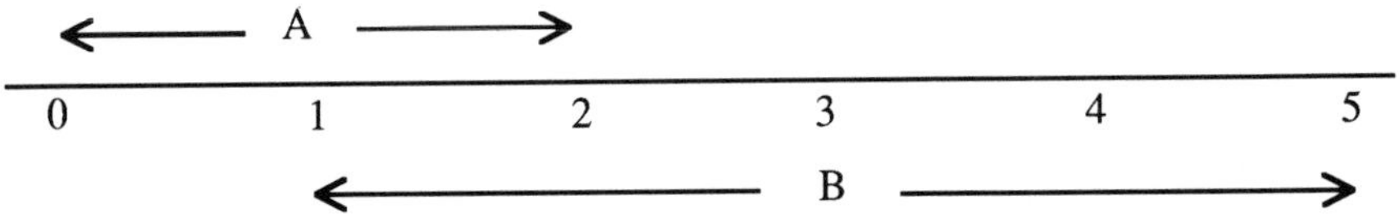

Here $d_A(B)$ = (the furthest we can move in A, away from B) = $d(0,1) = 1$. But $d_B(A) = d(2,5) = 3$, and so $d(A,B) = \max(1,3) = 3$.

(2) On the real line again, $A = [2,4]$, $B = [1,6]$.

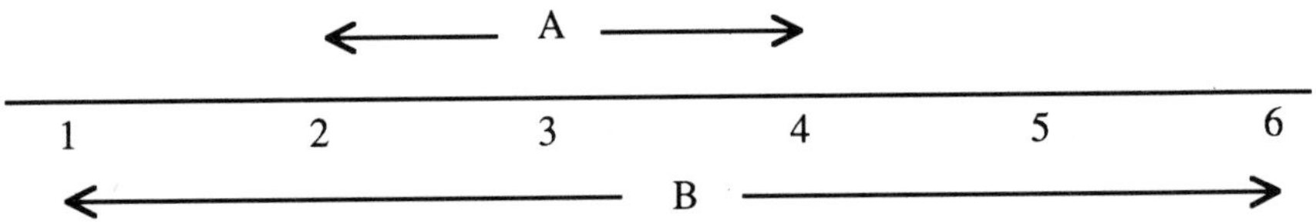

Since $A \subseteq B$ we have $d_A(B) = 0$ (Lemma 13.5). We cannot get away from B by moving around in A. On the other hand, B is not a subset of A, and correspondingly $d_B(A) = d(6,4) = 2$. Finally $d(A,B) = \max(0,2) = 2$.

(3) **The Cantor set**
For more details see Section 10.3.2 (cf. Remark 12.63).

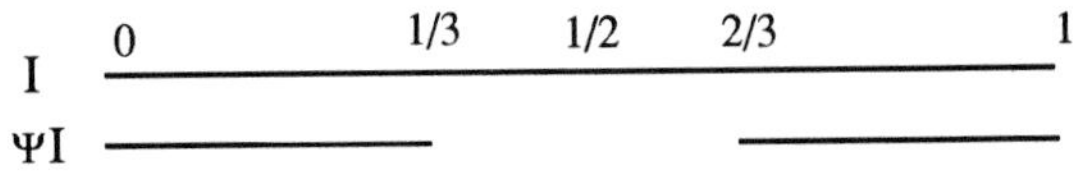

We calculate $d(I,\Psi I)$, where I is the unit interval [0,1]. With $\psi_1(x) = x/3$, $\psi_2(x) = x/3+2/3$, we have $\Psi I = \psi_1 I \cup \psi_2 I = [0,1/3] \cup [2/3,1] \subseteq I$. Thus $d_{\Psi I}(I) = 0$ (Lemma 13.5) and $d(I,\Psi I) = d_I(\Psi I) = d(1/2,1/3) = 1/6$.

(4) **The Sierpinski gasket** (cf. Figure 13.1) Let E be (the edges of) an equilateral triangle of side 1, with origin at lower left vertex.

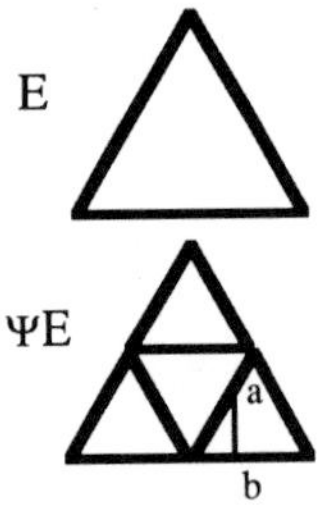

For this version we may take $\psi_1(\mathbf{x}) = \mathbf{x}/2$, $\psi_2(\mathbf{x}) = \mathbf{x}/2+(1/2,0)$ $\psi_3(x) = \mathbf{x}/2+(1/4)(1,\sqrt{3})$. Thus ΨE is a superset of E as indicated, so $d_E(\Psi E) = 0$. How far away from E can we get by moving in ΨE? To get away at all we must move to an edge of the central inner triangle. The furthest we can then get from the outer triangle E is represented by the distance $|ab|$ shown as a thin line. Thus $d(E,\Psi E) = |ab| = (1/4)$ (Height of triangle E).

EXERCISES Calculate the following Hausdorff distances.

(a) $d([1,3],[7,9])$, $d([2,5],[-1,7])$, $d([2,6],[5,7])$,

(b) $d(I,\Psi I)$ for the Koch snowflake curve,

(c) $d(\Psi I, \Psi^2 I)$ in the Cantor set construction of Example 13.7(3)
(d) $d(\Psi E, \Psi^2 E)$ in the Sierpinski construction of Example 13.7(4)

Having established that the Hausdorff distance makes $\mathcal{H}(\mathbf{R}^n)$ into a metric space, we make the first link with contractive maps. Later we will be ready to apply the famous Contraction Mapping/Fixed Point Theorem 13.14 to get what we want. The following theorem could equally well be stated for a general metric space X, but we'll concentrate on the main focus of interest, namely $\mathbf{R}^n$. Our similitudes with ratio less than 1 are included as a special case of the ψ_i.

THEOREM 13.8 Let $\psi_1, .., \psi_N$ be contractive maps with ratios r_i. Then formula (13.1),

$$\Psi E = (\psi_1 E) \cup (\psi_2 E) \cup ... \cup (\psi_N E)$$

defines a contractive map of $\mathcal{H}(\mathbf{R}^n)$ with ratio $r = max(r_1, ..., r_N)$.

Proof For simplicity we will take N = 2. To prove this theorem we express $d(\Psi E, \Psi F)$ in terms of distances between subsets such as $\psi_1 E$, $\psi_1 F$, and to this end we introduce the temporary notation $A = A_1 \cup A_2$, $B = B_1 \cup B_2$ where all six sets are in $\mathcal{H}(\mathbf{R}^n)$, that is they are nonempty compact subsets of $\mathbf{R}^n$. We claim that

$$d(A,B) \le \text{Max}(d(A_1,B_1), d(A_2,B_2)). \tag{13.8}$$

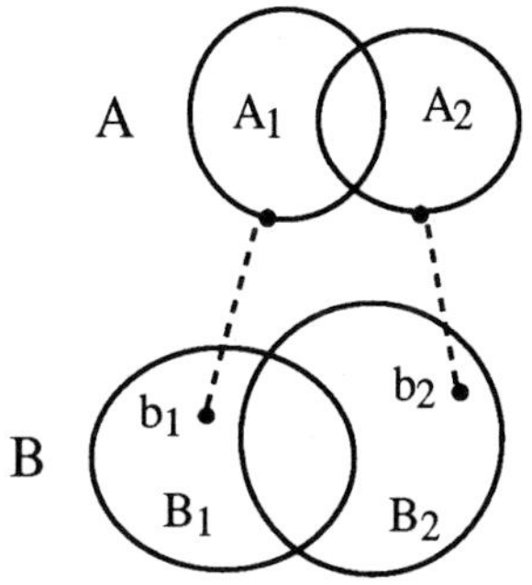

To prove this, let $b_i \in B_i$ for i = 1, 2. Then we have

$$\begin{aligned} d(b_1,A) &= \min_{a \in A} d(b_1,a), && \text{by definition} \\ &\le \min_{a \in A_1} d(b_1,a), && \text{since } A_1 \subseteq A, \\ &= d(b_1,A_1), && \text{by definition.} \end{aligned}$$

Hence $d_{B_1}(A) \le d_{B_1}(A_1)$ (*)

Now we extend this as follows

$$\begin{aligned} d_B(A) &= \max_{b \in B} d(b,A) && \text{by definition,} \\ &= \max\, d_{B_1}(A), d_{B_2}(A), && \text{as } B = B_1 \cup B_2, \\ &= \max\, d_{B_1}(A_1), d_{B_2}(A_2), && \text{by (*).} \\ d_A(B) &\le \max\, d_{A_1}(B_1), d_{A_2}(B_2), && \text{similarly.} \end{aligned}$$

Hence from the definition of d(A,B), assertion (13.8) does hold. We must now apply it to an arbitrary pair of sets E, F in $\mathcal{H}(\mathbf{R}^n)$, with $\Psi E = (\psi_1 E) \cup (\psi_2 E)$ and similarly for F. We have (we will not verify that $r = \max(r_1,r_2)$ is *least* possible):

$$\begin{aligned} d(\Psi E, \Psi F) &\le \max\, d(\psi_1 E, \psi_1 F), d(\psi_2 E, \psi_2 F), \quad \text{by (13.8),} \\ &\le \max\, r_1\, d(E,F),\ r_2\, d(E,F), \\ &\le \max(r_1, r_2)\, d(E,F). \end{aligned}$$

13.2 Euclidean space is complete

In this section we shall explain the meaning of completeness for a metric space, why we need this property, and why $\mathbf{R}^n$ has it. It should be mentioned that compactness is a stronger condition which we shall frequently call upon, but the Fixed Point (or Contraction Mapping) Theorem 13.14, which we shall prove and use, needs only completeness, which $\mathbf{R}^n$ possesses without being compact. The relation between the two properties is resolved in Theorem 13.30. Some references relevant to this section are Barnsley (1988), Falconer (1986, 1990) and Hutchinson (1981).

13.2.1 The Fixed Point Theorem, and n-space

We recall that a *fixed point* of a transformation $f: X \to X$ is a point e of X for which $f(e) = e$. We then say f *fixes* e. The theorem in question had many intriguing applications before its significance for fractals emerged, and we give some of these in the next section, en route. But now for the initial machinery.

DEFINITION 13.9 A sequence $\{x_n\}$ in a metric space X is a *Cauchy sequence* if, for any $\varepsilon > 0$, there is an integer N such that $d(x_n,x_m) < \varepsilon$ whenever $m,n \geq N$. The space X is *complete* if every Cauchy sequence converges (to a point in X).

REMARKS AND EXAMPLES 13.10

(1) **A convergent sequence is Cauchy** Let $x_n \to x$ in the space X; then informally, if points get closer to x, they get closer to each other. Formally, if $\varepsilon > 0$ we can choose N so that $d(x_n, x) < \varepsilon/2$ if $n \geq N$. Thus we have $d(x_n, x_m) \leq d(x_n, x) + d(x, x_m) < \varepsilon$ whenever $m, n \geq N$

(2) **A Cauchy sequence is bounded**, by the following instructive argument. With $\varepsilon = 1$ in the definition we have an integer N such that $d(x_n,x_m) < 1$ for all $m,n \geq N$. Hence if $B = \text{Max}(1, d(x_1,x_N), d(x_2,x_N), \ldots , d(x_{N-1},x_N))$ then $d(x_n,x_N) \leq B$ for all $n \in \mathbf{N}$.

(3) **What stops a Cauchy sequence converging?** Example: the sequence $\{1/n\}$ in the subspace (0,1) of $\mathbf{R}$. Since $x_n \to 0$, the sequence is Cauchy by (1) but, unfortunately it doesn't count as convergent because 0 is not in (0,1). This exemplifies the whole story. By a surprising theorem (Willard, 1970), *every Cauchy sequence in X that does not converge is a convergent sequence in a larger space Y.*

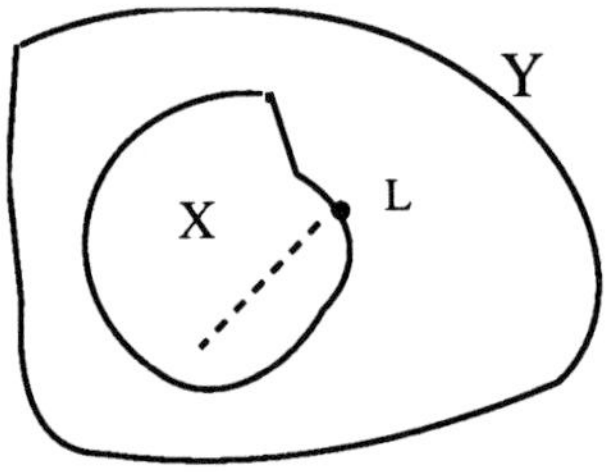

Figure 13.4

(4) **Completeness** We have just shown that the interval (0,1) is not complete by citing a non-convergent Cauchy sequence $\{1/n\}$ in that space. We see in retrospect that examples of non-complete spaces are provided by all non-closed intervals in $\mathbf{R}$. This anticipates Theorem 13.11, since happily $\mathbf{R}$ itself is complete (Theorem 13.12). A quite different kind of example, involving no intervals at all, is the subspace $\mathbf{Q}$ of rational numbers in $\mathbf{R}$. For example there is a sequence of rationals $x_n \to \pi$, but π is emphatically not rational (contrary to the impression sometimes gained from the use of approximations). cf. Example 11.17(3).

THEOREM 13.11 Let X be a complete metric space. Then a subspace is complete if and only if it is closed.

Proof Let A be a closed subspace of X. Then a Cauchy sequence $\{x_n\}$ in A is also in the complete space X, so has a limit $x \in X$. But A is closed and therefore contains all its limit points, which include x. Thus A is complete. The converse is similar, and left as the next exercise.

EXERCISE Prove that a complete subspace of a complete space is also a closed subset.

*THEOREM 13.12 The real line **R** is a complete metric space.*

Proof Let $\{x_n\}$ be Cauchy sequence in **R**. By Remark 13.10(2) the sequence is bounded, and so all x_n lie in some interval [-D,D]. Now, one half of this interval, [-D,0] or [0,D], must contain infinitely many members of the sequence. Call it $[a_1,b_1]$. In turn, one half of $[a_1,b_1]$ must contain infinitely many x_n's. Say $[a_2,b_2]$. Continuing thus, we have for n = 1,2,3,...

$$a_{n-1} \le a_n, \quad b_n \le b_{n-1}, \quad b_n - a_n = (1/2)^n\, 2D. \qquad (*)$$

Let $A = \{a_n\}$, $B = \{b_n\}$; then A is nonempty and bounded above by D, so has a least upper bound which we shall call a (see Definition 12.6). Similarly B has a greatest lower bound b. Thus $a_n \le a \le b \le b_n$, implying $b-a \le b_n-a_n$ But this is only possible if b = a, since b_n-a_n can be made arbitrarily small, by (*). As the reader may now guess, the rest of the proof consists in showing that *a* turns out to be the limit of the sequence $\{x_n\}$.

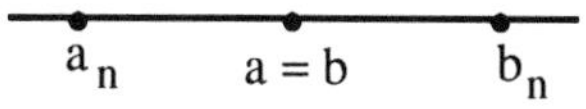

Let $\varepsilon > 0$. Then, since $\{x_n\}$ is Cauchy, there is an integer N such that

$$|x_k - x_m| \le \varepsilon/2 \quad \text{if } k,m \ge N \qquad (**)$$

And referring to N above, we show that

$$x_t \in (a - \varepsilon/2, a + \varepsilon/2) \quad \text{for some } t > N \qquad (***)$$

To establish this we at last use the infinity properties we have set up. Note first that, by (*), for large enough n we have $b_n-a_n < \varepsilon/2$. It follows that $[a_n,b_n]$ is a subset of the interval $(a - \varepsilon/2, a + \varepsilon/2)$, which therefore contains infinitely many members of $\{x_n\}$ (the diagram above makes this easier to see). Hence it contains some x_t outside the finite list $x_1,x_2, ..,x_N$ and we have proved (***). Finally, we have for any $n > N$,

$$\begin{aligned} |x_n - a| &\le |x_n - x_t| + |x_t - a|, \text{ by the triangle inequality,} \\ &\le \varepsilon/2 + \varepsilon/2. \quad \text{by (**) and (***),} \\ &= \varepsilon, \text{ which completes the proof.} \end{aligned}$$

EXAMPLE 13.13 We emphasise that every interval in **R** which is a closed set is complete (by Theorems 13.11, 13.12). Examples include both finite and infinite intervals, such as $(-\infty, 2]$, $[3,6]$ and $[5,\infty)$, but not $(4,5]$ or $(-\infty,3)$.

THEOREM 13.14 ***Banach's Fixed Point Theorem*** *(the Contraction Mapping Theorem). Let T be a contraction mapping on a complete metric space S, with ratio not exceeding r, $0 \le r < 1$. Then*

(a) T has a unique fixed point e $(T(x) = x$ for $x = e$, uniquely).

(b) For any x_0 in S, the sequence $\{T^n x_0\}$ converges to the fixed point.

(c) We have the following estimates for the distance from the fixed point after n applications of T.

$$d(x_n, e) \le \frac{r}{1-r} d(x_{n-1}, x_n) \quad (n \ge 1) \tag{13.9}$$

$$d(x_n, e) \le \frac{r^n}{1-r} d(x_0, x_1) \quad (n \ge 0) \tag{13.10}$$

Proof Let x_0 be an arbitrary point of S and write $x_n = T^n(x_0)$. Thus, starting with x_0 and applying T repeatedly we obtain successive points $x_0, x_1, x_2, .., x_n, ..$ The proof of (a), (b) consists of showing that the sequence $\{x_n\}$ is Cauchy, that its consequent limit is a fixed point of T, and that T cannot have more than one fixed point. Note that we use the argument that for $p,q \ge 1$, $d(x_p,x_q) = d(Tx_{p-1},Tx_{q-1}) \le r d(x_{p-1},x_{q-1})$, with both subscripts reducing by 1 each time the argument is applied. We have for $m > n \ge 0$,

$$\begin{aligned} d(x_n,x_m) &= d(T^n(x_0),T^m(x_0)), \\ &= d(T^n(x_0),T^n\, T^{m-n}(x_0)), \\ &\le r^n\, d(x_0,T^{m-n}(x_0)), \\ &= r^n\, d(x_0,x_{m-n}), \\ &\le r^n \{d(x_0,x_1) + d(x_1,x_2) + ... + d(x_{m-n-1},x_{m-n})\}, \text{ by} \end{aligned}$$

the triangle inequality applied repeatedly,

$$\begin{aligned} &\le r^n\, d(x_0,x_1)\, \{1 + r + r^2 + ... + r^{m-n-1}\}, \\ &\le r^n\, d(x_0,x_1)\, \{1 + r + r^2 + ... \}, \quad \text{(infinite series)} \\ &= r^n\, d(x_0,x_1) / (1-r), \text{ the sum of the geometric series} \end{aligned}$$

being $1/(1-r)$ (cf. Examples 11.15(4)).

But the last expression can be made arbitrarily small by taking m,n sufficiently large, so $\{x_n\}$ is Cauchy and, since S is complete, we have $x_n \to e$ for some e in S. We must show that *e is necessarily a fixed point.* Since T is contractive and therefore continuous, $x_n \to e$ implies $T(x_n) \to T(e)$ (Definition 11.33(b)). That is, $x_{n+1} \to T(e)$. But $x_{n+1} \to e$, so we may conclude that $e = T(e)$ as required. For *Uniqueness,* suppose that a,b are both fixed points. Then $d(a,b) = d(T(a),T(b)) \le r\, d(a,b)$, whence $(1-r)\, d(a,b) = 0$ with $1-r \ne 0$, implying $d(a,b) = 0$ and hence $a = b$.

(c) To prove (13.9) we use similar arguments to the above, with $m > n \ge 1$,

$$\begin{aligned} d(x_n,x_m) &\le d(x_n,x_{n+1}) + ... + d(x_{m-1},x_m) \\ &\le d(x_{n-1},x_n)(r + r^2 + ... + r^{m-n}) \\ &\le d(x_{n-1},x_n)\, r/(1-r). \end{aligned}$$

Now let $m \to \infty$, so that $x_m \to e$. Then since d is continuous in each variable (Theorem 11.42), $d(x_n,x_m) \to d(x_n,e)$. Since the last right hand side of the inequality remains constant, we have proved (13.9), from which the deduction of (13.10) is an appropriate exercise for the reader.

EXERCISE Deduce (13.10) from (13.9) in one line.

EXAMPLE 13.15 Show that f(x) = (x+1)/2 is a contraction map on [0,1] and find the fixed point.

Solution One should not miss the point that f is contractive because it may be re-expressed as $f(x) = x/2 + 1/2$; this simple expression shows too that f is a dilation with ratio 1/2 followed by a translation of 1/2. It shows too that f maps [0,1] onto itself. By Theorem 13.14, f has a fixed point in [0,1], this interval being complete by Example 13.13. We find the fixed point simply by $f(x) = x \Leftrightarrow x+1 = 2x \Leftrightarrow x = 1$. For more general equations of type $f(x) = 0$, their solution by the Fixed Point Theorem, and comparison with Newton's method, see Applications 13.19.

We shall deduce the completeness of $\mathbf{R}^n$ from that of $\mathbf{R}$, then give a first application to the plane. Having done so, we shall give an illustration of the power of these results not only by solving polynomial equations but by deducing existence and uniqueness of the solution of a well known type of differential equation in Section 13.2.2. We then proceed with our main application, to fractals, in Section 13.3.

THEOREM 13.16 Euclidean n-space $\mathbf{R}^n$ is complete.

Proof Let $\{\mathbf{x}_k\}$ be a Cauchy sequence in $\mathbf{R}^n$. Using superscripts to denote not powers but coordinate positions we write $\mathbf{x}_k = (x_k^1, x_k^2, \ldots, x_k^n)$. We use the completeness of $\mathbf{R}$ by noting that, for any $\mathbf{x}_k$, $\mathbf{x}_m$ and any coordinate position i,

$$d(x_k^i, x_m^i) = |x_k^i - x_m^i| \le \sqrt{\sum_{j=1}^{n} (x_k^j - x_m^j)^2} = d(\mathbf{x}_k, \mathbf{x}_m) \qquad (*)$$

Let $\varepsilon > 0$ be given. Then since $\{\mathbf{x}_k\}$ is Cauchy we have for some N,

$$d(\mathbf{x}_k, \mathbf{x}_m) < \varepsilon, \quad \text{for all } k,m \ge N.$$

Hence by (*),

$$d(x_k^i, x_m^i) < \varepsilon, \quad \text{for all } k,m \ge N.$$

Thus $\{x_k^i\}$ $(k = 1,2,\ldots)$ is a Cauchy sequence in the complete space $\mathbf{R}$ and so (Definition 13.9), has a limit a_i as $k \to \infty$. Since this holds for all $1 \le i \le n$, we have by Example 11.41(5) that $\mathbf{x}_k \to \mathbf{a}$, with coordinates $(a_1, \ldots, a_n)$. Thus we have proved that $\mathbf{R}^n$ is complete.

REMARKS 13.17 The same proof works using the 'Manhattan' or 'box' topology distance (11.5): $d(x,y) = \max d(x_i,y_i)$ $(1 \le i \le n)$ for a product space, in terms of distances in the factor spaces, here assumed complete. Indeed, the product is complete if and only if each factor is complete (Gemignani, 1967). Notice that this gives $\mathbf{R}^n$ complete for two choices of metric (distance). This is surprising because, although convergence depends only on the topology, completeness depends on the choice of metric. An illustration is close at hand. The open interval (0,1) is not complete, yet is homeomorphic to the complete space $\mathbf{R}$. This is possible because a homeomorphism is allowed to stretch a finite interval to an infinite one, as the reader is invited to explore below.

EXERCISE Construct a homeomorphism and its inverse between (0,1) and $\mathbf{R}$ (try the exponential function e^x).

EXAMPLE 13.18 We use Part (b) of the Fixed Point Theorem, 13.14, to locate the unique fixed point of a linear contractive map of the plane. A point starting anywhere must converge to this point.

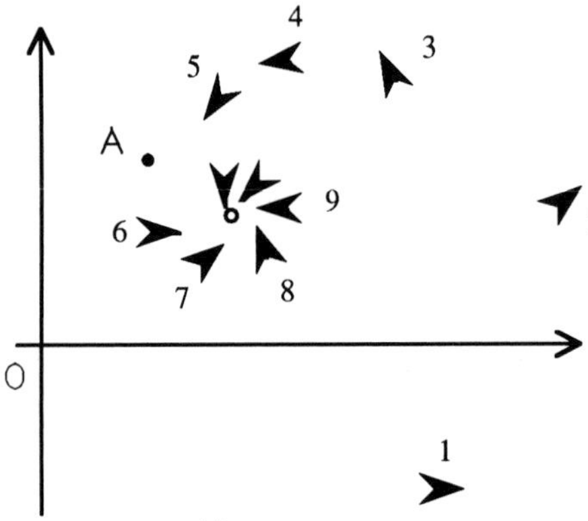

(a)

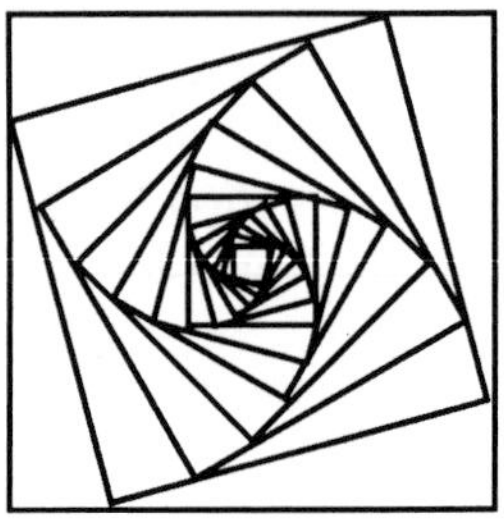

(b)

Figure 13.5 Iterations of a contractive map f carrying an object towards the fixed point. (a) f is rotation of 60° about A then vertical contraction in ratio 1/2, with a small O representing the fixed point. (b) A classical picture. f is rotation through 15° about the centre of the given starting set (the outer square) followed by dilation in ratio 4/5 with the same centre.

13.2.2 Solving equations by the Fixed Point Theorem

APPLICATIONS 13.19 One of the simplest situations to which we may apply the Fixed Point/Contractivity Theorem is the solution of an equation $f(x) = 0$, where f is a real function with a root α in some known interval [a,b]. The method is as follows.

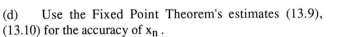

(a) Find a map g(x) so that $f(e) = 0$ if and only if e is a *fixed point* of g(x) (i.e. $g(e) = e$).

(b) Ensure that g(x) is contractive, by bounding the derivative g'(x), as exemplified below.

(c) Improve on an initial estimate x_0 for the root/fixed point in [a,b] by calculating successively $x_1, x_2, x_3, \ldots$, where $x_{n+1} = g(x_n)$.

(d) Use the Fixed Point Theorem's estimates (13.9), (13.10) for the accuracy of x_n.

EXAMPLE 13.20 We solve $f(x) = x^3 + 2x - 1 = 0$, via steps (a) to (d).

(a) In one class of methods we let

$$g(x) = x - \lambda f(x), \quad 0 < \lambda \le 1,$$
$$\text{so that } g(x) = x \Leftrightarrow f(x) = 0.$$

Here $f(0) = -1$, $f(1) = 2$, so f(x) has a root in the interval $I = [0,1]$ by the Intermediate

Value Theorem, Example 12.41(3).

(b) *(Contractivity.)* We recall the Mean Value Theorem of elementary Calculus: if $f:[a,b] \to \mathbf{R}$ is differentiable then there exists c in [a,b] such that $(f(b) - f(a))/(b - a) = f'(c)$, the prime denoting a derivative. For any distinct points x, y in I the Mean Value Theorem gives $(g(x) - g(y))/(x - y) = g'(c)$ for some c in I. Hence in absolute values $|g(x) - g(y)| = |g'(c)|\,|x - y|$. We may adjust λ as follows to keep $|g'(c)|$ small. Differentiating, we obtain $f'(x) = 3x^2 + 2$, $g'(x) = 1 - \lambda f'(x)$; therefore on I we have $2 \le f'(x) \le 5$, implying $1 - 5\lambda \le g'(x) \le 1 - 2\lambda$. An obvious choice for λ is 1/5, giving $|g(x) - g(y)| \le (3/5)\,|x - y|$. Thus g(x) is contractive, with ratio $r \le 3/5$.

(c) Starting with $x_0 = 0$, we obtain in succession, to three decimal places, 0.2, 0.318, 0.385, 0.419, 0.437.

(d) How good is this? The actual root to 3 decimal places is 0.453, so that after the five iterations we are out by 0.016. The error bound estimated by (13.10) from the values of x_0 and x_1 only is $(3/5)^5(5/2)\,(0.2) = 0.039$, which overestimates the error $d(x_5,e)$ by a factor of two (39 = 2 x 16 approx.). The bound of (13.9), estimated from the last two iterates x_4, x_5, is $(3/5)(5/2)\,(0.018) = 0.027$, and is thus superior.

EXAMPLE 13.21 We optimise the constant λ in Example 13.20. Referring to part(b) we consider the graphs of $1 - 5\lambda$ and $1 - 2\lambda$ between which $g'(x)$ lies. The lowest bound for $|g'(x)|$ occurs when $1 - 5\lambda = -(1 - 2\lambda)$, or $\lambda = 2/7$, giving $|g'(x)| \le 3/7$, which is better than the earlier 3/5. For comparison purposes we start the iteration as before with $x_0 = 0$. We obtain $x_5 = 0.452$ with an error of 0.001, which is superior to the 0.016 from our earlier naive choice of 1/5 for λ.

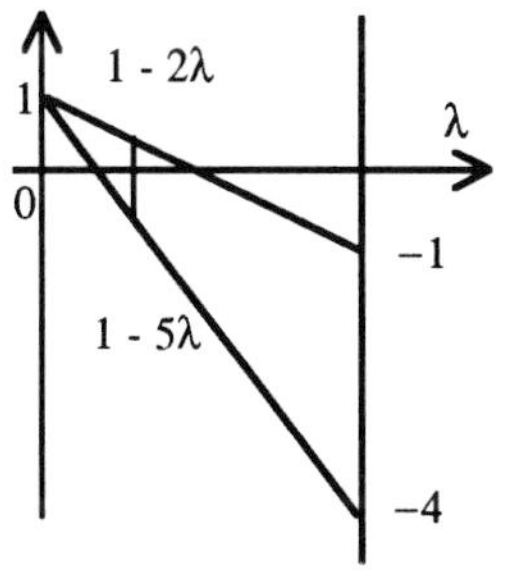

EXAMPLE 13.22 λ varying: Newton's method in Example 13.20.

Suppose we allow λ to vary with x; can we then push down $|g'(x)|$ still further? The answer is *yes*, and the best known way to do it is known as *Newton's method*. For this we take $\lambda(x) = 1/f'(x)$, as suggested by Figure 13.6, in which AP is tangent to the curve $y = f(x)$, and so $\tan\phi = |PB|/|AB|$, giving $x_{n+1} = x_n - |AB| = x_n - |PB|/\tan\phi = x_n - f(x_n)/f'(x_n)$. With the system of Newton's method,

$$x_{n+1} = x_n - f(x_n)/f'(x_n),$$

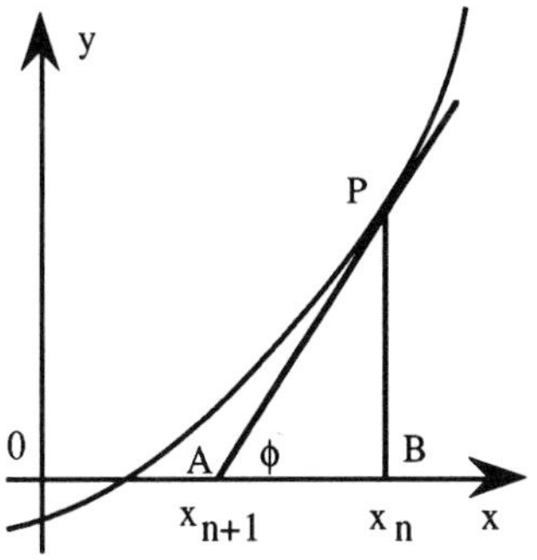

Figure 13.6 Newton's Method.

we repeat the iterations for $f(x) = x^3 + 2x - 1$ with the same starting point $x_0 = 0$. The result is that we get in succession 0.5, 0.45455, 0.45340. That is, just three iterations suffice to give the solution to five decimal places, a result far superior to the fixed λ method.

The results of Examples 13.20 to 13.22 are compared shortly in Figure 13.7 below, over five iterations. To see why Newton's method can (essentially) always be made to work, differentiate $g(x) = x - f(x)/f'(x)$ to obtain

$$g'(x) = f(x)f''(x)/(f'(x))^2.$$

So provided we start with an interval [a,b] on which $f''(x)$ exists and is continuous, with $f'(x)$ nonzero, we can guarantee that $g'(x) \to 0$ as x approaches the root since then f(x) approaches zero. Therefore we can get $g'(x)$ as small as desired by finding a sufficiently small interval around the root. Such an interval may be determined by calculating $f(y_i)$ for successive closely spaced points y_i until the sign of f(x) changes. For more on Newton's method (also known as the Newton-Raphson method), see a basic Calculus text such as Swokowski (1979). The complex case and its connection with fractals in the plane may be found in Section 16.4 of this text and Peitgen and Richter(1986), Peitgen and Saupe(1988), Barnsley(1988).

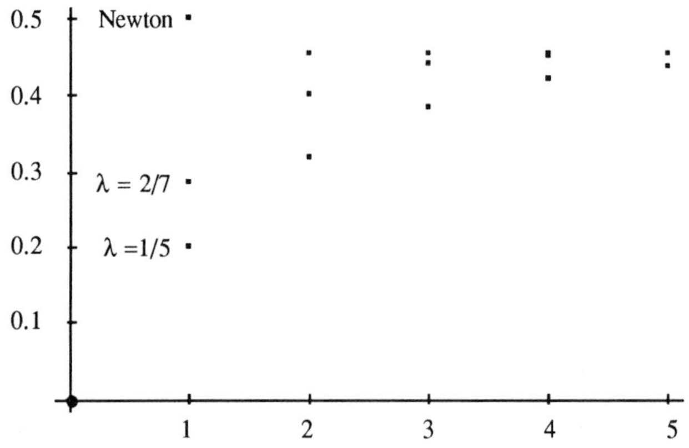

Figure 13.7 Convergence after five iterations, to a root of $x^3 + 2x - 1 = 0$. Three methods compared, all based on the Fixed Point Theorem. The fastest is Newton's method, the top line of dots, accurate to five decimal places after three iterations. The next is $\lambda = 2/7$, the bottom line is $\lambda = 1/5$. The starting value is zero in all cases.

EXERCISE Starting from $x = -2$, how many iterations are required with Newton's method to obtain a solution of $x^3 + 2x - 1 = 0$ correct to 5 decimal places?

APPLICATIONS 13.23 The Fixed Point Theorem, 13.14, has a surprise application to differential (and integral) equations. It may be used to demonstrate existence and uniqueness of solutions for many classes of such equations. It may not always give the fastest or most elegant method of solution but it does guarantee that any solution we may find by trickery, ingenuity or otherwise, is the solution. Also, not to be overlooked, if we opt for the iterative solution given in the theorem then it gives us bounds on the error (we used these bounds in Example 13.20). Consider the differential equation

$$\frac{dy}{dx} = f(x,y), \quad \text{with boundary condition} \quad y(x_0) = y_0, \tag{13.11}$$

where (x,y) lies in the rectangle D: $|x - x_0| \le a$, $|y - y_0| \le b$. Now we need a step of imagination, for we require a space whose points are functions g(x). We start with the space S consisting of all continuous functions $[x_0\text{-}a, x_0\text{+}a] \to \mathbf{R}$, with metric

$$d(g,h) \quad = \quad \max_x |g(x) - h(x)|. \tag{13.12}$$

The maximum exists because $g(x)\text{-}h(x)$ is a continuous function on a compact set, and it can be shown that S, with this metric, is a complete space (see the next exercise, and Theorem 13.33. On non-compact sets we replace max by sup). Elementary calculus shows that the differential equation (13.11) with which we started is equivalent to

$$y(x) \quad = \quad y_0 \;+\; \int_{x_0}^{x} f(t,y(t))\, dt \tag{13.13}$$

and guided by this we define a map $T: S \to S$ by letting $T(y(x))$ be the right hand side of (13.13). Then trivially $y(x)$ is a solution if and only if it is fixed by T, that is, $y(x) = T(y(x))$. But to apply the Fixed Point Theorem we need contractivity. Now, a standard requirement for such a differential equation is that it satisfies a so-called *Lipschitz condition*

$$|f(x,y_1) - f(x,y_2)| \quad \leq \quad M|y_1 - y_2| \tag{13.14}$$

over the rectangle D. And whatever the finite size of the constant M, we can convert (13.14) into a contractivity condition for the map T, as follows. Since D is compact, there is a constant c for which

$$|f(x,y)| \quad \leq \quad c \qquad \text{for all } (x,y) \text{ in D.} \tag{13.15}$$

Let r be any number in the range $0 < r < \min(1/M, a, b/c)$. Then the discussion above applies with x in the smaller interval given by $|x\text{-}x_0| \leq r < a$. Now with the constant function $y_0(x) = y_0$ for all x, the ball $B = \{y(x) \in S\colon\ d(y(x), y_0(x)) \leq cr\}$ is a closed subspace of the complete space S (Example 11.11), hence is itself complete (Theorem 13.11). Furthermore T sends B to itself, since we have for each x,

$$|T(y(x)) - y_0(x)| \quad \leq \quad \int_{x_0}^{x} |f(t, y(t))|\,dt \quad \leq \quad c|x - x_0| \quad \leq \quad cr,$$

in which the first inequality arises from the observation that

$$\left|\int_{x_0}^{x} g(t)\, dt\right| \quad \leq \quad \int_{x_0}^{x} |g(t)|\; dt,$$

the second is from (13.15), and the whole implies that $d(Ty(x), y_0(x)) \leq cr$ as required. Finally, T is contractive as a transformation of B, for

$$\begin{aligned}
|Ty_1(x) - Ty_2(x)| &\leq \int_{x_0}^{x} |f(t,y_1(t)) \;-\; f(t,y_2(t))|\,dt \\
&\leq \int_{x_0}^{x} M|y_1(t) \;-\; y_2(t)|\,dt, \quad \text{by (13.13)} \\
&\leq M|x - x_0| \max_t |y_1(t) - y_2(t)| \\
&\leq M\,r\, d(y_1(x), y_2(x))
\end{aligned}$$

and $Mr < 1$ by definition of r. Thus by the Fixed Point Theorem our differential equation (13.11) has a unique solution, possibly requiring the points (x,y) to lie in a smaller rectangle than the original D. This result is known as *Picard's Theorem*. Further details and a particular case may be found in Giles (1987).

EXERCISE Prove that formula (13.12) yields the Triangle inequality: $d(f,h) \leq d(f,g) + d(g,h)$.

FURTHER READING Bryant (1990) contains many applications of the Fixed Point Theorem.

13.3 Proof of the main result

We have shown that the Hausdorff distance d(A,B) makes the 'space of fractals' $\mathcal{H}(\mathbf{R}^n)$ into a metric space, and that $\Psi E = (\psi_1 E) \cup (\psi_2 E) \cup \ldots \cup (\psi_N E)$ gives a contractive map on it. Further, we have shown that a contractive map T on a complete space S has a unique fixed point e, with $T^n x_0 \to e$ for any point x_0 in S. What remains is the highly nontrivial task of proving that $\mathcal{H}(\mathbf{R}^n)$ is complete, and hence that $\Psi^n E_0$ has a unique limit for any starting set E_0, namely the fixed point of Ψ.

DEFINITION 13.24 Let $\{A_n\}$ be a sequence in $\mathcal{H}(X)$. That is, A_n is a nonempty compact subset of the metric space X. Then $\{x_n \in A_n\}$ denotes a sequence $\{x_n\}$ in X such that $x_n \in A_n$. For $A \in \mathcal{H}(X)$ and $\delta \geq 0$ we define a superset $A + \delta$ of A (written A_δ in some texts) by

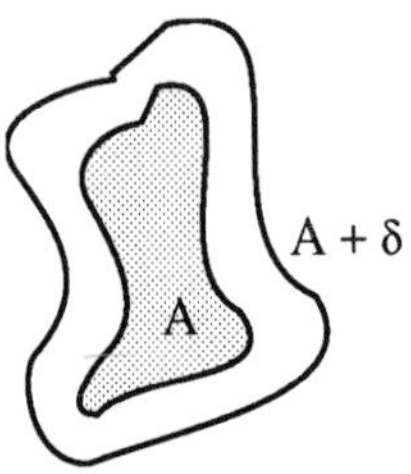

$$A + \delta = \{x \in X: d(x,A) \leq \delta\}$$
$$= \{x \in X: d(x,a) \leq \delta \text{ for some } a \in A\},$$

where the equality holds because $d(x,A) = d(x,a_0)$ for some a_0 in A (Lemma 13.2).

LEMMA 13.25 For $A,B \in \mathcal{H}(X)$ and any $\varepsilon > 0$, we have

(i) $d_A(B) \leq \varepsilon \quad \Leftrightarrow \quad A \subseteq B + \varepsilon$,

(ii) $d(A,B) \leq \varepsilon \quad \Leftrightarrow \quad A \subseteq B + \varepsilon$, and $B \subseteq A + \varepsilon$.

Proof (i) Suppose that $d_A(B) \leq \varepsilon$. Let $a \in A$. Then we have the inequalities $d(a,B) \leq \max_x d(x,B)\ (x \in A) = d_A(B) \leq \varepsilon$. Hence $a \in B + \varepsilon$ by Definition 13.24. So $A \subseteq B + \varepsilon$. Now (ii) follows from (i) and the definition of d(A,B).

LEMMA 13.26 (Sequence Extension.) Suppose $\{A_n\}$ is a Cauchy sequence in $\mathcal{H}(X)$ and $0 < n_1 < n_2 < \ldots$ are integers. Then any Cauchy sequence $\{x_{n_i} \in A_{n_i}\}$ of points in X extends to a Cauchy sequence $\{x_n \in A_n\}$. This converges to a point a if and only if the subsequence does so.

Proof For each n, $1 \leq n \leq n_1$ we have by Lemma 13.2 the point to set distance $d(x_{n_1}, A_n) = d(x_{n_1}, x_n)$ for some $x_n \in A_n$. When $n = n_1$ we have $x_n = x_{n_1}$ uniquely because $d(x_{n_1}, y) = d(x_{n_1}, A_{n_1}) = 0$ implies $y = x_{n_1}$. Similarly for integers m in the range $n_1 < m \leq n_2$, with $d(x_{n_2}, A_m) = d(x_{n_2},x_m)$, and so on. Thus we have extended the sequence, and now must prove the result is Cauchy. Let $\varepsilon > 0$; then since both $\{x_{n_i}\}$ and $\{A_n\}$ are Cauchy, we have for some integers M, N,

$$d(A_r,A_s) \le \varepsilon/3, \quad \text{if } r,s \ge N, \tag{*}$$

$$d(x_{n_r},x_{n_s}) \le \varepsilon/3, \quad \text{if } r,s \ge M. \tag{**}$$

Let $m,n \ge N$. Then m,n must both fit into the infinite sequence $0 < n_1 < n_2 < \ldots$, say $n_{j-1} < m \le n_j$, $n_{k-1} < n \le n_k$, and we can and do choose m,n so large that in addition $j,k \ge M$. Then, by definition of x_m and of $d(A,B)$, $d(x_{n_j},x_m) = d(x_{n_j},A_m) \le d(A_{n_j},A_m) \le \varepsilon/3$, by (*). This plus a similar argument gives a bound $\varepsilon/3$ for the first and third terms on the right of:

$$d(x_m,x_n) \le d(x_m,x_{n_j}) + d(x_{n_j},x_{n_k}) + d(x_{n_k},x_n),$$

whilst the second term is bounded by $\varepsilon/3$, because $j,k \ge M$. and so (**) applies. Thus $d(x_m,x_n) \le \varepsilon$ and the proof is complete, the last sentence of its statement being left as the exercise below.

EXERCISE Let $\{x_n\}$ be a Cauchy sequence in a metric space S, with $\{x_{n_i}\}$ as a subsequence. Let x be in S. Prove that $x_n \to x$ if and only if $x_{n_i} \to x$.

We have arrived at the toughest proof of this Chapter. It uses many of the ideas and results on topology we have built up so far, especially those relating to compactness. It naturally makes critical use of Cauchy sequences. We follow the general approach of Barnsley(1988).

THEOREM 13.27 The space of fractals $S = \mathcal{H}(\mathbf{R}^n)$ *is complete. The limit of a Cauchy sequence* $\{A_n\}$ *in S is*

$$A = \{x: x \text{ is the limit of a Cauchy sequence } \{x_n \in A_n\}\}. \tag{13.16}$$

Proof The proof consists in showing that, with A_n and A as given we have $A_n \to A$ which, by definition, means $d(A_n,A) \to 0$ in the Hausdorff metric. But $d(A_n,A)$ itself is only defined when not only A_n but also A is a nonempty compact subset of $\mathbf{R}^n$. In this case compact is equivalent by Theorem 12.26 to bounded and closed. Thus the proof is in four parts. (a) A is nonempty, (b) A is closed, (c) A is bounded, and finally (d) $A_n \to A$. For ease of reference, the eleven displayed statements in the proof are labelled simply (1) to (11).

(a) *A is nonempty.* We have to construct just one Cauchy sequence $\{x_n \in A_n\}$. It will have a limit because it is in $\mathbf{R}^n$, and $\mathbf{R}^n$ is complete (Theorem 13.16). Now, since the sequence of sets $\{A_n\}$ is given to be Cauchy, there is an integer m_1 such that $d(A_r, A_s) < 1/2$ if $r,s \ge m_1$. By the same token, there is an integer $m_2 > m_1$ such that $d(A_r, A_s) < 1/2^2$ if $r,s \ge m_2$. The process continues, giving integers $0 < m_1 < m_2 < \ldots$ such that

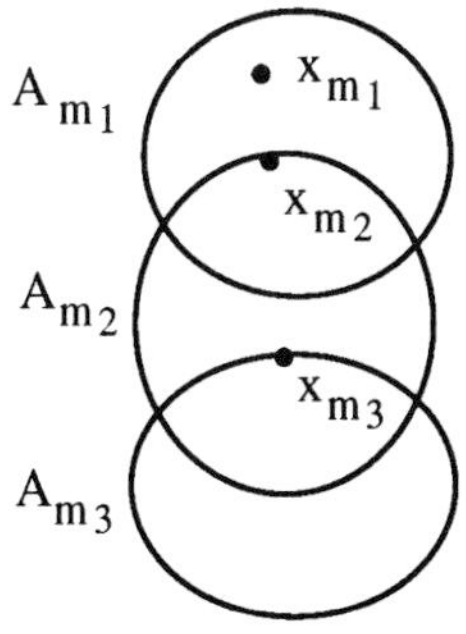

$$d(A_m,A_n) < \frac{1}{2^i}, \quad \text{if } m, n > m_i. \tag{1}$$

Let x_{m_1} be a point of A_{m_1}. Since by (1), $d(A_{m_1}, A_{m_2}) < 1/2$, there is $x_{m_2} \in A_{m_2}$ with $d(x_{m_1}, x_{m_2}) \leq 1/2$. Since $d(A_{m_2}, A_{m_3}) < 1/4$, there is $x_{m_3} \in A_{m_3}$ with $d(x_{m_2}, x_{m_3}) \leq 1/4$. Continuing in this way we obtain a sequence

$$\{x_{m_i} \in A_{m_i}\}, \quad \text{with } d(x_{m_i}, x_{m_{i+1}}) \leq \frac{1}{2i}. \tag{2}$$

It suffices to show this is Cauchy, since the Sequence Extension Lemma, 13.26, then exhibits it as part of a Cauchy sequence $\{x_n \in A_n\}$. So let $\varepsilon > 0$. We claim that for some integer N_ε,

$$\sum_{i = N_\varepsilon}^{\infty} \frac{1}{2^i} < \varepsilon. \tag{3}$$

The reason is simple, but not necessarily obvious. Let $S_n = 1 + r + r^2 + ... + r^{n-1}$ with $0 < r < 1$. Then $S_n = (1 - r^n)/(1 - r)$ by Table 11.2, with limit $\sigma = 1/(1-r)$ as $n \to \infty$. Hence $\sigma - S_n = r^n/(1 - r)$ can be made arbitrarily small, say less than ε, by taking n sufficiently large, say $n \geq N_\varepsilon$. Setting $r = 1/2$, we obtain statement (3). Thus whenever $k, j \geq N_\varepsilon$ we have

$$\begin{aligned} d(x_{m_k}, x_{m_j}) &\leq d(x_{m_k}, x_{m_{k+1}}) + d(x_{m_{k+1}}, x_{m_{k+2}}) + ... + d(x_{m_{j-1}}, x_{m_j}) \\ &\qquad \text{by the triangle inequality,} \\ &< \sum_{i = N_\varepsilon}^{\infty} \frac{1}{2^i}, \qquad \text{by (2),} \\ &< \varepsilon, \qquad \text{by (3).} \end{aligned}$$

Hence $\{x_{m_i} \in A_{m_i}\}$ is Cauchy. Finally, it extends (Lemma 13.26) to the required sequence $\{x_n \in A_n\}$.

(b) *A is closed.* We prove this by showing that A contains all its limit points (Test 11.19). That is, for an arbitrary sequence $\{a_n\}$ in A with limit a, we have $a \in A$. From the definition of A each a_n is the limit of a Cauchy sequence $\{x_{n_i} \in A_i\}$ $(i = 1, 2, 3, ...)$, as depicted below.

$$\begin{array}{ccccccc} A_1 & A_2 & A_3 & \cdots\cdots & & A \\ x_{11} & x_{12} & x_{13} & \cdots\cdots & \to & a_1 \\ x_{21} & x_{22} & x_{23} & \cdots\cdots & \to & a_2 \\ x_{31} & x_{32} & x_{33} & \cdots\cdots & \to & a_3 \\ & & & & & \downarrow \\ \cdots & \cdots & \cdots & & & \\ & & & & & a \end{array}$$

Now, since $a_n \to a$, there are integers $0 < n_1 < n_2 < ...$ such that

$$d(a, a_{n_i}) \leq 1/i. \tag{4}$$

And since $x_{n_i} \to a_n$, there is for each n_i, an integer m_i such that

$$d(a_{n_i}, x_{n_i, m_i}) \leq 1/i. \tag{5}$$

And on applying the triangle inequality to (4) and (5),

$$d(a, x_{n_i,m_i}) \le 2/i. \qquad (6)$$

Now we must be careful. There can be many n_i's paired with the same integer m_i, as the graph below indicates.

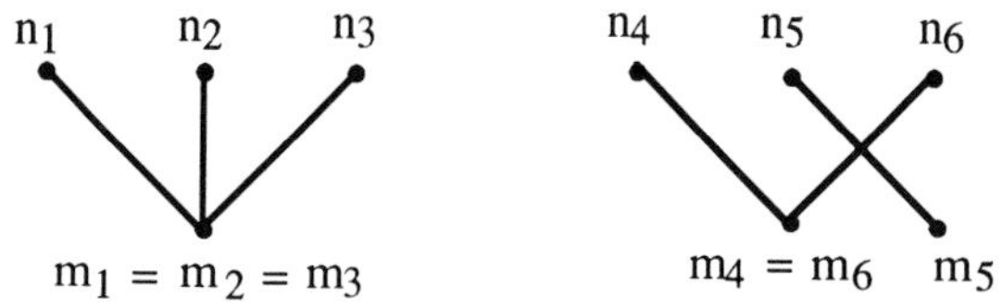

We write $y_{m_i} = x_{n_s,m_i}$ with n_s as small as possible (the graph makes clear that we may suppose $s \ge i$). If there are only finitely many m_i's altogether, say $m_1, \dots, m_k$ then $d(y_{m_k},a) \le 2/s$ for infinitely many values of s, so $d(y_{m_k},a) = 0$. In any case $y_{m_i} \in A_{m_i}$ and $y_{m_i} \to a$ (by (6)). Finally Lemma 13.26 extends this to a Cauchy sequence $\{y_n \in A_n\}$, with the same limit a, and since A consists of the limits of all convergent Cauchy sequences $\{x_n \in A_n\}$ we have $a \in A$ as required.

(c) *A is bounded.* We first show that for any $\varepsilon > 0$, there is N such that

$$A \subseteq A_n + \varepsilon, \quad \text{for all } n \ge N. \qquad (7)$$

Since $\{A_n\}$ is Cauchy we may choose N such that

$$d(A_m,A_n) \le \varepsilon, \quad \text{for all } m, n \ge N. \qquad (8)$$

Fix $n \ge N$ and let $a \in A$. We prove that $a \in A_n + \varepsilon$. By definition of A, there is a Cauchy sequence $\{a_n \in A_n\}$ with limit a. Thus we can argue from (8) and Lemma 13.25 that for any $m \ge N$, $a_m \in A_m \subseteq A_n + \varepsilon$. But A_n is a compact subset of $\mathbf{R}^n$, by definition, so is bounded and closed (Theorem 12.26). Therefore so is $A_n + \varepsilon$ (an exercise). So the fact that $a_m \to a$ implies $a \in A_n + \varepsilon$. This establishes (7). But since $A_n + \varepsilon$ is bounded, so is its subset A (see Definition 12.1).

(d) $A_n \to A$. We have shown that A is nonempty and compact, hence a member of $S = \mathcal{H}(\mathbf{R}^n)$ and a candidate for the limit of $\{A_n\}$. Let $\varepsilon > 0$. Then $d(A,A_n) \le \varepsilon$ if and only if both $A \subseteq A_n + \varepsilon$ and $A_n \subseteq A + \varepsilon$ (Lemma 13.25). The first inclusion, for sufficiently large n, is implied by (7). We must establish the second, $A_n \subseteq A + \varepsilon$. Now, since $\{A_n\}$ is Cauchy there is an integer N such that for $m, n \ge N$ we have $d(A_m,A_n) \le \varepsilon/2$, and so

$$A_m \subseteq A_n + \varepsilon/2 \quad (m, n \ge N). \qquad (9)$$

Fix $n \ge N$ and let $y \in A_n$. Then the proof is completed by deducing that $y \in A + \varepsilon$. Again since $\{A_n\}$ is Cauchy, there are integers n_i satisfying $n < n_1 < n_2 < \dots$ such that for each $s = 1,2,3, \dots$

$$A_m \subseteq A_k + \varepsilon/2^{s+1} \quad \text{if } m, k \ge n_s. \qquad (10)$$

By (9), since $n, n_1 \ge N$ we have $A_{n_1} \subseteq A_n + \varepsilon/2$. So by definition of "$A + \varepsilon$" and the fact that $y \in A_n$, there is $x_{n_1} \in A_{n_1}$ with $d(y,x_{n_1}) \le \varepsilon/2$. Now apply (10) repeatedly. With values $s = 1$, $m = n_1$, $k = n_2$ we have that, since $x_{n_1} \in A_{n_1}$,

$$\begin{aligned} &\text{there is } x_{n_2} \in A_{n_2} \text{ with } d(x_{n_1},x_{n_2}) \leq \varepsilon/2^2. \\ \text{Similarly} \quad &\text{there is } x_{n_3} \in A_{n_3} \text{ with } d(x_{n_2},x_{n_3}) \leq \varepsilon/2^3. \\ &\ldots\ldots\ldots\ldots\ldots\ldots\ldots\ldots\ldots\ldots \\ &\text{there is } x_{n_s} \in A_{n_s} \text{ with } d(x_{n_{s-1}},x_{n_s}) \leq \varepsilon/2^s. \end{aligned}$$

By the triangle inequality $d(y,x_{n_s})$ is less than or equal to the sum of these distances including $\varepsilon/2$, so

$$d(y,x_{n_s}) \leq \varepsilon(1/2 + 1/2^2 + \ldots + 1/2^s) < \varepsilon. \tag{11}$$

The block of inequalities leading to (11) also yields $d(x_{n_i},x_{n_j}) \leq \varepsilon / 2^i$ for $n_j \geq n_i$, showing that $\{x_{n_i}\}$ is Cauchy and therefore converges to some limit $x \in A$. But by (11), y is within ε of x_{n_s} for all s = 1, 2, 3, .. It follows that $d(y,x) \leq \varepsilon$, and hence $y \in A + \varepsilon$. Since y is an arbitrary element of A_n, we may conclude that $A_n \subseteq A + \varepsilon$, and the proof of Theorem 13.27 is complete.

EXERCISE Show that if A is a compact subset of $\mathbf{R}^n$ and $\varepsilon > 0$, then so is $A+\varepsilon$.

Now we draw together the threads to get the payoff for all our hard work.

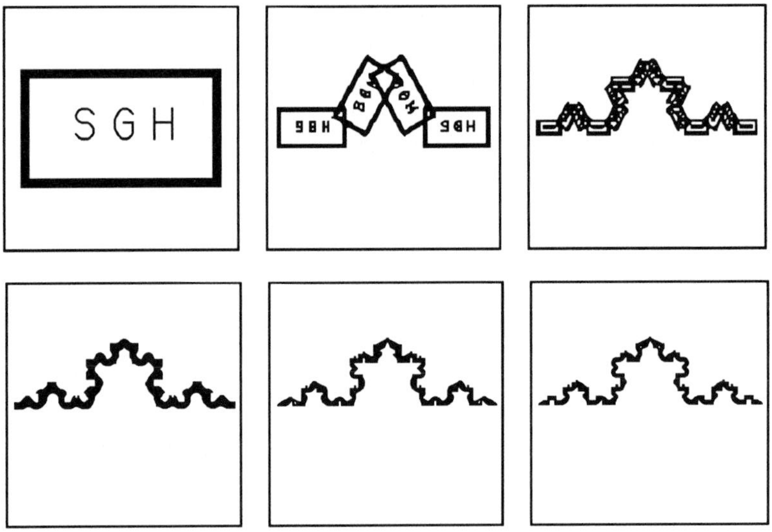

Figure 13.8(a) The Koch curve from an unusual starting set.

THEOREM 13.28 ***'Fractal limits exist and are unique'.***
Let E_0 be a nonempty bounded and closed subset of $\mathbf{R}^n$. Let $\psi_1, \ldots, \psi_N$ be contractive transformations of $\mathbf{R}^n$ with respective ratios r_i. Define as usual Ψ: $\mathcal{H}(\mathbf{R}^n) \to \mathcal{H}(\mathbf{R}^n)$ by $\Psi(E) = \psi_1 E \cup \ldots \cup \psi_N E$. Then Ψ is contractive, with ratio $r = \min(r_1, \ldots, r_N)$ and $\{\Psi^k(E_0)\}$ has a limit $\mathcal{A}$ in $\mathcal{H}(\mathbf{R}^n)$ as $k \to \infty$ (in the Hausdorff metric) which is independent of the choice of E_0. Further, $\mathcal{A}$ is the unique element in $\mathcal{H}(\mathbf{R}^n)$ with $\Psi(\mathcal{A}) = \mathcal{A}$.

Proof We have (at last) a contractive map $T = \Psi$ (Theorem 13.8) on a complete space S =

$\mathcal{H}(\mathbf{R}^n)$ (Theorem 13.27), and so may apply the Fixed Point Theorem to deduce that $\{\Psi^k(E_0)\}$ has a limit $\mathcal{A}$ in $\mathcal{H}(\mathbf{R}^n)$ which does not depend on the starting set E_0. Furthermore $\mathcal{A}$ is characterised uniquely by being a fixed point, $\Psi(\mathcal{A}) = \mathcal{A}$.

EXAMPLE 13.29 Here we use the same starting set E for the Koch curve and Sierpinski gasket, and it has no connection with either. The particular features of each are embodied in its corresponding transformation Ψ as predicted by Theorem 13.28, and in Figure 13.8 (a),(b) we show iterations of that transformation producing a sequence of sets which get closer and closer to the desired limit set $\mathcal{A}$.

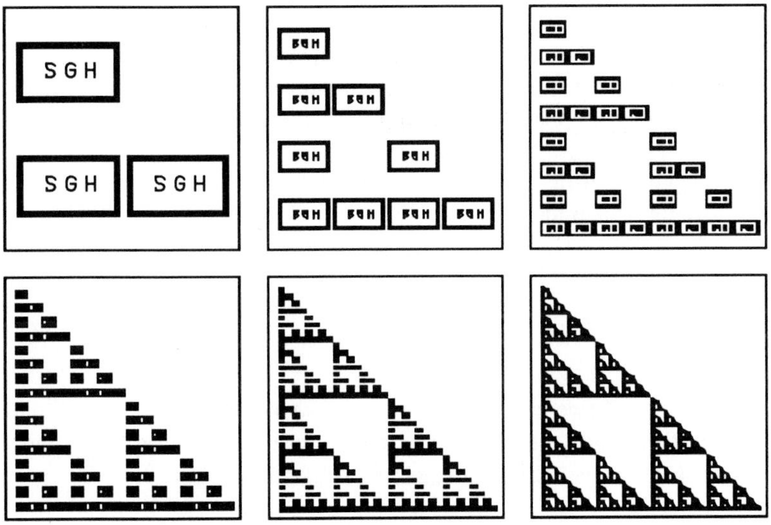

Figure 13.8(b) The Sierpinski gasket from the same starting set as (a). See Figure 14.1 for further illustrations.

13.4 Some loose ends tied

13.4.1 Compactness, completeness and uniform processes

We first clear up the relationship between completeness, important in our application of Hausdorff distance to the convergence of a sequence of sets, and the stronger property of compactness upon which much also depends.

THEOREM 13.30 A metric space X is compact if and only if it is both complete and totally bounded.

Proof Let X be compact. Then X is sequentially compact (every sequence has a convergent subsequence) by Theorem 12.23, hence totally bounded by Theorem 12.22. For the completeness of X we must show that an arbitrary Cauchy sequence $\{x_n\}$ converges. Now, X being sequentially compact, there is a convergent subsequence, say $x_{n_i} \to x$; but the Cauchy property ensures that $x_n \to x$ also (an exercise).

Conversely, suppose X is complete and totally bounded. To show that X is sequentially compact and hence compact we prove that any sequence $\{x_n\}$ in X has a convergent subsequence. But since X is complete a Cauchy sequence suffices. By total boundedness X is covered by a finite set of open balls of radius 1/2, so one (at least) of them contains infinitely many points of $\{x_n\}$, forming a subsequence

$$S_2 = \{x_{21}, x_{22}, x_{23}, \dots\},$$

where subscript 2 relates to the radius 1/2. Invoking total boundedness again gives a ball of radius 1/3 containing a subsequence of S_2, say

$$S_3 = \{x_{31}, x_{32}, x_{33}, \dots\}.$$

We continue this process and abstract a 'diagonal 'subsequence $\{y_n = x_{n,n}\}$, which we claim is Cauchy. For if $\varepsilon > 0$ we may choose an integer N so that $2/N < \varepsilon$ and then all y_n with $n \geq N$ lie in the same open ball of radius 1/N so are within distance ε of each other.

Uniform convergence and continuity We now set up the proof of Theorem 13.33, required in proving that under reasonable assumptions a Julia set is actually a curve (Theorem 16.54). Let $T = \{f: X \to \mathbf{R}\}$, the set of *all* real functions on the compact metric space X. Within T lies the set S of *continuous* functions. It is quite easy to show that

$$d(f,g) = \max_{x \in X} |f(x) - g(x)| \tag{13.17}$$

gives a metric on S and T (we have already assumed so in applying the Fixed Point Theorem to the solution of differential equations). The maximum exists because X is compact and d is continuous. Let us verify the triangle inequality for functions f,g,h.

$$\begin{aligned} |f(x) - h(x)| &\leq |f(x) - g(x)| + |g(x) - h(x)|, \quad \text{(triangle ineqality in } \mathbf{R}), \\ \text{hence} \quad d(f,h) &\leq \max\{|f(x) - g(x)| + |g(x) - h(x)|\}, \\ &\leq \max |f(x) - g(x)| + \max |g(x) - h(x)|, \\ &= d(f,g) + d(g,h). \end{aligned}$$

EXAMPLE 13.31 Let f, g: $[0,1] \to \mathbf{R}$ where $f(x) = x$, $g(x) = x^2 + 6x + 13$. We calculate that $d(f,g) = \max |x^2 + 6x + 13| = \max |(x+3)^2 + 4| = 20$.

Now let us unpack a little the meaning of $f_n \to f$ in the space T. For any $\varepsilon > 0$ there is an integer N such that $n \geq N \Rightarrow d(f_n,f) < \varepsilon \Rightarrow \max |f_n(x) - f(x)| < \varepsilon$. Therefore :

$$\text{for any } \varepsilon > 0 \text{ there is an integer N such that if } n \geq N \text{ then}$$
$$|f_n(x) - f(x)| < \varepsilon \text{ for all x in X.} \tag{13.18}$$

Property (13.18) is called *uniform convergence* of the sequence $\{f_n\}$. It is used also in Section 16.2.2 on Julia sets. The idea is that one integer N gives the inequality simultaneously, or 'uniformly' for all points x in X. Notice the implication that $f_n(x) \to f(x)$ for each x. The next 'uniformity' is over all *pairs* x,y in X.

LEMMA 13.32 A continuous function $f: X \to \mathbf{R}$ (X compact) is uniformly continuous, that is

$$\textit{for any } \varepsilon > 0 \textit{ there is a number } \delta > 0 \textit{ such that}$$
$$d(x,y) < \delta \Rightarrow |f(x) - f(y)| < \varepsilon \text{ (for all x,y in X).} \tag{13.19}$$

Proof Let $\varepsilon > 0$ and consider the open intervals $I_z = (f(z) - \varepsilon/2, f(z) + \varepsilon/2)$ for all z in X. Since z is in $f^{-1}(I_z)$ the set of all such inverse images is an open covering of the compact set X, and so has (Theorem 12.19) a Lebesgue number δ. But for any x,y in X with $d(x,y) < \delta$ the 2-element set $\{x,y\}$ has diameter less than δ and so lies (by definition of δ) in some inverse image $f^{-1}(I_z)$. Hence f(x), f(y) lie in I_z and $|f(x) - f(y)| < \varepsilon$.

Although we have not chosen to state it more generally, Lemma 13.32 is true with **R** replaced by any metric space Y, the proof being essentially the same. A similar comment holds for the following result we have been aiming for.

THEOREM 13.33 Let X be a compact metric space.
(a) If the functions $\{f_n: X \to \mathbf{R}\}$ are continuous and $f_n \to f$ then f is continuous,
(b) The space S of continuous functions $g: X \to \mathbf{R}$ is complete.

Proof Let $f_n \to f$. If f is to be continuous it will be uniformly continuous, and it is convenient simply to prove this, in the form (13.19). So let $\varepsilon > 0$ be given. Since $f_n \to f$ uniformly, (13.18), and each f_n is uniformly continuous there is an integer N and real number $\delta > 0$ for which the following two assertions are true.

$$|f_N(z) - f(z)| < \varepsilon/3 \quad \text{(for all z in X)}, \tag{*}$$
$$d(x,y) < \delta \quad \Rightarrow \quad |f_N(x) - f_N(y)| < \varepsilon/3 \quad \text{(for all x,y in X)}. \tag{**}$$

Let $x,y \in X$ satisfy $d(x,y) < \delta$. Then by the triangle inequality in **R**,

$$\begin{aligned} |f(x) - f(y)| &\le |f(x) - f_N(x)| + |f_N(x) - f_N(y)| + |f_N(y) - f(y)|, \\ &< \varepsilon/3 + \varepsilon/3 + \varepsilon/3, \end{aligned}$$

by (*) and (**). Thus f is uniformly continuous, hence continuous. This proves part (a), of which Part (b) is simply a formalised statement.

REMARK 13.34 As a special case of Theorem 13.33 the space of continuous real functions on a closed interval [a,b] is complete, a result anticipated in Applications 13.23 of the Fixed Point Theorem to differential equations. A similar proof enables us to replace **R** by any metric space Y, covering the case $[0,1] \to \mathbf{R}^2$, and leading to a proof of continuity for curves such as the Dragon, Sierpinski, and the plane-filling curves, all of which are uniformly attained limits of a sequence of curves (see e.g. Edgar, 1990). A third kind of uniformity, *uniform boundedness* appears briefly but importantly in connection with the Random Iteration Algorithm in Chapter 15 (see Remark 15.15).

Approximation by step functions A *step function* (or *simple function)* is one whose image is a finite set. The word 'step' comes from its general appearance in the common case $f: [\alpha,\beta] \to \mathbf{R}$, exemplified in Figure 13.9. For more details and an example see the application, again to the Random Iteration Algorithm, in Section 15.3.2.

THEOREM 13.35 Any continuous real function on a compact metric space X can be approximated with arbitrary precision by step functions. That is, if $f: X \to \mathbf{R}$ is continuous and X compact then there is a sequence of step functions $\{f_n\}$ with $f_n \to f$.

Proof Let $\varepsilon > 0$ be given. Since X is compact, f attains a minimum a and maximum b and lies within the closed interval [a,b]. We divide [a,b] into n subintervals of equal width $D = (b - a)/n$, where n is chosen so large that $D < \varepsilon$. We avoid duplicating endpoints of these intervals, to be denoted I_i, by defining

$$I_1 = [a, a + D], \text{ and } I_i = (a + (i-1)D, a + iD] \text{ for } 2 \le i \le n.$$

Since the I_i are thus disjoint, but include all of [a,b], the inverse images $X_i = f^{-1}(I_i)$ are disjoint and cover X, so we may choose $x_i \in X_i$ $(1 \le i \le n)$ and without contradiction define $f_n: X \to \mathbf{R}$ by $f_n(x) = f(x_i)$ if $x \in X_i$. Then for each x in X we have

$$d(f_n,f) = \max |f_n(x) - f(x)| \le D < \varepsilon.$$

This gives the sequence $\{f_n\}$ of step functions, with $f_n \to f$ as required.

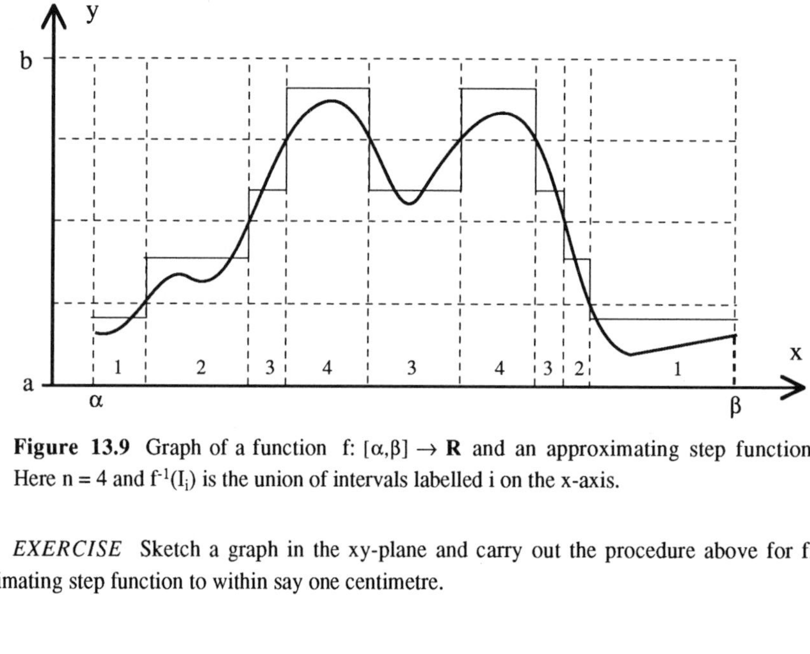

Figure 13.9 Graph of a function $f: [\alpha,\beta] \to \mathbf{R}$ and an approximating step function. Here n = 4 and $f^{-1}(I_i)$ is the union of intervals labelled i on the x-axis.

EXERCISE Sketch a graph in the xy-plane and carry out the procedure above for finding an approximating step function to within say one centimetre.

13.4.2 The Fundamental Theorem of Algebra by winding numbers

We have repeatedly called upon a result known as the Fundamental Theorem of Algebra. Now we are ready to prove it (repeated below for convenience),

every non-constant polynomial p(z) with real or complex coefficients has a root α, $p(\alpha) = 0$. (13.20)

Winding numbers Let $\gamma: [0,1] \to \mathbf{C}$ be a closed curve (loop) which does not pass through the point A. As t increases from 0 to 1 the radius vector AP from A to $\gamma(t)$ rotates until P is back at its original position $\gamma(0)$. See for example Figure 13.10(a). On the journey P may even visit $\gamma(0)$ several times, AP may swing back and forth, but when t = 1 is reached the net rotation (anticlockwise counting positive) is a whole number n of turns; we call n the *winding number* $w(\gamma,A)$ of γ about A.

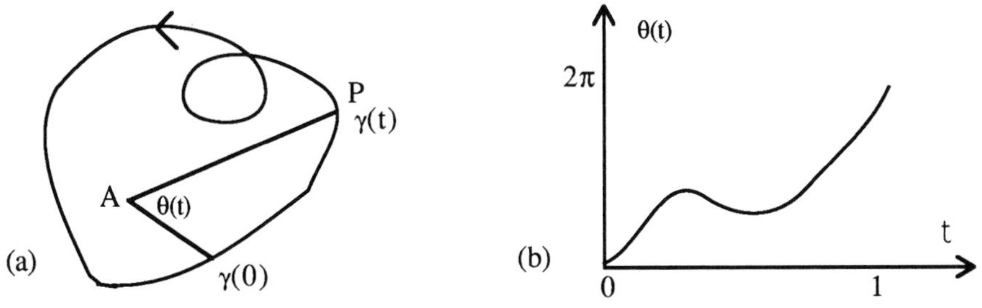

Figure 13.10 Defining the winding number (see text). Graph (b) represents the variation of θ(t) as t increases from 0 to 1 and P moves round the curve γ in (a).

We ensure that the *rotation angle* θ(t) between AP and its initial direction is a unique number (although adding angular multiples of 2π leaves the direction of AP unchanged) by specifying that θ(0) = 0 and that θ changes continuously as AP rotates. Notice how the inner loop of curve γ in Figure 13.10(a) causes the value of θ(t) to go up, down, and up again, in its graph as depicted in Figure 13.10(b). Alternatively if A is the origin we may retain uniqueness by taking the value of the argument angle arg g(0) which lies in the interval (-π,π]. We then have the formulae

$$w(\gamma,A) = [\theta(1) - \theta(0)]/2\pi, \qquad (13.21A)$$
$$w(\gamma,O) = [\arg \gamma(1) - \arg \gamma(0)]/2\pi. \qquad (13.21B)$$

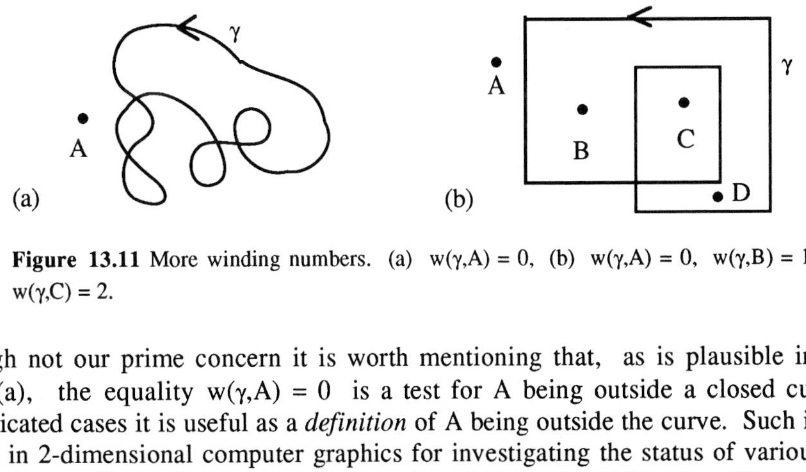

Figure 13.11 More winding numbers. (a) w(γ,A) = 0, (b) w(γ,A) = 0, w(γ,B) = 1, w(γ,C) = 2.

Though not our prime concern it is worth mentioning that, as is plausible in Figure 13.11(a), the equality w(γ,A) = 0 is a test for A being outside a closed curve. In complicated cases it is useful as a *definition* of A being outside the curve. Such ideas are useful in 2-dimensional computer graphics for investigating the status of various points relative to a self-crossing polygon such as that of Figure 13.11(b). See Kilgour (1987a, 1987b) for example. Indeed, by Theorem 12.43 every point in the same connected component of $\mathbf{C}\setminus\gamma(I)$ has the same winding number, in accordance with continuity of the map $\mathbf{C}\setminus\gamma(I) \to \mathbf{N}$ given by $A \to w(\gamma,A)$ (cf. Stewart & Tall, 1990).

EXERCISE Determine the winding number of the point D in Figure 13.11(b) [the answer may be checked by the sentence immediately above].

LEMMA 13.36 If the closed curve γ (i.e. its image) lies inside an open disc and A is a point outside then

$$w(\gamma,A) = 0.$$

Proof No two values of q(t) can differ by as much as π (see the diagram).

Proof of the Fundamental Theorem, (13.20). We suppose the result is false and obtain a contradiction using winding numbers. Thus we suppose there is a complex polynomial p(z) of degree $n \geq 1$ satisfying $p(z) \neq 0$ for all complex numbers z. Let S_r be the circle of radius r and centre the origin. Then p(z) defines a continuous map from **C** to **C** sending S_r in the first copy of **C** to a closed curve $\gamma = \gamma_r$ in the second. That is, $\gamma(t) = p(re^{2\pi it})$ for t in I (= [0,1]). This is shown in Figure 13.12. Since p(z) is never zero the curve γ does not pass through the second origin, so the winding number $w(\gamma,O)$ is well-defined. There are three steps to a contradiction. We prove each in turn.

(1) For r sufficiently small the winding number is 0.
(2) For r sufficiently large the winding number is n, a nonzero integer.
(3) The winding number does not vary with r.

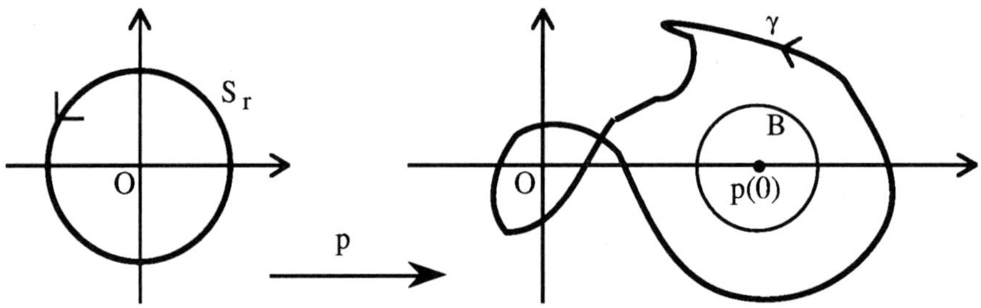

Figure 13.12 p(z) sends the left circle to a curve g in the second complex plane.

Proof of (1) Since p(0) is different from the origin O it centres an open disc B which excludes O (shown in Figure 13.12). But p is continuous and so maps S_r into B for sufficiently small r. By Lemma 12.36, the winding number is 0.
Proof of (2) The constant term of the polynomial p(z) equals p(0) and so is nonzero. Further, dividing all terms by the coefficient of z^n does not affect the roos of p. Thus we may write

$$\begin{aligned} p(z) &= z^n + a_1 z^{n-1} + a_2 z^{n-2} + \dots + a_n \quad (a_n \neq 0) \\ &= z^n(1 + a_1 z^{-1} + \dots + a_n z^{-n}) \\ &= z^n\, q(z), \text{ say,} \end{aligned}$$

where q(z) for sufficiently large r (= |z|) is close to the point z = 1, lying within an open disc centred at (1,0) which is small enough to exclude the origin. Thus writing for brevity $z(t) = re^{2\pi it}$ we have by Lemma 13.36 that $\arg q(z(1)) = \arg q(z(0))$, and

$$\begin{aligned} w(\gamma,O) &= [\arg p(z(1)) - \arg p(z(0))] / 2\pi \\ &= [\arg z(1)^n q(z(1)) - \arg z(0)^n q(z(0))] / 2\pi \\ &= [\arg z(1)^n + \arg q(z(1)) - \arg z(0)^n - \arg q(z(0))] / 2\pi \\ &= [\arg r^n e^{2\pi int} - \arg r^n] / 2\pi = [2\pi n - 0] / 2\pi = n. \end{aligned}$$

Proof of (3) Let $\theta_1(t)$, $\theta_2(t)$ be the rotation angles with respect to the origin for the curves given by radii r_1, r_2 of the circle S_r. The basic idea of the proof is that if $\theta_1(t)$, $\theta_2(t)$ stay sufficiently close as t increases from 0 to 1 they must yield the same winding number, and this may be achieved by taking $|r_1 - r_2|$ small enough. See Figure 13.13. We show that $w(\gamma,O)$ is unchanged as r increases from say a to b ($a < b$) by taking this increase in sufficiently small steps of size D so that w is unchanged over each step.

We need D to work for all values $a \le r \le b$ simultaneously and, without going into details, the existence of such D is ensured by compactness of the annular region defined by these values of r,θ and continuity of p(z). In effect we have a continuous map $[a,b] \to \mathbf{N}$ given by $r \to w(\gamma,O)$ which must be constant because the continuous image of a connected set is connected (cf. Example 12.44). This gives the required contradiction since according to (1) and (2) the function takes distinct values 0 and $n > 0$. Thus the Fundamental Theorem of Algebra is proved.

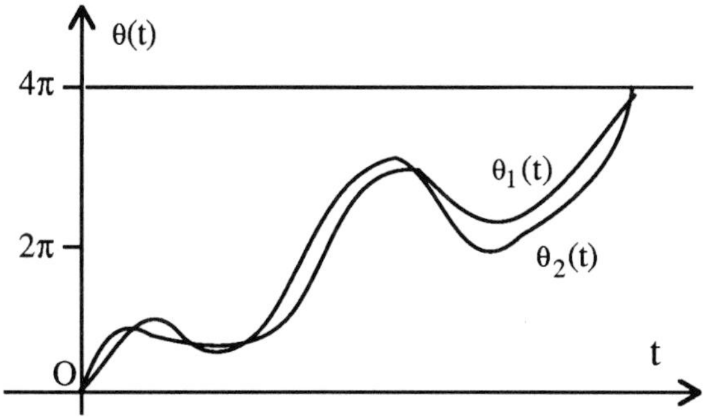

Figure 13.13 If $\theta_1(t)$, $\theta_2(t)$ stay close as t increases from 0 to 1 then they must finish at the same multiple of 2π.

EXERCISES 13

---

1 Draw the first three stages of an equilateral Sierpinski gasket, starting with a filled-in square.

2 √ Let x be a point of a subset A of a metric space. Show that the point to set distance d(x,A) is zero (One line: see (13.6)).

3 Calculate the distance of the point (3,4) from the circle $x^2 + y^2 - 2x - 4y = 14$.

4 Calculate the distance of the point (1,2,1) in 3-space from (a) the plane $2x-3y+4 = 0$, (b) the line $x/2 = (y-1)/3 = z/4$ (cf. Example 13.3).

5 Deduce the last assertion of Lemma 13.5 from the first (one line of proof).

6 √ Calculate the set to set distances d([2,6],[14,18]) and d([6,15],[-3,21]).

7 Determine the Hausdorff distances between the plane sets given by A: $x^2 + y^2 \le 16$, and B: $(x-3)^2 + (-4)^2 \le 9$, noting the values of $d_A(B)$ and $d_B(A)$ separately.

8 Verify the triangle inequality for the Hausdorff distances between the compact sets A, B of Exercise 7 above and the line segment C: $x = 5$, $-5 \le y \le 5$.

9 Calculate $d(\Psi I, \Psi^2 I)$ and $d(\Psi^2 I, \Psi^3 I)$ in the Cantor set construction (see Example 13.7(3)). Guess at an expression for $d(\Psi^n I, \Psi^{n+1} I)$. Can you now justify it? (b) Deduce from the triangle inequality that for $k,m \geq 1$, $d(\Psi^k I, \Psi^{k+m} I) \leq (1/2)\Sigma_i(1/3)^i \quad (k+1 \leq i \leq k+m) \leq (1/3)^k/4$, and hence that $\{\Psi^k I\}$ is a Cauchy sequence.

10 Calculate $d(\Psi E, \Psi^2 E)$ in the Sierpinski construction (isosceles right angled triangle version with equal sides of unit length). Do this for starting sets (a) the sides of the triangle, (b) the filled-in triangle. Extras: carry out the steps corresponding to Exercise 9(b).

11 √ Prove that a complete subspace of a complete space is also a closed subset (see Section 13.2.1, and in particular Theorem 13.11).

12 √ By considering intervals on the real line, give an example of a Cauchy sequence in a space X which does not converge, and a larger space in which it does.

13 √ Which of the following spaces are complete: $(0,1]$, $(-\infty,2]$, $[1,5]\cup(6,7]$, $(0,\infty)$? Must an interval be closed to be complete?

14 √ For the Fixed Point Theorem deduce (13.10), the second bound for $d(x_n,e)$, from the first (one line suffices).

15 √ Construct a homeomorphism between (0,1) and **R**, specifying also the inverse function. Why does the existence of such a mapping show that completeness is not topologically invariant?

16 √ Find the fixed point of the plane transformation $f(\mathbf{x}) = (3/4)R_O(\pi/4)(\mathbf{x}) + (1,2)$, stating why it is known in advance that such a point exists. Verify your answer roughly, in a diagram, by finding iterates first of the origin and then of another point.

17 Show that the continuous function $f: \mathbf{R} \to \mathbf{R}$, $f(x) = x(x-3)$, is not contractive, but nevertheless has a fixed point. How does this point arise as the intersection of two graphs in the plane?

18 (a) Let $f(x) = x^3 + 2x^2 - 1$. By calculating $f(x)$ for $x = 0,1,2, \ldots$ find an interval which must contain a real root of $f(x)$ (use the Intermediate Value Theorem, Example 12.41(3)). Determine this root correct to five decimal places by Newton's method (Example 13.22), using the error bounds given in The Fixed Point Theorem to demonstrate your accuracy.
(b) Repeat for $f(x) = x^5 - 3x + 1$.

19 Prove the distance formula (13.12) for functions satisfies the Axioms (Definition 11.1) for a metric space. Find $d(f,g)$, where $f,g: [0,\pi] \to \mathbf{R}$ are defined by $f(x) = \sin x$, and $g(x) = 1 + \cos x$.

20 Let $\{x_n\}$ be a Cauchy sequence in a metric space S, with a subsequence $\{x_{n_i}\}$. Let $x \in S$. Prove that $x_n \to x$ if and only if $x_{n_i} \to x$.

21 Prove that if A is a compact subset of $\mathbf{R}^n$ and $\varepsilon > 0$, then $A + \varepsilon$ is also a compact subset (see Definition 13.24).

22 Write a computer program to construct the Sierpinski gasket from several different starting sets. Now add a routine to print out the Hausdorff distance between successive iterates of the starting set.

23 Find the winding number of curve γ in Figure 13.11, about a point in each component of $\mathbf{C} \setminus \gamma(I)$.

Chapter 14 ITERATED FUNCTION SYSTEMS

The main result of the previous chapter, Theorem 13.28, gives an iterative method for constructing fractals from a finite set of contractive maps, as originally laid down by Hutchinson (1981). The method was developed and publicised under the title iterated function systems (IFS's) principally by Barnsley and co-workers who obtained impressively lifelike images both of scenes from nature and of the human face. See for example Barnsley and Demko (1985), Barnsley and Elton (1988), Barnsley and Sloan (1988), and the textbook of Barnsley (1988). See also Mandelbrot (1986), Edgar (1990), and Falconer (1990). The possibilities of image compression (storing an image economically) caught the attention of optical engineers, as evidenced by the survey article of Brammer (1989). One suggested reason as to why this iterative approach should be so successful is that, as far as the human eye is concerned such scenes contain less information than one might think (but no one approach is best for all situations. cf. Foley et al, 1990).

The purpose of this chapter is to offer knowledge and geometrical insight relevant to iterated function systems. In Section 14.1 we review some notation, the basis of the method, and discuss the speed of convergence to a desired image. Section 14.2 is devoted to affine transformations, the ones we shall require: their classification, how to predict their effect, and how to identify them by their effect. Section 14.3 is a tutorial on finding an iterated function system to produce a given image. Typically the reader is asked to consider a picture, form an opinion, then read the discussion containing an 'answer'. We begin with simple cases in which it is known that two transformations suffice, and work up to the collage method for general images. This chapter contains much less material of a technical nature than for example chapters eleven to thirteen.

14.1 Basic ideas - key examples

The foundations for this approach are in Chapters 11 to 13, Chapter 10 is introductory, whilst many results on plane transformations from earlier chapters will be extremely useful.

In this context we revert from letter Ψ to W for maps and keep fairly closely to the notation of Barnsley. We recall that here in Part 3 the composition of maps fg means 'do g then f. The latest map or corresponding matrix is written on the left. For example, rather than writing $[x_1 \ x_2] = [y_1 \ y_2]AB$, where A, B are transformation matrices, we use the transposed version

$$\begin{bmatrix} x_1 \\ x_2 \end{bmatrix} = B^T A^T \begin{bmatrix} y_1 \\ y_2 \end{bmatrix}.$$

To pass between the two systems we simply transpose corresponding matrices and reverse the order, as exemplified in Table 14.3.

DEFINITION 14.1 An *iterated function system* or IFS for short, is a collection of a complete metric space X, together with a finite set of contractive mappings $w_n: X \to X$ $(1 \le n \le N)$ with respective contractivity factors r_n. Thus $|w_n(\mathbf{x}) - w_n(\mathbf{y})| \le r_n|\mathbf{x} - \mathbf{y}|$. It is often convenient to write an IFS formally as $\{X; w_1, w_2, \dots, w_N\}$ or, somewhat more briefly, as $\{X; w_{1\text{-}N}\}$. We introduced as early as Section 10.3.1 the associated map of subsets $W: \mathcal{H}(X) \to \mathcal{H}(X)$, given by

$$W(E) = w_1E \cup w_2E \cup \dots \cup w_nE \quad \textit{(collage map)}, \tag{14.1}$$

where $\mathcal{H}(X)$ is the collection of all nonempty compact subsets of X. For a reminder on how this works out see Figures 10.14 to 10.16 and 13.8. The map W itself is contractive, with ratio $r = \max\{r_1, r_2, \dots, r_n\}$, by Theorem 13.8. In this text (as mentioned earlier) W is called the *collage map* to alert us to the fact that W(E) is formed as a union or collage of sets (14.1). This union is of course itself a set. Sometimes $\mathcal{H}(X)$ is referred to as the 'space of fractals in X' (but note that not all members of X are fractals).

DEFINITION 14.2 The **attractor** of an IFS is the unique set $\mathcal{A}$ for which $W^n(E_0) \to \mathcal{A}$ for every starting set E_0 (see Theorem 13.28 and Figure 13.8). The term *attractor* is chosen to suggest the movement of E_0 towards $\mathcal{A}$ under successive applications of W. By contrast, $\mathcal{A}$ is also the unique set in $\mathcal{H}(X)$ which is not changed by W, $W(\mathcal{A}) = \mathcal{A}$, and from this important perspective it is often called the *invariant set* of the IFS. This chapter is about starting with an 'image set' F and finding an IFS whose attractor is close to F.

IFS codes From now on X will be the plane $\mathbf{R}^2$ or a subset. If X is obvious from the context we may abbreviate the IFS to $\{w_1, w_2, \dots, w_N\}$. Another shortening is $\{w_{1\text{-}N}\}$. We assume henceforth that a coordinate system in the plane is given, and that all the maps w_i are affine, where a transformation w is *affine* if it may be represented by a matrix A and translation $\mathbf{t}$ as $w(\mathbf{x}) = A\mathbf{x} + \mathbf{t}$, or

$$w\begin{bmatrix} x \\ y \end{bmatrix} = \begin{bmatrix} a & b \\ c & d \end{bmatrix}\begin{bmatrix} x \\ y \end{bmatrix} + \begin{bmatrix} e \\ f \end{bmatrix}. \tag{14.2}$$

The *code* of w is the 6-tuple (a,b,c,d,e,f), and the *code of an IFS* is a table whose rows are the codes of $w_1, \dots, w_N$. This table relieves us of the need to write out a large number of matrices. If necessary we subscript the coefficients for w_i as $a_i \dots f_i$. A valuable feature of an IFS is the small number of constants involved, considering what it may produce, as we see in Figure 14.1.

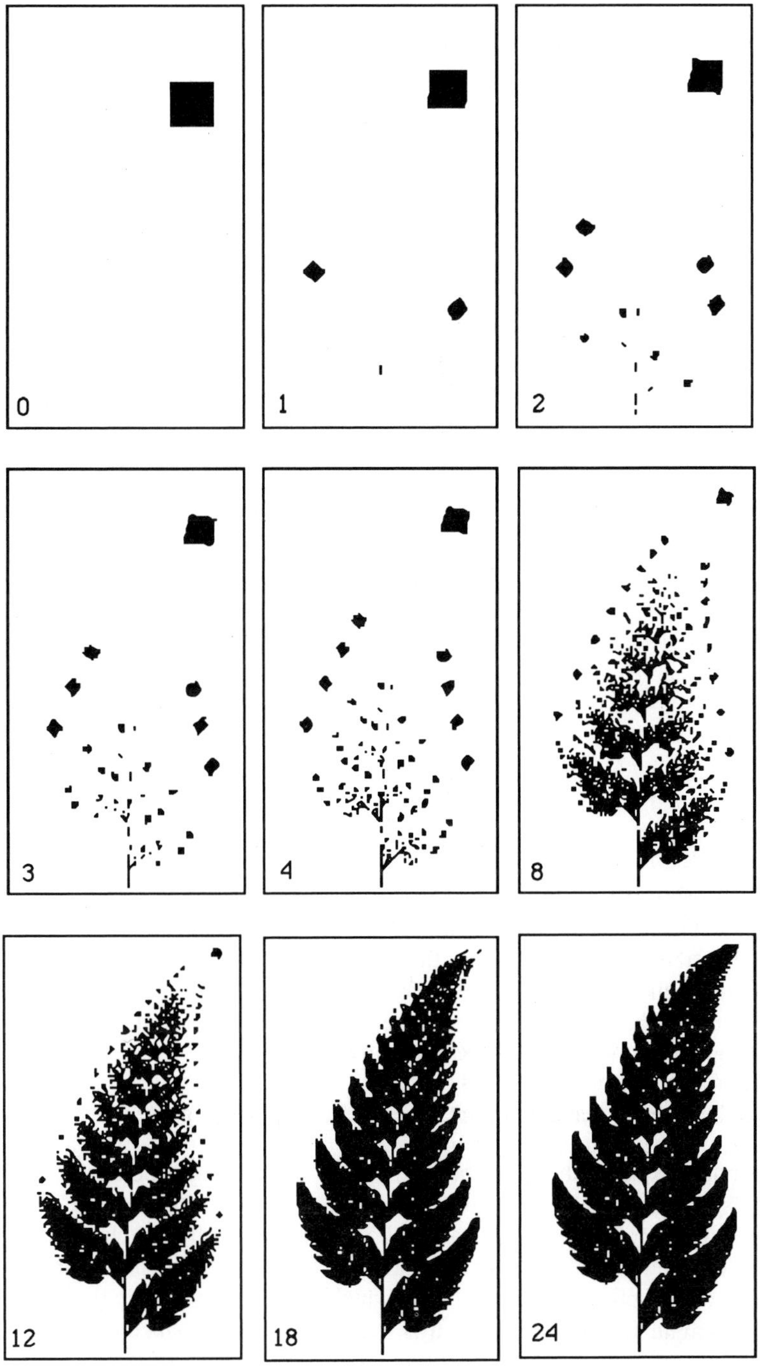

Figure 14.1 Barnsley's fern, obtained from the IFS code of Table 14.2. Starting with a small black square, the sets E_i converging to the fern are given recursively by $W(E) = w_1(E) \cup w_2(E) \cup w_3(E) \cup w_4(E)$. In each frame the number of iterations it represents is given in the lower left hand corner.

EXAMPLES 14.3 (1) The right-angled Sierpinski gasket of Figure 13.1, with shorter sides of length 2, results from the IFS $\{\mathbf{R}^2; w_1, w_2, w_3\}$, where $w_1(\mathbf{x}) = \mathbf{x}/2$, $w_2(\mathbf{x}) = \mathbf{x}/2 + (1,0)$, $w_3(\mathbf{x}) = \mathbf{x}/2 + (0,1)$. By writing out one of the matrix expressions (to get the idea), say

$$w_2\begin{bmatrix} x \\ y \end{bmatrix} = \begin{bmatrix} 1/2 & 0 \\ 0 & 1/2 \end{bmatrix}\begin{bmatrix} x \\ y \end{bmatrix} + \begin{bmatrix} 1 \\ 0 \end{bmatrix},$$

we see that the code of this Sierpinski IFS is that shown in Table 14.1.

TABLE 14.1

IFS code for the Sierpinski gasket.

	a	b	c	d	e	f
w_1	1/2	0	0	1/2	0	0
w_2	1/2	0	0	1/2	1	0
w_3	1/2	0	0	1/2	0	1

(2) In Table 14.2 appears Barnsley's remarkable IFS code for a fern, with the result shown in Figure 14.1. These numbers were obtained by the methods of Section 14.3.4.

TABLE 14.2

IFS code for Barnsley's fern. All entries should be divided by 100.

	a	b	c	d	e	f
w_1	0	0	0	16	0	0
w_2	85	4	- 4	85	0	160
w_3	20	- 26	23	22	0	160
w_4	- 15	28	26	24	0	44

EXERCISE Write down an IFS code to produce a Sierpinski gasket based on the triangle with coordinates (0,0), (4,0), (5,3). Each map should put a 1/2 sized copy of the main triangle at one of its vertices, similarly to (10.11).

How fast is the process? In Figure 14.1 a small black square is taken as starting set E_0 and by E_{24} we reach $\mathcal{A}$ within the accuracy allowed by screen resolution. The square was chosen to illustrate the process rather than to facilitate it - we see easily how one piece becomes four, each characterising a transformation w_i (cf Theorem 14.10). Did we thereby greatly slow down the speed of convergence to $\mathcal{A}$? The Fixed Point Theorem upon which our conclusion that $E_n \to \mathcal{A}$ is based provides a bound

$$d(E_n,\mathcal{A}) \le r^n\, d(E_0,E_1)/(1-r). \tag{14.3}$$

The most important thing about this bound is that it decreases geometrically as n increases. That is, it is scaled down by a factor $r < 1$ each time we go to the next iteration. Thus although $d(E_0,E_1)$ is rather large here, about 3/5 the height of a frame (check this!), its effect should wear off after a small number of iterations. To apply the bound we use a formula for the ratio ρ of a contractive affine map (14.2) which is derived in exactly the same way as the numerical Example 12.30 (notice that it is independent of e,f since translation preserves distances):

$$\rho = \sqrt{\alpha + \beta + \sqrt{(\alpha - \beta)^2 + \gamma^2}}, \tag{14.4}$$

where $\alpha = (a^2+c^2)/2$, $\beta = (b^2+d^2)/2$, $\gamma = ab+cd$.

In this case we obtain ratio 0.85 for w_2 and less for the others, so this is the value of r for

(14.3). Since r^{24} = 1/50 approximately, the bound is somewhat pessimistic in this case, but then most of the maps w_i have much lower ratios than w_2, so this is to be expected. Happily, as observed, we have a close representation of the attractor by stage 24.

POSTSCRIPT (Alternative forms.) (1) A restricted class of affine transformations may conveniently be written in terms of complex numbers, namely

Translation by a complex number a	$z \to z+a$
Rotation of θ about the origin	$z \to ze^{i\theta}$
Uniform scaling in ratio r > 0	$z \to rz$
Reflection in the x-axis	$z \to \bar{z}$.

Compositions of these form the class of similarities - uniform scaling combined with an isometry. (2) In Section 7.4.2 we showed how to work with plane isometries, including translations, by means of 3 x 3 matrices. This goes through unchanged for affine transformations; we simply allow the 2 x 2 part to vary arbitrarily. The reader is recommended to try out some of the worked examples of the present chapter using this approach.

14.2 The classification of affine maps

Recalling the overall aim of reproducing natural scenes by a small iterated function system, this is the point at which we should arm ourselves with more information about affine maps. What are all possible results of an affine map, what is the effect of a map specified by a row of the IFS code table, and how do we determine an affine map to do a particular task? Since isometries (distance-preserving maps) are a special case of affine maps we shall first review relevant properties of isometries, then see how much further the affine case can take us.

THEOREM 14.4 (From Theorems 1.1, 1.5.) An isometry g of the plane is determined by (i) its effect on any two points and whether it is sense preserving or sense reversing, or (ii) by its effect on the vertices of any triangle. Further, g must be one of the following.

(a) *A translation* T_a: $\mathbf{x} \to \mathbf{x} + \mathbf{a}$.

(b) *A rotation* $R_P(\theta)$ *about a point P, through signed angle θ, with anticlockwise as positive direction.*

(c) *A reflection* $R_{\mathbf{m}}$ *in a line* $\mathbf{m}$. *The subscript* $\mathbf{m}$ *may be replaced by symbols defining a line thus:* R_{AB}, $R_{y=2x}$, $R_{x\text{-axis}}$.

(d) *A glide* $R_{\mathbf{m}}T_{\mathbf{a}} = T_{\mathbf{a}}R_{\mathbf{m}}$, *where vector* $\mathbf{a}$ *is parallel to line* $\mathbf{m}$.

TABLE 14.3 The matrix A for some isometries of the form $\mathbf{x} \to A\mathbf{x}$ (obtained by transposing the matrices of (7.26), (7.28)).

$R_O(\theta)$	$R_{x\text{-axis}}$	$R_{y = x\tan\theta}$
$\begin{bmatrix} \cos\theta & -\sin\theta \\ \sin\theta & \cos\theta \end{bmatrix}$	$\begin{bmatrix} 1 & 0 \\ 0 & -1 \end{bmatrix}$	$\begin{bmatrix} \cos 2\theta & \sin 2\theta \\ \sin 2\theta & -\cos 2\theta \end{bmatrix}$

EXAMPLE 14.5 Find the IFS code for a rotation of 90 degrees about the point E(1,3) in the plane.

Solution Apart from memorising a general formula, Theorem 2.4 gives us one good way to do this. We translate the plane so as to send E to the origin, rotate about the origin itself, by the required angle, then translate the origin back to E. With **e** as position vector of E, the translation sending O to E is $T_{OE} = T_{\mathbf{e}}$, with inverse $T_{-\mathbf{e}}$. Noting that $T_{-\mathbf{e}}(x) = \mathbf{x}-\mathbf{e}$ and writing $R = R_O(\pi/2)$, we obtain the required map as

$$T_{\mathbf{e}} R\, T_{-\mathbf{e}}(\mathbf{x}) \quad = \quad T_{\mathbf{e}} R(\mathbf{x}-\mathbf{e}) \quad = \quad R(\mathbf{x}-\mathbf{e}) + \mathbf{e} \quad = \quad R(\mathbf{x}) - R(\mathbf{e}) + \mathbf{e}$$

$$= \begin{bmatrix} 0 & -1 \\ 1 & 0 \end{bmatrix}\begin{bmatrix} x \\ y \end{bmatrix} - \begin{bmatrix} 0 & -1 \\ 1 & 0 \end{bmatrix}\begin{bmatrix} 1 \\ 3 \end{bmatrix} + \begin{bmatrix} 1 \\ 3 \end{bmatrix}$$

$$= \begin{bmatrix} 0 & -1 \\ 1 & 0 \end{bmatrix}\begin{bmatrix} x \\ y \end{bmatrix} + \begin{bmatrix} 4 \\ 2 \end{bmatrix}.$$

The code is thus (a,b,c,d,e,f) = (0,-1,1,0,4,2). We state for future use the formula implicitly discovered en route for transformation S and translation vector **e**:

$$T_{\mathbf{e}} S\, T_{-\mathbf{e}}(\mathbf{x}) \quad = \quad S(\mathbf{x} - \mathbf{e}) + \mathbf{e}. \tag{14.5}$$

EXERCISE Find the IFS code for reflection in the line $y = x+2$.

14.2.1 Two affine maps which are not isometries

DEFINITION 14.6 The *coordinate scaling transformation* (w.r.t. the x, y axes) *with parameters r, s* is the map T(x,y) = (rx, sy), or in matrix form

$$T\begin{bmatrix} x \\ y \end{bmatrix} = \begin{bmatrix} r & 0 \\ 0 & s \end{bmatrix}\begin{bmatrix} x \\ y \end{bmatrix},$$

where we adopt the convention that r,s are non-negative, so that (by definition) directions are not reversed by a scaling. Thus horizontal line segments are 'stretched' in the ratio r and vertical ones in the ratio s. Of course, if for example $0 < r < 1$, the horizontal effect is actually a contraction. Case r = s is dilation, or *uniform scaling*. However we want to allow scaling with respect to arbitrary perpendicular axes along say <u>AB</u>, <u>AC</u> (origin A), with parameters r,s. With X, Y as coordinates in this system the transformation is T(X,Y) = (rX,sY). We call A the *centre* of T. We require T in terms of the original coordinates x,y, and this could be obtained by expressing X,Y in terms of x,y.

However we prefer the equivalent geometrical viewpoint (cf. the comment above Example 8.2) that, if g is an isometry mapping the x and y-axes to lie along AB, AC respectively, and S is the coordinate scaling S(x,y) = (rx,sy) , then the required transformation is $T(\mathbf{x}) = gSg^{-1}(\mathbf{x})$. Informally speaking, we map everything to the old axes, do the scaling there, then transfer the scaled object back to axes AB, AC (cf. Example 14.5). We are using again the standard ghg^{-1} trick of Theorem 2.4. Some rotation may well be involved, but we have all the tools we need for scaling, as the next example shows.

EXAMPLE 14.7 Given the points A(4,2), B(5,5), C(1,3), find the code of the coordinate scaling transformation T with centre A, axes along the perpendicular segments AB, AC, and parameters 2,3.

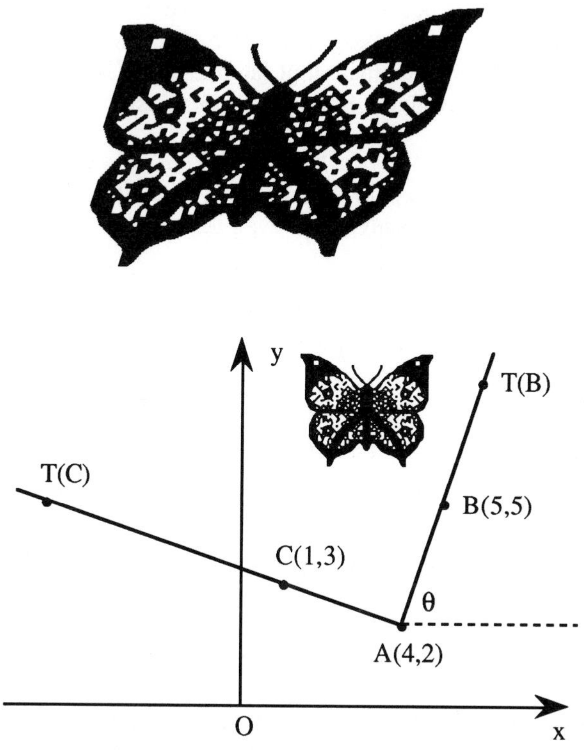

Figure 14.2 Coordinate scaling map T, centred at A, which doubles distances parallel to AB and trebles them parallel to AC. The effect on a butterfly is shown.

Solution For the isometry $g = T_{\mathbf{a}} R_O(\theta)$ sending O to A and Ox, Oy along AB, AC we note that $\underline{AB} = (1,3)$, of length $\sqrt{(10)}$. Hence $\cos\theta = 1/\sqrt{(10)}$, $\sin\theta = 3/\sqrt{(10)}$, and the matrix of $R_O(\theta)$ is, by Table 14.3,

$$\begin{bmatrix} \cos\theta & -\sin\theta \\ \sin\theta & \cos\theta \end{bmatrix} = \frac{1}{\sqrt{10}}\begin{bmatrix} 1 & -3 \\ 3 & 1 \end{bmatrix}.$$

The coordinate scaling map S with parameters 2,3 relative to the x,y-axes has matrix diag{2,3}. We note also that $g^{-1} = R_O(-\theta)T_{-\mathbf{a}}$ and $\mathbf{x}\text{-}\mathbf{a} = (x-4, y-2)$. The required transformation T is therefore given by

$$\begin{aligned} T(\mathbf{x}) = gSg^{-1}(\mathbf{x}) &= T_{\mathbf{a}}\,[R_O(\theta)SR_O(-\theta)]\,T_{-\mathbf{a}}(\mathbf{x}) \\ &= R_O(\theta)SR_O(-\theta)(\mathbf{x}-\mathbf{a}) + \mathbf{a} \qquad \text{by (14.5)} \\ &= \frac{1}{\sqrt{10}}\begin{bmatrix} 1 & -3 \\ 3 & 1 \end{bmatrix}\begin{bmatrix} 2 & 0 \\ 0 & 3 \end{bmatrix}\frac{1}{\sqrt{10}}\begin{bmatrix} 1 & 3 \\ -3 & 1 \end{bmatrix}\begin{bmatrix} x-4 \\ y-2 \end{bmatrix} + \begin{bmatrix} 4 \\ 2 \end{bmatrix} \\ &= \frac{1}{10}\begin{bmatrix} 29 & -3 \\ -3 & 21 \end{bmatrix}\begin{bmatrix} x-4 \\ y-2 \end{bmatrix} + \begin{bmatrix} 4 \\ 2 \end{bmatrix} \\ &= \frac{1}{10}\begin{bmatrix} 29 & -3 \\ -3 & 21 \end{bmatrix}\begin{bmatrix} x \\ y \end{bmatrix} - \begin{bmatrix} 7 \\ 1 \end{bmatrix}. \end{aligned}$$

Thus the code is (1/10)(29,-3,-3,21,-70,-10). As a check we note from Figure 14.2 that the geometry requires T(A) = A because A is the centre of T, also T(B) = (6,8) because as line segments $\underline{AT(B)} = 2\underline{AB}$, and similarly T(C) = (-5,5). These are given correctly by the matrix form of T above and, in anticipation of later results (Theorem 14.10), we remark that correctness on three non collinear points suffices to establish the correctness of the calculated code.

EXERCISE Find the IFS code for the scaling transformation with parameters 3,4 with respect to the x,y axes rotated through 45°. [Your matrix should have determinant 1.]

DEFINITION 14.8 A ***shear*** along the x-axis with parameter α is (we recall) the transformation T(x,y) = (x+αy, y). In matrix form

$$T\begin{bmatrix}x\\y\end{bmatrix} = \begin{bmatrix}x+\alpha y\\y\end{bmatrix} = \begin{bmatrix}1 & \alpha\\0 & 1\end{bmatrix}\begin{bmatrix}x\\y\end{bmatrix},$$

in which points are moved parallel to the x-axis in proportion to their signed distance above it, α being the constant of proportionality. Note that points above the x-axis are those to its left as a directed line, and are moved in the *positive* x-direction if α > 0, whilst those below/right are moved in the *negative* direction. These directions are reversed if α < 0. A shear can also take place with respect to (*along*) any directed line or segment, called its *axis*, on similar principles to that of coordinate scaling, as we illustrate in the example following.

EXAMPLE 14.9 Given the points A(1,3), B(3,4) find the code for a shear of parameter 1, along AB. First determine T(O), T(A), T(B) independently of the code.

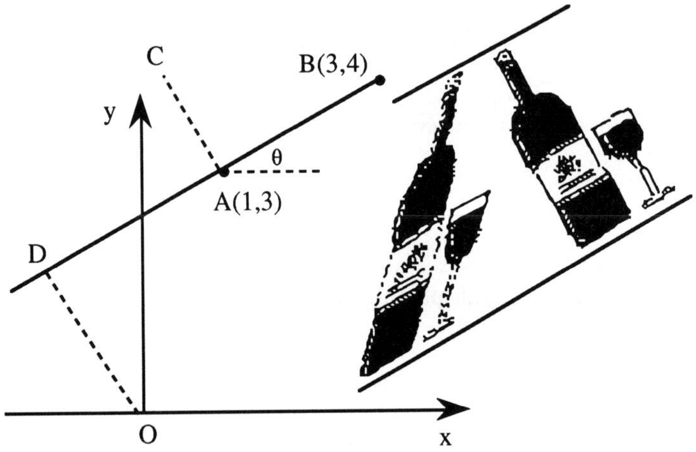

Figure 14.3 Shear along AB with parameter 1. Points above AB are moved to the right and those below are moved leftwards, parallel to AB. The effect on bottle and glass, showing the originals and their images. Notice that a segment parallel to AB is moved to an equal segment, exemplified by the bottom of a bottle.

Solution By definition, A and B are fixed by T. On the other hand O, being below the directed line AB is sent 'backwards' a distance equal to 1.|OD|. Recalling that two lines are perpendicular if and only if the product of their gradients is -1, we observe that $\underline{AB}$ = (2,1), with slope 1/2, so OD has slope -2 and hence equation y = -2x, whilst the line AB has equation y-3 = (1/2)(x-1). Hence D is (-1, 2) and |OD| = √5. A unit vector in direction AB is <u>AB</u>/ |AB| = (2,1)/√5, so the position vector of T(O) is given by **e** = -1.|OD| (2,1)/√5 = (-2,-1).

For the code, consider <u>AB</u>, <u>AC</u> as defining coordinate axes at A, where <u>AB</u> is perpendicular to <u>AC</u> and C is to the left of directed line segment <u>AB</u>, which makes, say, angle θ with the positive x-axis. We require the translation vector $T_{OA} = T_{\mathbf{a}}$ which sends the origin to A. As in the coordinate scaling case, let g = $T_{\mathbf{a}}$ $R_O(\theta)$, rotating the x,y-axes then translating them to lie along <u>AB</u>, <u>AC</u>. The shear S along the x-axis with parameter 1, and the rotation $R_O(\theta)$ have respective matrices

$$\begin{bmatrix}1 & 1\\ 0 & 1\end{bmatrix} \quad \text{and} \quad \frac{1}{\sqrt{5}}\begin{bmatrix}2 & -1\\ 1 & 2\end{bmatrix},$$

so the required transformation is $T(\mathbf{x}) = gSg^{-1}(\mathbf{x}) = T_{\mathbf{a}}\,[R_O(\theta)SR_O(-\theta)]\,T_{-\mathbf{a}}(\mathbf{x})$, with

$$T\begin{bmatrix}x\\ y\end{bmatrix} = \frac{1}{\sqrt{5}}\begin{bmatrix}2 & -1\\ 1 & 2\end{bmatrix}\begin{bmatrix}1 & 1\\ 0 & 1\end{bmatrix}\frac{1}{\sqrt{5}}\begin{bmatrix}2 & 1\\ -1 & 2\end{bmatrix}\begin{bmatrix}x-1\\ y-3\end{bmatrix} + \begin{bmatrix}1\\ 3\end{bmatrix}, \quad \text{by (14.5)},$$

$$= \frac{1}{5}\begin{bmatrix}3 & 4\\ -1 & 7\end{bmatrix}\begin{bmatrix}x\\ y\end{bmatrix} - \begin{bmatrix}2\\ 1\end{bmatrix} \quad \text{(cf. Example 14.7).}$$

Thus the code is (1/5)(3,4,-1,7,-10,-5), giving the same T(A), T(B), T(O) as before.

SUMMARY To find the matrix of a shear T along any given line m we may first map that line to the x-axis by an isometry (called for convenience g^{-1} above), perform a shear along this axis, then apply the inverse isometry (called g above). Note that m is characterised by being the line fixed by the shear T. It is time to combine such statements into a general one. Let S be

a rotation with centre the origin, or
a shear or reflection with respect to the x-axis, or
a coordinate scaling with respect to the x,y-axis, centre the origin.

Then:

The transformation of the same type relative to new centre/axes which are the images of the old under an isometry g is gSg^{-1}. (14.6)

EXERCISE Find the IFS code for Example 14.9, with the parameter changed to 2. Verify the answer similarly (the calculation is the same up to a certain stage - use this fact).

14.2.2 How affine transformations work

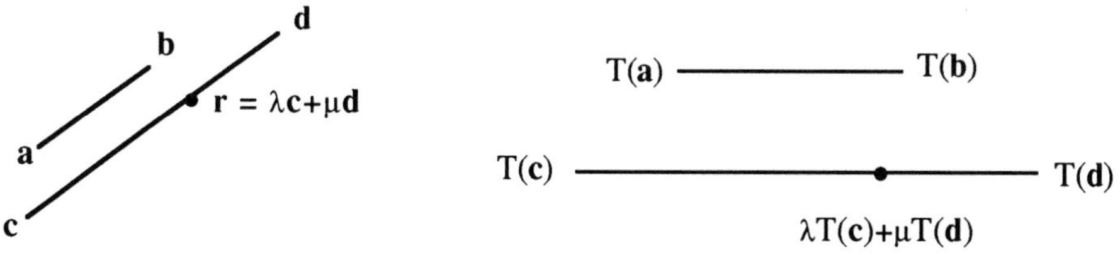

Figure 14.4 An affine transformation sends parallel line segments AB, CD with lengths in ratio ρ, to another such pair. Here ρ = 2, whilst λ = 1/3, μ = 2/3.

THEOREM 14.10 (Properties of an affine transformation.)

(a) An affine transformation $T(\mathbf{x}) = A\mathbf{x} + \mathbf{t}$ *is uniquely determined by its effect on the vertices of any triangle. Conversely, for any two triangles ABC, DEF there is a unique affine transformation sending A,B,C to D,E,F respectively. Similar statements hold also for parallelograms.*

(b) If AB and CD are parallel line segments with $\underline{AB} = \rho\underline{CD}$, *then so are their images under T. In particular, T sends*

lines to lines,

parallelograms to parallelograms, and

preserves the ratios of distances along a line

(c) The following are equivalent : (i) T maps the plane into a line, (ii) T maps some triangle into collinear points, (iii) The matrix of T has zero determinant.

Proof of Theorem 14.10. First, the following observations.

The line through points $\boldsymbol{a}, \boldsymbol{b}$ *is the set* $\{\lambda\boldsymbol{a} + \mu\boldsymbol{b}: \lambda + \mu = 1\}$. (14.7)

If $\lambda + \mu = 1$ *then* $T(\lambda\boldsymbol{a} + \mu\boldsymbol{b}) = \lambda T(\boldsymbol{a}) + \mu T(\boldsymbol{b})$. (14.8)

We begin by justifying (14.7) and (14.8). Note that, for example, $\mathbf{a}$ and $T(\mathbf{a})$ are the position vectors of respective points denoted A, T(A), though we often identify a point and its position vector. (14.7) holds because any point R on the line divides the segment AB in *some* ratio m: n, so by the Section formula (1.3) $\mathbf{r} = \lambda\mathbf{a} + \mu\mathbf{b}$ with $\lambda = n/(m+n)$, $\mu = m/(m+n)$; and conversely $\mathbf{r} = \lambda\mathbf{a} + \mu\mathbf{b}$, with $\lambda+\mu = 1$, is the point on AB dividing it in the ratio $\mu : \lambda$. For (14.8) we have, from the definition of T in terms of a matrix A, $T(\lambda\mathbf{a} + \mu\mathbf{b}) = A(\lambda\mathbf{a} + \mu\mathbf{b}) + \mathbf{t} = \lambda(A\mathbf{a} + \mathbf{t}) + \mu(A\mathbf{b} + \mathbf{t})$ (using $\lambda + \mu = 1$) $= \lambda T(\mathbf{a}) + \mu T(\mathbf{b})$, as asserted. Hence by (14.7) T sends the line through $\mathbf{a}$, $\mathbf{b}$ to the line through $T(\mathbf{a})$, $T(\mathbf{b})$. Now we prove (b), (a), (c) in that order.

(b) For the effect of T on parallel line segments AB, CD we note that $\mathbf{b}-\mathbf{a} = \rho(\mathbf{d}-\mathbf{c})$ for some number ρ, whence $T(\mathbf{b}) - T(\mathbf{a}) = A\mathbf{b} - A\mathbf{a}$ (the $\mathbf{t}$'s cancel) $= A(\mathbf{b}-\mathbf{a}) = \rho A(\mathbf{d}-\mathbf{c}) = \rho(T(\mathbf{d}) - T(\mathbf{c}))$, as required.

(a) We show that T is uniquely determined by its effect on the vertices $\mathbf{a}$, $\mathbf{b}$, $\mathbf{c}$ of any triangle. Let $\mathbf{r}$ be any other point. and consider Figure 14.5 below.

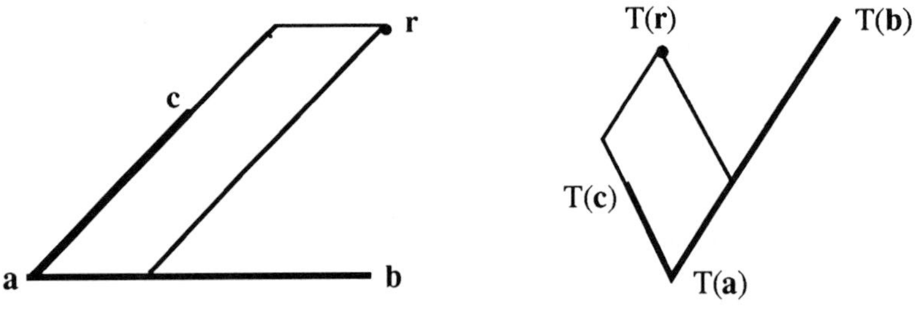

Figure 14.5 An affine transformation maps parallelograms to parallelogams.

By drawing lines through any point R, parallel to AB, AC, we obtain R as the vertex opposite A in a parallelogram (the case R on the line through AB or AC is handled by part (b)). Since T preserves parallel line segments and their ratios, the image triangle T(A),

T(B), T(C) determines the image parallelogram, and hence T(R). Conversely, suppose we want T to map triangle vertices A, B, C onto triangle vertices D, E, F. That is, we require matrix A and translation vector **t** such that $A\mathbf{a}+\mathbf{t} = \mathbf{d}$, $A\mathbf{b}+\mathbf{t} = \mathbf{e}$, $A\mathbf{c}+\mathbf{t} = \mathbf{f}$.

Subtracting the third equation from the first two in turn we get $A\mathbf{x}_1 = \mathbf{y}_1$, $A\mathbf{x}_2 = \mathbf{y}_2$, where **t** is eliminated and $\mathbf{x}_1 = \mathbf{a}-\mathbf{c}$, $\mathbf{x}_2 = \mathbf{b}-\mathbf{c}$, $\mathbf{y}_1 = \mathbf{d}-\mathbf{f}$, $\mathbf{y}_2 = \mathbf{e}-\mathbf{f}$. We combine column vectors $\mathbf{x}_1$, $\mathbf{x}_2$ into a 2 by 2 matrix $[\mathbf{x}_1\ \mathbf{x}_2]$, which is invertible because **a**,**b**,**c** are not collinear and therefore $\mathbf{x}_1$ is not a multiple of $\mathbf{x}_2$ (see Section 7.2.2). Combining the subtraction equations gives $A[\mathbf{x}_1\ \mathbf{x}_2] = [\mathbf{y}_1\ \mathbf{y}_2]$, whence the useful explicit formula

$$A = [\mathbf{y}_1\ \mathbf{y}_2][\mathbf{x}_1\ \mathbf{x}_2]^{-1}, \text{ with } \mathbf{t} = A\mathbf{a}-\mathbf{d}. \tag{14.9}$$

(c) We are to prove equivalence of the three propositions *(i) T maps the plane into a line, (ii) T maps some triangle into collinear points, (iii) The matrix of T has zero determinant.* We shall do so by a circle of implications (ii) ⇒ (i) ⇒ (iii) ⇒ (ii) as follows. For *(ii) ⇒ (i)* we refer to Figure 14.5. Let triangle ABC be mapped to a line. Just as in the proof of (a) we view any point R of the plane as the vertex opposite A in a parallelogram with sides along AB, AC. But since ABC is mapped to a line, so is the parallelogram, and in particular the point R.

For *(i) ⇒ (iii),* assume that (i) holds. Let $\mathbf{e}_1 = [1\ 0]^T$, $\mathbf{e}_2 = [0\ 1]^T$ as column vectors. Then by hypothesis $T(\mathbf{0})$, $T(\mathbf{e}_1)$, $T(\mathbf{e}_2)$ lie on a line, so that $\lambda(T(\mathbf{e}_1) - T(\mathbf{0})) = \mu(T(\mathbf{e}_2) - T(\mathbf{0}))$ for some $\lambda, \mu \in \mathbf{R}$. But the formula $T(\mathbf{x}) = A\mathbf{x} + \mathbf{t}$ gives

$$T(\mathbf{e}_1) - T(\mathbf{0}) = A\mathbf{e}_1 = [a\ c]^T, \qquad T(\mathbf{e}_2) - T(\mathbf{0}) = A\mathbf{e}_2 = [b\ d]^T. \tag{14.10}$$

Thus λ times the first column $[a\ c]^T$ of A equals μ times $[b\ d]^T$, the second, so by determinant Rule 7.20(5) A has zero determinant. For *(iii) ⇒ (ii)* we have the following sequence of implications.

$$\begin{aligned} \det A = 0 \quad &\Rightarrow \quad bc = ad \\ &\Rightarrow \quad b[a\ c]^T = a[b\ d]^T, && \text{since } ba = ab, \\ &\Rightarrow \quad b(T(\mathbf{e}_1) - T(\mathbf{0})) = a(T(\mathbf{e}_2) - T(\mathbf{0})), && \text{by (14.10)}, \\ &\Rightarrow \quad T(\mathbf{0}), T(\mathbf{e}_1), T(\mathbf{e}_2) \text{ are collinear,} \end{aligned}$$

and so T maps the triangle with vertices $\mathbf{0}$, $\mathbf{e}_1$, $\mathbf{e}_2$ onto a straight line.

EXERCISE Use Theorem 14.10 and (14.9) to find an affine transformation which maps the plane onto the line $y = 3x+4$. As a check, the determinant should be zero, by the Theorem just proved.

APPLICATION 14.11 (1) (defining the transformations.) By Theorem 14.10, we may define a collection of affine transformations w_i by starting with a fixed rectangle D and specifying the parallelograms $w_i(D)$. This gives a very handy visual representation, especially on a computer screen (cf. Barnsley's *Desktop Fractal Design* program). Usually, as in Example 14.12 to follow, we standardise on a rectangle with sides along the x,y-axes.

(2) The reader may have felt that the butterfly of Example 14.7 had been subject to shear in spite of the change being produced by coordinate scaling alone. The diagram given below illustrates a rectangle being distorted into the dotted one which we would at least in geometrical terms call subject to shear. Yet the distortion is accomplished by only a vertical coordinate scaling of ratio 3/2. To take account of this in considering the effect of a given transformation T we will normally refer to the presence of shear only if T produces shear in a

rectangle with sides parallel to the coordinate axes.That is, if the matrix A of T maps unit vectors $\mathbf{e}_1 = (1,0)$ and $\mathbf{e}_2 = (0,1)$ into a pair of non-perpendicular vectors (cf. the next example and Theorem 14.14)). Equivalently, by (14.10), the columns of A are not orthogonal.

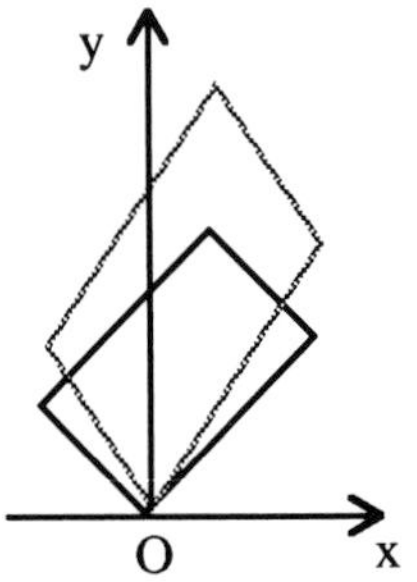

EXAMPLE 14.12 Referring to Figure 14.6, we calculate the code for the IFS $\{w_1, w_2, w_3, w_4\}$ with w_i determined by the parallelogram of that label, into which it maps the 80 x 60 rectangle. The parallelogram with label w_4 is 'degenerate', that is, it is a line segment.
A transformation is often easiest to determine through several stages. Further, it is usually expedient to leave translation until last since the matrix for rotations and reflections fixing the origin are easy to write down, and similarly for a shear fixing the x or y-axis. A suitable order of attack is therefore as follows.

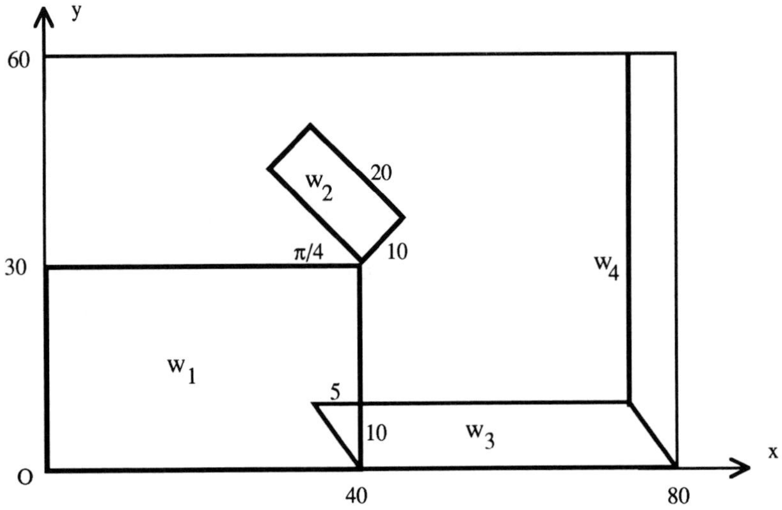

Figure 14.6 Affine transformations w_1 to w_4 are defined by their effect on a single rectangle, here 80 by 60 units. The parallelogram-shaped image under w_i is so labelled, but in the case of w_4 is degenerate, i.e. a line segment.

1. Perform suitable coordinate scaling, to get the correct base and height for the image (this involves choosing one side to regard as base).
2. Perform a shear along the x or y axis if the image of the standard rectangle is not a rectangle.
3. Perform rotation or reflection if necessary.
4. Translate the image into position.

This takes care of the image figure if it is not a line segment, but this case is easily handled (see below). Note that $w_1(\mathbf{x}) = (1/2)\mathbf{x}$. This apart, here is what we require before translation - for w_2: scale then rotate clockwise by $\pi/4$, for w_3: scale then shear, for w_4: scale then set the x coordinate to zero. The matrix products and IFS code are given below.

$$w_2(\mathbf{x}) = \frac{1}{\sqrt{2}}\begin{bmatrix} 1 & 1 \\ -1 & 1 \end{bmatrix}\begin{bmatrix} 1/4 & 0 \\ 0 & 1/6 \end{bmatrix}\mathbf{x} + \begin{bmatrix} 40 \\ 30 \end{bmatrix},$$

$$w_3(\mathbf{x}) = \begin{bmatrix} 1 & -1/2 \\ 0 & 1 \end{bmatrix}\begin{bmatrix} 1/2 & 0 \\ 0 & 1/6 \end{bmatrix}\mathbf{x} + \begin{bmatrix} 40 \\ 0 \end{bmatrix},$$

$$w_4(\mathbf{x}) = \begin{bmatrix} 0 & 0 \\ 0 & 5/6 \end{bmatrix}\mathbf{x} + \begin{bmatrix} 75 \\ 10 \end{bmatrix}.$$

TABLE 14.4

IFS code for Example 14.12.

	a	b	c	d	e	f
w_1	1/2	0	0	1/2	0	0
w_2	$1/8\sqrt{2}$	$-1/3\sqrt{2}$	$1/8\sqrt{2}$	$1/3\sqrt{2}$	40	30
w_3	1/2	-1/12	0	1/6	40	0
w_4	0	0	0	5/6	75	10

The upside down screen Suppose we have our IFS code nicely worked out and then find that, as is often so, the y-axis of the computer screen points downwards rather than upwards, with the x-axis at the top of the screen (CB rather than OA in the diagram of the next exercise). Our attractor would thus come out upside down, reflected in a horizontal line $y = h/2$ say, halfway down the screen. To express our original transformation $T(\mathbf{x}) = A\mathbf{x} + \mathbf{t}$ in terms of the new coordinates we must reflect, sending the new to the old, perform T, then reflect back to new coordinates. That is, the transformation becomes $T' = RTR$, where the reflection $R(x,y) = (x,h-y)$ satisfies $R^2 = I$ and so is its own inverse. We have $R(\mathbf{x}) = B\mathbf{x} + \mathbf{u}$, where $B = \text{diag}\{1,-1\}$, and $\mathbf{u} = [0\ h]^T$. Combining these, $RTR(\mathbf{x}) = RT(B\mathbf{x} + \mathbf{u}) = R(AB\mathbf{x} + A\mathbf{u} + \mathbf{t})$, which simplifies to $BAB\mathbf{x} + BA\mathbf{u} + B\mathbf{t} + \mathbf{u}$, and so, with $e' = bh+e$, $f' = h(1-d) - f$,

$$T'\begin{bmatrix} x \\ y \end{bmatrix} = \begin{bmatrix} a & -b \\ -c & d \end{bmatrix}\begin{bmatrix} x \\ y \end{bmatrix} + \begin{bmatrix} e' \\ f' \end{bmatrix}, \qquad (14.11)$$

The most important conclusion is the simplest. We must change the sign of the off-diagonal elements b,c of our original matrix A. For example, the w_2 code in Table 14.4 with upside down screen of height 300 units becomes (1/2, 1/12, 0, 1/6, 15, 250).

EXERCISE Express as a composition the affine transformation sending rectangle OABC below to the shaded parallelogram, following stages 1 to 4 of Example 14.12. Check the effect on points O, A, C. What does your expression become in upside down coordinates?

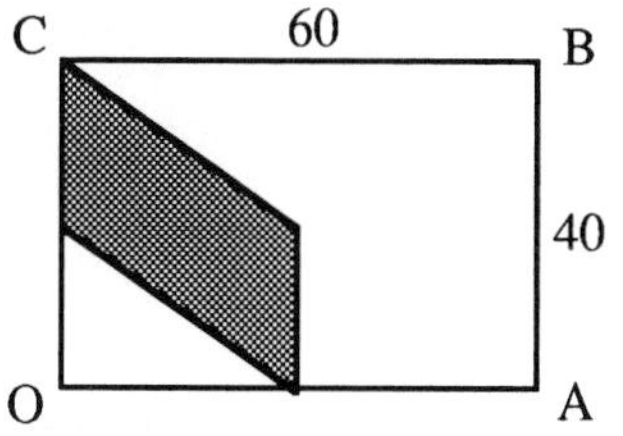

REMARK 14.13 (**Determinants**) (1) *A check on calculation.* Notice that a shear always preserves areas, since the areas of parallelograms with the same base and height are equal. Also, a coordinate scaling with parameters r,s multiplies the area by the product rs. It will then follow from Part (ii) of the next theorem that the shear and scaling transformations have respective determinants 1, rs. Thus we have the following useful check on our calculations of codes.

Transformation	Determinant
REFLECTION	-1
ROTATION, SHEAR	1
r,s COORDINATE SCALING	rs

(2) *A check on* ***Sense.*** In the case T has nonzero determinant, every triangle is mapped onto a triangle and so we can define whether the sense of an ordered triple ABC is preserved or reversed. It may be seen geometrically that a shear or scaling always preserves the sense, and so may be described as direct (cf. Examples 14.7, 14.9). Since these have positive determinant, we have that, unless it is pure translation, *an invertible affine transformation is direct or indirect according as its determinant is positive or negative.*

(3) *Warning.* Note the effect on its determinant when we multiply a matrix by a scalar: $\det \lambda A = \lambda^n \det A$, if A is n by n (by Rule 7.20(2)). Thus the shear of Example 14.9 has matrix $\frac{1}{5}\begin{bmatrix} 3 & 4 \\ -1 & 7 \end{bmatrix}$ and hence determinant $\frac{1}{25}(21+4) = 1$.

(4) *Agreement.* We often use the technique of calculating a matrix as a product BAB^{-1}, as in Example 14.9 just cited. The reader should be clear that this modification to matrix A leaves its determinant unchanged because of the determinant product formula $|PQ| = |P||Q|$ (Rule 7.20(4)). Thus $|BAB^{-1}| = |B||A||B^{-1}| = |B^{-1}||B||A| = |B^{-1}B||A| = |A|$.

(5) *Recapitulation*: determinant formula for the area of a triangle (Corollary 7.34B).

$$\text{Area of triangle ABC} = \frac{1}{2} \text{ absolute value of} \begin{vmatrix} 1 & 1 & 1 \\ a_1 & b_1 & c_1 \\ a_2 & b_2 & c_2 \end{vmatrix}.$$

THEOREM 14.14 Let $T(x) = Ax + t$ be an affine transformation with $A \neq 0$. Then
(i) T is invertible (has an inverse) if and only if $\det A \neq 0$.
(ii) T scales all areas by a factor $|\det A|$.
(iii) A is the product of a coordinate scale, shear, and reflection or rotation, which may be taken in that order.
(iv) A may be written

$$A = \begin{bmatrix} r_1\cos\theta_1 & -r_2\sin\theta_2 \\ r_1\sin\theta_1 & r_2\cos\theta_2 \end{bmatrix} = \begin{bmatrix} \cos\theta_1 & \sin\theta_2 \\ \sin\theta_1 & \cos\theta_2 \end{bmatrix}\begin{bmatrix} r_1 & 0 \\ 0 & r_2 \end{bmatrix} \quad (14.12)$$

where r_1, θ_1 and $r_2, \theta_2 + \pi/2$ are polar coordinates for column vectors 1,2 of A. Thus θ_1, θ_2 are the angles between unit vectors $\mathbf{e}_1, \mathbf{e}_2$ along the positive x,y axes and their respective images $A\mathbf{e}_1, A\mathbf{e}_2$, as shown in Figure 14.7. Further, if $r_1 = r_2 = 1$ then A is a rotation matrix if θ_1, θ_2 are equal and a reflection matrix if they differ by π.

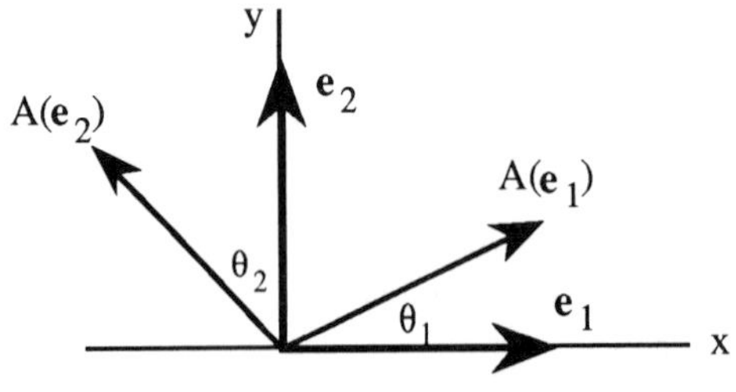

Figure 14.7 The effect of an affine transformation in the form (14.12).

Proof (i) Since translations are invertible we have: $x \to \mathbf{A}x+\mathbf{t}$ is invertible $\Leftrightarrow$ $x \to \mathbf{A}x$ is invertible $\Leftrightarrow$ $\det A \neq 0$ (using Theorem 14.10 (a), (c)). For (ii) the result holds trivially in case $\det A = 0$, since T maps the plane onto a line (Theorem 14.10(c)) and hence multiplies all areas by 0. Let $\det A \neq 0$. It suffices to prove the result for triangular areas, since the plane can be divided into equilateral triangles of arbitrarily small uniform size by the tesselation {3,6} (see Figure 5.2). Since translation preserves areas we need only consider the effect of A on any triangle with a vertex at the origin. But by Lemma 4.2 such a triangle has its area multiplied by $|\det A|$.

(iii) We build up T by steps 1 to 4 of Example 14.12. This gives an alternative approach to (ii), without Lemma 4.2: an isometry, shear or scaling transformation multiplies the area by $|\det A|$, hence so do their products, for $\det(AB) = (\det A)(\det B)$.

(iv) For a reminder on polar coordinates, see Section 1.2.4. If the second column vector of matrix A has polar coordinates r_2, ϕ we simply write $\phi = \theta + \pi/2$ and use the formulae $\cos(\theta+\pi/2) = -\sin\theta$, $\sin(\theta+\pi/2) = \cos\theta$. This gives the expressions (14.9) for A. Now we observe that $A\mathbf{e}_1$ is the first column of A which, with polar coordinates (r_1,θ_1), is at angle θ_1 with $\mathbf{e}_1$ and the positive x-axis. On the other hand $A\mathbf{e}_2$, the second column of A, with polar coordinates $(r_2, \theta_2 + \pi/2)$, is at angle $\theta_2 + \pi/2$ with $\mathbf{e}_1$ and so at θ_2 with $\mathbf{e}_2$ and the positive y-axis, as shown in Figure 14.7. For the last part set $r_1 = r_2 = 1$ in (14.12). With $\theta_2 = \theta_1 = \theta$ we obtain the rotation matrix of Table 14.3. But if we set $\theta_1 = \theta$ and $\theta_2 = \theta + \pi$ then the relations $\sin(\theta + \pi) = -\cos\theta$, $\cos(\theta + \pi) = -\sin\theta$ dictate that the matrix we get is that of reflection in the line $y = x \tan\theta/2$, according to Table 14.3.

EXERCISE Use the determinant formula of Remark 14.13 to show that transformations of shear or coordinate scaling type multiply the area of a triangle by $|\det A|$.

EXAMPLE 14.15 We apply the previous theorem to the fern code of Example 14.3, whose attractor $\mathcal{A}$ appears in Figure 14.1. In Section 14.3 we will study the ways in which the transformations w_i relate to the attractor, but here we comment briefly on this aspect.

w_1 Here $w_1(x,y) = (0, 0.16y)$ collapses everything onto the y-axis and reduces it vertically in ratio 0.16. This part contributes the stem.

w_2 $A = \begin{bmatrix} 0.85 & 0.04 \\ -0.04 & 0.85 \end{bmatrix}$ The column vectors have equal length 0.8509, and are perpendicular. Also $\det A > 0$. Thus A gives dilation in ratio 0.85 followed by rotation through $\theta = \tan^{-1}(-0.04/0.85) = -2.7^o$. This contributes the main part of the fern, curving it slightly to the right.

w_3

$A = \begin{bmatrix} 0.2 & -0.26 \\ 0.23 & 0.22 \end{bmatrix}$

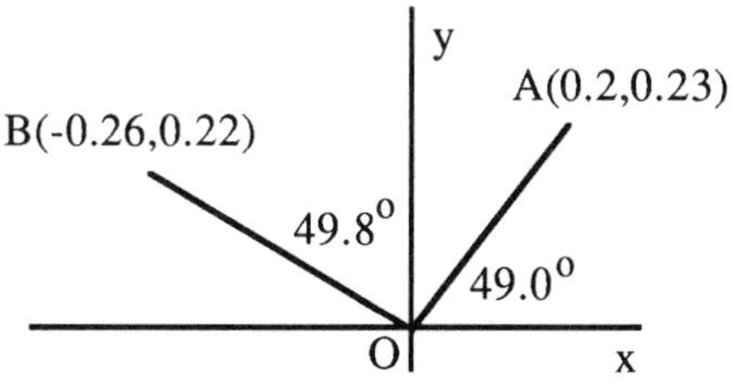

We refer to (14.7) and Figure 14.7. Since angle BOA is 0.8^o more than a right angle, a small amount of shear is present. From $\det A > 0$, we see that no reflection is involved, but rotation through close to 49°. Further, $|OA| = 0.30$, $|OB| = 0.34$, but the small shear corresponding to 0.8^o does not account for this inequality, and therefore we have non-uniform scaling with parameters 0.30, 0.34 (approximately). These conclusions suggest, on our inspecting Figure 14.1, that $w_3(\mathcal{A})$ is the lower left hand leaf of the fern.

w_4

$$A = \begin{bmatrix} -0.15 & 0.28 \\ 0.26 & 0.24 \end{bmatrix}$$

$$\theta_1 = 120^{\circ} \qquad \theta_2 = 50^{\circ}$$

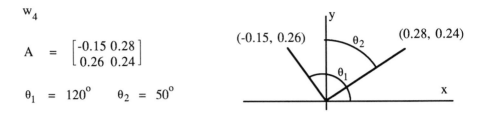

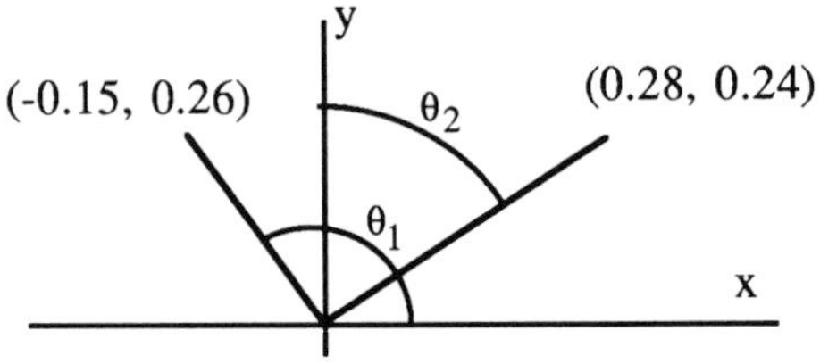

The column vectors are at an angle of about 80°, so some shear is included. The presence of reflection rather than rotation is shown by the opposite senses of θ_1 and θ_2, and is confirmed by $\det A < 0$. This suggests that $w_4(\mathcal{A})$ is the lower right hand leaf in the fern of Figure 14.1.

EXERCISE Given that w_3 and w_4 account for the lower two leaves in Example 14.15, how would you use det A to decide which is which?

14.2.3 Factorising rotations into shears

We recall the extremely potent fact from Part 1, that a plane rotation centred at point P is the product of reflections in two mirror lines through P, and that the direction of one mirror may be chosen arbitrarily. An analogous fact, useful for rotating bit maps, is given in Foley et al (1990). This is essentially that a rotation is the product of two shears. An interesting difference is that, having chosen the first shear direction arbitrarily, we may take the other at right angles. Thus the shear axes may be taken as coordinate axes, giving the matrices the simplest possible form. We shall give a proof of this proposition, since useful geometrical insights emerge thereby.

THEOREM 14.16 A rotation of less than one right angle in either direction is the product of two shears, along perpendicular axes through the rotation centre, followed by a coordinate scaling. The direction of one axis may be chosen arbitrarily. With coordinate axes along the shear axes, the corresponding matrix decomposition is

$$\begin{bmatrix} \cos\theta & -\sin\theta \\ \sin\theta & \cos\theta \end{bmatrix} = \begin{bmatrix} 1/\cos\theta & 0 \\ 0 & \cos\theta \end{bmatrix} \begin{bmatrix} 1 & -\sin\theta\cos\theta \\ 0 & 1 \end{bmatrix} \begin{bmatrix} 1 & 0 \\ \tan\theta & 1 \end{bmatrix}. \qquad (14.13)$$

Proof Notice that, given the explicit matrix decomposition to consider, we can establish the result simply by multiplying the matrices. What we shall do here is to show how the decomposition arises from geometrical considerations. This will indicate how developments of the result may be obtained. Take coordinate axes with origin at the rotation centre, the x-direction being an arbitrary choice. Since an affine transformation is determined by its effect on any parallelogram, we will know that we have the right one if it rotates a unit square with one vertex at the origin, through the appropriate angle θ. A handy dodge allowing the required shears to be along the x, y axes and hence to have simple matrices, is to start with the unit square OABC as in Figure 14.8, pre-rotated backwards by θ. The rotation we seek brings it back into a standard position with two edges along the axes. We perform shears parallel to the axes which together rotate the square through angle θ, turning it into a rectangle, needing only a coordinate scaling in the x and y directions to restore it to a unit square

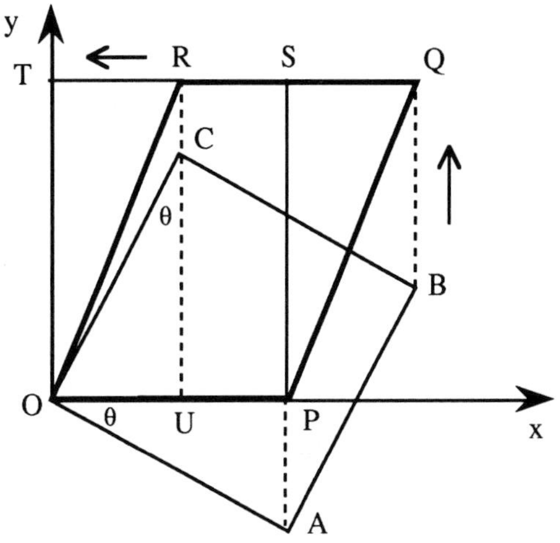

Figure 14.8 Performing a rotation by two shears and a rescaling. The unit square OABC is transformed to parallelogram OPQR by a vertical shear, then to rectangle OPST by a horizontal shear.

STEP 1 Perform a shear with axis Oy, sending A vertically to a point P on the x-axis. Then B, C move vertically to Q, R say, as depicted, and the unit square is transformed to parallelogram OPQR. The parameter is $\alpha = |AP| / |OP| = \tan\theta$. Therefore the shear sends $C(\sin\theta, \cos\theta)$ to R with coordinates

$$\begin{bmatrix} 1 & 0 \\ \tan\theta & 1 \end{bmatrix} \begin{bmatrix} \sin\theta \\ \cos\theta \end{bmatrix} = \begin{bmatrix} \sin\theta \\ \sec\theta \end{bmatrix}.$$

STEP 2 Perform a shear with axis Ox, sending R to a point T on the y-axis. Then OPQR becomes a rectangle OPST, since TOP is a right angle by construction. Now, since this shear sends $R(\sin\theta, \sec\theta)$ to $T(0, \sec\theta)$ the parameter β is such that the equality below holds and so $\sin\theta + \beta \sec\theta = 0$, or $\beta = -\sin\theta \cos\theta$.

$$\begin{bmatrix} 1 & \beta \\ 0 & 1 \end{bmatrix} \begin{bmatrix} \sin\theta \\ \sec\theta \end{bmatrix} = \begin{bmatrix} 0 \\ \sec\theta \end{bmatrix}$$

STEP 3 The coordinate scaling parameters required for converting rectangle OPST to a square of side 1 are $r = 1/|OP| = 1/\cos\theta$ (from triangle OAP), and $s = 1/|OT| = \cos\theta$. Finally, writing out the standard matrix forms for the three transformations we have used, we obtain the decomposition (14.13).

EXERCISE Draw a square in the plane so that a vertical coordinate scaling turns it into a sheared rectangle **or** factorise the rotation about O through 60° into shears and coordinate scaling.

14.3 Finding an IFS for a given image

We first gain insight by building things up, then practice finding the component transformations from given fractal images. The Collage Theorem (14.20) noted by Barnsley is a simple but vital implication of the Fixed Point Theorem which points the way to automating this. Note however that we can often find more than one IFS with the same attractor, especially where there is symmetry. Again the Sierpinski gasket is a useful example. Besides (10.11) the equilateral case has an IFS implied by its initiator-generator construction in Figure 10.7. By uniqueness of the *attractor*, the latter IFS must give Sierpinski whether we start with a line segment or other compact set. A nice exercise is to find either a third IFS for Sierpinski or to find a second one for the Cantor set. Remember $W(\mathcal{C}) = \mathcal{C}$ defines the result uniquely.

14.3.1 Condensation

Here is an important tool in the drive to produce the scenes we want. Suppose that in storing information from which an image is to be reproduced we are prepared to include a small subimage C, defined say by a bit pattern. This subimage might represent a tree trunk which we want to come out just that way in a fractal tree. In the technique of condensation, shortly defined, C is 'reset' at each stage of the iteration and so is part of the final image.

DEFINITION 14.17 Let C be a compact figure in the plane. Then $w_0: \mathcal{H}(\mathbf{R}^2) \to \mathcal{H}(\mathbf{R}^2)$, given by $w_0(E) = C$ for any set E, is called a *condensation transformation with condensation set C*. The idea is that w_0 'condenses' every set into just one, namely C. Notice that w_0 is actually a contraction mapping, not of $\mathbf{R}^2$ but of $\mathcal{H}(\mathbf{R}^2)$, with ratio 0. This is because $d(w_0(A),w_0(B)) = d(C,C) = 0$ for every A,B in $\mathcal{H}(\mathbf{R}^2)$. Thus there must be a unique fixed point (= set) and this is trivially C since $w_0(C) = C$ (every other set is changed by w_0). Adding w_0 to an IFS we obtain an IFS *with condensation* $\{w_0, w_1, .. , w_N\}$, where $W(E) = w_0(E) \cup w_1(E) \cup ... \cup w_N(E)$ is our map for iteration, a contraction map with ratio $\max(0,r_1, .. , r_N)$. Of course this equals $\max(r_1, .. , r_N)$. Thus $C = w_0(C)$ is a part of each iterate $W^n(E_0)$. Unless otherwise stated, $E_0 = C$ will be the starting set.

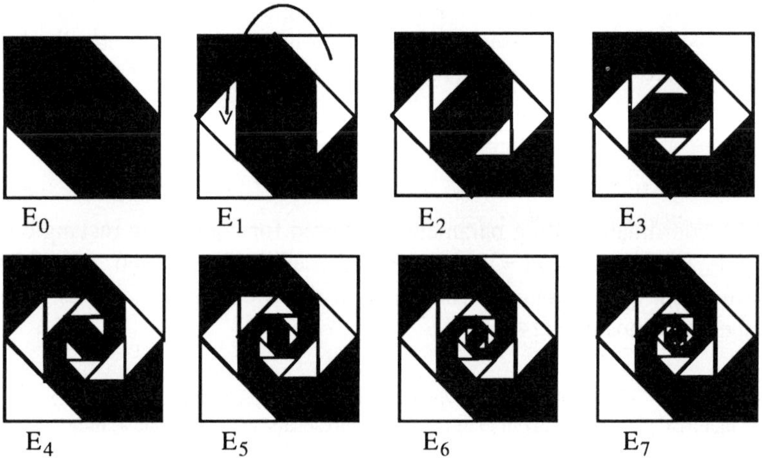

Figure 14.9 Successive iterations E_i on a black background, from IFS $\{w_0, w_1)$ with condensation set C, the union of two white triangles. w_1 is a scaling with ratio $1/\sqrt{2}$ followed by rotation through angle $3\pi/4$. See Example 14.18.

*EX*AMPLE 14.18 (1) (Figure 14.9) We describe how an IFS {w0,w1} has attractor approximately E_7 of Figure 14.9, shown as white on a black background. The starting and condensation set $E_0 = C$ consists of two white triangles at opposite corners of a unit square centred at the origin. The map w_1 is scaling by factor $1/\sqrt{2}$ followed by rotation of $3\pi/4$ about the origin. Thus $w_1(E_0)$ consists of the smaller pair of white triangles shown in E_1, their origin via w_1 suggested by the arrow, whilst $w_0(E_0) = C =$ two white triangles. Altogether $E_1 = W(E_0)$ consists of two pairs of triangles. To get E_2 we start as before with the large pair of triangles $w_0(E_1) = C$, then add in a scaled rotated copy of E_1, namely two more pairs of triangles. By E_3 the original triangles of E_0 have been rotated and scaled three times and are the smallest of the four pairs. In summary

$$
\begin{aligned}
E_0 &= C = \text{two white triangles}\\
E_1 &= C \cup (\text{two white triangles scaled and rotated by } w_1)\\
E_2 &= C \cup (\text{four white triangles scaled and rotated by } w_1)\\
E_3 &= C \cup (\text{six white triangles scaled and rotated by } w_1), \text{ and so on.}
\end{aligned}
$$

(2) In Figure 14.10 we build a tree using a condensation set to preserve the tree trunk $C = E_0$, of height 1 unit, using the IFS with condensation (w_0, w_1, w_2) where, with $c = \cos30°$, $s = \sin30°$,

$$w_1\begin{bmatrix}x\\y\end{bmatrix} = (3/4)\begin{bmatrix}c & -s\\ s & c\end{bmatrix}\begin{bmatrix}x\\y\end{bmatrix} + \begin{bmatrix}0\\1\end{bmatrix}, \qquad w_2\begin{bmatrix}x\\y\end{bmatrix} = (3/4)\begin{bmatrix}c & s\\ -s & c\end{bmatrix}\begin{bmatrix}x\\y\end{bmatrix} + \begin{bmatrix}0\\1\end{bmatrix}.$$

In $E_1 = w_0(E_0) \cup w_1(E_0) \cup w_2(E_0)$, w_1 places on top of the trunk a 3/4 size version of itself, related 30° anticlockwise, and w_2 does the same in a clockwise direction. In forming E_2, we again start with the trunk, but now add to it scaled rotated versions of E_1. The reader is invited to follow the formation of E_3 and E_4 as depicted below.

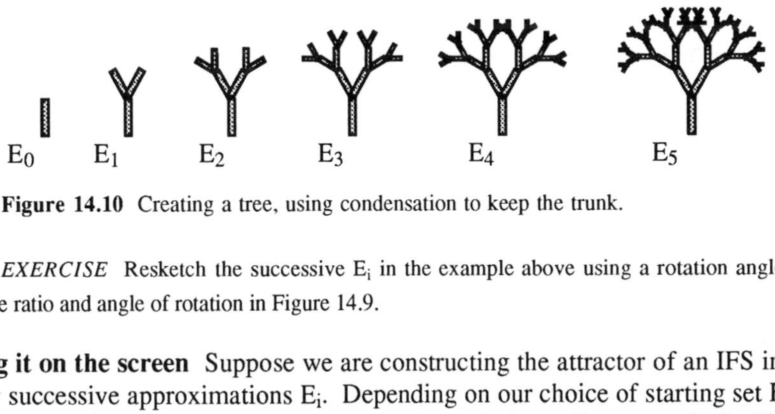

Figure 14.10 Creating a tree, using condensation to keep the trunk.

EXERCISE Resketch the successive E_i in the example above using a rotation angle of 45° **or** verify the ratio and angle of rotation in Figure 14.9.

Getting it on the screen Suppose we are constructing the attractor of an IFS in the usual way by successive approximations E_i. Depending on our choice of starting set E_0 we may find parts of E_1, E_2, .. lying ouside the drawing window. For example in Figure 14.1, constructing the fern, the black square showed a marked tendency to overshoot the frame. That this could be rectified by experimentation is a consequence of the result that

in an IFS $\{\mathbf{R}^n; w_{1\text{-}N}\}$ we may replace $\mathbf{R}^n$ by a bounded and closed (=compact) subset K containing any chosen set E_0. (14.14)

Let us call the starting set E, dropping the usual zero subscript, and let F denote an arbitrary member set of $\mathcal{H}(\mathbf{R}^n)$. As usual, let, $W(F) = w_1(F) \cup w_2(F) \cup .. \cup w_N(F)$. We form a new IFS $\{\mathbf{R}^n; w_0, w_1, w_2, \ldots, w_N\}$, where w_0 has condensation set E, and we write $W_1(F) = w_0(F) \cup W(F)$. Noting that $w_0(F) = E$ and that $f(A \cup B) = f(A) \cup f(B)$ for any function on sets A, B, we have

$$W_1(E) = w_0(E) \cup W(E) = E \cup W(E),$$
$$W_1^2(E) = w_0(E \cup W(E)) \cup W(E \cup W(E)) = E \cup W(E) \cup W^2(E),$$
$$\cdots\cdots\cdots\cdots$$
$$W_1^k(E) = E \cup W(E) \cup \ldots \cup W^k(E).$$

By Theorem 13.28 the sequence $\{W_1^k(E)\}$ has limit a compact nonempty subset K, as $k \to \infty$. On the other hand, K is the infinite union $E \cup W(E) \cup W^2(E) \cup \ldots$, which is the set of all points x in $\mathbf{R}^n$ for which $x \in W^k(E)$ for some $k \geq 0$, and so is mapped to itself by the w_i. For if $x \in K$ then $x \in W^m(E)$ for some integer m, and so $w_i(x) \in W^{m+1}(E)$ which is a subset of K. By construction, E lies within K, and we have proved the existence of a set K with the desired properties.

Thus suitably enlarging the area in which we construct E_0, E_1.. will guarantee success. However the size of our screen/frame may be fixed, so what this amounts to is a change of scale and perhaps a change of origin to lessen the need for scaling. To reduce the image in the ratio λ we multiply the translation parts e,f by λ and leave a,b,c,d alone. With new origin $\mathbf{a}$, $w(\mathbf{x}) = A\mathbf{x}+\mathbf{t}$ becomes $w(\mathbf{x}) = A\mathbf{x} + (A-I)\mathbf{a} + \mathbf{t}$. Alternatively we move the origin of screen coordinates. In practice a suitable K may best be found by experimentation, perhaps starting with the first few steps of the constuction. In many cases a suitable K is easy to see.

The Cantor set is constructed with K and E equal to the unit interval; for the Sierpinski gasket we may use a solid triangle as both K, E. It is natural in such situations to regard K as the space on which the affine transformations w_i act, writing for example $\{[0,1]; w_1, w_2\}$ as the IFS in the Cantor case. More generally we may write $\{K; w_{1\text{-}N}\}$ or $\{X: w_{1\text{-}N}\}$, where K, X are compact subsets of $\mathbf{R}^n$.

14.3.2 From attractor to IFS - first steps

In the previous section we exemplified starting with an IFS and determining its attractor by successive approximations $E_n = W^n(E_0)$. Now we take the reverse direction. We start with a set $\mathcal{A}$ and find an IFS whose attractor is this set. This is done by using the invariant aspect of $\mathcal{A}$ (Theorem 13.28, Definition 14.2), that if

$$\mathcal{A} = w_1(\mathcal{A}) \cup w_2(\mathcal{A}) \cup \ldots \cup w_N(\mathcal{A}) \quad (= W(\mathcal{A})),$$

then $\mathcal{A}$ is the attractor of the IFS $\{w_{1\text{-}N}\}$. The condition is in other words that $\mathcal{A}$ can be expressed as a union ('collage') of transformed copies $w_i(\mathcal{A})$ of itself, where w_i is of affine or condensation type. (We usually label a condensation map as w_0. There is no need for more than one such.) In this section we keep to N = 2.

EXAMPLE 14.19 Given the hint that each of the images in Figure 14.11 is the attractor of an IFS with just two maps, we deduce what those maps could be.
First observation: both appear to be formed from repetitions of a motif, which diminish in size and spiral towards a centre O.
Second observation: each such image is about nine tenths the size of its predecessor.
Third observation: the ninth repetition is 180 degrees round from the starter. Thus it is likely that these repetitions are the images of the starter under successive applications of $w_2(\mathbf{x}) = 9/10\ R_O(\pi/9)(\mathbf{x})$.

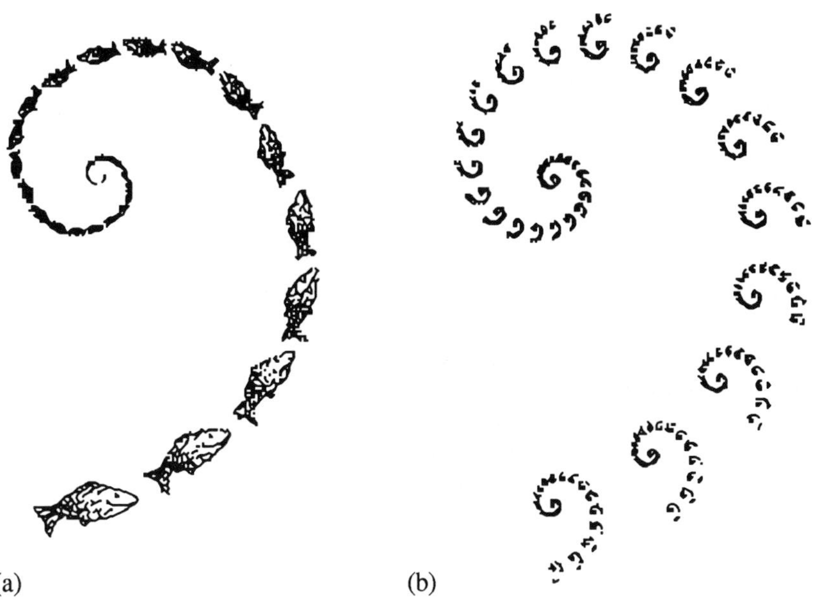

(a) (b)

Figure 14.11 Condensation vs its absence. Which of (a), (b) uses it?

Assuming the third observation is accurate, each of (a) and (b) may be viewed as a 9/10 sized rotated copy of itself, $w_1(\mathcal{A})$, together with its bottom motif. In case(a) this motif is a fish, which we see cannot be made from an affine transformation of the whole. Therefore it must be put in place by a condensation map w_0, with $w_0(A)$ = fish. In Case (b) the bottom motif *is* a scaled down copy of the whole. We measure the scaling factor as 1/5. With the centre as origin, the scaling must be followed by a downwards translation of about two inches for correct positioning, which is accomplished by a map $w_2(\mathbf{x}) = \mathbf{x}/5 + (0,-2)$. Now we have our conclusion.

Case (a): $\mathcal{A} = w_0(\mathcal{A}) \cup w_1(\mathcal{A})$, so $\mathcal{A}$ is the attractor of $\{w_0,w_1\}$,
Case (b): $\mathcal{A} = w_1(\mathcal{A}) \cup w_2(\mathcal{A})$, so $\mathcal{A}$ is the attractor of $\{w_1,w_2\}$.

But suppose we had been only roughly right? This important question is dealt with in Section 14.3.4. Meanwhile in the examples to follow we will often need to identify an affine map by its visible geometrical effect. It is helpful to recall that such a map is determined by its action on any three points not in a straight line or, in the case of an isometry, by any two points and whether it is direct or indirect. A direct isometry fixing some point is a rotation and an indirect is a reflection. For further recapitulation see Section 1.3.2, Theorem 14.4 and Theorem 14.10. A simple but useful rule is

to identify an affine transformation, follow its action on the most distinctive and/or large feature to be seen. (14.15)

EXERCISE What does Figure 14.11 become if the rotation is replaced by a horizontal translation (try a telegraph pole as starting set).

EXAMPLE 14.20 Now we see some other kinds of attractor that can be obtained from an IFS with just two maps. The purpose is that the reader may gain insight by first forming an opinion, firm or provisional, as to what maps will produce an attractor, then reading the relevant text. Try Figure 14.12(a) on the right before reading on. Its a good habit to look for a way to apply (14.15) every time.

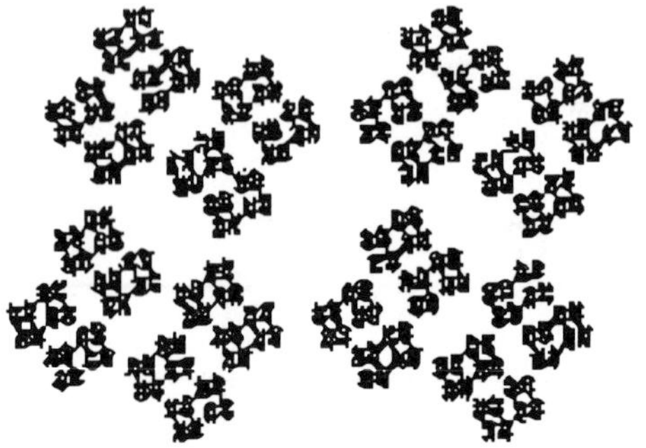

Figure 14.12(a)

(1) In Figure 14.12(a) the image may seem at first glance to require an IFS of four maps, but it may also be seen as consisting of a left and right half, congruent by a horizontal translation $T_{\mathbf{a}}$ (e.g. $T_{\mathbf{a}}$ maps the left half to the right). As measurement shows, the left half is a 70% sized copy of the whole, rotated by just under 80°. Thus we may write $w_1(\mathbf{x}) = (7/10)R_O(80\pi/180)(\mathbf{x}) + \mathbf{t}$, $w_2(\mathbf{x}) = w_1(\mathbf{x}) + \mathbf{a}$, where $\mathbf{t}$ is some translation depending on the position of the origin O.

(2) *(First consider Figure 14.12(b).)* Like its predecessor Figure 14.12(b) consists recognisably of a left and a right half congruent by a horizontal translation. There is a small optical illusion: each half appears to be a different shape from the whole, rather elongated. This impression is corrected when we rotate the page by some 70° clockwise. The reduction is a uniform 70%, with a rotation of 45°. Note the spiral effect whose beginning is represented by A → B → C → D, a consequence of the angular increment (can you see how it arises?). Since an affine transformation is defined by its effect on three non-collinear points, the A to D sequence is one way to find the code of w_1, using formula (14.9).

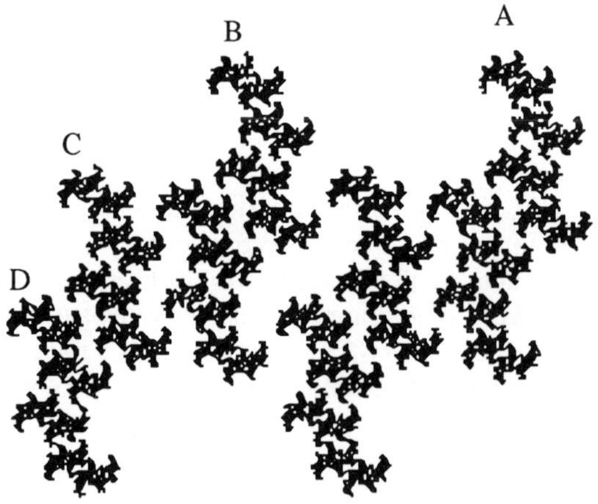

Figure 14.12(b)

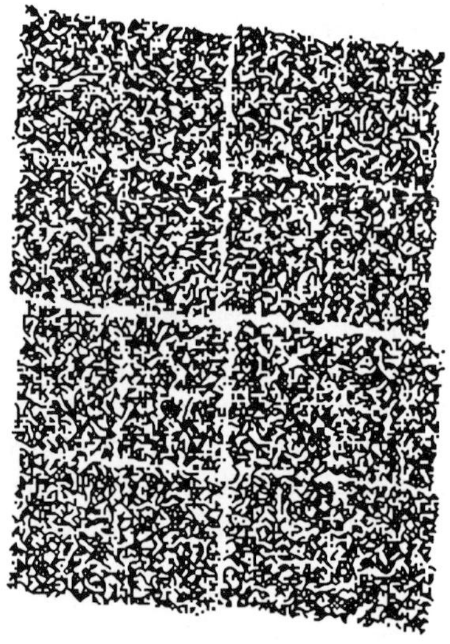

Figure 14.12(c)

(3) Figure 14.12(c) consists of a top and a bottom half. Each is approximately the whole scaled down in the ratio 7/10 and turned through a right angle; but not quite. Although the

halves are in line vertically, the overall slope of the upper boundary, for example, shows that a small amount of shear is present.

EXERCISE Use formula (14.9) to find the codes for Figure 14.12(c). By applying it to a rectangle, express w_1 as a product of rotation, non-uniform scaling, and shear in the x-direction.

14.3.3 Recognising 3-transformation cases

To get a start in identifying when a set A is the attractor of an IFS $\{w_1,w_2,w_3\}$ and finding the codes we impose restrictions on the maps which nevertheless allow some 30 to 40 attractors reasonably regarded as distinct. We refer to Figure 14.13, in which the large perimeter square has side 2 units. We take advantage of having enumerated all isometries sending a square onto itself (the dihedral group, Section 2.4). For a square of side 1, centre Q, these are $S_0, S_1, .., S_7$ where for $i = 0,1,2,3$ S_i is rotation of $i\pi/2$ about Q and for $i = 4,5,6,7$ it is reflection in QP_i (thus S_0 is the identity). The diagram below right recalls this notation. Each w_k maps the large square onto the small one labelled k, as follows.

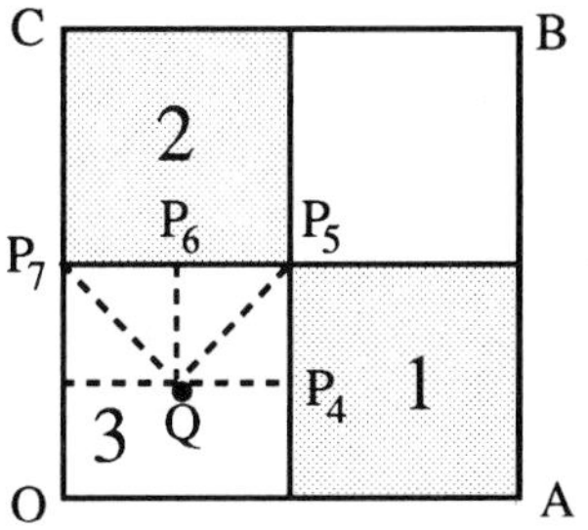

Figure 14.13

w_1 : scales large square down to square 3 ($\mathbf{x} \to \mathbf{x}/2$),
sends square 3 to itself by some S_i (8 choices),
translates square 3 to square 1 (the map $T_{(1,0)}$).

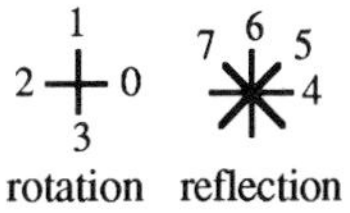

w_2 is similar but translates square 3 to square 2, whilst w_3 is simply the first line. The case in which w_1 uses S_i and w_2 uses S_j will be labelled Case ij. Thus Case 00 is a Sierpinski gasket. Codes are given in Table 14.5. Note that $R_O(3\pi/2) = R_O(-\pi/2)$.

EXAMPLE 14.21 Figure 14.14 shows four attractors, in each of whose IFS $\{w_1,w_2,w_3\}$ only one map uses reflection or rotation. The reader is invited to identify the maps used, then read the text following.

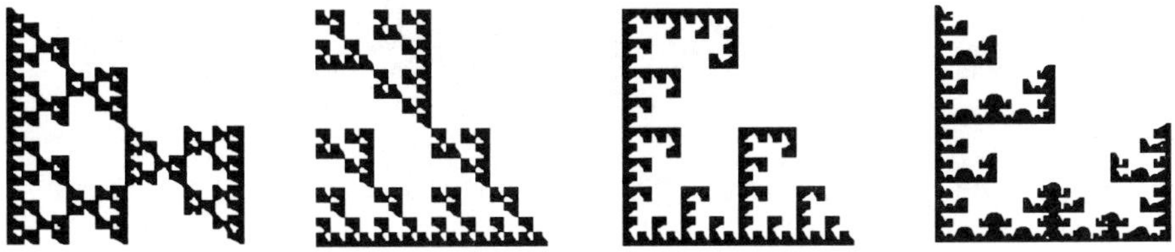

(a) (b) (c) (d)

Figure 14.14 Four attractors with IFS of form $\{w_1,w_2,w_3\}$.

We know in advance that the attractor is made up of three transformed copies of itself, lying in squares 1 to 3. Part 3 (i.e. the portion of the attractor lying in square 3) is only scaled, and we must compare the other two with this. One will be different. Looking at Case (a) we see that part 2 is the same, whilst part 1 is a 180 degree rotated copy. Thus the transformation we are looking for is a 1/2 turn S_2, and $w_1 = T_{(1,0)}R_Q(\pi)w_3$.

(a)	w_1 uses a 1/2 turn	Case 20,
(b)	w_2 uses reflection in QP_7	Case 07,
(c)	w_2 uses $3\pi/2$ rotation	Case 03,
(d)	w_1 uses reflection in QP_6	Case 60.

EXAMPLE 14.22 In Figure 14.15 we give some cases in which both w_1 and w_2 may involve a reflection or rotation. The reader is urged to take a little time spotting the nature of these maps before checking the answer in the text which follows.

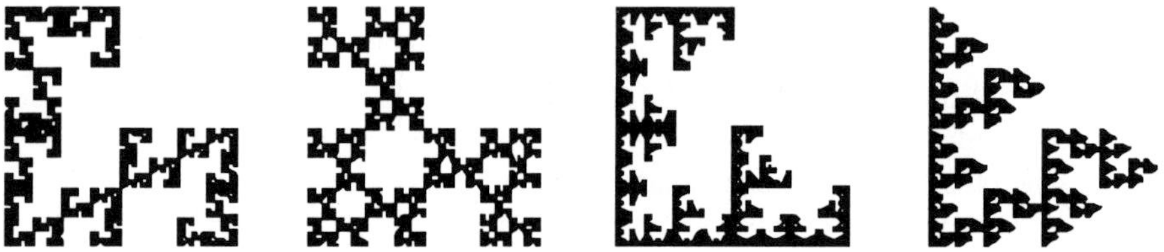

(a) (b) (c) (d)

Figure 14.15 Four more attractors with IFS of form $\{w_1,w_2,w_3\}$.

We give the solutions in the form of four Case numbers run together in order (a) to (d): 23275440. The codes may be determined from Table 14.5.

EXAMPLE 14.23 Now we allow any or all of our maps to involve more than scaling /translation. It is interesting to see the effect of allowing w_3 in particular to be more general. Can you identify the maps used in the IFS of each attractor shown in Figure 14.16? Can you explain the similarities in overall structure in terms of these maps. The answer is given in an extension of the previous notation to triples ijk identifying w_1,w_2,w_3 respectively, where the triples are run into each other in order corresponding to (a), (b), (c), (d): 012032112123.

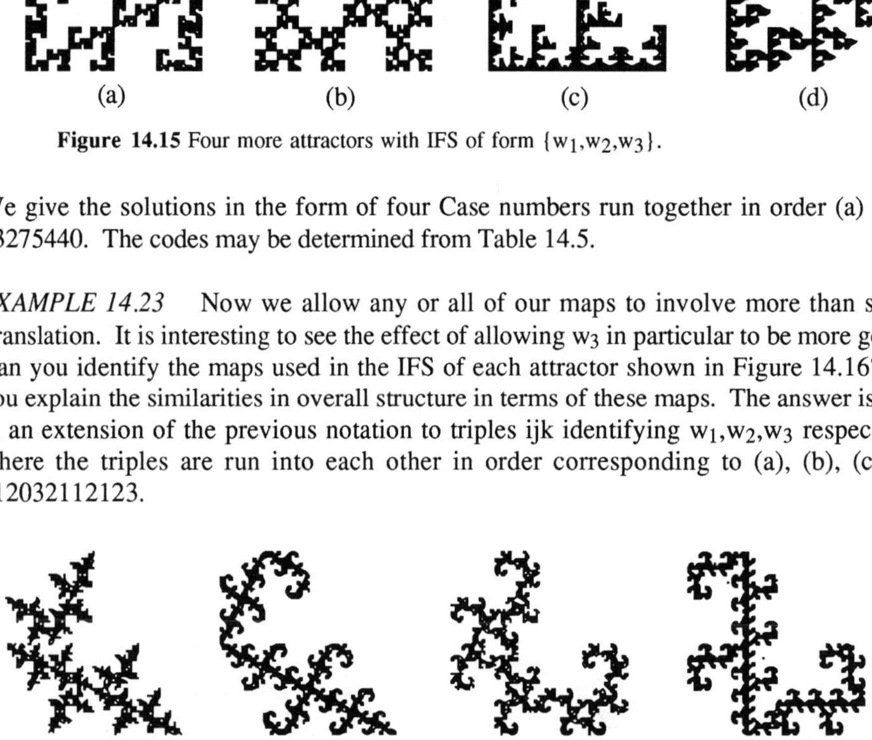

(a) (b) (c) (d)

Figure 14.16 Four attractors with IFS $\{w_1,w_2,w_3\}$ in which two or all of the maps involve rotation.

EXAMPLE 14.24 (Computing Table 14.5.) Here is a sample of how a code may be calculated in this series of examples. Suppose we have Case 41 with $w_2 = T_{(0,1)}S_1w_3$. Recalling that an affine transformation is uniquely determined by its action on a square we may recompose w_2 as the following sequence, in which rotation is performed about the origin O instead of about Q (see Figure 14.13 and the diagram below): $w_2 = T_{(1,1)}R_O(\pi)w_3$. This gives part of line 2 in Table 14.5.

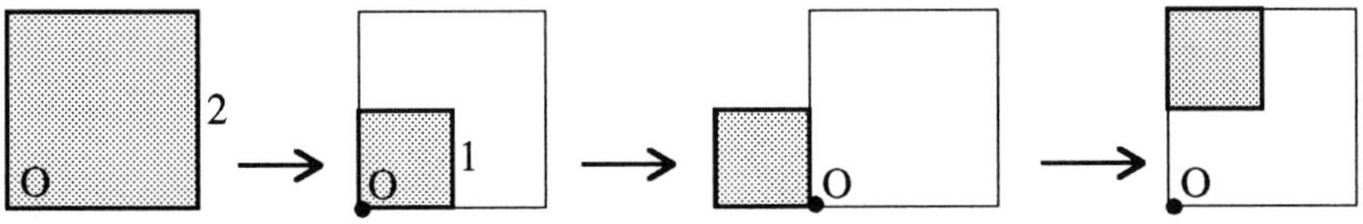

TABLE 14.5 (1) Codes for w_1, w_2 in Examples 14.21 to 14.23 (a,b,c,d are the same for w_1, w_2) with origin moved from Q to O. (2) (bracketed) coefficients for x-axis along CB, y-axis down along CO, screen height 2units. NB: scaling changes e,f only.

	Rotation	Matrix entries x 2				w_1 translations		w_2 translations	
i	/reflection	2a	2b	2c	2d	e	f	e	f
0	identity	1	0	0	1	1 (1)	0 (1)	0 (0)	1 (0)
1	$R_o(\pi/2)$	0	-1 (1)	1 (-1)	0	2 (1)	0 (2)	1 (0)	1 (1)
2	$R_o(\pi)$	-1	0	0	-1	2 (2)	1 (2)	1 (1)	2 (1)
3	$R_o(-\pi/2)$	0	1 (-1)	-1 (1)	0	1 (2)	1 (1)	0 (1)	2 (0)
4	$R_{y=0}$	1	0	0	-1	1 (1)	1 (2)	0 (0)	2 (1)
5	$R_{y=x}$	0	1 (-1)	1 (-1)	0	1 (2)	0 (2)	0 (1)	1 (1)
6	$R_{x=0}$	-1	0	0	1	2 (2)	0 (1)	1 (1)	1 (0)
7	$R_{y=-x}$	0	-1 (1)	-1 (1)	0	2 (1)	1 (1)	1 (0)	2 (0)

EXERCISE Recompose $w_1 = T_{(1,0)}S_4w_3$ by the method of Example 14.24 (Table 14.5).

EXERCISE From Table 14.5 infer the IFS code for Case 27 (answer in Table 14.6).

EXERCISE Independently calculate line 3 of Table 14.5.

EXAMPLE 14.25 (More general atractors with N = 3.) The two examples of Figure 14.17 below, in a slightly different format from before, are still reasonably easy to analyse for finding an IFS. In (a) we need to see how the anvil is made up of three small anvils. In (b) the Sierpinski arrow tile is made of an attractor and its mirror image.

(a)

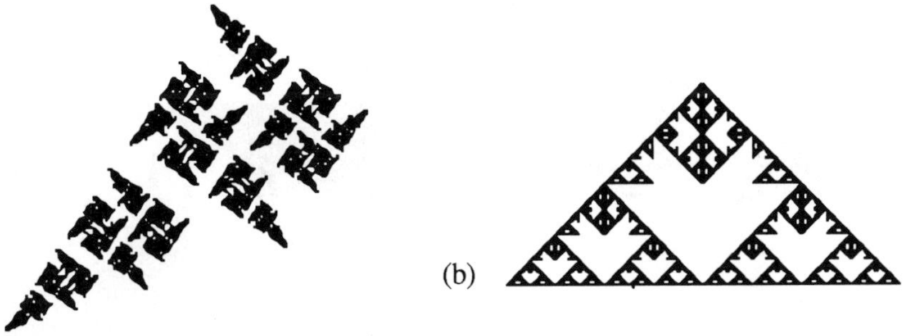

(b)

Figure 14.17 (a) the anvil, (b) a Sierpinski arrow tile.

TABLE 14.6
IFS code for Case 27
with y-axis down,80 pixels
per unit, and screen height
160 pixels (divide a,b,c,d by 100).

	a	b	c	d	e	f
w_1	-50	0	0	-50	160	160
w_2	0	50	50	0	0	0
w_3	50	0	0	50	0	80

EXAMPLE 14.26 (N = 3 with condensation.) Except for the condensation map the attractor shown in Figure 14.18 has an IFS identical to an earlier case in this chapter. Can you see the other attractor?

Figure 14.18 Tree of baseball players.

EXAMPLE 14.27 (some subleties with N = 3.) (1) Look briefly at Figure 14.19(a) , the snowflake, and try to give an IFS to produce this attractor. A natural first thought is to obtain this as three purely translated 1/2 sized copies of itself. Yet this, we already know gives a Sierpinski gasket (see (10.11)) and so cannot be correct here. We have met a subtlety that sometimes arises, and a potential explanation for the occasional baffling mystery (it may play this role in some later 'unseen' examples). Closer inspection reveals that the proposed 1/2 sized copies are not correctly oriented, but must be given a half turn.

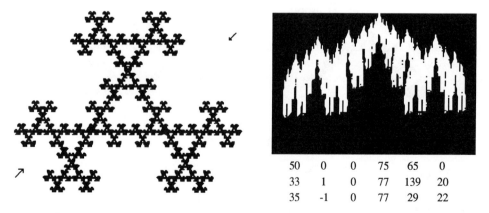

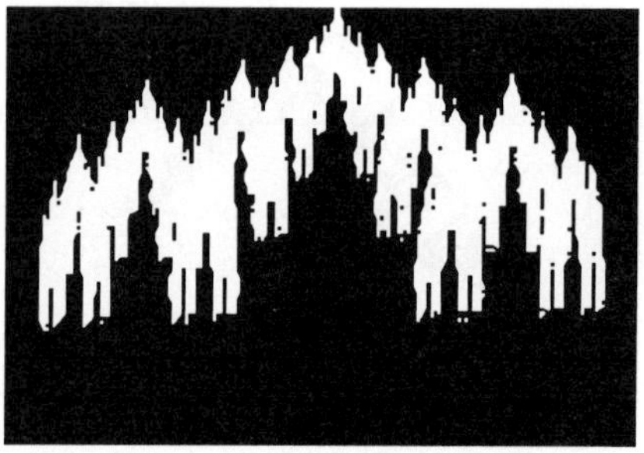

50	0	0	75	65	0
33	1	0	77	139	20
35	-1	0	77	29	22

Figure 14.19 (a) The snowflake, (b) people (white on black), Moscow by night (black on white). Codes for (b) are shown in the usual format.

Two arrows by the figure draw attention to the relevant features. Any doubts may be erased by manipulating an actual reduction on top of the page. Notice that an ambiguity is also exemplified in the representation of a set of maps by their effects on a standard rectangle, for the rectangle images here, shown on the right look identical to those in the Sierpinski case.

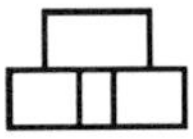

(2) Figure 14.19(b) was obtained by experimentation. In its original white on black form this represented a small crowd. But when we regard black as the foreground colour, something quite different emerges (to switch to seeing this is the 'gestalt' experience). Try to see how the three maps given by their codes relate to the outcome.

14.3.4 Growing trees and other objects

In earlier sections we sought insight into what kinds of attractor could be obtained from an iterated function system of up to three maps. The reader was invited to study the attractor and discover in what way it could be seen as a collage of transformed copies of itself. Now we open up the field. Presented with an arbitrary image, what are our chances of representing it as the attractor of an IFS? At one extreme, if we may use as many maps as we have screen pixels, we simply scale down the given image to a dot then translate the dot to each pixel position occupied by the original image. Each map consists of scaling followed by translation. But then the idea of an IFS has not helped; it would be more economical of memory space to store the address of each pixel to be lit.

Suppose on the other hand that we can tolerate some discrepancy between the given image, which we will call F, and the attractor $\mathcal{A}$ we will produce from our IFS. The issue becomes: can we represent F acceptably closely as the attractor of an IFS which is small enough to be worthwhile in terms of storage economy and/or other benefits? Benefits could include reproducing the image fast, at different sizes and resolutions, and with methods of grey or colour shading (see Section 15.3). Some successively less demanding criteria for $\mathcal{A}$ being close enough to F are:

to the human eye, F and $\mathcal{A}$ look identical, (14.16)

$\mathcal{A}$ is acceptable as a copy of F because it differs in sufficiently small details, (14.17)

though not satisfactory as a reproduction of the original, $\mathcal{A}$ is similar enough for its intended use. (14.18)

An example of (3) is that F is a tree (cloud, flower, ..) and we only need $\mathcal{A}$ to look like the same kind of tree. One application at this level could be flight simulation over a forest. Again, F may be simply a stepping off point to find something interesting or attractive of roughly the same ilk. So how do we set about it? We

lay reduced, possibly reshaped, copies of F over itself, aiming to express F as exactly their union, or 'collage'. (14.19)

Each copy is to be the image $w_i(F)$ ($i = 1, .., N$) of a contractive affine transformation of F, and when we succeed we have $F = w_1(F) \cup .. \cup w_N(F)$ $(= W(F))$ which, we recall, guarantees that $F = \mathcal{A}$, the attractor of $\{w_{1-N}\}$. But given that, apart from enormous luck, F does not equal W(F), what then? Can a small error result in a hopeless discrepancy between F and $\mathcal{A}$ (remember, $W^n(F) \to \mathcal{A}$ whatever F is). The fact is that the IFS method can be made to work because the answer is essentially NO, by the error bound (13.10) in the Fixed Point Theorem. Translated to the present context this result says that if we have expressed F as the required collage within reasonable accuracy, say $d(F, W(F)) \le \varepsilon$, then $\mathcal{A}$ is reasonably close to F in the sense that $d(F, \mathcal{A}) \le \varepsilon/(1-r)$, where r is the ratio of W. This conclusion is called the Collage Theorem in Barnsley(1988). We state a result formally.

THEOREM 14.28 Let F be in $\mathcal{H}(\mathbf{R}^2)$ and let $\{w_{1-N}\}$ be an IFS with ratio $r < 1$ and attractor $\mathcal{A}$. Write as usual $W(F) = w_1(F) \cup .. \cup w_N(F)$, and let $\varepsilon > 0$ be given.

$$\text{If } F = W(F) \text{ then } F = \mathcal{A};$$
$$\text{if } d(F, W(F)) \le \varepsilon \text{ then } d(F, \mathcal{A}) \le \varepsilon/(1-r). \tag{14.20}$$

Proof The first conlusion has already appeared as Theorem 13.28 and is restated here to provide contrast and context. For the second we consider the complete metric space $S = \mathcal{H}(\mathbf{R}^2)$ (Theorem 13.27). We have a contractive mapping T = W on S, with ratio r, fixed point $e = \mathcal{A}$, initial point $x_0 = F$ and by definition $x_{n+1} = T(x_n)$. We invoke the bound (13.10) of the Fixed Point Theorem in case n = 0, obtaining $d(x_0,e) \le d(x_0,x_1)/(1 - r)$, or here $d(F,\mathcal{A}) \le d(F,W(F))/(1 - r) \le \varepsilon/(1 - r)$.

EXAMPLE 14.29 (Making the collage.) How far can we improve on making up an image from dots, for the sketched face of Figure 14.20(a)? It is roughly the case that

(1) each feature, nose mouth or eye, is a non-uniformly scaled copy of the whole,
(2) the perimeter consists of 8 straight line segments.

(a) Original face F (b) F as a 12-piece collage (c) Attractor $\mathcal{A}$ of the IFS defined by the collage

Figure 14.20 Finding an IFS with attractor close to the starting image.

We frame the face by an invisible rectangle with vertical and horizontal sides just touching it. Now each of the 12 maps required is specified by its effect on this frame, and its coefficients a-f calculated by (14.9) (see Table 14.8 on page 360). For the line segments we observe that a horizontal contraction sending the frame onto a rectangle of width say 2 pixels maps the face into a vertical line segment. This is scaled, rotated and placed into each required position in turn. However we do not need to carry out the process of composing maps because an affine transformation is determined by the final images of any three vertices of the frame (Theorem 14.10). These are what we record, making the 2-pixel width extend vertically or horizontally as is most suitable for segment direction. For each feature we map the frame into a rectangle or more general parallelogram as fits best.

The resulting collage is shown in Figure 14.20(b). Notice that the features are not simply rectangles, for the reason that the face itself is not. Also, the original features, taken together, are mapped into a sort of filling of each feature in (b), slightly different in each case. This is appropriate for the eyes in the figure (cf. (14.17)). It arguably improves on the original bare nose and mouth (cf. (14.18)). We now combine the 12 maps from the collage into an IFS and obtain the attractor by successive iteration, $W^n(F) \to \mathcal{A}$. This is of course Figure 14.20(c) and happily does have a fair degree of resemblance to the collage and similarly to F itself.

Numerical limits The bound (14.20) limits the discrepancy between (a) and (c) of Figure 14.20 to a multiple 1/(1-r) of that between (a) and (b). Here r is the ratio of W, which is the maximum ratio of any collage map. This occurs when there is the least reduction in size: r = (greatest length of a line segment)/(height of frame) = 3/5. The distance (13.7) between (a) and (b) is by definition the greatest distance of any point in (a) from (b) or point in (b) from (a), where the distance of a point x from a set A equals min d(x,a) ($a \in A$). By inspection this is about 1.5mm and so the distance from original face (a) to attractor (c) cannot exceed (1.5)/(1 - 3/5), or 3.75mm. With such a discrepancy the attractor could be hopelesly distorted as a copy of F, but this laxity is not surprising because the overall ratio r we use in the bound is a worst case scenario. Most of the 12 ratios are below half of our 3/5 and four of them well below that. However this does bring out the idea that for best results we should map the frame to smaller rectangles in such a way as to minimise the ratio in each case. Here for example we would always use the longer side of the frame in making line segments.

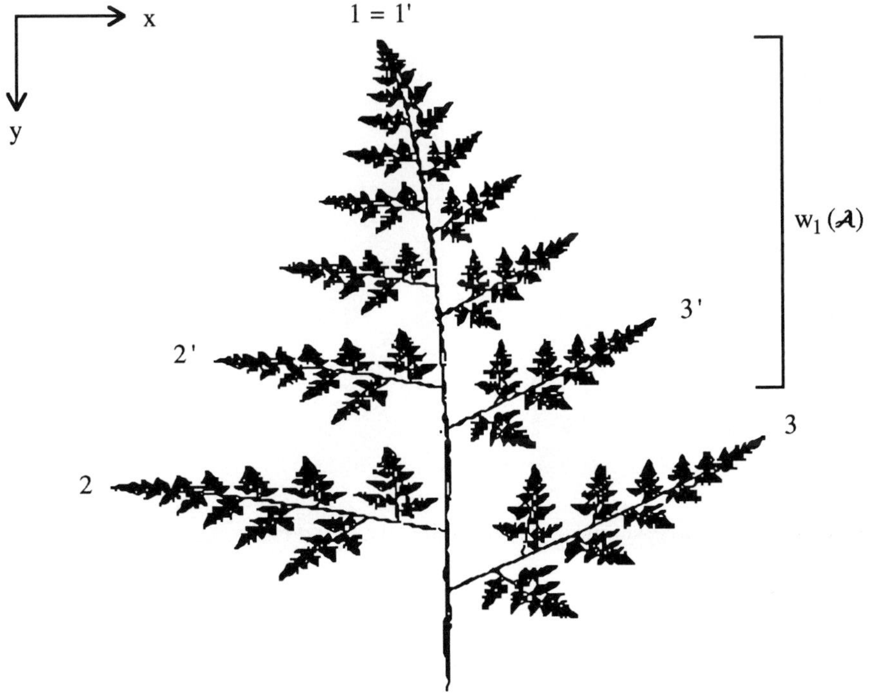

Figure 14.21 Fern represented as a collage $w_1(\mathcal{A}) \cup w_2(\mathcal{A}) \cup w_3(\mathcal{A}) \cup w_4(\mathcal{A})$, with contributions w_1: the main body from the top down, excluding the lower two leaves; w_2: the lower left leaf; w_3: the lower right leaf; w_4: the stem downwards from just above the junction with lower right leaf. The code is given in Table 14.7

EXAMPLE 14.30 Prime examples of (14.22) are many trees and treelike structures such as leaves and ferns. Figure 14.21 shows (let us suppose) a digitised impression of a natural fern, which we wish to obtain as attractor $\mathcal{A}$ of an iterated function system. As is usually the case with such objects, we can represent a major part by a single transformed copy $w_1(\mathcal{A})$, with only a modest size reduction. Here it seems likely that w_1 should fix 1 = 1' and map points 2 to 2' and 3 to 3' as indicated. Then we may determine w_1 uniquely from (14.9). In fact the lower left and right leaves are transformed copies $w_2(\mathcal{A})$, $w_3(\mathcal{A})$, and the part of the stem to which they connect is $w_4(\mathcal{A})$, with codes as in Table 14.7. (For a hint concerning the leaves, see Figure 14.22.) These numbers are calculated for a computer screen with y-axis pointing downwards. Thus with the axes of Figure 14.21 the reader should obtain the same numbers, within a margin of error, except for the translation parts e,f, which depend on the scale and particular positioning of the figure. In this case the the collage is thus $\mathcal{A} = w_1(\mathcal{A}) \cup w_2(\mathcal{A}) \cup w_3(\mathcal{A}) \cup w_4(\mathcal{A})$.

EXERCISE Determine the affine transformations w_2, w_3, w_4 of Figure 14.21 (answers are in Table 14.7).

EXAMPLE 14.31 Having obtained the 'global' transformation w_1 that works for Figure 14.21, we may experiment by varying the shape of the leaves $w_2(\mathcal{A})$, $w_3(\mathcal{A})$, resulting in the quite different looking images (attractors) of Figure 14.22, yet still having the gentle curve upward and to the left.

Figure 14.22 Two derivatives of Figure 14.21, with w_1 identical, and variations on w_2, w_3 (the stem is excluded here). In the second we may identify w_3 by its mapping points 1, 2, 1' to 1', 2', 1" respectively.

EXERCISE Find iterated function systems to produce the attractors of Figure 14.22 by taking suitable coordinates and applying (14.9).

EXAMPLE 14.32 In Figure 14.23(a) we show a leaf which is the attractor of an IFS of four maps. Simply changing the vertical translation component f in the map for the lower right leaflet gives (b). The result suggests a tree blowing in the wind. In Figure 14.24 we look from a different point of view; what sort of maps does the leaf use as compared with the fern of Figure 14.21? The maps corresponding to different parts of these natural objects may be compared via the parallelograms which are the maps' images of a given rectangle.

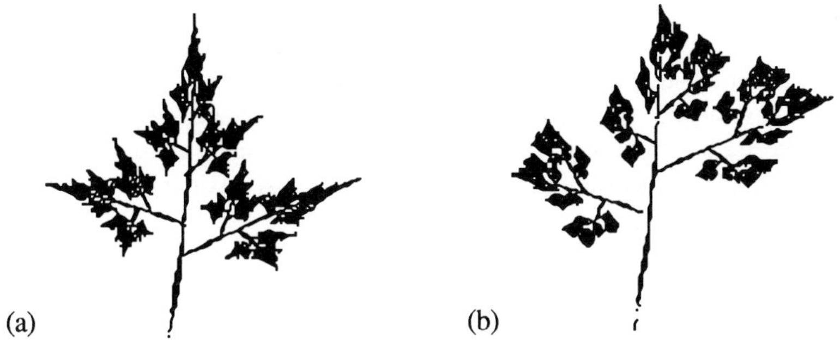

Figure 14.23 (a) A leaf made from an IFS with four maps, and (b) 'blowing in the wind', the new image after a change in the vertical translation part of the map for the lower right leaflet.

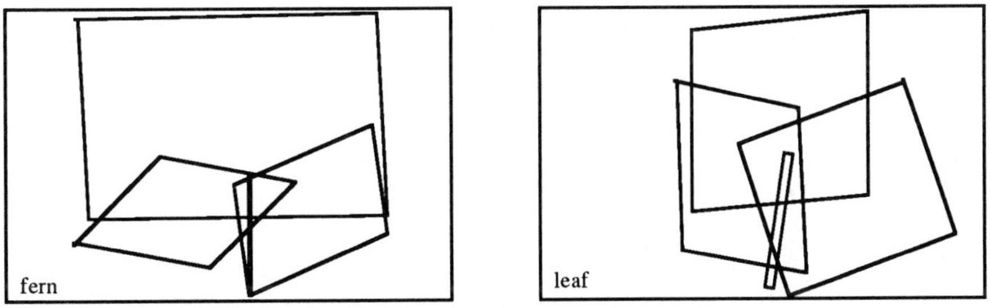

Figure 14.24 We show the maps of the IFS by their effect on a given rectangle where the attractor is (a) the fern of Figure 14.21, (b) the leaf of Figure 14.23(a).

What next? Some of the most successful applications of the collage method illustrated in Example 14.29 have been to natural objects such as trees, ferns, flowers, grass, clouds and so on. The extent of success is gratifying, and two possible contributory reasons for it may be

with enough visual clues we tend to see things as we expect them to be, (14.21)

structures in nature often repeat at one level after another. (14.22)

Some of the striking scenes produced as IFS attractors by Barnsley (1988) and associates are (with approximate numbers of maps): a sunflower field (100), the Black forest (120), Andes Indian girl from the National Geographic magazine (160), Monterey coast (180) and, last but not least, an arctic fox - all in colour (see Section 15.3). They used the following result to make a series of frames of fractal objects, each slightly different from its predecessor, and hence produced film of moving clouds for example. The proof is based on the fact that if X is compact then so is X x [0,1] and hence any continuous image of the latter (Theorems 12.16, 12.24).

THEOREM 14.33 Let $\{X; w_{1\text{-}N}\}$ be an IFS and let each $w_i = w_i(t)$ vary continuously with a parameter $t \in [0,1]$. Then the attractor $\mathcal{A} = \mathcal{A}(t)$ varies continuously with t.

The continuous variation of w_i means the continuous variation of its six coefficients. Changes in the attractor are measured as usual in the Hausdorff metric. The parameter may belong more generally to any compact metric space, say a square in the plane, so that we vary two real parameters t_1, t_2. Or we might use N parameters, each causing changes in just one of the transformations w_i. It is interesting that such a continuous change can nevertheless cause a sudden jump in the fractal dimension, as demonstrated by Falconer (1990, page 127).

TABLE 14.7

IFS code for Figure 14.21. All entries should be divided by 100

	a	b	c	d	e	f
w_1	68	4	-1	71	40	3
w_2	20	51	-19	9	36	128
w_3	3	-51	24	21	212	63
w_4	1	0	0	42	139	92

TABLE 14.8

IFS code for the face of Figure 14.20.

(Divide a,b,c,d by 100.)

	a	b	c	d	e	f
w_1	36	0	0	2.3	14	10.8
w_2	2.6	-16	0	62	15.8	4.2
w_3	2.6	4.6	0	30	-0.5	61.7
w_4	38	0	7	2.3	4	90.7
w_5	45	0	-7	2.3	33	97.7
w_6	2.6	-8	0	32.2	75.9	61.5
w_7	0	4.6	2.6	46	71.5	19.9
w_8	0	-35.6	2.6	-14.9	75.9	25.6
w_9	22.4	0	0	5.7	12	24.4
w_{10}	22.4	0	0	6.9	46	27.2
w_{11}	11.8	0	0	19.5	32	40.9
w_{12}	34.2	0	0	8	20	73.1

Exercises in identifying the IFS of an attractor (cf. (14.15))

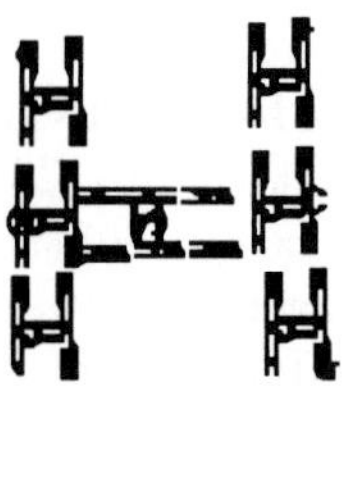

(a) An easy one. What seven transformations produce this attractor?

(b) How many transformations are needed for this one? Describe them briefly.

(c) What became of the third transformation of this ex-Sierpinski gasket? (A decisive aid here could be (14.15)).

(d) Can you recreate this cheese with 4 transformations?

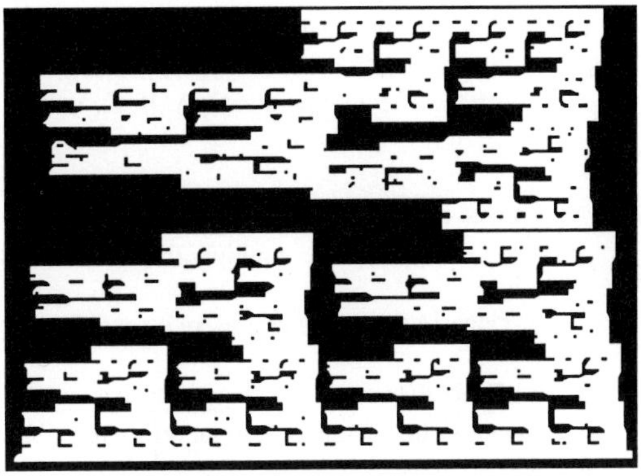

(e) Ships at anchor. What 3 transformations will create this scene?

(f) Right: Barnsley's castle fractal. What transformations involving only scaling and translation produce this?

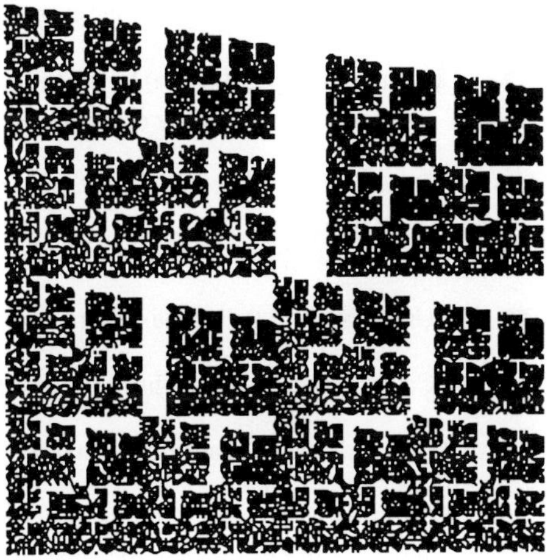

Figure 14.25 Exercises in identifying the IFS of an attractor.

EXERCISES 14

1 √ Write down an IFS code to produce a Sierpinski gasket based on the triangle with coordinates (0,0), (4,0), (5,3).

2 √ Find the IFS code for reflection in the line $y = x+2$.

3 Find the IFS code for the scaling transformation with parameters 3,4 with respect to the x,y axes rotated through 45°. [Your matrix should have determinant 1.]

4 Find the IFS code for the shear transformation of Example 14.9, with the parameter changed to 2. Verify the answer similarly. [The calculation is the same up to a certain stage - use this fact.]

5 √ Use Theorem 14.10 and (14.2) to find an affine transformation which maps the plane onto the line $y = 3x+4$. Is the determinant correct (Theorem 14.10 again)?

6 √ Express as a composition the affine transformation sending rectangle OABC below to the shaded parallelogram, following stages 1 to 4 of Example 14.12. Check the effect on points O, A, B, C.

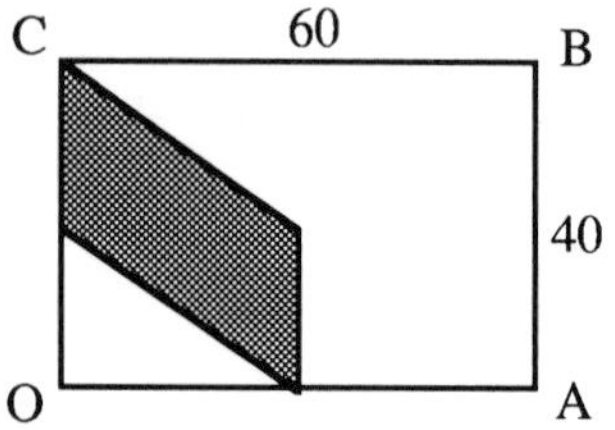

7 Use the determinant formula (14.6) to show that transformations of shear or coordinate scaling type along the x and y axes multiply the area of a triangle by |det A| (Rules 7.20 may help).

8 √ In Table 14.8, which maps make essential use of reflection?

9 (a) Draw a square in the plane in such a way that a vertical coordinate scaling turns it into a sheared rectangle **or** factorise the rotation about O through 60° into shears and coordinate scaling.

10 Verify the ratio and angle of rotation in Figure 14.9.

11 Sketch the successive E_i for the example in Figure 14.10, with the rotation angle changed to 45^0.

12 √ What does Figure 14.11(a) become if the rotation is replaced by a North Easterly translation and the fish by a telegraph pole as condensation set?

13 √ Determine the affine transformations w_2, w_3, w_4 of Figure 14.21 (answers in Table 14.7).

14 Find iterated function systems to produce the attractors of Figures 14.17 (no condensation).

15 √ Use Table 14.5 to find the IFS code for Case 27 of Figure 14.13 (answer is in Table 14.6).

16 Calculate independently, lines 3 and 7 of Table 14.5.

17 √ Find an IFS with condensation to produce the baseball players of Figure 14.18.

18 (**Further exercises**) Let T be the plane affine transformation of rotation through a right angle about the origin followed by reflection in the line y = x+2. Express T(x) as a composition in matrix form for (a) the system in which transformations are written in the order of their performance, (b) the reverse order.

19 Find the IFS code for a shear with parameter 3 which fixes the line y = x (choose your direction). Draw a diagram to indicate its effect.

20 Find the code for the coordinate scaling transformation with centre A(1,1), which doubles distances in the direction of AB, where B is (3,5).

21 Use Theorem 14.10 to show that an affine transformation is invertible if and only if it does not map the whole plane onto a line.

22 Show that if the rows of the matrix A of an affine transformation are orthogonal vectors then A is the product of a diagonal matrix and an orthogonal matrix.

23 Use the determinant formula (14.6) to verify that the area of a triangle is not changed by rotation, reflection, or translation (Rules 7.20 may help).

24 Express in 3 by 3 matrix form the shear with axis AB and parameter 3, for A (1,2) and B(3,5).

Chapter 15 ADDRESSES, MEASURES, AND THE RANDOM ITERATION ALGORITHM

This chapter is mostly about the Random Iteration Algorithm of Barnsley and Demko (1985) for constructing the attractor $\mathcal{A}$ of an iterated function system, and the intimately related idea of addresses on $\mathcal{A}$. In Section 15.1 we illustrate addressing schemes for a set and show how the notion adapts naturally for the attractor of an IFS. One consequence is that the attractor is approximated arbitrarily closely by 'periodic' points - a hint towards its construction. Section 15.2 offers a viewpoint on why the Random Iteration Algorithm works, and an approach to speeding it up via certain sequences arising in the mathematics of communications.

In Section 15.3 we review a second aspect of the Algorithm: it may be used not only to draw the attractor of an IFS but to render it - to allocate variation of light, shade and colour. The user chooses a probability for each map of the IFS, and with the maps these numbers define a unique measure; that is, in effect, a way to distribute shade, redness, or the spectrum itself - whatever we decide shall be distributed. It is hoped that the reader will find the discussion succint but not overly brief! A similar remark applies to Section 15.4, where Hausdorff dimension is covered, now that measures have been introduced.

Note: the set of all addresses for points of an attractor is called the Cantor set on N symbols in Hutchinson (1981) and code space Σ in Barnsley (1988). Retaining the symbol Σ we prefer on balance to call it simply *address space* (the heading of Section 15.1.2) for the obvious reason, and to *remind* us, that it consists of addresses (it was on similar grounds that we denoted the map W of (14.1) as the collage map).

15.1 From address space to periodic points

15.1.1 Addressing schemes

An *addressing scheme* in the present context is simply a system for addressing points of a set. The addressing map is the scheme we will introduce more formally in the next section, after leading up to it with some examples.

EXAMPLE 15.1 Suppose we wish to specify the position of a small object within a square box B in the plane. As a first approximation we may partition B into four sub-boxes labelled 1 to 4 according to the arrangement ('scheme') of Figure 15.1(a), where the object • is in sub-box number 2. Call this box B_2.

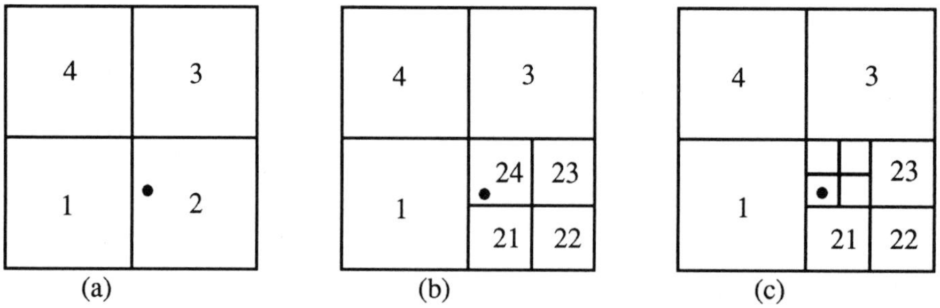

Figure 15.1 Scheme for recursively subdividing a box to obtain address label for a small object, here a dot, with address 241.

For more accuracy, subdivide square 2 by the same scheme, moving round anticlockwise as shown in Figure 15.1(b). At this second level, the box number is 4, so call this box B_{24}, and say it has address 24. In a third level of subdivision we find the object in box number 1, called B_{241} with address 241. Thus the object's position is given approximately by the seqence 241 of symbols from the set or *alphabet* {1,2,3,4}, and we can obtain any desired accuracy even for a single point by using a sufficiently long sequence (cf. Quadtrees. See for example Foley et al (1990)). In this sense every point has an exact address, consisting of an infinite sequence of symbols.

What has this to do with iterated function systems? First notice that boxes B_1 to B_4 are the respective images of the original box B, a unit square with origin at lower left corner, under the plane maps $w_1(\mathbf{x}) = \mathbf{x}/2$, $w_2(\mathbf{x}) = \mathbf{x}/2 + (1/2,0)$, $w_3(\mathbf{x}) = \mathbf{x}/2 + (1/2, 1/2)$, $w_4(\mathbf{x}) = \mathbf{x}/2 + (0,1/2)$. Figure 15.2 helps us to see that we obtain B_{241} in terms of these maps by first applying w_1 to B, then w_4, then w_2. That is, in the reverse order to which B_{241} was built.

Having said this, we have the happy coincidence of order of digits in the identical regions $B_{241} = w_2w_4w_1(B)$. Thus each point in B is located with arbitrary accuracy by a sufficiently long sequence abc... of symbols from {1,2,3,4}, by being in the region $w_aw_bw_c \ldots (B)$. Notice that points on the boundary between two boxes have at least two possible addresses (see Notation 15.3). Finally, the attractor $\mathcal{A}$ of the IFS $\{B; w_{1\text{-}4}\}$ is the whole of B for the simple reasons that $B = w_1(B) \cup .. \cup w_4(B) = W(B)$ and that $W(\mathcal{A}) = \mathcal{A}$ defines the attractor uniquely (see e.g. Definitions 14.1 and 14.2).

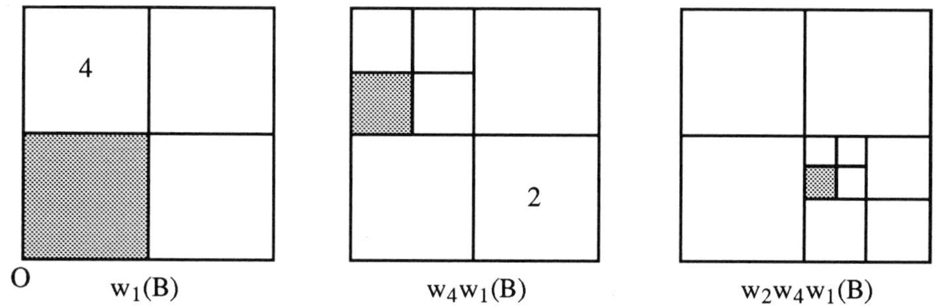

Figure 15.2 Shaded stages show that the area with address 241 equals $w_2w_4w_1(B)$.

EXERCISE Locate the point (0.6,0.7) to within 1/8 in both coordinate by a sequence of symbols as in Example 15.1.

EXAMPLE 15.2 (Decimal expansions.) In the previous scheme we partitioned a square into four half-sized clones of itself, then did the same for each clone, and so on. We are doing an analogous operation in one dimension when we write real numbers in 'decimal form' to any base. A convenient example is base three, the ternary expansion, for numbers in the unit interval I = [0,1].

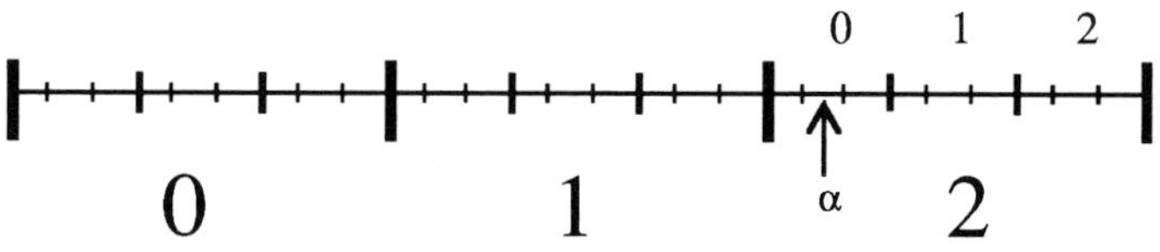

Figure 15.3 Addressing scheme for the ternary expansion of numbers.

We label successive 1/3 sized copies of I by 0,1,2. Thus a number α in the small arrowed interval has expansion beginning 0.201..., implying that

$$\alpha = \frac{2}{3^1} + \frac{0}{3^2} + \frac{1}{3^3} + \ldots\ldots$$

The corresponding maps are $w_i(x) = x/3 + i/3$, $i = 0,1,2$, and the interval containing α is $w_2w_0w_1(I)$. The IFS $\{I; w_{1\text{-}3}\}$ has attractor the whole of I since I = W(I).

EXERCISE Use a suitable addressing scheme to find the first three digits in both the binary and base 5 representations of 0.8.

NOTATION 15.3 Notice that, in Example 15.2, the point 1/3 is in the boundary of two reduced clones of I and as a result has the two addresses 0.1 and 0.02222.... The latter may be written $0.0\overline{2}$ by the convention in which indefinite repetition of symbols a..c is indicated by a bar: $\overline{a..c}$. Thus 5312312312... becomes $5\overline{312}$, where the bar covers 312 only.

The next step We have used addresses for IFS attractors which are standard objects of Euclidean geometry - a square and a line segment. Now we consider addresses on two 'classical' attractors which illustrate beautifully a step beyond this, already foreshadowed in the Cantor set constructions of Section 10.3.2.

EXAMPLE 15.4 The Cantor set C, Construction 10.13. Referring to Figure 15.3, we omit the middle third from the interval I, by using only the labels 0,2. Equivalently we obtain the points whose ternary expansion has no digit 1, in agreement with Construction 10.14 for C.

EXAMPLE 15.5 For the Sierpinski gasket, we start with a solid equilateral triangle Δ with vertices labelled 1,2,3 and centre of mass labelled 0. Let w_i be dilation with ratio 1/2 and centre the point i ($0 \le i \le 3$). Then the IFS $\{\Delta; w_{0\text{-}3}\}$ has attractor Δ, since $W(\Delta) = \Delta$, and gives an addressing scheme for Δ analogous to that for the square B of Example 15.1. On the other hand, $\{\Delta; w_{1\text{-}3}\}$ has attractor the Sierpinski gasket with outer vertices 1,2,3, since omitting the symbol 0 from the addresses has the effect of deleting recursively the 'middle fourth' triangle.

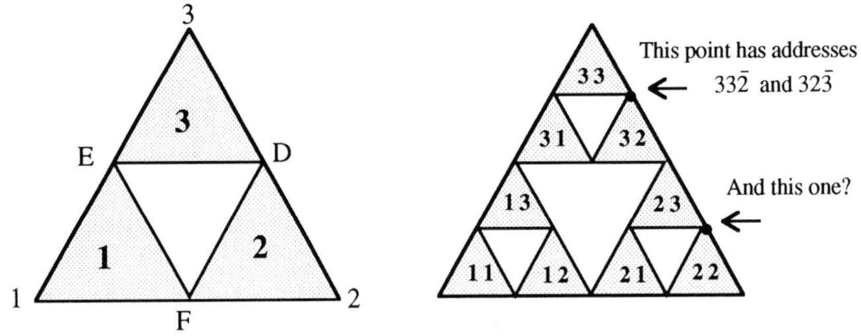

Figure 15.4 The addressing scheme that leads to the points of the Sierpinski gasket. The area labelled i is $w_i(\Delta)$, whilst ik denotes $w_i w_k(\Delta)$.

Thus every point of the gasket can be approximated arbitrarily closely by an address which is an infinite sequence. It is important to appreciate that for example, all points with addresses 1... are in the subtriangle $w_1(\Delta)$ of Δ, all those of type 13... are in $w_1w_3(\Delta)$, a subtriangle of $w_1(\Delta)$ and so on, as we indicate by the labels in Figure 15.4. By repeatedly choosing the same subtriangle number as we construct an address, we can home in on one vertex of, say $w_3w_2(\Delta)$. The point labelled 33$\bar{2}$ (that is, 3322222....) has this and the other address shown, because it can be approached from within either trangular area 33 or 32. A similar addressing scheme applies to the Sierpinski gasket for any shape of triangle.

EXERCISE Give the address sequences for points D, E, F and the question mark, in Figure 15.4.

EXAMPLE 15.6 Addresses for some parts of the fern of Figure 14.21 are shown in Figure 15.5. How the maps relate to the attractor is described in Example 14.30. Each integer or finite sequence of integers refers to the part of the attractor whose addresses begin that way. The region denoted 12 is $w_1w_2(\mathcal{A})$, and so on.

EXERCISE Find examples of areas in Figure 15.5 whose respective addresses require two, three, four and five digits. State these addresses.

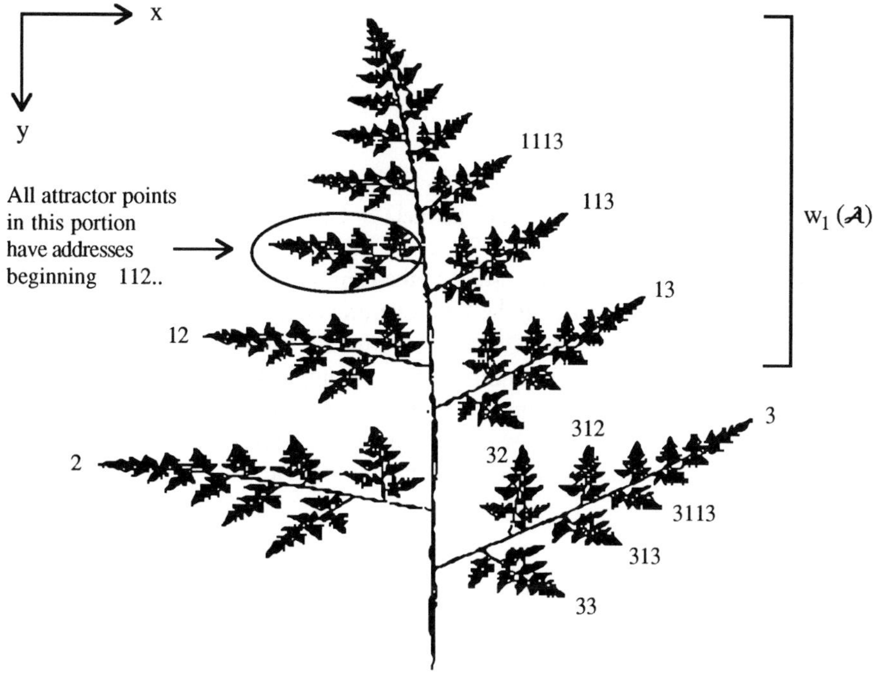

Figure 15.5 Addresses for areas of the fern-shaped attractor of Figure 14.21 and Table 14.7. For example, all points in the lowest left leaf of the lowest right leaf have addresses beginning 32, since they together form the subset $w_3w_2(\mathcal{A})$ of the attractor. To recap: $w_2(\mathcal{A})$, $w_3(\mathcal{A})$ are the lower left and right leaves, whilst $w_1(\mathcal{A})$ is the rest, apart from a small piece of the stem corresponding to w_4.

Extending the notation begun in Example 15.1, the box B, we express the portion of the attractor whose addresses begin with some finite sequence ab..z as

$$\mathcal{A}_{ab..z} \quad = \quad w_aw_b \,..\, w_z(\mathcal{A}). \tag{15.1}$$

Figure 15.4 illustrates for the Sierpinski case, with attractor Δ, that $\Delta = \Delta_1 \cup \Delta_2 \cup \Delta_3 = (\Delta_{11} \cup \Delta_{12} \cup \Delta_{13}) \cup (\Delta_{21} \cup \Delta_{22} \cup \Delta_{23}) \cup (\Delta_{31} \cup \Delta_{32} \cup \Delta_{33}) = \cup \Delta_{ij}$ $(1 \le i,j \le 3)$, a union of nine parts. Carrying out a similar subdivision process for the attractor $\mathcal{A}$ of an IFS of N maps, we obtain

$$\mathcal{A} \;=\; \cup \mathcal{A}_{ij} \;\; (1 \le i,j \le N), \qquad \mathcal{A} \;=\; \cup \mathcal{A}_{ijk} \;\; (1 \le i,j,k \le N) \tag{15.2}$$

and so on. This will be very useful in for example Section 15.2.2 on why the Random Iteration Algorithm works. Another illustration of it is Example 15.6, in which the 'tree' is divided into branches, which in turn are divided into sub branches, as often as we wish.

PROJECT (Pascal's triangle mod 2.) Can you explain the following phenomenon? We form Pascal's triangle of numbers up to say 10 rows, beginning as indicated on the right, in which the sum of adjacent numbers in a row gives the one centred below them in the next row. Now replace every odd number by a dot and delete the rest. The result is a 'Sierpinski gasket' which grows as we add more rows. This is a 'cellular automaton' process - see Willson (1986).

1
1 1
1 2 1
1 3 3 1

15.1.2 Address space

DEFINITION 15.7 The *address space* of an IFS $(X, w_{1\text{-}N})$ is the metric space (Σ, d), where Σ consists of all infinite sequences $\sigma = \sigma_1, \sigma_2, \sigma_3, ..$ of symbols σ_i from the set $\{1,2, ... , N\}$ and the distance between two sequences σ, τ is

$$d(\sigma,\tau) = \sum_{n=1}^{\infty} \frac{|\sigma_n - \tau_n|}{(N+1)^n}. \tag{15.3}$$

The factor (N+1), as distinct from N, corresponds to omitting the middle third in the Cantor set (N=2), and the middle fourth triangle in the Sierpinski gasket (N=3). We keep N parts out of a total of N+1. We verify that d satisfies the metric space axioms (Definition 11.1), show that (Σ,d) satisfies a stronger condition than topological equivalence with a Cantor type set, and then construct a continuous map $\phi: \Sigma \to \mathcal{A}$ from the address space of an IFS onto its attractor. This map ϕ both formalises the notion of addresses for points on a fractal attractor and gives an important tool for investigating that attractor. Some surprising and useful results emerge.

EXAMPLE 15.8 With N = 4, we find the distance between points $\overline{23}$ and $\overline{31}$ in code space on four symbols. By the formula of (15.3) this is

$$\begin{aligned} d(232323... , 313131...) &= \frac{1}{5} + \frac{2}{5^2} + \frac{1}{5^3} + \frac{2}{5^4} + ... \\ &= \frac{1}{5}(1+x+x^2+ ..) + \frac{2}{25}(1+x+x^2+ ..), \text{ where } x = \frac{1}{25} \\ &= \frac{7}{25} \cdot \frac{1}{1-1/25} = \frac{7}{24}. \end{aligned}$$

THEOREM 15.9 The address space (Σ,d) of an IFS is a metric space.

Proof Since the distance (15.3) is defined as a limit, our first task is to check that that limit exists. Write

$$S_k = S_k(\sigma,\tau) = \sum_{n=1}^{k} \frac{|\sigma_n - \tau_n|}{(N+1)^n}. \tag{15.4}$$

Then (15.3) says that $d(\sigma,\tau) = \lim_{k\to\infty} S_k$. But $S_1 \le S_2 \le ...$ since $|\sigma_n - \tau_n| \ge 0$, so by a standard test for convergence (Table 11.2(9)), the limit exists if the sequence $\{S_k\}$ is bounded above. But since $|\sigma_n - \tau_n| \le (N+1)$ we have, with $x = 1/(N+1)$,

$$S_k \le \sum_{n=1}^{k} \frac{N+1}{(N+1)^n} \le 1 + x + x^2 + .. = 1/(1-x).$$

Thus $d(\sigma,\tau)$ is well-defined. We must verify that the three axioms of a metric space hold (Definition 11.1). *Axiom 1* : We have $|\sigma_n - \tau_n| \ge 0$, moreover $|\sigma_n - \tau_n| = 0$ implies $\sigma_n = \tau_n$ ($n \in \mathbf{N}$). Therefore (a) $d(\sigma,\tau) \ge 0$ and (b) $d(\sigma,\tau) = 0 \Rightarrow |\sigma_n - \tau_n| = 0$ ($n \in \mathbf{N}$) $\Rightarrow \sigma_n = \tau_n$ ($n \in \mathbf{N}$) $\Rightarrow \sigma = \tau$. This verifies Axiom 1. *Axiom 2* states that $d(\tau,\sigma) = d(\sigma,\tau)$, and holds because $|\tau_n-\sigma_n| = |\sigma_n-\tau_n|$ for all $n \in \mathbf{N}$. *Axiom 3* is the triangle inequality. Let ω be another member of Σ. Then the triangle inequality for real numbers gives for each $n \in \mathbf{N}$, $|\sigma_n-\tau_n| \le |\sigma_n-\omega_n| + |\omega_n-\tau_n|$. So (notation of (15.4)), $S_k(\sigma,\tau) \le S_k(\sigma,\omega) + S_k(\omega,\tau)$. It follows on our letting $k \to \infty$ that $d(\sigma,\tau) \le d(\sigma,\omega) + d(\omega,\tau)$, as required. The result we have used here is that if three sequences $\{a_k\}$, $\{b_k\}$, $\{c_k\}$ with respective limits a, b, c satisfy $a_k \leq b_k + c_k$ for all $k \in \mathbf{N}$ then $a \leq b + c$ (Table 11.2(8)). The proof is complete.

EXERCISE Verify the triangle inequality for the points $1\overline{2}$, $3\overline{2}$, $3\overline{1}$ in Σ, when N = 3.

DEFINITION 15.10 Two metric spaces (X_1, d_1) and (X_2, d_2) are *metrically equivalent* if there is a bounded map $f: X_1 \to X_2$ with a bounded inverse g. Since bounded maps are continuous (Theorem 11.43) f and g are also continuous and invertible, so X_1, X_2 are homeomorphic, or topologically equivalent. One respect in which metric equivalence is the stronger condition on X_1, X_2 is that it forbids deforming one into the other by an 'infinite stretch'. For example the finite interval (0,1) is stretched to the infinite interval $(1,\infty)$ by the homeomorphism $f(x) = 1/x$, with inverse $g(y) = 1/y$, but there can be no bounded map f: $(0,1) \to (1,\infty)$ since d(x,y) can be arbitrarily large for pairs x, y in $(1,\infty)$. Of course f need not actually preserve distances.

REMARK 15.11 Consider the addressing scheme for points of the unit interval I which results from dividing I into N+1 equal parts labelled 0,1,2, ... , N. Through this scheme the map given by

$$\sigma_1\sigma_2\sigma_3 .. \to 0.\sigma_1\sigma_2\sigma_3 .. = \sum_{n=1}^{\infty} \frac{\sigma_n}{(N+1)^n} \tag{15.5}$$

is a bijection f of Σ onto the subset C_N of points in I whose expansion to base N+1 has no digit 0. We shall prove that f is a metric equivalence. This is very interesting since, as we shall shortly prove, the same address space may be used to address fractals of widely differing geometries (Theorem 15.17). The compactness of the Cantor set was established in Example 12.17(2).

Notice that C_N is the attractor of the IFS $\{[0,1];\ w_n(x) = (x+n)/(N+1):\ 1 \leq n \leq N\}$, with $w_n(I) = [n/(N+1), (n+1)/(N+1)]$. (Reason: $W(C_N) = C_N$.) At each stage we omit the bottom 1/(N+1)'th of all subintervals remaining. The name *generalised Cantor* (or even just Cantor) set is applied to such a set as C_N above in which I is divided into N+1 parts, possibly unequal, and the part in say the r'th position consistently omitted.

THEOREM 15.12 Address space Σ is metrically equivalent by the map f of (15.5) to a generalised Cantor set, and so is also compact.

Proof During this proof we shall denote the metric on Σ by d_1 and that on C_N by d_2. Thus

$$d_2(0.\sigma_1\sigma_2.., 0.\tau_1\tau_2 ..) = |\Sigma a_n|, \text{ where } a_n = (\sigma_n - \tau_n)/(N+1)^n. \tag{15.6}$$

We are to prove (Definition 15.10) that f and its inverse are bounded. We claim that it suffices to show that for all σ,τ in Σ

$$d_2(d(\sigma), f(\tau)) \leq d_1(\sigma,\tau) \leq (2N-1)d_2(f(\sigma), f(\tau)). \tag{15.7}$$

since then f is bounded according to the first inequality, and so is f^{-1} by the second because it is equivalent to

$$d_1(f^{-1}f(\sigma), f^{-1}f\tau)) \leq (2N-1)d_2(f(\sigma), f(\tau))$$

and σ,τ being arbitrary implies that $f(\sigma)$, $f(\tau)$ are arbitrary. Now we prove (15.7). Since the series (15.3) for d_1 converges we have by Table 11.2 (19) that

$$d_2(f(\sigma), f(\tau)) = |\Sigma a_n| \le \Sigma |a_n| = d_1(\sigma,\tau),$$

establishing the first inequality of (15.7). For the second, suppose the k'th place is the first in which σ,τ disagree. That is, $a_n = 0$ if $n < k$ but $|a_k| > 0$. Notice that for every $n \in \mathbf{N}$, $|\sigma_n - \tau_n| \le N-1$ and hence $|a_n| \le (N-1)/(N+1)^n$. Therefore we may argue as follows:

$$d_2(\sigma,\tau) = \left| a_k + \sum_{n=k+1}^{\infty} a_n \right|$$

$$\ge |a_k| - \left| \sum_{n=k+1}^{\infty} a_n \right| \quad \text{(since } |a+b| \ge |a| - |b| \text{ for a,b in R)}$$

$$\ge |a_k| - \sum_{n=k+1}^{\infty} |a_n| \quad \text{(by Table 11.2(19) applied to the series starting at } a_{k+1}\text{)}$$

$$\ge |a_k| - \sum_{n=k+1}^{\infty} \frac{N-1}{(N+1)^n} \quad \text{(since } |a_n| \le (N-1)/(N+1)^n \text{)}$$

$$= |a_k| - (N-1)/(N(N+1)^k) \quad \text{(the second term being the sum of the geometric series above it).}$$

On the other hand,

$$d_1(\sigma,\tau) = |a_k| + \sum_{n=k+1}^{\infty} |a_n| \le |a_k| + (N-1)/N(N+1)^k,$$

on summing the same geometric series as before, with again $|a_n| \le (N-1)/(N+1)^n$. As a result, $d_1(\sigma,\tau) \le (2N-1)d_2(\sigma,\tau)$ holds provided

$$|a_k| + (N-1)/N(N+1)^k \le (2N-1)\{|a_k| - (N-1)/N(N+1)^k\}.$$

But this simplifies to $|a_k| \ge 1/(N+1)^k$, which is itself a consequence of $\sigma_k \ne \tau_k$. Thus (15.7) is established and the proof is complete.

EXAMPLE 15.13 A Cantor set with N = 3. Removing the 'lower fourth', the first few stages are :

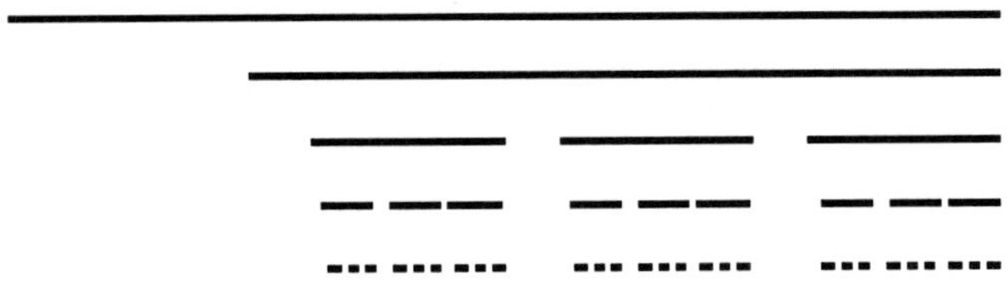

EXERCISE Draw the first three stages of the (generalised) Cantor set obtained recursively by dividing an interval into four parts and deleting the lowest but one part.

15.1.3 The addressing map

Let $\{K; w_{1-N}\}$ be an IFS. We assume K is compact, as we may by (14.14). In general we don't have a metric equivalence from the address space Σ of an IFS to its attractor $\mathcal{A}$, as we did in the Cantor type. What we have so far, as described in Section 15.1, is a way of passing from an address σ to a point $\phi(\sigma)$ by letting the sequence define successive subdivisions of $\mathcal{A}$ which contain the point ever more closely. This is a version of the *addressing map* $\phi: \Sigma \to \mathcal{A}$. It may be characterised as based on the 'invariant' property $\mathcal{A} = W(\mathcal{A})$. We require an equivalent (as we shall show) definition of ϕ based on $W^n(E_0) \to \mathcal{A}$ for any starting set E_0, the 'attractor' aspect of $\mathcal{A}$ (cf. Definition 14.2). In this we choose any x in K and apply (ad infinitum) maps w_i with subscripts in an order given by the sequence σ. This is illustrated in Example 15.18. The formal definition of ϕ, and the proof of its non-dependence on the choice of x in K, are in Theorem 15.17. The definition is essentially due to Hutchinson (1981), but we follow the approach of Barnsley (1988) in working via an intermediate definition: for $\sigma \in \Sigma$, $n \in \mathbf{N}$, and $x \in K$, let

$$\phi(\sigma,n,x) \quad = \quad w_{\sigma_1} w_{\sigma_2} \ldots\ldots w_{\sigma_n}(x)\,. \tag{15.8}$$

It is helpful to have two lemmas on the 'Calculus' of $\phi(\sigma,n,x)$. The first allows us to replace the integer m in $\phi(\sigma,m,x)$ by a smaller one n, if we also replace x by an unknown point x_1.

LEMMA 15.14 Let an iterated function system $\{K; w_{1\text{-}N}\}$ have address space Σ, and contraction ratio r. If $\sigma \in \Sigma$, $x,y \in K$, and $m \geq n$ in $\mathbf{N}$, we have for constant λ depending only on K:

$$\phi(\sigma,m,x) \quad = \quad \phi(\sigma,n,x_1), \quad \text{for some } x_1 \in K, \tag{15.9}$$

$$d(\phi(\sigma,m,x),\ \phi(\sigma,n,y)) \quad \leq \quad \lambda r^n. \tag{15.10}$$

Proof For (15.9) with m = n there is nothing to prove. If m > n we have by definition $\phi(\sigma,m,x) = w_{\sigma_1} \ldots\ldots w_{\sigma_n}(w_{\sigma_{n+1}} \cdots w_{\sigma_m}(x)) = \phi(\sigma,n,x_1)$, where $x_1 = w_{\sigma_{n+1}} \cdots w_{\sigma_m}(x)$. Hence (15.9), which shows in turn that the left hand side of (15.10) equals the distance $d(\phi(\sigma,n,x_1), \phi(\sigma,n,y))$ for some x_1 in K. Now the relation $d(w_i(x), w_i(y)) \leq r\, d(x,y)$ is applied repeatedly to get an upper bound $r^n d(x_1,y)$. But since K is compact and d is continuous (Theorem 11.42), $d(x_1,y)$ has a maximum λ for all $x_1, y \in K$. Hence the result.

REMARK 15.15 (15.10) is very welcome and very powerful because the inequality is uniform in x, y. That is, it is true for all pairs x,y simultaneously. As a notational point, we could drop the apparent restriction m > n and replace λr^n by $r^{\max(m,n)}$. The idea of addresses $\sigma,\tau \in \Sigma$ agreeing up to the n'th place is important here. For example σ = 53452626... and τ = 5342635... agree up to the third place, but $\sigma_4 = 5$, $\tau_4 = 2$ so the agreement stops there. We continue from time to time, as in the next Lemma, to need the sum of a geometric series $1+x+x^2+\ldots = 1/(1-x)$.

LEMMA 15.16 Let $\sigma,\tau \in \Sigma$, the address space of an IFS $\{K; w_{1\text{-}N}\}$. If σ and τ agree in the first n places then

$$d(\sigma,\tau) \quad < \quad \frac{1}{(N+1)^n}, \tag{15.11}$$

and if

$$d(\sigma,\tau) \quad < \quad \sum_{m=n+2}^{\infty} \frac{N}{(N+1)^m} \quad = \quad \frac{1}{(N+1)^{n+1}} \tag{15.12}$$

then σ,τ agree up to the n'th place. Agreement up to $n \leq m$ places implies

$$\phi(\sigma,m,x) \quad = \quad \phi(\tau,n,x_1), \quad \text{for some } x_1 \in K, \tag{15.13}$$

and

$$d(\phi(\sigma,m,x),\ \phi(\tau,n,y)) \ \leq \ \lambda r^n, \ \text{for some constant, } \lambda. \tag{15.14}$$

Proof The proof of (15.11) is left as the next exercise, being very similar to that of (15.12). The middle term of (15.12) is $N/(N+1)^{n+2}$ times the standard geometric series 1+x+.. with $x = 1/(N+1)$, hence the equality. If σ_n differs from τ_n then we have the chain of inequalities $|\sigma_n-\tau_n|/(N+1)^n \geq 1/(N+1)^n > 1/(N+1)^{n+1}$, so the given condition fails to hold. Also, $\sigma_m \neq \tau_m$ with $m < n$ produces an even bigger infringement. Hence the condition of (15.12) implies that σ, τ agree up to the n'th place. Now we suppose that they do so agree and deduce (15.13) and (15.14). We have for some $x_1 \in K$: $\phi(\sigma,m,x) = \phi(\sigma,n,x_1)$ (by (15.9)) $= w_{\sigma_1} \ldots w_{\sigma_n}(x_1)$ (by definition) $= w_{\tau_1} \ldots w_{\tau_n}(x)$ (by the agreement up to n places) $= \phi(\tau,n,x_1)$, hence (15.13). Finally $d(\phi(\sigma,m,x), \phi(\tau,n,y)) = d(\phi(\tau,n,x_1), \phi(\tau,n,y))$ (by (15.13)) $\leq \lambda r^n$ for some constant λ, by (15.10) with $m = n$, $\sigma = \tau$. Hence (15.14) holds.

EXERCISE (a) Prove statement (15.11) **or** (b) verify it for the points $132\overline{4}$ and $13\overline{242}$ of Σ, in case $N = 4$.

THEOREM 15.17 Let $\{K; w_{1-N}\}$ be an iterated function system with attractor $\mathcal{A}$ and address space Σ. Then the addressing map

$$\phi: \Sigma \to \mathcal{A}, \quad \textit{where} \quad \phi(\sigma) = \lim_{n\to\infty} \phi(\sigma,n,x) \qquad (x \in K) \tag{15.15}$$

is well-defined, independent of the choice of $x \in K$, continuous and onto.

Proof For $x \in K$, $\sigma \in \Sigma$, we have a sequence $\{\phi(\sigma,n,x) \in W^n(K)\}$, and since $r < 1$ this sequence is Cauchy by (15.10) with $y = x$. It has a limit L in $\mathbf{R}^n$ because $\mathbf{R}^n$ is complete (Theorem 13.16). But $\mathcal{A}$ consists precisely of all limits of Cauchy sequences of the form $\{a_n \in W^n(K)\}$ by Theorem 13.27, so $L \in \mathcal{A}$. Thus $\phi(\sigma) = L$ is well-defined. Further, L is independent of the choice of x, for by (15.10) $d(\phi(\sigma,n,x), \phi(\sigma,n,y)) \to 0$ as $n \to \infty$ for any pair x,y in K.

ϕ is continuous. Let $\varepsilon > 0$. We must specify how close σ, τ must be to ensure that $d(\phi(\sigma), \phi(\tau)) < \varepsilon$. The clue lies in (15.12). Suppose $d(\sigma,\tau) < 1/(N+1)^{n+1}$, so that σ,τ agree in the first n places. Choose n so large that $\lambda r^n < \varepsilon$ in (15.14). The following inequality for any $m > n$ is obtained by starting with the left hand side, using (15.9) to reduce both m's to n, and then applying (15.14) with $m = n$:

$$d(\phi(\sigma,m,x)), \phi(\tau,m,x)) \leq \lambda r^n. \tag{15.16}$$

Let $m \to \infty$. Then $\phi(\sigma,m,x) \to \phi(\sigma)$, $\phi(\tau,m,x) \to \phi(\tau)$ and, because d is continuous (Theorem 11.42) the left hand side of (15.16) has limit $d(\phi(\sigma), \phi(\tau)) \leq \lambda r^n$ which is less than ε by our choice of n. Thus ϕ is continuous.

ϕ is onto. Let $a \in \mathcal{A}$. We must find $\sigma \in \Sigma$ with $\phi(\sigma) = a$. Let x be any point of K. Then by Theorem 13.27, a is the limit of a Cauchy sequence $\{a_n \in W^n(\{x\})\}$. Thus for each n, we have $a_n = w_{\sigma_1} \ldots\ldots w_{\sigma_n}(x)$ for some $\sigma = \sigma^{(n)}$ in Σ, or equivalently $a_n = \phi(\sigma^{(n)},n, x)$. Now $\{\sigma^{(n)}\}$ is itself a sequence of elements of Σ. Since Σ is compact (Theorem 15.12) this infinite sequence contains a convergent subsequence $\tau^{(n)} \to \tau$, say (Corollary 12.12). Thus if $\tau^{(n)}$ and τ agree up to just the first $\alpha(n)$ places then $\alpha(n) \to \infty$, and therefore

$$\phi(\tau) = \lim_{m\to\infty} \phi(\tau, \alpha(m), x) = \lim_{m\to\infty} \phi(\tau^{\alpha(m)}, \alpha(m), x).$$

But this is the limit of a subsequence of $\{a_n\}$ and so has the same limit as $\{a_n\}$. That is, $\phi(\tau) = a$. The proof of the Theorem is complete.

EXAMPLE 15.18 We compute $\phi(\sigma)$ for some periodic sequences σ, on a Sierpinski gasket. For $\phi(\overline{21})$, we may select *any* point **x** and compute the limit of $(w_2w_1)^n(\mathbf{x})$ as $n \to \infty$. This is an important application of the theorem we have just proved. With $w_i(\mathbf{y}) = (1/2)(\mathbf{y} + \mathbf{a}_i)$ in Figure 15.6, where $\mathbf{a}_i$ is the position vector of A_i, we obtain:

$$\begin{aligned} w_2w_1(\mathbf{x}) &= \tfrac{1}{2}\,[\mathbf{a}_2 + \tfrac{1}{2}\,(\mathbf{a}_1+\mathbf{x})] = \tfrac{1}{4}\,\mathbf{a}_1 + \tfrac{1}{2}\,\mathbf{a}_2 + \tfrac{1}{4}\,\mathbf{x}, \\ (w_2w_1)^n(\mathbf{x}) &= (\tfrac{1}{4}\,\mathbf{a}_1 + \tfrac{1}{2}\,\mathbf{a}_2)(1 + \tfrac{1}{4} + \ldots + (\tfrac{1}{4})^{n-1}) + (\tfrac{1}{4})^n\,\mathbf{x} \\ &= \tfrac{1}{3}\,(\mathbf{a}_1 + 2\mathbf{a}_2)(1 - 4^{-n}) + 4^{-n}\,\mathbf{x}, \end{aligned}$$

on summing the geometric series. Letting $n \to \infty$ we obtain $\phi(\overline{21}) = (1/3)(\mathbf{a}_1 + 2\mathbf{a}_2)$, independently of the choice of **x**. This is seen in Figure 15.6, where we start from an arbitrary point $\mathbf{x} = \mathbf{z}_0$. Writing $\mathbf{z}_n = (w_2w_1)^n(\mathbf{z}_0)$ we get $\mathbf{z}_n \to (1/3)(\mathbf{a}_1 + 2\mathbf{a}_2)$ as predicted above.

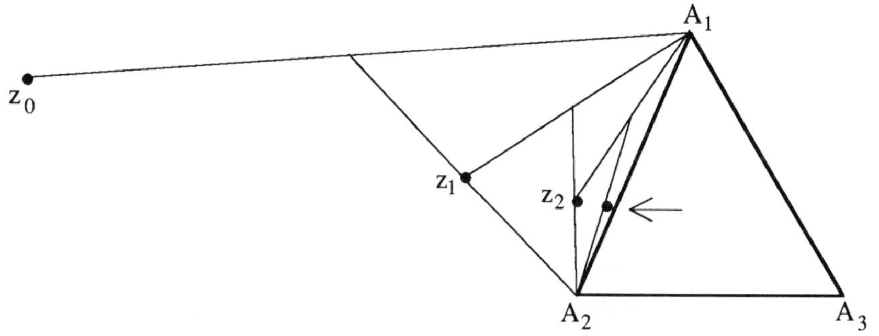

Figure 15.6 Finding $\phi(\overline{21})$ for the Sierpinski gasket in the triangle $A_1A_2\,A_3$. This limit is the point (arrowed) on A_1A_2 dividing it in the ratio 2:1.

Notice that $\phi(\overline{21})$ divides A_1A_2 in the ratio 2:1; this is a case of the section formula (1.3) that $\mathbf{r} = (n\mathbf{a}+m\mathbf{b})/(m+n)$ for the point on AB dividing it in the ratio m : n. (Note the switch between m,n for the numerator.) We can now mark in the $f(\overline{ji})$ $(i \neq j)$, of which three are shown in Figure 15.7.

EXERCISE Calculate $\phi(\overline{13})$ for the Sierpinski gasket (Figure 15.7 gives a check).

THEOREM 15.19 The two constructions for the addressing map (see Section 15.1 and (15.15)) coincide.

Proof Let $\{K;\ w_{1\text{-}N}\}$ be an IFS. It suffices to show that for any $\sigma = (\sigma_i)$ in Σ and $n \in N$ the set of points whose addresses beginning $\sigma_1\sigma_2 .. \sigma_n$ are the same in both constructions. We need a result which will also be useful in the next section. Keeping ϕ for the map of (15.15), let $\tau \in \Sigma$ and $i \in \{1,2,..,N\}$. We claim that

$$w_i\,\phi(\tau) = \phi(i\tau). \qquad (15.17)$$

To prove this, note that $\phi(i\tau,n+1,a) = w_iw_{\tau_1}\,w_{\tau_2}\,\ldots\,w_{\tau_n}\,(a) = w_i\phi(\tau,n,a)$. Let $n \to \infty$. Then, since w_i is continuous, we have $w_i\phi(\tau,n,a) \to w_i\phi(\tau)$. But $\phi(i\tau,n+1,a) \to \phi(i\tau)$, so the result follows. The argument is now that

$$\begin{aligned}
\mathcal{A}_{\sigma_1 \cdots \sigma_n} &= \{w_{\sigma_1} \ldots\ldots w_{\sigma_n}(x) : \quad x \in \mathcal{A}\} && \text{by (15.1)} \\
&= \{w_{\sigma_1} \ldots\ldots w_{\sigma_n}(x) : \quad x = \phi(\tau), \quad \tau \in \Sigma\} && \text{(f is onto)} \\
&= \{\phi(\sigma_1\sigma_2 \ldots \sigma_n\tau) : \quad \tau \in \Sigma\}. && \text{by (15.17)}
\end{aligned}$$

That is, the points whose addresses begin $\sigma_1\sigma_2 \ldots \sigma_n$ are the same in both constructions.

15.1.4 Periodic points

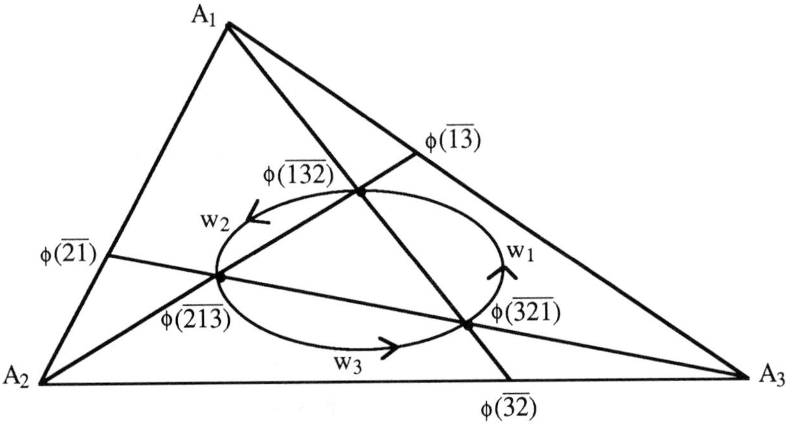

Figure 15.7 Images of the addressing map, in the Sierpinski Gasket. Notice the effect of the w_i on the inner triangle of points. They are examples of periodic points.

Now we determine $\phi(\overline{321})$, starting from the expression for $w_2w_1(\mathbf{x})$.

$$\begin{aligned}
w_3w_2w_1(\mathbf{x}) &= \tfrac{1}{8}\,\mathbf{a}_1 + \tfrac{1}{4}\,\mathbf{a}_2 + \tfrac{1}{2}\,\mathbf{a}_3 + \tfrac{1}{8}\,\mathbf{x} \\
(w_3w_2w_1)^n(\mathbf{x}) &= \tfrac{1}{8}\,(\mathbf{a}_1 + 2\mathbf{a}_2 + 4\mathbf{a}_3)(1 + \tfrac{1}{8} + \ldots + (\tfrac{1}{8})^{n-1}) + (\tfrac{1}{8})^n\,\mathbf{x}, \\
\phi(\overline{321}) &= \tfrac{1}{7}\,(\mathbf{a}_1 + 2\mathbf{a}_2 + 4\mathbf{a}_3) \\
&= \frac{1}{7}\left[3\left(\frac{\mathbf{a}_1 + 2\mathbf{a}_2}{3}\right) + 4\mathbf{a}_3\right] \quad = \quad \frac{1}{7}\left[\mathbf{a}_1 + 6\left(\frac{\mathbf{a}_2 + 2\mathbf{a}_3}{3}\right)\right].
\end{aligned}$$

Thus by the section formula again, $\phi(\overline{321})$ is the intersection of the join of A_3 to $\phi(\overline{21})$ with the join of A_1 to $\phi(\overline{32})$, dividing these segments in respective ratios 3:4 and 6:1, as represented in Figure 15.7. By permuting $1 \to 2 \to 3 \to 1$ we may now mark in $\phi(\overline{132})$ and $\phi(\overline{213})$. Now w_1 by its definition maps $\phi(\overline{321})$ to $\phi(\overline{132})$ because $d(A_1, \phi(\overline{132})) = (1/2)d(A_1, \phi(\overline{321}))$, and similarly for w_2 and w_3. Hence the arrows round the triangle of such points. In fact this is part of a wider phenomenon for all attractors, and the three points in question are periodic, of period three, according to the definition below.

DEFINITION 15.20 A point a in the attractor $\mathcal{A}$ of an IFS, is *periodic* if, for some finite sequence of IFS maps w_{σ_i},

$$w_{\sigma_1} w_{\sigma_2} \cdots w_{\sigma_n}(a) = a. \tag{15.18}$$

The *period* of a is the least $n \in \mathbf{N}$ for which an equation of type (15.18) is true. Now for an example that helps us to cash in on periodicity.

EXAMPLE 15.21 A point of an attractor is periodic if and only if it has a periodic address.

Proof Let $a \in A$ be a periodic point, in the notation of (15.18), and write $\sigma = \overline{\sigma_1\sigma_2 \dots \sigma_n}$. Then we have $\phi(\sigma) = \lim_{m\to\infty} \phi(\sigma,m,a) = \lim_{p\to\infty} \phi(\sigma,np,a) = \lim_{p\to\infty} (\sigma_1\sigma_2 \dots \sigma_n)^p(a) = a$. Thus a has a periodic address σ. Conversely, let $a = \phi(\sigma)$ where σ is periodic, say $\sigma = \overline{\sigma_1\sigma_2 \dots \sigma_n}$. Then, from (15.17), $w_{\sigma_1} w_{\sigma_2} \dots w_{\sigma_n}(a) = \phi(\sigma_1\sigma_2 \dots \sigma_n \sigma) = \phi(\sigma) = a$. Finally, a is a periodic point by (15.18).

EXERCISE Use (15.17) to derive the formula $\phi(213\sigma) = w_2w_1w_3\, \phi(\sigma)$.

Periodic points are dense We will now use the addressing map φ to show that every point in the attractor of an IFS may be approximated with arbitrary precision by periodic points. In other language, the set of periodic points is dense in $\mathcal{A}$ (its closure equals $\mathcal{A}$, Definition 11.22). Thus we may expect periodic points to play a key role in a successful screen representation of $\mathcal{A}$.

First we show that *the periodic points of address space Σ are dense in Σ*. Thus, let $\sigma \in \Sigma$ and $\varepsilon > 0$. We have to find a *periodic* address τ within distance ε of σ. For this, choose n so large that $1/(N+1)^n < \varepsilon$. Then according to (15.11) any sequence τ agreeing with σ up to the n'th place will satisfy $d(\sigma,\tau) < \varepsilon$. If $\sigma = \sigma_1\sigma_2 \dots$ then a suitable periodic sequence is $\tau = \overline{\sigma_1\sigma_2 \dots \sigma_n}$.

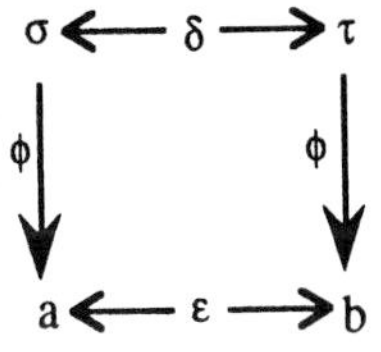

Now we make crucial use of φ. Let $a \in \mathcal{A}$ and $\varepsilon > 0$. Then we seek a *periodic* point $b \in \mathcal{A}$ such that $d(a,b) < \varepsilon$. Since φ is onto, a has some address σ. That is, $a = \phi(\sigma)$. Because φ is continuous, the point $b = \phi(\tau)$ is within distance ε of a for all τ within a certain distance δ of σ. But we have just shown that the periodic points of Σ are dense, so we may choose τ to be periodic. But then b is periodic too, by Example 15.21. We have proved the following result.

THEOREM 15.22 The set of periodic points in an attractor is dense.

EXERCISE Given an IFS, why must a periodic point of the attractor be the fixed point of a contractive map? (Use (15.17) and Example 15.21.) Deduce a possible (if inefficient) way to generate a computer picture of the attractor (use Theorem 15.22).

15.2 The Random Iteration Algorithm

15.2.1 Introduction

We recall that the *deterministic (or collage) algorithm* for finding the attractor of an IFS, enshrined in Definition 14.2, requires us to compute at each stage the collage of images $w_1(E) \cup \dots \cup w_N(E)$ from the previous stage E. By contrast, in the Random Iteration Algorithm (or RIA) below we calculate at each stage just one new point x_{n+1} from its predecessor x_n, by $x_{n+1} = w_i(x_n)$ with a randomly chosen i from 1,2, ... ,N. And it works, given a large number of iterations - say 40,000. Beneath the dancing iterated point the attractor emerges miraculously from the mist. After a formal description of the RIA and some examples we will be ready to show why it is so successful, using results of topology and address space.

DEFINITION 15.23 **The Random Iteration Algorithm.** Given the IFS $\{X; w_{1\text{-}N}\}$ we first associate with each w_i a probability $p_i = D_i/D$, calculated from the coefficients a_i to f_i in the map w_i by $D_i = |a_i d_i - b_i c_i|$ and $D = D_1 + ... + D_N$. Here D_i is the modulus of the determinant of the matrix of w_i as explained below.
Iteration Choose an initial point $x_0 \in X$. Compute successive points $x_{n+1} = w_r(x_n)$ where at each stage r is given one of the values 1, 2, ..., N subject to: the probability that r = i is p_i.

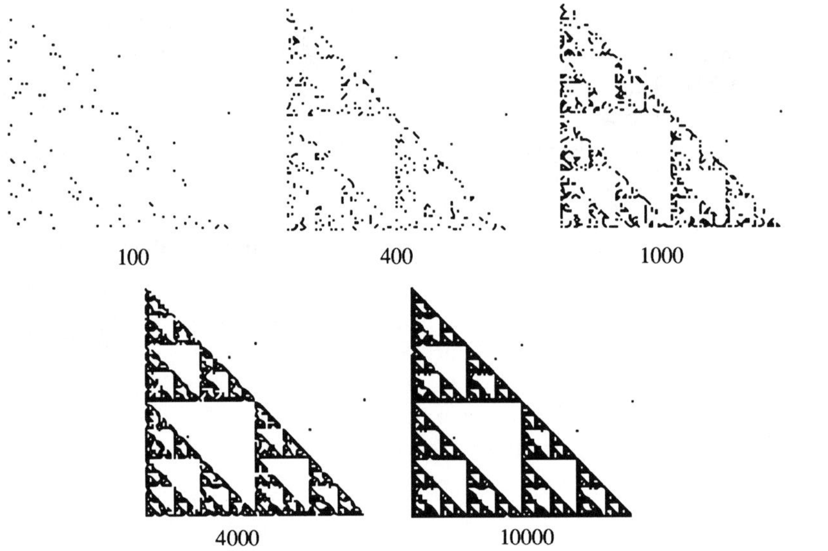

Figure 15.8 Sierpinski Gasket after various stages of the RIA.

Intuitively, we run through the choices so that each w_i appears with a frequency proportional to the area D_i (Theorem 14.14(ii)) of the image under w_i of a square of unit area. Thus the transformations responsible for producing the most area are allowed the most points. However, we can't afford to take this quite literally in the case w_i maps everything onto a line, for then $D_i = 0$ and the line (perhaps a plant stem) never appears. Instead we set p_i to a small value, say $p_i = 0.01$ or less. This was done for w_1 in Example 14.3.

EXAMPLE 15.24 If the RIA really does work, then the following simple construction should produce a Sierpinski gasket with vertices A_1, A_2, A_3, after a small number of points not yet on the attractor (cf. Figure 15.8).

(1) Choose three points A_1, A_2, A_3 not in the same straight line, and a starting point x_0.

(2) Select a number r = 1,2 or 3 at random (e.g. by computer's random number generator, or a throw of a dice). Then x_1 is the midpoint of segment $A_r x_0$. In the same way, find x_2 from x_1, and so on (cf. Figure 15.6).

EXERCISE State why the above construction must give Sierpinski, assuming the RIA does work. Deduce the order of the first few choices in Figure 15.8, by geometrical considerations.

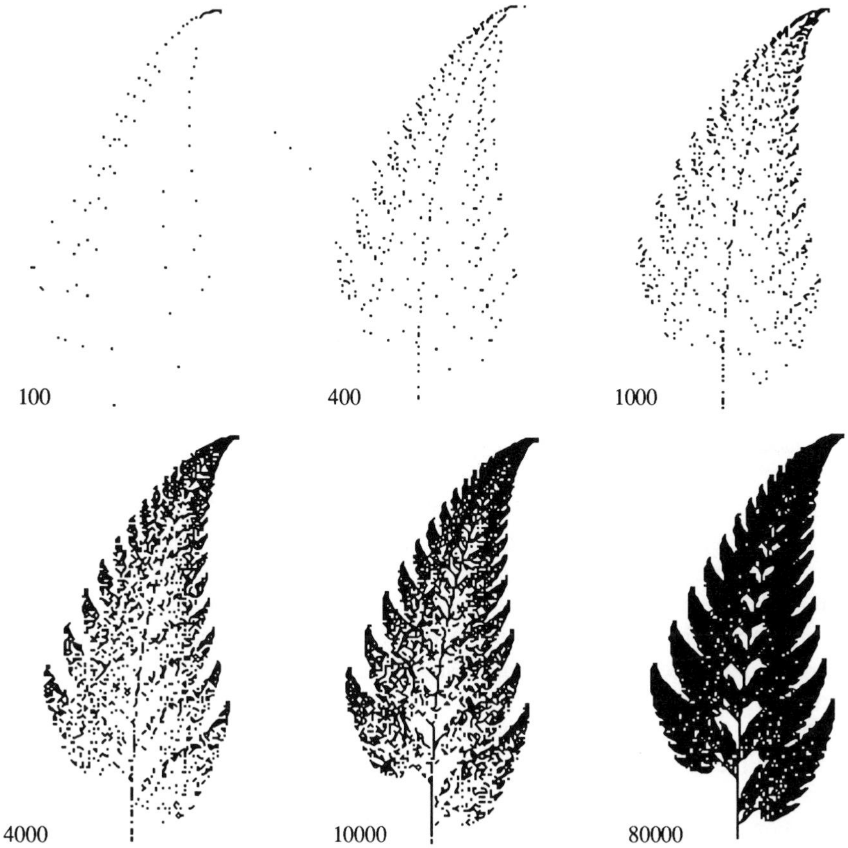

Figure 15.9 The fern of Figure 14.1 after various stages of the Random Iteration Algorithm. The few extraneous points are shown only in the first frame, Naturally more iterations are required for a full image than in the 'simpler' Sierpinski case. Compare the collage method in Figure 14.1 for the same attractor.

15.2.2 Why should it work?

PROBLEM 1 **Getting started.** We cannot guarantee that our starting point x_0 is actually on the attractor $\mathcal{A}$. However, we will deduce from earlier results that, given any small tolerance ε, say one tenth of a pixel diameter, all iterates x_n after a certain stage k will be within ε of points on the attractor. cf. Figure 15.10. This gives us the basis for lighting up the pixels by which the attractor may be represented - our objective in practical terms. From Definition 14.2, with W: $\mathcal{H}(X) \to \mathcal{H}(X)$ as the usual collage $W(E) = w_1(E) \cup \ldots \cup W_N(E)$, we have $W^n(E) \to \mathcal{A}$ for any starting set E_0. Let E_0 be the single point $\{x_0\}$. Then there is an integer k such that for all $n \geq k$ we have $d(W^n(\{x_0\}), \mathcal{A}) < \varepsilon$, where d is the usual Hausdorff distance (13.7). But x_n has the form $w_{\sigma_1} w_{\sigma_2} \ldots w_{\sigma_n}(x_0)$, which is in $W^n(\{x_0\})$, and therefore $d(x_n,A) < \varepsilon$. Thus x_n is within ε of some point a_n of the attractor, provided $n \geq k$. In practice k = 40 should be quite adequate.

PROBLEM 2 **Inaccuracy**. What about cumulative errors in computing an orbit? Fortunately the construction is self-correcting in that whatever potentially inaccurate point x_m we obtain at some intermediate stage in the process, it remains true that $W^n(E_0) \to \mathcal{A}$ if E_0

is the single point x_m. Also if x_{n+1} be accurately calculated from a possibly erroneous x_n then it is closer to $\mathcal{A}$ than x_n is, for if $a \in \mathcal{A}$ and $w_i(a) = b$, then $d(x_{n+1},b) = d(w_i(x_n), w(a)) \le r_i d(x_n,a)$.

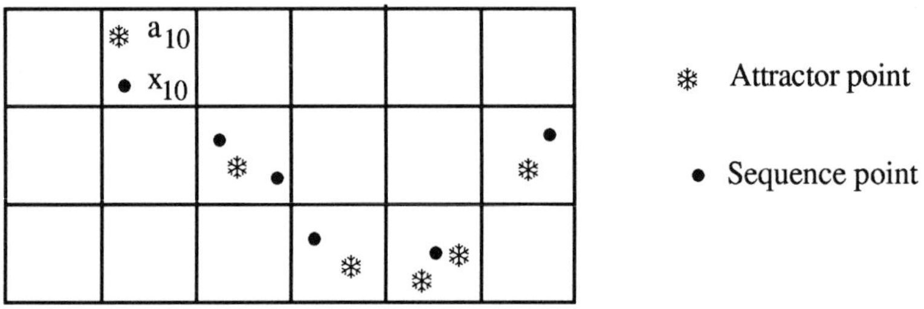

Figure 15.10 Each square denotes the extent of a pixel. Each point of the attractor has a sequence point close to it.

PROBLEM 3 **Distribution.** Given that the pixels we do light up are near enough correct, suppose all our hits are concentrated in certain parts of the attractor, and/or wasted in visiting the same places many times over? Thus only part of the attractor appears. This question is crucial. We give two answers. The second is based on measure theory and has fascinating implications. It is found in Section 15.3. The first and immediate answer is a finite version of the elegant and seminal result Theorem 15.22 that periodic points are dense in the attractor.

The essential idea used to prove that result was that any address and hence any $a \in \mathcal{A}$ can be approximated arbitrarily closely by getting the first k digits right for large enough k. After the k'th symbol, such a sequence may be continued in any way, and the approximation (15.11) still holds. It was nice to repeat the first k symbols ad infinitum so as to make a periodic sequence, but we don't *have* to do it that way. Suppose we run the RIA for 10,000 points. What is this 'badly distributed' horror we want to avoid? Answer: a significant proportion of points of $\mathcal{A}$ having no point of the RIA sequence $\{x_n\}$ near enough. The problem is solved if every point of $\mathcal{A}$ has points of $\{x_n\}$ within some small specified distance ε. So let us begin by supposing we have run the first forty points, and start counting with $x_0 \in \mathcal{A}$. Then we require that the finite sequence $X = \{x_n\}$ be *ε-dense* in $\mathcal{A}$, according to the following definition.

DEFINITION 15.25 Let X, A be compact nonempty subsets of a metric space, and $\varepsilon > 0$. We say *X is ε-dense in A* if

(1) $X \subseteq A$, and
(2) $d(X,A) \le \varepsilon$.

Note that (2) is equivalent to $d_A(X) \le \varepsilon$, since $X \subseteq A$ implies $d_X(A) = 0$. Hence in our case $X = \{x_n\}$ being ε-dense in $\mathcal{A}$ implies for any $a \in \mathcal{A}$:

$$\min_n d(a,x_n) = d(a,X) \le d_{\mathcal{A}}(X) \le \varepsilon. \tag{15.19}$$

That is, any $a_i \in \mathcal{A}$ has some point x_i of the sequence within distance ε, which is what we wanted. Here is the result on which a solution to Problem 3 is based. For it we recall that the diameter of a compact set A is $\operatorname{diam}(A) = \max d(x,y)$ $(x,y \in A)$.

THEOREM 15.26 Let the IFS $\{K; w_{1\text{-}N}\}$ have ratio r, and let x_0 be a point on the attractor $\mathcal{A}$. Suppose the finite sequence $\sigma = \sigma_1\sigma_2 \dots \sigma_s$ contains all finite sequences of length k, over $\{1,2, \dots ,N\}$, and is used to produce an RIA sequence of points $X = \{x_n\}$, defined by $x_{n+1} = w_{\sigma_n}(x_n)$. Then $\{x_n\}$ is ε-dense in $\mathcal{A}$, where

$$\varepsilon \ \le \ r^k \, diam(\mathcal{A}). \tag{15.20}$$

Proof Following the ideas of the addressing scheme, we establish the result by expressing $\mathcal{A}$ as a union of sets of diameter not exceeding r^k diam($\mathcal{A}$), each containing a point of $\{x_n\}$.

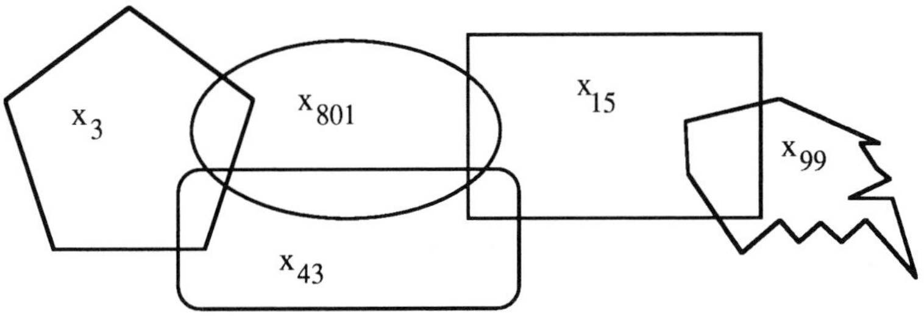

Figure 15.11 $\mathcal{A}$ as a union of sets of diameter not exceeding r^k diam($\mathcal{A}$), each containing a point of $\{x_n\}$.

It suffices to consider the case $k = 2$, for the general case is entirely similar. As in Section 15.1 we write $\mathcal{A}_i = w_i(\mathcal{A})$, $\mathcal{A}_{ij} = w_iw_j(\mathcal{A})$, and so on. Let $x,y \in \mathcal{A}_{ij}$. Then $x = w_iw_j(x')$, $y = w_iw_j(y')$, for some x',y' in $\mathcal{A}$ and we may argue thus: $d(x,y) = d(w_iw_j(x'), w_iw_j(y')) \le r\, d(w_j(x'), w_j(y')) \le r^2 d(x', y') \le r^2$ diam($\mathcal{A}$). In summary, recalling also (15.2), we have,

$$\mathcal{A} = \bigcup_{i,j=1}^{N} \mathcal{A}_{ij}, \qquad \text{diam}(\mathcal{A}_{ij}) \le r^2\text{diam}(\mathcal{A}). \tag{15.21}$$

Write $X = \{x_n\}$ and let a be a point of $\mathcal{A}$. From the first equality, $a \in \mathcal{A}_{ij}$ for some pair i,j. But σ contains all N^2 2-digit sequences, so we may write $\sigma = \dots ji\dots$, where $\sigma_v = i$, $\sigma_{v-1} = j$ for some v. Then with σ_1 applied first, $x_v = w_iw_j(w_{\sigma_{v-2}} \cdots w_{\sigma_1}(x_0))$, which is in $\mathcal{A}_{ij}$ because $x_0 \in \mathcal{A}$ implies that $w_{\sigma_{v-2}} \cdots w_{\sigma_1}(x_0)$ is in $\mathcal{A}$. Therefore

$d(a,X)$	$\le$	$d(a,x_v)$,	by Definition 13.1 for d(a,X)
	$\le$	diam($\mathcal{A}_{ij}$),	since $a, x_v \in \mathcal{A}_{ij}$
	$\le$	r^2diam($\mathcal{A}$),	by (15.21).

Since this inequality holds independently of the choice of $a \in \mathcal{A}$, we have finally that $d_{\mathcal{A}}(X) \le r^2$ diam($\mathcal{A}$) as required.

PROBLEM 3 SOLVED Although Theorem 15.26 specifies $x_0 \in A$, the last comment in Problem 2 implies that the sequence we actually get will be negligibly different from the $\{x_n\}$ of this Theorem and so will do equally well. That said, how long must the sequence be? For a given IFS attractor there is a suitably large k for acceptable accuracy, according to Theorem 15.26, and a long enough random sequence will contain all or near enough all sequences of size k. But just how long is 'enough'? Here is a sequence (spaced only for readability) that contains all sequences of size $k = 4$, where $N = 3$.

111121 132122 231133 121332 212123 233231 233331
113112 313332 112213 122331 313232 232132 222111 (15.22)

The number of 4-digit sequences is $3^4 = 81$, and each must start in the big sequence at a new position. This involves a *minimum* of 81 digits, plus three to complete the last 4-digit sequence, giving a total of 84. This minimum length is exactly what we have exhibited here. How such extremal situations may be achieved by a recursive construction is described in the next section. Right now we state the general formula, an easy generalisation from our example, and given as the exercise following.

THEOREM 15.27 If a sequence of digits from {1,2, .. ,N} contains every sequence of length k, then it has size at least $N^k + k - 1$.

EXERCISE Find in sequence (15.22) the 4-digit sequences 1122, 2222, 3333, 1231, 3131. Obtain the length formula of Theorem 15.27 by imitating the argument given for the case N = 3, k = 4.

EXAMPLE 15.28 Suppose we have an IFS $\{X; w_{1-4}\}$ with contraction factor $r = 1/2$, for which the attractor $\mathcal{A}$ lies within a square of 200 by 200 pixels on a computer screen. With pixel size as unit of length we have $\text{diam}(\mathcal{A}) \le 200\sqrt{2}$, say 283. How large should k be to ensure that every point of $\mathcal{A}$ has a sequence point within one pixel's distance? We require $(1/2)^k 283 < 1$, so with $2^8 = 256$, the value $k = 8$ will probably suffice in practice. From Theorem 15.27, the RIA sequence must have length at least $4^8 + 3 = 65{,}539$. On the other hand, a random sequence of this precise length is unlikely to be so optimally constructed as to actually include all 8-digit sequences.

What we have is a tradeoff. The lack of perfection is offset in the RIA by causing the digits to appear in proportion to the requirement of covering the attractor evenly, as distinct from within some tolerance. We choose a particular w_i more often if its images are to cover greater area. The possibilites of tradeoff are well illustrated by the fern of Figure 15.9, whose diameter is comparable to that of the present example. In that case, although the greatest contraction ratio of any w_i is as high as $r = 0.85$, the others are much less, and the final result is that 80,000 steps are used, compared to our idealised 65,539 (but cf. Figure 15.14).

15.2.3 M-sequences and the RIA

We show to construct a shortest possible sequence which will guarantee a given accuracy in the RIA. Consider first the case $N = p$, a prime number, such as 2,3,5,7,11, .. (divisible only by itself and 1). The digits $\{1,2, \dots, p\}$ or more usually $\{0,1,2, \dots, p-1\}$ represent the set Z_p of integers *reduced mod p*; that is, with the relation $p = 0$ imposed. Thus if $p = 5$ we may write $-2 = 5-2 = 3$. The most familiar case is $p = 2$, where we obtain the binary digits $Z_2 = \{0,1\}$, with $1+1 = 0$, and so $-1 = +1$. The sequences we require are obtained from (certain) polynomials with coefficients in Z_p. It will be convenient in the sequel to write such a polynomial, of degree k, as

$$f(x) = x^k - a_1x^{k-1} \dots - a_{k-1}x - a_k, \tag{15.23}$$

where we usually omit any term with coefficient zero. Since the coefficient of x^k is 1 by definition, we may represent f(x) by its coefficients $a_1a_2...a_k$, written in that order, with leading zeros optionally omitted. Of course k must then be given to avoid ambiguity, as in Table 15.1. Thus $x^4 - 2x^2 - 1$ becomes 0201, or just 201. It is important to note that highest powers and their coefficients go to the left. Given f(x), we define the *corresponding sequence* $\sigma = \sigma_0\sigma_1 \ldots$ to begin with k zeros, followed by a single 1, and thereafter

$$\sigma_n = a_1\sigma_{n-1} + a_2\sigma_{n-2} + \ldots + a_k\sigma_{n-k} \quad (n > k), \tag{15.24}$$

up to a total of $p^k + k - 1$ digits, the length required by Theorem 15.27. We will shortly show how to choose f(x) so that all possible sequences of length k appear in σ.

EXAMPLE 15.29 Let p = 2, k = 4, and $f(x) = x^4 - x^2 - 1$, with coefficients 0101. Then $\sigma_n = \sigma_{n-2} + \sigma_{n-4}$, the sum of the digits two back and four back (a helpful viewpoint for calculating) and σ = 00001010001010001.... But since a digit is determined recursively by the previous k by (15.24), it follows that whenever a sequence of k successive digits recurs, so do those following, and the sequence (if continued) is periodic. So we have here, after the initial zero, a sequence of period 6, namely the repetitions of 000101. Thus, however long we continue σ, we include only 7 of the 16 4-digit binary sequences posible, namely 0000, 0001, 0010, 0101, 1010, 0100, 1000. What we need is a sequence of period 15. Such is called an *M-sequence* (M for maximal), according to the following definition.

DEFINITION 15.30 If the sequence σ obtained from the mod p polynomial f(x) by (15.21) has period p^k-1 then we call σ an *M-sequence* and say that f(x) is *primitive.*

REMARKS 15.31 Strictly speaking, the M-sequence starts on our second digit, and continues indefinitely. The recursion formula (15.24) has k digits 00...01 as initial values. Each of the p^k-1 digits in a complete M-sequence period heads a *different* subsequence of k successive digits (why?); this excludes 00...0, which is catered for by our extra 0 at the start. In this way, choosing f(x) to be primitive results in a shortest possible sequence containing all p^k sequences of length k, as required for the accuracy $\varepsilon \le r^k \operatorname{diam}(\mathcal{A})$ of (15.20). Table 15.1 provides suitable polynomial coefficients for various values of k and p.

TABLE 15.1 Coefficients $a_1a_2 \ldots a_k$ for the recursion
$\sigma_n = a_1\sigma_{n-1} + a_2\sigma_{n-2} + \ldots + a_k\sigma_{n-k}$ (n > k), giving an M-sequence of integers mod p.

k	3	4	5	6	7	8	9	10	11
mod 2	11	11	101	11	11	1100011	10001	1001	101
mod 3	12	11	12	11	102				
mod 5	23	423	12						

	k	coefficients	k	coefficients	k	coefficients
mod 2	12	10011001	15	11	18	10000001
continued	13	11011	16	101101	19	1100011
	14	1100000000011	17	1001	20	1001

EXERCISE Use TABLE 15.1 to find a shortest possible sequence containing all 4-digit binary numbers.

EXAMPLE 15.32 (Sierpinski again.) In Figure 15.12 we compare results for the standard RIA versus the M-sequence method. The attractor's outline is a right angled triangle of side 100 pixels, with diameter taken as 142 units. We have N = p = 3 and contraction ratio r =

1/2. With σ from Table 15.1 the accuracy and sequence lengths L for k = 3, ... , 7 are shown below.

k	3	4	5	6	7
$\varepsilon = 2^{-k}\text{diam}(\mathcal{A})$	17.75	8.88	4.44	2.22	1.11
$L = 3^k+k-1$	29	84	247	734	2193

For example if k = 5 we read the relevant polynomial mod 3 as 00012, giving the recursion $\sigma_n = \sigma_{n-4} + 2\sigma_{n-5}$ and the sequence 00000100012001110100212.. . The high proportion of 0's early on results from the initial k and our (usual) choice of polynomial with as many leading zeros as possible, and few 1's. No 5-digit sequence is repeated unless we continue beyond the prescribed 247 digits (two extra are used below). A consequence is that the first few iterates home in on one vertex of the gasket.

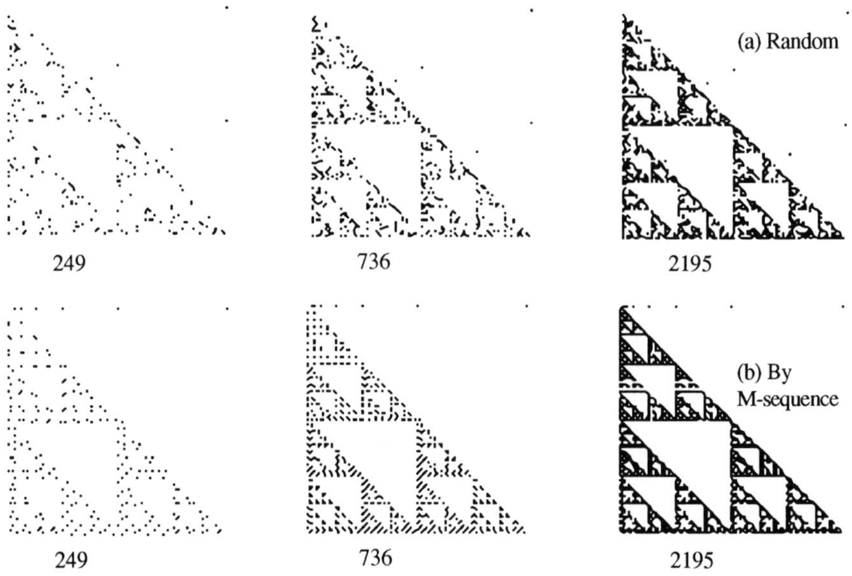

Figure 15.12 Comparison of results from (a) random iterations, (b) M-sequence iterations, in constructing the Sierpinski gasket one point at a time.

CONCLUSIONS 15.33 At every stage shown in Figure 15.12 the M-sequence method gives superior results to the standard RIA. This can be expected whenever N is obligingly a prime number and each $w_i(A)$ has the same area and so should receive the same number of points for uniform coverage. A random sequence of length p^k+k-1 cannot be expected to be optimised for length k subsequences in the same way as an M-sequence, but comes into its own when some areas have a high ratio to others and therefore some digits should appear say ten times as often as others, as in the fern case (see Figure 15.9 and Table 14.2).

On the other hand the M-sequence method can be adapted to a frequency ratio of, for example two, by taking large enough p and using the same transformation w_i for more than one digit value. Alternatively we may do everything in binary, say with 000, ..., 111 representing decimal 0 to 7, and ensuring that all binary words of length 3k occur. All this requires further experimentation. In addition we may investigate theoretically how an optimal sequence for a given IFS attractor may be generated (author's work in progress).

FURTHER DETAILS Useful references on M-sequences are McEliece (1987), and Lidl and Niederreiter (1986), whose Tables C and F may be used to extend the present Table 15.1 (but note that the signs must be changed). It can be shown that a primitive polynomial must be *irreducible* that is, must have no factor of lower positive degree. For example mod 2 (where + and - coincide), x^2+x+1 and x^3+x+1 are primitive, but x^2+1 is not even irreducible, since it equals $(x+1)^2$. On the other hand $x^6 + x^3 + 1$ is irreducible but not primitive. The existence and applications of irreducible and/or primitive polynomials, especially those with few nonzero coefficients, and other properties, is a fast expanding topic of research (see e.g. Cohen(1989)).

PROJECT Generate a sequence to produce a fern from Table 14.2 by using an M-sequence on digits 1,2,3 with a 4 for the stem inserted say after every 100 sequence digits. Compare results with those from a computer's random number generator, for a given number of iterations.

15.3 Why measure theory?

A measure in its historical technical sense is a way of distributing something - anything that can be quantified - over an area or more general space. Thus in *rendering*, i.e. distributing light, shade or colour, we are specifying a measure. There are many approaches: ray tracing (Glassner, 1989), digital halftoning (Ulichney, 1987), displacement methods (Blinn, 1978), texture mapping (Heckbert, 1989), to name only a few. For an overview under the heading of image synthesis see Joy et al (1988). However it is probably safe to say that workers in these fields do not normally think in terms of mathematical meaure theory. Fiume and Fournier (1984, 1989) propose a general framework for using measures in computer graphics, and time will clarify its appropriateness and usefulness.

By contrast we are dealing here with an approach through measures for iterated function systems in which a, perhaps controversial, issue, is just how general it can be made. Interestingly Hutchinson (1981) had argued that it should be easier to 'use' invariant sets, i.e. attractors of sets of contraction maps such as IFS's, if further natural structure were imposed; in particular, measures: and rendering. He laid the groundwork for this, including the measure-distinguishing metric to which subsequent writers have attached his name, and a contractive transformation on measures which is the key to having a unique measure associated with an IFS - called the Markov operator in Barnsley and Demko (1985). The latter set up a framework allowing the maps of an IFS to be if desired the solutions $w_1(z)$ .. $w_N(z)$ of an equation relating complex w, z, thus giving a new approach to measures on, and generation of, Julia sets (we touch on this in (16.20); see Barnsley(1988) for applications).

15.3.1 What measures are about

We will concentrate on applications in the plane or computer screen. Roughly, a measure is a rule for allocating or associating an amount of something to each of a collection of areas, or subsets. That 'something' could be

Rainfall	Ink
Area	Dots
Mass	Light intensity
Hours of sunshine	Shade of green

The second column exemplifies our concern here. Imagine dots from the RIA (Random Iteration Algorithm) raining down on the attractor $\mathcal{A}$ of the IFS, shading it in. We will determine a measure that controls how the process develops with time, and what the result will be. In the Algorithm as given in Definition 15.23, the probability p_i was fixed as D_i/D, the proportion of the attractor $\mathcal{A}$ covered by $w_i(\mathcal{A})$. Henceforth this will be simply the default value, in an *IFS with probabilites* $\{X: w_{1\text{-}N}; p_{1\text{-}N}\}$, subject only to $p_i > 0$ $(1 \le i \le N)$ and $\sum p_i = 1$.

It is by changing the parameters p_i that we can achieve varied lighting effects. And similarly for distributing shades of colour over the attractor. We'll suppose there is a fixed amount of 1 unit to distribute. Then if one area's share is increased, another gets less. We will denote the amount allocated to any set B by $\mu(B)$, and require the following important rules to hold (the last two follow from the first - see the exercise following):

$$\mu(A \cup B) = \mu(A) + \mu(B), \quad \text{provided that } A \cap B = \emptyset, \tag{15.25}$$
$$A \subseteq B \Rightarrow \mu(A) \le \mu(B), \tag{15.26}$$
$$\mu(\emptyset) = 0. \tag{15.27}$$

EXERCISE Notice that (15.25) implies (15.27): $\mu(A) = \mu(A \cup \emptyset) = \mu(A) + \mu(\emptyset)$, and hence $\mu(\emptyset) = 0$. Deduce also (15.26) by expressing B as the union of disjoint sets A, B\A.

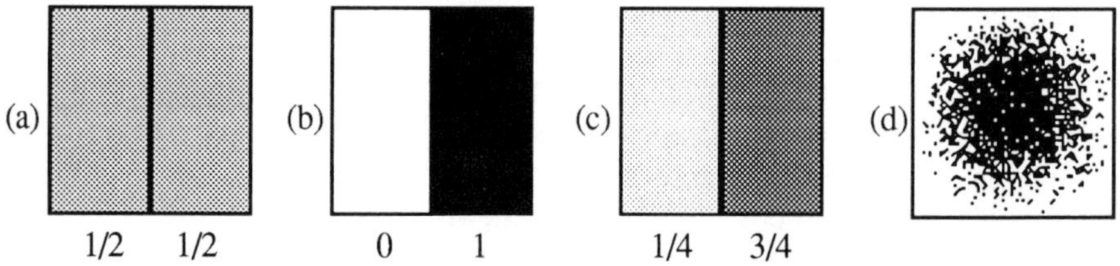

Figure 15.13 (a), (b), (c) Some ways to distribute one unit of ink over a square divided into two disjoint subsets, where the amount of ink in each subset is given. (d) A distribution requiring division into many subsets.

We will see in Sections 15.3.3 and 15.3.4 how to make the p_i determine μ uniquely. Suppose we apply the RIA to an iterated function system with attractor $\mathcal{A}$. Here is one viewpoint: the sequence of points output, $x_0, x_1, x_2, \ldots x_n \in \mathcal{A}$, will be suitably distributed if every subset of X contains the right proportion of these points. This is because our including every subset allows as fine a subdivision of the plane as we like. Compare Figure 15.13. What works well however is to take a slightly restricted collection of subsets. We start with all open discs, however small, and enlarge this collection in a manner soon to be described (Definition 15.34), resulting in a collection $\mathcal{B}$ called the *Borel subsets*. Let N(B,n) denote the actual number of the n+1 points x_i which fall in Borel set B. Then the proportion falling there is N(B,n)/(n+1), and the work of Elton (1987) shows that

$$\frac{N(B,n)}{n+1} \longrightarrow \mu(B), \qquad \text{as } n \to \infty, \tag{15.28}$$

with probability 1. That is, in practice, the actual proportion must get arbitrarily close to the required proportion as the number of iterations increases. This is independent of the specific choice of map used to derive x_{i+1} from x_i, provided it is chosen randomly as specified in Definition 15.23. Now we fill in some details.

	DISC 1		DISC 2
steps	ratio	steps	ratio
2000	0.196	1000	0.086
4000	0.204	2000	0.098
6000	0.198	3000	0.104
8000	0.193	4000	0.100
10000	0.201	5000	0.102
12000	0.204	6000	0.100
14000	0.209	7000	0.101
16000	0.210	8000	0.101
18000	0.206	9000	0.100
20000	0.210	10000	0.101

Figure 15.14 The proportion of iterated points falling in two discs. Note that, although disc 1 covers the smaller portion of the attractor, it has double the hits. This suggests that the allocation $p_i = D_i/D$ could be much improved.

DEFINITION 15.34 The collection $\mathbf{B}$ of all *Borel sets* B of a metric space X consists of:

(1) the open sets, namely all unions of open discs,
(2) the closed sets, that is the complements of open sets,
(3) all sets formed from (1), (2) by taking complements, countable unions, and countable intersections.

We recall that *countable* means 'can be put in correspondence with the integers', so that a *countable union* of sets has the form $A_1 \cup A_2 \cup \ldots = \cup_n A_n$ $(n = 0, 1, 2, \ldots)$.

EXAMPLES 15.35 (Some Borel sets.) (1) *On the real line* $\mathbf{R}$ all open intervals and all closed intervals are Borel sets. Note that the complement of one Borel set in another is included, for $A \backslash B = A \cap B^c$. Intersecting closed intervals with open ones gives the half open intervals, for example $(0,2) \cap [1,5] = [1,2)$, so they are Borel sets too. Also, since every point in $\mathbf{R}$ is a closed set, all countable subsets $\{y_1, y_2, ..\}$ are Borel sets.

(2) *In the plane.* We have all open or closed discs, their interiors, boundaries and intersections, and the same for rectangles. Thus we include a great variety of 'partly open' sets. Line segments are included too.

EXERCISE Write down a Borel subset of the plane which is neither open nor closed.

The reader is entitled to ask 'what sets are not Borel sets?'. The answer is too complicated to be worth developing here. Indeed, specialised texts are frequently content with simply proving that non-Borel sets must exist, without giving an explicit construction. The numbers $\mu(B)$ together constitute a function $\mu: \mathbf{B} \to [0,\infty)$ satisfying (15.25) (*additivity*), and $\mu(X) = 1$ (*normalisation*). Such a function on $\mathbf{B}$ is called a (normalised) *Borel measure* if it further satisfies

$$\mu\left(\bigcup_n A_n\right) = \sum_n \mu(A_n) \qquad (15.29)$$

for every countable collection $\{A_n\}$ of Borel subsets of X which are *mutually disjoint* (that is, $A_n \cap A_m = \emptyset$ if $n \neq m$). The infinite sum converges because of (15.26) and an upper bound of 1 (see Exercise 24 at the end of the chapter). The rest of Section 15.3 is mainly a quest for the Holy Grail of μ for an iterated function system. We find it in two ways:

ABSTRACTLY - as the unique fixed point of a contraction mapping,
CONCRETELY - in terms of the parameters p_i and the maps of the IFS.

15.3.2 Measures and integrals

We need to establish the connection between a Borel measure μ and a corresponding integral.

DEFINITION 15.36 The *characteristic function* $\chi_A: X \to \mathbf{R}$, of a subset A of a compact metric space X, is given by $\chi_A(x) = 1$ if $x \in A$, otherwise 0. A *simple function* $f: X \to \mathbf{R}$ has the form

$$f(x) = \sum_{i=1}^{m} c_i \, \chi_{B_i}(x), \tag{15.30}$$

where the c_i are real constants and the B_i are Borel sets forming a partition of X. That is, $X = B_1 \cup B_2 \cup \ldots \cup B_m$, with $B_i \cap B_j = \emptyset$ $(i \neq j)$. Thus f may be described as piecewise constant, taking the value c_1 for $x \in B_1$, the value c_2 for $x \in B_2$, and so on. A typical graph is shown in Figure 15.15.

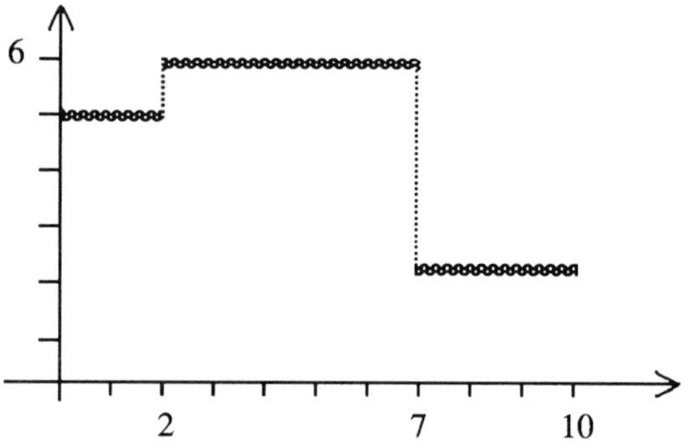

Figure 15.15 The graph of the simple function which equals 5 for $0 \leq x < 2$, 6 for $2 \leq x < 7$, and 2 for $7 \leq x \leq 10$. (Vertical dotted lines strictly not part of graph.)

For given μ, we now define the *integral of f with respect to μ* as

$$\int_X f(x)\, d\mu = \sum_{i=1}^{m} c_i \, \mu(B_i). \tag{15.31}$$

EXAMPLE 15.37 Let $X = [0,10]$, partitioned into Borel subsets $B_1 = [0,2)$, $B_2 = [2,7)$, $B_3 = [7,10]$. Define a Borel measure on X by $\mu([a,b]) = (1/10)(b - a)$, and similarly for open and half-open intervals in X. This implies that any single point x has measure zero; for example we have by (15.25): $\mu([0,x)) + \mu(\{x\}) = \mu([0,x]) = \mu([0,x))$. It follows that any countable subset has measure zero. The simple function $f = 5\chi_{B_1} + 6\chi_{B_2} + 2\chi_{B_3}$, has a graph as depicted in Figure 15.15. According to (15.31) the integral of f with respect to μ is

$5\mu(B_1) + 6\mu(B_2) + 2\mu(B_3) = 5(1/10)(2-0) + 6(1/10)(7-2) + 2(1/10)(10-7) = 4.6.$

The next step is to extend the definition (15.31) to a *continuous* function f(x) via a sequence of simple functions f_n converging to f, where the distance between functions is that of (13.12), namely $d(f_n,f) = \max |f_n(x) - f(x)|$ $(x \in X)$. Thus $f_n \to f$ entails $f_n(x) \to f(x)$, as $n \to \infty$, for each x in X. We then define

$$\int_X f(x)\, d\mu = \lim_{n\to\infty} \int_X f_n(x)\, d\mu . \quad (15.32)$$

We showed that such a sequence $\{f_n\}$ always exists (Theorem 13.35). To put it another way, every continuous function can be approximated to arbitrary precision by a simple function. The right hand limit of (15.32) always exists, as the limit of a Cauchy sequence, essentially because f_m and f_n, for large m,n, are close to f and hence to each other. Similarly it is independent of the choice of $\{f_n\}$, for if $\{f_n\}$, $\{g_n\}$ both have limit f then their difference is arbitrarily small for sufficiently large n and hence so are their integrals. Here is an example, again in **R**.

EXAMPLE 15.38 Let $f(x) = x^2$ on $X = [0,1]$ For each $n \geq 2$ we partition X into n intervals, which are Borel subsets: $B_1 = [0, 1/n)$, and $B_m = [(m-1)/n, m/n]$ for $m = 2, 3, \ldots, n$. Define the measure of an interval to be the distance between its endpoints. Now we are ready to define a sequence of simple functions by

$$f_n(x) = \sum_{m=1}^{n} f(\tfrac{m}{n})\, \chi_{B_m} \quad (15.33)$$

for which the graph of f_3 is shown in Figure 15.16 below.

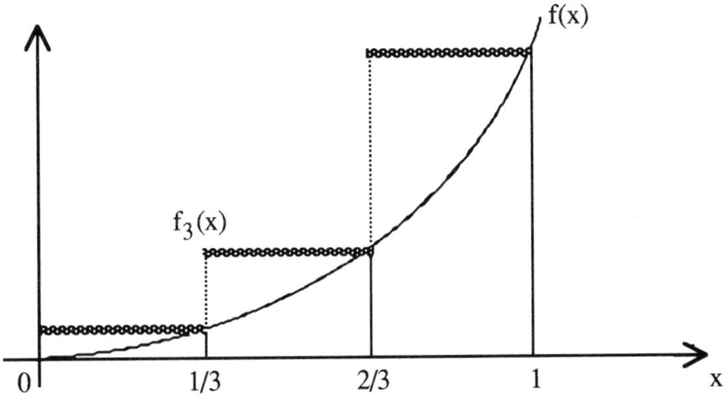

Figure 15.16 The staircase represents $f_3(x)$, for $f(x) = x^2$, as defined in (15.30).

Now let us prove that $f_n \to f$ as required. We have

$$\begin{aligned} d(f_n,f) &= \max_{x\in X} |f_n(x) - f(x)| = f(1) - f_n\left(\tfrac{n-1}{n}\right) \quad \text{(cf. Figure 15.16)} \\ &= 1 - (1 - \tfrac{1}{n})^2 = \tfrac{2}{n} - \tfrac{1}{n^2}, \end{aligned}$$

which does indeed tend to 0 as $n \to \infty$, and so $f_n \to f$. Now for the integral. We defined $\mu(B_m) = 1/n$, the distance between endpoints of B_m $(1 \leq m \leq n)$, so (15.31) works out as (again, see Figure 15.16),

$$\int_X f_n(x)\, d\mu = \sum_{m=1}^{n} \left(\frac{m}{n}\right)^2 \frac{1}{n} = \frac{1}{n^3} \sum_{m=1}^{n} m^2$$

$$= \tfrac{1}{6}(1 + \tfrac{1}{n})(2 + \tfrac{1}{n}), \quad \text{since} \sum_{m=1}^{n} m^2 = \tfrac{n}{6}(n+1)(2n+1).$$

So by (15.32), $\int_X f(x)\, d\mu = \lim_{n\to\infty} \int_X f_n(x)\, d\mu = \frac{1}{6} \cdot 2 = \frac{1}{3}.$

The reader may notice that this special case works out in a similar way, and to the same answer, as the usual integral of a real function done from first principles (cf. Swokowski, 1979).

EXERCISE Repeat Example 15.38 for $f(x) = x^2+1$. Check your answer by ordinary integration.

15.3.3 The measure as a fixed point

For this section, see especially Hutchinson (1981). Now we can introduce the metric space $\mathcal{P}(X)$ which exhibits the sought measure as the fixed point of a contraction mapping. The points of $\mathcal{P}(X)$ consist of all Borel measures on X, and the distance between two measures μ,ν is defined by their effect on functions, through the *Hutchinson metric*,

$$d_H(\mu,\nu) = \sup_f \left\{ \int_X f\, d\mu - \int_X f\, d\nu \ : \ f: X \to \mathbf{R}, \ |f| \le 1 \right\} \qquad (15.34)$$

where f is bounded, sup denotes the supremum or least upper bound (Definition 12.4), and $|f|$ is the norm, or minimum bound ratio, of Note 11.44, corresponding to the contraction ratio in the context of IFS's. Thus $|f(x) - f(y)| \le |f|\, d(x,y)$ $(x,y \in X)$. We state without proof the following important result from Hutchinson (1981).

THEOREM 15.39 $\mathcal{P}(X)$ is a compact metric space.

To define the crucial contraction mapping M, we first remark that the inverse image of one Borel set is another. More exactly, if $w: X \to X$ is a continuous map of a compact metric space X, and B is a Borel subset of X, then so is $w^{-1}(B)$. In the case B is actually open, $w^{-1}(B)$ is open and hence Borel, by Definition 11.34 for continuity. The other cases of B are left as the next exercise.

DEFINITION 15.40 The map $M: \mathcal{P}(X) \to \mathcal{P}(X)$ associated with an IFS $\{X; w_{1\text{-}N}; p_{1\text{-}N}\}$ is given by

$$M(\nu) = p_1\, \nu\, w_1^{-1} + p_2\, \nu\, w_2^{-1} + .. + p_N\, \nu\, w_N^{-1}. \qquad (15.35)$$

We validate this definition by showing that the right hand side ρ of (15.35) is a (normalised) Borel measure. That is, for disjoint Borel sets A, B: (1) $\rho(B) \in [0,\infty)$, (2) $\rho(A \cup B) = \rho(A) + \rho(B)$ provided $A \cap B = \emptyset$ (we omit details of the infinite case), (3) $\rho(X) = 1$.

Proof For (1), we already know $w_i^{-1}(B)$ must be Borel, $1 \le i \le N$, and since ν is by assumption a Borel measure we have $\nu(w_i^{-1}(B)) \in [0,\infty)$. But all $p_i \ge 0$ and therefore

$\Sigma p_i v w_i^{-1}(B) \in [0,\infty)$. Part (3) is a nice little exercise using the facts that $w_i^{-1}(X) = X$ and $\Sigma p_i = 1$. For Part (2), let $A \cap B = \emptyset$. Then

$$\begin{aligned}
\rho(A\cup B) &= \Sigma_i\, p_i v w_i^{-1}(A\cup B) \\
&= \Sigma_i\, p_i v\,(w_i^{-1}A \cup w_i^{-1}B), && \text{by Lemma 11.36} \\
&= \Sigma_i\, p_i\,(\, v(w_i^{-1}A) + v(w_i^{-1}B)\,), && \text{by (15.25)} \\
&= \Sigma_i\, p_i v w_i^{-1}(A) + \Sigma_i\, p_i v w_i^{-1}(B) \\
&= \rho(A) + \rho(B) && \text{by definition.}
\end{aligned}$$

THEOREM 15.41 (Hutchinson, 1981) For an IFS $\{X; w_{1\text{-}N}; p_{1\text{-}N}\}$ with contraction ratio $r < 1$, the map M is a contraction mapping (also with ratio r). Hence there is a unique measure $\mu \in \mathcal{P}(X)$ fixed by M.

DEFINITION 15.42 The unique measure μ fixed by M is called the *invariant measure* of the associated IFS.

Note that 'hence' in Theorem 15.41 refers to our old friend the Banach Fixed Point Theorem (or Contraction Mapping Theorem), 13.14, which predicts the existence of μ. We see in the next section that this same theorem gives a way to determine μ in terms of the parameters p_i.

EXERCISE Show that if X is compact and $w: X \to X$ is continuous, then the inverse image of a Borel set is another Borel set. [Note how w^{-1} acts on complements, unions, and intersections. See e.g. Table 11.4.]

15.3.4 Finding and using the invariant measure

According to the Fixed Point Theorem, the invariant measure may be found by starting with any measure, however simple, and applying the map M repeatedly. We'll see that this works beautifully with an IFS. The general case appears far easier if we begin with the very first IFS of this Chapter (Example 15.1), in which the attractor is not a fern, Sierpinski gasket or other fractal, but a filled in square B.

EXAMPLE 15.43 The IFS is $\{B; w_{1\text{-}4}; p_{1\text{-}4}\}$, where w_i is uniform scaling with centre the i'th vertex of B and ratio 1/2, as depicted in Figure 15.17. We write $B_i = w_i(B)$, $B_{ik} = w_i w_k(B)$, and so on. Note that i appears before k on both sides of the equals sign but that w_k is applied before w_i. Nevertheless B_3, for example, is the union of B_{31}, B_{32}, B_{33}, and B_{34}. The second subscript refers to the second level of subdivision of B.

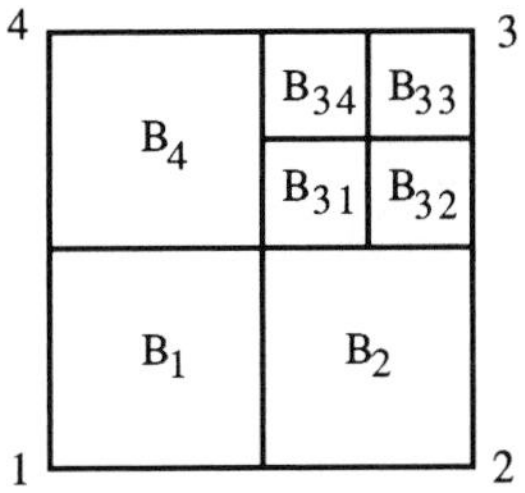

Figure 15.17

Suppose B has unit area and define (almost) the simplest possible measure μ_0 on B by $\mu_0(A) = \text{area}(A)$ for A an open disc in B. Then the same holds for any Borel set A after we follow Definition 15.34 and the additive rule (15.25). Without going into details, the measure of a set equals the measure of its closure and so the boundary has measure zero (see Exercise 25 at the end of the chapter). Since for example B_1, B_2 intersect only on their boundaries, we may neglect $B_1 \cap B_2$ in calculating measures.

Returning to the ink metaphor, we are distributing one unit of ink over B, and μ_0

distributes it in proportion to area. We use formula (15.35) to determine the sequence of measures $\mu_0, \mu_1, \ldots$ with $\mu_{n+1} = M(\mu_n)$, starting from μ_0. They give increasingly intricate ways in which to ink in the square, depending on the choices of p_1, p_2, p_3, p_4, and at the same time $\mu_n \to \mu$, the fixed 'point' of M. A key observation is that, apart from boundary points, w_1 maps no point of B into $w_2(B)$. So $w_1^{-1}(w_2B)$ is either the empty set or a nonempty subset of the boundary. In any event, $\tau(w_1^{-1}(w_2B)) = 0$ for every measure τ. More generally, for any $A \subseteq B$ and for every measure τ,

$$\tau(w_i^{-1}(w_k(A)) = \begin{cases} 0 & \text{if } i \neq k, \\ \tau(A) & \text{if } i = k. \end{cases} \qquad (15.36)$$

We may now compute as follows.

$$\begin{aligned} \mu_1(B_k) &= \Sigma_i\, p_i\, \mu_0\, w_i^{-1}(w_k(B)) \\ &= p_k\, \mu_0(B), && \text{since } \mu_0\, w_i^{-1}(w_k(B)) = 0,\ i \neq k, \\ & && \text{by (15.36) with } A = B. \\ &= p_k, && \text{since } \mu_0(B) = 1. \\ \mu_2(B_{rs}) &= \Sigma_i\, p_i\, \mu_1\, w_i^{-1}(B_{rs}) \\ &= \Sigma_i\, p_i\, \mu_1\, w_i^{-1}(w_r(B_s)) \\ &= p_r \mu_1(B_s), && \text{since } \mu_1\, w_i^{-1}(w_r(B_s)) = 0,\ i \neq r, \\ & && \text{by (15.36) with } A = B_s. \\ &= p_r p_s. \end{aligned}$$

μ_0: Distribution proportional to area,
μ_1: Uses the first subdivision of B, allocating amount p_i to B_i,
μ_2: Uses the second subdivision of B, with B_{rs} receiving amount $p_r p_s$.
...... and so on. We note that the total ink on B_i remains constant over successive μ_n, but is shared between the subdivisions of B_i. For example, after B_1 is subdivided into B_{11}, B_{12}, B_{13}, B_{14} its total ink is $p_1p_1 + p_1p_2 + p_1p_3 + p_1p_4$, which equals $p_1\Sigma_i p_i = p_1$, since $\Sigma_i p_i = 1$. Thus $\mu(B_i) = \mu_1(B_i)$. How the ink is redistributed by successive μ_n is illustrated in Figure 15.18, for the case $p_1 = 1/6$, $p_2 = 2/6$, $p_3 = 1/6$, $p_4 = 2/6$. An inductive proof may be modelled on the above arguments to show (n being the length of the subscript ik..z):

$$\mu(B_{ik\ldots z}) = \mu_n(B_{ik\ldots z}) = p_i p_k \cdots p_z. \qquad (15.37)$$

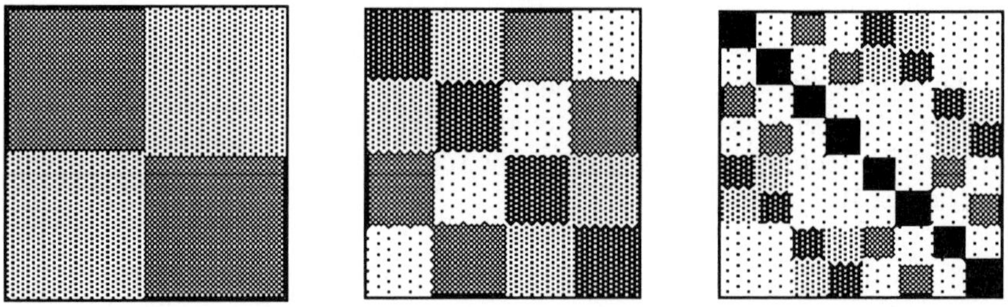

Figure 15.18 The three patchworks represent the effect of successive refinements μ_1, μ_2, μ_3 leading to the invariant measure μ, in case $p_1 = 1/6$, $p_2 = 2/6$, $p_3 = 1/6$, $p_4 = 2/6$ of Example 15.43.

EXERCISE In the notation of Example 15.43 above: (a) prove that $\mu_3(B_{rst}) = p_r p_s p_t$ by using the corresponding formulae for μ_1, μ_2 **or** (b) estimate how many points you would expect to have landed in each of B_1, B_{23}, B_{214} after 36000 iterations of the Random Iteration Algorithm [see (15.28)].

The result of running the RIA with the example probabilities p_i, whose influence is indicated in Figure 15.18, is shown below in Figure 15.19. We see a varying density of dots in which the structure of μ_1 and μ_2 can be discerned, with traces of μ_3.

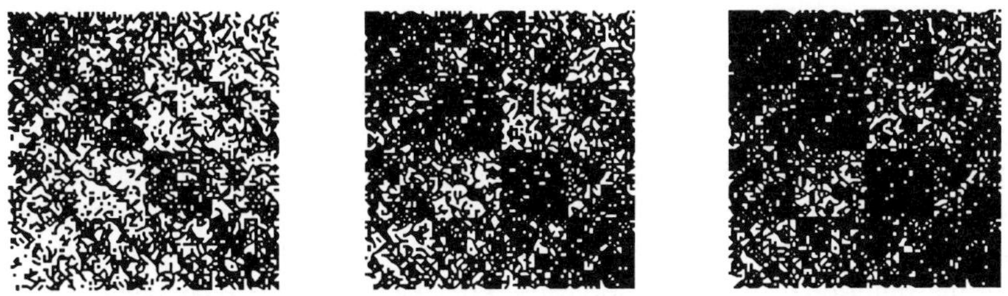

10000 20000 30000

Figure 15.19 The Box IFS of Example 15.43, with $p_1 = 1/6$, $p_2 = 2/6$, $p_3 = 1/6$, $p_4 = 2/6$. Result after various numbers of steps of the Random Iteration Algorithm.

It is salutary to realise that we can obtain such a pattern only during the construction process. For the attractor is a filled-in square, and that is what we will eventually get, with all trace of μ lost. The invariant measure controls the way in which the image builds up, the proportion of points landing in any (Borel) set A being more and more accurately $\mu(A)$. However, this can still give interesting effects, as illustrated in the next example.

The general case For an IFS in which the $w_i(\mathcal{A})$ intersect at most on their boundaries (15.36) applies and the calculation of Example 15.43 goes through. Without this condition some equalities of (15.37) may fail but we can still deduce the weaker result $\mu(\mathcal{A}_{ik..z}) \geq p_i p_k .. p_z$. Calculating μ on arbitrarily fine subdivisions $\mathcal{A}_{ik..z}$ is still possible in principle (Barnsley and Demko, 1985) but more important is that the p_i do determine μ (the problem of pressing interest is to work back from μ to the p_i).

EXAMPLE 15.44 Here we apply a standard 20000 iterations of the RIA for the 'Frizzy' attractor whose IFS code is given in Table 15.2. We compare results for three combinations of probabilites, shown as cases (a), (b), (c) in Figure 15.20 below.

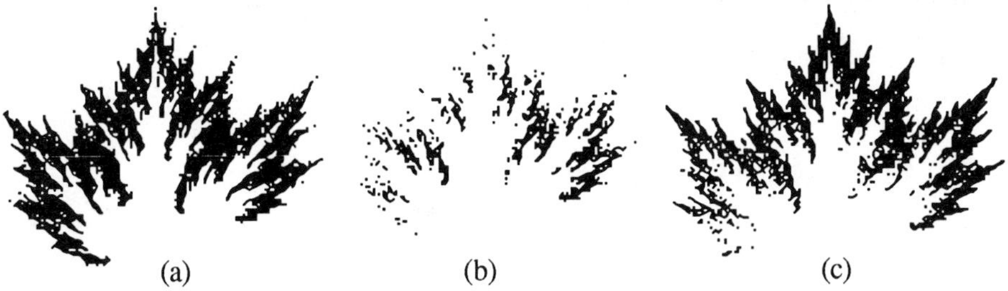

(a) (b) (c)

Figure 15.20 A version of Barnsley's 'Frizzy', with probabilities (a) all equal to 1/3, (b) 0.1, 0.8, 0.1 in some order, (c) 0.6, 0.3, 0.1 in some order.

EXERCISE For Figure 15.20 (b), (c) can you say to which transformations of Table 15.2 each probability applies? The number of iterations in each case is 20000.

TABLE 15.2

IFS code for Figure 15.20
a to d should be divided by 100

	a	b	c	d	e	f
w_1	50	0	0	75	64	0
w_2	26	-50	23	57	163	10
w_3	26	50	-23	57	28	69

METHOD 15.45 **Rendering by the RIA**. Although cases (a) to (c) of Figure 15.20 can be distinguished, it is still true that, as in the example preceding it, the eventual result is the attractor, independently of our choice of probabilities. However there is another way to proceed. For each pixel p we count the number of points n_p which arrive after a given number n_0 of iterations, and use this count to decide the pixel's grey or colour shading. A previously prepared table or 'colour assignment function' allocates to the pixel a colour corresponding to the number $c = n_p/n_0$ lying between 0 and 1. It may be worthwhile instead counting the number n_g of hits on a small group g of pixels and realising the value n_g/n_0 by adjusting the individual pixels of the group. For example some increasing shade values might be realised by (see e.g. Ulichney, 1987).

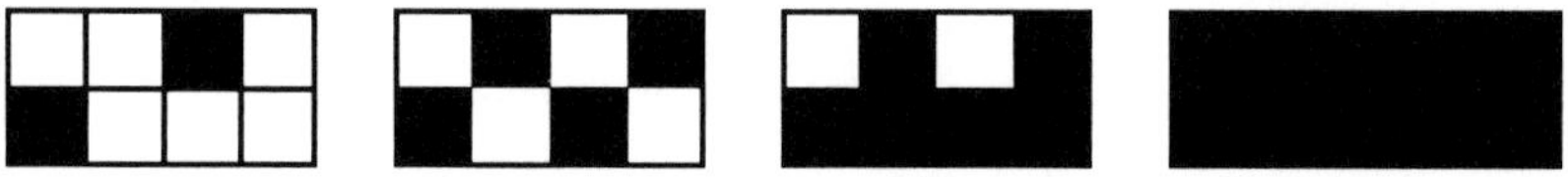

Similarly the range of colours may be increased. Here are the main degrees of freedom available in order to represent a coloured image by the IFS method.

(1) Segment the image. This might be to achieve a restricted colour spectrum in each piece, or to ensure that each piece requires shades of only one colour.
(2) Find an IFS for each part by the collage method (14.19).
(3) Add redundant maps to allow greater adjustment in rendering.
(4) Use a condensation set (Definition 14.17), perhaps consisting of several parts (a leaf, a flower, smoke, ..), preferably defined by an IFS.
(5) Experiment with probabilities for the IFS's, aiming for the desired colour effect. This may be systematised to some extent, analogously to the collage method for maps. The bound (13.10) gives a corresponding bound for how far out the result of a trial set of p_i will be.
(6) Construct and vary a colour assignment table for the IFS in each segment.

For more information and illustrations see Barnsley and Demko (1985), Barnsley and Elton (1988), Barnsley and Sloan (1988), Barnsley (1988), and especially Barnsley, Jacquin, Malassenet, Reuter, and Sloan (1988).

15.4 Hausdorff dimension

The dimension invented in 1919 by Hausdorff is defined through measures and so, like them, is based on ever more intricate subdivisions. For this reason alone we might guess it would be useful for making precise what we mean by 'fractal', though this is easier to see in retrospect. It occupied a perhaps undeservedly obscure place even in the mathematical world until its relevance to fractals (not to say *their* relevance) was highlighted by Mandelbrot's definition of a fractal as a set whose Hausdorff dimension exceeds its topological dimension.

We have opted for the definition of a set as fractal if the two dimensions differ, which occurs in particular if the Hausdorff dimension is not an integer (the other being integral by definition). It is not clear that the final satisfactory definition has been found (cf. Edgar, 1990).

Hausdorff dimension is defined for any set, unlike similarity dimension, which applies only to sets E in Euclidean space $\mathbf{R}^n$ which are self-similar. That is, they satisfy $E = w_1(E) \cup w_2(E) \cup .. \cup w_N(E)$, where the maps w are similarities of $\mathbf{R}^n$, namely dilation (uniform scaling) combined with an isometry. Equivalently they satisfy the scaling relation $d(w(x), w(y)) = r\, d(x,y)$, where r is the similarity ratio, $0 < r < 1$. Examples are the Koch curve and Sierpinski gasket but not the ferns of Figures 14.1 and 14.21. However similarity dimension is very important because it is not only easy to calculate, by formula (10.12), but coincides with Hausdorff dimension for self-similar sets (Theorem 15.54) under a mild restriction. Note: in this section all sets will be in $\mathbf{R}^n$.

DEFINITION 15.46 We recall that if a subset A of $\mathbf{R}$ is bounded above then there is a number sup A, the supremum or least upper bound of A. If A is bounded below we have inf A, the infimum or greatest lower bound of A. The diameter diam(E) or $|E|$ of a bounded subset of $\mathbf{R}^n$ is $\sup d(x,y)$ $(x,y \in E)$. A *δ-cover* of a set E is a countable family of sets $\{V_i\}$ which cover E, i.e. $E \subseteq V_1 \cup V_2 \cup ...$, and whose diameter $|V_i|$ satisfies $0 < |V_i| \leq \delta$. Unlike in our study of compact sets, the V_i need not be open. Hausdorff dimension is conveniently defined in *three stages*. We begin by defining for $E \subseteq \mathbf{R}^n$, $s \geq 0$ and $\delta > 0$,

Stage 1
$$H_\delta^s(E) = \inf \sum_{i=1}^{\infty} |V_i|^s \qquad (15.38)$$

where the infimum is taken over all δ-covers of E. The notation contains two further implications. Although the sum is written with an ∞ sign, we allow the possibility that the covering is finite, when we may think of all but a finite number of the V_i being the empty set. More importantly, it may happen that all the sums considered in (15.38) are infinite. We then say, in an extension of previous notation, that the infimum $H_\delta^s(E)$ is infinite, or $H_\delta^s(E) = \infty$.

Stage 2 (Hausdorff measure.) As δ decreases, fewer coverings qualify, and so the infimum in (15.38) is nondecreasing. Hence if $H_\delta^s(E)$ is bounded above it has a finite limit as $\delta \to 0$, otherwise $H_\delta^s(E) \to \infty$ (cf. Table 11.2(9)). Now we define *Hausdorff s-dimensional measure* by

$$H^s(E) = \lim_{\delta \to 0} H_\delta^s(E), \qquad (15.39)$$

writing $H^s(E) = \infty$ if a finite limit does not exist. It may be verified that H^s is a measure on the subsets of $\mathbf{R}^n$, meaning that if $A, B, V_1, V_2, .. \subseteq \mathbf{R}^n$ then

$$H^s(\emptyset) = 0, \quad A \subseteq B \Rightarrow H^s(A) \leq H^s(B), \text{ and} \qquad (15.40)$$

$$H^s(V_1 \cup V_2 \cup ...) \leq H^s(V_1) + H^s(V_2) + .. \text{ if } V_i \cap V_j = \emptyset \text{ for } i \neq j, \qquad (15.41)$$

the latter condition holding with strict equality in the case of Borel sets. Omitting most of the verification, we will show that $H^s(A \cup B) = H^s(A) + H^s(B)$ if A, B are disjoint nonempty compact (= bounded and closed) sets. Since we will let $\delta \to 0$ we may at this stage insist that $\delta < \min d(x,y)$ $(x \in A, y \in B)$, the latter being a positive number (an easy exercise). It follows that no set in a δ-cover of $A \cup B$ can intersect both A and B, so a δ-cover of $A \cup B$ consists of a δ-cover $\{V_i\}$ of A and a δ-cover $\{W_i\}$ of B, and we have

$$\begin{aligned} H^s(A\cup B) &= \lim_{\delta\to 0}\ \inf\{\sum_{i=1}^{\infty} |V_i|^s + \sum_{i=1}^{\infty} |W_i|^s\} \\ &= \lim_{\delta\to 0}\ \{\inf\sum_{i=1}^{\infty} |V_i|^s + \inf\sum_{i=1}^{\infty} |W_i|^s\} \\ &= \lim_{\delta\to 0}\ \inf\sum_{i=1}^{\infty} |V_i|^s + \lim_{\delta\to 0}\ \inf\sum_{i=1}^{\infty} |W_i|^s \\ &= H^s(A) + H^s(B). \end{aligned}$$

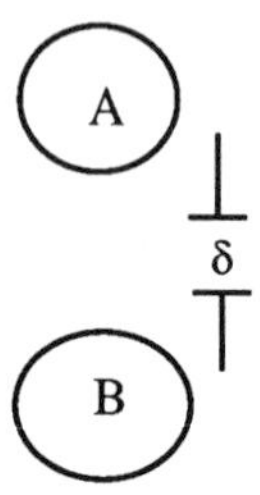

EXAMPLES 15.47 (1) We claim that if E is a single point then $H^0(E) = 1$. For, if $\{V_i\}$ is a δ-cover of E then since each $|V_i|^0 = 1$ we have $H^0(E)$ as lim inf of the number of sets in a δ-cover of E, i.e. the limit of the constant 1 as $\delta \to 0$, which is of course 1.

(2) If E is an infinite set then $H^0(E) = \infty$. For, E contains arbitrarily large unions of 1-point sets (each a Borel set), and since equality holds in (14.41) for these unions, $H^0(E)$ is greater than any multiple of $H^0(\text{point})$ (=1).

(3) Consider $H^1(I)$, where I is the unit interval. If $\{V_i\}$ is a δ-cover of I, then whatever the (positive) value of δ we have $1 \le \sum|V_i|$, so $1 \le \inf\sum|V_i|$. Thus if $\{W_i\}$ is a covering by closed intervals end to end then $1 \le \inf\sum|V_i| \le \sum|W_i| = 1$, and so $H^1(I) = \lim\inf\sum|V_i| = 1$. The argument extends to show that 1-dimensional Hausdorff measure gives the length of any smooth curve.

(4) In the plane H^2 gives a constant multiple π/4 of the area of a set and similarly for H^n and n-space in general, though we won't go into the case N > 2 here.

An important idea related to a set having further detail at every level of magnification is that of a *scaling property*. We are familiar with magnification by a factor r causing length, area, and volume to be multiplied by respective factors r, r^2, r^3. The Hausdorff measure H^s conveniently scales by r^s. Writing $rE = \{rx: x \in E\}$ we have as a special case of the theorem to follow:

$$H^s(rE) = r^sH^s(E). \qquad (15.42)$$

THEOREM 15.48 Let r > 0. If a subset E of $\mathbf{R}^n$ *and map* $f: E \to \mathbf{R}^n$ *satisfy*

$$|f(x) - f(y)| \le r|x - y| \quad (x,y \in E), \qquad (15.43)$$

$$\textit{then} \quad H^s(f(E)) \le r^sH^s(E). \qquad (15.44)$$

Equality in (15.43) implies equality in (15.44). In particular, the s-dimensional Hausdorff measure of a set is preserved by isometries and by uniform scaling.

Proof Assume that (15.43) holds and let $\{V_i\}$ be a δ-cover of E. Then $|f(E\cap V_i)| \le r|E\cap V_i| \le r|V_i|$ shows that $\{f(E\cap V_i)\}$ is a rδ-cover of f(E) and $\sum |f(E\cap V_i)|^s \le r^s \sum|V_i|^s$. Thus for every δ-cover of E there is an ε-cover of f(E) with $\varepsilon = r\delta$, and we have $H_\delta{}^s(f(E)) \le r^sH_\delta{}^s(E)$. Letting $\varepsilon \to 0$ and hence $\delta \to 0$ we obtain (15.44). With equality in (15.43) the restricted map $E \to f(E)$ is bijective, because $f(x) = f(y)$ implies $|x - y| = 0$ and so $x = y$. Hence it has an inverse g and we may write $x = g(a)$, $y = g(b)$ for unique a,b in f(E) to obtain for all a,b in f(E): $|fg(a) - fg(b)| = r\,|g(a) - g(b)|$, or $|g(a) - g(b)| = (1/r)\,|a - b|$. Hence by (15.43) applied to the map $g: f(E) \to E$ ($\subseteq \mathbf{R}^n$) we have $H^s(gf(E)) \le$

$(1/r)^s H^s(f(E))$, or $H^s(f(E)) \geq r^s H^s(E)$. Taken with (15.44) this implies the desired equality.

*Stage 3 (**Hausdorff dimension**)* The Hausdorff dimension $\dim_H(E)$ of a set E is based upon the idea that as s increases from 0, $H^s(E)$ suddenly jumps down from a positive number or infinity, to 0, and we can define $d_H(E)$ to be the value of s where this occurs. Let $0 < \delta < 1$ and $t > s \geq 0$. If $\{V_i\}$ is a δ-cover of E then $|V_i|^t = |V_i|^{t-s} |V_i|^s \leq \delta^{t-s}|V_i|^s$, and so $\sum |V_i|^t \leq \delta^{t-s} \sum |V_i|^s$. Hence $H_\delta^s(E) \leq \delta^{t-s} H^s(E)$ and, letting $\delta \to 0$, we may conclude tthat

$$\text{if } H^s(E) < \infty \text{ (is finite) then } H^t(E) = 0 \text{ for } t > s. \tag{15.45}$$

Example 15.47(2) shows that every infinite set E has $H^0(E) = \infty$, but (15.45) tells us that, when s increases from 0, as soon as $H^s(E)$ becomes finite it jumps to 0 (cf. Figure 15.21). We may legitimately define the *Hausdorff dimension* as the 'jump point' (interpreted as ∞ if the jump never occurs)

$$\dim_H(E) = \inf\{s: H^s(E) = 0\}, \tag{15.46}$$

whence

$$\text{if } 0 < H^s(E) < \infty \text{ then } \dim_H(E) = s. \tag{15.46'}$$

EXAMPLES 15.49 (1) Since $H^0(\text{point}) = 1$ by Example 15.47(1), the Hausdorff dimension of a point is 0, by (15.46').

(2) Let E be a square of side 1 in the plane. Since E contains a smooth curve of infinite length whose 1-dimensional Hausdorff measure is therefore infinite by Example 15.47(3), we have by (15.40) that $H^1(E) = \infty$. Further, $H^2(E)$ is the positive number $\pi/4$ (see Example 15.47(4)). By (15.45) the graph of H^s is as portrayed in the figure, a jump occurring at s = 2. Thus $\dim_H(E) = 2$. [In more detail $H^s(E)$ is infinite if s < 2, equals 2 if s = 2, and is zero if s > 2.]

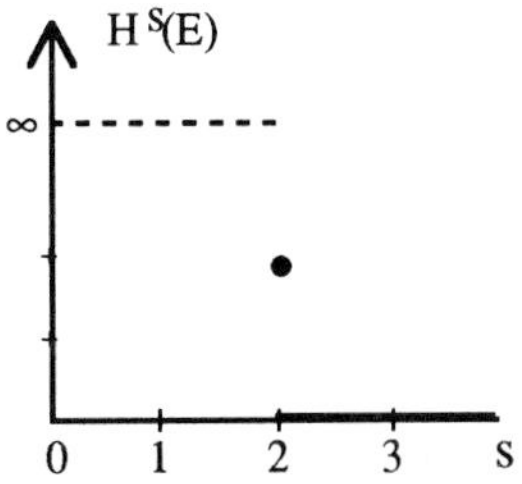

Figure 15.21

(3) *If $E \subseteq F$ then $\dim_H(E) \leq \dim_H(F)$.* For, $H^s(E) \leq H^s(F)$ by (15.40), whence $H^s(F) = 0 \Rightarrow H^s(E) = 0$. Now apply the definition, (15.46).

(4) Any open set in the plane has Hausdorff dimension at least 2 by (3), since it contains an open disc, which we know has Hausdorff dimension 2.

THEOREM 15.50 Let r > 0. If $E \subseteq \mathbf{R}^n$ and $f: E \to \mathbf{R}^m$ satisfy

$$|f(x) - f(y)| \leq r|x - y| \quad (x,y \in E), \tag{15.47}$$

then $\dim_H(f(E)) \leq \dim_H(E)$.

Proof Let (15.47) hold. If $s > \dim_H(E)$ then by Theorem 15.48 we have the argument $H^s(f(E)) \leq r^s H^s(E) = 0$, whence the result by (15.46).

COROLLARY 15.51 Let $E \subseteq \mathbf{R}^n$ and $f: \mathbf{R}^n \to \mathbf{R}^m$ satisfy

$$r_1|x - y| \leq |f(x) - f(y)| \leq r_2|x - y| \quad (x,y \in E) \tag{15.48}$$

for positive constants r_1, r_2. Then $\dim_H(f(E)) = \dim_H(E)$. In particular, Hausdorff dimension is unchanged by isometries, uniform scaling, or similarity.

COROLLARY 15.52 A subset of $\mathbf{R}^n$ *with Hausdorff dimension less than 1 is totally disconnected.*

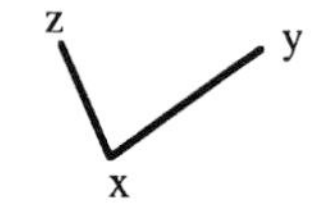

Proof It suffices to show that arbitrary distinct points x,y in such a set E must be in different connected components of E. Define a map $f: \mathbf{R}^n \to [0,\infty)$ by $f(z) = |x-z|$. Then by the triangle inequality in $\mathbf{R}^n$, $|f(z) - f(w)| = ||x-z| - |x-w|| \le |z-w|$, the inequality following from $|x-w| \le |x-z| + |z-w|$ and the same with z and w interchanged. Now $\dim_H(f(E)) \le \dim_H(E) < 1$ by Theorem 15.50, and so $H^1(f(E)) = 0$. It follows from Example 15.49(3) that f(E) contains no line segment, for this would be a subset of dimension 1. In particular, f(x) being zero and f(y) nonzero, it cannot include the line segment from f(x) to f(y). Hence $f(x) < c < f(y)$ for some c. Since f(x), f(y) are thus in different connected components of $\mathbf{R}\backslash\{c\}$, it follows that x, y are in different components of E (f is continuous, being bounded, and so maps connected components to connected components, see Theorems 11.43 and 12.43). Hence E is totally disconnected.

REMARK In applying this result the easiest way to find examples is to start with self similar attractors $\mathcal{A}$ for, as we shall see, their Hausdorff dimension equals their similarity dimension provided the various parts $\mathcal{A}_i$ do not overlap too much. We state the theorem on the basis of the 'open set condition' and then show the sufficiency of a more easily verified condition which is satisfied in very many examples of interest. First we require a lemma.

LEMMA 15.53 For arbitrary numbers $a_1, a_2, .., a_N$ *and* $k \in N$ *we have*

$$(x_1 + x_2 + .. + x_N)^k = \sum_{J_k} x_{i_1}x_{i_2} .. x_{i_k},$$

summing over the sequences of subscripts in the set J_k *of all k- term sequences of integers* i_r *from the set {1, 2, .., N}.*

Proof The left hand side is the product of k copies of $(x_1+x_2+ .. +x_N)$ written one after the other. This is the sum of all products found by taking one element in turn from each bracketed expression.

THEOREM 15.54 If $E \subseteq \mathbf{R}^n$ *is self-similar and its defining similarities* w_i *satisfy the open set condition, that for some nonempty bounded open set U*

$$w_i(U) \subseteq U \ (1 \le i \le N) \text{ and } w_i(U) \cap w_j(U) = \emptyset \ (i \ne j) \tag{15.49}$$

then the Hausdorff dimension of E equals its similarity dimension, namely the unique value d such that (with similarity ratios r_i*),*

$$r_1{}^d + r_2{}^d + .. + r_N{}^d = 1. \tag{15.50}$$

Proof (The result is essentially due to Moran (1946).) The method of proof is to show that $0 < H^d(E) \le |E|^d$, from which the result follows in the usual way from (15.45) and (15.46). E is of course the attractor, generally denoted $\mathcal{A}$, of the IFS $\{w_{1\text{-}N}\}$. In the present notation we have from (15.1), (15.2)

$$E_{ab..z} = w_a w_b .. w_z(E) \tag{15.51}$$

$$E = \bigcup E_{i_1 \dots i_k} \quad (i_1 \dots i_k \in J_k), \quad \text{a covering of } E, \tag{15.52}$$

$$|E_{i_1 \dots i_k}| = r_{i_1} \dots r_{i_k} |E|. \tag{15.53}$$

With a view to a δ-cover of E, we observe the consequences

$$\begin{aligned} \sum_{J_k} |E_{i_1 \dots i_k}|^d &= \sum_{J_k} (r_{i_1} \dots r_{i_k})^d |E|^d \\ &= \sum_{J_k} (r_{i_1}^d \dots r_{i_k}^d) |E|^d \\ &= (r_1^d + r_2^d + \dots + r_N^d)^k |E|^d, \quad \text{by Lemma 15.53 with } x_i = r_i^d \\ &= |E|^d, \quad \text{by (15.50).} \end{aligned}$$

For any positive δ we obtain a δ-cover $\{E_{i_1 \dots i_k}\}$ by choosing k so that

$$|E_{i_1 \dots i_k}| \le (\max(r_1, \dots, r_N))^k |E| \le \delta.$$

It follows that $H_\delta^d(E) \le |E|^d$ for all $\delta > 0$, and hence $H^d(E) \le |E|^d$ as was to be proved. It remains to show that $H^d(E) > 0$. This may seem innocuous enough, but takes considerably longer than the first part. We omit it and refer to for example Falconer (1985, 1990).

REMARK 15.55 A self-similar set with defining maps w_{1-N} satisfies the open set condition (15.49) if the *boundary intersection condition* (BIC) holds, namely that for some bounded set F which has nonempty interior, i.e. contains a disc, we have

$$w_i(F) \subseteq F \ (1 \le i \le N) \text{ and the sets } w_i(F) \text{ intersect, if at all, only on their boundaries.} \tag{15.54}$$

To prove this implication, suppose the BIC holds. Since the interior of a set and its boundary are disjoint (by definition) the interior of the sets $w_i(F)$ cannot intersect. And since each map w_i is a homeomorphism by virtue of being a similarity, sending boundary to boundary and interior to interior (see (11.19A)), we take U to be the interior of F, which is nonempty by hypothesis and bounded because F is bounded. Now the open set condition is satisfied with the specified set U.

EXAMPLES 15.56 (1) The Cantor set $\mathcal{C}$ with similarities $w_1(x) = x/3$, $w_2(x) = x/3 + 2/3$, acting on the unit interval I. Then the BIC is sastisfied with F = I. In fact $w_1(I)$ and $w_2(I)$ do not intersect at all. Thus by Theorem 15.54 $\mathcal{C}$ has Hausdorff dimension equal to its similarity dimension, calculated in Section 10.3.2 as log2/log3, or approximately 0.63. Since this is not an integer we have confirmed that $\mathcal{C}$ is indeed a fractal according to Definition 10.18. Furthermore this dimension is less than 1, so Corollary 15.52 gives another proof that $\mathcal{C}$ is totally disconnected as we concluded in Example 12.57.

(2) Another old friend, the Sierpinski gasket, satisfies the BIC of (15.54) in a very natural way, with F being the perimeter triangle Δ filled in. In the diagram the darkened triangles represent the sets $w_i(\Delta)$. Thus its Hausdorff dimension equals its similarity dimension log3/log2, a noninteger, and again we confirm a fractal.

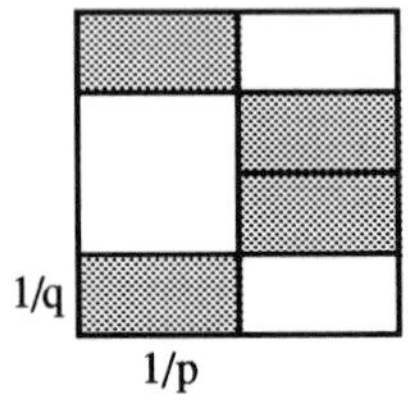

CONSTRUCTION 15.57 We conclude this section with a formula due to Falconer (1990) which gives Hausdorff dimension for some fractals which are not self-similar. For positive integers $p < q$, divide a unit square E_0 into an array of equal rectangles, p horizontally and q vertically. Form a subcollection of the rectangles (say those shaded in the diagram). Each small rectangle is the image of E_0 under a unique affine transformation w_i consisting of translation and nonuniform scaling only (cf. Theorem 14.10). These transformations form an iterated function system $\{w_{1-N}\}$. If N_j denotes the number of rectangles taken in column j, for $1 \le j \le p$, then the attractor $\mathcal{A}$ of the IFS has Hausdorff dimension

$$\dim_H(\mathcal{A}) \quad = \quad \log\left(\sum_{j=1}^{p} N_j^{\log p/\log q}\right)\frac{1}{\log p}. \qquad (15.55)$$

For many results and calculations on Hausdorff dimension in the non-self-similar case see e.g. Edgar (1990) or Falconer (1990).

EXAMPLE 15.56 Using the rectangles indicated above we have $p = 2$, $q = 4$, $N_1 = 2 = N_2$, $\log p/\log q = 1/2$, and

$$\dim_H(\mathcal{A}) = \log(2\sqrt{2})/\log 2, \text{ by (15.55).}$$
$$= 1.5.$$

It is an easy but instructive exercise to trace the not-quite self-similarity of this simple attractor which is nevertheless a fractal.

EXERCISES 15

---

1 Locate the point (0.6,0.7) to within 1/8 in both coordinates by a sequence of symbols as in Example 15.1.

2 √ Use a suitable addressing scheme to find the first three digits in both the binary and base 5 representations of 0.8.

3 √ Write down address sequences for points D, E, F and the question mark, in Figure 15.4.

4 Find examples of areas in Figure 15.5 whose respective addresses require two, three, four and five digits. State these addresses.

5 √ Verify the triangle inequality for the points $1\overline{2}$, $3\overline{2}$, $3\overline{1}$ in Σ, when $N = 3$ (use formula (15.3)).

6 Draw the first three stages of the (generalised) Cantor set obtained recursively by dividing an interval into four parts and deleting the lowest but one part.

7 (a) Prove statement (15.11) by summing a geometric series, **or** (b) verify it for the points $132\overline{4}$ and $13\overline{242}$ of Σ, in case $N = 4$.

8 √ Calculate $\phi(\overline{13})$ for the Sierpinski gasket (cf. Example 15.18). You can guess the answer from Figure 15.7.

9 √ Use (15.17) to derive the formula $\phi(213\sigma) = w_2w_1w_3\,\phi(\sigma)$.

10 √ State why the construction of Example 15.24 must give Sierpinski, assuming the RIA does work. Deduce the order of the first few choices in Figure 15.8. Now write a small program to perform the construction. How many extraneous points appear?

11 Find in sequence (15.19) the 4-digit sequences 1122, 2222, 3333, 1231, 3131. Obtain the length formula of Theorem 15.27 by imitating the argument given in the case N = 3, k = 4.

12 √ Use Table 15.1 to find a shortest possible sequence containing all 4-digit binary numbers.

13 √ Notice that (15.25) implies (15.27), for $\mu(A) = \mu(A \cup \emptyset) = \mu(A) + \mu(\emptyset)$, and hence $\mu(\emptyset) = 0$. Deduce also (15.26) by expressing B as the union of disjoint sets A, B\A.

14 √ Write down explicitly a Borel subset of the plane which is neither open nor closed.

15 Repeat Example 15.38 for $f(x) = x^2+1$. Check your answer by ordinary integration.

16 √ Show that if X is compact and w: X → X is continuous, then the inverse image of a Borel set is another Borel set. [Note how w^{-1} acts on complements, unions, and intersections. See e.g. Table 11.4.]

17 We use the notation of Example 15.43. (a) Prove that $\mu_3(B_{rst}) = p_rp_sp_t$ by using the corresponding formulae for μ_1, μ_2 **or** (b) estimate how many points you would expect to have landed in each of B_1, B_{23}, B_{214} after 36000 iterations of the Random Iteration Algorithm [see (15.28)].

18 **(Further Exercises)** Find the point in the Sierpinski gasket with address $333\overline{1}$. Does it have another address?

19 Find the parts of the attractor of Figure 15.5 with addresses 1212, 2133, 11111113.

20 Verify the triangle inequality in code space with N = 4 for the points $\overline{2}$, $213\overline{4}$, $3\overline{21}$.

21 Calculate $\phi(\overline{231})$ for the Sierpinski gasket in terms of the position vectors of the bounding triangle. Show that this point is periodic and determine its orbit. Exhibit these points as the intersections in pairs, of three lines, as is done in Figure 15.7.

22 Use Table 15.1 to find a shortest sequence containing all 3-digit sequences from the symbols 1,2,3,4 by starting with a binary sequence of length 6. If the contraction ratio for an associated IFS is 1/3, what bound can be given for $d(\mathcal{A},\{x_n\})$?

23 √ Find a primitive polynomial mod 2 of degree five beside that given in Table 15.1.

24 Prove that, if $\{A_n\}$ $(n \in \mathbf{N})$ are mutually disjoint Borel subsets of a compact metric space X and $\mu: \mathcal{B} \to [0,]$ satisfies $\mu(A \cup B) = \mu(A) + \mu(B)$ for any disjoint Borel sets A,B, then the infinite sum $\Sigma\,\mu(A_n)$ converges. You may find Table 11.2(9) useful.

25 Prove that, for a Borel measure μ, a Borel set B, its interior and its closure all have the same measure, and the boundary has measure zero.

26 Prove that an open set cannot have zero Borel measure.

27 Repeat Example 15.38 for $f(x) = x^3$, representing f(x) as the limit of a sequence of simple functions and hence finding its integral over the unit interval.

28 **Project** (a) Use program 15.1 to run the Random Iteration Algorithm for the fern of Table 14.1, trying out different combinations of probabilities. (b) Modify the program to compute points by using an M-sequence from Table 15.1 and compare results from the standard RIA for the same numbers of iterations. (c) Try using a binary M-sequence that allows you to give higher frequency to some symbols than others. Can you improve on the performance of the usual RIA?

How to use Program 15.1 (see next page)

The program shows an image produced by the Random Iteration Algorithm, at a sequence of stages determined by the user. It is compiled by Think Pascal 2.0 or 3.0 and is designed to be usable on a variety of Macintosh screens, the window and image size being adjusted automatically in procedure *setUp*. For example, the user may choose to get the scale and origin right for an IFS on a MacPlus then produce a larger image on a MacII with no further work. As given, the program draws the Sierpinski gasket, but this is easily changed (see below).

Operation At each stage, enter q to quit, a title of at least two characters to save the current stage in Macpaint form, or c to continue. The number of iterations so far is printed on screen. On *continue*, you are asked for the number of iterations to be done before the next stop for further instructions.

Varying the IFS We give the adaptions required for producing the fern stages of Figure 15.9, from which it is clear what to do in general.

(1) Replace 'setSierp' by say 'setFern' in procedures setSierp and setUp.

(2) Replace the three lines beginning code(..)by four corresponding to Table 14.2 (page 332), where the last constant of each line, the probability, is calculated as specified in Definition 15.23. Reset the origin and scale. The replacement lines are thus:

```
ox:= 150;          scale:= 40;
code(1, 0, 0, 0, 0.16, 0, 0, 0.01);
code(2, 0.85, 0.04, -0.04, 0.85, 0, 1.6, 0.85);
code(3, 0.2, -0.26, 0.23, 0.22, 0, 1.6, 0.07);
code(4, -0.15, 0.28, 0.26, 0.24, 0, 0.44, 0.07);
```

```
Program program15;
{Paints the attractor of an iterated function system}
{by the Random Iteration Algorithm}
const  IFS = 14;          {up to 14 functions}
type   subs = 1..IFS;
var
  x, y, newx, newy, scale : real;
  k: subs;  str: string;   n: integer;
  bx, by : integer;          {screen bounds}
  ox, oy: integer;           {origin}
  Numits, Count: Longint;
  a, b, c, d, e, f, p: array[SUBS] of real;
  DrawArea, TextArea: Rect;
procedure WhatNow;
begin
  repeat
    ShowText;
    writeln('Enter q to quit ');
    writeln('title to save ');
    writeln('or c to continue');
    repeat
      readln(str)
      until (str = 'q') or (length(str) > 1) or (str = 'c');
      if str = 'q' then  HALT;        {Stop program}
      if length(str) > 1 then
        begin
          showdrawing;  SaveDrawing(str);
          ShowText;
        end;
    until str = 'c';
    ShowText;        Writeln('Nr of steps?');
    Read(Numits);  Showdrawing;
end;
function RND (r: integer): integer;
begin
  Rnd := ((Random + 32768) mod r) + 1;
end;
procedure Pset (x, y: real);
begin
  MoveTo(Round(x+ox), Round(by-oy-y));
  Line(0, 0);  {y+oy for upright y-axis}
end;
procedure code (i: SUBS;
            a1, b1, c1, d1, e1, f1, p1: real);
begin
  a[i] := a1;  b[i] := b1;  c[i] := c1;
  d[i] := d1;  e[i] := e1;  f[i] := f1;  p[i] := p1;
end;
procedure setSierp;        {or other IFS code}
begin
  {reset origin and/or scale here if required}
  scale:= 200;                 {large size}
  code(1, 1 / 2, 0, 0, 1 / 2, 0, 0, 1 / 3);
  code(2, 1 / 2, 0, 0, 1 / 2, 1, 0, 1 / 3);
  code(3, 1 / 2, 0, 0, 1 / 2, 0, 1, 1 / 3);
end;
procedure SetUP;
begin
  bx := ScreenBits.Bounds.right - 10;
  by := ScreenBits.Bounds.bottom - 10;
  SetRect(DrawArea, 10, 40, bx - 180, by);
  SetDrawingRect(DrawArea);
  SetRect(TextArea, bx - 160, 40, bx, by);
  SetTextRect(TextArea);
  Numits := 0;   Count := 0;   str := '';
  ox := 20;  oy := 60;          {default origin}
  scale := 100;                 {default scale}
  setSierp;                     {new origin/scale?}
  scale:= scale*(by-50)/420; {adjust to screen size}
end;
procedure whichMap (var k: subs);
var
  sum, rn: real;
begin
  rn := (rnd(1000)) / 1000;
  k := 1;  sum := p[1];
  while rn > sum do
    begin
      k := k + 1;  sum := sum + p[k];
    end;
end;
begin  {main program}
  SetUp;  ShowDrawing;
  x := 100;  y := 100;  {first point}
  pset(x, y);                 {plot it}
  repeat
    WhatNow;
    for n := 1 to numits do
      begin
        whichMap(k);
        newx := a[k] * x + b[k] * y + e[k] * scale;
        newy := c[k] * x + d[k] * y + f[k] * scale;
        x := newx;  y := newy;
        pset(x, y);  {adjust proc if y-axis up}
      end;
    count := count + numits;
    ShowText;
    Writeln(count, ' steps done');
  until str = 'q';
end.
```

Chapter 16 JULIA, MANDELBROT, AND BEYOND

Our final topic in this text is the how and why of spectacular computer graphical effects obtained by representing, in the complex plane, Julia sets and the intimately related set of Mandelbrot (1980). It is salutary that, in spite of the brilliant pioneering work by Julia (1918) and Fatou (1919) earlier this century, the Dynamics of iterated complex functions simply did not catch the interest even of the mathematical community until its visual potential was brought out.

16.1 The dynamics of iterated complex functions

The complex numbers **C** were introduced in Chapter 8 and their basic properties developed in Chapter 9. There is a well-developed theory on those transformations of the plane which can be expressed as functions of a single, but complex, variable, with powerful applications in Science and Engineering. We shall sketch a reasonable minimum for the present purpose. For proofs and for more information, see Ahlfors (1966), Priestley (1990), Stewart and Tall (1990), and for the wider applications Churchill (1960). The reader may find it helpful to bear in mind some properties of the *modulus* $|z| = \sqrt{(x^2 + y^2)}$ of a complex number $z = x+\mathbf{i}y$ which we shall call upon repeatedly to good effect throughout this chapter. For any z,w in C: $|zw| = |z||w|$, hence $|w/z| = |w|/|z|$ $(z \neq 0)$ and $|z^n| = |z|^n$; also the two forms of the triangle inequality: $|(|z| - |w|)| \le |z + w| \le |z| + |w|$. The topological foundations of Chapters 11 to 13 will play a key role, and it may be useful to refer back.

16.1.1 Complex variables

Examples of functions of a complex variable are easily generated from the real case. We have polynomials such as $f(z) = z^2+3$, rational functions such as $3z/(z^2-4)$ (defined for all $z \neq \pm 2$) and infinite series such as $e^z = 1 + z + z^2/2! + z^3/3! + \ldots$, the exponential function. We still have $1 + z + z^2 + \ldots + z^{n-1} = (1-z^n)/(1-z)$ the sum of a geometric series. Its infinite form $1 + z + z^2 + \ldots = 1/(1-z)$ is valid for $|z| < 1$, since then $|z^n| = |z|^n \to 0$ as $n \to \infty$. It is a special case of the *Binomial theorem* for a positive or negative integer n

$$(1 + z)^n = 1 + nz + \frac{n(n-1)}{2!} z^2 + \frac{n(n-1)(n-2)}{3!} z^3 + \ldots \qquad (16.1)$$

valid for $|z| < 1$ if n is negative, otherwise for all n. Polynomials, rational functions, and convergent series may be differentiated as in the real case, subject to the usual product, quotient, and chain rules, but the consequences are more profound. Here is the formal definition.

DEFINITION 16.1 Let U be an open set in **C**. A complex function $f: U \to \mathbf{C}$ is *differentiable* or *analytic* at a point z_0 of U if the *derivative*

$$f'(z_0) = \lim_{z \to z_0} \frac{f(z) - f(z_0)}{z - z_0} \quad (z \in U) \qquad (16.2)$$

exists. We call f *analytic on U*, or say that *f: U → **C** is analytic,* if f is analytic at each point of U. We say f is analytic on a non-open set A to mean that f is defined on some open set U containing A and is analytic at the points of A. This is convenient if the focus is on A and U is known to exist. We emphasise that the limit in (16.2) is to be the same regardless of how z approaches z_0 (in the real case it can only approach from the left or right). We have kept all possibilites open by insisting that z_0 is in an open set and hence centres an open disc on which f is defined. Otherwise differentiablility could mean one thing on a boundary and another in an interior (cf. Figure 16.1).

THEOREM 16.2 Let f(z) be analytic at z_0. Then for some $r > 0$ we have

$$f(z) = \sum_{n=0}^{\infty} a_n (z - z_0)^n \qquad (16.3)$$

$$f'(z) = \sum_{n=1}^{\infty} n a_n (z - z_0)^{n-1} \qquad (16.4)$$

where the complex coefficients a_n are unique, the expansions hold for $|z - z_0| < r$, and the derivative is also analytic. Conversely, a series of the form (16.3) convergent for $|z - z_0| < r$ defines an analytic function there.

DEFINITION 16.3 We call (16.3) the Taylor *expansion of f(z) about z_0.*

EXAMPLE 16.4 To verify that the rational function $f(z) = 1/z^2$ is analytic on $U = \mathbf{C} \setminus \{0\}$, let $z_0 \neq 0$. Then on simplification $[f(z) - f(z_0)] / (z - z_0) = -(z_0 + z)/z^2 z_0^2$ which, happily, tends to $-2/z_0^3$ no matter how z tends to z_0. Thus $f'(z) = -2/z^3$ on U. By Theorem 16.2 we can expand $1/z^2$ about any complex point other than the origin, and however we compute such an expansion the answer must be the same, since it is unique. We shall expand about $z_0 = 1$, by writing z as the binomial $1+(z-1)$ and applying (16.1). The result is then valid when $|z-1| < 1$. It is

$$z^{-2} = 1 - 2(z-1) + \frac{(-2)(-3)}{2!}(z-1)^2 + .. = 1-2(z-1)+3(z-1)^2-4(z-1)^3+...$$

EXERCISE Expand $1/(z-1)^2$ about $z_0 = 3$ by writing $z-1 = 2+(z-3) = 2(1 + (z-3)/2)$. Now check your answer by differentiating an expansion of $1/(z-1)$.

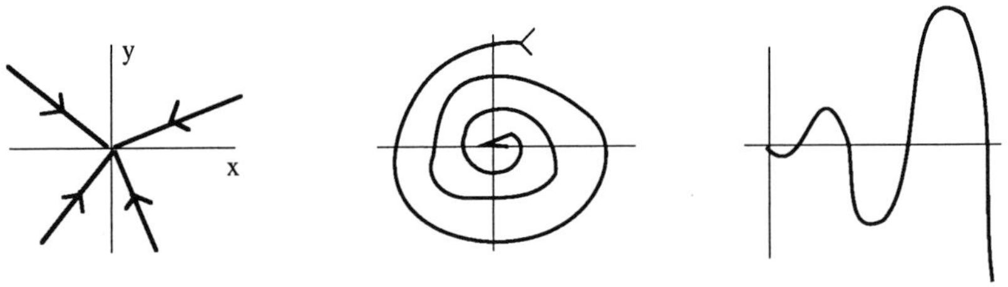

Figure 16.1 Some ways we may have $z \to 0$, described by z(t). (a) $z(t) = te^{i\alpha}$ (α constant), (b) $z(t) = te^{2\pi it}$, (c) $z(t) = (t, t\sin(2\pi t))$.

It is interesting to note the formula $a_n = f^{(n)}(z_0)/n!$ for the coefficients in (16.3). It yields the same coefficients as in the real case for the functions sinz, cosz and e^z, valid over the whole complex plane. Now here are three special properties of analytic complex functions. Note that if f is analytic (= differentiable) at z_0 then f is continuous at z_0, as in the real case, for if $(f(z)-f(z_0))/(z-z_0) \to \lambda$, a finite constant, as $z \to z_0$, then $f(z)-f(z_0) \to 0$.

THEOREM 16.5 Let f(z) be analytic on a set V.
(a) If f is non-constant, then it maps open sets to open sets.
(b) If V is compact, |f(z)| attains its maximum on the boundary of V.
(c) If V is open and connected, and f(z) is constant on an open subset of V, then f is constant on the whole of V.

The significance of these results will appear later, but here are some observations. With regard to (a), continuity of f means that if a set B is open then so is the inverse image $f^{-1}(B)$, whereas analyticity adds that if A is open then so is f(A). Assertion (b) is the *Maximum Modulus Theorem*: We already know that compactness of V and continuity of f ensure that |f(z)| attains a maximum somewhere on V (Theorem 12.28), but here, unlike the situation for real variables, we require no extra condition on derivatives to ensure that this maximum occurs on the boundary. This is illustrated in the exercise following. A nice implication of (c) is that if two analytic functions f,g on an open set V agree on an open subset U, no matter how small, then they agree on the whole of V, *provided* V is connected. The proof is that the difference function f-g is zero on U and hence on V. This is one reason why the extra hypothesis of connectedness can be important and for sometimes giving a special name to open sets which are also connected - usually *domain* (Ahlfors' *region*) - not to be confused with the domain X of a function h: X → Y, for which we shall reserve the term.

EXERCISE Let $V = \{x+iy: -2 \le x,y \le 2\}$. Verify that |f(z)| attains its maximum off the boundary in case $f(x+iy) = (4-x^2)(4-y^2)$, but on the boundary in the case of the analytic function g(x+iy) =

z^2. [It follows that f is not an analytic function of z.]

THEOREM 16.6A (The Inverse Function Theorem for analytic functions.) If f(z) is analytic at z_0 and $f'(z_0) \neq 0$, then f is 1-1 on some open neighbourhood V of z_0 and the inverse mapping $f^{-1}: f(V) \to V$ is analytic.

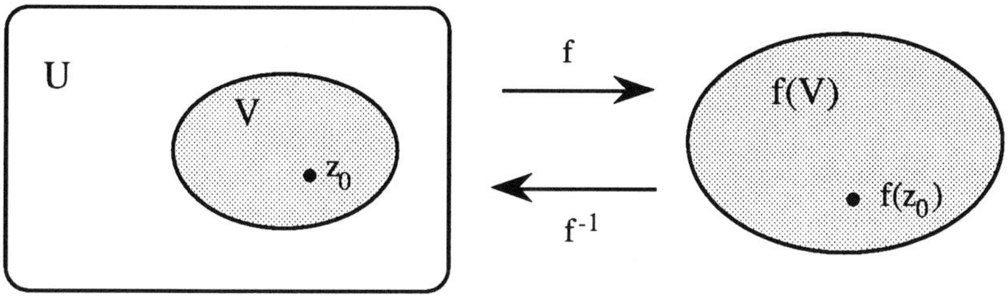

Figure 16.2 Analytic map with local inverse near a point z_0.

For the next theorem we recall that a simply connected set is basically one without holes, equivalent in the extended plane (see Table 16.2 and preceding remarks) to a set which is both connected and has connected complement. For discussion of this concept see Definition 12.59ff. In particular, a homeomorphic image of an open or closed disc in the plane is simply connected.

THEOREM 16.6B (Blanchard, 1984, Lemma 5.9). Suppose R is a rational function on **C** *and U is a simply connected open set containing no critical value of R (i.e. a value $R(z_0)$ with $R'(z_0) = 0$). Then if $R(\alpha) = \beta$, with $\beta \in U$, there exists an analytic inverse S to R, defined on U, such that $S(\beta) = \alpha$.*

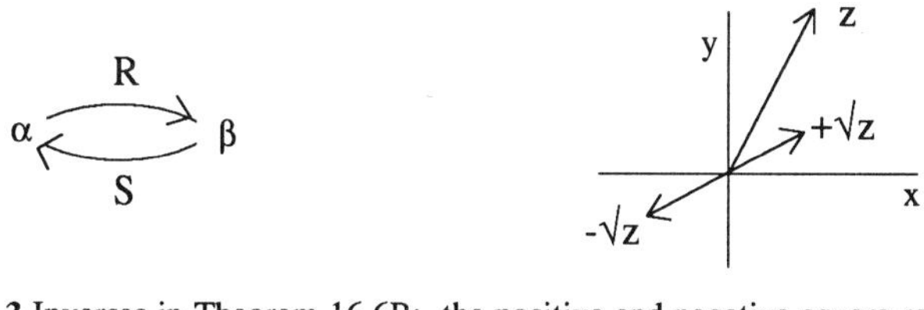

Figure 16.3 Inverses in Theorem 16.6B; the positive and negative square roots of z.

DEFINITION 16.7 We recall from Chapter 9 that every nonzero complex number z has exactly two square roots and that each is the negative of the other. Sometimes it is useful to know which one we are talking about and so we define the *positive square root* $+\sqrt{z}$ *of* z to be the one with positive real part or, if z is purely imaginary (has zero real part), the one with positive imaginary part.

EXERCISE Use a diagram to show why, if z is nonzero and we take the positive square root, then $|1+\sqrt{z}| > 1$. Verify this by calculation for $z = \mathbf{i}$.

EXAMPLE 16.8 **The square root mapping(s).** The function $f(z) = z^2$ has $|f'(z)| = |2z|$, which differs from zero except at the origin, so near any $z_0 \neq 0$, f(z) has an analytic inverse function g(w), according to Theorem 16.6A. Let $f(z_0) = w_0$. Then $f(-z_0) = w_0$ too. From the possibilities for a continuous inverse function, $g(re^{i\theta}) = \pm(\sqrt{r})e^{i\theta/2}$ $(0 \leq \theta < 2\pi)$, we have to choose the one with $g(w_0) = +z_0$. However, by allowing w to move far enough, we finish on the other function, as illustrated in Figure 16.4(a). More details follow the diagram.

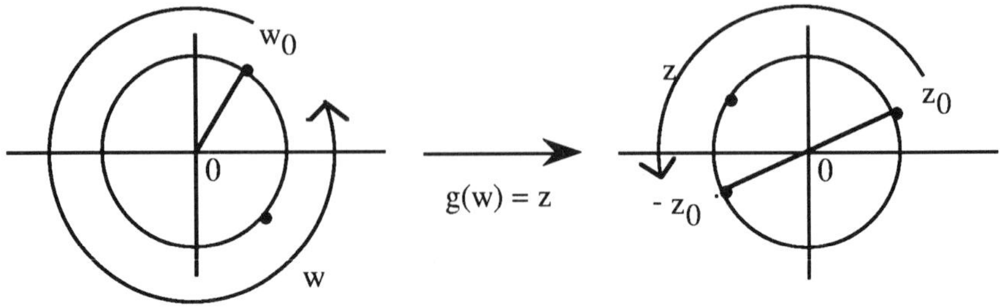

Figure 16.4(a) The branch of the square root map g(w), inverse to $f(z) = z^2$, sending w_0 to z_0 rather than to its negative. By the time w has traversed a complete loop (not necessarily a circle) around the origin, from w_0 and back to w_0, we are mapping w_0 to $-z_0$, on the other branch.

From the viewpoint of Theorem 16.6B there are two analytic inverse functions to f(z), defined on any simply connected subset of $\mathbf{C}\backslash\{0\}$. We normally choose that subset as a slit plane, obtained from **C** by deleting any infinite radius vector $\{(x,mx):\ x \geq 0\}$. For example, with $m = 0$ we restrict θ to $0 < \theta < 2\pi$. The two functions, called *branches of the square root function*, may be written $\pm g$, where $g(re^{i\theta}) = (\sqrt{r})e^{i\theta/2}$ and g(r) is the positive square root. We extend the domain of definition a little, first adding the origin with $g(0) = 0$. The result is not analytic at 0 but it is continuous there.

Now we take the non-negative x-axis as slit but close it by allowing $0 \leq \theta < 2\pi$ (with $r > 0$). The result is well-defined on the whole plane, continuous in the variable $\theta \in [0,\pi)$, but not, *as a function on the space* **C**, continuous on the slit. Indeed, when a moving point crosses the positive x-axis from above, θ jumps from 0 to 2π, $e^{i\theta/2}$ jumps from e^{i0} (= 1) to $e^{i\pi}$ (= -1). cf. Figure 16.4(a). Note that g maps all the points of a radius vector $\theta = \alpha$ onto another radius vector $\theta = \alpha/2$. The consequences of the above are interesting and useful. They give some important results about Mandelbrot and Julia sets, proved in Section 16.3.4. Here we observe the convenience that with the domain of g thus extended we may write for any subset A of the plane $f^{-1}(A) = g(A) \cup (-g)(A)$, a set symmetrical under a half turn about the origin. This is illustrated in Figure 16.4(b) below.

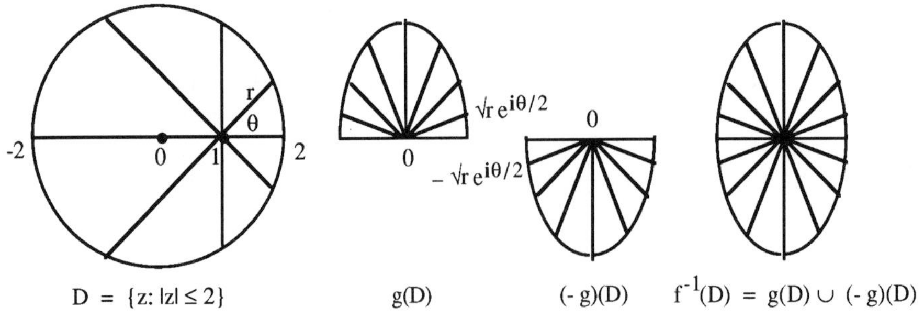

Figure 16.4(b) With $f(z) = z^2 + 1$ the inverse image $f^{-1}(D)$ of a disc D is the union $g(D) \cup (-g)(D)$, where $\pm g(w)$ are the branches of $\sqrt{(w-1)}$.

EXAMPLE 16.9 (Differentiating $\sqrt{z}$.) By Theorem 16.6A the inverse function $g(w) = +\sqrt{w}$ of $f(z) = z^2$ (=w) is analytic where it is defined (inverses are unique where they exist). Since the laws of differentiation apply, as noted earlier, we have $dg/dw = 1/(df/dz) = 1/2z = 1/2\sqrt{w}$, as we would obtain in the real case. The same argument yields $d(-g)/dw = -1/2\sqrt{w}$.

16.1.2 Iterated maps of the complex plane

The special effects we are interested in arise from the dynamics of iterated transformations of the plane which are given by analytic functions of a complex variable. What sort of things happen when we start with an initial point z_0 in the complex plane and follow its *(forward) orbit* $\{z_0, z_1, z_2, ...\}$ under such a function f(z). This is an example of the important class of *discrete* dynamical systems, in that z depends, not on a continously changing variable, but on a discrete one, its subscript (see e.g. Devaney, 1989). Here $z_n = f(z_{n-1}) = f^n(z_0)$ $(n \geq 1)$ and f^n is the n-fold composition of f with itself, f^0 being the identity map. Of crucial importance too, is the *inverse orbit* $\{f^{-1}(z_0), f^{-2}(z_0), ...\}$, where we generalise $f^{-1}(z_0)$ to $f^{-n}(z_0) = \{z: f^n(z) = z_0\}$ $(n \geq 1)$. It is both an aid in proving results and a method of construction (cf. Construction 16.46). Notice that $f^n(f^{-n}(z_0)) = z_0$ and that $f^{-n}(f^n(z_0))$ *contains* z_0.

Of special interest and influence on the global picture as we vary z_0 is the effect of iterating with f near a fixed point. That is, near a point α satisfying $f(\alpha) = \alpha$. For the Taylor expansion (16.3) of f(z) about α, we first set $z_0 = \alpha$. The series now satisfies $f(\alpha) = a_0$ and $f'(\alpha) = a_1$ so, noting that $f(\alpha) = \alpha$ and setting $\lambda = f'(\alpha)$, we obtain

$$f(z) \quad = \quad \alpha + \lambda(z - \alpha) + a_2(z - \alpha)^2 + ... \qquad (16.5)$$

We call λ the *eigenvalue* of the fixed point α with respect to f(z). The reason for this terminology is that around α as origin we have to first approximation $f(z) = \lambda z$, analogously to the matrix equation for eigenvalues $\mathbf{x}M = \lambda\mathbf{x}$. In each case, applying the transformation in question multiplies a vector by a scalar λ. In the present case the first (= linear) approximation is $f(z) - f(\alpha) = \lambda(z - \alpha)$, and so $|f(z) - f(\alpha)| = |\lambda||z - \alpha|$. Thus, what happens near α depends on the eigenvalue. If $|\lambda| < 1$ then f tends to move points towards α, and so we call α an *attractive* fixed point, or *attractor*. If $|\lambda| > 1$ we have the reverse effect and α is a *repeller*. The complete list of possibilites is given in Table 16.1. The indifferent type will be considered later.

TABLE 16.1 Classification of the behaviour of an iterated function f near a fixed point α in terms of the eigenvalue $\lambda = f'(\alpha)$. Note that α is an attractor if and only if $f^n(z) \to \alpha$ as $n \to \infty$ for some point z.

Case of λ	Type of fixed point α	Behaviour for $\lvert z-\alpha \rvert$ sufficiently small	
$\lvert\lambda\rvert < 1$ $\lambda = 0$	Attractor Super attractor		$\lvert f(z) - \alpha\rvert < \lvert z - \alpha\rvert$
$\lvert\lambda\rvert = 1$	Indifferent		$\lvert f(z) - \alpha\rvert = \lvert z - \alpha\rvert$
$\lvert\lambda\rvert > 1$	Repeller		$\lvert f(z) - \alpha\rvert > \lvert z - \alpha\rvert$

EXAMPLE 16.10 (1) We find the fixed points and their natures for $f(z) = z^2 - \mathbf{i}z + \mathbf{i}$. Here $f(z) = z \Leftrightarrow z^2 - \mathbf{i}z + \mathbf{i} - z = 0 \Leftrightarrow (z-1)(z-\mathbf{i}) = 0$, giving fixed points 1 and $\mathbf{i}$. For z = 1, the eigenvalue is $\lambda = f'(1) = (2z-\mathbf{i})_{z=1} = 2-\mathbf{i}$, so $|\lambda| = \sqrt{5}$ and we have a *repeller*. At the other fixed point, $\lambda = (2z-\mathbf{i})_{z=\mathbf{i}} = \mathbf{i}$, hence this one is of *indifferent type*, in the notation of Table 16.1.

(2) If f is analytic with inverse g on an open set around a fixed point α of f (and hence of

g) then α is attractive for f $\Leftrightarrow$ α is repelling for g.
Proof Differentiate both sides of $fg(z) = z$ to get $f'(g(z))g'(z) = 1$, and so $f'(\alpha)g'(\alpha) = 1$. Thus $|f'(\alpha)| < 1 \Leftrightarrow |g'(\alpha)| > 1$.

DEFINITION 16.11 Given that α is an attractor for the function f(z), the collection of all points drawn ultimately to α is called its *basin of attraction,*

$$A(\alpha) = \{z \in \mathbf{C}: f^n(z) \to \alpha \text{ as } n \to \infty\}. \tag{16.6}$$

We observe that if α is an attractive fixed point of f(z), then $f^k(z) \in A(\alpha)$ for some k implies z is in $A(\alpha)$. If an attractive basin is not connected we often wish to consider the *immediate basin of attraction* $A_0(\alpha)$, namely the connected component of $A(\alpha)$ which contains α itself. It follows from the next theorem that not only $A(\alpha)$ but $A_0(\alpha)$ is an open set. The immediate basin is first used in Example 16.20.

THEOREM 16.12 A basin of attraction is an open set.

Proof Since α is attractive, all points within a sufficiently small distance r from α will converge to α under repeated iterations of f. In other words we have $\alpha \in D \subseteq A(\alpha)$ for a small open disc D. Let z be in $A(\alpha)$. We must show that z lies within an open set contained in $A(\alpha)$. But $f^n(z)$ is in D for some n, so z is contained in the n'th inverse image $f^{-n}(D)$, which is open by the continuity of f, and lies in $A(\alpha)$ because D does (N.B. $f^n(f^{-n}(D)) = D$).

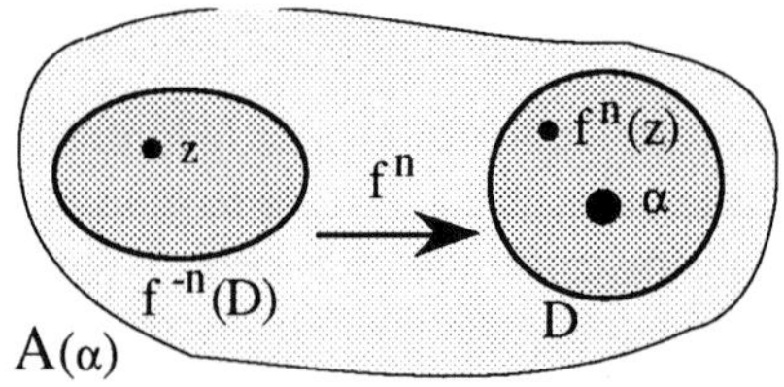

Figure 16.5 $A(\alpha)$ is an open set.

EXAMPLE 16.13 Let $f(z) = z^2$, so that $f^n(z) = z^{2^n}$. This is the simplest function of type $f(z) = z^2+c$, and it will prove instructive to see how the geometry changes, sometimes dramatically, as c is altered. In our case c = 0 the fixed points are a repeller z = 1, since $f'(1) = 2$, and a superattractor z = 0. The basin of attraction of 0 is

$$A(0) = \{z \in \mathbf{C}: z^{2^n} \to 0 \text{ as } n \to \infty\} = \{z \in \mathbf{C}: |z| < 1\}.$$

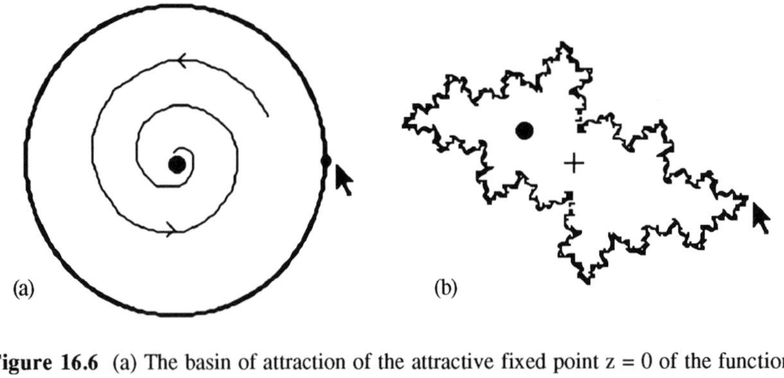

Figure 16.6 (a) The basin of attraction of the attractive fixed point z = 0 of the function $f(z) = z^2$ (interior of a unit circle centred at the origin). The unique repelling fixed point is z = 1 (arrowed). Points spiral in towards z = 0. (b) Compare case $f(z) = z^2 - 0.5 + 0.5i$, drawn to the same scale, with '+' denoting the origin. Now $-0.41 + 0.28i$ is the attractive fixed point, whilst the unique repelling fixed point (arrowed) is $1.41 - 0.28i$.

Thus A(0) is open as predicted by Theorem 16.12. It is in fact the open unit disc. Notice that we can easily identify the boundary $\partial A(0)$ as the unit circle, which is also the boundary of the set for which $|f^n(z)| \to \infty$ as $n \to \infty$, namely $\{z \in \mathbf{C}: |z| > 1\}$. We shall see below how '∞' can be creatively used so that the latter set is regarded as a basin of attraction $A(\infty)$. Then in this case, $\partial A(0) = \partial A(\infty)$. This turns out to be part of something more general, and very useful in practice. In Figure 16.6 we compare this case with $f(z) = z^2 + c$ for c fairly small. Now $\partial A(0)$ is no longer a circle, but is nevertheless a closed curve without self-intersections.

EXERCISE Let $c = (1/2)(-1+\mathbf{i})$. Verify that the attractive and repelling fixed points of $z^2 + c$ are approximately as given under Figure 16.6 (b).

EXERCISE Show that the fixed points of $f(z) = z^2 + \mathbf{i}$ are both repellers. [Use the formula for the roots of a quadratic equation, Remarks 9.16. $f'(z)$ has imaginary part ± 1.26 approx. at these points.]

Using infinity Working with the complex plane, we are so far *coping* with infinity. The idea can be used much more creatively if we append to **C** an extra point labelled '∞'. The result, with the provisos to follow, is called the *extended* complex plane, $\mathbf{C} \cup \{\infty\}$, or $\overline{\mathbf{C}}$. Appropriate rules governing '∞' are deduced via stereographic projection p from $S^2 \backslash \{NP\}$ to **C**, as portrayed in Figure 16.7, where a point z′ of the 2-sphere, different from the North pole NP, is mapped bijectively to the point z (unprimed) in which a straight line from NP to z′ meets the plane. We identify $\mathbf{C} \cup \{\infty\}$ with the whole of the 2-sphere

$$S^2 \quad = \quad \{(x,y,z) \in \mathbf{R}^3: \ (x^2 + y^2 + (z-1)^2 = 1\}, \qquad (16.7)$$

with ∞ corresponding to NP. With this identification S^2 is often called the *Riemann sphere.* Here the sphere touches the plane with South pole SP at the origin - another choice is to take the sphere centre at the origin.

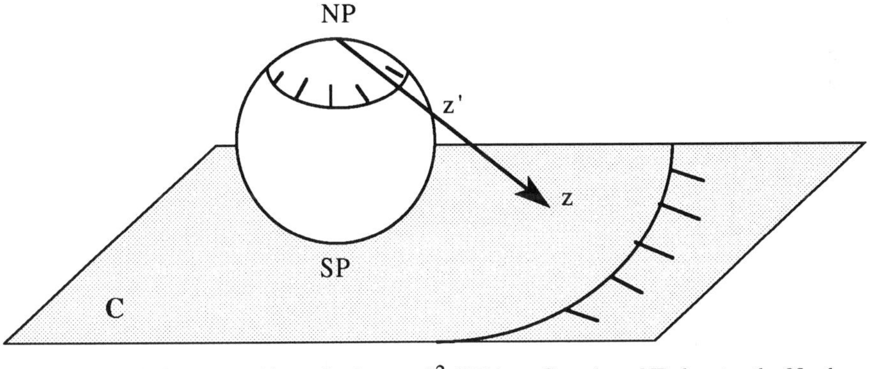

Figure 16.7 Stereographic projection $p: S^2\text{-}\{NP\} \to \mathbf{C}$, where NP denotes the North pole, and the sphere S^2 is tangent to **C** with South pole at the origin. The *interior* of a small disc round NP is mapped to the *exterior* of a large disc around the origin.

The key idea is that for any sequence $\{z_n\}$ in **C** we have $|z_n| \to \infty$ in the ordinary sense (it becomes arbitrarily large as n increases) if and only if $z_n' \to NP$ on the sphere. This leads to the translations given in Table 16.2, of statements involving the symbol '∞' of the extended complex plane. With these rules this extra point is shown as no different from any other when we transfer the action over to S^2, since any point may be chosen to play the role of North pole. We emphasise that a function, variable, or sequence tends to ∞ in the extended plane if and only if its modulus tends to infinity (becomes arbitrarily large). The lemma after Table 16.2 is useful for calculating with ∞.

TABLE 16.2 Expressions involving '∞' in the extended complex plane

	Expression	Equivalent
1	$z \to \infty$	$\lvert z\rvert \to \infty$
2	$f(\infty)$	$\lim_{\lvert z\rvert\to\infty} f(z)$, if this exists
3	$f(\alpha) = \infty$	$f(z) \to \infty$ as $z \to \alpha$
4	$f(\infty) = \infty$	$f(z) \to \infty$ as $z \to \infty$
5	$A(\infty)$	$\{z \in \mathbf{C}: f^n(z) \to \infty \text{ as } n \to \infty\}$

LEMMA 16.14 Let f(z) be a polynomial or rational function. Define $g(z) = 1/f(1/z)$. Then ∞ is a fixed point of f if and only if 0 is a fixed point of g, and in the affirmative case the two points have the same type (attractive, indifferent, repelling).

Proof We have

$$\begin{aligned} f(\infty) = \infty \quad &\Leftrightarrow \quad f(z) \to \infty \quad \text{as } z \to \infty \\ &\Leftrightarrow \quad f(1/z) \to \infty \quad \text{as } z \to 0 \\ &\Leftrightarrow \quad g(z) \to 0 \quad \text{as } z \to 0. \end{aligned}$$

The last part follows, essentially because $z \to 1/z$ switches 0 and ∞ and under the identification of $\mathbf{C}\cup\{\infty\}$ with S^2 it maps, homeomorphically, open sets containing NP to open sets containing SP. We omit further details, but see Example 16.64 later.

EXAMPLES 16.15 (1) $f(z) = z^2/(2z^2 - 1)$ satisfies $f(\infty) = 1/2$. To see this we write $f(z) = 1/(2 - 1/z^2)$ and apply line 2 of Table 16.2.

(2) $f(z) = 3z^3/(z^2+1)$ satisfies $f(\pm\mathbf{i}) = \infty$ by line 3 of the table. It has ∞ as a fixed point by line 4, since $f(z) \to \infty$ as $z \to \infty$. For a comparison we will try lemma 16.14. Write $g(z) = 1/f(1/z) = (z^{-2} + 1)/3z^{-3} = (z + z^3)/3$. Hence $g(0) = 0$ and so $f(\infty) = \infty$. In this case some may prefer one method and some another.

(3) Every complex polynomial $p(z)$, of degree at least two has ∞ as an attractive fixed point. Fixed, because $\lvert p(z)\rvert \to \infty$ as $\lvert z\rvert \to \infty$ (see Table 16.2, line 4), and attractive by a generalisation of the following argument in the case $f(z) = z^2 + z - 1$. We first give a 'barehanded method' (the alternative approach with Lemma 16.14 will follow).This is a nice application of some facts recalled at the start of Section 16.1: for any z,w in **C** we have $\lvert w/z\rvert = \lvert w\rvert/\lvert z\rvert$ $(z \neq 0)$, and $\lvert(\lvert z\rvert - \lvert w\rvert)\rvert \le \lvert z + w\rvert \le \lvert z\rvert + \lvert w\rvert$. Let z be any point with $\lvert z\rvert \ge 3$. Then

$$\begin{aligned} \lvert f(z)\rvert / \lvert z\rvert &= \lvert f(z)/z\rvert &&= \lvert z + 1 - 1/z\rvert \\ &\ge \lvert z+1\rvert - \lvert 1/z\rvert &&\ge \lvert z\rvert - 1 - \lvert 1/z\rvert \\ &\ge 3 - 1 - 1/3 &&= 5/3. \end{aligned}$$

Thus each iteration $w \to f(w)$ multiplies a modulus by at least 5/3, with the consequence that $\lvert f^n(z)\rvert \ge (5/3)^n \lvert z\rvert$, which tends to infinity.

Proof (3) by Lemma 16.14. Write $g(z) = 1/f(1/z) = 1/(z^{-2} + z^{-1} - 1) = z^2/(1+z-z^2)$. Now $g(0) = 0$ so $f(\infty) = \infty$. Also $g'(z) = [(1+z-z^2)2z - z^2(1-2z)]/(1+z-z^2)^2$, whence $g'(0) = 0$ (we need not simplify $g'(z)$), and ∞ is an attractive fixed point.

(4) If for a fixed positive $\delta > 0$, a complex function $R(z)$ satisfies $\lvert R(z)/z\rvert \ge 1+\delta$ for all

sufficiently large z, say $|z| \geq M$, then ∞ is an attractive fixed point of R(z). This follows by (3) with the last 5/3 replaced by $1+\delta$ (cf. Lemma 16.14).

(5) For a rational function p(z)/q(z) with degree p greater than degree q, ∞ is a fixed point but need not be attractive. Consider $R(z) = (2z^3+1)/3z^2$. Guided by Lemma 16.14 we write $S(z) = 1/R(1/z) = 3z^{-2}/(2z^{-3}+1) = 3z/(2+z^3)$. We obtain $S(0) = 0$, $S'(0) = 3/2$ (> 1). Hence ∞ is a repelling fixed point of R(z). However if the degree of p(z) exceeds the degree of q(z) by at least 2 then ∞ is attractive.

EXERCISE Let $R(z) = (3z^2 + 4)/(5z^2 + 2z)$. Use Table 16.2 to determine $R(\infty)$ and the points w for which $R(w) = \infty$ **or** show that $f(z) = z^3 + 2z + 1$ has ∞ as an attractive fixed point either by using a chain of inequalites as in Example 16.15 (3), or by Lemma 16.14.

Periodic points We cannot guarantee the presence of attractive *fixed points*, and results will be proved for the natural generalisation to *periodic points*, described next.

DEFINITION 16.16 Let $f^p(z_0) = z_0$ for a complex analytic function f(z), with p the least positive integer for which the equality holds. Then we call z_0 a *periodic point (of f) of period p*, and the sequence $\gamma = \{z_0, z_1, \ldots, z_{p-1}\}$ a *fixed p-cycle*. Here as usual $z_{n+1} = f(z_n)$. Notice that each point of γ is a fixed point of the map f^p, and as such has an eigenvalue.

THEOREM 16.17 All points of a fixed p-cycle of f(z) have the same eigenvalue for f^p.

Proof We first prove a useful general result for any point z_0 and integer $n \geq 2$:

$$(f^n)'(z_0) = f'(z_0)\, f'(z_1) \ldots f'(z_{n-1}). \tag{16.8}$$

We have $(f^n)'(z_0) = (f^{n-1}.f)'(z_0) = (f^{n-1})'(f(z_0))\, f'(z_0)$, by the Chain Rule for differentiation. This both proves (16.8) in case $n = 2$, and gives the inductive step from n-1 to n. In particular, (16.8) yields $(f^p)'(z_i) = f'(z_i)\, f'(z_{i+1}) \ldots f'(z_{i+p-1})$ which, with z_0 of period p, gives the same product with factors in different cyclic orders, for each i, $1 \leq i \leq p$.

EXAMPLE 16.18 If z_0 is a fixed point of g(z) then by (16.8): $(g^n)'(z_0) = (g'(z_0))^n$.

DEFINITION 16.19 A periodic point z_0 of f(z) (or the corresponding p-cycle γ) is called *attractive* if $|\lambda| < 1$ for the eigenvalue $\lambda = |(f^p)'(z_0)|$. [Similarly for superattractive, indifferent, repelling, with $|\lambda| = 0$, $|\lambda| = 1$, $|\lambda| > 1$.] The *basin of attraction* of γ is

$$A(\gamma) = A(z_0) \cup A(z_1) \cup \ldots \cup A(z_{p-1}), \tag{16.9}$$

the union of the basins, with respect to f^p, of each point of the cycle. As in the next example for $p = 2$, when an iterate enters $A(z_0)$, say, it will cycle round the $A(z_i)$ in turn, and each time it visits a particular $A(z_i)$ it forms the next member of a sequence which tends to z_i. The reason:

$$\begin{aligned} z \in A(z_i) &\Rightarrow (f^p)^n(z) \to z_i \text{ as } n \to \infty \\ &\Rightarrow f[(f^p)^n(z)] \to f(z_i), && \text{since f is continuous} \\ &\Rightarrow (f^p)^n(f(z)) \to z_{i+1}, && \text{since } f^r.f^s = f^s.f^r \quad (r, s \in \mathbf{N}) \\ &\Rightarrow f(z) \in A(z_{i+1}). \end{aligned}$$

EXAMPLE 16.20 We shall find the fixed 2-cycles of $f(z) = z^2-1$. Now, $f^2(z) = z \Leftrightarrow (z^2-1)^2 - 1 = z$, or equivalently $z^4 - 2z^2 - z = 0$. This gives four points, but, importantly, two of them must be the fixed points of f(z), namely the solutions of $z^2 - z - 1 = 0$. Dividing out by this quadratic we obtain $f^2(z) = z$ in the form $z(z+1)(z^2-z-1) = 0$. There is thus a unique fixed 2-cycle $\gamma = \{0, -1\}$. A check is that $f(0) = -1$ and $f(-1) = 0$. The common eigenvalue is $\lambda = (f^2)'(0) = (4z^3 - 4z)_{z=0} = 0$. Thus the 2-cycle is superattractive. The basin of attaction is shown in Figure 16.8 of the next section, where the example continues. This time $\partial A(\infty) = \partial A(\gamma)$.

EXERCISE Show that the fixed points of Example 16.20 are both repellers.

16.2 Julia sets

16.2.1 Introducing the Julia set

Julia sets were invented by Gaston Julia in 1914, long before the Mandelbrot set was thought of (though Julia would surely have been delighted by Mandelbrot's idea).

DEFINITION 16.21 The *Julia set* of a complex function with ∞ as an attractive fixed point is the boundary $J(f) = \partial A(\infty)$. We shall define here for later use the *filled-in Julia set* $K(f) = C \setminus A(\infty)$. Where f is known from the context we may simply write J or K. Notice that $J = \partial K$ since the boundary of a set equals the boundary of its complement.

We have chosen to make our primary definition of Julia sets one which depends on f(z) having ∞ as an attractive fixed point, although the theory developed by Julia and Fatou applies to the wider class of all rational functions. However this choice seems the most accessible of several possibilities, to which it will in due course be shown equivalent, and which do apply to rational functions. In particular though, the present definition of J as boundary applies to polynomials of degree at least two (Example 16.15(3)), for which most of the spectacular colour effects and intricacy associated with Julia sets are already present. Indeed we get a more than adequate sample of theory and effect from degree two, the topic of Section 16.3.

We begin with examples, and establish foundations in the next two sections. Thus, consider $f(z) = z^2$ of Example 16.13 and Figure 16.6(a), where A(0) and $A(\infty)$ are respectively the points within and outside the unit circle S^1, and

$$J = \partial A(\infty) = S^1 = \partial A(0). \qquad (16.10)$$

In Figure 16.6(b), with $f(z) = z^2+c$ and c small, the Julia set is a very complicated but nevertheless non-crossing distortion of S^1. The finite attractive fixed point has moved from the origin to a nearby point α (both marked by a heavy dot), but we still have a common boundary property, $J = \partial A(\infty) = \partial A(\alpha)$. We will show that this holds for any finite attractive fixed point of a polynomial p(z), leading in Section 16.2.5 to the Boundary Scanning Method for computer generation of J.

EXAMPLE 16.20 continued For a highly nontrivial example in degree 2 consider the Julia set of $f(z) = z^2 - 1$, shown in Figure 16.8(a). Notice how outlying regions are mapped from region to region by f until they reach the region containing -1, or that containing 0, whereupon they alternate between the two.

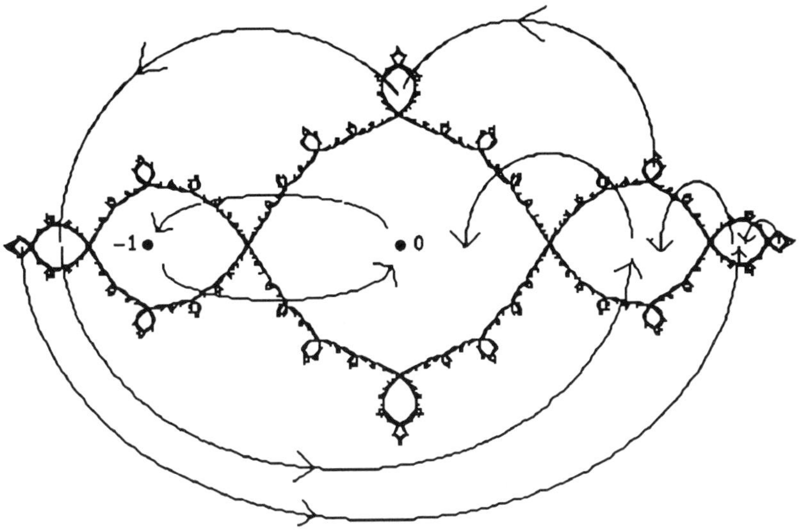

Figure 16.8(a) The Julia set of $f(z) = z^2 - 1$ is the curve shown above (cf. Example 16.20), with attractive 2-cycle $\{-1,0\}$. It bounds an infinite number of connected regions. Each region is mapped completely into another by f(z) (see arrows), since the continuous image of a connected set is connected (Theorem 12.36).

The darkened regions in Figure 16.8(b) below represent the basin of attraction A(-1) of the point -1 under the composition map f^2. They constitute those points of the plane which are mapped after some even number of applications of f into the dark region containing -1. This region is the immediate basin of attraction $A_0(-1)$, namely the connected component of A(-1) which contains -1 itself (Definition 16.11). The remaining regions bounded by J form the basin of attraction of the point 0 under f^2.

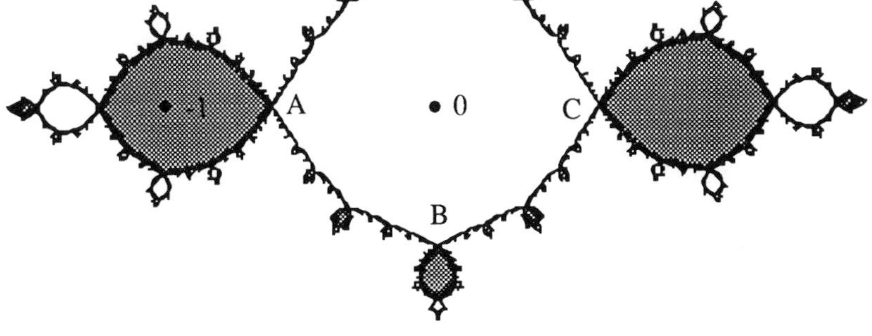

Figure 16.8(b) Here we show darkened the regions which are part of the basin of attraction of $z = -1$ under f^2, namely those which follow an even number of arrows to enter the region containing -1. Every region is in the basin of attraction of -1 or of 0. Thus the union of the regions is the basin of attraction of the fixed 2-cycle $\gamma = \{-1,0\}$, and the Julia set J(f) equals $\partial A(\gamma)$.

Their points are characterised by being mapped into the central white region $A_0(0)$ by some even number of iterations of f. Equivalently, an odd number of iterations of f maps them into the other immediate basin, $A_0(-1)$, since f maps $A_0(0)$ to $A_0(-1)$ and vice versa. The union of all the regions referred, to$A(\gamma) = A(-1) \cup A(0)$, is by definition the basin of attraction with f mapping every region of A(-1) to a region of A(0), and vice versa. It appears, as we shall later prove, that $J = \partial A(\gamma)$ (Theorem 16.43). Much less obvious is that J is the boundary of the union of the dark regions alone, as will follow from $J(f) = J(f^2)$ (Theorem 16.37). Indeed, not only the noted points A,B,C,D in Figure 16.8(b), but *every* point of J is a common boundary point of a white and a dark region. Thus it is that there is further detail at every level of magnification.

EXERCISE Let $f(z) = z^2 - 7/8$. Without writing down the fixed points explicitly, find the fixed 2-cycle of f and show that it is attractive. [The eigenvalue is 1/2.] **or** Make a rough copy of Figure 16.8(a). Without consulting its companion, Figure 16.8(b), darken as many regions as you can deduce are in the attractive basin of 0 (under f^2).

In Sections 16.2.3 and 16.2.4 we prove some crucial basic results about Julia sets. In particular we prove some results on which their computer graphical generation is based. To do so we must lead up to their somewhat technical classical definition, which we will show is equivalent to the one adopted earlier ($\partial A(\infty)$, Definition 16.21). The results are summarised in Table 16.3 at the end of the chapter. Meanwhile, here are the 'big three', where α is *any* attractive fixed point and γ *any* attractive cycle. The first suggests that every point of J is in several regions simultaneously, hence that J is very complicated and probably a fractal (cf. Mandelbrot, 1983). It gives us the Boundary Scanning Method for constructing J (Construction 16.45).

$$J(f) = \partial A(\alpha) = \partial A(\gamma) \tag{16.11}$$

The set of repelling periodic points of f is dense in J(f) (16.12)

If $z_0 \in J(f)$ then the *inverse orbit* $\bigcup_{n=1}^{\infty} f^{-n}(z_0)$ is dense in J(f). (16.13)

EXAMPLE 16.22 We saw that $J(z^2)$ is the unit circle, S^1. Thus by (16.12) the repelling periodic points of $f(z) = z^2$ must be dense in this circle. Here is an explicit calculation to verify this. Firstly every (2^n-1)'th root of unity w is periodic repelling, for $f^n(w) = w^{2^n} = w$, and $|(f^n)'(w)| = |2^n w^{2^n-1}| = 2^n > 1$. Let $\alpha \in S^1$ and $\varepsilon > 0$. Since the (2^n-1)'th roots of unity consist of $2^n - 1$ points equally spaced round the circle, there is one within distance ε of α for sufficiently large n. Thus the repelling periodic points of f are dense in the circle S^1. This also illustrates the value of considering periodic points as well as fixed ones.

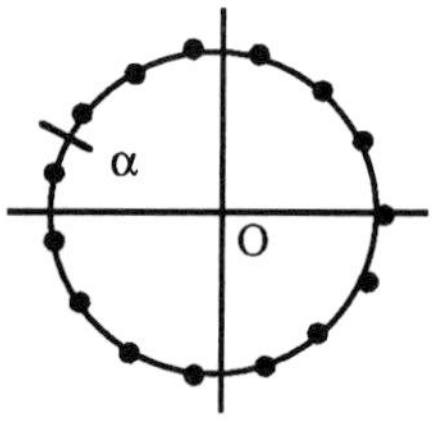

Figure 16.9 Any point α on S^1 has a (2^n-1)'th root close . Here n = 4.

As just exemplified, (16.12) tells us that every repelling periodic point is in J and that every point of J has such points arbitrarily close. Thus there are plenty around to be discovered. This suggests that we try to determine a repelling (preferably) fixed point of f(z) as initial point z_0 of J, then use the third statement to obtain a dense subset of J by iterating backwards (the Inverse Iteration Method, Construction 16.44). Notice that if for example $f(z) = z^2 + c$, then in general $f^{-1}(z_0)$ consists of the two solutions of $f(z) = z_0$, which we may write as $\pm\sqrt{(z_0 - c)}$, whilst $f^{-2}(z_0)$ consists of the four solutions of $z^2 + c = \pm\sqrt{(z_0 - c)}$, and so on. More on this under the method itself.

EXAMPLE 16.23 Let $f(z) = z^2\text{-}\mathbf{i}z+\mathbf{i}$. We use (16.12 to find a point in J(f) then obtain three more by (16.13). We find f(z) = z ⇔ (z-1)(z-**i**) = 0, hence fixed points 1,**i**. Then $f'(\mathbf{i}) = (2z\text{-}\mathbf{i})_{z=\mathbf{i}} = \mathbf{i}$, of modulus 1; but $f'(1) = 2\text{-}\mathbf{i}$, of modulus $\sqrt{5}$, so $1 \in J$. Now we calculate inverse images. If $z \in f^{-1}(1)$ then $f(z) = 1$, $z^2\text{-}\mathbf{i}z+\mathbf{i}\text{-}1 = 0$. One solution must be z = 1 since this is a fixed point, the other is new: $-1+\mathbf{i} \in J$. Iterating back a stage further, $f(z) = -1+\mathbf{i}$ gives $z^2\text{-}\mathbf{i}z+1 = 0$, and so two more points $z = (1/2)(1 \pm \sqrt{5})\mathbf{i}$ in J. Thus we have

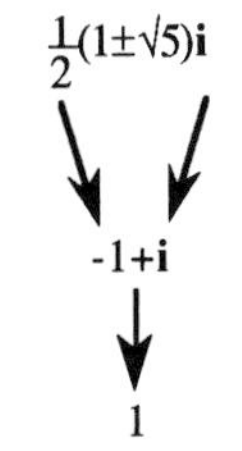

Figure 16.10

$$f^{-1}(1) = \{1, -1+\mathbf{i}\} \qquad f^{-2}(1) = \{1, -1+\mathbf{i}, (1/2)(1 \pm \sqrt{5})\mathbf{i}\}.$$

EXERCISE Find $f^{-3}(1)$ in Example 16.23.

EXAMPLE 16.24 We claim that $f(z) = z^2 + c$ has a repelling fixed point unless $c = 1/4$. For, a root $\alpha = (1/2)(1 \pm\sqrt{(1\text{-}4c)})$ of $f(z) = z$ has eigenvalue λ with $|\lambda| = 2|\alpha|$, which equals $|1 \pm\sqrt{(1\text{-}4c)}|$. And taking the positive square root, Definition 16.7, we discover that $|\lambda| > 1$ unless $1\text{-}4c = 0$, $c = 1/4$, when both roots equal 1/2 with eigenvalue 1. We can show directly that 1/2 is in the Julia set in this case (see Exercise 34 at the chapter's end).

16.2.2 Normal families

In three short sections, 16.2.2 to 16.2.4 we will prove some satisfying facts about Julia sets. They are listed as items 1 to 6 in Table 16.3 at the end of the chapter, and may be referred to as required without the need to work through their proofs, which are slightly more demanding than most in Chapter 16. A Julia set J(f), however defined, has to do with iterates f^n of a complex analytic function f on an open set U. Such iterates form a special type of family $\{F_n: U \to C\}$ in which $F_n(z) = f^n(z)$, and we need to investigate when, and in what sense, $\{F_n\}$ converges.

DEFINITION 16.25 We say $\{F_n\}$ *converges uniformly* on a set V if either

(1) $F_n \to F$ (F analytic) as $n \to \infty$,

or (2) $F_n \to \infty$ uniformly as $n \to \infty$,

with the usual metric $d(F_n,F) = \sup_{z \in V} |F_n(z) - F(z)|$.

Here F(z) is any analytic function; the meaning of 'uniformly' in (2) is that, given any number M, however large, there is an integer N such that $|F_n(z)| \geq M$ *simultaneously for all* $z \in V$, whenever $n \geq N$. Notice that an analogous property holds in (1), for if we are given $\varepsilon > 0$ and sufficiently large N, then $|F_n(z) - F(z)| \leq d(F_n,F) < \varepsilon$, for all $z \in V$. Indeed the other way to express this is to say that $F_n \to F$ uniformly on V (see below Example 13.31).

EXAMPLE 16.26 If f(z) is a polynomial of degree at least two then for some radius r, we have $|f(z)| \geq 2|z|$ on the open set $V = \{Z: |z| > r\}$. This may be proved by the 'barehanded' method in Example 16.15(3). Thus $f^n \to \infty$ uniformly on V. However we also need the weaker convergence defined below.

DEFINITION 16.27 Given a family $\{F_n: V \to \mathbf{C}\}$ we shall say that $F_n \to F$ *pointwise*, if $F_n(z) \to F(z)$ $(z \in V)$ as $n \to \infty$. Similarly with ∞ replacing F and F(z). We say $\{F_n\}$ *converges* to mean that either holds.

EXAMPLE 16.28 (Uniform versus non-uniform convergence.) Let U be the open set given by $|z| < 1$ and define $F_n(z) = 3z/(3-z^n)$. Then for every z in U we have $z^n \to 0$ as $n \to \infty$ and so $F_n \to F$ pointwise, where $F(z) = z$.

*Convergence of F_n is **not** uniform on U (in this example).* We will establish this by proving that, with $\varepsilon = 1/4$ and any given integer n,

$$|F_n(z) - F(z)| \geq \varepsilon \quad \text{for } \textit{some } z \text{ in } U, \tag{16.14}$$

for the displayed part contradicts "$|F_n(z) - F(z)| < \varepsilon$ for *all* z in U". Now, the equality $|F_n(z) - F(z)| = |z^{n+1}/(3-z^n)|$, with z restricted to real values, gives us a continuous function $g: [0,1] \to \mathbf{R}$ with $g(0) = 0$, $g(1) = 1/2$. It follows that there is a number z_0 in the open interval (0,1), hence in U, for which $g(z_0) = 1/4$ (otherwise $g([0,1])$ would be disconnected: this is a version of the Intermediate Value Theorem of Example 12.41). We have found the value $z = z_0$ to satisfy (16.14), so convergence is not uniform. But much can be salvaged by means of compact sets.

$F_n \to F$ uniformly on all compact subsets of U. A compact subset of U is bounded and closed and so lies within a closed disc D_r: $|z| \leq r$ for some $r < 1$. Let $\varepsilon > 0$ be given. and suppose without loss of generality that $\varepsilon < 1$. We shall obtain $|z|^n < \varepsilon$ by taking $(1/|z|)^n > 1/\varepsilon$, or $n > \log(1/\varepsilon)/\log(1/|z|)$. Thus $|z^{n+1}| < \varepsilon$ and $|3-z^n| > 3 - |z^n| > 1$, so that we have $|F_n(z) - F(z)| < \varepsilon$. This inequality holds simultaneously for all z in D_r provided, since $|x| \leq r$, that we take $n > \log(1/e)/\log(1/r)$. We have shown that in this example not only does $F_n \to F$ (pointwise) but that the convergence is uniform on every compact subset of U. Such a property enables the following useful result to be stated.

THEOREM 16.29 Let $\{F_n: U \to \mathbf{C}\}$ be a family of complex analytic functions. If $F_n \to F$ (pointwise) and the convergence is uniform on compact subsets then the derivatives satisfy $F_n' \to F'$ in the same sense. If $F_n \to F$ uniformly on U itself then likewise does $F_n' \to F'$.

CONVENTION 16.30 When we say that $\{F_n: U \to \mathbf{C}\}$ converges uniformly on compact subsets it will be implied also that F_n converges pointwise on all of U. Now we are ready to define a concept crucial for the next section.

DEFINITION 16.31 The family $\{F_n: U \to \mathbf{C}\}$ is *normal* on an open subset V of U if every sequence of functions from this family has a subsequence which converges uniformly on every compact subset of V. $\{F_n\}$ is *normal at a point z_0* if it is normal on some open set V containing z_0. (Notice that $\{F_n\}$ is then normal at every point of V.) Thus one normal family is $\{F_n\}$ in Example 16.28, for $\{F_n\}$ itself converges uniformly on compact subsets of U and therefore so do all its subsequences.

We have a sort of 'double take': since $\{F_n\}$ is itself a sequence we are really asking about convergence of a subsequence of a subsequence of $\{F_n\}$. However this causes no difficulty in practice. For instance the 'family' of functions $\{z^n\}$ has a subsequence $\{z^{2n}\}$ of which a subsequence is $\{z^{6n}\}$. The deep result upon which the next section is based, and upon which the theory of Julia sets depends, is *Montel's Theorem*: that if $\{F_n: U \to \mathbf{C}\}$ is *not* a normal family then it spreads out U across the entire complex plane, with the possible exception of one point. Put otherwise, the functions F_n between them take all complex values except possibly one.

THEOREM 16.32 (Proved by Montel, 1927) Suppose the family of complex analytic functions $\{F_n; U \to \mathbf{C}\}$ is not normal. Then

$$\bigcup_{n=1}^{\infty} F_n(U) = \mathbf{C} \text{ (possibly excluding one point)}. \qquad (16.15)$$

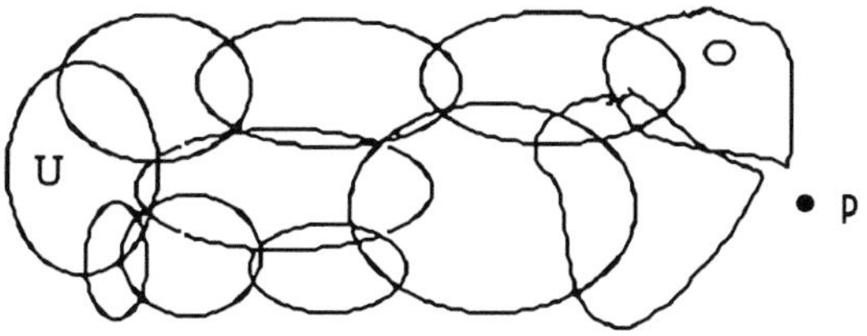

Figure 16.11 If $\{f^n: U \to \mathbf{C}\}$ is *not* normal then the images $\{f^n U\}$ cover the plane, excluding a maximum of one point (Montel's Theorem).

EXAMPLE 16.33 Let $f(z) = \lambda z$, with $|\lambda| > 1$. Thus $f^n(z) = \lambda^n z$. Let U be an open subset of **C**, as usual. All depends on whether or not 0 is in U.
Case $0 \notin U$. We claim that $\{f^n: U \to \mathbf{C}\}$ is normal. For, in any compact and hence closed subset V of U, there is a least value $r > 0$ of $|z|$, and so $|f^n(z)| \geq |\lambda|^n r$ for all z in V simultaneously. Thus $f^n \to \infty$ uniformly on V, by Definition 16.25.

Case $0 \in U$. The statement that $f^n \to \infty$ on all compact subsets V of U is no longer true, since $f^n(0) = 0$ and we can choose V to contain 0. Furthermore, $f^n \to f$ (f analytic) is ruled out because for any $z \neq 0$ in U we have $|f^n(z)| \to \infty$. Thus $\{f^n\}$ is **not** normal on U. Now we may prove Montel's Theorem for this special case by showing that

$$\bigcup_{n=1}^{\infty} f^n(U) = \mathbf{C}.$$

Since U is open and contains 0, it contains all z with $|z| < r$, for some $r > 0$. Let z_0 be in $\mathbf{C} \setminus \{0\}$. It suffices to find z with $|z| < r$, and $n \in \mathbf{N}$, such that $\lambda^n z = z_0$. That is, $z = z_0/\lambda^n$. We take n so large that $|z_0|/|\lambda|^n < r$, and then z lies in U as required.

EXERCISE Let $f(z) = \lambda z$ with $|\lambda| < 1$. Show that $\{f^n\}$ is normal on every open set U by showing it converges uniformly to the constant function 0 on every compact set.

16.2.3 Implications of the classical definition of Julia set

Now we are ready to define the classical version of the Julia set, here denoted by $J_0(f)$, and to derive important properties, before proving that this is equivalent to our preferred definition. As before, we shall sometimes drop the parentheses if there is no ambiguity as to f. In this section and the next we concentrate on the case f(z) is a polynomial, with some comment on the transition to a rational function R(z). Firstly, the well-tried way to ensure R(z) is defined everywhere is to work with $R: \overline{\mathbf{C}} \to \overline{\mathbf{C}}$, replacing **C** by $\overline{\mathbf{C}}$ in the definition of

J. In fact Theorems 16.36 and 16.37 go through unchanged. Lemma 16.38, on which Lemma 16.39 also depends, allows two exceptional points by a slightly more general version of Montel's theorem than we stated, with ∞ as a possible point (Blanchard, 1984).

DEFINITION 16.34 (The Julia and Fatou sets.)

$$J_0(f) = \{z \in C: \ \{f^n\} \text{ is not normal at } z\}$$
$$= \{z \in C: \ \{f^n\} \text{ is normal on } no \text{ open set containing } z\} \quad (16.16)$$

$$F_0(f) = C \setminus J_0(f) \quad (\text{the Fatou set})$$
$$= \{z \in C: \ \{f^n\} \text{ is normal on } some \text{ open set containing } z\} \quad (16.17)$$

REMARKS 16.35 (1) $F_0(f)$ is open , from the second form of its definition in (16.17), so $J_0(f)$ is closed.
(2) If B is closed then $A \subseteq B$ implies $\overline{A} \subseteq B$ (since $\overline{A} \subseteq \overline{B} = B$, see (11.10) and Table 11.3(10)).
(3) In Example 16.33, Case $0 \in U$, the sequence $\{f^n\}$ was normal on no open set containing the origin 0. Thus $0 \in J_0(f)$ by (16.16). The Case $0 \notin U$ brought out that if $z \neq 0$ then $\{f^n\}$ *is* normal on an open set containing z, hence $z \in F_0(f)$ by (16.17). We conclude that $J_0(f) = \{0\}$ when $f = \lambda z$ with $|\lambda| > 1$, a rather uninteresting Julia set. By the exercise following that Example, $\{f^n\}$ is normal at every point of the plane in case $|\lambda| < 1$, giving $J_0(f)$ as the empty set. Consequently Julia sets of polynomials $f(z) = az+b$ will not be considered further.

EXERCISE Deduce from Example 16.26 that $J_0(f)$ is bounded, by proving $J_0(f) \subseteq C\backslash V$.

THEOREM 16.36 $J_0(f)$ is forward and backward invariant, that is,

$$f(J_0) = J_0 = f^{-1}(J_0) \quad (16.18)$$

Proof It is simpler, and it suffices, to prove (16.18) with J_0 replaced by its complement F_0. The result is then a consequence of inclusions (1) $F_0 \subseteq f(F_0)$, (2) $F_0 \supseteq f(F_0)$, (3) $F_0 \subseteq f^{-1}(F_0)$, (4) $F_0 \supseteq f^{-1}(F_0)$. Of these, (2) and (3) are logically equivalent. We shall prove (4), the rest being similar. Let $w \in f^{-1}(F_0)$. Then the image $z = f(w)$ is in F_0, so $\{f^n\}$ is normal on an open set V containing z. We prove that $w \in F_0$ by showing that $\{f^n\}$ is normal on the open set $f^{-1}(V)$ containing w.

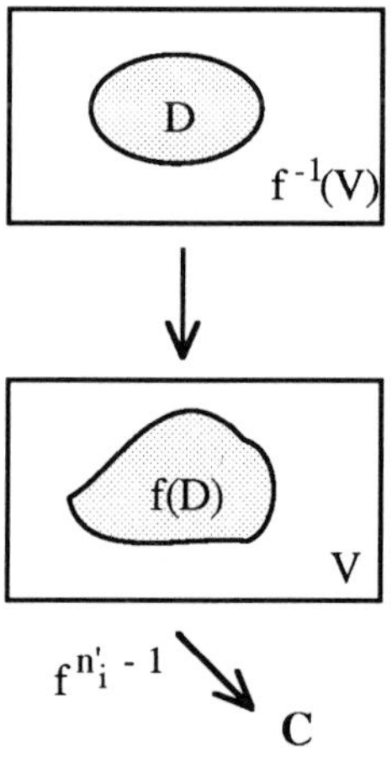

Figure 16.12

Let $\{f^{n_i}\}$ be a subsequence of $\{f^n\}$. Then so is $\{f^{n_i-1}\}$, which therefore contains a subsequence $\{f^{n_i'-1}\}$ uniformly convergent on compact subsets of V. Let D be a compact subset of $f^{-1}(V)$. Then f(D) is a compact subset of V (Theorem 12.15) and so $\{f^{n_i'-1}\}$ is uniformly convergent on f(D). Therefore (see Figure 16.12) $\{f^{n_i'}\}$ is uniformly convergent on D. This establishes (4). For the rest, we note that if U is open then not only $f^{-1}(U)$ but also f(U) is open (Theorem 16.5), since f is analytic.

The next result brings out further the subsequence aspect of normality.

THEOREM 16.37 $J_0(f^p) = J_0(f)$, *for* $p = 1, 2, 3, \ldots$.

Proof As in the previous proof, it is helpful to work with the complement F_0 of J_0. Firstly, $F_0(f) \subseteq F_0(f^p)$, for if every subsequence of $\{f^n\}$ has a subsequence uniformly convergent on a given set V then the same holds for $\{f^{np}\}$, i.e. for $\{(f^p)^n\}$. Now for $F_0(f) \supseteq F_0(f^p)$. We first observe that if a family of functions $\{F_n\}$ is uniformly convergent on a compact set D then so is the family $\{G.F_n\}$ for any continuous G(z). Thus, let $\{f^{np}\}$ be normal on an open set V; then so also is $\{f^{np+s}\} = \{f^s.f^{np}\}$ for each of $s = 1, 2, \ldots, p-1$. Consider a subsequence S (by definition infinite) of $\{f^n\}$. If S contained only finitely many members of each of the p sequences $\{f^{np+s}\}$, $0 \le s \le p-1$, then S would itself be finite. Therefore S contains an infinite subsequence of $\{f^{np+s}\}$ for some s, which sequence, by normality of $\{f^{np+s}\}$, has a subsequence uniformly convergent on compact subsets of V. Thus $\{f^n\}$ is normal as required, and $F_0(f) \supseteq F_0(f^p)$.

LEMMA 16.38 Let $w \in J_0(f)$. *Then for any open set U containing w,*

$$\bigcup_{n=1}^{\infty} f^n(U) = \mathbf{C} \text{ (except possibly for one point)} \qquad (16.19)$$

Any such exceptional point is not in $J_0(f)$.

Proof Since w is in J_0, the family $\{f^n\}$ is not normal at w (see (16.16)), hence not normal on U. Now (16.19) follows from Montel's Theorem, 16.32. Now suppose v is the exceptional point omitted in the infinite union W of (16.19) above. We must show that $\{f^n\}$ *is* normal at v, so that $v \notin J_0$. Note that $f(W) \subseteq W$, so if $f(z) = v$ then $z \notin W$. But since $\mathbf{C} \backslash W = \{v\}$, we have $z = v$. Thus the only solution of the equation $f(z) - v = 0$ is v. So by the Fundamental Theorem of Algebra (13.20), $f(z)-v = A(z-v)^d$ for some constant A, where f(z) is, by assumption, a polynomial of degree $d \ge 2$. Suppose z lies in the open disc $D = \{z: |z-v|^{d-1} < 1/|2A|\}$, centre v. Then $|f(z)-v| < (1/2)|z-v|$, hence $f^n(z)$ converges uniformly to v on all subsets of D and $\{f^n\}$ is normal at v. Thus $v \notin J_0(f)$, as required.

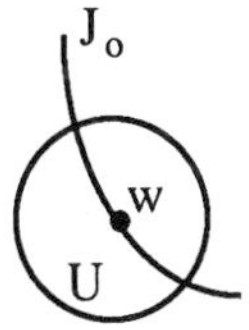

Figure 16.13

LEMMA 16.39 $J_0(f)$ *has no isolated points.*

Proof A point $w \in J_0$ is by definition isolated if some open set U contains w but no other point of J_0. We must show that this cannot occur. That is, if $w \in J_0$ then any open set U containing w has other points of J_0 besides w (cf. Figure 16.13). Since $J_0(f) = J_0(f^p)$ by Theorem 16.37, we may regard the case of periodic points as subsumed under fixed points, and divide consideration between cases (a) w is a fixed point of f, (b) it is not. We omit further details, but cf. Falconer (1990), Blanchard(1984).

16.2.4 Proofs of three main results

First we give the basis of the Inverse Iteration Method for Julia sets. As before the proofs are given for a polynomial f(z). However the three results hold if f is a rational function. Theorems 16.40 and 16.43 here depend on the polynomial hypothesis through Lemma 16.38, whilst Theorem 16.42 needs a more complicated version of the family $\{h_n\}$ and of Montel's Theorem.

THEOREM 16.40 If $z \in J_0(f)$ *then* $\bigcup_{k=1}^{\infty} f^{-k}(z)$ *is dense in* J_0.

Proof If $z \in J_0(f)$ then $f^{-k}(z) \subseteq J_0(f)$ for $k = 1, 2, \ldots$, by backward invariance, Theorem 16.36. Hence the given union W, and therefore its closure $\overline{W}$ are contained in the closed set $J_0(f)$ (cf. Remarks 16.35(2)). It remains to show that, conversely, any given $w \in J_0(f)$ is in $\overline{W}$. Let U be an open set containing w, as in Figure 16.13. By Theorem 16.38, w is in $f^k(U)$ for some $k \geq 1$ (w not being an omitted exceptional point, since w is in $J_0(f)$). Hence $f^{-k}(w)$ intersects U. Thus any open set U containing w intersects W, satisfying a standard criterion for $w \in \overline{W}$ (Tests 11.18, 11.19).

NOTATION 16.41 Let $\mathbf{P} = \mathbf{P}(f)$ denote the set of all repelling periodic points of f. The following result shows their importance and is a powerful tool for reaching the main goal of this section, Theorem 16.43.

THEOREM 16.42 For a polynomial f(z), the repelling periodic points are dense in $J_0(f)$. *That is,* $J_0(f) = \overline{\mathbf{P}}$.

Proof (1) We show first that $\overline{\mathbf{P}} \subseteq J_0(f)$. Let $w \in \mathbf{P}$, of period $p \geq 1$. Then w is a repelling fixed point of $g = f^p$, so that by Theorem 16.37 $J_0(f) = J_0(g)$, and we must show that $\{g^n\}$ is not normal at w. Suppose it is (we shall obtain a contradiction). Then w is in an open set V on which a subsequence $\{g^{n_i}\}$ converges uniformly on every compact subset, not to infinity since $g^k(w) = w$ $(k = 1,2, \ldots)$, but to an analytic function g_0. According to Theorem 16.29 we may differentiate and obtain $(g^{n_i})'(z) \to (g_0)'(z)$ for all z in V. But since $g(w) = w$ we have by the Chain Rule (cf. Example 16.18) $|(g^{n_i})'(w)| = |g'(w)|^{n_i}$, which tends to infinity because g is repelling, that is $|g'(w)| > 1$. This contradiction shows that $w \in J_0(g) = J_0(f)$. Thus $\mathbf{P} \subseteq J_0(f)$ and, because J_0 is closed, $\overline{\mathbf{P}} \subseteq J_0(f)$ as required (cf. Remark 16.35(2)).

(2) Now we show that $J_0 \subseteq \overline{\mathbf{P}}$. Define

$$W = \{w \in J_0\colon\ f(z) = w \text{ for some } z \neq w \text{ with } f'(z) \neq 0\}$$

Thus W results by deleting from J_0 those points $w = f(z)$ for which $z \neq w$ but $f'(z) = 0$, and the number of these points is finite, not exceeding the degree of f(z). Further, being in J_0, each such point is non-isolated by Lemma 16.39, so has points of W arbitrarily close, and so is in $\overline{W}$. Hence $\overline{W} = J_0$, and it remains to prove that $\overline{W} \subseteq \overline{\mathbf{P}}$, or simply $W \subseteq \overline{\mathbf{P}}$ (since $\overline{\mathbf{P}}$ is closed).

(3) The proof that $W \subseteq \overline{\mathbf{P}}$. Let $w \in W$. Then by definition of W there is a point z with $f(z) = w$, $z \neq w$, $f'(z) \neq 0$. By the Inverse Function Theorem, 16.6A, f has an analytic inverse f^{-1} on some open set V containing w. Again, because $z \neq w$ we can choose V so small that V and $f^{-1}(V)$ do not meet, so that we have $f^{-1}\colon V \to \mathbf{C}\backslash V$ with $f(f^{-1}(v)) = v$ for all $v \in V$. See Figure 16.14.

Therefore the family of functions

$$g_n(v) = \frac{f^n(v) - v}{f^{-1}(v) - v} \qquad (v \in V)$$

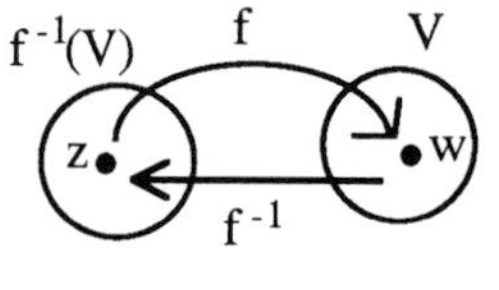

Figure 16.14

is well-defined and analytic. Now, $w \in \overline{\mathbf{P}}$ will follow if every open set containing w meets **P** (Definition 11.20, Test 11.18). Let U be such an open set. We may take $U \subseteq V$. Since $w \in J_0$, the family $\{f^n\}$ and hence $\{g_n\}$ is not normal on U (note that the denominator of g_n does not vary with n). By Montel's Theorem, 16.32, $g_n(v)$ must take the value 0 or 1 for some n, and $v \in U$, giving respectively $f^n(v) = v$ or $f^{n+1}(v) = v$. Thus U contains a periodic point. We need it to be repelling. And it is, for no point in V is mapped back into V by f since V and $f^{-1}(V)$ do not intersect. It follows that $w \in \overline{\mathbf{P}}$ and the proof is complete, since w was an arbitrary point of W.

Finally, our definition of J as $\partial A(\infty)$ will be shown to be equivalent to the classical one J_0, and thus to share all the properties we have just proved for J_0. Furthermore J is the boundary of the basin of attraction of every attractive fixed point or attractive cycle.

THEOREM 16.43 Let f(z) have attractive fixed points $\alpha, \beta, \ldots,$ *and attractive fixed cycles* $\gamma, \delta, \ldots$. *Then*

$$\begin{aligned} J(f) &= \partial A(\infty) \quad \text{(by definition)} \\ &= \partial A(\alpha) = \partial A(\beta) = \ldots\ldots \\ &= \partial A(\gamma) = \partial A(\delta) = \ldots\ldots = J_0(f). \end{aligned}$$

Proof (1) Our main task is to prove that $J_0(f) = \partial A(\alpha)$ for any attractive fixed point α. The rest will quickly follow. We first show that $J_0(f) \subseteq \partial A(\alpha)$. Let $w \in J_0$. Then by forward invariance (Theorem 16.36) $f^k(w) \in J_0(f)$ (for all $k \in \mathbf{N}$), a set in which the repelling points are dense by Theorem 16.42. Thus $f^k(w)$ cannot converge to an attractive fixed point, and we have $w \notin A(\alpha)$. On the other hand, if U is any open set containing the point w of J_0 (see e.g. Figure 16.13), then $f^k(U)$ intersects $A(\alpha)$ for some k by the 'spreading' Lemma 16.38. So some point $z \neq w$ in U satisfies $f^k(z) \in A(\alpha)$, implying z itself is in $A(\alpha)$. Since therefore every open set around w intersects $A(\alpha)$ we have w in the closure of this set. Then since w is not in $A(\alpha)$ itself we have w in $\partial A(\alpha)$ as required.

(2) To prove that $\partial A(\alpha) \subseteq J_0(f)$, let $z \in \partial A(\alpha)$. We suppose $z \notin J_0(f)$ and obtain a contradiction. By definition of J_0 we have z within an open set V on which $\{f^n\}$ has a uniformly convergent subsequence. We may take V to be connected, if necessary relabelling as V the connected component containing z. Now, $U = V \cap A(\alpha)$ is open, being the intersection of two open sets, and it is nonempty since it contains z. See Figure 16.15.

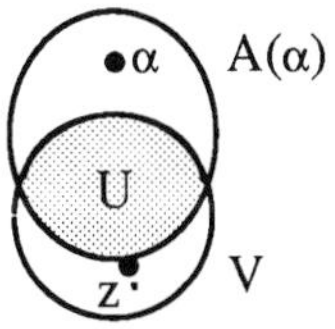

Figure 16.15

On $U \subseteq A(\alpha)$, the subsequence converges to the constant function α. It follows that the limit function is constant on the whole of V, for an analytic function constant on any open subset (here U) of a connected open set (here V) is constant on the latter set (Theorem 16.5). We conclude that all points of V are eventually mapped into $A(\alpha)$ by iterates of f. But this entails $V \subseteq A(\alpha)$. Thus z lies within an open subset V of $A(\alpha)$, contradicting $z \in \partial A(\alpha)$. This completes the proof that $J_0(f) = \partial A(\alpha)$.

(3) $J_0 = \partial A(\alpha)$ holds also for $\alpha = '\infty'$ in the extended complex plane, since we may view the action as taking place on the 2-sphere, where the North pole corresponds to '∞' but is like any other point (cf. Figure 16.7).

(4) Consider an attractive p-cycle $\gamma = \{z_0, z_1, \ldots, z_{p-1}\}$. We have $J_0(f) = J_0(f^p)$ (Theorem 16.37) $= \partial A(z_0) = \partial A(z_1) = \ldots = \partial A(z_{p-1})$ (by (1)), where the basins of attraction are taken with respect to f^p. Therefore all these equal $\partial A(\gamma)$, the boundary, by

definition, of the union of the disjoint open basins $A(z_i)$. The proof of this key result is complete.

EXERCISE Assuming that $J = \partial A(\alpha) = \partial A(\infty)$, where α and ∞ are attractive fixed points of a polynomial $f(z)$, deduce that $f(J)$ and $f^{-1}(J)$ are in J.

16.2.5 Constructing the Julia set

We use the identifying abbreviations of Peitgen and Saupe (1988) for the various methods, for polynomial, rational, or even more general functions. See this reference for further details and extensions. The 'IIM' is especially suited to $f(z) = z^2+c$ (equivalent to any quadratic - cf. remarks heading section 16.3), and is illustrated for this case.

CONSTRUCTION 16.44 ***IIM - The Inverse Iteration Method****. We iterate backwards from a starting point z_0 in the Julia set.*

(1) Calculate the fixed points of $f(z) = z^2+c$ and take z_0 as the one with modulus greater than 1/2. Such exists unless $c = 1/4$, when we take $z_0 = 1/2$. Alternatively, start with any point (except 0 if $c = 0$) and depend on spotting spurious points among the first few produced by iteration (see below).

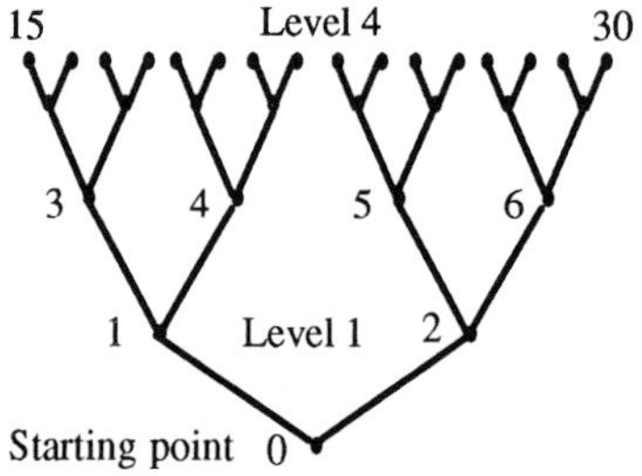

Figure 16.16 Tree representing the pre-images generated for the IIM.

(2) Iterate backwards: for each point z_i so far calculated, obtain new ones as the roots of $f(z) = z_i$. Calculate level by level, where points of level k are those calculated by solving k equations (see Figure 16.16). Stop when the image is satisfactory or after allotted time.

BASIS of the IIM The idea is that if z is in J then every point of J has some inverse iterate of z arbitrarily close, by Theorem 16.40. (1) Example 16.24 shows that one of the fixed points of $f(z) = z^2 + c$ is a repeller and so by Theorem 16.42 is in J, unless $c = 1/4$. A different argument shows that in this case the double root 1/2 of $f(z) = z$ is in J. Convergence to J from most starting points occurs, because the process is equivalent to employing an iterated function system (Definition 14.1), albeit nonlinear, with maps

$$w_1(z) = \sqrt{(z - c)}, \quad w_2(z) = -\sqrt{(z - c)} \qquad (16.20)$$

where any set A of points so far computed yields a larger set $w_1(A) \cup w_2(A)$. For the required contraction property note that w_1 is the composition of a translation $z \to z-c$ with a map $re^{i\theta} \to (\sqrt{r})\, e^{i\theta/2}$, so w_1 is certainly contractive whenever $r = |z-c| > 1$. Barnsley (1988) explores this viewpoint in detail.

(2) After k steps of the IIM we have up to 2^k pre-images, corresponding to the vertices of the tree in Figure 16.16. This number rapidly becomes very large as k increases, and a problem with the method is that some parts of J may be hit excessively often and others too rarely, resulting in a patchy image. To alleviate this, one modified Inverse Iteration Method (MIIM) adds the proviso:

> Divide the region considered into a lattice of small squares. Iterate no more from points of a square after the square has been hit a pre-determined number of times, say 10 times. (16.21)

CONSTRUCTION 16.45 **BSM - the Boundary Scanning Method.** Start with a lattice of small squares (as before, they could be screen pixels). Choose a large distance R and number of iterations N. Go through the vertices of the squares row by row, labelling a point v as type ∞ if $|f^k(v)| > R$ for some $k \le N$, otherwise type 0. Now darken each square that has vertices of both types.

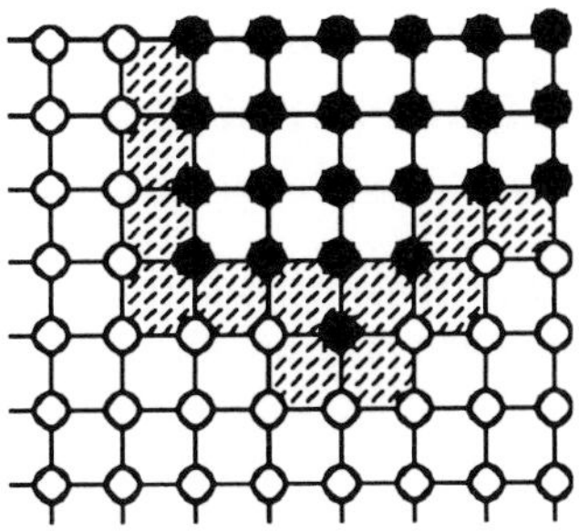

Figure 16.17 BSM, with black dots representing ∞. A square is shaded if its vertices include both types. The result is the Julia set.

BASIS By Definition 16.21 we have $J = \partial A(\infty) = \partial K$, where $K = C\backslash A(\infty)$, the filled-in Julia set. As an approximation $|f^k(v)| > R$ (some $k \le N$) implies that $v \in A(\infty)$, and otherwise $v \in K$. Thus we take a square having vertices of both types to belong to the common boundary J of $A(\infty)$ and K.

CONSTRUCTION 16.46 **LSM/J - The Level Set Method for J.** Also called the *Escape Time Method,* this causes J to stand out against a spectrum of colour bands, approaching from without or within. We first divide the region considered into a lattice of small squares such as screen pixels, allocating a representative point v within each square (say the centre). Choose a number N of iterations (say 100), and number the colours you will use from 1 to N, periodically if necessary. For example allocate 1-10 to one colour, 11-20 to another, and so on.

(A) *Approaching J from the outside*. Choose a large radius R. If $f^N(v)$ is inside the disc $\{z: |z| \le R\}$ then colour the corresponding square black ('no escape'), otherwise, if $f^k(v)$ is the first iterate to emerge, give colour k to that square.

(B) *Approaching J from the inside.* This requires an attractive fixed point α. Choose a small number ε. Let D be the disc $D = \{z: |z - \alpha| < \varepsilon\}$. If $f^N(v)$ is outside D, colour the point v black (say), otherwise, if $f^k(v)$ is the first iterate to enter D, give colour k to the corresponding square.

THE BASIS OF LEVEL SET METHODS Approach (A) above depends on $J = \partial A(\infty)$ and (B) on $J = \partial A(\alpha)$ (Theorem 16.43) for an attractive fixed point α. Thus the LSM may be regarded as a variant of the BSM. On the whole, the LSM is more powerful. It is very useful to observe that the two approaches have in common that we measure the number k(v,T) of iterations applied to a point v in order to enter a certain *target set* T. Cases (A), (B) have respective target sets $T = \{z: |z| > R\}$, the complement of the cited disc, and $T = \{z: |z - \alpha| < \varepsilon\}$, the disc itself. It is helpful to intuition to call k(v,T) the *escape time* of v. The *set of level k* consists of those points with escape time k, allocated the same colour in this method. The method may be extended not only to the Mandelbrot set (Construction 16.51 but to a variety of rational maps and target sets, including an approach to Escher-type tilings (see Peitgen & Saupe, 1988). It is sometimes useful to formalise a little more by specifying a source set for the points to be iterated, such as $|z| \le 2$ for M.

EXERCISE Produce a variant of Figure 16.17 by labelling the vertices differently and filling in the squares for J according to the algorithm.

16.3 Variety of Julia sets charted by the Mandelbrot set

For reasons of space (and time) we restrict to f(z) being a quadratic polynomial. We shall comment later on what happens in more general cases, but even this first step beyond the uninteresting linear case has proved a rich source of the remarkable. A pleasant fact is that we lose nothing by taking $f(z) = f_c(z) = z^2 + c$, where c is a real or complex constant. The reason is that every quadratic may be converted to this form by a linear change of variables $w = az+b$, and such a transformation is geometrically composed of no more than uniform scaling, rotation, and translation (for more on this, see Example 16.63). It will be found that all Julia sets $J_c = J(f_c)$ are symmetrical under a half turn about the origin (can you see why?). For the symmetry of more general Julia sets, see Beardon (1990).

16.3.1 A brief anatomy of M

The Mandelbrot set M was originally defined as the set of points c for which the Julia set $J(f_c)$ is connected (Mandelbrot, 1980). It comes as a surprise that this is exactly the set of points for which $f_c^n(0)$ does *not* tend to infinity as $n \to \infty$ (Brolin, 1965), which fact is the basis of the Level Set Method (Construction 16.51) for constructing pictures of M and much else related. We give correspondingly two definitions of M. Their equivalence, along with the total disconnectedness of J for values of c outside M, will be proved in Section 16.3.4 as Theorems 16.59 and 16.61.

DEFINITION 16.47 $\quad M = \{c \in \mathbf{C}: J(f_c) \text{ is connected}\}$.

DEFINITION 16.48 $\quad M = \{c \in \mathbf{C}: f_c^n(0) \not\to \infty \text{ as } n \to \infty\}$.

M is invaluable in charting how the structure of J(f) changes as c moves across the complex plane. Here is a brief *anatomy of M (cf. Figure 16.18)*.

1. The main body of M is a filled-in cardioid.
2. A series of circular buds surround the main body, attached tangentially. Each bud is similarly surrounded, and so on.
3. From the buds there sprout fine branching antennae-like structures, each carrying miniature copies of the whole of M.
4. M is contained in a circle of radius 2 about the origin, and is connected.

As implied by items 2,3 above, there are further details of M to explore at every level of magnification. Right now we shall prove item 4 (first part), and a second useful practical point that, in deciding whether or not $f_c^n(0) \to \infty$, we may view infinity as the outside of a circle of radius 3 (Theorem 16.50). We use this information in Construction 16.51. Note that $f_c(0) = c$, so we may replace $f_c^n(0)$ by $f_c^n(c)$ in Definition 16.48 . Now we shall prove a lemma, itself independently useful from time to time as we proceed, and which yields Theorem 16.50.

LEMMA 16.49 (a) If $|c| > 2$ *then* $f_c^n(0) \to \infty$ *as* $n \to \infty$, *(b) if* $|c| \le |z|$ *and* $|z| \ge 3$ *then* $|f_c(z)/z| \ge 2$, *(c) if* $|c| \le 2$ *and* $|f_c^k(0)| \ge 3$ *for some* $k \in \mathbf{N}$, *then* $c \notin M$.

Proof (a) Let $|c| = 2+\delta$ $(\delta > 0)$. Since iterations of f yield $0 \to c \to f_c(c) \to ..$ it suffices, as we shall see, to show that $|f(z)/|z| \geq 1+\delta$ provided $|z| \geq |c|$. Let $|z| \geq |c|$ and hence $|c/z| = |c|/|z| \leq 1$. Using the inequality $|u+v| \geq |(|u| - |v|)|$ for $u,v \in \mathbf{C}$ we have $|f(z)|/|z| = |f(z)/z| = |z + c/z| \geq |(|z| - |c/z|)| \geq 2+\delta - 1 = 1+\delta$. Thus applying f to iterates of c multiplies their moduli by a factor of at least $(1+\delta)$. In particular we have $|f_c{}^n(c)| \geq |c|(1+\delta)^n$, which tends to infinity with n.

(b) Let $|c| \leq |z|$ and $|z| \geq 3$. Similarly to Part (a), $|f(z)/z| \geq |(|z| - |c/z|)| \geq 3\text{-}1$.

(c) Let $|c| \leq 2$ and $|f_c{}^k(0)| \geq 3$. Then by Part (b) the moduli of iterates from $f_c{}^k(0)$ onwards is multiplied by at least 2 when f_c is applied, and so $f_c{}^n(0) \to \infty$ as $n \to \infty$.

THEOREM 16.50 (a) the Mandelbrot set M lies within a disc of radius 2 at the origin, (b) if $|f_c{}^k(0)| \geq 3$ *for some k, then* $c \notin$ M.

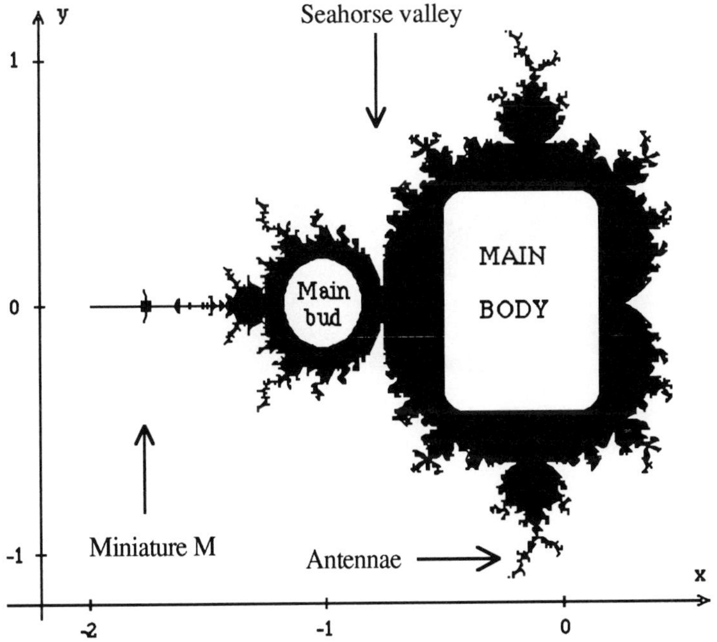

Figure 16.18 The Mandelbrot set M in the complex plane, with $|z| \leq 2$ as in Theorem 16.50. Seahorse valley and miniature M are areas named from their appearance under magnification (see Figure 16.21 and colour plates). For antennae see also Figure 16.22(b).

CONSTRUCTION 16.51 **LSM/M - The Level Set Method for M.** We emphasise that this is also known as the escape time method for obtaining coloured bands which converge on M, as well as being a case of the Level Set Method described below Construction 16.46. We'll first state it in a self-contained form, guided by Theorem 16.50. Divide the region $|z| \leq 2$ into a lattice of small squares such as screen pixels, choosing systematically a point c, such as the centre, within each square. Choose a number N of iterations (say 100) and number the colours to be used from 1 to N, periodically if necessary. For example allocate 1-10 to one colour, 11-20 to another, and so on. If $|f_c{}^N(c)| \leq 3$ then colour the corresponding square black. Otherwise, if $f_c{}^k(c)$ is the first iterate of c to emerge from $\{z: |z| \leq 3\}$ then allocate colour k to that square. The result is M in black surrounded by an often intricate colour network.

REMARK 16.52 As a Level Set Method the above uses target set $T = \{z: |z| > 3\}$ and source set $\{z: |z| \le 2\}$. Restricting the colours to black and white can nonetheless yield striking and worthwhile pictures, such as that used to mark the 1987 centenary of the American Mathematical Society. In the light of items (1) to (3) in '*Anatomy of M*', blowups of M are naturally very interesting, and render it most surprising that M should be connected, as it is by a Theorem of Douady and Hubbard (1982). The proof is sketched in Section 16.3.4.

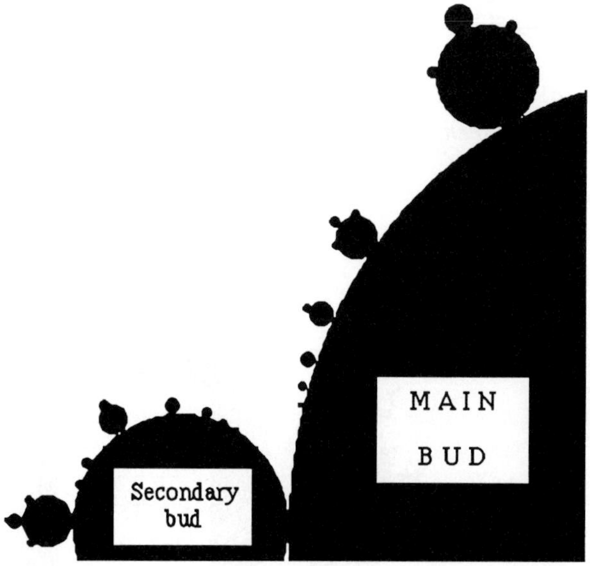

Figure 16.19 Part of the Mandelbrot set to left of the main body, showing how buds grow upon each other. An infinitude of buds exists within this area. The 'antennae' are omitted.

EXERCISE With $f(z) = z^2 + c$, show that if $|c| \le 2$ and $|z| \ge 4$ then $|f(z)/z| \ge 7/2$, by the method of proof of Lemma 16.49(b), **or** write a computer program to implement the LSM for the Mandelbrot set. How many stages can you get of bud upon bud?

16.3.2 The Mandelbrot set as dictionary

The Mandelbrot set M acts as a look-up table for Julia sets J_c of f_c, at several levels.

1 M divides Julia sets into two dramatically different categories (see Figure 16.23 and Section 16.3.4).

J is connected $c \in M$	J is totally disconnected $c \notin M$

2 *A smaller subdivision.* For c in the main body of M we have a unique attractive fixed point and J_c is a simple closed curve (see Section 16.3.4). The unit circle (c = 0) and one other case were shown in Figure 16.6. More interestingly, each bud has an associated period $p \ge 2$, some cases being indicated in Figure 16.20. For c in this bud f_c has a unique

attractive p-cycle, and J_c bounds its basin of attraction. Figures 16.8 (a) and (b) illustrate J_c in case $p = 2$ (with $c = -1$). Julia sets for other values of p are found in Section 16.3.3, along with proofs of some pertinent results.

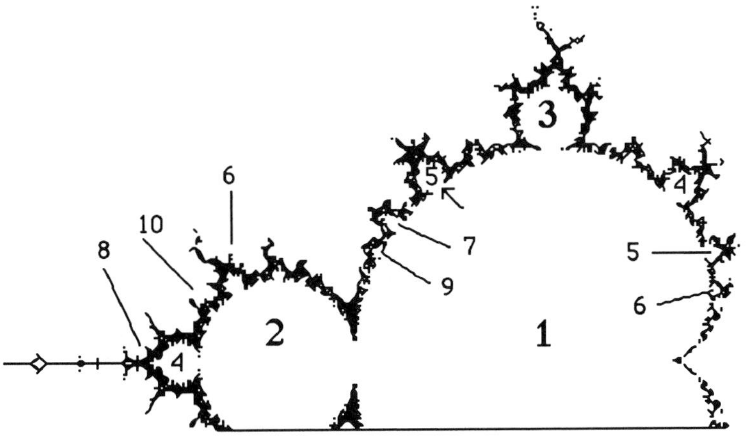

Figure 16.20 The periods of attractive orbits of f_c for c in various parts of M.

3 *Under magnification, an area of M round c is very similar to J_c itself.* We illustrate this to a first approximation in Figure 16.21, where (a) shows a detail from 'Seahorse valley', deep in the top cleft between the main bud and main body of M (see Figure 16.18). The Julia set of $c = -0.745 + 0.113002\mathbf{i}$ from that region appears in Figure 16.21(b), where the seahorse tail of (a) is a recurring theme. Some very detailed further comparisons are brought out in Peitgen-Saupe (1988). See also the colour Plates. It might be argued that M actually contains every connected Julia set, in that each feature of every Julia set seems to appear in M, at some level of magnification or other.

EXERCISE Use your LSM program to find a bud period not shown in Figure 16.20.

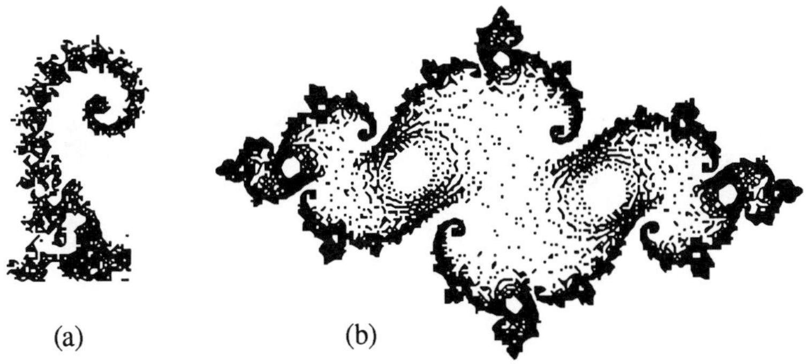

Figure 16.21 (a) A tail from 'seahorse valley' in the Mandelbrot set, (b) The Julia set of a value of c in that region, $c = -0.745 + 0.113002\mathbf{i}$. This is inside M, at about 0.000002 from the boundary, and J is nearly (but not quite) disconnected.

4 *A boundary effect - Siegel discs.* For c on the boundary of a bud or the main body of M (not on an antenna) the Julia set has a fixed point α which is indifferent. This category

might be considered a 'boundary' between attractive and repelling, according to the classification of Table 16.1. We refer to Figure 16.22(a) for an example. Infinity is the only other fixed point. All points in the connected interior regions bounded by J are eventually iterated into the region containing α, where each lands on a circle and continues round it forever. The set of all such circles forms a disc - named after its discoverer C. L. Siegel (1942).

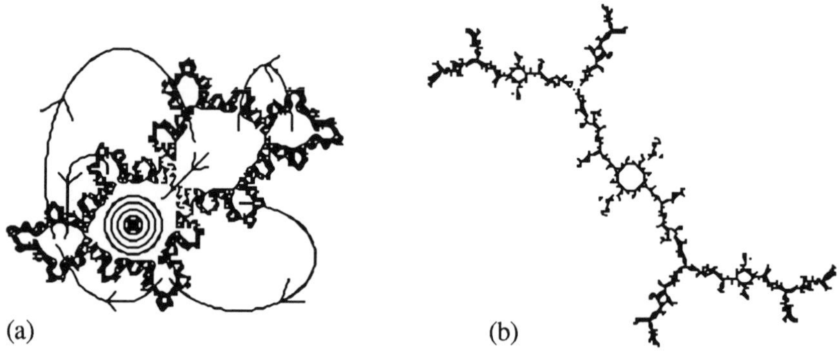

Figure 16.22 (a) Julia set with a Siegel disc, on which all points of the enclosed regions eventually land, then circle forever. Here c = -0.39054 - 0.58679**i**. (b) Julia set when c lies in a miniature copy of M on an antenna. For this case we take c = -0.15652 +1.03225**i**.

5 *The antennae.* For c in an antenna the Julia set has a similar dendritic (= tree-like) form to that part of M. Further, if c is in one of the miniature copies of M carried by the antennae, as in the case of Figure 16.22(b), then there are added to a dendritic part infinitely many copies of the Julia set from the corresponding value of c in the main part of M.

6 *The case of c outside M.* Now J is totally disconnected by Theorem 16.61, though it can present a variety of appearances, as illustrated in Figure 16.23. Each new level of magnification reveals further disconnections not apparent on inspection at the previous level.

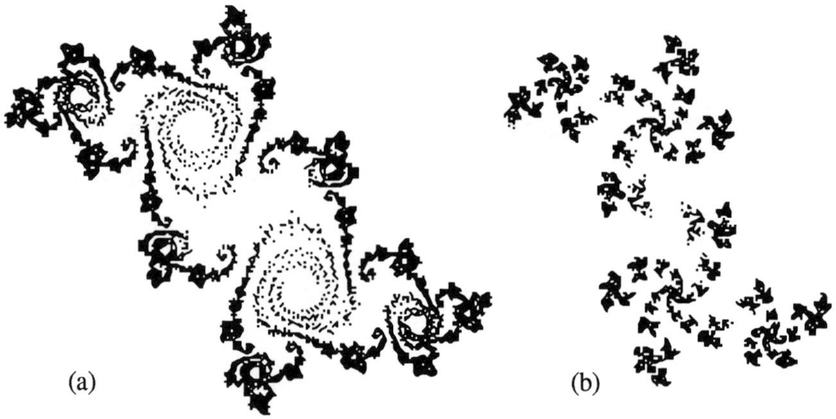

Figure 16.23 Julia sets for c outside the Mandelbrot set. Each appears to consist of a finite number of connected pieces but is in fact totally disconnected, by Theorem16.57. Every connected-looking piece will become at least two as magnification increases. (a) c = -0.194+0.6557**i**, (b) c = 0.11031-0.67037**i**.

EXERCISE Using your computer program for J, construct the Julia set of Figure 16.23. Magnify a part that looks solid until it splits visibly into subunits.

16.3.3 Julia sets and p-cycles

First a fundamental fact which clears the ground considerably. We continue often to abbreviate f_c simply to f.

THEOREM 16.53 f_c has at most one finite attractive fixed point or attractive cycle.

Proof Consider first the case of period $p = 1$, with α a finite attractive fixed point of f_c. We need only prove that c is in the basin of attraction $A(\alpha)$, for a second attractive fixed point β would entail $c \in A(\beta)$, imputing two different limits to c under iteration. We proceed by supposing that $c \notin A(\alpha)$ and obtaining a contradiction in two stages.
(1) Our assumption implies that $f_c^n(c)$ does not tend to α, and so no iterate $f_c^n(c)$ can enter $A(\alpha)$. We show that these are precisely the iterates which are critical values $f^n(z)$ - those $f^n(z_0)$ for which $(f^n)'(z_0) = 0$. The Chain Rule gives $(f^n)'(z_0) = f'(z_0)\ldots\ldots f'(z_{n-1})$ (see (16.8), where $z_i = f^i(z_0)$. Since $f_c'(z) = 2z$, this product is zero if and only if $z_i = 0$, for some $0 \le i \le n-1$. But then $f^n(z_0) = f^{n-i}(z_i) = f^{n-i}(0) = f^r(c)$, for $r \ge 0$. Thus $A(\alpha)$ contains no critical value of any f_c^n.

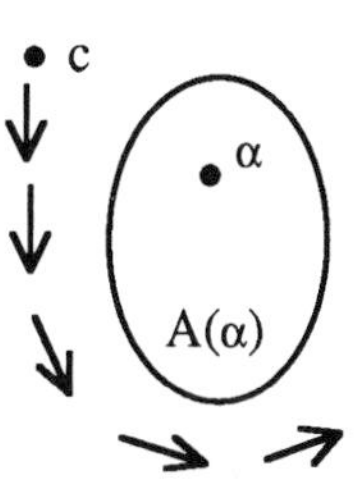

Figure 16.24 Here the iterates of c avoid A(α).

(2) If $c = 0$ then by Example 16.13 $A(\alpha)$ is the open unit disc and we already have a contradiction $c \in A(\alpha)$. So let $c \neq 0$. Within the open set $A(\alpha)$, α centres an open disc U. Since U is simply connected, containing no critical value of f, and $f_c(\alpha) = \alpha$, we may apply the Inverse Function Theorem 16.6B to obtain a map f^{-1} on U inverse to f_c, with $f^{-1}(\alpha) = \alpha$. Here f^{-1} and f_c are inverse analytic homeomorphisms between U and $f^{-1}(U)$ with $f^{-1}(U)$ simply connected and contained in $A(\alpha)$. Hence we may continue the process indefinitely, to get a family of analytic functions $\{f^{-n}: U \to \mathbf{C}\}$. And because $f^{-n}(U)$ is within $A(\alpha)$ for all n, this is a normal family by Montel's Theorem, 16.32, and so $\alpha \notin J(f^{-1})$ by (16.17). But this contradicts the fact that α is a repelling point for f^{-1}, being attracting for f, and so is in $J(f^{-1})$ (see Example 16.10(2) and Theorem 16.42). This contradiction shows that , after all, c is in $A(\alpha)$, proving the theorem in case $p = 1$. Finally, since $J(f^p) = J(f)$ by Theorem 16.37, the case of an attractive *cycle* is covered too.

EXAMPLE 16.54 **The main body of M.** We show that f_c has an attractive fixed point if and only if c lies within the region bounded by a certain cardioid curve (path of a fixed point on one circle rolling round another). Write $f = f_c$. Then $f(z) = z^2 + c$, $f'(z) = 2z$. A fixed point is a solution of $z^2 - z + c = 0$, namely $(1/2)(1 \pm w)$, where w may be either square root of $1-4c$. Now, $(1/2)(1+w)$ is attractive $\Leftrightarrow |1+w| < 1 \Leftrightarrow 1+w = re^{i\theta}$, i.e. $w = re^{i\theta} - 1$, for some r,θ with $0 \le \theta \le 2\pi$ and $0 \le r < 1$. So the condition for at least one of the fixed points to be attractive is that at least one of $\pm w$ equals $re^{i\theta} - 1$, with r,θ as stated. But this is equivalent to $w^2 = (re^{i\theta} - 1)^2$. With $w^2 = 1-4c$ we obtain $c = (1/4)(2re^{i\theta} - r^2e^{2i\theta})$. Consequently the condition is that c lie in the interior of the region bounded by the cardioid curve

$$z = (1/4)(2e^{i\theta} - e^{2i\theta}) \quad (0 \le \theta \le 2\pi) \qquad (16.22)$$

This is the region we call the *main body* of the Mandelbrot set. Examples of the Julia set for

J in this region are found in Figure 16.6.

EXERCISE Write a computer program to draw the boundary of the main body of M, using the cardioid equation **or** prove that the boundary is indeed a cardioid.

EXAMPLE 16.55 **The main bud of M.** It turns out that, as we shall prove, this bud is precisely the region of c-values for which f_c has an attractive orbit of period 2. The points z_0, z_1 of a 2-cycle (not necessarily attractive) satisfy the fourth degree equation $f^2(z) - z = 0$. However it is important to observe that so do the fixed points, the solutions of $f(z)-z = 0$. Hence z_0 and z_1 are the roots of the quadratic expressed as a quotient: $(f^2(z) - z)/(f(z)-z) = ((z^2+c)^2 + c - z)/(z^2+c-z) = z^2+z+c+1$. We recall from Theorem 16.17 that $(f^2)'(z)$ takes the same value at z_0 and z_1. In either case

$$\begin{aligned}(f^2)'(z) &= 4z(z^2+c) \\ &= 4z(-z-1) \quad (= -4(z^2+z)), && \text{since } z^2+z+c+1 = 0 \\ &= 4(c+1), && \text{for the same reason.}\end{aligned}$$

So the 2-cycle is attractive $\Leftrightarrow$ $|(f^2)'(z_0)| < 1$ $\Leftrightarrow$ $|c+1| < 1/4$. Thus the values of c for which f_c has an attractive 2-cycle constitute the interior of a disc of radius 1/4 centred at the point (-1,0). This is the *main bud* of M. Figure 16.8(a) contains an example of the Julia set for c in this bud.

EXAMPLE 16.56 **Buds of period p > 2.** As we remarked in the previous Section, each bud has an associated period for the corresponding Julia sets. In Figure 16.25 below we represent the change in J as c moves from the main body into a bud of period five via the bud's germination point (the journey itself is suggested by an arrow in Figure 16.20).

(a) c near the bud. One attractive fixed point, but change on the way. (b) c at a bud junction. Fixed point about to split into a 5 cycle. (c) c inside the bud. An attractive 5-cycle (basin of attraction shaded). (d) c far across the bud. The basin is more spiky.

Figure 16.25 Four Julia sets of f_c as c moves from the main body of M into a bud.

In case (b) of Figure 16.25 the attractive fixed point is said to be *marginally stable*, for sufficiently small changes in c leave it as a fixed point. However by stage (c), with c within the bud, it has split or 'bifurcated' into a fixed 5-cycle $\gamma = \{z_0, z_1, \ldots, z_4\}$. Now J bounds an infinite family of regions which together form the basin of attraction $A(\gamma)$, the union of the basins of attraction (under f^5) of the points z_i. Each of these basins has its immediate basin $A_0(z_i)$, namely the component containing z_i. In Figure 16.25(c) these connected pieces form five petals (shaded), whose boundaries meet at the position of the former fixed point. The action of f permutes them cyclically. On the other hand every region bounded by J, no matter how small or remote, is eventually 'brought in from the cold', mapped into one of these petals under iterations of f (cf. discussion of a $p = 2$ case beginning above Figure 16.8). However, it should not be assumed that in general the p immediate basins (under f^p) have a common boundary point (see below).

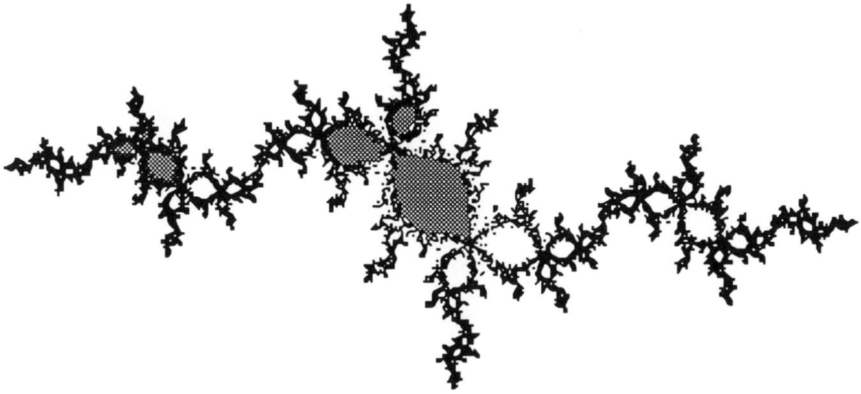

Figure 16.26 Julia set of an attractive cycle of period $6 = 2 \times 3$, with c in a bud off the main bud. The immediate basin of attraction consists of two triples.

In Figure 16.26 we show a Julia set for c in a period six bud growing directly off the main bud, whose period is 2 (see Figure 16.20). Noting that $6 = 2 \times 3$, we may view the secondary bud as contributing the factor 3 on its own account, especially as the six petals occur in two triples, each triple having a common boundary point. Note, consistently with this, the position in Figure 16.20 of the bud with period $10 = 2 \times 5$. We conclude with a remarkable result of Guckenheimer and McGehee (1988). For further information on properties of J see Peitgen and Richter (1986), Peitgen and Saupe (1988), or the technical work of Sullivan (1982ff).

THEOREM 16.57 The diameter of a bud characterising an attractive p-cycle is proportional to $1/p^2$.

EXERCISE Test Theorem 16.57 by estimating the diameters of buds in Figure 16.20 (in the MS of this text the diameter in centimetres equals approximately $10/p^2$).

16.3.4 Four sketch proofs with common theme

Let $f(z) = f_c(z) = z^2+c$. In this section we establish the equivalence of Definitions 16.47 and 16.48 for the Mandelbrot set. That is, M is simultaneously the set of points c for which J_c is connected, and the set for which $f_c^n(0)$ does not tend to infinity. Further, if c is not in M then J_c is not only disconnected, it is totally disconnected (i.e has no subset of more than one point connected). Thus as c moves outwards across the boundary of M the Julia set explodes, and there are impressive videos to demonstrate this. Yet a connected Julia set is not just an aggregate of points, it is a curve, and we deal here with the case of f having a single attractive fixed point (f cannot have more than one, by Theorem 16.53). We sketch too the proof that M itself is connected, introducing the important concept of equipotential curves around J and M.

We begin with a lemma extending Example 16.8 on the square root function to the present context. The two branches $\pm\sqrt{(z-c)}$ of $f^{-1}(z)$ will be denoted by $\pm g(z)$. Notice that the inverse image $f^{-1}(S)$ of a curve S may be expressed as $g(S) \cup (-g)(S)$, and so is symmetrical under a 1/2 turn about the origin, as (we observed) is J itself.

LEMMA 16.58 Let S be a simple closed curve. Then, depending on the position of c, there are three categories for $f^{-1}(S)$

(a) c inside S

$f^{-1}(S)$ is a simple closed curve

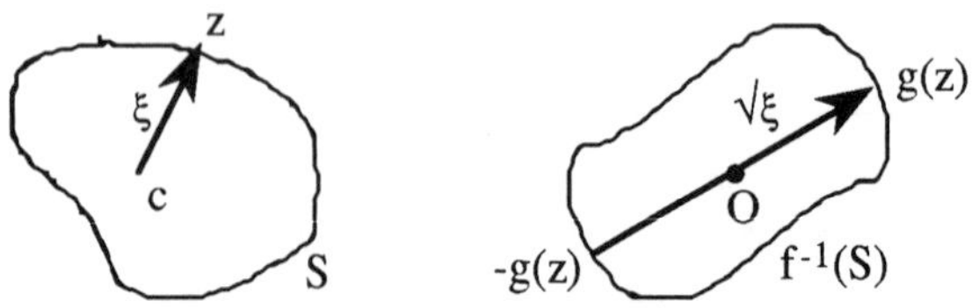

(b) c is on S

$f^{-1}(S)$ is a figure of eight

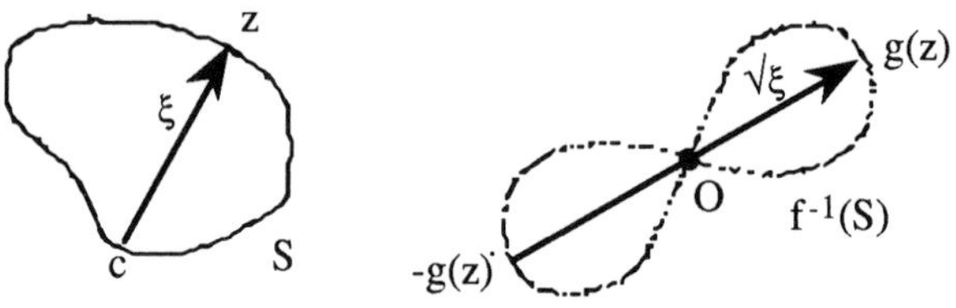

(c) c outside S

$f^{-1}(S)$ consists of two disjoint simple closed curves

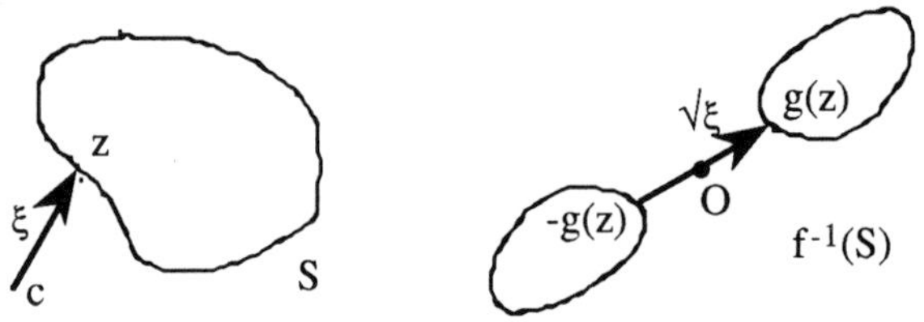

Figure 16.27 The three cases of $f^{-1}(S)$ for a simple closed curve S.

Let D be the interior of (the region bounded by) S. Then $f^{-1}(D)$ is the interior of $f^{-1}(S)$, which in Cases (b), (c) is the union of the interiors of the two loops.

EXERCISE Let D be the disc of radius 2 at the origin and $f(z) = z^2+c$. Sketch roughly the inverse image $f^{-1}(D)$ in the cases c = 1, -2, -3.

THEOREM 16.59 If $f^n(0) \not\to \infty$ as $n \to \infty$ then J_c is connected.

Proof Let c be such that $f_n(0)$ does not iterate to infinity. Then for some R, which we may take as at least 3, we have $|f^n(0)| < R$ for all $n \in \mathbf{N}$. Let S_0 be the circle of radius R at the origin. We construct a series of simple closed curves S_n by $S_{n+1} = f^{-1}(S_n)$. The S_n will converge onto J_c from outside as illustrated in Figure 16.28. Here are some preliminary facts.

(1) All iterates $f^n(0)$ lie inside S_0.

(2) We have $|c| \leq 2$ because (Lemma 16.49(a)) $|c| > 2$ implies $f^n(0) \to \infty$, which is contrary to our hypothesis. Thus c is inside S_0, we have Case(a) of Lemma 16.58, and S_1 is a simple closed curve.

(3) S_1 lies inside S_0. For if z lies on S_0 then $|z-c| \leq |z|+|c| < R+3$, implying, since $R \geq 3$, that $\sqrt{|z-c|} < R$.

We need to show that for $n = 0,1,2, ..$ both c and S_{n+1} are inside S_n. By (2), (3) it is true if $n = 0$. The step from general n to n+1 is similar to that from 0 to 1, which we now give. By Lemma 16.58, f^{-1} maps the interior of S_0 into the interior of S_1. But $f(c)$ $(= f^2(0))$ and S_1 are in the interior of S_0. Therefore both $f^{-1}(f(c))$, which includes c, and S_2 $(= f^{-1}(S_1))$, are in the interior of S_1 as required.

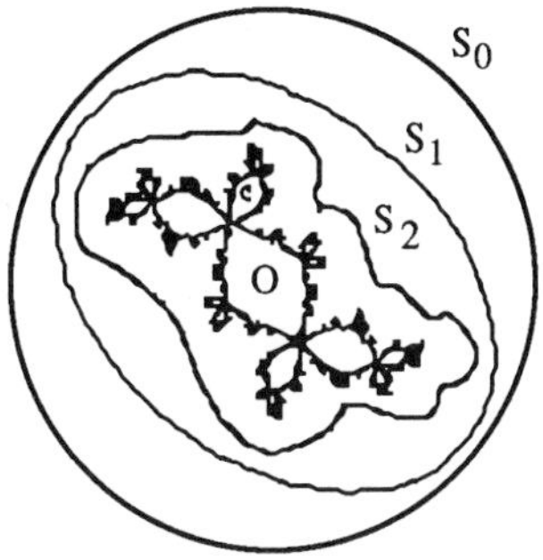

Figure 16.28 Simple closed curves converging onto a Julia set which is therefore connected.

Let D_n consist of S_n and its interior, and define D to be the intersection of all D_n. We claim that $D = \mathbf{C} \setminus A(\infty)$, the filled-in Julia set. To prove this, take the complements. Then $z \in \mathbf{C} \setminus D \Leftrightarrow$ z is outside some $D_n \Leftrightarrow f^n(z)$ is outside S_0 for some n $\Leftrightarrow z \in A(\infty)$. Note for the last equivalence that points z outside S_0 iterate to infinity in consequence of $|c| \leq 2$ and $|z| \geq 3$ (cf. Lemma 16.49(b)). Since a set and its complement have the same boundary we have $J = \partial A(\infty) = \partial D$. By Theorem 12.64, J is connected because each D_n is homeomorphic to a closed disc.

THEOREM 16.60 Let $f_c(z)$ have a single finite attractive fixed point. Then J is a simple closed curve but has no well-defined tangent line.

Proof Let f continue to denote f_c. Note that f cannot have more than one attractive fixed point α, by Theorem 16.53, and we have shown that in this case c is within the cardioid-shaped main body of M (Example 16.54). To simplify the discussion we shall assume further that $|c| < 1/4$. We proved above that M is connected if $f^n(0)$ does not tend to infinity, by using a shrinking series of simple closed curves converging to J from the outside. This time we start from within $A(\alpha)$ with an expanding series of such curves which approach its boundary J.

(1) Let S_1 be the circle of radius 1/2 around the origin and define $S_{n+1} = f^{-1}(S_n)$, for $n = 1,2,3, ...$. As an attractive fixed point α satisfies $1 > |f'(\alpha)| = |2\alpha|$, so α is inside S_1. Furthermore S_1 is inside $A(\alpha)$ because we have the equality $\alpha^2+c = \alpha$ (α being a fixed point) and therefore with z on S_1, $(f(z) - \alpha)/(z - \alpha) = (z^2 + c - \alpha)/(z - \alpha) = z + \alpha$, and further, $|z + \alpha| \leq |z| + |\alpha| < 1/2 + |\alpha| < 1$, implying that the iterates of z tend to α. Moreover, since $f^{n-1}(S_n) = S_1$, we have S_n also inside $A(\alpha)$. This is a good moment to refer to figure 16.29 for illustration.

(2) Because c is inside S_1 we have case (a) of Lemma 16.58, so S_2 is a simple closed curve. Now, S_2 lies outside S_1 by the chain of implications

$$z \in S_1 \Rightarrow |z-c| \geq |z|-|c| > 1/2 - 1/4 = 1/4 \Rightarrow |g(z)| > 1/2.$$

Thus c is inside S_2 also, and S_3 is a simple closed curve by Lemma 16.58(a). Again, by this Lemma, f^{-1} maps the exterior of S_1 (which includes S_2) to the exterior of S_2 and so S_3 is outside S_2. And so on. S_{n+1} is always a simple closed curve outside S_n, with α and c inside the innermost curve S_1.

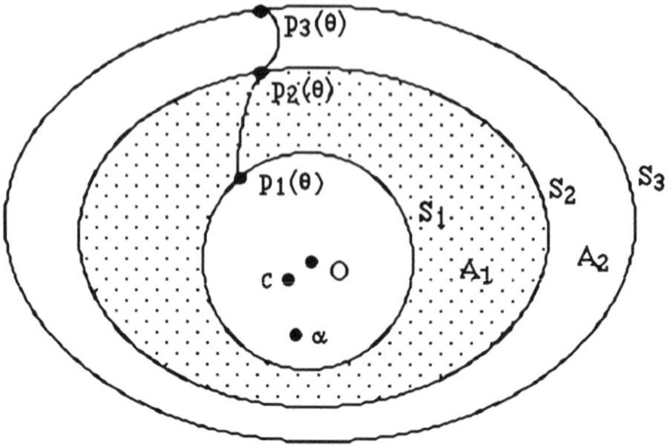

Figure 16.29 An expanding series of simple closed curves approaching J.

(3) In particular f^{-1} maps the closed annular region A_1 bounded by S_1 and S_2 to the annular region A_2 between S_2 and S_3. Let ϕ: $\{re^{i\theta} : 1 \le r \le 2, \ \theta \in \mathbf{R}\} \to A_1$ be a homeomorphism from a standard annulus, mapping boundaries $r = 1$ and $r = 2$ onto the corresponding inner and outer boundaries S_1, S_2. Write $p_r(\theta) = \phi(re^{i\theta})$. As θ varies, $p_1(\theta)$ takes us round S_1, whereas with θ fixed $p_r(\theta)$ gives a continuous curve from $p_1(\theta)$ on S_1 to $p_2(\theta)$ on S_2. Now we use $\pm g$ to extend $p_r(\theta)$ over $2 \le r \le 3$, with $p_3(\theta)$ lying on S_3. Proceeding thus we obtain a sequence of continuous functions $p_n(\theta)$, $n = 1,2, \ldots$.

(4) Each point of $\partial A(\alpha)$ is the limit of a sequence $p_n(\theta)$ as $n \to \infty$, for some θ in the closed interval $[0, 2\pi]$. Thus the $p_n(\theta)$ converge to a function $p(\theta)$ whose points are those of $\partial A(\alpha) = J$. By Theorem 13.33, $p(\theta)$ is continuous if the convergence is *uniform*. That is, given $\varepsilon > 0$, there is an integer N such that $|p_n(\theta) - p(\theta)| < \varepsilon$ for all θ *simultaneously*, if $n > N$. This does hold, as a consequence of the fact $|f'(z)| \ge d$ for some $d > 1$ when z is outside S_2. We omit details and the proof that $p(\theta)$ has no self-crossings and no tangent. See for example Devaney (1989) or Falconer (1990).

EXERCISE Show that if $|c| < 1/4$ then $f(z) = z^2 + c$ has an attractive fixed point, by determining the product of the roots of $f(z) = z$.

THEOREM 16.61 If $f_c^n(0) \to \infty$ then J_c is totally disconnected.

Proof Writing $f = f_c$, let $f^n(0) \to \infty$ as $n \to \infty$. We shall exhibit the total disconnectedness of $J = J_c$ by an infinite bisection process based on Lemma 16.58. As usual in this section we define a series of curves, which we shall call $S_0, S_1, \ldots$, with S_{n+1} as the inverse image $f^{-1}(S_n)$. Let S_0 be a circle around the origin, with radius R chosen, as we will show it may be, to satisfy the following.

(i) S_1 lies inside S_0,
(ii) points outside S_0 iterate to infinity under f,
(iii) for some q, $f^k(0)$ is inside S_0 if $k < q$, on S_0 if $k = q$, and outside if $k > q$.

Firstly, let $R \ge 3$, $R > |c|$. If $z \in S_0$ we have $|z| = R$ and $|g(z)|^2 = |z-c| \le |z| + |c| < 2R < R^2$, as required for (i). Also, when $|c| \le |z|$ and $|z| \ge 3$ we have by Lemma 16.49(b) that $|f(z)|/|z| \ge 2$. Hence outside S_0 not only does $f^n(z) \to \infty$, but $|f^n(z)|$ is strictly increasing with n. Thus R exists to satisfy conditions (i) to (iii), given that $f^n(0) \to \infty$, for these iterates must eventually reach the region $|z| \ge 3$. Since c is inside S_0 we know from Lemma

16.58(a) that S_1 is a simple closed curve and that f^{-1} maps the interior of S_0 (which contains S_1) to the interior of S_1. Hence we also have that S_2 is in the interior of S_1

The argument can be continued, so S_{n+1} is inside S_n for $n = 1,2,3, ..$. But now there are two crucial differences from the previous pair of proofs. Because of (ii) each S_n and its exterior are in $A(\infty)$, whereas $J = \partial A(\infty)$ lies inside each S_n. When the construction starts we have c inside S_0, but after a while we come to S_{q-1}, which contains c because $f^{q-1}(c) = f^q(0)$, a point of S_0 (by (iii)). Now we have case (b) of the lemma, and S_q is a figure of eight (cf. Figure 16.30). This is where the bisection of J begins.

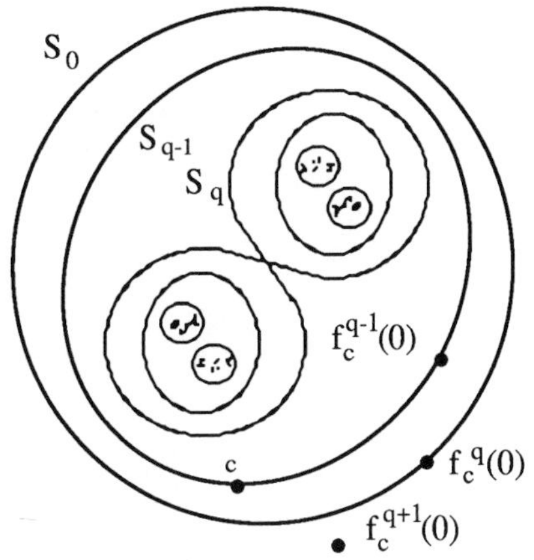

Figure 16.30 Bisecting J.

Both loops $\pm g(S_{q-1})$ of S_q contain points of J, because J is inside S_{q-1} and $f^{-1}(J) = J$ (Theorem 16.36). Since the interiors of the loops are disjoint, they disconnect J. At the next stage, S_q being inside S_{q-1}, we have c outside S_q. Thus Case (c) of Lemma 16.58 arises and S_{q+1} consists of two disjoint loops. Similarly for $S_{q+2}, S_{q+3},..,$ each stage disconnecting the parts of J from the previous stage. Thus it is that J is totally disconnected, for every pair of points u,v on J can ultimately be separated by open sets U,V. That is, $u \in U$, $v \in V$, but U and V are disjoint (we shall let this amount of detail suffice).

OBSERVATION We now know that the following is true for J when $c \notin M$.

(1) J is totally disconnected
(2) J is compact - since J is bounded (see the proof above and Figure 16.30), and closed, by Remark 16.35(1). This suffices, by Theorem 12.26.
(3) J is perfect - that is it is closed and has no isolated points (see Lemma 16.39).

Therefore by Remark 12.58 we are entitled to draw the conclusion that J, although spread, albeit thinly, over an area, is nevertheless homeomorphic to the standard Cantor set, a subset of the real line, indeed of the interval [0,1]. For this reason, the Julia set in the disconnected case is often described as a 'Cantor dust'. In fact we can identify the Cantor connection more closely, for we already have the setup for a Cantor type addressing scheme (Section 15.1) on two symbols 0,2 at the end of the proof above, in which the next stage is formed by bisecting all parts of the previous one. Now we come to Douady & Hubbard's (1982) result on M that, contrary to appearances, we have:

THEOREM 16.62 The Mandelbrot set M is connected.

The main part of the proof consists in establishing that M can be reached from the outside by a shrinking series of simple closed curves; the connectedness of M then follows as it did for J in the case $f^n(0)$ does not tend to infinity with n (Theorem 16.59). But, it may be objected, we have already used such curves in the escape time method, to produce colour bands around M and to make it stand out. However, no matter how accurately we may produce these curves, and no matter how close to M, this falls short of a proof that such curves exist arbitrarily close to M, or that they must always be simple and closed. Indeed, these very demonstrations serve to heighten the impression that M cannot be connected.

A key idea in the successful theoretical construction is that of 'equipotential' curves. Even knowing little about electrostatics, let us accept that if the closed unit disc D is given an electric charge, uniformly distributed, then a certain function $\phi(x,y)$ called a 'potential' function is constant on any concentric circle S outside D.

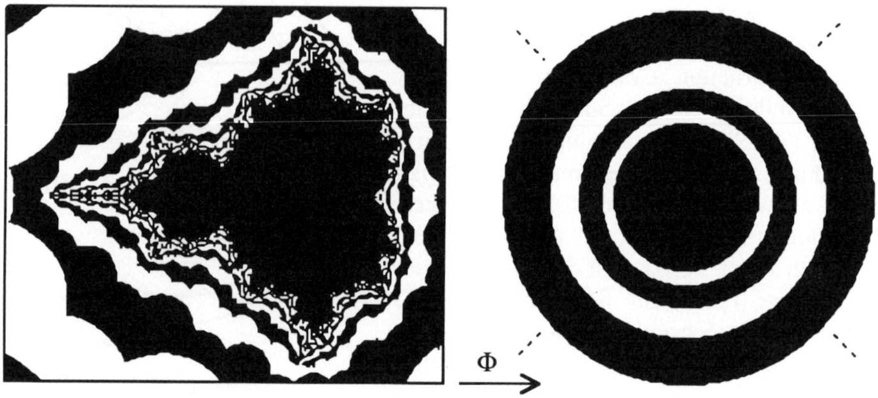

Figure 16.31 Equipotential curves around M corresponding to concentric circles around the closed unit disc.

The hard thing is to transfer equipotential circles around D to their counterparts around M. In view of the intricacy of M's boundary this was a considerable achievement of Douady and Hubbard, which they carried out by means of a map Φ between the exterior of M and that of D, where

$$\Phi\colon \mathbf{C}\setminus M \to \mathbf{C}\setminus D \qquad (16.23)$$

is analytic, with analytic inverse Φ^{-1}. Thus, corresponding to circles S around D we have curves $C = \Phi^{-1}(S)$ around M, which are simple closed curves, or 'circle like', since they are homeomorphic images of circles. A function G(c), to qualify as a potential function for the curves C, must be constant on each C. Equivalently G(c) must be constant as $\Phi(c)$ moves round a circle, i.e. whilst $|\Phi(c)|$ is constant. The simplest choice is therefore $G(c) = |\Phi(c)|$, but we take its logarithm to slow down the rate of change with respect to $|c|$ to a level found convenient. That is, we define the potential function as

$$G(c) = \log|\Phi(c)|. \qquad (16.24)$$

A natural question now is, how do these equipotential curves relate to the curves of constant escape-time? The answer is that we can assign an escape time to each equipotential curve in such a way that the two sets of curves move roughly in tandem. More technically, we define the (continuous) escape-time by E by $E(c) = -\log_2(G(c))$, constant on equipotential curves, and then with target set $T = \{z: |z| > 1/\varepsilon\}$ and corresponding escape-time $L(c;T)$ we have a bound on $|E(c) - L(c,T)|$ which is uniform, that is it depends on c but not on ε.
We refer to Peitgen & Saupe (1988) for two further methods for constructing M and J which follow on from (16.24). The first is analogous to the LSM, but uses a potential function instead of escape times. This is the continuous potential method, or CPM. The second uses an estimate for the distance of a point to M or J and so fills up disc by disc the region *not* in the set. No method is best for every situation, and the variety of methods has been valuable for producing a very wide range of excellent pictures.

16.4 Coordinate change and Newton's method

An important use of iterating a function is the famed Newton's method (or Newton-Raphson method) for solving an equation $g(x) = 0$, introduced briefly in Chapter 13 (Example 13.22). We recall the method is to solve an equation $g(x) = 0$ by iteration with Newton's function

$$N(x) = x - g(x)/g'(x), \qquad (16.25)$$

from a suitable starting value x_0. Normally g(x) is a real function of a real variable x and x_0 is chosen to be real. But the method is well-defined if g is a complex analytic (i.e differentiable) function. Could it help, even for real g, to use a non-real starting value? If α is a solution then the set of all starting points leading to α is by definition the basin of attraction $A(\alpha) = \{z \in C: N^n(z) \to \alpha\}$, so we might regard the Mandelbrot and Julia sets we have so far investigated as depicting the convergence properties of Newton's method for certain functions g(z), where $N(z) = z - g(z)/g'(z) = z^2+c$. Unfortunately such g(z) do not exist in a recognisable form, so we shall not pursue this further, but rather follow up Newton's method in its own right. To this end, and to illustrate some techniques used in the wider theory of dynamics of iterated maps, we include a short study on what may be gained by a change of coordinates $z \to w = \Phi(z)$, where $\Phi: C \to C$ is a homeomorphism with Φ and Φ^{-1} differentiable, or more briefly a *diffeomorphism*.

Julia sets for rational maps The classical definition in terms of normal families is hard to grasp, but because we were hitherto dealing with polynomials we were able to use $J = \partial A(\infty)$ as definition of the Julia set of a map f(z) and then to prove (albeit making use of the classical definition en route) that (a) $J = \partial A(\gamma)$ for γ any attractive cycle, including the special case of a fixed point, (b) the set of repelling points of f is dense in J, and (c) given any point α of J, the union of all $f^{-n}(\alpha)$ is dense in J.

Although with J classically defined the proofs of these results extend to the case of a rational map R(z), it is not true for general rational maps that ∞ is attractive, even if it is a fixed point (see Example 16.15(5)). We shall compromise by *defining* J to be the closure of the repelling fixed points (cf. Devaney, 1989), and assuming property (c). Thus the coordinate change Φ maps the dynamics of the z-plane onto the w-plane, and in particular

$$\begin{aligned} \Phi(\text{repeller } \alpha) &= \text{repeller } \Phi(\alpha) \\ \Phi(\text{attractive fixed point } \alpha) &= \text{attractive fixed point } \Phi(\alpha) \\ \Phi(\text{basin of attraction of } \alpha) &= \text{basin of attraction of } \Phi(\alpha) \\ \Phi(\text{Julia set of } R(z)) &= \text{Julia set of } \Phi.N.\Phi^{-1}(w) \text{ (see below).} \end{aligned}$$

The reason for the last statement is that the change of coordinates converts a map N(z) in the z-plane to $\Phi.N.\Phi^{-1}(w)$ in the w-plane, as depicted in Figure 16.32. Let us write $R(z) = h(z)/k(z)$, where h,k are polynomials with no common complex factor. Then Table 16.2 tells us that $R(z_0) = \infty$ if $k(z_0) = 0$, $R(\infty) = 0$ if degree h < degree k, and ∞ is a fixed point of R if degree h > degree k.

EXAMPLE 16.63 **Converting quadratics**. We detail how an arbitrary quadratic $q(z) = az^2 + 2bz + d$ $(a \neq 0)$ may be simplified by a linear change of coordinates $w = \Phi(z) = az+b$ to the form $p(z) = z^2 + c$, where a, b are the same throughout and $c = ad-b^2+b$. Figure 16.32 show how the process works for general Φ and q(z). It is called a *commutative diagram* to mean that all compositions taking us from one given point to another are equal. Thus $p = \Phi.q.\Phi^{-1}$, or equivalently $\Phi q = q\Phi$. Noting the implication in the present case that $z = (w-b)/a = \Phi^{-1}(w)$. We have

$$\begin{aligned} p(w) &= \Phi.q.\Phi^{-1}(w) \\ &= \Phi.q((w-b)/a) \\ &= \Phi\left(a(\tfrac{w-b}{a})^2 + 2b(\tfrac{w-b}{a}) + d\right) \\ &= \Phi\left(\tfrac{1}{a}[w^2 - 2bw + b^2 + 2bw - 2b^2 + ad]\right) \\ &= \Phi\left(\tfrac{1}{a}[w^2 - b^2 + ad]\right) \\ &= w^2 - b^2 + ad + b \\ &= w^2 + c, \quad \text{where } c = ad - b^2 + b. \end{aligned}$$

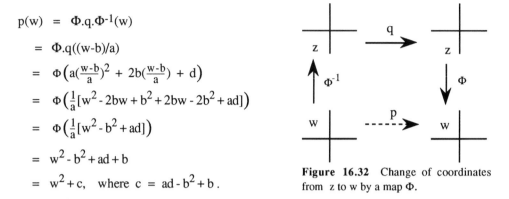

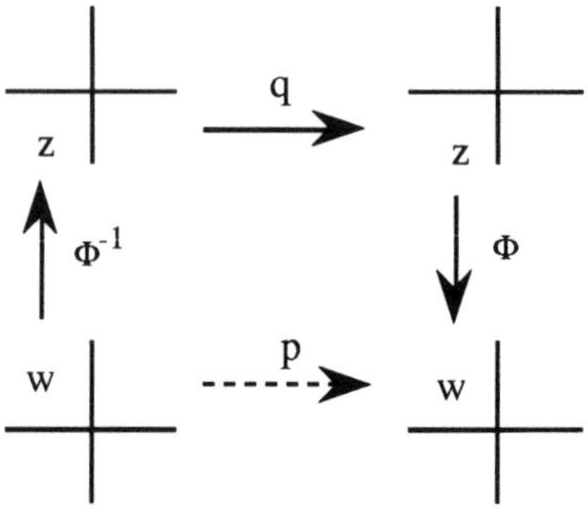

Figure 16.32 Change of coordinates from z to w by a map Φ.

EXERCISE Transform $q(z) = z(z-1)$ to the form $z^2 + c$ by a linear change of coordinates.

It would be nice to obtain $p(w) = w^2$, but we can't guarantee $c = 0$ with a linear transformation. In the next example we introduce a powerful type of transformation which will achieve this and much more.

EXAMPLE 16.64 **Möbius transformations**. The coordinate transformation

$$w = \frac{az+b}{cz+d} \quad (ad \neq bc) \tag{16.26}$$

is called a *bilinear, linear fractional, or Möbius* transformation. The conditions in parenthesis ensure that it is invertible. Again we work with the extended complex plane and invoke Table 16.2. Thus $w(-d/c) = \infty$, $w(\infty) = a/c$, and the inverse map is

$$z = \Phi^{-1}(w) = (dw-b)/(-cw+a). \tag{16.27}$$

Notice that Φ is a composition of maps of the following types

$$z \to z+\alpha \text{ (translation)}, \qquad z \to \beta z \text{ (similarity)}$$
$$z \to 1/\bar{z}, \text{ i.e. } re^{i\theta} \to (1/r)e^{i\theta} \text{ (inversion)}$$
$$z \to \bar{z} \text{ (reflection in the x-axis).}$$

THEOREM 16.65 A Möbius transformation maps lines and circles to lines and circles (a circle may be mapped to a line and vice-versa).

Proof For the above list of transformation types, it is quickly verified that the result holds for translations, similarities and reflections, so we only need consider inversion, for which $\Phi(x + iy) = 1/(x - iy) = (x + iy)/(x^2+y^2) = \xi + i\eta$, say. Then $\xi = x/(x^2+y^2)$, $\eta = y/(x^2+y^2)$. For the image of a line under Φ we have (with $u,v,w \in \mathbf{R}$): $ux+vy = w \Leftrightarrow u\xi+v\eta = w(\xi^2+\eta^2)$, and the latter defines a line if $w = 0$, otherwise a circle. On the other hand, starting with a circle of radius R ($a,b \in \mathbf{R}$) we obtain $(x-a)^2 + (y-b)^2 = R^2 \Leftrightarrow x^2+y^2 -2(ax+by) = R^2 - a^2 - b^2$ (= d, say) $\Leftrightarrow 1 -2(a\xi+b\eta) = d(\xi^2 + \eta^2)$, which is again a line or a circle.

EXAMPLE 16.66 We find the image of the upper half-plane H: $y > 0$, under the transformation $w = (z+\mathbf{i})/(z-\mathbf{i})$. Notice that the transformation is uniquely determined by its effect on the three points $0,1,\infty$. It is a useful standard technique to capitalise on this. We have $0 \to -1$, $1 \to (1+\mathbf{i})/(1-\mathbf{i}) = \mathbf{i}$ (a useful check: this image has modulus $\sqrt{2}/\sqrt{2} = 1$), and $\infty \to 1$.

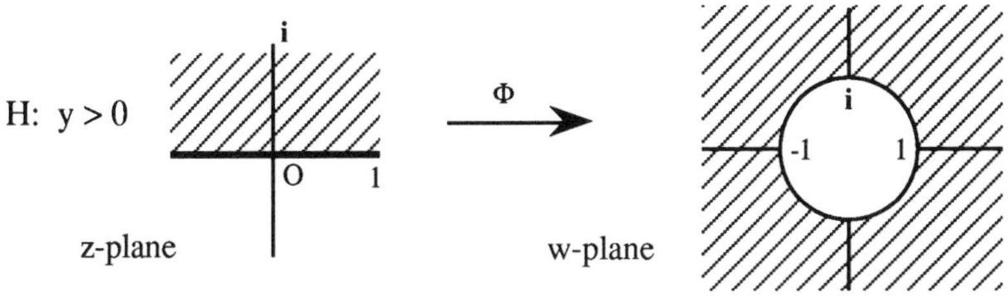

Figure 16.33 $w = \Phi(z) = (z+\mathbf{i})/(z-\mathbf{i})$ maps the x-axis to the unit circle and the upper half-plane to its exterior.

(1) The boundary of H is the x-axis, which contains the points $0,1,\infty$. By Theorem 16.65 Φ sends the x-axis to a line or circle containing the image points -1, $\mathbf{i}$, 1. No line contains these points, but they lie on a unique circle, namely the unit circle S^1, which is therefore the image of the x-axis.
(2) Now we make a nice use of topology. Since H is a connected component of **C** with x-axis removed, the image $\Phi(H)$ is a connected component of $\mathbf{C}\backslash S^1$ (Φ being a homeomorphism), namely either the interior or the exterior of S^1. Furthermore we can easily determine which is the case by computing the image of a single point of H. An extremely convenient choice is $\Phi(\mathbf{i}) = \infty$, a point emphatically exterior to S^1. Finally therefore, $\Phi(H)$ is the exterior $\{z: |z| > 1\}$ of S^1.
(3) In this easy case we can conveniently give a direct calculation of the image thus: z is in H $\Leftrightarrow$ z is nearer to $\mathbf{i}$ than to $-\mathbf{i}$ $\Leftrightarrow$ $|z - \mathbf{i}| < |z + \mathbf{i}|$ $\Leftrightarrow$ $1 < |z + \mathbf{i}| / |z - \mathbf{i}|$ ($= |w|$).

EXERCISE What does the transformation $w = (z-\mathbf{i})/(z+\mathbf{i})$ do to the lower half-plane $y < 0$?

EXAMPLE 16.67 **Newton's method for quadratics.** We have seen that any quadratic polynomial may be reduced to the form $p(z) = z^2-c$ (the minus sign is convenient here) by a linear change of coordinates. We determine for Newton's iterative method the attractive basin of each complex root $\pm\sqrt{c}$. Here we iterate with the rational function

$$N(z) = z - p(z)/p'(z) = (z^2 + c)/2z. \qquad (16.28)$$

Notice that apart from ∞ the fixed points, given by $N(z) = z$, are the roots $\pm\sqrt{c}$ as we would expect. For their *type* we have $N'(z) = (z^2 - c)/2z^2$, so the roots are superattractive. But now let us use a Möbius transformation to map the dynamics to an equivalent system which is easier to handle. We guess that it is a good idea to send $\pm\sqrt{c}$ to the points 0, ∞, which is accomplished for example by $w = \Phi(z) = (z + \sqrt{c})/(z - \sqrt{c})$. The inverse is $\Phi^{-1}(w) = (-w\sqrt{c} - \sqrt{c})/(-w + 1) = \sqrt{c}(w + 1)/(w - 1)$, by formula (16.27). If $N(z)$ becomes $M(w)$ then (cf. Figure 16.32, where $q(z)$ becomes $p(w)$):

$$\begin{aligned} M(w) &= \Phi.N.\Phi^{-1}(w) = \Phi.N\left(\sqrt{c}.\tfrac{w+1}{w-1}\right) \\ &= \Phi\left(\sqrt{c}.\tfrac{w^2+1}{w^2-1}\right), \quad \text{since } N(z) = (z^2+c)/2z, \\ &= \frac{(w^2+1)/(w^2-1)+1}{(w^2+1)/(w^2-1)-1}, \quad \text{since the } \sqrt{c}\text{'s cancel}, \\ &= w^2, \end{aligned}$$

as we might possibly have guessed. We have already dealt with this case in Example 16.13, and know that $J = S^1$, with interior $A(0)$ and exterior $A(\infty)$. cf. Figure 16.34 (right).

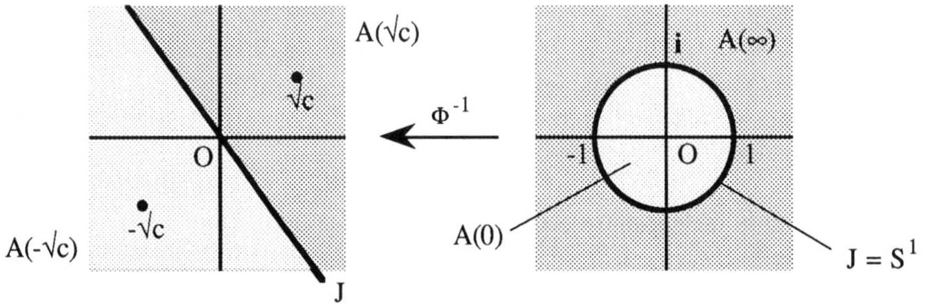

Figure 16.34 Transforming the attractive basins and Julia set of $f(w) = w^2$ (right) back to the original context in the z-plane (left).

Transforming back to the z-plane we obtain:

$\Phi^{-1}(1)$	$= \infty$	therefore $\Phi^{-1}(S^1)$ is a line,
$\Phi^{-1}(-1)$	$= 0$	therefore this line contains the origin,
$\Phi^{-1}(i)$	$= -i\sqrt{c}$	a complex number at right angles to $\sqrt{c}$.

Thus $J = \Phi^{-1}(S^1)$ is the perpendicular bisector of the line segment joining $-\sqrt{c}$ to $\sqrt{c}$. Further, by a connected components argument similar to that in Example 16.66, we conclude that $A(\pm\sqrt{c})$ are the half-planes on opposite sides of J, as depicted in Figure 16.34. A check is that $\Phi^{-1}(0) = -\sqrt{c}$.

Newton's method for $z^3 - 1 = 0$ The roots are known to be the three cube roots of unity $1, \omega, \omega^2$ where $\omega = e^{2\pi i/3}$. We expect that, due to symmetry, the attractive basins of the roots are the connected regions separated by the darkened lines of Figure 16.35 (b), bisecting the edges of the triangle with the roots as vertices. If our hypothesis is correct, the union of these dark lines is the Julia set. It is true that the origin is 3-cornered, that is, it lies in the boundaries of all three basins. But, as we shall show in the next theorem, every point of J is 3-cornered, and so the apparently simple situation is almost unimaginably complicated. Perhaps it is not surprising that, in his own day, Cayley was unable to unravel the dynamics of Newton's method even for the present case of a cubic equation. The function for iteration is

$$N(z) = z - (z^3 - 1)/3z^2 = (2z^3 + 1)/3z^2, \quad \text{with} \tag{16.29}$$

$$N'(z) = 2(z^3 - 1)/3z^3.$$

Thus $N'(z) = 0$ at the cube roots of unity, which are therefore superattractive.

EXERCISE Prove that a root α of an analytic function f(z) with $f'(\alpha) \neq 0$, is a superattractive fixed point of the Newton function $N(z) = z - f(z)/f'(z)$.

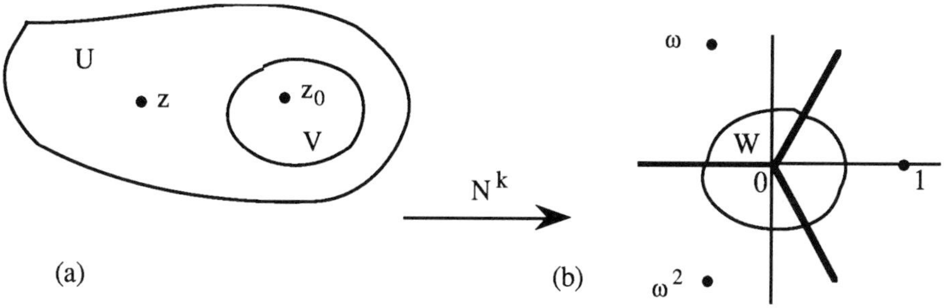

Figure 16.35 Diagram for proof of Theorem 16.68 below: under the Newton iteration function N(z), every point of the Julia set is in the boundary of the basin of attraction for all three cube roots of unity.

THEOREM 16.68 In the Julia set of Newton's function (16.29) for the iterative solution of z^3-1, every point is 3-cornered. That is, every point is in the boundary of each root's basin of attraction.

Proof Recall that in the case of a rational function N(z) we defined the Julia set to be the closure of the set of repelling fixed points, and assumed the result that the set of all inverse iterates $N^{-n}(\alpha)$ of a point in J is dense in J. The task we have set ourselves is to deduce Theorem 16.68 on that basis. The proof is in three stages.

(1) We claim that $0 \in J$. Now under N we have $0 \to \infty$ $(\to \infty)$ so since $N^{-1}(J)$ is in J it suffices to show that $\infty \in J$. This will follow if the fixed point ∞ is repelling (not attractive). It *is* repelling because $|N(z)/z| = |2/3 + 1/3z^3| \leq 7/9$ for sufficiently large z (say $|z| > 4$), so that the image of z on S^2 (see Figure 16.7) is iterated away from the North pole NP when it approaches NP sufficiently closely.

(2) 0 is 3-cornered. To show this, let the 1/3 turn transformation D of the plane be defined by $D(z) = \omega z$ ($\omega = e^{2\pi i/3}$), then $N.D(z) = (2\omega^3 z^3 + 1)/3\omega^2 z^2 = \omega N(z) = D.N(z)$. Therefore the change of coordinates $z \to \omega z$, transforming N into $D.N.D^{-1}$, simply replaces N by itself.

(3) The 3-corneredness of 0 is transferred by some N^k to any point of J as follows. Let z be a point of J and let U be an open set containing z, as depicted in Figure 16.35(a). Since $\{N^{-n}(0)\}$ is dense in J there is a point z_0 of J in U, with $N^k(z_0) = 0$ for some integer k. By the Chain Rule (16.8) $(N^k)'(z_0) = N'(z_0)N'(z_1)... N'(z_{k-1})$, which is nonzero since $N'(z) = 0 \Leftrightarrow z^3 = 1 \Leftrightarrow N(z) = z$. Hence by Theorem 16.6A, N^k has an analytic inverse g on a neighbourhood V of z_0, and N^k: $V \to W$ where $W = N^k(V)$, is an analytic homeomorphism. Since g maps boundaries to boundaries (see (11.19A)), the fact that 0 is in the boundary of all three basins of attraction implies the same for z_0 (= g(0)). Therefore the neighbourhood U of z_0 contains points from all three *basins*. But since U was an arbitrary neighbourhood of z, it follows that z itself is in all three boundaries.

Note. The interweaving of the three basins of attraction for Newton's method on $z^3 - 1$ is shown in the Colour Plate section.

TABLE 16.3 Some properties of Julia and Mandelbrot sets

f(z): a polynomial of degree at least two, or a rational function g(z)/h(z), in which g, h have no common factor and max(degree g, degree h) ≥ 2. Any of 4 to 6 may be used to define the Julia set of f.

α:	an attractive fixed point of f
γ:	an attractive p-cycle of f
$A(\alpha)$	the attractive basin of α
$A(\gamma)$	the attractive basin of a point of γ, with respect to f^p
P	the set of repelling periodic points of f
J(f)	the *Julia set* of f
F(f)	the *Fatou set* $\mathbf{C} \setminus J(f)$ of f

1 J is *perfect* : closed, with no isolated points.

2 J is *completely invariant*: $f(J) = J = f^{-1}(J)$.

3 $J(f^r) = J(f) \quad (r \geq 2)$.

4 The *inverse orbit* $\bigcup_{n=1}^{\infty} f^{-n}(z_0)$ is dense in J(f), for any $z_0 \in J(f)$.

5 $J(f) = \partial A(\alpha) = \partial A(\gamma)$.

6 **P** is dense in J.

EXAMPLE Newton's method. To solve f(x) = 0 we iterate $N(z) = z - f(z)/f'(z)$. Every point of J is in the boundary of the basin of attraction of each solution.

The quadratic case $f(z) = f_c(z) = z^2+c, \quad J(f) = J_c$.

Define $M = \{c \in \mathbf{C}: J(f_c) \text{ is connected}\}$, the Mandelbrot set.

7 $M = \{c \in \mathbf{C}: f_c^n(0) \not\rightarrow \infty \text{ as } n \rightarrow \infty\}$.

8 M is connected (and lies in a disc of radius 2 about the origin).

9 if c is not in M then J is totally disconnected and is a Cantor set.

10 The main body of M is a filled-in cardioid. A series of circular buds surround the main body, attached tangentially. Each bud is similarly surrounded, and so on. From the buds there sprout fine branching antennae-like structures, each carrying miniature copies of the whole of M.

11 Under magnification, an area of M round c is very similar to J_c itself.

12 *If c is in the main body of M* then f_c has a single finite attractive fixed point, and J is a simple closed curve but has no well-defined tangent line.

13 *If c is in a bud of M* then f_c has an attractive p-cycle ($p \geq 2$). The diameter of the bud is proportional to $1/p^2$. J_c bounds infinitely many closed regions, mapped to each other with period p by f_c.

EXERCISES 16

1 Expand $1/(z-1)^3$ about $z_0 = 3$ by writing $z-1 = 2+(z-3) = 2(1 + (z-3)/2)$. Now check your answer for the first few terms by differentiating an expansion of $1/(z-1)^2$ about $z_0 = 3$.

2 Let $V = \{x+iy: -2 \le x,y \le 2\}$. Verify that $|f(z)|$ attains its maximum off the boundary in case $f(x+iy) = (4 - x^2)(4 - y^2)$, but on the boundary in the case of the analytic function $g(x+iy) = z^2$. [It follows that f(z) is not an analytic function of z.]

3 Use a diagram to show how it is that, if z is nonzero and we take the positive square root, then $|1+\sqrt{z}| > 1$. Verify this by calculation for $z = \mathbf{i}$.

4 Show that the fixedpoints of $f(z) = z^2 + \mathbf{i}$ are both repellers. [Use the formula for the roots of a quadratic equation. $f'(z)$ has imaginary part ± 1.26 approx. at these points.]

5 √ Verify that the attractive and repelling fixed points for $f(z) = z^2 + c$ with $c = -0.5 + 0.5\mathbf{i}$, are approximately as given under Figure 16.6 (b).

6 √ Let $R(z) = (3z^2 + 4)/(5z^2 + 2z)$. Use Table 16.2 to determine $R(\infty)$ and the points w for which $R(w) = \infty$.

7 Show that $f(z) = z^3 + 2z + 1$ has ∞ as an attractive fixed point by using a chain of inequalites as in Example 16.15 (3), or by Lemma 16.14.

8 √ Show that the fixed points of Example 16.20 are both repellers.

9 √ Let $f(z) = z^2 - 7/8$. Without writing down the fixed points explicitly, find the fixed 2-cycle of f and show that it is attractive. [The eigenvalue is 1/2.]

10 Make a rough copy of Figure 16.8(a). Without consulting its companion, Figure 16.8(b), darken as many regions as you can deduce are in the attractive basin of 0 (under f^2).

11 Find $f^{-3}(1)$ in Example 16.23.

12 Why does normality at every point of an open set V not imply normality on V? [Hint: focus on compact subsets.]

13 Let $f(z) = \lambda z$ with $|\lambda| < 1$. Show that $\{f^n\}$ is normal on every open set U by showing it converges uniformly to the constant function 0 on every compact set.

14 Deduce from Example 16.26 that $J_0(f)$ is bounded, by showing that $J_0(f) \subseteq \mathbf{C}\backslash V$.

15 √ Assuming that $J = \partial A(\infty)$, where ∞ is an attractive fixed point of a polynomial f(z), deduce that $f(J) \subseteq J$.

16 Produce a variant of Figure 16.17 by labelling the vertices differently and filling in the squares for J according to the algorithm.

17 With $f(z) = z^2 + c$, show that if $|c| \le 2$ and $|z| \ge 4$ then $|f(z)/z| \ge 7/2$, by the method of proof of Lemma 16.49(b).

18 Write a computer program to implement the LSM for the Mandelbrot set. How many stages can you get of bud upon bud?

19 Use your LSM program to find a bud period not shown in Figure 16.20.

20 Using your computer program for J, construct the Julia set of Figure 16.23. Magnify a part that looks solid until it splits visibly into subunits.

21 Write a computer program to draw the boundary of the main body of M, using the cardioid equation **or** prove that the boundary is indeed a cardioid.

22 Test Theorem 16.57 by estimating the radii of buds in Figure 16.20.

23 Let D be the disc of radius 2 at the origin and $f(z) = z^2+c$. Sketch roughly the inverse image $f^{-1}(D)$ in the cases $c = 1, -2, -3$ (see Lemma 16.58).

24 √ Show that if $|c| < 1/4$ then $f(z) = z^2 + c$ has an attractive fixed point, by determining the product of the roots of $f(z) = z$.

25 √ Transform the quadratic $q(z) = z(z-1)$ into the form $z^2 + c$ by a linear change of coordinates.

26 √ What does the transformation $w = (z-\mathbf{i})/(z+\mathbf{i})$ do to the lower half-plane $y < 0$?

27 √ Prove that a root α of an analytic function $f(z)$ with $f'(\alpha) \neq 0$, is a superattractive fixed point of the Newton function $N(z) = z - f(z)/f'(z)$.

28 (**Further exercises**) Let stereographic projection be from the North pole of a unit sphere whose centre is at the origin in **C**. Find the image of that circle in the sphere, whose plane has a normal vector (1,2,1) and is at distance 1/2 from the origin.

29 (a) Find a bilinear transformation which sends points above the line $x-y = 5$ to the exterior of the unit circle. (b) Find the bilinear transformation which sends 0 to 1, 1 to ∞, and ∞ to 2. What is its effect on the line $x+y = 1$? What is the image of the interior of the unit circle?

30 What especially simple bilinear transformation interchanges 0 and ∞? Use it to determine the nature of ∞ as a fixed point of (a) $z^3 + 2z + 1$, (b) $(z^2 - 1)/z$, (c) $(2z^2 + 3)/(z + 1)$ (see Lemma 16.14).

31 Let $f(z)$ be a real function of a complex variable which is differentiable at $z = a$. Show that $f'(a) = 0$, by considering $(f(a+h) - f(a))/h$ (a) with h real, (b) with h purely imaginary.

32 Show that on its domain of definition, $g(z) = \sqrt{(z-c)}$ has derivative $1/2\sqrt{(z-c)}$ by differentiating the composition f.g, where $f(x) = z^2 + c$.

33 Find out whether some bud of period 10 on the main bud of the Mandelbrot set has a Julia set like this: the components of its basin of attraction are grouped in two fives or five twos (Figure 16.26 has the components grouped in two threes).

34 √ Prove that the indifferent fixed point 1/2 of $f(z) = z^2 + 1/4$ is in $J = \partial A(\infty)$. [Show that for any $\delta > 0$, $f(1/2 + \delta) > 1 + \delta/2$ and $f^n(1/2 + \delta) \geq (1 + \delta/2)^n$, and hence 1/2 has points of $A(\infty)$ arbitrarily close.]

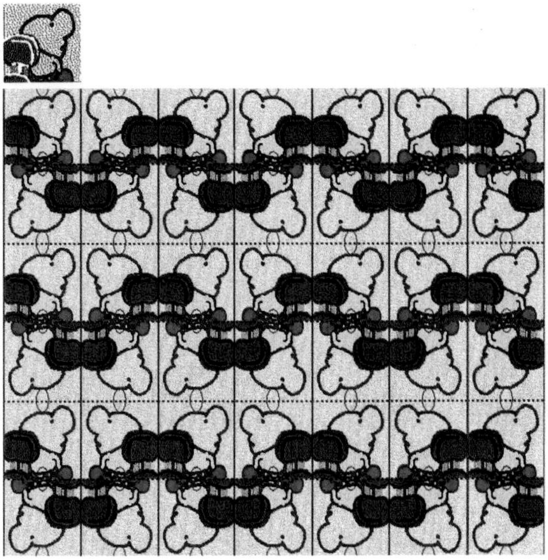

Plate 1. The filled-in fundamental region top left is replicated so as to give a plane pattern of type pmg. Some of the pattern's symmetries are exhibited. Mirror lines are continuous, glide lines dotted, and each small ellipse marks a point of 2-fold symmetry (symmetry under a 180 degree turn). The theory is given in Sections 6.4.3 and 6.4.4. Computer generation by David Ebert.

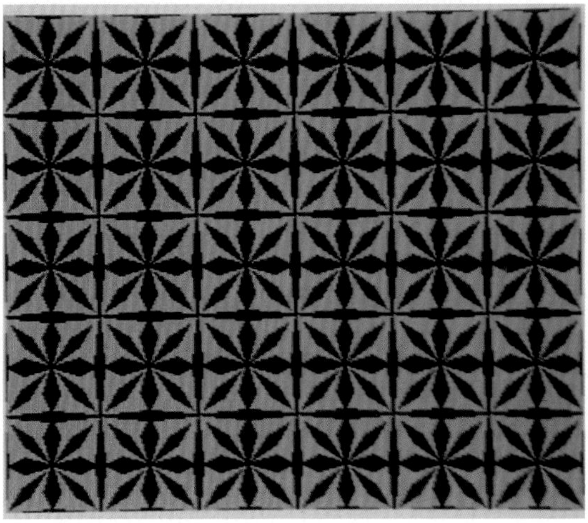

Plate 2. Plausible design for a wall tile, obtained by a 'suck it and see' approach. Produced from a quickly drawn motif in a fundamental region, with computer replication into a pmg type plane pattern (see Section 5.5).

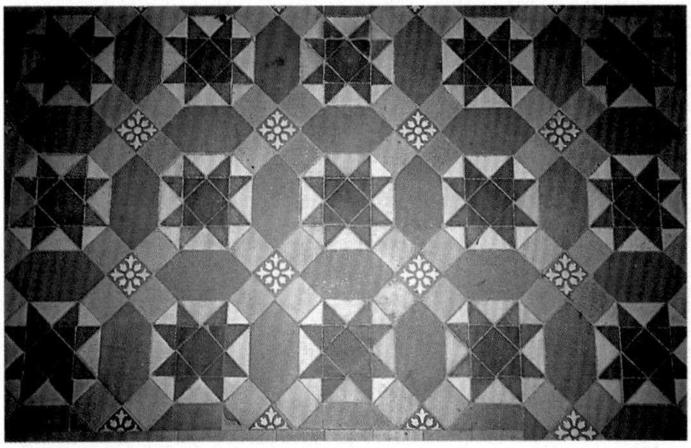

Plate 3. Hall floor pattern from a block of flats in Glasgow, Scotland. With Plate 2, this p4m pattern helps to suggest the variety allowed in each type. (An Art History comment: typical of Soviet Central Asia.) Photograph by Herbert Runcimen.

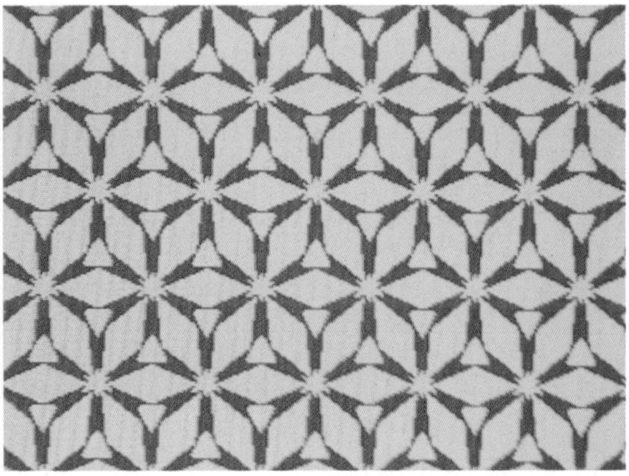

Plate 4. Computer generated plane pattern of type p6m. The symmetry thus includes 2-, 3- and 6-fold centres of symmetry, together with mirror and glide lines (see Section 5.6).

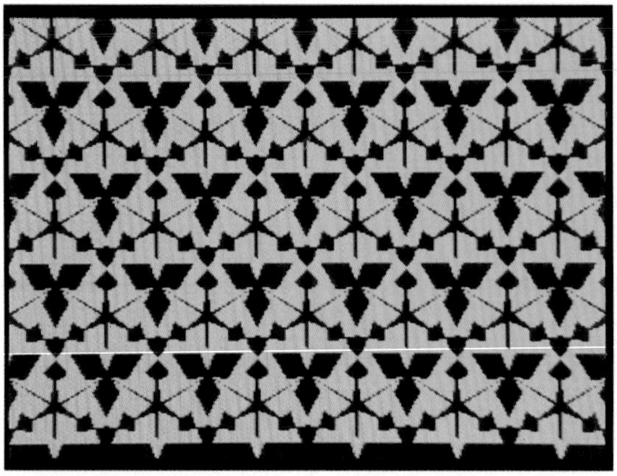

Plate 5. This plane pattern is symmetrical under certain 1/3 turns, but no 1/6 or 1/2 turns, and has mirror and glide lines in three directions. Its type is p3m1.

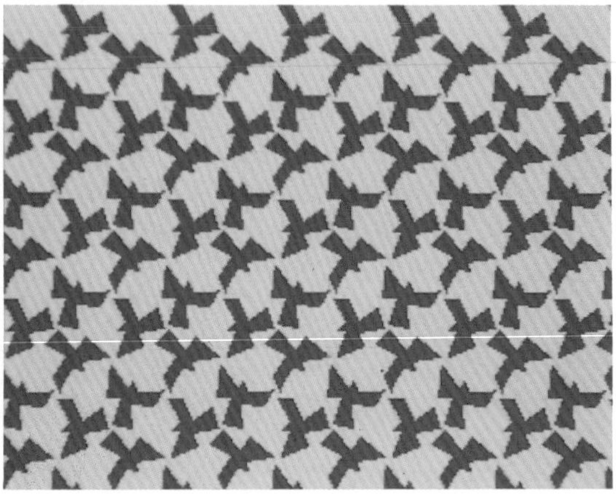

Plate 6. The dark creatures are easy to spot in this p3 pattern. Can you pick out the others?

Plate 7. This fractal fern (or is it a tree?) is the attractor of an iterated function system and, correspondingly, is a 'collage' or union of transformed copies of itself, each shown in a different colour. cf. Figure 14.21.

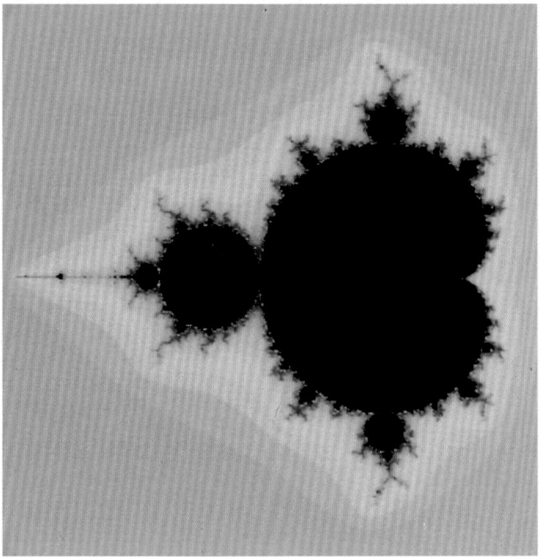

Plate 8. The Mandelbrot set M with some exterior colour bands.

Plate 9. *Seahorse valley* – a closeup of the 'V' between the main bud (largest disc) and cardioid-shaped main body of M. The seahorses right of the V show remarkable further detail in plates 11–16.

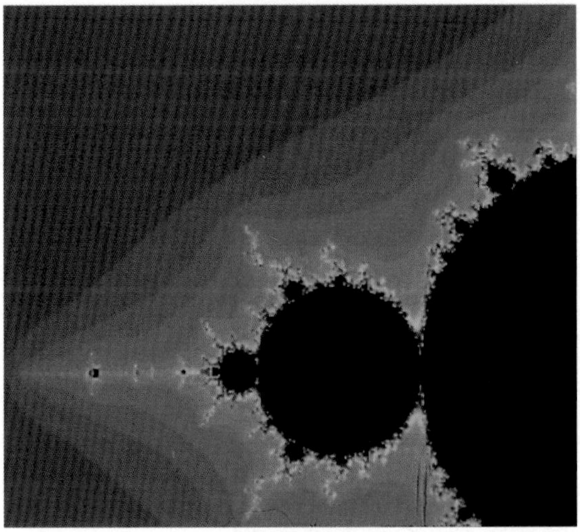

Plate 10. Part of the main bud of M (*not* the main body), indicating a succession of bud upon bud to the left, ad infinitum. The horizontal spike, or skewer, carries a complete miniature copy of M itself (cf. Plate 16).

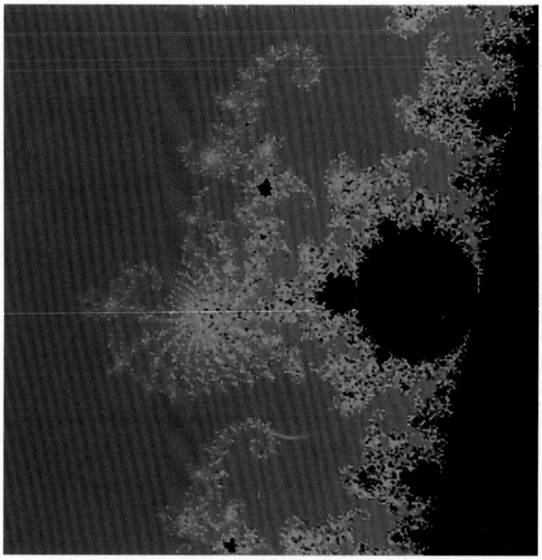

Plate 11. Blow up of a seahorse from Plate 9, with see-through effect. We begin to see that the boundary of the Mandelbrot set is very complicated indeed, yet not a mish-mash.

Plate 12. Magnification by 2 of Plate 11, this time with Chinese magic lantern effect. Notice the black eye, to be shown with more detail and colour in Plate 13.

Plate 13. Blow up of the seahorse eye of Plates 11, 12, spawning yet further seahorses on a smaller scale [David Ebert].

Plate 14. Tail of the seahorse from Plates 11, 12.

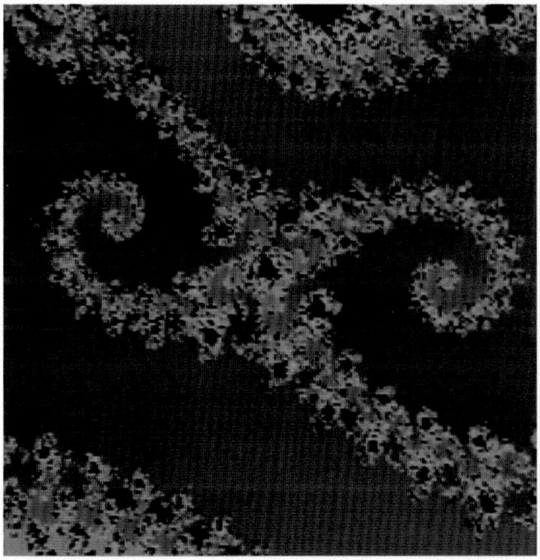

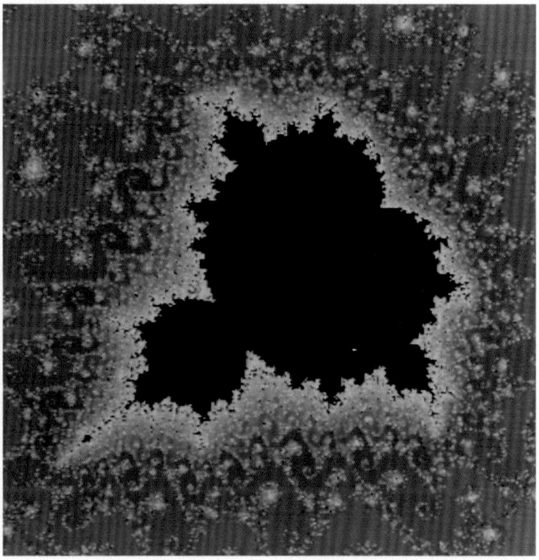

Plate 15. Blow up of part of the seahorse tail in Plate 14. The central black 'triangle' is really a complete miniscule Mandelbrot set.

Plate 16. A minute copy of the Mandelbrot set within itself from Plate 15, shown in greater detail.

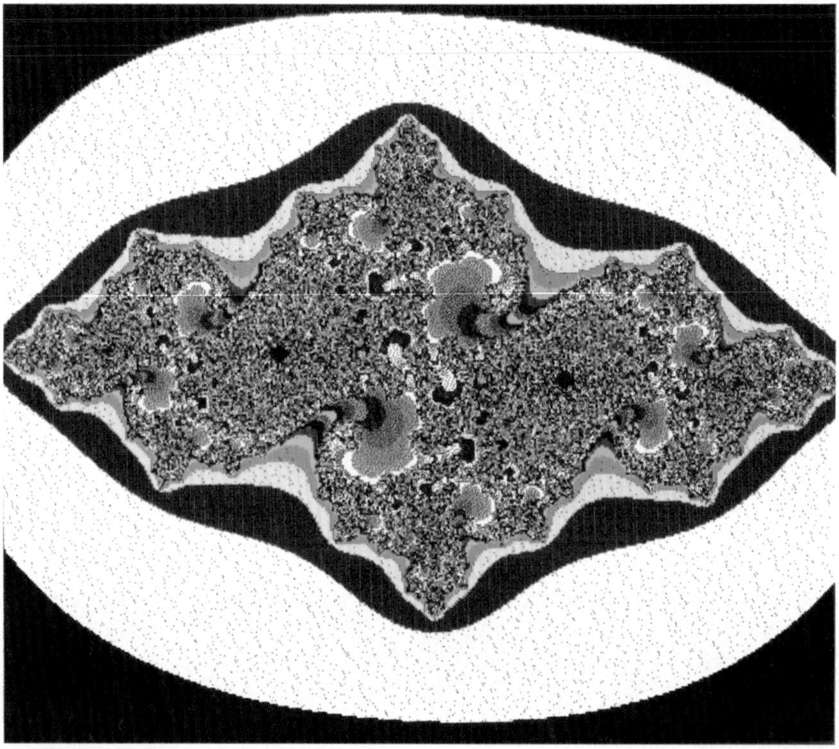

Plates 17–19. Three versions of the Julia set of $f_c(z) = z^2 + c$, with c taking the value –0.74543 + 0.11301**i**, a point just within the main body of the Mandelbrot set. [Plate 17 is by David Ebert.]

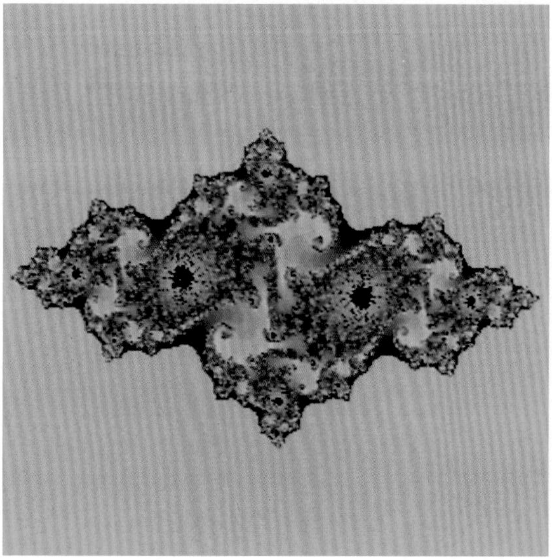

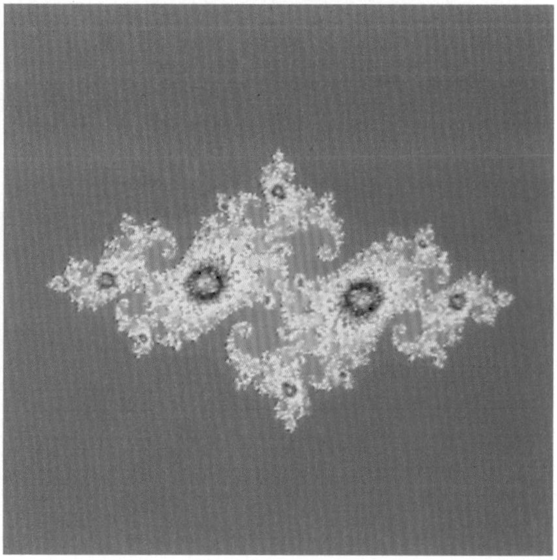

An Art Historical view (James Brown)

Plate 17: Typical 1960s' record cover.

Plate 18: Reminiscent of Anglo Saxon jewellery on 'interlacing serpent' theme.

Plate 19: Turn of the century jewellery, perhaps Viennese.

Plates 20–22. Julia sets with period 3.

Plate 20 (right). Julia set of f_c, with c in a bud of associated period 3.

Plate 21 (below). Julia set of f_c, where c is in a mini Mandelbrot set on an antenna of the original M, and is chosen similarly situated to the c of Plate 20. Notice the miniscule copies of itself on the 'antennae' round J, with each copy looking like Plate 20 rotated.

Plate 22 (below right). Julia set of f_c, with c in the mini-Mandelbrot set on the left skewer of M, similarly situated to the c of Plate 20. Like Plate 21, it consists of variations on the 'standard' J of Plate 20.

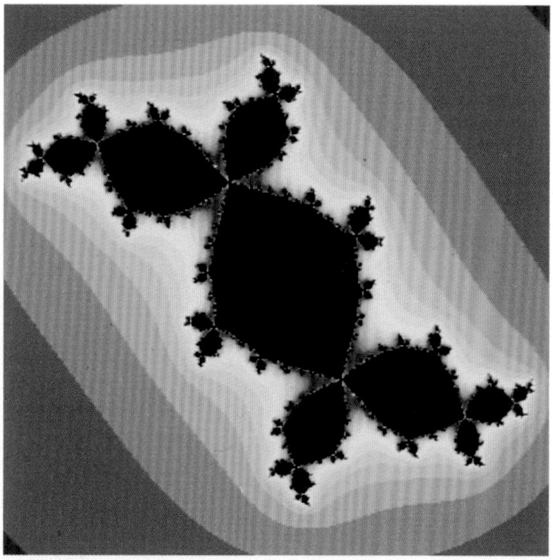

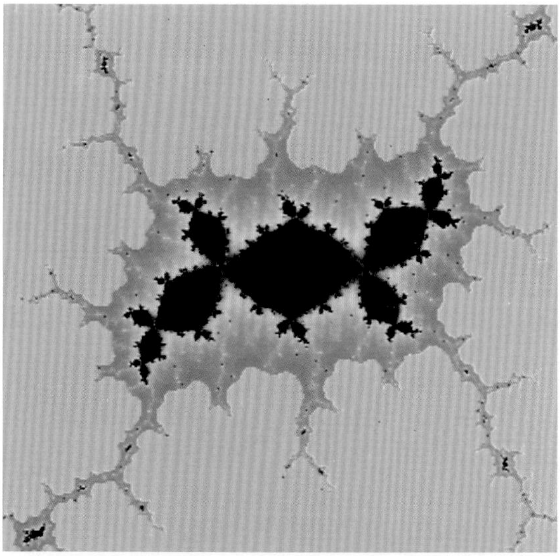

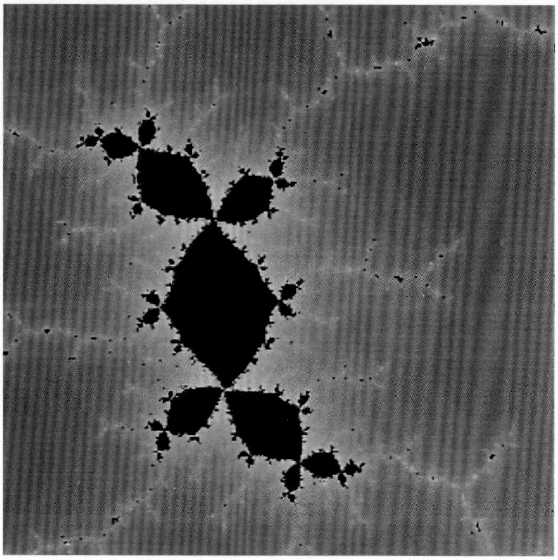

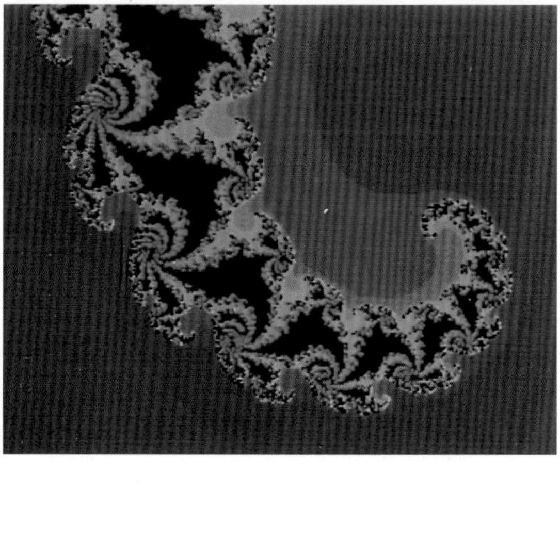

Plate 23. Julia set of a point c in a bud of the Mandelbrot set with period 10: blow-up of a typical piece (cf. Figure 16.20).

Plate 24. Highly magnified part of M from seahorse valley [by Michael Snyder].

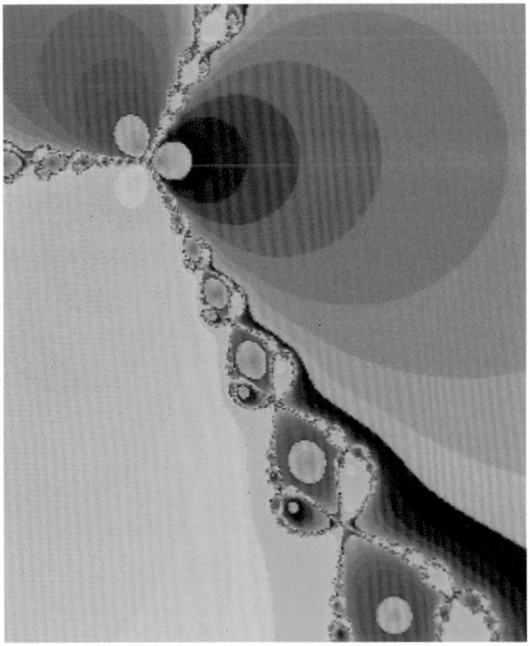

Plate 25. Illustration of Newton's iterative method of solution in case $z^3 = 1$. The basin of attraction of each root is shown in a different colour. Notice the (infinitely) complex intermingling of the basins. A remarkable result (Theorem 16.68) states that a boundary point of any one basin must also be a boundary point of the other two.

REFERENCES

Ahlfors L.V. (1966) Complex analysis. *McGraw-Hill.*

Avis D. and Doskas M. (1988) Algorithms for higher dimensional stabbing problems. *NATO ASI series Vol. F40, Theoretical foundations of computer graphics and CAD, (Ed. R. A. Earnshaw), Springer-Verlag Berlin Heidelberg.*

Barnsley M.F. (1987) Fractal modelling of real world images. *In: The science of fractal images, eds H-O Peitgen and D Saupe, Springer-Verlag1988.*

Barnsley M.F. (1988) Fractals everywhere. *Academic Press.*

Barnsley M.F. and Demko S. (1985) Iterated function systems and the global construction of fractals. *Proc. Royal Soc. London A399, 243-275.*

Barnsley M.F. and Elton J. (1988) A new class of Markov processes for image encoding. *Journal of Applied probability 20, 14-32.*

Barnsley M.F. and Sloan A.D. (1988) A better way to compress images. *Byte magazine (Jan. 1988) 215-223.*

Barnsley M.F., Jacquin A., Malassenet F., Reuter L., and Sloan A.D. (1988) Harnessing chaos for image synthesis. *SIGGRAPH 1988 Proceedings. Computer graphics (22) (1988), 131-140.*

Barsky B.A. (1988) Computer graphics and geometric modeling using Beta splines. *Springer-Verlag.*

Bartels R.H., Beatty J.C. & Barsky B.A. (1987) Introduction to splines for use in computer graphics and geometric modeling. *Morgan Kaufman Pubs., Inc., Los Altos, CA.*

Baumgart B.G. (1974) Geometric modeling for computer vision. *PhD thesis, Reprint AIM-249, STAN-CS-74-463, Computer Science Department, Stanford University, Palo Alto, CA, USA.*

Beardon A.F. (1990) Symmetries of Julia sets. Bull. London Math. Soc. 22(1990), 576-582.

Becker K-H and Dorfler M. (1990) Dynamical systems and fractals. Translated by I. Stewart. *Cambridge University Press.*

Bézier P. (1972) Numerical control. *In: Mathematics and applications. Wiley.*

Birkhoff G. and Mac Lane S. (1963) A survey of modern Algebra. *Macmillan.*

Blackett D.W. (1967) Elementary topology. *Academic Press.*

Blanchard P. (1984) Complex analytical dynamics on the Riemann sphere. *Bull. Amer. Math. Soc. 11 , 85-141.*

Blinn J.F. (1978) Simulation of wrinkled surfaces. In *SIGGRAPH 1978 Proceedings. Computer graphics 12 (1978), 286-292.*

Brammer R.F. (1989) Unified image computing based on fractals and chaos model techniques. *Optical engineering 28 , 726-734.*

Brolin H.(1965) Invariant sets under iteration of Rational functions. *Arkiv for Matematik 6, 103-144.*

Bryant V. (1990) Metric spaces: iteration and application. *Cambridge University Press.*

Burger P. and Gillies D. (1989) Interactive computer graphics. *Addison-Wesley .*

Cayley A. (1845) *On certain results relating to quaternions.* Philosophical magazine 26, 141-145.

Cherbit G. (1990) Fractals: Non-integral dimensions and applications. *Wiley, Chichester, England.*

Churchill R.V. (1960) Complex variables and applications. *McGraw-Hill.*

Cohen S. D. (1989) Windmill polynomials over fields of characteristic two. *Monatshefte für Mathematik 107, 291-301.*

Conway J.H. and Sloane N.A.J. (1988) *Sphere packings, lattices, and groups. Springer-Verlag.*

Coxeter H. S. M. (1973) Regular Polytopes. 2nd ed. Collier-Macmillan, New York, 1963; 3rd ed., Dover, New York, 1973.

Coxeter H. S. M. (1974) Regular Complex Polytopes. *Cambridge University Press, Cambridge, England.*

Coxeter H. S. M. (1987) (Co-editor) M. C. Escher: Art and Science. *Proceedings of the International Congress on M.C. Escher, Rome, 1985. Elsevier Science Pub. Co. Inc., New York (2nd ed.).*

Coxeter H.S.M. and Moser W.O.J. (1980) Generators and relations for discrete groups *(4th ed.). Springer-Verlag.*

Critchlow K. (1976) Islamic patterns. An analytical and cosmological approach. *Schocken books, New York, 1976. Thames & Hudson, London, 1976.*

Crowe D.W. (1981) The geometry of African art III: the smoking pipes of Begho. In: *The geometric vein (The Coxeter Festschrift), C.Davis et al., eds. Springer-Verlag, New York.*

Davis C. and Knuth D.E. (1970) Number representations and dragon curves. *Journal of Recreational mathematics 3, 66-81 and 133-149.*

Dekking F.M. (1982) Recurrent sets. *Advances in Mathematics 44 , 78-104.*

Demko S., Hodges L., and Naylor B. (1985) Construction of fractal objects with iterated function systems. *SIGGRAPH 1985 Proceedings. Computer Graphics 19(3), 271-278.*

Devaney B. (1989) The harmony guide to colourful machine knitting. *Lyric books Ltd, Hodder & Stoughton.*

Devaney R.L. (1989) An Introduction to Chaotic dynamical systems. *Addison-Wesley.*

Dobkin D.P. (1988) Computational geometry - then and now. *In NATO ASI series F40 (Ed. R.A.Earnshaw). Springer-Verlag.*

Douady A. and Hubbard J.H. (1982) Iteration des polynomes quadratiques complexes. *C.R.Acad.Sc. Paris 294, 123-126.*

Edgar G.A. (1990) Measure, topology, and fractal geometry. *Springer-Verlag.*

Edge C., Higgins D., and Thomson C (1988) *Theoretical studies of the electrostatic potential of some enzyme inhibitors using computer graphics techniques.* J. Molecular graphics 6, 171-177.

Elton J. (1987) An ergodic theorem for iterated maps. *Journal of ergodic theory and dynamical systems 7, 481-488.*

Escher M. C (1989) Escher on Escher - Exploring the infinite. *Meulenhoff International, Amsterdam, 1986. Harry N. Abrams Inc., New York.*

Euler L. (1758) Du movement de rotation des corps solides autour d'un axe variable. In:

Opera Omnia, Ser. secunda, v. 8, Orell Füsli Turiei, Lausanne.

Falconer K.J. (1985,1986) The geometry of fractal sets. *Cambridge University Press.*

Falconer K.J. (1990) Fractal geometry: Mathematical foundations and applications. *Wiley & Sons, Chichester.*

Fatou P. (1919) Sur les équations fonctionelles. *Bull. Soc. Math.,France 47(1919), 161-271.*

Faux I.D. and Pratt M.J. (1987) Computational geometry for design and manufacture. *Ellis Horwood, Chichester. Wiley, Chichester, 1987 (6th printing).*

Field R. (1988) Geometric patterns from Roman mosaics. *Tarquin Publications, Stradbroke, Diss, Norfolk, England.*

Fiume E.L. (1989) The mathematical structure of raster graphics. *Academic Press.*

Fiume E.L. and Fournier A. (1984) A programme for the development of a mathematical theory of computer graphics. *Proceedings of Graphics Interface '84, 251-256.*

Foley J. D., van Dam A., Feiner S.K., and Hughes J.F. (1990) Computer graphics, principles and practice. *Addison-Wesley .*

Gasson P. C. (1983) Geometry of spatial forms. *Ellis Horwood, Wiley.*

Gemignani M.C. (1967) Elementary topology. *Addison-Wesley.*

Gilbert W.J. (1982) Fractal geometries derived from complex bases. *Math. Intelligencer 4, 78-86.*

Giles J.R. (1987) Introduction to the analysis of metric spaces. *Cambridge University Press.*

Glassner A.S. (1989) (Ed) An introduction to ray tracing. Academic Press, London.

Gleick J. (1988) Chaos : making a new science. *Viking Penguin*

GrünBaum B. and Shephard G. C. (1987) Tilings and patterns. *Freeman, New York.*

Guckenheimer J. and McGehee R. (1988) A proof of the Mandelbrot N^2 conjecture. *Report of the Mittag-Leffler Institute, Djursholm, Sweden.*

Hamilton W.R. (1844) On quaternions: Or on a new system of imaginaries in algebra. *Philosophical magazine 25, 10-13.*

Heckbert P.S. (1989) Fundamentals of texture mapping and image warping. *Rept. UCB/CSD 89/516. Computer Science Division, University of California, Berkeley, California 94720.*

Heise R. and MacDonald B.A. (1989) Quaternions and motion interpolation: *A tutorial. Proceedings of CG International '89. Eds. R.A. Earnshaw & B. Wyvill, Springer-Verlag.*

Heyting A. and Freudenthal H. (1975) Collected works of L.E.J. Brouwer. *North Holland-Elsevier.*

Hocking J.G. and Young G.S. (1961) Topology. *Addison-Wesley.*

Hoggar S.G. (1982) t-designs in projective spaces, *European Journal of Combinatorics 3 (1982), 233-254.*

Hughes P.C. (1986) Spacecraft attitudes & dynamics. *Wiley .*

Husemoller D. (1966) Fibre bundles. *McGraw-Hill.*

Hutchinson J.E. (1981) Fractals and self similarity. *Indiana University Mathematics Journal 30 , 713-747.*

Joy K.I., Grant C.W., Max N.L., and Hatfield L. (1988) Tutorial on Image Synthesis. *Computer Society Press (IEEE).*

Julia G. (1918) Sur l'iteration des fonctions rationelles. *J. Math. Pure Appl. 8, 47-245.*

Kaye B.H. (1989) A random walk through fractal dimensions. *VCH publishers (Cambridge, New York).*

Kelley J.L. (1964) General Topology. *Van Nostrand.*

Kennedy H.C. (1973) Selected works of G. Peano. *Toronto University Press.*

Kilgour A.C. (1987a) Unifying vector and polygon algorithms for scan conversion and clipping. *Computing Science research report CSC/87/R7, University of Glasgow.*

Kilgour A.C. (1987b) Polygon processing for VLSI pattern generation. In R.A Earnshaw and D.F.Rogers (eds): State of the art in computer graphics. *Springer Verlag.*

Knuth D. (1980) The art of computer programming, Volume 2. *Addison Wesley.*

Le Chenadec, Philippe (1986) Canonical forms in finitely presented algebras, *Pitman.*

Lidl R. and Niederreiter H. (1986) Introduction to finite fields and their applications. *Cambridge University Press.*

Lindenmayer A. and Prusinkiewicz P. (1990). The algorithmic beauty of plants. *Springer-Verlag.*

Lockwood E.H. and Macmillan R.H. (1978) Geometric symmetry. *Cambridge University Press.*

Macgillavry C.H. (1976) Symmetry aspects of M.C. Escher's periodic drawings. *2nd ed. (International union of crystallography). Bohn, Scheltema & Holkema, Utrecht, The Netherlands.*

Mandelbrot B. (1980) Fractal aspects of the iteration of $z \rightarrow \lambda z(1-z)$ and z. *Ann. New York Acad. Sci. 357, 249-259.*

Mandelbrot B. (1983) The fractal geometry of nature. *W H Freeman.*

Mandelbrot B. (1986) Self-affine fractal sets. In *Fractals in Physics (Eds L. Pietronero and E. Tosatti), North -Holland, Amsterdam.*

Mäntylä M. (1988) Introduction to solid modeling. *Computer Science Press, Rockville, MD, USA.*

Maunder C.R.F. (1970) Algebraic Topology. *Van Nostrand Reinhold.*

McEliece R. J. (1987) Finite fields for computer scientists and engineers. *Kluwer.*

McGregor J. and Watt A. (1984) The art of microcomputer graphics. *Addison-Wesley.*

Miller W. (1972) Symmetry groups and their applications, *Academic Press.*

Montel P. (1927) Leçons sur les familles normales. *Gunther-villars, Paris.*

Montesinos J. M. (1987) Classical tessellations and three-manifolds. *Springer-Verlag.*

Moran P.A.P (1946) Additive functions of intervals and Hausdorff measure. *Proc. Cam. Phil. Soc. 42, 15-23.*

Murphy I.S. (1984) Basic mathematical analysis. *Arklay publishers, Stirling, Scotland.*

Murphy I.S. (1989) Calculus for Scientists and Engineers. *Arklay Publishers, Stirling, Scotland.*

Niven I. and Zuckerman H. S. (1980) An introduction to the theory of numbers. (4th edn) *Wiley.*

Norton V.A. (1982) Generalisation and display of geometric fractals in 3-D. *Computer Graphics 16, 61-67.*

Oliver J. (1979) Polysymetrics. *Tarquin Publications, Stradbroke, Diss Norfolk, England.*

Patterson J.W., Hoggar S.G. and Logie J.L. (1991) Inverse displacement mapping. *Computer graphics forum 10(1991), 129-139.*

Peitgen H-O and Saupe D. (eds) (1988) The science of fractals images. *Springer-Verlag.*

Peitgen H.O. and Richter P.H. (1986) The beauty of fractals. *Springer-Verlag.*

Phillips F.C. (1971) Introduction to crystallography. Oliver & Boyd.

Porteous I.R. (1969) Topological Geometry. *Van Nostrand Reinhold.*

Press W.H. et al (1988) Numerical recipes in C. *Cambridge University Press.*

Priestley H.A. (1990) Introduction to complex analysis. *Oxford University Press.*

Ranuchi E.R. and Teeters J. L. (1977) Creating Escher type drawings. *Creative Puplications, Oak Lawn, Illinois, USA. Jonathan Press, Great Tey, Colchester, England.*

Richardson L.F. (1961) The problem of contiguity: an appendix of statistics of deadly quarrels. *General Systems Yearbook 6, 139-187.*

Rogers D.F. and Adams J.A. (1990) Mathematical elements for computer graphics (2nd. ed.). *McGraw Hill.*

Rudin W. (1978) Real & complex analysis. *McGraw Hill, New York, 1966; Tata McGraw-Hill, New Delhi, 1978.*

Schattschneider D. and Walker W. (1982) M. C. Escher kaleidocycles. *Tarquin Publications, Stradbroke, Diss, Norfolk, England.*

Schroeder M.R. (1986) Number theory in science and communication. *Springer-Verlag.*

Schwarze J. et al (1990) Cubic and quartic roots (etc.). *In Glassner A.S. (ed.) 'Graphics gems', p.403-422. Academic Press.*

Schwarzenberger R.L.E. (1980) N-dimensional crystallography. *Research notes in mathematics, Pitman.*

Shamos M.I. (1978) Computational complexity. PhD dissertation, Yale University.

Shoemake K. (1985) Animating rotation with quaternion curves. *SIGGRAPH 85 Proceedings. Computer Graphics 19 (1985), 245-254.*

Shoemake K. (1987) Quaternion calculus and fast animation. *SIGGRAPH 87 Tutorial 10. Computer animation: 3D motion specification and control.*

Siegel C.L. (1942) Iteration of analytic functions. *Ann. Math. 43, 607-612.*

Simmons G.F. (1963) Introduction to topology and modern analysis. *McGraw-Hill.*

Stewart I. and Tall D. (1990) Complex analysis. *Cambridge University Press.*

Sullivan D. (1982ff) Quasi-conformal homeomorphisms and dynamics I. II, III. *Preprint, IHES, France.*

Sutherland W.A. (1975) Intoduction to metric and topological spaces. *Oxford University Press.*

Swokowski E.W. (1979) Calculus with analytic geometry. *(Wadsworth International Student Edition) Prindle, Weber and Schmidt.*

Ulichney R. (1987) Digital halftoning. *MIT Press, Cambridge (Massachusetts) and London.*

von Koch H. (1904) Sur une courbe continue sans tangents, obtenue par une construction géométrique élémentaire. *Arkiv för Matematik, Astronomi och Fysik 1, 681-704.*

Voss R.F. (1988) Fractals in nature: From characterisation to simulation. In *"The science of fractal images". ed. Peitgen H-O and Saupe D, Springer-Verlag.*

Watt A. (1990) Fundamentals of three-dimensional computer graphics. Addison-Wesley.

Whitelaw T.A. (1988) An introduction to abstract algebra (2nd edn.). *Blackie (Glasgow and London).*

Whitelaw T.A. (1991) An introduction to linear algebra (2nd edn.). *Blackie (Glasgow and London).*

Willard S. (1970) General topology. *Addison-Wesley.*

Willson S.J. (1986) A use of cellular automata to obtain families of fractals. In *Chaotic dynamics and fractals. Academic Press.*

Symbols

$\lvert\lambda\rvert$	Absolute value of a number λ	66
$\lvert AB\rvert$, $\lvert\mathbf{a}\rvert$	Length of line segment AB, length of vector **a**	5
$\underline{AB}$	Line segment directed from point A to B	5
$A(a_1,a_2)$	Point A with Cartesian coordinates (a_1,a_2)	6
$\mathbf{a} = (a_1,a_2)$	General vector **a** or *position vector* of point A (see also next page)	6
$\mathbf{a.b}$	Scalar product of vectors **a**,**b**	117
$\mathbf{a} \times \mathbf{b}$	Vector product of vectors **a**,**b**	128
$[\mathbf{a},\mathbf{b},\mathbf{c}]$	Scalar triple product of vectors **a**,**b**,**c**	129
$g: X \to Y$	Transformation or more general function (mapping) from X to Y	8, 251
P^g and $g(P)$	Image of point (or more general object) under transformation g	9
P'	As above, with g understood	9
T_{AB}	The translation that sends point A to point B	9
$T_{\mathbf{a}}$	The translation given by $\mathbf{x} \to \mathbf{x}+\mathbf{a}$	9
$R_A(\phi)$	Rotation in the plane about point A, through signed angle ϕ, counting anticlockwise as positive	10
$R_A(m/n)$	Rotation as above, through the fraction m/n of a 360 degree turn	10
$R_{\mathbf{a}}(\phi)$, $R_{AB}(\phi)$	Rotation ϕ in 3-space about an axis in direction of vector **a**, about directed axis $\underline{AB}$	156
$R_{\boldsymbol{m}}$, R_{AB},	(In the plane) Reflection in mirror line $\boldsymbol{m}$, in line through A,B	10, 11
$R_{ax+by=c}$	(In the plane) Reflection in line with given equation	11
R_Π, R_{ABC}	Reflection in the plane Π, in the plane through points A,B,C	154
$R_{\mathbf{u}}$	Reflection in plane through the origin perpendicular to **u**	154
I	The identity isometry (or more general transformation)	10
	The identity element of a group	38
	The identity matrix	121
g^{-1}	The inverse of an isometry g, group element g, or more general transformation	30
h^g	The product $g^{-1}hg$, for transformations or group elements g,h	31
D_{2n}	The Dihedral group of order 2n	35
C_n	The cyclic group of order n	36
S_n	The group of all permutations of n objects,	206
A_n	The group of even permutations of n objects	206
$Gp\{g_1,..,g_n\}$	The group generated by the elements g_i	37
F	Pattern (figure) in the plane	47
G	The group of symmetries of a plane figure	3, 47
T	The group of all translation symmetries of a plane pattern	49
$\mathcal{P}$	The point group of a plane group	84
N	The net of a plane group	49
$\mathcal{F}$	The fundamental region of a plane group	103
N	The set of natural numbers 1,2,3, ...	21
Z	The set of all integers ...-2,-1,0,1,2,...	21
Q	The rational numbers m/n	21
R	The real numbers	21
$\{m,n\}$	Regular tiling of the plane (n regular m-gons meet at point)	93
$x \in A$	x is a member of set A	241
$A \subseteq B$	A is a subset of B	241

$A \cup B$, $A \cap B$	Union, intersection of two sets	241
A^c, $B \backslash A$	Complement of set A, its complement in B	241
$\emptyset$	The empty set	241
A^0, $\overline{A}$, ∂A	Interior, closure, boundary of subset A of a space	250
A'	Derived set of A	248
$A \times B$	Cartesian product of sets (or product space)	243
$\mathbf{R}^n$	Euclidean n-space	119
$\mathbf{i},\mathbf{j},\mathbf{k}$	Unit vectors defining coordinate axes in 3-space	115
	Along with 1, a basis for the quaternions	191
$\mathbf{e}_1,\dots,\mathbf{e}_n$	Standard basis vectors for n-space	120
δ_{ik}	The Kronecker delta, equal to 1 if i=k, otherwise 0	120
a_{ik} or $(A)_{ik}$	Entry in row i, column k of matrix A	121
$\mathrm{diag}\{d_1,\dots,d_n\}$	The square matrix whose diagonal elements are d_i, the rest 0	122
A^T	The transpose of matrix A (the rows are rewritten as columns)	123
$\|A\|$ or det A	The determinant of a square matrix A	124
A^{-1}, adj A	The inverse of a square matrix A, its adjoint	126
M_g	3 x 3 matrix for plane isometry g	137
O(n),	The group of orthogonal matrices	128
SO(n)	The group of *special* (determinant 1) orthogonal matrices	167
GL(n,**R**)	General linear group	258
Tr A	The trace (sum of the diagonal elements a_{ii}) of a matrix A	162
E_{ik}	Matrix whose i,k entry is 1, and the rest 0	169
C	The complex numbers	159
$z = x+y\mathbf{i}$	Complex number (see also Section 9.1)	160
$\|z\|$	Modulus of complex number z	160
Re z, Im z	Real part, imaginary part of z	182
$\bar{z}$	Conjugate of z	182
arg(z)	Argument (angle) of z	182
$e^{i\theta}$	The complex number $\cos\theta + \mathbf{i}\sin\theta$	185
r,θ	Polar coordinates	184
τ, σ	The golden ratio and its algebraic conjugate	189
H	The quaternions	192
a	The quaternion $a_0 + a_1\mathbf{i} + a_2\mathbf{j} + a_3\mathbf{k}$	191
S**a**, V**a** (or **a**´)	Scalar part a_0, vector part $a_1\mathbf{i} + a_2\mathbf{j} + a_3\mathbf{k}$ of quaternion **a**	192
$\bar{\mathbf{a}}$	Conjugate $a_0 - \mathbf{a}'$ of quaternion **a**	192
$\|\mathbf{a}\|$	Norm $\sqrt{(\mathbf{a}\bar{\mathbf{a}})}$ of quaternion **a**	192
Q	The quaternion group $\{\pm 1, \pm\mathbf{i}, \pm\mathbf{j}, \pm\mathbf{k}\}$	196
$e^{\mathbf{I}\theta}$	The quaternion $\cos\theta + \mathbf{I}\sin\theta$	196
M_L, M_R	Matrices of the transformations in 4-space given by left, right multiplication by a quaternion	198
M(**a**)	Matrix of 3-d rotation given in quaternions by $\mathbf{x} \to \mathbf{a}\mathbf{x}\mathbf{a}^{-1}$	200
double(**a**,**b**), bisect(**a**,**b**)	Certain points of the great arc through quaternions **a**,**b** on the unit sphere in 4-space	213
$\mathcal{K}$	Snowflake curve of Helga von Koch	219
$\mathcal{C}$	Cantor set	230
D	Similarity dimension	233
(a,b), [a,b]	Open, closed interval on real line	230
[a,b)	Half-open interval	243
$B_{\mathbf{a}}(r)$, $B_{\mathbf{a}}[r]$	Open ball, closed ball with centre **a**, radius r	238
$S_{\mathbf{a}}(r)$	Sphere with centre **a**, radius r	238

Selected answers

Chapter 1

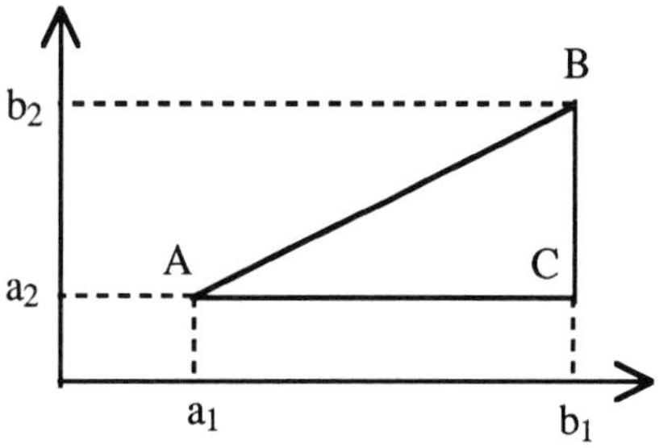

2 (i) Symmetries leaving unmoved the central point A: rotations about A through multiples of a 1/6 turn, reflection in any of the six lines of symmetry through A.
(ii) By Pythagoras, $|AB|^2 = |AC|^2 + |BC|^2$
$= (b_1 - a_1)^2 + (b_2 - a_2)^2$.
Now take the positive square root of each side.

(iii) Here a_1, b_1 label directed line segments.

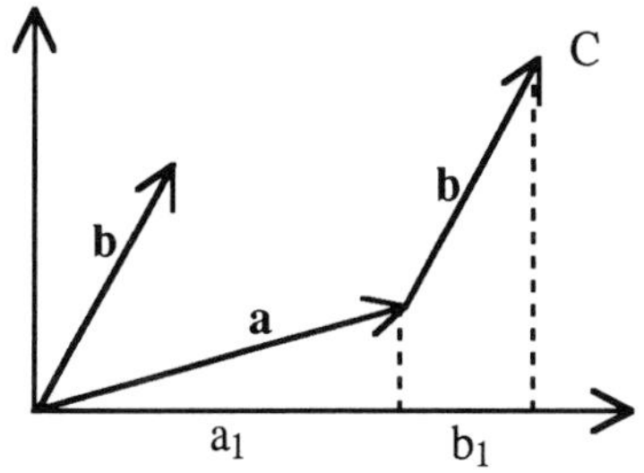

Since $\mathbf{a} + \mathbf{b} = \underline{OC}$, it follows that its first component, the distance horizontally from the origin to C, equals $a_1 + b_1$. Similarly the second component is $a_2 + b_2$.

5 $R_A(1/2).R_m$ is a composition of a direct and an indirect isometry, so it is indirect, by Remark 1.17, hence a glide or reflection, by Theorem 1.18. By Theorem 1.10 it is determined by its effect on A, A'. We have $A \to A \to A'$ and $B' \to B \to B$. An indirect isometry achieving this is a glide along AB with translation part 2$\underline{AB}$. By uniqueness, this must be the desired composition. [In chapter 2 we give a systematic approach via reflections.]

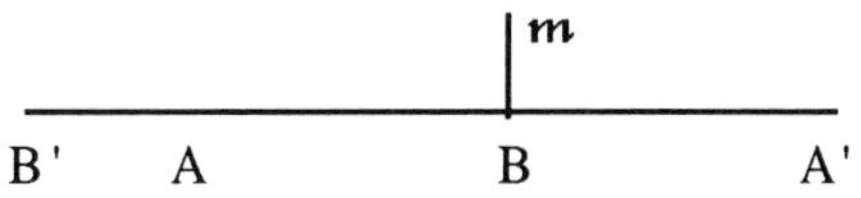

6 $(T_{\mathbf{a}})^n = T_{n\mathbf{a}}$. The rotation is through 5 x 3 x (3/10) = 4 1/2 turns. The same *isometry* is achieved by a 1/2 turn.
7 Components $2\sqrt{2}$ along OB and $2\sqrt{2}$ perpendicular to OB.
8 (i) Reflection in mirror x = a gives, by (1.6), $R_{x=a}(x) = 2a-x$. Hence this reflection followed by one in the line x = a+d gives $x \to 2a-x \to 2(a+d) - (2a-x) = x+2d$. (ii) $R_{OX}.R_{OY} = R_O(1/2)$.

11 $R_C(1/3).R_B(1/3)$ is direct (Remark 1.17) so is a rotation or translation (Theorem 1.18), determined by its effect on A,C (Theorem 1.10). Now, $A \to D \to A$, hence rotation about A, and $C \to C \to E$, hence 2/3 turn.

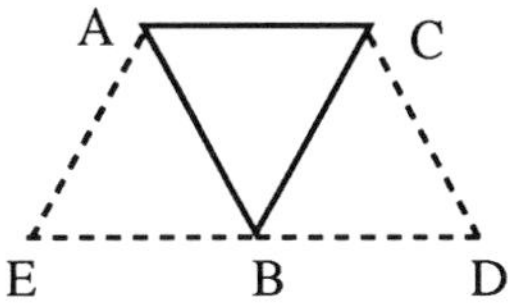

13 Let P(x,y) be reflected into $Q(x_Q,y_Q)$. By the hint, PR has slope b/a, hence $\underline{PR}$ = d(a,b) for some d, and $\underline{OR}$ = (x,y) + d(a,b). Since R is on aX+bY = 1 we have a(x+da) + b(y+db) = 1, whence $d = (1-ax-by)/(a^2+b^2)$. By definition of reflection, $\underline{OQ} = \underline{OP} + 2\underline{PR}$ =

$$(x,y) + 2(1-ax-by)(a,b)/(a^2+b^2).$$

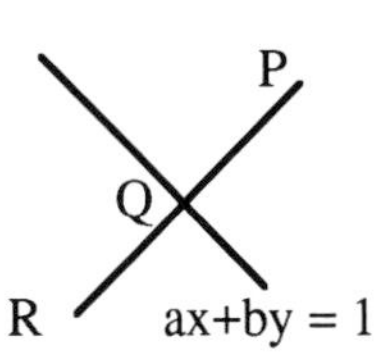

That is, $(a^2+b^2)x_Q = (b^2-a^2)x - 2aby + 2a$ and $(a^2+b^2)y_Q = (a^2-b^2)x - 2abx + 2b$.

Chapter 2

2 (i) $R_B(1/3)\,R_A(1/3) = R_{BC}R_{BA}.\,R_{BA}R_{CA} = R_{BC}.\,R_{CA} = R_C(-1/3)$

(ii) $T_{CA}.\,R_A(1/3) = R_{BD}R_{EA}.\,R_{EA}R_{GA} = R_{BD}.\,R_{GA} = R_G(1/3)$

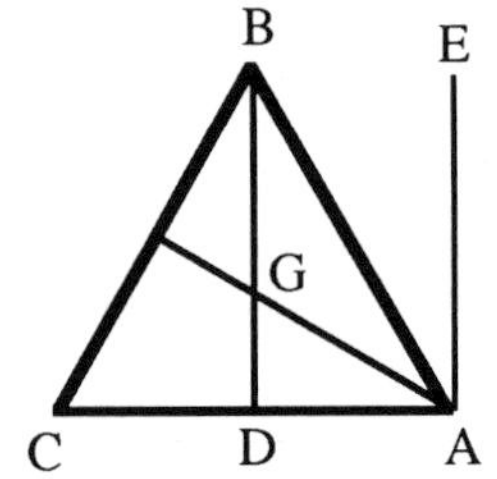

5 The composition of three reflections is an indirect isometry (cf. Remark 1.17) and is therefore a glide or reflection (cf. Theorem 1.18). With four reflections the result is direct, hence a translation or rotation.

8 The order of a 2/7 turn g is 7, so the required powers are 2, 6, and 5 (only the second called for change).

9 $(R_mR_n)^2 = I$ means $R_mR_nR_mR_n = I$. Multiply on the left and on the right of each side by R_m. We get $R_m{}^2R_nR_mR_nR_m = R_mIR_m$ and, using $R_m{}^2 = I$ simplifies this to the required result $R_nR_mR_nR_m = I$. If m,n were parallel then R_mR_n would be a translation and so would its square, which therefore could not equal I (we assume m,n do not coincide). On the other hand, R_mR_n is rotation, which must be a 1/2 turn if its square equals I. But then $(R_nR_m)^2$ is the inverse rotation, also a 1/2 turn squared, so also equals I.

10 $R_mR_nR_p$ has inverse $R_pR_nR_m$, by (2.9).

14 (a) D_{10}, (b) D_{12}, (c) C_4.

15 By (2.9), $(g^r)^{-1} = (g^{-1})^r$, so we have $g^r = I \Leftrightarrow (g^r)^{-1} = I \Leftrightarrow (g^{-1})^r = I$. Therefore g and its inverse have the same order. For the last part, since C_{14} has an element of order 14 but D_{14} does not (cf. Section 1.4), the groups cannot be isomorphic.

Chapter 3

1 r1, r1m, r2, r2mg, r11g.

2 r11m, r1, r11g, r2mg, r2mm, r1m, r2

Chapter 4

1 2-fold, at the meeting of two heads, wings, or tails.

2 Figure 4.2: at the meeting of two heads, wings, or tails. Figure 1.1: star centres.

6 (a), (b) parallelogram, (c) hexagonal, (d) square, (e) rectangular, (f) centred rectangular, (g) rectangular.

Chapter 5

1 (a) pm, (b) pgg, (c) p4, (d) p3, (e) p6, (f) p31m.

2 (a) p1, (b) cm, (c) p3m1, (d) pmg, (e) p4m, treating thickened edges as thin (otherwise pm), (f) p6m.

3 (a) pmm, (b) p2, (c) pg, (d) cmm, (e) p4g, (f) p6m (treating all lines alike).

Chapter 6

1 C_{12} and D_{12} are not isomorphic, since C_{12} contains an element of order 12, unlike D_{12}. The symmetry group of a letter 's' is {T,I}, where T is a 1/2 turn and $T^2 = I$. This is isomorphic to the symmetry group of a letter 'A', consisting of a single reflection R and the identity. The only isomorphism sends T to R, but it does not send rotations to rotations, so the groups are not *equivalent*.

4 The interior angle of a regular n-gon has angle $\pi - 2\pi/n$, and the m angles at a vertex must sum to 2π. That is, $m(\pi - 2\pi/n) = 2\pi$. One easy way to find all possible integer solutions $m,n \geq 3$ is to rewrite the equation as $mn-2m = 2n$, and add 4 to both sides so as to get the factorised form $(m-2)(n-2) = 4$. Then each of m-2, n-2 is a divisor 1,2,4 of 4, allowing (m,n) = (3,6), (4,4) or (6,3). These values are realised by the well-known regular tilings by hexagons, squares, or triangles.

13 The type is p6

14 For lines 1,2 see answer to Chapter 1, Exercise 8.

Chapter 7

2 The triple is right handed; and each pair has zero inner product, so is at right angles.

3 The angle has cosine $1/\sqrt{3}$ so is about 55 degrees.

5 (i) $[(AB)^T]_{ik} = (AB)_{ki} =$ (row k of A).(column i of B)
$=$ (row i of B^T).(column k of A^T) $= (B^TA^T)_{ik}$. Hence $(AB)^T = B^TA^T$.

(iii) $(A^TB - B^TA)^T = (A^TB)^T - (B^TA)^T = B^TA - A^TB$ (by (i)) $= -(A^TB - B^TA)$.

6 The inverse of diag{2,-1,3} is diag{1/2,-1,1/3}, (i) If $A^4 = I$ then $|A|^4 = 1$ so $|A| = \pm 1$. If complex numbers are allowed we can also have $\pm\mathbf{i}$. (ii) $A.A^3 = I$ implies $A^{-1} = A^3$. An example is $\begin{vmatrix} 0 & 1 \\ -1 & 0 \end{vmatrix}$.

9 Matrix multiplication is defined and associative. The identity I is in O(n), and the inverse of an orthogonal matrix is also orthogonal.

10 (1/2)(1,-1,-1,1). The determinant is -1.

11 (a) Right, (b) left, (c) coplanar, (d) right.

12 $\begin{vmatrix} 2 & -5 \\ -3 & -40 \end{vmatrix} = -95$ so the rotation is clockwise.

13 $[\alpha\mathbf{a} + \beta\mathbf{b},\mathbf{c},\mathbf{d}] = (\alpha\mathbf{a} + \beta\mathbf{b}).(\mathbf{c} \times \mathbf{d}) = \alpha\mathbf{a}.(\mathbf{c} \times \mathbf{d}) + \beta\mathbf{b}.(\mathbf{c} \times \mathbf{d})$, which equals $\alpha[\mathbf{a},\mathbf{c},\mathbf{d}] + \beta[\mathbf{b},\mathbf{c},\mathbf{d}]$ by definition. The last two follow by cyclic symmetry. Using these formulae gives $[\mathbf{a}+\mathbf{b},\mathbf{b}+\mathbf{c},\mathbf{c}+\mathbf{a}]$ as the sum of eight terms $[\mathbf{p},\mathbf{q},\mathbf{r}]$ of which six equal 0 because two of $\mathbf{p},\mathbf{q},\mathbf{r}$ coincide and the other two are equal by cyclic symmetry.

16 By Theorem 2.1 the 1/2 turn may be obtained as reflection in line y = b followed by reflection in x = a. Using formula (1.6) we have $(x,y) \to (x,2b-y) \to (2a-x,2b-y)$.

17 $\begin{bmatrix} 0 & 1 & 0 \\ -1 & 0 & 0 \\ 2a & 0 & 1 \end{bmatrix} = \begin{bmatrix} 0 & 1 & 0 \\ -1 & 0 & 0 \\ 0 & 0 & 1 \end{bmatrix}\begin{bmatrix} 1 & 0 & 0 \\ 0 & 1 & 0 \\ 2a & 0 & 1 \end{bmatrix}$ hence a 1/4 turn about the origin followed by translation through (2a,0).

19 $\begin{bmatrix} 1/2 & \sqrt{3}/2 & 0 \\ -\sqrt{3}/2 & 1/2 & 0 \\ 4 & 0 & 1 \end{bmatrix}$ The composition of the transformation matries is the matrix A on the left. The 2 x 2 part is the matrix of a 1/6 turn. The centre (a,b) satisfies [a b 1]A = [a b 1], so is $(2,2\sqrt{3})$.

20 Resolve the translation along and perpendicular to the mirror line.

Chapter 8

1 (a) $\begin{bmatrix} 3 & 2 & 1 \\ -1 & 0 & -1 \\ 0 & 1 & 1 \end{bmatrix}$, (b) $\begin{bmatrix} 1 & 0 & 1 \\ 0 & 1 & 1 \\ 1 & -1 & 0 \end{bmatrix}$, (c) $\frac{1}{\sqrt{2}}\begin{bmatrix} 1 & 0 & 1 \\ -1 & 0 & 1 \\ 0 & 1 & 0 \end{bmatrix}$

The matrices in cases (b), (c) are obtained by Theorem 8.5. For (c) we note that by linearity $T(\mathbf{i}+\mathbf{j}) = \sqrt{2}\mathbf{k}$, $T(\mathbf{i}-\mathbf{j}) = \sqrt{2}\mathbf{i}$ implies $T(2\mathbf{i}) = \sqrt{2}\mathbf{k} + \sqrt{2}\mathbf{i}$ and so $T(\mathbf{i}) = (\mathbf{k}+\mathbf{i})/\sqrt{2}$. Similarly $T(\mathbf{j}) = (\mathbf{k}-\mathbf{i})/\sqrt{2}$. This gives an isometry the matrix has orthonormal rows and so is orthogonal (Section 7.24). Cases (a), (b) are not isometries, for the matrix rows are not even unit vectors.

5 (a) The matrix of the transformation has negative determinant, so orientations are reversed. (b) The matrix M has $|M| = 0$. In accordance with Rule 7.20 (5) the rows are dependent, in fact row 3 = row 1 + row 2. Since these are the images of **i**,**j**,**k**, all 3-space is mapped onto the plane consisting of linear combinations of the first two rows. (c) The inverse map sends **i**,**j**,**k** to **j**+**k**, **k**+**i**, **i**+**j** respectively, for which the matrix has positive determinant. Hence both the inverse and the original preserve orientation.

8 By formula (8.10), $R_u(x,y,z) = (-x,y,z)$, $R_v(x,y,z) = (-y,-x,z)$, and $R_w(x,y,z) = ((x,-z,-y)$. Hence we can make the composition $(x,y,z) \to (-x,y,z) \to (-y,x,z) \to (y,x,z)$, interchanging the x,y coordinates. Hence we can also change the sign of the y coordinate. Invoking R_w, we can change the sign of any coordinate and interchange any two. The orbit therefore consists of $(\pm 2,0,0)$, $(0,\pm 2,0)$, $(0,0,\pm 2)$, the vertices of an octahedron (or the face centres of a certain cube centred at the origin).

14 The first matrix, A, has negative determinant, so must be reflection and have an eigenvalue -1 corresponding to say [x y z] as eigenvector. But it is easier to use (8.11): we may take as normal vector any row of A-I which is not zero (i.e. not all zeros). Using 7A-7I to avoid fractions we obtain (-4,-6,2).

The second matrix, B, is therefore rotation, so its axis **x** is an eigenvector of B with eigenvalue 1, and hence equation $\mathbf{x}[B - I] = 0$. But again we have a read off method from Corollary 8.52: an axis vector from the skew part S of B. Unfortunately B is actually symmetric and S = 0, but in this case the corollary gives any nonzero row of B+I as axis vector. For example (8,4,8). (This is the cae of a 1/2 turn. Check: $2\cos\phi + 1 = \text{trace } B = -1$, hence $\cos\phi = -1$, $\phi = \pi$.)

16 (a) Write $r = \sqrt{3}$. By (8.12) the matrix M for $R_k(1/3)R_j(1/3)$, and its skew-symmetric part S are

$$M = \frac{1}{2}\begin{bmatrix} -1 & r & 0 \\ -r & -1 & 0 \\ 0 & 0 & 2 \end{bmatrix} \frac{1}{2}\begin{bmatrix} -1 & 0 & -r \\ 0 & 2 & 0 \\ r & 0 & -1 \end{bmatrix} = \frac{1}{4}\begin{bmatrix} 1 & 2r & r \\ r & -2 & 3 \\ 2r & 0 & -2 \end{bmatrix}, \quad S = \frac{1}{8}\begin{bmatrix} 0 & r & -r \\ -r & 0 & 3 \\ r & -3 & 0 \end{bmatrix}$$

By Corollary 8.52 applied to S, an axis vector is (3,r,r), or more simply $\mathbf{a} = (r,1,1)$. For the angle ϕ of rotation we have by Theorem 8.42, $2\cos\phi + 1 = \text{trace } M = -3/4$, $\cos\phi = -7/8$. This determines ϕ up to sign, which is that of the determinant $[\mathbf{a},\mathbf{v},\mathbf{v}M]$ for any vector **v** not parallel to **a**. We take $\mathbf{v} = (0,0,1)$ and obtain the value $[\mathbf{a},\mathbf{v},\mathbf{v}M] = r/2 > 0$. Thus ϕ is the positive angle $\cos^{-1}(-7/8)$, or about 151 degrees.

Chapter 9

4 (i) Use $\overline{z/w} = \bar{z}/\bar{w}$. (ii) Use $|z/w| = |z|/|w| = 1$ as clue. The answer is **i** by trial.

5 $x^2 - y^2 + 2x = 2xy - 2y$ gives $z = 0, -2, 1\pm i\sqrt{3}$.

7 $2e^{5\pi i/6}$, $\sqrt{2}\, e^{i\pi/4}$, $\sqrt{2}\, e^{-i\pi/4}$, $6\sqrt{3}\, e^{i\pi/6}$. By the binomial theorem $(\mathbf{i} - \sqrt{3})^4$ has the expansion $\mathbf{i}^4 - 4\mathbf{i}^3\sqrt{3} + 6\mathbf{i}^2.3 - 4\mathbf{i}.3\sqrt{3} + 9$, which simplifies to $-8 - 8\mathbf{i}\sqrt{3}$. Calculating it by De Moivre's Theorem: $(2e^{5\pi i/6})^4 = 16\, e^{10\pi i/3} = 16\, e^{-2\pi i/3} = 16(\cos(2\pi/3) - \mathbf{i}\sin(2\pi/3))$ $= -8 - 8\mathbf{i}\sqrt{3}$, as before.

25 (i) Up to a scalar factor the needed quaternion product is $(1-\mathbf{i}+\mathbf{j}-\mathbf{k})(-1+\mathbf{i}) = 2(\mathbf{i}-\mathbf{j})$. Here $\cos\phi = 0$ and we have a 1/2 turn about OP where P(1,-1,0) lies on a vertical edge of the cube. (ii) $(1+\mathbf{j})(\mathbf{i}-\mathbf{k}) = -2\mathbf{k}$, hence a 1/2 turn about the z-axis.

Chapter 10

1 Let Greatfract and Littlefract have rulers of respective lengths $\varepsilon = r,s$. Assuming the Richardson's graph to be a straight line of slope -3/10 we have $L = A\,\varepsilon^{-3/10}$, hence 160/185 $= (As^{-3/10}) / (Ar^{-3/10}) = (r/s)^{3/10}$. From this, $r/s = (160/185)^{10/3} = 0.62..$. Thus the explanation is that the Greatfract ruler is about 62% the length of the Littlefract.

10 (i) With initiator OP, where P is (1,0), we may take the maps as $R_O(-\pi/4)(\mathbf{x}/2\sqrt{2})$,

$R_O(\pi/4)(\mathbf{x}/\surd 2) + (1/4)(1,-1)$, $R_O(3\pi/4)(\mathbf{x}/2\surd 2) + (1,0)$. (ii) $\Sigma r_i{}^D = 1$ gives $4x^2 + x = 1$, where $x = (1/2)^D$. Hence, approximately, $x = 0.39$ and $D = 1.36$.

Chapter 11

3 In **R** the interval (0,1) is open but [0,1) is not. In any metric space, a 1-point set is closed because its complement is open (apply the definition of open).

4 An open line segment PQ is not open, for a point of PQ is not contained in an open disk lying within PQ (no disks do). But PQ is not closed because its complement is not open: for example the point P (outside open segment PQ) is not in an open disk lying entirely *outside* PQ.

6 Open triangles, for example.

9 Every real number is a limit point of the rationals.

10 The point 1.

11 Closure [0,3], interior $(0,1)\cup(1,3)$, boundary {0,1,3}.

14 Bijective.

21 A closed in X implies A^c open in X and hence $A^c \times X$ open in X x X (see (11.4)). Therefore the complement A x X and similarly X x B, is closed in X x X. Since A x B equals the intersection $(A \times X) \cap (X \times B)$, it is closed.

22 The function det: {n x n matrices} $\to$ **R** is continuous. (a) This set is $\det^{-1}(\{1\})$, the inverse image of the closed set {1} (see Exercise 3), so it is closed. (b) This set is closed because it equals $\det^{-1}(\{1\}) \cup \det^{-1}(\{-1\})$.

25 f: $(0,1) \to$ **R** given by $f(x) = 1/x$, is continuous but not bounded.

37 (iii) Write $C = X \setminus (A\cup B)$. Then $\partial(A\cup B) = \overline{A\cup B} \cap \overline{C} = (\overline{A} \cup \overline{B}) \cap \overline{C}$ $= (\overline{A} \cap \overline{C}) \cup (\overline{B} \cap \overline{C}) \subseteq (\overline{A} \cap \overline{X\setminus A}) \cup (\overline{B} \cap \overline{X\setminus B}) = \partial A \cup \partial B$.

Chapter 11

1 The function $(x-2)/(x-1) = 1 - 1/(x-1)$ takes the value 1/2 at $x = 3$ and then stays less than 1 but approaches 1 arbitrarily closely. The supremeum of set A is therefore 1.

3 Suppose A,B are compact subsets of space X. Let $\mathcal{A}$ be a family of open sets that covers $A\cup B$. We must extract a finite subcover. Since $\mathcal{A}$ covers A, so does some finite subfamily $\mathcal{A}_1$. Similarly , some finite subfamily $\mathcal{A}_2$ covers B. Therefore the finite subfamily $\mathcal{A}_1\cup\mathcal{A}_2$ covers $A\cup B$. Thus $A\cup B$ is compact. Analogously we prove $A\cap B$ is compact. The set **N** is not compact because **N** itself is a cover by open sets with no finite subcover.

6 $f(A\cup B) = f(A)\cup f(B)$ (cf. Table 11.4).

7 The space P is the image of compact set D under the continuous map $D \to D/R$.

8 Since translation preserves lengths we need only consider $f(x,y) = (2x-3,5x+y)$. By the method of Example 12.30, the minimum bound ratio is about 5.4 (NB: there is a formula based on this method, (14.4)).

9 The maximum value of $f = x^2 + y^2 + z^2$ is found on the boundary of the tetrahedron since the derivatives of f can be zero only at the vertex (0,0,0), not in the interior. (cf. Application 12.31). A similar argument applies to each face then to its boundary edges; the the maximum is at a vertex. The greatest vertex value is $f(2,-3,7) = 62$.

10 Open or closed balls in $\mathbf{R}^n$ are connected, by Theorem 12.37, because each point is on a ray from itself to the origin.

11 Choose a point x different from the origin. We can join any point to x by a finite sequence of line segments. Apply Theorem 12.37.

13 Any closed curve removed from the sphere leaves a disconnected set, but in the torus, removal of the circular boundary of a cross-section leaves a connected set.

14 The homeomorphism $(x,y) \to (x,e^y)$, sends the connected set $\mathbf{R}^2$ onto H^+.

16 (i) The Platonic solids S are path-connected because they are convex: if A,B are points of S then the line segment AB lies in S. (ii) The projective plane P is path-connected because D is path-connected and $D \to D/R = P$ is onto (see Exercise 7).

17 The torus is connected (i) because it is path connected (vary the angles in turn, in Example 11.48), or alternatively (ii) because it is the continuous image of a connected set (Example 11.57).

Chapter 13

2 Let x be in A. Then $0 \le d(x,A) \le d(x,x) = 0$.

6 $d([2,6],[14,18]) = 12$, $d([6,15],[-3,21]) = 9$.

11 Let A be a complete subspace of a complete space S. Let x be a limit point of A. We must show that x is in A. For each n in **N**, the ball $B_x(1/n)$ contains a point x_n of A, so that $x_n \to x$ in X and the sequence $\{x_n\}$ is Cauchy. Since A is given to be complete, the limit x is in A itself. Hence x is closed.

12 Let $x_n = 1/n$. Then $\{x_n\}$ is a sequence in $A = (0,1)$. Since, in the larger space **R**, the sequence has a limit, it is Cauchy. But, as a sequence in A, it does not converge, because this limit is not in A.

13 Complete: $(-\infty,2]$. By Exercise 11, an interval must be *closed* in **R**, to be complete.

14 In (13.9): $d(x_{n-1},x_n) = d(Tx_{n-2},Tx_{n-1}) \le rd(x_{n-2},x_{n-1}) \le ... \le r^{n-1}d(x_0,x_1)$.

15 One homeomorphism from (0,1) to **R** is h = gf, where f: $(0,1) \to (0,\infty)$ with $y = f(x) = x/(1-x)$ and g: $(0,\infty) \to$ **R** with $g(y) = \log y$. Then $h(x) = \log(x/(1-x))$ and $h^{-1}(z) = f^{-1}g^{-1}(z)$. We have $g^{-1}(z) = e^z$, and $y(1-x) = x$ gives $f^{-1}(y) = x = y/(1+y)$, hence $h^{-1}(z) = e^z/(1 + e^z)$. Completeness is not topologically invariant because: (0,1) and **R** are topologically equivalent yet **R** is complete and (0,1) is not.

16 f(x) must have a fixed point because it is a contractive transformation (ratio 3/4) on the complete space $\mathbf{R}^2$. For the final part we solve $\mathbf{x} = (3/4)R_o(\pi/4)(\mathbf{x}) + (1,2)$.

Chapter 14

1 $w_1(\mathbf{x}) = \mathbf{x}/2$, $w_2(\mathbf{x}) = (1/2)(\mathbf{x} + (4,0)) = \mathbf{x}/2 + (2,0)$, $w_3(\mathbf{x}) = \mathbf{x}/2 + (5,3)/2$.

2 Reflection in the line y = x simply interchanges x and y coordinates, so reflection in y = x + 2 is the composition $(x,y) \to (x,y-2) \to (y-2,x) \to (y-2,x+2)$. In matrix form this is

$$\begin{bmatrix} 0 & 1 \\ 1 & 0 \end{bmatrix}\begin{bmatrix} x \\ y \end{bmatrix} + \begin{bmatrix} -2 \\ 2 \end{bmatrix},$$ so the code is (0,1,1,0,-2,2).

5 We must map three non-collinear points onto three distinct points of line $y = 3x + 4$, say by $T(0,0) = (0,4)$, $T(1,0) = (1,7)$, $T(0,1) = (-1,1)$. With T defined by (14.2) this immediately gives the code (1,-1,3,-3,0,4). The determinant is 0, as it should be by Theorem 14.10(c), criterion (iii). Note that we could alternatively use formula (14.9).

6 The stages are (1) Scale towards O by $\mathbf{x} \to \mathbf{x}/2$, (2) shear downwards so that when x = 30 y has decreased by 20: $(x,y) \to (x, y - 2x/3)$, (3) translate upwards into the shaded area by (0,20). The code is (1/2,0,-1/3,1/2,0,20).

8 However the map is decomposed, reflections cannot be avoided if the determinant is negative, other otherwise they can (coordinate scaling is not allowed to introduce a disguised reflection via negative prameters). Thus an essential reflection is present only in w_7.

12 A line of telegraph poles disappearing into the distance.

13 See Table 14.7. **15** See Table 14.6.

17 As for Figure 14.10, with tree trunk replaced by baseball player as condensation set.

Chapter 15

2 0.8 is greater than1/2 and 3/4 but less than 7/8, so the first three digits of its binary expansion are 110. Since 0.5 = 4/5 its base 5 expansion is 400... .

3 D : 233... or 322... , E: 133... or 311... , F: 122... or 211... . The queried point is 22333... or 23222... .

5 *The distances*: $d(1\bar{2},3\bar{2}) = 2/4 = 1/2$. $d(3\bar{2},3\bar{1}) = 0/4 + 1/4^2 + 1/4^3 + ... = 1/12$, $d(1\bar{2},3\bar{1}) = 2/4 + 1/4^2 + 1/4^3 + ... = 7/12$. Since none of these distances exceeds the sum of the other two, the triangle inequality is satisfied.

8 $\phi(\bar{13}) = (1/3)(\mathbf{a}_3 + 2\mathbf{a}_1)$.

9 $\phi(213\sigma) = \phi(2(13\sigma)) = w_2\,\phi(13\sigma) = w_2w_1\,\phi(3\sigma) = w_2w_1w_3\,\phi(\sigma)$.

10 The process gives the Sierpinski gasket Δ with vertices $A_1A_2A_3$ because the middle of segment A_rx_0 is $w_r(x_0)$, and $\Delta = w_1(\Delta) \cup w_2(\Delta) \cup w_3(\Delta)$. In Figure 15.8, label the vertices counterclockwise from the top (as in Figure 15.7). Assuming x_0 is the furthest extraneous point to the right, the first few choices of w_i are given by 1312.

12 The 19-bit sequence 00001... continues by recursion from the polynomial of Table 15.1 with coefficients 0011, namely $a_n = a_{n-3} + a_{n-4}$. We get 0000100110101111000.

13 From $B = A \cup (B\backslash A)$, we have by (15.25), $\mu(B) = \mu(A) + \mu(B\backslash A) \geq \mu(A)$.

14 *Example* $\{(x,y): 1 \leq x \leq 2,\ 1 < y < 3\}$, the intersection of a closed with an open set.

16 w^{-1} 'preserves' the properties of being open, closed, a complement, a countable union, a countable intersection. See Table 11.4.

23 Another primitive polynomial mod 2 is $1 + x^2 + x^5$.

Chapter 16

5 The fixed points are the solutions of $f(z) = z$, i.e. of $z^2 - z + c = 0$, $c = (-1+\mathbf{i})/2$. Hence $z = (1/2)(-1 \pm \sqrt{1-4c}) = (1/2)(-1 \pm \sqrt{3-2\mathbf{i}})$. To find the square root of $3-2\mathbf{i}$ we put it into polar form $re^{i\theta}$. To do so we first plot (3, -2) in the plane (= argand diagram), then read off the values $r = \sqrt{13}$, $\theta = -\tan^{-1}(2/3) = -33.69°$. By De Moivre's Theorem $\sqrt{3-2\mathbf{i}} = 13^{1/4}e^{i\theta/2} = 1.90(\cos 16.85° - \mathbf{i}\sin 16.85°) = 1.82 - 0.55\mathbf{i}$ (the positive square root of Definition 16.7). This gives the fixed points as $z = 1.41 - 0.28\mathbf{i}$ and $-0.41 + 0.28\mathbf{i}$. The first point is a repeller, since its eigenvalue modulus $|f'(z)| = |2z|$ exceeds 1. We need not calculate this exactly: the conclusion is clear since even the real part exceeds 1. For the second point $|2z| < 1$, giving an attractor.

6 (i) $R(z) = (3 + 4/z^2)/(5 + 2/z) \to 3/5$ as $|z| \to \infty$. Hence $R(\infty) = 3/5$. (ii) $R(z) = (3z^2 + 4) / z(5z + 2)$, which tends to infinity precisely when $z \to 0$ or $z \to -2/5$, hence $R(0) = \infty$, $R(-2/5) = \infty$.

8 The fixed points are the roots of $z^2 - z - 1 = 0$, namely $(1/2)(1\pm\sqrt{5})$. For the eigenvalues, $|2z| = |1\pm\sqrt{5})| > 1$, so that both are repellers.

9 We use the method of Example 16.20 with $f(z) = z^2 - 7/8$. The points of a fixed 2-cycle are those roots of $f^2(z) = z$ which are not also roots of $f(z) = z$. We have $f^2(z) = z \Leftrightarrow (z^2 - 7/8)^2 - 7/8 = z \Leftrightarrow 64z^4 - 112z^2 - 64z - 7 = 0$, and $f(z) = z \Leftrightarrow 8z^2 - 8z - 7 = 0$. Dividing the quartic polynomial by the quadratic we obtain the 2-cycle as the roots of

$$8z^2 + 8z + 1 = 0, \qquad (1)$$

namely $(1/4)(-2\pm\sqrt{2})$. But by Theorem 16.17 the eigenvalue (of f^2) is the same for both roots, so we may expect to find it by using (1) without direct substitution of a root. In fact we have $(f^2)'(z) = 4z(z^2 - 7/8) = 4z(-z-1)$ (by (1)) $= -4(z^2+z) = 4/8$ (by (1)), showing that the 2-cycle is attractive.

15 Assuming that $J = \partial A(\infty)$, we show that $f(J)$ is in J. Let $x \in J$ be given. That is (a) x is not in $A(\infty)$, (b) x has points of $A(\infty)$ arbitrarily close. We must deduce the same for f(x). Firstly, f(x) is not in $A(\infty)$, for otherwise we would have x in $A(\infty)$. Let $\delta > 0$ be given. We must show that f(x) has points of $A(\infty)$ within distance δ of itself. Let y be a point of $A(\infty)$; then so is f(y). But since f is continuous, f(y) is within δ of f(x) provided y is sufficiently close to x. By (b) such y exists in $A(\infty)$, so we have proved (b) for f(x) and thus shown that f(x) is in $A(\infty)$. Since x was an arbitrary point of J we have $f(J) \subseteq J$.

24 The fixed points a,b satisfy $z^2 - z + c = (z - a)(z - b) = 0$, whence $|a|\,|b| = |ab| = |c| < 1/4$. Thus at least one of the eigenvalues' modulus $|2a|$ or $|2b|$, is less than 1, giving an attractive fixed point.

25 By the method of Example 16.63 the quadratic becomes $w^2 - 3/4$.

26 $w = (z-\mathbf{i})/(z+\mathbf{i})$. We compute $w(\infty) = 1$, $w(0) = -1$, $w(1) = -\mathbf{i}$, so w maps the x-axis to the circle $|w| = 1$. Since $w(-\mathbf{i}) = \infty$, the lower half-plane is sent to the exterior of the circle.

27 We have $N(z) = z - f(z)/f'(z)$, and $N'(z) = 1 - [f'(z)^2 - f(z)f''(z)]/f'(z)^2$. From $f(\alpha) = 0$, $f'(\alpha) \neq 0$ follows $N'(\alpha) = 1 - f'(\alpha)^2 / f'(\alpha)^2 = 0$. That is, α is superattractive.

34 By the suggested argument, 1/2 has points of $A(\infty)$ arbitrarily close, and so 1/2 is in the closure $\overline{A(\infty)}$. But since 1/2 is not in $A(\infty)$ itself we have, by definition of closure and boundary, $1/2 \in \overline{A(\infty)} \setminus A(\infty) = \partial A(\infty) = J$.

Index